Applications in Economics

Indicates global example   Continued on the next page. See inside back cover for Chapters 22–34.

Applications in Economics

Continued from the previous page

See inside back cover for Chapters 22–34   Indicates global example

ECONOMICS

SECOND EDITION

ECONOMICS

Paul Krugman | Robin Wells

Princeton University

WORTH PUBLISHERS

Senior Publishers: Catherine Woods and Craig Bleyer

Acquisitions Editor: Sarah Dorger

Senior Marketing Manager: Scott Guile

Executive Development Editor: Sharon Balbos

Development Editor: Marilyn Freedman

Senior Consultant: Andreas Bentz

Consultant: Kathryn Graddy

Consulting Editor: Paul Shensa

Development Editor, Media, Supplements: Marie McHale

Assistant Editor: Tom Acox

Director of Market Research and Development: Steven Rigolosi

Associate Managing Editor: Tracey Kuehn

Project Editor: Anthony Calcara

Art Director and Interior Designer: Babs Reingold

Cover Designers: Babs Reingold and Lyndall Culbertson

Layout Designer: Lee Ann McKevitt

Illustrations: TSI Graphics and Lyndall Culbertson

Photo Editors: Cecilia Varas, Donna Ranieri

Photo Researchers: Elyse Rieder and Julie Tesser

Production Manager: Barbara Anne Seixas

Composition: TSI Graphics

Printing and Binding: RR Donnelley

ISBN-13: 978-0-7167-7158-6
ISBN-10: 0-7167-7158-6

Library of Congress Control Number: 2009920558

Worth Publishers
41 Madison Avenue
New York, NY 10010

www.worthpublishers.com

Cover Photo Credits

Image of seated group on front: *Comstock/Jupiter Images;* **First Row:** Colorful buildings: *Photodisc;* Sunflowers: *Photodisc;* Highways: *Fotosearch;* Cityscape: *Photodisc;* Golden Gate Bridge: *Photodisc;* Wiretubes: *Digitalvision;* Car-factory: *Digital Vision;* Bike rider: *Flat Earth Images;* **Second Row:** Little girl: *Photodisc;* Tires: *Photodisc;* Grocers: *Photodisc;* Trees: *Photodisc;* Couple buying car: *Photodisc;* Red Factory shot: *Digitalvision;* Ships: *Photodisc;* Vancover Skyline: *Photodisc;* **Third Row:** Cars in traffic: *PhotoDisc;* Farmer on tractor: *Photodisc;* Pipes in oil field: *Photodisc;* Tugboat: *Flat Earth Images;* Squash: *Photodisc;* Mom and Baby: *Photodisc;* Machine Worker: *Digitalvision;* Cargo: *Photodisc;* **Fourth Row:** Boy with flowers: *Photodisc;* Oil well: *Photodisc;* Flowers in a field: *Stockbyte;* Engineers: *PhotoDisc;* Oil Refinery at Night: *Digitalvision;* Double-decker bus: *Flat Earth Images;* Lambs: *Photodisc;* Fruit-stand: *Photodisc;* **Fifth Row:** Cornstalks: *Stockbyte;* Sewage treatment plant: *Digital Vision;* Evening dining: *Photodisc;* Woman smiling: *Photodisc;* We Deliver Sign: *Photodisc;* Surgeon: *Stockbyte;* Steam: *Photodisc;* Ship: *Photodisc;* **Sixth Row:** Oil Refinery: *Photodisc;* Fleamarket: *Photodisc;* Windmill: *Photodisc;* Depression: *Imagebank/Getty Images;* Logs on truck: *Photodisc;* Baskets: *Photodisc;* Cows: *Stockbyte;* Pineapples: *Photodisc;* **Seventh Row:** Hybrid car: *istockphoto;* Hay in snow: *Photodisc;* Bridge: *PhotoDisc;* Woman in pink scarf: *Photodisc;* Vegetable stand: *Photodisc;* Gas prices: *Photodisc;* Concrete Mixer: *PhotoDisc;* Trying on glasses: *Photodisc;* **Eight Row:** Steam: *PhotoDisc;* NY Stock Exchange: *Image Source;* Espresso Bar: *Photodisc;* Oil pump and pipes: *Photodisc;* Fisher: *Photodisc;* Logging: *Photodisc;* Father and Son: *Photodisc;* Flags: *Photodisc;* **Ninth Row:** Woman wearing purple scarf: *Photodisc;* Towing Logs: *Photodisc;* Oil Refinery: *Photodisc;* Tokyo Stock Exchange: *Media Bakery;* Doctor: *Stockbyte;* Railroad Crossing: *PhotoDisc;* Currency: *Photodisc;* Hong Kong Intersection: *Photodisc*

Text Credits

Chapter 6, Source information for Table 6-1 on page 147: *Eggs, beef:* Kuo S. Huang and Biing-Hwan Lin, Estimation of Food Demand and Nutrient Elasticities from Household Survey Data, United States Department of Agriculture Economic Research Service Technical Bulletin, No. 1887 (Washington, DC: U.S. Department of Agriculture, 2000); ***Stationery, gasoline, airline travel, foreign travel:*** H. S. Houthakker and Lester D. Taylor, *Consumer Demand in the United States, 1929–1970: Analyses and Projections* (Cambridge, MA: Harvard University Press, 1966); ***Housing, restaurant meals:*** H. S. Houthakker and Lester D. Taylor, *Consumer Demand in the United States: Analyses and Projections,* 2nd ed. (Cambridge, MA: Harvard University Press, 1970). **Chapter 12, Source information for "Economics in Action" on page 310:** www.ercb.com, Dr. Dobb's Electronic Review of Computer Books. **Chapter 17, Source article for "Economics in Action" on page 439:** M. Gross, J.L. Sindelar, J. Mullahy, and R. Anderson, Policy Watch: Alcohol and Cigarette Taxes, *Journal of Economic Perspectives, 7,* 211–222, 1993. **Chapter 20, Source article of "For Inquiring Minds" box on page 501:** C. Camerer et al., Labor Supply of New York City Cab Drivers: One Day at a Time. *Quarterly Journal of Economics,* 112, 407–471, 1997. **Chapter 20, Source article of "For Inquiring Minds" box on page 511:** Nancy Stokey, A Quantitative Model of the British Industrial Revolution, 1780–1850. *Carnegie-Rochester Conference Series on Public Policy,* 55, 55–109, 2001. **Chapter 21, Source article of "For Inquiring Minds" box on page 557:** Joe Nocera, "Can We Turn Off Our Emotions When Investing?" *New York Times,* September 29, 2007. Retrieved from: http://www.nytimes.com/2007/09/29/business/29nocera.html?_r=1&scp=1&sq=nocera%20Zweig&st=cse&oref=slogin

To beginning students everywhere, which we all were at one time.

About the Authors

Paul Krugman, recipient of the 2008 Nobel Memorial Prize in Economic Sciences, is Professor of Economics at Princeton University, where he regularly teaches the principles course. He received his BA from Yale and his PhD from MIT. Prior to his current position, he taught at Yale, Stanford, and MIT. He also spent a year on the staff of the Council of Economic Advisers in 1982–1983. His research is mainly in the area of international trade, where he is one of the founders of the "new trade theory," which focuses on increasing returns and imperfect competition. He also works in international finance, with a concentration in currency crises. In 1991, Krugman received the American Economic Association's John Bates Clark medal. In addition to his teaching and academic research, Krugman writes extensively for nontechnical audiences. Krugman is a regular op-ed columnist for the *New York Times.* His latest trade books, both best sellers, include *The Return of Depression Economics and the Crisis of 2008,* a history of recent economic troubles and their implications for economic policy, and *The Conscience of a Liberal,* a study of the political economy of economic inequality and its relationship with political polarization from the Gilded Age to the present. His earlier books, *Peddling Prosperity* and *The Age of Diminished Expectations,* have become modern classics.

Robin Wells was a Lecturer and Researcher in Economics at Princeton University. She received her BA from the University of Chicago and her PhD from the University of California at Berkeley; she then did postdoctoral work at MIT. She has taught at the University of Michigan, the University of Southampton (United Kingdom), Stanford, and MIT. The subject of her teaching and research is the theory of organizations and incentives.

brief contents

contents

Preface

"If you want to be listened to, you should put in time listening."

Marge Piercy

FROM PAUL AND ROBIN

We both believe that a successful second edition is an exercise in listening. Writing a successful first edition is largely a matter of capitalizing on one's strengths, but writing a successful second edition means listening to those who used the first edition and using that feedback to address one's oversights and misjudgments. In many ways, writing a second edition can be as challenging as writing a first edition.

We've been fortunate to have a devoted group of adopters and reviewers to help guide us in this revision. Their input has prompted us to undertake a major reorganization of the microeconomics chapters, moving to a more traditional sequence. While there were good theoretical reasons behind the first edition chapter sequence, in which the producer theory chapters preceded the consumer theory chapters, we learned from our reviewers that a more traditional sequence of chapters better served adopters' pedagogical objectives.

As for the macroeconomics chapters, we planned from the beginning to make significant revisions to incorporate reviewer suggestions. Even if little had changed in the real economy, these chapters would have been recognizably different from those in the first edition. But, what we (and our harried editors) didn't expect was that we would be revising our macroeconomics chapters in the midst of the greatest financial crisis in decades, possibly since the Great Depression, with many forecasters predicting the worst U.S. recession in a quarter century. For us (and, dare we say, for our adopters), the timing of the unfortunate events of 2008 was fortunate, allowing us to incorporate those events into this edition.

We believe that the momentous events of 2008 validate the pedagogical approach toward macroeconomics that we took in the first edition. In the preface to that edition we argued that a principles text should emphasize the way economics applies to the real world. When applied to macroeconomics, this approach means giving full and early coverage to the macroeconomics of the business cycle. We contrasted our approach with that of some other principles texts that, for whatever reasons—such as a sense that the business cycle is a less "fundamental" concern than, say, the price level, or a reluctance to emphasize issues that have been the center of extensive controversy—give the short run short shrift, relegating it to a few chapters at the end of the book. In fact, even before the crisis broke, we had planned to strengthen our coverage of the short run by providing an early discussion of the key issues of unemployment and inflation, and by placing an even stronger emphasis on the role and importance of aggregate spending. The crisis has reinforced our belief that one of the core purposes of a macroeconomics text should be to show students how macroeconomic models shed light on short-run economic developments.

In this revision, we've eliminated some chapters, written three new ones, devised a new feature, updated extensively (adding many new applications and cases), and, where needed, simplified. We've also responded to a demand for hearing more of our unique voice. As you peruse the second edition, you'll see the extent of the changes. It is no exaggeration to say that the second edition you are holding in your hands is a significant revision of this book.

However, the principles that guided us in writing the first edition have not changed. In the second edition, we've aimed to keep the writing fresh and lively. We find that, like Paul's *New York Times* readers, students are able to more easily absorb economic concepts when they enjoy what they are reading. In addition, we've maintained our commitment to help students go beyond a "one-model-fits-all" version of economics. As we stated in the first edition, "To achieve deeper levels of understanding of the real world through economics, students must learn to appreciate the kinds of trade-offs and ambiguities that economists and policy makers face when applying their models to real-world problems. We believe this approach will make students more insightful and more effective participants in our common economic, social, and political lives." The events that have occurred over the past few years, since the first edition was written, lead us to believe more than ever in this approach to teaching economics.

The Second Edition: What's New?

Although the first edition was a resounding success, quickly becoming one of the top-selling economics textbooks, there is always room for improvement. In preparing this new edition, every single chapter was carefully evaluated and revised, many of them significantly, to clarify explanations, streamline and reorganize content when necessary, and update. We hope that these revisions lead to a more successful teaching experience for you. We look forward to your comments.

New Chapter 7, "Taxes" Material that previously appeared in the various contexts of quotas, elasticity, and consumer and producer surplus has been consolidated into a single early chapter. This change allows an instructor to give a comprehensive overview of the economics of taxation, with early applications of concepts from supply and demand, consumer and producer surplus, and elasticity.

New Chapter 19, "The Economics of the Welfare State" The new chapter on the welfare state, although optional for many of you, covers a topic that is deeply important to us and is at the heart of much of today's political debates. It is also a response to those who have asked to hear more of our unique voice in the book. The chapter focuses on timely topics such as the economics of health care and federal entitlement spending, carefully presenting the arguments for both expanding the welfare state and for reducing it. As in Paul's *New York Times* columns, this chapter takes a complex topic and reduces it to its essential elements, illuminating the intellectual foundations of our policy choices. In addition, this chapter provides a timely and engaging examination of the challenges that economists and policy makers face when applying economic concepts to daily realities. We believe that this chapter and the new examples of SCHIP (The State Children's Health Insurance Program), poverty in the world's rich nations, a comparison of the welfare state in France and the United States, and much more will motivate students to think more deeply about economic trade-offs, social welfare, and the political process.

New Chapter 24, "Unemployment and Inflation" Adopters and reviewers urged us to offer an early, comprehensive overview of the key problems of short-run macroeconomics. We responded by creating Chapter 24, "Unemployment and Inflation," which immediately follows preliminary chapters that introduce macroeconomics as a subject and explain how macroeconomic aggregates are measured. Chapter 24 is *not* about the Phillips curve, which is discussed in Chapter 32. Instead, the new chapter shows students how inflation and unemployment are measured and why they matter, providing a context for the discussion of macroeconomic policy.

New "Global Comparison" Boxed Feature In the first edition we made extensive use of international examples—policies and events in countries other than the United States—to illustrate key concepts. Adopters and reviewers were enthusiastic about this globalization of the narrative, and we decided to make international comparisons a regular feature of the book. Most chapters now contain a Global Comparison boxed feature that uses data from several countries to give students an international perspective on a fundamental concept or issue. For example, the Chapter 7 Global Comparison, "You Think You

Pay High Taxes?" (p. 189), compares tax rates in the United States to those in other advanced countries, giving students a more informed view of U.S. tax policy. Chapter 23, "Tracking the Macroeconomy," contains the Global Comparison "GDP and the Meaning of Life" (p. 602), which compares real GDP per capita with polling data on "life satisfaction."

We believe that the Global Comparisons help show students how looking at the wide range of international experience, not only at that of the United States, expands our understanding of economics. For a complete list of Global Comparison boxes, see the inside front and back covers.

An Even Stronger Focus on Global Issues Throughout In addition to the new Global Comparison feature, we've enhanced our focus on global issues in two more ways. First, the international trade chapter (Chapter 8) has been moved up in the sequence to give students an early grounding in the importance of comparative advantage and trade. Second, we include globally focused examples in virtually every chapter of this book. Some of our favorites include the Chapter 8 For Inquiring Minds, "Chinese Pants Explosion" (p. 217), a discussion of the significant distributional consequences arising from the elimination of a U.S. quota on imports of Chinese pants, and the Economics in Action, "The Doha Deadlock," in that same chapter (p. 219), which explains why world trade negotiations have stalled. Later in the book there is the Chapter 17 Economics in Action, "Cap and Trade" (p. 445), which discusses the European Union's mandatory cap and trade scheme for greenhouse gases, as well as the Chapter 30 For Inquiring Minds, "Who Gets the Interest on the Fed's Assets?" (p. 816), which discusses the impact on the money supply of forged $100 bills allegedly printed in North Korea. Throughout the text, global examples are highlighted with an orange globe stamp. For a list of all such examples, see the inside front and back covers.

Even More on Policy and Timely Coverage of the Current Financial Crisis Taking advantage of current events, the new edition of *Economics* offers an even stronger discussion of real-world policy. A sampling includes our evaluation of greenhouse gas emissions and economic growth around the world, our discussion of the fight over the shape of the 2008 U.S. fiscal stimulus package, and our coverage of the debate over the extent to which America's trade deficit was a benign by-product of a "global savings glut."

The strengthening of the policy focus is especially relevant in two chapters: Chapter 19, "The Economics of the Welfare State," one of our new chapters, which discusses the health care crisis and proposals for reform, and Chapter 30, "Money, Banking, and the Federal Reserve

System." In the first edition Chapter 30 was mainly a discussion of long-established Federal Reserve operating procedures that no one expected to change very much. Now, however, there are radical changes in how the Fed operates, taking place before our eyes in order to confront the ongoing financial crisis and economic fallout—and this new edition follows the action. We are particularly excited about the new final section in this chapter, "An Overview of the Twenty-First Century American Banking System" (p. 818), which gives an overview of the behavior and regulation of the American banking system and concludes with a very timely Economics in Action titled "The 2008 Crisis and the Fed" (p. 824).

A New, More Teacher-Friendly Chapter Organization The most substantive change in the book includes the new organization of microeconomics chapters, reflecting a more traditional sequence. We've also reorganized our chapters on aggregate expenditure (Chapter 27) and aggregate demand and aggregate supply (Chapter 28) in the macroeconomics section to offer a more straightforward demand-side approach.

Organizational changes in this second edition include the following:

➤ **Tax coverage has been consolidated into a single new chapter.** Our first edition treatment of taxes had been spread across several chapters. The second edition consolidates the material into one early chapter: Chapter 7, "Taxes."

➤ **Consumer theory now precedes producer theory, so that the market structure chapters are grouped together.** Although many instructors choose not to teach consumer theory, the majority of those who do cover it before producer theory. In response, we've rearranged the chapters so that consumer theory (Chapters 10 and 11) now precedes producer theory (Chapters 12 and 13). As a result, chapters on perfectly competitive industries are now immediately followed by the monopoly, oligopoly, and monopolistic competition chapters (Chapters 14, 15, and 16), allowing a continuous treatment of industrial organization.

➤ **The international trade chapter appears earlier.** Along with adding the new "Global Comparison" feature, described on the next page, placing international trade (Chapter 8) earlier greatly enhances the international focus of the text.

➤ **The consumer and producer surplus chapter has been moved earlier to follow the supply-and-demand chapter.** This change allows for an earlier introduction to the modern tools of consumer and producer surplus, giving readers a better sense of the efficiency of markets and what happens under price ceilings and price floors. We believe this change results in better motivation and clearer exposition of the benefits of competitive markets (see Chapters 3 and 4.)

➤ **Optional chapters on factors markets and risk have been moved later.** While some instructors will find these chapters very useful to teach, placing these optional chapters at the end of the microeconomics portion of the text improves the pedagogical flow of core material. (See Chapters 20 and 21.)

➤ **The chapter on aggregate expenditure has been moved up to precede the chapter on aggregate demand and aggregate supply (AD-AS).** Most teachers cover aggregate expenditure first. This change reflects classroom reality and makes the macro sections of the book even more accessible. (See Chapters 27 and 28.)

➤ **Full, intuitive coverage of the multiplier has moved into the chapter on aggregate expenditure.** Coverage of the multiplier is now the first major section in Chapter 27 on aggregate expenditure. Instructors can skip the rest of the chapter, if they prefer, but it's now easier for instructors who want to use the income-expenditure approach to dive right in.

➤ **Aggregate demand is covered before aggregate supply within the AD-AS chapter.** This is a more logical reorganization of content in Chapter 28 now that aggregate expenditure precedes coverage of the AD-AS model. It is also the way teachers report that they teach the AD-AS model.

Advantages of This Book

Although a lot is new in this second edition, our basic approach to textbook writing remains the same:

➤ **Chapters build intuition through realistic examples.** In every chapter, we use real-world examples, stories, applications, and case studies to teach the core concepts and motivate student learning. The best way to introduce concepts and reinforce them is through real-world examples; students simply relate more easily to them.

➤ **Pedagogical features reinforce learning.** We've crafted what we believe are a genuinely helpful set of features that are described in the next section, "Tools for Learning."

➤ **Chapters are accessible and entertaining.** We use a fluid and friendly writing style to make concepts accessible. Whenever possible, we use examples that are familiar to students: choosing which course to take, buying a used textbook, deciding where to eat at the food court in the local shopping mall, or the similarity between a household's budget and a country's balance of payments.

▶ **Although easy to understand, the book also prepares students for further coursework.** Too often, instructors find that selecting a textbook means choosing between two unappealing alternatives: a textbook that is "easy to teach" but leaves major gaps in students' understanding, or a textbook that is "hard to teach" but adequately prepares students for future coursework. We offer an easy-to-understand textbook that offers the best of both worlds.

Tools for Learning

Every chapter is structured around a common set of features that help students learn while keeping them engaged.

Opening Story   Each chapter opens with a compelling story that often extends through the entire chapter. Stories were chosen to accomplish three things: to illustrate important concepts in the chapter, to build intuition with realistic examples, and to encourage students to read on and learn more. For example, Chapter 3 uses the price of coffee at the local Starbucks and the supply of coffee beans to teach the supply and demand model. Chapter 22 uses the Great Depression and the financial crisis of 2007–2008 to set the stage for the field of macroeconomics as a whole. Because each chapter is introduced with a real-world story, students are drawn in and can relate more easily to the material. A complete list of opening stories appears on the inside front and back covers.

"What You Will Learn in This Chapter"   Following every opening story is a preview of the chapter in an easy-to-review bulleted list format that alerts students to critical concepts and chapter objectives.

"Economics in Action" Case Studies   In addition to the vivid stories that open every chapter, we conclude virtually every major text section with still more examples: a real-world case study called Economics in Action. This much-lauded feature provides a short but compelling application of the major concept just covered in that section. Students experience an immediate payoff when they can apply concepts they've just read about to real phenomena. For example, in Chapter 4, we use the case of eBay, the online auctioneer, to communicate the concept of efficiency (p. 110). In Chapter 26 we use the rise and fall of the housing bubble—an event that has touched many students' lives—to illustrate financial fluctuations (p. 697). For a list of all the Economics in Action cases, see the inside front and back covers and the table of contents.

Unique End-of-Section Review: "Quick Review" and "Check Your Understanding" Questions   Every Economics in Action case study is followed by two opportunities for review: a Quick Review and Check Your Understanding questions. Because jargon and abstract concepts can quickly overwhelm the principles student, the Quick Reviews (short, bulleted summaries of key concepts) help ensure that students understand what they have just read. Then the Check Your Understanding questions (a short set of review questions with solutions at the back of the book) allow students to immediately test their understanding of a section. If they're not getting the answers to the questions right, it's a clear signal for them to go back and reread before moving on.

We've received a lot of positive feedback about this end-of-section pedagogy that encourages students to apply what they've learned (via the Economics in Action) and then review it (with the Quick Reviews and Check Your Understanding questions).

Boxed Features   We include three types of boxes:

"For Inquiring Minds": To further our goal of helping students build intuition with real-world examples and infuse chapters with our voice, every chapter contains one or more For Inquiring Minds boxes. In these boxes, concepts are applied to real-world events in unexpected and sometimes surprising ways, generating a sense of the power and breadth of economics. These boxes show students that economics can be fun despite being labeled "the dismal science." In a Chapter 18 box on water bottling in Maine, students learn how one of America's favorite bottled waters, Poland Spring, is at the center of a dispute over the management of a common resource (p. 471). In a Chapter 25 box, students learn how famous economists once warned—wrongly—that Britain's prosperity would end when it started running low on coal (p. 665). For a list of all For Inquiring Minds boxes, see the inside front and back covers and the table of contents.

"Global Comparison": As explained earlier, in this new box we explore concepts using real data to illustrate how and why countries reach different economic outcomes.

"Pitfalls": Certain concepts are prone to be misunderstood when students begin their study of economics. We alert students to these mistakes in the Pitfalls boxes. Here common misunderstandings are spelled out and corrected. For example, in a Chapter 3 Pitfalls, we clarify the difference between demand and quantity demanded (p. 66). In a Chapter 29 Pitfalls, we take on the all-too-common confusion between deficits and debt (p. 784). For an overview of all the Pitfalls boxes in chapters, see the table of contents.

Definitions of Key Terms   Every key term is defined in the text and then again in the margin, making it easy for students to study and review.

"A Look Ahead" Each chapter ends with A Look Ahead, a short overview of what lies ahead in upcoming chapters. This conclusion provides students with a sense of continuity among chapters.

End-of-Chapter Review In addition to the opportunities for review at the end of every major section, each chapter ends with a brief but complete summary of the key concepts, a list of key terms, and a comprehensive set of end-of-chapter problems. Users and reviewers alike have praised the problem sets for how effectively they test intuition as well as the ability to calculate important variables. We have also responded to requests for more problems drawn from real life by adding news- and data-based problems to every second edition chapter.

The Organization of This Book and How to Use It

This book is organized as a series of building blocks in which conceptual material learned at one stage is built upon and then integrated into the conceptual material covered in the next stage. And our organization remains flexible: we recognize that a number of chapters will be considered optional and that many instructors will prefer to teach the chapters using a different order. Chapters and sections have been written to incorporate a degree of flexibility in the sequence in which they are taught, without sacrificing conceptual continuity. Following is a walk-through of coverage in the second edition.

Part 1: What Is Economics? The **Introduction** initiates students into the study of economics in the context of a shopping trip on any given Sunday in everyday America. It provides students with definitions of basic terms such as *economics,* the *invisible hand,* and *market structure* and serves as a "tour d'horizon" of economics, explaining the difference between microeconomics and macroeconomics. It is followed by **Chapter 1, "First Principles,"** with its 12 principles underlying the study of economics: four principles of individual choice, covering concepts such as opportunity cost, marginal analysis, and incentives; five principles of interaction between individuals, covering concepts such as gains from trade, market efficiency, and market failure; and three principles of economy-wide interaction, covering concepts that underlie the multiplier effect, recession and inflation, and macroeconomic policy. In later chapters, we build intuition by referring to these principles in the explanation of specific models. Students learn that these 12 principles form a cohesive conceptual foundation for all of economics.

Chapter 2, "Economic Models: Trade-offs and Trade," shows students how to think like economists by using two models—the production possibility frontier and

comparative advantage. It gives students an early introduction to gains from trade and to international comparisons. The **Chapter 2 appendix** offers a comprehensive math and graphing review that provides a solid foundation for later material in the book.

Part 2: Supply and Demand Chapter 3, "Supply and Demand," begins with an all-new opening story that uses the market for coffee beans to illustrate supply and demand, market equilibrium, and surplus and shortage. Students learn how the demand and supply curves of coffee beans shift in response to events such as changes in consumer tastes and changes in global coffee production. By showing how increases in the cost of a cappuccino at Starbucks can be traced to drought in Vietnam, we introduce students to standard material in a way that is fresh and compelling. The story is supplemented with a Global Comparison on gas prices that shows how differences in gas prices across countries have led to different consumer choices. Through examples such as the market for used textbooks and eBay, students learn how markets increase welfare in **Chapter 4, "Consumer and Producer Surplus."** This revised chapter contains an expanded discussion of market efficiency and the ways in which markets fail, addressing topics such as the role of prices as signals and property rights. A new For Inquiring Minds on the best mechanism for allocating transplant organs prompts students to think about nonmarket allocation systems and how they compare to markets.

Chapter 5, "The Market Strikes Back," covers various types of market interventions and their consequences: price and quantity controls, inefficiency, and deadweight loss. Through tangible examples such as New York City rent-control regulations and New York City taxi licenses, as well as rent control in Mumbai, India, and shopping in Hugo Chavez's Venezuela, the costs generated by attempts to control markets are made real to students. **Chapter 6, "Elasticity,"** introduces the various elasticity measures. It contains a new opening story on the flu vaccine shortage of 2004–2005. Through a discussion of how patients and vaccine suppliers responded to a sudden shortfall of available flu vaccine, students are given a real-world example of how markets respond to events.

Part 3: Individuals and Markets In new **Chapter 7, "Taxes,"** we aggregate material on taxation that had previously appeared in several first edition chapters. Basic tax analysis is covered, along with a review of the burden of taxation and considerations of equity versus efficiency. The chapter also provides an in-depth overview of the structure of taxation, current tax policy, and public spending in the United States. The chapter on taxes is paired with **Chapter 8, "International Trade,"** which now appears much earlier in the sequence. The chapter's new opening story on conflict arising from increased importation of shrimp into the United States builds on the material in Chapter 2 on comparative advantage and trade. Here we trace the sources of comparative advantage, consider tariffs and quotas, and explore the politics of trade protection. We also provide in-depth coverage on the controversy over imports from low-wage countries.

Part 4: Economics and Decision Making **Chapter 9, "Making Decisions,"** is unique and important because microeconomics is fundamentally a science of how to make decisions. In the chapter we focus on developing an understanding of how decisions should be made in any context rather than placing the emphasis on comprehending the consequences of decisions. We want students to be able to distinguish between what is and what isn't a marginal decision, and to do that, we have included an entire section on "either–or" versus "how much" decisions—a distinction that is particularly useful when students are asked to compare a firm's output decision to its entry/exit decision. In this chapter we also reprise the concept of opportunity cost, present a thorough treatment of marginal analysis, explain the concept of sunk cost, and cover present value. This chapter will help students develop a deeper intuition about the common conceptual foundations of microeconomic models, and it will serve as a valuable foundation for the following four chapters on consumer and producer theory.

Part 5: The Consumer Chapters on consumer theory now precede the chapters on producer theory. **Chapter 10, "The Rational Consumer,"** provides a complete treatment of consumer behavior for instructors who don't cover indifference curves. There is a simple, intuitive exposition of the budget line, the optimal consumption choice, diminishing marginal utility, and income and substitution effects and their relationship to market demand. Students learn, for example, that a budget line constructed using prices is much like a Weight Watchers' diet plan constructed using a "point" system. **Chapter 11, "Consumer Preferences and Consumer Choice,"** offers a more detailed treatment for those who wish to cover indifference curves. It contains an analysis of the optimal consumption choice using the marginal rate of substitution as well as income and substitution effects. An Economics in Action on the relationship between music file downloads and albums prompts students to think more deeply about the problem of classifying a pair of goods as substitutes rather than complements.

Part 6: The Production Decision In **Chapter 12, "Behind the Supply Curve: Inputs and Costs,"** we develop the production function and the various cost measures of the firm. There is an extensive discussion of the difference between average cost and marginal cost, illustrated by examples such as a student's grade point average. **Chapter**

13, "Perfect Competition and the Supply Curve," explains the output decision of the perfectly competitive firm, its entry/exit decision, the industry supply curve, and the equilibrium of a perfectly competitive market. Here, a timely Economics in Action on the ethanol-driven rise in the demand for corn and the accompanying rise in the cost of inputs for corn production provides students with a real-world illustration of the adjustment to long-term equilibrium in a competitive industry.

Part 7: Market Structure: Beyond Perfect Competition The market structure chapters now appear consecutively. **Chapter 14, "Monopoly,"** provides a full treatment of monopoly, including topics such as price discrimination and the welfare effects of monopoly. We provide an array of compelling examples, such as De Beers diamonds, price manipulation by California power companies, and airline ticket-pricing. A Global Comparison features an analysis of why Americans pay higher prices for prescription drugs. In **Chapter 15, "Oligopoly,"** we present basic game theory in both a one-shot and repeated-game context, as well as an integrated treatment of the kinked demand curve model. The models are applied to a wide set of actual examples, such as Archer Daniels Midland, a European vitamin cartel, OPEC, and airline ticket-pricing wars. We've expanded our treatment of antitrust policy, enhancing it with a discussion of the differences between American and European enforcement policies. In **Chapter 16, "Monopolistic Competition and Product Differentiation,"** students are brought face to face early on with an example of monopolistic competition that is a familiar feature of their lives: the food court at the local mall. We go on to cover entry and exit, efficiency considerations, and advertising in monopolistic competition.

Part 8: Microeconomics and Public Policy **Chapter 17, "Externalities,"** covers negative externalities and solutions to them, such as Coasian private trades, emissions taxes, and a system of tradable permits. We also examine positive externalities, technological spillovers, and the resulting arguments for industrial policy. We've added a new section, "Network Externalities," with an Economics in Action on the Microsoft case, which brings to life the unique qualities and challenges posed by goods like software and music downloads. **Chapter 18, "Public Goods and Common Resources,"** makes an immediate impression by opening with the story of how "The Great Stink" of 1858 compelled Londoners to build a public sewer system. Students learn how to classify goods into four categories (private goods, common resources, public goods, and artificially scarce goods) based on two dimensions: excludability and rivalry in consumption. With this system, they can develop an intuitive understanding of why some goods but not others can be efficiently managed by markets. New **Chapter 19, "The Economics of the**

Welfare State," provides a comprehensive overview of the American welfare state as well as its philosophical foundations. Sure to pique students' interests is a section on the American health care system, written with Paul's signature lucidity. It also provides a cogent analysis of the problem of poverty and the issue of income inequality.

Part 9: Factor Markets and Risk **Chapter 20, "Factor Markets and the Distribution of Income,"** covers the competitive factor market model and the factor distribution of income. It also contains modifications and alternative interpretations of the labor market: the efficiency-wage model of the labor market and the influences of education, discrimination, and market power. For instructors who covered indifference curves in Chapter 11, the **Chapter 20 appendix** offers a detailed examination of the labor–leisure trade-off and the backward-bending labor supply curve.

In **Chapter 21, "Uncertainty, Risk, and Private Information,"** we explain attitudes toward risk in a careful and methodical way, grounded in the basic concept of diminishing marginal utility. This allows us to analyze a simple competitive insurance market and to examine the benefits and limits of diversification. Next comes an easily comprehensible and intuitive presentation of private information in the context of adverse selection and moral hazard, with illustrations drawn from the market for used cars (lemons) and franchising. Instructors have told us how easy it is to teach this chapter and how much it helps to enlighten students about the relevance of economics to their everyday lives.

A Word about Organization in the Macroeconomics Section The history of macroeconomic theory is one in which short-run and long-run issues vie for priority. Two issues are particularly tricky. First, should long-run economic growth be covered early or later, after the business cycle has been discussed? Second, should classical, full-employment analysis of the price level come before or after business cycle analysis?

We've made long-run growth the fourth chapter in the sequence because we feel that an early discussion of the long-run growth of real GDP helps students understand why the business cycle involves fluctuations around an upward trend. We have, however, structured the subsequent short-run analysis (Chapters 27 and 28) in a way that allows instructors to reverse this order, deferring our chapter on long-run growth (Chapter 25) until later in the course.

However, we've taken a firmer stand when it comes to the second question. As explained previously, we believe that the fundamental approach of this book—to tie macroeconomics to real-world concerns—requires that a discussion of the short-run effects of demand and supply shocks come before a discussion of the classical model. If students begin their study of macroeconomics with mod-

els in which monetary policy has no effect on aggregate output, they will get the impression that what they are learning in the classroom is irrelevant to the real world. In this book we explain early why demand shocks have no effect on output in the long run, but we don't emphasize the long-run neutrality of money before describing how monetary and fiscal policy work in the short run.

We believe that the diffidence with which some textbooks approach the short run is partly driven by reluctance to enter an area that was marked by fierce debates in the 1970s and 1980s. But the ferocity of those debates, like double-digit inflation, has receded into the past. Yes, there are still serious disputes about macroeconomic theory and policy. But as we explain in Chapter 33, "Macroeconomics: Events and Ideas," there is also far more consensus than in the past. Students are best served by a book that emphasizes the macroeconomic issues that matter most to public debate rather than downplays these issues out of fear of stepping into contentious areas. That's why we have chosen to provide an extended early discussion of the short-run effects of demand and supply shocks and the role of fiscal and monetary policy in responding to these shocks.

Part 10: Introduction to Macroeconomics **Chapter 22, "Macroeconomics: The Big Picture,"** introduces the big ideas in macroeconomics. Starting with the story of the Great Depression, this chapter provides a quick overview of recessions and expansions, employment and unemployment, long-run growth, inflation versus deflation, and the open economy. An Economics in Action contrasts the vastly different policy responses of Herbert Hoover and George W. Bush in reaction to a slumping economy, giving students an understanding of where macroeconomics came from and how greatly it has changed over the past 80 years. A new Global Comparison on international business cycles shows students how deeply interrelated the world's major economies are.

Chapter 23, "Tracking the Macroeconomy," explains how the numbers macroeconomists use are calculated, and why. We start with a real-world example of how an estimate of real GDP helped save a country from policy mistakes, then turn to the basics of national income accounting and price indexes.

Chapter 24, "Unemployment and Inflation," is a new chapter introduced in response to the comments of adopters and reviewers who wanted to see one chapter devoted to these topics fairly early in the macro portion of the book. It covers the measurement of unemployment, the reasons why unemployment is positive even when the economy is booming, and the problems posed by inflation. Through the case studies, students will learn why unemployment is low in America's mountain states but high in the former East Germany. An Economics in

Action on Israel during the 1980s gives students an understanding of the challenges faced by those living under high inflation.

Part 11: Long-Run Economic Growth Chapter 25, "Long-Run Economic Growth,"

starts with a discussion of the dramatic increase in average height to illustrate the human significance of economic growth. When we turn to economic data, we emphasize an international perspective—economic growth is a story about the world as a whole, not just the United States. The chapter uses a streamlined approach to the aggregate production function to present an analysis of the sources of economic growth and the reasons some countries have been more successful than others. Here, we cover India's recent economic takeoff in a new Economics in Action. A new Global Comparison contrasts the different experiences of the United States and Europe in incorporating new technologies and the effects on their growth rates.

Chapter 26, "Savings, Investment Spending, and the Financial System," introduces students to financial markets and institutions. We group it with Chapter 25 in this part because it highlights the role of these markets and institutions in economic growth. Chapter 26 is also, however, integral to short-run analysis, for two reasons. First, its analysis of the market for loanable funds and the determination of interest rates provides an analytical tool that will be helpful for understanding monetary policy, international capital flows, and other topics covered later in the book. Second, its discussion of financial institutions provides crucial background for our later discussion of money and banking—a subject that has become unexpectedly exciting lately! America's low savings rate is examined in a new Global Comparison, and students will learn about the recent housing bubble in a new Economics in Action.

Part 12: Short-Run Economic Fluctuations Part 12

on the short run begins with **Chapter 27, "Income and Expenditure."** Here we use real-world data to delve into the determinants of consumer and investment spending, introduce the famous 45-degree diagram, and explain the logic of the multiplier. These are topics that have taken on new importance in today's economy, and we have responded to instructors' comments by moving this chapter ahead of *AD-AS* and making it a core rather than an optional chapter. It has been streamlined and begins with an intuitive discussion of the multiplier before moving to the graphical approach. Through the new Economics in Action, "The Multiplier and the Great Depression," students will learn how a collapse in investment spending led to a collapse in consumer spending during the Great Depression. The chapter also contains a new Economics in Action that illustrates how the Fed's low interest rate policies of the 1990s fed the U.S. housing boom (and eventually the U.S. housing bubble). For instructors who

would like more algebraic detail, the **Chapter 27 appendix** shows how to derive the multiplier algebraically.

In **Chapter 28, "Aggregate Demand and Aggregate Supply,"** we continue our introduction to short-run macroeconomics with a traditional focus on the aggregate price level. This chapter uses a traditional approach to *AD-AS* in order to better focus on the important distinction between the private sector's behavior and the effects of policy responses on that behavior. Furthermore, the chapter emphasizes a crucial insight: the economy's ability to correct itself in the long run. This chapter's opening story covers the economic slump of 1979–1982, which startled Americans with its combination of recession and inflation. This leads into an analysis of how both demand shocks and supply shocks affect the economy. In analyzing supply shocks, we emphasize positive shocks, such as the productivity surge of the late 1990s, as well as negative shocks, and a new Global Comparison discusses the supply shock posed by rising commodity prices in 2007–2008. The chapter concludes with the key insight that demand shocks affect only output in the short run.

Part 13: Stabilization Policy One insight that

emerged from the Great Depression and from Keynes's analysis is that there is a role for using monetary and fiscal policy to manage the ups and downs of the business cycle. Accordingly, **Chapter 29, "Fiscal Policy,"** starts with a discussion of the tense negotiations over a U.S. stimulus package in early 2008. This leads into an analysis of the role of discretionary fiscal policy. We also cover automatic stabilizers—using the woes of Europe's "stability pact" to illustrate their importance—and long-run issues of debt and solvency. In a new Global Comparison, "The American Way of Debt," students will see a comparison of the ratios of debt-to-GDP of the United States to those of other advanced countries. The **Chapter 29 appendix** shows how to introduce taxes into the analysis. It shows more specifically than the main text how the size of the multiplier depends on the tax rate, and it provides an intuitive explanation, in terms of successive rounds of spending, of how taxes reduce the size of the multiplier.

The next two chapters address monetary policy. **Chapter 30, "Money, Banking, and the Federal Reserve System,"** covers the roles of money, the ways in which banks create money, and the structure and role of the Federal Reserve and other central banks. We use episodes from U.S. history together with the story of the creation of the euro to illustrate how money and monetary institutions have evolved. A completely new section analyzes the role of the "shadow," or "parallel," banking system that played such a large role in the 2008 financial crisis, as well as provides an overview of U.S. financial crises from 1907 onward. **Chapter 31, "Monetary Policy,"** covers the role of Federal Reserve policy in driving interest rates and aggregate demand. In the real-world examples, we took full advantage of the dramatic recent developments in monetary policy, which make it easier than ever before to illustrate what the Federal Reserve does. We also made a special effort to build a bridge between the short run and the long run. For example, we carefully explain how the Federal Reserve can set the interest rate in the short run, even though that rate reflects the supply and demand for savings in the long run. Instructors of advanced students may want to teach the **Chapter 31 Appendix,** which explains how the liquidity preference and loanable funds models of the interest rate can both be true. A new For Inquiring Minds covers an especially timely topic: how fear affects the spreads between interest rates. A new Global Comparison illustrates for students how various countries set their monetary policy by inflation targeting.

Chapter 32, **"Inflation, Disinflation, and Deflation,"** covers the causes and consequences of inflation, the large cost disinflation imposes on the economy, and the danger that deflation leads the economy into a liquidity trap. We illustrate the problems that a "zero bound" poses for monetary policy using the examples of Japan during the 1990s and the U.S. economy in late 2008. As we explain, these issues, dormant for more than half a century after the Great Depression, surfaced in Japan in the 1990s and have had a major impact on policy thinking, forcing the Fed to adopt unconventional monetary policy. From a new Economics in Action on Zimbabwe, students learn that hyperinflation remains a real possibility in the twenty-first century. And the difficulty of getting rid of persistent inflation is demonstrated with a new Global Comparison that contrasts experiences with disinflation around the world.

Part 14: Events and Ideas We recognize that many instructors will find that there's only enough time to cover core chapters through Chapter 32 on inflation. For those with enough time, however, Part 14 (and Part 15, along with Chapter 25 on long-run growth, for instructors who choose to cover it later) broadens the analysis. Part 14 offers a brief history of macroeconomic thought.

Macroeconomics has always been a field in flux, with new policy issues constantly arising and traditional views often challenged. **Chapter 33, "Macroeconomics: Events and Ideas,"** provides a unique overview of the history of macroeconomic thought, set in the context of changing policy concerns, then turns to a description of the current state of macroeconomic debates. Here, again, we are able to incorporate current events, including an Economics in Action on the quandary that asset bubbles and their aftermath pose for the Fed.

Part 15: The Open Economy Part 15, also for those with time to cover it, takes the analysis into international economics. **Chapter 34, "Open-Economy Macroeconomics,"** analyzes the special issues raised for macroeconomics by the open economy. We frame the discussion with real-world concerns: the weak dollar, China's accumulation of dollar reserves, and debates about adopting the euro. A new For Inquiring Minds addresses the question of whether there is a global glut of savings. For instructors and students who want to delve more deeply into international macroeconomics, we provide a supplemental chapter—available on the web, at www.worthpublishers.com/krugmanwells, and in booklet form. This chapter, **"Currencies and Crises,"** takes students into the world of currency speculation and international financial crises, with an emphasis on the dramatic events that have unfolded in developing countries during the past decade.

What's Core, What's Optional?

To help with lecture planning, on the next page we list the chapters we view as core and those that could be considered optional—with helpful explanatory annotations for each optional chapter.

Supplements and Media

Worth Publishers is pleased to offer an enhanced and completely revised supplements and media package to accompany this textbook. The package has been crafted to help instructors teach their principles course and to give students the tools to develop their skills in economics.

For Instructors

Instructor's Resource Manual with Solutions Manual
The Instructor's Resource Manual, written by Margaret Ray, University of Mary Washington, is a resource meant to provide materials and tips to enhance the classroom experience. The Instructor's Resource Manual provides the following:

➤ Chapter-by-chapter learning objectives

➤ Chapter outlines

➤ Teaching tips and ideas that include:

  ➤ Hints on how to create student interest

  ➤ Tips on presenting the material in class

➤ Discussion of the examples used in the text, including points to emphasize with your students

➤ Activities that can be conducted in or out of the classroom

➤ Hints for dealing with common misunderstandings that are typical among students

WHAT'S CORE, WHAT'S OPTIONAL: MICROECONOMICS

Core	Optional
	Introduction: The Ordinary Business of Life
1. First Principles	
2. Economic Models: Trade-offs and Trade	Chapter 2 Appendix: Graphs in Economics
	A comprehensive review of graphing and math for students who would find such a refresher helpful. This appendix is more detailed than most because our goal is to reduce students' difficulty in grasping the concepts found in this book as well as to better prepare them for economic literacy in the real world.
3. Supply and Demand	
4. Consumer and Producer Surplus	
5. The Market Strikes Back	
6. Elasticity	
7. Taxes	
	8. International Trade
	This chapter recaps comparative advantage, considers tariffs and quotas, and explores the politics of trade protection. Coverage here links back to the international coverage in Chapter 2.
9. Making Decisions	
10. The Rational Consumer	
	11. Consumer Preferences and Consumer Choice
	This chapter offers a more detailed treatment of consumer behavior for instructors who wish to cover indifference curves.
12. Behind the Supply Curve: Inputs and Costs	
13. Perfect Competition and the Supply Curve	
14. Monopoly	
15. Oligopoly	
16. Monopolistic Competition and Product Differentiation	
17. Externalities	
18. Public Goods and Common Resources	
	19. The Economics of the Welfare State
	A unique chapter that gives a succinct overview of the American welfare state and its intellectual foundation. It provides a brief introduction to the economics of health care provision, as well as addresses the topics of poverty and income inequality.
	20. Factor Markets and the Distribution of Income Plus Appendix: Indifference Curve Analysis of Labor Supply
	For instructors who want to go into more depth, this chapter covers the efficiency-wage model of the labor market as well as the influences of education, discrimination, and market power. The appendix examines the labor–leisure trade-off and the backward-bending labor supply curve.
	21. Uncertainty, Risk, and Private Information
	This unique, applied chapter explains attitudes toward risk, examines the benefits and limits of diversification, and considers private information in the context of adverse selection and moral hazard.

WHAT'S CORE, WHAT'S OPTIONAL: MACROECONOMICS

Core	Optional
22. Macroeconomics: The Big Picture	
23. Tracking the Macroeconomy	
24. Unemployment and Inflation	
25. Long-Run Economic Growth	
26. Savings, Investment Spending, and the Financial System	
27. Income and Expenditure	**Chapter 27 Appendix: Deriving the Multiplier Algebraically** A rigorous and mathematical approach to deriving the multiplier.
28. Aggregate Demand and Aggregate Supply	
29. Fiscal Policy	**Chapter 29 Appendix: Taxes and the Multiplier** A rigorous derivation of the role of taxes in reducing the size of the multiplier and acting as an automatic stabilizer.
30. Money, Banking, and the Federal Reserve System	
31. Monetary Policy	**Chapter 31 Appendix: Reconciling the Two Models of the Interest Rate** Most macroeconomics texts, including this one, emphasize two different approaches to thinking about interest rates. In long-run discussions, the loanable funds model describes the interest rate as matching the supply and demand of lending. In short-run discussions, the liquidity preference approach focuses on the supply and demand for money. Despite appearances, these are not contradictory approaches—both are true. This appendix explains why.
32. Inflation, Disinflation, and Deflation	33. Macroeconomics: Events and Ideas A chapter for instructors who like to cover the history of economic ideas and the current state of policy debate. It offers a unique survey of changing macroeconomic thought. 34. Open-Economy Macroeconomics A chapter for instructors who want to take a more international approach. It covers the ways in which capital flows affect financial markets, the importance of exchange rates and exchange rate regimes, and the effects of monetary policy changes under fixed and floating rates.

➤ Web resources

➤ Solutions manual with detailed solutions to all of the end-of-chapter problems from the textbook

Printed Test Bank *Coordinator and Consultant:* Doris Bennett, Jacksonville State University. *Contributing Authors:* Eric R. Dodge, Rivers Institute at Hanover College; Sarah Ghosh, University of Scranton; Solina Lindahl, California Polytechnic State University; and Janice Yee, Worcester State College. The Test Bank provides a wide range of questions appropriate for assessing your students' comprehension, interpretation, analysis, and synthesis skills. Totaling more than 8,000 questions, the Test Bank offers multiple-choice, true/false, and short-answer questions designed for comprehensive coverage of the text concepts. Questions have been checked for continuity with the text content, overall usability, and accuracy.

The Test Bank features include the following:

➤ To aid instructors in building tests, each question has been categorized according to its general *degree of difficulty.* The three levels are: *easy, moderate,* and *difficult.*

 ➤ *Easy* questions require students to recognize concepts and definitions. These are questions that can be answered by direct reference to the textbook.

 ➤ *Moderate* questions require some analysis on the student's part.

 ➤ *Difficult* questions usually require more detailed analysis by the student.

➤ Each question has also been categorized according to a *skill descriptor.* These include: *Fact-Based, Definitional, Concept-Based, Critical-Thinking,* and *Analytical-Thinking.*

 ➤ *Fact-Based Questions* require students to identify facts presented in the text.

 ➤ *Definitional Questions* require students to define an economic term or concept.

 ➤ *Concept-Based Questions* require a straightforward knowledge of basic concepts.

 ➤ *Critical-Thinking Questions* require the student to apply a concept to a particular situation.

 ➤ *Analytical-Thinking Questions* require another level of analysis to answer the question. Students must be able to apply a concept and use this knowledge for further analysis of a situation or scenario.

➤ To further aid instructors in building tests, each question is conveniently cross-referenced to the appropriate topic heading in the textbook. Questions are presented in the order in which concepts are presented in the text.

➤ The Test Bank includes questions with tables that students must analyze to solve for numerical answers. It contains questions based on the graphs that appear in the book. These questions ask students to use the graphical models developed in the textbook and to interpret the information presented in the graph. Selected questions are paired with scenarios to reinforce comprehension.

➤ Questions have been designed to correlate with the various questions in the text. *Study Guide Questions* are also available in each chapter. This is a unique set of 25–30 questions per chapter that are parallel to the *Chapter Review Questions* in the printed Study Guide. These questions focus on the key concepts from the text that students should grasp after reading the chapter. These questions reflect the types of questions that the students have likely already worked through in homework assignments or in self-testing. These questions can also be used for testing or for brief in-class quizzes.

Diploma 6 Computerized Test Bank The Krugman/Wells printed Test Banks are also available in CD-ROM format for both Windows and Macintosh users. WebCT and Blackboard-formatted versions of the Test Bank are also available on the CD-ROM. With Diploma, you can easily write and edit questions as well as create and print tests. You can sort questions according to various information fields and scramble questions to create different versions of your tests. You can preview and reformat tests before printing them. Tests can be printed in a wide range of formats. The software's unique synthesis of flexible word-processing and database features creates a program that is extremely intuitive and capable.

Lecture PowerPoint Presentation Created by Can Erbil, Brandeis University, the enhanced PowerPoint presentation slides are designed to assist you with lecture preparation and presentations. The slides are organized by topic and contain graphs, data tables, and bulleted lists of key concepts suitable for lecture presentation. Key figures from the text are replicated and animated to demonstrate how they build. *Notes to the Instructor* are now also included to provide added tips, class exercises, examples, and explanations to enhance classroom presentations. The slides have been designed to allow for easy editing of graphs and text. These slides can be customized to suit your individual needs by adding your own data, questions, and lecture notes. These files may be accessed on the instructor's side of the website or on the Instructor's Resource CD-ROM.

Instructor's Resource CD-ROM Using the Instructor's Resource CD-ROM, you can easily build classroom presentations or enhance your online courses.

This CD-ROM contains all text figures (in JPEG and PPT formats), PowerPoint lecture slides, and detailed solutions to all end-of-chapter problems. You can choose from the various resources, edit, and save for use in your classroom. The Instructor's Resource CD-ROM includes:

➤ **Instructor's Resource Manual** (PDF): containing chapter-by-chapter learning objectives, chapter outlines, teaching tips, examples used in the text, activities, hints for dealing with common student misunderstandings, and web resources.

➤ **Solutions Manual** (PDF): including detailed solutions to all of the end-of-chapter problems from the textbook.

➤ **Lecture PowerPoint Presentations** (PPT): PowerPoint slides including graphs, data tables, and bulleted lists of key concepts suitable for lecture presentation.

➤ **Images from the Textbook** (JPEG): a complete set of textbook images in high-res and low-res JPEG formats.

➤ **Illustration PowerPoint Slides** (PPT): a complete set of figures and tables from the textbook in PPT format.

For Students

Study Guide Prepared by Elizabeth Sawyer-Kelly, University of Wisconsin, Madison, the Study Guide reinforces the topics and key concepts covered in the text. For each chapter, the Study Guide is organized as follows:

➤ *Before You Read the Chapter*

  ➤ Summary: an opening paragraph that provides a brief overview of the chapter.

  ➤ Objectives: a numbered list outlining and describing the material that the student should have learned in the chapter. These objectives can be easily used as a study tool for students.

  ➤ Key Terms: a list of boldface key terms with their definitions—including room for note-taking.

➤ *After You Read the Chapter*

  ➤ Tips: numbered list of learning tips with graphical analysis.

  ➤ Problems and Exercises: a set of 10 to 15 comprehensive problems.

➤ *Before You Take the Test*

  ➤ Chapter Review Questions: a set of 30 multiple-choice questions that focus on the key concepts from the text students should grasp after reading the

chapter. These questions are designed for student exam preparation. A parallel set of these questions is also available to instructors in the Test Bank.

➤ *Answer Key*

  ➤ Answers to Problems and Exercises: detailed solutions to the problems and exercises in the Study Guide.

  ➤ Answers to Chapter Review Questions: solutions to the multiple-choice questions in the Study Guide—along with thorough explanations.

ONLINE OFFERINGS
VERSION 2.0

Companion Website for Students and Instructors
www.worthpublishers.com/krugmanwells
The companion website for the Krugman/Wells text offers valuable tools for both the instructor and students.

For instructors, the site gives you the ability to track students' interaction with the site and gives you access to additional instructor resources.

The following instructor resources are available:

➤ **Quiz Gradebook:** The site gives you the ability to track students' work by accessing an online gradebook. Instructors also have the option to have student results e-mailed directly to them. All student answers to the Self-Test Quizzes are saved in this online database. Student responses and interactions with the Graphing Exercises are also tracked and stored.

➤ **Lecture PowerPoint Presentations:** Instructors have access to helpful lecture material in PowerPoint format. These PowerPoint slides are designed to assist instructors with lecture preparation and presentation.

➤ **Illustration PowerPoint Slides:** A complete set of figures and tables from the textbook in PowerPoint format is available.

➤ **Images from the Textbook:** Instructors have access to a complete set of figures and tables from the textbook in high-res and low-res JPEG formats. The textbook art has been processed for "high-resolution" (150 dpi). These figures and photographs have been especially formatted for maximum readability in large lecture halls and follow standards that were set and tested in a real university auditorium.

➤ **Instructor's Resource Manual:** Instructors have access to the files for the Instructor's Resource Manual.

➤ **Solutions Manual:** Instructors have access to the files for the detailed solutions to the text's end-of-chapter problems.

For students, the site offers many opportunities for self-testing and review.

The following resources are available for students:

> **Self-Test Quizzes:** This quizzing engine provides 20 multiple-choice questions per chapter. Immediate and appropriate feedback is provided to students along with topic references for further review. The questions as well as the answer choices are randomized to give students a different quiz with every refresh of the screen.

> **Key Term Flashcards:** Students can test themselves on the key terms with these pop-up electronic flashcards.

> **Graphing Exercises:** Selected graphs from the textbook have been animated in a Flash format. Working with these animated figures enhances student understanding of the effects of concepts such as the shifts or movements of the curves. Every interactive graph is accompanied by questions that quiz students on key concepts from the textbook and provide instructors with feedback on student progress.

> **Web Links:** Created and continually updated by Jules Kaplan, University of Colorado–Boulder, these Web Links allow students to easily and effectively locate outside resources and readings that relate to topics covered in the textbook. They list web addresses that hotlink to relevant websites; each URL is accompanied by a detailed description of the site and its relevance to each chapter. This allows students to conduct research and explore related readings on specific topics with ease. Also hotlinked are relevant articles by Paul Krugman.

> **Aplia**

Aplia, founded by Paul Romer, Stanford University, is the first web-based company to integrate pedagogical features from a textbook with interactive media. Aplia and Worth Publishers were the first to offer an Integrated Text Solution and all Aplia tools. The features of the Krugman/Wells text have been combined with Aplia's interactive media to save time for professors and encourage students to exert more effort in their learning. The structure adheres to that of the Krugman/Wells text and works consistently within the Aplia framework. The Krugman/Wells Aplia ITS offers a content section, followed up by an application (*Economics in Action*), a Quick Review, and a short quiz (*Check Your Understanding*). With this structure, students are presented bite-sized, easily digestible portions of content and are immediately tested on that material before moving on.

The integrated online version of the Aplia media and the Krugman/Wells text includes:

> Extra problem sets (derived from in-chapter questions in the book) suitable for homework and keyed to specific topics from each chapter

> Regularly updated news analyses

> Real-time online simulations of market interactions

> Interactive tutorials to assist with math and graphing

> Instant online reports that allow instructors to target student trouble areas more efficiently

With Aplia, you retain complete control and flexibility for your course. You choose the content you want students to cover, and you decide how to organize it. You decide whether online activities are practice (ungraded or graded).

For a preview of Aplia materials and to learn more, visit http://www.aplia.com/worth.

WebCT E-pack The Krugman/Wells WebCT E-packs enable you to create a thorough, interactive, and pedagogically sound online course or course website. The Krugman/Wells E-pack provides you with online materials that facilitate critical thinking and learning, including Test Bank material, quizzes, links, and graphing exercises. Best of all, this material is preprogrammed and fully functional in the WebCT environment. Prebuilt materials eliminate hours of course-preparation work and offer significant support as you develop your online course.

Blackboard The Krugman/Wells Blackboard Course Cartridge allows you to combine Blackboard's popular tools and easy-to-use interface with the Krugman/Wells' text-specific resources: Test Bank material, quizzes, links, and graphing exercises. The result is an interactive, comprehensive online course that allows for effortless implementation, management, and use. The Worth electronic files are organized and prebuilt to work within the Blackboard software and can be easily downloaded from the Blackboard content showcases directly onto your department server.

VERSION 3.0—AVAILABLE WITH KRUGMAN/WELLS ECONOMICS FOR FALL 2010 CLASSES

EconPortal

EconPortal is the digital gateway to Krugman/Wells *Economics*, designed to enrich your course, help you organize and better utilize resources, and improve your students' understanding of economics. EconPortal provides a powerful, easy-to-use, completely customizable teaching and learning management system complete with the following:

> **An Interactive eBook with Embedded Learning Resources and Enhanced Assessment:** The eBook's functionality will provide for highlighting, note-taking, graph and example enlargements, a fully searchable glossary, as well as a full text search. You can customize any eBook page with comments, external web links, and supplemental resources. Unlike most eBooks, which are static pages of text, this interactive eBook will bring the book to life with embedded icons that link directly to resources that include *Tutorials, Graphing Exercises,* and *Quizzes.*

  > Student Tutorials will be available in coordination with key topics in the text. The tutorials are meant to provide a detailed, guided tour through a specific concept (such as shift of a curve vs. movement along a curve). They will cover topics that students typically have trouble understanding or concepts that require more class time to fully explain. They'll bring these concepts to life with pictures, animations, and useful worked-out examples. These tutorials would be available to students as a self-guided resource. *Optional* assessment will be tied to each tutorial to assess whether students have grasped the concepts presented. You can choose how to use the tutorials to best meet your students' needs. Assigning these tutorials ensures that valuable class time isn't spent on remediation of topics already covered.

> **A Personalized Study Plan for Students Featuring Diagnostic Quizzing:** A Personalized Study Plan is available to assess students' knowledge of the material and to guide further study. Students will be asked to take the PSP: Self-Check Quiz after they have read the chapter and before they come to the lecture that discusses that chapter. Once they've taken the quiz, they can view their Personalized Study Plan based on the quiz results. This Personalized Study Plan will provide a path to the appropriate eBook materials and resources for further study and exploration.

> **A Fully Integrated Learning Management System:** The EconPortal is meant to be a one-stop shop for all the resources tied to the book. The system will carefully integrate the teaching and learning resources for the book into an easy-to-use system. The Assignment Center organizes preloaded assignments centered on a comprehensive course outline, but it also provides the flexibility for you to add your own assignments.

EconPortal will enable you to create assignments from a variety of question types to prepare self-graded homework, quizzes, or tests. Assignments may be created from the following:

> End-of-Chapter Quiz Questions: The Krugman/Wells end-of-chapter problems will be available in a self-graded format—perfect for quick in-class quizzes or homework assignments. The questions have been carefully edited to ensure that they maintain the integrity of the text's end-of-chapter problems.

> Algorithmic Questions: A question generator will be available that allows the variables of each question to be algorithmically generated—an ideal resource for creating randomized sets of quizzes and for ensuring that students get as much practice as they need.

> Graphing Questions: Pulled from our graphing tool engine, EconPortal can provide electronically gradable graphing-related problems. Students will be asked to draw their response to a question, and the software will grade that response. These graphing exercises are meant to replicate the pencil-and-paper experience of drawing graphs—with the bonus to you of not having to hand-grade each assignment!

> Multipart Assignments: This allows a great degree of flexibility in assigning sections of the eBook, Tutorials, Quizzes, or any resources available within the EconPortal as one complete assignment for your students to complete.

> Test Bank Questions: Assignments can be generated by pulling from the pool of Krugman/Wells Test Bank questions.

The EconPortal's Assignment Center will allow you to select your preferred policies for scheduling, maximum attempts, time limitations, feedback, and more. A wizard will guide you through the creation of assignments. You can assign and track any aspect of your students' EconPortal. The Gradebook will capture your students' results and allow for easily exporting reports.

The ready-to-use course can save you many hours of preparation time. It is fully customizable and highly interactive.

ADDITIONAL OFFERINGS

i>clicker

Developed by a team of University of Illinois physicists, i>clicker is the most flexible and most reliable classroom response system available. It is the only solution created *for* educators, *by* educators, with continuous product improvements made through direct classroom testing and faculty feedback. You'll love i>clicker no matter your level of technical expertise because the focus is on *your* teaching, *not the technology*. To learn more about packaging i>clicker with this textbook, please contact your local sales rep or visit www.iclicker.com.

Wall Street Journal Edition For adopters of the Krugman/Wells text, Worth Publishers and the *Wall Street Journal* are offering a 15-week subscription to students at a tremendous savings. Professors also receive their own free *Wall Street Journal* subscription plus additional instructor supplements created exclusively by the *Wall Street Journal*. Please contact your local sales rep for more information or go to the *Wall Street Journal* online at www.wsj.com.

Financial Times Edition For adopters of the Krugman/Wells text, Worth Publishers and the *Financial Times* are offering a 15-week subscription to students at a tremendous savings. Professors also receive their own free *Financial Times* subscription for one year. Students and professors may access research and archived information at www.ft.com.

Dismal Scientist A high-powered business database and analysis service comes to the classroom! Dismal Scientist offers real-time monitoring of the global economy, produced locally by economists and professionals at Economy.com's London, Sydney, and West Chester offices. Dismal Scientist is *free* when packaged with the Krugman/Wells text. Please contact your local sales rep for more information or go to www.economy.com.

The Economist Subscription *The Economist* has partnered with Worth Publishers to create an exclusive offer we believe will enhance the classroom experience. Students get 15 issues of *The Economist* for just $15. That's an 85% savings off the cover price. Faculty receive a complimentary 15-week subscription when 10 or more students purchase a subscription.

Inside and outside the classroom, *The Economist* provides a global perspective that helps students keep abreast of what's going on in the world and gives insight into how the world views the United States. *The Economist* ignites dialogue, encourages debate, and enables readers to form well-reasoned opinions—all while providing a deep understanding of key political, social, and business issues. Supplement your textbook with the knowledge and insight that only *The Economist* can provide.

Each subscription include the following:

- Special Reports: Approximately 20 times a year, *The Economist* publishes a Special Report providing in-depth analysis that highlights a specific country, industry, or hot-button issue.

- Technology Quarterly Supplements: Published four times a year, these supplements analyze new technology that could potentially transform lives, business models, industries, governments, and financial markets.

- Economist.com: Receive free and unlimited access with your print subscription. Included on the website are the following:

  - Searchable Archive: offers subscribers full access to 28,000+ articles.

  - Exclusive Online Research Tools: including articles by Subject, Back grounders, Surveys, Economics A–Z, Style Guide, Weekly Indicators, and Currency Converter.

  - The Full Audio Edition: offers the entire magazine for download or subscribers can choose favorite sections for download.

  - *The Economist* Debate Series: brings the essence of Oxford-style debate into an interactive online forum. Your participation shapes the contest and your votes decide the winner. As a subscriber you can sign up for moderator alerts for upcoming debates.

  - Today's Views: includes daily columns and an economics debate.

  - Daily Columns: feature articles that are exclusively available online, covering views on business, the market, personal technology, the arts, and much more.

  - Correspondent's Diary: covers an *Economist* writer's experiences and opinions from a different country each week.

  - Blogs on economics and U.S. and European politics.

To get 15 issues of *The Economist* for only $15, go to: www.economistacademic.com/worth.

Acknowledgments

We are indebted to the following reviewers, focus group participants, and other consultants for their suggestions and advice on the first edition:

Ashley Abramson, *Barstow College;* Lee Adkins, *Oklahoma State University;* Terry Alexander, *Iowa State University;* Elena Alvarez, *State University of New York, Albany;* David A. Anderson, *Centre College;* Charles Antholt, *Western Washington University;* Richard Ball, *Haverford University;* Sheryl Ball, *Virginia Polytechnic Institute and State University;* Charles L. Ballard, *Michigan State University;* Richard Barrett, *University of Montana;*

Daniel Barszcz, *College of DuPage;* Leon Battista, *Bronx Community College;* Richard Beil, *Auburn University;* Charles A. Bennett, *Gannon University;* Andreas Bentz, *Dartmouth College;* Harmanna Bloemen, *Houston Community College;* Edward Blomdahl, *Bridgewater State College;* John Bockino, *Suffolk County Community College;* Michael Bordo, *Rutgers University, NBER;* Ellen Bowen, *Fisher College, New Bedford;* Michael Brace, *Jamestown Community College;* James Bradley, Jr., *University of South Carolina;* William Branch, *University of Oregon;* Michael Brandl, *University of Texas, Austin;* Anne Bresnock, *University of California, Los Angeles;* Kathleen Bromley, *Monroe Community College;* Bruce Brown, *California State Polytechnic University, Pomona;* John Buck, *Jacksonville University;* Raymonda Burgman, *University of Southern Florida;* Charles Callahan, III, *State University of New York, College at Brockport;* William Carlisle, *University of Utah;* Kevin Carlson, *University of Massachusetts, Boston;* Leonard A. Carlson, *Emory University;* Fred Carstensen, *University of Connecticut;* Shirley Cassing, *University of Pittsburgh;* Ramon Castillo-Ponce, *California State University, Los Angeles;* Emily Chamlee-Wright, *Beloit College;* Anthony Chan, *Santa Monica College;* Yuna Chen, *South Georgia College;* Maryanne Clifford, *Eastern Connecticut State University;* Jim Cobbe, *Florida State University;* Gregory Colman, *Pace University;* Barbara Connolly, *Westchester Community College;* Tom Cooper, *Georgetown College;* Eleanor D. Craig, *University of Delaware;* James Craven, *Clark College;* Tom Creahan, *Morehead State University;* Sarah Culver, *University of Alabama;* Will Cummings, *Grossmont College;* Rosemary Thomas Cunningham, *Agnes Scott College;* James Cypher, *California State University, Fresno;* Susan Dadres, *Southern Methodist University;* Ardeshir Dalal, *Northern Illinois University;* Rosa Lea Danielson, *College of DuPage;* Stephen Davis, *University of Minnesota, Crookston;* A. Edward Day, *University of Texas, Dallas;* Stephen J. DeCanio, *University of California, Santa Barbara;* Tom DelGiudice, *Hofstra University;* J. Bradford DeLong, *University of California, Berkeley;* Arna Desser, *United States Naval Academy;* Asif Dowla, *St. Mary's College of Maryland;* James Dulgeroff, *San Bernardino Valley Community College;* Tom Duston, *Keene State College;* Debra Dwyer, *State University of New York, Stony Brook;* Dorsey Dyer, *Davidson County Community College;* Jim Eden, *Portland Community College;* Mary Edwards, *St. Cloud State University;* Fritz Efaw, *University of Tennessee at Chattanooga;* Herb Elliot, *Alan Hancock College;* Michael Ellis, *New Mexico State University;* Can Erbil, *Brandeis University;* Joe Essuman, *University of Wisconsin, Waukesha;* David W. Findlay, *Colby College;* Chuck Fischer, *Pittsburgh State University;* Eric Fisher, *The Ohio State University;* David Flath, *North Carolina State University;* Oliver Franke, *Athabasca University;* Rhona Free, *Eastern Connecticut State University;* Yee Tien Fu,

Stanford University; Susan Gale, *New York University;* Yoram Gelman, *Lehman College, The City University of New York;* E. B. Gendel, *Woodbury College;* Doug Gentry, *St. Mary's College;* Sarah Ghosh, *University of Scranton;* J. Robert Gillette, *University of Kentucky;* Lynn G. Gillette, *University of Kentucky;* James N. Giordano, *Villanova University;* Robert Godby, *University of Wyoming;* David Goodwin, *University of New Brunswick;* Richard Gosselin, *Houston Community College, Central Campus;* Patricia Graham, *University of Northern Colorado;* Kathleen Greer Rossman, *Birmingham Southern College;* Lisa Grobar, *California State University, Long Beach;* Philip Grossman, *St. Cloud State University;* Wayne Grove, *Syracuse University;* Eleanor Gubins, *Rosemont College;* Jang-Ting Guo, *University of California, Riverside;* Alan Haight, *State University of New York, Cortland;* Jonathan Hamilton, *University of Florida;* Gautam Hazarika, *University of Texas, Brownsville;* Tom Head, *George Fox University;* Julie Heath, *University of Memphis;* Susan Helper, *Case Western Reserve University;* Jill M. Hendrickson, *University of the South;* Gus Herring, *Brookhaven College;* Paul Hettler, *Duquesne University;* Roger Hewett, *Drake University;* Hart Hodges, *Western Washington University;* Jill Holman, *University of Wisconsin, Milwaukee;* David Horlacher, *Middlebury College;* Robert Horn, *James Madison University;* Scott Houser, *California State University, Fresno;* Yu Hsing, *Southeastern Louisiana University;* Ray Hubbard, *Central Georgia Technical College;* Patrik T. Hultberg, *University of Wyoming;* Murat Iyigun, *University of Colorado;* Habib Jam, *Rowan University;* Nancy Jianakoplos, *Colorado State University;* Bruce Johnson, *Centre College;* Donn Johnson, *Quinnipiac University;* Louis Johnston, *College of St. Benedict/St. John's University;* James Jozefowicz, *Indiana University of Pennsylvania;* Jack Julian, *Indiana University of Pennsylvania;* Elia Kacapyr, *Ithaca College;* Soheila Kahkashan, *Towson University;* Matthew Kahn, *Columbia University;* Charles Kaplan, *St. Joseph's College;* Bentzil Kasper, *Broome Community College;* Barry Keating, *University of Notre Dame;* Diane Keenan, *Cerritos College;* Bill Kerby, *California State University, Sacramento;* Farida Khan, *University of Wisconsin, Parkside;* Kyoo Kim, *Bowling Green University;* Philip King, *San Francisco State University;* Sharmila King, *University of the Pacific;* Kent Klitgaard, *Wells College;* Sinan Koont, *Dickinson College;* Kala Krishna, *Penn State University, NBER;* Kenneth Kriz, *University of Nebraska, Omaha;* Margaret Landman, *Bridgewater State College;* Tom Larson, *California State University, Los Angeles;* Susan K. Laury, *Georgia State University;* Bill Lee, *St. Mary's College;* Jim Lee, *Texas A&M University, Corpus Christi;* Tony Lima, *California State University, Hayward;* Delores Linton, *Tarrant County College, Northwest;* Rolf Lokke, *Albuquerque Academy;* Ellen Magenheim, *Swarthmore College;* Diana McCoy, *Truckee Meadows Community College;* Rachel McCulloch,

Brandeis University; Diego Mendez-Carbajo, *Illinois Wesleyan University;* Juan Mendoza, *State University of New York, Buffalo;* Jeffrey Michael, *Towson University;* Garrett Milam, *Ryerson University;* Robert Miller, *Fisher College, New Bedford Campus;* Michael Milligan, *Front Range Community College;* Cathy Miners, *Fairfield University;* Larry Miners, *Fairfield University;* Jenny Minier, *University of Miami;* Ida A. Mirzaie, *John Carroll University;* Kristen Monaco, *California State University, Long Beach;* Marie Mora, *University of Texas, Pan American;* Peter B. Morgan, *University of Michigan;* W. Douglas Morgan, *University of California, Santa Barbara;* James Mueller, *Alma College;* Ranganath Murthy, *Bucknell University;* Nelson Nagai, *San Joaquin Delta College;* Gerardo Nebbia, *Glendale College;* Anthony Negbenebor, *Gardner-Webb University;* John A. Neri, *University of Maryland;* Joseph Nowakowski, *Muskingum College;* Seamus O'Cleireacain, *Columbia University/State University of New York, Purchase;* William O'Dea, *State University of New York, Oneonta;* Charles Okeke, *Community College of Southern Nevada;* Martha Olney, *University of California, Berkeley;* Douglas Orr, *Eastern Washington University;* Kimberley Ott, *Kent State University, Salem Campus;* Philip Packard, *St. Mary's College;* Chris Papageorgiou, *Louisiana State University;* Jamie Pelley, *Mary Baldwin College;* Mary K. Perkins, *Howard University;* Brian Peterson, *Central College;* John Pharr, *Dallas County Community College;* Raymond E. Polchow, *Zane State College;* Ernest Poole, *Fashion Institute of Technology;* Kevin Quinn, *Bowling Green State University;* Jeffrey Racine, *University of South Florida;* Matthew Rafferty, *Quinnipiac University;* Reza Ramazani, *St. Michael's College;* Dixie Watts Reaves, *Virginia Polytechnic Institute and State University;* Charles Reichheld, *Cuyahoga Community College;* Siobhán Reilly, *Mills College;* Thomas Rhoads, *Towson University;* Libby Rittenberg, *Colorado College;* Malcolm Robinson, *Thomas More College;* Charles Rock, *Rollins College;* Michael Rolleigh, *Williams College;* Richard Romano, *Broome Community College;* Christina Romer, *University of California, Berkeley;* Jeff Romine, *University of Colorado, Denver;* Bernie Rose, *Rocky Mountain College;* Patricia Rottschaefer, *California State University, Fullerton;* Dan Rubenson, *Southern Oregon University;* Jeff Rubin, *Rutgers University;* Lynda Rush, *California State Polytechnic University, Pomona;* Henry D. Ryder, *Gloucester County College;* Martin Sabo, *Community College of Denver;* Sara Saderion, *Houston Community College, Southwest;* Allen Sanderson, *University of Chicago;* Rolando Santos, *Lakeland Community College;* Christine Sauer, *University of New Mexico;* George Sawdy, *Providence College;* Elizabeth Sawyer-Kelly, *University of Wisconsin, Madison;* Edward Sayre, *Agnes Scott College;* Richard Schatz, *Whitworth College;* Ted Scheinman, *Mt. Hood Community College;* Robert Schwab, *University of Maryland;* Stanley Sedo, *University of Maryland;* Kathleen Segerson, *University of Connecticut;* Russell Settle, *University of Delaware;* Anna Shostya, *Pace University;* Eugene Silberberg, *University of Washington;* Millicent Sites, *Carson-Newman College;* Bill Smith, *University of Memphis;* Herrick Smith, *Nease High School;* Marcia S. Snyder, *College of Charleston;* John Solow, *University of Iowa;* John Somers, *Portland Community College;* Jim Spellicy, *Lowell High School;* David E. Spencer, *Brigham Young University;* Denise Stanley, *California State University, Fullerton;* Martha A. Starr, *American University;* Richard Startz, *University of Washington;* Kurt Stephenson, *Virginia Tech;* Jill Stowe, *Texas A&M University, Austin;* Charles Stull, *Kalamazoo College;* Laddie Sula, *Loras College;* Rodney Swanson, *University of California, Los Angeles;* David Switzer, *University of Northern Michigan;* Jason Taylor, *University of Virginia;* Mark Thoma, *University of California, San Diego;* J. Ross Thomas, *Albuquerque Technical Vocational Institute;* Deborah Thorsen, *Palm Beach Community College;* Andrew Toole, *Cook College/Rutgers University;* Karen Travis, *Pacific Lutheran University;* Brian Trinque, *University of Texas, Austin;* Arienne Turner, *Fullerton College;* Anthony Uremovic, *Joliet Junior College;* Abu Wahid, *Tennessee State University;* Jane Wallace, *University of Pittsburgh;* Tom Watkins, *Eastern Kentucky University;* Stephan Weiler, *Colorado State University;* Maurice Weinrobe, *Clark University;* Robert Whaples, *Wake Forest University;* Jonathan B. Wight, *University of Richmond;* Mark Wohar, *University of Nebraska, Omaha;* Larry Wolfenbarger, *Macon State College;* Gary Wolfram, *Hillsdale College;* William C. Wood, *James Madison University;* James Woods, *Portland State University;* Mickey Wu, *Coe College;* Ranita Wyatt, *Dallas Community College;* Cemile Yavas, *Pennsylvania State University;* Lou Zaera, *Fashion Institute of Technology;* Paul Zak, *Claremont Graduate University;* and Andrea Zanter, *Hillsborough Community College, Dale Mabry Campus.*

Our deep appreciation and heartfelt thanks to the following reviewers, class-testers, survey participants, and other contributors whose input helped us shape this second edition.

Carlos Aguilar, *El Paso Community College*

Terence Alexander, *Iowa State University*

Morris Altman, *University of Saskatchewan*

Farhad Ameen, *State University of New York, Westchester Community College*

Christopher P. Ball, *Quinnipiac University*

Sue Bartlett, *University of South Florida*

Scott Beaulier, *Mercer University*

David Bernotas, *University of Georgia*

Marc Bilodeau, *Indiana University and Purdue University, Indianapolis*

Kelly Blanchard, *Purdue University*

Anne Bresnock, *California State Polytechnic University*

Douglas M. Brown, *Georgetown University*

Joseph Calhoun, *Florida State University*

Douglas Campbell, *University of Memphis*

Kevin Carlson, *University of Massachusetts, Boston*

Andrew J. Cassey, *Washington State University*

Shirley Cassing, *University of Pittsburgh*

Sewin Chan, *New York University*

Mitchell M. Charkiewicz, *Central Connecticut State University*

Joni S. Charles, *Texas State University, San Marcos*

Adhip Chaudhuri, *Georgetown University*

Eric P. Chiang, *Florida Atlantic University*

Hayley H. Chouinard, *Washington State University*

Kenny Christianson, *Binghamton University*

Lisa Citron, *Cascadia Community College*

Steven L. Cobb, *University of North Texas*

Barbara Z. Connolly, *Westchester Community College*

Stephen Conroy, *University of San Diego*

Thomas E. Cooper, *Georgetown University*

Cesar Corredor, *Texas A&M University and University of Texas, Tyler*

Jim F. Couch, *University of Northern Alabama*

Daniel Daly, *Regis University*

H. Evren Damar, *Pacific Lutheran University*

Antony Davies, *Duquesne University*

Greg Delemeester, *Marietta College*

Patrick Dolenc, *Keene State College*

Christine Doyle-Burke, *Framingham State College*

Ding Du, *South Dakota State University*

Jerry Dunn, *Southwestern Oklahoma State University*

Robert R. Dunn, *Washington and Jefferson College*

Ann Eike, *University of Kentucky*

Tisha L. N. Emerson, *Baylor University*

Hadi Salehi Esfahani, *University of Illinois*

William Feipel, *Illinois Central College*

Rudy Fichtenbaum, *Wright State University*

David W. Findlay, *Colby College*

Mary Flannery, *University of California, Santa Cruz*

Robert Francis, *Shoreline Community College*

Shelby Frost, *Georgia State University*

Frank Gallant, *George Fox University*

Robert Gazzale, *Williams College*

Robert Godby, *University of Wyoming*

Michael Goode, *Central Piedmont Community College*

Douglas E. Goodman, *University of Puget Sound*

Marvin Gordon, *University of Illinois at Chicago*

Kathryn Graddy, *Brandeis University*

Alan Day Haight, *State University of New York, Cortland*

Mehdi Haririan, *Bloomsburg University*

Clyde A. Haulman, *College of William and Mary*

Richard R. Hawkins, *University of West Florida*

Mickey A. Hepner, *University of Central Oklahoma*

Michael Hilmer, *San Diego State University*

Tia Hilmer, *San Diego State University*

Jane Himarios, *University of Texas, Arlington*

Jim Holcomb, *University of Texas, El Paso*

Don Holley, *Boise State University*

Alexander Holmes, *University of Oklahoma*

Julie Holzner, *Los Angeles City College*

Robert N. Horn, *James Madison University*

Steven Husted, *University of Pittsburgh*

John O. Ifediora, *University of Wisconsin, Platteville*

Hiro Ito, *Portland State University*

Mike Javanmard, *Rio Hondo Community College*

Robert T. Jerome, *James Madison University*

Shirley Johnson-Lans, *Vassar College*

David Kalist, *Shippensburg University*

Lillian Kamal, *Northwestern University*

Roger T. Kaufman, *Smith College*

Herb Kessel, *St. Michael's College*

Rehim Kılıç, *Georgia Institute of Technology*

Grace Kim, *University of Michigan, Dearborn*

Michael Kimmitt, *University of Hawaii, Manoa*

Robert Kling, *Colorado State University*

Sherrie Kossoudji, *University of Michigan*

Charles Kroncke, *College of Mount Saint Joseph*

Reuben Kyle, *Middle Tennessee State University (retired)*

Katherine Lande-Schmeiser, *University of Minnesota, Twin Cities*

David Lehr, *Longwood College*

Mary Jane Lenon, *Providence College*

Mary H. Lesser, *Iona College*

Solina Lindahl, *California Polytechnic State University, San Luis Obispo*

Haiyong Liu, *East Carolina University*

Jane S. Lopus, *California State University, East Bay*

María José Luengo-Prado, *Northeastern University*

Rotua Lumbantobing, *North Carolina State University*

Ed Lyell, *Adams State College*

John Marangos, *Colorado State University*

Ralph D. May, *Southwestern Oklahoma State University*

Wayne McCaffery, *University of Wisconsin, Madison*

Larry McRae, *Appalachian State University*

Mary Ruth J. McRae, *Appalachian State University*

Ellen E. Meade, *American University*

Meghan Millea, *Mississippi State University*

Norman C. Miller, *Miami University (of Ohio)*

Khan A. Mohabbat, *Northern Illinois University*

Myra L. Moore, *University of Georgia*

Jay Morris, *Champlain College in Burlington*

Akira Motomura, *Stonehill College*

Kevin J. Murphy, *Oakland University*

Robert Murphy, *Boston College*

Ranganath Murthy, *Bucknell University*

Anthony Myatt, *University of New Brunswick, Canada*

Randy A. Nelson, *Colby College*

Charles Newton, *Houston Community College*

Daniel X. Nguyen, *Purdue University*

Dmitri Nizovtsev, *Washburn University*

Thomas A. Odegaard, *Baylor University*

Constantin Ogloblin, *Georgia Southern University*

Charles C. Okeke, *College of Southern Nevada*

Terry Olson, *Truman State University*

Una Okonkwo Osili, *Indiana University and Purdue University, Indianapolis*

Maxwell Oteng, *University of California, Davis*

P. Marcelo Oviedo, *Iowa State University*

Jeff Owen, *Gustavus Adolphus College*

James Palmieri, *Simpson College*

Walter G. Park, *American University*

Elliott Parker, *University of Nevada, Reno*

Michael Perelman, *California State University, Chico*

Nathan Perry, *Utah State University*

Dean Peterson, *Seattle University*

Ken Peterson, *Furman University*

Paul Pieper, *University of Illinois at Chicago*

Dennis L. Placone, *Clemson University*

Michael Polcen, *Northern Virginia Community College*

Raymond A. Polchow, *Zane State College*

Linnea Polgreen, *University of Iowa*

Michael A. Quinn, *Bentley University*

Eileen Rabach, *Santa Monica College*

Matthew Rafferty, *Quinnipiac University*

Jaishankar Raman, *Valparaiso University*

Margaret Ray, *Mary Washington College*

Helen Roberts, *University of Illinois, Chicago*

Jeffrey Rubin, *Rutgers University, New Brunswick*

Rose M. Rubin, *University of Memphis*

Lynda Rush, *California State Polytechnic University, Pomona*

Michael Ryan, *Western Michigan University*

Sara Saderion, *Houston Community College*

Djavad Salehi-Isfahani, *Virginia Tech*

Elizabeth Sawyer-Kelly, *University of Wisconsin, Madison*

Jesse A. Schwartz, *Kennesaw State University*

Chad Settle, *University of Tulsa*

Steve Shapiro, *University of North Florida*

Robert L. Shoffner III, *Central Piedmont Community College*

Joseph Sicilian, *University of Kansas*

Judy Smrha, *Baker University*

John Solow, *University of Iowa*

John Somers, *Portland Community College*

Stephen Stageberg, *University of Mary Washington*

Monty Stanford, *DeVry University*

Rebecca Stein, *University of Pennsylvania*

William K. Tabb, *Queens College, City University of New York (retired)*

Sarinda Taengnoi, *University of Wisconsin, Oshkosh*

Henry Terrell, *University of Maryland*

Rebecca Achée Thornton, *University of Houston*

Michael Toma, *Armstrong Atlantic State University*

Brian Trinque, *University of Texas, Austin*

Boone A. Turchi, *University of North Carolina, Chapel Hill*

Nora Underwood, *University of Central Florida*

J. S. Uppal, *State University of New York, Albany*

John Vahaly, *University of Louisville*

Jose J. Vazquez-Cognet, *University of Illinois at Urbana-Champaign*

Daniel Vazzana, *Georgetown College*

Roger H. von Haefen, *North Carolina State University*

Andreas Waldkirch, *Colby College*

Christopher Waller, *University of Notre Dame*

Gregory Wassall, *Northeastern University*

Robert Whaples, *Wake Forest University*

Thomas White, *Assumption College*

Jennifer P. Wissink, *Cornell University*

Mark Witte, *Northwestern University*

Kristen M. Wolfe, *St. Johns River Community College*

Larry Wolfenbarger, *Macon State College*

Louise B. Wolitz, *University of Texas, Austin*

Gavin Wright, *Stanford University*

Bill Yang, *Georgia Southern University*

Jason Zimmerman, *South Dakota State University*

We must also thank the many people at Worth Publishers for their contributions and the talented team of consultants and contributors they assembled to work with us. As in the first edition, Andreas Bentz did yeoman's work, granting us the ability to focus on larger issues because we could trust him to focus on the details. More than ever we count ourselves fortunate to have found Andreas. Development editor Marilyn Freedman's sharp eye and commonsense appraisals were critical inputs in this significant revision, helping us to sort out the pedagogical issues as before. Many thanks to Kathryn Graddy, Brandeis University, for her invaluable contributions to this revision. Katy also brought us Charles Brendon, who assisted us with extremely quick and thorough data research, as well as Nikhil Agarwal and Chanont Banternghansa, who helped with the important work of devising problem sets. Special thanks go to Eric P. Chiang, Florida Atlantic University, Myra L. Moore, University of Georgia, and Kathryn Graddy for the sharp eye and astonishing attention to detail that they brought to their ongoing role as reviewers of page proof. Special thanks, too, to David W. Findlay, Colby College, for his close review of pages in both editions. And, for their insightful reading of chapters in page proof, many thanks to Carlos Aguilar, El Paso Community College; Chanont Banternghansa; Kevin Carlson, University of Massachusetts, Boston; Hiro Ito, Portland State University; Robert Murphy, Boston College; Helen Roberts, University of Illinois, Chicago; Nora Underwood, University of Central

Florida; and, of course, Jose J. Vazquez-Cognet, University of Illinois at Urbana-Champaign.

Craig Bleyer, publisher at Worth, has brought so much to both editions of this book. His sales savvy and incredibly thorough understanding of the textbook market helped to make the first edition a huge success. Most recently, we've relied on Craig's keen instincts in developing our revision strategy for the second edition. Elizabeth Widdicombe, president of Freeman and Worth, and Catherine Woods, publisher at Worth, played important roles in planning for this revision. We have Liz to thank for the idea that became our Global Comparison box. And special thanks to Paul Shensa, who, many moons ago, suggested that we write this book; most recently, we've been thrilled to have Paul's wisdom and expertise on hand to help with market research and planning for the revision.

Once again, we have had an incredible production and design team on this book, people whose hard work, creativity, dedication, and patience continue to amaze us. Thank you all: Tracey Kuehn and Anthony Calcara for producing this book; Babs Reingold and Lyndall Culbertson for the beautiful interior design and the absolutely spectacular cover; Lee McKevitt, who lays out pages like no other; Karen Osborne, for her thoughtful copyedit; Barbara Seixas, who worked her magic once again on the manufacturing end and despite the vagaries of the project schedule; Cecilia Varas, Donna Ranieri, Elyse Rieder, Julie Tesser, and Ted Szczepanski for photo research; Stacey Alexander, Laura McGinn, and Jenny Chiu for coordinating the production on all supplemental materials; and Tom Acox, assistant editor extraordinaire. It is a thrill to behold a book that one has written; but it's a particularly special thrill to behold a book so beautifully published.

Many thanks to Sarah Dorger and Marie McHale for devising and coordinating the impressive collection of media and supplements that accompany our book. Thanks to the incredible team of supplements writers and coordinators who worked with them on the supplements and media package. And we would be remiss if we didn't also thank Sarah for her helpful editorial suggestions and market insights during the revision process.

Thanks to Scott Guile, marketing manager, for his tireless advocacy of this book; to Steve Rigolosi, director of market development, for his many contributions; to Bruce Kaplan for his support of the sales effort on both editions; and to Tom Kling for his critical role in launching this book in the sales department.

And most of all, special thanks to Sharon Balbos, executive development editor on this edition as well as the first edition. Much of the success of this book is owed to Sharon's dedication and professionalism. As always, she kept her cool through some rough spots. Sharon, we're not sure we deserved an editor as good as you, but we're sure that everyone involved, as well as our adopters and readers, have been made better off by your presence.

Paul Krugman

Robin Wells

ECONOMICS

Introduction: The Ordinary Business of Life

ANY GIVEN SUNDAY

I T'S SUNDAY AFTERNOON IN THE SPRING OF 2008, and Route 1 in central New Jersey is a busy place. Thousands of people crowd the shopping malls that line the road for 20 miles, all the way from Trenton to New Brunswick. Most of the shoppers are cheerful—and why not? The stores in those malls offer an extraordinary range of choice; you can buy everything from sophisticated electronic equipment to fashionable

The scene along Route 1 on this spring day is, of course, perfectly ordinary—very much like the scene along hundreds of other stretches of road, all across America, that same afternoon. And the discipline of economics is mainly concerned with ordinary things. As the great nineteenth-century economist Alfred Marshall put it, economics is "a study of mankind in the ordinary business of life."

Delivering the goods: the market economy in action

Robert Landau/Corbis

clothes to organic carrots. There are probably 100,000 distinct items available along that stretch of road. And most of these items are not luxury goods that only the rich can afford; they are products that millions of Americans can and do purchase every day.

What can economics say about this "ordinary business"? Quite a lot, it turns out. What we'll see in this book is that even familiar scenes of economic life pose some very important questions—questions that economics can help answer. Among these questions are:

- How does our economic system work? That is, how does it manage to deliver the goods?

- When and why does our economic system go astray, leading people into counterproductive behavior?

- Why are there ups and downs in the economy? That is, why does the economy sometimes have a "bad year"?

- Finally, why is the long run mainly a story of ups rather than downs? That is, why has America, along with other advanced nations, become so much richer over time?

Let's take a look at these questions and offer a brief preview of what you will learn in this book.

The Invisible Hand

That ordinary scene in central New Jersey would not have looked at all ordinary to an American from colonial times—say, one of the patriots who helped George Washington win the Battle of Trenton in 1776. At the time, Trenton was a small village, and farms lined the route of Washington's epic night march from Trenton to Princeton—a march that took him right past the future site of the giant Quakerbridge shopping mall.

Imagine that you could transport an American from the colonial period forward in time to our own era. (Isn't that the plot of a movie? Several, actually.) What would this time-traveler find amazing?

Surely the most amazing thing would be the sheer prosperity of modern America—the range of goods and services that ordinary families can afford. Looking at all that wealth, our transplanted colonial would wonder, "How can I get some of that?" Or perhaps he would ask himself, "How can my society get some of that?"

The answer is that to get this kind of prosperity, you need a well-functioning system for coordinating productive activities—the activities that create the goods and services people want and get them to the people who want them. That kind of system is what we mean when we talk about the **economy.** And **economics** is the social science that studies the production, distribution, and consumption of goods and services.

An economy succeeds to the extent that it, literally, delivers the goods. A time-traveler from the eighteenth century—or even from 1950—would be amazed at how many goods and services the modern American economy delivers and at how many people can afford them. Compared with any past economy and with all but a few other countries today, America has an incredibly high standard of living.

So our economy must be doing something right, and the time-traveler might want to compliment the person in charge. But guess what? There isn't anyone in charge. The United States has a **market economy,** in which production and consumption are the result of decentralized decisions by many firms and individuals. There is no central authority telling people what to produce or where to ship it. Each individual producer makes what he or she thinks will be most profitable; each consumer buys what he or she chooses.

The alternative to a market economy is a *command economy,* in which there *is* a central authority making decisions about production and consumption. Command economies have been tried, most notably in the Soviet Union between 1917 and 1991. But they didn't work very well. Producers in the Soviet Union routinely found themselves unable to produce because they did not have crucial raw materials, or they succeeded in producing but then found that nobody wanted their products. Consumers were often unable to find necessary items—command economies are famous for long lines at shops.

Market economies, however, are able to coordinate even highly complex activities and to reliably provide consumers with the goods and services they want. Indeed, people quite casually trust their lives to the market system: residents of any major city would starve in days if the unplanned yet somehow orderly actions of thousands of businesses did not deliver a steady supply of food. Surprisingly, the unplanned "chaos" of a market economy turns out to be far more orderly than the "planning" of a command economy.

In 1776, in a famous passage in his book *The Wealth of Nations,* the pioneering Scottish economist Adam Smith wrote about how individuals, in pursuing their own

An **economy** is a system for coordinating society's productive activities.

Economics is the social science that studies the production, distribution, and consumption of goods and services.

A **market economy** is an economy in which decisions about production and consumption are made by individual producers and consumers.

interests, often end up serving the interests of society as a whole. Of a businessman whose pursuit of profit makes the nation wealthier, Smith wrote: "[H]e intends only his own gain, and he is in this, as in many other cases, led by an invisible hand to promote an end which was no part of his intention." Ever since, economists have used the term **invisible hand** to refer to the way a market economy manages to harness the power of self-interest for the good of society.

The study of how individuals make decisions and how these decisions interact is called **microeconomics.** One of the key themes in microeconomics is the validity of Adam Smith's insight: individuals pursuing their own interests often do promote the interests of society as a whole.

So part of the answer to our time-traveler's question—"How can my society achieve the kind of prosperity you take for granted?"—is that his society should learn to appreciate the virtues of a market economy and the power of the invisible hand.

But the invisible hand isn't always our friend. It's also important to understand when and why the individual pursuit of self-interest can lead to counterproductive behavior.

ECONOMICS THROUGH THE AGES

My Benefit, Your Cost

One thing that our time-traveler would not admire about modern Route 1 is the traffic. In fact, although most things have gotten better in America over time, traffic congestion has gotten a lot worse.

When traffic is congested, each driver is imposing a cost on all the other drivers on the road—he is literally getting in their way (and they are getting in his way). This cost can be substantial: in major metropolitan areas, each time someone drives to work, instead of taking public transportation or working at home, he can easily impose $15 or more in hidden costs on other drivers. Yet when deciding whether or not to drive, commuters have no incentive to take the costs they impose on others into account.

Traffic congestion is a familiar example of a much broader problem: sometimes the individual pursuit of one's own interest, instead of promoting the interests of society as a whole, can actually make society worse off. When this happens, it is known as **market failure.** Other important examples of market failure involve air and water pollution as well as the overexploitation of natural resources such as fish and forests.

The good news, as you will learn as you use this book to study microeconomics, is that economic analysis can be used to diagnose cases of market failure. And often, economic analysis can also be used to devise solutions for the problem.

The **invisible hand** refers to the way in which the individual pursuit of self-interest can lead to good results for society as a whole.

Microeconomics is the branch of economics that studies how people make decisions and how these decisions interact.

When the individual pursuit of self-interest leads to bad results for society as a whole, there is **market failure.**

Good Times, Bad Times

Route 1 was bustling on that day in 2008. But if you'd visited the malls in 2002, the scene wouldn't have been quite as cheerful. That's because New Jersey's economy, along with that of the United States as a whole, was somewhat depressed in 2002: in early 2001, businesses began laying off workers in large numbers, and employment didn't start bouncing back until the summer of 2003.

A **recession** is a downturn in the economy.

Macroeconomics is the branch of economics that is concerned with overall ups and downs in the economy.

Economic growth is the growing ability of the economy to produce goods and services.

Such troubled periods are a regular feature of modern economies. The fact is that the economy does not always run smoothly: it experiences *fluctuations,* a series of ups and downs. By middle age, a typical American will have experienced three or four downs, known as **recessions.** (The U.S. economy experienced serious recessions beginning in 1973, 1981, 1990, and 2001.) During a severe recession, millions of workers may be laid off.

Like market failure, recessions are a fact of life; but also like market failure, they are a problem for which economic analysis offers some solutions. Recessions are one of the main concerns of the branch of economics known as **macroeconomics,** which is concerned with the overall ups and downs of the economy. If you study macroeconomics, you will learn how economists explain recessions and how government policies can be used to minimize the damage from economic fluctuations.

Despite the occasional recession, however, over the long run the story of the U.S. economy contains many more ups than downs. And that long-run ascent is the subject of our final question.

Onward and Upward

At the beginning of the twentieth century, most Americans lived under conditions that we would now think of as extreme poverty. Only 10 percent of homes had flush toilets, only 8 percent had central heating, only 2 percent had electricity, and almost nobody had a car, let alone a washing machine or air conditioning.

Such comparisons are a stark reminder of how much our lives have been changed by **economic growth,** the growing ability of the economy to produce goods and services.

Why does the economy grow over time? And why does economic growth occur faster in some times and places than in others? These are key questions for economics because economic growth is a good thing, as those shoppers on Route 1 can attest, and most of us want more of it.

An Engine for Discovery

We hope we have convinced you that the "ordinary business of life" is really quite extraordinary, if you stop to think about it, and that it can lead us to ask some very interesting and important questions.

In this book, we will describe the answers economists have given to these questions. But this book, like economics as a whole, isn't a list of answers: it's an introduction to a discipline, a way to address questions like those we have just asked. Or as Alfred Marshall, who described economics as a study of the "ordinary business of life," put it: "Economics . . . is not a body of concrete truth, but an engine for the discovery of concrete truth."

So let's turn the key and start the ignition.

www.worthpublishers.com/krugmanwells

>> First Principles

COMMON GROUND

THE ANNUAL MEETING OF THE AMERICAN Economic Association draws thousands of economists, young and old, famous and obscure. There are booksellers, business meetings, and quite a few job interviews. But mainly the economists gather to talk and listen. During the busiest times, 60 or more presentations may be taking place simultaneously, on questions that range from the future of the stock market to who does the cooking in two-earner families.

What do these people have in common? An expert on the stock market probably knows very little about the economics of housework, and vice versa. Yet an economist who wanders into the wrong seminar and ends up listening to presentations on some unfamiliar topic is nonetheless likely to hear much that is familiar. The reason is that all economic analysis is based on a set of common principles that apply to many different issues.

Some of these principles involve *individual choice*—for economics is, first of all, about the choices that individuals make. Do you choose to work over the summer or take a backpacking trip? Do you buy a new CD or go to a movie? These decisions involve *making a choice* from among a limited number of alternatives—limited because no one can have everything that he or she wants. Every question in economics at its most basic level involves individuals making choices.

One must choose.

But to understand how an economy works, you need to understand more than how individuals make choices. None of us are Robinson Crusoe, alone on an island—we must make decisions in an environment that is shaped by the decisions of others. Indeed, in a modern economy even the simplest decisions you make—say, what to have for breakfast—are shaped by the decisions of thousands of other people, from the banana grower in Costa Rica who decided to grow the fruit you eat to the farmer in Iowa who provided the corn in your cornflakes. And because each of us in a market economy depends on so many others—and they, in turn, depend on us—our choices interact. So although all economics at a basic level is about individual choice, in order to understand how market economies behave we must also understand economic *interaction*—how my choices affect your choices, and vice versa.

Many important economic interactions can be understood by looking at the markets for individual goods, like the market for corn. But an economy as a whole has its ups and downs—and we therefore need to understand economy-wide interactions as well as the more limited interactions that occur in individual markets.

In this chapter, we will look at twelve basic principles of economics—four principles involving individual choice, five involving the way individual choices interact, and three more involving economy-wide interactions.

Individual Choice: The Core of Economics

Every economic issue involves, at its most basic level, **individual choice**—decisions by an individual about what to do and what *not* to do. In fact, you might say that it isn't economics if it isn't about choice.

Step into a big store like a Wal-Mart or Target. There are thousands of different products available, and it is extremely unlikely that you—or anyone else—could afford to buy everything you might want to have. And anyway, there's only so much space in your dorm room or apartment. So will you buy another bookcase or a mini-refrigerator? Given limitations on your budget and your living space, you must choose which products to buy and which to leave on the shelf.

The fact that those products are on the shelf in the first place involves choice—the store manager chose to put them there, and the manufacturers of the products chose to produce them. All economic activities involve individual choice.

Four economic principles underlie the economics of individual choice, as shown in Table 1-1. We'll now examine each of these principles in more detail.

Resources Are Scarce

You can't always get what you want. Everyone would like to have a beautiful house in a great location (and help with the housecleaning), two or three luxury cars, and frequent vacations in fancy hotels. But even in a rich country like the United States, not many families can afford all that. So they must make choices—whether to go to Disney World this year or buy a better car, whether to make do with a small backyard or accept a longer commute in order to live where land is cheaper.

Limited income isn't the only thing that keeps people from having everything they want. Time is also in limited supply: there are only 24 hours in a day. And because the time we have is limited, choosing to spend time on one activity also means choosing not to spend time on a different activity—spending time studying for an exam means forgoing a night at the movies. Indeed, many people are so limited by the number of hours in the day that they are willing to trade money for time. For example, convenience stores normally charge higher prices than a regular supermarket. But they fulfill a valuable role by catering to time-pressured customers who would rather pay more than travel farther to the supermarket.

Why do individuals have to make choices? The ultimate reason is that *resources are scarce*. A **resource** is anything that can be used to produce something else. Lists of the economy's resources usually begin with land, labor (the time of workers), capital (machinery, buildings, and other man-made productive assets), and human capital (the educational achievements and skills of workers). A resource is **scarce** when there's not enough of the resource available to satisfy all the various ways a society wants to use it. There are many scarce resources. These include natural resources—resources that come from the physical environment, such as minerals, lumber, and petroleum. There is also a limited quantity of human resources—labor, skill, and intelligence. And in a growing world economy with a rapidly increasing human population, even clean air and water have become scarce resources.

Just as individuals must make choices, the scarcity of resources means that society as a whole must make choices. One way for a society to make choices is simply to allow them to emerge as the result of many individual choices, which is what usually happens in a market economy. For example, Americans as a group have only so many

TABLE 1-1

Principles That Underlie the Economics of Individual Choice

1. Resources are scarce.

2. The real cost of something is what you must give up to get it.

3. "How much?" is a decision at the margin.

4. People usually exploit opportunities to make themselves better off.

Individual choice is the decision by an individual of what to do, which necessarily involves a decision of what not to do.

A **resource** is anything that can be used to produce something else.

Resources are **scarce**—there is not enough of the resources available to satisfy all the various ways a society wants to use them.

hours in a week: how many of those hours will they spend going to supermarkets to get lower prices, rather than saving time by shopping at convenience stores? The answer is the sum of individual decisions: each of the millions of individuals in the economy makes his or her own choice about where to shop, and the overall choice is simply the sum of those individual decisions.

But for various reasons, there are some decisions that a society decides are best not left to individual choice. For example, the authors live in an area that until recently was mainly farmland but is now being rapidly built up. Most local residents feel that the community would be a more pleasant place to live if some of the land were left undeveloped. But no individual has an incentive to keep his or her land as open space, rather than sell it to a developer. So a trend has emerged in many communities across the United States of local governments purchasing undeveloped land and preserving it as open space. We'll see in later chapters why decisions about how to use scarce resources are often best left to individuals but sometimes should be made at a higher, community-wide, level.

The Real Cost of Something Is What You Must Give Up to Get It

It is the last term before you graduate, and your class schedule allows you to take only one elective. There are two, however, that you would really like to take: History of Jazz and Beginning Tennis.

Suppose you decide to take the History of Jazz course. What's the cost of that decision? It is the fact that you can't take Beginning Tennis, your next best alternative choice. Economists call that kind of cost—what you must give up in order to get an item you want—the **opportunity cost** of that item. So the opportunity cost of taking the History of Jazz class is the enjoyment you would have derived from the Beginning Tennis class.

The concept of opportunity cost is crucial to understanding individual choice because, in the end, all costs are opportunity costs. That's because every choice you make means forgoing some other alternative. Sometimes critics claim that economists are concerned only with costs and benefits that can be measured in dollars and cents. But that is not true. Much economic analysis involves cases like our elective course example, where it costs no extra tuition to take one elective course—that is, there is no direct monetary cost. Nonetheless, the elective you choose has an opportunity cost— the other desirable elective course that you must forgo because your limited time permits taking only one. More specifically, the opportunity cost of a choice is what you forgo by not choosing your next best alternative.

You might think that opportunity cost is an add-on—that is, something *additional* to the monetary cost of an item. Suppose that an elective class costs additional tuition of $750; now there is a monetary cost to taking History of Jazz. Is the opportunity cost of taking that course something separate from that monetary cost?

Well, consider two cases. First, suppose that taking Beginning Tennis also costs $750. In this case, you would have to spend that $750 no matter which class you take. So what you give up to take the History of Jazz class is still the Beginning Tennis class, period—you would have to spend that $750 either way. But suppose there isn't any fee for the tennis class. In that case, what you give up to take the jazz class is the enjoyment from the tennis class *plus* the enjoyment that you could have gained from spending the $750 on other things.

Either way, the real cost of taking your preferred class is what you must give up to get it. As you expand the set of decisions that underlie each choice—whether to take an elective or not, whether to finish this term or not, whether to drop out or not— you'll realize that *all* costs are ultimately opportunity costs.

Sometimes the money you have to pay for something is a good indication of its opportunity cost. But many times it is not. One very important example of how poorly monetary cost can indicate opportunity cost is the cost of attending college. Tuition

The real cost of an item is its **opportunity cost**: what you must give up in order to get it.

Got a Penny?

At many cash registers—for example, the one downstairs in our college cafeteria—there is a little basket full of pennies. People are encouraged to use the basket to round their purchases up or down: if it costs $5.02, you give the cashier $5 and take two pennies from the basket; if it costs $4.99, you pay $5 and the cashier throws in a penny. It makes everyone's life a bit easier. Of course, it would be easier still if we just abolished the penny, a step that some economists have urged.

But then why do we have pennies in the first place? If it's too small a sum to worry about, why calculate prices that exactly?

The answer is that a penny wasn't always such a negligible sum: the purchasing power of a penny has been greatly reduced by inflation, a general rise in the prices of all goods and services over time. Forty years ago, a penny had more purchasing power than a nickel does today.

Why does this matter? Well, remember the saying: "A penny saved is a penny earned." But there are other ways to earn money, so you must decide whether saving a penny is a productive use of your time. Could you earn more by devoting that time to other uses?

Sixty years ago, the average wage was about $1.20 an hour. A penny was equivalent to 30 seconds' worth of work—it was worth saving a penny if doing so took less than 30 seconds. But wages have risen along with overall prices, so that the average worker is now paid more than $17 per hour. A penny is therefore equivalent to just over 2 seconds of work—and so it's not worth the opportunity cost of the time it takes to worry about a penny more or less.

In short, the rising opportunity cost of time in terms of money has turned a penny from a useful coin into a nuisance.

LeBron James understood the concept of opportunity cost.

and housing are major monetary expenses for most students; but even if these things were free, attending college would still be an expensive proposition because most college students, if they were not in college, would have a job. That is, by going to college, students *forgo* the income they could have made if they had worked instead. This means that the opportunity cost of attending college is what you pay for tuition and housing *plus* the forgone income you would have earned in a job.

It's easy to see that the opportunity cost of going to college is especially high for people who could be earning a lot during what would otherwise have been their college years. That is why star athletes like LeBron James often skip college. Some, like Tiger Woods, leave before graduating.

"How Much?" Is a Decision at the Margin

Some important decisions involve an "either-or" choice—for example, you decide either to go to college or to begin working; you decide either to take economics or to take something else. But other important decisions involve "how much" choices—for example, if you are taking both economics and chemistry this semester, you must decide how much time to spend studying for each. When it comes to understanding "how much" decisions, economics has an important insight to offer: "how much" is a decision made *at the margin*.

Suppose you are taking both economics and chemistry. And suppose you are a pre-med student, so that your grade in chemistry matters more to you than your grade in economics. Does that therefore imply that you should spend *all* your study time on chemistry and wing it on the economics exam? Probably not; even if you think your chemistry grade is more important, you should put some effort into studying for economics.

Spending more time studying for economics involves a benefit (a higher expected grade in that course) and a cost (you could have spent that time doing something else, such as studying to get a higher grade in chemistry). That is, your decision involves a **trade-off**—a comparison of costs and benefits.

How do you decide this kind of "how much" question? The typical answer is that you make the decision a bit at a time, by asking how you should spend the next hour. Say both exams are on the same day, and the night before you spend time reviewing your notes for both courses. At 6:00 P.M., you decide that it's a good idea to spend at least an hour on each course. At 8:00 P.M., you decide you'd better spend another

You make a **trade-off** when you compare the costs with the benefits of doing something.

hour on each course. At 10:00 P.M., you are getting tired and figure you have one more hour to study before bed—chemistry or economics? If you are pre-med, it's likely to be chemistry; if you are pre-MBA, it's likely to be economics.

Note how you've made the decision to allocate your time: at each point the question is whether or not to spend *one more hour* on either course. And in deciding whether to spend another hour studying for chemistry, you weigh the costs (an hour forgone of studying for economics or an hour forgone of sleeping) versus the benefits (a likely increase in your chemistry grade). As long as the benefit of studying one more hour for chemistry outweighs the cost, you should choose to study for that additional hour.

Decisions of this type—what to do with your next hour, what to do with your next dollar, and so on—are **marginal decisions.** They involve making trade-offs *at the margin:* comparing the costs and benefits of doing a little bit more of an activity versus doing a little bit less. The study of such decisions is known as **marginal analysis.**

Many of the questions that we face in economics—as well as in real life—involve marginal analysis: How many workers should I hire in my shop? At what mileage should I change the oil in my car? What is an acceptable rate of negative side effects from a new medicine? Marginal analysis plays a central role in economics because it is the key to deciding "how much" of an activity to do.

> Decisions about whether to do a bit more or a bit less of an activity are **marginal decisions.** The study of such decisions is known as **marginal analysis.**
>
> An **incentive** is anything that offers rewards to people who change their behavior.

People Usually Exploit Opportunities to Make Themselves Better Off

One day, while listening to the morning financial news, the authors heard a great tip about how to park cheaply in Manhattan. Garages in the Wall Street area charge as much as $30 per day. But according to the newscaster, some people had found a better way: instead of parking in a garage, they had their oil changed at the Manhattan Jiffy Lube, where it costs $19.95 to change your oil—and they keep your car all day!

It's a great story, but unfortunately it turned out not to be true—in fact, there is no Jiffy Lube in Manhattan. But if there were, you can be sure there would be a lot of oil changes there. Why? Because when people are offered opportunities to make themselves better off, they normally take them—and if they could find a way to park their car all day for $19.95 rather than $30, they would.

When you try to predict how individuals will behave in an economic situation, it is a very good bet that they will exploit opportunities to make themselves better off. Furthermore, individuals will *continue* to exploit these opportunities until they have been fully exhausted—that is, people will exploit opportunities until those opportunities have been fully exploited.

If there really was a Manhattan Jiffy Lube and an oil change really was a cheap way to park your car, we can safely predict that before long the waiting list for oil changes would be weeks, if not months.

In fact, the principle that people will exploit opportunities to make themselves better off is the basis of *all* predictions by economists about individual behavior. If the earnings of those who get MBAs soar while the earnings of those who get law degrees decline, we can expect more students to go to business school and fewer to go to law school. If the price of gasoline rises and stays high for an extended period of time, we can expect people to buy smaller cars with higher gas mileage—making themselves better off in the presence of higher gas prices by driving more fuel-efficient cars.

When changes in the available opportunities offer rewards to those who change their behavior, we say that people face new **incentives.** If the price of parking in Manhattan rises, those who can find alternative ways to get to their Wall Street jobs will save money by doing so—and so we can expect fewer people to drive to work.

One last point: economists tend to be skeptical of any attempt to change people's behavior that *doesn't* change their incentives. For example, a plan that calls on manufacturers to reduce pollution voluntarily probably won't be effective; a plan that gives them a financial incentive to reduce pollution is a lot more likely to work.

Pay for Grades?

The true reward for learning is, of course, the learning itself. But teachers and schools often feel that it's worth throwing in a few extras. Elementary school students who do well get gold stars; at higher levels, students who score well on tests may receive trophies, plaques, or even gift certificates.

But what about cash?

A few years ago, some Florida schools stirred widespread debate by offering actual cash bonuses to students who scored high on the state's standardized exams. At Parrott Middle School, which offered the highest amounts, an eighth-grader with a top score on an exam received a $50 savings bond.

Many people questioned the monetary awards. In fact, the great majority of teachers feel that cash rewards for learning are a bad idea—the dollar amounts can't be made large enough to give students a real sense of how important their education is, and they make learning seem like work-for-pay. So why did the schools engage in the practice?

The answer, it turns out, is that the previous year the state government had introduced a pay-for-performance scheme for schools: schools whose students earned high marks on the state exams received extra state funds. The problem arose of how to motivate the students to take the exams as seriously as the school

administrators did. Parrott's principal defended the pay-for-grades practice by pointing out that good students would often "Christmas tree" their exams—ignore the questions and fill out the bubble sheets in the shape of Christmas trees. With large sums of money for the school at stake, he decided to set aside his misgivings and pay students to do well on the exams.

Does paying students for grades lead to higher grades? Interviews with students suggest that it does spur at least some students to try harder on state exams. And some Florida schools that have introduced rewards for good grades on state exams report substantial improvements in student performance.

Individual Choice: Summing It Up

We have just seen that there are four basic principles of individual choice:

- *Resources are scarce.* It is always necessary to make choices.
- *The real cost of something is what you must give up to get it.* All costs are opportunity costs.
- *"How much?" is a decision at the margin.* Usually the question is not "whether" but "how much." And that is a question whose answer hinges on the costs and benefits of doing a bit more or a bit less.
- *People usually exploit opportunities to make themselves better off.* As a result, people will respond to incentives.

So are we ready to do economics? Not yet—because most of the interesting things that happen in the economy are the result not merely of individual choices but of the way in which individual choices *interact*.

➤ECONOMICS IN ACTION

A Woman's Work

One of the great social transformations of the twentieth century was the change in the nature of women's work. In 1900, only 6 percent of married women worked for pay outside the home. By 2005, the number was about 60 percent.

What caused this transformation? Changing attitudes toward work outside the home certainly played a role: in the first half of the twentieth century, it was often considered improper for a married woman to work outside the home if she could afford not to, whereas today it is considered normal. But an important driving force was the invention and growing availability of home appliances, especially washing machines. Before these appliances became available, housework was an extremely laborious task—much more so than a full-time job. In 1945, government researchers clocked a farm wife as she did the weekly wash by hand; she spent 4 hours washing clothes and 4½ hours ironing, and she walked more than a mile. Then she was equipped with a washing machine; the same wash took 41 minutes, ironing was reduced to 1¾ hours, and the distance walked was reduced by 90 percent.

The point is that in pre-appliance days, the opportunity cost of working outside the home was very high: it was something women typically did only in the face of dire financial necessity. With modern appliances, the opportunities available to women changed—and the rest is history. ▲

> > > > > > > > > > > >

► CHECK YOUR UNDERSTANDING 1-1

1. Explain how each of the following situations illustrates one of the four principles of individual choice.
   a. You are on your third trip to a restaurant's all-you-can-eat dessert buffet and are feeling very full. Although it would cost you no additional money, you forgo a slice of coconut cream pie but have a slice of chocolate cake.
   b. Even if there were more resources in the world, there would still be scarcity.
   c. Different teaching assistants teach several Economics 101 tutorials. Those taught by the teaching assistants with the best reputations fill up quickly, with spaces left unfilled in the ones taught by assistants with poor reputations.
   d. To decide how many hours per week to exercise, you compare the health benefits of one more hour of exercise to the effect on your grades of one less hour spent studying.

2. You make $45,000 per year at your current job with Whiz Kids Consultants. You are considering a job offer from Brainiacs, Inc., which will pay you $50,000 per year. Which of the following are elements of the opportunity cost of accepting the new job at Brainiacs, Inc.?
   a. The increased time spent commuting to your new job
   b. The $45,000 salary from your old job
   c. The more spacious office at your new job

Solutions appear at back of book.

Interaction: How Economies Work

As we learned in the Introduction, an economy is a system for coordinating the productive activities of many people. In a market economy, such as the one we live in, that coordination takes place without any coordinator: each individual makes his or her own choices. Yet those choices are by no means independent of each other: each individual's opportunities, and hence choices, depend to a large extent on the choices made by other people. So to understand how a market economy behaves, we have to examine this **interaction** in which my choices affect your choices, and vice versa.

When studying economic interaction, we quickly learn that the end result of individual choices may be quite different from what any one individual intends.

For example, over the past century farmers in the United States have eagerly adopted new farming techniques and crop strains that have reduced their costs and increased their yields. Clearly, it's in the interest of each farmer to keep up with the latest farming techniques. But the end result of each farmer trying to increase his or her own income has actually been to drive many farmers out of business. Because American farmers have been so successful at producing larger yields, agricultural prices have steadily fallen. These falling prices have reduced the incomes of many farmers, and as a result fewer and fewer people find farming worth doing. That is, an individual farmer who plants a better variety of corn is better off; but when many farmers plant a better variety of corn, the result may be to make farmers as a group worse off.

A farmer who plants a new, more productive corn variety doesn't just grow more corn. Such a farmer also affects the market for corn through the increased yields attained, with consequences that will be felt by other farmers, consumers, and beyond.

Just as there are four economic principles that fall under the theme of choice, there are five principles that fall under the theme of interaction. These five principles are summarized in Table 1-2. We will now examine each of these principles more closely.

Interaction of choices—my choices affect your choices, and vice versa—is a feature of most economic situations. The results of this interaction are often quite different from what the individuals intend.

TABLE 1-2

Principles That Underlie the Interaction of Individual Choices

1. There are gains from trade.

2. Markets move toward equilibrium.

3. Resources should be used as efficiently as possible to achieve society's goals.

4. Markets usually lead to efficiency.

5. When markets don't achieve efficiency, government intervention can improve society's welfare.

In a market economy, individuals engage in **trade:** they provide goods and services to others and receive goods and services in return.

There are **gains from trade:** people can get more of what they want through trade than they could if they tried to be self-sufficient. This increase in output is due to **specialization:** each person specializes in the task that he or she is good at performing.

There Are Gains from Trade

Why do the choices I make interact with the choices you make? A family could try to take care of all its own needs—growing its own food, sewing its own clothing, providing itself with entertainment, writing its own economics textbooks. But trying to live that way would be very hard. The key to a much better standard of living for everyone is **trade,** in which people divide tasks among themselves and each person provides a good or service that other people want in return for different goods and services that he or she wants.

The reason we have an economy, not many self-sufficient individuals, is that there are **gains from trade:** by dividing tasks and trading, two people (or 6 billion people) can each get more of what they want than they could get by being self-sufficient. Gains from trade arise, in particular, from this division of tasks, which economists call **specialization**—a situation in which different people each engage in a different task.

The advantages of specialization, and the resulting gains from trade, were the starting point for Adam Smith's 1776 book *The Wealth of Nations,* which many regard as the beginning of economics as a discipline. Smith's book begins with a description of an eighteenth-century pin factory where, rather than each of the 10 workers making a pin from start to finish, each worker specialized in one of the many steps in pin-making:

> One man draws out the wire, another straights it, a third cuts it, a fourth points it, a fifth grinds it at the top for receiving the head; to make the head requires two or three distinct operations; to put it on, is a particular business, to whiten the pins is another; it is even a trade by itself to put them into the paper; and the important business of making a pin is, in this manner, divided into about eighteen distinct operations. . . . Those ten persons, therefore, could make among them upwards of forty-eight thousand pins in a day. But if they had all wrought separately and independently, and without any of them having been educated to this particular business, they certainly could not each of them have made twenty, perhaps not one pin a day. . . .

"I hunt and she gathers—otherwise we couldn't make ends meet."

The same principle applies when we look at how people divide tasks among themselves and trade in an economy. *The economy, as a whole, can produce more when each person specializes in a task and trades with others.*

The benefits of specialization are the reason a person typically chooses only one career. It takes many years of study and experience to become a doctor; it also takes many years of study and experience to become a commercial airline pilot. Many doctors might well have had the potential to become excellent pilots, and vice versa; but it is very unlikely that anyone who decided to pursue both careers would be as good a pilot or as good a doctor as someone who decided at the beginning to specialize in that field. So it is to everyone's advantage that individuals specialize in their career choices.

Markets are what allow a doctor and a pilot to specialize in their own fields. Because markets for commercial flights and for doctors' services exist, a doctor is assured that she can find a flight and a pilot is assured that he can find a doctor. As long as individuals know that they can find the goods and services that they want in the market, they are willing to forgo self-sufficiency and are willing to specialize. But what assures people that markets will deliver what they want? The answer to that question leads us to our second principle of how individual choices interact.

Markets Move Toward Equilibrium

It's a busy afternoon at the supermarket; there are long lines at the checkout counters. Then one of the previously closed cash registers opens. What happens?

The first thing that happens, of course, is a rush to that register. After a couple of minutes, however, things will have settled down; shoppers will have rearranged themselves so that the line at the newly opened register is about the same length as the lines at all the other registers.

How do we know that? We know from our fourth principle of individual choice that people will exploit opportunities to make themselves better off. This means that people will rush to the newly opened register in order to save time standing in line. And things will settle down when shoppers can no longer improve their position by switching lines—that is, when the opportunities to make themselves better off have all been exploited.

A story about supermarket checkout lines may seem to have little to do with how individual choices interact, but in fact it illustrates an important principle. A situation in which individuals cannot make themselves better off by doing something different—the situation in which all the checkout lines are the same length—is what economists call an **equilibrium.** An economic situation is in equilibrium when no individual would be better off doing something different.

Recall the story about the mythical Jiffy Lube, where it was supposedly cheaper to leave your car for an oil change than to pay for parking. If that opportunity had really existed and people were still paying $30 to park in garages, the situation would *not* have been an equilibrium. And that should have been a giveaway that the story couldn't be true. In reality, people would have seized an opportunity to park cheaply, just as they seize opportunities to save time at the checkout line. And in so doing they would have eliminated the opportunity! Either it would have become very hard to get an appointment for an oil change or the price of a lube job would have increased to the point that it was no longer an attractive option (unless you really needed a lube job).

As we will see, markets usually reach equilibrium via changes in prices, which rise or fall until no opportunities for individuals to make themselves better off remain.

The concept of equilibrium is extremely helpful in understanding economic interactions because it provides a way of cutting through the sometimes complex details of those interactions. To understand what happens when a new line is opened at a supermarket, you don't need to worry about exactly how shoppers rearrange themselves, who moves ahead of whom, which register just opened, and so on. What you need to know is that any time there is a change, the situation will move to an equilibrium.

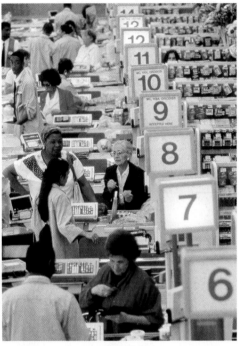

Rhoda Sydney/Photo Edit

Witness equilibrium in action at the checkout lines in your neighborhood supermarket.

An economic situation is in **equilibrium** when no individual would be better off doing something different.

Choosing Sides

Why do people in America drive on the right side of the road? Of course, it's the law. But long before it was the law, it was an equilibrium.

Before there were formal traffic laws, there were informal "rules of the road," practices that everyone expected everyone else to follow. These rules included an understanding that people would normally keep to one side of the road. In some places, such as England, the rule was to keep to the left; in others, such as France, it was to keep to the right.

Why would some places choose the right and others, the left? That's not completely clear, although it may have

depended on the dominant form of traffic. Men riding horses and carrying swords on their left hip preferred to ride on the left (think about getting on or off the horse, and you'll see why). On the other hand, right-handed people walking but leading horses apparently preferred to walk on the right.

In any case, once a rule of the road was established, there were strong incentives for each individual to stay on the "usual" side of the road: those who didn't would keep colliding with oncoming traffic. So once established, the rule of the road would be self-enforcing—that is, it would be an equilibrium. Nowadays, of

course, which side you drive on is determined by law; some countries have even changed sides (Sweden went from left to right in 1967). But what about pedestrians? There are no laws—but there are informal rules. In the United States, urban pedestrians normally keep to the right. But if you should happen to visit a country where people drive on the left, watch out: people who drive on the left also typically walk on the left. So when in a foreign country, do as the locals do. You won't be arrested if you walk on the right, but you will be worse off than if you accept the equilibrium and walk on the left.

An economy is **efficient** if it takes all opportunities to make some people better off without making other people worse off.

Equity means that everyone gets his or her fair share. Since people can disagree about what's "fair," equity isn't as well defined a concept as efficiency.

The fact that markets move toward equilibrium is why we can depend on them to work in a predictable way. In fact, we can trust markets to supply us with the essentials of life. For example, people who live in big cities can be sure that the supermarket shelves will always be fully stocked. Why? Because if some merchants who distribute food *didn't* make deliveries, a big profit opportunity would be created for any merchant who did—and there would be a rush to supply food, just like the rush to a newly opened cash register. So the market ensures that food will always be available for city dwellers. And, returning to our previous principle, this allows city dwellers to be city dwellers—to specialize in doing city jobs rather than living on farms and growing their own food.

A market economy also allows people to achieve gains from trade. But how do we know how well such an economy is doing? The next principle gives us a standard to use in evaluating an economy's performance.

Resources Should Be Used as Efficiently as Possible to Achieve Society's Goals

Suppose you are taking a course in which the classroom is too small for the number of students—many people are forced to stand or sit on the floor—despite the fact that large, empty classrooms are available nearby. You would say, correctly, that this is no way to run a college. Economists would call this an *inefficient* use of resources.

But if an inefficient use of resources is undesirable, just what does it mean to use resources *efficiently*? You might imagine that the efficient use of resources has something to do with money, maybe that it is measured in dollars-and-cents terms. But in economics, as in life, money is only a means to other ends. The measure that economists really care about is not money but people's happiness or welfare. Economists say that *an economy's resources are used efficiently when they are used in a way that has fully exploited all opportunities to make everyone better off*. To put it another way, an economy is **efficient** if it takes all opportunities to make some people better off without making other people worse off.

In our classroom example, there clearly was a way to make everyone better off—moving the class to a larger room would make people in the class better off without hurting anyone else in the college. Assigning the course to the smaller classroom was an inefficient use of the college's resources, whereas assigning the course to the larger classroom would have been an efficient use of the college's resources.

When an economy is efficient, it is producing the maximum gains from trade possible given the resources available. Why? Because there is no way to rearrange how resources are used in a way that can make everyone better off. When an economy is efficient, one person can be made better off by rearranging how resources are used *only* by making someone else worse off. In our classroom example, if all larger classrooms were already occupied, the college would have been run in an efficient way: your class could be made better off by moving to a larger classroom only by making people in the larger classroom worse off by making them move to a smaller classroom.

Should economic policy makers always strive to achieve economic efficiency? Well, not quite, because efficiency is not the only criterion by which to evaluate an economy. People also care about issues of fairness, or **equity.** And there is typically a trade-off between equity and efficiency: policies that promote equity often come at a cost of decreased efficiency in the economy, and vice versa.

To see this, consider the case of disabled-designated parking spaces in public parking lots. Many people have great difficulty walking due to age or disability, so it seems only fair to assign closer parking spaces specifically for their use. You may have noticed, however, that a certain amount of inefficiency is involved. To make sure that there is always an appropriate space available should a disabled person want one, there are typically quite a number of disabled-designated spaces. So at any one time there are typically more such spaces available than there are disabled people who want one. As a result, desirable parking spaces are unused. (And the temptation for nondisabled people to use them is so great that we must be dissuaded by fear of getting a ticket.) So, short of hiring parking valets to allocate spaces, there is a conflict between *equity,* making life "fairer" for disabled people, and *efficiency,* making sure that all opportunities to make people better off have been fully exploited by never letting close-in parking spaces go unused.

Exactly how far policy makers should go in promoting equity over efficiency is a difficult question that goes to the heart of the political process. As such, it is not a question that economists can answer. What is important for economists, however, is always to seek to use the economy's resources as efficiently as possible in the pursuit of society's goals, whatever those goals may be.

Markets Usually Lead to Efficiency

No branch of the U.S. government is entrusted with ensuring the general economic efficiency of our market economy—we don't have agents who go around making sure that brain surgeons aren't plowing fields, that Minnesota farmers aren't trying to grow oranges, that prime beachfront property isn't taken up by used-car dealerships, that colleges aren't wasting valuable classroom space. The government doesn't need to enforce efficiency because in most cases the invisible hand does the job.

In other words, the incentives built into a market economy already ensure that resources are usually put to good use, that opportunities to make people better off are not wasted. If a college were known for its habit of crowding students into small classrooms while large classrooms go unused, it would soon find its enrollment dropping, putting the jobs of its administrators at risk. The "market" for college students would respond in a way that induces administrators to run the college efficiently.

A detailed explanation of why markets are usually very good at making sure that resources are used well will have to wait until we have studied how markets actually work. But the most basic reason is that in a market economy, in which individuals are free to choose what to consume and what to produce, opportunities for mutual gain are normally taken. If there is a way in which some people can be made better off, people will usually be able to take advantage of that opportunity. And that is exactly what defines efficiency: all the opportunities to make some people better off without making other people worse off have been exploited.

As we learned in the Introduction, however, there are exceptions to this principle that markets are generally efficient. In cases of *market failure,* the individual pursuit of self-interest found in markets makes society worse off—that is, the market outcome is inefficient. And, as we will see in examining the next principle, when markets fail, government intervention can help. But short of instances of market failure, the general rule is that markets are a remarkably good way of organizing an economy.

When Markets Don't Achieve Efficiency, Government Intervention Can Improve Society's Welfare

Let's recall from the Introduction the nature of the market failure caused by traffic congestion—a commuter driving to work has no incentive to take into account the cost that his or her action inflicts on other drivers in the form of increased traffic congestion. There are several possible remedies to this situation; examples include charging road tolls, subsidizing the cost of public transportation, and taxing sales of gasoline to individual drivers. All these remedies work by changing the incentives of would-be drivers—motivating them to drive less and use alternative transportation. But they also share another feature: each relies on government intervention in the market.

This brings us to our fifth and last principle of interaction: *When markets don't achieve efficiency, government intervention can improve society's welfare.* That is, when markets go wrong, an appropriately designed government policy can sometimes move society closer to an efficient outcome by changing how society's resources are used.

A very important branch of economics is devoted to studying why markets fail and what policies should be adopted to improve social welfare. We will study these problems and their remedies in depth in later chapters, but here we give a brief overview of three principal ways in which they fail:

- Individual actions have *side effects* that are not properly taken into account by the market. An example is an action that causes pollution.

- One party prevents mutually beneficial trades from occurring in an attempt to capture a greater share of resources for itself. An example is a drug company that keeps its prices so high that some people who would benefit from their drugs cannot afford to buy them.

- Some goods, by their very nature, are unsuited for efficient management by markets. An example of such a good is air traffic control.

An important part of your education in economics is learning to identify not just when markets work but also when they don't work—and to judge what government policies are appropriate in each situation.

➤ECONOMICS IN ACTION

Restoring Equilibrium on the Freeways

Back in 1994 a powerful earthquake struck the Los Angeles area, causing several freeway bridges to collapse and thereby disrupting the normal commuting routes of hundreds of thousands of drivers. The events that followed offer a particularly clear example of interdependent decision making—in this case, the decisions of commuters about how to get to work.

In the immediate aftermath of the earthquake, there was great concern about the impact on traffic, since motorists would now have to crowd onto alternative routes or detour around the blockages by using city streets. Public officials and news programs warned commuters to expect massive delays and urged them to avoid unnecessary travel, reschedule their work to commute before or after the rush, or use mass transit. These warnings were unexpectedly effective. In fact, so many people heeded them that in the first few days following the quake, those who maintained their regular commuting routine actually found the drive to and from work faster than before.

Of course, this situation could not last. As word spread that traffic was actually not bad at all, people abandoned their less convenient new commuting methods and reverted to their cars—and traffic got steadily worse. Within a few weeks after the quake, serious traffic jams had appeared. After a few more weeks, however, the situation stabilized: the reality of worse-than-usual congestion discouraged enough drivers to prevent the nightmare of citywide gridlock from materializing. Los Angeles traffic, in short, had settled into a new equilibrium, in which each commuter was making the best choice he or she could, given what everyone else was doing.

This was not, by the way, the end of the story: fears that the city would strangle on traffic led local authorities to repair the roads with record speed. Within only 18 months after the quake, all the freeways were back to normal, ready for the next one. ▲

< < < < < < < < < < < <

➤ CHECK YOUR UNDERSTANDING 1-2

1. Explain how each of the following situations illustrates one of the five principles of interaction.
   a. Using the college website, any student who wants to sell a used textbook for at least $30 is able to sell it to someone who is willing to pay $30.
   b. At a college tutoring co-op, students can arrange to provide tutoring in subjects they are good in (like economics) in return for receiving tutoring in subjects they are poor in (like philosophy).

   c. The local municipality imposes a law that requires bars and nightclubs near residential areas to keep their noise levels below a certain threshold.

   d. To provide better care for low-income patients, the local municipality has decided to close some underutilized neighborhood clinics and shift funds to the main hospital.

   e. On the college website, books of a given title with approximately the same level of wear and tear sell for about the same price.

2. Which of the following describes an equilibrium situation? Which does not? Explain your answer.

   a. The restaurants across the street from the university dining hall serve better-tasting and cheaper meals than those served at the university dining hall. The vast majority of students continue to eat at the dining hall.

   b. You currently take the subway to work. Although taking the bus is cheaper, the ride takes longer. So you are willing to pay the higher subway fare in order to save time.

Solutions appear at back of book.

Economy-Wide Interactions

As we mentioned in the Introduction, the economy as a whole has its ups and downs. For example, business in America's shopping malls was somewhat depressed in 2002, because the economy hadn't fully recovered from the 2001 recession. To understand recessions, we need to understand economy-wide interactions, and understanding the big picture of the economy requires understanding three more important economic principles. Those three economy-wide principles are summarized in Table 1-3.

One Person's Spending Is Another Person's Income

In 2001, corporations that had been buying a lot of computers, software, and other high-tech supplies in the late 1990s suddenly decided to cut back on their purchases. The result, economists agree, was a recession caused mainly by these cuts in business investment spending. As we mentioned in the previous chapter, this was followed by a sharp drop-off in spending at the nation's retail stores.

But why should a cut in spending by businesses mean empty stores in the shopping malls? After all, malls are places where families, not businesses, do their shopping. The answer is that lower business spending led to lower incomes throughout the economy, because people who had been making those computers or designing that software either lost their jobs or were forced to take pay cuts. And as incomes fell, so did spending by consumers.

This story illustrates a general principle: *One person's spending is another person's income.* In a market economy, people make a living selling things—including their labor—to other people. If some group in the economy decides, for whatever reason, to spend more, the income of other groups will rise. If some group decides to spend less, the income of other groups will fall.

Because one person's spending is another person's income, a chain reaction of changes in spending behavior tends to have repercussions that spread through the economy. For example, a cut in business investment spending, like the one that happened in 2001, leads to reduced family incomes; families respond by reducing consumer spending; this leads to another round of income cuts; and so on. These repercussions play an important role in our understanding of recessions and recoveries.

Overall Spending Sometimes Gets Out of Line With the Economy's Productive Capacity

Macroeconomics emerged as a separate branch of economics in the 1930s, when a collapse of consumer and business spending, a crisis in the banking industry, and other factors led to a plunge in overall spending. This plunge in spending, in turn, led to a period of very high unemployment known as the Great Depression.

TABLE 1-3

Principles That Underlie Economy-Wide Interactions

1. One person's spending is another person's income.

2. Overall spending sometimes gets out of line with the economy's productive capacity.

3. Government policies can change spending.

The lesson economists learned from the troubles of the 1930s is that overall spending—the amount of goods and services that consumers and businesses want to buy—sometimes doesn't match the amount of goods and services the economy is capable of producing. In the 1930s, spending fell far short of what was needed to keep American workers employed, and the result was a severe economic slump. In fact, shortfalls in spending are responsible for most, though not all, recessions—although nothing like the Great Depression has happened since the 1930s.

It's also possible for overall spending to be too high. In that case, the economy experiences *inflation,* a rise in prices throughout the economy. This rise in prices occurs because when the amount that people want to buy outstrips the supply, producers can raise their prices and still find willing customers.

Government Policies Can Change Spending

Overall spending sometimes gets out of line with the economy's productive capacity. But can anything be done about that? Yes, a lot. Government policies can have strong effects on spending.

For one thing, the government itself does a lot of spending on everything from military equipment to education—and it can choose to do more or less. The government can also vary how much it collects from the public in taxes, which in turn affects how much income consumers and businesses have left to spend. And the government's control of the quantity of money in circulation, it turns out, gives it another powerful tool with which to affect total spending. Government spending, taxes, and control of money are the tools of *macroeconomic policy.*

Modern governments deploy these tools of macroeconomic policy in an effort to manage overall spending in the economy, trying to steer it between the perils of recession and inflation. These efforts aren't always successful—recessions still happen, and so do periods of inflation. But it's widely believed that the growing sophistication of macroeconomic policy is an important reason why the United States and other major economies seem to be more stable today than they were in the past.

➤ECONOMICS IN ACTION

Adventures in Babysitting

The website myarmylifetoo.com, which offers advice to army families, suggests that parents join a babysitting cooperative—an arrangement that is common in many walks of life. In a babysitting cooperative, a number of parents exchange babysitting services rather than hire someone to babysit. But how do these organizations make sure that everyone does their fair share of the work? As myarmylifetoo.com explains, "Instead of money, most co-ops exchange tickets or points. When you need a sitter, you call a friend on the list, and you pay them with tickets. You earn tickets by babysitting other children within the co-op."

In other words, a babysitting co-op is a miniature economy in which people buy and sell babysitting services. And it happens to be a type of economy that can have macroeconomic problems! A famous article titled "Monetary Theory and the Great Capitol Hill Babysitting Co-Op Crisis," published in 1977, described the troubles of a babysitting cooperative that issued too few tickets. Bear in mind that, on average, people in a babysitting co-op want to have a reserve of tickets stashed away in case they need to go out several times before they can replenish their stash by doing some more babysitting.

In this case, because there weren't that many tickets out there to begin with, most parents were anxious to add to their reserves by babysitting but reluctant to run them down by going out. But one parent's decision to go out was another's chance to babysit, so it became difficult to earn tickets. Knowing this, parents became even more reluctant to use their reserves except on special occasions.

In short, the co-op had fallen into a recession.

Recessions in the larger, nonbabysitting economy are a bit more complicated than this, but the troubles of the Capitol Hill babysitting co-op demonstrate two of our three principles of economy-wide interactions. One person's spending is another person's income: opportunities to babysit arose only to the extent that other people went out. And an economy can suffer from too little spending: when not enough people were willing to go out, everyone was frustrated at the lack of babysitting opportunities.

And what about government policies to change spending? Actually, the Capitol Hill co-op did that, too. Eventually, it solved its problem by handing out more tickets, and with increased reserves, people were willing to go out more. ▲

> **CHECK YOUR UNDERSTANDING** 1-3

1. Explain how each of the following examples illustrates one of the three principles of economy-wide interactions.
   a. The White House urged Congress to pass major tax cuts in the spring of 2001, when it became clear that the U.S. economy was experiencing a slump.
   b. Oil companies are investing heavily in projects that will extract oil from the "oil sands" of Canada. In Edmonton, Alberta, near the projects, restaurants and other consumer businesses are booming.
   c. In the mid-2000s, Spain, which was experiencing a big housing boom, also had the highest inflation rate in Europe.

Solutions appear at back of book.

[**>> A LOOK AHEAD** •••

The twelve basic principles we have described lie behind almost all economic analysis. Although they can be immediately helpful in understanding many situations, they are usually not enough. Applying the principles to real economic issues takes one more step.

That step is the creation of *models*—simplified representations of economic situations. Models must be realistic enough to provide real-world guidance but simple enough to allow us to clearly see the implications of the principles described in this chapter. So our next step is to show how models are used to actually do economic analysis.]

SUMMARY

1. All economic analysis is based on a list of basic principles. These principles apply to three levels of economic understanding. First, we must understand how individuals make choices; second, we must understand how these choices interact; and third, we must understand how the economy functions overall.

2. Everyone has to make choices about what to do and what *not* to do. **Individual choice** is the basis of economics—if it doesn't involve choice, it isn't economics.

3. The reason choices must be made is that **resources**—anything that can be used to produce something else—are **scarce.** Individuals are limited in their choices by money and time; economies are limited by their supplies of human and natural resources.

4. Because you must choose among limited alternatives, the true cost of anything is what you must give up to get it—all costs are **opportunity costs.**

5. Many economic decisions involve questions not of "whether" but of "how much"—how much to spend on some good, how much to produce, and so on. Such decisions must be taken by performing a **trade-off** at the margin—by comparing the costs and benefits of doing a bit more or a bit less. Decisions of this type are called **marginal decisions,** and the study of them, **marginal analysis,** plays a central role in economics.

6. The study of how people *should* make decisions is also a good way to understand actual behavior. Individuals usually exploit opportunities to make themselves better off.

If opportunities change, so does behavior: people respond to **incentives.**

7. **Interaction**—my choices depend on your choices, and vice versa—adds another level to economic understanding. When individuals interact, the end result may be different from what anyone intends.

8. The reason for interaction is that there are **gains from trade:** by engaging in the **trade** of goods and services with one another, the members of an economy can all be made better off. Underlying gains from trade are the advantages of **specialization,** of having individuals specialize in the tasks they are good at.

9. Economies normally move toward **equilibrium**—a situation in which no individual can make himself or herself better off by taking a different action.

10. An economy is **efficient** if all opportunities to make some people better off without making other people worse off are taken. Resources should be used as efficiently as possible to achieve society's goals. But efficiency is not the sole way to evaluate an economy: **equity,** or fairness, is also desirable, and there is often a trade-off between equity and efficiency.

11. Markets usually lead to efficiency, with some well-defined exceptions.

12. When markets fail and do not achieve efficiency, government intervention can improve society's welfare.

13. One person's spending is another person's income.

14. Overall spending in the economy can get out of line with the economy's productive capacity, leading to recession or inflation.

15. Governments have the ability to strongly affect overall spending, an ability they use in an effort to steer the economy between recession and inflation.

KEY TERMS

Individual choice, p. 6
Resource, p. 6
Scarce, p. 6
Opportunity cost, p. 7
Trade-off, p. 8

Marginal decisions, p. 9
Marginal analysis, p. 9
Incentive, p. 9
Interaction, p. 11
Trade, p. 12

Gains from trade, p. 12
Specialization, p. 12
Equilibrium, p. 13
Efficient, p. 14
Equity, p. 14

PROBLEMS

1. In each of the following situations, identify which of the twelve principles is at work.

   a. You choose to shop at the local discount store rather than paying a higher price for the same merchandise at the local department store.

   b. On your spring break trip, your budget is limited to $35 a day.

   c. The student union provides a website on which departing students can sell items such as used books, appliances, and furniture rather than giving them away to their roommates as they formerly did.

   d. After a hurricane did extensive damage to homes on the island of St. Crispin, homeowners wanted to purchase many more building materials and hire many more workers than were available on the island. As a result, prices for goods and services rose dramatically across the board.

   e. You buy a used textbook from your roommate. Your roommate uses the money to buy songs from iTunes.

   f. You decide how many cups of coffee to have when studying the night before an exam by considering how much more work you can do by having another cup versus how jittery it will make you feel.

   g. There is limited lab space available to do the project required in Chemistry 101. The lab supervisor assigns lab time to each student based on when that student is able to come.

   h. You realize that you can graduate a semester early by forgoing a semester of study abroad.

   i. At the student union, there is a bulletin board on which people advertise used items for sale, such as bicycles. Once you have adjusted for differences in quality, all the bikes sell for about the same price.

   j. You are better at performing lab experiments, and your lab partner is better at writing lab reports. So the two of you agree that you will do all the experiments, and she will write up all the reports.

   k. State governments mandate that it is illegal to drive without passing a driving exam.

   l. Your parents' after-tax income has increased because of a tax cut passed by Congress. They therefore increase your allowance, which you spend on a spring break vacation.

2. Describe some of the opportunity costs when you decide to do the following.

   a. Attend college instead of taking a job

b. Watch a movie instead of studying for an exam

c. Ride the bus instead of driving your car

3. Liza needs to buy a textbook for the next economics class. The price at the college bookstore is $65. One online site offers it for $55 and another site, for $57. All prices include sales tax. The accompanying table indicates the typical shipping and handling charges for the textbook ordered online.

Shipping method	Delivery time	Charge
Standard shipping	3–7 days	$3.99
Second-day air	2 business days	8.98
Next-day air	1 business day	13.98

a. What is the opportunity cost of buying online instead of at the bookstore? Note that if you buy the book online, you must wait to get it.

b. Show the relevant choices for this student. What determines which of these options the student will choose?

4. Use the concept of opportunity cost to explain the following.

a. More people choose to get graduate degrees when the job market is poor.

b. More people choose to do their own home repairs when the economy is slow and hourly wages are down.

c. There are more parks in suburban than in urban areas.

d. Convenience stores, which have higher prices than supermarkets, cater to busy people.

e. Fewer students enroll in classes that meet before 10:00 A.M.

5. In the following examples, state how you would use the principle of marginal analysis to make a decision.

a. Deciding how many days to wait before doing your laundry

b. Deciding how much library research to do before writing your term paper

c. Deciding how many bags of chips to eat

d. Deciding how many lectures of a class to skip

6. This morning you made the following individual choices: you bought a bagel and coffee at the local café, you drove to school in your car during rush hour, and you typed your roommate's term paper because you are a fast typist—in return for which she will do your laundry for a month. For each of these actions, describe how your individual choices interacted with the individual choices made by others. Were other people left better off or worse off by your choices in each case?

7. The Hatfield family lives on the east side of the Hatatoochie River, and the McCoy family lives on the west side. Each family's diet consists of fried chicken and corn-on-the-cob, and each is self-sufficient, raising their own chickens and growing their own corn. Explain the conditions under which each of the following would be true.

a. The two families are made better off when the Hatfields specialize in raising chickens, the McCoys specialize in growing corn, and the two families trade.

b. The two families are made better off when the McCoys specialize in raising chickens, the Hatfields specialize in growing corn, and the two families trade.

8. Which of the following situations describes an equilibrium? Which does not? If the situation does not describe an equilibrium, what would an equilibrium look like?

a. Many people regularly commute from the suburbs to downtown Pleasantville. Due to traffic congestion, the trip takes 30 minutes when you travel by highway but only 15 minutes when you go by side streets.

b. At the intersection of Main and Broadway are two gas stations. One station charges $3.00 per gallon for regular gas and the other charges $2.85 per gallon. Customers can get service immediately at the first station but must wait in a long line at the second.

c. Every student enrolled in Economics 101 must also attend a weekly tutorial. This year there are two sections offered: section A and section B, which meet at the same time in adjoining classrooms and are taught by equally competent instructors. Section A is overcrowded, with people sitting on the floor and often unable to see the chalkboard. Section B has many empty seats.

9. In each of the following cases, explain whether you think the situation is efficient or not. If it is not efficient, why not? What actions would make the situation efficient?

a. Electricity is included in the rent at your dorm. Some residents in your dorm leave lights, computers, and appliances on when they are not in their rooms.

b. Although they cost the same amount to prepare, the cafeteria in your dorm consistently provides too many dishes that diners don't like, such as tofu casserole, and too few dishes that diners do like, such as roast turkey with dressing.

c. The enrollment for a particular course exceeds the spaces available. Some students who need to take this course to complete their major are unable to get a space even though others who are taking it as an elective do get a space.

10. Discuss the efficiency and equity implications of each of the following policies. How would you go about balancing the concerns of equity and efficiency in these areas?

a. The government pays the full tuition for every college student to study whatever subject he or she wishes.

b. When people lose their jobs, the government provides unemployment benefits until they find new ones.

11. Governments often adopt certain policies in order to promote desired behavior among their citizens. For each of the following policies, determine what the incentive is and what behavior the government wishes to promote. In each case, why do you think that the government might wish to change people's behavior, rather than allow their actions to be solely determined by individual choice?

a. A tax of $5 per pack is imposed on cigarettes.

b. The government pays parents $100 when their child is vaccinated for measles.

c. The government pays college students to tutor children from low-income families.

d. The government imposes a tax on the amount of air pollution that a company discharges.

12. In each of the following situations, explain how government intervention could improve society's welfare by changing people's incentives. In what sense is the market going wrong?

a. Pollution from auto emissions has reached unhealthy levels.

b. Everyone in Woodville would be better off if streetlights were installed in the town. But no individual resident is willing to pay for installation of a streetlight in front of his or her house because it is impossible to recoup the cost by charging other residents for the benefit they receive from it.

13. In his January 31, 2007, speech on the state of the economy, President George W. Bush said that "Since we enacted major tax relief into law in 2003, our economy has created nearly 7.2 million new jobs. Our economy has expanded by more than 13 percent." Which two of the three principles of economy-wide interaction are at work in this statement?

14. In August 2007, a sharp downturn in the U.S. housing market reduced the income of many who worked in the home construction industry. A *Wall Street Journal* news article reported that Wal-Mart's wire-transfer business was likely to suffer because many construction workers are Hispanics who regularly send part of their wages back to relatives in their home countries via Wal-Mart. With this information, use one of the principles of economy-wide interaction to trace a chain of links that explains how reduced spending for U.S. home purchases is likely to affect the performance of the Mexican economy.

15. In 2005, Hurricane Katrina caused massive destruction to the U.S. Gulf Coast. Tens of thousands of people lost their homes and possessions. Even those who weren't directly affected by the destruction were hurt because businesses and jobs dried up. Using one of the principles of economy-wide interaction, explain how government intervention can help in this situation.

16. During the Great Depression, food was left to rot in the fields or fields that had once been actively cultivated were left fallow. Use one of the principles of economy-wide interaction to explain how this could have occurred.

 www.worthpublishers.com/krugmanwells

>> Economic Models: Trade-offs and Trade

TUNNEL VISION

IN 1901 WILBUR AND ORVILLE WRIGHT BUILT something that would change the world. No, not the airplane—their successful flight at Kitty Hawk would come two years later. What made the Wright brothers true visionaries was their wind tunnel, an apparatus that let them experiment with many different designs for wings and control surfaces. These experiments gave them the knowledge that would make heavier-than-air flight possible.

A miniature airplane sitting motionless in a wind tunnel isn't the same thing as an actual aircraft in flight. But it is a very useful model of a flying plane—a simplified representation of the real thing that can be used to answer crucial questions, such as how much lift a given wing shape will generate at a given airspeed.

Needless to say, testing an airplane design in a wind tunnel is cheaper and safer than building a full-scale version and hoping it will fly. More generally, models play a crucial role in almost all scientific research—economics very much included.

In fact, you could say that economic theory consists mainly of a collection of models, a series of simplified representations of economic reality that allow us to understand a variety of economic issues. In this chapter, we will look at two economic models that are crucially important in their own right and also illustrate why such models are so useful. We'll conclude with a look at how economists actually use models in their work.

Landow Photos

Clearly, the Wright brothers believed in their model.

WHAT YOU WILL LEARN IN THIS CHAPTER:

➤ Why **models**—simplified representations of reality—play a crucial role in economics

➤ Two simple but important models: the **production possibility frontier** and **comparative advantage**

➤ The **circular-flow diagram**, a schematic representation of the economy

➤ The difference between **positive economics**, which tries to

describe the economy and predict its behavior, and **normative economics**, which tries to prescribe economic policy

➤ When economists agree and why they sometimes disagree

A **model** is a simplified representation of a real situation that is used to better understand real-life situations.

The **other things equal assumption** means that all other relevant factors remain unchanged.

Models in Economics: Some Important Examples

A **model** is any simplified representation of reality that is used to better understand real-life situations. But how do we create a simplified representation of an economic situation?

One possibility—an economist's equivalent of a wind tunnel—is to find or create a real but simplified economy. For example, economists interested in the economic role of money have studied the system of exchange that developed in World War II prison camps, in which cigarettes became a universally accepted form of payment even among prisoners who didn't smoke.

Another possibility is to simulate the workings of the economy on a computer. For example, when changes in tax law are proposed, government officials use *tax models*—large mathematical computer programs—to assess how the proposed changes would affect different types of people.

Models are important because their simplicity allows economists to focus on the effects of only one change at a time. That is, they allow us to hold everything else constant and study how one change affects the overall economic outcome. So an important assumption when building economic models is the **other things equal assumption,** which means that all other relevant factors remain unchanged.

But you can't always find or create a small-scale version of the whole economy, and a computer program is only as good as the data it uses. (Programmers have a saying: garbage in, garbage out.) For many purposes, the most effective form of economic modeling is the construction of "thought experiments": simplified, hypothetical versions of real-life situations.

In Chapter 1 we illustrated the concept of equilibrium with the example of how customers at a supermarket would rearrange themselves when a new cash register opens. Though we didn't say it, this was an example of a simple model—an imaginary

FOR INQUIRING MINDS

Models for Money

What's an economic model worth, anyway? In some cases, quite a lot of money.

Although many economic models are developed for purely scientific purposes, others are developed to help governments make economic policies. And there is a growing business in developing economic models to help corporations make decisions.

Who models for money? There are dozens of consulting firms that use models to predict future trends, offer advice based on their models, or develop custom models for business and government clients. A notable example is Global Insight, the world's biggest economic consulting firm. It was created by a merger between Data Resources, Inc., founded by professors from Harvard and MIT, and Wharton Economic Forecasting Associates, founded by professors at the University of Pennsylvania.

One particularly lucrative branch of economics is finance theory, which helps investors figure out what assets, such as shares in a company, are worth. Finance theorists often become highly paid "rocket scientists" at big Wall Street firms because financial models demand a high level of technical expertise.

Unfortunately, the most famous business application of finance theory came spectacularly to grief. In 1994 a group of Wall Street traders teamed up with famous finance theorists—including two Nobel Prize winners—to form Long-Term Capital Management (LTCM), a fund that used sophisticated financial models to invest the money of wealthy clients. At first, the fund did very well. But in 1998 bad economic news from all over the world— with countries as disparate as Russia, Japan, and Brazil in financial trouble at the same time—inflicted huge losses on LTCM's investments. For a few anxious days, many people feared not only that the fund would collapse but also that it would bring many other companies down with it. Thanks in part to a rescue operation organized by government officials, this did not happen; but LTCM was closed a few months later, having lost millions of dollars and with some of its investors losing most of the money they had put in.

What went wrong? Partly it was bad luck. But experienced hands also faulted the economists at LTCM for taking too many risks. Although LTCM's models indicated that a run of bad news like the one that actually happened was extremely unlikely, a sensible economist knows that sometimes even the best model misses important possibilities.

Interestingly, a similar phenomenon occurred in the summer of 2007, when problems in the financial market for home mortgage loans caused severe losses for several investment funds. It turns out that these funds had made the same mistake as LTCM—omitting from their models the possibility of a severe downturn in the home mortgage loan market.

supermarket, in which many details were ignored (what are the customers buying? never mind), that could be used to answer a "what if" question: what if another cash register were opened?

As the cash register story showed, it is often possible to describe and analyze a useful economic model in plain English. However, because much of economics involves changes in quantities—in the price of a product, the number of units produced, or the number of workers employed in its production—economists often find that using some mathematics helps clarify an issue. In particular, a numerical example, a simple equation, or—especially—a graph can be key to understanding an economic concept.

Whatever form it takes, a good economic model can be a tremendous aid to understanding. The best way to grasp this point is to consider some simple but important economic models and what they tell us. First, we will look at the *production possibility frontier,* a model that helps economists think about the trade-offs every economy faces. Then we will turn to *comparative advantage,* a model that clarifies the principle of gains from trade—trade both between individuals and between countries. In addition, we'll examine the *circular-flow diagram,* a schematic representation that helps us understand how flows of money, goods, and services are channeled through the economy.

In discussing these models, we make considerable use of graphs to represent mathematical relationships. Such graphs will play an important role throughout this book. If you are already familiar with the use of graphs, the material that follows should not present any problem. If you are not, this would be a good time to turn to the appendix of this chapter, which provides a brief introduction to the use of graphs in economics.

> The **production possibility frontier** illustrates the trade-offs facing an economy that produces only two goods. It shows the maximum quantity of one good that can be produced for any given quantity produced of the other.

Trade-offs: The Production Possibility Frontier

The hit movie *Cast Away,* starring Tom Hanks, was an update of the classic story of Robinson Crusoe, the hero of Daniel Defoe's eighteenth-century novel. Hanks played the sole survivor of a plane crash, stranded on a remote island. As in the original story of Robinson Crusoe, the character played by Hanks had limited resources: the natural resources of the island, a few items he managed to salvage from the plane, and, of course, his own time and effort. With only these resources, he had to make a life. In effect, he became a one-man economy.

The first principle of economics we introduced in Chapter 1 was that resources are scarce and that, as a result, any economy—whether it contains one person or millions of people—faces trade-offs. For example, if a castaway devotes resources to catching fish, he cannot use those same resources to gather coconuts.

To think about the trade-offs that face any economy, economists often use the model known as the **production possibility frontier.** The idea behind this model is to improve our understanding of trade-offs by considering a simplified economy that produces only two goods. This simplification enables us to show the trade-off graphically.

Figure 2-1 on the next page shows a hypothetical production possibility frontier for Tom, a castaway alone on an island, who must make a trade-off between production of fish and production of coconuts. The frontier—the line in the diagram—shows the maximum quantity of fish Tom can catch during a week *given* the quantity of coconuts he gathers, and vice versa. That is, it answers questions of the form, "What is the maximum quantity of fish Tom can catch if he also gathers 9 (or 15, or 30) coconuts?"

There is a crucial distinction between points *inside* or *on* the production possibility frontier (the shaded area) and *outside* the frontier. If a production point lies inside or on the frontier—like point C, at which Tom catches 20 fish and gathers 9 coconuts—it is feasible. After all, the frontier tells us that if Tom catches 20 fish, he could also gather a maximum of 15 coconuts, so he could

What to do? Even a castaway faces trade-offs.

FIGURE 2-1

The Production Possibility Frontier

The production possibility frontier illustrates the trade-offs facing an economy that produces two goods. It shows the maximum quantity of one good that can be produced given the quantity of the other good produced. Here, the maximum quantity of coconuts that Tom can gather depends on the quantity of fish he catches, and vice versa. His feasible production is shown by the area *inside* or *on* the curve. Production at point *C* is feasible but not efficient. Points *A* and *B* are feasible and efficient in production, but point *D* is not feasible.

certainly gather 9 coconuts. However, a production point that lies outside the frontier—such as the hypothetical production point *D*, where Tom catches 40 fish and gathers 30 coconuts—isn't feasible. (In this case, Tom could catch 40 fish and gather no coconuts *or* he could gather 30 coconuts and catch no fish, but he can't do both.)

In Figure 2-1 the production possibility frontier intersects the horizontal axis at 40 fish. This means that if Tom devoted all his resources to catching fish, he would catch 40 fish per week but would have no resources left over to gather coconuts. The production possibility frontier intersects the vertical axis at 30 coconuts. This means that if Tom devoted all his resources to gathering coconuts, he could gather 30 coconuts per week but would have no resources left over to catch fish.

The figure also shows less extreme trade-offs. For example, if Tom decides to catch 20 fish, he is able to gather at most 15 coconuts; this production choice is illustrated by point *A*. If Tom decides to catch 28 fish, he can gather at most only 9 coconuts, as shown by point *B*.

Thinking in terms of a production possibility frontier simplifies the complexities of reality. The real-world economy produces millions of different goods. Even a castaway on an island would produce more than two different items (for example, he would need clothing and housing as well as food). But in this model we imagine an economy that produces only two goods.

By simplifying reality, however, the production possibility frontier helps us understand some aspects of the real economy better than we could without the model: efficiency, opportunity cost, and economic growth.

Efficiency First of all, the production possibility frontier is a good way to illustrate the general economic concept of *efficiency*. Recall from Chapter 1 that an economy is efficient if there are no missed opportunities—there is no way to make some people better off without making other people worse off.

One key element of efficiency is that there are no missed opportunities in production—there is no way to produce more of one good without producing less of other goods. As long as Tom is on the production possibility frontier, his production is efficient. At point *A*, the 15 coconuts he gathers are the maximum quantity he can get *given* that he has chosen to catch 20 fish; at point *B*, the 9 coconuts he gathers are the maximum he can get *given* his choice to catch 28 fish; and so on. If an economy is producing at a point on its production possibility frontier, we say that the economy is *efficient in production*.

But suppose that for some reason Tom was at point *C*, producing 20 fish and 9 coconuts. Then this one-person economy would definitely not be efficient in production, and would therefore be *inefficient:* it could be producing more of both goods. Another example of this occurs when people are involuntarily unemployed: they want to work but are unable to find jobs. When that happens, the economy is not efficient in production because it could be producing more output if these people were employed.

Although the production possibility frontier helps clarify what it means for an economy to be efficient in production, it's important to understand that efficiency in production is only *part* of what's required for the economy as a whole to be efficient. Efficiency also requires that the economy allocate its resources so that consumers are as well off as possible. If an economy does this, we say that it is *efficient in allocation.* To see why efficiency in allocation is as important as efficiency in production, notice that points A and B in Figure 2-1 both represent situations in which the economy is efficient in production, because in each case it can't produce more of one good without producing less of the other. But these two situations may not be equally desirable. Suppose that Tom prefers point *B* to point *A*—that is, he would rather consume 28 fish and 9 coconuts than 20 fish and 15 coconuts. Then point *A* is inefficient from the point of view of the economy as a whole: it's possible to make Tom better off without making anyone else worse off. (Of course, in this castaway economy there isn't anyone else: Tom is all alone.)

This example shows that efficiency for the economy as a whole requires *both* efficiency in production and efficiency in allocation: to be efficient, an economy must produce as much of each good as it can given the production of other goods, and it must also produce the mix of goods that people want to consume. In the real world, command economies, such as the former Soviet Union, were notorious for inefficiency in allocation. For example, it was common for consumers to find a store stocked with a few odd items of merchandise, but lacking such basics as soap and toilet paper.

Opportunity Cost The production possibility frontier is also useful as a reminder of the fundamental point that the true cost of any good is not just the amount of money it costs to buy, but everything else in addition to money that must be given up in order to get that good—the *opportunity cost.* If, for example, Tom decides to go from point *A* to point *B*, he will produce 8 more fish but 6 fewer coconuts. So the opportunity cost of those 8 fish is the 6 coconuts not gathered. Since 8 extra fish have an opportunity cost of 6 coconuts, each 1 fish has an opportunity cost of $6/8 = 3/4$ of a coconut.

Is the opportunity cost of an extra fish in terms of coconuts always the same, no matter how many fish Tom catches? In the example illustrated by Figure 2-1, the answer is yes. If Tom increases his catch from 28 to 40 fish, the number of coconuts he gathers falls from 9 to zero. So his opportunity cost per additional fish is $9/12 = 3/4$ of a coconut, the same as it was when he went from 20 fish caught to 28. However, the fact that in this example the opportunity cost of an additional fish in terms of coconuts is always the same is a result of an assumption we've made, an assumption that's reflected in how Figure 2-1 is drawn. Specifically, whenever we assume that the opportunity cost of an additional unit of a good doesn't change regardless of the output mix, the production possibility frontier is a straight line.

Moreover, as you might have already guessed, the slope of a straight-line production possibility frontier is equal to the opportunity cost—specifically, the opportunity cost for the good measured on the horizontal axis in terms of the good measured on the vertical axis. In Figure 2-1, the production possibility frontier has a *constant slope* of $-3/4$, implying that Tom faces a *constant opportunity cost* for 1 fish equal to $3/4$ of a coconut. (A review of how to calculate the slope of a straight line is found in this chapter's appendix.) This is the simplest case, but the production possibility frontier model can also be used to examine situations in which opportunity costs change as the mix of output changes.

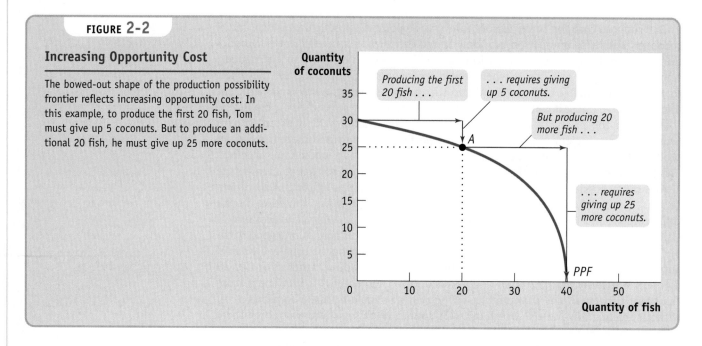

FIGURE 2-2

Increasing Opportunity Cost

The bowed-out shape of the production possibility frontier reflects increasing opportunity cost. In this example, to produce the first 20 fish, Tom must give up 5 coconuts. But to produce an additional 20 fish, he must give up 25 more coconuts.

Producing the first 20 fish . . .

. . . requires giving up 5 coconuts.

But producing 20 more fish . . .

. . . requires giving up 25 more coconuts.

PPF

Figure 2-2 illustrates a different assumption, a case in which Tom faces *increasing opportunity cost.* Here, the more fish he catches, the more coconuts he has to give up to catch an additional fish, and vice versa. For example, to go from producing zero fish to producing 20 fish, he has to give up 5 coconuts. That is, the opportunity cost of those 20 fish is 5 coconuts. But to increase his fish production to 40—that is, to produce an additional 20 fish—he must give up 25 more coconuts, a much higher opportunity cost. As you can see in Figure 2-2, when opportunity costs are increasing rather than constant, the production possibility frontier is a bowed-out curve rather than a straight line.

Although it's often useful to work with the simple assumption that the production possibility frontier is a straight line, economists believe that in reality opportunity costs are typically increasing. When only a small amount of a good is produced, the opportunity cost of producing that good is relatively low because the economy needs to use only those resources that are especially well suited for its production. For example, if an economy grows only a small amount of corn, that corn can be grown in places where the soil and climate are perfect for corn-growing but less suitable for growing anything else, like wheat. So growing that corn involves giving up only a small amount of potential wheat output. Once the economy grows a lot of corn, however, land that is well suited for wheat but isn't so great for corn must be used to produce corn anyway. As a result, the additional corn production involves sacrificing considerably more wheat production. In other words, as more of a good is produced, its opportunity cost typically rises because well-suited inputs are used up and less adaptable inputs must be used instead.

Economic Growth Finally, the production possibility frontier helps us understand what it means to talk about *economic growth.* We introduced the concept of economic growth in the Introduction, defining it as *the growing ability of the economy to produce goods and services.* As we saw, economic growth is one of the fundamental features of the real economy. But are we really justified in saying that the economy has grown over time? After all, although the U.S. economy produces more of many things than it did a century ago, it produces less of other things—for example, horse-drawn carriages. Production of many goods, in other words, is actually down. So how can we say for sure that the economy as a whole has grown?

The answer, illustrated in Figure 2-3, is that economic growth means an *expansion of the economy's production possibilities:* the economy *can* produce more of everything. For example, if Tom's production is initially at point *A* (20 fish and 25 coconuts),

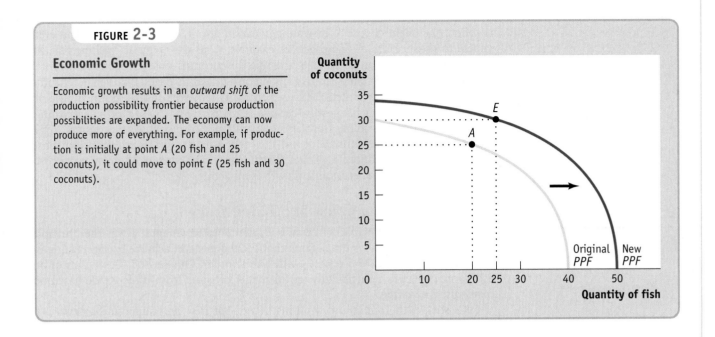

FIGURE 2-3

Economic Growth

Economic growth results in an *outward shift* of the production possibility frontier because production possibilities are expanded. The economy can now produce more of everything. For example, if production is initially at point *A* (20 fish and 25 coconuts), it could move to point *E* (25 fish and 30 coconuts).

economic growth means that he could move to point *E* (25 fish and 30 coconuts). *E* lies outside the original frontier; so in the production possibility frontier model, growth is shown as an outward shift of the frontier.

What can lead the production possibility frontier to shift outward? There are basically two sources of economic growth. One is an increase in the economy's **factors of production,** the resources used to produce goods and services. Economists usually use the term *factor of production* to refer to a resource that is not used up in production. For example, workers use sewing machines to convert cloth into shirts; the workers and the sewing machines are factors of production, but the cloth is not. Once a shirt is made, a worker and a sewing machine can be used to make another shirt; but the cloth used to make one shirt cannot be used to make another. Broadly speaking, the main factors of production are the resources land, labor, capital, and human capital. Land is a resource supplied by nature; labor is the economy's pool of workers; capital refers to "created" resources such as machines and buildings; and human capital refers to the educational achievements and skills of the labor force, which enhance its productivity. Of course, each of these is really a category rather than a single factor: land in North Dakota is quite different from land in Florida.

To see how adding to an economy's factors of production leads to economic growth, suppose that Tom finds a fishing net washed ashore on the beach that is larger than the net he currently uses. The fishing net is a factor of production, a resource he can use to produce more fish in the course of a day spent fishing. We can't say how many more fish Tom will catch; that depends on how much time he decides to spend fishing now that he has the larger net. But because the larger net makes his fishing more productive, he can catch more fish without reducing the number of coconuts he gathers, or gather more coconuts without reducing his fish catch. So his production possibility frontier shifts outward.

The other source of economic growth is progress in **technology,** the technical means for the production of goods and services. Suppose Tom figures out a better way either to catch fish or to gather coconuts—say, by inventing a fishing hook or a wagon for transporting coconuts. Either invention would shift his production possibility frontier outward. In real-world economies, innovations in the techniques we use to produce goods and services have been a crucial force behind economic growth.

Again, economic growth means an increase in what the economy *can* produce. What the economy actually produces depends on the choices people make. After his production possibilities expand, Tom might not choose to produce both more fish and more

Factors of production are resources used to produce goods and services.

Technology is the technical means for producing goods and services.

coconuts—he might choose to increase production of only one good, or he might even choose to produce less of one good. For example, if he gets better at catching fish, he might decide to go on an all-fish diet and skip the coconuts—just as the introduction of motor vehicles led most people to give up on horse-drawn carriages. But even if, for some reason, he chooses to produce either fewer coconuts or fewer fish than before, we would still say that his economy has grown—because he *could* have produced more of everything.

The production possibility frontier is a very simplified model of an economy. Yet it teaches us important lessons about real-life economies. It gives us our first clear sense of what constitutes economic efficiency, it illustrates the concept of opportunity cost, and it makes clear what economic growth is all about.

Comparative Advantage and Gains from Trade

Among the twelve principles of economics described in Chapter 1 was the principle of *gains from trade*—the mutual gains that individuals can achieve by specializing in doing different things and trading with one another. Our second illustration of an economic model is a particularly useful model of gains from trade—trade based on *comparative advantage*.

Let's stick with Tom stranded on his island, but now let's suppose that a second castaway, who just happens to be named Hank, is washed ashore. Can they benefit from trading with each other?

It's obvious that there will be potential gains from trade if the two castaways do different things particularly well. For example, if Tom is a skilled fisherman and Hank is very good at climbing trees, clearly it makes sense for Tom to catch fish and Hank to gather coconuts—and for the two men to trade the products of their efforts.

But one of the most important insights in all of economics is that there are gains from trade even if one of the trading parties isn't especially good at anything. Suppose, for example, that Hank is less well suited to primitive life than Tom; he's not nearly as good at catching fish, and compared to Tom even his coconut-gathering leaves something to be desired. Nonetheless, what we'll see is that both Tom and Hank can live better by trading with each other than either could alone.

For the purposes of this example, let's go back to the simpler case of straight-line production possibility frontiers. Tom's production possibilities are represented by the

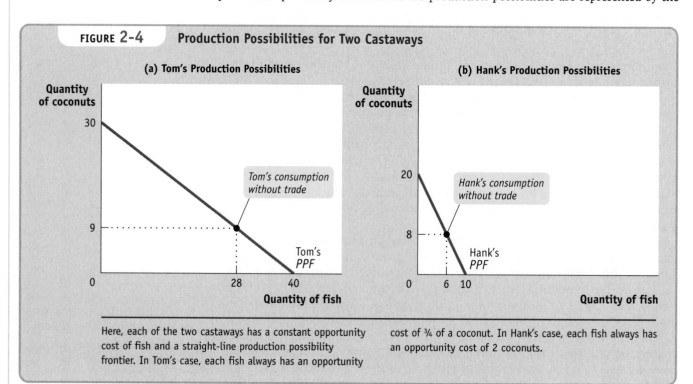

FIGURE 2-4   **Production Possibilities for Two Castaways**

Here, each of the two castaways has a constant opportunity cost of fish and a straight-line production possibility frontier. In Tom's case, each fish always has an opportunity cost of ¾ of a coconut. In Hank's case, each fish always has an opportunity cost of 2 coconuts.

production possibility frontier in panel (a) of Figure 2-4, which is the same as the production possibility frontier in Figure 2-1. According to this diagram, Tom could catch 40 fish, but only if he gathered no coconuts, and could gather 30 coconuts, but only if he caught no fish, as before. Recall that this means that the slope of his production possibility frontier is −¾: his opportunity cost of 1 fish is ¾ of a coconut.

Panel (b) of Figure 2-4 shows Hank's production possibilities. Like Tom's, Hank's production possibility frontier is a straight line, implying a constant opportunity cost of fish in terms of coconuts. His production possibility frontier has a constant slope of −2. Hank is less productive all around: at most he can produce 10 fish or 20 coconuts. But he is particularly bad at fishing; whereas Tom sacrifices ¾ of a coconut per fish caught, for Hank the opportunity cost of a fish is 2 whole coconuts. Table 2-1 summarizes the two castaways' opportunity costs of fish and coconuts.

> An individual has a **comparative advantage** in producing a good or service if the opportunity cost of producing the good or service is lower for that individual than for other people.

TABLE 2-1

Tom's and Hank's Opportunity Costs of Fish and Coconuts

	Tom's Opportunity Cost	Hank's Opportunity Cost
One fish	3/4 coconut	2 coconuts
One coconut	4/3 fish	1/2 fish

Now, Tom and Hank could go their separate ways, each living on his own side of the island, catching his own fish and gathering his own coconuts. Let's suppose that they start out that way and make the consumption choices shown in Figure 2-4: in the absence of trade, Tom consumes 28 fish and 9 coconuts per week, while Hank consumes 6 fish and 8 coconuts.

But is this the best they can do? No, it isn't. Given that the two castaways have different opportunity costs, they can strike a deal that makes both of them better off.

Table 2-2 shows how such a deal works: Tom specializes in the production of fish, catching 40 per week, and gives 10 to Hank. Meanwhile, Hank specializes in the production of coconuts, gathering 20 per week, and gives 10 to Tom. The result is shown in Figure 2-5 on the next page. Tom now consumes more of both goods than before: instead of 28 fish and 9 coconuts, he consumes 30 fish and 10 coconuts. And Hank also consumes more, going from 6 fish and 8 coconuts to 10 fish and 10 coconuts. As Table 2-2 also shows, both Tom and Hank experience gains from trade: Tom's consumption of fish increases by two, and his consumption of coconuts increases by one. Hank's consumption of fish increases by four, and his consumption of coconuts increases by two.

So both castaways are better off when they each specialize in what they are good at and trade. It's a good idea for Tom to catch the fish for both of them because his opportunity cost of a fish is only ¾ of a coconut not gathered versus 2 coconuts for Hank. Correspondingly, it's a good idea for Hank to gather coconuts for both of them.

Or we could put it the other way around: Because Tom is so good at catching fish, his opportunity cost of gathering coconuts is high: ⁴⁄₃ of a fish not caught for every coconut gathered. Because Hank is a pretty poor fisherman, his opportunity cost of gathering coconuts is much less, only ½ of a fish per coconut.

What we would say in this case is that Tom has a comparative advantage in catching fish and Hank has a comparative advantage in gathering coconuts. An individual has a **comparative advantage** in producing something if the opportunity cost of that production is lower for that individual than for other people. In other words, Hank has a comparative advantage over Tom in producing a particular good or service if Hank's opportunity cost of producing that good or service is lower than Tom's.

TABLE 2-2

How the Castaways Gain from Trade

		Without Trade		With Trade		Gains from Trade
		Production	Consumption	Production	Consumption	
Tom	Fish	28	28	40	30	+2
	Coconuts	9	9	0	10	+1
Hank	Fish	6	6	0	10	+4
	Coconuts	8	8	20	10	+2

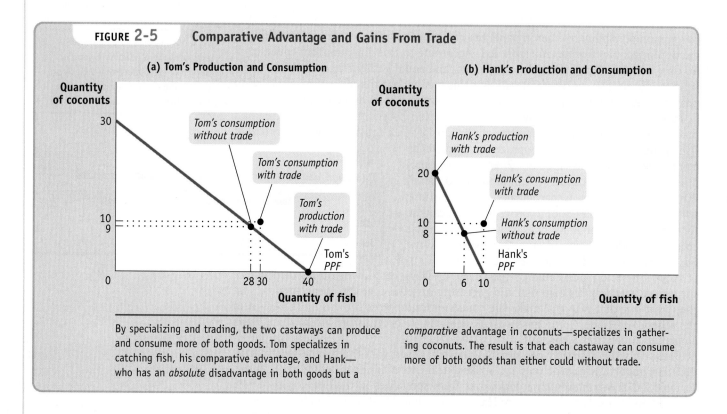

FIGURE **2-5** **Comparative Advantage and Gains From Trade**

(a) Tom's Production and Consumption

(b) Hank's Production and Consumption

By specializing and trading, the two castaways can produce and consume more of both goods. Tom specializes in catching fish, his comparative advantage, and Hank—who has an *absolute* disadvantage in both goods but a *comparative* advantage in coconuts—specializes in gathering coconuts. The result is that each castaway can consume more of both goods than either could without trade.

One point of clarification before we proceed further. You may have wondered why Tom and Hank traded 10 fish for 10 coconuts. Why not some other deal, like trading 15 coconuts for 5 fish? The answer to that question has two parts. First, there may indeed be deals other than 10 fish for 10 coconuts that Tom and Hank are willing to agree to. Second, there are some deals that we can, however, safely rule out—one like 15 coconuts for 5 fish. To understand why, reexamine Table 2-1 and consider Hank first. When Hank works on his own without trading with Tom, his opportunity cost of 1 fish is 2 coconuts. Therefore, it's clear that Hank will not accept any deal with Tom in which he must give up more than 2 coconuts per fish—otherwise, he's better off not trading at all. So we can rule out a deal that requires Hank to pay 3 coconuts per fish—such as trading 15 coconuts for 5 fish. But Hank will accept a trade in which he pays less than 2 coconuts per fish—such as paying 1 coconut for 1 fish. Likewise, Tom will reject a deal that requires him to give up more than 4/3 of a fish per coconut. For example, Tom would refuse a trade that required him to give up 10 fish for 6 coconuts. But he will accept a deal where he pays less than 4/3 of a fish per coconut—and 1 fish for 1 coconut works. You can check for yourself why a trade of 1 fish for 1.5 coconuts would also be acceptable to both Tom and Hank. So the point to remember is that Tom and Hank will be willing to engage in a trade only if the "price" of the good each person is obtaining from the trade is less than his own opportunity cost of producing the good himself. Moreover, that's a general statement that is true whenever two parties trade voluntarily.

The story of Tom and Hank clearly simplifies reality. Yet it teaches us some very important lessons that apply to the real economy, too.

First, the model provides a clear illustration of the gains from trade: by agreeing to specialize and provide goods to each other, Tom and Hank can produce more and therefore both be better off than if they tried to be self-sufficient.

Second, the model demonstrates a very important point that is often overlooked in real-world arguments: as long as people have different opportunity costs, *everyone has a comparative advantage in something, and everyone has a comparative disadvantage in something.*

Notice that in our example Tom is actually better than Hank at producing both goods: Tom can catch more fish in a week, and he can also gather more coconuts. That is, Tom has an **absolute advantage** in both activities: he can produce more output with a given amount of input (in this case, his time) than Hank. You might therefore be tempted to think that Tom has nothing to gain from trading with the less competent Hank.

But we've just seen that Tom can indeed benefit from a deal with Hank because *comparative,* not *absolute,* advantage is the basis for mutual gain. It doesn't matter that it takes Hank more time to gather a coconut; what matters is that for him the opportunity cost of that coconut in terms of fish is lower. So Hank, despite his absolute disadvantage, even in coconuts, has a comparative advantage in coconut-gathering. Meanwhile Tom, who can use his time better by catching fish, has a comparative *dis*advantage in coconut-gathering.

If comparative advantage were relevant only to castaways, it might not be that interesting. In fact, however, the idea of comparative advantage applies to many activities in the economy. Perhaps its most important application is to trade—not between individuals, but between countries. So let's look briefly at how the model of comparative advantage helps in understanding both the causes and the effects of international trade.

Comparative Advantage and International Trade

Look at the label on a manufactured good sold in the United States, and there's a good chance you will find that it was produced in some other country—in China, or Japan, or even in Canada, eh? On the other side, many U.S. industries sell a large fraction of their output overseas. (This is particularly true of agriculture, high technology, and entertainment.)

Should all this international exchange of goods and services be celebrated, or is it cause for concern? Politicians and the public often question the desirability of international trade, arguing that the nation should produce goods for itself rather than buying them from foreigners. Industries around the world demand protection from foreign competition: Japanese farmers want to keep out American rice, American steelworkers want to keep out European steel. And these demands are often supported by public opinion.

Economists, however, have a very positive view of international trade. Why? Because they view it in terms of comparative advantage.

Figure 2-6 on the next page shows, with a simple example, how international trade can be interpreted in terms of comparative advantage. Although the example as constructed is hypothetical, it is based on an actual pattern of international trade: American exports of pork to Canada and Canadian exports of aircraft to the United States. Panels (a) and (b) illustrate hypothetical production possibility frontiers for the United States and Canada, with pork measured on the horizontal axis and aircraft measured on the vertical axis. The U.S. production possibility frontier is flatter than the Canadian frontier, implying that producing one more ton of pork costs a lot fewer aircraft in the United States than it does in Canada. This means that the United States has a comparative advantage in pork and Canada has a comparative advantage in aircraft.

Although the consumption points in Figure 2-6 are hypothetical, they illustrate a general principle: just like the example of Tom and Hank, the United States and Canada can both achieve mutual gains from trade. If the United States concentrates on producing pork and ships some of its output to Canada, while Canada concentrates on aircraft and ships some of its output to the United States, both countries can consume more than if they insisted on being self-sufficient.

> An individual has an **absolute advantage** in an activity if he or she can do it better than other people. Having an absolute advantage is not the same thing as having a comparative advantage.

PITFALLS

MISUNDERSTANDING COMPARATIVE ADVANTAGE

Students do it, pundits do it, and politicians do it all the time: they confuse *comparative* advantage with *absolute* advantage. For example, back in the 1980s, when the U.S. economy seemed to be lagging behind that of Japan, one often heard commentators warn that if we didn't improve our productivity, we would soon have no comparative advantage in anything.

What those commentators meant was that we would have no *absolute* advantage in anything—that there might come a time when the Japanese were better at everything than we were. (It didn't turn out that way, but that's another story.) And they had the idea that in that case we would no longer be able to benefit from trade with Japan.

But just as Hank is able to benefit from trade with Tom (and vice versa) despite the fact that Tom is better at everything, nations can still gain from trade even if they are less productive in all industries than the countries they trade with.

FIGURE 2-6   Comparative Advantage and International Trade

(a) U.S. Production Possibility Frontier

(b) Canadian Production Possibility Frontier

In this hypothetical example, Canada and the United States produce only two goods: pork and aircraft. Aircraft are measured on the vertical axis and pork on the horizontal axis. Panel (a) shows the U.S. production possibility frontier. It is relatively flat, implying that the United States has a comparative advantage in pork production. Panel (b) shows the Canadian production possibility frontier. It is relatively steep, implying that Canada has a comparative advantage in aircraft production. Just like two individuals, both countries gain from specialization and trade.

Moreover, these mutual gains don't depend on each country being better at producing one kind of good. Even if one country has, say, higher output per person-hour in both industries—that is, even if one country has an absolute advantage in both industries—there are still mutual gains from trade.

 GLOBAL COMPARISON   **PAJAMA REPUBLICS**

Poor countries tend to have low productivity in clothing manufacture, but even lower productivity in other industries (see the upcoming Economics in Action). As a result, they have a comparative advantage in clothing production, which actually dominates the industries of some very poor countries. An official from one such country once joked, "We are not a banana republic—we are a pajama republic."

This figure, which compares per capita income (the total income of the country divided by the size of the population) with the share of the clothing industry in manufacturing employment, shows just how strong this effect is.

According to a U.S. Department of Commerce assessment, Bangladesh's clothing industry has "low productivity, largely low literacy levels, frequent labor unrest, and outdated technology." Yet it devotes most of its manufacturing workforce to clothing, the sector in which it nonetheless has a *comparative* advantage because its productivity in nonclothing industries is even lower. The same assessment describes Costa Rica as having "relatively high productivity" in clothing—yet a much smaller and declining fraction of Costa Rica's workforce is employed in clothing production. That's because productivity in nonclothing industries is somewhat higher in Costa Rica than in Bangladesh.

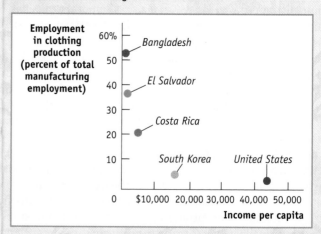

Source: World Bank, World Development Indicators; Nicita A. and M. Olarreaga "Trade, Production and Protection 1976–2004," *World Bank Economic Review* 21 no. 1 (2007): 165–171.

Transactions: The Circular-Flow Diagram

The little economy created by Tom and Hank on their island lacks many features of the modern American economy. For one thing, though millions of Americans are self-employed, most workers are employed by someone else, usually a company with hundreds or thousands of employees. Also, Tom and Hank engage only in the simplest of economic transactions, **barter,** in which an individual directly trades a good or service he or she has for a good or service he or she wants. In the modern economy, simple barter is rare: usually people trade goods or services for money—pieces of colored paper with no inherent value—and then trade those pieces of colored paper for the goods or services they want. That is, they sell goods or services and buy other goods or services.

And they both sell and buy a lot of different things. The U.S. economy is a vastly complex entity, with more than a hundred million workers employed by millions of companies, producing millions of different goods and services. Yet you can learn some very important things about the economy by considering the simple graphic shown in Figure 2-7, the **circular-flow diagram.** This diagram represents the transactions that take place in an economy by two kinds of flows around a circle: flows of physical things such as goods, services, labor, or raw materials in one direction, and flows of money that pay for these physical things in the opposite direction. In this case the physical flows are shown in yellow, the money flows in green.

The simplest circular-flow diagram illustrates an economy that contains only two kinds of "inhabitants": **households** and **firms.** A household consists of either an individual or a group of people (usually, but not necessarily, a family) that share their income. A firm is an organization (usually, but not necessarily, a corporation) that produces goods and services for sale—and that employs members of households.

As you can see in Figure 2-7, there are two kinds of markets in this simple economy. On one side (here the left side) there are **markets for goods and services** in which households buy the goods and services they want from firms. This produces a flow of goods and services to households and a return flow of money to firms.

On the other side, there are **factor markets** in which firms buy the resources they need to produce goods and services. Recall from earlier in the chapter that the main factors of production are land, labor, capital, and human capital.

Trade takes the form of **barter** when people directly exchange goods or services that they have for goods or services that they want.

The **circular-flow diagram** represents the transactions in an economy by flows around a circle.

A **household** is a person or a group of people that share their income.

A **firm** is an organization that produces goods and services for sale.

Firms sell goods and services that they produce to households in **markets for goods and services.**

Firms buy the resources they need to produce goods and services in **factor markets.**

FIGURE 2-7

The Circular-Flow Diagram

This diagram represents the flows of money and goods and services in the economy. In the markets for goods and services, households purchase goods and services from firms, generating a flow of money to the firms and a flow of goods and services to the households. The money flows back to households as firms purchase factors of production from the households in factor markets.

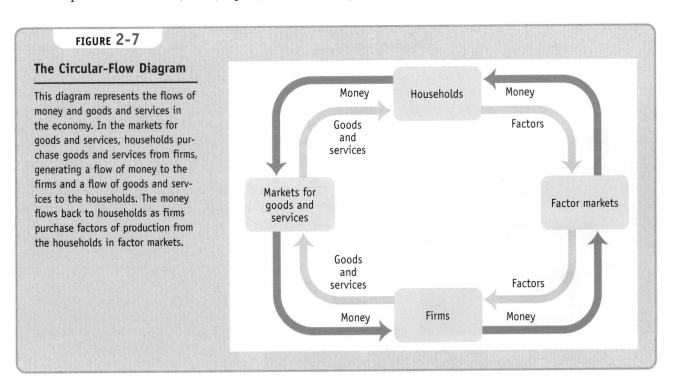

An economy's **income distribution** is the way in which total income is divided among the owners of the various factors of production.

The factor market most of us know best is the *labor market*, in which workers are paid for their time. Besides labor, we can think of households as owning and selling the other factors of production to firms. For example, when a corporation pays dividends to its stockholders, who are members of households, it is in effect paying them for the use of the machines and buildings that ultimately belong to those investors. In this case, the transactions are occurring in the *capital market,* the market in which capital is bought and sold. As we'll examine in detail later, factor markets ultimately determine an economy's **income distribution,** how the total income created in an economy is allocated between less skilled workers, highly skilled workers, and the owners of capital and land.

The circular-flow diagram ignores a number of real-world complications in the interests of simplicity. A few examples:

- In the real world, the distinction between firms and households isn't always that clear-cut. Consider a small, family-run business—a farm, a shop, a small hotel. Is this a firm or a household? A more complete picture would include a separate box for family businesses.

- Many of the sales firms make are not to households but to other firms; for example, steel companies sell mainly to other companies such as auto manufacturers, not to households. A more complete picture would include these flows of goods, services, and money within the business sector.

- The figure doesn't show the government, which in the real world diverts quite a lot of money out of the circular flow in the form of taxes but also injects a lot of money back into the flow in the form of spending.

Figure 2-7, in other words, is by no means a complete picture either of all the types of inhabitants of the real economy or of all the flows of money and physical items that take place among these inhabitants.

Despite its simplicity, the circular-flow diagram is a very useful aid to thinking about the economy.

►ECONOMICS IN ACTION

Rich Nation, Poor Nation

Try taking off your clothes—at a suitable time and in a suitable place, of course—and take a look at the labels inside that say where they were made. It's a very good bet that much, if not most, of your clothing was manufactured overseas, in a country that is much poorer than the United States—say, in El Salvador, Sri Lanka, or Bangladesh.

Why are these countries so much poorer than we are? The immediate reason is that their economies are much less *productive*—firms in these countries are just not able to produce as much from a given quantity of resources as comparable firms in the United States or other wealthy countries. Why countries differ so much in productivity is a deep question—indeed, one of the main questions that preoccupy economists. But in any case, the difference in productivity is a fact.

But if the economies of these countries are so much less productive than ours, how is it that they make so much of our clothing? Why don't we do it for ourselves?

The answer is "comparative advantage." Just about every industry in Bangladesh is much less productive than the corresponding industry in the United States. But the productivity difference between rich and poor countries varies across goods; it is very large in the production of sophisticated goods like aircraft but not that large in the production of simpler goods like clothing. So Bangladesh's position with regard to clothing production is like Hank's position with respect to coconut-gathering: he's not as good at it as his fellow castaway, but it's the thing he does comparatively well.

Although less productive than American workers, Bangladeshi workers have a comparative advantage in clothing production.

Bangladesh, though it is at an absolute disadvantage compared with the United States in almost everything, has a comparative advantage in clothing production. This means that both the United States and Bangladesh are able to consume more because they specialize in producing different things, with Bangladesh supplying our clothing and the United States supplying Bangladesh with more sophisticated goods. ▲

> > > > > > > > > > > >

> ### CHECK YOUR UNDERSTANDING 2-1

1. True or false? Explain your answer.
   a. An increase in the amount of resources available to Tom for use in producing coconuts and fish does not change his production possibility frontier.
   b. A technological change that allows Tom to catch more fish for any amount of coconuts gathered results in a change in his production possibility frontier.
   c. The production possibility frontier is useful because it illustrates how much of one good an economy must give up to get more of another good regardless of whether resources are being used efficiently.

2. In Italy, an automobile can be produced by 8 workers in one day and a washing machine by 3 workers in one day. In the United States, an automobile can be produced by 6 workers in one day, and a washing machine by 2 workers in one day.
   a. Which country has an absolute advantage in the production of automobiles? In washing machines?
   b. Which country has a comparative advantage in the production of washing machines? In automobiles?
   c. What pattern of specialization results in the greatest gains from trade between the two countries?

3. Explain why Tom and Hank are willing to engage in a trade of 1 fish for 1.5 coconuts.

4. Use the circular-flow diagram to explain how an increase in the amount of money spent by households results in an increase in the number of jobs in the economy. Describe in words what the circular-flow diagram predicts.

Solutions appear at back of book.

Using Models

Economics, we have now learned, is mainly a matter of creating models that draw on a set of basic principles but add some more specific assumptions that allow the modeler to apply those principles to a particular situation. But what do economists actually *do* with their models?

Positive versus Normative Economics

Imagine that you are an economic adviser to the governor of your state. What kinds of questions might the governor ask you to answer?

Well, here are three possible questions:

1. How much revenue will the tolls on the state turnpike yield next year?

2. How much would that revenue increase if the toll were raised from $1 to $1.50?

3. Should the toll be raised, bearing in mind that a toll increase will reduce traffic and air pollution near the road but will impose some financial hardship on frequent commuters?

There is a big difference between the first two questions and the third one. The first two are questions about facts. Your forecast of next year's toll collection will be proved right or wrong when the numbers actually come in. Your estimate of the impact of a change in the toll is a little harder to check—revenue depends on other factors besides the toll, and it may be hard to disentangle the causes of any change in revenue. Still, in principle there is only one right answer.

But the question of whether tolls should be raised may not have a "right" answer—two people who agree on the effects of a higher toll could still disagree about whether raising the toll is a good idea. For example, someone who lives near the turnpike but doesn't commute on it will care a lot about noise and air pollution but not so much about commuting costs. A regular commuter who doesn't live near the turnpike will have the opposite priorities.

This example highlights a key distinction between two roles of economic analysis. Analysis that tries to answer questions about the way the world works, which have definite right and wrong answers, is known as **positive economics.** In contrast, analysis that involves saying how the world *should* work is known as **normative economics.** To put it another way, positive economics is about description, normative economics is about prescription.

Positive economics occupies most of the time and effort of the economics profession. And models play a crucial role in almost all positive economics. As we mentioned earlier, the U.S. government uses a computer model to assess proposed changes in national tax policy, and many state governments have similar models to assess the effects of their own tax policy.

It's worth noting that there is a subtle but important difference between the first and second questions we imagined the governor asking. Question 1 asked for a simple prediction about next year's revenue—a **forecast.** Question 2 was a "what if" question, asking how revenue would change if the tax law were to change. Economists are often called upon to answer both types of questions, but models are especially useful for answering "what if" questions.

The answers to such questions often serve as a guide to policy, but they are still predictions, not prescriptions. That is, they tell you what will happen if a policy is changed; they don't tell you whether or not that result is good. Suppose that your economic model tells you that the governor's proposed increase in highway tolls will raise property values in communities near the road but will hurt people who must use the turnpike to get to work. Does that make this proposed toll increase a good idea or a bad one? It depends on whom you ask. As we've just seen, someone who is very concerned with the communities near the road will support the increase, but someone who is very concerned with the welfare of drivers will feel differently. That's a value judgment—it's not a question of economic analysis.

Still, economists often do engage in normative economics and give policy advice. How can they do this when there may be no "right" answer?

One answer is that economists are also citizens, and we all have our opinions. But economic analysis can often be used to show that some policies are clearly better than others, regardless of anyone's opinions.

Suppose that policies A and B achieve the same goal, but policy A makes everyone better off than policy B—or at least makes some people better off without making other people worse off. Then A is clearly more efficient than B. That's not a value judgment: we're talking about how best to achieve a goal, not about the goal itself.

For example, two different policies have been used to help low-income families obtain housing: rent control, which limits the rents landlords are allowed to charge, and rent subsidies, which provide families with additional money to pay rent. Almost all economists agree that subsidies are the more efficient policy. (In Chapter 5 we'll see why this is so.) And so the great majority of economists, whatever their personal politics, favor subsidies over rent control.

When policies can be clearly ranked in this way, then economists generally agree. But it is no secret that economists sometimes disagree.

When and Why Economists Disagree

Economists have a reputation for arguing with each other. Where does this reputation come from?

One important answer is that media coverage tends to exaggerate the real differences in views among economists. If nearly all economists agree on an issue—for example, the proposition that rent controls lead to housing shortages—reporters and editors are likely to conclude that there is no story worth covering, and so the professional consensus tends to go unreported. But when there is some issue on which prominent economists take opposing sides on the same issue—for example, whether cutting taxes right now would help the economy—that does make a good news story. So you hear much more about the areas of disagreement within economics than you do about the large areas of agreement.

It is also worth remembering that economics is, unavoidably, often tied up in politics. On a number of issues powerful interest groups know what opinions they want to hear; they therefore have an incentive to find and promote economists who profess those opinions, giving these economists a prominence and visibility out of proportion to their support among their colleagues.

But although the appearance of disagreement among economists exceeds the reality, it remains true that economists often *do* disagree about important things. For example, some very respected economists argue vehemently that the U.S. government should replace the income tax with a *value-added tax* (a national sales tax, which is the main source of government revenue in many European countries). Other equally respected economists disagree. Why this difference of opinion?

One important source of differences is in values: as in any diverse group of individuals, reasonable people can differ. In comparison to an income tax, a value-added tax typically falls more heavily on people of modest means. So an economist who values a society with more social and income equality for its own sake will tend to oppose a value-added tax. An economist with different values will be less likely to oppose it.

A second important source of differences arises from economic modeling. Because economists base their conclusions on models, which are simplified representations of reality, two economists can legitimately disagree about which simplifications are appropriate—and therefore arrive at different conclusions.

Suppose that the U.S. government was considering introducing a value-added tax. Economist A may rely on a model that focuses on the administrative costs of tax systems—that is, the costs of monitoring, processing papers, collecting the tax, and so on. This economist might then point to the well-known high costs of administering a value-added tax and argue against the change. But economist B may think that the right way to approach the question is to ignore the administrative costs and focus on how the proposed law would change savings behavior. This economist might point to studies suggesting that value-added taxes promote higher consumer saving, a desirable result.

FOR INQUIRING MINDS

When Economists Agree

"If all the economists in the world were laid end to end, they still couldn't reach a conclusion." So goes one popular economist joke. But do economists really disagree that much?

Not according to a classic survey of members of the American Economic Association, reported in the May 1992 issue of the *American Economic Review*. The authors asked respondents to agree or disagree with a number of statements about the economy; what they found was a high level of agreement among professional economists on many of the statements. At the top, with more than 90 percent of the economists agreeing, were "Tariffs and import quotas usually reduce general economic welfare" and "A ceiling on rents reduces the quantity and quality of housing available." What's striking about these two statements is that many noneconomists disagree: tariffs and import quotas to keep out foreign-produced goods are favored by many voters, and proposals to do away with rent control in cities like New York and San Francisco have met fierce political opposition.

So is the stereotype of quarreling economists a myth? Not entirely: economists do disagree quite a lot on some issues, especially in macroeconomics. But there is a large area of common ground.

Because the economists have used different models—that is, made different simplifying assumptions—they arrive at different conclusions. And so the two economists may find themselves on different sides of the issue.

Most such disputes are eventually resolved by the accumulation of evidence showing which of the various models proposed by economists does a better job of fitting the facts. However, in economics, as in any science, it can take a long time before research settles important disputes—decades, in some cases. And since the economy is always changing, in ways that make old models invalid or raise new policy questions, there are always new issues on which economists disagree. The policy maker must then decide which economist to believe.

The important point is that economic analysis is a method, not a set of conclusions.

►ECONOMICS IN ACTION

Economists in Government

Many economists are mainly engaged in teaching and research. But quite a few economists have a more direct hand in events.

As described earlier in the chapter (For Inquiring Minds, "Models for Money"), economists play a significant role in the business world, especially in the financial industry. But the most striking involvement of economists in the "real" world is their extensive participation in government.

This shouldn't be surprising: one of the most important functions of government is to make economic policy, and almost every government policy decision must take economic effects into consideration. So governments around the world employ economists in a variety of roles.

In the U.S. government, a key role is played by the Council of Economic Advisers, a branch of the Executive Office (that is, the staff of the President) whose sole purpose is to advise the White House on economic matters and to prepare the annual Economic Report of the President. Unlike most employees in government agencies, the majority of the economists at the Council are not long-term civil servants; instead, they are mainly professors on leave for one or two years from their universities. Many of the nation's best-known economists have served on the Council of Economic Advisers at some point during their careers.

Economists also play an important role in many other parts of the U.S. government. Indeed, as the Bureau of Labor Statistics *Occupational Outlook Handbook* says, "Government employed 58 percent of economists in a wide range of government agencies." Needless to say, the Bureau of Labor Statistics is itself a major employer of economists. And economists dominate the staff of the Federal Reserve, a government agency that controls the supply of money in the economy and is crucial to its operation.

It's also worth noting that economists play an especially important role in two international organizations headquartered in Washington, D.C.: the International Monetary Fund, which provides advice and loans to countries experiencing economic difficulties, and the World Bank, which provides advice and loans to promote long-term economic development.

Do all these economists in government disagree with each other all the time? Are their positions largely dictated by political affiliation? The answer to both questions is no. Although there are important disputes over economic issues in government, and politics inevitably plays some role, there is broad agreement among economists on many issues, and most economists in government try very hard to assess issues as objectively as possible. ▲

< < < < < < < < < < < <

>>QUICK REVIEW

➤ Economists do mostly **positive economics,** analysis of the way the world works, in which there are definite right and wrong answers and which involve making **forecasts.** But in **normative economics,** which makes prescriptions about how things ought to be, there are often no right answers and only value judgments.

➤ Economists do disagree—though not as much as legend has it—for two main reasons. One, they may disagree about which simplifications to make in a model. Two, economists may disagree—like everyone else—about values.

> **CHECK YOUR UNDERSTANDING** 2-2

1. Which of the following statements is a positive statement? Which is a normative statement?
   a. Society should take measures to prevent people from engaging in dangerous personal behavior.
   b. People who engage in dangerous personal behavior impose higher costs on society through higher medical costs.

2. True or false? Explain your answer.
   a. Policy choice A and policy choice B attempt to achieve the same social goal. Policy choice A, however, results in a much less efficient use of resources than policy choice B. Therefore, economists are more likely to agree on choosing policy choice B.
   b. When two economists disagree on the desirability of a policy, it's typically because one of them has made a mistake.
   c. Policy makers can always use economics to figure out which goals a society should try to achieve.

Solutions appear at back of book.

[>> **A LOOK** AHEAD •••

This chapter has given you a first view of what it means to do economics, starting with the general idea of models as a way to make sense of a complicated world and then moving on to two simple introductory models.

To get a real sense of how economic analysis works, however, and to show just how useful such analysis can be, we need to move on to a more powerful model. In the next two chapters we will study the quintessential economic model, one that has an amazing ability to make sense of many policy issues, predict the effects of many forces, and change the way you look at the world. That model is known as "supply and demand."]

SUMMARY ••■

1. Almost all economics is based on **models,** "thought experiments" or simplified versions of reality, many of which use mathematical tools such as graphs. An important assumption in economic models is the **other things equal assumption,** which allows analysis of the effect of a change in one factor by holding all other relevant factors unchanged.

2. One important economic model is the **production possibility frontier.** It illustrates: *opportunity cost* (showing how much less of one good can be produced if more of the other good is produced); *efficiency* (an economy is efficient in production if it produces on the production possibility frontier and efficient in allocation if it produces the mix of goods and services that people want to consume); and *economic growth* (an outward shift of the production possibility frontier). There are two basic sources of growth: an increase in **factors of production,** resources such as land, labor, capital, and human capital, inputs that are not used up in production, and improved **technology.**

3. Another important model is **comparative advantage,** which explains the source of gains from trade between individuals and countries. Everyone has a comparative advantage in something—some good or service in which that person has a lower opportunity cost than everyone

else. But it is often confused with **absolute advantage,** an ability to produce a particular good or service better than anyone else. This confusion leads some to erroneously conclude that there are no gains from trade between people or countries.

4. In the simplest economies people **barter**—trade goods and services for one another—rather than trade them for money, as in a modern economy. The **circular-flow diagram** represents transactions within the economy as flows of goods, services, and money between **households** and **firms.** These transactions occur in **markets for goods and services** and **factor markets,** markets for **factors of production**—land, labor, capital, and human capital. It is useful in understanding how spending, production, employment, income, and growth are related in the economy. Ultimately, factor markets determine the economy's **income distribution,** how an economy's total income is allocated to the owners of the factors of production.

5. Economists use economic models for both **positive economics,** which describes how the economy works, and for **normative economics,** which prescribes how the economy *should* work. Positive economics often involves making **forecasts.** Economists can determine correct answers for positive questions, but typically not

for normative questions, which involve value judgments. The exceptions are when policies designed to achieve a certain prescription can be clearly ranked in terms of efficiency.

6. There are two main reasons economists disagree. One, they may disagree about which simplifications to make in a model. Two, economists may disagree—like everyone else—about values.

KEY TERMS

Model, p. 24
Other things equal assumption, p. 24
Production possibility frontier, p. 25
Factors of production, p. 29
Technology, p. 29
Comparative advantage, p. 31

Absolute advantage, p. 33
Barter, p. 35
Circular-flow diagram, p. 35
Household, p. 35
Firm, p. 35
Markets for goods and services, p. 35

Factor markets, p. 35
Income distribution, p. 36
Positive economics, p. 38
Normative economics, p. 38
Forecast, p. 38

PROBLEMS

1. Two important industries on the island of Bermuda are fishing and tourism. According to data from the World Resources Institute and the Bermuda Department of Statistics, in the year 2000 the 307 registered fishermen in Bermuda caught 286 metric tons of marine fish. And the 3,409 people employed by hotels produced 538,000 hotel stays (measured by the number of visitor arrivals). Suppose that this production point is efficient in production. Assume also that the opportunity cost of one additional metric ton of fish is 2,000 hotel stays and that this opportunity cost is constant (the opportunity cost does not change).

   a. If all 307 registered fishermen were to be employed by hotels (in addition to the 3,409 people already working in hotels), how many hotel stays could Bermuda produce?

   b. If all 3,409 hotel employees were to become fishermen (in addition to the 307 fishermen already working in the fishing industry), how many metric tons of fish could Bermuda produce?

   c. Draw a production possibility frontier for Bermuda, with fish on the horizontal axis and hotel stays on the vertical axis, and label Bermuda's actual production point for the year 2000.

2. Atlantis is a small, isolated island in the South Atlantic. The inhabitants grow potatoes and catch fish. The accompanying table shows the maximum annual output combinations of potatoes and fish that can be produced. Obviously, given their limited resources and available technology, as they use more of their resources for potato production, there are fewer resources available for catching fish.

Maximum annual output options	Quantity of potatoes (pounds)	Quantity of fish (pounds)
A	1,000	0
B	800	300
C	600	500
D	400	600
E	200	650
F	0	675

   a. Draw a production possibility frontier with potatoes on the horizontal axis and fish on the vertical axis illustrating these options, showing points A-F.

   b. Can Atlantis produce 500 pounds of fish and 800 pounds of potatoes? Explain. Where would this point lie relative to the production possibility frontier?

   c. What is the opportunity cost of increasing the annual output of potatoes from 600 to 800 pounds?

   d. What is the opportunity cost of increasing the annual output of potatoes from 200 to 400 pounds?

   e. Can you explain why the answers to parts c and d are not the same? What does this imply about the slope of the production possibility frontier?

3. According to data from the U.S. Department of Agriculture's National Agricultural Statistics Service, 124 million acres of land in the United States were used for wheat or corn farming in 2004. Of those 124 million acres, farmers used 50 million acres to grow 2.158 billion bushels of wheat and 74 million acres of land to grow 11.807 billion bushels of corn. Suppose that U.S. wheat and corn farming is efficient in production. At that production point, the opportunity cost of producing one additional bushel of wheat is 1.7 fewer bushels of corn. However, farmers have increasing opportunity costs, so that additional bushels of wheat have an opportunity cost greater than 1.7 bushels of corn. For each of the following production points, decide whether that production point is (i) feasible and efficient in production, (ii) feasible but not efficient in production, (iii) not feasible, or (iv) unclear as to whether or not it is feasible.

   a. Farmers use 40 million acres of land to produce 1.8 billion bushels of wheat, and they use 60 million acres of land to produce 9 billion bushels of corn. The remaining 24 million acres are left unused.

   b. From their original production point, farmers transfer 40 million acres of land from corn to wheat production. They now produce 3.158 billion bushels of wheat and 10.107 bushels of corn.

   c. Farmers reduce their production of wheat to 2 billion bushels and increase their production of corn to 12.044

billion bushels. Along the production possibility frontier, the opportunity cost of going from 11.807 billion bushels of corn to 12.044 billion bushels of corn is 0.666 bushel of wheat per bushel of corn.

4. In the ancient country of Roma, only two goods, spaghetti and meatballs, are produced. There are two tribes in Roma, the Tivoli and the Frivoli. By themselves, the Tivoli each month can produce either 30 pounds of spaghetti and no meatballs, or 50 pounds of meatballs and no spaghetti, or any combination in between. The Frivoli, by themselves, each month can produce 40 pounds of spaghetti and no meatballs, or 30 pounds of meatballs and no spaghetti, or any combination in between.

   a. Assume that all production possibility frontiers are straight lines. Draw one diagram showing the monthly production possibility frontier for the Tivoli and another showing the monthly production possibility frontier for the Frivoli. Show how you calculated them.

   b. Which tribe has the comparative advantage in spaghetti production? In meatball production?

   In A.D. 100 the Frivoli discover a new technique for making meatballs that doubles the quantity of meatballs they can produce each month.

   c. Draw the new monthly production possibility frontier for the Frivoli.

   d. After the innovation, which tribe now has an absolute advantage in producing meatballs? In producing spaghetti? Which has the comparative advantage in meatball production? In spaghetti production?

5. According to the U.S. Census Bureau, in July 2006 the United States exported aircraft worth $1 billion to China and imported aircraft worth only $19,000 from China. During the same month, however, the United States imported $83 million worth of men's trousers, slacks, and jeans from China but exported only $8,000 worth of trousers, slacks, and jeans to China. Using what you have learned about how trade is determined by comparative advantage, answer the following questions.

   a. Which country has the comparative advantage in aircraft production? In production of trousers, slacks, and jeans?

   b. Can you determine which country has the absolute advantage in aircraft production? In production of trousers, slacks, and jeans?

6. Peter Pundit, an economics reporter, states that the European Union (EU) is increasing its productivity very rapidly in all industries. He claims that this productivity advance is so rapid that output from the EU in these industries will soon exceed that of the United States and, as a result, the United States will no longer benefit from trade with the EU.

   a. Do you think Peter Pundit is correct or not? If not, what do you think is the source of his mistake?

   b. If the EU and the United States continue to trade, what do you think will characterize the goods that the EU exports to the United States and the goods that the United States exports to the EU?

7. You are in charge of allocating residents to your dormitory's baseball and basketball teams. You are down to the last four people, two of whom must be allocated to baseball and two to basketball. The accompanying table gives each person's batting average and free-throw average.

Name	Batting average	Free-throw average
Kelley	70%	60%
Jackie	50%	50%
Curt	10%	30%
Gerry	80%	70%

   a. Explain how you would use the concept of comparative advantage to allocate the players. Begin by establishing each player's opportunity cost of free throws in terms of batting average.

   b. Why is it likely that the other basketball players will be unhappy about this arrangement but the other baseball players will be satisfied? Nonetheless, why would an economist say that this is an efficient way to allocate players for your dormitory's sports teams?

8. The inhabitants of the fictional economy of Atlantis use money in the form of cowry shells. Draw a circular-flow diagram showing households and firms. Firms produce potatoes and fish, and households buy potatoes and fish. Households also provide the land and labor to firms. Identify where in the flows of cowry shells or physical things (goods and services, or resources) each of the following impacts would occur. Describe how this impact spreads around the circle.

   a. A devastating hurricane floods many of the potato fields.

   b. A very productive fishing season yields a very large number of fish caught.

   c. The inhabitants of Atlantis discover Shakira and spend several days a month at dancing festivals.

9. An economist might say that colleges and universities "produce" education, using faculty members and students as inputs. According to this line of reasoning, education is then "consumed" by households. Construct a circular-flow diagram to represent the sector of the economy devoted to college education: colleges and universities represent firms, and households both consume education and provide faculty and students to universities. What are the relevant markets in this diagram? What is being bought and sold in each direction? What would happen in the diagram if the government decided to subsidize 50% of all college students' tuition?

10. Your dormitory roommate plays loud music most of the time; you, however, would prefer more peace and quiet. You suggest that she buy some earphones. She responds that although she would be happy to use earphones, she has many other things that she would prefer to spend her money on right now. You discuss this situation with a friend who is an economics major. The following exchange takes place:
   He: How much would it cost to buy earphones?
   You: $15.

He: How much do you value having some peace and quiet for the rest of the semester?

You: $30.

He: It is efficient for you to buy the earphones and give them to your roommate. You gain more than you lose; the benefit exceeds the cost. You should do that.

You: It just isn't fair that I have to pay for the earphones when I'm not the one making the noise.

a. Which parts of this conversation contain positive statements and which parts contain normative statements?

b. Compose an argument supporting your viewpoint that your roommate should be the one to change her behavior. Similarly, compose an argument from the viewpoint of your roommate that you should be the one to buy the earphones. If your dormitory has a policy that gives residents the unlimited right to play music, whose argument is likely to win? If your dormitory has a rule that a person must stop playing music whenever a roommate complains, whose argument is likely to win?

11. A representative of the American clothing industry recently made the following statement: "Workers in Asia often work in sweatshop conditions earning only pennies an hour. American workers are more productive and as a result earn higher wages. In order to preserve the dignity of the American workplace, the government should enact legislation banning imports of low-wage Asian clothing."

a. Which parts of this quote are positive statements? Which parts are normative statements?

b. Is the policy that is being advocated consistent with the preceding statements about the wages and productivities of American and Asian workers?

c. Would such a policy make some Americans better off without making any other Americans worse off? That is, would this policy be efficient from the viewpoint of all Americans?

d. Would low-wage Asian workers benefit from or be hurt by such a policy?

12. Are the following statements true or false? Explain your answers.

a. "When people must pay higher taxes on their wage earnings, it reduces their incentive to work" is a positive statement.

b. "We should lower taxes to encourage more work" is a positive statement.

c. Economics cannot always be used to completely decide what society ought to do.

d. "The system of public education in this country generates greater benefits to society than the cost of running the system" is a normative statement.

e. All disagreements among economists are generated by the media.

13. Evaluate the following statement: "It is easier to build an economic model that accurately reflects events that have already occurred than to build an economic model to forecast future events." Do you think that this is true or not? Why? What does this imply about the difficulties of building good economic models?

14. Economists who work for the government are often called on to make policy recommendations. Why do you think it is important for the public to be able to differentiate normative statements from positive statements in these recommendations?

15. The mayor of Gotham City, worried about a potential epidemic of deadly influenza this winter, asks an economic adviser the following series of questions. Determine whether a question requires the economic adviser to make a positive assessment or a normative assessment.

a. How much vaccine will be in stock in the city by the end of November?

b. If we offer to pay 10% more per dose to the pharmaceutical companies providing the vaccines, will they provide additional doses?

c. If there is a shortage of vaccine in the city, whom should we vaccinate first—the elderly or the very young? (Assume that a person from one group has an equal likelihood of dying from influenza as a person from the other group.)

d. If the city charges $25 per shot, how many people will pay?

e. If the city charges $25 per shot, it will make a profit of $10 per shot, money that can go to pay for inoculating poor people. Should the city engage in such a scheme?

16. Assess the following statement: "If economists just had enough data, they could solve all policy questions in a way that maximizes the social good. There would be no need for divisive political debates, such as whether the government should provide free medical care for all."

 www.worthpublishers.com/krugmanwells

> Chapter 2 Appendix:
> Graphs in Economics

Getting the Picture

Whether you're reading about economics in the *Wall Street Journal* or in your economics textbook, you will see many graphs. Visual images can make it much easier to understand verbal descriptions, numerical information, or ideas. In economics, graphs are the type of visual image used to facilitate understanding. To fully understand the ideas and information being discussed, you need to be familiar with how to interpret these visual aids. This appendix explains how graphs are constructed and interpreted and how they are used in economics.

> A quantity that can take on more than one value is called a **variable**.

Graphs, Variables, and Economic Models

One reason to attend college is that a bachelor's degree provides access to higher-paying jobs. Additional degrees, such as MBAs or law degrees, increase earnings even more. If you were to read an article about the relationship between educational attainment and income, you would probably see a graph showing the income levels for workers with different amounts of education. And this graph would depict the idea that, in general, more education increases income. This graph, like most of those in economics, would depict the relationship between two economic variables. A **variable** is a quantity that can take on more than one value, such as the number of years of education a person has, the price of a can of soda, or a household's income.

As you learned in this chapter, economic analysis relies heavily on *models*, simplified descriptions of real situations. Most economic models describe the relationship between two variables, simplified by holding constant other variables that may affect the relationship. For example, an economic model might describe the relationship between the price of a can of soda and the number of cans of soda that consumers will buy, assuming that everything else that affects consumers' purchases of soda stays constant. This type of model can be described mathematically or verbally, but illustrating the relationship in a graph makes it easier to understand. Next we show how graphs that depict economic models are constructed and interpreted.

How Graphs Work

Most graphs in economics are based on a grid built around two perpendicular lines that show the values of two variables, helping you visualize the relationship between them. So a first step in understanding the use of such graphs is to see how this system works.

Two-Variable Graphs

Figure 2A-1 on the next page shows a typical two-variable graph. It illustrates the data in the accompanying table on outside temperature and the number of sodas a typical vendor can expect to sell at a baseball stadium during one game. The first column shows the values of outside temperature (the first variable) and the second column shows the values of the number of sodas sold (the second variable). Five combinations or pairs of the two variables are shown, each denoted by *A* through *E* in the third column.

Now let's turn to graphing the data in this table. In any two-variable graph, one variable is called the *x*-variable and the other is called the *y*-variable. Here we have made outside temperature the *x*-variable and number of sodas sold the *y*-variable. The

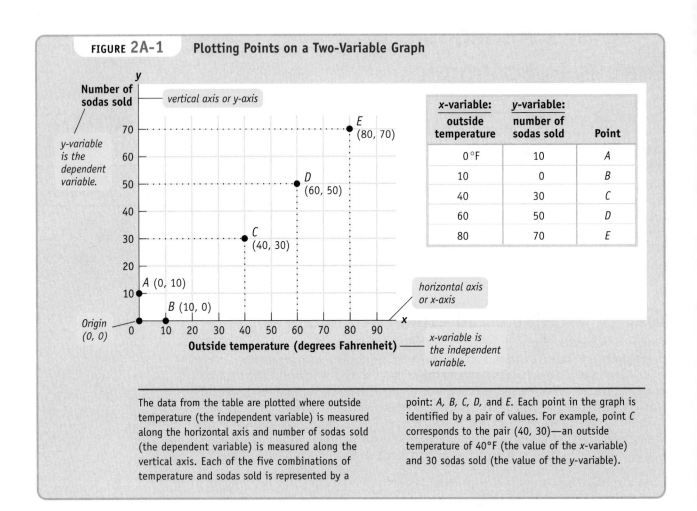

FIGURE 2A-1   Plotting Points on a Two-Variable Graph

x-variable: outside temperature	y-variable: number of sodas sold	Point
0 °F	10	A
10	0	B
40	30	C
60	50	D
80	70	E

The data from the table are plotted where outside temperature (the independent variable) is measured along the horizontal axis and number of sodas sold (the dependent variable) is measured along the vertical axis. Each of the five combinations of temperature and sodas sold is represented by a point: *A, B, C, D,* and *E.* Each point in the graph is identified by a pair of values. For example, point *C* corresponds to the pair (40, 30)—an outside temperature of 40°F (the value of the *x*-variable) and 30 sodas sold (the value of the *y*-variable).

The line along which values of the *x*-variable are measured is called the **horizontal axis** or **x-axis**. The line along which values of the *y*-variable are measured is called the **vertical axis** or **y-axis**. The point where the axes of a two-variable graph meet is the **origin**.

A **causal relationship** exists between two variables when the value taken by one variable directly influences or determines the value taken by the other variable. In a causal relationship, the determining variable is called the **independent variable**; the variable it determines is called the **dependent variable**.

solid horizontal line in the graph is called the **horizontal axis** or **x-axis,** and values of the *x*-variable—outside temperature—are measured along it. Similarly, the solid vertical line in the graph is called the **vertical axis** or **y-axis,** and values of the *y*-variable—number of sodas sold—are measured along it. At the **origin,** the point where the two axes meet, each variable is equal to zero. As you move rightward from the origin along the *x*-axis, values of the *x*-variable are positive and increasing. As you move up from the origin along the *y*-axis, values of the *y*-variable are positive and increasing.

You can plot each of the five points *A* through *E* on this graph by using a pair of numbers—the values that the *x*-variable and the *y*-variable take on for a given point. In Figure 2A-1, at point *C*, the *x*-variable takes on the value 40 and the *y*-variable takes on the value 30. You plot point *C* by drawing a line straight up from 40 on the *x*-axis and a horizontal line across from 30 on the *y*-axis. We write point *C* as (40, 30). We write the origin as (0, 0).

Looking at point *A* and point *B* in Figure 2A-1, you can see that when one of the variables for a point has a value of zero, it will lie on one of the axes. If the value of the *x*-variable is zero, the point will lie on the vertical axis, like point *A*. If the value of the *y*-variable is zero, the point will lie on the horizontal axis, like point *B*.

Most graphs that depict relationships between two economic variables represent a **causal relationship,** a relationship in which the value taken by one variable directly influences or determines the value taken by the other variable. In a causal relationship, the determining variable is called the **independent variable;** the variable it determines is called the **dependent variable.** In our example of soda sales, the outside temperature is the independent variable. It directly influences the number of sodas that are sold, the dependent variable in this case.

By convention, we put the independent variable on the horizontal axis and the dependent variable on the vertical axis. Figure 2A-1 is constructed consistent with this convention; the independent variable (outside temperature) is on the horizontal axis and the dependent variable (number of sodas sold) is on the vertical axis. An important exception to this convention is in graphs showing the economic relationship between the price of a product and quantity of the product: although price is generally the independent variable that determines quantity, it is always measured on the vertical axis.

> A **curve** is a line on a graph that depicts a relationship between two variables. It may be either a straight line or a curved line. If the curve is a straight line, the variables have a **linear relationship**. If the curve is not a straight line, the variables have a **nonlinear relationship**.

Curves on a Graph

Panel (a) of Figure 2A-2 contains some of the same information as Figure 2A-1, with a line drawn through the points *B*, *C*, *D*, and *E*. Such a line on a graph is called a **curve,** regardless of whether it is a straight line or a curved line. If the curve that shows the relationship between two variables is a straight line, or linear, the variables have a **linear relationship.** When the curve is not a straight line, or nonlinear, the variables have a **nonlinear relationship.**

A point on a curve indicates the value of the *y*-variable for a specific value of the *x*-variable. For example, point *D* indicates that at a temperature of 60°F, a vendor can expect to sell 50 sodas. The shape and orientation of a curve reveal the general nature of the relationship between the two variables. The upward tilt of the curve in panel (a) of Figure 2A-2 suggests that vendors can expect to sell more sodas at higher outside temperatures.

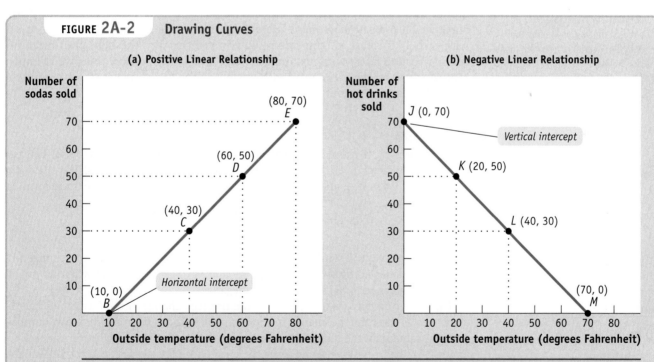

FIGURE 2A-2   Drawing Curves

The curve in panel (a) illustrates the relationship between the two variables, outside temperature and number of sodas sold. The two variables have a positive linear relationship: positive because the curve has an upward tilt, and linear because it is a straight line. It implies that an increase in the *x*-variable (outside temperature) leads to an increase in the *y*-variable (number of sodas sold). The curve in panel (b) is also a straight line, but it tilts downward. The two variables here, outside temperature and number of hot drinks sold, have a negative linear relationship: an increase in the *x*-variable (outside temperature) leads to a decrease in the *y*-variable (number of hot drinks sold). The curve in panel (a) has a horizontal intercept at point *B*, where it hits the horizontal axis. The curve in panel (b) has a vertical intercept at point *J*, where it hits the vertical axis, and a horizontal intercept at point *M*, where it hits the horizontal axis.

When variables are related this way—that is, when an increase in one variable is associated with an increase in the other variable—the variables are said to have a **positive relationship.** It is illustrated by a curve that slopes upward from left to right. Because this curve is also linear, the relationship between outside temperature and number of sodas sold illustrated by the curve in panel (a) of Figure 2A-2 is a positive linear relationship.

When an increase in one variable is associated with a decrease in the other variable, the two variables are said to have a **negative relationship.** It is illustrated by a curve that slopes downward from left to right, like the curve in panel (b) of Figure 2A-2. Because this curve is also linear, the relationship it depicts is a negative linear relationship. Two variables that might have such a relationship are the outside temperature and the number of hot drinks a vendor can expect to sell at a baseball stadium.

Return for a moment to the curve in panel (a) of Figure 2A-2 and you can see that it hits the horizontal axis at point B. This point, known as the **horizontal intercept,** shows the value of the *x*-variable when the value of the *y*-variable is zero. In panel (b) of Figure 2A-2, the curve hits the vertical axis at point J. This point, called the **vertical intercept,** indicates the value of the *y*-variable when the value of the *x*-variable is zero.

A Key Concept: The Slope of a Curve

The **slope** of a line or curve is a measure of how steep it is and indicates how sensitive the *y*-variable is to a change in the *x*-variable. In our example of outside temperature and the number of cans of soda a vendor can expect to sell, the slope of the curve would indicate how many more cans of soda the vendor could expect to sell with each 1° increase in temperature. Interpreted this way, the slope gives meaningful information. Even without numbers for *x* and *y*, it is possible to arrive at important conclusions about the relationship between the two variables by examining the slope of a curve at various points.

The Slope of a Linear Curve

Along a linear curve the slope, or steepness, is measured by dividing the "rise" between two points on the curve by the "run" between those same two points. The rise is the amount that *y* changes, and the run is the amount that *x* changes. Here is the formula:

$$\frac{\text{Change in } y}{\text{Change in } x} = \frac{\Delta y}{\Delta x} = \text{Slope}$$

In the formula, the symbol Δ (the Greek uppercase delta) stands for "change in." When a variable increases, the change in that variable is positive; when a variable decreases, the change in that variable is negative.

The slope of a curve is positive when the rise (the change in the *y*-variable) has the same sign as the run (the change in the *x*-variable). That's because when two numbers have the same sign, the ratio of those two numbers is positive. The curve in panel (a) of Figure 2A-2 has a positive slope: along the curve, both the *y*-variable and the *x*-variable increase. The slope of a curve is negative when the rise and the run have different signs. That's because when two numbers have different signs, the ratio of those two numbers is negative. The curve in panel (b) of Figure 2A-2 has a negative slope: along the curve, an increase in the *x*-variable is associated with a decrease in the *y*-variable.

Figure 2A-3 illustrates how to calculate the slope of a linear curve. Let's focus first on panel (a). From point A to point B the value of the *y*-variable changes from 25 to 20 and the value of the *x*-variable changes from 10 to 20. So the slope of the line between these two points is:

$$\frac{\text{Change in } y}{\text{Change in } x} = \frac{\Delta y}{\Delta x} = \frac{-5}{10} = -\frac{1}{2} = -0.5$$

FIGURE 2A-3 Calculating the Slope

Panels (a) and (b) show two linear curves. Between points A and B on the curve in panel (a), the change in y (the rise) is −5 and the change in x (the run) is 10. So the slope from A to B is $\frac{\Delta y}{\Delta x} = \frac{-5}{10} = -\frac{1}{2} = -0.5$, where the negative sign indicates that the curve is downward sloping. In panel (b), the curve has a slope from A to B of $\frac{\Delta y}{\Delta x} = \frac{10}{2} = 5$. The slope from C to D is

$\frac{\Delta y}{\Delta x} = \frac{20}{4} = 5$. The slope is positive, indicating that the curve is upward sloping. Furthermore, the slope between A and B is the same as the slope between C and D, making this a linear curve. The slope of a linear curve is constant: it is the same regardless of where it is calculated along the curve.

Because a straight line is equally steep at all points, the slope of a straight line is the same at all points. In other words, a straight line has a constant slope. You can check this by calculating the slope of the linear curve between points A and B and between points C and D in panel (b) of Figure 2A-3.

Between A and B: $\qquad\qquad\qquad \frac{\Delta y}{\Delta x} = \frac{10}{2} = 5$

Between C and D: $\qquad\qquad\qquad \frac{\Delta y}{\Delta x} = \frac{20}{4} = 5$

Horizontal and Vertical Curves and Their Slopes

When a curve is horizontal, the value of the y-variable along that curve never changes—it is constant. Everywhere along the curve, the change in y is zero. Now, zero divided by any number is zero. So, regardless of the value of the change in x, the slope of a horizontal curve is always zero.

If a curve is vertical, the value of the x-variable along the curve never changes—it is constant. Everywhere along the curve, the change in x is zero. This means that the slope of a vertical line is a ratio with zero in the denominator. A ratio with zero in the denominator is equal to infinity—that is, an infinitely large number. So the slope of a vertical line is equal to infinity.

A vertical or a horizontal curve has a special implication: it means that the x-variable and the y-variable are unrelated. Two variables are unrelated when a change in one variable (the independent variable) has no effect on the other variable (the dependent variable). Or to put it a slightly different way, two variables are unrelated when the dependent variable is constant regardless of the value of the independent variable. If, as is usual, the y-variable is the dependent variable, the curve is horizontal. If the dependent variable is the x-variable, the curve is vertical.

> A **nonlinear curve** is one in which the slope is not the same between every pair of points.

The Slope of a Nonlinear Curve

A **nonlinear curve** is one in which the slope changes as you move along it. Panels (a), (b), (c), and (d) of Figure 2A-4 show various nonlinear curves. Panels (a) and (b) show nonlinear curves whose slopes change as you move along them, but the slopes always remain positive. Although both curves tilt upward, the curve in panel

FIGURE 2A-4   Nonlinear Curves

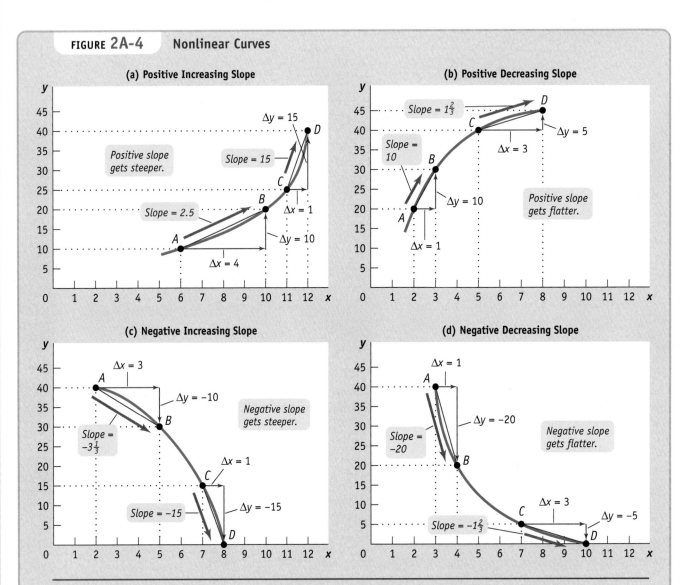

In panel (a) the slope of the curve from A to B is $\frac{\Delta y}{\Delta x} = \frac{10}{4} = 2.5$, and from C to D it is $\frac{\Delta y}{\Delta x} = \frac{15}{1} = 15$. The slope is positive and increasing; it gets steeper as you move to the right. In panel (b) the slope of the curve from A to B is $\frac{\Delta y}{\Delta x} = \frac{10}{1} = 10$, and from C to D it is $\frac{\Delta y}{\Delta x} = \frac{5}{3} = 1\frac{2}{3}$. The slope is positive and decreasing; it gets flatter as you move to the right. In panel (c) the slope from A to B is $\frac{\Delta y}{\Delta x} = \frac{-10}{3} = -3\frac{1}{3}$, and from C to D it is $\frac{\Delta y}{\Delta x} = \frac{-15}{1} = -15$. The slope is negative and increasing;

it gets steeper as you move to the right. And in panel (d) the slope from A to B is $\frac{\Delta y}{\Delta x} = \frac{-20}{1} = -20$, and from C to D it is $\frac{\Delta y}{\Delta x} = \frac{-5}{3} = -1\frac{2}{3}$. The slope is negative and decreasing; it gets flatter as you move to the right. The slope in each case has been calculated by using the arc method—that is, by drawing a straight line connecting two points along a curve. The average slope between those two points is equal to the slope of the straight line between those two points.

(a) gets steeper as you move from left to right in contrast to the curve in panel (b), which gets flatter. A curve that is upward sloping and gets steeper, as in panel (a), is said to have *positive increasing* slope. A curve that is upward sloping but gets flatter, as in panel (b), is said to have *positive decreasing* slope.

When we calculate the slope along these nonlinear curves, we obtain different values for the slope at different points. How the slope changes along the curve determines the curve's shape. For example, in panel (a) of Figure 2A-4, the slope of the curve is a positive number that steadily increases as you move from left to right, whereas in panel (b), the slope is a positive number that steadily decreases.

The slopes of the curves in panels (c) and (d) are negative numbers. Economists often prefer to express a negative number as its **absolute value,** which is the value of the negative number without the minus sign. In general, we denote the absolute value of a number by two parallel bars around the number; for example, the absolute value of −4 is written as |−4| = 4. In panel (c), the absolute value of the slope steadily increases as you move from left to right. The curve therefore has *negative increasing* slope. And in panel (d), the absolute value of the slope of the curve steadily decreases along the curve. This curve therefore has *negative decreasing* slope.

Calculating the Slope Along a Nonlinear Curve

We've just seen that along a nonlinear curve, the value of the slope depends on where you are on that curve. So how do you calculate the slope of a nonlinear curve? We will focus on two methods: the *arc method* and the *point method*.

The Arc Method of Calculating the Slope
An arc of a curve is some piece or segment of that curve. For example, panel (a) of Figure 2A-4 shows an arc consisting of the segment of the curve between points A and B. To calculate the slope along a nonlinear curve using the arc method, you draw a straight line between the two endpoints of the arc. The slope of that straight line is a measure of the average slope of the curve between those two end-points. You can see from panel (a) of Figure 2A-4 that the straight line drawn between points A and B increases along the x-axis from 6 to 10 (so that $\Delta x = 4$) as it increases along the y-axis from 10 to 20 (so that $\Delta y = 10$). Therefore the slope of the straight line connecting points A and B is:

$$\frac{\Delta y}{\Delta x} = \frac{10}{4} = 2.5$$

This means that the average slope of the curve between points A and B is 2.5.

Now consider the arc on the same curve between points C and D. A straight line drawn through these two points increases along the x-axis from 11 to 12 ($\Delta x = 1$) as it increases along the y-axis from 25 to 40 ($\Delta y = 15$). So the average slope between points C and D is:

$$\frac{\Delta y}{\Delta x} = \frac{15}{1} = 15$$

Therefore the average slope between points C and D is larger than the average slope between points A and B. These calculations verify what we have already observed— that this upward-tilted curve gets steeper as you move from left to right and therefore has positive increasing slope.

The Point Method of Calculating the Slope
The point method calculates the slope of a nonlinear curve at a specific point on that curve. Figure 2A-5 on the next page illustrates how to calculate the slope at point B on the curve. First, we draw a straight line that just touches the curve at point B. Such a line is called a **tangent line:** the fact that it just touches the curve at point B and does not touch the curve at any other point on the curve means that the straight line is *tangent* to the curve at point B. The slope of this tangent line is equal to the slope of the nonlinear curve at point B.

The **absolute value** of a negative number is the value of the negative number without the minus sign.

A **tangent line** is a straight line that just touches, or is tangent to, a nonlinear curve at a particular point. The slope of the tangent line is equal to the slope of the nonlinear curve at that point.

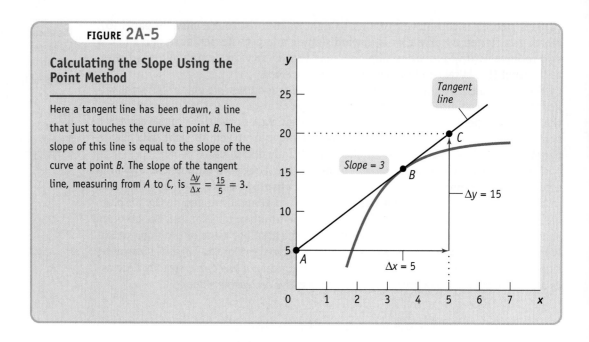

You can see from Figure 2A-5 how the slope of the tangent line is calculated: from point *A* to point *C*, the change in *y* is 15 and the change in *x* is 5, generating a slope of:

$$\frac{\Delta y}{\Delta x} = \frac{15}{5} = 3$$

By the point method, the slope of the curve at point *B* is equal to 3.

A natural question to ask at this point is how to determine which method to use—the arc method or the point method—in calculating the slope of a nonlinear curve. The answer depends on the curve itself and the data used to construct it. You use the arc method when you don't have enough information to be able to draw a smooth curve. For example, suppose that in panel (a) of Figure 2A-4 you have only the data represented by points *A*, *C*, and *D* and don't have the data represented by point *B* or any of the rest of the curve. Clearly, then, you can't use the point method to calculate the slope at point *B*; you would have to use the arc method to approximate the slope of the curve in this area by drawing a straight line between points *A* and *C*. But if you have sufficient data to draw the smooth curve shown in panel (a) of Figure 2A-4, then you could use the point method to calculate the slope at point *B*—and at every other point along the curve as well.

Maximum and Minimum Points

The slope of a nonlinear curve can change from positive to negative or vice versa. When the slope of a curve changes from positive to negative, it creates what is called a *maximum* point of the curve. When the slope of a curve changes from negative to positive, it creates a *minimum* point.

Panel (a) of Figure 2A-6 illustrates a curve in which the slope changes from positive to negative as you move from left to right. When *x* is between 0 and 50, the slope of the curve is positive. At *x* equal to 50, the curve attains its highest value of *y* along the curve. This point is called the **maximum** of the curve. When *x* exceeds 50, the slope becomes negative as the curve turns downward. Many important curves in economics, such as the curve that represents how the profit of a firm changes as it produces more output, are hill-shaped like this.

A nonlinear curve may have a **maximum** point, the highest point along the curve. At the maximum, the slope of the curve changes from positive to negative.

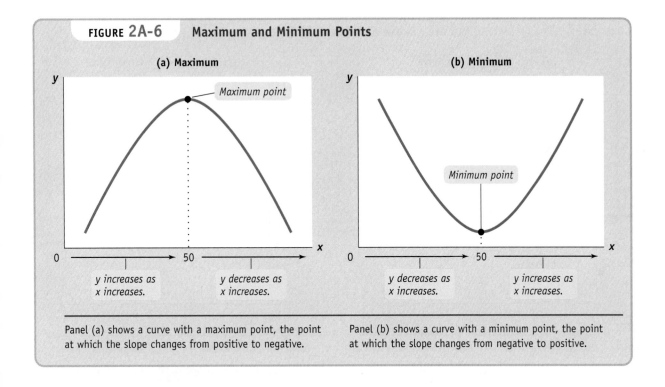

FIGURE 2A-6 **Maximum and Minimum Points**

(a) Maximum

Maximum point

0   50

y increases as x increases.   *y decreases as x increases.*

(b) Minimum

Minimum point

0   50

y decreases as x increases.   *y increases as x increases.*

Panel (a) shows a curve with a maximum point, the point at which the slope changes from positive to negative.

Panel (b) shows a curve with a minimum point, the point at which the slope changes from negative to positive.

In contrast, the curve shown in panel (b) of Figure 2A-6 is U-shaped: it has a slope that changes from negative to positive. At *x* equal to 50, the curve reaches its lowest point—the smallest value of *y* along the curve. This point is called the **minimum** of the curve. Various important curves in economics, such as the curve that represents how the costs of some firms change as output increases, are U-shaped like this.

Calculating the Area Below or Above a Curve

Sometimes it is useful to be able to measure the size of the area below or above a curve. We will encounter one such case in Chapter 4. To keep things simple, we'll only calculate the area below or above a linear curve.

How large is the shaded area below the linear curve in panel (a) of Figure 2A-7 on the next page? First note that this area has the shape of a right triangle. A right triangle is a triangle that has two sides that make a right angle with each other. We will refer to one of these sides as the *height* of the triangle and the other side as the *base* of the triangle. For our purposes, it doesn't matter which of these two sides we refer to as the base and which as the height. Calculating the area of a right triangle is straightforward: multiply the height of the triangle by the base of the triangle, and divide the result by 2. The height of the triangle in panel (a) of Figure 2A-7 is 10 – 4 = 6. And the base of the triangle is 3 – 0 = 3. So the area of that triangle is

$$\frac{6 \times 3}{2} = 9$$

How about the shaded area above the linear curve in panel (b) of Figure 2A-7? We can use the same formula to calculate the area of this right triangle. The height of the triangle is 8 – 2 = 6. And the base of the triangle is 4 – 0 = 4. So the area of that triangle is

$$\frac{6 \times 4}{2} = 12$$

A nonlinear curve may have a **minimum** point, the lowest point along the curve. At the minimum, the slope of the curve changes from negative to positive.

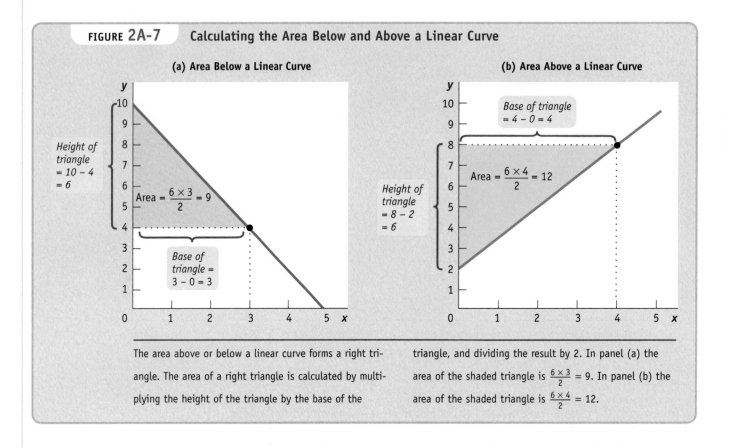

FIGURE 2A-7   Calculating the Area Below and Above a Linear Curve

(a) Area Below a Linear Curve

(b) Area Above a Linear Curve

The area above or below a linear curve forms a right triangle. The area of a right triangle is calculated by multiplying the height of the triangle by the base of the triangle, and dividing the result by 2. In panel (a) the area of the shaded triangle is $\frac{6 \times 3}{2} = 9$. In panel (b) the area of the shaded triangle is $\frac{6 \times 4}{2} = 12$.

Graphs That Depict Numerical Information

Graphs can also be used as a convenient way to summarize and display data without assuming some underlying causal relationship. Graphs that simply display numerical information are called *numerical graphs*. Here we will consider four types of numerical graphs: *time-series graphs*, *scatter diagrams*, *pie charts*, and *bar graphs*. These are widely used to display real, empirical data about different economic variables because they often help economists and policy makers identify patterns or trends in the economy. But as we will also see, you must be careful not to misinterpret or draw unwarranted conclusions from numerical graphs. That is, you must be aware of both the usefulness and the limitations of numerical graphs.

Types of Numerical Graphs

You have probably seen graphs in newspapers that show what has happened over time to economic variables such as the unemployment rate or stock prices. A **time-series graph** has successive dates on the horizontal axis and the values of a variable that occurred on those dates on the vertical axis. For example, Figure 2A-8 shows the unemployment rate in the United States from 1989 to late 2006. A line connecting the points that correspond to the unemployment rate for each month during those years gives a clear idea of the overall trend in unemployment over these years.

Figure 2A-9 is an example of a different kind of numerical graph. It represents information from a sample of 158 countries on average life expectancy and gross national product (GNP) per capita—a rough measure of a country's standard of living. Each point here indicates an average resident's life expectancy and the log of GNP per capita for a given country. (Economists have found that the log of GNP rather than the simple level of GNP is more closely tied to average life expectancy.)

A **time-series graph** has dates on the horizontal axis and values of a variable that occurred on those dates on the vertical axis.

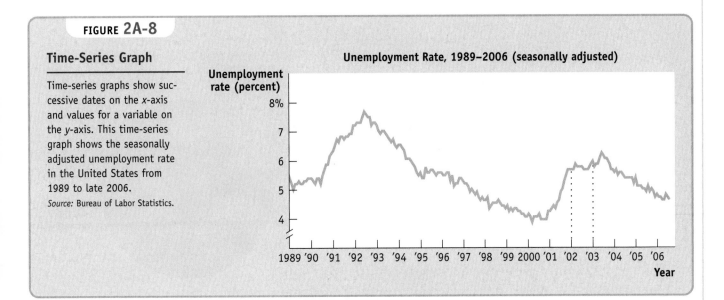

FIGURE 2A-8

Time-Series Graph

Time-series graphs show successive dates on the *x*-axis and values for a variable on the *y*-axis. This time-series graph shows the seasonally adjusted unemployment rate in the United States from 1989 to late 2006.

Source: Bureau of Labor Statistics.

Unemployment Rate, 1989–2006 (seasonally adjusted)

The points lying in the upper right of the graph, which show combinations of high life expectancy and high log GNP per capita, represent economically advanced countries such as the United States. Points lying in the bottom left of the graph, which show combinations of low life expectancy and low log GNP per capita, represent economically less advanced countries such as Afghanistan and Sierra Leone. The pattern of points indicates that there is a positive relationship between life expectancy and log GNP per capita: on the whole, people live longer in countries with a higher standard of living. This type of graph is called a **scatter diagram,** a diagram in which each point corresponds to an actual observation of the *x*-variable and the *y*-variable. In scatter diagrams, a curve is typically fitted to the scatter of points; that is, a curve is drawn that approximates as closely as possible the general relationship between the variables. As you can see, the fitted curve in Figure 2A-9 is upward-sloping, indicating the underlying positive relationship between the two variables. Scatter diagrams are often used to show how a general relationship can be inferred from a set of data.

A **scatter diagram** shows points that correspond to actual observations of the *x*- and *y*-variables. A curve is usually fitted to the scatter of points.

FIGURE 2A-9

Scatter Diagram

In a scatter diagram, each point represents the corresponding values of the *x*- and *y*-variables for a given observation. Here, each point indicates the observed average life expectancy and the log of GNP per capita of a given country for a sample of 158 countries. The upward-sloping fitted line here is the best approximation of the general relationship between the two variables.

Source: Eduard Bos et al., *Health, Nutrition, and Population Indicators: A Statistical Handbook* (Washington, DC: World Bank, 1999).

Standard of Living and Average Life Expectancy

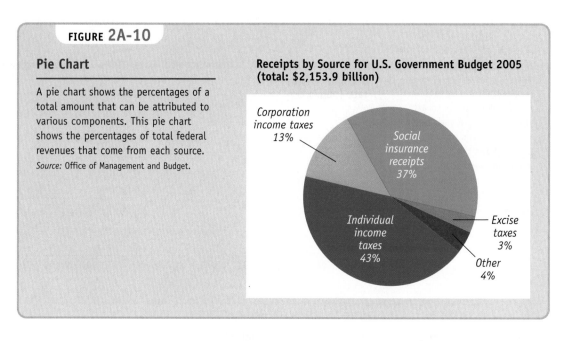

FIGURE 2A-10

Pie Chart

A pie chart shows the percentages of a total amount that can be attributed to various components. This pie chart shows the percentages of total federal revenues that come from each source.

Source: Office of Management and Budget.

Receipts by Source for U.S. Government Budget 2005 (total: $2,153.9 billion)

A **pie chart** shows the share of a total amount that is accounted for by various components, usually expressed in percentages. For example, Figure 2A-10 is a pie chart that depicts the various sources of revenue for the U.S. government budget in 2005, expressed in percentages of the total revenue amount, $2,153.9 billion. As you can see, social insurance receipts (the revenues collected to fund Social Security, Medicare, and unemployment insurance) accounted for 37% of total government revenue and individual income tax receipts accounted for 43%.

Bar graphs use bars of various heights or lengths to indicate values of a variable. In the bar graph in Figure 2A-11, the bars show the percent change in the number of unemployed workers in the United States from 2001 to 2002, separately for White, Black or African-American, and Asian workers. Exact values of the variable that is being measured may be written at the end of the bar, as in this figure. For instance, the number of unemployed Asian workers in the United States increased by 35% between 2001 and 2002. But even without the precise values, comparing the heights or lengths of the bars can give useful insight into the relative magnitudes of the different values of the variable.

A **pie chart** shows how some total is divided among its components, usually expressed in percentages.

A **bar graph** uses bars of varying height or length to show the comparative sizes of different observations of a variable.

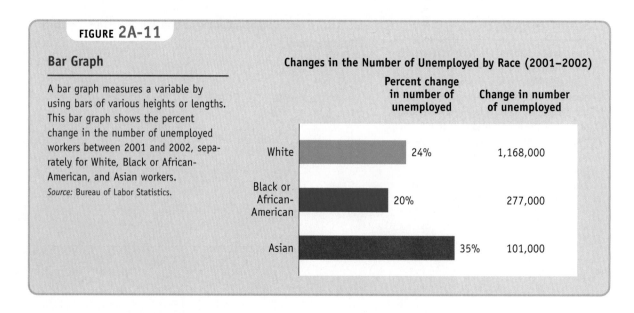

FIGURE 2A-11

Bar Graph

A bar graph measures a variable by using bars of various heights or lengths. This bar graph shows the percent change in the number of unemployed workers between 2001 and 2002, separately for White, Black or African-American, and Asian workers.

Source: Bureau of Labor Statistics.

Changes in the Number of Unemployed by Race (2001–2002)

	Percent change in number of unemployed	Change in number of unemployed
White	24%	1,168,000
Black or African-American	20%	277,000
Asian	35%	101,000

Problems in Interpreting Numerical Graphs

Although the beginning of this appendix emphasized that graphs are visual images that make ideas or information easier to understand, graphs can be constructed (intentionally or unintentionally) in ways that are misleading and can lead to inaccurate conclusions. This section raises some issues that you should be aware of when you interpret graphs.

Features of Construction Before drawing any conclusions about what a numerical graph implies, you should pay attention to the scale, or size of increments, shown on the axes. Small increments tend to visually exaggerate changes in the variables, whereas large increments tend to visually diminish them. So the scale used in construction of a graph can influence your interpretation of the significance of the changes it illustrates—perhaps in an unwarranted way.

Take, for example, Figure 2A-12, which shows the unemployment rate in the United States in 2002 using a 0.1% scale. You can see that the unemployment rate rose from 5.6% at the beginning of 2002 to 6.0% by the end of the year. Here, the rise of 0.4% in the unemployment rate looks enormous and could lead a policy maker to conclude that it was a relatively significant event. But if you go back and reexamine Figure 2A-8, which shows the unemployment rate in the United States from 1989 to late 2006, you can see that this would be a misguided conclusion. Figure 2A-8 includes the same data shown in Figure 2A-12, but it is constructed with a 1% scale rather than a 0.1% scale. From it you can see that the rise of 0.4% in the unemployment rate during 2002 was, in fact, a relatively insignificant event, at least compared to the rise in unemployment during 1990 or during 2001. This comparison shows that if you are not careful to factor in the choice of scale in interpreting a graph, you can arrive at very different, and possibly misguided, conclusions.

Related to the choice of scale is the use of *truncation* in constructing a graph. An axis is **truncated** when part of the range is omitted. This is indicated by two slashes (//) in the axis near the origin. You can see that the vertical axis of Figure 2A-12 has been truncated—the range of values from 0 to 5.6 has been omitted and a // appears in the axis. Truncation saves space in the presentation of a graph and allows smaller increments to be used in constructing it. As a result, changes in the variable depicted on a graph that has been truncated appear larger compared to a graph that has not been truncated and that uses larger increments.

> An axis is **truncated** when some of the values on the axis are omitted, usually to save space.

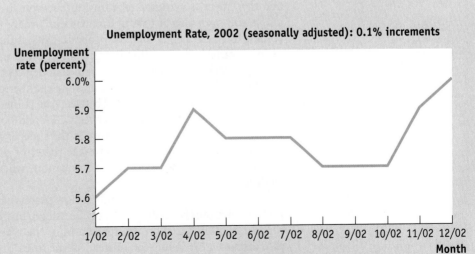

FIGURE 2A-12

Interpreting Graphs: The Effect of Scale

Some of the same data for the year 2002 used in Figure 2A-8 are represented here, except that here they are shown using 0.1% increments rather than 1% increments. As a result of this change in scale, the rise in the unemployment rate during 2002 looks much larger in this figure compared to Figure 2A-8.

Source: Bureau of Labor Statistics.

An **omitted variable** is an unobserved variable that, through its influence on other variables, creates the erroneous appearance of a direct causal relationship among those variables.

The error of **reverse causality** is committed when the true direction of causality between two variables is reversed.

You must also pay close attention to exactly what a graph is illustrating. For example, in Figure 2A-11, you should recognize that what is being shown here are percentage changes in the number of unemployed, not numerical changes. The unemployment rate for Asian workers increased by the highest percentage, 35% in this example. If you confused numerical changes with percentage changes, you would erroneously conclude that the greatest number of newly unemployed workers were Asian. But, in fact, a correct interpretation of Figure 2A-11 shows that the greatest number of newly unemployed workers were White: the total number of unemployed White workers grew by 1,168,000 workers, which is greater than the increase in the number of unemployed Asian workers, which is 101,000 in this example. Although there was a higher percentage increase in the number of unemployed Asian workers, the number of unemployed Asian workers in the United States in 2001 was much smaller than the number of unemployed White workers, leading to a smaller number of newly unemployed Asian workers than White workers.

Omitted Variables From a scatter diagram that shows two variables moving either positively or negatively in relation to each other, it is easy to conclude that there is a causal relationship. But relationships between two variables are not always due to direct cause and effect. Quite possibly an observed relationship between two variables is due to the *unobserved* effect of a third variable on each of the other two variables. An unobserved variable that, through its influence on other variables, creates the erroneous appearance of a direct causal relationship among those variables is called an **omitted variable.** For example, in New England, a greater amount of snowfall during a given week will typically cause people to buy more snow shovels. It will also cause people to buy more de-icer fluid. But if you omitted the influence of the snowfall and simply plotted the number of snow shovels sold versus the number of bottles of de-icer fluid sold, you would produce a scatter diagram that showed an upward tilt in the pattern of points, indicating a positive relationship between snow shovels sold and de-icer fluid sold. To attribute a causal relationship between these two variables, however, is misguided; more snow shovels sold do not cause more de-icer fluid to be sold, or vice versa. They move together because they are both influenced by a third, determining, variable—the weekly snowfall, which is the omitted variable in this case. So before assuming that a pattern in a scatter diagram implies a cause-and-effect relationship, it is important to consider whether the pattern is instead the result of an omitted variable. Or to put it succinctly: correlation is not causation.

Reverse Causality Even when you are confident that there is no omitted variable and that there is a causal relationship between two variables shown in a numerical graph, you must also be careful that you don't make the mistake of **reverse causality**—coming to an erroneous conclusion about which is the dependent and which is the independent variable by reversing the true direction of causality between the two variables. For example, imagine a scatter diagram that depicts the grade point averages (GPAs) of 20 of your classmates on one axis and the number of hours that each of them spends studying on the other. A line fitted between the points will probably have a positive slope, showing a positive relationship between GPA and hours of studying. We could reasonably infer that hours spent studying is the independent variable and that GPA is the dependent variable. But you could make the error of reverse causality: you could infer that a high GPA causes a student to study more, whereas a low GPA causes a student to study less.

The significance of understanding how graphs can mislead or be incorrectly interpreted is not purely academic. Policy decisions, business decisions, and political arguments are often based on interpretation of the types of numerical graphs that we've just discussed. Problems of misleading features of construction, omitted variables, and reverse causality can lead to very important and undesirable consequences.

PROBLEMS ···■

1. Study the four accompanying diagrams. Consider the following statements and indicate which diagram matches each statement. Which variable would appear on the horizontal and which on the vertical axis? In each of these statements, is the slope positive, negative, zero, or infinity?

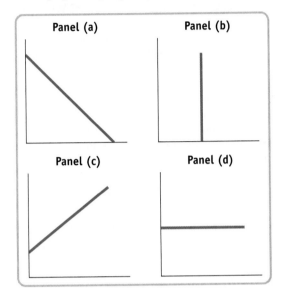

Panel (a)   Panel (b)

Panel (c)   Panel (d)

a. If the price of movies increases, fewer consumers go to see movies.

b. More experienced workers typically have higher incomes than less experienced workers.

c. Whatever the temperature outside, Americans consume the same number of hot dogs per day.

d. Consumers buy more frozen yogurt when the price of ice cream goes up.

e. Research finds no relationship between the number of diet books purchased and the number of pounds lost by the average dieter.

f. Regardless of its price, Americans buy the same quantity of salt.

2. During the Reagan administration, economist Arthur Laffer argued in favor of lowering income tax rates in order to increase tax revenues. Like most economists, he believed that at tax rates above a certain level, tax revenue would fall because high taxes would discourage some people from working and that people would refuse to work at all if they received no income after paying taxes. This relationship between tax rates and tax revenue is graphically summarized in what is widely known as the Laffer curve. Plot the Laffer curve relationship assuming that it has the shape of a nonlinear curve. The following questions will help you construct the graph.

a. Which is the independent variable? Which is the dependent variable? On which axis do you therefore measure the income tax rate? On which axis do you measure income tax revenue?

b. What would tax revenue be at a 0% income tax rate?

c. The maximum possible income tax rate is 100%. What would tax revenue be at a 100% income tax rate?

d. Estimates now show that the maximum point on the Laffer curve is (approximately) at a tax rate of 80%. For tax rates less than 80%, how would you describe the relationship between the tax rate and tax revenue, and how is this relationship reflected in the slope? For tax rates higher than 80%, how would you describe the relationship between the tax rate and tax revenue, and how is this relationship reflected in the slope?

3. In the accompanying figures, the numbers on the axes have been lost. All you know is that the units shown on the vertical axis are the same as the units on the horizontal axis.

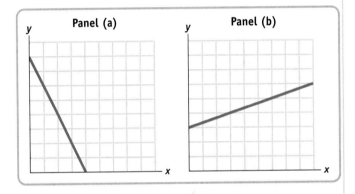

Panel (a)   Panel (b)

a. In panel (a), what is the slope of the line? Show that the slope is constant along the line.

b. In panel (b), what is the slope of the line? Show that the slope is constant along the line.

4. Answer each of the following questions by drawing a schematic diagram.

a. Taking measurements of the slope of a curve at three points farther and farther to the right along the horizontal axis, the slope of the curve changes from −0.3, to −0.8, to −2.5, measured by the point method. Draw a schematic diagram of this curve. How would you describe the relationship illustrated in your diagram?

b. Taking measurements of the slope of a curve at five points farther and farther to the right along the horizontal axis, the slope of the curve changes from 1.5, to 0.5, to 0, to −0.5, to −1.5, measured by the point method. Draw a schematic diagram of this curve. Does it have a maximum or a minimum?

5. For each of the accompanying diagrams, calculate the area of the shaded right triangle.

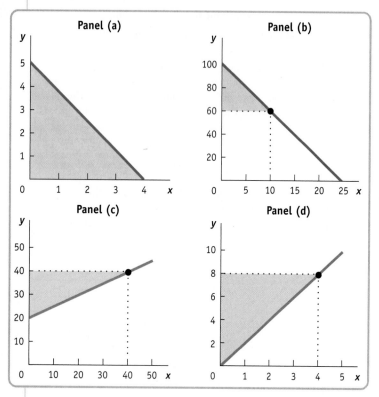

6. The base of a right triangle is 10, and its area is 20. What is the height of this right triangle?

7. The accompanying table shows the relationship between workers' hours of work per week and their hourly wage rate. Apart from the fact that they receive a different hourly wage rate and work different hours, these five workers are otherwise identical.

Name	Quantity of labor (hours per week)	Wage rate (per hour)
Athena	30	$15
Boris	35	30
Curt	37	45
Diego	36	60
Emily	32	75

a. Which variable is the independent variable? Which is the dependent variable?

b. Draw a scatter diagram illustrating this relationship. Draw a (nonlinear) curve that connects the points. Put the hourly wage rate on the vertical axis.

c. As the wage rate increases from $15 to $30, how does the number of hours worked respond according to the relationship depicted here? What is the average slope of the curve between Athena's and Boris's data points using the arc method?

d. As the wage rate increases from $60 to $75, how does the number of hours worked respond according to the relationship depicted here? What is the average slope of the curve between Diego's and Emily's data points using the arc method?

8. Studies have found a relationship between a country's yearly rate of economic growth and the yearly rate of increase in airborne pollutants. It is believed that a higher rate of economic growth allows a country's residents to have more cars and travel more, thereby releasing more airborne pollutants.

a. Which variable is the independent variable? Which is the dependent variable?

b. Suppose that in the country of Sudland, when the yearly rate of economic growth fell from 3.0% to 1.5%, the yearly rate of increase in airborne pollutants fell from 6% to 5%. What is the average slope of a nonlinear curve between these points using the arc method?

c. Now suppose that when the yearly rate of economic growth rose from 3.5% to 4.5%, the yearly rate of increase in airborne pollutants rose from 5.5% to 7.5%. What is the average slope of a nonlinear curve between these two points using the arc method?

d. How would you describe the relationship between the two variables here?

9. An insurance company has found that the severity of property damage in a fire is positively related to the number of firefighters arriving at the scene.

a. Draw a diagram that depicts this finding with number of firefighters on the horizontal axis and amount of property damage on the vertical axis. What is the argument made by this diagram? Suppose you reverse what is measured on the two axes. What is the argument made then?

b. In order to reduce its payouts to policyholders, should the insurance company therefore ask the city to send fewer firefighters to any fire?

10. The accompanying table illustrates annual salaries and income tax owed by five individuals. Apart from the fact that they receive different salaries and owe different amounts of income tax, these five individuals are otherwise identical.

Name	Annual salary	Annual income tax owed
Susan	$22,000	$3,304
Eduardo	63,000	14,317
John	3,000	454
Camila	94,000	23,927
Peter	37,000	7,020

a. If you were to plot these points on a graph, what would be the average slope of the curve between the points for Eduardo's and Camila's salaries and taxes using the arc method? How would you interpret this value for slope?

b. What is the average slope of the curve between the points for John's and Susan's salaries and taxes using the arc method? How would you interpret that value for slope?

c. What happens to the slope as salary increases? What does this relationship imply about how the level of income taxes affects a person's incentive to earn a higher salary?

> Supply and Demand

WAKE UP AND DON'T SMELL THE COFFEE

FOR THOSE WHO NEED A CAPPUCCINO, MOCHA latte, or frappuccino to get through the day, coffee drinking can become an expensive habit. And on October 6, 2006, the habit got a little more expensive. On that day Starbucks raised its drink prices for the first time in six years. The average price of coffee beverages at the world's leading chain of coffeehouses rose about 11 cents per cup.

Starbucks had kept its prices unchanged for six years. So what compelled them to finally raise their prices in the fall of 2006? Mainly the fact that the cost of a major ingredient—coffee beans—had gone up significantly. In fact, coffee bean prices doubled between 2002 and 2006.

Who decided to raise the prices of coffee beans? Nobody: prices went up because of events outside anyone's control. Specifically, the main cause of rising bean prices was a significant decline in the supply of coffee beans from the world's two leading coffee exporters: Brazil and Vietnam. (Yes, Vietnam: since the 1990s, a

country best known to Americans as a place we fought a war has become a coffee-growing giant.) In Brazil, the decline in supply was a delayed reaction to low prices earlier in the decade, which led coffee growers to cut back on planting. In Vietnam, the problem was weather: a prolonged drought sharply reduced coffee harvests.

And a lower supply of coffee beans from Vietnam or Brazil inevitably translates into a higher price of coffee on Main Street. It's just a matter of supply and demand.

What do we mean by that? Many people use "supply and demand" as a sort of catchphrase to mean "the laws of the marketplace at work." To economists, however, the concept of supply and demand has a precise meaning: it is a *model of how a market behaves* that is extremely useful for understanding many—but not all—markets.

In this chapter, we lay out the pieces that make up the *supply and demand model*, put them together, and show how this model can be used to understand how many—but not all—markets behave.

Reduced coffee bean production in Vietnam inevitably translates into higher coffee prices at your local Starbucks.

Supply and Demand: A Model of a Competitive Market

Coffee bean sellers and coffee bean buyers constitute a market—a group of producers and consumers who exchange a good or service for payment. In this chapter, we'll focus on a particular type of market known as a *competitive market*. Roughly, a **competitive market** is a market in which there are many buyers and sellers of the same good or service. More precisely, the key feature of a competitive market is that no individual's actions have a noticeable effect on the price at which the good or service is sold. It's important to understand, however, that this is not an accurate description of every market. For example, it's not an accurate description of the market for cola beverages. That's because in the market for cola beverages, Coca-Cola and Pepsi account for such a large proportion of total sales that they are able to influence the price at which cola beverages are bought and sold. But it is an accurate description of the market for coffee beans. The global marketplace for coffee beans is so huge that even a coffee retailer as large as Starbucks accounts for only a tiny fraction of transactions, making it unable to influence the price at which coffee beans are bought and sold.

It's a little hard to explain why competitive markets are different from other markets until we've seen how a competitive market works. So let's take a rain check—we'll return to that issue at the end of this chapter. For now, let's just say that it's easier to model competitive markets than other markets. When taking an exam, it's always a good strategy to begin by answering the easier questions. In this book, we're going to do the same thing. So we will start with competitive markets.

When a market is competitive, its behavior is well described by the **supply and demand model.** Because many markets *are* competitive, the supply and demand model is a very useful one indeed.

There are five key elements in this model:

■ The *demand curve*

■ The *supply curve*

■ The set of factors that cause the demand curve to shift and the set of factors that cause the supply curve to shift

■ The *market equilibrium,* which includes the *equilibrium price* and *equilibrium quantity*

■ The way the market equilibrium changes when the supply curve or demand curve shifts

To understand the supply and demand model, we will examine each of these elements.

The Demand Curve

How many pounds of coffee beans do consumers around the world want to buy in a given year? You might at first think that we can answer this question by looking at the total number of cups of coffee drunk around the world each day and the amount of coffee beans it takes to brew a cup, then multiplying by 365. But that's not enough to answer the question, because how many pounds of coffee beans consumers want

A **competitive market** is a market in which there are many buyers and sellers of the same good or service, none of whom can influence the price at which the good or service is sold.

The **supply and demand model** is a model of how a competitive market works.

to buy—and therefore how much coffee people want to drink—depends on the price of coffee beans. When the price of coffee rises, as it did in 2006, some people drink less of it, perhaps switching completely to other caffeinated beverages, such as tea or Coca-Cola. (Yes, there are people who drink Coke in the morning.) In general, the quantity of coffee beans, or of any good or service that people want to buy, depends on the price. The higher the price, the less of the good or service people want to purchase; alternatively, the lower the price, the more they want to purchase.

So the answer to the question "How many pounds of coffee beans do consumers want to buy?" depends on the price of coffee beans. If you don't yet know what the price will be, you can start by making a table of how many pounds of coffee beans people would want to buy at a number of different prices. Such a table is known as a *demand schedule*. This, in turn, can be used to draw a *demand curve*, which is one of the key elements of the supply and demand model.

> A **demand schedule** shows how much of a good or service consumers will want to buy at different prices.

The Demand Schedule and the Demand Curve

A **demand schedule** is a table showing how much of a good or service consumers will want to buy at different prices. At the right of Figure 3-1, we show a hypothetical demand schedule for coffee beans. It's hypothetical in that it doesn't use actual data on the world demand for coffee beans and it assumes that all coffee beans are of equal quality (with our apologies to coffee connoisseurs).

According to the table, if coffee beans cost $1 a pound, consumers around the world will want to purchase 10 billion pounds of coffee beans over the course of a year. If the price is $1.25 a pound, they will want to buy only 8.9 billion pounds; if

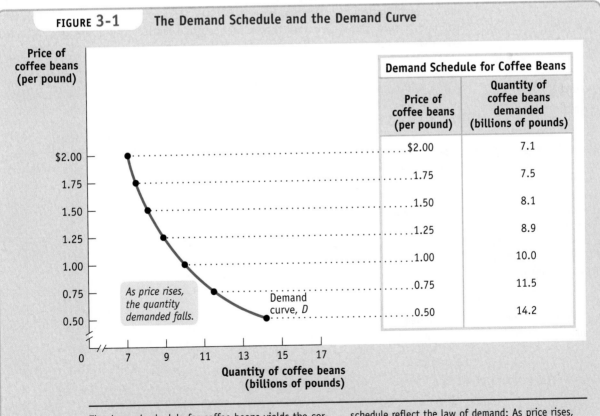

FIGURE 3-1 The Demand Schedule and the Demand Curve

As price rises, the quantity demanded falls.

Demand curve, D

Demand Schedule for Coffee Beans

Price of coffee beans (per pound)	Quantity of coffee beans demanded (billions of pounds)
$2.00	7.1
1.75	7.5
1.50	8.1
1.25	8.9
1.00	10.0
0.75	11.5
0.50	14.2

The demand schedule for coffee beans yields the corresponding demand curve, which shows how much of a good or service consumers want to buy at any given price. The demand curve and the demand schedule reflect the law of demand: As price rises, the quantity demanded falls. Similarly, a decrease in price raises the quantity demanded. As a result, the demand curve is downward sloping.

The **quantity demanded** is the actual amount of a good or service consumers are willing to buy at some specific price.

A **demand curve** is a graphical representation of the demand schedule. It shows the relationship between quantity demanded and price.

The **law of demand** says that a higher price for a good or service, other things equal, leads people to demand a smaller quantity of that good or service.

the price is only $0.75 a pound, they will want to buy 11.5 billion pounds; and so on. So the higher the price, the fewer pounds of coffee beans consumers will want to purchase. In other words, as the price rises, the **quantity demanded** of coffee beans—the actual amount consumers are willing to buy at some specific price—falls.

The graph in Figure 3-1 is a visual representation of the information in the table. (You might want to review the discussion of graphs in economics in the appendix to Chapter 2.) The vertical axis shows the price of a pound of coffee beans and the horizontal axis shows the quantity of coffee beans. Each point on the graph corresponds to one of the entries in the table. The curve that connects these points is a **demand curve.** A demand curve is a graphical representation of the demand schedule, another way of showing the relationship between the quantity demanded and price.

Note that the demand curve shown in Figure 3-1 slopes downward. This reflects the general proposition that a higher price reduces the quantity demanded. For example, some people who drink two cups of coffee a day when beans are $1 per pound will cut down to one cup when beans are $2 per pound. Similarly, some who drink one cup when beans are $1 a pound will drink tea instead if the price doubles to $2 per pound and so on. In the real world, demand curves almost always *do* slope downward. (The exceptions are so rare that for practical purposes we can ignore them.) Generally, the proposition that a higher price for a good, *other things equal*, leads people to demand a smaller quantity of that good is so reliable that economists are willing to call it a "law"—the **law of demand.**

Shifts of the Demand Curve

Even though coffee prices were a lot higher in 2006 than they had been in 2002, total world consumption of coffee was higher in 2006. How can we reconcile this fact with the law of demand, which says that a higher price reduces the quantity demanded, other things equal?

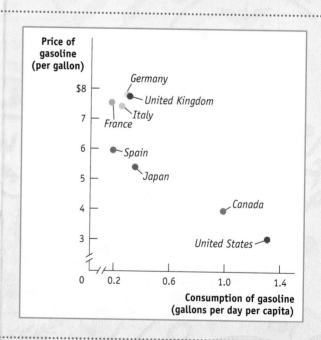

GLOBAL COMPARISON **PAY MORE, PUMP LESS**

For a real-world illustration of the law of demand, consider how gasoline consumption varies according to the prices consumers pay at the pump. Because of high taxes, gasoline and diesel fuel are more than twice as expensive in most European countries as in the United States. According to the law of demand, this should lead Europeans to buy less gasoline than Americans—and they do. As you can see from the figure, per person, Europeans consume less than half as much fuel as Americans, mainly because they drive smaller cars with better mileage.

Prices aren't the only factor affecting fuel consumption, but they're probably the main cause of the difference between European and American fuel consumption per person.

Source: U.S. Energy Information Administration, 2007.

The answer lies in the crucial phrase *other things equal*. In this case, other things weren't equal: the world had changed between 2002 and 2006, in ways that increased the quantity of coffee demanded at any given price. For one thing, the world's population, and therefore the number of potential coffee drinkers, increased. In addition, the growing popularity of different types of coffee beverages, like lattes and cappuccinos, led to an increase in the quantity demanded at any given price. Figure 3-2 illustrates this phenomenon using the demand schedule and demand curve for coffee beans. (As before, the numbers in Figure 3-2 are hypothetical.)

The table in Figure 3-2 shows two demand schedules. The first is a demand schedule for 2002, the same one shown in Figure 3-1. The second is a demand schedule for 2006. It differs from the 2002 demand schedule due to factors such as a larger population and the greater popularity of lattes, factors that led to an increase in the quantity of coffee beans demanded at any given price. So at each price the 2006 schedule shows a larger quantity demanded than the 2002 schedule. For example, the quantity of coffee beans consumers wanted to buy at a price of $1 per pound increased from 10 billion to 12 billion pounds per year, the quantity demanded at $1.25 per pound went from 8.9 billion to 10.7 billion pounds, and so on.

What is clear from this example is that the changes that occurred between 2002 and 2006 generated a *new* demand schedule, one in which the quantity demanded was greater at any given price than in the original demand schedule. The two curves in Figure 3-2 show the same information graphically. As you can see, the demand schedule for 2006 corresponds to a new demand curve, D_2, that is to the right of the demand curve for 2002, D_1. This **shift of the demand curve** shows the change in the quantity demanded at any given price, represented by the change in position of the original demand curve D_1 to its new location at D_2.

> A **shift of the demand curve** is a change in the quantity demanded at any given price, represented by the change of the original demand curve to a new position, denoted by a new demand curve.

FIGURE 3-2   An Increase in Demand

Demand Schedules for Coffee Beans		
Price of coffee beans (per pound)	Quantity of coffee beans demanded (billions of pounds)	
	in 2002	in 2006
$2.00	7.1	8.5
1.75	7.5	9.0
1.50	8.1	9.7
1.25	8.9	10.7
1.00	10.0	12.0
0.75	11.5	13.8
0.50	14.2	17.0

An increase in the population and other factors generate an increase in demand—a rise in the quantity demanded at any given price. This is represented by the two demand schedules—one showing demand in 2002, before the rise in population, the other showing demand in 2006, after the rise in population—and their corresponding demand curves. The increase in demand shifts the demand curve to the right.

FIGURE 3-3

Movement Along the Demand Curve Versus Shift of the Demand Curve

The rise in quantity demanded when going from point *A* to point *B* reflects a movement along the demand curve: it is the result of a fall in the price of the good. The rise in quantity demanded when going from point *A* to point *C* reflects a shift of the demand curve: it is the result of a rise in the quantity demanded at any given price.

PITFALLS

DEMAND VERSUS QUANTITY DEMANDED

When economists say "an increase in demand," they mean a rightward shift of the demand curve, and when they say "a decrease in demand," they mean a leftward shift of the demand curve—that is, when they're being careful. In ordinary speech most people, including professional economists, use the word *demand* casually. For example, an economist might say "the demand for air travel has doubled over the past 15 years, partly because of falling air fares" when he or she really means that the *quantity demanded* has doubled.

It's OK to be a bit sloppy in ordinary conversation. But when you're doing economic analysis, it's important to make the distinction between changes in the quantity demanded, which involve movements along a demand curve, and shifts of the demand curve. Sometimes students end up writing something like this: "If demand increases, the price will go up, but that will lead to a fall in demand, which pushes the price down . . ." and then go around in circles. If you make a clear distinction between changes in *demand*, which mean shifts of the demand curve, and changes in *quantity demanded*, you can avoid a lot of confusion.

It's crucial to make the distinction between such shifts of the demand curve and **movements along the demand curve,** changes in the quantity demanded of a good that result from a change in that good's price. Figure 3-3 illustrates the difference.

The movement from point *A* to point *B* is a movement along the demand curve: the quantity demanded rises due to a fall in price as you move down D_1. Here, a fall in the price of coffee beans from $1.50 to $1 per pound generates a rise in the quantity demanded from 8.1 billion to 10 billion pounds per year. But the quantity demanded can also rise when the price is unchanged if there is an *increase in demand*—a rightward shift of the demand curve. This is illustrated in Figure 3-3 by the shift of the demand curve from D_1 to D_2. Holding the price constant at $1.50 a pound, the quantity demanded rises from 8.1 billion pounds at point *A* on D_1 to 9.7 billion pounds at point *C* on D_2.

When economists say "the demand for *X* increased" or "the demand for *Y* decreased," they mean that the demand curve for *X* or *Y* shifted—*not* that the quantity demanded rose or fell because of a change in the price.

Understanding Shifts of the Demand Curve

Figure 3-4 illustrates the two basic ways in which demand curves can shift. When economists talk about an "increase in demand," they mean a *rightward* shift of the demand curve: at any given price, consumers demand a larger quantity of the good or service than before. This is shown by the rightward shift of the original demand curve D_1 to D_2. And when economists talk about a "decrease in demand," they mean a *leftward* shift of the demand curve: at any given price, consumers demand a smaller quantity of the good or service than before. This is shown by the leftward shift of the original demand curve D_1 to D_3.

A **movement along the demand curve** is a change in the quantity demanded of a good that is the result of a change in that good's price.

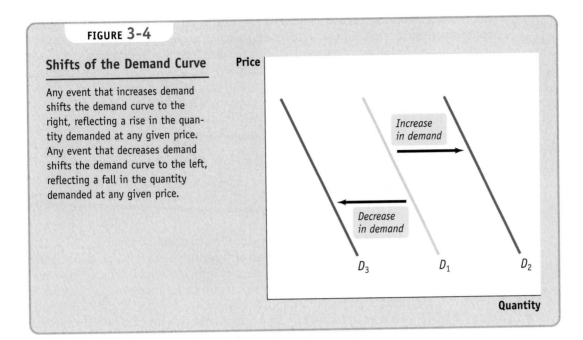

FIGURE 3-4

Shifts of the Demand Curve

Any event that increases demand shifts the demand curve to the right, reflecting a rise in the quantity demanded at any given price. Any event that decreases demand shifts the demand curve to the left, reflecting a fall in the quantity demanded at any given price.

What caused the demand curve for coffee beans to shift? We have already mentioned two reasons: changes in population and a change in the popularity of coffee beverages. If you think about it, you can come up with other things that would be likely to shift the demand curve for coffee beans. For example, suppose that the price of tea rises. This will induce some people who previously drank tea to drink coffee instead, increasing the demand for coffee beans.

Economists believe that there are five principal factors that shift the demand curve for a good or service:

- Changes in the prices of related goods or services
- Changes in income
- Changes in tastes
- Changes in expectations
- Changes in the number of consumers

Although this is not an exhaustive list, it contains the five most important factors that can shift demand curves. So when we say that the quantity of a good or service demanded falls as its price rises, *other things equal*, we are in fact stating that the factors that shift demand are remaining unchanged. Let's now explore, in more detail, how those factors shift the demand curve.

Changes in the Prices of Related Goods or Services While there's nothing quite like a good cup of coffee to start your day, a cup or two of strong tea isn't a bad alternative. Tea is what economists call a *substitute* for coffee. A pair of goods are **substitutes** if a rise in the price of one good (coffee) makes consumers more willing to buy the other good (tea). Substitutes are usually goods that in some way serve a similar function: concerts and theater plays, muffins and doughnuts, train rides and air flights. A rise in the price of the alternative good induces some consumers to purchase the original good *instead* of it, shifting demand for the original good to the right.

But sometimes a fall in the price of one good makes consumers *more* willing to buy another good. Such pairs of goods are known as **complements.** Complements are usually goods that in some sense are consumed together: computers and software, cappuccinos and croissants, cars and gasoline. Because consumers like to consume a good and its complement together, a change in the price of one of the goods will affect the demand for its complement. In particular, when the price of one good

Two goods are **substitutes** if a rise in the price of one of the goods leads to an increase in the demand for the other good.

Two goods are **complements** if a rise in the price of one good leads to a decrease in the demand for the other good.

rises, the demand for its complement decreases, shifting the demand curve for the complement to the left. So the October 2006 rise in Starbucks' cappuccino prices is likely to have precipitated a leftward shift of the demand curve for croissants, as people consumed fewer cappuccinos and croissants. Likewise, when the price of one good falls, the quantity demanded of its complement rises, shifting the demand curve for the complement to the right. This means that if, for some reason, the price of cappuccinos falls, we should see a rightward shift of the demand curve for croissants as people consume more cappuccinos and croissants.

Changes in Income When individuals have more income, they are normally more likely to purchase a good at any given price. For example, if a family's income rises, it is more likely to take that summer trip to Disney World—and therefore also more likely to buy plane tickets. So a rise in consumer incomes will cause the demand curves for most goods to shift to the right.

Why do we say "most goods," not "all goods"? Most goods are **normal goods**—the demand for them increases when consumer income rises. However, the demand for some products falls when income rises. Goods for which demand decreases when income rises are known as **inferior goods.** Usually an inferior good is one that is considered less desirable than more expensive alternatives—such as a bus ride versus a taxi ride. When they can afford to, people stop buying an inferior good and switch their consumption to the preferred, more expensive alternative. So when a good is inferior, a rise in income shifts the demand curve to the left. And, not surprisingly, a fall in income shifts the demand curve to the right.

One example of the distinction between normal and inferior goods that has drawn considerable attention in the business press is the difference between so-called casual-dining restaurants such as Applebee's or Olive Garden and fast-food chains such as McDonald's and KFC. When Americans' income rises, they tend to eat out more at casual-dining restaurants. However, some of this increased dining out comes at the expense of fast-food venues—to some extent, people visit McDonald's less once they can afford to move upscale. So casual dining is a normal good, while fast-food consumption appears to be an inferior good.

Changes in Tastes Why do people want what they want? Fortunately, we don't need to answer that question—we just need to acknowledge that people have certain preferences, or tastes, that determine what they choose to consume and that these tastes can change. Economists usually lump together changes in demand due to fads, beliefs, cultural shifts, and so on under the heading of changes in *tastes* or *preferences*.

For example, once upon a time men wore hats. Up until around World War II, a respectable man wasn't fully dressed unless he wore a dignified hat along with his suit. But the returning GIs adopted a more informal style, perhaps due to the rigors of the war. And President Eisenhower, who had been supreme commander of Allied Forces before becoming president, often went hatless. After World War II, it was clear that the demand curve for hats had shifted leftward, reflecting a decrease in the demand for hats.

We've already mentioned one way in which changing tastes played a role in the increase in the demand for coffee beans from 2002 to 2006: the increase in the popularity of coffee beverages such as lattes and cappuccinos. In addition, there was another route by which changing tastes increased worldwide demand for coffee beans: the switch by consumers in traditionally tea-drinking countries to coffee. "In 1999," reported *Roast* magazine, "the ratio of Russian tea drinkers to coffee drinkers was five to one. In 2005, the ratio is roughly two to one."

Economists have little to say about the forces that influence consumers' tastes. (Although marketers and advertisers have plenty to say about them!) However, a *change* in tastes has a predictable impact on demand. When tastes change in favor of a good, more people want to buy it at any given price, so the demand curve shifts to the right. When tastes change against a good, fewer people want to buy it at any given price, so the demand curve shifts to the left.

Changes in Expectations When consumers have some choice about when to make a purchase, current demand for a good is often affected by expectations about its future price. For example, savvy shoppers often wait for seasonal sales—say, buying next year's holiday gifts during the post-holiday markdowns. In this case, expectations of a future drop in price lead to a decrease in demand today. Alternatively, expectations of a future rise in price are likely to cause an increase in demand today. For example, savvy shoppers, knowing that Starbucks was going to increase the price of its coffee beans on October 6, 2006, would stock up on Starbucks coffee beans before that date.

Expected changes in future income can also lead to changes in demand: if you expect your income to rise in the future, you will typically borrow today and increase your demand for certain goods; and if you expect your income to fall in the future, you are likely to save today and reduce your demand for some goods.

Changes in the Number of Consumers As we've already noted, one of the reasons for rising coffee demand between 2002 and 2006 was a growing world population. Because of population growth, overall demand for coffee would have risen even if each individual coffee-drinker's demand for coffee had remained unchanged.

Let's introduce a new concept: the **individual demand curve,** which shows the relationship between quantity demanded and price for an individual consumer. For example, suppose that Darla is a consumer of coffee beans and that panel (a) of Figure 3-5 shows how many pounds of coffee beans she will buy per year at any given price per pound. Then D_{Darla} is Darla's individual demand curve.

The *market demand curve* shows how the combined quantity demanded by all consumers depends on the market price of that good. (Most of the time, when economists refer to the demand curve, they mean the market demand curve.) The market demand curve is the *horizontal sum* of the individual demand curves of all

An **individual demand curve** illustrates the relationship between quantity demanded and price for an individual consumer.

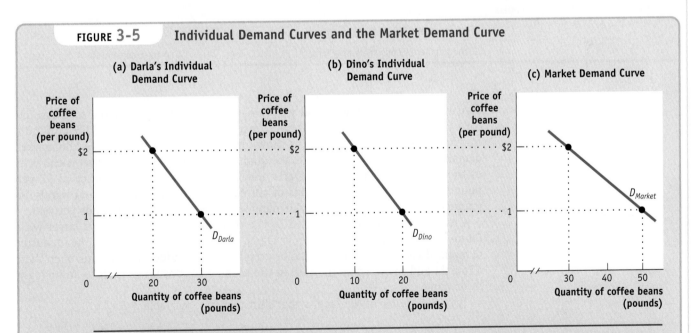

FIGURE 3-5   Individual Demand Curves and the Market Demand Curve

Darla and Dino are the only two consumers of coffee beans in the market. Panel (a) shows Darla's individual demand curve: the number of pounds of coffee beans she will buy per year at any given price. Panel (b) shows Dino's individual demand curve. Given that Darla and Dino are the only two consumers, the *market demand curve,* which shows the quantity of coffee demanded by all consumers at any given price, is shown in panel (c). The market demand curve is the *horizontal sum* of the individual demand curves of all consumers. In this case, at any given price, the quantity demanded by the market is the sum of the quantities demanded by Darla and Dino.

TABLE **3-1**

Factors That Shift Demand

Changes in the prices of related goods or services		
If *A* and *B* are **substitutes** . . .	. . . and the price of *B* rises, . . .	. . . demand for *A* increases.
	. . . and the price of *B* falls, . . .	. . . demand for *A* decreases.
If *A* and *B* are **complements** . . .	. . . and the price of *B* rises, . . .	. . . demand for *A* decreases.
	. . . and the price of *B* falls, . . .	. . . demand for *A* increases.
Changes in income		
If *A* is a **normal good** . . .	. . . and income rises, . . .	. . . demand for *A* increases.
	. . . and income falls, . . .	. . . demand for *A* decreases.
If *A* is an **inferior good** . . .	. . . and income rises, . . .	. . . demand for *A* decreases.
	. . . and income falls, . . .	. . . demand for *A* increases.
Changes in tastes		
	If tastes change in favor of *A*, . . .	. . . demand for *A* increases.
	If tastes change against *A*, . . .	. . . demand for *A* decreases.
Changes in expectations		
	If the price of *A* is expected to rise in the future, . . .	. . . demand for *A* increases today.
	If the price of *A* is expected to fall in the future, . . .	. . . demand for *A* decreases today.
If *A* is a **normal good** . . .	. . . and income is expected to rise in the future, . . .	. . . demand for *A* may increase today.
	. . . and income is expected to fall in the future, . . .	. . . demand for *A* may decrease today.
If *A* is an **inferior good** . . .	. . . and income is expected to rise in the future, . . .	. . . demand for *A* may decrease today.
	. . . and income is expected to fall in the future, . . .	. . . demand for *A* may increase today.
Changes in the number of consumers		
	If the number of consumers of *A* rises, . . .	. . . market demand for *A* increases.
	If the number of consumers of *A* falls, . . .	. . . market demand for *A* decreases.

consumers in that market. To see what we mean by the term *horizontal sum*, assume for a moment that there are only two consumers of coffee, Darla and Dino. Dino's individual demand curve, D_{Dino}, is shown in panel (b). Panel (c) shows the market demand curve. At any given price, the quantity demanded by the market is the sum of the quantities demanded by Darla and Dino. For example, at a price of $2 per pound, Darla demands 20 pounds of coffee beans per year and Dino demands 10 pounds per year. So the quantity demanded by the market is 30 pounds per year.

Clearly, the quantity demanded by the market at any given price is larger with Dino present than it would be if Darla was the only consumer. The quantity demanded at any given price would be even larger if we added a third consumer, then a fourth, and so on. So an increase in the number of consumers leads to an increase in demand.

For an overview of the factors that shift demand, see Table 3-1.

►*ECONOMICS IN ACTION*

Beating the Traffic

All big cities have traffic problems, and many local authorities try to discourage driving in the crowded city center. If we think of an auto trip to the city center as a good that people consume, we can use the economics of demand to analyze anti-traffic policies.

One common strategy of local governments is to reduce the demand for auto trips by lowering the prices of substitutes. Many metropolitan areas subsidize bus and rail service, hoping to lure commuters out of their cars.

An alternative strategy is to raise the price of complements: several major U.S. cities impose high taxes on commercial parking garages, both to raise revenue and to discourage people from driving into the city. Short time limits on parking meters, combined with vigilant parking enforcement, is a related tactic.

However, few cities have been willing to adopt the politically controversial direct approach: reducing congestion by raising the price of driving. So it was a shock when, in 2003, London imposed a "congestion charge" on all cars entering the city center during business hours—currently £8 (about $16) for drivers who pay on the same day they travel.

Compliance is monitored with automatic cameras that photograph license plates. People can either pay the charge in advance or pay it by midnight of the day they have driven. If they pay on the day after they have driven, the charge increases to £10 (about $20). And if they don't pay and are caught, a fine of £120 (about $240) is imposed for each transgression. (A full description of the rules can be found at www.cclondon.com.)

Not surprisingly, the result of the new policy confirms the law of demand: three years after the charge was put in place, traffic in central London was about 10 percent lower than before the charge. In February 2007, the British government doubled the area of London covered by the congestion charge, and it suggested that it might institute congestion charging across the country by 2015. Several American and European municipalities, having seen the success of London's congestion charge, have said that they are seriously considering adopting a congestion charge as well. ▲

> > > > > > > > > > > >

► CHECK YOUR UNDERSTANDING 3-1

1. Explain whether each of the following events represents (i) a *shift of* the demand curve or (ii) a *movement along* the demand curve.
   a. A store owner finds that customers are willing to pay more for umbrellas on rainy days.
   b. When XYZ Telecom, a long-distance telephone service provider, offered reduced rates on weekends, its volume of weekend calling increased sharply.
   c. People buy more long-stem roses the week of Valentine's Day, even though the prices are higher than at other times during the year.
   d. The sharp rise in the price of gasoline leads many commuters to join carpools in order to reduce their gasoline purchases.

Solutions appear at back of book.

The Supply Curve

Some parts of the world are especially well suited to growing coffee beans, which is why, as the lyrics of an old song put it, "There's an awful lot of coffee in Brazil." But even in Brazil, some land is better suited to growing coffee than other land. Whether Brazilian farmers restrict their coffee-growing to only the most ideal locations or expand it to less suitable land depends on the price they expect to get for their beans. Moreover, there are many other areas in the world where coffee beans could be grown—such as Madagascar and Vietnam. Whether farmers there actually grow coffee depends, again, on the price.

So just as the quantity of coffee beans that consumers want to buy depends on the price they have to pay, the quantity that producers are willing to produce and sell—the **quantity supplied**—depends on the price they are offered.

The Supply Schedule and the Supply Curve

The table in Figure 3-6 on the next page shows how the quantity of coffee beans made available varies with the price—that is, it shows a hypothetical **supply schedule** for coffee beans.

QUICK REVIEW

➤ The **supply and demand model** is a model of a **competitive market**—one in which there are many buyers and sellers of the same good or service.
➤ The **demand schedule** shows how the **quantity demanded** changes as the price changes. This relationship is illustrated by a **demand curve.**
➤ The **law of demand** asserts that demand curves normally slope downward—that is, a higher price reduces the quantity demanded.
➤ Increases or decreases in demand correspond to **shifts of the demand curve.** An increase in demand is a rightward shift: the quantity demanded rises for any given price. A decrease in demand is a leftward shift: the quantity demanded falls for any given price. A change in price results in a **movement along the demand curve**—a change in the quantity demanded.
➤ The five main factors that can shift the demand curve are changes in (1) the price of a related good, such as a **substitute** or a **complement,** (2) income, (3) tastes, (4) expectations, and (5) the number of consumers.
➤ The market demand curve is the horizontal sum of the **individual demand curves** of all consumers in the market.

The **quantity supplied** is the actual amount of a good or service producers are willing to sell at some specific price.

A **supply schedule** shows how much of a good or service producers will supply at different prices.

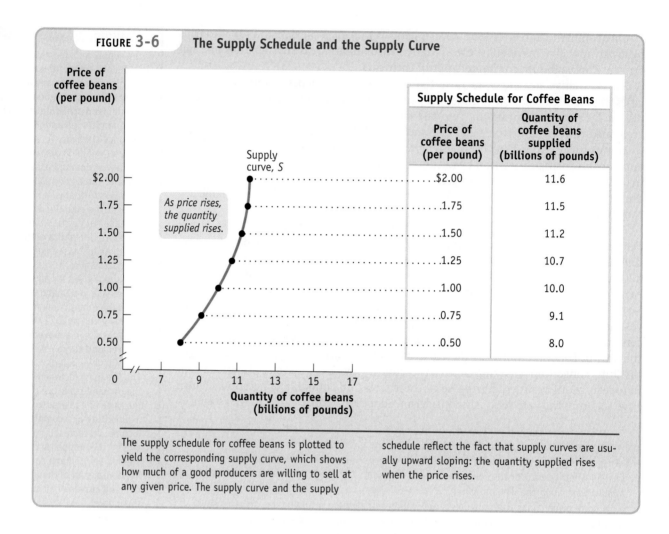

FIGURE 3-6 The Supply Schedule and the Supply Curve

Price of coffee beans (per pound)

Supply curve, *S*

As price rises, the quantity supplied rises.

Quantity of coffee beans (billions of pounds)

Supply Schedule for Coffee Beans	
Price of coffee beans (per pound)	Quantity of coffee beans supplied (billions of pounds)
$2.00	11.6
1.75	11.5
1.50	11.2
1.25	10.7
1.00	10.0
0.75	9.1
0.50	8.0

The supply schedule for coffee beans is plotted to yield the corresponding supply curve, which shows how much of a good producers are willing to sell at any given price. The supply curve and the supply schedule reflect the fact that supply curves are usually upward sloping: the quantity supplied rises when the price rises.

A supply schedule works the same way as the demand schedule shown in Figure 3-1: in this case, the table shows the quantity of coffee beans farmers are willing to sell at different prices. At a price of $0.50 per pound, farmers are willing to sell only 8 billion pounds of coffee beans per year. At $0.75 per pound, they're willing to sell 9.1 billion pounds. At $1, they're willing to sell 10 billion pounds, and so on.

In the same way that a demand schedule can be represented graphically by a demand curve, a supply schedule can be represented by a **supply curve,** as shown in Figure 3-6. Each point on the curve represents an entry from the table.

Suppose that the price of coffee beans rises from $1 to $1.25; we can see that the quantity of coffee beans farmers are willing to sell rises from 10 billion to 10.7 billion pounds. This is the normal situation for a supply curve, reflecting the general proposition that a higher price leads to a higher quantity supplied. So just as demand curves normally slope downward, supply curves normally slope upward: the higher the price being offered, the more of any good or service producers will be willing to sell.

Shifts of the Supply Curve

Compared to earlier trends, coffee beans were unusually cheap in the early years of the twenty-first century. One reason was the emergence of new coffee bean-producing countries, which began competing with the traditional sources in Latin

A **supply curve** shows the relationship between quantity supplied and price.

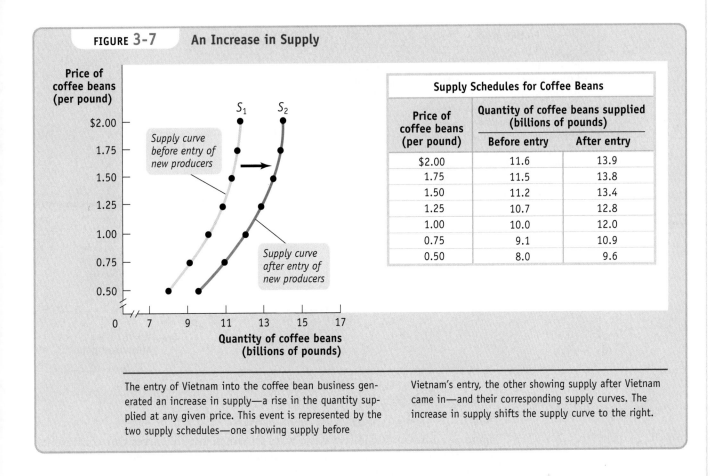

FIGURE 3-7   An Increase in Supply

Supply Schedules for Coffee Beans

Price of coffee beans (per pound)	Quantity of coffee beans supplied (billions of pounds)	
	Before entry	After entry
$2.00	11.6	13.9
1.75	11.5	13.8
1.50	11.2	13.4
1.25	10.7	12.8
1.00	10.0	12.0
0.75	9.1	10.9
0.50	8.0	9.6

The entry of Vietnam into the coffee bean business generated an increase in supply—a rise in the quantity supplied at any given price. This event is represented by the two supply schedules—one showing supply before Vietnam's entry, the other showing supply after Vietnam came in—and their corresponding supply curves. The increase in supply shifts the supply curve to the right.

America. Vietnam, in particular, emerged as a big new source of coffee beans. Figure 3-7 illustrates this event in terms of the supply schedule and the supply curve for coffee beans.

The table in Figure 3-7 shows two supply schedules. The schedule before new producers such as Vietnam arrived on the scene is the same one as in Figure 3-6. The second schedule shows the supply of coffee beans *after* the entry of new producers. Just as a change in demand schedules leads to a shift of the demand curve, a change in supply schedules leads to a **shift of the supply curve**—a change in the quantity supplied at any given price. This is shown in Figure 3-7 by the shift of the supply curve before the entry of the new producers, S_1, to its new position after the entry of the new producers, S_2. Notice that S_2 lies to the right of S_1, a reflection of the fact that quantity supplied increases at any given price.

As in the analysis of demand, it's crucial to draw a distinction between such shifts of the supply curve and **movements along the supply curve**—changes in the quantity supplied that result from a change in price. We can see this difference in Figure 3-8 on the next page. The movement from point A to point B is a movement along the supply curve: the quantity supplied rises along S_1 due to a rise in price. Here, a rise in price from $1 to $1.50 leads to a rise in the quantity supplied from 10 billion to 11.2 billion pounds of coffee beans. But the quantity supplied can also rise when the price is unchanged if there is an increase in supply—a rightward shift of the supply curve. This is shown by the rightward shift of the supply curve from S_1 to S_2. Holding price constant at $1, the quantity supplied rises from 10 billion pounds at point A on S_1 to 12 billion pounds at point C on S_2.

A **shift of the supply curve** is a change in the quantity supplied of a good or service at any given price. It is represented by the change of the original supply curve to a new position, denoted by a new supply curve.

A **movement along the supply curve** is a change in the quantity supplied of a good that is the result of a change in that good's price.

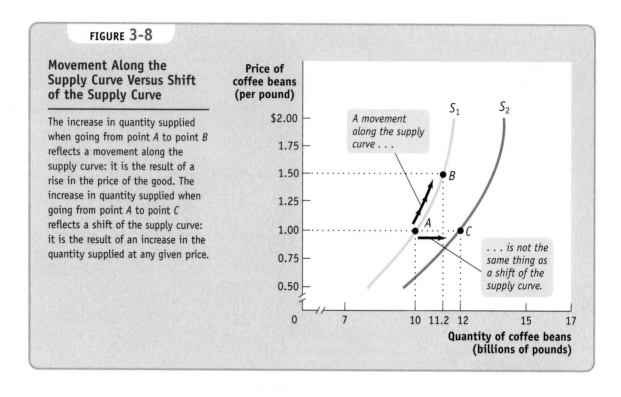

FIGURE 3-8

Movement Along the Supply Curve Versus Shift of the Supply Curve

The increase in quantity supplied when going from point *A* to point *B* reflects a movement along the supply curve: it is the result of a rise in the price of the good. The increase in quantity supplied when going from point *A* to point *C* reflects a shift of the supply curve: it is the result of an increase in the quantity supplied at any given price.

Understanding Shifts of the Supply Curve

Figure 3-9 illustrates the two basic ways in which supply curves can shift. When economists talk about an "increase in supply," they mean a *rightward* shift of the supply curve: at any given price, producers supply a larger quantity of the good than before. This is shown in Figure 3-9 by the rightward shift of the original supply curve S_1 to S_2. And when economists talk about a "decrease in supply," they mean a *leftward* shift of the supply curve: at any given price, producers supply a smaller quantity of the good than before. This is represented by the leftward shift of S_1 to S_3.

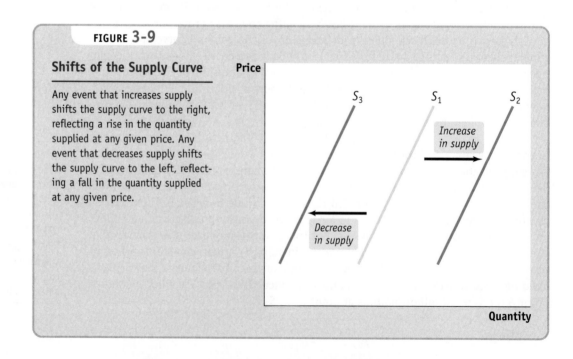

FIGURE 3-9

Shifts of the Supply Curve

Any event that increases supply shifts the supply curve to the right, reflecting a rise in the quantity supplied at any given price. Any event that decreases supply shifts the supply curve to the left, reflecting a fall in the quantity supplied at any given price.

Economists believe that shifts of the supply curve for a good or service are mainly the result of five factors (though, as in the case of demand, there are other possible causes):

An **input** is a good or service that is used to produce another good or service.

- Changes in input prices
- Changes in the prices of related goods or services
- Changes in technology
- Changes in expectations
- Changes in the number of producers

Changes in Input Prices To produce output, you need inputs. For example, to make vanilla ice cream, you need vanilla beans, cream, sugar, and so on. An **input** is any good or service that is used to produce another good or service. Inputs, like output, have prices. And an increase in the price of an input makes the production of the final good more costly for those who produce and sell it. So producers are less willing to supply the final good at any given price, and the supply curve shifts to the left. For example, newspaper publishers buy large quantities of newsprint (the paper on which newspapers are printed). When newsprint prices rose sharply in 1994–1995, the supply of newspapers fell: several newspapers went out of business and a number of new publishing ventures were canceled. Similarly, a fall in the price of an input makes the production of the final good less costly for sellers. They are more willing to supply the good at any given price, and the supply curve shifts to the right.

Changes in the Prices of Related Goods or Services A single producer often produces a mix of goods rather than a single product. For example, an oil refinery produces gasoline from crude oil, but it also produces heating oil and other products from the same raw material. When a producer sells several products, the quantity of any one good it is willing to supply at any given price depends on the prices of its other co-produced goods. This effect can run in either direction. An oil refiner will supply less gasoline at any given price when the price of heating oil rises, shifting the supply curve for gasoline to the left. But it will supply more gasoline at any given price when the price of heating oil falls, shifting the supply curve for gasoline to the right. This means that gasoline and other co-produced oil products are *substitutes in production* for refiners. In contrast, due to the nature of the production process, other goods can be *complements in production*. For example, producers of crude oil—oil-well drillers—often find that oil wells also produce natural gas as a by-product of oil extraction. The higher the price at which a driller can sell its natural gas, the more oil wells it will drill and the more oil it will supply at any given price for oil. As a result, natural gas is a complement in production for crude oil.

Changes in Technology When economists talk about "technology," they don't necessarily mean high technology—they mean all the methods people can use to turn inputs into useful goods and services. In that sense, the whole complex sequence of activities that turn corn from an Iowa farm into cornflakes on your breakfast table is technology. And when a better technology becomes available, reducing the cost of production—that is, letting a producer spend less on inputs yet produce the same output—supply increases, and the supply curve shifts to the right. For example, an improved strain of corn that is more resistant to disease makes farmers willing to supply more corn at any given price.

Changes in Expectations Just as changes in expectations can shift the demand curve, they can also shift the supply curve. When suppliers have some choice about when they put their good up for sale, changes in the expected future price of the good can lead a supplier to supply less or more of the good today. For example, consider the fact that gasoline and other oil products are often stored for significant periods of time at oil refineries before being sold to consumers. In fact, storage is normally part of producers' business strategy. Knowing that the demand for gasoline

An **individual supply curve** illustrates the relationship between quantity supplied and price for an individual producer.

peaks in the summer, oil refiners normally store some of their gasoline produced during the spring for summer sale. Similarly, knowing that the demand for heating oil peaks in the winter, they normally store some of their heating oil produced during the fall for winter sale. In each case, there's a decision to be made between selling the product now versus storing it for later sale. Which choice a producer makes depends on a comparison of the current price versus the expected future price. This example illustrates how changes in expectations can alter supply: an increase in the anticipated future price of a good or service reduces supply today, a leftward shift of the supply curve. But a fall in the anticipated future price increases supply today, a rightward shift of the supply curve.

Changes in the Number of Producers Just as changes in the number of consumers affect the demand curve, changes in the number of producers affect the supply curve. Let's examine the **individual supply curve,** which shows the relationship between quantity supplied and price for an individual producer. For example, suppose that Mr. Figueroa is a Brazilian coffee farmer and that panel (a) of Figure 3-10 shows how many pounds of beans he will supply per year at any given price. Then $S_{Figueroa}$ is his individual supply curve.

The *market supply curve* shows how the combined total quantity supplied by all individual producers in the market depends on the market price of that good. Just as the market demand curve is the horizontal sum of the individual demand curves of all consumers, the market supply curve is the horizontal sum of the individual supply curves of all producers. Assume for a moment that there are only two producers of coffee beans, Mr. Figueroa and Mr. Bien Pho, a Vietnamese coffee farmer. Mr. Bien Pho's individual supply curve is shown in panel (b). Panel (c) shows the market supply curve. At any given price, the quantity supplied to the market is the sum of the quantities supplied by Mr. Figueroa and Mr. Bien Pho. For example, at a price of $2 per pound, Mr. Figueroa supplies 3,000 pounds of coffee beans per year and Mr. Bien Pho supplies 2,000 pounds per year, making the quantity supplied to the market 5,000 pounds.

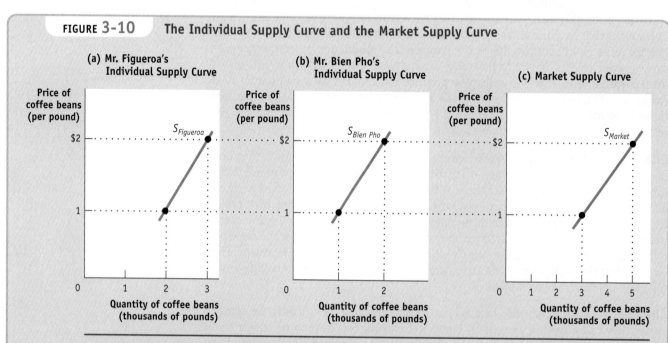

FIGURE 3-10   **The Individual Supply Curve and the Market Supply Curve**

Panel (a) shows the individual supply curve for Mr. Figueroa, $S_{Figueroa}$, the quantity of coffee beans he will sell at any given price. Panel (b) shows the individual supply curve for Mr. Bien Pho, $S_{Bien\ Pho}$. The market supply curve, which shows the quantity of coffee beans supplied by all producers at any given price, is shown in panel (c). The market supply curve is the horizontal sum of the individual supply curves of all producers.

TABLE **3-2**

Factors That Shift Supply

Changes in input prices		
	If the price of an input used to produce *A* rises, . . .	. . . supply of *A* decreases.
	If the price of an input used to produce *A* falls, . . .	. . . supply of *A* increases.
Changes in the prices of related goods or services		
If *A* and *B* are **substitutes in production** . . .	. . . and the price of *B* rises, . . .	. . . supply of *A* decreases.
	. . . and the price of *B* falls, . . .	. . . supply of *A* increases.
If *A* and *B* are **complements in production** . . .	. . . and the price of *B* rises, . . .	. . . supply of *A* increases.
	. . . and the price of *B* falls, . . .	. . . supply of *A* decreases.
Changes in technology		
	If the technology used to produce *A* improves, . . .	. . . supply of *A* increases.
Changes in expectations		
	If the price of *A* is expected to rise in the future, . . .	. . . supply of *A* decreases today.
	If the price of *A* is expected to fall in the future, . . .	. . . supply of *A* increases today.
Changes in the number of producers		
	If the number of producers of *A* rises, . . .	. . . market supply of *A* increases.
	If the number of producers of *A* falls, . . .	. . . market supply of *A* decreases.

Clearly, the quantity supplied to the market at any given price is larger with Mr. Bien Pho present than it would be if Mr. Figueroa was the only supplier. The quantity supplied at a given price would be even larger if we added a third producer, then a fourth, and so on. So an increase in the number of producers leads to an increase in supply and a rightward shift of the supply curve.

For an overview of the factors that shift supply, see Table 3-2.

➤ECONOMICS IN ACTION

Only Creatures Small and Pampered

During the 1970s, British television featured a popular show titled *All Creatures Great and Small*. It chronicled the real life of James Herriot, a country veterinarian who tended to cows, pigs, sheep, horses, and the occasional house pet, often under arduous conditions, in rural England during the 1930s. The show made it clear that in those days the local vet was a critical member of farming communities, saving valuable farm animals and helping farmers survive financially. And it was also clear that Mr. Herriot considered his life's work well spent.

But that was then and this is now. According to a 2007 article in the *New York Times*, the United States has experienced a severe decline in the number of farm veterinarians over the past two decades. The source of the problem is competition. As the number of household pets has increased and the incomes of pet owners have grown, the demand for pet veterinarians has increased sharply. As a result, vets are being drawn away from the business of caring for farm animals into the more lucrative business of caring for pets. As one vet stated, she began her career caring for farm animals but changed her mind after "doing a C-section on a cow and it's 50 bucks. Do a C-section on a Chihuahua and you get $300. It's the money. I hate to say that."

How can we translate this into supply and demand curves? Farm veterinary services and pet veterinary services are like gasoline and fuel oil: they're related goods that are substitutes in production. A veterinarian typically specializes in one type of practice or the other, and that decision often depends on the going price for the service.

- The **supply schedule** shows how the **quantity supplied** depends on the price. The relationship between the two is illustrated by the **supply curve.**
- Supply curves are normally upward sloping: at a higher price, producers are willing to supply more of a good or service.
- A change in price results in a **movement along the supply curve** and a change in the quantity supplied.
- As with demand, increases or decreases in supply correspond to **shifts of the supply curve.** An increase in supply is a rightward shift: the quantity supplied rises for any given price. A decrease in supply is a leftward shift: the quantity supplied falls for any given price.
- The five main factors that can shift the supply curve are changes in (1) input prices, (2) prices of related goods or services, (3) technology, (4) expectations, and (5) number of producers.
- The market supply curve is the horizontal sum of the **individual supply curves** of all producers in the market.

America's growing pet population, combined with the increased willingness of doting owners to spend on their companions' care, has driven up the price of pet veterinary services. As a result, fewer and fewer veterinarians have gone into farm animal practice. So the supply curve of farm veterinarians has shifted leftward—fewer farm veterinarians are offering their services at any given price.

In the end, farmers understand that it is all a matter of dollars and cents—that they get fewer veterinarians because they are unwilling to pay more. As one farmer, who had recently lost an expensive cow due to the unavailability of a veterinarian, stated, "The fact that there's nothing you can do, you accept it as a business expense now. You didn't used to. If you have livestock, sooner or later you're going to have deadstock." (Although we should note that this farmer *could* have chosen to pay more for a vet who would have then saved his cow.) ▲

< < < < < < < < < < < <

> ► **CHECK YOUR UNDERSTANDING** 3-2

1. Explain whether each of the following events represents (i) a *shift of* the supply curve or (ii) a *movement along* the supply curve.
   a. More homeowners put their houses up for sale during a real estate boom that causes house prices to rise.
   b. Many strawberry farmers open temporary roadside stands during harvest season, even though prices are usually low at that time.
   c. Immediately after the school year begins, fast-food chains must raise wages, which represent the price of labor, to attract workers.
   d. Many construction workers temporarily move to areas that have suffered hurricane damage, lured by higher wages.
   e. Since new technologies have made it possible to build larger cruise ships (which are cheaper to run per passenger), Caribbean cruise lines have offered more cabins, at lower prices, than before.

Solutions appear at back of book.

Supply, Demand, and Equilibrium

We have now covered the first three key elements in the supply and demand model: the demand curve, the supply curve, and the set of factors that shift each curve. The next step is to put these elements together to show how they can be used to predict the actual price at which the good is bought and sold, as well as the actual quantity transacted.

What determines the price at which a good or service is bought and sold? What determines the quantity transacted of the good or service? In Chapter 1 we learned the general principle that *markets move toward equilibrium*, a situation in which no individual would be better off taking a different action. In the case of a competitive market, we can be more specific: a competitive market is in equilibrium when the price has moved to a level at which the quantity of a good demanded equals the quantity of that good supplied. At that price, no individual seller could make herself better off by offering to sell either more or less of the good and no individual buyer could make himself better off by offering to buy more or less of the good. In other words, at the market equilibrium, price has moved to a level that exactly matches the quantity demanded by consumers to the quantity supplied by sellers.

The price that matches the quantity supplied and the quantity demanded is the **equilibrium price;** the quantity bought and sold at that price is the **equilibrium quantity.** The equilibrium price is also known as the **market-clearing price:** it is the price that "clears the market" by ensuring that every buyer willing to pay that price finds a seller willing to sell at that price, and vice versa. So how do we find the equilibrium price and quantity?

A competitive market is in equilibrium when price has moved to a level at which the quantity of a good or service demanded equals the quantity of that good or service supplied. The price at which this takes place is the **equilibrium price,** also referred to as the **market-clearing price.** The quantity of the good or service bought and sold at that price is the **equilibrium quantity.**

BOUGHT AND SOLD?

We have been talking about the price at which a good or service is bought *and* sold, as if the two were the same. But shouldn't we make a distinction between the price received by sellers and the price paid by buyers? In principle, yes; but it is helpful at this point to sacrifice a bit of realism in the interest of simplicity—by assuming away the difference between the prices received by sellers and those paid by buyers. In reality, there is often a middleman—someone who brings buyers and sellers together—who buys from suppliers, then sells to consumers at a markup, for example, coffee

merchants who buy from coffee growers and sell to consumers. The growers generally receive less than those who eventually buy the coffee beans pay. No mystery there: that difference is how coffee merchants or any other middlemen make a living. In many markets, however, the difference between the buying and selling price is quite small. So it's not a bad approximation to think of the price paid by buyers as being the *same* as the price received by sellers. And that is what we assume in this chapter.

Finding the Equilibrium Price and Quantity

The easiest way to determine the equilibrium price and quantity in a market is by putting the supply curve and the demand curve on the same diagram. Since the supply curve shows the quantity supplied at any given price and the demand curve shows the quantity demanded at any given price, the price at which the two curves cross is the equilibrium price: the price at which quantity supplied equals quantity demanded.

Figure 3-11 combines the demand curve from Figure 3-1 and the supply curve from Figure 3-6. They *intersect* at point *E*, which is the equilibrium of this market; that is, $1 is the equilibrium price and 10 billion pounds is the equilibrium quantity.

FIGURE 3-11

Market Equilibrium

Market equilibrium occurs at point *E*, where the supply curve and the demand curve intersect. In equilibrium, the quantity demanded is equal to the quantity supplied. In this market, the equilibrium price is $1 per pound and the equilibrium quantity is 10 billion pounds per year.

There is a **surplus** of a good or service when the quantity supplied exceeds the quantity demanded. Surpluses occur when the price is above its equilibrium level.

Let's confirm that point *E* fits our definition of equilibrium. At a price of $1 per pound, coffee bean producers are willing to sell 10 billion pounds a year and coffee bean consumers want to buy 10 billion pounds a year. So at the price of $1 a pound, the quantity of coffee beans supplied equals the quantity demanded. Notice that at any other price the market would not clear: every willing buyer would not be able to find a willing seller, or vice versa. More specifically, if the price were more than $1, the quantity supplied would exceed the quantity demanded; if the price were less than $1, the quantity demanded would exceed the quantity supplied.

The model of supply and demand, then, predicts that given the demand and supply curves shown in Figure 3-11, 10 billion pounds of coffee beans would change hands at a price of $1 per pound. But how can we be sure that the market will arrive at the equilibrium price? We begin by answering three simple questions:

1. Why do all sales and purchases in a market take place at the same price?
2. Why does the market price fall if it is above the equilibrium price?
3. Why does the market price rise if it is below the equilibrium price?

Why Do All Sales and Purchases in a Market Take Place at the Same Price?

There are some markets where the same good can sell for many different prices, depending on who is selling or who is buying. For example, have you ever bought a souvenir in a "tourist trap" and then seen the same item on sale somewhere else (perhaps even in the shop next door) for a lower price? Because tourists don't know which shops offer the best deals and don't have time for comparison shopping, sellers in tourist areas can charge different prices for the same good.

But in any market where the buyers and sellers have both been around for some time, sales and purchases tend to converge at a generally uniform price, so that we can safely talk about *the* market price. It's easy to see why. Suppose a seller offered a potential buyer a price noticeably above what the buyer knew other people to be paying. The buyer would clearly be better off shopping elsewhere—unless the seller was prepared to offer a better deal. Conversely, a seller would not be willing to sell for significantly less than the amount he knew most buyers were paying; he would be better off waiting to get a more reasonable customer. So in any well-established, ongoing market, all sellers receive and all buyers pay approximately the same price. This is what we call the *market price*.

Why Does the Market Price Fall If It Is Above the Equilibrium Price?

Suppose the supply and demand curves are as shown in Figure 3-11 but the market price is above the equilibrium level of $1—say, $1.50. This situation is illustrated in Figure 3-12. Why can't the price stay there?

As the figure shows, at a price of $1.50 there would be more coffee beans available than consumers wanted to buy: 11.2 billion pounds, versus 8.1 billion pounds. The difference of 3.1 billion pounds is the **surplus**—also known as the *excess supply*—of coffee beans at $1.50.

This surplus means that some coffee producers are frustrated: at the current price, they cannot find consumers who want to buy their coffee beans. The surplus offers an incentive for those frustrated would-be sellers to offer a lower price in order to poach business from other producers and entice more consumers to buy. The result of this price cutting will be to push the prevailing price down until it reaches the equilibrium price. So the price of a good will fall whenever there is a surplus—that is, whenever the market price is above its equilibrium level.

FIGURE 3-12

Price Above Its Equilibrium Level Creates a Surplus

The market price of $1.50 is above the equilibrium price of $1. This creates a surplus: at a price of $1.50, producers would like to sell 11.2 billion pounds but consumers want to buy only 8.1 billion pounds, so there is a surplus of 3.1 billion pounds. This surplus will push the price down until it reaches the equilibrium price of $1.

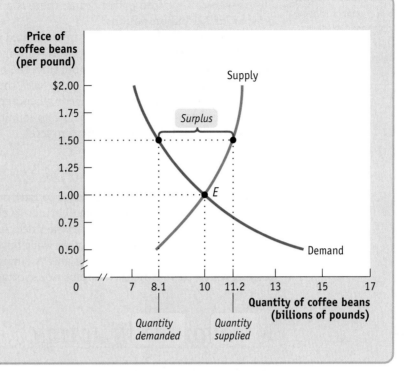

Why Does the Market Price Rise if It Is Below the Equilibrium Price?

Now suppose the price is below its equilibrium level—say, at $0.75 per pound, as shown in Figure 3-13. In this case, the quantity demanded, 11.5 billion pounds, exceeds the quantity supplied, 9.1 billion pounds, implying that there are would-be

FIGURE 3-13

Price Below Its Equilibrium Level Creates a Shortage

The market price of $0.75 is below the equilibrium price of $1. This creates a shortage: consumers want to buy 11.5 billion pounds, but only 9.1 billion pounds are for sale, so there is a shortage of 2.4 billion pounds. This shortage will push the price up until it reaches the equilibrium price of $1.

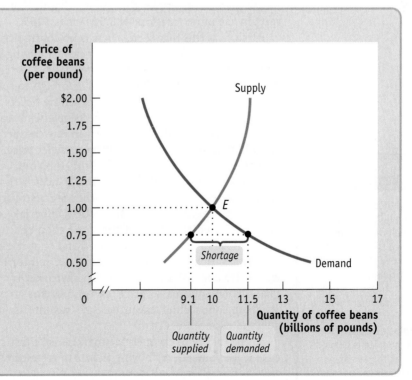

There is a **shortage** of a good or service when the quantity demanded exceeds the quantity supplied. Shortages occur when the price is below its equilibrium level.

buyers who cannot find coffee beans: there is a **shortage,** also known as an *excess demand*, of 2.4 billion pounds.

When there is a shortage, there are frustrated would-be buyers—people who want to purchase coffee beans but cannot find willing sellers at the current price. In this situation, either buyers will offer more than the prevailing price or sellers will realize that they can charge higher prices. Either way, the result is to drive up the prevailing price. This bidding up of prices happens whenever there are shortages—and there will be shortages whenever the price is below its equilibrium level. So the market price will always rise if it is below the equilibrium level.

Using Equilibrium to Describe Markets

We have now seen that a market tends to have a single price, the equilibrium price. If the market price is above the equilibrium level, the ensuing surplus leads buyers and sellers to take actions that lower the price. And if the market price is below the equilibrium level, the ensuing shortage leads buyers and sellers to take actions that raise the price. So the market price always *moves toward* the equilibrium price, the price at which there is neither surplus nor shortage. ▲

►*ECONOMICS IN ACTION*

The Price of Admission

The market equilibrium, so the theory goes, is pretty egalitarian because the equilibrium price applies to everyone. That is, all buyers pay the same price—the equilibrium price—and all sellers receive that same price. But is this realistic?

The market for concert tickets is an example that seems to contradict the theory—there's one price at the box office, and there's another price (typically much higher) for the same event on Internet sites where people who already have tickets resell them, such as StubHub.com or eBay. For example, compare the box office price for a recent Justin Timberlake concert in Miami, Florida, to the StubHub.com price for seats in the same location: $88.50 versus $155.

Puzzling as this may seem, there is no contradiction once we take opportunity costs and tastes into account. For major events, buying tickets from the box office means waiting in very long lines. Ticket buyers who use Internet resellers have decided that the opportunity cost of their time is too high to spend waiting in line. And for those major events with online box offices selling tickets at face value, tickets often sell out within minutes. In this case, some people who want to go to the concert badly but have missed out on the opportunity to buy cheaper tickets from the online box office are willing to pay the higher Internet reseller price.

Not only that, perusing the StubHub.com website you can see that markets really do move to equilibrium. You'll notice that the prices quoted by different sellers for seats close to one another are also very close: $184.99 versus $185 for seats on the main floor of the Justin Timberlake concert. As the competitive market model predicts, units of the same good end up selling for the same price. And prices move in response to demand and supply. According to an article in the *New York Times,* tickets on StubHub.com can sell for less than the face value for events with little appeal, while prices can skyrocket for events that are in high demand. (The article quotes a price of $3,530 for a recent Madonna concert.) Even StubHub.com's chief executive says his site is "the embodiment of supply-and-demand economics."

So the theory of competitive markets isn't just speculation. If you want to experience it for yourself, try buying tickets to a concert. ▲

►► QUICK REVIEW

➢ Price in a competitive market moves to the **equilibrium price,** or **market-clearing price,** where the quantity supplied is equal to the quantity demanded. This quantity is the **equilibrium quantity.**

➢ All sales and purchases in a market take place at the same price. If the price is above its equilibrium level, there is a **surplus** that drives the price down. If the price is below its equilibrium level, there is a **shortage** that drives the price up.

< < < < < < < < < < < <

► CHECK YOUR UNDERSTANDING 3-3

1. In the following three situations, the market is initially in equilibrium. After each event described below, does a surplus or shortage exist at the original equilibrium price? What will happen to the equilibrium price as a result?
  a. 2005 was a very good year for California wine-grape growers, who produced a bumper crop.
  b. After a hurricane, Florida hoteliers often find that many people cancel their upcoming vacations, leaving them with empty hotel rooms.
  c. After a heavy snowfall, many people want to buy secondhand snowblowers at the local tool shop.

Solutions appear at back of book.

Changes in Supply and Demand

The emergence of Vietnam as a major coffee-producing country came as a surprise, but the subsequent fall in the price of coffee beans was no surprise at all. Suddenly the quantity of coffee beans available at any given price rose—that is, there was an increase in supply. Predictably, an increase in supply lowers the equilibrium price.

The entry of Vietnamese producers into the coffee bean business was an example of an event that shifted the supply curve for a good without having much effect on the demand curve. There are many such events. There are also events that shift the demand curve without shifting the supply curve. For example, a medical report that chocolate is good for you increases the demand for chocolate but does not affect the supply. That is, events often shift either the supply curve or the demand curve, but not both; it is therefore useful to ask what happens in each case.

We have seen that when a curve shifts, the equilibrium price and quantity change. We will now concentrate on exactly how the shift of a curve alters the equilibrium price and quantity.

What Happens When the Demand Curve Shifts

Coffee and tea are substitutes: if the price of tea rises, the demand for coffee will increase, and if the price of tea falls, the demand for coffee will decrease. But how does the price of tea affect the *market equilibrium* for coffee?

Figure 3-14 on the next page shows the effect of a rise in the price of tea on the market for coffee. The rise in the price of tea increases the demand for coffee. Point E_1 shows the equilibrium corresponding to the original demand curve, with P_1 the equilibrium price and Q_1 the equilibrium quantity bought and sold.

An increase in demand is indicated by a *rightward* shift of the demand curve from D_1 to D_2. At the original market price P_1, this market is no longer in equilibrium: a shortage occurs because the quantity demanded exceeds the quantity supplied. So the price of coffee rises and generates an increase in the quantity supplied, an upward *movement along the supply curve*. A new equilibrium is established at point E_2, with a higher equilibrium price, P_2, and higher equilibrium quantity, Q_2. This sequence of events reflects a general principle: *When demand for a good or service increases, the equilibrium price and the equilibrium quantity of the good or service both rise.*

What would happen in the reverse case, a fall in the price of tea? A fall in the price of tea reduces the demand for coffee, shifting the demand curve to the *left*. At the original price, a surplus occurs as quantity supplied exceeds quantity demanded. The price falls and leads to a decrease in the quantity supplied, resulting in a lower equilibrium price and a lower equilibrium quantity. This illustrates another general principle: *When demand for a good or service decreases, the equilibrium price and the equilibrium quantity of the good or service both fall.*

To summarize how a market responds to a change in demand: *An increase in demand leads to a rise in both the equilibrium price and the equilibrium quantity. A decrease in demand leads to a fall in both the equilibrium price and the equilibrium quantity.*

FIGURE 3-14

Equilibrium and Shifts of the Demand Curve

The original equilibrium in the market for coffee is at E_1, at the intersection of the supply curve and the original demand curve, D_1. A rise in the price of tea, a substitute, shifts the demand curve rightward to D_2. A shortage exists at the original price, P_1, causing both the price and quantity supplied to rise, a movement along the supply curve. A new equilibrium is reached at E_2, with a higher equilibrium price, P_2, and a higher equilibrium quantity, Q_2. When demand for a good or service increases, the equilibrium price and the equilibrium quantity of the good or service both rise.

What Happens When the Supply Curve Shifts

In the real world, it is a bit easier to predict changes in supply than changes in demand. Physical factors that affect supply, like the availability of inputs, are easier to get a handle on than the fickle tastes that affect demand. Still, with supply as with demand, what we can best predict are the *effects* of shifts of the supply curve.

As we mentioned in this chapter's opening story, a prolonged drought in Vietnam sharply reduced its supply of coffee beans. Figure 3-15 shows how this shift affected the market equilibrium. The original equilibrium is at E_1, the point of intersection of the original supply curve, S_1, and the demand curve, with an equilibrium price P_1 and

FIGURE 3-15

Equilibrium and Shifts of the Supply Curve

The original equilibrium in the market for coffee beans is at E_1. A drought causes a fall in the supply of coffee beans and shifts the supply curve leftward from S_1 to S_2. A new equilibrium is established at E_2, with a higher equilibrium price, P_2, and a lower equilibrium quantity, Q_2.

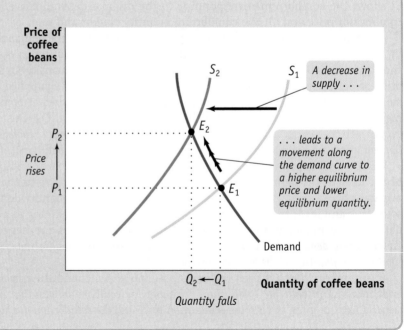

equilibrium quantity Q_1. As a result of the drought, supply falls and S_1 shifts *leftward* to S_2. At the original price P_1, a shortage of coffee beans now exists and the market is no longer in equilibrium. The shortage causes a rise in price and a fall in quantity demanded, an upward movement along the demand curve. The new equilibrium is at E_2, with an equilibrium price P_2, and an equilibrium quantity Q_2. In the new equilibrium E_2, the price is higher and the equilibrium quantity lower than before. This may be stated as a general principle: *When supply of a good or service decreases, the equilibrium price of the good or service rises and the equilibrium quantity of the good or service falls.*

What happens to the market when supply increases? An increase in supply leads to a *rightward* shift of the supply curve. At the original price, a surplus now exists; as a result, the equilibrium price falls and the quantity demanded rises. This describes what happened to the market for coffee beans when Vietnam entered the field. We can formulate a general principle: *When supply of a good or service increases, the equilibrium price of the good or service falls and the equilibrium quantity of the good or service rises.*

To summarize how a market responds to a change in supply: *An increase in supply leads to a fall in the equilibrium price and a rise in the equilibrium quantity. A decrease in supply leads to a rise in the equilibrium price and a fall in the equilibrium quantity.*

Simultaneous Shifts of Supply and Demand Curves

Finally, it sometimes happens that events shift *both* the demand and supply curves at the same time. This is not unusual; in real life, supply curves and demand curves for many goods and services typically shift quite often because the economic environment continually changes. Figure 3-16 illustrates two examples of simultaneous shifts. In both panels there is an increase in demand—that is, a rightward shift of the demand curve, from D_1 to D_2—say, for example, representing the increase in the demand for

> ### PITFALLS
>
> #### WHICH CURVE IS IT, ANYWAY?
> When the price of some good or service changes, in general, we can say that this reflects a change in either supply or demand. But it is easy to get confused about which one. A helpful clue is the direction of change in the quantity. If the quantity sold changes in the *same* direction as the price—for example, if both the price and the quantity rise—this suggests that the demand curve has shifted. If the price and the quantity move in *opposite* directions, the likely cause is a shift of the supply curve.

FIGURE 3-16   Simultaneous Shifts of the Demand and Supply Curves

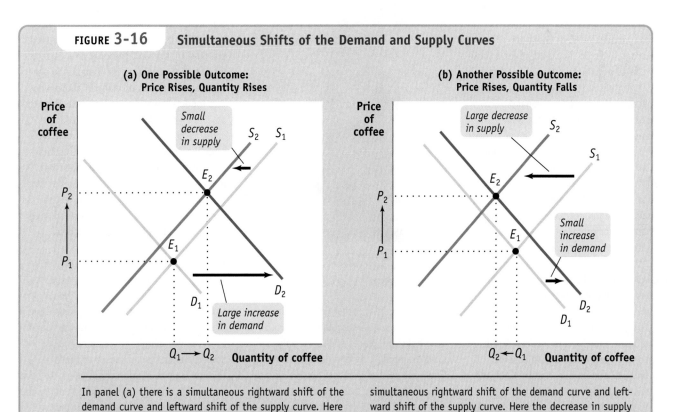

In panel (a) there is a simultaneous rightward shift of the demand curve and leftward shift of the supply curve. Here the increase in demand is relatively larger than the decrease in supply, so the equilibrium price and equilibrium quantity both rise. In panel (b) there is also a simultaneous rightward shift of the demand curve and leftward shift of the supply curve. Here the decrease in supply is relatively larger than the increase in demand, so the equilibrium price rises and the equilibrium quantity falls.

coffee due to changing tastes. Notice that the rightward shift in panel (a) is larger than the one in panel (b): we can suppose that panel (a) represents a year in which many more people than usual choose to drink double lattes and panel (b) represents a normal year. Both panels also show a decrease in supply—that is, a leftward shift of the supply curve from S_1 to S_2. Also notice that the leftward shift in panel (b) is relatively larger than the one in panel (a): we can suppose that panel (b) represents the effect of a particularly extreme drought in Vietnam and panel (a) represents the effect of a much less severe weather event.

In both cases, the equilibrium price rises from P_1 to P_2, as the equilibrium moves from E_1 to E_2. But what happens to the equilibrium quantity, the quantity of coffee bought and sold? In panel (a) the increase in demand is large relative to the decrease in supply, and the equilibrium quantity rises as a result. In panel (b), the decrease in supply is large relative to the increase in demand, and the equilibrium quantity falls as a result. That is, when demand increases and supply decreases, the actual quantity bought and sold can go either way, depending on *how much* the demand and supply curves have shifted.

In general, when supply and demand shift in opposite directions, we can't predict what the ultimate effect will be on the quantity bought and sold. What we can say is that a curve that shifts a disproportionately greater distance than the other curve will have a disproportionately greater effect on the quantity bought and sold. That said,

FOR INQUIRING MINDS

Tribulations on the Runway

You probably don't spend much time worrying about the trials and tribulations of fashion models. Most of them don't lead glamorous lives; in fact, except for a lucky few, life as a fashion model today can be very trying and not very lucrative. And it's all because of supply and demand.

Consider the case of Bianca Gomez, a willowy 18-year-old from Los Angeles, with green eyes, honey-colored hair, and flawless skin, whose experience was detailed in a 2007 article in the *Wall Street Journal*. Bianca began modeling while still in high school, earning about $30,000 in modeling fees during her senior year. Having attracted the interest of some top designers in New York, she moved there after graduation, hoping to land jobs in leading fashion houses and photo-shoots for leading fashion magazines.

But once in New York, Bianca entered the global market for fashion models. And it wasn't very pretty. Due to the ease of transmitting photos over the Internet and the relatively low cost of international travel, top fashion centers such as New York and Milan, Italy, are now deluged with beautiful young women from all over the world, eagerly trying to make it as models.

Bianca Gomez on the runway before intense global competition got her thinking about switching careers.

Although Russians, other Eastern Europeans, and Brazilians are particularly numerous, some hail from places such as Kazakhstan and Mozambique. As one designer said, "There are so many models now. . . .There are just thousands every year."

Returning to our (less glamorous) economic model of supply and demand, the influx of aspiring fashion models from around the world can be represented by a

rightward shift of the supply curve in the market for fashion models, which would by itself tend to lower the price paid to models. And that wasn't the only change in the market. Unfortunately for Bianca and others like her, the tastes of many of those who hire models have changed as well. Over the past few years, fashion magazines have come to prefer using celebrities such as Angelina Jolie on their pages rather than anonymous models, believing that their readers connect better with a familiar face. This amounts to a leftward shift of the demand curve for models—again reducing the equilibrium price paid to models.

This was borne out in Bianca's experiences. After paying her rent, her transportation, all her modeling expenses, and 20% of her earnings to her modeling agency (which markets her to prospective clients and books her jobs), Bianca found that she was barely breaking even. Sometimes she even had to dip into savings from her high school years. To save money, she ate macaroni and hot dogs; she traveled to auditions, often four or five in one day, by subway. As the *Wall Street Journal* reported, Bianca was seriously considering quitting modeling altogether.

we can make the following prediction about the outcome when the supply and demand curves shift in opposite directions:

- When demand increases and supply decreases, the equilibrium price rises but the change in the equilibrium quantity is ambiguous.

- When demand decreases and supply increases, the equilibrium price falls but the change in the equilibrium quantity is ambiguous.

But suppose that the demand and supply curves shift in the same direction. This was the case in the global market for coffee beans, where both supply and demand have increased over the past decade. Can we safely make any predictions about the changes in price and quantity? In this situation, the change in quantity bought and sold can be predicted but the change in price is ambiguous. The two possible outcomes when the supply and demand curves shift in the same direction (which you should check for yourself) are as follows:

- When both demand and supply increase, the equilibrium quantity increases but the change in equilibrium price is ambiguous.

- When both demand and supply decrease, the equilibrium quantity decreases but the change in equilibrium price is ambiguous.

➤ECONOMICS IN ACTION

The Great Tortilla Crisis

"Thousands in Mexico City protest rising food prices." So read the headline in the *New York Times* on February 1, 2007. Specifically, the demonstrators were protesting a sharp rise in the price of tortillas, a staple food of Mexico's poor, which had gone from 25 cents a pound to between 35 and 45 cents a pound in just a few months.

Why were tortilla prices soaring? It was a classic example of what happens to equilibrium prices when supply falls. Tortillas are made from corn; much of Mexico's corn is imported from the United States, with the price of corn in both countries basically set in the U.S. corn market. And U.S. corn prices were rising rapidly thanks to surging demand in a new market: the market for ethanol.

Ethanol's big break came with the Energy Policy Act of 2005, which mandated the use of a large quantity of "renewable" fuels starting in 2006, and rising steadily thereafter. In practice, that meant increased use of ethanol. Ethanol producers rushed to build new production facilities and quickly began buying lots of corn. The result was a rightward shift of the demand curve for corn, leading to a sharp rise in the price of corn. And since corn is an input in the production of tortillas, a sharp rise in the price of corn led to a fall in the supply of tortillas and higher prices for tortilla consumers.

The increase in the price of corn was good news in Iowa, where farmers began planting more corn than ever before. But it was bad news for Mexican consumers, who found themselves paying more for their tortillas. ▲

> > > > > > > > > > > >

➤ CHECK YOUR UNDERSTANDING 3-4

1. In each of the following examples, determine (i) the market in question; (ii) whether a shift in demand or supply occurred, the direction of the shift, and what induced the shift; and (iii) the effect of the shift on the equilibrium price and the equilibrium quantity.
   a. As the price of gasoline fell in the United States during the 1990s, more people bought large cars.
   b. As technological innovation has lowered the cost of recycling used paper, fresh paper made from recycled stock is used more frequently.
   c. When a local cable company offers cheaper pay-per-view films, local movie theaters have more unfilled seats.

➤➤QUICK REVIEW

- Changes in the equilibrium price and quantity in a market result from shifts of the supply curve, the demand curve, or both.
- An increase in demand increases both the equilibrium price and the equilibrium quantity. A decrease in demand pushes both the equilibrium price and the equilibrium quantity down.
- An increase in supply drives the equilibrium price down but increases the equilibrium quantity. A decrease in supply raises the equilibrium price but reduces the equilibrium quantity.
- Often the fluctuations in markets involve shifts of both the supply and demand curves. When they shift in the same direction, the change in equilibrium quantity is predictable but the change in equilibrium price is not. When they move in opposite directions, the change in equilibrium price is predictable but the change in equilibrium quantity is not. When there are simultaneous shifts of the demand and supply curves, the curve that shifts the greater distance has a greater effect on the change in equilibrium price and quantity.

2. Periodically, a computer chip maker like Intel introduces a new chip that is faster than the previous one. In response, demand for computers using the earlier chip decreases as customers put off purchases in anticipation of machines containing the new chip. Simultaneously, computer makers increase their production of computers containing the earlier chip in order to clear out their stocks of those chips.

Draw two diagrams of the market for computers containing the earlier chip: (a) one in which the equilibrium quantity falls in response to these events and (b) one in which the equilibrium quantity rises. What happens to the equilibrium price in each diagram?

Solutions appear at back of book.

Competitive Markets—And Others

Early in this chapter, we defined a competitive market and explained that the supply and demand framework is a model of competitive markets. But we took a rain check on the question of why it matters whether or not a market is competitive. Now that we've seen how the supply and demand model works, we can offer some explanation.

To understand why competitive markets are different from other markets, compare the problems facing two individuals: a wheat farmer who must decide whether to grow more wheat, and the president of a giant aluminum company—say, Alcoa—who must decide whether to produce more aluminum.

For the wheat farmer, the question is simply whether the extra wheat can be sold at a price high enough to justify the extra production cost. The farmer need not worry about whether producing more wheat will affect the price of the wheat he or she was already planning to grow. That's because the wheat market is competitive. There are thousands of wheat farmers, and no one farmer's decision will have much impact on the market price.

For the Alcoa executive, things are not that simple because the aluminum market is *not* competitive. There are only a few big players, including Alcoa, and each of them is well aware that its actions *do* have a noticeable impact on the market price. This adds a whole new level of complexity to the decisions producers have to make. Alcoa can't decide whether or not to produce more aluminum just by asking whether the additional product will sell for more than it costs to make. The company also has to ask whether producing more aluminum will drive down the market price and reduce its *profit*, its net gain from producing and selling its output.

When a market is competitive, individuals can base decisions on less complicated analyses than those used in a noncompetitive market. This in turn means that it's easier for economists to build a model of a competitive market than of a noncompetitive market.

Don't take this to mean that economic analysis has nothing to say about noncompetitive markets. On the contrary, economists can offer some very important insights into how other kinds of markets work. But those insights require other models, which we will learn about later in this text. In the next chapter, we will focus on how competitive markets benefit producers and consumers.

[>> A LOOK AHEAD ···

We've now developed a model that explains how markets arrive at prices and why markets "work" in the sense that buyers can almost always find sellers, and vice versa.

But what we haven't yet explained is what motivates buyers and sellers to participate in markets. In the next chapter, we'll study how a competitive market allocates gains—and potentially losses—to buyers and sellers. And we'll discover a surprisingly strong result: under certain conditions, a competitive market maximizes the total gains to buyers from consuming and to sellers from producing.]

SUMMARY

1. The **supply and demand model** illustrates how a **competitive market,** one with many buyers and sellers, none of whom can influence the market price, works.

2. The **demand schedule** shows the **quantity demanded** at each price and is represented graphically by a **demand curve.** The **law of demand** says that demand curves slope downward; that is, a higher price for a good or service leads people to demand a smaller quantity, other things equal.

3. A **movement along the demand curve** occurs when a price change leads to a change in the quantity demanded. When economists talk of increasing or decreasing demand, they mean **shifts of the demand curve**—a change in the quantity demanded at any given price. An increase in demand causes a rightward shift of the demand curve. A decrease in demand causes a leftward shift.

4. There are five main factors that shift the demand curve:
   - A change in the prices of related goods or services, such as **substitutes** or **complements**
   - A change in income: when income rises, the demand for **normal goods** increases and the demand for **inferior goods** decreases.
   - A change in tastes
   - A change in expectations
   - A change in the number of consumers

5. The market demand curve for a good or service is the horizontal sum of the **individual demand curves** of all consumers in the market.

6. The **supply schedule** shows the **quantity supplied** at each price and is represented graphically by a **supply curve.** Supply curves usually slope upward.

7. A **movement along the supply curve** occurs when a price change leads to a change in the quantity supplied. When economists talk of increasing or decreasing supply, they mean **shifts of the supply curve**—a change in

the quantity supplied at any given price. An increase in supply causes a rightward shift of the supply curve. A decrease in supply causes a leftward shift.

8. There are five main factors that shift the supply curve:
   - A change in **input** prices
   - A change in the prices of related goods and services
   - A change in technology
   - A change in expectations
   - A change in the number of producers

9. The market supply curve for a good or service is the horizontal sum of the **individual supply curves** of all producers in the market.

10. The supply and demand model is based on the principle that the price in a market moves to its **equilibrium price,** or **market-clearing price,** the price at which the quantity demanded is equal to the quantity supplied. This quantity is the **equilibrium quantity.** When the price is above its market-clearing level, there is a **surplus** that pushes the price down. When the price is below its market-clearing level, there is a **shortage** that pushes the price up.

11. An increase in demand increases both the equilibrium price and the equilibrium quantity; a decrease in demand has the opposite effect. An increase in supply reduces the equilibrium price and increases the equilibrium quantity; a decrease in supply has the opposite effect.

12. Shifts of the demand curve and the supply curve can happen simultaneously. When they shift in opposite directions, the change in equilibrium price is predictable but the change in equilibrium quantity is not. When they shift in the same direction, the change in equilibrium quantity is predictable but the change in equilibrium price is not. In general, the curve that shifts the greater distance has a greater effect on the changes in equilibrium price and quantity.

KEY TERMS

Competitive market, p. 62
Supply and demand model, p. 62
Demand schedule, p. 63
Quantity demanded, p. 64
Demand curve, p. 64
Law of demand, p. 64
Shift of the demand curve, p. 65
Movement along the demand curve, p. 66
Substitutes, p. 67

Complements, p. 67
Normal good, p. 68
Inferior good, p. 68
Individual demand curve, p. 69
Quantity supplied, p. 71
Supply schedule, p. 71
Supply curve, p. 72
Shift of the supply curve, p. 73
Movement along the supply curve, p. 73

Input, p. 75
Individual supply curve, p. 76
Equilibrium price, p. 78
Equilibrium quantity, p. 78
Market-clearing price, p. 78
Surplus, p. 80
Shortage, p. 82

PROBLEMS

1. A survey indicated that chocolate is Americans' favorite ice cream flavor. For each of the following, indicate the possible effects on demand, supply, or both as well as equilibrium price and quantity of chocolate ice cream.

   a. A severe drought in the Midwest causes dairy farmers to reduce the number of milk-producing cattle in their herds by a third. These dairy farmers supply cream that is used to manufacture chocolate ice cream.

   b. A new report by the American Medical Association reveals that chocolate does, in fact, have significant health benefits.

   c. The discovery of cheaper synthetic vanilla flavoring lowers the price of vanilla ice cream.

   d. New technology for mixing and freezing ice cream lowers manufacturers' costs of producing chocolate ice cream.

2. In a supply and demand diagram, draw the shift of the demand curve for hamburgers in your hometown due to the following events. In each case show the effect on equilibrium price and quantity.

   a. The price of tacos increases.

   b. All hamburger sellers raise the price of their french fries.

   c. Income falls in town. Assume that hamburgers are a normal good for most people.

   d. Income falls in town. Assume that hamburgers are an inferior good for most people.

   e. Hot dog stands cut the price of hot dogs.

3. The market for many goods changes in predictable ways according to the time of year, in response to events such as holidays, vacation times, seasonal changes in production, and so on. Using supply and demand, explain the change in price in each of the following cases. Note that supply and demand may shift simultaneously.

   a. Lobster prices usually fall during the summer peak lobster harvest season, despite the fact that people like to eat lobster during the summer more than at any other time of year.

   b. The price of a Christmas tree is lower after Christmas than before but fewer trees are sold.

   c. The price of a round-trip ticket to Paris on Air France falls by more than $200 after the end of school vacation in September. This happens despite the fact that generally worsening weather increases the cost of operating flights to Paris, and Air France therefore reduces the number of flights to Paris at any given price.

4. Show in a diagram the effect on the demand curve, the supply curve, the equilibrium price, and the equilibrium quantity of each of the following events.

   a. The market for newspapers in your town

   Case 1: The salaries of journalists go up.

   Case 2: There is a big news event in your town, which is reported in the newspapers.

   b. The market for St. Louis Rams cotton T-shirts

   Case 1: The Rams win the Super Bowl.

   Case 2: The price of cotton increases.

   c. The market for bagels

   Case 1: People realize how fattening bagels are.

   Case 2: People have less time to make themselves a cooked breakfast.

   d. The market for the Krugman and Wells economics textbook

   Case 1: Your professor makes it required reading for all of his or her students.

   Case 2: Printing costs for textbooks are lowered by the use of synthetic paper.

5. The U.S. Department of Agriculture reported that in 1997 each person in the United States consumed an average of 41 gallons of soft drinks (nondiet) at an average price of $2 per gallon. Assume that, at a price of $1.50 per gallon, each individual consumer would demand 50 gallons of soft drinks. The U.S. population in 1997 was 267 million. From this information about the individual demand schedule, calculate the market demand schedule for soft drinks for the prices of $1.50 and $2 per gallon.

6. Suppose that the supply schedule of Maine lobsters is as follows:

Price of lobster (per pound)	Quantity of lobster supplied (pounds)
$25	800
20	700
15	600
10	500
5	400

Suppose that Maine lobsters can be sold only in the United States. The U.S. demand schedule for Maine lobsters is as follows:

Price of lobster (per pound)	Quantity of lobster demanded (pounds)
$25	200
20	400
15	600
10	800
5	1,000

   a. Draw the demand curve and the supply curve for Maine lobsters. What are the equilibrium price and quantity of lobsters?

Now suppose that Maine lobsters can be sold in France. The French demand schedule for Maine lobsters is as follows:

Price of lobster (per pound)	Quantity of lobster demanded (pounds)
$25	100
20	300
15	500
10	700
5	900

b. What is the demand schedule for Maine lobsters now that French consumers can also buy them? Draw a supply and demand diagram that illustrates the new equilibrium price and quantity of lobsters. What will happen to the price at which fishermen can sell lobster? What will happen to the price paid by U.S. consumers? What will happen to the quantity consumed by U.S. consumers?

7. Find the flaws in reasoning in the following statements, paying particular attention to the distinction between shifts of and movements along the supply and demand curves. Draw a diagram to illustrate what actually happens in each situation.

a. "A technological innovation that lowers the cost of producing a good might seem at first to result in a reduction in the price of the good to consumers. But a fall in price will increase demand for the good, and higher demand will send the price up again. It is not certain, therefore, that an innovation will really reduce price in the end."

b. "A study shows that eating a clove of garlic a day can help prevent heart disease, causing many consumers to demand more garlic. This increase in demand results in a rise in the price of garlic. Consumers, seeing that the price of garlic has gone up, reduce their demand for garlic. This causes the demand for garlic to decrease and the price of garlic to fall. Therefore, the ultimate effect of the study on the price of garlic is uncertain."

8. The following table shows a demand schedule for a normal good.

Price	Quantity demanded
$23	70
21	90
19	110
17	130

a. Do you think that the increase in quantity demanded (say, from 90 to 110 in the table) when price decreases (from $21 to $19) is due to a rise in consumers' income? Explain clearly (and briefly) why or why not.

b. Now suppose that the good is an inferior good. Would the demand schedule still be valid for an inferior good?

c. Lastly, assume you do not know whether the good is normal or inferior. Devise an experiment that would allow you to determine which one it was. Explain.

9. According to the *New York Times* (November 18, 2006), the number of car producers in China is increasing rapidly. The newspaper reports that "China has more car brands now than the United States. . . . But while car sales have climbed 38 percent in the first three quarters of this year, automakers have increased their output even faster, causing fierce competition and a slow erosion in prices." At the same time, Chinese consumers' incomes have risen. Assume that cars are a normal good. Use a diagram of the supply and demand curves for cars in China to explain what has happened in the Chinese car market.

10. Aaron Hank is a star hitter for the Bay City baseball team. He is close to breaking the major league record for home runs hit during one season, and it is widely anticipated that in the next game he will break that record. As a result, tickets for the team's next game have been a hot commodity. But today it is announced that, due to a knee injury, he will not in fact play in the team's next game. Assume that season ticket-holders are able to resell their tickets if they wish. Use supply and demand diagrams to explain the following.

a. Show the case in which this announcement results in a lower equilibrium price and a lower equilibrium quantity than before the announcement.

b. Show the case in which this announcement results in a lower equilibrium price and a higher equilibrium quantity than before the announcement.

c. What accounts for whether case a or case b occurs?

d. Suppose that a scalper had secretly learned before the announcement that Aaron Hank would not play in the next game. What actions do you think he would take?

11. In *Rolling Stone* magazine, several fans and rock stars, including Pearl Jam, were bemoaning the high price of concert tickets. One superstar argued, "It just isn't worth $75 to see me play. No one should have to pay that much to go to a concert." Assume this star sold out arenas around the country at an average ticket price of $75.

a. How would you evaluate the arguments that ticket prices are too high?

b. Suppose that due to this star's protests, ticket prices were lowered to $50. In what sense is this price too low? Draw a diagram using supply and demand curves to support your argument.

c. Suppose Pearl Jam really wanted to bring down ticket prices. Since the band controls the supply of its services, what do you recommend they do? Explain using a supply and demand diagram.

d. Suppose the band's next CD was a total dud. Do you think they would still have to worry about ticket prices being too high? Why or why not? Draw a supply and demand diagram to support your argument.

e. Suppose the group announced their next tour was going to be their last. What effect would this likely have on the demand for and price of tickets? Illustrate with a supply and demand diagram.

12. The accompanying table gives the annual U.S. demand and supply schedules for pickup trucks.

Price of truck	Quantity of trucks demanded (millions)	Quantity of trucks supplied (millions)
$20,000	20	14
25,000	18	15
30,000	16	16
35,000	14	17
40,000	12	18

a. Plot the demand and supply curves using these schedules. Indicate the equilibrium price and quantity on your diagram.

b. Suppose the tires used on pickup trucks are found to be defective. What would you expect to happen in the market for pickup trucks? Show this on your diagram.

c. Suppose that the U.S. Department of Transportation imposes costly regulations on manufacturers that cause them to reduce supply by one-third at any given price. Calculate and plot the new supply schedule and indicate the new equilibrium price and quantity on your diagram.

13. After several years of decline, the market for handmade acoustic guitars is making a comeback. These guitars are usually made in small workshops employing relatively few highly skilled luthiers. Assess the impact on the equilibrium price and quantity of handmade acoustic guitars as a result of each of the following events. In your answers indicate which curve(s) shift(s) and in which direction.

a. Environmentalists succeed in having the use of Brazilian rosewood banned in the United States, forcing luthiers to seek out alternative, more costly woods.

b. A foreign producer reengineers the guitar-making process and floods the market with identical guitars.

c. Music featuring handmade acoustic guitars makes a comeback as audiences tire of heavy metal and grunge music.

d. The country goes into a deep recession and the income of the average American falls sharply.

14. *Demand twisters:* Sketch and explain the demand relationship in each of the following statements.

a. I would never buy a Britney Spears CD! You couldn't even give me one for nothing.

b. I generally buy a bit more coffee as the price falls. But once the price falls to $2 per pound, I'll buy out the entire stock of the supermarket.

c. I spend more on orange juice even as the price rises. (Does this mean that I must be violating the law of demand?)

d. Due to a tuition rise, most students at a college find themselves with less disposable income. Almost all of them eat more frequently at the school cafeteria and less often at restaurants, even though prices at the cafeteria have risen, too. (This one requires that you draw both the demand and the supply curves for school cafeteria meals.)

15. Will Shakespeare is a struggling playwright in sixteenth-century London. As the price he receives for writing a play increases, he is willing to write more plays. For the following situations, use a diagram to illustrate how each event affects the equilibrium price and quantity in the market for Shakespeare's plays.

a. The playwright Christopher Marlowe, Shakespeare's chief rival, is killed in a bar brawl.

b. The bubonic plague, a deadly infectious disease, breaks out in London.

c. To celebrate the defeat of the Spanish Armada, Queen Elizabeth declares several weeks of festivities, which involves commissioning new plays.

16. The small town of Middling experiences a sudden doubling of the birth rate. After three years, the birth rate returns to normal. Use a diagram to illustrate the effect of these events on the following.

a. The market for an hour of babysitting services in Middling today

b. The market for an hour of babysitting services 14 years into the future, after the birth rate has returned to normal, by which time children born today are old enough to work as babysitters

c. The market for an hour of babysitting services 30 years into the future, when children born today are likely to be having children of their own

17. Use a diagram to illustrate how each of the following events affects the equilibrium price and quantity of pizza.

a. The price of mozzarella cheese rises.

b. The health hazards of hamburgers are widely publicized.

c. The price of tomato sauce falls.

d. The incomes of consumers rise and pizza is an inferior good.

e. Consumers expect the price of pizza to fall next week.

18. Although he was a prolific artist, Pablo Picasso painted only 1,000 canvases during his "Blue Period." Picasso is now dead, and all of his Blue Period works are currently on display in museums and private galleries throughout Europe and the United States.

a. Draw a supply curve for Picasso Blue Period works. Why is this supply curve different from ones you have seen?

b. Given the supply curve from part a, the price of a Picasso Blue Period work will be entirely dependent on what factor(s)? Draw a diagram showing how the equilibrium price of such a work is determined.

c. Suppose rich art collectors decide that it is essential to acquire Picasso Blue Period art for their collections. Show the impact of this on the market for these paintings.

19. Draw the appropriate curve in each of the following cases. Is it like or unlike the curves you have seen so far? Explain.

a. The demand for cardiac bypass surgery, given that the government pays the full cost for any patient

b. The demand for elective cosmetic plastic surgery, given that the patient pays the full cost

c. The supply of reproductions of Rembrandt paintings

>> Consumer and Producer Surplus

MAKING GAINS BY THE BOOK

THERE IS A LIVELY MARKET IN SECOND-HAND college textbooks. At the end of each term, some students who took a course decide that the money they can make by selling their used books is worth more to them than keeping the books. And some students who are taking the course next term prefer to buy a somewhat battered but less expensive used textbook rather than pay full price for a new one.

Textbook publishers and authors are not happy about these transactions, because they cut into sales of new books. But both the students who sell used books and those who buy them clearly benefit from the existence of the market. That is why many college bookstores facilitate their trade, buying used textbooks and selling them alongside the new books.

How much am I willing to pay for that used textbook?

But can we put a number on what used textbook buyers and sellers gain from these transactions? Can we answer the question, "*How much* do the buyers and sellers of textbooks gain from the existence of the used-book market?"

Yes, we can. In this chapter we will see how to measure benefits, such as those to buyers of used textbooks,

from being able to purchase a good—known as *consumer surplus*. And we will see that there is a corresponding measure, *producer surplus*, of the benefits sellers receive from being able to sell a good.

The concepts of consumer surplus and producer surplus are extremely useful for analyzing a wide variety of economic issues. They let us calculate how much benefit producers and consumers receive from the existence of a market. They also allow us to calculate how the welfare of consumers and producers is affected by changes in market prices. Such calculations play a crucial role in evaluating many economic policies.

What information do we need to calculate consumer and producer surplus? Surprisingly, all we need are the demand and supply curves for a good. That is, the supply and demand model isn't just a model of how a competitive market works—it's also a model of how much consumers and producers gain from participating in that market. So our first step will be to learn how consumer and producer surplus can be derived from the demand and supply curves. We will then see how these concepts can be applied to actual economic issues.

Consumer Surplus and the Demand Curve

The market in used textbooks is a big business in terms of dollars and cents—approximately $1.9 billion in 2004–2005. More importantly for us, it is a convenient starting point for developing the concepts of consumer and producer surplus. We'll use the concepts of consumer and producer surplus to understand exactly how buyers and sellers benefit from a competitive market and how big those benefits are. In addition, these concepts play important roles in analyzing what happens when competitive markets don't work well or there is interference in the market.

So let's begin by looking at the market for used textbooks, starting with the buyers. The key point, as we'll see in a minute, is that the demand curve is derived from their tastes or preferences—and that those same preferences also determine how much they gain from the opportunity to buy used books.

Willingness to Pay and the Demand Curve

A used book is not as good as a new book—it will be battered and coffee-stained, may include someone else's highlighting, and may not be completely up to date. How much this bothers you depends on your preferences. Some potential buyers would prefer to buy the used book even if it is only slightly cheaper than a new one, while others would buy the used book only if it is considerably cheaper. Let's define a potential buyer's **willingness to pay** as the maximum price at which he or she would buy a good, in this case a used textbook. An individual won't buy the good if it costs more than this amount but is eager to do so if it costs less. If the price is just equal to an individual's willingness to pay, he or she is indifferent between buying and not buying. For the sake of simplicity, we'll assume that the individual buys the good in this case.

The table in Figure 4-1 shows five potential buyers of a used book that costs $100 new, listed in order of their willingness to pay. At one extreme is Aleisha, who will buy a second-hand book even if the price is as high as $59. Brad is less willing to have a used book and will buy one only if the price is $45 or less. Claudia is willing to pay only $35 and Darren, only $25. And Edwina, who really doesn't like the idea of a used book, will buy one only if it costs no more than $10.

How many of these five students will actually buy a used book? It depends on the price. If the price of a used book is $55, only Aleisha buys one; if the price is $40, Aleisha and Brad both buy used books, and so on. So the information in the table can be used to construct the *demand schedule* for used textbooks.

As we saw in Chapter 3, we can use this demand schedule to derive the market demand curve shown in Figure 4-1. Because we are considering only a small number of consumers, this curve doesn't look like the smooth demand curves of Chapter 3, where markets contained hundreds or thousands of consumers. This demand curve is step-shaped, with alternating horizontal and vertical segments. Each horizontal segment—each step—corresponds to one potential buyer's willingness to pay. However, we'll see shortly that for the analysis of consumer surplus it doesn't matter whether the demand curve is step-shaped, as in this figure, or whether there are many consumers, making the curve smooth.

A consumer's **willingness to pay** for a good is the maximum price at which he or she would buy that good.

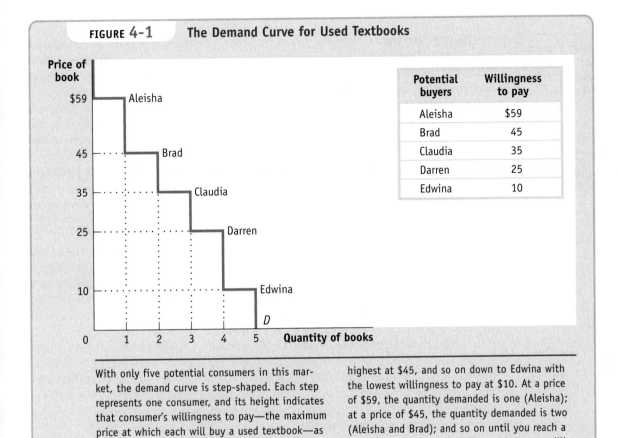

FIGURE 4-1   The Demand Curve for Used Textbooks

Potential buyers	Willingness to pay
Aleisha	$59
Brad	45
Claudia	35
Darren	25
Edwina	10

With only five potential consumers in this market, the demand curve is step-shaped. Each step represents one consumer, and its height indicates that consumer's willingness to pay—the maximum price at which each will buy a used textbook—as indicated in the table. Aleisha has the highest willingness to pay at $59, Brad has the next highest at $45, and so on down to Edwina with the lowest willingness to pay at $10. At a price of $59, the quantity demanded is one (Aleisha); at a price of $45, the quantity demanded is two (Aleisha and Brad); and so on until you reach a price of $10, at which all five students are willing to purchase a book.

Willingness to Pay and Consumer Surplus

Suppose that the campus bookstore makes used textbooks available at a price of $30. In that case Aleisha, Brad, and Claudia will buy books. Do they gain from their purchases, and if so, how much?

The answer, shown in Table 4-1, is that each student who purchases a book does achieve a net gain but that the amount of the gain differs among students.

Aleisha would have been willing to pay $59, so her net gain is $59 − $30 = $29. Brad would have been willing to pay $45, so his net gain is $45 − $30 = $15. Claudia would have been willing to pay $35, so her net gain is $35 − $30 = $5. Darren and Edwina, however, won't be willing to buy a used book at a price of $30, so they neither gain nor lose.

TABLE 4-1

Consumer Surplus When the Price of a Used Textbook Is $30

Potential buyer	Willingness to pay	Price paid	Individual consumer surplus = Willingness to pay − Price paid
Aleisha	$59	$30	$29
Brad	45	30	15
Claudia	35	30	5
Darren	25	—	—
Edwina	10	—	—
All buyers			**Total consumer surplus = $49**

Individual consumer surplus is the net gain to an individual buyer from the purchase of a good. It is equal to the difference between the buyer's willingness to pay and the price paid.

Total consumer surplus is the sum of the individual consumer surpluses of all the buyers of a good in a market.

The term **consumer surplus** is often used to refer to both individual and to total consumer surplus.

The net gain that a buyer achieves from the purchase of a good is called that buyer's **individual consumer surplus.** What we learn from this example is that whenever a buyer pays a price less than his or her willingness to pay, the buyer achieves some individual consumer surplus.

The sum of the individual consumer surpluses achieved by all the buyers of a good is known as the **total consumer surplus** achieved in the market. In Table 4-1, the total consumer surplus is the sum of the individual consumer surpluses achieved by Aleisha, Brad, and Claudia: $29 + $15 + $5 = $49.

Economists often use the term **consumer surplus** to refer to both individual and total consumer surplus. We will follow this practice; it will always be clear in context whether we are referring to the consumer surplus achieved by an individual or by all buyers.

Total consumer surplus can be represented graphically. Figure 4-2 reproduces the demand curve from Figure 4-1. Each step in that demand curve is one book wide and represents one consumer. For example, the height of Aleisha's step is $59, her willingness to pay. This step forms the top of a rectangle, with $30—the price she actually pays for a book—forming the bottom. The area of Aleisha's rectangle, ($59 − $30) × 1 = $29, is her consumer surplus from purchasing one book at $30. So the individual consumer surplus Aleisha gains is the *area of the dark blue rectangle* shown in Figure 4-2.

In addition to Aleisha, Brad and Claudia will also each buy a book when the price is $30. Like Aleisha, they benefit from their purchases, though not as much, because they each have a lower willingness to pay. Figure 4-2 also shows the consumer surplus gained by Brad and Claudia; again, this can be measured by the areas of the appropriate rectangles. Darren and Edwina, because they do not buy books at a price of $30, receive no consumer surplus.

The total consumer surplus achieved in this market is just the sum of the individual consumer surpluses received by Aleisha, Brad, and Claudia. So total consumer surplus is equal to the combined area of the three rectangles—the entire shaded area in Figure 4-2. Another way to say this is that total consumer surplus is equal to the area below the demand curve but above the price.

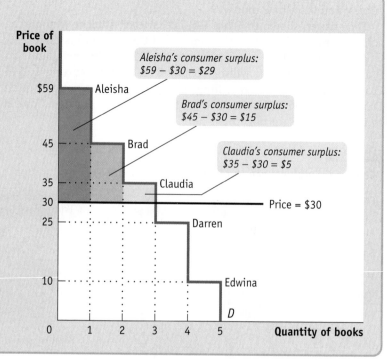

FIGURE 4-2

Consumer Surplus in the Used-Textbook Market

At a price of $30, Aleisha, Brad, and Claudia each buy a book but Darren and Edwina do not. Aleisha, Brad, and Claudia get individual consumer surpluses equal to the difference between their willingness to pay and the price, illustrated by the areas of the shaded rectangles. Both Darren and Edwina have a willingness to pay less than $30, so they are unwilling to buy a book in this market; they receive zero consumer surplus. The total consumer surplus is given by the entire shaded area—the sum of the individual consumer surpluses of Aleisha, Brad, and Claudia—equal to $29 + $15 + $5 = $49.

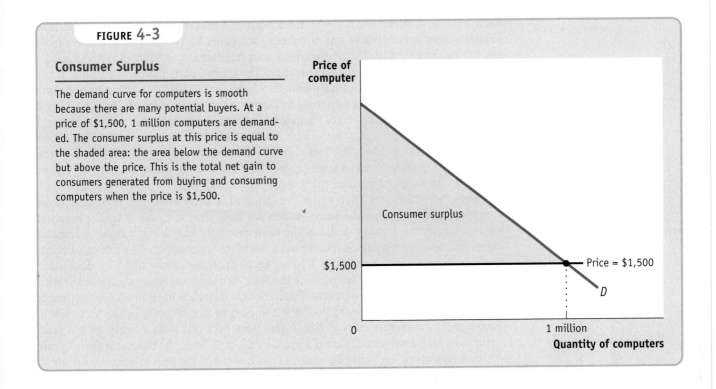

FIGURE 4-3

Consumer Surplus

The demand curve for computers is smooth because there are many potential buyers. At a price of $1,500, 1 million computers are demanded. The consumer surplus at this price is equal to the shaded area: the area below the demand curve but above the price. This is the total net gain to consumers generated from buying and consuming computers when the price is $1,500.

This illustrates the following general principle: *The total consumer surplus generated by purchases of a good at a given price is equal to the area below the demand curve but above that price.* The same principle applies regardless of the number of consumers.

When we consider large markets, this graphical representation becomes extremely helpful. Consider, for example, the sales of personal computers to millions of potential buyers. Each potential buyer has a maximum price that he or she is willing to pay. With so many potential buyers, the demand curve will be smooth, like the one shown in Figure 4-3.

Suppose that at a price of $1,500, a total of 1 million computers are purchased. How much do consumers gain from being able to buy those 1 million computers? We could answer that question by calculating the individual consumer surplus of each buyer and then adding these numbers up to arrive at a total. But it is much easier just to look at Figure 4-3 and use the fact that total consumer surplus is equal to the shaded area. As in our original example, consumer surplus is equal to the area below the demand curve but above the price. (You can refresh your memory on how to calculate the area of a right triangle by turning to the appendix to Chapter 2.)

How Changing Prices Affect Consumer Surplus

It is often important to know how much consumer surplus *changes* when the price changes. For example, we may want to know how much consumers are hurt if a frost in Florida drives up orange prices or how much consumers gain if the introduction of fish farming makes salmon steaks less expensive. The same approach we have used to derive consumer surplus can be used to answer questions about how changes in prices affect consumers.

Let's return to the example of the market for used textbooks. Suppose that the bookstore decided to sell used textbooks for $20 instead of $30. How much would this fall in price increase consumer surplus?

The answer is illustrated in Figure 4-4 on the next page. As shown in the figure, there are two parts to the increase in consumer surplus. The first part, shaded dark blue, is the gain of those who would have bought books even at the higher price of $30.

Each of the students who would have bought books at $30—Aleisha, Brad, and Claudia—now pays $10 less, and therefore each gains $10 in consumer surplus from the fall in price to $20. So the dark blue area represents the $10 × 3 = $30 increase in consumer surplus to those three buyers. The second part, shaded light blue, is the gain to those who would not have bought a book at $30 but are willing to pay more than $20. In this case that gain goes to Darren, who would not have bought a book at $30 but does buy one at $20. He gains $5—the difference between his willingness to pay of $25 and the new price of $20. So the light blue area represents a further $5 gain in consumer surplus. The total increase in consumer surplus is the sum of the shaded areas, $35. Likewise, a rise in price from $20 to $30 would decrease consumer surplus by an amount equal to the sum of the shaded areas.

Figure 4-4 illustrates that when the price of a good falls, the area under the demand curve but above the price—which we have seen is equal to total consumer surplus—increases. Figure 4-5 shows the same result for the case of a smooth demand curve, the demand for personal computers. Here we assume that the price of computers falls from $5,000 to $1,500, leading to an increase in the quantity demanded from 200,000 to 1 million units. As in the used-textbook example, we divide the gain in consumer surplus into two parts. The dark blue rectangle in Figure 4-5 corresponds to the dark blue area in Figure 4-4: it is the gain to the 200,000 people who would have bought computers even at the higher price of $5,000. As a result of the price reduction, each receives additional surplus of $3,500. The light blue triangle in Figure 4-5 corresponds to the light blue area in Figure 4-4: it is the gain to people who would not have bought the good at the higher price but are willing to do so at a price of $1,500. For example, the light blue triangle includes the gain to someone who would have been willing to pay $2,000 for a computer and therefore gains $500 in consumer surplus when it is possible to buy a computer for only $1,500. As before, the total gain in consumer surplus is the sum of the shaded areas, the increase in the area under the demand curve but above the price.

FIGURE 4-4

Consumer Surplus and a Fall in the Price of Used Textbooks

There are two parts to the increase in consumer surplus generated by a fall in price from $30 to $20. The first is given by the dark blue rectangle: each person who would have bought at the original price of $30—Aleisha, Brad, and Claudia—receives an increase in consumer surplus equal to the total reduction in price, $10. So the area of the dark blue rectangle corresponds to an amount equal to 3 × $10 = $30. The second part is given by the light blue area: the increase in consumer surplus for those who would *not* have bought at the original price of $30 but who buy at the new price of $20—namely, Darren. Darren's willingness to pay is $25, so he now receives consumer surplus of $5. The total increase in consumer surplus is 3 × $10 + $5 = $35, represented by the sum of the shaded areas. Likewise, a rise in price from $20 to $30 would decrease consumer surplus by an amount equal to the sum of the shaded areas.

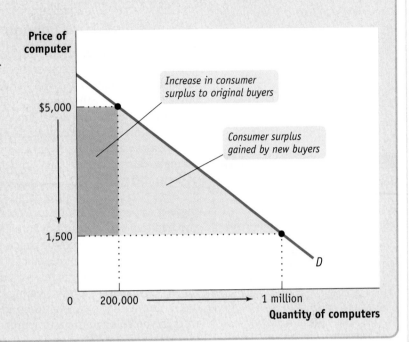

FIGURE 4-5

A Fall in the Price Increases Consumer Surplus

A fall in the price of a computer from $5,000 to $1,500 leads to an increase in the quantity demanded and an increase in consumer surplus. The change in total consumer surplus is given by the sum of the shaded areas: the total area below the demand curve and between the old and new prices. Here, the dark blue area represents the increase in consumer surplus for the 200,000 consumers who would have bought a computer at the original price of $5,000; they each receive an increase in consumer surplus of $3,500. The light blue area represents the increase in consumer surplus for those willing to buy at a price equal to or greater than $1,500 but less than $5,000. Similarly, a rise in the price of a computer from $1,500 to $5,000 generates a decrease in consumer surplus equal to the sum of the two shaded areas.

What would happen if the price of a good were to rise instead of fall? We would do the same analysis in reverse. Suppose, for example, that for some reason the price of computers rises from $1,500 to $5,000. This would lead to a fall in consumer surplus, equal to the sum of the shaded areas in Figure 4-5. This loss consists of two parts. The dark blue rectangle represents the loss to consumers who would still buy a computer, even at a price of $5,000. The light blue triangle represents the loss to consumers who decide not to buy a computer at the higher price.

FOR INQUIRING MINDS

A Matter of Life and Death

Each year, about 4,000 people in the United States die while waiting for a kidney transplant. In 2007, some 70,000 more were wait-listed. Since the number of those in need of a kidney far exceeds availability, what is the best way to allocate available organs? A market isn't feasible. For understandable reasons, the sale of human body parts is illegal in this country. So the task of establishing a protocol for these situations has fallen to the nonprofit group United Network for Organ Sharing (UNOS).

Under current UNOS guidelines, a donated kidney goes to the person who has been waiting the longest. According to this system, an available kidney would go to a 75-year-old who has been waiting for 2 years instead of to a 25-year-old who has been

waiting 6 months, even though the 25-year-old will likely live longer and benefit from the transplanted organ for a longer period of time.

To address this issue, UNOS is devising a new set of guidelines based on a concept it calls "net benefit." According to these new guidelines, kidneys would be allocated on the basis of who will receive the greatest net benefit, where net benefit is measured as the expected increase in lifespan from the transplant. And age is by far the biggest predictor of how long someone will live after a transplant. For example, a typical 25-year-old diabetic will gain an extra 8.7 years of life from a transplant, but a typical 55-year-old diabetic will gain only 3.6 extra years. Under the current system,

based on waiting times, transplants lead to about 44,000 extra years of life for recipients; under the new system, that number would jump to 55,000 extra years. The share of kidneys going to those in their 20s would triple; the share going to those 60 and older would be halved.

What does this have to do with consumer surplus? As you may have guessed, the UNOS concept of "net benefit" is a lot like individual consumer surplus—the individual consumer surplus generated from getting a new kidney. In essence, UNOS has devised a system that allocates donated kidneys according to who gets the greatest individual consumer surplus. In terms of results, then, its proposed "net benefit" system operates a lot like a competitive market.

►*ECONOMICS IN ACTION*

When Money Isn't Enough

The key insight we get from the concept of consumer surplus is that purchases yield a net benefit to the consumer, because the consumer typically pays a price less than his or her willingness to pay for the good. Another way to say this is that the right to buy a good at the going price is a valuable thing in itself.

Most of the time we don't think about the value associated with the right to buy a good. In a market economy, we take it for granted that we can buy whatever we want, as long as we are willing to pay the market price. But that hasn't always been true. For example, during World War II the demands of wartime production created shortages of consumer goods when these goods were sold at pre-war prices. Rather than allow prices to rise, government officials created a system of rationing many goods. To buy sugar, meat, coffee, gasoline, and many other goods, you not only had to pay cash; you also had to present stamps or coupons from special books issued to each family by the government. These pieces of paper, which represented the right to buy goods at the government-regulated price, quickly became valuable commodities in themselves. As a result, illegal markets in meat stamps and gasoline coupons sprang into existence. Moreover, criminals began stealing coupons and even counterfeiting stamps.

The funny thing was that even if you had bought a gasoline coupon on the illegal market, you still had to pay to purchase gasoline. So what you were buying on the illegal market was not the good but *the right to buy the good* at the government-regulated price. That is, people who bought ration coupons on the illegal market were paying for the right to get some consumer surplus. ▲

◄ < < < < < < < < < < <

> **CHECK YOUR UNDERSTANDING** 4-1

1. Consider the market for cheese-stuffed jalapeno peppers. There are two consumers, Casey and Josey, and their willingness to pay for each pepper is given in the accompanying table. (Neither is willing to consume more than 4 peppers at any price.) Use the table (i) to construct the demand schedule for peppers for prices of $0.00, $0.10, and so on, up to $0.90, and (ii) to calculate the total consumer surplus when the price of a pepper is $0.40.

Quantity of peppers	Casey's willingness to pay	Josey's willingness to pay
1st pepper	$0.90	$0.80
2nd pepper	0.70	0.60
3rd pepper	0.50	0.40
4th pepper	0.30	0.30

Solutions appear at back of book.

Producer Surplus and the Supply Curve

Just as some buyers of a good would have been willing to pay more for their purchase than the price they actually pay, some sellers of a good would have been willing to sell it for less than the price they actually receive. We can therefore carry out an analysis of producer surplus and the supply curve that is almost exactly parallel to that of consumer surplus and the demand curve.

Cost and Producer Surplus

Consider a group of students who are potential sellers of used textbooks. Because they have different preferences, the various potential sellers differ in the price at which they are willing to sell their books. The table in Figure 4-6 shows the prices at which several different students would be willing to sell. Andrew is willing to sell the book as long as he can get at least $5; Betty won't sell unless she can get at least $15; Carlos, unless he can get $25; Donna, unless she can get $35; Engelbert, unless he can get $45.

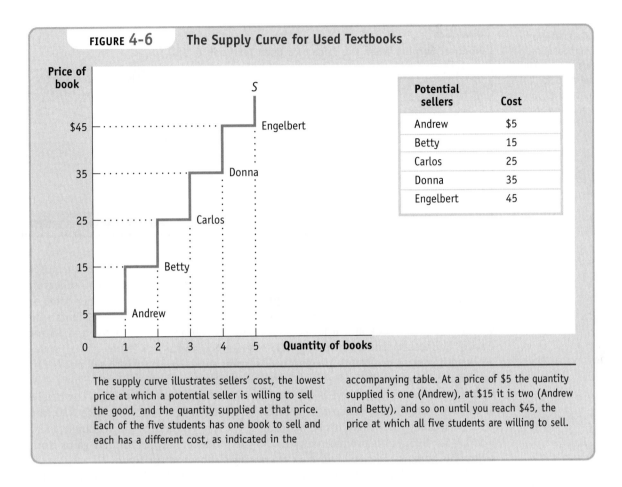

FIGURE 4-6   The Supply Curve for Used Textbooks

Potential sellers	Cost
Andrew	$5
Betty	15
Carlos	25
Donna	35
Engelbert	45

The supply curve illustrates sellers' cost, the lowest price at which a potential seller is willing to sell the good, and the quantity supplied at that price. Each of the five students has one book to sell and each has a different cost, as indicated in the accompanying table. At a price of $5 the quantity supplied is one (Andrew), at $15 it is two (Andrew and Betty), and so on until you reach $45, the price at which all five students are willing to sell.

The lowest price at which a potential seller is willing to sell has a special name in economics: it is called the seller's **cost.** So Andrew's cost is $5, Betty's is $15, and so on.

Using the term *cost*, which people normally associate with the monetary cost of producing a good, may sound a little strange when applied to sellers of used textbooks. The students don't have to manufacture the books, so it doesn't cost the student who sells a book anything to make that book available for sale, does it?

Yes, it does. A student who sells a book won't have it later, as part of his or her personal collection. So there is an *opportunity cost* to selling a textbook, even if the owner has completed the course for which it was required. And remember that one of the basic principles of economics is that the true measure of the cost of doing something is always its opportunity cost. That is, the real cost of something is what you must give up to get it.

So it is good economics to talk of the minimum price at which someone will sell a good as the "cost" of selling that good, even if he or she doesn't spend any money to make the good available for sale. Of course, in most real-world markets the sellers are also those who produce the good and therefore *do* spend money to make the good available for sale. In this case the cost of making the good available for sale *includes* monetary costs, but it may also include other opportunity costs.

Getting back to the example, suppose that Andrew sells his book for $30. Clearly he has gained from the transaction: he would have been willing to sell for only $5, so he has gained $25. This net gain, the difference between the price he actually gets and his cost—the minimum price at which he would have been willing to sell—is known as his **individual producer surplus.**

Just as we derived the demand curve from the willingness to pay of different consumers, we can derive the supply curve from the cost of different producers. The step-shaped curve in Figure 4-6 shows the supply curve implied by the costs shown in the accompanying table. At a price less than $5, none of the students are willing to sell; at a price between $5 and $15, only Andrew is willing to sell, and so on.

A seller's **cost** is the lowest price at which he or she is willing to sell a good.

Individual producer surplus is the net gain to an individual seller from selling a good. It is equal to the difference between the price received and the seller's cost.

Total producer surplus in a market is the sum of the individual producer surpluses of all the sellers of a good in a market. Economists use the term **producer surplus** to refer both to individual and to total producer surplus.

TABLE 4-2

Producer Surplus When the Price of a Used Textbook Is $30

Potential seller	Cost	Price received	Individual producer surplus = Price received − Cost
Andrew	$5	$30	$25
Betty	15	30	15
Carlos	25	30	5
Donna	35	—	—
Engelbert	45	—	—
All sellers			**Total producer surplus = $45**

As in the case of consumer surplus, we can add the individual producer surpluses of sellers to calculate the **total producer surplus,** the total net gain to all sellers in the market. Economists use the term **producer surplus** to refer to either total or individual producer surplus. Table 4-2 shows the net gain to each of the students who would sell a used book at a price of $30: $25 for Andrew, $15 for Betty, and $5 for Carlos. The total producer surplus is $25 + $15 + $5 = $45.

As with consumer surplus, the producer surplus gained by those who sell books can be represented graphically. Figure 4-7 reproduces the supply curve from Figure 4-6. Each step in that supply curve is one book wide and represents one seller. The height of Andrew's step is $5, his cost. This forms the bottom of a rectangle, with $30, the price he actually receives for his book, forming the top. The area of this rectangle, ($30 − $5) × 1 = $25, is his producer surplus. So the producer surplus Andrew gains from selling his book is the *area of the dark red rectangle* shown in the figure.

Let's assume that the campus bookstore is willing to buy all the used copies of this book that students are willing to sell at a price of $30. Then, in addition to Andrew, Betty and Carlos will also sell their books. They will also benefit from their sales, though not as much as Andrew, because they have higher costs. Andrew, as we have

FIGURE 4-7

Producer Surplus in the Used-Textbook Market

At a price of $30, Andrew, Betty, and Carlos each sell a book but Donna and Engelbert do not. Andrew, Betty, and Carlos get individual producer surpluses equal to the difference between the price and their cost, illustrated here by the shaded rectangles. Donna and Engelbert each have a cost that is greater than the price of $30, so they are unwilling to sell a book and so receive zero producer surplus. The total producer surplus is given by the entire shaded area, the sum of the individual producer surpluses of Andrew, Betty, and Carlos, equal to $25 + $15 + $5 = $45.

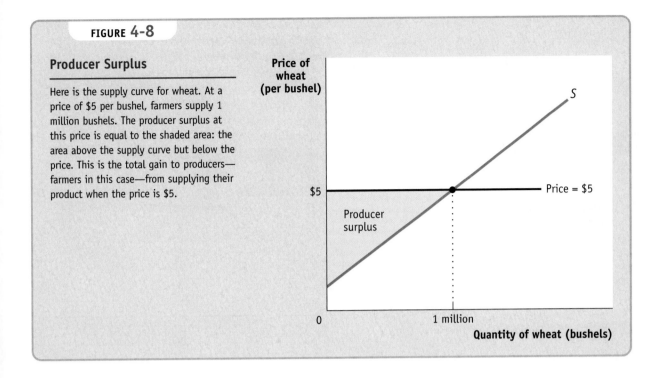

FIGURE 4-8

Producer Surplus

Here is the supply curve for wheat. At a price of $5 per bushel, farmers supply 1 million bushels. The producer surplus at this price is equal to the shaded area: the area above the supply curve but below the price. This is the total gain to producers—farmers in this case—from supplying their product when the price is $5.

Price of wheat (per bushel)

$5

Producer surplus

Price = $5

S

0

1 million

Quantity of wheat (bushels)

seen, gains $25. Betty gains a smaller amount: since her cost is $15, she gains only $15. Carlos gains even less, only $5.

Again, as with consumer surplus, we have a general rule for determining the total producer surplus from sales of a good: *The total producer surplus from sales of a good at a given price is the area above the supply curve but below that price.*

This rule applies both to examples like the one shown in Figure 4-7, where there are a small number of producers and a step-shaped supply curve, and to more realistic examples, where there are many producers and the supply curve is more or less smooth.

Consider, for example, the supply of wheat. Figure 4-8 shows how producer surplus depends on the price per bushel. Suppose that, as shown in the figure, the price is $5 per bushel and farmers supply 1 million bushels. What is the benefit to the farmers from selling their wheat at a price of $5? Their producer surplus is equal to the shaded area in the figure—the area above the supply curve but below the price of $5 per bushel.

How Changing Prices Affect Producer Surplus

As in the case of consumer surplus, a change in price alters producer surplus. However, although a fall in price increases consumer surplus, it reduces producer surplus. Similarly, a rise in price reduces consumer surplus but increases producer surplus.

To see this, let's first consider a rise in the price of the good. Producers of the good will experience an increase in producer surplus, though not all producers gain the same amount. Some producers would have produced the good even at the original price; they will gain the entire price increase on every unit they produce. Other producers will enter the market because of the higher price; they will gain only the difference between the new price and their cost.

Figure 4-9 on the next page is the supply counterpart of Figure 4-5. It shows the effect on producer surplus of a rise in the price of wheat from $5 to $7 per bushel. The increase in producer surplus is the sum of the shaded areas, which consists of two parts. First, there is a dark red rectangle corresponding to the gains to those farmers who would have supplied wheat even at the original $5 price. Second, there is an additional light red

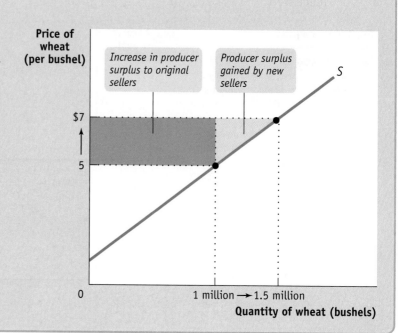

FIGURE 4-9

A Rise in the Price Increases Producer Surplus

A rise in the price of wheat from $5 to $7 leads to an increase in the quantity supplied and an increase in producer surplus. The change in total producer surplus is given by the sum of the shaded areas: the total area above the supply curve but between the old and new prices. The dark red area represents the gain to the farmers who would have supplied 1 million bushels at the original price of $5; they each receive an increase in producer surplus of $2 for each of those bushels. The triangular light red area represents the increase in producer surplus achieved by the farmers who supply the additional 500,000 bushels because of the higher price. Similarly, a fall in the price of wheat generates a reduction in producer surplus equal to the sum of the shaded areas.

triangle that corresponds to the gains to those farmers who would not have supplied wheat at the original price but are drawn into the market by the higher price.

If the price were to fall from $7 to $5 per bushel, the story would run in reverse. The sum of the shaded areas would now be the decline in producer surplus, the decrease in the area above the supply curve but below the price. The loss would consist of two parts, the loss to farmers who would still grow wheat at a price of $5 (the dark red rectangle) and the loss to farmers who decide to no longer grow wheat because of the lower price (the light red triangle).

►ECONOMICS IN ACTION

When the Corn Is High

The average value of farmland in Iowa hit a record high in 2006. A lot of people, it seems, wanted to be Iowa farmers. And there was no mystery why: it was all about the ethanol.

Let's explain: ethanol—the same kind of alcohol that's in beer and other alcoholic drinks—can also fuel automobiles. And in recent years government policy, at both the federal and state levels, has encouraged the use of gasoline that contains a percentage of ethanol. There are a couple of reasons for this policy, including some benefits in fighting air pollution and the hope that using more ethanol will reduce U.S. dependence on imported oil.

But where is the ethanol to come from? Ethanol advocates look to the example of Brazil, which has shifted much of its fuel consumption from gasoline to ethanol. Brazil gets its ethanol by fermenting sugarcane, then distilling out the alcohol. The United States can't follow the same strategy: we don't grow enough sugarcane to satisfy our own sweet tooths, let alone run our cars. But we do produce an awful lot of corn. And corn can also be turned into ethanol.

One result of the shift to ethanol fuel has been a rise in the demand for corn, leading to a surge in corn prices, which rose from $1.85 a bushel in late 2005 to about $4 a bushel in early 2007. And there's no place like Iowa for growing corn. Iowa farmers gained from high prices both because they could sell the corn they would have grown even at lower prices for more money, and because they could shift land away from other crops—especially soybeans—to corn.

What does this have to do with the price of land? A person who buys a farm in Iowa buys the producer surplus that farm generates. And higher prices for corn, which raise the producer surplus of Iowa farmers, make Iowa farmland more valuable. According to the U.S. Department of Agriculture, Iowa farmland went from an average of $1,800 per acre in 2000 to $2,930 per acre in 2006, a 63% increase. ▲

> > > > > > > > > > > >

▶ CHECK YOUR UNDERSTANDING 4-2

1. Consider the market for cheese-stuffed jalapeno peppers. There are two producers, Cara and Jamie, and their costs of producing each pepper are given in the accompanying table. (Neither is willing to produce more than 4 peppers at any price.) Use the table (i) to construct the supply schedule for peppers for prices of $0.00, $0.10, and so on, up to $0.90, and (ii) to calculate the total producer surplus when the price of a pepper is $0.70.

Quantity of peppers	Cara's cost	Jamie's cost
1st pepper	$0.10	$0.30
2nd pepper	0.10	0.50
3rd pepper	0.40	0.70
4th pepper	0.60	0.90

Solutions appear at back of book.

Consumer Surplus, Producer Surplus, and the Gains from Trade

One of the 12 core principles of economics we introduced in Chapter 1 is that markets are a remarkably effective way to organize economic activity: they generally make society as well off as possible given the available resources. The concepts of consumer surplus and producer surplus can help us deepen our understanding of why this is so.

The Gains from Trade

Let's return to the market in used textbooks, but now consider a much bigger market—say, one at a large state university. There are many potential buyers and sellers, so the market is competitive. Let's line up incoming students who are potential buyers of a book in order of their willingness to pay, so that the entering student with the highest willingness to pay is potential buyer number 1, the student with the next highest willingness to pay is number 2, and so on. Then we can use their willingness to pay to derive a demand curve like the one in Figure 4-10 on the next page. Similarly, we can line up outgoing students, who are potential sellers of the book, in order of their cost, starting with the student with the lowest cost, then the student with the next lowest cost, and so on, to derive a supply curve like the one shown in the same figure.

As we have drawn the curves, the market reaches equilibrium at a price of $30 per book, and 1,000 books are bought and sold at that price. The two shaded triangles show the consumer surplus (blue) and the producer surplus (red) generated by this market. The sum of consumer and producer surplus is known as the **total surplus** generated in a market.

The striking thing about this picture is that both consumers and producers gain—that is, both consumers and producers are better off because there is a market in this good. But this should come as no surprise—it illustrates another core principle of economics: *There are gains from trade.* These gains from trade are the reason everyone is better off participating in a market economy than they would be if each individual tried to be self-sufficient.

But are we as well off as we could be? This brings us to the question of the efficiency of markets.

The **total surplus** generated in a market is the total net gain to consumers and producers from trading in the market. It is the sum of the producer and the consumer surplus.

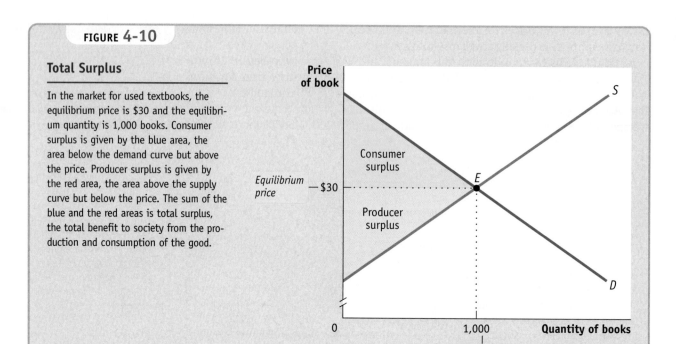

FIGURE 4-10

Total Surplus

In the market for used textbooks, the equilibrium price is $30 and the equilibrium quantity is 1,000 books. Consumer surplus is given by the blue area, the area below the demand curve but above the price. Producer surplus is given by the red area, the area above the supply curve but below the price. The sum of the blue and the red areas is total surplus, the total benefit to society from the production and consumption of the good.

The Efficiency of Markets

Markets produce gains from trade, but in Chapter 1 we made an even bigger claim: that markets are usually *efficient*. That is, we claimed that once the market has produced its gains from trade, there is no way to make some people better off without making other people worse off, except under some well-defined conditions.

The analysis of consumer and producer surplus helps us understand why markets are usually efficient. To gain more intuition into why this is so, consider the fact that market equilibrium is just *one* way of deciding who consumes the good and who sells the good. There are other possible ways of making that decision. Consider, for example, the case of kidney transplants, discussed earlier in For Inquiring Minds. There you learned that available kidneys currently go to the people who have been waiting the longest, rather than to those most likely to benefit from the organ for longer. To address this inefficiency, a new set of guidelines is being devised to determine eligibility for a kidney transplant based on "net benefit," a concept an awful lot like consumer surplus: kidneys would be allocated largely on the basis of who will benefit from them the most.

Similarly, imagine a committee charged with improving on the market equilibrium by deciding who gets and who gives up a used textbook. The committee's ultimate goal: to bypass the market outcome and come up with another arrangement that would produce higher total surplus.

Let's consider the three ways in which the committee might try to increase the total surplus:

1. Reallocate consumption among consumers
2. Reallocate sales among sellers
3. Change the quantity traded

Reallocate Consumption Among Consumers The committee might try to increase total surplus by selling books to different consumers. Figure 4-11 shows why this will result in lower surplus compared to the market equilibrium outcome. Points *A* and *B* show the positions on the demand curve of two potential buyers of used books, Ana and Bob. As we can see from the figure, Ana is willing to pay $35 for a book, but

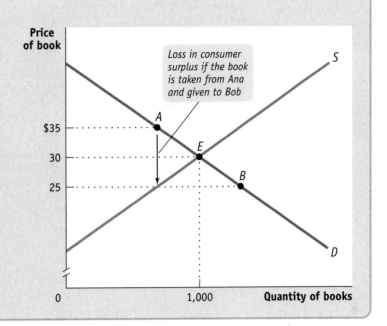

FIGURE 4-11

Reallocating Consumption Lowers Consumer Surplus

Ana (point *A*) has a willingness to pay of $35. Bob (point *B*) has a willingness to pay of only $25. At the market equilibrium price of $30, Ana purchases a book but Bob does not. If we rearrange consumption by taking a book from Ana and giving it to Bob, consumer surplus declines by $10 and, as a result, total surplus declines by $10. The market equilibrium generates the highest possible consumer surplus by ensuring that those who consume the good are those who most value it.

Bob is willing to pay only $25. Since the market equilibrium price is $30, under the market outcome Ana gets a book and Bob does not.

Now suppose the committee reallocates consumption. This would mean taking the book away from Ana and giving it to Bob. Since the book is worth $35 to Ana but only $25 to Bob, this change *reduces total consumer surplus* by $35 − $25 = $10. Moreover, this result doesn't depend on which two students we pick. Every student who buys a book in the market equilibrium has a willingness to pay of $30 or more, and every student who doesn't buy a book has a willingness to pay of less than $30. So reallocating the good among consumers always means taking a book away from a student who values it more and giving it to one who values it less. This necessarily reduces total consumer surplus.

Reallocate Sales Among Sellers The committee might try to increase total surplus by altering who sells their books, taking sales away from sellers who would have sold their books in the market equilibrium and instead compelling those who would not have sold their books in the market equilibrium to sell them. Figure 4-12 on the next page shows why this will result in lower surplus. Here points *X* and *Y* show the positions on the supply curve of Xavier, who has a cost of $25, and Yvonne, who has a cost of $35. At the equilibrium market price of $30, Xavier would sell his book but Yvonne would not sell hers. If the committee reallocated sales, forcing Xavier to keep his book and Yvonne to sell hers, total producer surplus would be reduced by $35 − $25 = $10. Again, it doesn't matter which two students we choose. Any student who sells a book in the market equilibrium has a lower cost than any student who keeps a book. So reallocating sales among sellers necessarily increases total cost and reduces total producer surplus.

Change the Quantity Traded The committee might try to increase total surplus by compelling students to trade either more books or fewer books than the market equilibrium quantity. Figure 4-13 on the next page shows why this will result in lower surplus. It shows all four students: potential buyers Ana and Bob, and potential sellers Xavier and Yvonne. To reduce sales, the committee will have to prevent a transaction that would have occurred in the market equilibrium—that is, prevent Xavier from selling to Ana. Since Ana is willing to pay $35 and Xavier's cost is $25, preventing this transaction reduces total surplus by $35 − $25 = $10. Once again, this result doesn't depend on which two students we pick: any student who would have sold the book in the market equilibrium has a cost of $30 or less, and any student who would

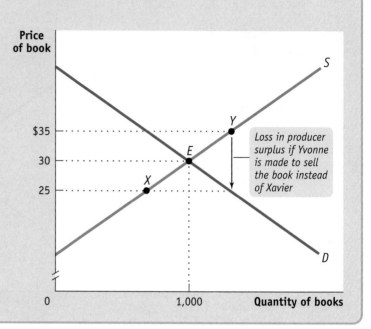

FIGURE 4-12

Reallocating Sales Lowers Producer Surplus

Yvonne (point Y) has a cost of $35, $10 more than Xavier (point X), who has a cost of $25. At the market equilibrium price of $30, Xavier sells a book but Yvonne does not. If we rearrange sales by preventing Xavier from selling his book and compelling Yvonne to sell hers, producer surplus declines by $10 and, as a result, total surplus declines by $10. The market equilibrium generates the highest possible producer surplus by assuring that those who sell the good are those who most value the right to sell it.

have purchased the book in the market equilibrium has a willingness to pay of $30 or more. So preventing any sale that would have occurred in the market equilibrium necessarily reduces total surplus.

Finally, the committee might try to increase sales by forcing Yvonne, who would not have sold her book in the market equilibrium, to sell it to someone like Bob, who would not have bought a book in the market equilibrium. Because Yvonne's cost is $35, but Bob is only willing to pay $25, this transaction reduces total surplus by $10. And once again it doesn't matter which two students we pick—anyone who wouldn't have bought the book has a willingness to pay of less than $30, and anyone who wouldn't have sold has a cost of more than $30.

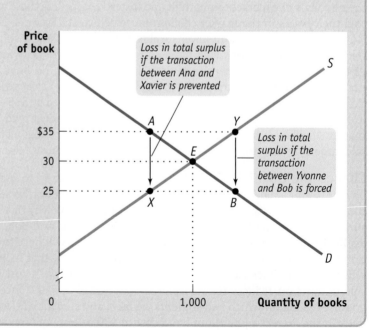

FIGURE 4-13

Changing the Quantity Lowers Total Surplus

If Xavier (point X) were prevented from selling his book to someone like Ana (point A), total surplus would fall by $10, the difference between Ana's willingness to pay ($35) and Xavier's cost ($25). This means that total surplus falls whenever fewer than 1,000 books—the equilibrium quantity—are transacted. Likewise, if Yvonne (point Y) were compelled to sell her book to someone like Bob (point B), total surplus would also fall by $10, the difference between Yvonne's cost ($35) and Bob's willingness to pay ($25). This means that total surplus falls whenever more than 1,000 books are transacted. These two examples show that at market equilibrium, all mutually beneficial transactions—and only mutually beneficial transactions—occur.

The key point to remember is that once this market is in equilibrium, there is no way to increase the gains from trade. Any other outcome reduces total surplus. (This is why UNOS is trying, with its new guidelines based on "net benefit," to reproduce the allocation of donated kidneys that would occur if there were a market for the organs.) We can summarize our results by stating that an efficient market performs four important functions:

1. It allocates consumption of the good to the potential buyers who most value it, as indicated by the fact that they have the highest willingness to pay.

2. It allocates sales to the potential sellers who most value the right to sell the good, as indicated by the fact that they have the lowest cost.

3. It ensures that every consumer who makes a purchase values the good more than every seller who makes a sale, so that all transactions are mutually beneficial.

4. It ensures that every potential buyer who doesn't make a purchase values the good less than every potential seller who doesn't make a sale, so that no mutually beneficial transactions are missed.

There are three caveats, however. First, although a market may be efficient, it isn't necessarily *fair*. In fact, fairness, or *equity*, is often in conflict with efficiency. We'll discuss this next.

The second caveat is that markets sometimes *fail*. As we mentioned in Chapter 1, under some well-defined conditions, markets can fail to deliver efficiency. When this occurs, markets no longer maximize total surplus. We provide a brief overview of why markets fail at the end of this chapter, reserving a more detailed analysis for later chapters.

Third, even when the market equilibrium maximizes total surplus, this does not mean that it results in the best outcome for every *individual* consumer and producer. Other things equal, each buyer would like to pay a lower price and each seller would like to receive a higher price. So if the government were to intervene in the market—say, by lowering the price below the equilibrium price to make consumers happy or by raising the price above the equilibrium price to make producers happy—the outcome would no longer be efficient. Although some people would be happier, society as a whole would be worse off because total surplus would be lower.

Maximizing total surplus at your local hardware store.

Equity and Efficiency

For many patients who need kidney transplants, the proposed UNOS guidelines, covered earlier, will be unwelcome news. Those who had waited years for a transplant will no doubt find these guidelines, which give precedence to younger patients, . . . well . . . unfair. And the guidelines raise other questions about fairness: Why limit potential transplant recipients to Americans? Why include younger patients with other chronic diseases? Why not give precedence to those who have made recognized contributions to society? And so on.

The point is that efficiency is about *how to achieve goals, not what those goals should be*. For example, UNOS decided that its goal is to maximize the life span of kidney recipients. Some might have argued for a different goal, and efficiency does not address which goal is the best. *What efficiency does address is the best way to achieve a goal once it has been determined*—in this case, using the UNOS concept of "net benefit."

It's easy to get carried away with the idea that markets are always right and that economic policies that interfere with efficiency are bad. But that would be misguided because there is another factor to consider: society cares about equity, or what's "fair." As we discussed in Chapter 1, there is often a trade-off between equity and efficiency: policies that promote equity often come at the cost of decreased efficiency, and policies that promote efficiency often result in decreased equity. So it's important to realize that a society's choice to sacrifice some efficiency for the sake of equity, however it defines equity, is a valid one. And it's important to understand that fairness, unlike efficiency, can be very hard to define. Fairness is a concept about which well-intentioned people often disagree.

➤ECONOMICS IN ACTION

eBay and eFficiency

Garage sales are an old American tradition: they are a way for people to sell items they don't want to others who have some use for them, to the benefit of both parties. But

"I got it from eBay"

many potentially beneficial trades are missed. For all Mr. Smith knows, there is someone 1,000 miles away who would really love that 1930s gramophone he has in the basement; for all Ms. Jones knows, there is someone 1,000 miles away who has that 1930s gramophone she has always wanted. When garage sales are the only means by which buyers and sellers meet, there is no way for people like Mr. Smith and Ms. Jones to find each other.

Enter eBay, the online auction service. eBay was founded in 1995 by Pierre Omidyar, a programmer whose fiancée was a collector of Pez candy dispensers and wanted a way to find potential sellers. The company, which says that its mission is "to help practically anyone trade practically anything on earth," provides a way for would-be buyers and would-be sellers of unique or used items to find each other, even if they don't live in the same neighborhood or even the same city.

The potential gains from trade were evidently large: by late 2007, eBay had 83.2 million active users, and in 2007, $60 billion in goods were bought and sold using the service. The Omidyars now possess a large collection of Pez dispensers. They are also billionaires. ▲

< < < < < < < < < < < <

>> QUICK REVIEW

➤ **Total surplus** measures the gains from trade in a market.

➤ Markets are efficient except under some well-defined conditions. We can demonstrate the efficiency of a market by considering what happens to total surplus if we start from the equilibrium and reallocate consumption, reallocate sales, or change the quantity traded. Any outcome other than the market equilibrium reduces total surplus, which means that the market equilibrium is efficient.

➤ Because society cares about equity, government intervention in a market that reduces efficiency while increasing equity can be justified.

➤ CHECK YOUR UNDERSTANDING 4-3

1. Using the tables in Check Your Understanding 4-1 and 4-2, find the equilibrium price and quantity in the market for cheese-stuffed jalapeno peppers. What is total surplus in the equilibrium in this market, and who receives it?

2. Show how each of the following three actions reduces total surplus:
   a. Having Josey consume one less pepper, and Casey one more pepper, than in the market equilibrium
   b. Having Cara produce one less pepper, and Jamie one more pepper, than in the market equilibrium
   c. Having Josey consume one less pepper, and Cara produce one less pepper, than in the market equilibrium

3. Suppose UNOS alters its guidelines for the allocation of donated kidneys, no longer relying solely on the concept of "net benefit" but also giving preference to patients with small children. If "total surplus" in this case is defined to be the total life span of kidney recipients, is this new guideline likely to reduce, increase, or leave total surplus unchanged? How might you justify this new guideline?

Solutions appear at back of book.

A Market Economy

As we learned earlier in the book, in a market economy decisions about production and consumption are made via markets. In fact, the economy as a whole is made up of many *interrelated markets*. Up until now, to learn how markets work we've been examining a single market—the market for used textbooks. But in reality, consumers and producers do not make decisions in isolated markets. For example, a student's decision in the market for used textbooks might be affected by how much interest must be paid on a student loan; thus, the decision in the used textbook market would be influenced by what is going on in the market for money.

We know that an efficient market equilibrium maximizes total surplus—the gains to buyers and sellers in that market. Is there a comparable result for an economy as a whole, an economy composed of a vast number of individual markets? The answer is yes, but with qualifications. When each and every market in the economy maximizes total surplus, then the economy as a whole is efficient. This is a very important result: just as it is impossible to make someone better off without making other people worse off in a single market when it is efficient, it is impossible to improve upon the outcome of a market economy when each and every market in that economy is efficient. However, it is important to realize that this is a *theoretical* result: it is virtually impossible to find an economy in which every market is efficient. For now, let's examine why markets and market economies typically work so well. Once we understand why, we can then briefly address why markets sometimes get it wrong.

Why Markets Typically Work So Well

Economists have written volumes about why markets are an effective way to organize an economy. In the end, well-functioning markets owe their effectiveness to two powerful features: *property rights* and the role of prices as *economic signals*.

By **property rights** we mean a system in which valuable items in the economy have specific owners who can dispose of them as they choose. In a system of property rights, by purchasing a good you receive "ownership rights": the right to use and dispose of the good as you see fit. Property rights are what make the mutually beneficial transactions in the used-textbook market, or any market, possible.

To see why property rights are crucial, imagine that students do not have full property rights in their textbooks and are prohibited from reselling them when the semester ends. This restriction on property rights would prevent many mutually beneficial transactions. Some students would be stuck with textbooks they will never reread when they would be much happier receiving some cash instead. Other students would be forced to pay full price for brand-new books when they would be happier getting slightly battered copies at a lower price.

Once a system of well-defined property rights is in place, the second necessary feature of well-functioning markets—prices as economic signals—can operate. An **economic signal** is any piece of information that helps people make better economic decisions. There are thousands of signals that businesses watch in the real world. For example, business forecasters say that sales of cardboard boxes are a good early indicator of changes in industrial production: if businesses are buying lots of cardboard boxes, you can be sure that they will soon increase their production.

But prices are far and away the most important signals in a market economy, because they convey essential information about other people's costs and their willingness to pay. If the equilibrium price of used books is $30, this in effect tells everyone both that there are consumers willing to pay $30 and up and that there are potential sellers with a cost of $30 or less. The signal given by the market price ensures that total surplus is maximized by telling people whether to buy books, sell books, or do nothing at all. Each potential seller with a cost of $30 or less learns from the market price that it's a good idea to sell her book; if she has a higher cost, it's a good idea to keep it. Likewise, each consumer willing to pay $30 or more learns from the market price that it's a good idea to buy a book; if he is unwilling to pay $30, then it's a good idea not to buy a book.

This example shows that the market price "signals" to consumers with a willingness to pay equal to or more than the market price that they should buy the good, just as it signals to producers with a cost equal to or less than the market price that they should sell the good. And since, in equilibrium, the quantity demanded equals the quantity supplied, all willing consumers will find willing sellers.

Prices can sometimes fail as economic signals. Sometimes a price is not an accurate indicator of how desirable a good is. When there is uncertainty about the quality of a good, price alone may not be an accurate indicator of the value of the good. For example, you can't infer from the price alone whether a used car is good or a

Property rights are the rights of owners of valuable items, whether resources or goods, to dispose of those items as they choose.

An **economic signal** is any piece of information that helps people make better economic decisions.

A market or an economy is **inefficient** if there are missed opportunities: some people could be made better off without making other people worse off.

Market failure occurs when a market fails to be efficient.

"lemon." In fact, a well-known problem in economics is "the market for lemons," a market in which prices don't work well as economic signals. (We'll learn about the market for lemons in Chapter 21.)

A Few Words of Caution

As we've seen, markets are an amazingly effective way to organize economic activity. But as we've noted, markets can sometimes get it wrong. We first learned about this in Chapter 1 in our fifth principle of interaction: *When markets don't achieve efficiency, government intervention can improve society's welfare.* When markets are **inefficient,** there are missed opportunities—ways in which production or consumption can be rearranged that would make some people better off without making other people worse off. In other words, there are gains from trade that go unrealized: total surplus could be increased. And when a market or markets are inefficient, the economy in which they are embedded is also inefficient.

Markets can be rendered inefficient for a number of reasons. Two of the most important are a lack of property rights and inaccuracy of prices as economic signals. When a market is inefficient, we have what is known as **market failure.** We will examine various types of market failure in later chapters; for now, let's review the three main ways in which markets sometimes fall short of efficiency.

First, markets can fail when, in an attempt to capture more surplus, one party prevents mutually beneficial trades from occurring. This situation arises, for instance, when a market contains only a single seller of a good, known as a *monopolist.* In this case, the assumption we have relied on in supply and demand analysis—that no individual buyer or seller can have a noticeable effect on the market price—is no longer valid; the monopolist can determine the market price. As we'll see in Chapter 14, this gives rise to inefficiency as a monopolist manipulates the market price in order to increase profits, thereby preventing mutually beneficial trades from occurring.

Second, actions of individuals sometimes have side effects on the welfare of others that markets don't take into account. In economics, these side effects are known as *externalities,* and the best-known example is pollution. We can think of the problem of pollution as a problem of incomplete property rights; for example, existing property rights don't guarantee a right to ownership of clean air. We'll see in Chapter 17 that pollution and other externalities also give rise to inefficiency.

Third, markets for some goods fail because these goods, by their very nature, are unsuited for efficient management by markets. In Chapter 21, we will analyze goods that fall into this category because of problems of *private information*—information about a good that some people possess but others don't. The seller of a used car that is a "lemon" may have information that is unknown to potential buyers. In cases like this where there is private information, prices don't always accurately reflect true value. In Chapter 18, we will encounter other types of goods that fall into the category of being unsuited for efficient management by markets—*public goods, common resources, and artificially scarce goods.* Markets for these goods fail because of problems in limiting people's access to and consumption of the good; examples are fish in the sea and trees in the Amazonian rainforest. In these instances, markets generally fail due to incomplete property rights.

But even with these caveats, it's remarkable how well markets work at maximizing the gains from trade.

►*ECONOMICS IN ACTION*

A Great Leap—Backward

Economies in which a central planner, rather than markets, makes consumption and production decisions are known as *planned economies.* Russia (formerly part of the U.S.S.R.), many Eastern European countries, and several Southeast Asian countries once had planned economies, and countries such as India and Brazil once had significant parts of their economies under central planning. China still does today.

Planned economies are notorious for their inefficiency, and what is probably the most compelling example of that is the so-called Great Leap Forward, an ambitious economic plan instituted in China during the late 1950s by its leader Mao Zedong. Its intention was to speed up the country's industrialization. Key to this plan was a shift from urban to rural manufacturing: farming villages were supposed to start producing heavy industrial goods such as steel.

Unfortunately, the plan backfired. Diverting farmers from their usual work led to a sharp fall in food production. Meanwhile, because raw materials for steel, such as coal and iron ore, were sent to ill-equipped and inexperienced rural producers rather than to urban factories, industrial output declined as well. The plan, in short, led to a fall in the production of everything in China.

Because China was a very poor country to start with, the results were catastrophic. The famine that followed is estimated to have reduced China's population by as much as 30 million. ▲

> > > > > > > > > > > > >

> ► **CHECK YOUR UNDERSTANDING** 4-4

1. In some states that are rich in natural resources, such as oil, the law separates the right to above-ground use of the land from the right to drill below ground (called "mineral rights"). Someone who owns both the above-ground rights and the mineral rights can sell the two rights separately. Explain how this division of the property rights enhances efficiency compared to a situation in which the two rights must always be sold together.

2. Suppose that in the market for used textbooks the equilibrium price is $30, but it is mistakenly announced that the equilibrium price is $300. How does this affect the efficiency of the market? Be specific.

3. What is wrong with the following statement? "Markets are always the best way to organize economic activity. Any policies that interfere with markets reduce society's welfare."

Solutions appear at back of book.

>> **QUICK REVIEW**

► In a market economy, markets are interrelated. When each and every market in an economy is efficient, the economy as a whole is efficient. But in the real world, some markets in a market economy will almost certainly fail to be efficient.

► A system of **property rights** and the operation of prices as **economic signals** are two key factors that enable a market to be efficient. But under conditions in which property rights are incomplete or prices give inaccurate economic signals, markets can fail.

► Under certain conditions, **market failure** occurs and the market is **inefficient**: gains to trade are unrealized. The three principal ways in which markets fail are the prevention of mutually beneficial transactions caused by one party's attempt to capture more surplus, side effects that aren't properly accounted for, and problems in the nature of the goods themselves.

[►► **A LOOK** AHEAD •••

We have now seen how to measure the gains producers and consumers receive by trading in a market, and we've also seen that, subject to certain caveats, a market equilibrium maximizes these gains. Nonetheless, governments sometimes object to the equilibrium price or equilibrium quantity arising from an efficient market, and they intervene to change the result. In the next chapter, we'll describe the usually unpleasant consequences of attempts to tell efficient markets what to do.]

SUMMARY ....■

1. The **willingness to pay** of each individual consumer determines the demand curve. When price is less than or equal to the willingness to pay, the potential consumer purchases the good. The difference between willingness to pay and price is the net gain to the consumer, the **individual consumer surplus.**

2. **Total consumer surplus** in a market, the sum of all individual consumer surpluses in a market, is equal to the area below the market demand curve but above the price. A rise in the price of a good reduces consumer surplus; a fall in the price increases consumer surplus. The term **consumer surplus** is often used to refer to both individual and total consumer surplus.

3. The **cost** of each potential producer, the lowest price at which he or she is willing to supply a unit of that good, determines the supply curve. If the price of a good is above a producer's cost, a sale generates a net gain to the producer, known as the **individual producer surplus.**

4. **Total producer surplus** in a market, the sum of the individual producer surpluses in a market, is equal to the area above the market supply curve but below the price. A rise in the price of a good increases producer surplus; a fall in the price reduces producer surplus. The term **producer surplus** is often used to refer to both individual and total producer surplus.

5. **Total surplus,** the total gain to society from the production and consumption of a good, is the sum of consumer and producer surplus.

6. Usually, markets are efficient and achieve the maximum total surplus. Any possible reallocation of consumption or sales, or change in the quantity bought and sold, reduces total surplus. However, society also cares about equity. So government intervention in a market that reduces efficiency but increases equity can be a valid choice by society.

7. An economy composed of efficient markets is also efficient, although this is virtually impossible to achieve in reality. The keys to the efficiency of a market economy are **property rights** and the operation of prices as **economic signals.** Under certain conditions, **market failure** occurs, making a market **inefficient.** Three principal sources of market failure are: attempts to capture more surplus that create inefficiencies, side effects of some transactions, and problems in the nature of the good.

KEY TERMS

Willingness to pay, p. 94
Individual consumer surplus, p. 96
Total consumer surplus, p. 96
Consumer surplus, p. 96
Cost, p. 101

Individual producer surplus, p. 101
Total producer surplus, p. 102
Producer surplus, p. 102
Total surplus, p. 105
Property rights, p. 111

Economic signal, p. 111
Inefficient, p. 112
Market failure, p. 112

PROBLEMS

1. Determine the amount of consumer surplus generated in each of the following situations.

   a. Leon goes to the clothing store to buy a new T-shirt, for which he is willing to pay up to $10. He picks out one he likes with a price tag of exactly $10. When he is paying for it, he learns that the T-shirt has been discounted by 50%.

   b. Alberto goes to the CD store hoping to find a used copy of *Nirvana's Greatest Hits* for up to $10. The store has one copy selling for $10, which he purchases.

   c. After soccer practice, Stacey is willing to pay $2 for a bottle of mineral water. The 7-Eleven sells mineral water for $2.25 per bottle, so she declines to purchase it.

2. Determine the amount of producer surplus generated in each of the following situations.

   a. Gordon lists his old Lionel electric trains on eBay. He sets a minimum acceptable price, known as his *reserve price,* of $75. After five days of bidding, the final high bid is exactly $75. He accepts the bid.

   b. So-Hee advertises her car for sale in the used-car section of the student newspaper for $2,000, but she is willing to sell the car for any price higher than $1,500. The best offer she gets is $1,200, which she declines.

   c. Sanjay likes his job so much that he would be willing to do it for free. However, his annual salary is $80,000.

3. There are six potential consumers of computer games, each willing to buy only one game. Consumer 1 is willing to pay $40 for a computer game, consumer 2 is willing to pay $35, consumer 3 is willing to pay $30, consumer 4 is willing to pay $25, consumer 5 is willing to pay $20, and consumer 6 is willing to pay $15.

   a. Suppose the market price is $29. What is the total consumer surplus?

   b. The market price decreases to $19. What is the total consumer surplus now?

   c. When the price fell from $29 to $19, how much did each consumer's individual consumer surplus change? How does total consumer surplus change?

4. a. In an auction, potential buyers compete for a good by submitting bids. Adam Galinsky, a social psychologist at Northwestern University, compared eBay auctions in which the same good was sold. He found that, on average, the higher the number of bidders, the higher the sales price. For example, in two auctions of identical iPods, the one with the higher number of bidders brought a higher selling price. According to Galinsky, this explains why smart sellers on eBay set absurdly low opening prices (the lowest price that the seller will accept), such as 1 cent for a new iPod. Use the concepts of consumer and producer surplus to explain Galinsky's reasoning.

   b. You are considering selling your vintage 1969 convertible Volkswagen Beetle. If the car is in good condition, it is worth a lot; if it is in poor condition, it is useful only as scrap. Assume that your car is in excellent condition but that it costs a potential buyer $500 for an inspection to learn the car's condition. Use what you learned in part a to explain whether or not you should pay for an inspection and share the results with all interested buyers.

5. According to the Bureau of Transportation Statistics, due to an increase in demand, the average domestic airline fare increased from $367.17 in the fourth quarter of 2005 to $381.99 in the first quarter of 2006, an increase of $14.82.

The number of passenger tickets sold in the fourth quarter of 2005 was 178.1 million. Over the same period, the airlines' costs remained roughly the same: the price of jet fuel averaged around $1.85 per gallon in both quarters (Source: Energy Information Administration), and airline pilots' salaries remained roughly the same (according to the Bureau of Labor Statistics, they averaged $135,040 per year in 2005).

Can you determine precisely by how much producer surplus has increased as a result of the $14.82 increase in the average fare? If you cannot be precise, can you determine whether it will be less than, or more than, a specific amount?

6. Hollywood screenwriters negotiate a new agreement with movie producers stipulating that they will receive 10% of the revenue from every video rental of a movie they authored. They have no such agreement for movies shown on pay-per-view television.

   a. When the new writers' agreement comes into effect, what will happen in the market for video rentals—that is, will supply or demand shift, and how? As a result, how will consumer surplus in the market for video rentals change? Illustrate with a diagram. Do you think the writers' agreement will be popular with consumers who rent videos?

   b. Consumers consider video rentals and pay-per-view movies substitutable to some extent. When the new writers' agreement comes into effect, what will happen in the market for pay-per-view movies—that is, will supply or demand shift, and how? As a result, how will producer surplus in the market for pay-per-view movies change? Illustrate with a diagram. Do you think the writers' agreement will be popular with cable television companies that show pay-per-view movies?

7. The accompanying table shows the supply and demand schedules for used copies of the first edition of this textbook. The supply schedule is derived from offers at amazon.com. The demand schedule is hypothetical.

Price of book	Quantity of books demanded	Quantity of books supplied
$60	30	0
65	27	3
70	25	7
75	20	7
80	17	8
85	15	15
90	12	16
95	9	17
100	8	29
105	2	31
110	0	34

   a. Calculate consumer and producer surplus at the equilibrium in this market.

   b. Now the second edition of this textbook becomes available. As a result, the willingness to pay of each potential buyer for a second-hand copy of the first edition falls by $20. In a table, show the new demand schedule and again calculate consumer and producer surplus at the new equilibrium.

8. On Thursday nights, a local restaurant has a pasta special. Ari likes the restaurant's pasta, and his willingness to pay for each serving is shown in the accompanying table.

Quantity of pasta (servings)	Willingness to pay for pasta (per serving)
1	$10
2	8
3	6
4	4
5	2
6	0

   a. If the price of a serving of pasta is $4, how many servings will Ari buy? How much consumer surplus does he receive?

   b. The following week, Ari is back at the restaurant again, but now the price of a serving of pasta is $6. By how much does his consumer surplus decrease compared to the previous week?

   c. One week later, he goes to the restaurant again. He discovers that the restaurant is offering an "all-you-can-eat" special for $25. How much pasta will Ari eat, and how much consumer surplus does he receive now?

   d. Suppose you own the restaurant and Ari is a "typical" customer. What is the highest price you can charge for the "all-you-can-eat" special and still attract customers?

9. You are the manager of Fun World, a small amusement park. The accompanying diagram shows the demand curve of a typical customer at Fun World.

   a. Suppose that the price of each ride is $5. At that price, how much consumer surplus does an individual consumer get? (Recall that the area of a right triangle is 1/2 × the height of the triangle × the base of the triangle.)

b. Suppose that Fun World considers charging an admission fee, even though it maintains the price of each ride at $5. What is the maximum admission fee it could charge? (Assume that all potential customers have enough money to pay the fee.)

c. Suppose that Fun World lowered the price of each ride to zero. How much consumer surplus does an individual consumer get? What is the maximum admission fee Fun World could charge?

10. The accompanying diagram illustrates a taxi driver's individual supply curve (assume that each taxi ride is the same distance).

a. Suppose the city sets the price of taxi rides at $4 per ride, and at $4 the taxi driver is able to sell as many taxi rides as he desires. What is this taxi driver's producer surplus? (Recall that the area of a right triangle is $\frac{1}{2} \times$ the height of the triangle $\times$ the base of the triangle.)

b. Suppose that the city keeps the price of a taxi ride set at $4, but it decides to charge taxi drivers a "licensing fee." What is the maximum licensing fee the city could extract from this taxi driver?

c. Suppose that the city allowed the price of taxi rides to increase to $8 per ride. Again assume that, at this price, the taxi driver sells as many rides as he is willing to offer. How much producer surplus does an individual taxi driver now get? What is the maximum licensing fee the city could charge this taxi driver?

11. On November 18, 2006, the *New York Times* reported that "The Universal Music Group, the world's largest music company, filed a copyright infringement lawsuit yesterday against MySpace, the popular social networking Web site, for allowing users to upload and download songs and music videos. . . . In court papers, Universal noted that unauthorized copies of music and video from one of its biggest acts, U2, were easily available on the site, as is material from an unreleased album by the rap star Jay-Z." Allowing Internet users to download music and video for free limits Universal's right to dispose of the music and video as it chooses; in particular, it limits Universal's right to give access to its music only to those who have paid for it. In other words, it limits Universal's property rights.

a. If everyone were to obtain music and video content for free from websites such as MySpace, instead of paying Universal, what would Universal's producer surplus be from music sales? What are the implications for Universal's incentive to produce music and video content in the future?

b. If Universal loses the lawsuit and music can be freely downloaded from the Internet, what do you think will happen to mutually beneficial transactions (the producing and buying of music) in the future?

 www.worthpublishers.com/krugmanwells

The Market Strikes Back

BIG CITY, NOT-SO-BRIGHT IDEAS

NEW YORK CITY IS A PLACE WHERE YOU CAN find almost anything—that is, almost anything, except a taxicab when you need one or a decent apartment at a rent you can afford. You might think that New York's notorious shortages of cabs and apartments are the inevitable price of big-city living. However, they are largely the product of government policies—specifically, of government policies that have, one way or another, tried to prevail over the market forces of supply and demand.

In Chapter 3, we learned the principle that a market moves to equilibrium—that the market price rises or falls to the level at which the quantity of a good that people are willing to supply is equal to the quantity that other people demand. In Chapter 4, we

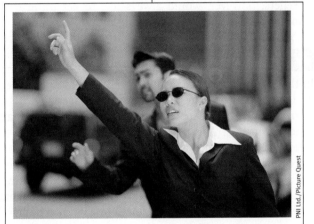

New York City: an empty taxi is hard to find.

learned that markets are typically efficient: at equilibrium a market typically maximizes the gains from trade—that is, the sum of consumer and producer surplus. We also learned in Chapter 4 that government intervention in a market can sometimes be justified on the grounds of equity or when the market itself is inefficient. But it's important to note that governments also frequently intervene in markets without these justifications, often to please powerful interests.

Whenever a government tries to dictate either a market price or a market quantity that's different from the equilibrium price or quantity, the market strikes back in

predictable ways. Our ability to predict what will happen when governments try to defy supply and demand shows the power and usefulness of supply and demand analysis itself.

The shortages of apartments and taxicabs in New York are particular examples that illuminate what happens when the logic of the market is defied. New York's housing shortage is the result of *rent control,* a law that prevents landlords from raising rents except when specifically given permission. Rent control was introduced during World War II to protect the interests of tenants, and it still remains in force. Many other American cities have had rent control at one time or another, but with the notable exceptions of New York and San Francisco, these controls have largely been done away with. Similarly, New York's limited supply of taxis is the result of a licensing system introduced in the 1930s. New York taxi licenses are known as "medallions," and only taxis with medallions are allowed to pick up passengers. Although this system was originally intended to protect the interests of both drivers and customers, it has generated a shortage of taxis in the city. The number of medallions remained fixed for nearly 60 years, with no significant increase until 2004.

In this chapter, we begin by examining what happens when governments try to control prices in a competitive market, keeping the price in a market either below its equilibrium level—a *price ceiling* such as rent control—or above it—a *price floor* such as the minimum wage paid to workers in many countries. We then turn to schemes such as taxi medallions that attempt to dictate the quantity of a good bought and sold.

WHAT YOU WILL LEARN IN THIS CHAPTER:

➤ The meaning of **price controls** and **quantity controls,** two kinds of government intervention in markets

➤ How price and quantity controls create problems and can make a market inefficient

➤ What **deadweight loss** is

➤ Why the predictable side effects of intervention in markets often lead economists to be skeptical of its usefulness

➤ Who benefits and who loses from market interventions, and why they are used despite their well-known problems

---

Why Governments Control Prices

You learned in Chapter 3 that a market moves to equilibrium—that is, the market price moves to the level at which the quantity supplied equals the quantity demanded. But this equilibrium price does not necessarily please either buyers or sellers.

After all, buyers would always like to pay less if they could, and sometimes they can make a strong moral or political case that they should pay lower prices. For example, what if the equilibrium between supply and demand for apartments in a major city leads to rental rates that an average working person can't afford? In that case, a government might well be under pressure to impose limits on the rents landlords can charge.

Sellers, however, would always like to get more money for what they sell, and sometimes they can make a strong moral or political case that they should receive higher prices. For example, consider the labor market: the price for an hour of a worker's time is the wage rate. What if the equilibrium between supply and demand for less skilled workers leads to wage rates that yield an income below the poverty level? In that case, a government might well be pressured to require employers to pay a rate no lower than some specified minimum wage.

In other words, there is often a strong political demand for governments to intervene in markets. And powerful interests can make a compelling case that a market intervention favoring them is "fair." When a government intervenes to regulate prices, we say that it imposes **price controls.** These controls typically take the form either of an upper limit, a **price ceiling,** or a lower limit, a **price floor.**

Unfortunately, it's not that easy to tell a market what to do. As we will now see, when a government tries to legislate prices—whether it legislates them *down* by imposing a price ceiling or *up* by imposing a price floor—there are certain predictable and unpleasant side effects.

We make an important assumption in this chapter: the markets in question are efficient before price controls are imposed. As we noted in Chapter 4, markets can sometimes be inefficient—for example, a market dominated by a monopolist, a single seller who has the power to influence the market price. When markets are inefficient, price controls don't necessarily cause problems and can potentially move the market closer to efficiency. In practice, however, price controls often *are* imposed on efficient markets—like the New York apartment market. And so the analysis in this chapter applies to many important real-world situations.

Price controls are legal restrictions on how high or low a market price may go. They can take two forms: a **price ceiling,** a maximum price sellers are allowed to charge for a good or service, or a **price floor,** a minimum price buyers are required to pay for a good or service.

Price Ceilings

Aside from rent control, there are not many price ceilings in the United States today. But at times they have been widespread. Price ceilings are typically imposed during crises—wars, harvest failures, natural disasters—because these events often lead to sudden price increases that hurt many people but produce big gains for a lucky few.

The U.S. government imposed ceilings on many prices during World War II: the war sharply increased demand for raw materials, such as aluminum and steel, and price controls prevented those with access to these raw materials from earning huge profits. Price controls on oil were imposed in 1973, when an embargo by Arab oil-exporting countries seemed likely to generate huge profits for U.S. oil companies. Price controls were imposed on California's wholesale electricity market in 2001, when a shortage created big profits for a few power-generating companies but led to higher electricity bills for consumers.

Rent control in New York is, believe it or not, a legacy of World War II: it was imposed because wartime production produced an economic boom, which increased demand for apartments at a time when the labor and raw materials that might have been used to build them were being used to win the war instead. Although most price controls were removed soon after the war ended, New York's rent limits were retained and gradually extended to buildings not previously covered, leading to some very strange situations.

You can rent a one-bedroom apartment in Manhattan on fairly short notice—if you are able and willing to pay several thousand dollars a month and live in a less-than-desirable area. Yet some people pay only a small fraction of this for comparable apartments, and others pay hardly more for bigger apartments in better locations.

Aside from producing great deals for some renters, however, what are the broader consequences of New York's rent-control system? To answer this question, we turn to the model we developed in Chapter 3: the supply and demand model.

Modeling a Price Ceiling

To see what can go wrong when a government imposes a price ceiling on an efficient market, consider Figure 5-1, which shows a simplified model of the market for apartments in New York. For the sake of simplicity, we imagine that all apartments are

FIGURE 5-1   **The Market for Apartments in the Absence of Government Controls**

Monthly rent (per apartment)	Quantity of apartments (millions)	
	Quantity demanded	Quantity supplied
$1,400	1.6	2.4
1,300	1.7	2.3
1,200	1.8	2.2
1,100	1.9	2.1
1,000	2.0	2.0
900	2.1	1.9
800	2.2	1.8
700	2.3	1.7
600	2.4	1.6

Without government intervention, the market for apartments reaches equilibrium at point E with a market rent of $1,000 per month and 2 million apartments rented.

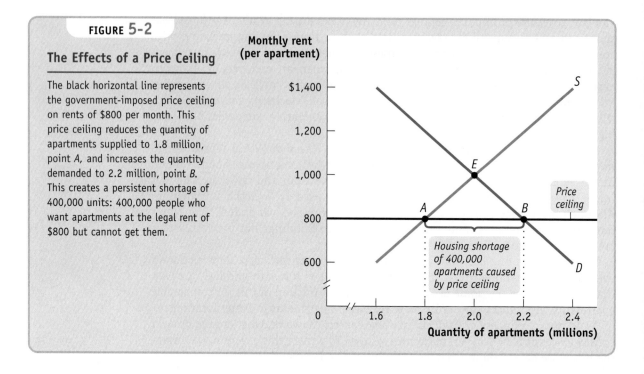

FIGURE 5-2

The Effects of a Price Ceiling

The black horizontal line represents the government-imposed price ceiling on rents of $800 per month. This price ceiling reduces the quantity of apartments supplied to 1.8 million, point A, and increases the quantity demanded to 2.2 million, point B. This creates a persistent shortage of 400,000 units: 400,000 people who want apartments at the legal rent of $800 but cannot get them.

exactly the same and so would rent for the same price in an unregulated market. The table in the figure shows the demand and supply schedules; the demand and supply curves are shown on the left. We show the quantity of apartments on the horizontal axis and the monthly rent per apartment on the vertical axis. You can see that in an unregulated market the equilibrium would be at point *E:* 2 million apartments would be rented for $1,000 each per month.

Now suppose that the government imposes a price ceiling, limiting rents to a price below the equilibrium price—say, no more than $800.

Figure 5-2 shows the effect of the price ceiling, represented by the line at $800. At the enforced rental rate of $800, landlords have less incentive to offer apartments, so they won't be willing to supply as many as they would at the equilibrium rate of $1,000. They will choose point A on the supply curve, offering only 1.8 million apartments for rent, 200,000 fewer than in the unregulated market. At the same time, more people will want to rent apartments at a price of $800 than at the equilibrium price of $1,000; as shown at point B on the demand curve, at a monthly rent of $800 the quantity of apartments demanded rises to 2.2 million, 200,000 more than in the unregulated market and 400,000 more than are actually available at the price of $800. So there is now a persistent shortage of rental housing: at that price, 400,000 more people want to rent than are able to find apartments.

Do price ceilings always cause shortages? No. If a price ceiling is set above the equilibrium price, it won't have any effect. Suppose that the equilibrium rental rate on apartments is $1,000 per month and the city government sets a ceiling of $1,200. Who cares? In this case, the price ceiling won't be binding—it won't actually constrain market behavior—and it will have no effect.

How a Price Ceiling Causes Inefficiency

The housing shortage shown in Figure 5-2 is not merely annoying: like any shortage induced by price controls, it can be seriously harmful because it leads to inefficiency. In other words, there are gains from trade that go unrealized. Rent control, like all price ceilings, creates inefficiency in at least four distinct ways. It reduces the quantity of apartments rented below the efficient level; it typically leads to misallocation of apartments among would-be renters; it leads to wasted time and effort as people search for apartments; and it leads landlords to maintain apartments in inefficiently low quality or condition. In addition to inefficiency, price ceilings give rise to illegal behavior as people try to circumvent them.

Deadweight loss is the loss in total surplus that occurs whenever an action or a policy reduces the quantity transacted below the efficient market equilibrium quantity.

Inefficiently Low Quantity   In Chapter 4 we learned that the market equilibrium of an efficient market leads to the "right" quantity of a good or service being bought and sold—that is, the quantity that maximizes the sum of producer and consumer surplus. Because rent controls reduce the number of apartments supplied, they reduce the number of apartments rented, too. Figure 5-3 shows the implications for total surplus. Recall that total surplus is the sum of the area above the supply curve and below the demand curve. If the only effect of rent control was to reduce the number of apartments available, it would cause a loss of surplus equal to the area of the shaded triangle in the figure. The area represented by that triangle has a special name in economics, **deadweight loss:** the lost surplus associated with the transactions that no longer occur due to the market intervention. In this example, the deadweight loss is the lost surplus associated with the apartment rentals that no longer occur due to the price ceiling, a loss that is experienced by both disappointed renters and frustrated landlords. Economists often call triangles like the one in Figure 5-3 a *deadweight-loss triangle.*

Deadweight loss is a key concept in economics, one that we will encounter whenever an action or a policy leads to a reduction in the quantity transacted below the efficient market equilibrium quantity. It is important to realize that deadweight loss is a *loss to society*—it is a reduction in total surplus, a loss in surplus that accrues to no one as a gain. It is not the same as a loss in surplus to one person that then accrues as a gain to someone else, what an economist would call a *transfer of surplus* from one person to another. For an example of how a price ceiling leads to a transfer of surplus between renters and landlords and the deadweight loss that arises, see For Inquiring Minds on the next page.

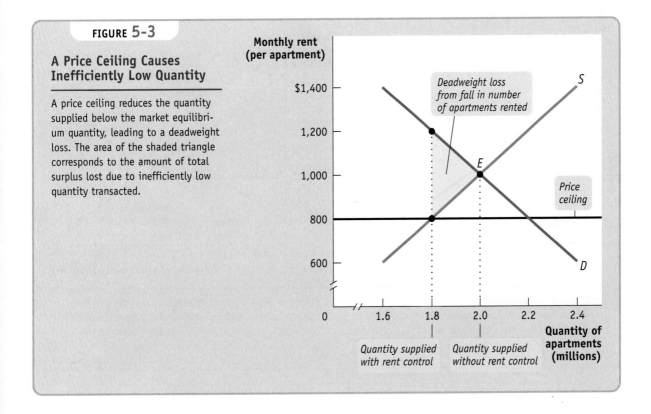

FIGURE 5-3

A Price Ceiling Causes Inefficiently Low Quantity

A price ceiling reduces the quantity supplied below the market equilibrium quantity, leading to a deadweight loss. The area of the shaded triangle corresponds to the amount of total surplus lost due to inefficiently low quantity transacted.

Winners, Losers, and Rent Control

Price controls create winners and losers: some people benefit from the policy but others are made worse off.

In New York City, some of the biggest beneficiaries of rent control are affluent tenants who have lived for decades in choice apartments that would now command very high rents. These winners include celebrities like the pop singer Cyndi Lauper, who in 2005 was paying only $989 a month for an apartment that would have been worth $3,750 if unregulated. There is also the classic case of the actress Mia Farrow's apartment, which, when it lost its rent-control status, rose from the bargain rate of $2,900 per month to $8,000. Ironically, in cases like these, the losers are the working-class renters the system was intended to help.

We can use the concepts of consumer and producer surplus, which you learned about in Chapter 4, to evaluate graphically the winners and the losers from rent control. Panel (a) of Figure 5-4 shows the con-

sumer surplus and producer surplus in the equilibrium of the unregulated market for apartments—before rent control. Recall that the consumer surplus, represented by the area below the demand curve and above the price, is the total net gain to consumers in the market equilibrium. Likewise, producer surplus, represented by the area above the supply curve and below the price, is the total net gain to producers in the market equilibrium.

Panel (b) of this figure shows the consumer and producer surplus in the market after the price ceiling of $800 has been imposed. As you can see, for those consumers who can still obtain apartments under rent control, consumer surplus has increased. These renters are clearly winners: those who obtain an apartment at $800, paying $200 less than the unregulated market price. These people receive a direct transfer of surplus from landlords in the form of lower rent. But not all renters win:

there are fewer apartments to rent now than if the market had remained unregulated, making it hard, if not impossible, for some to find a place to call home. Without direct calculation of the surpluses gained and lost, it is generally unclear whether renters as a whole are made better or worse off by rent control. What we can say is that the greater the deadweight loss—the larger the reduction in the quantity of apartments rented—the more likely it is that renters as a whole lose.

However, we can say unambiguously that landlords are worse off: producer surplus has clearly decreased. Landlords who continue to rent out their apartments get $200 a month less in rent, and others withdraw their apartments from the market altogether. The deadweight-loss triangle, shaded yellow in panel (b), represents the value lost to both renters and landlords from rentals that essentially vanish thanks to rent control.

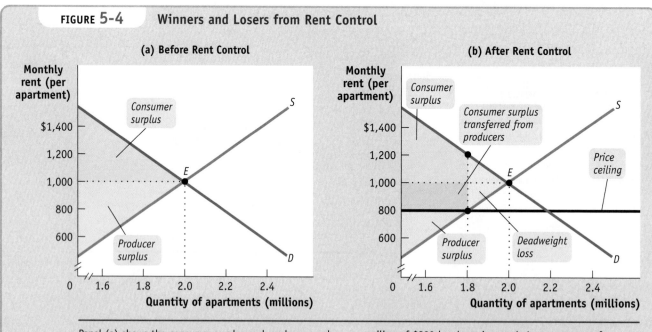

FIGURE 5-4   Winners and Losers from Rent Control

Panel (a) shows the consumer surplus and producer surplus in the equilibrium of the unregulated market for apartments—before rent control. Panel (b) shows the consumer and producer surplus in the market after a price

ceiling of $800 has been imposed. As you can see, for those consumers who can still obtain apartments under rent control, consumer surplus has increased but producer surplus and total surplus have decreased.

Deadweight loss is not the only type of inefficiency that arises from a price ceiling. The types of inefficiency created by rent control go beyond reducing the quantity of apartments available. These additional inefficiencies—inefficient allocation to consumers, wasted resources, and inefficiently low quality—lead to a loss of surplus over and above the deadweight loss.

Inefficient Allocation to Consumers Rent control doesn't just lead to too few apartments being available. It can also lead to misallocation of the apartments that are available: people who badly need a place to live may not be able to find an apartment, while some apartments may be occupied by people with much less urgent needs.

In the case shown in Figure 5-2, 2.2 million people would like to rent an apartment at $800 per month, but only 1.8 million apartments are available. Of those 2.2 million who are seeking an apartment, some want an apartment badly and are willing to pay a high price to get one. Others have a less urgent need and are only willing to pay a low price, perhaps because they have alternative housing. An efficient allocation of apartments would reflect these differences: people who really want an apartment will get one and people who aren't all that anxious to find an apartment won't. In an inefficient distribution of apartments, the opposite will happen: some people who are not especially anxious to find an apartment will get one and others who are very anxious to find an apartment won't. Because people usually get apartments through luck or personal connections under rent control, it generally results in an **inefficient allocation to consumers** of the few apartments available.

To see the inefficiency involved, consider the plight of the Lees, a family with young children who have no alternative housing and would be willing to pay up to $1,500 for an apartment—but are unable to find one. Also consider George, a retiree who lives most of the year in Florida but still has a lease on the New York apartment he moved into 40 years ago. George pays $800 per month for this apartment, but if the rent were even slightly more—say, $850—he would give it up and stay with his children when he is in New York.

This allocation of apartments—George has one and the Lees do not—is a missed opportunity: there is a way to make the Lees and George both better off at no additional cost. The Lees would be happy to pay George, say, $1,200 a month to sublease his apartment, which he would happily accept since the apartment is worth no more than $849 a month to him. George would prefer the money he gets from the Lees to keeping his apartment; the Lees would prefer to have the apartment rather than the money. So both would be made better off by this transaction—and nobody else would be made worse off.

Generally, if people who really want apartments could sublease them from people who are less eager to live there, both those who gain apartments and those who trade their occupancy for money would be better off. However, subletting is illegal under rent control because it would occur at prices above the price ceiling. The fact that subletting is illegal doesn't mean it never happens. In fact, chasing down illegal subletting is a major business for New York private investigators. A 2007 report in the *New York Times* described how private investigators use hidden cameras and other tricks to prove that the legal tenants in rent-controlled apartments actually live in the suburbs, or even in other states, and have sublet their apartments at two or three times the controlled rent. This subletting is a kind of illegal activity, which we will discuss shortly. For now, just notice that landlords' pursuit of illegal subletting surely discourages the practice, so there isn't enough subletting to eliminate the inefficient allocation of apartments.

Wasted Resources Another reason a price ceiling causes inefficiency is that it leads to **wasted resources**: people expend money, effort, and time to cope with the shortages caused by the price ceiling. Back in 1979, U.S. price controls on gasoline led to shortages that forced millions of Americans to spend hours each week waiting in lines

---

Price ceilings often lead to inefficiency in the form of **inefficient allocation to consumers**: people who want the good badly and are willing to pay a high price don't get it, and those who care relatively little about the good and are only willing to pay a low price do get it.

Price ceilings typically lead to inefficiency in the form of **wasted resources**: people expend money, effort, and time to cope with the shortages caused by the price ceiling.

> Price ceilings often lead to inefficiency in that the goods being offered are of **inefficiently low quality**: sellers offer low-quality goods at a low price even though buyers would prefer a higher quality at a higher price.

at gas stations. The opportunity cost of the time spent in gas lines—the wages not earned, the leisure time not enjoyed—constituted wasted resources from the point of view of consumers and of the economy as a whole. Because of rent control, the Lees will spend all their spare time for several months searching for an apartment, time they would rather have spent working or in family activities. That is, there is an opportunity cost to the Lees' prolonged search for an apartment—the leisure or income they had to forgo. If the market for apartments worked freely, the Lees would quickly find an apartment at the equilibrium rent of $1,000, leaving them time to earn more or to enjoy themselves—an outcome that would make them better off without making anyone else worse off. Again, rent control creates missed opportunities.

Inefficiently Low Quality Yet another way a price ceiling causes inefficiency is by causing goods to be of inefficiently low quality. **Inefficiently low quality** means that sellers offer low-quality goods at a low price even though buyers would rather have higher quality and are willing to pay a higher price for it.

Again, consider rent control. Landlords have no incentive to provide better conditions because they cannot raise rents to cover their repair costs but are able to find tenants easily. In many cases, tenants would be willing to pay much more for improved conditions than it would cost for the landlord to provide them—for example, the upgrade of an antiquated electrical system that cannot safely run air conditioners or computers. But

FOR INQUIRING MINDS

Rent Control, Mumbai Style

How far would you go to keep a rent-controlled apartment? Some tenants in the city of Mumbai, India, went very far indeed. According to a *Wall Street Journal* article, in May 2006 three people were killed when four floors in a rent-controlled apartment building in Mumbai collapsed. Despite demands by the city government to vacate the deteriorated building, 58 other tenants refused to leave. They stayed put even after having their electricity and water shut off, being locked out of their apartments, and surviving a police raid on the building. Tenants camped out on the building's veranda, vowing not to give up.

Not all of these tenants were desperately poor and lacking other options. One rent-controlled tenant is the owner of a thriving textile business who was paying a total of $8.50 a month for a spacious two-bedroom apartment. (Luxury apartments in Mumbai can go for thousands of dollars a month.)

Although it's a world away, the dynamics of rent control in Mumbai are a lot like those in New York (although Mumbai has clearly had a much more extreme experience). Rent control began in Mumbai in 1947, to address a critical shortage of

In Mumbai, rent control has led to a steep deterioration in housing quality.

housing caused by a flood of refugees fleeing conflict between Hindus and Muslims. Clearly intended to be a temporary measure, it was so popular politically that it has been extended 20 times and now applies to about 60% of the buildings in the city's center. Tenants pass apartments on to their heirs or sell the right to occupy to other tenants. Despite the fact that land prices in Mumbai surged more than 30% in 2005, landlords of rent-controlled buildings have suffered financially, with the result that across the city prime buildings have been abandoned to decay, even though half of the city's 12 million residents live in slums because of a lack of new housing.

Christie Johnson/Chicago Tribune/MCT/Newscom

any additional payment for such improvements would be legally considered a rent increase, which is prohibited. Indeed, rent-controlled apartments are notoriously badly maintained, rarely painted, subject to frequent electrical and plumbing problems, sometimes even hazardous to inhabit. As one former manager of Manhattan buildings described: "At unregulated apartments we'd do most things that the tenants requested. But on the rent-regulated units, we did absolutely only what the law required. . . . We had a perverse incentive to make those tenants unhappy. With regulated apartments, the ultimate objective is to get people out of the building."

This whole situation is a missed opportunity—some tenants would be happy to pay for better conditions, and landlords would be happy to provide them for payment. But such an exchange would occur only if the market were allowed to operate freely.

Black Markets And that leads us to a last aspect of price ceilings: the incentive they provide for illegal activities, specifically the emergence of **black markets.** We have already described one kind of black market activity—illegal subletting by tenants. But it does not stop there. Clearly, there is a temptation for a landlord to say to a potential tenant, "Look, you can have the place if you slip me an extra few hundred in cash each month"—and for the tenant to agree, if he or she is one of those people who would be willing to pay much more than the maximum legal rent.

What's wrong with black markets? In general, it's a bad thing if people break *any* law, because it encourages disrespect for the law in general. Worse yet, in this case illegal activity worsens the position of those who try to be honest. If the Lees are scrupulous about upholding the rent-control law but other people—who may need an apartment less than the Lees—are willing to bribe landlords, the Lees may *never* find an apartment.

> A **black market** is a market in which goods or services are bought and sold illegally—either because it is illegal to sell them at all or because the prices charged are legally prohibited by a price ceiling.

So Why Are There Price Ceilings?

We have seen three common results of price ceilings:

- A persistent shortage of the good
- Inefficiency arising from this persistent shortage in the form of inefficiently low quantity (deadweight loss), inefficient allocation of the good to consumers, resources wasted in searching for the good, and the inefficiently low quality of the good offered for sale
- The emergence of illegal, black market activity

Given these unpleasant consequences, why do governments still sometimes impose price ceilings? Why does rent control, in particular, persist in New York?

One answer is that although price ceilings may have adverse effects, they do benefit some people. In practice, New York's rent-control rules—which are more complex than our simple model—hurt most residents but give a small minority of renters much cheaper housing than they would get in an unregulated market. And those who benefit from the controls are typically better organized and more vocal than those who are harmed by them.

Also, when price ceilings have been in effect for a long time, buyers may not have a realistic idea of what would happen without them. In our previous example, the rental rate in an unregulated market (Figure 5-1) would be only 25% higher than in the regulated market (Figure 5-2): $1,000 instead of $800. But how would renters know that? Indeed, they might have heard about black market transactions at much higher prices—the Lees or some other family paying George $1,200 or more—and would not realize that these black market prices are much higher than the price that would prevail in a fully unregulated market.

A last answer is that government officials often do not understand supply and demand analysis! It is a great mistake to suppose that economic policies in the real world are always sensible or well informed.

➤ECONOMICS IN ACTION

Hard Shopping in Caracas

Supermarket shopping in Caracas, Venezuela, reported the *New York Times* in February 2007, "is a bizarre experience. Shelves are fully stocked with Scotch whiskey, Argentine wines and imported cheeses like brie and Camembert, but basic staples like black beans and desirable cuts of beef like sirloin are often absent." Why? Because of price controls.

Since 1998, Venezuela has been governed by Hugo Chavez, a populist president who has routinely denounced the nation's economic elite and pursued policies favoring the poor and working classes. Among those policies were price controls on basic foods such as beans, sugar, beef, and chicken, intended to hold down the cost of living. These policies led to sporadic shortages beginning in 2003, but the shortages became much more severe in 2006. On one side, generous government policies led to higher spending by consumers and sharply rising prices for goods that weren't subject to price controls. The result was a big increase in demand for price-controlled goods. On the other side, a sharp decline in the value of Venezuela's currency led to a fall in imports of foreign food. The result was empty shelves in the nation's food stores.

The Venezuelan government responded by accusing food producers, wholesalers, and grocers of profiteering, threatening to seize control of supermarkets if they didn't make more food available. Yet even Mercal, a government-owned grocery chain, had empty shelves.

The government also instituted rationing, restricting shoppers' purchases of sugar to two large bags. Predictably, reported the *Times,* "a black market in sugar has developed among street vendors."

All in all, food shortages in Venezuela offer a textbook example both of why governments sometimes think price ceilings would be a good idea and of why they're usually wrong. ▲

< < < < < < < < < < <

➤ CHECK YOUR UNDERSTANDING 5-1

1. On game days, homeowners near Middletown University's stadium used to rent parking spaces in their driveways to fans at a going rate of $11. A new town ordinance now sets a maximum parking fee of $7. Use the accompanying supply and demand diagram to explain how each of the following corresponds to a price-ceiling concept.

   a. Some homeowners now think it's not worth the hassle to rent out spaces.

   b. Some fans who used to carpool to the game now drive alone.

   c. Some fans can't find parking and leave without seeing the game.

   Explain how each of the following adverse effects arises from the price ceiling.

   d. Some fans now arrive several hours early to find parking.

   e. Friends of homeowners near the stadium regularly attend games, even if they aren't big fans. But some serious fans have given up because of the parking situation.

   f. Some homeowners rent spaces for more than $7 but pretend that the buyers are nonpaying friends or family.

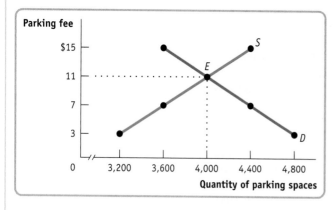

2. True or false? Explain your answer. A price ceiling below the equilibrium price of an otherwise efficient market does the following:

   a. Increases quantity supplied

   b. Makes some people who want to consume the good worse off

   c. Makes all producers worse off

3. Which of the following create deadweight loss? Which do not and are simply a transfer of surplus from one person to another? Explain your answer.

a. You have been evicted from your rent-controlled apartment after the landlord discovered your pet boa constrictor. The apartment is quickly rented to someone else at the same price. You and the new renter do not necessarily have the same willingness to pay for the apartment.

b. In a contest, you won a ticket to a jazz concert. But you can't go to the concert because of an exam, and the terms of the contest do not allow you to sell the ticket or give it to someone else. Would your answer to this question change if you could not sell the ticket but could give it to someone else?

c. Your school's dean of students, who is a proponent of a low-fat diet, decrees that ice cream can no longer be served on campus.

d. Your ice cream cone falls on the ground and your dog eats it. (Take the liberty of counting your dog as a member of society, and that, if he could, your dog would be willing to pay the same amount for the ice cream cone as you.)

Solutions appear at back of book.

> The **minimum wage** is a legal floor on the wage rate, which is the market price of labor.

Price Floors

Sometimes governments intervene to push market prices up instead of down. *Price floors* have been widely legislated for agricultural products, such as wheat and milk, as a way to support the incomes of farmers. Historically, there were also price floors on such services as trucking and air travel, although these were phased out by the U.S. government in the 1970s. If you have ever worked in a fast-food restaurant, you are likely to have encountered a price floor: governments in the United States and many other countries maintain a lower limit on the hourly wage rate of a worker's labor—that is, a floor on the price of labor—called the **minimum wage.**

Just like price ceilings, price floors are intended to help some people but generate predictable and undesirable side effects. Figure 5-5 shows hypothetical supply and demand curves for butter. Left to itself, the market would move to equilibrium at

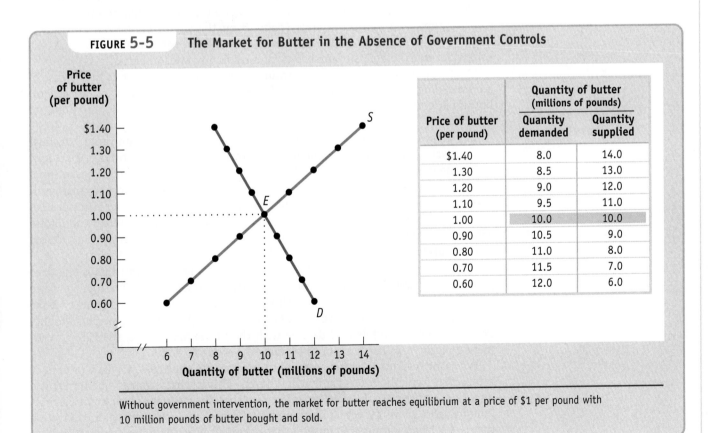

FIGURE 5-5   The Market for Butter in the Absence of Government Controls

Price of butter (per pound)	Quantity of butter (millions of pounds)	
	Quantity demanded	Quantity supplied
$1.40	8.0	14.0
1.30	8.5	13.0
1.20	9.0	12.0
1.10	9.5	11.0
1.00	10.0	10.0
0.90	10.5	9.0
0.80	11.0	8.0
0.70	11.5	7.0
0.60	12.0	6.0

Without government intervention, the market for butter reaches equilibrium at a price of $1 per pound with 10 million pounds of butter bought and sold.

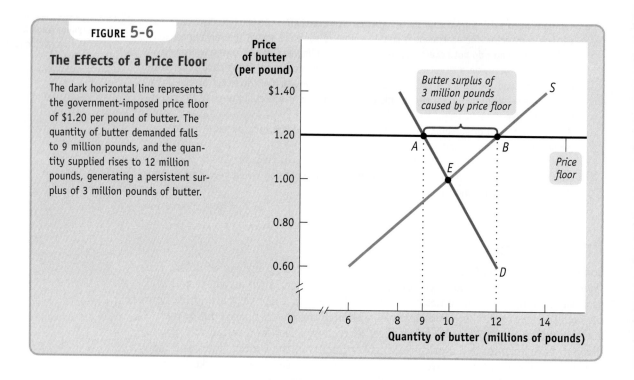

FIGURE 5-6

The Effects of a Price Floor

The dark horizontal line represents the government-imposed price floor of $1.20 per pound of butter. The quantity of butter demanded falls to 9 million pounds, and the quantity supplied rises to 12 million pounds, generating a persistent surplus of 3 million pounds of butter.

point *E*, with 10 million pounds of butter bought and sold at a price of $1 per pound.

Now suppose that the government, in order to help dairy farmers, imposes a price floor on butter of $1.20 per pound. Its effects are shown in Figure 5-6, where the line at $1.20 represents the price floor. At a price of $1.20 per pound, producers would want to supply 12 million pounds (point *B* on the supply curve) but consumers would want to buy only 9 million pounds (point *A* on the demand curve). So the price floor leads to a persistent surplus of 3 million pounds of butter.

Does a price floor always lead to an unwanted surplus? No. Just as in the case of a price ceiling, the floor may not be binding—that is, it may be irrelevant. If the equilibrium price of butter is $1 per pound but the floor is set at only $0.80, the floor has no effect.

But suppose that a price floor is binding: what happens to the unwanted surplus? The answer depends on government policy. In the case of agricultural price floors, governments buy up unwanted surplus. As a result, the U.S. government has at times found itself warehousing thousands of tons of butter, cheese, and other farm products. (The European Commission, which administers price floors for a number of European countries, once found itself the owner of a so-called butter mountain, equal in weight to the entire population of Austria.) The government then has to find a way to dispose of these unwanted goods.

Some countries pay exporters to sell products at a loss overseas; this is standard procedure for the European Union. The United States gives surplus food away to schools, which use the products in school lunches (see For Inquiring Minds on the next page). In some cases, governments have actually destroyed the surplus production. To avoid the problem of dealing with the unwanted surplus, the U.S. government typically pays farmers not to produce the products at all.

When the government is not prepared to purchase the unwanted surplus, a price floor means that would-be sellers cannot find buyers. This is what happens when there is a price floor on the wage rate paid for an hour of labor, the *minimum wage*: when the minimum wage is above the equilibrium wage rate, some people who are willing to work—that is, sell labor—cannot find buyers—that is, employers—willing to give them jobs.

Price Floors and School Lunches

When you were in grade school, did your school offer free or very cheap lunches? If so, you were probably a beneficiary of price floors.

Where did all the cheap food come from? During the 1930s, when the U.S. economy was going through the Great Depression, a prolonged economic slump, prices were low and farmers were suffering severely. In an effort to help rural Americans, the U.S. government imposed price floors on a number of agricultural products. The system of agricultural price floors—officially called price support programs—continues to this day. Among the products subject to price support are sugar and various dairy products; at times grains, beef, and pork have also had a minimum price.

The big problem with any attempt to impose a price floor is that it creates a surplus. To some extent the U.S. Department of Agriculture has tried to head off surpluses by taking steps to reduce supply; for example, by paying farmers *not* to grow crops. As a last resort, however, the U.S. government has been willing to buy up the surplus, taking the excess supply off the market.

But then what? The government has to find a way to get rid of the agricultural products it has bought. It can't just sell them: that would depress market prices, forcing the government to buy the stuff right back. So it has to give it away in ways that don't depress market prices. One of the ways it does this is by giving surplus food, free, to school lunch programs.

These gifts are known as "bonus foods." Along with financial aid, bonus foods are what allow many school districts to provide free or very cheap lunches to their students. Is this a story with a happy ending?

Not really. Nutritionists, concerned about growing child obesity in the United States, place part of the blame on those bonus foods. Schools get whatever the government has too much of—and that has tended to include a lot of dairy products, beef, and corn, and not much in the way of fresh vegetables or fruit. As a result, school lunches that make extensive use of bonus foods tend to be very high in fat and calories. So this is a case in which there is such a thing as a free lunch—but this lunch may be bad for your health.

How a Price Floor Causes Inefficiency

The persistent surplus that results from a price floor creates missed opportunities—inefficiencies—that resemble those created by the shortage that results from a price ceiling. These include deadweight loss from inefficiently low quantity, inefficient allocation of sales among sellers, wasted resources, inefficiently high quality, and the temptation to break the law by selling below the legal price.

Inefficiently Low Quantity Because a price floor raises the price of a good to consumers, it reduces the quantity of that good demanded; because sellers can't sell more units of a good than buyers are willing to buy, a price floor reduces the quantity of a good bought and sold below the market equilibrium quantity and leads to a deadweight loss. Notice that this is the *same* effect as a price ceiling. You might be tempted to think that a price floor and a price ceiling have opposite effects, but both have the effect of reducing the quantity of a good bought and sold (see Pitfalls to the right).

Since the equilibrium of an efficient market maximizes the sum of consumer and producer surplus, a price floor that reduces the quantity below the equilibrium quantity reduces total surplus. Figure 5-7 on the next page shows the implications for total surplus of a price floor on the price of butter. Total surplus is the sum of the area above the supply curve and below the demand curve. By reducing the quantity of butter sold, a price floor causes a deadweight loss equal to the area of the shaded triangle in the figure. As in the case of a price ceiling, however, deadweight loss is only one of the forms of inefficiency that the price control creates.

CEILINGS, FLOORS, AND QUANTITIES

A price ceiling pushes the price of a good *down*. A price floor pushes the price of a good *up*. So it's easy to assume that the effects of a price floor are the opposite of the effects of a price ceiling. In particular, if a price ceiling reduces the quantity of a good bought and sold, doesn't a price floor increase the quantity?

No, it doesn't. In fact, both floors and ceilings reduce the quantity bought and sold. Why? When the quantity of a good supplied isn't equal to the quantity demanded, the actual quantity sold is determined by the "short side" of the market—whichever quantity is less. If sellers don't want to sell as much as buyers want to buy, it's the sellers who determine the actual quantity sold, because buyers can't force unwilling sellers to sell. If buyers don't want to buy as much as sellers want to sell, it's the buyers who determine the actual quantity sold, because sellers can't force unwilling buyers to buy.

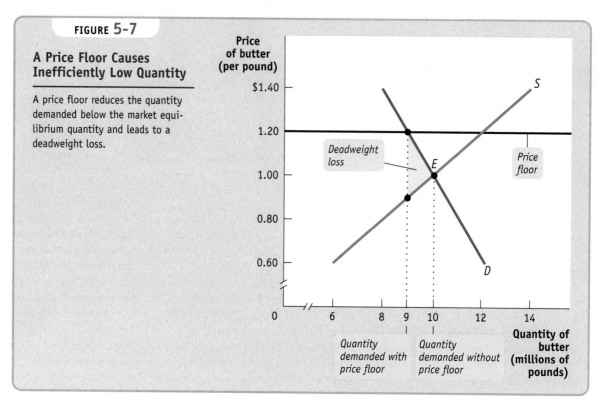

FIGURE 5-7

A Price Floor Causes Inefficiently Low Quantity

A price floor reduces the quantity demanded below the market equilibrium quantity and leads to a deadweight loss.

Inefficient Allocation of Sales Among Sellers

Like a price ceiling, a price floor can lead to *inefficient allocation*—but in this case **inefficient allocation of sales among sellers** rather than inefficient allocation to consumers.

An episode from the Belgian movie *Rosetta,* a realistic fictional story, illustrates the problem of inefficient allocation of selling opportunities quite well. Like many European countries, Belgium has a high minimum wage, and jobs for young people are scarce. At one point Rosetta, a young woman who is very anxious to work, loses her job at a fast-food stand because the owner of the stand replaces her with his son—a very reluctant worker. Rosetta would be willing to work for less money, and with the money he would save, the owner could give his son an allowance and let him do something else. But to hire Rosetta for less than the minimum wage would be illegal.

Wasted Resources

Also like a price ceiling, a price floor generates inefficiency by *wasting resources*. The most graphic examples involve government purchases of the unwanted surpluses of agricultural products caused by price floors. The surplus production is sometimes destroyed, which is pure waste; in other cases the stored produce goes, as officials euphemistically put it, "out of condition" and must be thrown away.

Price floors also lead to wasted time and effort. Consider the minimum wage. Would-be workers who spend many hours searching for jobs, or waiting in line in the hope of getting jobs, play the same role in the case of price floors as hapless families searching for apartments in the case of price ceilings.

Inefficiently High Quality

Again like price ceilings, price floors lead to inefficiency in the quality of goods produced.

We saw that when there is a price ceiling, suppliers produce products that are of inefficiently low quality: buyers prefer higher-quality products and are willing to pay for them, but sellers refuse to improve the quality of their products because the price ceiling prevents their being compensated for doing so. This same logic applies to price floors, but in reverse: suppliers offer goods of **inefficiently high quality.**

How can this be? Isn't high quality a good thing? Yes, but only if it is worth the cost. Suppose that suppliers spend a lot to make goods of very high quality but that this quality isn't worth much to consumers, who would rather receive the money spent on that quality in the form of a lower price. This represents a missed opportunity: suppliers and buyers could make a mutually beneficial deal in which buyers got goods of lower quality for a much lower price.

Price floors lead to **inefficient allocation of sales among sellers:** those who would be willing to sell the good at the lowest price are not always those who actually manage to sell it.

Price floors often lead to inefficiency in that goods of **inefficiently high quality** are offered: sellers offer high-quality goods at a high price, even though buyers would prefer a lower quality at a lower price.

A good example of the inefficiency of excessive quality comes from the days when transatlantic airfares were set artificially high by international treaty. Forbidden to compete for customers by offering lower ticket prices, airlines instead offered expensive services, like lavish in-flight meals that went largely uneaten. At one point the regulators tried to restrict this practice by defining maximum service standards—for example, that snack service should consist of no more than a sandwich. One airline then introduced what it called a "Scandinavian Sandwich," a towering affair that forced the convening of another conference to define *sandwich*. All of this was wasteful, especially considering that what passengers really wanted was less food and lower airfares.

Since the deregulation of U.S. airlines in the 1970s, American passengers have experienced a large decrease in ticket prices accompanied by a decrease in the quality of in-flight service—smaller seats, lower-quality food, and so on. Everyone complains about the service—but thanks to lower fares, the number of people flying on U.S. carriers has grown several hundred percent since airline deregulation.

Illegal Activity Finally, like price ceilings, price floors provide incentives for illegal activity. For example, in countries where the minimum wage is far above the equilibrium wage rate, workers desperate for jobs sometimes agree to work off the books for employers who conceal their employment from the government—or bribe the government inspectors. This practice, known in Europe as "black labor," is especially common in Southern European countries such as Italy and Spain (see Economics in Action on the next page).

So Why Are There Price Floors?

To sum up, a price floor creates various negative side effects:

- A persistent surplus of the good
- Inefficiency arising from the persistent surplus in the form of inefficiently low quantity (deadweight loss), inefficient allocation of sales among sellers, wasted resources, and an inefficiently high level of quality offered by suppliers
- The temptation to engage in illegal activity, particularly bribery and corruption of government officials

GLOBAL COMPARISON   CHECK OUT OUR LOW, LOW WAGES!

The minimum wage rate in the United States, as you can see in this graph, is actually quite low compared with other rich countries. Since minimum wages are set in national currency—the British minimum wage is set in British pounds, the French minimum wage is set in euros, and so on—the comparison depends on the exchange rate on any given day. As of November 1, 2007, Australia had a minimum wage about twice as high as the U.S. rate, with Ireland and France not far behind. You can see one effect of this difference in the supermarket checkout line. In the United States there is usually someone to bag your groceries—someone typically paid the minimum wage or at best slightly more. In Europe, where hiring a bagger is a lot more expensive, you're almost always expected to do the bagging yourself.

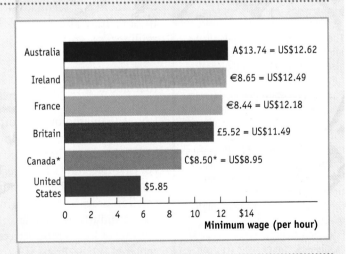

Source: Department of Enterprise, Trade and Employment (Ireland); Ministere du Travail, des Relations Sociales et de la Solidarite (France); Australian Fair Pay Commission (Australia); Department for Business, Enterprise and Regulatory Reform (Britain); Human Resources and Social Development Canada (Canada); Department of Labor (U.S.); Federal Reserve Bank of St. Louis (exchange rates as of 11/1/2007).

*The Canadian minimum wage varies by province from C$7.25 to C$8.50.

So why do governments impose price floors when they have so many negative side effects? The reasons are similar to those for imposing price ceilings. Government officials often disregard warnings about the consequences of price floors either because they believe that the relevant market is poorly described by the supply and demand model or, more often, because they do not understand the model. Above all, just as price ceilings are often imposed because they benefit some influential buyers of a good, price floors are often imposed because they benefit some influential sellers.

➤ *ECONOMICS IN ACTION*

"Black Labor" in Southern Europe

The best-known example of a price floor is the minimum wage. Most economists believe, however, that the minimum wage has relatively little effect on the job market in the United States, mainly because the floor is set so low. In 1968, the U.S. minimum wage was 53% of the average wage of blue-collar workers; by 2005, it had fallen to about 32%.

The situation is different, however, in many European countries, where minimum wages have been set much higher than in the United States. This has happened despite the fact that workers in most European countries are somewhat less productive than their American counterparts, which means that the equilibrium wage in Europe—the wage that would clear the labor market—is probably lower in Europe than in the United States. Moreover, European countries often require employers to pay for health and retirement benefits, which are more extensive and so more costly than comparable American benefits. These mandated benefits make the actual cost of employing a European worker considerably more than the worker's paycheck.

The result is that in Europe the price floor on labor is definitely binding: the minimum wage is well above the wage rate that would make the quantity of labor supplied by workers equal to the quantity of labor demanded by employers.

The persistent surplus that results from this price floor appears in the form of high unemployment—millions of workers, especially young workers, seek jobs but cannot find them. In countries where the enforcement of labor laws is lax, however, there is a second, entirely predictable result: widespread evasion of the law. In both Italy and Spain, officials believe there are hundreds of thousands, if not millions, of workers who are employed by companies that pay them less than the legal minimum, fail to provide the required health and retirement benefits, or both. In many cases the jobs are simply unreported: Spanish economists estimate that about a third of the country's reported unemployed are in the black labor market—working at unreported jobs. In fact, Spaniards waiting to collect checks from the unemployment office have been known to complain about the long lines that keep them from getting back to work!

Employers in these countries have also found legal ways to evade the wage floor. For example, Italy's labor regulations apply only to companies with 15 or more workers. This gives a big cost advantage to small Italian firms, many of which remain small in order to avoid paying higher wages and benefits. And sure enough, in some Italian industries there is an astonishing proliferation of tiny companies. For example, one of Italy's most successful industries is the manufacture of fine woolen cloth, centered in the Prato region. The average textile firm in that region employs only four workers! ▲

➤➤ **QUICK REVIEW**

➤ The most familiar price floor is the **minimum wage.** Price floors are also commonly imposed on agricultural goods.
➤ A price floor above the equilibrium price benefits successful sellers but causes predictable adverse effects such as a persistent surplus, which leads to four kinds of inefficiencies: deadweight loss from inefficiently low quantities, **inefficient allocation of sales among sellers,** wasted resources, and **inefficiently high quality.**
➤ Price floors encourage illegal activity, such as workers who work off the books, often leading to official corruption.

1. The state legislature mandates a price floor for gasoline of P_F per gallon. Assess the following statements and illustrate your answer using the figure provided.

   a. Proponents of the law claim it will increase the income of gas station owners. Opponents claim it will hurt gas station owners because they will lose customers.

   b. Proponents claim consumers will be better off because gas stations will provide better service. Opponents claim consumers will be generally worse off because they prefer to buy gas at cheaper prices.

   c. Proponents claim that they are helping gas station owners without hurting anyone else. Opponents claim that consumers are hurt and will end up doing things like buying gas in a nearby state or on the black market.

   Solutions appear at back of book.

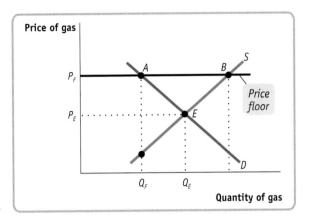

Controlling Quantities

In the 1930s, New York City instituted a system of licensing for taxicabs: only taxis with a "medallion" were allowed to pick up passengers. Because this system was intended to assure quality, medallion owners were supposed to maintain certain standards, including safety and cleanliness. A total of 11,787 medallions were issued, with taxi owners paying $10 for each medallion.

In 1995, there were still only 11,787 licensed taxicabs in New York, even though the city had meanwhile become the financial capital of the world, a place where hundreds of thousands of people in a hurry tried to hail a cab every day. (An additional 400 medallions were issued in 1995, and after several rounds of sales of additional medallions, today there are 13,089 medallions.)

The result of this restriction on the number of taxis was that a New York City taxi medallion became very valuable: if you wanted to operate a taxi in New York, you had to lease a medallion from someone else or buy one for a going price of several hundred thousand dollars.

It turns out that this story is not unique; other cities introduced similar medallion systems in the 1930s and, like New York, have issued few new medallions since. In San Francisco and Boston, as in New York, taxi medallions trade for six-figure prices.

A taxi medallion system is a form of **quantity control**, or **quota**, by which the government regulates the quantity of a good that can be bought and sold rather than the price at which it is transacted. The total amount of the good that can be transacted under the quantity control is called the **quota limit**. Typically, the government limits quantity in a market by issuing **licenses;** only people with a license can legally supply the good. A taxi medallion is just such a license. The government of New York City limits the number of taxi rides that can be sold by limiting the number of taxis to only those who hold medallions. There are many other cases of quantity controls, ranging from limits on how much foreign currency (for instance, British pounds or Mexican pesos) people are allowed to buy to the quantity of clams New Jersey fishing boats are allowed to catch. Notice, by the way, that although there are price controls on both sides of the equilibrium price—price ceilings and price floors—in the real world, quantity controls always set an upper, not a lower, limit on quantities. After all, nobody can be forced to buy or sell more than they want to!

A **quantity control,** or **quota,** is an upper limit on the quantity of some good that can be bought or sold. The total amount of the good that can be legally transacted is the **quota limit.**

A **license** gives its owner the right to supply a good.

The **demand price** of a given quantity is the price at which consumers will demand that quantity.

Some attempts to control quantities are undertaken for good economic reasons, some for bad ones. In many cases, as we will see, quantity controls introduced to address a temporary problem become politically hard to remove later because the beneficiaries don't want them abolished, even after the original reason for their existence is long gone. But whatever the reasons for such controls, they have certain predictable—and usually undesirable—economic consequences.

The Anatomy of Quantity Controls

To understand why a New York taxi medallion is worth so much money, we consider a simplified version of the market for taxi rides, shown in Figure 5-8. Just as we assumed in the analysis of rent control that all apartments are the same, we now suppose that all taxi rides are the same—ignoring the real-world complication that some taxi rides are longer, and so more expensive, than others. The table in the figure shows supply and demand schedules. The equilibrium—indicated by point E in the figure and by the shaded entries in the table—is a fare of $5 per ride, with 10 million rides taken per year. (You'll see in a minute why we present the equilibrium this way.)

The New York medallion system limits the number of taxis, but each taxi driver can offer as many rides as he or she can manage. (Now you know why New York taxi drivers are so aggressive!) To simplify our analysis, however, we will assume that a medallion system limits the number of taxi rides that can legally be given to 8 million per year.

Until now, we have derived the demand curve by answering questions of the form: "How many taxi rides will passengers want to take if the price is $5 per ride?" But it is possible to reverse the question and ask instead: "At what price will consumers want to buy 10 million rides per year?" The price at which consumers want to buy a given quantity—in this case, 10 million rides at $5 per ride—is the **demand price** of that quantity. You can see from the demand schedule in Figure 5-8 that the demand price of 6 million rides is $7 per ride, the demand price of 7 million rides is $6.50 per ride, and so on.

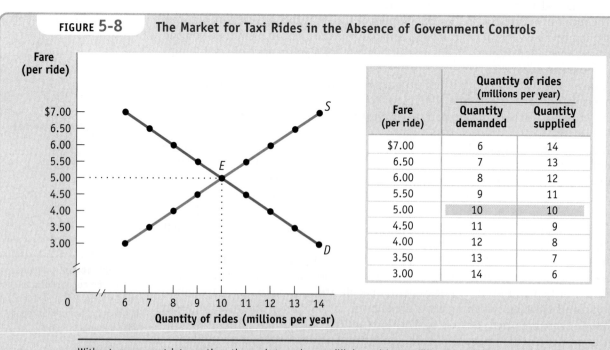

FIGURE 5-8   The Market for Taxi Rides in the Absence of Government Controls

Fare (per ride)	Quantity of rides (millions per year)	
	Quantity demanded	Quantity supplied
$7.00	6	14
6.50	7	13
6.00	8	12
5.50	9	11
5.00	10	10
4.50	11	9
4.00	12	8
3.50	13	7
3.00	14	6

Without government intervention, the market reaches equilibrium with 10 million rides taken per year at a fare of $5 per ride.

Similarly, the supply curve represents the answer to questions of the form: "How many taxi rides would taxi drivers supply at a price of $5 each?" But we can also reverse this question to ask: "At what price will suppliers be willing to supply 10 million rides per year?" The price at which suppliers will supply a given quantity—in this case, 10 million rides at $5 per ride—is the **supply price** of that quantity. We can see from the supply schedule in Figure 5-8 that the supply price of 6 million rides is $3 per ride, the supply price of 7 million rides is $3.50 per ride, and so on.

Now we are ready to analyze a quota. We have assumed that the city government limits the quantity of taxi rides to 8 million per year. Medallions, each of which carries the right to provide a certain number of taxi rides per year, are made available to selected people in such a way that a total of 8 million rides will be provided. Medallion holders may then either drive their own taxis or rent their medallions to others for a fee.

Figure 5-9 shows the resulting market for taxi rides, with the black vertical line at 8 million rides per year representing the quota limit. Because the quantity of rides is limited to 8 million, consumers must be at point *A* on the demand curve, corresponding to the shaded entry in the demand schedule: the demand price of 8 million rides is $6 per ride. Meanwhile, taxi drivers must be at point *B* on the supply curve, corresponding to the shaded entry in the supply schedule: the supply price of 8 million rides is $4 per ride.

But how can the price received by taxi drivers be $4 when the price paid by taxi riders is $6? The answer is that in addition to the market in taxi rides, there is also a market in medallions. Medallion-holders may not always want to drive their taxis: they may be ill or on vacation. Those who do not want to drive their own taxis will sell the right to use the medallion to someone else. So we need to consider two sets of transactions here, and so two prices: (1) the transactions in taxi rides and the price

> The **supply price** of a given quantity is the price at which producers will supply that quantity.

FIGURE 5-9   **Effect of a Quota on the Market for Taxi Rides**

Fare (per ride)	Quantity of rides (millions per year)	
	Quantity demanded	Quantity supplied
$7.00	6	14
6.50	7	13
6.00	8	12
5.50	9	11
5.00	10	10
4.50	11	9
4.00	12	8
3.50	13	7
3.00	14	6

The table shows the demand price and the supply price corresponding to each quantity: the price at which that quantity would be demanded and supplied, respectively. The city government imposes a quota of 8 million rides by selling licenses for only 8 million rides, represented by the black vertical line. The price paid by consumers rises to $6 per ride, the demand price of 8 million rides, shown by point *A*. The supply price of 8 million rides is only $4 per ride, shown by point *B*. The difference between these two prices is the quota rent per ride, the earnings that accrue to the owner of a license. The quota rent drives a wedge between the demand price and the supply price. And since the quota discourages mutually beneficial transactions, it creates a deadweight loss equal to the shaded triangle.

A quantity control, or quota, drives a **wedge** between the demand price and the supply price of a good; that is, the price paid by buyers ends up being higher than that received by sellers. The difference between the demand and supply price at the quota limit is the **quota rent,** the earnings that accrue to the license-holder from ownership of the right to sell the good. It is equal to the market price of the license when the licenses are traded.

at which these will occur, and (2) the transactions in medallions and the price at which these will occur. It turns out that since we are looking at two markets, the $4 and $6 prices will both be right.

To see how this all works, consider two imaginary New York taxi drivers, Sunil and Harriet. Sunil has a medallion but can't use it because he's recovering from a severely sprained wrist. So he's looking to rent his medallion out to someone else. Harriet doesn't have a medallion but would like to rent one. Furthermore, at any point in time there are many other people like Harriet who would like to rent a medallion. Suppose Sunil agrees to rent his medallion to Harriet. To make things simple, assume that any driver can give only one ride per day and that Sunil is renting his medallion to Harriet for one day. What rental price will they agree on?

To answer this question, we need to look at the transactions from the viewpoints of both drivers. Once she has the medallion, Harriet knows she can make $6 per day—the demand price of a ride under the quota. And she is willing to rent the medallion only if she makes at least $4 per day—the supply price of a ride under the quota. So Sunil cannot demand a rent of more than $2—the difference between $6 and $4. And if Harriet offered Sunil less than $2—say, $1.50—there would be other eager drivers willing to offer him more, up to $2. So, in order to get the medallion, Harriet must offer Sunil at least $2. Since the rent can be no more than $2 and no less than $2, it must be exactly $2.

It is no coincidence that $2 is exactly the difference between $6, the demand price of 8 million rides, and $4, the supply price of 8 million rides. In every case in which the supply of a good is legally restricted, there is a **wedge** between the demand price of the quantity transacted and the supply price of the quantity transacted. This wedge, illustrated by the double-headed arrow in Figure 5-9, has a special name: the **quota rent.** It is the earnings that accrue to the license-holder from ownership of a valuable commodity, the license. In the case of Sunil and Harriet, the quota rent of $2 goes to Sunil because he owns the license, and the remaining $4 from the total fare of $6 goes to Harriet.

So Figure 5-9 also illustrates the quota rent in the market for New York taxi rides. The quota limits the quantity of rides to 8 million per year, a quantity at which the demand price of $6 exceeds the supply price of $4. The wedge between these two prices, $2, is the quota rent that results from the restrictions placed on the quantity of taxi rides in this market.

But wait a second. What if Sunil doesn't rent out his medallion? What if he uses it himself? Doesn't this mean that he gets a price of $6? No, not really. Even if Sunil doesn't rent out his medallion, he could have rented it out, which means that the medallion has an *opportunity cost* of $2: if Sunil decides to use his own medallion and drive his own taxi rather than renting his medallion to Harriet, the $2 represents his opportunity cost of not renting out his medallion. That is, the $2 quota rent is now the rental income he forgoes by driving his own taxi. In effect, Sunil is in two businesses—the taxi-driving business and the medallion-renting business. He makes $4 per ride from driving his taxi and $2 per ride from renting out his medallion. It doesn't make any difference that in this particular case he has rented his medallion to himself! So regardless of whether the medallion owner uses the medallion himself or herself, or rents it to others, it is a valuable asset. And this is represented in the going price for a New York City taxi medallion: in February 2008, it was around $429,000.

Notice, by the way, that quotas—like price ceilings and price floors—don't always have a real effect. If the quota were set at 12 million rides—that is, above the equilibrium quantity in an unregulated market—it would have no effect because it would not be binding.

The Costs of Quantity Controls

Like price controls, quantity controls can have some predictable and undesirable side effects. The first is the by-now-familiar problem of inefficiency due to missed opportunities: quantity controls create deadweight loss by preventing mutually beneficial transactions from occurring, transactions that would benefit both buyers and sellers.

Looking back at Figure 5-9, you can see that starting at the quota limit of 8 million rides, New Yorkers would be willing to pay at least $5.50 per ride for an additional 1 million rides and that taxi drivers would be willing to provide those rides as long as they got at least $4.50 per ride. These are rides that would have taken place if there were no quota limit. The same is true for the next 1 million rides: New Yorkers would be willing to pay at least $5 per ride when the quantity of rides is increased from 9 to 10 million, and taxi drivers would be willing to provide those rides as long as they got at least $5 per ride. Again, these rides would have occurred without the quota limit. Only when the market has reached the unregulated market equilibrium quantity of 10 million rides are there no "missed-opportunity rides"—the quota limit of 8 million rides has caused 2 million "missed-opportunity rides." Generally, *as long as the demand price of a given quantity exceeds the supply price, there is a deadweight loss.* A buyer would be willing to buy the good at a price that the seller would be willing to accept, but such a transaction does not occur because it is forbidden by the quota. The deadweight loss arising from the 2 million in missed-opportunity rides is represented by the shaded triangle in Figure 5-9.

And because there are transactions that people would like to make but are not allowed to, quantity controls generate an incentive to evade them or even to break the law. New York's taxi industry again provides clear examples. Taxi regulation applies only to those drivers who are hailed by passengers on the street. A car service that makes prearranged pickups does not need a medallion. As a result, such hired cars provide much of the service that might otherwise be provided by taxis, as in other cities. In addition, there are substantial numbers of unlicensed cabs that simply defy the law by picking up passengers without a medallion. Because these cabs are illegal, their drivers are completely unregulated, and they generate a disproportionately large share of traffic accidents in New York City.

In fact, in 2004 the hardships caused by the limited number of New York taxis led city leaders to authorize an increase in the number of licensed taxis. In a series of sales, the city sold almost 1,000 new medallions, to bring the total number up to the current 13,089 medallions—a move that certainly cheered New York riders. But those who already owned medallions were less happy with the increase; they understood that the nearly 1,000 new taxis would reduce or eliminate the shortage of taxis. As a result, taxi drivers anticipated a decline in their revenues as they would no longer always be assured of finding willing customers. And, in turn, the value of a medallion would fall. So to placate the medallion owners, city officials also raised taxi fares: by 25% in 2004, and again—by a smaller percentage—in 2006. Although taxis are now easier to find, a ride now costs more—and that price increase slightly diminished the newfound cheer of New York taxi riders.

In sum, quantity controls typically create the following undesirable side effects:

- Deadweight loss because some mutually beneficial transactions don't occur

- Incentives for illegal activities

►*ECONOMICS IN ACTION*

The Clams of New Jersey

Forget the refineries along the Jersey Turnpike; one industry that New Jersey *really* dominates is clam fishing. In 2005 the Garden State supplied 71% of the country's surf clams, whose tongues are used in fried-clam dinners, and 92% of the quahogs, which are used to make clam chowder.

In the 1980s, however, excessive fishing threatened to wipe out New Jersey's clam beds. To save the resource, the U.S. government introduced a clam quota, which sets an overall limit on the number of bushels of clams that may be caught and allocates licenses to owners of fishing boats based on their historical catches.

Notice, by the way, that this is an example of a quota that is probably justified by broader economic and environmental considerations—unlike the New York taxicab quota, which has long since lost any economic rationale. Still, whatever its rationale, the New Jersey clam quota works the same way as any other quota.

Once the quota system was established, many boat owners stopped fishing for clams. They realized that rather than operate a boat part time, it was more profitable to sell or rent their licenses to someone else, who could then assemble enough licenses to operate a boat full time. Today, there are about 50 New Jersey boats fishing for clams; the license required to operate one is worth more than the boat itself. ▲

‹ ‹ ‹ ‹ ‹ ‹ ‹ ‹ ‹ ‹ ‹ ‹

➤ CHECK YOUR UNDERSTANDING 5-3

1. Suppose that the supply and demand for taxi rides is given by Figure 5-8 but the quota is set at 6 million rides instead of 8 million. Find the following and indicate them on Figure 5-8.
   a. The price of a ride
   b. The quota rent
   c. The deadweight loss
   d. Suppose the quota limit on taxi rides is increased to 9 million. What happens to the quota rent? To the deadweight loss?

2. Assume that the quota limit is 8 million rides. Suppose demand decreases due to a decline in tourism. What is the smallest parallel leftward shift in demand that would result in the quota no longer having an effect on the market? Illustrate your answer using Figure 5-8.

Solutions appear at back of book.

[>> A LOOK AHEAD •••

It's important to remember that the supply and demand model isn't a static model, limited to describing a market at only one point in time. Instead, it can also be used to understand how markets change over time in response to events. To understand the relationship between an event and the magnitude of its effect on a market, we now turn to the concept that's the subject of the next chapter, elasticity.]

SUMMARY

1. Even when a market is efficient, governments often intervene to pursue greater fairness or to please a powerful interest group. Interventions can take the form of **price controls** or quantity controls, both of which generate predictable and undesirable side effects consisting of various forms of inefficiency and illegal activity.

2. A **price ceiling,** a maximum market price below the equilibrium price, benefits successful buyers but creates persistent shortages. Because the price is maintained below the equilibrium price, the quantity demanded is increased and the quantity supplied is decreased compared to the equilibrium quantity. This leads to predictable problems: inefficiencies in the form of **deadweight loss** from inefficiently low quantity, **inefficient allocation to consumers, wasted resources,** and **inefficiently low quality.** It also encourages illegal activity as people turn to **black markets** to get the good. Because of these problems, price ceilings have generally lost favor as an economic policy tool. But some governments continue to impose them either because they don't understand the effects or because the price ceilings benefit some influential group.

3. A **price floor,** a minimum market price above the equilibrium price, benefits successful sellers but creates persistent surplus. Because the price is maintained above the equilibrium price, the quantity demanded is decreased and the quantity supplied is increased compared to the equilibrium quantity. This leads to predictable problems: inefficiencies in the form of deadweight loss from inefficiently low quantity, **inefficient allocation of sales among sellers,** wasted resources, and **inefficiently high quality.** It also encourages illegal activity and black markets. The most well known kind of price floor is the **minimum wage,** but price floors are also commonly applied to agricultural products.

4. **Quantity controls,** or **quotas,** limit the quantity of a good that can be bought or sold. The quantity allowed for sale is the **quota limit.** The government issues **licenses** to individuals, the right to sell a given quantity of the good. The owner of a license earns a **quota rent,** earnings that accrue from ownership of the right to sell the good. It is equal to the difference between the **demand price** at the quota limit, what consumers are willing to pay for that

quantity, and the **supply price** at the quota limit, what suppliers are willing to accept for that quantity. Economists say that a quota drives a **wedge** between the demand price and the supply price; this wedge is equal to the quota rent. Quantity controls lead to deadweight loss in addition to encouraging illegal activity.

KEY TERMS

Price controls, p. 118
Price ceiling, p. 118
Price floor, p. 118
Deadweight loss, p. 121
Inefficient allocation to consumers, p. 123
Wasted resources, p. 123
Inefficiently low quality, p. 124

Black markets, p. 125
Minimum wage, p. 127
Inefficient allocation of sales among sellers, p. 130
Inefficiently high quality, p. 130
Quantity control, p. 133
Quota, p. 133

Quota limit, p. 133
License, p. 133
Demand price, p. 134
Supply price, p. 135
Wedge, p. 136
Quota rent, p. 136

PROBLEMS

1. Suppose it is decided that rent control in New York City will be abolished and that market rents will now prevail. Assume that all rental units are identical and so are offered at the same rent. To address the plight of residents who may be unable to pay the market rent, an income supplement will be paid to all low-income households equal to the difference between the old controlled rent and the new market rent.

   a. Use a diagram to show the effect on the rental market of the elimination of rent control. What will happen to the quality and quantity of rental housing supplied?

   b. Use a second diagram to show the additional effect of the income-supplement policy on the market. What effect does it have on the market rent and quantity of rental housing supplied in comparison to your answers to part a?

   c. Are tenants better or worse off as a result of these policies? Are landlords better or worse off? Is society as a whole better or worse off?

   d. From a political standpoint, why do you think cities have been more likely to resort to rent control rather than a policy of income supplements to help low-income people pay for housing?

2. In order to ingratiate himself with voters, the mayor of Gotham City decides to lower the price of taxi rides. Assume, for simplicity, that all taxi rides are the same distance and therefore cost the same. The accompanying table shows the demand and supply schedules for taxi rides.

Fare (per ride)	Quantity of rides (millions per year)	
	Quantity demanded	Quantity supplied
$7.00	10	12
6.50	11	11
6.00	12	10
5.50	13	9
5.00	14	8
4.50	15	7

   a. Assume that there are no restrictions on the number of taxi rides that can be supplied (there is no medallion system). Find the equilibrium price and quantity.

   b. Suppose that the mayor sets a price ceiling at $5.50. How large is the shortage of rides? Illustrate with a diagram. Who loses and who benefits from this policy?

   c. Suppose that the stock market crashes and, as a result, people in Gotham City are poorer. This reduces the quantity of taxi rides demanded by 6 million rides per year at any given price. What effect will the mayor's new policy have now? Illustrate with a diagram.

   d. Suppose that the stock market rises and the demand for taxi rides returns to normal (that is, returns to the demand schedule given in the table). The mayor now decides to ingratiate himself with taxi drivers. He announces a policy in which operating licenses are given to existing taxi drivers; the number of licenses is restricted such that only 10 million rides per year can be given. Illustrate the effect of this policy on the market, and indicate the resulting price and quantity transacted. What is the quota rent per ride?

3. In the late eighteenth century, the price of bread in New York City was controlled, set at a predetermined price above the market price.

   a. Draw a diagram showing the effect of the policy. Did the policy act as a price ceiling or a price floor?

   b. What kinds of inefficiencies were likely to have arisen when the controlled price of bread was above the market price? Explain in detail.

   One year during this period, a poor wheat harvest caused a leftward shift in the supply of bread and therefore an increase in its market price. New York bakers found that the controlled price of bread in New York was below the market price.

   c. Draw a diagram showing the effect of the price control on the market for bread during this one-year period. Did the policy act as a price ceiling or a price floor?

d. What kinds of inefficiencies do you think occurred during this period? Explain in detail.

4. The U.S. Department of Agriculture (USDA) administers the price floor for milk, set at $0.10 per pound of milk. (The price floor is officially set at $9.90 per hundredweight of milk. One hundredweight is 100 pounds.) At that price, according to data from the USDA, the quantity of milk produced in 2003 by U.S. producers was 170 billion pounds, and the quantity demanded was 169 billion pounds. To support the price of milk at the price floor, the USDA had to buy up 1 billion pounds of milk. The accompanying diagram shows supply and demand curves illustrating the market for milk.

a. In the absence of a price floor, how much consumer surplus is created? How much producer surplus? What is the total surplus?

b. With the price floor at $0.10 per pound of milk, consumers buy 169 billion pounds of milk. How much consumer surplus is created now?

c. With the price floor at $0.10 per pound of milk, producers sell 170 billion pounds of milk (some to consumers and some to the USDA). How much producer surplus is created now?

d. How much money does the USDA spend on buying up surplus milk?

e. Taxes must be collected to pay for the purchases of surplus milk by the USDA. As a result, total surplus (producer plus consumer) is reduced by the amount the USDA spent on buying surplus milk. Using your answers for parts b–d, what is the total surplus when there is a price floor? How does this compare to the total surplus without a price floor from part a?

5. The accompanying table shows hypothetical demand and supply schedules for milk per year. The U.S. government decides that the incomes of dairy farmers should be maintained at a level that allows the traditional family dairy farm to survive. So it implements a price floor of $1 per pint by buying surplus milk until the market price is $1 per pint.

Price of milk (per pint)	Quantity of milk (millions of pints per year)	
	Quantity demanded	Quantity supplied
$1.20	550	850
1.10	600	800
1.00	650	750
0.90	700	700
0.80	750	650

a. In a diagram, show the deadweight loss from the inefficiently low quantity bought and sold.

b. How much surplus milk will be produced as a result of this policy?

c. What will be the cost to the government of this policy?

d. Since milk is an important source of protein and calcium, the government decides to provide the surplus milk it purchases to elementary schools at a price of only $0.60 per pint. Assume that schools will buy any amount of milk available at this low price. But parents now reduce their purchases of milk at any price by 50 million pints per year because they know their children are getting milk at school. How much will the dairy program now cost the government?

e. Explain how inefficiencies in the form of inefficient allocation to sellers and wasted resources arise from this policy.

6. As noted in the text, European governments tend to make greater use of price controls than does the U.S. government. For example, the French government sets minimum starting yearly wages for new hires who have completed *le bac*, certification roughly equivalent to a high school diploma. The demand schedule for new hires with *le bac* and the supply schedule for similarly credentialed new job seekers are given in the accompanying table. The price here—given in euros, the currency used in France—is the same as the yearly wage.

Wage (per year)	Quantity demanded (new job offers per year)	Quantity supplied (new job seekers per year)
€45,000	200,000	325,000
40,000	220,000	320,000
35,000	250,000	310,000
30,000	290,000	290,000
25,000	370,000	200,000

a. In the absence of government interference, what are the equilibrium wage and number of graduates hired per year? Illustrate with a diagram. Will there be anyone seeking a job at the equilibrium wage who is unable to find one—that is, will there be anyone who is involuntarily unemployed?

b. Suppose the French government sets a minimum yearly wage of €35,000. Is there any involuntary unemployment at this wage? If so, how much? Illustrate with a diagram. What if the minimum wage is set at €40,000? Also illustrate with a diagram.

c. Given your answer to part b and the information in the table, what do you think is the relationship between the level of involuntary unemployment and the level of the minimum wage? Who benefits from such a policy? Who loses? What is the missed opportunity here?

7. Until recently, the standard number of hours worked per week for a full-time job in France was 39 hours, just as in the United States. But in response to social unrest over high levels of involuntary unemployment, the French government instituted a 35-hour workweek—a worker could not work more than 35 hours per week even if both the worker and employer wanted it. The motivation behind this policy was that if current employees worked fewer hours, employers would be forced to hire more new workers. Assume that it is costly for employers to train new workers. French employers were greatly opposed to this policy and threatened to move their operations to neighboring countries that did not have such employment restrictions. Can you explain their attitude? Give an example of both an inefficiency and an illegal activity that are likely to arise from this policy.

8. For the last 70 years the U.S. government has used price supports to provide income assistance to American farmers. To implement these price supports, at times the government has used price floors, which it maintains by buying up the surplus farm products. At other times, it has used target prices, a policy by which the government gives the farmer an amount equal to the difference between the market price and the target price for each unit sold. Consider the market for corn depicted in the accompanying diagram.

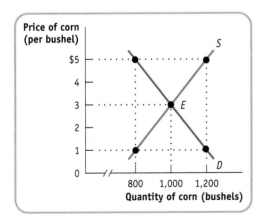

a. If the government sets a price floor of $5 per bushel, how many bushels of corn are produced? How many are purchased by consumers? By the government? How much does the program cost the government? How much revenue do corn farmers receive?

b. Suppose the government sets a target price of $5 per bushel for any quantity supplied up to 1,000 bushels. How many bushels of corn are purchased by consumers and at what price? By the government? How much does the

program cost the government? How much revenue do corn farmers receive?

c. Which of these programs (in parts a and b) costs corn consumers more? Which program costs the government more? Explain.

d. Is one of these policies less inefficient than the other? Explain.

9. The waters off the North Atlantic coast were once teeming with fish. Now, due to overfishing by the commercial fishing industry, the stocks of fish are seriously depleted. In 1991, the National Marine Fishery Service of the U.S. government implemented a quota to allow fish stocks to recover. The quota limited the amount of swordfish caught per year by all U.S.-licensed fishing boats to 7 million pounds. As soon as the U.S. fishing fleet had met the quota limit, the swordfish catch was closed down for the rest of the year. The accompanying table gives the hypothetical demand and supply schedules for swordfish caught in the United States per year.

Price of swordfish (per pound)	Quantity of swordfish (millions of pounds per year)	
	Quantity demanded	Quantity supplied
$20	6	15
18	7	13
16	8	11
14	9	9
12	10	7

a. Use a diagram to show the effect of the quota on the market for swordfish in 1991. In your diagram, illustrate the deadweight loss from inefficiently low quantity.

b. How do you think fishermen will change how they fish in response to this policy?

10. In Maine, you must have a license to harvest lobster commercially; these licenses are issued yearly. The state of Maine is concerned about the dwindling supplies of lobsters found off its coast. The state fishery department has decided to place a yearly quota of 80,000 pounds of lobsters harvested in all Maine waters. It has also decided to give licenses this year only to those fishermen who had licenses last year. The accompanying diagram shows the demand and supply curves for Maine lobsters.

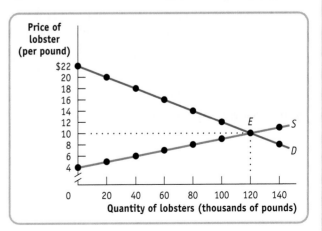

a. In the absence of government restrictions, what are the equilibrium price and quantity?

b. What is the *demand price* at which consumers wish to purchase 80,000 pounds of lobsters?

c. What is the *supply price* at which suppliers are willing to supply 80,000 pounds of lobsters?

d. What is the *quota rent* per pound of lobster when 80,000 pounds are sold? Illustrate the quota rent and the deadweight loss on the diagram.

e. Explain a transaction that benefits both buyer and seller but is prevented by the quota restriction.

11. The Venezuelan government has imposed a price ceiling on the retail price of roasted coffee beans. The accompanying diagram shows the market for coffee beans. In the absence of price controls, the equilibrium is at point *E*, with an equilibrium price of P_E and an equilibrium quantity bought and sold of Q_E.

a. Show the consumer and producer surplus before the introduction of the price ceiling.

After the introduction of the price ceiling, the price falls to P_C and the quantity bought and sold falls to Q_C.

b. Show the consumer surplus after the introduction of the price ceiling (assuming that the consumers with the highest willingness to pay get to buy the available coffee beans; that is, assuming that there is no inefficient allocation to consumers).

c. Show the producer surplus after the introduction of the price ceiling (assuming that the producers with the lowest cost get to sell their coffee beans; that is, assuming that there is no inefficient allocation of sales among producers).

d. Using the diagram, show how much of what was producer surplus before the introduction of the price ceiling has been transferred to consumers as a result of the price ceiling?

e. Using the diagram, show how much of what was total surplus before the introduction of the price ceiling has been lost? That is, how great is the deadweight loss?

12. The accompanying diagram shows data from the U.S. Bureau of Labor Statistics on the average price of an airline ticket in the United States from 1975 until 1985, adjusted to eliminate the effect of *inflation* (the general increase in the prices of all goods over time). In 1978, the United States Airline Deregulation Act removed the price floor on airline fares, and it also allowed the airlines greater flexibility to offer new routes.

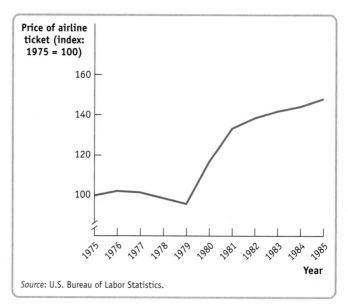

Source: U.S. Bureau of Labor Statistics.

a. Looking at the data on airline ticket prices in the diagram, do you think the price floor that existed before 1978 was binding or nonbinding? That is, do you think it was set above or below the equilibrium price? Draw a supply and demand diagram, showing where the price floor that existed before 1978 was in relation to the equilibrium price.

b. Most economists agree that the average airline ticket price per mile traveled actually *fell* as a result of the Airline Deregulation Act. How might you reconcile that view with what you see in the diagram?

>> Elasticity

MORE PRECIOUS THAN A FLU SHOT

ANIC WAS THE ONLY WORD TO DESCRIBE THE situation at hospitals, clinics, and nursing homes across America in October 2004. Early that month, Chiron Corporation, one of only two suppliers of flu vaccine for the entire U.S. market, announced that contamination problems would force the closure of its manufacturing plant. With that closure, the U.S. supply of vaccine for the 2004–2005 flu season was suddenly cut in half, from 100 million to 50 million doses. Because making flu vaccine is a costly and time-consuming process, no more doses could be made to replace Chiron's lost output. And since every country jealously guards its supply of flu vaccine for its own citizens, none could be obtained from other countries.

If you've ever had a real case of the flu, you know just how unpleasant an experience it is. And it can be worse than unpleasant: every year the flu kills around 36,000 Americans and sends another 200,000 to the hospital. Victims are most commonly children, seniors, or those with compromised immune systems. In a normal flu season, this part of the population, along with health care workers, are immunized first.

But the flu vaccine shortfall of 2004 upended those plans. As news of it spread, there was a rush to get the

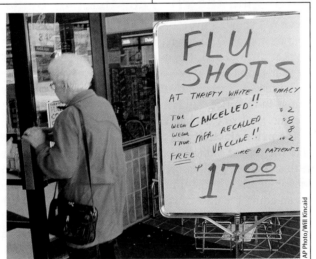

A shortage of flu vaccine created panic during the flu season of 2004.

shots. People lined up in the middle of the night at the few locations that had somehow obtained the vaccine and were offering it at a reasonable price: the crowds included seniors with oxygen tanks, parents with sleeping children, and others in wheelchairs. Meanwhile, some pharmaceutical distributors—the companies that obtain vaccine from manufacturers and then distribute it to hospitals and pharmacies—detected a profit-making opportunity in the frenzy. One company, Med-Stat, which normally charged $8.50 for a dose, began charging $90, more than 10 times the normal price. A survey of pharmacists found that price-gouging was fairly widespread.

Although most people refused or were unable to pay such a high price for the vaccine, many others undoubtedly did. Med-Stat judged, correctly, that consumers of the vaccine were relatively *unresponsive* to price; that is, the large increase in the price of the vaccine left the quantity demanded by consumers relatively unchanged.

Clearly, the demand for flu vaccine is unusual in this respect. For many, getting vaccinated meant the difference between life and death. Let's consider a very different and less urgent scenario. Suppose, for example, that the supply of a particular type of breakfast cereal was halved due to manufacturing problems. It would be extremely unlikely, if not impossible, to find a consumer willing to pay 10 times the original price for a box of this particular cereal. In other words, consumers of breakfast cereal are much more responsive to price than consumers of flu vaccine. But how do we define *responsiveness*?

Economists measure responsiveness of consumers to price with a particular number, called the *price elasticity of demand*. In this chapter we will show how the price elasticity of demand is calculated and why it is the best measure of how the quantity demanded responds to changes in price. We will then see that the price elasticity of demand is only one of a family of related concepts, including the *income elasticity of demand* and the *price elasticity of supply*.

WHAT YOU WILL LEARN IN THIS CHAPTER:

➤ The definition of **elasticity**, a measure of responsiveness to changes in prices or incomes

➤ The importance of the **price elasticity of demand**, which measures the responsiveness of the quantity demanded to changes in price

➤ The meaning and importance of the **income elasticity of demand**, a measure of the responsiveness of demand to changes in income

➤ How the **cross-price elasticity of demand** measures the responsiveness of demand for one good to changes in the price of another good.

➤ The significance of the **price elasticity of supply**, which measures the responsiveness of the quantity supplied to changes in price

➤ The factors that influence the size of these various elasticities

Defining and Measuring Elasticity

In order for Flunomics, a hypothetical flu vaccine distributor, to know whether it could raise its revenue by significantly raising the price of its flu vaccine during the 2004 flu vaccine panic, it would have to know the *price elasticity of demand* for flu vaccinations.

Calculating the Price Elasticity of Demand

Figure 6-1 shows a hypothetical demand curve for flu vaccinations. At a price of $20 per vaccination, consumers would demand 10 million vaccinations per year (point *A*); at a price of $21, the quantity demanded would fall to 9.9 million vaccinations per year (point *B*).

Figure 6-1, then, tells us the change in the quantity demanded for a particular change in the price. But how can we turn this into a measure of price responsiveness? The answer is to calculate the *price elasticity of demand*.

The **price elasticity of demand** compares the *percent change in quantity demanded* to the *percent change in price* as we move along the demand curve. As we'll see later in this chapter, the reason economists use percent changes is to get a measure that doesn't depend on the units in which a good is measured (say, a child-size dose versus an adult-size dose of vaccine). But before we get to that, let's look at how elasticity is calculated.

To calculate the price elasticity of demand, we first calculate the *percent change in the quantity demanded* and the corresponding *percent change in the price* as we move along the demand curve. These are defined as follows:

$$\textbf{(6-1)} \quad \% \text{ change in quantity demanded} = \frac{\text{Change in quantity demanded}}{\text{Initial quantity demanded}} \times 100$$

and

$$\textbf{(6-2)} \quad \% \text{ change in price} = \frac{\text{Change in price}}{\text{Initial price}} \times 100$$

The **price elasticity of demand** is the ratio of the percent change in the quantity demanded to the percent change in the price as we move along the demand curve (dropping the minus sign).

In Figure 6-1, we see that when the price rises from $20 to $21, the quantity demanded falls from 10 million to 9.9 million vaccinations, yielding a change in

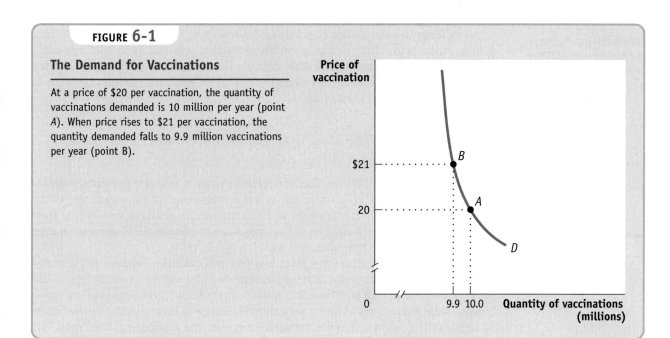

FIGURE 6-1

The Demand for Vaccinations

At a price of $20 per vaccination, the quantity of vaccinations demanded is 10 million per year (point A). When price rises to $21 per vaccination, the quantity demanded falls to 9.9 million vaccinations per year (point B).

the quantity demanded of 0.1 million vaccinations. So the percent change in the quantity demanded is

$$\% \text{ change in quantity demanded} = \frac{-0.1 \text{ million vaccinations}}{10 \text{ million vaccinations}} \times 100 = -1\%$$

The initial price is $20 and the change in the price is $1, so the percent change in price is

$$\% \text{ change in price} = \frac{\$1}{\$20} \times 100 = 5\%$$

To calculate the price elasticity of demand, we find the ratio of the percent change in the quantity demanded to the percent change in the price:

(6-3) $\text{Price elasticity of demand} = \dfrac{\% \text{ change in quantity demanded}}{\% \text{ change in price}}$

In Figure 6-1, the price elasticity of demand is therefore

$$\text{Price elasticity of demand} = \frac{1\%}{5\%} = 0.2$$

The *law of demand* says that demand curves are downward sloping, so price and quantity demanded always move in opposite directions. In other words, a positive percent change in price (a rise in price) leads to a negative percent change in the quantity demanded; a negative percent change in price (a fall in price) leads to a positive percent change in the quantity demanded. This means that the price elasticity of demand is, in strictly mathematical terms, a negative number. However, it is inconvenient to repeatedly write a minus sign. So when economists talk about the price elasticity of demand, they usually drop the minus sign and report the absolute value of the price elasticity of demand. In this case, for example, economists would usually say "the price elasticity of demand is 0.2," taking it for granted that you understand they mean *minus* 0.2. We follow this convention here.

The larger the price elasticity of demand, the more responsive the quantity demanded is to the price. When the price elasticity of demand is large—when consumers change their quantity demanded by a large percentage compared with the percent change in the price—economists say that demand is highly elastic.

The **midpoint method** is a technique for calculating the percent change. In this approach, we calculate changes in a variable compared with the average, or midpoint, of the starting and final values.

As we'll see shortly, a price elasticity of 0.2 indicates a small response of quantity demanded to price. That is, the quantity demanded will fall by a relatively small amount when price rises. This is what economists call *inelastic* demand. And inelastic demand was exactly what Flunomics needed for its strategy to increase revenue by raising the price of its flu vaccines.

An Alternative Way to Calculate Elasticities: the Midpoint Method

Price elasticity of demand compares the *percent change in quantity demanded* with the *percent change in price*. When we look at some other elasticities, which we will do shortly, we'll see why it is important to focus on percent changes. But at this point we need to discuss a technical issue that arises when you calculate percent changes in variables and how economists deal with it.

The best way to understand the issue is with a real example. Suppose you were trying to estimate the price elasticity of demand for gasoline by comparing gasoline prices and consumption in different countries. Because of high taxes, gasoline usually costs about three times as much per gallon in Europe as it does in the United States. So what is the percent difference between American and European gas prices?

Well, it depends on which way you measure it. Because the price of gasoline in Europe is approximately three higher than in the United States, it is 200 percent higher. Because the price of gasoline in the United States is one-third as high as in Europe, it is 66.7 percent lower.

This is a nuisance: we'd like to have a percent measure of the difference in prices that doesn't depend on which way you measure it. A good way to avoid computing different elasticities for rising and falling prices is to use the *midpoint method*.

The **midpoint method** replaces the usual definition of the percent change in a variable, *X*, with a slightly different definition:

$$\textbf{(6-4)} \quad \% \text{ change in } X = \frac{\text{Change in } X}{\text{Average value of } X} \times 100$$

where the average value of *X* is defined as

$$\text{Average value of } X = \frac{\text{Starting value of } X + \text{Final value of } X}{2}$$

When calculating the price elasticity of demand using the midpoint method, both the percent change in the price and the percent change in the quantity demanded are found using this method. To see how this method works, suppose you have the following data for some good:

	Price	Quantity demanded
Situation A	$0.90	1,100
Situation B	$1.10	900

To calculate the percent change in quantity going from situation A to situation B, we compare the change in the quantity demanded—a fall of 200 units—with the *average* of the quantity demanded in the two situations. So we calculate

$$\% \text{ change in quantity demanded} = \frac{-200}{(1{,}100 + 900)/2} \times 100 = \frac{-200}{1{,}000} \times 100 = -20\%$$

In the same way, we calculate

$$\% \text{ change in price} = \frac{\$0.20}{(\$0.90 + \$1.10)/2} \times 100 = \frac{\$0.20}{\$1.00} \times 100 = 20\%$$

So in this case we would calculate the price elasticity of demand to be

$$\text{Price elasticity of demand} = \frac{\text{\% change in quantity demanded}}{\text{\% change in price}} = \frac{20\%}{20\%} = 1$$

again dropping the minus sign.

The important point is that we would get the same result, a price elasticity of demand of 1, whether we go up the demand curve from situation A to situation B or down from situation B to situation A.

To arrive at a more general formula for price elasticity of demand, suppose that we have data for two points on a demand curve. At point 1 the quantity demanded and price are (Q_1, P_1); at point 2 they are (Q_2, P_2). Then the formula for calculating the price elasticity of demand is:

(6-5) $\text{Price elasticity of demand} = \dfrac{\dfrac{Q_2 - Q_1}{(Q_1 + Q_2)/2}}{\dfrac{P_2 - P_1}{(P_1 + P_2)/2}}$

As before, when reporting a price elasticity of demand calculated by the midpoint method, we drop the minus sign and report the absolute value.

➤ECONOMICS IN ACTION

Estimating Elasticities

You might think it's easy to estimate price elasticities of demand from real-world data: just compare percent changes in prices with percent changes in quantities demanded. Unfortunately, it's rarely that simple because changes in price aren't the only thing affecting changes in the quantity demanded: other factors—such as changes in income, changes in population, and changes in the prices of other goods—shift the demand curve, thereby changing the quantity demanded at any given price. To estimate price elasticities of demand, economists must use careful statistical analysis to separate the influence of these different factors, holding other things equal.

The most comprehensive effort to estimate price elasticities of demand was a mammoth study by the economists Hendrik S. Houthakker and Lester D. Taylor. Some of their results are summarized in Table 6-1. These estimates show a wide range of price elasticities. There are some goods, like eggs, for which demand hardly responds at all to changes in the price; there are other goods, most notably foreign travel, for which the quantity demanded is very sensitive to the price.

Notice that Table 6-1 is divided into two parts: inelastic and elastic demand. We'll explain in the next section the significance of that division. ▲

TABLE 6-1

Some Estimated Price Elasticities of Demand

Good	Price elasticity of demand
Inelastic demand	
Eggs	0.1
Beef	0.4
Stationery	0.5
Gasoline	0.5
Elastic demand	
Housing	1.2
Restaurant meals	2.3
Airline travel	2.4
Foreign travel	4.1

Please find source information on the copyright page.

> > > > > > > > > > > >

► CHECK YOUR UNDERSTANDING 6-1

1. The price of strawberries falls from $1.50 to $1.00 per carton and the quantity demanded goes from 100,000 to 200,000 cartons. Use the midpoint method to find the price elasticity of demand.

2. At the present level of consumption, 4,000 movie tickets, and at the current price, $5 per ticket, the price elasticity of demand for movie tickets is 1. Using the midpoint method, calculate the percentage by which the owners of movie theaters must reduce price in order to sell 5,000 tickets.

3. The price elasticity of demand for ice-cream sandwiches is 1.2 at the current price of $0.50 per sandwich and the current consumption level of 100,000 sandwiches. Calculate the change in the quantity demanded when price rises by $0.05. Use Equations 6-1 and 6-2 to calculate percent changes and Equation 6-3 to relate price elasticity of demand to the percent changes.

Solutions appear at back of book.

>> QUICK REVIEW

➤ The **price elasticity of demand** is equal to the percent change in the quantity demanded divided by the percent change in the price as you move along the demand curve (dropping the minus sign).

➤ In practice, percent changes are best measured using the **midpoint method,** in which the percent change in each variable is calculated using the average of starting and final values.

Demand is **perfectly inelastic** when the quantity demanded does not respond at all to changes in the price. When demand is perfectly inelastic, the demand curve is a vertical line.

Interpreting the Price Elasticity of Demand

Med-Stat and other pharmaceutical distributors believed they could sharply drive up flu vaccine prices in the face of a shortage because the price elasticity of vaccine demand was low. But what does that mean? How low does a price elasticity have to be for us to classify it as low? How high does it have to be for us to consider it high? And what determines whether the price elasticity of demand is high or low, anyway?

To answer these questions, we need to look more deeply at the price elasticity of demand.

How Elastic Is Elastic?

As a first step toward classifying price elasticities of demand, let's look at the extreme cases.

First, consider the demand for a good when people pay no attention to the price—say, shoelaces. Suppose that consumers will buy 1 billion pairs of shoelaces per year regardless of the price. In this case, the demand curve for shoelaces would look like the curve shown in panel (a) of Figure 6-2: it would be a vertical line at 1 billion pairs of shoelaces. Since the percent change in the quantity demanded is zero for *any* change in the price, the price elasticity of demand in this case is zero. The case of a zero price elasticity of demand is known as **perfectly inelastic demand.**

The opposite extreme occurs when even a tiny rise in the price will cause the quantity demanded to drop to zero or even a tiny fall in the price will cause the quantity demanded to get extremely large. Panel (b) of Figure 6-2 shows the case of pink tennis balls; we suppose that tennis players really don't care what color their balls are and that other colors, such as neon green and vivid yellow, are available at $5 per dozen balls. In this case, consumers will buy no pink balls if they cost more than $5 per dozen but will buy only pink balls if they cost less than $5. The demand curve will therefore be a horizontal line at a price of $5 per dozen balls. As you move back and forth along this line, there is a change in the quantity demanded but no change in the price. Roughly

FIGURE 6-2 Two Extreme Cases of Price Elasticity of Demand

Panel (a) shows a perfectly inelastic demand curve, which is a vertical line. The quantity of shoelaces demanded is always 1 billion pairs, regardless of price. As a result, the price elasticity of demand is zero—the quantity demanded is unaffected by the price. Panel (b) shows a perfectly elastic demand curve, which is a horizontal line. At a price of $5, consumers will buy any quantity of pink tennis balls, but will buy none at a price above $5. If the price falls below $5, they will buy an extremely large number of pink tennis balls and none of any other color.

speaking, when you divide a number by zero, you get infinity, denoted by the symbol ∞. So a horizontal demand curve implies an infinite price elasticity of demand. When the price elasticity of demand is infinite, economists say that demand is **perfectly elastic.**

The price elasticity of demand for the vast majority of goods is somewhere between these two extreme cases. Economists use one main criterion for classifying these intermediate cases: they ask whether the price elasticity of demand is greater or less than 1. When the price elasticity of demand is greater than 1, economists say that demand is **elastic.** When the price elasticity of demand is less than 1, they say that demand is **inelastic.** The borderline case is **unit-elastic demand,** where the price elasticity of demand is—surprise—exactly 1.

To see why a price elasticity of demand equal to 1 is a useful dividing line, let's consider a hypothetical example: a toll bridge operated by the state highway department. Other things equal, the number of drivers who use the bridge depends on the toll, the price the highway department charges for crossing the bridge: the higher the toll, the fewer the drivers who use the bridge.

Figure 6-3 shows three hypothetical demand curves—one in which demand is unit-elastic, one in which it is inelastic, and one in which it is elastic. In each case, point

Demand is **perfectly elastic** when any price increase will cause the quantity demanded to drop to zero. When demand is perfectly elastic, the demand curve is a horizontal line.

Demand is **elastic** if the price elasticity of demand is greater than 1, **inelastic** if the price elasticity of demand is less than 1, and **unit-elastic** if the price elasticity of demand is exactly 1.

FIGURE 6-3 — Unit-Elastic Demand, Inelastic Demand, and Elastic Demand

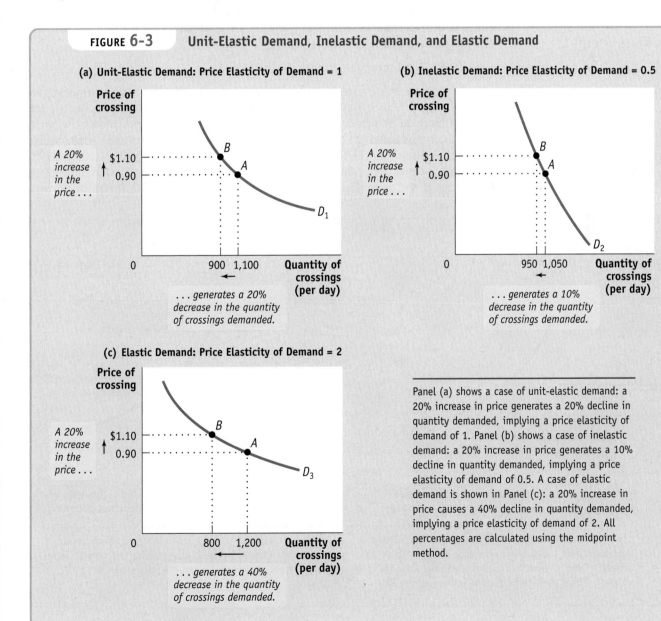

(a) Unit-Elastic Demand: Price Elasticity of Demand = 1

A 20% increase in the price . . . generates a 20% decrease in the quantity of crossings demanded.

(b) Inelastic Demand: Price Elasticity of Demand = 0.5

A 20% increase in the price . . . generates a 10% decrease in the quantity of crossings demanded.

(c) Elastic Demand: Price Elasticity of Demand = 2

A 20% increase in the price . . . generates a 40% decrease in the quantity of crossings demanded.

Panel (a) shows a case of unit-elastic demand: a 20% increase in price generates a 20% decline in quantity demanded, implying a price elasticity of demand of 1. Panel (b) shows a case of inelastic demand: a 20% increase in price generates a 10% decline in quantity demanded, implying a price elasticity of demand of 0.5. A case of elastic demand is shown in Panel (c): a 20% increase in price causes a 40% decline in quantity demanded, implying a price elasticity of demand of 2. All percentages are calculated using the midpoint method.

The **total revenue** is the total value of sales of a good or service. It is equal to the price multiplied by the quantity sold.

A shows the quantity demanded if the toll is $0.90 and point *B* shows the quantity demanded if the toll is $1.10. An increase in the toll from $0.90 to $1.10 is an increase of 20% if we use the midpoint method to calculate percent changes.

Panel (a) shows what happens when the toll is raised from $0.90 to $1.10 and the demand curve is unit-elastic. Here the 20% price rise leads to a fall in the quantity of cars using the bridge each day from 1,100 to 900, which is a 20% decline (again using the midpoint method). So the price elasticity of demand is 20%/20% = 1.

Panel (b) shows a case of inelastic demand when the toll is raised from $0.90 to $1.10. The same 20% price rise reduces the quantity demanded from 1,050 to 950. That's only a 10% decline, so in this case the price elasticity of demand is 10%/20% = 0.5.

Panel (c) shows a case of elastic demand when the toll is raised from $0.90 to $1.10. The 20% price increase causes the quantity demanded to fall from 1,200 to 800—a 40% decline, so the price elasticity of demand is 40%/20% = 2.

Why does it matter whether demand is unit-elastic, inelastic, or elastic? Because this classification predicts how changes in the price of a good will affect the *total revenue* earned by producers from the sale of that good. In many real-life situations, such as the one faced by Med-Stat, it is crucial to know how price changes affect total revenue. **Total revenue** is defined as the total value of sales of a good or service: the price multiplied by the quantity sold.

(6-6)   Total revenue = Price × Quantity sold

Total revenue has a useful graphical representation that can help us understand why knowing the price elasticity of demand is crucial when we ask whether a price rise will increase or reduce total revenue. Panel (a) of Figure 6-4 shows the same demand curve as panel (a) of Figure 6-3. We see that 1,100 drivers will use the bridge if the toll is $0.90. So the total revenue at a price of $0.90 is $0.90 × 1,100 = $990. This value is equal to the area of the green rectangle, which is drawn with the bottom left corner at the point (0, 0) and the top right corner at (1,100, 0.90). In general,

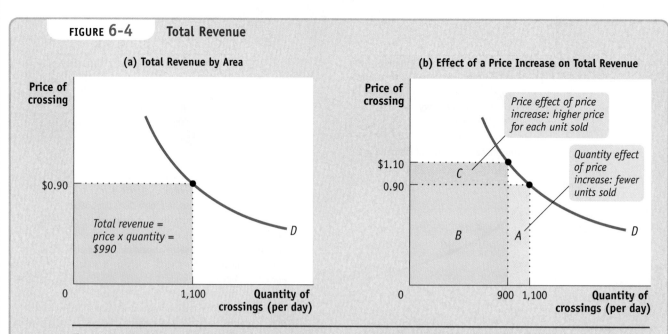

FIGURE 6-4   **Total Revenue**

(a) Total Revenue by Area

Price of crossing

$0.90

Total revenue = price x quantity = $990

0

1,100

Quantity of crossings (per day)

D

(b) Effect of a Price Increase on Total Revenue

Price of crossing

Price effect of price increase: higher price for each unit sold

Quantity effect of price increase: fewer units sold

$1.10

0.90

C

B   *A*

D

0

900 1,100

Quantity of crossings (per day)

The green rectangle in panel (a) represents total revenue generated from 1,100 drivers who each pay a toll of $0.90. Panel (b) shows how total revenue is affected when the price increases from $0.90 to $1.10. Due to the quantity effect, total revenue falls by area *A*. Due to the price effect, total revenue increases by the area *C*. In general, the overall effect can go either way, depending on the price elasticity of demand.

the total revenue at any given price is equal to the area of a rectangle whose height is the price and whose width is the quantity demanded at that price.

To get an idea of why total revenue is important, consider the following scenario. Suppose that the toll on the bridge is currently $0.90 but that the highway department must raise extra money for road repairs. One way to do this is to raise the toll on the bridge. But this plan might backfire, since a higher toll will reduce the number of drivers who use the bridge. And if traffic on the bridge dropped a lot, a higher toll would actually reduce total revenue instead of increasing it. So it's important for the highway department to know how drivers will respond to a toll increase.

We can see graphically how the toll increase affects total bridge revenue by examining panel (b) of Figure 6-4. At a toll of $0.90, total revenue is given by the sum of the areas A and B. After the toll is raised to $1.10, total revenue is given by the sum of areas B and C. So when the toll is raised, revenue represented by area A is lost but revenue represented by area C is gained. These two areas have important interpretations. Area C represents the revenue gain that comes from the additional $0.20 paid by drivers who continue to use the bridge. That is, the 900 who continue to use the bridge contribute an additional $0.20 × 900 = $180 per day to total revenue, represented by area C. But 200 drivers who would have used the bridge at a price of $0.90 no longer do so, generating a loss to total revenue of $0.90 × 200 = $180 per day, represented by area A. (In this particular example, because demand is unit-elastic—the same as in panel (a) of Figure 6-3 —the rise in the toll has no effect on total revenue; areas A and B are the same size.)

Except in the rare case of a good with perfectly elastic or perfectly inelastic demand, when a seller raises the price of a good, two countervailing effects are present:

- *A price effect.* After a price increase, each unit sold sells at a higher price, which tends to raise revenue.

- *A quantity effect.* After a price increase, fewer units are sold, which tends to lower revenue.

But then, you may ask, what is the net ultimate effect on total revenue: does it go up or down? The answer is that, in general, the effect on total revenue can go either way—a price rise may either increase total revenue or lower it. If the price effect, which tends to raise total revenue, is the stronger of the two effects, then total revenue goes up. If the quantity effect, which tends to reduce total revenue, is the stronger, then total revenue goes down. And if the strengths of the two effects are exactly equal—as in our toll bridge example, where a $180 gain offsets a $180 loss— total revenue is unchanged by the price increase.

The price elasticity of demand tells us what happens to total revenue when price changes: its size determines which effect—the price effect or the quantity effect—is stronger. Specifically:

- If demand for a good is *unit-elastic* (the price elasticity of demand is 1), an increase in price does not change total revenue. In this case, the quantity effect and the price effect exactly offset each other.

- If demand for a good is *inelastic* (the price elasticity of demand is less than 1), a higher price increases total revenue. In this case, the price effect is stronger than the quantity effect.

- If demand for a good is *elastic* (the price elasticity of demand is greater than 1), an increase in price reduces total revenue. In this case, the quantity effect is stronger than the price effect.

Table 6-2 on the next page shows how the effect of a price increase on total revenue depends on the price elasticity of demand, using the same data as in Figure 6-3. An increase in the price from $0.90 to $1.10 leaves total revenue unchanged at $990 when demand is unit-elastic. When demand is inelastic, the price effect dominates the quantity effect; the same price increase leads to an increase in total revenue

TABLE 6-2

Price Elasticity of Demand and Total Revenue

	Price of crossing = $0.90	Price of crossing = $1.10
Unit-elastic demand (price elasticity of demand = 1)		
Quantity demanded	1,100	900
Total revenue	$990	$990
Inelastic demand (price elasticity of demand = 0.5)		
Quantity demanded	1,050	950
Total revenue	$945	$1,045
Elastic demand (price elasticity of demand = 2)		
Quantity demanded	1,200	800
Total revenue	$1,080	$880

from $945 to $1,045. And when demand is elastic, the quantity effect dominates the price effect; the price increase leads to a decline in total revenue from $1,080 to $880.

The price elasticity of demand also predicts the effect of a *fall* in price on total revenue. When the price falls, the same two countervailing effects are present, but they work in the opposite directions as compared to the case of a price rise. There is the price effect of a lower price per unit sold, which tends to lower revenue. This is countered by the quantity effect of more units sold, which tends to raise revenue. Which effect dominates depends on the price elasticity. Here is a quick summary:

- When demand is *unit-elastic,* the two effects exactly balance; so a fall in price has no effect on total revenue.

- When demand is *inelastic,* the price effect dominates the quantity effect; so a fall in price reduces total revenue.

- When demand is *elastic,* the quantity effect dominates the price effect; so a fall in price increases total revenue.

Price Elasticity Along the Demand Curve

Suppose an economist says that "the price elasticity of demand for coffee is 0.25." What he or she means is that *at the current price* the elasticity is 0.25. In the previous discussion of the toll bridge, what we were really describing was the elasticity *at the price* of $0.90. Why this qualification? Because for the vast majority of demand curves, the price elasticity of demand at one point along the curve is different from the price elasticity of demand at other points along the same curve.

To see this, consider the table in Figure 6-5, which shows a hypothetical demand schedule. It also shows in the last column the total revenue generated at each price and quantity combination in the demand schedule. The upper panel of the graph in Figure 6-5 shows the corresponding demand curve. The lower panel illustrates the same data on total revenue: the height of a bar at each quantity demanded—which corresponds to a particular price—measures the total revenue generated at that price.

In Figure 6-5, you can see that when the price is low, raising the price increases total revenue: starting at a price of $1, raising the price to $2 increases total revenue from $9 to $16. This means that when the price is low, demand is inelastic. Moreover, you can see that demand is inelastic on the entire section of the demand curve from a price of $0 to a price of $5.

When the price is high, however, raising it further reduces total revenue: starting at a price of $8, raising the price to $9 reduces total revenue, from $16 to $9. This

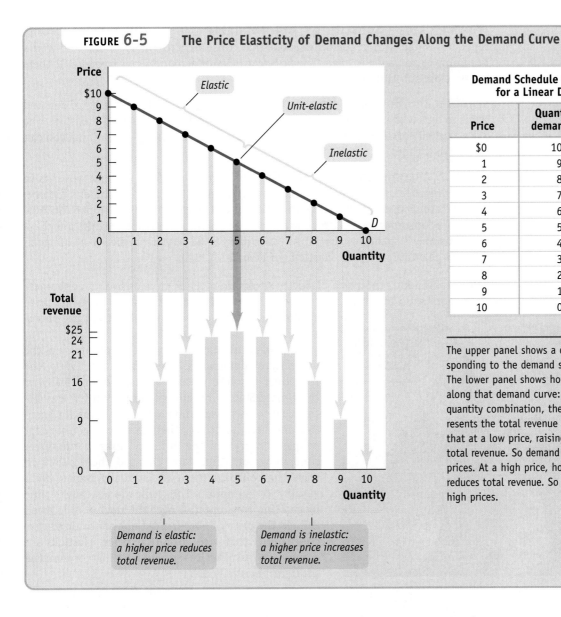

FIGURE 6-5 The Price Elasticity of Demand Changes Along the Demand Curve

Demand Schedule and Total Revenue for a Linear Demand Curve		
Price	Quantity demanded	Total revenue
$0	10	$0
1	9	9
2	8	16
3	7	21
4	6	24
5	5	25
6	4	24
7	3	21
8	2	16
9	1	9
10	0	0

The upper panel shows a demand curve corresponding to the demand schedule in the table. The lower panel shows how total revenue changes along that demand curve: at each price and quantity combination, the height of the bar represents the total revenue generated. You can see that at a low price, raising the price increases total revenue. So demand is inelastic at low prices. At a high price, however, a rise in price reduces total revenue. So demand is elastic at high prices.

Demand is elastic: a higher price reduces total revenue.

Demand is inelastic: a higher price increases total revenue.

means that when the price is high, demand is elastic. Furthermore, you can see that demand is elastic over the section of the demand curve from a price of $5 to $10.

For the vast majority of goods, the price elasticity of demand changes along the demand curve. So whenever you measure a good's elasticity, you are really measuring it at a particular point or section of the good's demand curve.

What Factors Determine the Price Elasticity of Demand?

The flu vaccine shortfall of 2004–2005 allowed vaccine distributors to significantly raise their prices for two important reasons: there were no substitutes, and for many people the vaccine was a medical necessity. People responded in various ways. Some paid the high prices, and some traveled to Canada and other countries to get vaccinated. Some simply did without (and over time often changed their habits to avoid catching the flu, such as eating out less often and avoiding mass transit). This experience illustrates the four main factors that determine elasticity: whether close substitutes are available, whether the good is a necessity or a luxury, the share of income a consumer spends on the good, and how much time has elapsed since the price change. We'll briefly examine each of these factors.

Whether Close Substitutes Are Available The price elasticity of demand tends to be high if there are other goods that consumers regard as similar and would be willing to consume instead. The price elasticity of demand tends to be low if there are no close substitutes.

Whether the Good Is a Necessity or a Luxury The price elasticity of demand tends to be low if a good is something you must have, like a life-saving medicine. The price elasticity of demand tends to be high if the good is a luxury—something you can easily live without.

Share of Income Spent on the Good The price elasticity of demand tends to be low when spending on a good accounts for a small share of a consumer's income. In that case, a significant change in the price of the good has little impact on how much the consumer spends. In contrast, when a good accounts for a significant share of a consumer's spending, the consumer is likely to be very responsive to a change in price. In this case, the price elasticity of demand is high.

Time In general, the price elasticity of demand tends to increase as consumers have more time to adjust to a price change. This means that the long-run price elasticity of demand is often higher than the short-run elasticity.

A good illustration of the effect of time on the elasticity of demand is drawn from the 1970s, the first time gasoline prices increased dramatically in the United States. Initially, consumption fell very little because there were no close substitutes for gasoline and because driving their cars was necessary for people to carry out the ordinary tasks of life. Over time, however, Americans changed their habits in ways that enabled them to gradually reduce their gasoline consumption. The result was a steady decline in gasoline consumption over the next decade, even though the price of gasoline did not continue to rise, confirming that the long-run price elasticity of demand for gasoline was indeed much larger than the short-run elasticity.

Mike Thompson, Detroit Free Press. Reprinted by permission.

►ECONOMICS IN ACTION

Responding to Your Tuition Bill

College costs more than ever—and not just because of overall inflation. Tuition has been rising faster than the overall cost of living for years. But does rising tuition keep people from going to college? Two studies found that the answer depends on the type of college. Both studies assessed how responsive the decision to go to college is to a change in tuition.

A 1988 study found that a 3% increase in tuition led to an approximately 2% fall in the number of students enrolled at four-year institutions, giving a price elasticity of demand of 0.67 (2%/3%). In the case of two-year institutions, the study found a significantly higher response: a 3% increase in tuition led to a 2.7% fall in enrollments, giving a price elasticity of demand of 0.9. In other words, the enrollment decision for students at two-year colleges was significantly more responsive to price than for students at four-year colleges. The result: students at two-year colleges are more likely to forgo getting a degree because of tuition costs than students at four-year colleges.

A 1999 study confirmed this pattern. In comparison to four-year colleges, it found that two-year college enrollment rates were significantly more responsive to changes in state financial aid (a decline in aid leading to a decline in enrollments), a predictable effect given these students' greater sensitivity to the cost of tuition. Another piece of evidence suggests that students at two-year colleges are more likely to be paying their own way and making a trade-off between attending college versus working: the study found that enrollments at two-year colleges are much more responsive to changes in the unemployment rate (an increase in the unemployment rate leading to an increase in enrollments) than enrollments at four-year colleges. So is the cost of tuition a barrier to getting a college degree in the United States? Yes, but more so at two-year colleges than at four-year colleges.

Interestingly, the 1999 study found that for both two-year and four-year colleges, price sensitivity of demand had fallen somewhat since the 1988 study. One possible explanation is that because the value of a college education has risen considerably over time, fewer people forgo college, even if tuition goes up. (See source note on copyright page.) ▲

> > > > > > > > > > > > >

➤ CHECK YOUR UNDERSTANDING 6-2

1. For each case, choose the condition that characterizes demand: elastic demand, inelastic demand, or unit-elastic demand.
   a. Total revenue decreases when price increases.
   b. The additional revenue generated by an increase in quantity sold is exactly offset by revenue lost from the fall in price received per unit.
   c. Total revenue falls when output increases.
   d. Producers in an industry find they can increase their total revenues by working together to reduce industry output.
2. For the following goods, what is the elasticity of demand? Explain. What is the shape of the demand curve?
   a. Demand by a snake-bite victim for an antidote
   b. Demand by students for green erasers

Solutions appear at back of book.

Other Demand Elasticities

The quantity of a good demanded depends not only on the price of that good but also on other variables. In particular, demand curves shift because of changes in the prices of related goods and changes in consumers' incomes. It is often important to have a measure of these other effects, and the best measures are—you guessed it—elasticities. Specifically, we can best measure how the demand for a good is affected by prices of other goods using a measure called the *cross-price elasticity of demand,* and we can best measure how demand is affected by changes in income using the *income elasticity of demand.*

The Cross-Price Elasticity of Demand

In Chapter 3 you learned that the demand for a good is often affected by the prices of other, related goods—goods that are substitutes or complements. There you saw that a change in the price of a related good shifts the demand curve of the original good, reflecting a change in the quantity demanded at any given price. The strength of such a "cross" effect on demand can be measured by the **cross-price elasticity of demand,** defined as the ratio of the percent change in the quantity demanded of one good to the percent change in the price of the other.

The **cross-price elasticity of demand** between two goods measures the effect of the change in one good's price on the quantity demanded of the other good. It is equal to the percent change in the quantity demanded of one good divided by the percent change in the other good's price.

The **income elasticity of demand** is the percent change in the quantity of a good demanded when a consumer's income changes divided by the percent change in the consumer's income.

(6-7) Cross-price elasticity of demand between goods A and B

$$= \frac{\% \text{ change in quantity of A demanded}}{\% \text{ change in price of B}}$$

When two goods are substitutes, like hot dogs and hamburgers, the cross-price elasticity of demand is positive: a rise in the price of hot dogs increases the demand for hamburgers—that is, it causes a rightward shift of the demand curve for hamburgers. If the goods are close substitutes, the cross-price elasticity will be positive and large; if they are not close substitutes, the cross-price elasticity will be positive and small. So when the cross-price elasticity of demand is positive, its size is a measure of how closely substitutable the two goods are.

When two goods are complements, like hot dogs and hot dog buns, the cross-price elasticity is negative: a rise in the price of hot dogs decreases the demand for hot dog buns—that is, it causes a leftward shift of the demand curve for hot dog buns. As with substitutes, the size of the cross-price elasticity of demand between two complements tells us how strongly complementary they are: if the cross-price elasticity is only slightly below zero, they are weak complements; if it is very negative, they are strong complements.

Note that in the case of the cross-price elasticity of demand, the sign (plus or minus) is very important: it tells us whether the two goods are complements or substitutes. So we cannot drop the minus sign as we did for the price elasticity of demand.

Our discussion of the cross-price elasticity of demand is a useful place to return to a point we made earlier: elasticity is a *unit-free* measure—that is, it doesn't depend on the units in which goods are measured.

To see the potential problem, suppose someone told you that "if the price of hot dog buns rises by $0.30, Americans will buy 10 million fewer hot dogs this year." If you've ever bought hot dog buns, you'll immediately wonder: is that a $0.30 increase in the price *per bun,* or is it a $0.30 increase in the price *per package* (buns are usually sold by the dozen)? It makes a big difference what units we are talking about! However, if someone says that the cross-price elasticity of demand between buns and hot dogs is –0.3, it doesn't matter whether buns are sold individually or by the package. So elasticity is defined as a ratio of percent changes, as a way of making sure that confusion over units doesn't arise.

The Income Elasticity of Demand

The **income elasticity of demand** is a measure of how much the demand for a good is affected by changes in consumers' incomes. It allows us to determine whether a good is a normal or inferior good as well as to measure how intensely the demand for the good responds to changes in income.

(6-8) Income elasticity of demand $= \dfrac{\% \text{ change in quantity demanded}}{\% \text{ change in income}}$

Just as the cross-price elasticity of demand between two goods can be either positive or negative, depending on whether the goods are substitutes or complements, the income elasticity of demand for a good can also be either positive or negative. Recall from Chapter 3 that goods can be either *normal goods,* for which demand increases when income rises, or *inferior goods,* for which demand decreases when income rises. These definitions relate directly to the sign of the income elasticity of demand:

- When the income elasticity of demand is positive, the good is a normal good—that is, the quantity demanded at any given price increases as income increases.

- When the income elasticity of demand is negative, the good is an inferior good—that is, the quantity demanded at any given price decreases as income increases.

Where Have All the Farmers Gone?

What percentage of Americans live on farms? Sad to say, the U.S. government no longer publishes that number. In 1991 the official percentage was 1.9, but in that year the government decided it was no longer a meaningful indicator of the size of the agricultural sector because a large proportion of those who live on farms actually make their living doing something else. But in the days of the Founding Fathers, the great majority of Americans lived on farms. As recently as the 1940s, one American in six—or approximately 17%—still did.

Why do so few people now live and work on farms in the United States? There are two main reasons, both involving elasticities.

First, the income elasticity of demand for food is much less than 1—it is income-inelastic. As consumers grow richer, other things equal, spending on food rises less than income. As a result, as the U.S. economy has grown, the share of income it spends on food—and therefore the share of total U.S. income earned by farmers—has fallen.

Second, agriculture has been a technologically progressive sector for approximately 150 years in the United States, with steadily increasing yields over time. You might think that technological progress would be good for farmers. But competition among farmers means that technological progress leads to lower food prices. Meanwhile, the demand for food is price-inelastic, so falling prices of agricultural goods, other things equal, reduce the total revenue of farmers. That's right: progress in farming is good for consumers but bad for farmers.

The combination of these effects explains the relative decline of farming. Even if farming weren't such a technologically progressive sector, the low income elasticity of demand for food would ensure that the income of farmers grows more slowly than the economy as a whole. The combination of rapid technological progress in farming with price-inelastic demand for farm products reinforces this effect, further reducing the growth of farm income. In short, the U.S. farm sector has been a victim of success—the U.S. economy's success as a whole (which reduces the importance of spending on food) and its own success in increasing yields.

Economists often use estimates of the income elasticity of demand to predict which industries will grow most rapidly as the incomes of consumers grow over time. In doing this, they often find it useful to make a further distinction among normal goods, identifying which are *income-elastic* and which are *income-inelastic*.

The demand for a good is **income-elastic** if the income elasticity of demand for that good is greater than 1. When income rises, the demand for income-elastic goods rises *faster* than income. Luxury goods such as second homes and international travel tend to be income-elastic. The demand for a good is **income-inelastic** if the income elasticity of demand for that good is positive but less than 1. When income rises, the demand for income-inelastic goods rises, but more slowly than income. Necessities such as food and clothing tend to be income-inelastic.

> The demand for a good is **income-elastic** if the income elasticity of demand for that good is greater than 1.
>
> The demand for a good is **income-inelastic** if the income elasticity of demand for that good is positive but less than 1.

GLOBAL COMPARISON   **FOOD'S BITE IN WORLD BUDGETS**

If the income elasticity of demand for food is less than 1, we would expect to find that people in poor countries spend a larger share of their income on food than people in rich countries. And that's exactly what the data show. In this graph, we compare per capita income—a country's total income, divided by the population—with the share of income that is spent on food. (To make the graph a manageable size, per capita income is measured as a percentage of U.S. per capita income.) In very poor countries, like Sri Lanka, people spend most of their income on food. In middle-income countries, like Israel, the share of spending that goes to food is much lower. And it's even lower in rich countries, like the United States.

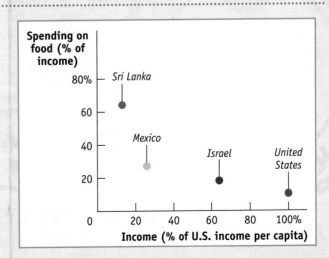

Data: Food shares from U.S. Department of Agriculture database. Income per capita from OECD, *The World Economy: Historical Statistics.*

►ECONOMICS IN ACTION

Spending It

The U.S. Bureau of Labor Statistics carries out extensive surveys of how families spend their incomes. This is not just a matter of intellectual curiosity. Quite a few government programs involve some adjustment for changes in the cost of living; to estimate those changes, the government must know how people spend their money. But an additional payoff to these surveys is data on the income elasticity of demand for various goods.

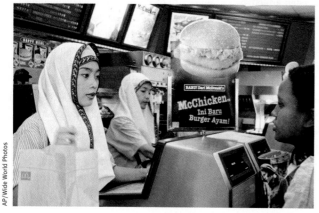

Judging from the activity at this busy McDonald's, incomes are rising in Jakarta, Indonesia.

What stands out from these studies? The classic result is that the income elasticity of demand for "food eaten at home" is considerably less than 1: as a family's income rises, the share of its income spent on food consumed at home falls. Correspondingly, the lower a family's income, the higher the share of income spent on food consumed at home. In poor countries, many families spend more than half their income on food consumed at home. Although the income elasticity of demand for "food eaten at home" is estimated at less than 0.5 in the United States, the income elasticity of demand for "food eaten away from home" (restaurant meals) is estimated to be much higher—close to 1. Families with higher incomes eat out more often and at fancier places. In 1950, about 19% of U.S. income was spent on food consumed at home, a number that has dropped to 7% today. But over the same time period, the share of U.S. income spent on food away from home has stayed constant at 5%. In fact, a sure sign of rising income levels in developing countries is the arrival of fast-food restaurants that cater to newly affluent customers. For example, McDonald's can now be found in Jakarta, Shanghai, and Mumbai.

There is one clear example of an inferior good found in the surveys: rental housing. Families with higher income actually spend less on rent than families with lower income, because they are much more likely to own their own homes. And the category identified as "other housing"—which basically means second homes—is highly income-elastic. Only higher-income families can afford a vacation home at all, so "other housing" has an income elasticity of demand greater than 1. ▲

< < < < < < < < < < < <

> ►► **QUICK REVIEW**

> ➤ Goods are substitutes when the **cross-price elasticity of demand** is positive. Goods are complements when the cross-price elasticity of demand is negative.
> ➤ Inferior goods have a negative **income elasticity of demand.** Most goods are normal goods, which have a positive income elasticity of demand.
> ➤ Normal goods may be either **income-elastic,** with an income elasticity of demand greater than 1, or **income-inelastic,** with an income elasticity of demand that is positive but less than 1.

> ► **CHECK YOUR UNDERSTANDING** **6-3**

1. After Chelsea's income increased from $12,000 to $18,000 a year, her purchases of CDs increased from 10 to 40 CDs a year. Calculate Chelsea's income elasticity of demand for CDs using the midpoint method.

2. Expensive restaurant meals are income-elastic goods for most people, including Sanjay. Suppose his income falls by 10% this year. What can you predict about the change in Sanjay's consumption of expensive restaurant meals?

3. As the price of margarine rises by 20%, a manufacturer of baked goods increases its quantity of butter demanded by 5%. Calculate the cross-price elasticity of demand between butter and margarine. Are butter and margarine substitutes or complements for this manufacturer?

Solutions appear at back of book.

The Price Elasticity of Supply

In the wake of the flu vaccine shortfall of 2004, attempts by vaccine distributors to drive up the price of vaccines would have been much less effective if a higher price had induced a large increase in the output of flu vaccines by flu vaccine manufacturers other than Chiron. In fact, if the rise in price had precipitated a significant increase in flu vaccine production, the price would have been pushed back down. But that didn't happen because, as we mentioned earlier, it would have been far too costly and technically difficult to produce more vaccine for the 2004–2005 flu season. (In reality, the production of flu vaccine is begun a year before it is to be distributed.) This was another critical element in the ability of some flu vaccine distributors, like Med-Stat, to get significantly higher prices for their product: a low responsiveness in the quantity of output supplied to the higher price of flu vaccine by flu vaccine producers. To measure the response of producers to price changes, we need a measure parallel to the price elasticity of demand—the *price elasticity of supply*.

The **price elasticity of supply** is a measure of the responsiveness of the quantity of a good supplied to the price of that good. It is the ratio of the percent change in the quantity supplied to the percent change in the price as we move along the supply curve.

Measuring the Price Elasticity of Supply

The **price elasticity of supply** is defined the same way as the price elasticity of demand (although there is no minus sign to be eliminated here):

(6-9)   Price elasticity of supply $= \dfrac{\%\ \text{change in quantity supplied}}{\%\ \text{change in price}}$

The only difference is that here we consider movements along the supply curve rather than movements along the demand curve.

Suppose that the price of tomatoes rises by 10%. If the quantity of tomatoes supplied also increases by 10% in response, the price elasticity of supply of tomatoes is 1 (10%/10%) and supply is unit-elastic. If the quantity supplied increases by 5%, the price elasticity of supply is 0.5 and supply is inelastic; if the quantity increases by 20%, the price elasticity of supply is 2 and supply is elastic.

As in the case of demand, the extreme values of the price elasticity of supply have a simple graphical representation. Panel (a) of Figure 6-6 shows the supply of cell phone frequencies, the portion of the radio spectrum that is suitable for sending and receiving cell phone signals. Governments own the right to sell the use of this part

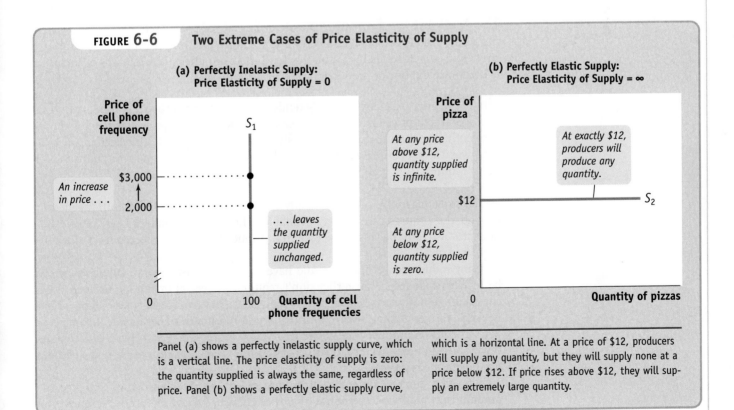

FIGURE 6-6   **Two Extreme Cases of Price Elasticity of Supply**

Panel (a) shows a perfectly inelastic supply curve, which is a vertical line. The price elasticity of supply is zero: the quantity supplied is always the same, regardless of price. Panel (b) shows a perfectly elastic supply curve, which is a horizontal line. At a price of $12, producers will supply any quantity, but they will supply none at a price below $12. If price rises above $12, they will supply an extremely large quantity.

There is **perfectly inelastic supply** when the price elasticity of supply is zero, so that changes in the price of the good have no effect on the quantity supplied. A perfectly inelastic supply curve is a vertical line.

There is **perfectly elastic supply** when even a tiny increase or reduction in the price will lead to very large changes in the quantity supplied, so that the price elasticity of supply is infinite. A perfectly elastic supply curve is a horizontal line.

of the radio spectrum to cell phone operators inside their borders. But governments can't increase or decrease the number of cell phone frequencies that they have to offer—for technical reasons, the quantity of frequencies suitable for cell phone operation is a fixed quantity. So the supply curve for cell phone frequencies is a vertical line, which we have assumed is set at the quantity of 100 frequencies. As you move up and down that curve, the change in the quantity supplied by the government is zero, whatever the change in price. So panel (a) illustrates a case in which the price elasticity of supply is zero. This is a case of **perfectly inelastic supply.**

Panel (b) shows the supply curve for pizza. We suppose that it costs $12 to produce a pizza, including all opportunity costs. At any price below $12, it would be unprofitable to produce pizza and all the pizza parlors in America would go out of business. Alternatively, there are many producers who could operate pizza parlors if they were profitable. The ingredients—flour, tomatoes, cheese—are plentiful. And if necessary, more tomatoes could be grown, more milk could be produced to make mozzarella, and so on. So any price above $12 would elicit an extremely large quantity of pizzas supplied. The implied supply curve is therefore a horizontal line at $12. Since even a tiny increase in the price would lead to a huge increase in the quantity supplied, the price elasticity of supply would be more or less infinite. This is a case of **perfectly elastic supply.**

As our cell phone frequencies and pizza examples suggest, real-world instances of both perfectly inelastic and perfectly elastic supply are easy to find—much easier than their counterparts in demand.

What Factors Determine the Price Elasticity of Supply?

Our examples tell us the main determinant of the price elasticity of supply: the availability of inputs. In addition, as with the price elasticity of demand, time may also play a role in the price elasticity of supply. Here we briefly summarize the two factors.

The Availability of Inputs The price elasticity of supply tends to be large when inputs are readily available and can be shifted into and out of production at a relatively low cost. It tends to be small when inputs are difficult to obtain—and can be shifted into and out of production only at a relatively high cost.

Time The price elasticity of supply tends to grow larger as producers have more time to respond to a price change. This means that the long-run price elasticity of supply is often higher than the short-run elasticity. (In the case of the flu vaccine shortfall, time was the crucial element because flu vaccine must be grown in cultures over many months.)

The price elasticity of pizza supply is very high because the inputs needed to expand the industry are readily available. The price elasticity of cell phone frequencies is zero because an essential input—the radio spectrum—cannot be increased at all.

Many industries are like pizza and have large price elasticities of supply: they can be readily expanded because they don't require any special or unique resources. On the other hand, the price elasticity of supply is usually substantially less than perfectly elastic for goods that involve limited natural resources: minerals like gold or copper, agricultural products like coffee that flourish only on certain types of land, and renewable resources like ocean fish that can only be exploited up to a point without destroying the resource.

But given enough time, producers are often able to significantly change the amount they produce in response to a price change, even when production involves a limited natural resource. For example, consider again the effects of a surge in flu vaccine prices, but this time focus on the supply response. If the price were to rise to $90 per vaccination and stay there for a number of years, there would almost certainly be a substantial increase in flu vaccine production. Producers such as Chiron would eventually respond by increasing the size of their manufacturing plants, hiring more lab technicians, and so on. But significantly enlarging the capacity of a biotech manufacturing lab takes several years, not weeks or months or even a single year.

For this reason, economists often make a distinction between the short-run elasticity of supply, usually referring to a few weeks or months, and the long-run elasticity of supply, usually referring to several years. In most industries, the long-run elasticity of supply is larger than the short-run elasticity.

➤ECONOMICS IN ACTION

European Farm Surpluses

One of the policies we analyzed in Chapter 5 was the imposition of a *price floor,* a lower limit below which price of a good could not fall. We saw that price floors are often used by governments to support the incomes of farmers but create large unwanted surpluses of farm products. The most dramatic example of this is found in the European Union, where price floors have created a "butter mountain," a "wine lake," and so on.

Were European politicians unaware that their price floors would create huge surpluses? They probably knew that surpluses would arise but underestimated the price elasticity of agricultural supply. In fact, when the agricultural price supports were put in place, many analysts thought they were unlikely to lead to big increases in production. After all, European countries are densely populated and there was little new land available for cultivation.

What the analysts failed to realize, however, was how much farm production could expand by adding other resources, especially fertilizer and pesticides which were readily available. So although European farm acreage didn't increase much in response to the imposition of price floors, European farm production did! ▲

> > > > > > > > > > > >

➤➤QUICK REVIEW

➤ The **price elasticity of supply** is the percent change in the quantity supplied divided by the percent change in the price.

➤ Under **perfectly inelastic supply,** the quantity supplied is completely unresponsive to price and the supply curve is a vertical line. Under **perfectly elastic supply,** the supply curve is horizontal at some specific price. If the price falls below that level, the quantity supplied is zero. If the price rises above that level, the quantity supplied is infinite.

➤ The price elasticity of supply depends on the availability of inputs, the ease of shifting inputs into and out of alternative uses, and on the period of time that has elapsed since the price change.

➤ CHECK YOUR UNDERSTANDING 6-4

1. Using the midpoint method, calculate the price elasticity of supply for web-design services when the price per hour rises from $100 to $150 and the number of hours transacted increases from 300,000 hours to 500,000. Is supply elastic, inelastic, or unit-elastic?

2. True or false? If the demand for milk rose, then, in the long run, milk-drinkers would be better off if supply was elastic rather than inelastic.

3. True or false? Long-run price elasticities of supply are generally larger than short-run price elasticities of supply. As a result, the short-run supply curves are generally flatter than the long-run supply curves.

4. True or false? When supply is perfectly elastic, changes in demand have no effect on price.

Solutions appear at back of book.

An Elasticity Menagerie

We've just run through quite a few different elasticities. Keeping them all straight can be a challenge. So in Table 6-3 on the next page we provide a summary of all the elasticities we have discussed and their implications.

TABLE **6-3**

An Elasticity Menagerie

Name	Possible values	Significance
Price elasticity of demand $= \dfrac{\text{\% change in quantity demanded}}{\text{\% change in price}}$ (dropping the minus sign)		
Perfectly inelastic demand	0	Price has no effect on quantity demanded (vertical demand curve).
Inelastic demand	Between 0 and 1	A rise in price increases total revenue.
Unit-elastic demand	Exactly 1	Changes in price have no effect on total revenue.
Elastic demand	Greater than 1, less than ∞	A rise in price reduces total revenue.
Perfectly elastic demand	∞	A rise in price causes quantity demanded to fall to 0. A fall in price leads to an infinite quantity demanded (horizontal demand curve).
Cross-price elasticity of demand $= \dfrac{\text{\% change in quantity } \textit{of one good } \text{demanded}}{\text{\% change in price } \textit{of another good}}$		
Complements	Negative	Quantity demanded of one good falls when the price of another rises.
Substitutes	Positive	Quantity demanded of one good rises when the price of another rises.
Income elasticity of demand $= \dfrac{\text{\% change in quantity demanded}}{\text{\% change in income}}$		
Inferior good	Negative	Quantity demanded falls when income rises.
Normal good, income-inelastic	Positive, less than 1	Quantity demanded rises when income rises, but not as rapidly as income.
Normal good, income-elastic	Greater than 1	Quantity demanded rises when income rises, and more rapidly than income.
Price elasticity of supply $= \dfrac{\text{\% change in quantity supplied}}{\text{\% change in price}}$		
Perfectly inelastic supply	0	Price has no effect on quantity supplied (vertical supply curve).
	Greater than 0, less than ∞	Ordinary upward-sloping supply curve.
Perfectly elastic supply	∞	Any fall in price causes quantity supplied to fall to 0. Any rise in price elicits an infinite quantity supplied (horizontal supply curve).

[>> A LOOK AHEAD •••

The concept of elasticity deepens our understanding of supply and demand, helping us to predict changes in equilibrium prices and quantities in response to events. For example, we now know why vaccine distributors could significantly raise the market price of flu vaccine during the 2004–2005 flu season—because both supply and demand for flu vaccine were inelastic. Using the concept of income elasticity, we've also learned how changes in the incomes of consumers affect the demand for a good. With this we can explain why you'd rather be a fast-food producer than a farmer in a country where incomes are growing quickly.

But there is even more to learn with the help of elasticities. In the next chapter, we'll see that elasticities are vitally important for tax policy: in determining how much revenue is gained by imposing a tax, in determining who actually pays the cost of the tax, and in predicting how much inefficiency is caused by a tax.]

SUMMARY

1. Many economic questions depend on the size of consumer or producer responses to changes in prices or other variables. *Elasticity* is a general measure of responsiveness that can be used to answer such questions.

2. The **price elasticity of demand**—the percent change in the quantity demanded divided by the percent change in the price (dropping the minus sign)—is a measure of the responsiveness of the quantity demanded to changes in the price. In practical calculations, it is usually best to use the **midpoint method,** which calculates percent changes in prices and quantities based on the average of starting and final values.

3. The responsiveness of the quantity demanded to price can range from **perfectly inelastic demand,** where the quantity demanded is unaffected by the price, to **perfectly elastic demand,** where there is a unique price at which consumers will buy as much or as little as they are offered. When demand is perfectly inelastic, the demand curve is a vertical line; when it is perfectly elastic, the demand curve is a horizontal line.

4. The price elasticity of demand is classified according to whether it is more or less than 1. If it is greater than 1, demand is **elastic;** if it is less than 1, demand is **inelastic;** if it is exactly 1, demand is **unit-elastic.** This classification determines how **total revenue,** the total value of sales, changes when the price changes. If demand is elastic, total revenue falls when the price increases and rises when the price decreases. If demand is inelastic, total revenue rises when the price increases and falls when the price decreases.

5. The price elasticity of demand depends on whether there are close substitutes for the good in question, whether the good is a necessity or a luxury, the share of income spent on the good, and the length of time that has elapsed since the price change.

6. The **cross-price elasticity of demand** measures the effect of a change in one good's price on the quantity of another good demanded. The cross-price elasticity of demand can be positive, in which case the goods are substitutes, or negative, in which case they are complements.

7. The **income elasticity of demand** is the percent change in the quantity of a good demanded when a consumer's income changes divided by the percent change in income. The income elasticity of demand indicates how intensely the demand for a good responds to changes in income. It can be negative; in that case the good is an inferior good. Goods with positive income elasticities of demand are normal goods. If the income elasticity is greater than 1, a good is **income-elastic;** if it is positive and less than 1, the good is **income-inelastic.**

8. The **price elasticity of supply** is the percent change in the quantity of a good supplied divided by the percent change in the price. If the quantity supplied does not change at all, we have an instance of **perfectly inelastic supply;** the supply curve is a vertical line. If the quantity supplied is zero below some price but infinite above that price, we have an instance of **perfectly elastic supply;** the supply curve is a horizontal line.

9. The price elasticity of supply depends on the availability of resources to expand production and on time. It is higher when inputs are available at relatively low cost and the longer the time elapsed since the price change.

KEY TERMS

Price elasticity of demand, p. 144
Midpoint method, p. 146
Perfectly inelastic demand, p. 148
Perfectly elastic demand, p. 149
Elastic demand, p. 149

Inelastic demand, p. 149
Unit-elastic demand, p. 149
Total revenue, p. 150
Cross-price elasticity of demand, p. 155
Income elasticity of demand, p. 156

Income-elastic demand, p. 157
Income-inelastic demand, p. 157
Price elasticity of supply, p. 159
Perfectly inelastic supply, p. 160
Perfectly elastic supply, p. 160

PROBLEMS

1. Nile.com, the online bookseller, wants to increase its total revenue. One strategy is to offer a 10% discount on every book it sells. Nile.com knows that its customers can be divided into two distinct groups according to their likely responses to the discount. The accompanying table shows how the two groups respond to the discount.

	Group A (sales per week)	Group B (sales per week)
Volume of sales before the 10% discount	1.55 million	1.50 million
Volume of sales after the 10% discount	1.65 million	1.70 million

a. Using the midpoint method, calculate the price elasticities of demand for group A and group B.

b. Explain how the discount will affect total revenue from each group.

c. Suppose Nile.com knows which group each customer belongs to when he or she logs on and can choose whether or not to offer the 10% discount. If Nile.com wants to increase its total revenue, should discounts be offered to group A or to group B, to neither group, or to both groups?

2. Do you think the price elasticity of demand for Ford sport-utility vehicles (SUVs) will increase, decrease, or remain the same when each of the following events occurs? Explain your answer.

a. Other car manufacturers, such as General Motors, decide to make and sell SUVs.

b. SUVs produced in foreign countries are banned from the American market.

c. Due to ad campaigns, Americans believe that SUVs are much safer than ordinary passenger cars.

d. The time period over which you measure the elasticity lengthens. During that longer time, new models such as four-wheel-drive cargo vans appear.

3. U.S. winter wheat production increased dramatically in 1999 after a bumper harvest. The supply curve shifted rightward; as a result, the price decreased and the quantity demanded increased (a movement along the demand curve). The accompanying table describes what happened to prices and the quantity of wheat demanded.

	1998	1999
Quantity demanded (bushels)	1.74 billion	1.9 billion
Average price (per bushel)	$3.70	$2.72

a. Using the midpoint method, calculate the price elasticity of demand for winter wheat.

b. What is the total revenue for U.S. wheat farmers in 1998 and 1999?

c. Did the bumper harvest increase or decrease the total revenue of American wheat farmers? How could you have predicted this from your answer to part a?

4. The accompanying table gives part of the supply schedule for personal computers in the United States.

Price of computer	Quantity of computers supplied
$1,100	12,000
900	8,000

a. Calculate the price elasticity of supply when the price increases from $900 to $1,100 using the midpoint method.

b. Suppose firms produce 1,000 more computers at any given price due to improved technology. As price increases from $900 to $1,100, is the price elasticity of supply now greater than, less than, or the same as it was in part a?

c. Suppose a longer time period under consideration means that the quantity supplied at any given price is 20% higher than the figures given in the table. As price increases from $900 to $1,100, is the price elasticity of supply now greater than, less than, or the same as it was in part a?

5. The accompanying table lists the cross-price elasticities of demand for several goods, where the percent quantity change is measured for the first good of the pair, and the percent price change is measured for the second good.

Good	Cross-price elasticities of demand
Air-conditioning units and kilowatts of electricity	−0.34
Coke and Pepsi	+0.63
High-fuel-consuming sport-utility vehicles (SUVs) and gasoline	−0.28
McDonald's burgers and Burger King burgers	+0.82
Butter and margarine	+1.54

a. Explain the sign of each of the cross-price elasticities. What does it imply about the relationship between the two goods in question?

b. Compare the absolute values of the cross-price elasticities and explain their magnitudes. For example, why is the cross-price elasticity of McDonald's burgers and Burger King burgers less than the cross-price elasticity of butter and margarine?

c. Use the information in the table to calculate how a 5% increase in the price of Pepsi affects the quantity of Coke demanded.

d. Use the information in the table to calculate how a 10% decrease in the price of gasoline affects the quantity of SUVs demanded.

6. What can you conclude about the price elasticity of demand in each of the following statements?

a. "The pizza delivery business in this town is very competitive. I'd lose half my customers if I raised the price by as little as 10%."

b. "I owned both of the two Jerry Garcia autographed lithographs in existence. I sold one on eBay for a high price. But when I sold the second one, the price dropped by 80%."

c. "My economics professor has chosen to use the Krugman/Wells textbook for this class. I have no choice but to buy this book."

d. "I always spend a total of exactly $10 per week on coffee."

7. Take a linear demand curve like that shown in Figure 6-5, where the range of prices for which demand is elastic and inelastic is labeled. In each of the following scenarios, the supply curve shifts. Show along which portion of the demand curve (that is, the elastic or the inelastic portion) the supply curve must have shifted in order to generate the event described. In each case, show on the diagram the quantity effect and the price effect.

a. Recent attempts by the Colombian army to stop the flow of illegal drugs into the United States have actually benefited drug dealers.

b. New construction increased the number of seats in the football stadium and resulted in greater total revenue from box-office ticket sales.

c. A fall in input prices has led to higher output of Porsches. But total revenue for the Porsche Company has declined as a result.

8. The accompanying table shows the price and yearly quantity sold of souvenir T-shirts in the town of Crystal Lake according to the average income of the tourists visiting.

Price of T-shirt	Quantity of T-shirts demanded when average tourist income is $20,000	Quantity of T-shirts demanded when average tourist income is $30,000
$4	3,000	5,000
5	2,400	4,200
6	1,600	3,000
7	800	1,800

a. Using the midpoint method, calculate the price elasticity of demand when the price of a T-shirt rises from $5 to $6 and the average tourist income is $20,000. Also calculate it when the average tourist income is $30,000.

b. Using the midpoint method, calculate the income elasticity of demand when the price of a T-shirt is $4 and the average tourist income increases from $20,000 to $30,000. Also calculate it when the price is $7.

9. A recent study determined the following elasticities for Volkswagen Beetles:

Price elasticity of demand = 2
Income elasticity of demand = 1.5

The supply of Beetles is elastic. Based on this information, are the following statements true or false? Explain your reasoning.

a. A 10% increase in the price of a Beetle will reduce the quantity demanded by 20%.

b. An increase in consumer income will increase the price and quantity of Beetles sold. Since price elasticity of demand is greater than 1, total revenue will go down.

10. In each of the following cases, do you think the price elasticity of supply is (i) perfectly elastic; (ii) perfectly inelastic; (iii) elastic, but not perfectly elastic; or (iv) inelastic, but not perfectly inelastic? Explain using a diagram.

a. An increase in demand this summer for luxury cruises leads to a huge jump in the sales price of a cabin on the Queen Mary 2.

b. The price of a kilowatt of electricity is the same during periods of high electricity demand as during periods of low electricity demand.

c. Fewer people want to fly during February than during any other month. The airlines cancel about 10% of their flights as ticket prices fall about 20% during this month.

d. Owners of vacation homes in Maine rent them out during the summer. Due to the soft economy this year, a 30% decline in the price of a vacation rental leads more than half of homeowners to occupy their vacation homes themselves during the summer.

11. Use an elasticity concept to explain each of the following observations.

a. During economic booms, the number of new personal care businesses, such as gyms and tanning salons, is proportionately greater than the number of other new businesses, such as grocery stores.

b. Cement is the primary building material in Mexico. After new technology makes cement cheaper to produce, the supply curve for the Mexican cement industry becomes relatively flatter.

c. Some goods that were once considered luxuries, like a telephone, are now considered virtual necessities. As a result, the demand curve for telephone services has become steeper over time.

d. Consumers in a less developed country like Guatemala spend proportionately more of their income on equipment for producing things at home, like sewing machines, than consumers in a more developed country like Canada.

12. Taiwan is a major world supplier of semiconductor chips. A recent earthquake severely damaged the production facilities of Taiwanese chip-producing companies, sharply reducing the amount of chips they could produce.

a. Assume that the total revenue of a typical non-Taiwanese chip manufacturer rises due to these events. In terms of an elasticity, what must be true for this to happen?

Illustrate the change in total revenue with a diagram, indicating the price effect and the quantity effect of the Taiwan earthquake on this company's total revenue.

b. Now assume that the total revenue of a typical non-Taiwanese chip manufacturer falls due to these events. In terms of an elasticity, what must be true for this to happen? Illustrate the change in total revenue with a diagram, indicating the price effect and the quantity effect of the Taiwan earthquake on this company's total revenue.

13. There is a debate about whether sterile hypodermic needles should be passed out free of charge in cities with high drug use. Proponents argue that doing so will reduce the incidence of diseases, such as HIV/AIDS, that are often spread by needle sharing among drug users. Opponents believe that doing so will encourage more drug use by reducing the risks of this behavior. As an economist asked to assess the policy, you must know the following: (i) how responsive the spread of diseases like HIV/AIDS is to the price of sterile needles and (ii) how responsive drug use is to the price of sterile needles. Assuming that you know these two things, use the concepts of price elasticity of demand for sterile needles and the cross-price elasticity between drugs and sterile needles to answer the following questions.

a. In what circumstances do you believe this is a beneficial policy?

b. In what circumstances do you believe this is a bad policy?

14. Worldwide, the average coffee grower has increased the amount of acreage under cultivation over the past few years. The result has been that the average coffee plantation produces significantly more coffee than it did 10 to 20 years ago. Unfortunately for the growers, however, this has also been a period in which their total revenues have plunged. In terms of an elasticity, what must be true for these events to have occurred? Illustrate these events with a diagram, indicating the quantity effect and the price effect that gave rise to these events.

15. A recent report by the U.S. Centers for Disease Control and Prevention (CDC), published in the CDC's *Morbidity and Mortality Weekly Report,* studied the effect of an increase in the price of beer on the incidence of new cases of sexually transmitted disease in young adults. In particular, the researchers analyzed the responsiveness of gonorrhea cases to a tax-induced increase in the price of beer. The report concluded that "the . . . analysis suggested that a beer tax increase of $0.20 per six-pack could reduce overall gonorrhea rates by 8.9%." Assume that a six-pack costs $5.90 before the price increase. Use the midpoint method to determine the percent increase in the price of a six-pack, and then calculate the cross-price elasticity of demand between beer and incidence of gonorrhea. According to your estimate of this cross-price elasticity of demand, are beer and gonorrhea complements or substitutes?

16. The U.S. government is considering reducing the amount of carbon dioxide that firms are allowed to produce by issuing a limited number of tradable allowances for carbon dioxide (CO_2) emissions. In an April 25, 2007, report, the U.S. Congressional Budget Office (CBO) argues that "most of the cost of meeting a cap on CO_2 emissions would be borne by consumers, who would face persistently higher prices for products such as electricity and gasoline . . . poorer households would bear a larger burden relative to their income than wealthier households would." What assumption about one of the elasticities you learned about in this chapter has to be true for poorer households to be disproportionately affected?

17. According to a Honda press release on October 23, 2006, sales of the fuel-efficient four-cylinder Honda Civic rose by 7.1% from 2005 to 2006. Over the same period, according to data from the U.S. Energy Information Administration, the average price of regular gasoline rose from $2.27 per gallon to $2.57 per gallon. Using the midpoint method, calculate the cross-price elasticity of demand between Honda Civics and regular gasoline. According to your estimate of the cross-price elasticity, are the two goods complements or substitutes? Does your answer make sense?

www.worthpublishers.com/krugmanwells

chapter: 7

>> Taxes

A TAX RIOT

ON MARCH 31, 1990, HUNDREDS OF THOUSANDS of British citizens marched across London, protesting a new tax that had been introduced by Prime Minister Margaret Thatcher. As some protesters clashed with police, the initially peaceful demonstration turned into a riot, with hundreds injured. The violence came as a surprise, but maybe it shouldn't have: the tax had aroused angry opposition throughout Britain. Later that year, Mrs. Thatcher was forced to resign, and many observers believed that the tax controversy was the primary cause of her fall.

The tax at issue was officially known as the "Community Charge" but was popularly known as the "poll tax." Until 1989 local public services like street cleaning and trash collection had been financed with "the rates," a tax that depended on the value of a person's home. (Most local services in the United States are financed with similar property-based taxes.) Mrs. Thatcher, however, replaced these property taxes with a payment from each individual over the age of 18. Although the amount of the poll tax varied from town to town, every adult in a given town owed the same amount, regardless of income or the value of his or her property.

Supporters of the poll tax argued that it was more efficient than the tax it replaced. Because the old tax depended on the value of property, it discouraged people both from buying more expensive homes and from improving the homes they had. Supporters also argued that the poll tax was fair, because the cost of providing local public services depended mainly on how many people lived in a town, not on how rich those people were.

But opponents argued that the poll tax was extremely unfair because it did not take into account differences in people's ability to pay—a single mother who worked as a waitress and a millionaire stockbroker owed the same amount if they lived in the same town.

One moral of this story is that making tax policy isn't easy—in fact, if you are a politician, it can be dangerous

Margaret Thatcher and these protesters differed sharply over the fairness of the poll tax.

to your professional health. But the story also illustrates some crucial issues in tax policy—issues that economic models help clarify.

Taxes are necessary: all governments need money to function. Without taxes, governments could not provide the services we want, from national defense to public parks. But taxes have a cost that normally exceeds the money actually paid to the government. That's because taxes distort incentives to engage in mutually beneficial transactions. For example, as mentioned above, Britain's "rates" discouraged homeowners from improving their homes. So

one principle used for guiding tax policy is *efficiency*: taxes should be designed to distort incentives as little as possible. But efficiency is not the only concern when designing tax rates. As the British government learned from the poll tax riot, it's also important that a tax be seen as *fair*. Tax policy always involves striking a balance between the pursuit of efficiency and the pursuit of perceived fairness.

In this chapter, we will look at the economics of tax policy and show how attempts to make the best of the trade-off between efficiency and fairness influence the design of actual tax systems.

WHAT YOU WILL LEARN IN THIS CHAPTER:

➤ The effects of taxes on supply and demand

➤ What determines who really bears the burden of a tax

➤ The costs and benefits of taxes, and why taxes impose a cost that is larger than the tax revenue they raise

➤ The difference between progressive and regressive taxes and the trade-off between tax equity and tax efficiency.

➤ The structure of the U.S. tax system

The Economics of Taxes: A Preliminary View

To understand the economics of taxes, it's helpful to look at a simple type of tax known as an **excise tax**—a tax charged on each unit of a good or service that is sold. Most tax revenue in the United States comes from other kinds of taxes, which we'll describe later in this chapter. But excise taxes are common. For example, there are excise taxes on gasoline, cigarettes, and foreign-made trucks, and many local governments impose excise taxes on services such as hotel room rentals. The lessons we'll learn from studying excise taxes apply to other, more complex taxes as well.

The Effect of an Excise Tax on Quantities and Prices

Suppose that the supply and demand for hotel rooms in the city of Potterville are as shown in Figure 7-1. We'll make the simplifying assumption that all hotel rooms are the same. In the absence of taxes, the equilibrium price of a room is $80 per night and the equilibrium quantity of hotel rooms rented is 10,000 per night.

Now suppose that Potterville's government imposes an excise tax of $40 per night on hotel rooms—that is, every time a room is rented for the night, the owner of the hotel must pay the city $40. For example, if a customer pays $80, $40 is collected as a tax, leaving the hotel owner with only $40. As a result, hotel owners are less willing to supply rooms at any given price.

What does this imply about the supply curve for hotel rooms in Potterville? To answer this question, we must compare the incentives of hotel owners *pre-tax* (before the tax is levied) to their incentives *post-tax* (after the tax is levied). From Figure 7-1 we know that pre-tax, hotel owners are willing to supply 5,000 rooms per night at a price of $60 per room. But after the $40 tax per room is levied, they are willing to supply the same amount, 5,000 rooms, only if they receive $100 per room—$60 for themselves plus $40 paid to the city as tax. In other words, in order for hotel owners to be willing to supply the same quantity post-tax as they would have pre-tax, they must receive an additional $40 per room, the amount of the tax. This implies that the post-tax supply curve shifts up by the amount of the tax compared to the pre-tax supply

An **excise tax** is a tax on sales of a good or service.

FIGURE 7-1

The Supply and Demand for Hotel Rooms in Potterville

In the absence of taxes, the equilibrium price of hotel rooms is $80 a night, and the equilibrium number of rooms rented is 10,000 per night, as shown by point *E*. The supply curve, *S*, shows the quantity supplied at any given price, pre-tax. At a price of $60 a night, hotel owners are willing to supply 5,000 rooms, point *B*. But post-tax, hotel owners are willing to supply the same quantity only at a price of $100: $60 for themselves plus $40 paid to the city as tax.

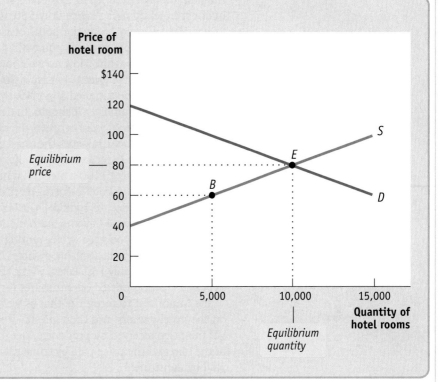

curve. At every quantity supplied, the supply price—the price that producers must receive to produce a given quantity—has increased by $40.

The upward shift of the supply curve caused by the tax is shown in Figure 7-2, where S_1 is the pre-tax supply curve and S_2 is the post-tax supply curve. As you can see, the market equilibrium moves from *E*, at the equilibrium price of $80 per room and 10,000 rooms rented each night, to *A*, at a market price of $100 per room and only 5,000 rooms rented each night. *A* is, of course, on both the demand curve *D* and

FIGURE 7-2

An Excise Tax Imposed on Hotel Owners

A $40 per room tax imposed on hotel owners shifts the supply curve from S_1 to S_2, an upward shift of $40. The equilibrium price of hotel rooms rises from $80 to $100 a night, and the equilibrium quantity of rooms rented falls from 10,000 to 5,000. Although hotel owners pay the tax, they actually bear only half the burden: the price they receive net of tax falls only $20, from $80 to $60. Guests who rent rooms bear the other half of the burden, because the price they pay rises by $20, from $80 to $100.

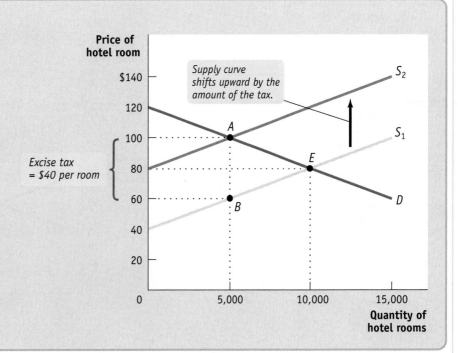

the new supply curve S_2. In this case, $100 is the demand price of 5,000 rooms—but in effect hotel owners receive only $60, when you account for the fact that they have to pay the $40 tax. From the point of view of hotel owners, it is as if they were on their original supply curve at point B.

Let's check this again. How do we know that 5,000 rooms will be supplied at a price of $100? Because the price *net of tax* is $60, and according to the original supply curve, 5,000 rooms will be supplied at a price of $60, as shown by point B in Figure 7-2.

Does this look familiar? It should. In Chapter 5 we described the effects of a quota on sales: a quota *drives a wedge* between the price paid by consumers and the price received by producers. An excise tax does the same thing. As a result of this wedge, consumers pay more and producers receive less. In our example, consumers—people who rent hotel rooms—end up paying $100 a night, $20 more than the pre-tax price of $80. At the same time, producers—the hotel owners—receive a price net of tax of $60 per room, $20 less than the pre-tax price. In addition, the tax creates missed opportunities: 5,000 potential consumers who would have rented hotel rooms—those willing to pay $80 but not $100 per night—are discouraged from renting rooms. Correspondingly, 5,000 rooms that would have been made available by hotel owners when they receive $80 are not offered when they receive only $60. Like a quota, this tax leads to inefficiency by distorting incentives and creating missed opportunities for mutually beneficial transactions.

It's important to recognize that as we've described it, Potterville's hotel tax is a tax on the hotel owners, not their guests—it's a tax on the producers, not the consumers. Yet the price received by producers, net of tax, is down by only $20, half the amount of the tax, and the price paid by consumers is up by $20. In effect, half the tax is being paid by consumers.

What would happen if the city levied a tax on consumers instead of producers? That is, suppose that instead of requiring hotel owners to pay $40 a night for each room they rent, the city required hotel *guests* to pay $40 for each night they stayed in a hotel. The answer is shown in Figure 7-3. If a hotel guest must pay a tax of $40 per night, then the price for a room paid by that guest must be reduced by $40 in order for the quantity of hotel rooms demanded post-tax to be the same as that demanded pre-tax. So the demand curve shifts *downward*, from D_1 to D_2, by the amount of the tax. At every quantity demanded, the demand price—the price that consumers must be offered

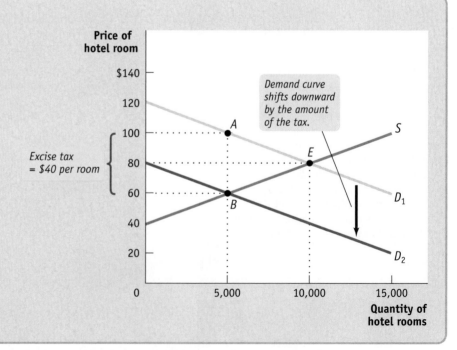

FIGURE 7-3

An Excise Tax Imposed on Hotel Guests

A $40 per room tax imposed on hotel guests shifts the demand curve from D_1 to D_2, a downward shift of $40. The equilibrium price of hotel rooms falls from $80 to $60 a night, and the quantity of rooms rented falls from 10,000 to 5,000. Although in this case the tax is officially paid by consumers, while in Figure 7-2 the tax was paid by producers, the outcome is the same: after taxes, hotel owners receive $60 per room but guests pay $100. This illustrates a general principle: *The incidence of an excise tax doesn't depend on whether consumers or producers officially pay the tax.*

to demand a given quantity—has fallen by $40. This shifts the equilibrium from *E* to *B*, where the market price of hotel rooms is $60 and 5,000 hotel rooms are bought and sold. In effect, hotel guests pay $100 when you include the tax. So from the point of view of guests, it is as if they were on their original demand curve at point *A*.

If you compare Figures 7-2 and 7-3, you will immediately notice that they show the same price effect. In each case, consumers pay an effective price of $100, producers receive an effective price of $60, and 5,000 hotel rooms are bought and sold. *In fact, it doesn't matter who officially pays the tax—the equilibrium outcome is the same.*

This insight illustrates a general principle of the economics of taxation: the **incidence** of a tax—who really bears the burden of the tax—is typically not a question you can answer by asking who writes the check to the government. In this particular case, a $40 tax on hotel rooms is reflected in a $20 increase in the price paid by consumers and a $20 decrease in the price received by producers. Here, regardless of whether the tax is levied on consumers or producers, the incidence of the tax is evenly split between them.

The **incidence** of a tax is a measure of who really pays it.

Price Elasticities and Tax Incidence

We've just learned that the incidence of an excise tax doesn't depend on who officially pays it. In the example shown in Figures 7-1 through 7-3, a tax on hotel rooms falls equally on consumers and producers, no matter who the tax is levied on. But it's important to note that this 50–50 split between consumers and producers is a result of our assumptions in this example. In the real world, the incidence of an excise tax usually falls unevenly between consumers and producers: one group bears more of the burden than the other.

What determines how the burden of an excise tax is allocated between consumers and producers? The answer depends on the shapes of the supply and the demand curves. *More specifically, the incidence of an excise tax depends on the price elasticity of supply and the price elasticity of demand.* We can see this by looking first at a case in which consumers pay most of an excise tax, then at a case in which producers pay most of the tax.

When an Excise Tax Is Paid Mainly by Consumers Figure 7-4 shows an excise tax that falls mainly on consumers: an excise tax on gasoline, which we set at $1 per gallon. (There really is a federal excise tax on gasoline, though it is actually only about $0.18 per gallon in the United States. In addition, states impose excise taxes between $0.08 and $0.31 per gallon.) According to Figure 7-4, in the absence of the tax, gasoline would sell for $2 per gallon.

FIGURE 7-4

An Excise Tax Paid Mainly by Consumers

The relatively steep demand curve here reflects a low price elasticity of demand for gasoline. The relatively flat supply curve reflects a high price elasticity of supply. The pre-tax price of a gallon of gasoline is $2.00, and a tax of $1.00 per gallon is imposed. The price paid by consumers rises by $0.95 to $2.95, reflecting the fact that most of the burden of the tax falls on consumers. Only a small portion of the tax is borne by producers: the price they receive falls by only $0.05 to $1.95.

Two key assumptions are reflected in the shapes of the supply and demand curves in Figure 7-4. First, the price elasticity of demand for gasoline is assumed to be very low, so the demand curve is relatively steep. Recall that a low price elasticity of demand means that the quantity demanded changes little in response to a change in price. Second, the price elasticity of supply of gasoline is assumed to be very high, so the supply curve is relatively flat. A high price elasticity of supply means that the quantity supplied changes a lot in response to a change in price.

We have just learned that an excise tax drives a wedge, equal to the size of the tax, between the price paid by consumers and the price received by producers. This wedge drives the price paid by consumers up and the price received by producers down. But as we can see from Figure 7-4, in this case those two effects are very unequal in size. The price received by producers falls only slightly, from $2.00 to $1.95, but the price paid by consumers rises by a lot, from $2.00 to $2.95. This means that consumers bear the greater share of the tax burden.

This example illustrates another general principle of taxation: *When the price elasticity of demand is low and the price elasticity of supply is high, the burden of an excise tax falls mainly on consumers.* Why? A low price elasticity of demand means that consumers have few substitutes and so little alternative to buying higher-priced gasoline. In contrast, a high price elasticity of supply results from the fact that producers have many production substitutes for their gasoline (that is, other uses for the crude oil from which gasoline is refined). This gives producers much greater flexibility in refusing to accept lower prices for their gasoline. And, not surprisingly, the party with the least flexibility—in this case, consumers—gets stuck paying most of the tax. This is a good description of how the burden of the main excise taxes actually collected in the United States today, such as those on cigarettes and alcoholic beverages, is allocated between consumers and producers.

When an Excise Tax Is Paid Mainly by Producers Figure 7-5 shows an example of an excise tax paid mainly by producers, a $5.00 per day tax on downtown parking in a small city. In the absence of the tax, the market equilibrium price of parking is $6.00 per day.

We've assumed in this case that the price elasticity of supply is very low because the lots used for parking have very few alternative uses. This makes the supply curve for parking spaces relatively steep. The price elasticity of demand, however, is assumed to be high: consumers can easily switch from the downtown spaces to other parking spaces a few minutes' walk from downtown, spaces that are not subject to the tax. This makes the demand curve relatively flat.

FIGURE 7-5

An Excise Tax Paid Mainly by Producers

The relatively flat demand curve here reflects a high price elasticity of demand for downtown parking, and the relatively steep supply curve results from a low price elasticity of supply. The pre-tax price of a daily parking space is $6.00 and a tax of $5.00 is imposed. The price received by producers falls a lot, to $1.50, reflecting the fact that they bear most of the tax burden. The price paid by consumers rises a small amount, $0.50, to $6.50, so they bear very little of the burden.

The tax drives a wedge between the price paid by consumers and the price received by producers. In this example, however, the tax causes the price paid by consumers to rise only slightly, from $6.00 to $6.50, but the price received by producers falls a lot, from $6.00 to $1.50. In the end, a consumer bears only $0.50 of the $5 tax burden, with a producer bearing the remaining $4.50.

Again, this example illustrates a general principle: *When the price elasticity of demand is high and the price elasticity of supply is low, the burden of an excise tax falls mainly on producers.* A real-world example is a tax on purchases of existing houses. Over the past few years in many American towns, house prices in desirable locations have risen significantly as well-off outsiders move in and purchase homes from the less well-off original occupants, a phenomenon called gentrification. Some of these towns have imposed taxes on house sales intended to extract money from the new arrivals. But this ignores the fact that the price elasticity of demand for houses in a particular town is often high, because potential buyers can choose to move to other towns. Furthermore, the price elasticity of supply is often low because most sellers must sell their houses due to job transfers or to provide funds for their retirement. So taxes on home purchases are actually paid mainly by the less well-off sellers—not, as town officials imagine, by wealthy buyers.

Putting It All Together We've just seen that when the price elasticity of supply is high and the price elasticity of demand is low, an excise tax falls mainly on consumers. And when the price elasticity of supply is low and the price elasticity of demand is high, an excise tax falls mainly on producers. This leads us to the general rule: *When the price elasticity of demand is higher than the price elasticity of supply, an excise tax falls mainly on producers. When the price elasticity of supply is higher than the price elasticity of demand, an excise tax falls mainly on consumers.* So elasticity—not who officially pays the tax—determines the incidence of an excise tax.

➤ECONOMICS IN ACTION

Who Pays the FICA?

Anyone who works for an employer receives a paycheck that itemizes not only the wages paid but also the money deducted from the paycheck for various taxes. For most people, one of the big deductions is *FICA*, also known as the payroll tax. *FICA*, which stands for the Federal Insurance Contributions Act, pays for the Social Security and Medicare systems, federal social insurance programs that provide income and medical care to retired and disabled Americans.

As of the time of writing, most American workers paid 7.65% of their earnings in FICA. But this is literally only the half of it: each employer is required to pay an amount equal to the contribution of his or her employee.

How should we think about FICA? Is it really shared equally by workers and employers? We can use our previous analysis to answer that question because FICA is like an excise tax—a tax on the sale and purchase of labor. Half of it is a tax levied on the sellers—that is, workers. The other half is a tax levied on the buyers—that is, employers.

But we already know that the incidence of a tax does not really depend on who actually makes out the check. Almost all economists agree that FICA is a tax actually paid by workers, not by their employers. The reason for this conclusion lies in a comparison of the price elasticities of the supply of labor by households and the demand for labor by firms. Evidence indicates that the price elasticity of demand for labor is quite high, at least 3. That is, an increase in average wages of 1% would lead to at least a 3% decline in the number of hours of work demanded by employers. Labor economists believe, however, that the price elasticity of supply of labor is very low. The reason is that although a fall in the wage rate reduces the incentive to work more hours, it also makes people poorer and less able to afford leisure time. The strength of this second effect is shown in the data: the number of hours people are willing to work falls very little—if at all—when the wage per hour goes down.

Our general rule of tax incidence says that when the price elasticity of demand is much higher than the price elasticity of supply, the burden of an excise tax falls mainly on the suppliers. So the FICA falls mainly on the suppliers of labor, that is, workers—even though on paper half the tax is paid by employers. In other words, the FICA is largely borne by workers in the form of lower wages, rather than by employers in lower profits.

This conclusion tells us something important about the American tax system: the FICA, rather than the much-maligned income tax, is the main tax burden on most families. FICA is 15.3% of all wages and salaries up to $102,000 per year (note that 7.65% + 7.65% = 15.3%). That is, the great majority of workers in the United States pay 15.3% of their wages in FICA. Only a minority of American families pay more than 15% of their income in income tax. In fact, according to estimates by the Congressional Budget Office, for more than 70% of families FICA is Uncle Sam's main bite out of their income. ▲

< < < < < < < < < < <

► CHECK YOUR UNDERSTANDING 7-1

1. Consider the market for butter, shown in the accompanying figure. The government imposes an excise tax of $0.30 per pound of butter. What is the price paid by consumers post-tax? What is the price received by producers post-tax? What is the quantity of butter transacted? How is the incidence of the tax allocated between consumers and producers? Show this on the figure.

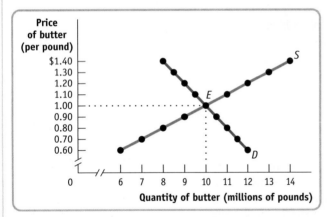

2. The demand for economics textbooks is very inelastic, but the supply is somewhat elastic. What does this imply about the incidence of an excise tax? Illustrate with a diagram.

3. True or false? When a substitute for a good is readily available to consumers, but it is difficult for producers to adjust the quantity of the good produced, then the burden of a tax on the good falls more heavily on producers.

4. The supply of bottled spring water is very inelastic, but the demand for it is somewhat elastic. What does this imply about the incidence of a tax? Illustrate with a diagram.

5. True or false? Other things equal, consumers would prefer to face a less elastic supply curve for a good or service when an excise tax is imposed.

Solutions appear at back of book.

The Benefits and Costs of Taxation

When a government is considering whether to impose a tax or how to design a tax system, it has to weigh the benefits of a tax against its costs. We don't usually think of a tax as something that provides benefits, but governments need money to provide things people want, such as national defense and health care for those unable to afford it. The benefit of a tax is the revenue it raises for the government to pay for these services. Unfortunately, this benefit comes at a cost—a cost that is normally larger than the amount consumers and producers pay. Let's look first at what determines how much money a tax raises, then at the costs a tax imposes.

The Revenue from an Excise Tax

How much revenue does the government collect from an excise tax? In our hotel tax example, the revenue is equal to the area of the shaded rectangle in Figure 7-6.

To see why this area represents the revenue collected by a $40 tax on hotel rooms, notice that the *height* of the rectangle is $40, equal to the tax per room. It is also, as

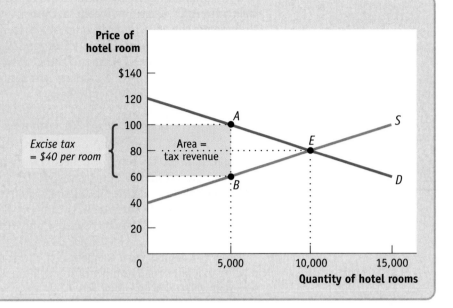

FIGURE 7-6

The Revenue from an Excise Tax

The revenue from a $40 excise tax on hotel rooms is $200,000, equal to the tax rate, $40—the size of the wedge that the tax drives between the supply price and the demand price—multiplied by the number of rooms rented, 5,000. This is equal to the area of the shaded rectangle.

we've seen, the size of the wedge that the tax drives between the supply price (the price received by producers) and the demand price (the price paid by consumers). Meanwhile, the *width* of the rectangle is 5,000 rooms, equal to the equilibrium quantity of rooms given the $40 tax. With that information, we can make the following calculations.

The tax revenue collected is:

$$\text{Tax revenue} = \$40 \text{ per room} \times 5{,}000 \text{ rooms} = \$200{,}000$$

The area of the shaded rectangle is:

$$\text{Area} = \text{Height} \times \text{Width} = \$40 \text{ per room} \times 5{,}000 \text{ rooms} = \$200{,}000$$

or,

$$\text{Tax revenue} = \text{Area of shaded rectangle}$$

This is a general principle: *The revenue collected by an excise tax is equal to the area of the rectangle whose height is the tax wedge between the supply and demand curves and whose width is the quantity transacted under the tax.*

Tax Rates and Revenue

In Figure 7-6, $40 per room is the *tax rate* on hotel rooms. A **tax rate** is the amount of tax levied per unit of whatever is being taxed. Sometimes tax rates are defined in terms of dollar amounts per unit of a good or service; for example, $2.46 per pack of cigarettes sold. In other cases, they are defined as a percentage of the price; for example, the payroll tax is 15.3% of a worker's earnings up to $102,000.

There's obviously a relationship between tax rates and revenue. That relationship is not, however, one-for-one. In general, doubling the excise tax rate on a good or service won't double the amount of revenue collected, because the tax increase will reduce the quantity of the good or service transacted. And the relationship between the level of the tax and the amount of revenue collected may not even be positive: in some cases raising the tax rate actually *reduces* the amount of revenue the government collects.

A **tax rate** is the amount of tax people are required to pay per unit of whatever is being taxed.

We can illustrate these points using our hotel room example. Figure 7-6 showed the revenue the government collects from a $40 tax on hotel rooms. Figure 7-7 shows the revenue the government would collect from two alternative tax rates—a lower tax of only $20 per room and a higher tax of $60 per room.

Panel (a) of Figure 7-7 shows the case of a $20 tax, equal to half the tax rate illustrated in Figure 7-6. At this lower tax rate, 7,500 rooms are rented, generating tax revenue of:

$$\text{Tax revenue} = \$20 \text{ per room} \times 7,500 \text{ rooms} = \$150,000$$

Recall that the tax revenue collected from a $40 tax rate is $200,000. So the revenue collected from a $20 tax rate, $150,000, is only 75% of the amount collected when the tax rate is twice as high ($150,000/$200,000 × 100 = 75%). To put it another way, a 100% increase in the tax rate from $20 to $40 per room leads to only a one-third, or 33.3%, increase in revenue, from $150,000 to $200,000 (($200,000 − $150,000)/$150,000 × 100 = 33.3%).

Panel (b) depicts what happens if the tax rate is raised from $40 to $60 per room, leading to a fall in the number of rooms rented from 5,000 to 2,500. The revenue collected at a $60 per room tax rate is:

$$\text{Tax revenue} = \$60 \text{ per room} \times 2,500 \text{ rooms} = \$150,000$$

This is also *less* than the revenue collected by a $40 per room tax. So raising the tax rate from $40 to $60 actually reduces revenue. More precisely, in this case raising the

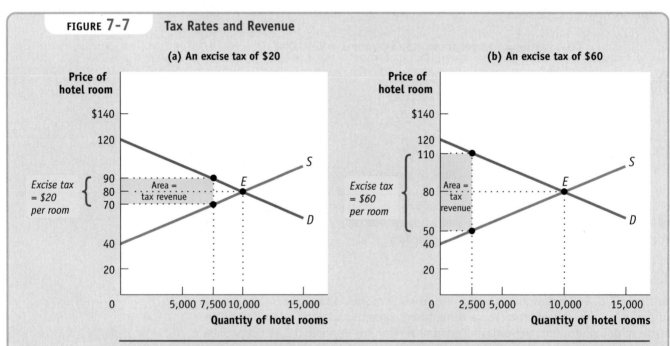

FIGURE 7-7 **Tax Rates and Revenue**

(a) An excise tax of $20

(b) An excise tax of $60

In general, doubling the excise tax rate on a good or service won't double the amount of revenue collected, because the tax increase will reduce the quantity of the good or service bought and sold. And the relationship between the level of the tax and the amount of revenue collected may not even be positive. Panel (a) shows the revenue raised by a tax rate of $20 per room, only half the tax rate in Figure 7-6. The tax revenue raised, equal to the area of the shaded rectangle, is $150,000, three-quarters as much as the revenue raised by a $40 tax rate. Panel (b) shows that the revenue raised by a $60 tax rate is also $150,000. So raising the tax rate from $40 to $60 actually *reduces* tax revenue.

tax rate by 50% (($60 − $40)/$40 × 100 = 50%) lowers the tax revenue by 25% (($150,000 − $200,000)/$200,000 × 100 = −25%). Why did this happen? It happened because the fall in tax revenue caused by the reduction in the number of rooms rented more than offset the increase in the tax revenue caused by the rise in the tax rate. In other words, setting a tax rate so high that it deters a significant number of transactions is likely to lead to a fall in tax revenue.

One way to think about the revenue effect of increasing an excise tax is that the tax increase affects tax revenue in two ways. On one side, the tax increase means that the government raises more revenue for each unit of the good sold, which other things equal would lead to a rise in tax revenue. On the other side, the tax increase reduces the quantity of sales, which other things equal would lead to a fall in tax revenue. The end result depends both on the price elasticities of supply and demand and on the initial level of the tax. If the price elasticities of both supply and demand are low, the tax increase won't reduce the quantity of the good sold very much, so that tax revenue will definitely rise. If the price elasticities are high, the result is less certain; if they are high enough, the tax reduces the quantity sold so much that tax revenue falls. Also, if the initial tax rate is low, the government doesn't lose much revenue from the decline in the quantity of the good sold, so the tax increase will definitely increase tax revenue. If the initial tax rate is high, the result is again less certain. Tax revenue is likely to fall or rise very little from a tax increase only in cases where the price elasticities are high and there is already a high tax rate.

The possibility that a higher tax rate can reduce tax revenue, and the corresponding possibility that cutting taxes can increase tax revenue, is a basic principle of taxation that policy makers take into account when setting tax rates. That is, when considering a tax created for the purpose of raising revenue (in contrast to taxes created to discourage undesirable behavior, known as "sin taxes"), a well-informed policy maker won't impose a tax rate so high that cutting the tax would increase revenue. In the real world, policy makers aren't always well informed, but they usually aren't complete fools either. That's why it's very hard to find real-world examples in which raising a tax reduced revenue or cutting a tax increased revenue. Nonetheless, the theoretical possibility that a tax reduction increases tax revenue has played an important role in the folklore of American politics. As explained in For Inquiring Minds, an economist who, in the 1970s, sketched on a napkin the figure of a revenue-increasing income tax reduction had a significant impact on the economic policies adopted in the United States in the 1980s.

FOR INQUIRING MINDS

The Laffer Curve

One afternoon in 1974, the economist Arthur Laffer got together in a cocktail lounge with Jude Wanniski, a writer for the *Wall Street Journal,* and Dick Cheney, who would later become vice president but at the time was the deputy White House chief of staff. During the course of their conversation, Laffer drew a diagram on a napkin that was intended to explain how tax cuts could sometimes lead to higher tax revenue. According to Laffer's diagram, raising tax rates initially increases revenue, but beyond a certain level revenue falls instead as tax rates continue to rise. That is, at some point tax rates are so high and reduce the number of transactions so greatly that tax revenues fall.

There was nothing new about this idea, but in later years that napkin became the stuff of legend. The editors of the *Wall Street Journal* began promoting the "Laffer curve" as a justification for tax cuts. And when Ronald Reagan took office in 1981, he used the Laffer curve to argue that his proposed cuts in income tax rates would not reduce the federal government's revenue.

So is there a Laffer curve? Yes—as a theoretical proposition it's definitely possible that tax rates could be so high that cutting taxes would increase revenue. But very few economists now believe that Reagan's tax cuts actually increased revenue, and real-world examples in which revenue and tax rates move in opposite directions are very hard to find. That's because it's rare to find an existing tax rate so high that reducing it leads to an increase in revenue.

The Costs of Taxation

What is the cost of a tax? You might be inclined to answer that it is the money taxpayers pay to the government. In other words, you might believe that the cost of a tax is the tax revenue collected. But suppose the government uses the tax revenue to provide services that taxpayers want. Or suppose that the government simply hands the tax revenue back to taxpayers. Would we say in those cases that the tax didn't actually cost anything?

No—because a tax, like a quota, prevents mutually beneficial transactions from occurring. Consider Figure 7-6 once more. Here, with a $40 tax on hotel rooms, guests pay $100 per room but hotel owners receive only $60 per room. Because of the wedge created by the tax, we know that some transactions don't occur that would have occurred without the tax. More specifically, we know from the supply and demand curves that there are some potential guests who would be willing to pay up to $90 per night and some hotel owners who would be willing to supply rooms if they received at least $70 per night. If these two sets of people were allowed to trade with each other without the tax, they would engage in mutually beneficial transactions—hotel rooms would be rented. But such deals would be illegal, because the $40 tax would not be paid. In our example, 5,000 potential hotel room rentals that would have occurred in the absence of the tax, to the mutual benefit of guests and hotel owners, do not take place because of the tax.

So an excise tax imposes costs over and above the tax revenue collected in the form of inefficiency, which occurs because the tax discourages mutually beneficial transactions. As we learned in Chapter 5, the cost to society of this kind of inefficiency—the value of the forgone mutually beneficial transactions—is called the deadweight loss. While all real-world taxes impose some deadweight loss, a badly designed tax imposes a larger deadweight loss than a well-designed one.

To measure the deadweight loss from a tax, we turn to the concepts of producer and consumer surplus. Figure 7-8 shows the effects of an excise tax on consumer and producer surplus. In the absence of the tax, the equilibrium is at E and the equilibrium price and quantity are P_E and Q_E, respectively. An excise tax drives a wedge equal to the amount of the tax between the price received by producers and the price paid by consumers, reducing the quantity sold. In this case, where the tax is T dollars per unit, the quantity sold falls to Q_T. The price paid by consumers rises to P_C, the

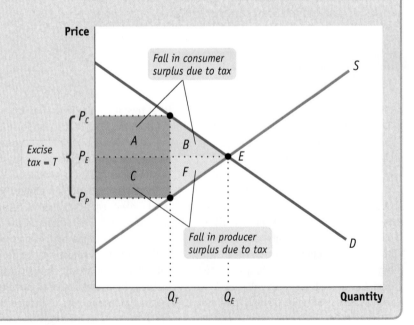

FIGURE 7-8

A Tax Reduces Consumer and Producer Surplus

Before the tax, the equilibrium price and quantity are P_E and Q_E, respectively. After an excise tax of T per unit is imposed, the price to consumers rises to P_C and consumer surplus falls by the sum of the dark blue rectangle, labeled A, and the light blue triangle, labeled B. The tax also causes the price to producers to fall to P_P; producer surplus falls by the sum of the dark red rectangle, labeled C, and the light red triangle, labeled F. The government receives revenue from the tax, $Q_T \times T$, which is given by the sum of the areas A and C. Areas B and F represent the losses to consumer and producer surplus that are not collected by the government as revenue; they are the deadweight loss to society of the tax.

demand price of the reduced quantity, Q_T, and the price received by producers falls to P_P, the supply price of that quantity. The difference between these prices, $P_C - P_P$, is equal to the excise tax, T.

Using the concepts of producer and consumer surplus, we can show exactly how much surplus producers and consumers lose as a result of the tax. From Figure 4-5 we learned that a fall in the price of a good generates a gain in consumer surplus that is equal to the sum of the areas of a rectangle and a triangle. Similarly, a price increase causes a loss to consumers that is represented by the sum of the areas of a rectangle and a triangle. So it's not surprising that in the case of an excise tax, the rise in the price paid by consumers causes a loss equal to the sum of the areas of a rectangle and a triangle: the dark blue rectangle labeled A and the area of the light blue triangle labeled B in Figure 7-8.

Meanwhile, the fall in the price received by producers leads to a fall in producer surplus. This, too, is equal to the sum of the areas of a rectangle and a triangle. The loss in producer surplus is the sum of the areas of the dark red rectangle labeled C and the light red triangle labeled F in Figure 7-8.

Of course, although consumers and producers are hurt by the tax, the government gains revenue. The revenue the government collects is equal to the tax per unit sold, T, multiplied by the quantity sold, Q_T. This revenue is equal to the area of a rectangle Q_T wide and T high. And we already have that rectangle in the figure: it is the sum of rectangles A and C. So the government gains part of what consumers and producers lose from an excise tax.

But a portion of the loss to producers and consumers from the tax is not offset by a gain to the government—specifically, the two triangles B and F. The deadweight loss caused by the tax is equal to the combined area of these two triangles. It represents the total surplus lost to society because of the tax—that is, the amount of surplus that would have been generated by transactions that now do not take place because of the tax.

Figure 7-9 is a version of Figure 7-8 that leaves out rectangles A (the surplus shifted from consumers to the government) and C (the surplus shifted from producers to the government) and shows only the deadweight loss, here drawn as a triangle shaded yellow. The base of that triangle is equal to the tax wedge, T; the height of the triangle is equal to the reduction in the quantity transacted due to the tax, $Q_E - Q_T$. Clearly, the

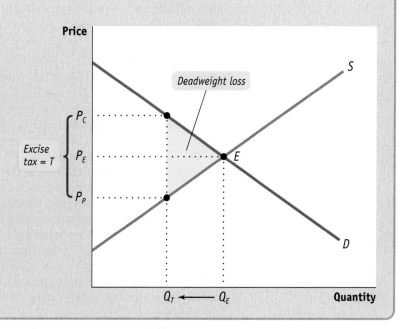

FIGURE 7-9

The Deadweight Loss of a Tax

A tax leads to a deadweight loss because it creates inefficiency: some mutually beneficial transactions never take place because of the tax, namely the transactions $Q_E - Q_T$. The yellow area here represents the value of the deadweight loss: it is the total surplus that would have been gained from the $Q_E - Q_T$ transactions. If the tax had not discouraged transactions—had the number of transactions remained at Q_E—no deadweight loss would have been incurred.

The **administrative costs** of a tax are the resources used by government to collect the tax, and by taxpayers to pay it, over and above the amount of the tax, as well as to evade it.

larger the tax wedge and the larger the reduction in the quantity transacted, the greater the inefficiency from the tax. But also note an important, contrasting point: if the excise tax somehow *didn't* reduce the quantity bought and sold in this market—if Q_T remained equal to Q_E after the tax was levied—the yellow triangle would disappear and the deadweight loss from the tax would be zero. This observation is simply the flip-side of the principle found earlier in the chapter: a tax causes inefficiency because it discourages mutually beneficial transactions between buyers and sellers. So if a tax does *not* discourage transactions, it causes no deadweight loss. In this case, the tax simply shifts surplus straight from consumers and producers to the government.

Using a triangle to measure deadweight loss is a technique used in many economic applications. For example, triangles are used to measure the deadweight loss produced by types of taxes other than excise taxes. They are also used to measure the deadweight loss produced by monopoly, another kind of market distortion. And deadweight-loss triangles are often used to evaluate the benefits and costs of public policies besides taxation—such as whether to impose stricter safety standards on a product.

In considering the total amount of inefficiency caused by a tax, we must also take into account something not shown in Figure 7-9: the resources actually used by the government to collect the tax, and by taxpayers to pay it, over and above the amount of the tax. These lost resources are called the **administrative costs** of the tax. The most familiar administrative cost of the U.S. tax system is the time individuals spend filling out their income tax forms or the money they spend on accountants to prepare their tax forms for them. (The latter is considered an inefficiency from the point of view of society because accountants could instead be performing other, non-tax-related services.) Included in the administrative costs that taxpayers incur are resources used to evade the tax, both legally and illegally. The costs of operating the Internal Revenue Service, the arm of the federal government tasked with collecting the federal income tax, are actually quite small in comparison to the administrative costs paid by taxpayers.

So the total inefficiency caused by a tax is the sum of its deadweight loss and its administrative costs. The general rule for economic policy is that, other things equal, a tax system should be designed to minimize the total inefficiency it imposes on society. In practice, other considerations also apply (as Margaret Thatcher learned), but this principle nonetheless gives valuable guidance. Administrative costs are usually well known, more or less determined by the current technology of collecting taxes (for example, filing paper returns versus filing electronically). But how can we predict the size of the deadweight loss associated with a given tax? Not surprisingly, as in our analysis of the incidence of a tax, the price elasticities of supply and demand play crucial roles in making such a prediction.

Elasticities and the Deadweight Loss of a Tax

We know that the deadweight loss from an excise tax arises because it prevents some mutually beneficial transactions from occurring. In particular, the producer and consumer surplus that is forgone because of these missing transactions is equal to the size of the deadweight loss itself. This means that the larger the number of transactions that are prevented by the tax, the larger the deadweight loss.

This fact gives us an important clue in understanding the relationship between elasticity and the size of the deadweight loss from a tax. Recall that when demand or supply is elastic, the quantity demanded or the quantity supplied is relatively responsive to changes in the price. So a tax imposed on a good for which either demand or supply, or both, is elastic will cause a relatively large decrease in the quantity transacted and a relatively large deadweight loss. And when we say that demand or supply is inelastic, we mean that the quantity demanded or the quantity supplied is relatively unresponsive to changes in the price. As a result, a tax imposed when demand or supply, or both, is inelastic will cause a relatively small decrease in the quantity transacted and a relatively small deadweight loss.

The four panels of Figure 7-10 illustrate the positive relationship between a good's price elasticity of either demand or supply and the deadweight loss from taxing that good. Each panel represents the same amount of tax imposed but on a different good; the size of the deadweight loss is given by the area of the shaded triangle. In panel (a), the deadweight-loss triangle is large because demand for this good is relatively elastic—a large number of transactions fail to occur because of the tax. In panel (b), the same supply curve is drawn as in panel (a), but demand for this good is relatively inelastic; as a result, the triangle is small because only a small number of transactions are forgone. Likewise, panels (c) and (d) contain the same demand curve but different supply curves. In panel (c), an elastic supply curve gives rise to a large

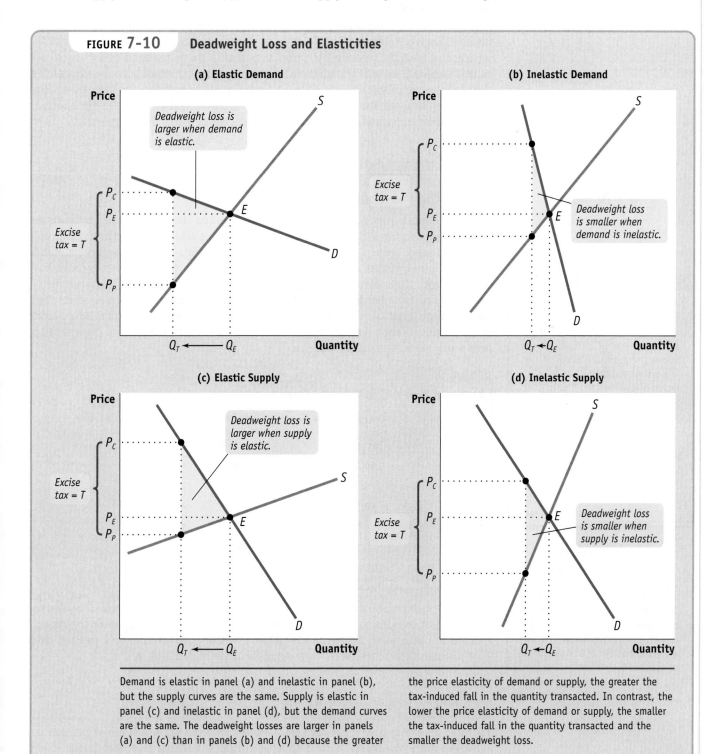

FIGURE 7-10   Deadweight Loss and Elasticities

Demand is elastic in panel (a) and inelastic in panel (b), but the supply curves are the same. Supply is elastic in panel (c) and inelastic in panel (d), but the demand curves are the same. The deadweight losses are larger in panels (a) and (c) than in panels (b) and (d) because the greater the price elasticity of demand or supply, the greater the tax-induced fall in the quantity transacted. In contrast, the lower the price elasticity of demand or supply, the smaller the tax-induced fall in the quantity transacted and the smaller the deadweight loss.

deadweight-loss triangle, but in panel (d) an inelastic supply curve gives rise to a small deadweight-loss triangle.

The implication of this result is clear: if you want to minimize the efficiency costs of taxation, you should choose to tax only those goods for which demand or supply, or both, is relatively inelastic. For such goods, a tax has little effect on behavior because behavior is relatively unresponsive to changes in the price. In the extreme case in which demand is perfectly inelastic (a vertical demand curve), the quantity demanded is unchanged by the imposition of the tax. As a result, the tax imposes no deadweight loss. Similarly, if supply is perfectly inelastic (a vertical supply curve), the quantity supplied is unchanged by the tax and there is also no deadweight loss. So if the goal in choosing whom to tax is to minimize deadweight loss, then taxes should be imposed on goods and services that have the most inelastic response—that is, goods and services for which consumers or producers will change their behavior the least in response to the tax. (Unless they have a tendency to riot, of course.) And this lesson carries a flip-side: using a tax to purposely decrease the amount of a harmful activity, such as underage drinking, will have the most impact when that activity is elastically demanded or supplied.

►ECONOMICS IN ACTION

Taxing the Marlboro Man

One of the most important excise taxes in the United States is the tax on cigarettes. The federal government imposes a tax of 39 cents a pack; state governments impose taxes that range from 7 cents a pack in South Carolina to $2.46 a pack in Rhode Island; and many cities impose further taxes. In general, tax rates on cigarettes have increased over time, because more and more governments have seen them not just as a source of revenue but as a way to discourage smoking. But the rise in cigarette taxes has not been gradual. Usually, once a state government decides to raise cigarette taxes, it raises them a lot—which provides economists with useful data on what happens when there is a big tax increase.

TABLE 7-1

Results of Increases in Cigarette Taxes

State	Year	Increase in tax (per pack)	New state tax (per pack)	Change in quantity transacted	Change in tax revenue
Utah	1997	$0.25	$0.52	−20.7%	+86.2%
Maryland	1999	0.30	0.66	−15.3	+52.6
California	1999	0.50	0.87	−18.9	+90.7
Michigan	1994	0.50	0.75	−20.8	+139.9
New York	2000	0.55	1.11	−20.2	+57.4

Source: M. C. Farrelly, C. T. Nimsch, and J. James, "State Cigarette Excise Taxes: Implications for Revenue and Tax Evasion," RTI International 2003.

Table 7-1 above shows the results of big increases in cigarette taxes. In each case, sales fell, just as our analysis predicts. Although it's theoretically possible for tax revenue to fall after such a large tax increase, in reality tax revenue rose in each case. That's because cigarettes have a low price elasticity of demand. ▲

< < < < < < < < < < < <

► CHECK YOUR UNDERSTANDING 7-2

1. The accompanying table shows five consumers' willingness to pay for one can of diet soda each as well as five producers' costs of selling one can of diet soda each. Each consumer buys at most one can of soda; each producer sells at most one can of soda. The government asks your advice about the effects of an excise tax of $0.40 per can of diet soda. Assume that there are no administrative costs from the tax.

a. Without the excise tax, what is the equilibrium price and the equilibrium quantity of soda transacted?

b. The excise tax raises the price paid by consumers post-tax to $0.60 and lowers the price received by producers post-tax to $0.20. With the excise tax, what is the quantity of soda transacted?

c. Without the excise tax, how much individual consumer surplus does each of the consumers gain? How much with the tax? How much total consumer surplus is lost as a result of the tax?

d. Without the excise tax, how much individual producer surplus does each of the producers gain? How much with the tax? How much total producer surplus is lost as a result of the tax?

e. How much government revenue does the excise tax create?

f. What is the deadweight loss from the imposition of this excise tax?

Consumer	Willingness to pay	Producer	Cost
Ana	$0.70	Zhang	$0.10
Bernice	0.60	Yves	0.20
Chizuko	0.50	Xavier	0.30
Dagmar	0.40	Walter	0.40
Ella	0.30	Vern	0.50

2. In each of the following cases, focus on the price elasticity of demand and use a diagram to illustrate the likely size—small or large—of the deadweight loss resulting from a tax. Explain your reasoning.

a. Gasoline

b. Milk chocolate bars

Solutions appear at back of book.

Tax Fairness and Tax Efficiency

We've just seen how economic analysis can be used to determine the inefficiency caused by a tax. It's clear that, other things equal, policy makers should choose a tax that creates less inefficiency over a tax that creates more. But that guideline still leaves policy makers with wide discretion in choosing what to tax and, consequently, who bears the burden of the tax. How should they exercise this discretion?

One answer is that policy makers should make the tax system fair. But what exactly does fairness mean? Moreover, however you define fairness, how should policy makers balance considerations of fairness versus considerations of efficiency?

Two Principles of Tax Fairness

Fairness, like beauty, is often in the eyes of the beholder. When it comes to taxes, however, most debates about fairness rely on one of two principles of tax fairness: the *benefits principle* and the *ability-to-pay principle*.

According to the **benefits principle** of tax fairness, those who benefit from public spending should bear the burden of the tax that pays for that spending. For example, those who benefit from a road should pay for that road's upkeep, those who fly on airplanes should pay for air traffic control, and so on. The benefits principle is the basis for some parts of the U.S. tax system. For example, revenue from the federal tax on gasoline is specifically reserved for the maintenance and improvement of federal roads, including the Interstate Highway System. In this way motorists, who benefit from the highway system, also pay for it.

The benefits principle is attractive from an economic point of view because it matches well with one of the major justifications for public spending—the theory of public goods, which will be covered in Chapter 18. This theory explains why government action is sometimes needed to provide people with goods that markets alone would not provide, goods like national defense. If that's the role of government, it seems natural to charge each person in proportion to the benefits he or she gets from those goods.

Practical considerations, however, make it impossible to base the entire tax system on the benefits principle. It would be too cumbersome to have a specific tax for each of the many distinct programs that the government offers. Also, attempts to base

According to the **benefits principle** of tax fairness, those who benefit from public spending should bear the burden of the tax that pays for that spending.

According to the **ability-to-pay principle** of tax fairness, those with greater ability to pay a tax should pay more tax.

A **lump-sum tax** is the same for everyone, regardless of any actions people take.

taxes on the benefits principle often conflict with the other major principle of tax fairness: the **ability-to-pay principle,** according to which those with greater ability to pay a tax should pay more.

The ability-to-pay principle is usually interpreted to mean that high-income individuals should pay more in taxes than low-income individuals. Often the ability-to-pay principle is used to argue not only that high-income individuals should pay more taxes but also that they should pay a higher *percentage* of their income in taxes. We'll consider the issue of how taxes vary as a percentage of income later.

The London protest described at the beginning of this chapter was basically a protest against the failure of the poll tax to take the ability-to-pay principle into account. In some parts of Britain, the poll tax was as high as £550 (equivalent to around $1,400 in today's dollars) per adult per year. For highly paid executives or professionals, £550 was not a lot of money. But for struggling British families, £550 per year was a crushing burden. It's not surprising that many people were upset that the new tax completely disregarded the ability-to-pay principle.

Equity versus Efficiency

Margaret Thatcher's poll tax was an example of a **lump-sum tax,** a tax that is the same for everyone regardless of any actions people take. It was widely perceived as much less fair than the tax structure it replaced, in which local taxes were proportional to property values. Under the old system, the highest local taxes were paid by the people with the most expensive houses. Because these people tended to be wealthy, they were also best able to bear the burden.

But the old system definitely distorted incentives to engage in mutually beneficial transactions and created deadweight loss. People who were considering home improvements knew that such improvements, by making their property more valuable, would increase their tax bills. The result, surely, was that some home improvements that would have taken place without the tax did not take place because of it.

In contrast, a lump-sum tax does not distort incentives. Because under a lump-sum tax people have to pay the same amount of tax regardless of their actions, it does not lead them to change their actions and therefore causes no deadweight loss. So lump-sum taxes, although unfair, are better than other taxes at promoting economic efficiency.

FOR INQUIRING MINDS

Killing the Lawyers

Perhaps Margaret Thatcher wouldn't have tried to impose a poll tax if she had remembered her English history. For it was the tripling of an existing poll tax that set off the great English peasant rebellion of 1381.

In that rebellion, peasants under the leadership of Wat Tyler marched on London to demand a repeal of the tax. One of their slogans was "The first thing to do is to kill all the lawyers." (Lawyers at that time were responsible for enforcing the tax.) The rebels did kill quite a few lawyers and tax collectors; they also burned part of

London and came close to taking King Richard II hostage. However, they dispersed after the king promised some concessions—a promise he promptly broke. After all, in 1381 royal promises to peasants didn't count: as the king declared before hanging Wat Tyler and the other rebel leaders, "Villeins ye are, and villeins ye shall remain." (*Villein* is a fourteenth-century English term for a peasant.)

Nonetheless, the fact that the rebellion came so close to success struck terror into the hearts of the English nobility, and it remained a cautionary tale for centuries.

A lesson from history: in 1381, English peasants revolted over unfair taxes.

A tax system can be made fairer by moving it in the direction of the benefits principle or the ability-to-pay principle. But this will come at a cost because the tax system will now tax people more heavily based on their actions, increasing the amount of deadweight loss. This observation reflects a general principle that we learned in Chapter 1: there is often a trade-off between equity and efficiency. Here, unless a tax system is badly designed, it can be made fairer only by sacrificing efficiency. Conversely, it can be made more efficient only by making it less fair. This means that there is normally a **trade-off between equity and efficiency** in the design of a tax system.

It's important to understand that economic analysis cannot say how much weight a tax system should give to equity and how much to efficiency. That choice is a value judgment, one we make through the political process.

> In a well-designed tax system, there is a **trade-off between equity and efficiency:** the system can be made more efficient only by making it less fair, and vice versa.

►ECONOMICS IN ACTION

Federal Tax Philosophy

What is the principle underlying the federal tax system? (By federal, we mean taxes collected by the federal government, as opposed to the taxes collected by state and local governments.) The answer is that it depends on the tax.

The best-known federal tax, accounting for about half of all federal revenue, is the income tax. The structure of the income tax reflects the ability-to-pay principle: families with low incomes pay little or no income tax. In fact, some families pay negative income tax: a program known as the Earned Income Tax Credit "tops up" or adds to the earnings of low-wage workers. Meanwhile, those with high incomes not only pay a lot of income tax, but must pay a larger share of their income in income taxes than the average family.

The second most important federal tax, FICA, also known as the payroll tax, is set up very differently. It was originally introduced in 1935 to pay for Social Security, a program that guarantees retirement income to qualifying older Americans and also provides benefits to workers who become disabled and to family members of workers who die. (Part of the payroll tax is now also used to pay for Medicare, a program that pays most medical bills of older Americans.) The Social Security system was set up to resemble a private insurance program: people pay into the system during their working years, then receive benefits based on their payments. And the tax more or less reflects the benefits principle: because the benefits of Social Security are mainly intended to assist lower- and middle-income people, and don't increase substantially for the rich, the Social Security tax is levied only on incomes up to a maximum level—$102,000 in 2008. (The Medicare portion of the payroll tax continues to be levied on incomes over $102,000.) As a result, a high-income family doesn't pay much more in payroll taxes than a middle-income family.

Table 7-2 illustrates the difference in the two taxes, using data from a Congressional Budget Office study. The study divided American families into quintiles: the bottom quintile is the poorest 20% of families, the second quintile is the next poorest 20%, and so on. The second column shows the share of total U.S. pre-tax income received by each quintile. The third column shows the share of total federal income tax collected that is paid by each quintile. As you can see, low-income families actually paid negative income tax through the Earned Income Tax Credit program. Even middle-income families paid a substantially smaller share of total income tax collected than their share of

TABLE **7-2**

Share of Pre-Tax Income, Federal Income Tax, and Payroll Tax, by Quintile in 2005

Income group	Percent of total pre-tax income received	Percent of total federal income tax paid	Percent of total payroll tax paid
Bottom quintile	4.0%	−2.9%	4.3%
Second quintile	8.5	−0.9	10.1
Third quintile	13.3	4.4	16.7
Fourth quintile	19.8	13.1	25.1
Top quintile	55.1	86.3	43.6

Source: Congressional Budget Office.

total income. In contrast, the fifth or top quintile, the richest 20% of families, paid a much higher share of total federal income tax collected compared with their share of total income. The fourth column shows the share of total payroll tax collected that is paid by each quintile, and the results are very different: the share of total payroll tax paid by the top quintile is substantially *less* than their share of total income. ▲

< < < < < < < < < < < <

> **CHECK YOUR UNDERSTANDING** 7-3

1. Assess each of the following taxes in terms of the benefits principle versus the ability-to-pay principle. What, if any, actions are distorted by the tax? Assume for simplicity in each case that the purchaser of the good bears 100% of the burden of the tax.

a. A federal tax of $500 for each new car purchased that finances highway safety programs

b. A local tax of 20% on hotel rooms that finances local government expenditures

c. A local tax of 1% on the assessed value of homes that finances local schools

d. A 1% sales tax on food that pays for government food safety regulation and inspection programs

Solutions appear at back of book.

Understanding the Tax System

An excise tax is the easiest tax to analyze, making it a good vehicle for understanding the general principles of tax analysis. However, in the United States today, excise taxes are actually a relatively minor source of government revenue. In this section, we develop a framework for understanding more general forms of taxation and look at some of the major taxes used in the United States.

Tax Bases and Tax Structure

Every tax consists of two pieces: a *base* and a *structure*. The **tax base** is the measure or value that determines how much tax an individual or firm pays. It is usually a monetary measure, like income or property value. The **tax structure** specifies how the tax depends on the tax base. It is usually expressed in percentage terms; for example, homeowners in some areas might pay taxes equal to 2% of the value of their homes.

Some important taxes and their tax bases are as follows:

■ **Income tax:** a tax that depends on the income of an individual or family from wages and investments

■ **Payroll tax:** a tax that depends on the earnings an employer pays to an employee

■ **Sales tax:** a tax that depends on the value of goods sold (also known as an excise tax)

■ **Profits tax:** a tax that depends on a firm's profits

■ **Property tax:** a tax that depends on the value of property, such as the value of a home

■ **Wealth tax:** a tax that depends on an individual's wealth

Once the tax base has been defined, the next question is how the tax depends on the base. The simplest tax structure is a **proportional tax,** also sometimes called a *flat tax,* which is the same percentage of the base regardless of the taxpayer's income or wealth. For example, a property tax that is set at 2% of the value of the property, whether the property is worth $10,000 or $10,000,000, is a proportional tax. Many taxes, however, are not proportional. Instead, different people pay different percentages, usually because the tax law tries to take account of either the benefits principle or the ability-to-pay principle.

The **tax base** is the measure or value, such as income or property value, that determines how much tax an individual or firm pays.

The **tax structure** specifies how the tax depends on the tax base.

An **income tax** is a tax on an individual's or family's income.

A **payroll tax** is a tax on the earnings an employer pays to an employee.

A **sales tax** is a tax on the value of goods sold.

A **profits tax** is a tax on a firm's profits.

A **property tax** is a tax on the value of property, such as the value of a home.

A **wealth tax** is a tax on an individual's wealth.

A **proportional tax** is the same percentage of the tax base regardless of the taxpayer's income or wealth.

Because taxes are ultimately paid out of income, economists classify taxes according to how they vary with the income of individuals. A tax that rises *more* than in proportion to income, so that high-income taxpayers pay a larger percentage of their income than low-income taxpayers, is a **progressive tax.** A tax that rises *less* than in proportion to income, so that higher-income taxpayers pay a smaller percentage of their income than low-income taxpayers, is a **regressive tax.** A proportional tax on income would be neither progressive nor regressive.

The U.S. tax system contains a mixture of progressive and regressive taxes, though it is somewhat progressive overall.

> A **progressive tax** takes a larger share of the income of high-income taxpayers than of low-income taxpayers.
>
> A **regressive tax** takes a smaller share of the income of high-income taxpayers than of low-income taxpayers.
>
> The **marginal tax rate** is the percentage of an increase in income that is taxed away.

Equity, Efficiency, and Progressive Taxation

Most, though not all, people view a progressive tax system as fairer than a regressive system. The reason is the ability-to-pay principle: a high-income family that pays 35% of its income in taxes is still left with a lot more money than a low-income family that pays only 15% in taxes. But attempts to make taxes strongly progressive run up against the trade-off between equity and efficiency.

To see why, consider a hypothetical example, illustrated in Table 7-3. We assume that there are two kinds of people in the nation of Taxmania: half of the population earns $40,000 a year and half earns $80,000, so the average income is $60,000 a year. We also assume that the Taxmanian government needs to collect one-fourth of that income—$15,000 a year per person—in taxes.

One way to raise this revenue would be through a proportional tax that takes one-fourth of everyone's income. The results of this proportional tax are shown in the second column of Table 7-3: after taxes, lower-income Taxmanians would be left with an income of $30,000 a year and higher-income Taxmanians, $60,000.

TABLE 7-3

Proportional versus Progressive Taxes in Taxmania

Pre-tax income	After-tax income with proportional taxation	After-tax income with progressive taxation
$40,000	$30,000	$40,000
$80,000	$60,000	$50,000

Even this system might have some negative effects on incentives. Suppose, for example, that finishing college improves a Taxmanian's chance of getting a higher-paying job. Some people who would invest time and effort in going to college in hopes of raising their income from $40,000 to $80,000, a $40,000 gain, might not bother if the potential gain is only $30,000, the after-tax difference in pay between a lower-paying and higher-paying job.

But a strongly progressive tax system could create a much bigger incentive problem. Suppose that the Taxmanian government decided to exempt the poorer half of the population from all taxes, but still wanted to raise the same amount of revenue. To do this, it would have to collect $30,000 from each individual earning $80,000 a year. As the third column of Table 7-3 shows, people earning $80,000 would then be left with income after taxes of $50,000—only $10,000 more than the after-tax income of people earning half as much. This would greatly reduce the incentive for people to invest time and effort to raise their earnings.

The point here is that any income tax system will tax away part of the gain an individual gets by moving up the income scale, reducing the incentive to earn more. But a progressive tax takes away a larger share of the gain than a proportional tax, creating a more adverse effect on incentives. In comparing the incentive effects of tax systems, economists often focus on the **marginal tax rate:** the percentage of an increase in income that is taxed away. In this example, the marginal tax rate on income above $40,000 is 25% with proportional taxation but 75% with progressive taxation.

Our hypothetical example is much more extreme than the reality of progressive taxation in the modern United States—although, as the upcoming Economics in Action explains, in previous years the marginal tax rates paid by high earners were very high indeed. However, these have moderated over time as concerns arose about the severe incentive effects of extremely progressive taxes. In short, the ability-to-pay principle pushes governments toward a highly progressive tax system, but efficiency considerations push them the other way.

TABLE 7-4

Major Taxes in the United States, 2006

Federal taxes ($ billion)		State and local taxes ($ billion)	
Income	$1,537.5	Income	$275.1
Payroll	901.6	Sales	415.4
Profits	373.1	Profits	62.4
		Property	367.8

Source: Department of Commerce, Bureau of Economic Analysis.

Taxes in the United States

Table 7-4 shows the revenue raised by major taxes in the United States in 2006. Some of the taxes are collected by the federal government and the others by state and local governments.

There is a major tax corresponding to five of the six tax bases we identified earlier. There are income taxes, payroll taxes, sales taxes, profits taxes, and property taxes, all of which play an important role in the overall tax system. The only item missing is a wealth tax. In fact, the United States does have a wealth tax, the *estate tax,* which depends on the value of someone's estate after he or she dies. But at the time of writing, the current law phases out the estate tax over a few years, and in any case it raises much less money than the taxes shown in the table.

In addition to the taxes shown, state and local governments collect substantial revenue from other sources as varied as driver's license fees and sewer charges. These fees and charges are an important part of the tax burden but very difficult to summarize or analyze.

Are the taxes in Table 7-4 progressive or regressive? It depends on the tax. The personal income tax is strongly progressive. The payroll tax, which, except for the Medicare portion, is paid only on earnings up to $102,000, is somewhat regressive. Sales taxes are generally regressive, because higher-income families save more of their income and thus spend a smaller share of it on taxable goods than do lower-income families. In addition, there are other taxes principally levied at the state and local level that are typically quite regressive: it costs the same amount to get a new driver's license no matter what your income is.

Overall, the taxes collected by the federal government are quite progressive. The second column of Table 7-5 shows estimates of the average federal tax rate paid by families at different levels of income earned in 2004. These estimates don't count just the money families pay directly. They also attempt to estimate the incidence of taxes directly paid by businesses, like the tax on corporate profits, which ultimately falls on individual shareholders. The table shows that the federal tax system is indeed progressive, with low-income families paying a relatively small share of their income in federal taxes and high-income families paying a greater share of their income.

Since 2000, the federal government has cut income taxes for most families. The largest cuts, both as a share of income and as a share of federal taxes collected, have gone to families with high incomes. As a result, the federal system is less progressive (at the time of writing) than it was in 2000 because the share of income paid by high-income families has fallen relative to the share paid by middle- and low-income families. And it will become even less progressive over the next few years, as some delayed pieces of the post-2000 tax cut legislation take effect. However, even after those changes, the federal tax system will remain progressive.

As the third column of Table 7-5 shows, however, taxes at the state and local levels are generally regressive. That's because the sales tax, the largest source of revenue for most states, is somewhat regressive, and other items, such as vehicle licensing fees, are strongly regressive.

Overall, the U.S. tax system is somewhat progressive, with the richest fifth of the population paying a somewhat higher share of income in taxes than families in the middle and the poorest fifth paying considerably less.

Yet there are important differences within the American tax system: the federal income tax is more progressive than the payroll tax, which can be seen from Table 7-2. And federal taxation is more progressive than state and local taxation.

TABLE 7-5

Federal, State, and Local Taxes as a Percentage of Income, by Income Category, 2004

Income group	Federal	State and local	Total
Bottom quintile	7.9%	11.8%	19.7%
Second quintile	11.4	11.9	23.3
Third quintile	15.8	11.2	27.0
Fourth quintile	18.7	11.0	29.8
Next 15%	21.1	10.5	31.6
Next 4%	22.5	9.7	32.2
Top 1%	24.6	8.2	32.8
Average	19.8	10.3	30.1

Source: Institute on Taxation and Economic Policy.

GLOBAL COMPARISON YOU THINK YOU PAY HIGH TAXES?

Everyone, everywhere complains about taxes. But citizens of the United States actually have less to complain about than citizens of most other wealthy countries.

To assess the overall level of taxes, economists usually calculate taxes as a share of *gross domestic product*—the total value of goods and services produced in a country. By this measure, as you can see in the accompanying figure, U.S. taxes are near the bottom of the scale. Even our neighbor Canada has significantly higher taxes. Tax rates in Europe, where governments need a lot of revenue to pay for extensive benefits such as guaranteed health care and generous unemployment benefits, are 50% to 100% higher than in the United States.

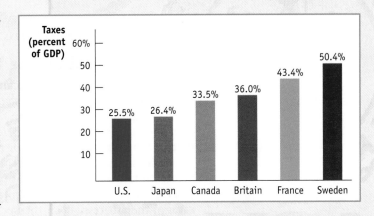

Source: OECD in Figures 2007.

Different Taxes, Different Principles

Why are some taxes progressive but others regressive? Can't the government make up its mind?

There are two main reasons for the mixture of regressive and progressive taxes in the U.S. system: the difference between levels of government and the fact that different taxes are based on different principles.

State and especially local governments generally do not make much effort to apply the ability-to-pay principle. This is largely because they are subject to *tax competition:* a state or local government that imposes high taxes on people with high incomes faces the prospect that those people may move to other locations where taxes are lower. This is much less of a concern at the national level, although a handful of very rich people have given up their U.S. citizenship to avoid paying U.S. taxes.

Although the federal government is in a better position than state or local governments to apply principles of fairness, it applies different principles to different taxes. We saw an example of this in the preceding Economics in Action. The most important tax, the federal income tax, is strongly progressive, reflecting the ability-to-pay principle. But the second most important tax, the federal payroll tax, is somewhat regressive,

FOR INQUIRING MINDS

Taxing Income versus Taxing Consumption

The U.S. government taxes people mainly on the money they *make,* not on the money they spend on consumption. Yet most tax experts argue that this policy badly distorts incentives. Someone who earns income and then invests that income for the future gets taxed twice: once on the original sum and again on any earnings made from the investment. So a system that taxes income rather than consumption discourages people from saving and investing, instead

providing an incentive to spend their income today. And encouraging saving and investing is an important policy goal, both because empirical data show that Americans tend to save too little for retirement and health expenses in their later years and because saving and investing contribute to economic growth.

Moving from a system that taxes income to one that taxes consumption would solve this problem. In fact, the governments of

many countries get much of their revenue from a value-added tax, or VAT, which acts like a national sales tax. In some countries VAT rates are very high; in Sweden, for example, the rate is 25%.

The United States does not have a value-added tax for two main reasons. One is that it is difficult, though not impossible, to make a consumption tax progressive. The other is that a VAT typically has very high administrative costs.

because most of it is linked to specific programs—Social Security and Medicare—and, reflecting the benefits principle, is levied more or less in proportion to the benefits received from these programs.

►*ECONOMICS IN ACTION*

The Top Marginal Income Tax Rate

The amount of money an American owes in federal income taxes is defined in terms of marginal tax rates on successively higher "brackets" of income. For example, in 2007 a single person paid 10% on the first $7,825 of taxable income (that is, income after subtracting exemptions and deductions); 15% on the next $24,050; and so on up to a top rate of 35% on his or her income, if any, over $349,700. Relatively few people (less than 1% of taxpayers) have incomes high enough to pay the top marginal rate. In fact, 77% of Americans pay no income tax or they fall into either the 10% or 15% bracket. But the top marginal income tax rate is often viewed as a useful indicator of the progressivity of the tax system, because it shows just how high a tax rate the U.S. government is willing to impose on the very affluent.

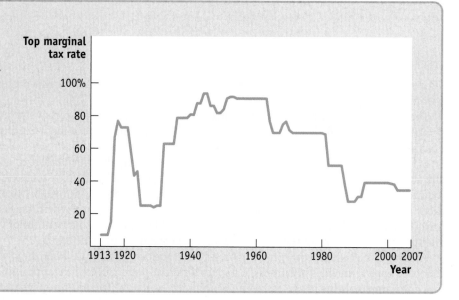

FIGURE 7-11

The Top Marginal Income Tax Rate

The marginal tax rate imposed on the highest income bracket has varied greatly over time. It shot up during the administration of Franklin Delano Roosevelt in the 1930s and 1940s, and it fell sharply during the administration of Ronald Reagan in the 1980s. The current top tax rate, 35%, is low by historical standards.

Source: U.S. Internal Revenue Service.

Figure 7-11 shows the top marginal income tax rate from 1913, when the U.S. government first imposed an income tax, to 2007. The first big increase in the top marginal rate came during World War I (1914) and was reversed after the war ended (1918). After that, the figure is dominated by two big changes: a huge increase in the top marginal rate during the administration of Franklin Roosevelt (1933–1945) and a sharp reduction during the administration of Ronald Reagan (1981–1989). By comparison, recent changes have been relatively small potatoes. ▲

< < < < < < < < < < <

► CHECK YOUR UNDERSTANDING 7-4

1. An income tax taxes 1% of the first $10,000 of income and 2% on all income above $10,000.
   a. What is the marginal tax rate for someone with income of $5,000? How much total tax does this person pay? How much is this as a percentage of his or her income?
   b. What is the marginal tax rate for someone with income of $20,000? How much total tax does this person pay? How much is this as a percentage of his or her income?
   c. Is this income tax proportional, progressive, or regressive?

2. When comparing households at different income levels, economists find that consumption spending grows more slowly than income. Assume that when income grows by 50%, from $10,000 to $15,000, consumption grows by 25%, from $8,000 to $10,000. Compare the percent of income paid in taxes by a family with $15,000 in income to that paid by a family with $10,000 in income under a 1% tax on consumption purchases. Is this a proportional, progressive, or regressive tax?

3. True or false? Explain your answers.
   a. Payroll taxes do not affect a person's incentive to take a job because they are paid by employers.
   b. A lump-sum tax is a proportional tax because it is the same amount for each person.

   Solutions appear at back of book.

[>> A LOOK AHEAD •••

The costs and benefits of taxation are often controversial—which is why economic analysis, which helps us understand those costs and benefits, is especially useful when it comes to tax policy. In the next chapter, we turn to a subject that may be even more controversial than taxes: international trade, which produces many benefits but also sometimes has important costs. We'll see how the comparative advantage model introduced in Chapter 2, together with the supply and demand model, can help us understand the effects of international trade.]

SUMMARY ···■

1. **Excise taxes**—taxes on the purchase or sale of a good—raise the price paid by consumers and reduce the price received by producers, driving a wedge between the two. The **incidence** of the tax—how the burden of the tax is divided between consumers and producers—does not depend on who officially pays the tax.

2. The incidence of an excise tax depends on the price elasticities of supply and demand. If the price elasticity of demand is higher than the price elasticity of supply, the tax falls mainly on producers; if the price elasticity of supply is higher than the price elasticity of demand, the tax falls mainly on consumers.

3. The tax revenue generated by a tax depends on the **tax rate** and on the number of units transacted with the tax. Excise taxes cause inefficiency in the form of deadweight loss because they discourage some mutually beneficial transactions. Taxes also impose **administrative costs:** resources used to collect the tax, to pay it (over and above the amount of the tax), and to evade it.

4. An excise tax generates revenue for the government but lowers total surplus. The loss in total surplus exceeds the tax revenue, resulting in a deadweight loss to society. This deadweight loss is represented by a triangle, the area of which equals the value of the transactions discouraged by the tax. The greater the elasticity of demand or supply, or both, the larger the deadweight loss from a tax. If either demand or supply is perfectly inelastic, there is no deadweight loss from a tax.

5. An efficient tax minimizes both the sum of the deadweight loss due to distorted incentives and the administrative costs of the tax. However, tax fairness, or tax equity, is also a goal of tax policy.

6. There are two major principles of tax fairness, the **benefits principle** and the **ability-to-pay principle.** The most efficient tax, a **lump-sum tax,** does not distort incentives but performs badly in terms of fairness. The fairest taxes in terms of the ability-to-pay principle, however, distort incentives the most and perform badly on efficiency grounds. So in a well-designed tax system, there is a **trade-off between equity and efficiency.**

7. Every tax consists of a **tax base,** which defines what is taxed, and a **tax structure,** which specifies how the tax depends on the tax base. Different tax bases give rise to different taxes—the **income tax, payroll tax, sales tax, profits tax, property tax,** and **wealth tax.** A **proportional tax** is the same percentage of the tax base for all taxpayers.

8. A tax is **progressive** if higher-income people pay a higher percentage of their income in taxes than lower-income people and **regressive** if they pay a lower percentage. Progressive taxes are often justified by the ability-to-pay principle. However, a highly progressive tax system significantly distorts incentives because it leads to a high **marginal tax rate,** the percentage of an increase in income that is taxed away, on high earners. The U.S. tax system is progressive overall, although it contains a mixture of progressive and regressive taxes.

KEY TERMS

Excise tax, p. 168
Incidence, p. 171
Tax rate, p. 175
Administrative costs, p. 180
Benefits principle, p. 183
Ability-to-pay principle, p. 184
Lump-sum tax, p. 184

Trade-off between equity and efficiency, p. 185
Tax base, p. 186
Tax structure, p. 186
Income tax, p. 186
Payroll tax, p. 186
Sales tax, p. 186

Profits tax, p. 186
Property tax, p. 186
Wealth tax, p. 186
Proportional tax, p. 186
Progressive tax, p. 187
Regressive tax, p. 187
Marginal tax rate, p. 187

PROBLEMS

1. The United States imposes an excise tax on the sale of domestic airline tickets. Let's assume that in 2006 the total excise tax was $5.80 per airline ticket (consisting of the $3.30 flight segment tax plus the $2.50 September 11 fee). According to data from the Bureau of Transportation Statistics, in 2006, 656 million passengers traveled on domestic airline trips at an average price of $389.08 per trip. The accompanying table shows the supply and demand schedules for airline trips. The quantity demanded at the average price of $389.08 is actual data; the rest is hypothetical.

Price of trip	Quantity of trips demanded (millions)	Quantity of trips supplied (millions)
$389.17	655	1,100
389.08	656	1,000
384.00	685	685
383.28	700	656
383.27	701	655

a. What is the government tax revenue in 2006 from the excise tax?

b. On January 1, 2007, the total excise tax increased to $5.90 per ticket. What is the equilibrium quantity of tickets transacted now? What is the average ticket price now? What is the 2007 government tax revenue?

c. Does this increase in the excise tax increase or decrease government tax revenue?

2. The U.S. government would like to help the American auto industry compete against foreign automakers that sell trucks in the United States. It can do this by imposing an excise tax on each foreign truck sold in the United States. The hypothetical pre-tax demand and supply schedules for imported trucks are given in the accompanying table.

Price of imported truck	Quantity of imported trucks (thousands)	
	Quantity demanded	Quantity supplied
$32,000	100	400
31,000	200	350
30,000	300	300
29,000	400	250
28,000	500	200
27,000	600	150

a. In the absence of government interference, what is the equilibrium price of an imported truck? The equilibrium quantity? Illustrate with a diagram.

b. Assume that the government imposes an excise tax of $3,000 per imported truck. Illustrate the effect of this excise tax in your diagram from part a. How many imported trucks are now purchased and at what price? How much does the foreign automaker receive per truck?

c. Calculate the government revenue raised by the excise tax in part b. Illustrate it on your diagram.

d. How does the excise tax on imported trucks benefit American automakers? Who does it hurt? How does inefficiency arise from this government policy?

3. In 1990, the United States began to levy a tax on sales of luxury cars. For simplicity, assume that the tax was an excise tax of $6,000 per car. The accompanying figure shows hypothetical demand and supply curves for luxury cars.

a. Under the tax, what is the price paid by consumers? What is the price received by producers? What is the government tax revenue from the excise tax?

Over time, the tax on luxury automobiles was slowly phased out (and completely eliminated in 2002). Suppose that the excise tax falls from $6,000 per car to $4,500 per car.

b. After the reduction in the excise tax from $6,000 to $4,500 per car, what is the price paid by consumers? What is the price received by producers? What is tax revenue now?

c. Compare the tax revenue created by the taxes in parts a and b. What accounts for the change in tax revenue from the reduction in the excise tax?

4. All states impose excise taxes on gasoline. According to data from the Federal Highway Administration, the state of California imposes an excise tax of $0.18 per gallon of gasoline. In 2005, gasoline sales in California totaled 15.6 billion gallons. What was California's tax revenue from the gasoline excise tax? If California doubled the excise tax, would tax revenue double? Why or why not?

5. In the United States, each state government can impose its own excise tax on the sale of cigarettes. Suppose that in the state of North Texarkana, the state government imposes a tax of $2.00 per pack sold within the state. In contrast, the neighboring state of South Texarkana imposes no excise tax on cigarettes. Assume that in both states the pre-tax price of a pack of cigarettes is $1.00. Assume that the total cost to a resident of North Texarkana to smuggle a pack of cigarettes from South Texarkana is $1.85 per pack. (This includes the cost of time, gasoline, and so on.) Assume that the supply curve for cigarettes is neither perfectly elastic nor perfectly inelastic.

a. Draw a diagram of the supply and demand curves for cigarettes in North Texarkana showing a situation in which it makes economic sense for a North Texarkanan to smuggle a pack of cigarettes from South Texarkana to North Texarkana. Explain your diagram.

b. Draw a corresponding diagram showing a situation in which it does not make economic sense for a North Texarkanan to smuggle a pack of cigarettes from South Texarkana to North Texarkana. Explain your diagram.

c. Suppose the demand for cigarettes in North Texarkana is perfectly inelastic. How high could the cost of smuggling a pack of cigarettes go until a North Texarkanan no longer found it profitable to smuggle?

d. Still assume that demand for cigarettes in North Texarkana is perfectly inelastic and that all smokers in North Texarkana are smuggling their cigarettes at a cost of $1.85 per pack, so no tax is paid. Is there any inefficiency in this situation? If so, how much per pack? Suppose chip-embedded cigarette packaging makes it impossible to smuggle cigarettes across the state border. Is there any inefficiency in this situation? If so, how much per pack?

6. In each of the following cases involving taxes, explain: (i) whether the incidence of the tax falls more heavily on consumers or producers, (ii) why government revenue raised from the tax is not a good indicator of the true cost of the tax, and (iii) how deadweight loss arises as a result of the tax.

a. The government imposes an excise tax on the sale of all college textbooks. Before the tax was imposed, 1 million textbooks were sold every year at a price of $50. After the tax is imposed, 600,000 books are sold yearly; students pay $55 per book, $30 of which publishers receive.

b. The government imposes an excise tax on the sale of all airline tickets. Before the tax was imposed, 3 million airline tickets were sold every year at a price of $500. After the tax is imposed, 1.5 million tickets are sold yearly; travelers pay $550 per ticket, $450 of which the airlines receive.

c. The government imposes an excise tax on the sale of all toothbrushes. Before the tax, 2 million toothbrushes were

sold every year at a price of $1.50. After the tax is imposed, 800,000 toothbrushes are sold every year; consumers pay $2 per toothbrush, $1.25 of which producers receive.

7. The accompanying diagram shows the market for cigarettes. The current equilibrium price per pack is $4, and every day 40 million packs of cigarettes are sold. In order to recover some of the health care costs associated with smoking, the government imposes a tax of $2 per pack. This will raise the equilibrium price to $5 per pack and reduce the equilibrium quantity to 30 million packs.

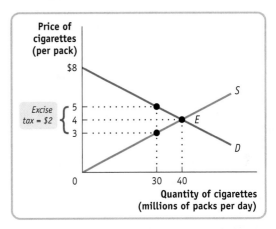

The economist working for the tobacco lobby claims that this tax will reduce consumer surplus for smokers by $40 million per day, since 40 million packs now cost $1 more per pack. The economist working for the lobby for sufferers of second-hand smoke argues that this is an enormous overestimate and that the reduction in consumer surplus will be only $30 million per day, since after the imposition of the tax only 30 million packs of cigarettes will be bought and each of these packs will now cost $1 more. They are both wrong. Why?

8. Consider the original market for pizza in Collegetown, illustrated in the accompanying table. Collegetown officials decide to impose an excise tax on pizza of $4 per pizza.

Price of pizza	Quantity of pizza demanded	Quantity of pizza supplied
$10	0	6
9	1	5
8	2	4
7	3	3
6	4	2
5	5	1
4	6	0
3	7	0
2	8	0
1	9	0

a. What is the quantity of pizza bought and sold after the imposition of the tax? What is the price paid by consumers? What is the price received by producers?

b. Calculate the consumer surplus and the producer surplus after the imposition of the tax. By how much has the imposition of the tax reduced consumer surplus? By how much has it reduced producer surplus?

c. How much tax revenue does Collegetown earn from this tax?

d. Calculate the deadweight loss from this tax.

9. The state needs to raise money, and the governor has a choice of imposing an excise tax of the same amount on one of two previously untaxed goods: the state can tax sales of either restaurant meals or gasoline. Both the demand for and the supply of restaurant meals are more elastic than the demand for and the supply of gasoline. If the governor wants to minimize the deadweight loss caused by the tax, which good should be taxed? For each good, draw a diagram that illustrates the deadweight loss from taxation.

10. Assume that the demand for gasoline is inelastic and supply is relatively elastic. The government imposes a sales tax on gasoline. The tax revenue is used to fund research into clean fuel alternatives to gasoline, which will improve the air we all breathe.

a. Who bears more of the burden of this tax, consumers or producers? Show in a diagram who bears how much of the excess burden.

b. Is this tax based on the benefits principle or the ability-to-pay principle? Explain.

11. Assess the following four tax policies in terms of the benefits principle versus the ability-to-pay principle.

a. A tax on gasoline that finances maintenance of state roads

b. An 8% tax on imported goods valued in excess of $800 per household brought in on passenger flights

c. Airline-flight landing fees that pay for air traffic control

d. A reduction in the amount of income tax paid based on the number of dependent children in the household

12. You are advising the government on how to pay for national defense. There are two proposals for a tax system to fund national defense. Under both proposals, the tax base is an individual's income. Under proposal A, all citizens pay exactly the same lump-sum tax, regardless of income. Under proposal B, individuals with higher incomes pay a greater proportion of their income in taxes.

a. Is the tax in proposal A progressive, proportional, or regressive? What about the tax in proposal B?

b. Is the tax in proposal A based on the ability-to-pay principle or on the benefits principle? What about the tax in proposal B?

c. In terms of efficiency, which tax is better? Explain.

13. Each of the following tax proposals has income as the tax base. In each case, calculate the marginal tax rate for each level of income. Then calculate the percentage of income paid in taxes for an individual with a pre-tax income of $5,000 and for an individual with a pre-tax income of $40,000. Classify the tax as being proportional, progressive, or regressive. (*Hint:* You can calculate the marginal tax rate as the percentage of an additional $1 in income that is taxed away.)

a. All income is taxed at 20%.

b. All income up to $10,000 is tax-free. All income above $10,000 is taxed at a constant rate of 20%.

c. All income between $0 and $10,000 is taxed at 10%. All income between $10,000 and $20,000 is taxed at 20%. All income higher than $20,000 is taxed at 30%.

d. Each individual who earns more than $10,000 pays a lump-sum tax of $10,000. If the individual's income is less than $10,000, that individual pays in taxes exactly what his or her income is.

e. Of the four tax policies, which is likely to cause the worst incentive problems? Explain.

14. In Transylvania the basic income tax system is fairly simple. The first 40,000 sylvers (the official currency of Transylvania) earned each year are free of income tax. Any additional income is taxed at a rate of 25%. In addition, every individual pays a social security tax, which is calculated as follows: all income up to 80,000 sylvers is taxed at an additional 20%, but there is no additional social security tax on income above 80,000 sylvers.

a. Calculate the marginal tax rates (including income tax and social security tax) for Transylvanians with the following levels of income: 20,000 sylvers, 40,000 sylvers, and 80,000 sylvers. (*Hint:* You can calculate the marginal tax rate as the percentage of an additional 1 sylver in income that is taxed away.)

b. Is the income tax in Transylvania progressive, regressive, or proportional? Is the social security tax progressive, regressive, or proportional?

c. Which income group's incentives are most adversely affected by the combined income and social security tax systems?

15. You work for the Council of Economic Advisers, providing economic advice to the White House. The president wants to overhaul the income tax system and asks your advice. Suppose that the current income tax system consists of a proportional tax of 10% on all income and that there is one person in the country who earns $110 million; everyone else earns less than $100 million. The president proposes a tax cut targeted at the very rich so that the new tax system would consist of a proportional tax of 10% on all income up to $100 million and a marginal tax rate of 0% (no tax) on income above $100 million. You are asked to evaluate this tax proposal.

a. For incomes of $100 million or less, is this tax system progressive, regressive, or proportional? For incomes of more than $100 million? Explain.

b. Would this tax system create more or less tax revenue, other things equal? Is this tax system more or less efficient than the current tax system? Explain.

www.worthpublishers.com/krugmanwells

International Trade

A SEAFOOD FIGHT

"FOR THE FIRST TIME IN RECORDED HISTORY, Americans are eating more shrimp than canned tuna." So declared the U.S. Commerce Department in a 2002 press release. Since then, shrimp consumption has pulled even further ahead: in 2005 the average American ate 4.1 pounds of shrimp, compared with only 3.1 pounds of canned tuna.

Where's all that shrimp coming from? Mainly from Asia and Latin America. Local entrepreneurs have taken advantage of a favorable climate, cheap labor, and large coastal tracts to produce huge quantities of "farmed" shrimp raised in ponds, shipping their catch mainly to Japan and the United States.

Is it a good thing that we now buy most of our shrimp from abroad? It's certainly a good thing from the point of view of America's shrimp-eaters, and the vast majority of economists would say that international trade is a good thing from the point of view of the nation as a whole. That is, economists say that international trade, in which

countries specialize in producing different goods and trade those goods with each other, is a source of mutual benefit to the countries involved. In Chapter 2 we laid out the basic principle that there are *gains from trade;* it's a principle that applies to countries as well as individuals.

But politicians and the public are often not convinced, in part because those who are hurt by foreign competition are often very effective at making their voices heard. In fact, in 2004 the U.S. government responded to complaints by domestic shrimp fishermen that they were facing unfair foreign competition. In response, the government imposed a tax on imports called a *tariff*—on shrimp from Vietnam, Thailand, and other shrimp-exporting nations.

Until now, we have analyzed the economy as if it were self-sufficient, as if the economy produces all the goods and services it consumes, and vice versa. This is, of course, true of the world economy as a whole. But it's not true of any individual country. Assuming self-sufficiency

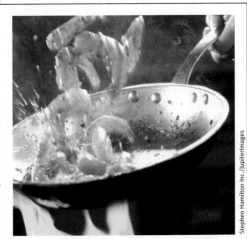

The mutual benefits of international trade are enjoyed by shrimp farmers in Bangkok, Thailand, and by American shrimp eaters.

195

would have been far more accurate 40 years ago, when the United States exported only a small fraction of what it produced and imported only a small fraction of what it consumed. Since then, however, both U.S. imports and exports have grown much faster than the U.S. economy as a whole. Moreover, compared to the United States, other countries engage in far more foreign trade relative to the size of their economies. To have a full picture of how national economies work, we must understand international trade.

This chapter examines the economics of international trade. We start from the model of comparative advantage, which, as we saw in Chapter 2, explains why there are gains from international trade. It's also important, however, to understand how some individuals, like U.S. shrimp producers, can be hurt by international trade. At the conclusion of the chapter, we'll examine the effects of policies, like the tariff on shrimp imports, that countries use to limit imports or promote exports, as well as how governments work together to overcome barriers to trade.

WHAT YOU WILL LEARN IN THIS CHAPTER:

➤ How comparative advantage leads to mutually beneficial international trade

➤ The sources of international comparative advantage

➤ Who gains and who loses from interna-

tional trade, and why the gains exceed the losses

➤ How **tariffs** and **import quotas** cause inefficiency and reduce total surplus

➤ Why governments often engage in **trade protection** to shelter domestic industries from imports and how **international trade agreements** counteract this

Comparative Advantage and International Trade

The United States buys shrimp—and many other goods and services—from other countries. At the same time, it sells many goods and services to other countries. Goods and services purchased from abroad are **imports;** goods and services sold abroad are **exports.**

As illustrated by the opening story, imports and exports have taken on an increasingly important role in the U.S. economy. Over the last 40 years, both imports into and exports from the United States have grown faster than the U.S. economy. Panel (a) of Figure 8-1 shows how the values of U.S. imports and exports have grown as a percentage of gross domestic product (GDP). Panel (b) shows imports and exports as a percentage of GDP for a number of countries. It shows that foreign trade is significantly more important for many other countries than it is for the United States. (Japan is the exception.)

Foreign trade isn't the only way countries interact economically. In the modern world, investors from one country often invest funds in another nation; many companies are multinational, with subsidiaries operating in several countries; and a growing number of individuals work in a country different from the one in which they were born. The growth of all these forms of economic linkages among countries is often called **globalization.**

In this chapter, however, we'll focus mainly on international trade. To understand why international trade occurs and why economists believe it is beneficial to the economy, we will first review the concept of comparative advantage.

Production Possibilities and Comparative Advantage, Revisited

To produce shrimp, any country must use resources—land, labor, capital, and so on—that could have been used to produce other things. The potential production of other goods a country must forgo to produce a ton of shrimp is the opportunity cost of that ton of shrimp.

Goods and services purchased from other countries are **imports;** goods and services sold to other countries are **exports.**

Globalization is the phenomenon of growing economic linkages among countries.

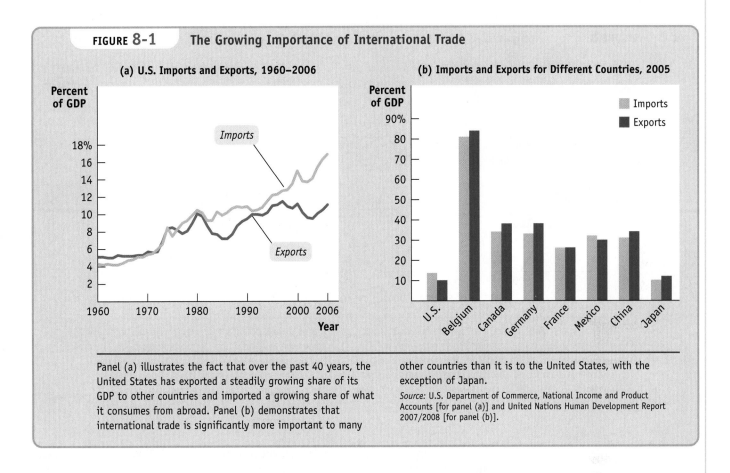

FIGURE 8-1   The Growing Importance of International Trade

Panel (a) illustrates the fact that over the past 40 years, the United States has exported a steadily growing share of its GDP to other countries and imported a growing share of what it consumes from abroad. Panel (b) demonstrates that international trade is significantly more important to many other countries than it is to the United States, with the exception of Japan.

Source: U.S. Department of Commerce, National Income and Product Accounts [for panel (a)] and United Nations Human Development Report 2007/2008 [for panel (b)].

It's a lot easier to produce shrimp in Vietnam, where the climate is nearly ideal and there's plenty of coastal land suitable for shellfish farming, than it is in the United States. Conversely, other goods are not produced as easily in Vietnam as in the United States. For example, Vietnam doesn't have the base of skilled workers and technological know-how that makes the United States so good at producing high-technology goods. So the opportunity cost of a ton of shrimp, in terms of other goods such as computers, is much less in Vietnam than it is in the United States.

So we say that Vietnam has a comparative advantage in producing shrimp. Let's repeat the definition of comparative advantage from Chapter 2: *a country has a comparative advantage in producing a good or service if the opportunity cost of producing the good or service is lower for that country than for other countries.*

Figure 8-2 on the next page provides a hypothetical numerical example of comparative advantage in international trade. We assume that only two goods are produced and consumed, shrimp and computers, and that there are only two countries in the world, the United States and Vietnam. The figure shows hypothetical production possibility frontiers for the United States and Vietnam. As in Chapter 2, we simplify the model by assuming that the production possibility frontiers are straight lines, as shown in Figure 2-1, rather than the more realistic bowed-out shape shown in Figure 2-2. The straight-line shape implies that the opportunity cost of a ton of shrimp in terms of computers in each country is constant—it does not depend on how many units of each good the country produces. The analysis of international trade under the assumption that opportunity costs are constant, which makes production possibility frontiers straight lines, is known as the **Ricardian model of international trade,** named after the English economist David Ricardo, who introduced this analysis in the early nineteenth century.

The **Ricardian model of international trade** analyzes international trade under the assumption that opportunity costs are constant.

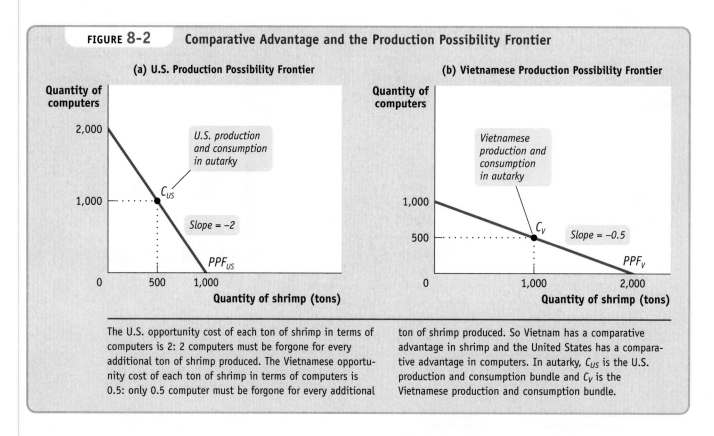

FIGURE 8-2 Comparative Advantage and the Production Possibility Frontier

The U.S. opportunity cost of each ton of shrimp in terms of computers is 2: 2 computers must be forgone for every additional ton of shrimp produced. The Vietnamese opportunity cost of each ton of shrimp in terms of computers is 0.5: only 0.5 computer must be forgone for every additional ton of shrimp produced. So Vietnam has a comparative advantage in shrimp and the United States has a comparative advantage in computers. In autarky, C_{US} is the U.S. production and consumption bundle and C_V is the Vietnamese production and consumption bundle.

Table 8-1 presents the same information shown in Figure 8-2. We assume that the United States can produce 1,000 tons of shrimp if it produces no computers or 2,000 computers if it produces no shrimp. Because we measure shrimp output in tons, the slope of the production possibility frontier in panel (a) is –2,000/1,000, or –2: to produce an additional ton of shrimp, the United States must forgo the production of 2 computers.

Similarly, we assume that Vietnam can produce 2,000 tons of shrimp if it produces no computers or 1,000 computers if it produces no shrimp. The slope of the production possibility frontier in panel (b) is –1,000/2,000, or –0.5: to produce an additional ton of shrimp, Vietnam must forgo the production of 0.5 computer.

Economists use the term **autarky** to describe a situation in which a country does not trade with other countries. We assume that in autarky the United States would choose to produce and consume 500 tons of shrimp and 1,000 computers. This autarky production and consumption bundle is shown by point C_{US} in panel (a) of

Autarky is a situation in which a country does not trade with other countries.

TABLE 8-1

Production Possibilities

(a) United States	Production	
	One possibility	Another possibility
Quantity of shrimp (tons)	1,000	0
Quantity of computers	0	2,000

(b) Vietnam	Production	
	One possibility	Another possibility
Quantity of shrimp (tons)	2,000	0
Quantity of computers	0	1,000

Figure 8-2. We also assume that in autarky Vietnam would choose to produce and consume 1,000 tons of shrimp and 500 computers, shown by point C_V in panel (b). The outcome in autarky is summarized in Table 8-2, where world production and consumption is the sum of U.S. and Vietnamese production and consumption.

If the countries trade with each other, they can do better than they can in autarky. In this example, Vietnam has a comparative advantage in the production of shrimp. That is, the opportunity cost of shrimp is lower in Vietnam than in the United States: 0.5 computer per ton of shrimp in Vietnam versus 2 computers per ton of shrimp in the United States. Conversely, the United States has a comparative advantage in the production of computers: to produce an additional computer, the United States must forgo the production of 0.5 ton of shrimp, but producing an additional computer in Vietnam requires forgoing the production of 2 tons of shrimp. International trade allows each country to specialize in producing the good in which it has a comparative advantage: computers in the United States, shrimp in Vietnam. As a result, each country is able to obtain the good in which it doesn't have a comparative advantage at a lower opportunity cost than if it produced the good itself. And that leads to gains for both when they trade.

TABLE 8-2

Production and Consumption Under Autarky

(a) United States	Production	Consumption
Quantity of shrimp (tons)	500	500
Quantity of computers	1,000	1,000
(b) Vietnam	**Production**	**Consumption**
Quantity of shrimp (tons)	1,000	1,000
Quantity of computers	500	500
(c) World (United States and Vietnam)	**Production**	**Consumption**
Quantity of shrimp (tons)	1,500	1,500
Quantity of computers	1,500	1,500

The Gains from International Trade

Figure 8-3 on the next page illustrates how both countries gain from specialization and trade. Again, panel (a) represents the United States and panel (b) represents Vietnam. As a result of international trade, the United States produces at point Q_{US}: 2,000 computers but no shrimp. Vietnam produces at Q_V: 2,000 tons of shrimp but no computers. The new production choices are given in the second column of Table 8-3.

By comparing Table 8-3 with Table 8-2, you can see that specialization increases total world production of *both* goods. In the absence of specialization, total world production consists of 1,500 computers and 1,500 tons of shrimp. After specialization, total world production rises to 2,000 computers and 2,000 tons of shrimp. These

TABLE 8-3

Production and Consumption After Specialization and Trade

(a) United States	Production	Consumption
Quantity of shrimp (tons)	0	750
Quantity of computers	2,000	1,250
(b) Vietnam	**Production**	**Consumption**
Quantity of shrimp (tons)	2,000	1,250
Quantity of computers	0	750
(c) World (United States and Vietnam)	**Production**	**Consumption**
Quantity of shrimp (tons)	2,000	2,000
Quantity of computers	2,000	2,000

goods can now be traded, with the United States consuming shrimp produced in Vietnam and Vietnam consuming computers produced in the United States. The result is that each country can consume more of *both* goods than it did in autarky.

In addition to showing production under trade, Figure 8-3 shows one of many possible pairs of consumption bundles for the United States and Vietnam, which is also given in Table 8-3. In this example, the United States moves from its autarky consumption of 1,000 computers and 500 tons of shrimp, shown by C_{US}, to consumption after trade of 1,250 computers and 750 tons of shrimp, represented by C'_{US}. Vietnam moves from its autarky consumption of 500 computers and 1,000 tons of shrimp, shown by C_V, to consumption after trade of 750 computers and 1,250 tons of shrimp, shown by C'_V.

What makes this possible is the fact that with international trade countries are no longer required to consume the same bundle of goods they produce. Each country

FIGURE 8-3   The Gains from International Trade

Trade increases world production of both goods, allowing both countries to consume more. Here, each country specializes its production as a result of trade: the United States produces at Q_{US} and Vietnam produces at Q_V. Total world production of computers has risen from 1,500 to 2,000 and of shrimp from 1,500 tons to 2,000 tons. The United States can now consume bundle C'_{US}, and Vietnam can now consume bundle C'_V—consumption bundles that were unattainable without trade.

produces at one point (Q_{US} for the United States, Q_V for Vietnam) but consumes at a different point (C'_{US} for the United States, C'_V for Vietnam). The difference reflects imports and exports: the 750 tons of shrimp the United States consumes are imported from Vietnam; the 750 computers Vietnam consumes are imported from the United States.

In this example we have simply assumed the post-trade consumption bundles of the two countries. In fact, the consumption choices of a country reflect both the preferences of its residents and the *relative prices*—the prices of one good in terms of another in international markets. Although we have not explicitly given the price of computers in terms of shrimp, that price is implicit in our example: Vietnam exports 750 tons of shrimp and receives 750 computers in return, so 1 ton of shrimp is traded for 1 computer. This tells us that the price of a computer on world markets must be equal to the price of 1 ton of shrimp in our example.

One requirement that the relative price must satisfy is that no country pays a relative price greater than its opportunity cost of obtaining the good in autarky. That is, the United States won't pay more than 2 computers for 1 ton of shrimp from Vietnam, and Vietnam won't pay more than 2 tons of shrimp for 1 computer from the United States. Once this requirement is satisfied, the actual relative price in international trade is determined by supply and demand—and we'll turn to supply and demand in international trade in the next section. However, first let's look more deeply into the nature of the gains from trade.

Comparative Advantage versus Absolute Advantage

It's easy to accept the idea that Vietnam has a comparative advantage in shrimp production: it has a tropical climate that's better suited to shrimp farming than that of the United States (even along the Gulf Coast), and it has a lot of usable coastal area. In other cases, however, it may be harder to understand why we import certain goods from abroad.

Consider, for example, U.S. trade with Bangladesh. We import a lot of clothing from Bangladesh—shirts, trousers, and so on. Yet there's nothing about the climate or resources of Bangladesh that makes it especially good at sewing shirts. In fact, it takes *fewer* hours of labor to produce a shirt in the United States than in Bangladesh.

Why, then, do we buy Bangladeshi shirts? Because the gains from trade depend on *comparative advantage,* not *absolute advantage.* Yes, it takes less labor to produce a shirt in the United States than in Bangladesh. That is, the productivity of Bangladeshi shirt workers is less than that of their U.S. counterparts. But what determines comparative advantage is not the amount of resources used to produce a good but the opportunity cost of that good—here, the quantity of other goods forgone in order to produce a shirt. And the opportunity cost of a shirt is lower in Bangladesh than in the United States.

Here's how it works: Bangladeshi workers have low productivity compared with U.S. workers in the shirt industry. But Bangladeshi workers have even lower productivity compared with U.S. workers in other industries. Because Bangladeshi labor productivity in industries other than shirt-making is very low, producing a shirt in Bangladesh, even though it takes a lot of labor, does not require forgoing the production of large quantities of other goods. In the United States, the opposite is true: very high productivity in other industries (such as high-technology goods) means that producing a shirt in the United States, even though it doesn't require much labor, requires sacrificing lots of other goods. So the opportunity cost of producing a shirt is less in Bangladesh than in the United States. Despite its lower labor productivity, Bangladesh has a comparative advantage in clothing production, although the United States has an absolute advantage.

Bangladesh's comparative advantage in clothing gets translated into an actual advantage on world markets through its wage rates. A country's wage rates, in general, reflect its labor productivity. In countries where labor is highly productive in many industries, employers are willing to pay high wages to attract workers, so competition among employers leads to an overall high wage rate. In countries where labor is less productive, competition for workers is less intense and wage rates are correspondingly lower.

As the Global Comparison on the next page shows, there is a strong relationship between overall levels of productivity and wage rates around the world. Because Bangladesh has generally low productivity, it has a relatively low wage rate. Low wages, in turn, give Bangladesh a cost advantage in producing goods where its productivity is only moderately low, like shirts. As a result, it's cheaper to produce shirts in Bangladesh than in the United States.

The kind of trade that takes place between low-wage, low-productivity economies like Bangladesh and high-wage, high-productivity economies like the United States gives rise to two common misperceptions. One, the *pauper labor fallacy,* is the belief that when a country with high wages imports goods produced by workers who are paid low wages, this must hurt the standard of living of workers in the importing country. The other, the *sweatshop labor fallacy,* is the belief that trade must be bad for workers in poor exporting countries because those workers are paid very low wages by our standards. Both fallacies miss the nature of gains from trade: it's to the advantage of *both* countries if the poorer, lower-wage country exports goods in which it has a comparative advantage, even if its cost advantage in these goods depends on low wages. That is, both countries are able to achieve a higher standard of living through trade.

It's particularly important to understand that buying a shirt made by someone who makes only 30 cents an hour doesn't necessarily imply that you're taking advantage of that person. It depends on the alternatives. Because workers in poor countries have low productivity across the board, they are offered low wages whether they produce goods exported to America or goods sold in local markets. A job that looks terrible by rich-country standards can be a step up for someone in a poor country. And international trade that depends on low-wage exports can nonetheless raise a country's standard of living. Bangladesh, in particular, would be much poorer than it is—possibly its citizens would even be starving—if it weren't able to export clothing based on its low wage rates.

GLOBAL COMPARISON
PRODUCTIVITY AND WAGES AROUND THE WORLD

Is it true that both the pauper labor argument and the sweatshop labor argument are fallacies? Yes, it is. The real explanation for low wages in poor countries is low overall productivity.

The graph shows estimates of labor productivity and wages in manufacturing industries for several countries in 2002. Note that both productivity and wages are expressed as percentages of U.S. productivity and wages (for example, wages and productivity in Japan are about 79% of those in the United States). You can see the very close relationship between productivity and wages. The relationship isn't perfect: Korea and Brazil in particular have somewhat lower wages than their productivity might lead you to expect, and the European Union has higher wages than predicted by its productivity. But simple comparisons of wages give a misleading sense of labor costs in poor countries: their low-wage advantage is mostly offset by low productivity.

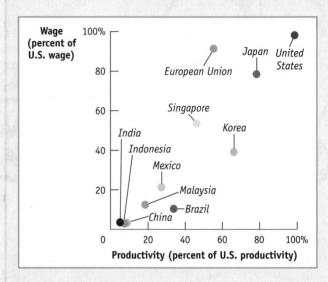

Source: Janet Ceglowski and Stephen Golub, "Just How Low Are China's Labour Costs?" *World Economy* vol. 30(4), p. 597–617 (2007).

Sources of Comparative Advantage

International trade is driven by comparative advantage, but where does comparative advantage come from? Economists who study international trade have found three main sources of comparative advantage: international differences in *climate,* international differences in *factor endowments,* and international differences in *technology.*

Differences in Climate A key reason the opportunity cost of producing shrimp in Vietnam is less than in the United States is that shrimp need warm water—Vietnam has plenty of that, but America doesn't. In general, differences in climate play a significant role in international trade. Tropical countries export tropical products like coffee, sugar, bananas, and, these days, shrimp. Countries in the temperate zones export crops like wheat and corn. Some trade is even driven by the difference in seasons between the northern and southern hemispheres: winter deliveries of Chilean grapes and New Zealand apples have become commonplace in U.S. and European supermarkets.

Differences in Factor Endowments Canada is a major exporter of forest products—lumber and products derived from lumber, like pulp and paper—to the United States. These exports don't reflect the special skill of Canadian lumberjacks. Canada has a comparative advantage in forest products because its forested area is much greater compared to the size of its labor force than the ratio of forestland to the labor force in the United States.

Forestland, like labor and capital, is a *factor of production:* an input used to produce goods and services. (Recall from Chapter 2 that the factors of production are land, labor, capital, and human capital.) Due to history and geography, the mix of available factors of production differs among countries, providing an important source of comparative advantage. The relationship between comparative advantage and factor availability is found in an influential model of international trade, the *Heckscher-Ohlin model,* developed by two Swedish economists in the first half of the twentieth century.

A key concept in the model is *factor intensity*. Producers use different ratios of factors of production in the production of different goods. For example, oil refineries use much more capital per worker than clothing factories. Economists use the term **factor intensity** to describe this difference among goods: oil refining is capital-intensive, because it tends to use a high ratio of capital to labor, but clothing manufacture is labor-intensive, because it tends to use a high ratio of labor to capital.

According to the **Heckscher–Ohlin model,** *a country will have a comparative advantage in a good whose production is intensive in the factors that are abundantly available in that country compared to other countries.* So a country that has a relative abundance of capital will have a comparative advantage in capital-intensive industries such as oil refining, but a country that has a relative abundance of labor will have a comparative advantage in labor-intensive industries such as clothing production. The basic intuition behind this result is simple and based on opportunity cost. The opportunity cost of a given factor—the value that the factor would generate in alternative uses—is low for a country when it is relatively abundant in that factor. (For example, in rainy parts of the United States, the opportunity cost of water for residences is low because there is a plentiful supply for other uses, such as agriculture.) So the opportunity cost of producing goods that are intensive in the use of an abundantly available factor is also low.

The most dramatic example of the validity of the Heckscher–Ohlin model is world trade in clothing. Clothing production is a labor-intensive activity: it doesn't take much physical capital, nor does it require a lot of human capital in the form of highly educated workers. So you would expect labor-abundant countries such as China and Bangladesh to have a comparative advantage in clothing production. And they do.

That much international trade is the result of differences in factor endowments helps explain another fact: international specialization of production is often *incomplete*. That is, a country often maintains some domestic production of a good that it imports. A good example of this is the United States and oil. Saudi Arabia exports oil to the United States because Saudi Arabia has an abundant supply of oil relative to its other factors of production; the United States exports medical devices to Saudi Arabia because it has an abundant supply of expertise in medical technology relative to its other factors of production. But the United States also produces some oil domestically because the size of its domestic oil reserves makes it economical to do so. In our demand and supply analysis in the next section, we'll consider incomplete specialization by a country to be the norm. We should emphasize, however, that the fact that countries often incompletely specialize does not in any way change the conclusion that there are gains from trade.

Differences in Technology

In the 1970s and 1980s, Japan became by far the world's largest exporter of automobiles, selling large numbers to the United States and the rest of the world. Japan's comparative advantage in automobiles wasn't the result of climate. Nor can it easily be attributed to differences in factor endowments: aside from a scarcity of land, Japan's mix of available factors is quite similar to that in other advanced countries. Instead, Japan's comparative advantage in automobiles was based on the superior production techniques developed by that country's manufacturers, which allowed them to produce more cars with a given amount of labor and capital than their American or European counterparts.

Japan's comparative advantage in automobiles was a case of comparative advantage caused by differences in technology—the techniques used in production.

The causes of differences in technology are somewhat mysterious. Sometimes they seem to be based on knowledge accumulated through experience—for example, Switzerland's comparative advantage in watches reflects a long tradition of watchmaking. Sometimes they are the result of a set of innovations that for some reason occur in one country but not in others. Technological advantage, however, is often

The **factor intensity** of production of a good is a measure of which factor is used in relatively greater quantities than other factors in production.

According to the **Heckscher–Ohlin model,** a country has a comparative advantage in a good whose production is intensive in the factors that are abundantly available in that country.

Increasing Returns to Scale and International Trade

Most analysis of international trade focuses on how differences between countries—differences in climate, factor endowments, and technology—create national comparative advantage. However, economists have also pointed out another reason for international trade: the role of *increasing returns to scale.*

Production of a good is characterized by increasing returns to scale if the productivity of labor and other resources used in production rises with the quantity of output. For example, in an industry characterized by increasing returns to scale, increasing output by 10% might require only 8% more labor and 9% more raw materials.

Examples of industries with increasing returns to scale include auto manufacturing, oil refining, and the production of jumbo jets, all of which require large outlays of capital. Increasing returns to scale (sometimes also called economies of scale) can give rise to monopoly, a situation in which an industry is composed of only one producer, because they give large firms an advantage over small ones.

But increasing returns to scale can also give rise to international trade. The logic runs as follows: if production of a good is characterized by increasing returns to scale, it makes sense to concentrate production in

only a few locations, so as to achieve a high level of production in each location. But that also means that the good is produced in only a few countries, which export that good to other countries. A commonly cited example is the North American auto industry: although both the United States and Canada produce automobiles and their components, each particular model or component tends to be produced in only one of the two countries and exported to the other. Increasing returns to scale probably play a large role in the trade in manufactured goods between advanced countries, which is about 25% of the total value of world trade.

transitory. American auto manufacturers have now closed much of the gap in productivity with their Japanese competitors; Europe's aircraft industry has closed a similar gap with the U.S. aircraft industry. At any given point in time, however, differences in technology are a major source of comparative advantage.

►*ECONOMICS IN ACTION*

Skill and Comparative Advantage

In 1953 U.S. workers were clearly better equipped with machinery than their counterparts in other countries. Most economists at the time thought that America's comparative advantage lay in capital-intensive goods. But Wassily Leontief made a surprising discovery: America's comparative advantage was something other than capital-intensive goods. In fact, goods that the United States exported were slightly less capital-intensive than goods the country imported. This discovery came to be known as the Leontief paradox, and it led to a sustained effort to make sense of U.S. trade patterns.

The main resolution of this paradox, it turns out, depends on the definition of *capital.* U.S. exports aren't intensive in *physical* capital—machines and buildings. Instead, they are *skill-intensive*—that is, they are intensive in *human* capital. U.S. exporting industries use a substantially higher ratio of highly educated workers to other workers than is found in U.S. industries that compete against imports. For example, one of America's biggest export sectors is aircraft; the aircraft industry employs large numbers of engineers and other people with graduate degrees relative to the number of manual laborers. Conversely, we import a lot of clothing, which is often produced by workers with little formal education.

In general, countries with highly educated workforces tend to export skill-intensive goods, while countries with less educated workforces tend to export goods whose production requires little skilled labor. Figure 8-4 illustrates this point by comparing the goods the United States imports from Germany, a country with a highly educated labor force, with the goods the United States imports from Bangladesh, where about half of the adult population is still illiterate. In each country industries are ranked, first, according to how skill-intensive they are. Next, for each industry, we calculate its share of exports to the United States. This allows us to plot, for each country, various industries according to

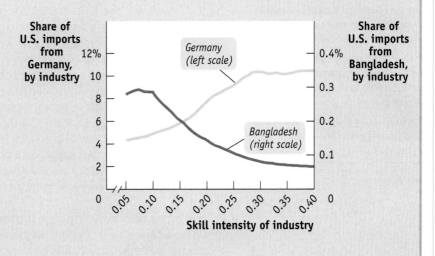

FIGURE 8-4

Education, Skill Intensity, and Trade

In this graph, increasing skill intensity is measured by moving from left to right along the horizontal axis. The vertical axes measure the share of exports from a given industry to the United States, with Germany on the left axis and Bangladesh on the right. The upward slope of the yellow curve illustrates the fact that as a German industry grows more skill-intensive, its share of exports to the United States also grows. In contrast, the downward slope of the brown curve shows that as a Bangladeshi industry grows less skill-intensive, its share of exports to the United States rises.

Source: John Romalis, "Factor Proportions and the Structure of Commodity Trade," *American Economic Review,* Vol. 94, No. 1, 2004.

their skill intensity and their share of exports to the United States. In Figure 8-4, the horizontal axis shows a measure of the skill intensity of different industries, and the vertical axes show the share of U.S. imports in each industry coming from Germany (on the left) and Bangladesh (on the right). As you can see, each country's exports to the United States reflect its skill level. The curve representing Germany slopes upward: the more skill-intensive a German industry is, the higher its share of exports to the United States. In contrast, the curve representing Bangladesh slopes downward: the less skill-intensive a Bangladeshi industry is, the higher its share of exports to the United States. ▲

> > > > > > > > > > > > >

▶ **CHECK YOUR UNDERSTANDING** 8-1

1. In the United States, the opportunity cost of 1 ton of corn is 50 bicycles. In China, the opportunity cost of 1 bicycle is 0.01 ton of corn.
   a. Determine the pattern of comparative advantage.
   b. In autarky, the United States can produce 200,000 bicycles if no corn is produced, and China can produce 3,000 tons of corn if no bicycles are produced. Draw each country's production possibility frontier assuming constant opportunity cost, with tons of corn on the vertical axis and bicycles on the horizontal axis.
   c. With trade, each country specializes its production. The United States consumes 1,000 tons of corn and 200,000 bicycles; China consumes 3,000 tons of corn and 100,000 bicycles. Indicate the production and consumption points on your diagrams, and use them to explain the gains from trade.

2. Explain the following patterns of trade using the Heckscher–Ohlin model.
   a. France exports wine to the United States, and the United States exports movies to France.
   b. Brazil exports shoes to the United States, and the United States exports shoe-making machinery to Brazil.

Solutions appear at back of book.

▶▶ **QUICK REVIEW**

➤ **Imports** and **exports** account for a growing share of the U.S. economy and the economies of many other countries.

➤ The growth of international trade and other international linkages is known as **globalization.**

➤ International trade is driven by comparative advantage. The **Ricardian model of international trade** shows that trade between two countries makes both countries better off than they would be in **autarky**—that is, there are gains from trade.

➤ The main sources of comparative advantage are international differences in climate, factor endowments, and technology.

➤ The **Heckscher–Ohlin model** shows how comparative advantage can arise from differences in factor endowments: goods differ in their **factor intensity,** and countries tend to export goods that are intensive in the factors they have in abundance.

Supply, Demand, and International Trade

Simple models of comparative advantage are helpful for understanding the fundamental causes of international trade. However, to analyze the effects of international trade at a more detailed level and to understand trade policy, it helps to return to the supply and demand model. We'll start by looking at the effects of imports on domestic producers and consumers, then turn to the effect of exports.

The **domestic demand curve** shows
how the quantity of a good demanded
by domestic consumers depends on the
price of that good.

The **domestic supply curve** shows how
the quantity of a good supplied by
domestic producers depends on the
price of that good.

The **world price** of a good is the price
at which that good can be bought or
sold abroad.

The Effects of Imports

Figure 8-5 shows the U.S. market for shrimp, ignoring international trade for a moment. It introduces a few new concepts: the *domestic demand curve,* the *domestic supply curve,* and the domestic or autarky price.

The **domestic demand curve** shows how the quantity of a good demanded by residents of a country depends on the price of that good. Why "domestic"? Because people living in other countries may demand the good, too. Once we introduce international trade, we need to distinguish between purchases of a good by domestic consumers and purchases by foreign consumers. So the domestic demand curve reflects only the demand of residents of our own country. Similarly, the **domestic supply curve** shows how the quantity of a good supplied by producers inside our own country depends on the price of that good. Once we introduce international trade, we need to distinguish between the supply of domestic producers and foreign supply—supply brought in from abroad.

In autarky, with no international trade in shrimp, the equilibrium in this market would be determined by the intersection of the domestic demand and domestic supply curves, point A. The equilibrium price of shrimp would be P_A, and the equilibrium quantity of shrimp produced and consumed would be Q_A. As always, both consumers and producers gain from the existence of the domestic market. In autarky, consumer surplus would be equal to the area of the blue-shaded triangle in Figure 8-5. Producer surplus would be equal to the area of the red-shaded triangle. And total surplus would be equal to the sum of these two shaded triangles.

Now let's imagine opening up this market to imports. To do this, we must make an assumption about the supply of imports. The simplest assumption, which we will adopt here, is that unlimited quantities of shrimp can be purchased from abroad at a fixed price, known as the **world price** of shrimp. Figure 8-6 shows a situation in which the world price of shrimp, P_W, is lower than the price of shrimp that would prevail in the domestic market in autarky, P_A.

Given that the world price is below the domestic price of shrimp, it is profitable for importers to buy shrimp abroad and resell it domestically. The imported shrimp increases the supply of shrimp in the domestic market, driving down the domestic

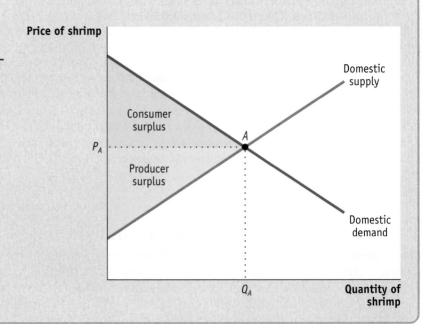

FIGURE 8-5

**Consumer and Producer Surplus
in Autarky**

In the absence of trade, domestic price is P_A, the autarky price at which the domestic supply curve and the domestic demand curve intersect. The quantity produced and consumed domestically is Q_A. Consumer surplus is represented by the blue-shaded area, and producer surplus is represented by the red-shaded area.

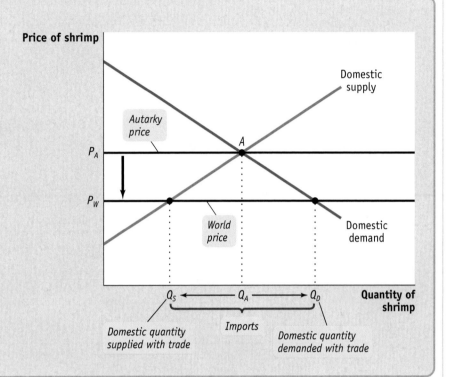

FIGURE 8-6

The Domestic Market with Imports

Here the world price of shrimp, P_W, is below the autarky price, P_A. When the economy is opened to international trade, imports enter the domestic market, and the domestic price falls from the autarky price, P_A, to the world price, P_W. As the price falls, the domestic quantity demanded rises from Q_A to Q_D and the domestic quantity supplied falls from Q_A to Q_S. The difference between domestic quantity demanded and domestic quantity supplied at P_W, the quantity $Q_D - Q_S$, is filled by imports.

market price. Shrimp will continue to be imported until the domestic price falls to a level equal to the world price.

The result is shown in Figure 8-6. Because of imports, the domestic price of shrimp falls from P_A to P_W. The quantity of shrimp demanded by domestic consumers rises from Q_A to Q_D, and the quantity supplied by domestic producers falls from Q_A to Q_S. The difference between the domestic quantity demanded and the domestic quantity supplied, $Q_D - Q_S$, is filled by imports.

Now let's turn to the effects of imports on consumer surplus and producer surplus. Because imports of shrimp lead to a fall in its domestic price, consumer surplus rises and producer surplus falls. Figure 8-7 on the next page shows how this works. We label four areas: W, X, Y, and Z. The autarky consumer surplus we identified in Figure 8-5 corresponds to W, and the autarky producer surplus corresponds to the sum of X and Y. The fall in the domestic price to the world price leads to an increase in consumer surplus; it increases by X and Z, so that consumer surplus now equals the sum of W, X, and Z. At the same time, producers lose X in surplus, so that producer surplus now equals only Y.

The table in Figure 8-7 summarizes the changes in consumer and producer surplus when the shrimp market is opened to imports. Consumers gain surplus equal to the areas $X + Z$. Producers lose surplus equal to X. So the sum of producer and consumer surplus—the total surplus generated in the shrimp market—increases by Z. As a result of trade, consumers gain and producers lose, but the gain to consumers exceeds the loss to producers.

This is an important result. We have just shown that opening up a market to imports leads to a net gain in total surplus, which is what we should have expected given the proposition that there are gains from international trade. However, we have also learned that although the country as a whole gains, some groups—in this case, domestic shrimp producers—lose as a result of international trade. As we'll see shortly, the fact that international trade typically creates losers as well as winners is crucial for understanding the politics of trade policy.

We turn next to the case in which a country exports a good.

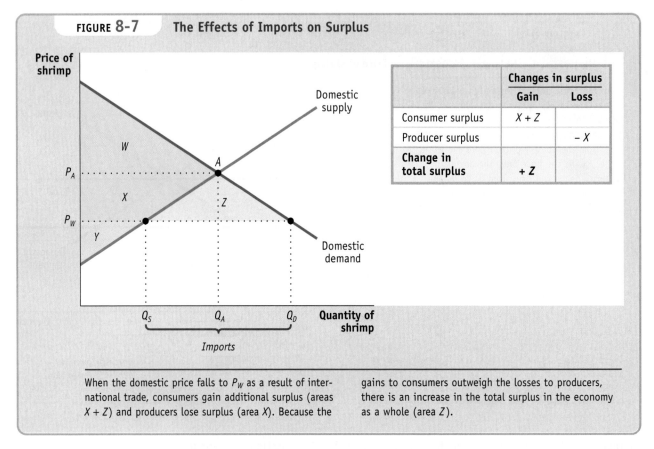

FIGURE 8-7 **The Effects of Imports on Surplus**

	Changes in surplus	
	Gain	**Loss**
Consumer surplus	$X + Z$	
Producer surplus		$- X$
Change in total surplus	**+ Z**	

When the domestic price falls to P_W as a result of international trade, consumers gain additional surplus (areas $X + Z$) and producers lose surplus (area X). Because the gains to consumers outweigh the losses to producers, there is an increase in the total surplus in the economy as a whole (area Z).

The Effects of Exports

Figure 8-8 shows the effects on a country when it exports a good, in this case computers. For this example, we assume that unlimited quantities of computers can be sold abroad at a given world price, P_W, which is higher than the price that would prevail in the domestic market in autarky, P_A.

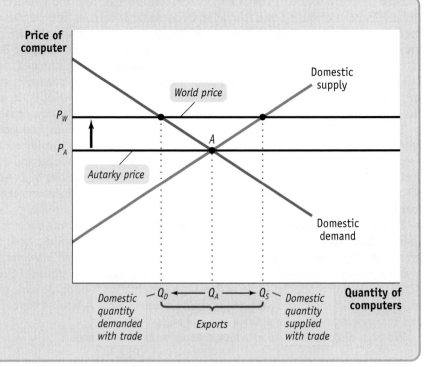

FIGURE 8-8

The Domestic Market with Exports

Here the world price, P_W, is greater than the autarky price, P_A. When the economy is opened to international trade, some of the domestic supply is now exported. The domestic price rises from the autarky price, P_A, to the world price, P_W. As the price rises, the domestic quantity demanded falls from Q_A to Q_D and the domestic quantity supplied rises from Q_A to Q_S. The portion of domestic production that is not consumed domestically, $Q_S - Q_D$, is exported.

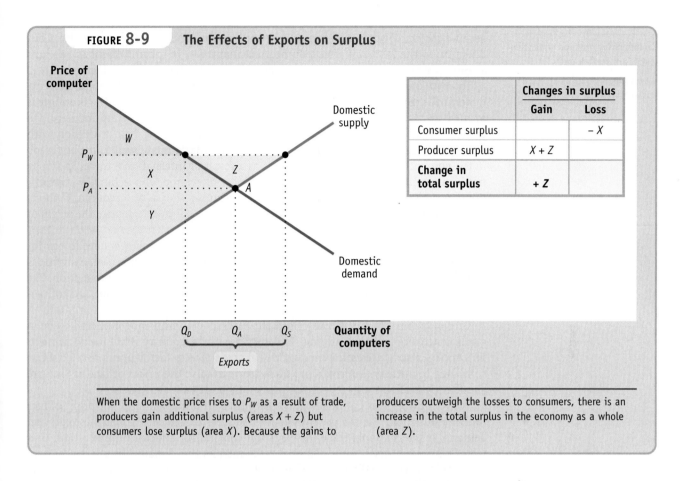

FIGURE 8-9 **The Effects of Exports on Surplus**

Price of computer

P_W
P_A

W
X
Z
Y
A

Domestic supply
Domestic demand

Q_D Q_A Q_S **Quantity of computers**

Exports

| | Changes in surplus | |
	Gain	Loss
Consumer surplus		– X
Producer surplus	X + Z	
Change in total surplus	**+ Z**	

When the domestic price rises to P_W as a result of trade, producers gain additional surplus (areas X + Z) but consumers lose surplus (area X). Because the gains to producers outweigh the losses to consumers, there is an increase in the total surplus in the economy as a whole (area Z).

The higher world price makes it profitable for exporters to buy computers domestically and sell them overseas. The purchases of domestic computers drive the domestic price up until it is equal to the world price. As a result, the quantity demanded by domestic consumers falls from Q_A to Q_D and the quantity supplied by domestic producers rises from Q_A to Q_S. This difference between domestic production and domestic consumption, $Q_S - Q_D$, is exported.

Like imports, exports lead to an overall gain in total surplus for the exporting country but also create losers as well as winners. Figure 8-9 shows the effects of computer exports on producer and consumer surplus. In the absence of trade, the price of computers would be P_A. Consumer surplus in the absence of trade is the sum of areas W and X, and producer surplus is area Y. As a result of trade, price rises from P_A to P_W, consumer surplus falls to W, and producer surplus rises to $Y + X + Z$. So producers gain $X + Z$, consumers lose X, and, as shown in the table accompanying the figure, the economy as a whole gains total surplus in the amount of Z.

We have learned, then, that imports of a particular good hurt domestic producers of that good but help domestic consumers, whereas exports of a particular good hurt domestic consumers but help domestic producers of that good. In each case, the gains are larger than the losses.

International Trade and Wages

So far we have focused on the effects of international trade on producers and consumers in a particular industry. For many purposes this is a very helpful approach. However, producers and consumers are not the only parts of society affected by trade—so are the owners of factors of production. In particular, the owners of labor, land, and capital employed in producing goods that are exported, or goods that compete with imported goods, can be deeply affected by trade. Moreover, the effects of trade aren't limited to just those industries that export or compete with imports

Exporting industries produce goods and services that are sold abroad.

Import-competing industries produce goods and services that are also imported.

because *factors of production can often move between industries.* So now we turn our attention to the long-run effects of international trade on income distribution—how a country's total income is allocated among its various factors of production.

To begin our analysis, consider the position of Maria, an accountant who currently works for the Crazy Cajun Shrimp Company, based in Louisiana. If the economy is opened up to imports of shrimp from Vietnam, the domestic shrimp industry will contract, and it will hire fewer accountants. But accounting is a profession with employment opportunities in many industries, and Maria might well find a better job in the computer industry, which expands as a result of international trade. So it may not be appropriate to think of her as a producer of shrimp who is hurt by competition from imported shrimp. Rather, we should think of her as an accountant who is affected by shrimp imports only to the extent that these imports change the wages of accountants in the economy as a whole.

The wage rate of accountants is a *factor price*—the price employers have to pay for the services of a factor of production. One key question about international trade is how it affects factor prices—not just narrowly defined factors of production like accountants, but broadly defined factors such as capital, unskilled labor, and college-educated labor.

Earlier in this chapter we described the Heckscher–Ohlin model of trade, which states that comparative advantage is determined by a country's factor endowment. This model also suggests how international trade affects factor prices in a country: compared to autarky, international trade tends to raise the prices of factors that are abundantly available and reduce the prices of factors that are scarce.

We won't work this out in detail, but the idea is intuitively simple. The prices of factors of production, like the prices of goods and services, are determined by supply and demand. If international trade increases the demand for a factor of production, that factor's price will rise; if international trade reduces the demand for a factor of production, that factor's price will fall. Now think of a country's industries as consisting of two kinds: **exporting industries,** which produce goods and services that are sold abroad, and **import-competing industries,** which produce goods and services that are also imported from abroad. Compared with autarky, international trade leads to higher production in exporting industries and lower production in import-competing industries. This indirectly increases the demand for the factors used by exporting industries and decreases the demand for factors used by import-competing industries. In addition, the Heckscher–Ohlin model says that a country tends to export goods that are intensive in its abundant factors and to import goods that are intensive in its scarce factors. So *international trade tends to increase the demand for factors that are abundant in our country compared with other countries, and to decrease the demand for factors that are scarce in our country compared with other countries.* As a result, *the prices of abundant factors tend to rise, and the prices of scarce factors tend to fall as international trade grows.* In other words, international trade tends to redistribute income toward a country's abundant factors and away from its less abundant factors.

The Economics in Action at the end of the preceding section pointed out that U.S. exports tend to be human-capital-intensive and U.S. imports tend to be unskilled-labor-intensive. This suggests that the effect of international trade on U.S. factor markets is to raise the wage rate of highly educated American workers and reduce the wage rate of unskilled American workers.

This effect has been a source of much concern in recent years. Wage inequality—the gap between the wages of high-paid and low-paid workers—has increased substantially over the last 25 years. Some economists believe that growing international trade is an important factor in that trend. If international trade has the effects predicted by the Heckscher–Ohlin model, its growth raises the wages of highly educated American workers, who already have relatively high wages, and lowers the wages of less educated American workers, who already have relatively low wages. But keep in mind another phenomenon: trade reduces the income inequality *between* countries as poor countries improve their standard of living by exporting to rich countries.

How important are these effects? In some historical episodes, the impacts of international trade on factor prices have been very large. As we explain in the Economics in Action that follows, the opening of transatlantic trade in the late nineteenth century had a large negative impact on land rents in Europe, hurting landowners but helping workers and owners of capital. The effects of trade on wages in the United States have generated considerable controversy in recent years. Most economists who have studied the issue agree that growing imports of labor-intensive products from newly industrializing economies, and the export of high-technology goods in return, have helped cause a widening wage gap between highly educated and less educated workers in this country. However, most economists believe that it is only one of several forces explaining growing wage inequality.

> An economy has **free trade** when the government does not attempt either to reduce or to increase the levels of exports and imports that occur naturally as a result of supply and demand.

►ECONOMICS IN ACTION

Trade, Wages, and Land Prices in the Nineteenth Century

Beginning around 1870, there was an explosive growth of world trade in agricultural products, based largely on the steam engine. Steam-powered ships could cross the ocean much more quickly and reliably than sailing ships. Until about 1860, steamships had higher costs than sailing ships, but after that costs dropped sharply. At the same time, steam-powered rail transport made it possible to bring grain and other bulk goods cheaply from the interior to ports. The result was that land-abundant countries—the United States, Canada, Argentina, Australia—began shipping large quantities of agricultural goods to the densely populated, land-scarce countries of Europe.

This opening up of international trade led to higher prices of agricultural products, such as wheat, in exporting countries and a decline in their prices in importing countries. Notably, the difference between wheat prices in the midwestern United States and England plunged.

The change in agricultural prices created winners and losers on both sides of the Atlantic as factor prices adjusted. In England, land prices fell by half compared with average wages; landowners found their purchasing power sharply reduced, but workers benefited from cheaper food. In the United States, the reverse happened: land prices doubled compared with wages. Landowners did very well, but workers found the purchasing power of their wages dented by rising food prices. ▲

> > > > > > > > > > > > >

► CHECK YOUR UNDERSTANDING 8-2

1. Due to a strike by truckers, trade in food between the United States and Mexico is halted. In autarky, the price of Mexican grapes is lower than that of U.S. grapes. Using a diagram of the U.S. domestic demand curve and the U.S. domestic supply curve for grapes, explain the effect of these events on the following.
   a. U.S. grape consumers' surplus
   b. U.S. grape producers' surplus
   c. U.S. total surplus

2. What effect do you think this event will have on Mexican grape producers? Mexican grape pickers? Mexican grape consumers? U.S. grape pickers?

Solutions appear at back of book.

The Effects of Trade Protection

Ever since David Ricardo laid out the principle of comparative advantage in the early nineteenth century, most economists have advocated **free trade.** That is, they have argued that government policy should not attempt either to reduce or to increase the levels of exports and imports that occur naturally as a result of supply and demand.

Policies that limit imports are known as **trade protection** or simply as **protection.**

A **tariff** is a tax levied on imports.

Despite the free-trade arguments of economists, however, many governments use taxes and other restrictions to limit imports. Much less frequently, governments offer subsidies to encourage exports. Policies that limit imports, usually with the goal of protecting domestic producers in import-competing industries from foreign competition, are known as **trade protection** or simply as **protection.**

Let's look at the two most common protectionist policies, tariffs and import quotas, then turn to the reasons governments follow these policies.

The Effects of a Tariff

A **tariff** is a form of excise tax, one that is levied only on sales of imported goods. For example, the U.S. government could declare that anyone bringing in shrimp from Vietnam must pay a tariff of $1,000 per ton. In the distant past, tariffs were an important source of government revenue because they were relatively easy to collect. But in the modern world, tariffs are usually intended to discourage imports and protect import-competing domestic producers rather than as a source of government revenue.

The tariff raises both the price received by domestic producers and the price paid by domestic consumers. Suppose, for example, that our country imports shrimp, and a ton of shrimp costs $2,000 on the world market. As we saw earlier, under free trade the domestic price would also be $2,000. But if a tariff of $1,000 per ton is imposed, the domestic price will rise to $3,000, because it won't be profitable to import shrimp unless the price in the domestic market is high enough to compensate importers for the cost of paying the tariff.

Figure 8-10 illustrates the effects of a tariff on shrimp imports. As before, we assume that P_W is the world price of shrimp. Before the tariff is imposed, imports have driven the domestic price down to P_W, so that pre-tariff domestic production is Q_S, pre-tariff domestic consumption is Q_D, and pre-tariff imports are $Q_D - Q_S$.

Now suppose that the government imposes a tariff on each ton of shrimp imported. As a consequence, it is no longer profitable to import shrimp unless the domestic

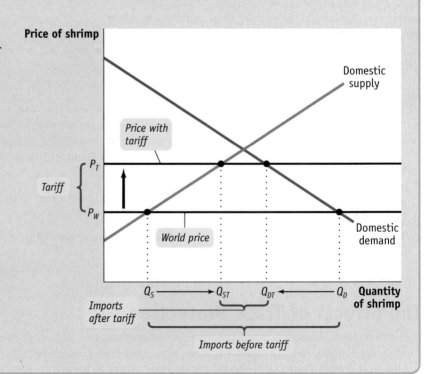

FIGURE 8-10

The Effect of a Tariff

A tariff raises the domestic price of the good from P_W to P_T. The domestic quantity demanded shrinks from Q_D to Q_{DT}, and the domestic quantity supplied increases from Q_S to Q_{ST}. As a result, imports—which had been $Q_D - Q_S$ before the tariff was imposed—shrink to $Q_{DT} - Q_{ST}$ after the tariff is imposed.

price received by the importer is greater than or equal to the world price *plus* the tariff. So the domestic price rises to P_T, which is equal to the world price, P_W, plus the tariff. Domestic production rises to Q_{ST}, domestic consumption falls to Q_{DT}, and imports fall to $Q_{DT} - Q_{ST}$.

A tariff, then, raises domestic prices, leading to increased domestic production and reduced domestic consumption compared to the situation under free trade. Figure 8-11 shows the effects on surplus. There are three effects. First, the higher domestic price increases producer surplus, a gain equal to area *A*. Second, the higher domestic price reduces consumer surplus, a reduction equal to the sum of areas *A, B, C,* and *D*. Finally, the tariff yields revenue to the government. How much revenue? The government collects the tariff—which, remember, is equal to the difference between P_T and P_W on each of the $Q_{DT} - Q_{ST}$ tons of shrimp imported. So total revenue is $(P_T - P_W) \times (Q_{DT} - Q_{ST})$. This is equal to area *C*.

The welfare effects of a tariff are summarized in the table in Figure 8-11. Producers gain, consumers lose, and the government gains. But consumer losses are greater than the sum of producer and government gains, leading to a net reduction in total surplus equal to areas *B + D*.

An excise tax creates inefficiency, or deadweight loss, because it prevents mutually beneficial trades from occurring. The same is true of a tariff, where the deadweight loss imposed on society is equal to the loss in total surplus represented by areas *B + D*. Tariffs generate deadweight losses because they create inefficiencies in two ways. First, some mutually beneficial trades go unexploited: some consumers who are willing to pay more than the world price, P_W, do not purchase the good, even though P_W is the true cost of a unit of the good to the economy. The cost of this inefficiency is represented in Figure 8-11 by area *D*. Second, the economy's resources are wasted on

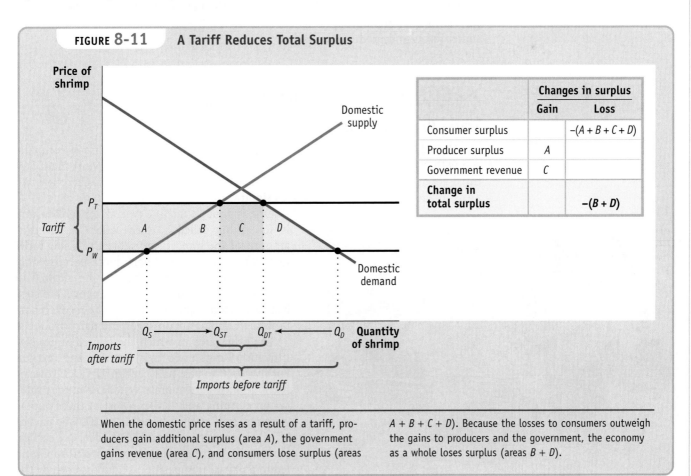

FIGURE 8-11   A Tariff Reduces Total Surplus

When the domestic price rises as a result of a tariff, producers gain additional surplus (area *A*), the government gains revenue (area *C*), and consumers lose surplus (areas *A + B + C + D*). Because the losses to consumers outweigh the gains to producers and the government, the economy as a whole loses surplus (areas *B + D*).

An **import quota** is a legal limit on the quantity of a good that can be imported.

inefficient production: some producers whose cost exceeds P_W produce the good, even though an additional unit of the good can be purchased abroad for P_W. The cost of this inefficiency is represented in Figure 8-11 by area B.

The Effects of an Import Quota

An **import quota,** another form of trade protection, is a legal limit on the quantity of a good that can be imported. For example, a U.S. import quota on Vietnamese shrimp might limit the quantity imported each year to 3 million tons. Import quotas are usually administered through licenses: a number of licenses are issued, each giving the license-holder the right to import a limited quantity of the good each year.

A quota on sales has the same effect as an excise tax, with one difference: the money that would otherwise have accrued to the government as tax revenue under an excise tax becomes license-holders' revenue under a quota—also known as quota rents. Similarly, an import quota has the same effect as a tariff, with one difference: the money that would otherwise have been government revenue becomes quota rents to license-holders. Look again at Figure 8-11. An import quota that limits imports to $Q_{DT} - Q_{ST}$ will raise the domestic price of shrimp by the same amount as the tariff we considered previously. That is, it will raise the domestic price from P_W to P_T. However, area C will now represent quota rents rather than government revenue.

Who receives import licenses and so collects the quota rents? In the case of U.S. import protection, the answer may surprise you: the most important import licenses—mainly for clothing, to a lesser extent for sugar—are granted to foreign governments.

Because the quota rents for most U.S. import quotas go to foreigners, the cost to the nation of such quotas is larger than that of a comparable tariff (a tariff that leads to the same level of imports). In Figure 8-11 the net loss to the United States from such an import quota would be equal to areas $B + C + D$, the difference between consumer losses and producer gains.

►*ECONOMICS IN ACTION*

Trade Protection in the United States

The United States today generally follows a policy of free trade, at least in comparison with other countries and also in comparison with its own past. Most manufactured goods are subject either to no tariff or to a low tariff. However, there are two areas in which the United States does significantly limit imports.

One is agriculture. The typical U.S. policy here is something called a "tariff quota." A certain amount of the imports are subject to a low tariff rate; this acts like an import quota because only importers that are license-holders are allowed to pay the low rate. Any additional imports are subject to a much higher tariff rate. The most important tariff quotas are on sugar and dairy products.

The other area in which the United States significantly limits imports is clothing and textiles. For most of the past half-century the U.S. government applied an elaborate system of import quotas on clothing and textiles. Most of these quotas were removed at the beginning of 2005 as part of a trade agreement reached a decade earlier. However, a surge of clothing exports from China led to a partial reimposition of quotas both by the United States and by European nations.

The peculiar thing about U.S. trade protection is that in most cases quota licenses are assigned to foreigners, often foreign governments. For example, rights to sell sugar in the United States are allotted to various exporting countries, which can then hand those rights out as they see fit. This means that the quota rents go overseas, greatly increasing the cost to the United States of the import limitations. In fact, according to some estimates, about 70% of the total cost of U.S. import restrictions comes not from deadweight loss but from the transfer of quota rents to foreigners.

Maybe the most important thing to know about U.S. trade protection, however, is that there isn't much of it. According to official U.S. estimates, the total economic cost of all quantifiable restrictions on imports is about $3.7 billion a year, or around one-fortieth of a percent of national income. Of this, about $1.9 billion comes from restrictions on clothing imports, $0.8 billion from restrictions on sugar, and $0.6 billion from restrictions on dairy. Everything else is small change. ▲

> > > > > > > > > > > > >

> ### CHECK YOUR UNDERSTANDING 8-3

1. Suppose the world price of butter is $0.50 per pound and the domestic price in autarky is $1.00 per pound. Use a diagram similar to Figure 8-10 to show the following.
   a. If there is free trade, domestic butter producers want the government to impose a tariff of no less than $0.50 per pound.
   b. What happens if a tariff greater than $0.50 per pound is imposed?
2. Suppose the government imposes an import quota rather than a tariff on butter. What quota limit would generate the same quantity of imports as a tariff of $0.50 per pound?

Solutions appear at back of book.

>> QUICK REVIEW

➤ Most economists advocate **free trade,** although many governments engage in **trade protection** of import-competing industries. The two most common protectionist policies are tariffs and import quotas. In rare instances, governments subsidize exporting industries.

➤ A **tariff** is a tax on imports. It raises the domestic price above the world price, leading to a fall in trade and domestic consumption and a rise in domestic production. Domestic producers and the government gain, but domestic consumer losses more than offset this gain, leading to deadweight loss.

➤ An **import quota** is a legal quantity limit on imports. Its effect is like that of a tariff, except that revenues—the quota rents—accrue to the license-holder, not to the domestic government.

The Political Economy of Trade Protection

We have seen that international trade produces mutual benefits to the countries that engage in it. We have also seen that tariffs and import quotas, although they produce winners as well as losers, reduce total surplus. Yet many countries continue to impose tariffs and import quotas as well as to enact other protectionist measures.

To understand why trade protection takes place, we will first look at some common justifications for protection. Then we will look at the politics of trade protection. Finally, we will look at an important feature of trade protection in today's world: tariffs and import quotas are the subject of international negotiation and are policed by international organizations.

Arguments for Trade Protection

Advocates for tariffs and import quotas offer a variety of arguments. Three common arguments are *national security, job creation,* and the *infant industry argument.*

The national security argument is based on the proposition that overseas sources of goods are vulnerable to disruption in times of international conflict; therefore, a country should protect domestic suppliers of crucial goods with the aim to be self-sufficient in those goods. In the 1960s, the United States—which had begun to import oil as domestic oil reserves ran low—had an import quota on oil, justified on national security grounds. Some people have argued that we should again have policies to discourage imports of oil, especially from the Middle East.

The job creation argument points to the additional jobs created in import-competing industries as a result of trade protection. Economists argue that these jobs are offset by the jobs lost elsewhere, such as industries that use imported inputs and now face higher input costs. But noneconomists don't always find this argument persuasive.

Finally, the infant industry argument, often raised in newly industrializing countries, holds that new industries require a temporary period of trade protection to get established. For example, in the 1950s many countries in Latin America imposed

International trade agreements are treaties in which a country promises to engage in less trade protection against the exports of other countries in return for a promise by other countries to do the same for its own exports.

The **North American Free Trade Agreement**, or **NAFTA**, is a trade agreement among the United States, Canada, and Mexico.

The **European Union**, or **EU**, is a customs union among 27 European nations.

tariffs and import quotas on manufactured goods, in an effort to switch from their traditional role as exporters of raw materials to a new status as industrial countries. In theory, the argument for infant industry protection can be compelling, particularly in high-tech industries that increase a country's overall skill level. Reality, however, is more complicated: it is most often industries that are politically influential that gain protection. In addition, governments tend to be poor predictors of the best emerging technologies. Finally, it is often very difficult to wean an industry from protection when it should be mature enough to stand on its own.

The Politics of Trade Protection

In reality, much trade protection has little to do with the arguments just described. Instead, it reflects the political influence of import-competing producers.

We've seen that a tariff or import quota leads to gains for import-competing producers and losses for consumers. Producers, however, usually have much more influence over trade policy decisions. The producers who compete with imports of a particular good are usually a smaller, more cohesive group than the consumers of that good.

An example is trade protection for sugar: the United States has an import quota on sugar, which on average leads to a domestic price about twice the world price. This quota is difficult to rationalize in terms of any economic argument. However, consumers rarely complain about the quota because they are unaware that it exists: because no individual consumer buys large amounts of sugar, the cost of the quota is only a few dollars per family each year, not enough to attract notice. But there are only a few thousand sugar growers in the United States. They are very aware of the benefits they receive from the quota and make sure that their representatives in Congress are also aware of their interest in the matter.

Given these political realities, it may seem surprising that trade is as free as it is. For example, the United States has low tariffs, and its import quotas are mainly confined to clothing and a few agricultural products. It would be nice to say that the main reason trade protection is so limited is that economists have convinced governments of the virtues of free trade. A more important reason, however, is the role of *international trade agreements*.

International Trade Agreements and the World Trade Organization

When a country engages in trade protection, it hurts two groups. We've already emphasized the adverse effect on domestic consumers, but protection also hurts foreign export industries. This means that countries care about each others' trade policies: the Canadian lumber industry has a strong interest in keeping U.S. tariffs on forest products low.

Because countries care about each others' trade policies, they engage in **international trade agreements**: treaties in which a country promises to engage in less trade protection against the exports of another country in return for a promise by the other country to do the same for its own exports. Most world trade is now governed by such agreements.

Some international trade agreements involve just two countries or a small group of countries. The United States, Canada, and Mexico are joined together by the **North American Free Trade Agreement,** or **NAFTA.** This agreement, signed in 1993, will eventually remove all barriers to trade among the three nations. In Europe, 27 nations are part of an even more comprehensive agreement, the **European Union** or **EU.** In NAFTA, the member countries set their own tariff rates against imports from other nonmember countries. The EU, however, is a *customs union*: tariffs are levied at the same rate on goods from outside the EU entering the union.

There are also global trade agreements covering most of the world. Such global agreements are overseen by the **World Trade Organization,** or **WTO,** an international organization composed of member countries, which plays two roles. First, it provides the framework for the massively complex negotiations involved in a major international trade agreement (the full text of the last major agreement, approved in 1994, was 24,000 pages long). Second, the WTO resolves disputes between its members. These disputes typically arise when one country claims that another country's policies violate its previous agreements. Currently, the WTO has 151 member countries, accounting for the bulk of world trade.

> The **World Trade Organization,** or **WTO,** oversees international trade agreements and rules on disputes between countries over those agreements.

Here are two examples that illustrate the WTO's role. First, in 1999 the WTO ruled that the European Union's import restrictions on bananas, which discriminate in favor of banana producers in former European colonies and against Central American banana producers, are in violation of international trade rules. The United States took the side of the Central American countries, and the dispute threatened to become a major source of conflict between the European Union and the United States. Europe is currently in the process of revising its system. A more recent example is the dispute between the United States and Brazil over American subsidies to its cotton farmers. These subsidies, in the amount of $3 to $4 billion a year, are illegal under WTO rules. Brazil argues that they artificially reduce the price of American cotton on world markets and hurt Brazilian cotton farmers. In 2005 the WTO ruled against the United States and in favor of Brazil, and the United States responded by cutting some export subsidies on cotton. However, in 2007, the WTO ruled that the United States had not done enough to fully comply, such as eliminating government loans to cotton farmers. At the time of writing, the United States has not yet replied to the WTO's ruling.

By the way, Vietnam and Thailand are both members of the WTO. Some students may wonder why, in that case, the rules don't prevent the United States from imposing tariffs on shrimp imports. The answer is that WTO rules do allow trade protection under certain circumstances. One circumstance is where the foreign competition is "unfair" under certain technical criteria. That's what the United States is alleging in the case of shrimp imports. Trade protection is also allowed as a temporary measure when a sudden surge of imports threatens to disrupt a domestic industry. The response to Chinese clothing exports, described in For Inquiring Minds, is an important recent example.

FOR INQUIRING MINDS

Chinese Pants Explosion

From 1973 onwards, most world trade in clothing was regulated by a complex system of export and import quotas known as the Multifiber Agreement. However, in 1994 the members of the World Trade Organization agreed to end restrictions on the clothing trade over the next decade. At the end of 2004, the remaining restrictions were removed, with dramatic results: clothing exports from China, a huge country with vast reserves of cheap labor that had relatively small export quotas under the old system, exploded. Exports of clothing from China to the United States in January 2005 were more than twice their level a year

earlier. Chinese exports of cotton trousers were up more than 1,000%.

The Chinese pants explosion provided clear evidence of the extent to which quotas had previously been restricting trade. It also produced urgent demands for temporary protection from clothing producers in importing countries. Within a few months, both the United States and the European Union imposed new restrictions on China's clothing exports to counteract the flood.

Surprisingly, these new restrictions didn't violate WTO rules. When China joined the WTO in 2001, it agreed to what is known, in trade policy jargon, as a "safeguard

mechanism": importing countries were granted the right to impose temporary limits on Chinese clothing exports in the event of an import surge. And that's just what they did.

You shouldn't be too cynical about this failure to achieve complete free trade in clothing. World trade negotiations have always been based on the principle that half a loaf is better than none, that it's better to have an agreement that allows politically sensitive industries to retain some protection than to insist on free trade purity. In spite of the restrictions imposed on China, world trade in clothing is much freer now than it was just a few years ago.

Offshore outsourcing takes place when businesses hire people in another country to perform various tasks.

The WTO is sometimes, with great exaggeration, described as a world government. In fact, it has no army, no police, and no direct enforcement power. The grain of truth in that description is that when a country joins the WTO, it agrees to accept the organization's judgments—and these judgments apply not only to tariffs and import quotas but also to domestic policies that the organization considers trade protection disguised under another name. So in joining the WTO a country does give up some of its sovereignty.

New Challenges to Globalization

The forward march of globalization over the past century is generally considered a major political and economic success. Economists and policy makers alike have viewed growing world trade, in particular, as a good thing. We would be remiss, however, if we failed to acknowledge that many people are having second thoughts about globalization. To a large extent, these second thoughts reflect two concerns shared by many economists: worries about the effects of globalization on inequality and worries that new developments, in particular the growth in *offshore outsourcing,* are increasing economic insecurity.

Globalization and Inequality We've already mentioned the implications of international trade for factor prices, such as wages: when wealthy countries like the United States export skill-intensive products like aircraft while importing labor-intensive products like clothing, they can expect to see the wage gap between more educated and less educated domestic workers widen. Thirty years ago, this wasn't too much of a concern, because most of the goods wealthy countries imported from poorer countries were raw materials or goods where comparative advantage depended on climate. Today, however, many manufactured goods are imported from relatively poor countries, with a potentially much larger effect on the distribution of income.

Trade with China, in particular, raises concerns among labor groups trying to maintain wage levels in rich countries. Although China has experienced spectacular economic growth since the economic reforms that began in the late 1970s, it remains a poor, low-wage country: wages in Chinese manufacturing are estimated to be only about 3% of U.S. wages. Meanwhile, imports from China have soared. In 1983 less than 1% of U.S. imports came from China; by 2007, the figure was more than 16%. There's not much question that these surging imports from China put at least some downward pressure on the wages of less educated American workers.

Outsourcing Chinese exports to the United States overwhelmingly consist of labor-intensive manufactured goods. However, some U.S. workers have recently found themselves facing a new form of international competition. *Outsourcing,* in which a company hires another company to perform some task, such as running the corporate computer system, is a long-standing business practice. Until recently, however, outsourcing was normally done locally, with a company hiring another company in the same city or country. Now, modern telecommunications increasingly makes it possible to engage in **offshore outsourcing,** in which businesses hire people in another country to perform various tasks. The classic example is call centers: the person answering the phone when you call a company's 1-800 help line may well be in India, which has taken the lead in attracting offshore outsourcing. Offshore outsourcing has also spread to fields such as software design and even health care: the radiologist examining your X-rays, like the person giving you computer help, may be on another continent.

Although offshore outsourcing has come as a shock to some U.S. workers, such as programmers whose jobs have been outsourced to India, it's still relatively small compared with more traditional trade. Some economists have warned, however, that millions or even tens of millions of workers who have never thought they could face foreign competition for their jobs may face unpleasant surprises in the not-too-distant future.

Concerns about income distribution and outsourcing, as we've said, are shared by many economists. There is also, however, widespread opposition to globalization in general, particularly among college students. In 1999, an attempt to start a major round of trade negotiations failed in part because the WTO meeting, in Seattle, was disrupted by antiglobalization demonstrators. However, the more important reason for its failure was disagreement among the countries represented.

What motivates the antiglobalization movement? To some extent it's the sweatshop labor fallacy: it's easy to get outraged about the low wages paid to the person who made your shirt, and harder to appreciate how much worse off that person would be if denied the opportunity to sell goods in rich countries' markets. It's also true, however, that the movement represents a backlash against supporters of globalization who have oversold its benefits. Countries in Latin America, in particular, were promised that reducing their tariff rates would produce an economic takeoff; instead, they have experienced disappointing results. Some groups, such as poor farmers facing new competition from imported food, ended up worse off.

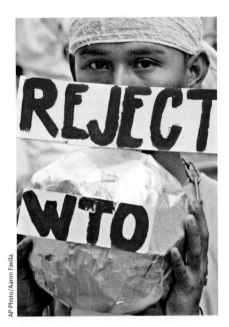

Angry protests regularly occur at annual meetings of the WTO.

Do these new challenges to globalization undermine the argument that international trade is a good thing? The great majority of economists would argue that the gains from reducing trade protection still exceed the losses. However, it has become more important than before to make sure that the gains from international trade are widely spread. And the politics of international trade is becoming increasingly difficult as the extent of trade has grown.

►*ECONOMICS IN ACTION*

The Doha Deadlock

Since the end of World War II there have been nine rounds of global trade negotiations. A trade round is a multiyear process in which negotiators from many countries cut complex deals on trade policy. For example, the eighth set of trade negotiations, known as the Uruguay Round, lasted from 1986 to 1994. That round created the World Trade Organization. It also involved a deal in which wealthy countries agreed to dismantle the system of import quotas restricting trade in clothing, and poorer countries agreed to new rules governing investment by multinational corporations, patent protection, and other matters.

The so-called Doha Round began with a formal ceremony in the Persian Gulf city of Doha, Qatar, in 2001. (The location was chosen in part because it was inaccessible to the demonstrators who had disrupted the 1999 WTO meeting in Seattle.) Trade officials then moved the meeting to Geneva, Switzerland, which is where most global negotiating takes place. Unfortunately, it went mostly downhill from there. By late 2007, talks appeared to be deadlocked.

Here's a quick summary of the deadlock: poorer countries, which still have substantial trade protection in manufactured goods, refused to reduce that protection without an agreement by rich countries, the Europeans in particular but the Americans as well, to reduce the substantial subsidies they give farmers. Because the farm lobbies in rich countries have a lot of political power, however, these countries weren't willing to make sufficient concessions.

>> QUICK REVIEW

➤ The three major justifications for trade protection are national security, job creation, and protection of infant industries.

➤ Despite the deadweight losses, import protections are often imposed because groups representing import-competing industries are smaller and more cohesive, and so more influential, than groups of consumers.

➤ To further trade liberalization, countries engage in **international trade agreements.** Some agreements are for only a small number of countries, such as the **North American Free Trade Agreement (NAFTA)** and the **European Union (EU).** The **World Trade Organization (WTO)** is a multinational organization that seeks to negotiate global trade agreements as well as referee trade disputes between members.

➤ Greater resistance to globalization has emerged over the past few years in response to a surge in imports from relatively poor countries and the **offshore outsourcing** of many jobs that had previously been considered safe from foreign competition.

At a deeper level, the latest trade round may simply be a victim of the success of previous rounds. Over the course of 50 years of trade negotiations, all the easy deals were made, and many of the pretty hard ones, too. What's left—above all, the subsidies received by politically powerful farmers—may simply not be negotiable.

It's important to realize, however, that even if the Doha Round fails, previous trade agreements will remain in force. The fact is that trade negotiations have produced a world in which trade is remarkably free by historical standards. ▲

< < < < < < < < < < < <

> CHECK YOUR UNDERSTANDING 8-4

1. In 2002 the United States imposed tariffs on steel imports, which are an input in a large number and variety of U.S. industries. Explain why political lobbying to eliminate these tariffs is more likely to be effective than political lobbying to eliminate tariffs on consumer goods such as sugar or clothing.

2. Over the years, the WTO has increasingly found itself adjudicating trade disputes that involve not just tariffs or quota restrictions but also restrictions based on quality, health, and environmental considerations. Why do you think this has occurred? What method would you, as a WTO official, use to decide whether a quality, health, or environmental restriction is in violation of a free-trade agreement?

Solutions appear at back of book.

[>> A LOOK AHEAD •••

As we move on to new topics, remember the insights learned in this chapter about the logic of comparative advantage and the gains from international trade. They will provide us with a deeper understanding of what drives the world economy and the reasons countries differ economically. In addition, the study of international trade teaches us how economic policies can create both winners and losers despite the fact that society as a whole gains, an important consideration in any study of how policies are actually made.]

SUMMARY ••• ∎

1. International trade is of growing importance to the United States and of even greater importance to most other countries. International trade, like trade among individuals, arises from comparative advantage: the opportunity cost of producing an additional unit of a good is lower in some countries than in others. Goods and services purchased abroad are **imports;** those sold abroad are **exports.** Foreign trade, like other economic linkages between countries, has been growing rapidly, a phenomenon called **globalization.**

2. The **Ricardian model of international trade** assumes that opportunity costs are constant. It shows that there are gains from trade: two countries are better off with trade than in **autarky.**

3. In practice, comparative advantage reflects differences between countries in climate, factor endowments, and technology. The **Heckscher–Ohlin model** shows how differences in factor endowments determine comparative advantage: goods differ in **factor intensity,** and

countries tend to export goods that are intensive in the factors they have in abundance.

4. The **domestic demand curve** and the **domestic supply curve** determine the price of a good in autarky. When international trade occurs, the domestic price is driven to equality with the **world price,** the price at which the good is bought and sold abroad.

5. If the world price is below the autarky price, a good is imported. This leads to an increase in consumer surplus, a fall in producer surplus, and a gain in total surplus. If the world price is above the autarky price, a good is exported. This leads to an increase in producer surplus, a fall in consumer surplus, and a gain in total surplus.

6. International trade leads to expansion in **exporting industries** and contraction in **import-competing industries.** This raises the domestic demand for abundant factors of production, reduces the demand for scarce factors, and so affects factor prices, such as wages.

7. Most economists advocate **free trade,** but in practice many governments engage in **trade protection.** The two most common forms of **protection** are tariffs and quotas. In rare occasions, export industries are subsidized.

8. A **tariff** is a tax levied on imports. It raises the domestic price above the world price, hurting consumers, benefiting domestic producers, and generating government revenue. As a result, total surplus falls. An **import quota** is a legal limit on the quantity of a good that can be imported. It has the same effects as a tariff, except that the revenue goes not to the government but to those who receive import licenses.

9. Although several popular arguments have been made in favor of trade protection, in practice the main reason for protection is probably political: import-competing industries are well organized and well informed about how they gain from trade protection, while consumers are unaware of the costs they pay. Still, U.S. trade is fairly free, mainly because of the role of **international trade agreements,** in which countries agree to reduce trade protection against each others' exports. The **North American Free Trade Agreement (NAFTA)** and the **European Union (EU)** cover a small number of countries. In contrast, the **World Trade Organization (WTO)** covers a much larger number of countries, accounting for the bulk of world trade. It oversees trade negotiations and adjudicates disputes among its members.

10. In the past few years, many concerns have been raised about the effects of globalization. One issue is the increase in income inequality due to the surge in imports from relatively poor countries over the past 20 years. Another concern is the increase in **offshore outsourcing,** as many jobs that were once considered safe from foreign competition have been moved abroad.

KEY TERMS

Imports, p. 196
Exports, p. 196
Globalization, p. 196
Ricardian model of international trade, p. 197
Autarky, p. 198
Factor intensity, p. 203
Heckscher–Ohlin model, p. 203

Domestic demand curve, p. 206
Domestic supply curve, p. 206
World price, p. 206
Exporting industries, p. 210
Import-competing industries, p. 210
Free trade, p. 211
Trade protection, p. 212
Protection, p. 212

Tariff, p. 212
Import quota, p. 214
International trade agreements, p. 216
North American Free Trade Agreement (NAFTA), p. 216
European Union (EU), p. 216
World Trade Organization (WTO), p. 217
Offshore outsourcing, p. 218

PROBLEMS

1. Assume Saudi Arabia and the United States face the production possibilities for oil and cars shown in the accompanying table.

Saudi Arabia		United States	
Quantity of oil (millions of barrels)	Quantity of cars (millions)	Quantity of oil (millions of barrels)	Quantity of cars (millions)
0	4	0	10.0
200	3	100	7.5
400	2	200	5.0
600	1	300	2.5
800	0	400	0

   a. What is the opportunity cost of producing a car in Saudi Arabia? In the United States? What is the opportunity cost of producing a barrel of oil in Saudi Arabia? In the United States?

   b. Which country has the comparative advantage in producing oil? In producing cars?

   c. Suppose that in autarky, Saudi Arabia produces 200 million barrels of oil and 3 million cars; similarly, that the United States produces 300 million barrels of oil and 2.5 million cars. Without trade, can Saudi Arabia produce more oil *and* more cars? Without trade, can the United States produce more oil *and* more cars?

2. The production possibilities for the United States and Saudi Arabia are given in Problem 1. Suppose now that each country specializes in the good in which it has the comparative advantage, and the two countries trade. Also assume that for each country the value of imports must equal the value of exports.

   a. What is the total quantity of oil produced? What is the total quantity of cars produced?

b. Is it possible for Saudi Arabia to consume 400 million barrels of oil and 5 million cars and for the United States to consume 400 million barrels of oil and 5 million cars?

c. Suppose that, in fact, Saudi Arabia consumes 300 million barrels of oil and 4 million cars and the United States consumes 500 million barrels of oil and 6 million cars. How many barrels of oil does the United States import? How many cars does the United States export? Suppose a car costs $10,000 on the world market. How much, then, does a barrel of oil cost on the world market?

3. Both Canada and the United States produce lumber and music CDs with constant opportunity costs. The United States can produce either 10 tons of lumber and no CDs, or 1,000 CDs and no lumber, or any combination in between. Canada can produce either 8 tons of lumber and no CDs, or 400 CDs and no lumber, or any combination in between.

a. Draw the U.S. and Canadian production possibility frontiers in two separate diagrams, with CDs on the horizontal axis and lumber on the vertical axis.

b. In autarky, if the United States wants to consume 500 CDs, how much lumber can it consume at most? Label this point *A* in your diagram. Similarly, if Canada wants to consume 1 ton of lumber, how many CDs can it consume in autarky? Label this point *C* in your diagram.

c. Which country has the absolute advantage in lumber production?

d. Which country has the comparative advantage in lumber production?

Suppose each country specializes in the good in which it has the comparative advantage, and there is trade.

e. How many CDs does the United States produce? How much lumber does Canada produce?

f. Is it possible for the United States to consume 500 CDs and 7 tons of lumber? Label this point *B* in your diagram. Is it possible for Canada at the same time to consume 500 CDs and 1 ton of lumber? Label this point *D* in your diagram.

4. For each of the following trade relationships, explain the likely source of the comparative advantage of each of the exporting countries.

a. The United States exports software to Venezuela, and Venezuela exports oil to the United States.

b. The United States exports airplanes to China, and China exports clothing to the United States.

c. The United States exports wheat to Colombia, and Colombia exports coffee to the United States.

5. The U.S. Census Bureau keeps statistics on U.S. imports and exports on its website. The following steps will take you to the foreign trade statistics. Use them to answer the questions below.

    (i) Go to the U.S. Census Bureau's website at www.census.gov

    (ii) Under the heading "Business & Industry," click "Foreign Trade"

    (iii) At the top of the page, click "Statistics"

    (iv) Click "Country/Product Trade Data"

    (v) Under the heading "North American Industry Classification System (NAICS)-Based," click "NAICS web application"

    (vi) In the drop-down menu "3-digit and 6-digit NAICS by country," select the product category you are interested in, and click "Go"

    (vii) In the drop-down menu "Select 6-digit NAICS," select the good or service you are interested in, and click "Go"

    (viii) In the drop-down menus that allow you to select a month and year, select "December" and "2006," and click "Go"

    (ix) The right side of the table now shows the import and export statistics for the entire year 2006. For the questions below on U.S. imports, use the column for "Consumption Imports, Customs Value Basis."

a. Look up data for U.S. imports of hats and caps: in step (vi), select "(315) Apparel & Accessories" and in step (vii), select "(315991) Hats and Caps." From which country do we import the most hats and caps? Which of the three sources of comparative advantage (climate, factor endowments, and technology) accounts for that country's comparative advantage in hat and cap production?

b. Look up data for U.S. imports of grapes: in step (vi), select "(111) Agricultural Products" and in step (vii), select "(111332) Grapes." From which country do we import the most grapes? Which of the three sources of comparative advantage (climate, factor endowments, and technology) accounts for that country's comparative advantage in grape production?

c. Look up data for U.S. imports of food product machinery: in step (vi), select "(333) Machinery, Except Electrical" and in step (vii), select "(333294) Food Product Machinery." From which country do we import the most food product machinery? Which of the three sources of comparative advantage (climate, factor endowments, and technology) accounts for that country's comparative advantage in food product machinery?

6. Compare the data for U.S. imports of hats and caps from China in 2006 that you found in Problem 5, with the same data for the year 2000. Repeat the steps outlined in Problem 5, but in step (viii) select "December" and "2000."

a. What has happened to the value of U.S. imports of hats and caps from China between 2000 and 2006?

b. What prediction does the Heckscher–Ohlin model make about the wages received by labor in China?

7. Shoes are labor-intensive and satellites are capital-intensive to produce. The United States has abundant capital. China has abundant labor. According to the Heckscher–Ohlin model,

which good will China export? Which good will the United States export? In the United States, what will happen to the price of labor (the wage) and to the price of capital?

8. Before the North American Free Trade Agreement (NAFTA) gradually eliminated import tariffs on goods, the autarky price of tomatoes in Mexico was below the world price and in the United States was above the world price. Similarly, the autarky price of poultry in Mexico was above the world price and in the United States was below the world price. Draw diagrams with domestic supply and demand curves for each country and each of the two goods. As a result of NAFTA, the United States now imports tomatoes from Mexico and the United States now exports poultry to Mexico. How would you expect the following groups to be affected?

a. Mexican and U.S. consumers of tomatoes. Illustrate the effect on consumer surplus in your diagram.

b. Mexican and U.S. producers of tomatoes. Illustrate the effect on producer surplus in your diagram.

c. Mexican and U.S. tomato workers.

d. Mexican and U.S. consumers of poultry. Illustrate the effect on consumer surplus in your diagram.

e. Mexican and U.S. producers of poultry. Illustrate the effect on producer surplus in your diagram.

f. Mexican and U.S. poultry workers.

9. The accompanying table indicates the U.S. domestic demand schedule and domestic supply schedule for commercial jet airplanes. Suppose that the world price of a commercial jet airplane is $100 million.

Price of jet (millions)	Quantity of jets demanded	Quantity of jets supplied
$120	100	1,000
110	150	900
100	200	800
90	250	700
80	300	600
70	350	500
60	400	400
50	450	300
40	500	200

a. In autarky, how many commercial jet airplanes does the United States produce, and at what price are they bought and sold?

b. With trade, what will the price for commercial jet airplanes be? Will the United States import or export airplanes? How many?

10. The accompanying table shows the U.S. domestic demand schedule and domestic supply schedule for oranges. Suppose that the world price of oranges is $0.30 per orange.

Price of orange	Quantity of oranges demanded (thousands)	Quantity of oranges supplied (thousands)
$1.00	2	11
0.90	4	10
0.80	6	9
0.70	8	8
0.60	10	7
0.50	12	6
0.40	14	5
0.30	16	4
0.20	18	3

a. Draw the U.S. domestic supply curve and domestic demand curve.

b. With free trade, how many oranges will the United States import or export?

Suppose that the U.S. government imposes a tariff on oranges of $0.20 per orange.

c. How many oranges will the United States import or export after introduction of the tariff?

d. In your diagram, shade the gain or loss to the economy as a whole from the introduction of this tariff.

11. The U.S. domestic demand schedule and domestic supply schedule for oranges was given in Problem 10. Suppose that the world price of oranges is $0.30. The United States introduces an import quota of 3,000 oranges and assigns the quota rents to foreign orange exporters.

a. Draw the domestic demand and supply curves.

b. What will the domestic price of oranges be after introduction of the quota?

c. What is the value of the quota rents that foreign exporters of oranges receive?

12. The accompanying diagram illustrates the U.S. domestic demand curve and domestic supply curve for beef.

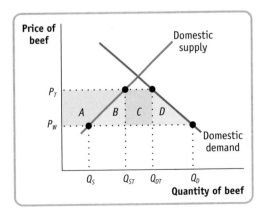

The world price of beef is P_W. The United States currently imposes an import tariff on beef, so the price of beef is P_T. Congress decides to eliminate the tariff. In terms of the areas marked in the diagram, answer the following questions.

a. What is the gain/loss in consumer surplus?

b. What is the gain/loss in producer surplus?

c. What is the gain/loss to the government?

d. What is the gain/loss to the economy as a whole?

13. As the United States has opened up to trade, it has lost many of its low-skill manufacturing jobs, but it has gained jobs in high-skill industries, such as the software industry. Explain whether the United States as a whole has been made better off by trade.

14. The United States is highly protective of its agricultural industry, imposing import tariffs, and sometimes quotas, on imports of agricultural goods. This chapter presented three arguments for trade protection. For each argument, discuss whether it is a valid justification for trade protection of U.S. agricultural products.

15. In World Trade Organization (WTO) negotiations, if a country agrees to reduce trade barriers (tariffs or quotas), it usually refers to this as a *concession* to other countries. Do you think that this terminology is appropriate?

16. Producers in import-competing industries often make the following argument: "Other countries have an advantage in production of certain goods purely because workers abroad are paid lower wages. In fact, American workers are much more productive than foreign workers. So import-competing industries need to be protected." Is this a valid argument? Explain your answer.

 www.worthpublishers.com/krugmanwells

chapter: 9

Making Decisions

A TALE OF TWO INVASIONS

On June 6, 1944, Allied soldiers stormed the beaches of Normandy, beginning the liberation of France from German rule. Long before the assault, however, Allied generals had to make a crucial decision: *where* would the soldiers land?

They had to make what we call an "either-or" decision. *Either* the invasion force could cross the English Channel at its narrowest point, Calais—which was what the Germans expected—*or* it could try to surprise the Germans by landing farther west, in Normandy. Since men and landing craft were in limited supply, the Allies could not do both. In fact, they chose to rely on surprise. The German defenses in Normandy were too weak to stop the landings, and the Allies went on to liberate France and win the war.

Thirty years earlier, at the beginning of World War I, German generals had to make a different kind of decision. They, too, planned to invade France,

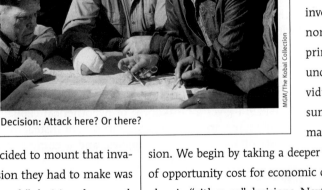

Decision: Attack here? Or there?

in this case by land, and had decided to mount that invasion through Belgium. The decision they had to make was not an "either-or" but a "how much" decision: *how much* of their army should be allocated to the invasion force, and how much should be used to defend Germany's border with France? The original plan, devised by General Alfred von Schlieffen, allocated most of the German army to the invasion force; on his deathbed, Schlieffen is supposed to have pleaded, "Keep the right wing [the invasion force] strong!" But his successor, General Helmuth von Moltke, weakened the plan: he reallocated to the defense some of the divisions that were supposed to race through Belgium. The weakened invasion force wasn't strong enough: the defending French army stopped it 30 miles from Paris. Most military historians believe that by allocating too few men to the attack, von Moltke cost Germany the war.

So Allied generals made the right decision in 1944; German generals made the wrong decision in 1914. The important point for this chapter is that in both cases the generals had to apply the same logic that applies to economic decisions, like consumption decisions by households and production decisions by businesses.

In this chapter we will survey the principles involved in making economic decisions. These principles will help us understand how any individual—whether a consumer or a producer—makes an economic decision. We begin by taking a deeper look at the significance of opportunity cost for economic decisions and the role it plays in "either-or" decisions. Next we turn to the problem of making "how much" decisions and the usefulness of *marginal analysis*. We then examine what kind of costs should be ignored in making a decision—costs that economists call *sunk costs*. We end by considering the concept of *present value* and its importance for making decisions when costs and benefits arrive at different times.

Opportunity Cost and Decisions

In Chapter 1 we introduced some core principles underlying economic decisions. We've just seen two of those principles at work in our tale of two invasions. The first is that *resources are scarce*—the invading Allies had a limited number of landing craft, and the invading Germans had a limited number of divisions. Because resources are scarce, the true cost of anything is its *opportunity cost*—that is, the real cost of something is what you must give up to get it. When making decisions, it is crucial to think in terms of opportunity cost, because the opportunity cost of an action is often considerably more than the cost of any outlays of money.

Explicit versus Implicit Costs

Suppose that, after graduating from college, you have two options: to go to school for an additional year to get an advanced degree or to take a job immediately. You would like to take the extra year in school but are concerned about the cost.

But what exactly is the cost of that additional year of school? Here is where it is important to remember the concept of opportunity cost: the cost of that year spent getting an advanced degree is what you forgo by not taking a job for that year. The opportunity cost of an additional year of school, like any cost, can be broken into two parts: the *explicit cost* of the year's schooling and the *implicit cost*.

An **explicit cost** is a cost that requires an outlay of money. For example, the explicit cost of the additional year of schooling includes tuition. An **implicit cost,** though, does not involve an outlay of money; instead, it is measured by the value, in dollar terms, of the benefits that are forgone. For example, the implicit cost of the year spent in school includes the income you would have earned if you had taken a job instead.

A common mistake, both in economic analysis and in real business situations, is to ignore implicit costs and focus exclusively on explicit costs. But often the implicit cost of an activity is quite substantial—indeed, sometimes it is much larger than the explicit cost.

Table 9-1 gives a breakdown of hypothetical explicit and implicit costs associated with spending an additional year in school instead of taking a job. The explicit cost consists of tuition, books, supplies, and a computer for doing assignments—all of

> An **explicit cost** is a cost that involves actually laying out money. An **implicit cost** does not require an outlay of money; it is measured by the value, in dollar terms, of benefits that are forgone.

TABLE 9-1

Opportunity Cost of an Additional Year of School

Explicit cost		Implicit cost	
Tuition	$7,000	Forgone salary	$35,000
Books and supplies	1,000		
Computer	1,500		
Total explicit cost	9,500	**Total implicit cost**	35,000
Total opportunity cost = Total explicit cost + Total implicit cost = $44,500			

Famous College Dropouts

What do Bill Gates, Tiger Woods, and Madonna have in common? None of them have a college degree.

Nobody doubts that all three are easily smart enough to have gotten their diplomas. However, each one made the rational decision that the implicit cost of getting a degree would have been too high—by their late teens, each had a very promising career that would have had to be put on hold to get a college degree. Madonna would have had to postpone her musical career; Woods would have had to put off winning one major golf tournament after another and becoming one of the world's best golfers; Gates would have had to delay developing the most successful and most lucrative software ever sold, Microsoft's computer operating system.

In fact, extremely successful people—especially those in careers like acting or athletics, where starting early in life is especially crucial—are often college dropouts. It's a simple matter of economics: the opportunity cost of their time at that stage in their lives is just too high to postpone their careers for a college degree.

which require you to spend money. The implicit cost is the salary you would have earned if you had taken a job instead. As you can see, the forgone salary is $35,000 and the explicit cost is $9,500, making the implicit cost more than three times as much as the explicit cost in this example. So ignoring the implicit cost of an action can lead to a seriously misguided decision.

A slightly different way of looking at the implicit cost in this example can deepen our understanding of opportunity cost. The forgone salary is the cost of using your own resources—your time—in going to school rather than working. The use of your *time* for more schooling, despite the fact that you don't have to spend any money, is still costly to you. This illustrates an important aspect of opportunity cost: in considering the cost of an activity, you should include the cost of using any of your own resources for that activity. You can calculate the cost of using your own resources by determining what they would have earned in their next best use.

Accounting Profit versus Economic Profit

As the example of going to school suggests, taking account of implicit as well as explicit costs can be very important for individuals making decisions. The same is true of businesses.

Consider the case of Babette's Cajun Café, a small restaurant in New Orleans. This year Babette made $100,000 in revenue. Out of that revenue, she paid her expenses: the cost of food ingredients and other supplies, the cost of wages for her employees, and the rent for her restaurant space. This year her expenses were $60,000. We assume that Babette owns her restaurant equipment—items such as appliances and furnishings. The question is: is Babette's restaurant profitable?

At first it might seem that the answer is obviously yes: she receives $100,000 from her customers and has expenses of only $60,000. Doesn't this mean that she has a profit of $40,000? Not according to her accountant, who reduces the number by $5,000 for the yearly *depreciation* (reduction in value) of the restaurant equipment. Depreciation occurs because equipment wears out over time. As a consequence, every few years Babette must replace her appliances and furnishings. The yearly depreciation amount reflects what an accountant estimates to be the reduction in the value of the machines due to wear and tear that year. This leaves $35,000, which is the business's **accounting profit.** Basically, the accounting profit of a business is its revenue minus its explicit cost and depreciation. The accounting profit is the number that Babette has to report on her income tax forms and that she would be obliged to report to anyone thinking of investing in her business.

Accounting profit is a very useful number, but suppose that Babette wants to decide whether to keep her restaurant open or do something else. To make this decision, she will need to calculate her **economic profit**—the revenue she receives minus

The **accounting profit** of a business is the business's revenue minus the explicit cost and depreciation.

The **economic profit** of a business is the business's revenue minus the opportunity cost of its resources. It is usually less than the accounting profit.

"I've done the numbers, and I will marry you."

her opportunity cost, which may include implicit as well as explicit costs. In general, when economists use the simple term *profit*, they are referring to economic profit. (We will adopt this simplification in later chapters of this book.)

Why does Babette's economic profit differ from her accounting profit? Because she may have implicit costs over and above the explicit cost her accountant has calculated. Businesses can face implicit costs for two reasons. First, a business's **capital**—its equipment, buildings, tools, inventory, and financial assets—could have been put to use in some other way. If the business owns its capital, it does not pay any money for its use, but it pays an implicit cost because it does not use the capital in some other way. Second, the owner devotes time and energy to the business that could have been used elsewhere—a particularly important factor in small businesses, whose owners tend to put in many long hours.

If Babette had rented her appliances and furnishings instead of owning them, their rent would have been an explicit cost. But because Babette owns her own equipment, she does not pay rent on them and her accountant deducts an estimate of their depreciation in the profit statement. However, this does not account for the opportunity cost of the equipment—what Babette forgoes by owning it. Suppose that instead of using the equipment in her own restaurant, the best alternative Babette has is to sell the equipment for $50,000 and put the money into a bank account where it would earn yearly interest of $3,000. This $3,000 is an implicit cost of running the business.

It is generally known as the **implicit cost of capital,** the opportunity cost of the capital used by a business; it reflects the income that could have been realized if the capital had been used in its next best alternative way. It is just as much a true cost as if Babette had rented her equipment instead of owning it.

Finally, Babette should take into account the opportunity cost of her own time. Suppose that instead of running her own restaurant, she could earn $34,000 as a chef in someone else's restaurant. That $34,000 is also an implicit cost of her business.

Table 9-2, in the column titled Case 1, summarizes the accounting for Babette's Cajun Café, taking both explicit and implicit costs into account. It turns out, unfortunately, that although the business makes an accounting profit of $35,000, its economic profit is actually negative. This means that Babette would be better off financially if she closed the restaurant and devoted her time and capital to something else. If, however, some of Babette's cost should fall sufficiently, she could earn a positive economic profit. In that case, she would be better off financially if she continued to operate the restaurant. Now consider the column titled Case 2: here we assume that what Babette could

The **capital** of a business is the value of its assets—equipment, buildings, tools, inventory, and financial assets.

The **implicit cost of capital** is the opportunity cost of the capital used by a business—the income the owner could have realized from that capital if it had been used in its next best alternative way.

TABLE 9-2

Profit at Babette's Cajun Café

	Case 1	Case 2
Revenue	$100,000	$100,000
Explicit cost	−60,000	−60,000
Depreciation	−5,000	−5,000
Accounting profit	**35,000**	**35,000**
Implicit cost of business		
Income Babette could have earned on capital used in the next best way	−3,000	−3,000
Income Babette could have earned as a chef in someone else's restaurant	−34,000	−30,000
Economic profit	**−2,000**	**+2,000**

earn as a chef employed by someone else has dropped to $30,000 (say, due to a soft labor market). In this case, her economic profit is now +$2,000: she is earning more than her explicit and implicit costs and she should keep her restaurant open.

In real life, discrepancies between accounting profit and economic profit are extremely common. As the following Economics in Action explains, this is a message that has found a receptive audience among real-world businesses.

►ECONOMICS IN ACTION

Farming in the Shadow of Suburbia

Beyond the sprawling suburbs, most of New England is covered by dense forest. But this is not the forest primeval: if you hike through the woods, you encounter many stone walls, relics of the region's agricultural past when stone walls enclosed fields and pastures. In 1880, more than half of New England's land was farmed; by 2006, the amount was down to 10%.

The remaining farms of New England are mainly located close to large metropolitan areas. There farmers get high prices for their produce from city dwellers who are willing to pay a premium for locally grown, extremely fresh fruits and vegetables.

But now even these farms are under economic pressure caused by a rise in the implicit cost of farming close to a metropolitan area. As metropolitan areas have expanded during the last two decades, farmers increasingly ask themselves whether they could do better by selling their land to property developers.

In 2006, the average value of an acre of farmland in the United States as a whole was $1,900; in Rhode Island, the most densely populated of the New England states, the average was $12,500. The Federal Reserve Bank of Boston has noted that "high land prices put intense pressure on the region's farms to generate incomes that are substantial enough to justify keeping the land in agriculture." The important point is that the pressure is intense even if the farmer owns the land because the land is a form of capital used to run the business. So maintaining the land as a farm instead of selling it to a developer constitutes a large implicit cost of capital. A fact provided by the U.S. Department of Agriculture (USDA) helps us put a dollar figure on the portion of the implicit cost of capital due to development pressure for some Rhode Island farms. In 2004, a USDA program designed to prevent development of Rhode Island farmland by paying owners for the "development rights" to their land paid an average of $4,949 per acre for those rights alone. By 2006, the amount had risen to $9,238.

About two-thirds of New England's farms remaining in business earn very little money. They are maintained as "rural residences" by people with other sources of income—not so much because they are commercially viable, but more out of a personal commitment and the satisfaction these people derive from farm life. Although many businesses have important implicit costs, they can also have important benefits to their owners that go beyond the revenue earned. ▲

> > > > > > > > > > > >

► CHECK YOUR UNDERSTANDING 9-1

1. Karma and Don run a furniture-refinishing business from their home. Which of the following represent an explicit cost of the business and which represent an implicit cost?
   a. Supplies such as paint stripper, varnish, polish, sandpaper, and so on
   b. Basement space that has been converted into a workroom
   c. Wages paid to a part-time helper
   d. A van that they inherited and use only for transporting furniture
   e. The job at a larger furniture restorer that Karma gave up in order to run the business

Solutions appear at back of book.

Making "How Much" Decisions: The Role of Marginal Analysis

As the story of the two wars at the beginning of this chapter demonstrated, there are two types of decisions: "either–or" decisions and "how much" decisions. To help you get a better sense of that distinction, Table 9-3 offers some examples of each kind of decision.

TABLE 9-3

"How Much" Versus "Either–Or" Decisions

"How much" decisions	"Either–or" decisions
How many days before you do your laundry?	Tide or Cheer?
How many miles do you go before an oil change in your car?	Buy a car or not?
How many jalapenos on your nachos?	An order of nachos or a sandwich?
How many workers should you hire in your company?	Run your own business or work for someone else?
How much should a patient take of a drug that generates side effects?	Prescribe drug A or drug B for your patients?
How many troops do you allocate to your invasion force?	Invade at Calais or in Normandy?

Although many decisions in economics are "either–or," many others are "how much." Not many people will stop driving if the price of gasoline goes up, but many people will drive less. How much less? A rise in corn prices won't necessarily persuade a lot of people to take up farming for the first time, but it will persuade farmers who were already growing corn to plant more. How much more?

To understand "how much" decisions, we use an approach known as *marginal analysis.* Marginal analysis involves comparing the benefit of doing a little bit more of some activity with the cost of doing a little bit more of that activity. The benefit of doing a little bit more of something is what economists call its *marginal benefit,* and the cost of doing a little bit more of something is what they call its *marginal cost.*

Why is this called "marginal" analysis? A margin is an edge; what you do in marginal analysis is push out the edge a bit and see whether that is a good move. We will study marginal analysis by considering a decision faced by Babette when she continues to run her restaurant—a decision faced by practically every person who has ever operated a restaurant as well. That is, just how large should your portion sizes be in order to maximize your profits? We'll begin by examining Babette's marginal cost.

Marginal Cost

In the restaurant business, food ingredients represent a relatively small share of the costs. According to a recent article, the cost of food accounts for only about one-third of the total cost of operating a restaurant. That's because food (at least in the United States) is relatively cheap. Other items, such as rent, electricity, employee wages, and so on (including, of course, the opportunity cost of the owner's time and the implicit cost of capital), represent the major share of an average restaurant's costs.

Generally, that's good news if you are a restaurant owner: it doesn't cost very much to increase the portion size of your meals. And customers are typically willing to pay more for bigger portions. However, as common sense tells us, there has to be a limit, even for customers with the hardiest appetites. The first step in finding the portion size that maximizes Babette's profits is to find the marginal cost of increasing her portion size.

For simplicity, we'll assume that Babette offers only one dish on her menu, spicy chicken wings, and that she serves the same number of customers every day. So Babette's only decision is how many chicken wings to include in each serving. As in almost all businesses, Babette has two types of costs. First, there are the costs of actually preparing and serving the food, such as ingredients, fuel, and employee wages. These costs vary according to how much food Babette serves. Second, there are the operating costs incurred regardless of how much food is prepared: the opportunity costs of her time and equipment (as well as depreciation) plus the cost of her rent. These costs are fixed and do not vary depending on how much food is prepared. So the total cost of each serving is equal to the cost of actually preparing the serving plus its share of the restaurant's operating cost. We'll assume that this share of the operating cost is equal to $4.00 per serving.

The second column of Table 9-4 shows how the total cost of one serving of chicken wings depends on the portion size. For a 1-wing serving, Babette incurs a cost of $4.80: $4.00 for that serving's share of the restaurant's fixed operating costs plus $0.80 for preparing the food. For a 2-wing serving, Babette's cost is $5.60: $4.00 for operating costs plus $1.60 for the food. At 6 wings, the cost of a serving is $8.80: $4.00 for operating costs plus $4.80 for the food.

The third column of Table 9-4 shows the cost Babette incurs for each *additional* chicken wing in a serving, calculated from information in the second column. Starting at a 0-wing serving (that is, an empty plate), it costs an additional $0.80 to serve the 1st wing; this number appears in the third column between the rows at 0 and 1 because $0.80 is the additional cost of going from a 0-wing to a 1-wing serving. Going from 1 to 2 wings, the next increment also costs an additional $0.80. So $0.80 appears in the third column between the rows at the 1st and 2nd wing, and so on.

The change in Babette's total cost of a serving when she increases her portion size by 1 wing is the **marginal cost** of the increase in portion size for spicy chicken wings. In general, the marginal cost of producing a good or service is the additional cost incurred by producing one more unit of that good or service.

The marginal costs shown in Table 9-4 have a clear and simple pattern. For every additional chicken wing per serving, Babette's marginal cost is $0.80. Babette's portion size decision has what economists call **constant marginal cost:** each chicken wing costs the same amount to produce as the previous one.

Figure 9-1 is a graphical representation of the third column in Table 9-4. The horizontal axis measures the quantity of chicken wings per serving, and the vertical axis measures the marginal cost of producing a chicken wing. The height of each shaded bar indicates the marginal cost incurred by producing a given quantity of chicken wings. Here, because the marginal cost is the same regardless of whether Babette is going from 0 to 1 wing or from 6 to 7 wings, each shaded bar in Figure 9-1 has the

> The **marginal cost** of producing a good or service is the additional cost incurred by producing one more unit of that good or service.
>
> Production of a good or service has **constant marginal cost** when each additional unit costs the same to produce as the previous one.

TABLE 9-4

Babette's Marginal Cost of Increasing Portion Size

Quantity of chicken wings	Total cost	Marginal cost (per wing)
0	$4.00	
		$0.80
1	4.80	
		0.80
2	5.60	
		0.80
3	6.40	
		0.80
4	7.20	
		0.80
5	8.00	
		0.80
6	8.80	
		0.80
7	9.60	

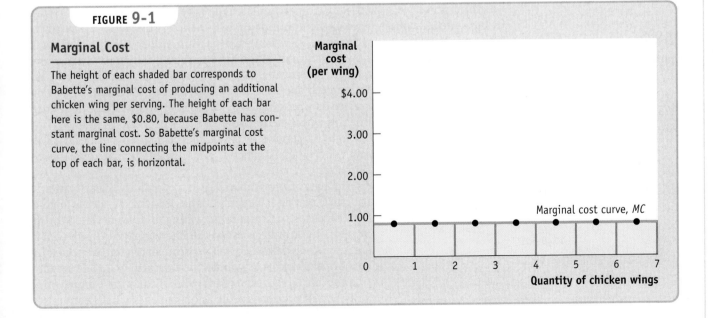

FIGURE 9-1

Marginal Cost

The height of each shaded bar corresponds to Babette's marginal cost of producing an additional chicken wing per serving. The height of each bar here is the same, $0.80, because Babette has constant marginal cost. So Babette's marginal cost curve, the line connecting the midpoints at the top of each bar, is horizontal.

Marginal cost (per wing)

$4.00

3.00

2.00

1.00

Marginal cost curve, MC

0   1   2   3   4   5   6   7

Quantity of chicken wings

TOTAL COST VERSUS MARGINAL COST

It can be easy to wrongly conclude that marginal cost and total cost must always move in the same direction. That is, if total cost is rising, then marginal cost must also be rising. Or if marginal cost is falling, then total cost must be falling as well. But the following example shows that this conclusion is incorrect.

Suppose that we change the numbers of our example: the marginal cost of the 1st chicken wing is still $0.80, but the marginal cost of the 2nd is now $0.70. In both instances, total cost increases as Babette increases her portion size: it goes from $4.00 to $4.80 when producing the 1st chicken wing and from $4.80 to $5.50 in producing the 2nd. But in this example marginal cost is *decreasing*: the marginal cost of the 2nd wing is less than the marginal cost of the 1st. So we have a case of increasing total cost and decreasing marginal cost. This shows us that, in fact, totals and marginals can sometimes move in opposite directions. What is true is that total cost increases whenever marginal cost is *positive,* regardless of whether it is increasing or decreasing.

same height. Consequently, the **marginal cost curve,** the red curve in Figure 9-1, which shows the relationship between marginal cost and the quantity of the good already produced, is a horizontal line at the value $0.80. It is shown in Figure 9-1 as the line connecting the midpoints at the top of each bar.

It's important to recognize that not all goods have constant marginal cost of production. In fact, constant marginal cost is more often the exception than the rule. For example, in the manufacture of a new model of car, production costs arise from the wages paid to workers to assemble the cars. It's likely that workers are slow to assemble the very first car of the new model on the assembly line because of its unfamiliarity. But as they assemble the 2nd, then the 3rd, and so on, they learn more about the new model and reduce the assembly time required per car. *Learning effects* like these lead to *decreasing marginal cost:* each unit costs less to produce than the previous unit because it takes less of workers' time to produce another unit. In this case, the marginal cost curve slopes downward.

It's also possible for marginal costs to rise. To understand this, suppose that autoworkers are now well experienced and producing 55 of the new-model cars each day, running the assembly line at a brisk pace. As they attempt to produce even more cars, they must speed up a bit more. But doing this takes a toll, in terms of a disproportionately greater number of mistakes and accidents. So, for example, the 56th car of the day costs more to produce than the 55th car, and so on. This is an example of **increasing marginal cost:** each unit of a good costs more to produce than the previous unit. Increasing marginal cost is illustrated by an upward-sloping marginal cost curve. As a company tries to produce more and more output with a limited amount of equipment and workers, it will typically reach a point of increasing marginal cost for additional units.

As our story indicates, it's not only possible for marginal costs to be decreasing or increasing, it's also possible for the same good to have some units over which marginal cost is decreasing, and later have some units over which it is increasing. (For a good like this, the marginal cost curve will be U-shaped. We'll discuss this in more detail in Chapter 12.) For now we'll stick to our simple example of constant marginal cost, and move on to the parallel concept of marginal benefit.

Marginal Benefit

Babette's customers enjoy her chicken wings and are willing to pay $4.30 for a 1-wing portion, $6.80 for a 2-wing portion, $8.30 for a 3-wing portion, and so on. The second column of Table 9-5 shows the total benefit to Babette for each serving of chicken wings according to portion size. Here, benefit is measured in terms of Babette's earnings. The third column of Table 9-5 shows the *marginal benefit* to Babette of increasing her portion size by 1 wing. It shows how the amount that a customer is willing to pay for another chicken wing depends on how large the serving already is. In general, the **marginal benefit** of producing a good or service is the additional benefit earned from producing one more unit of that good or service. Because it arises from enlarging a serving by 1 wing, each marginal benefit value in Table 9-5 appears between the rows associated with portion sizes.

The data from Table 9-5 have a fairly clear pattern. Babette's marginal benefit of the 1st wing served is high— $4.30—because customers are willing to pay that much for it. But in going from the 1st to the 2nd wing, it drops to $2.50 and continues falling for all subsequent 1-wing increases in portion size. In other words, the larger the current serving size, the less her customers are willing to pay for 1 more wing. So Babette's portion-size decision includes what economists

TABLE 9-5

Babette's Marginal Benefit of Increasing Portion Size

Quantity of chicken wings	Total benefit	Marginal benefit (per wing)
0	$0	
		$4.30
1	4.30	
		2.50
2	6.80	
		1.50
3	8.30	
		1.20
4	9.50	
		0.90
5	10.40	
		0.70
6	11.10	
		0.60
7	11.70	

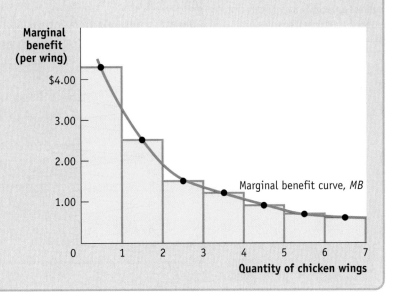

FIGURE 9-2

Marginal Benefit

The height of each shaded bar corresponds to Babette's marginal benefit of producing an additional chicken wing per serving. The height of each bar is lower than the one preceding it because Babette has decreasing marginal benefit. That is, the additional amount that Babette's customers are willing to pay for an additional chicken wing falls as the portion size gets larger and larger. As a result, Babette's marginal benefit curve, the curve connecting the midpoints at the top of each bar, slopes downward.

call **decreasing marginal benefit:** each additional increase in portion size yields less benefit than the previous increase. Or, to put it slightly differently, with decreasing marginal benefit, the marginal benefit of producing more of the good falls as the quantity already produced rises.

Just as marginal cost can be represented by a marginal cost curve, marginal benefit can be represented by a **marginal benefit curve,** shown in blue in Figure 9-2. The height of each bar shows the marginal benefit of each increase in the serving size. Here, the curve through the middle of each bar's top illustrates how the marginal benefit of a unit depends on the number of units that have already been produced.

Babette's marginal benefit curve slopes downward because she faces decreasing marginal benefit from increasing her portion size. Not all goods exhibit decreasing marginal benefit. In fact, there are many goods for which the marginal benefit of production is constant—that is, the additional benefit from producing one more unit is the same regardless of the number of units already produced. In later chapters where we study firms, we will see that the shape of a firm's marginal benefit curve from producing output has important implications for how it behaves within its industry. We'll also see in Chapters 12 and 13 why constant marginal benefit is considered the norm for many important industries. Now we are ready to see how the concepts of marginal benefit and marginal cost are brought together to answer the question of how large Babette's portion size should be.

Marginal Analysis

Table 9-6 on the next page shows the marginal cost and marginal benefit numbers from Tables 9-4 and 9-5. It also adds an additional column: the net gain to Babette from enlarging her portion size by 1 wing, equal to the difference between the marginal benefit and the marginal cost of that wing. Because every serving earns the same amount and costs the same amount to produce as every other serving, Babette maximizes her total profit by maximizing the net gain per serving.

We can use Table 9-6 to determine how many wings Babette should serve per portion. To see this, imagine that Babette serves 2-wing portions. We can immediately see that this is too small a quantity. If Babette increases her portion size by 1 wing, going from 2 to 3 wings, she earns a marginal benefit of $1.50 and incurs a marginal cost of only $0.80—so her net gain is $0.70. But even a 3-wing serving is still too small: if Babette increases the portion size from 3 to 4 wings, her marginal benefit is $1.20 and her marginal cost is only $0.80, for a net gain of $0.40.

The **marginal cost curve** shows how the cost of producing one more unit depends on the quantity that has already been produced.

Production of a good or service has **increasing marginal cost** when each additional unit costs more to produce than the previous one.

The **marginal benefit** of a good or service is the additional benefit derived from producing one more unit of that good or service.

There is **decreasing marginal benefit** from an activity when each additional unit of the activity produces less benefit than the previous unit.

The **marginal benefit curve** shows how the benefit from producing one more unit depends on the quantity that has already been produced.

The **optimal quantity** is the quantity that generates the maximum possible total net gain.

TABLE 9-6

Babette's Net Gain from Increasing Portion Size

Quantity of chicken wings	Marginal benefit (per wing)	Marginal cost (per wing)	Net gain (per wing)
0			
	$4.30	$0.80	$3.50
1			
	2.50	0.80	1.70
2			
	1.50	0.80	0.70
3			
	1.20	0.80	0.40
4			
	0.90	0.80	0.10
5			
	0.70	0.80	−0.10
6			
	0.60	0.80	−0.20
7			

A 7-wing portion, however, is too large. We can see this by looking at the net gain from going from a 6-wing to a 7-wing portion: the marginal benefit is $0.60, but the marginal cost is $0.80, resulting in a net gain of −$0.20. That is, Babette incurs a *loss* on the 7th wing. Even 6 wings is too many: by increasing the serving size from 5 to 6 wings, Babette incurs a marginal benefit of only $0.70 compared with a marginal cost of $0.80, making for a net gain of −$0.10 (that is, a loss of $0.10). She is best off choosing a serving size of 5 wings, the largest portion for which marginal benefit is at least as great as marginal cost.

The upshot is that Babette should choose a portion size of 5 wings—no more and no less. If the portion size is smaller than 5 wings, her marginal benefit from enlarging it by 1 wing is greater than her marginal cost; she would be passing up a net gain by not increasing her portion size. But if she chooses a portion size larger than 5 wings, her marginal benefit from the last wing is less than her marginal cost, resulting in a loss on the last wing. So 5 wings is the portion size that generates Babette's maximum possible total net gain, or profit, per serving; it is what economists call the **optimal quantity** of wings per serving.

Figure 9-3 shows graphically how the optimal quantity can be determined. Babette's marginal benefit and marginal cost curves are shown together. If Babette chooses a portion size smaller than 5 wings, the marginal benefit curve is *above* the marginal cost curve, so she can make herself better off by increasing her portion size; if she chooses a portion size larger than 5 wings, the marginal benefit curve is *below* the marginal cost curve, so she would be better off reducing her portion size.

The table in Figure 9-3 confirms our result. The second column repeats information from Table 9-6, showing marginal benefit minus marginal cost—or the net gain— per 1-wing increase in portion size per serving. The third column shows total net gain per serving according to portion size (the same as Babette's profit per serving according to portion size). The total net gain, or profit, of each serving of a given portion size is simply the sum of numbers in the second column up to and including that portion size. For example, the net gain is $3.50 for the 1st wing served and $1.70 for the 2nd wing. So the total net gain of a 2-wing portion size is $3.50 + $1.70 = $5.20, and the total net gain of a 3-wing portion size is $5.20 + $0.70 = $5.90. Our conclusion that 5 is the optimal portion size is confirmed by the fact that the greatest total net gain, or profit, $6.40, occurs when Babette chooses a 5-wing portion size.

The example of Babette's portion-size decision shows how you go about finding the optimal quantity: increase the quantity as long as the marginal benefit from one more unit is greater than the marginal cost, but stop before the marginal benefit becomes less than the marginal cost. In many cases, there is a simpler version of the decision

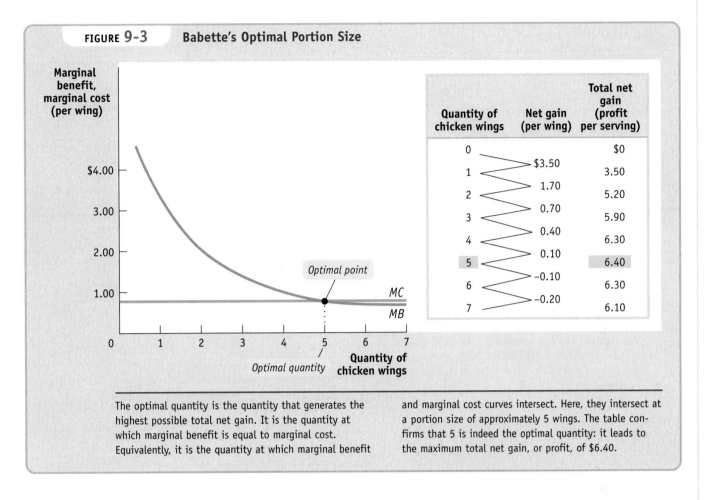

FIGURE 9-3   Babette's Optimal Portion Size

Quantity of chicken wings	Net gain (per wing)	Total net gain (profit per serving)
0		$0
1	$3.50	3.50
2	1.70	5.20
3	0.70	5.90
4	0.40	6.30
5	0.10	6.40
6	−0.10	6.30
7	−0.20	6.10

The optimal quantity is the quantity that generates the highest possible total net gain. It is the quantity at which marginal benefit is equal to marginal cost. Equivalently, it is the quantity at which marginal benefit and marginal cost curves intersect. Here, they intersect at a portion size of approximately 5 wings. The table confirms that 5 is indeed the optimal quantity: it leads to the maximum total net gain, or profit, of $6.40.

rule used to find the optimal quantity. When a "how much" decision involves relatively large quantities, the rule simplifies to this: *the optimal quantity is the quantity at which marginal benefit is equal to marginal cost.* To see why this is so, consider the example of a farmer who finds that her optimal quantity of wheat produced is 5,000 bushels. Typically, she will find that in going from 4,999 to 5,000 bushels, her marginal benefit is only very slightly greater than her marginal cost—that is, the difference between marginal benefit and marginal cost is close to zero. Similarly, in going from 5,000 to 5,001 bushels, her marginal cost is only very slightly greater than her marginal benefit—again, the difference between marginal cost and marginal benefit is very close to zero. So a simple rule for her in choosing the optimal quantity of wheat is to produce the quantity at which the difference between marginal benefit and marginal cost is approximately zero—that is, the quantity at which marginal benefit equals marginal cost.

Economists call this rule the **principle of marginal analysis.** It says that the optimal quantity of an activity is the quantity at which marginal benefit equals marginal cost. (In our example, the activity is producing chicken wing meals.) Graphically, the optimal quantity is the quantity of an activity at which the marginal benefit curve *intersects* the marginal cost curve. In fact, this graphical method works quite well even when the numbers involved aren't that large. For example, in Figure 9-3 the marginal benefit and marginal cost curves cross each other at approximately 5 wings—that is, marginal benefit approximately equals marginal cost at a portion size of 5 wings, which we have already seen is Babette's optimal portion size.

In fact, a straightforward application of marginal analysis explains why restaurant portion sizes in the United States are typically larger than those in other countries: because food is relatively cheap in the United States compared to other countries. That is, American restaurants have a lower marginal cost of increasing the portion size

The **principle of marginal analysis** says that the optimal quantity is the quantity at which marginal benefit is equal to marginal cost.

GLOBAL COMPARISON — PORTION SIZES

Health experts call it the "French Paradox." If you think French food is fattening, you're right: the French diet is, on average, higher in fat than the American diet. Yet the French themselves are considerably thinner than we are: in 2004, only 9.5% of French adults were classified as obese, compared with 33.2% of Americans.

What's the secret? It seems that the French simply eat less, largely because they eat smaller portions. This chart compares average portion sizes at food establishments in Paris and Philadelphia. In four cases, researchers looked at portions served by the same chain; in the other cases, they looked at comparable establishments, such as local pizza parlors. In every case but one, U.S. portions were bigger, in most cases much bigger.

Why are American portions so big? Probably because food is cheaper in the United States. At the margin, it makes sense for restaurants to offer big portions, since the additional cost of enlarging a portion is so small.

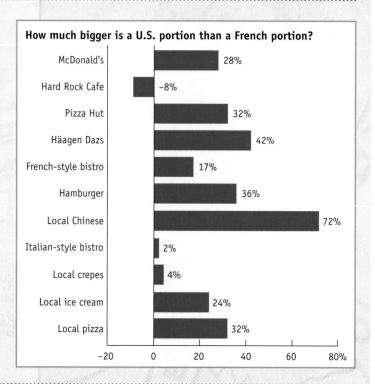

How much bigger is a U.S. portion than a French portion?

McDonald's	28%
Hard Rock Cafe	–8%
Pizza Hut	32%
Häagen Dazs	42%
French-style bistro	17%
Hamburger	36%
Local Chinese	72%
Italian-style bistro	2%
Local crepes	4%
Local ice cream	24%
Local pizza	32%

Source: Paul Rozin, Kimberly Kabnick, Erin Pete, Claude Fischler, and Christy Shields, "The Ecology of Eating," *Psychological Science* (September 2003): Vol. 14, pp. 450–454.

PITFALLS

MUDDLED AT THE MARGIN

The idea of setting marginal benefit *equal* to marginal cost sometimes confuses people. Aren't we trying to maximize the *difference* between benefits and costs? And don't we wipe out our gains by setting benefits and costs equal to each other? But what we are doing is setting *marginal,* not *total,* benefit and cost equal to each other.

Once again, the point is to maximize the total net gain from an activity. If the marginal benefit from the activity is greater than the marginal cost, doing a bit more will increase that gain. If the marginal benefit is less than the marginal cost, doing a bit less will increase the total net gain. So only when the *marginal* benefit and *marginal* cost are equal is the difference between *total* benefit and *total* cost at a maximum.

compared to other countries. (Why American food is cheaper is a matter of both government policy and natural resources—topics we'll touch on later.) As a recent newspaper article states: "So while it may cost a restaurant a few pennies to offer 25% more French fries, it can raise its prices much more than a few cents. The result is that larger portions are a reliable way to bolster the average check at restaurants." So if you've ever wondered why dieting seems to be a uniquely American obsession, the principle of marginal analysis can help provide the answer: it's to counteract the effects of our larger portion sizes.

A Principle with Many Uses

The principle of marginal analysis can be applied to just about any "how much" decision. Although we have focused until now on production decisions, marginal analysis is equally applicable to consumption decisions—decisions made by consumers. Furthermore, decisions where the benefits and costs are not expressed in dollars and cents can also be made using marginal analysis (as long as benefits and costs can be measured in some type of common units). Here are a few examples of decisions that are suitable for marginal analysis:

- A consumer, Jonah, has a consumption decision problem: given his weekly budget, how many restaurant meals to consume versus how many double-mocha lattes to consume at Starbucks. Specifically, he can consume a larger number of restaurant meals only by consuming a smaller number of double-mocha lattes; likewise, he can consume more double-mocha lattes only by consuming fewer restaurant meals. Jonah can use marginal analysis, weighing the marginal benefit and marginal cost of another restaurant meal versus the marginal benefit and marginal cost of another double-mocha latte, to find the optimal combination, the one that gives him the greatest satisfaction. (In fact, Chapter 10 will consider such consumption decision problems.)

■ A policy maker must decide how much to spend on improving highways, improvements that reduce traffic deaths. He can make this decision by comparing the marginal benefit to society of saving a life versus the marginal cost of doing so. The optimal level of spending on highway improvements is the level at which the marginal benefit and marginal cost of saving a life are equal. (If you think no price is too high to save a life, see the following Economics in Action.)

■ Many useful drugs have side effects that depend on the dosage. So a physician must consider the marginal cost, in terms of side effects, of increasing the dosage of a drug versus the marginal benefit of increasing the dosage in fighting disease. The optimal dosage level is the level at which the marginal benefit of disease amelioration and the marginal cost of side effects are equal.

►ECONOMICS IN ACTION

The Cost of a Life

What's the marginal benefit to society of saving a human life? You might be tempted to answer that human life is infinitely precious. But in the real world, resources are scarce, so we must decide how much to spend on saving lives since we cannot spend infinite amounts. After all, we could surely reduce highway deaths by dropping the speed limit on interstates to 40 miles per hour, but the cost of such a lower speed limit—in time and money—is more than most people are willing to pay.

Generally, people are reluctant to talk in a straightforward way about comparing the marginal cost of a life saved with the marginal benefit—it sounds too callous. Sometimes, however, the question becomes unavoidable.

For example, the cost of saving a life became an object of intense discussion in the United Kingdom after a horrible train crash near London's Paddington Station killed 31 people. There were accusations that the British government was spending too little on rail safety. However, the government estimated that improving rail safety would cost an additional $4.5 million per life saved. But if that amount was worth spending—that is, if the estimated marginal benefit of saving a life exceeded $4.5 million—then the implication was that the British government was spending far too little on *traffic safety*. That's because the estimated marginal cost per life saved through highway improvements was only $1.5 million, making it a much better deal than saving lives through greater rail safety. ▲

> > > > > > > > > > > >

► CHECK YOUR UNDERSTANDING 9-2

1. For each of the "how much" decisions listed in Table 9-3, describe the nature of the marginal cost and of the marginal benefit.

Quantity of chicken wings	Total cost
0	$4.00
1	4.25
2	4.40
3	4.50
4	4.65
5	4.90
6	5.35
7	6.20

2. Suppose that Babette's total cost of a serving according to portion size is now given by the data in the accompanying table. Assume that Babette's total benefit and marginal benefit remain as reported in Table 9-5.

Use this information to calculate: (i) Babette's new marginal cost; (ii) her new net gain; (iii) her new optimal serving size. What kind of marginal cost does Babette now have—constant, increasing, or decreasing?

Solutions appear at back of book.

This vet left law school to pursue his dream career. The cost for a year of law school was lost—a sunk cost. But he and his patients are now happy.

Sunk Costs

When making decisions, knowing what to ignore is important. Although we have devoted much attention in this chapter to costs that are important to take into account when making a decision, some costs should be ignored when doing so. In this section we will focus on the kinds of costs that people should ignore when making decisions—what economists call *sunk costs*—and why they should be ignored.

To gain some intuition, consider the following scenario. You own a car that is a few years old, and you have just replaced the brake pads at a cost of $250. But then you find out that the entire brake system is defective and also must be replaced. This will cost you an additional $1,500. Alternatively, you could sell the car and buy another of comparable quality, but with no brake defects, by spending an additional $1,600. What should you do: fix your old car, or sell it and buy another?

Some might say that you should take the latter option. After all, this line of reasoning goes, if you repair your car, you will end up having spent $1,750: $1,500 for the brake system and $250 for the brake pads. If you were instead to sell your old car and buy another, you would spend only $1,600.

But this reasoning, although it sounds plausible, is wrong. It is wrong because it ignores the fact that you have *already* spent $250 on brake pads, and that $250 is *nonrecoverable*. That is, having already been spent, the $250 cannot be recouped. Therefore, it should be ignored and should have no effect on your decision whether to repair your car and keep it or not. From a rational viewpoint, the real cost at this time of repairing and keeping your car is $1,500, not $1,750. So the correct decision is to repair your car and keep it rather than spend $1,600 on a new car.

In this example, the $250 that has already been spent and cannot be recovered is what economists call a **sunk cost.** Sunk costs should be ignored in making decisions about future actions because they have no influence on their actual costs and benefits. It's like the old saying, "There's no use crying over spilled milk": once something can't be recovered, it is irrelevant in making decisions about what to do in the future.

It is often psychologically hard to ignore sunk costs. And if, in fact, you haven't yet incurred the costs, then you should take them into consideration. That is, if you had known at the beginning that it would cost $1,750 to repair your car, then the right choice *at that time* would have been to buy a new car for $1,600. But once you have already paid the $250 for brake pads, you should no longer include it in your decision making about your next actions. It may be hard to accept that "bygones are bygones," but it is the right way to make a decision.

➤ECONOMICS IN ACTION

A Billion Here, a Billion There . . .

If there is any industry that exemplifies the principle that sunk costs don't matter, it has to be the biotech industry. Biotech firms use cutting-edge bioengineering techniques to combat disease. But according to Arthur Levinson, chief executive of Genentech, one of the largest and most successful biotech firms, biotechnology has been "one of the biggest money-losing industries in the history of mankind." He estimates that the industry has lost nearly $100 billion since 1976 (yes, that's "billion"). Of 342 publicly held American biotech firms, only 54 were profitable in 2006. However, this is not a tale of incompetence because the problem lies in the nature of the science. It takes about seven to eight years, on average, to develop and bring a new drug to the market. Moreover, there is a huge failure rate along the way, as only one in five drugs tested on humans ever gets to the market. The company Xoma is a case

A **sunk cost** is a cost that has already been incurred and is nonrecoverable. A sunk cost should be ignored in decisions about future actions.

in point: it has suffered setbacks on several drugs addressing diseases as varied as acne and complications from organ transplants. Since 1981, it has never earned a profit on one of its own drugs and has burned through more than $700 million dollars. Why does Xoma keep going? And, more importantly, why are investors willing to keep providing it with more money? It's because Xoma possesses a very promising technology and because shrewd investors understand the principle of sunk costs. ▲

> > > > > > > > > > > >

> **QUICK REVIEW**

> ➤ **Sunk costs** should be ignored in decisions regarding future actions. Because they have already been incurred and are nonrecoverable, they have no effect on future costs and benefits.

► **CHECK YOUR UNDERSTANDING 9-3**

1. You have decided to go into the ice-cream business and have bought a used ice-cream truck for $8,000. Now you are reconsidering. What is your sunk cost in the following scenarios?
 a. The truck cannot be resold.
 b. It can be resold, but only at a 50% discount.

2. You have gone through two years of medical school but are suddenly wondering whether you wouldn't be happier as a musician. Which of the following statements are potentially valid arguments and which are not?
 a. "I can't give up now, after all the time and money I've put in."
 b. "If I had thought about it from the beginning, I never would have gone to med school, so I should give it up now."
 c. "I wasted two years, but never mind—let's start from here."
 d. "My parents would kill me if I stopped now." (*Hint:* we're discussing *your* decision-making ability, not your parents'.)

Solutions appear at back of book.

The Concept of Present Value

In many cases, individuals must make decisions whose consequences extend some way into the future. For example, when you decide to attend college, you are committing yourself to years of study, which you expect will pay off for the rest of your life. So the decision to attend college is a decision to embark on a long-term project.

As we have already seen, the basic rule in deciding whether or not to undertake a project is that you should compare the benefits of that project with its costs, implicit as well as explicit. But making these comparisons can sometimes be difficult because the benefits and costs of a project may not arrive at the same time. Sometimes the costs of a project come at an earlier date than the benefits. For example, going to college involves large immediate costs: tuition, income forgone because you are in school, and so on. The benefits, such as a higher salary in your future career, come later, often much later. In other cases, the benefits of a project come at an earlier date than the costs. If you take out a loan to pay for a vacation cruise, the satisfaction of the vacation will come immediately, but the burden of making payments will come later.

But why is time an issue?

Borrowing, Lending, and Interest

In general, having a dollar today is worth more than having a dollar a year from now. To see why, let's consider two examples.

First, suppose that you get a new job that comes with a $1,000 bonus, which will be paid at the end of the first year. But you would like to spend the extra money now—say, on new clothes for work. Can you do that?

The answer is yes—you can borrow money today and use the bonus to repay the debt a year from now. But if that is your plan, you cannot borrow the full $1,000 today. You must borrow *less* than that, because a year from now you will have to repay the amount borrowed *plus interest*.

When someone borrows money for a year, the **interest rate** is the price, calculated as a percentage of the amount borrowed, charged by the lender.

Now consider a different scenario. Suppose that you are paid a bonus of $1,000 today, and you decide that you don't want to spend the money right now. What do you do with it? You put it in the bank; in effect, you are lending the $1,000 to the bank, which in turn lends it out to its customers who wish to borrow. At the end of a year, you will get *more* than $1,000 back—you will have the $1,000 plus the interest earned.

All of this means that having $1,000 today is worth more than having $1,000 a year from now. As any borrower and lender know, this is what allows a lender to charge a borrower interest on a loan: borrowers are willing to pay interest in order to have money today rather than wait to have the money until they have saved it from their own income. When someone borrows money for a year, the **interest rate** is the price, calculated as a percentage of the amount borrowed, charged by the lender. But the same principle applies regardless of whether money is borrowed for 1 month or 10 years and regardless of the amount: money in your pocket today is worth more than money in your pocket tomorrow. However, in practice we'll restrict ourselves to considering examples of 1 year and $1 in order to keep things simple.

For this reason, you can't evaluate a project just by adding up the costs and benefits when those costs and benefits arrive at different times. You must take time into account when evaluating the project because $1 that is paid to you today is worth more than $1 that is paid to you a year from now. Similarly, $1 that you must pay today is more burdensome to you than $1 that you must pay next year. Fortunately, there is a simple way to adjust for these complications so that we can correctly compare the value of dollars received and paid out at different times.

What we will now see is that the interest rate can be used to convert future benefits and costs into what economists call their *present values*. By using present values when evaluating a project, you can evaluate a project *as if* all its costs and benefits were occurring today rather than at different times. This allows people to "factor out" the complications created by time. We'll start by defining exactly what the concept of present value is.

Defining Present Value

The key to the concept of present value is to understand that you can use the interest rate to compare the value of a dollar realized today with the value of a dollar realized later. Why the interest rate? Because the interest rate correctly measures the cost to you of delaying the receipt of a dollar of benefit and, correspondingly, the benefit to you of delaying the payment of a dollar of cost. Let's illustrate this with some examples.

Suppose that you are evaluating whether or not to take a job in which your employer promises to pay you a bonus at the end of the first year. What is the value to you today of $1 of bonus money to be paid one year in the future? A slightly different way of asking the same question: what amount would you be willing to accept today as a substitute for receiving $1 one year from now?

To answer this question, begin by observing that you need *less* than $1 today in order to be assured of having $1 one year from now. Why? Because any money that you have today can be lent out at interest—say, by depositing it in a bank account so that the bank can then lend it out to its borrowers. This turns any amount you have today into a greater sum at the end of the year.

Let's work this out mathematically. We'll use the symbol r to represent the interest rate, expressed in decimal terms—that is, if the interest rate is 10%, then $r = 0.10$. If you lend out X, at the end of a year you will receive your X back, plus the interest on your X, which is $X \times r$. Thus, at the end of the year you will receive:

> **(9-1)** Amount received one year from now as a result of lending X today = $X + X \times r = X \times (1 + r)$

The next step is to find out how much you would have to lend out today to have $1 a year from now. To do that, we just need to set Equation 9-1 equal to $1 and solve for $X. That is, solving the following Equation 9-2 for $X:

(9-2) Condition satisfied when $1 is received one year from now as a result of lending $X today: $X \times (1 + r) = \$1$

Rearranging Equation 9-2 to solve for $X, the amount you need today in order to receive $1 one year from now:

(9-3) Amount lent today in order to receive $1 one year from now =
$X = \$1/(1 + r)$

This means that you would be willing to accept today the amount $X defined by Equation 9-3 for every $1 to be paid to you one year from now. The reason is that if you were to lend out $X today, you can be assured of receiving $1 one year from now. Returning to our original question, this also means that if someone promises to pay you a sum of money one year in the future, you are willing to accept today $X in place of every $1 to be paid one year from now.

Now let's solve Equation 9-3 for the value of $X. To do this we simply need to use the actual value of r (a value determined by the financial markets). Let's assume that the actual value of r is 10%, which means that $r = 0.10$. In that case:

(9-4) Value of $X when $r = 0.10$: $X = \$1/(1 + 0.10) = \$1/1.10 = \$0.91$

So you would be willing to accept $0.91 today in exchange for every $1 to be paid to you one year from now. Economists have a special name for $X—it's called the **present value** of $1. (Note that the present value of any given amount will change as the interest rate changes.)

To see that this technique works for evaluating future costs as well as evaluating future benefits, consider the following example. Suppose you enter into an agreement that obliges you to pay $1 one year from now—say, to pay off your student loan when you graduate in a year. How much money would you need today to ensure that you have $1 in a year? The answer is $X, the present value of $1, which in our example is $0.91. The reason $0.91 is the right answer is that if you lend it out for one year at an interest rate of 10%, you will receive $1 in return at the end. So if, for example, you must pay back $5,000 one year from now, then you need to deposit $5,000 × 0.91 = $4,550 into a bank account today earning an interest rate of 10% in order to have $5,000 one year from now. (There is a slight discrepancy due to rounding.) In other words, you need to have today the present value of $5,000, the amount $4,550, in order to be assured of paying off your debt in a year.

These examples show us that the present value concept provides a way to calculate the value today of $1 that is realized in the future—regardless of whether that $1 is realized as a benefit (the bonus) or a cost (the student loan payback). To evaluate a project today that has benefits, costs, or both to be realized in the future, we just use the relevant interest rate to convert those future dollars into their present values. In that way we have "factored out" the complication that time creates for decision making.

In the next section we will work out an example of using the present value concept to evaluate a project. But before we do that, it is worthwhile to note that the present value method can be used for projects in which the $1 is realized more than a year later—say, two, three, or even more years. Suppose you are considering a project that will pay you $1 *two* years from today. What is the value to you today of $1 received two years into the future? We can find the answer to that question by expanding our formula for present value.

Let's call $V the amount of money you need to lend today at an interest rate of r in order to have $1 in two years. So if you lend $V today, you will receive $V \times (1 + r)$ in one year. And if you *re-lend* that sum for yet another year, you will receive $V \times (1 + r) \times (1 + r) = V \times (1 + r)^2$ at the end of the second year. At the end of two years, $V will be worth $V \times (1 + r)^2$. In other words:

(9-5)   Amount received in one year from lending $V = V \times (1 + r)$
Amount received in two years from lending $V = V \times (1 + r) \times (1 + r)$
$= V \times (1 + r)^2$

and so on. For example, if $r = 0.10$, then $V \times (1.10)^2 = V \times (1.21)$.

Now we are ready to answer the question of what $1 realized two years in the future is worth today. In order for the amount lent today, $V, to be worth $1 two years from now, it must satisfy this formula:

(9-6)   Condition satisfied when $1 is received two years from now as a result of lending $V today: $V \times (1 + r)^2 = \$1$

Rearranging Equation 9-6, we can solve for $V:

(9-7)   Amount lent today in order to receive $1 two years from now =
$V = \$1 / (1 + r)^2$

Given $r = 0.10$ and using Equation 9-7, we arrive at $V = \$1/1.21 = \$0.83$. So when the interest rate is 10%, $1 realized two years from today is worth $0.83 today because by lending out $0.83 today you can be assured of having $1 in two years. And that means that the present value of $1 realized two years into the future is $0.83.

(9-8)   Present value of $1 realized two years from now = $V = \$1 / (1.10)^2$
$= \$1/1.21 = \$0.83$

From this example we can see how the present value concept can be expanded to a number of years even greater than two. If we ask what the present value of $1 realized N number of years into the future is, the answer is given by a generalization of the present value formula: it is equal to $\$1/(1 + r)^N$.

Using Present Value

Suppose you have to choose one of three hypothetical projects to undertake. Project A has an immediate payoff to you of $100, but project B requires that you put up $10 of your own money today in order to receive $115 a year from now. Project C gives you an immediate payoff of $119 but requires that you pay $20 a year from now. We'll assume that the annual interest rate is 10%—that is, $r = 0.10$.

The problem in evaluating these three projects is that their costs and benefits are realized at different times. That is, of course, where the concept of present value becomes extremely helpful: by using present value to convert any dollars realized in the future into today's value, you factor out the issue of time. When you

TABLE 9-7

The Net Present Value of Three Hypothetical Projects

Project	Dollars realized today	Dollars realized one year from today	Present value formula	Net present value given $r = 0.10$
A	$100	—	$100	$100.00
B	−$10	$115	−$10 + $115/(1 + r)	$94.55
C	$119	−$20	$119 − $20/(1 + r)	$100.82

The **net present value** of a project is the present value of current and future benefits minus the present value of current and future costs.

factor out the issue of time, you can calculate the **net present value** of a project—the present value of current and future benefits minus the present value of current and future costs. And the best project to undertake is the one with the highest net present value.

Table 9-7 shows how to calculate net present value for each of the three projects. The second and third columns show how many dollars are realized and when they are realized; costs are indicated by a minus sign. The fourth column shows the equations used to convert the flows of dollars into their present value, and the fifth column shows the actual amounts of the total net present value for each of the three projects.

For instance, to calculate the net present value of project B, we need to calculate the present value of $115 received in one year. The present value of $1 received in one year would be $1/(1 + r)$. So the present value of $115 is equal to $115 \times \$1/(1 + r)$; that is, $115/(1 + r)$. The net present value of project B is the present value of today's and future benefits minus the present value of today's and future costs: $-\$10 + \$115/(1 + r)$.

From the fifth column, we can immediately see which is the preferred project—it is project C. That's because it has the highest net present value, $100.82, which is higher than the net present value of project A ($100) and much higher than the net present value of project B ($94.55).

This example shows how important the concept of present value is. If we had failed to use the present value calculations and instead had simply added up the dollars generated by each of the three projects, we could have easily been misled into believing that project B was the best project and project C was the worst one.

►ECONOMICS IN ACTION

How Big Is That Jackpot, Anyway?

For a clear example of present value at work, consider the case of lottery jackpots.

On March 6, 2007, Mega Millions set the record for the largest jackpot ever in North America, for a payout of $390 million. Well, sort of. That $390 million was available only if you chose to take your winnings in the form of an "annuity," consisting of an annual payment for the next 26 years. If you wanted cash up front, the jackpot was only $233 million and change.

Why was Mega Millions so stingy about quick payoffs? It was all a matter of present value. If the winner had been willing to take the annuity, the lottery would have invested the jackpot money, buying U.S. government bonds (in effect lending the money to the federal government). The money would have been invested in such a way that the investments would pay just enough to pay the annuity. This worked, of course, because at the interest rates prevailing at the time, the present value of a $390 million annuity spread over 26 years was just about $233 million. To put it another way, the opportunity cost to the lottery of that annuity in present value terms was $233 million.

So why didn't they just call it a $233 million jackpot? Well, $390 million sounds more impressive! But it was really the same thing. ▲

< < < < < < < < < < < <

> CHECK YOUR UNDERSTANDING 9-4

1. Consider the three hypothetical projects shown in Table 9-7. This time, however, suppose that the interest rate is only 2%.
   a. Calculate the net present values of the three projects. Which one is now preferred?
   b. Explain why the preferred choice is different with a 2% interest rate than with a 10% rate.

Solutions appear at back of book.

[>> A LOOK AHEAD···

This chapter laid out the basic concepts that we need to understand economic decisions. These concepts, as we will soon see, provide the necessary tools for understanding not only the behavior behind the supply and demand curves but also the implications of markets for consumer and producer welfare.

But to get there we need a bit more context—we need to know more about the kinds of decisions that producers and consumers must make. We start with consumers: in the next two chapters, we will see how consumers can use marginal analysis to maximize the enjoyment they receive when choosing how much of various goods to consume while at the same time living within their incomes.]

SUMMARY

1. All economic decisions involve the allocation of scarce resources. Some decisions are "either-or" decisions, in which the question is whether or not to do something. Other decisions are "how much" decisions, in which the question is how much of a resource to put into a given activity.

2. The cost of using a resource for a particular activity is the opportunity cost of that resource. Some opportunity costs are **explicit costs;** they involve a direct payment of cash. Other opportunity costs, however, are **implicit costs;** they involve no outlay of money but represent the inflows of cash that are forgone. Both explicit and implicit costs should be taken into account in making decisions. Companies use **capital** and their owners' time. So companies should base decisions on **economic profit,** which takes into account implicit costs such as the opportunity cost of the owners' time and the **implicit cost of capital.** The **accounting profit,** which companies calculate for the purposes of taxes and public reporting, is often considerably larger than the economic profit because it includes only explicit costs and depreciation, not implicit costs.

3. A "how much" decision is made using marginal analysis, which involves comparing the benefit to the cost of doing an additional unit of an activity. The **marginal cost** of producing a good or service is the additional cost incurred by producing one more unit of that good or service. The **marginal benefit** of producing a good or service is the additional benefit earned by producing one more unit. The **marginal cost curve** is the graphical illustration of marginal cost, and the **marginal benefit curve** is the graphical illustration of marginal benefit.

4. In the case of **constant marginal cost,** each additional unit costs the same amount to produce as the unit before; this is represented by a horizontal marginal cost curve. However, marginal cost and marginal benefit typically depend on how much of the activity has already been done. With **increasing marginal cost,** each unit costs more to produce than the unit before and is represented by an upward-sloping marginal cost curve. In the case of **decreasing marginal benefit,** each additional unit produces a smaller benefit than the unit before and is represented by a downward-sloping marginal benefit curve.

5. The **optimal quantity** is the quantity that generates the maximum possible total net gain. According to the **principle of marginal analysis,** the optimal quantity is the quantity at which marginal benefit is equal to marginal cost. It is the quantity at which the marginal cost curve and the marginal benefit curve intersect.

6. A cost that has already been incurred and that is nonrecoverable is a **sunk cost.** Sunk costs should be ignored in decisions about future actions because they have no effect on future benefits and costs.

7. In order to evaluate a project in which costs or benefits are realized in the future, you must first transform them into their **present values** using the **interest rate,** *r*. The present value of $1 realized one year from now is $1/(1 + r)$, the amount of money you must lend out today to have $1 one year from now. Once this transformation is done, you should choose the project with the highest **net present value.**

KEY TERMS

Explicit cost, p. 226
Implicit cost, p. 226
Accounting profit, p. 227
Economic profit, p. 227
Capital, p. 228
Implicit cost of capital, p. 228
Marginal cost, p. 231

Constant marginal cost, p. 231
Marginal cost curve, p. 232
Increasing marginal cost, p. 232
Marginal benefit, p. 232
Decreasing marginal benefit, p. 233
Marginal benefit curve, p. 233

Optimal quantity, p. 234
Principle of marginal analysis, p. 235
Sunk cost, p. 238
Interest rate, p. 240
Present value, p. 241
Net present value, p. 243

PROBLEMS

1. Hiro owns and operates a small business that provides economic consulting services. During the year he spends $55,000 on travel to clients and other expenses, and the computer that he owns depreciates by $2,000. If he didn't use the computer, he could sell it and earn yearly interest of $100 on the money created through this sale. Hiro's total revenue for the year is $100,000. Instead of working as a consultant for the year, he could teach economics at a small local college and make a salary of $50,000.

    a. What is Hiro's accounting profit?

    b. What is Hiro's economic profit?

    c. Should Hiro continue working as a consultant, or should he teach economics instead?

2. Jackie owns and operates a web-design business. Her computing equipment depreciates by $5,000 per year. She runs the business out of a room in her home. If she didn't use the room as her business office, she could rent it out for $2,000 per year. Jackie knows that if she didn't run her own business, she could return to her previous job at a large software company that would pay her a salary of $60,000 per year. Jackie has no other expenses.

    a. How much total revenue does Jackie need to make in order to break even in the eyes of her accountant? That is, how much total revenue would give Jackie an accounting profit of just zero?

    b. How much total revenue does Jackie need to make in order for her to want to remain self-employed? That is, how much total revenue would give Jackie an economic profit of just zero?

3. You own and operate a bike store. Each year, you receive revenue of $200,000 from your bike sales, and it costs you $100,000 to obtain the bikes. In addition, you pay $20,000 for electricity, taxes, and other expenses per year. Instead of running the bike store, you could become an accountant and receive a yearly salary of $40,000. A large clothing retail chain wants to expand and offers to rent the store from you for $50,000 per year. How do you explain to your friends that despite making a profit, it is too costly for you to continue running your store?

4. Suppose you have just paid a nonrefundable fee of $1,000 for your meal plan for this academic term. This allows you to eat dinner in the cafeteria every evening.

    a. You are offered a part-time job in a restaurant where you can eat for free each evening. Your parents say that you should eat dinner in the cafeteria anyway, since you have already paid for those meals. Are your parents right? Explain why or why not.

    b. You are offered a part-time job in a different restaurant where, rather than being able to eat for free, you receive only a large discount on your meals. Each meal there will cost you $2; if you eat there each evening this semester, it will add up to $200. Your roommate says that you should eat in the restaurant since it costs less than the $1,000 that you paid for the meal plan. Is your roommate right? Explain why or why not.

5. You have bought a $10 ticket in advance for the college soccer game, a ticket that cannot be resold. You know that going to the soccer game will give you a benefit equal to $20. After you have bought the ticket, you hear that there will be a professional baseball post-season game at the same time. Tickets to the baseball game cost $20, and you know that going to the baseball game will give you a benefit equal to $35. You tell your friends the following: "If I had known about the baseball game before buying the ticket to the soccer game, I would have gone to the baseball game instead. But now that I already have the ticket to the soccer game, it's better for me to just go to the soccer game." Are you making the correct decision? Justify your answer by calculating the benefits and costs of your decision.

6. Amy, Bill, and Carla all mow lawns for money. Each of them operates a different lawn mower. The accompanying table shows the total cost to Amy, Bill, and Carla of mowing lawns.

Quantity of lawns mowed	Amy's total cost	Bill's total cost	Carla's total cost
0	$0	$0	$0
1	20	10	2
2	35	20	7
3	45	30	17
4	50	40	32
5	52	50	52
6	53	60	82

a. Calculate Amy's, Bill's, and Carla's marginal costs, and draw each of their marginal cost curves.

b. Who has increasing marginal cost, who has decreasing marginal cost, and who has constant marginal cost?

7. You are the manager of a gym, and you have to decide how many customers to admit each hour. Assume that each customer stays exactly one hour. Customers are costly to admit because they inflict wear and tear on the exercise equipment. Moreover, each additional customer generates more wear and tear than the customer before. As a result, the gym faces increasing marginal cost. The accompanying table shows the marginal costs associated with each number of customers per hour.

Quantity of customers per hour	Marginal cost of customer
0	
	$14.00
1	
	14.50
2	
	15.00
3	
	15.50
4	
	16.00
5	
	16.50
6	
	17.00
7	

a. Suppose that each customer pays $15.25 for a one-hour workout. Use the principle of marginal analysis to find the optimal number of customers that you should admit per hour.

b. You increase the price of a one-hour workout to $16.25. What is the optimal number of customers per hour that you should admit now?

8. Georgia and Lauren are economics students who go to a karate class together. Both have to choose how many classes to go to per week. Each class costs $20. The accompanying table shows Georgia's and Lauren's estimates of the marginal benefit that each of them gets from each class per week.

Quantity of classes	Lauren's marginal benefit of each class	Georgia's marginal benefit of each class
0		
	$23	$28
1		
	19	22
2		
	14	15
3		
	8	7
4		

a. Use marginal analysis to find Lauren's optimal number of karate classes per week. Explain your answer.

b. Use marginal analysis to find Georgia's optimal number of karate classes per week. Explain your answer.

9. The Centers for Disease Control and Prevention (CDC) recommended against vaccinating the whole population against the smallpox virus because the vaccination has undesirable, and sometimes fatal, side effects. Suppose the accompanying table gives the data that are available about the effects of a smallpox vaccination program.

Percent of population vaccinated	Deaths due to smallpox	Deaths due to vaccination side effects
0%	200	0
10	180	4
20	160	10
30	140	18
40	120	33
50	100	50
60	80	74

a. Calculate the marginal benefit (in terms of lives saved) and the marginal cost (in terms of lives lost) of each 10% increment of smallpox vaccination. Calculate the net gain for each 10% increment in population vaccinated.

b. Using marginal analysis, determine the optimal percentage of the population that should be vaccinated.

10. In 2007, the online medical journal *Circulation* published a study that analyzed the cost-effectiveness of standard-dosage versus high-dosage amounts of statins, drugs designed to lower cholesterol. Patients of approximately 60 years of age were divided into two groups: ACS, or acute coronary syndrome, patients who had recently suffered a heart attack or chest pains severe enough for hospitalization; and CAD, or stable coronary artery disease, patients who had less severe cases of heart disease. The benefit of a dose of statins was measured in terms of the number of additional years of lifespan lived in a quality way—or QALYs (Quality-Adjusted Life Years). The table below gives some data from the study, where for each group, the outcome from the standard dose was the baseline.

	ACS	CAD
Standard dose	Baseline	Baseline
High dose	Additional 0.35 QALY	Additional 0.096 QALY

In the following table, we have posed two assumptions about the value of a QALY: in the first case it is worth $30,000 and in the second case it is worth $50,000. We have assumed that ACS patients live an average of 6 additional years with the high dose than with the standard dose, and CAD patients live an average of 10 additional years with the high dose than with the standard dose. Both sets of patients must take the high dose for their entire future life span to receive the additional QALY benefits from it. We have also made two assumptions about the additional cost of a high dose versus a standard dose of statin: in the first case the high dose costs an additional $3.50 per day and in the second case the high dose costs an additional $1.25 per day. In the empty cells in the table, indicate whether the high dose therapy should be prescribed from weighing its marginal benefits and marginal costs. Explain

your choices. Disregard the fact that some benefits and costs arrive at different times. Also assume that all years have 365 days (i.e., no leap years).

	QALY = $30,000	QALY = $50,000
ACS (additional 6 years over standard dose; high dose costs additional $3.50/day)	?	?
ACS (additional 6 years over standard dose; high dose costs additional $1.25/day)	?	?
CAD (additional 10 years over standard dose; high dose costs additional $3.50/day)	?	?
CAD (additional 10 years over standard dose; high dose costs additional $1.25/day)	?	?

11. Patty delivers pizza using her own car, and she is paid according to the number of pizzas she delivers. The accompanying table shows Patty's total benefit and total cost when she works a specific number of hours.

Quantity of hours worked	Total benefit	Total cost
0	$0	$0
1	30	10
2	55	21
3	75	34
4	90	50
5	100	70

a. Use marginal analysis to determine Patty's optimal number of hours worked.

b. Calculate the total net gain to Patty from working 0 hours, 1 hour, 2 hours, and so on. Now suppose Patty chooses to work for 1 hour. Compare her total net gain from working for 1 hour with her total net gain from working the optimal number of hours. How much would she lose by working for only 1 hour?

12. Assume De Beers is the sole producer of diamonds. When it wants to sell more diamonds, it must lower its price in order to induce consumers to buy more. Furthermore, each additional diamond that is produced costs more than the previous one due to the difficulty of mining for diamonds. De Beers's total benefit schedule is given in the accompanying table, along with its total cost schedule.

Quantity of diamonds	Total benefit	Total cost
0	$0	$0
1	1,000	50
2	1,900	100
3	2,700	200
4	3,400	400
5	4,000	800
6	4,500	1,500
7	4,900	2,500
8	5,200	3,800

a. Draw the marginal cost curve and the marginal benefit curve and, from your diagram, graphically derive the optimal quantity of diamonds to produce.

b. Calculate the total net gain to De Beers from producing each quantity of diamonds. Which quantity gives De Beers the highest total net gain?

13. According to a report in the St. Louis (Missouri) *Post-Dispatch,* that city's main thoroughfare, Interstate 64, will be completely closed to traffic for two years, from January 2008 to December 2009, for reconstruction at a cost of $535 million. If the construction company were to keep the highway open for traffic during construction, the highway reconstruction project would take much longer and be more expensive. Suppose that construction would take four years if the highway were kept open, at a total cost of $800 million. The Missouri Department of Transportation had to make its decision in 2007, one year before the start of construction (so that the first payment is one year away). So the Missouri Department of Transportation had the following choices:

(i) Close Interstate 64 during construction, at an annual cost of $267.5 million per year for two years.

(ii) Keep Interstate 64 open during construction, at an annual cost of $200 million per year for four years.

a. Suppose the interest rate is 10%. Calculate the present value of the costs incurred under each plan. Which reconstruction plan is less expensive?

b. Now suppose the interest rate is 80%. Calculate the present value of the costs incurred under each plan. Which reconstruction plan is now less expensive?

14. You have won the state lottery. There are two ways in which you can receive your prize. You can either have $1 million in cash now, or you can have $1.2 million that is paid out as follows: $300,000 now, $300,000 in one year's time, $300,000 in two years' time, and $300,000 in three years' time. The interest rate is 20%. How would you prefer to receive your prize?

15. The drug company Pfizer is considering whether to invest in the development of a new cancer drug. Development will require an initial investment of $10 million now; beginning one year from now, the drug will generate annual profits of $4 million for three years.

a. If the interest rate is 12%, should Pfizer invest in the development of the new drug? Why or why not?

b. If the interest rate is 8%, should Pfizer invest in the development of the new drug? Why or why not?

 www.worthpublishers.com/krugmanwells

>> The Rational Consumer

A CLAM TOO FAR

TO ENTICE CUSTOMERS, RESTAURANTS SOMETIMES offer "all-you-can-eat" specials: all-you-can-eat salad bars, all-you-can-eat breakfast buffets, and all-you-can-eat fried-clam dinners.

But how can a restaurant owner who offers such a special be sure he won't be eaten out of business? If he charges $12.99 for an all-you-can-eat clam dinner, what prevents his average customer from wolfing down $30 worth of clams?

The answer is that even though every once in a while you see someone really take advantage of the offer—heaping a plate high with 30 or 40 fried clams—it's a rare occurrence. And even those of us who like fried clams shudder a bit at the sight. Five or even 10 fried clams can be a treat, but 30 clams is ridiculous. Anyone who pays for an all-you-can-eat meal wants to make the most of it, but a sensible person knows when one more clam would be one clam too many.

Notice that last sentence. We said that customers in a restaurant want to "make the most" of their meal; that sounds as if they are trying to maximize something. And we also said that they will stop when consuming one more

When is more of a good thing too much?

clam would be a mistake; that sounds as if they are making a marginal decision.

When, in later chapters, we analyze the behavior of *producers,* it makes sense to assume that they maximize profit. But what do consumers maximize? Isn't it all a matter of taste?

The answer is yes, it is a matter of taste—and economists can't say much about where tastes come from. But economists *can* say a lot about how a rational individual goes about satisfying his or her tastes. And that is in fact the way that economists think about consumer choice. They work with a model of a *rational consumer*—a consumer who knows what he or she wants and makes the most of the available opportunities.

In this chapter, we will show how to analyze the decisions of a rational consumer. We will begin by showing how the concept of *utility*—a measure of consumer satisfaction—allows us to begin thinking about rational consumer choice. We will then look at how *budget constraints* determine what a consumer can buy and how marginal analysis can be used to determine the consumption choice that maximizes utility. Finally, we will see how this analysis can be used to understand the law of demand and why the demand curve slopes downward.

Utility: Getting Satisfaction

When analyzing consumer behavior, we're talking about people trying to get what they want—that is, about subjective feelings. Yet there is no simple way to measure subjective feelings. How much satisfaction do I get from my third fried clam? Is it less or more than yours? Does it even make sense to ask the question?

Luckily, we don't need to make comparisons between your feelings and mine. All that is required to analyze consumer behavior is to suppose that each individual is trying to maximize some personal measure of the satisfaction gained from consumption of goods and services. That measure is known as the consumer's **utility,** a concept we use to understand behavior but don't expect to measure in practice. Nonetheless, we'll see that the assumption that consumers maximize utility helps us think clearly about consumer choice.

Utility and Consumption

An individual's utility depends on everything that individual consumes, from apples to Ziploc bags. The set of all the goods and services an individual consumes is known as the individual's **consumption bundle.** The relationship between an individual's consumption bundle and the total amount of utility it generates for that individual is known as the **utility function.** The utility function is a personal matter; two people with different tastes will have different utility functions. Someone who actually likes to consume 40 fried clams at a sitting must have a utility function that looks different from that of someone who would rather stop at 5 clams.

So we can think of consumers as using consumption to "produce" utility, much in the same way as in later chapters we will think of producers as using inputs to produce output. However, it's obvious that people do not have a little computer in their heads that calculates the utility generated by their consumption choices. Nonetheless, people must make choices, and they usually base them on at least a rough attempt to decide which choice will give them greater satisfaction. I can have either soup or salad with my dinner. Which will I enjoy more? I can go to Disney World this year or save the money toward buying a new car. Which will make me happier?

The concept of a utility function is just a way of representing the fact that people must make such choices and that they make those choices in a more or less rational way.

How do we measure utility? For the sake of simplicity, it is useful to suppose that we can measure utility in hypothetical units called—what else?—**utils.**

Figure 10-1 illustrates a utility function. It shows the total utility that Cassie, who likes fried clams, gets from an all-you-can-eat clam dinner. We suppose that her consumption bundle consists of a side of coleslaw, which comes with the meal, plus a number of clams to be determined. The table that accompanies the figure shows how Cassie's total utility depends on the number of clams; the curve in panel (a) of the figure shows that same information graphically.

Cassie's utility function slopes upward over most of the range shown, but it gets flatter as the number of clams consumed increases. And in this example it eventually turns downward. According to the information in the table in Figure 10-1, nine

---

The **utility** of a consumer is a measure of the satisfaction the consumer derives from consumption of goods and services.

An individual's **consumption bundle** is the collection of all the goods and services consumed by that individual.

An individual's **utility function** gives the total utility generated by his or her consumption bundle.

A **util** is a unit of utility.

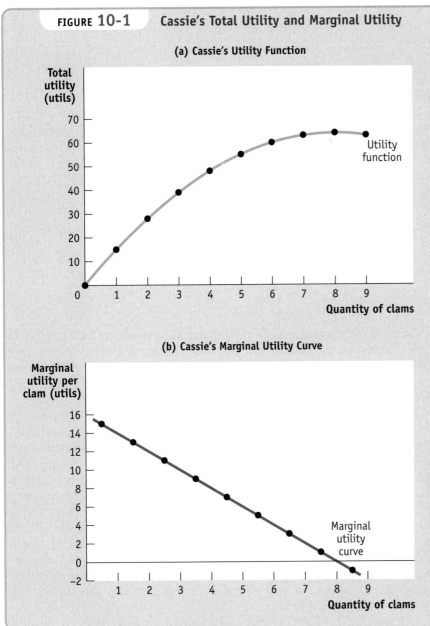

FIGURE **10-1**   Cassie's Total Utility and Marginal Utility

(a) Cassie's Utility Function

Quantity of clams	Total utility (utils)	Marginal utility per clam (utils)
0	0	
		15
1	15	
		13
2	28	
		11
3	39	
		9
4	48	
		7
5	55	
		5
6	60	
		3
7	63	
		1
8	64	
		−1
9	63	

(b) Cassie's Marginal Utility Curve

Panel (a) shows how Cassie's total utility depends on her consumption of fried clams. It increases until it reaches its maximum utility level of 64 utils at 8 clams consumed and decreases after that. Marginal utility is calculated in the table. Panel (b) shows the marginal utility curve, which slopes downward due to diminishing marginal utility. That is, each additional clam gives Cassie less utility than the previous clam.

clams is a clam too far. Adding that additional clam actually makes Cassie worse off: it would lower her total utility. If she's rational, of course, Cassie will realize that and not consume the ninth clam.

So when Cassie chooses how many clams to consume, she will make this decision by considering the *change* in her total utility from consuming one more clam. This illustrates the general point: to maximize *total* utility, consumers must focus on *marginal* utility.

The Principle of Diminishing Marginal Utility

In addition to showing how Cassie's total utility depends on the number of clams she consumes, the table in Figure 10-1 also shows the **marginal utility** generated by consuming each additional clam—that is, the *change* in total utility from consuming one additional clam. Panel (b) shows the implied **marginal utility curve.** Following our practice in Chapter 9 with the marginal benefit curve, the marginal utility curve is constructed by plotting points at the midpoint of the unit intervals.

The **marginal utility** of a good or service is the change in total utility generated by consuming one additional unit of that good or service. The **marginal utility curve** shows how marginal utility depends on the quantity of a good or service consumed.

Is Marginal Utility Really Diminishing?

Are all goods really subject to diminishing marginal utility? Of course not; there are a number of goods for which, at least over some range, marginal utility is surely *increasing*.

For example, there are goods that require some experience to enjoy. The first time you do it, downhill skiing involves a lot more fear than enjoyment—or so they say: the authors have never tried it! It only becomes a pleasurable activity if you do it enough to become reasonably competent. And even some less strenuous forms of consumption take practice; people who

are not accustomed to drinking coffee say it has a bitter taste and can't understand its appeal. (The authors, on the other hand, regard coffee as one of the basic food groups.)

Another example would be goods that only deliver positive utility if you buy enough. The great Victorian economist Alfred Marshall, who more or less invented the supply and demand model, gave the example of wallpaper: buying only enough to do half a room is worse than useless. If you need two rolls of wallpaper to finish a room, the marginal utility of the second

roll is larger than the marginal utility of the first roll.

So why does it make sense to assume diminishing marginal utility? For one thing, most goods don't suffer from these qualifications: nobody needs to learn to like ice cream. Also, although most people don't ski and some people don't drink coffee, those who do ski or drink coffee do enough of it that the marginal utility of one more ski run or one more cup is less than that of the last. So *in the relevant range* of consumption, marginal utility is still diminishing.

The marginal utility curve slopes downward: each successive clam adds less to total utility than the previous clam. This is reflected in the table: marginal utility falls from a high of 15 utils for the first clam consumed to −1 for the ninth clam consumed. The fact that the ninth clam has negative marginal utility means that consuming it actually reduces total utility. (Restaurants that offer all-you-can-eat meals depend on the proposition that you can have too much of a good thing.) Not all marginal utility curves eventually become negative. But it is generally accepted that marginal utility curves do slope downward—that consumption of most goods and services is subject to *diminishing marginal utility.*

The basic idea behind the **principle of diminishing marginal utility** is that the additional satisfaction a consumer gets from one more unit of a good or service declines as the amount of that good or service consumed rises. Or, to put it slightly differently, the more of a good or service you consume, the closer you are to being satiated—reaching a point at which an additional unit of the good adds nothing to your satisfaction. For someone who almost never gets to eat a banana, the occasional banana is a marvelous treat (as it was in Eastern Europe before the fall of communism, when bananas were very hard to find). For someone who eats them all the time, a banana is just, well, a banana.

The principle of diminishing marginal utility isn't always true. But it is true in the great majority of cases, enough to serve as a foundation for our analysis of consumer behavior.

►*ECONOMICS IN ACTION*

Oysters versus Chicken

Is a particular food a special treat, something you consume on special occasions? Or is it an ordinary, take-it-or-leave-it dish? The answer depends a lot on how much of that food people normally consume, which determines how much utility they get *at the margin* from having a bit more.

Consider chicken. Modern Americans eat a lot of chicken, so much that they regard it as nothing special. Yet this was not always the case. Traditionally chicken was a luxury dish because chickens were expensive to raise. Restaurant menus from two centuries ago show chicken dishes as the most expensive items listed. Even as

The **principle of diminishing marginal utility** says that each successive unit of a good or service consumed adds less to total utility than the previous unit.

recently as 1928, Herbert Hoover ran for president on the slogan "A chicken in every pot," a promise of great prosperity.

What changed the status of chicken was the emergence of new, technologically advanced methods for raising and processing the birds. (You don't want to know.) These methods made chicken abundant, cheap, and also—thanks to the principle of diminishing marginal utility—nothing to get excited about.

The reverse evolution took place for oysters. Not everyone likes oysters, or for that matter has ever tried them—they are definitely not ordinary food. But they are regarded as a delicacy by some; at restaurants that serve them, an oyster appetizer often costs more than the main course.

Yet oysters were once very cheap and abundant—and were regarded as poverty food. In *The Pickwick Papers* by Charles Dickens, published in the 1830s, the author remarks that "poverty and oysters always seem to go together."

What changed? Pollution, which destroyed many oyster beds, greatly reduced the supply, but human population growth greatly increased the demand. As a result, thanks to the principle of diminishing marginal utility, oysters went from being a common food, regarded as nothing special, to being a highly prized luxury good. ▲

> > > > > > > > > > > >

▶ CHECK YOUR UNDERSTANDING 10-1

1. Explain why a rational consumer who has diminishing marginal utility for a good would not consume an additional unit when it generates negative marginal utility, even when that unit is free.

2. Marta drinks three cups of coffee a day, for which she has diminishing marginal utility. Which of her three cups generates the greatest increase in total utility? Which generates the least?

3. In each of the following cases, does the consumer have diminishing, constant, or increasing marginal utility? Explain your answers.
   a. The more Mabel exercises, the more she enjoys each additional visit to the gym.
   b. Although Mei's classical CD collection is huge, her enjoyment from buying another CD has not changed as her collection has grown.
   c. When Dexter was a struggling student, his enjoyment from a good restaurant meal was greater than now, when he has them more frequently.

Solutions appear at back of book.

>> QUICK REVIEW

➤ **Utility** is a measure of a consumer's satisfaction from consumption, expressed in units of **utils.** Consumers try to maximize their utility. A consumer's **utility function** shows the relationship between the **consumption bundle** and the total utility it generates.

➤ To maximize utility, a consumer considers the **marginal utility** from consuming one more unit of a good or service, illustrated by the **marginal utility curve.**

➤ In the consumption of most goods and services, and for most people, the **principle of diminishing marginal utility** holds: each successive unit consumed adds less to total utility than the previous unit.

Budgets and Optimal Consumption

The principle of diminishing marginal utility explains why most people eventually reach a limit, even at an all-you-can-eat buffet where the cost of another clam is measured only in future indigestion. Under ordinary circumstances, however, it costs some additional resources to consume more of a good, and consumers must take that cost into account when making choices.

What do we mean by cost? As always, the fundamental measure of cost is *opportunity cost*. Because the amount of money a consumer can spend is limited, a decision to consume more of one good is also a decision to consume less of some other good.

Budget Constraints and Budget Lines

Consider Sammy, whose appetite is exclusively for clams and potatoes (there's no accounting for tastes). He has a weekly income of $20 and since, given his appetite, more of either good is better than less, he spends all of it on clams and potatoes. We will assume that clams cost $4 per pound and potatoes cost $2 per pound. What are his possible choices?

Whatever Sammy chooses, we know that the cost of his consumption bundle cannot exceed the amount of money he has to spend. That is,

(10-1) Expenditure on clams + Expenditure on potatoes ≤ Total income

A **budget constraint** requires that the cost of a consumer's consumption bundle be no more than the consumer's income.

A consumer's **consumption possibilities** is the set of all consumption bundles that can be consumed given the consumer's income and prevailing prices.

A consumer's **budget line** shows the consumption bundles available to a consumer who spends all of his or her income.

Consumers always have limited income, which constrains how much they can consume. So the requirement illustrated by Equation 10-1—that a consumer must choose a consumption bundle that costs no more than his or her income—is known as the consumer's **budget constraint.** It's a simple way of saying that a consumer can't spend more than the total amount of income available to him or her. In other words, consumption bundles are affordable when they obey the budget constraint. We call the set of all of Sammy's affordable consumption bundles his **consumption possibilities.** In general, whether or not a particular consumption bundle is included in a consumer's consumption possibilities depends on the consumer's income and the prices of goods and services.

Figure 10-2 shows Sammy's consumption possibilities. The quantity of clams in his consumption bundle is measured on the horizontal axis and the quantity of potatoes on the vertical axis. The downward-sloping line connecting points *A* through *F* shows which consumption bundles are affordable and which are not. Every bundle on or inside this line (the shaded area) is affordable; every bundle outside this line is unaffordable. As an example of one of the points, let's look at point *C*, representing 2 pounds of clams and 6 pounds of potatoes, and check whether it satisfies Sammy's budget constraint. The cost of bundle *C* is 6 pounds of potatoes × $2 per pound + 2 pounds of clams × $4 per pound = $12 + $8 = $20. So bundle *C* does indeed satisfy Sammy's budget constraint: it costs no more than his weekly income of $20. In fact, bundle *C* costs exactly as much as Sammy's income. By doing the arithmetic, you can check that all the other points lying on the downward-sloping line are also bundles at which Sammy spends all of his income.

The downward-sloping line has a special name, the **budget line.** It shows all the consumption bundles available to Sammy when he spends all of his income. It's

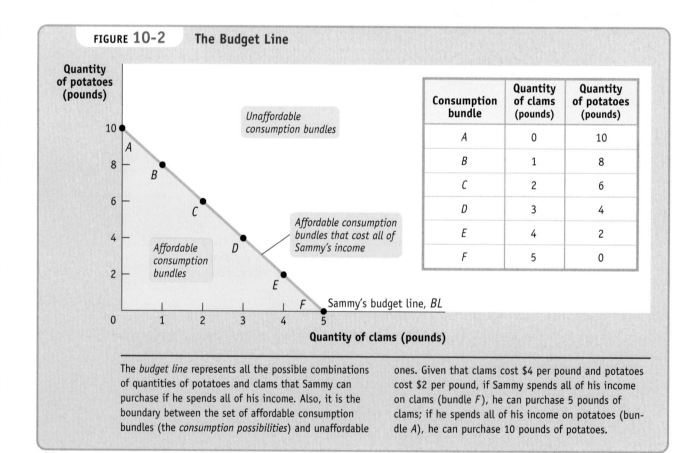

FIGURE 10-2   The Budget Line

Consumption bundle	Quantity of clams (pounds)	Quantity of potatoes (pounds)
A	0	10
B	1	8
C	2	6
D	3	4
E	4	2
F	5	0

The *budget line* represents all the possible combinations of quantities of potatoes and clams that Sammy can purchase if he spends all of his income. Also, it is the boundary between the set of affordable consumption bundles (the *consumption possibilities*) and unaffordable ones. Given that clams cost $4 per pound and potatoes cost $2 per pound, if Sammy spends all of his income on clams (bundle *F*), he can purchase 5 pounds of clams; if he spends all of his income on potatoes (bundle *A*), he can purchase 10 pounds of potatoes.

downward-sloping because when Sammy is consuming all of his income, say consuming at point A on the budget line, then in order to consume more clams he must consume fewer potatoes—that is, he must move to a point like B. In other words, when Sammy is on his budget line, the opportunity cost of consuming more clams is consuming fewer potatoes, and vice versa. As Figure 10-2 indicates, any consumption bundle that lies above the budget line is unaffordable.

Do we need to consider the other bundles in Sammy's consumption possibilities, the ones that lie *within* the shaded region in Figure 10-2 bounded by the budget line? The answer is, for all practical situations, no: as long as Sammy doesn't get satiated— that is, as long as his marginal utility from consuming either good is always positive— and he doesn't get any utility from saving income rather than spending it, then he will always choose to consume a bundle that lies on his budget line.

Given that $20 per week budget, what point on his budget line will Sammy choose?

Optimal Consumption Choice

Because Sammy has a budget constraint, which means that he will consume a consumption bundle on the budget line, a choice to consume a given quantity of clams also determines his potato consumption, and vice versa. We want to find the consumption bundle—the point on the budget line—that maximizes Sammy's total utility. This bundle is Sammy's **optimal consumption bundle,** the consumption bundle that maximizes his total utility given the budget constraint.

Table 10-1 shows how much utility Sammy gets from different levels of consumption of clams and potatoes, respectively. According to the table, Sammy has a healthy appetite; the more of either good he consumes, the higher his utility.

But because he has a limited budget, he must make a trade-off: the more pounds of clams he consumes, the fewer pounds of potatoes, and vice versa. That is, he must choose a point on his budget line.

Table 10-2 on the next page shows how his total utility varies for the different consumption bundles along his budget line. Each of six possible consumption bundles, *A* through *F* from Figure 10-2, is given in the first column. The second column shows the level of clam consumption corresponding to each choice. The third

> A consumer's **optimal consumption bundle** is the consumption bundle that maximizes the consumer's total utility given his or her budget constraint.

TABLE 10-1

Sammy's Utility from Clam and Potato Consumption

Utility from clam consumption		Utility from potato consumption	
Quantity of clams (pounds)	Utility from clams (utils)	Quantity of potatoes (pounds)	Utility from potatoes (utils)
0	0	0	0
1	15	1	11.5
2	25	2	21.4
3	31	3	29.8
4	34	4	36.8
5	36	5	42.5
		6	47.0
		7	50.5
		8	53.2
		9	55.2
		10	56.7

TABLE **10-2**

Sammy's Budget and Total Utility

Consumption bundle	Quantity of clams (pounds)	Utility from clams (utils)	Quantity of potatoes (pounds)	Utility from potatoes (utils)	Total utility (utils)
A	0	0	10	56.7	56.7
B	1	15	8	53.2	68.2
C	2	25	6	47.0	72.0
D	3	31	4	36.8	67.8
E	4	34	2	21.4	55.4
F	5	36	0	0	36.0

column shows the utility Sammy gets from consuming those clams. The fourth column shows the quantity of potatoes Sammy can afford *given* the level of clam consumption; this quantity goes down as his clam consumption goes up, because he is sliding down the budget line. The fifth column shows the utility he gets from consuming those potatoes. And the final column shows his *total utility*. In this example, Sammy's total utility is the sum of the utility he gets from clams and the utility he gets from potatoes.

Figure 10-3 gives a visual representation of the data shown in Table 10-2. Panel (a) shows Sammy's budget line, to remind us that when he decides to consume more clams he is also deciding to consume fewer potatoes. Panel (b) then shows how his total utility depends on that choice. The horizontal axis in panel (b) has two sets of labels: it shows both the quantity of clams, increasing from left to right, and the quantity of potatoes, increasing from right to left. The reason we can use the same axis to represent consumption of both goods is, of course, the budget line: the more pounds of clams Sammy consumes, the fewer pounds of potatoes he can afford, and vice versa.

Clearly, the consumption bundle that makes the best of the trade-off between clam consumption and potato consumption, the optimal consumption bundle, is the one that maximizes Sammy's total utility. That is, Sammy's optimal consumption bundle puts him at the top of the total utility curve.

As always, we can find the top of the curve by direct observation. We can see from Figure 10-3 that Sammy's total utility is maximized at point C—that his optimal consumption bundle contains 2 pounds of clams and 6 pounds of potatoes. But we know that we usually gain more insight into "how much" problems when we use marginal analysis. So in the next section we turn to representing and solving the optimal consumption choice problem with marginal analysis.

FOR INQUIRING MINDS

Food for Thought on Budget Constraints

Budget constraints aren't just about money. In fact, there are many other budget constraints affecting our lives. You face a budget constraint if you have a limited amount of closet space for your clothes. All of us face a budget constraint on time: there are only so many hours in the day.

And people trying to lose weight on the Weight Watchers plan face a budget constraint on the foods they eat.

The Weight Watchers plan assigns each food a certain number of "points." A scoop of ice cream gets 4 points, a slice of pizza 7 points, a cup of grapes 1 point. You are

allowed a maximum number of points each day but are free to choose which foods you eat. In other words, a dieter on the Weight Watchers plan is just like a consumer choosing a consumption bundle: points are the equivalent of prices, and the overall point limit is the equivalent of total income.

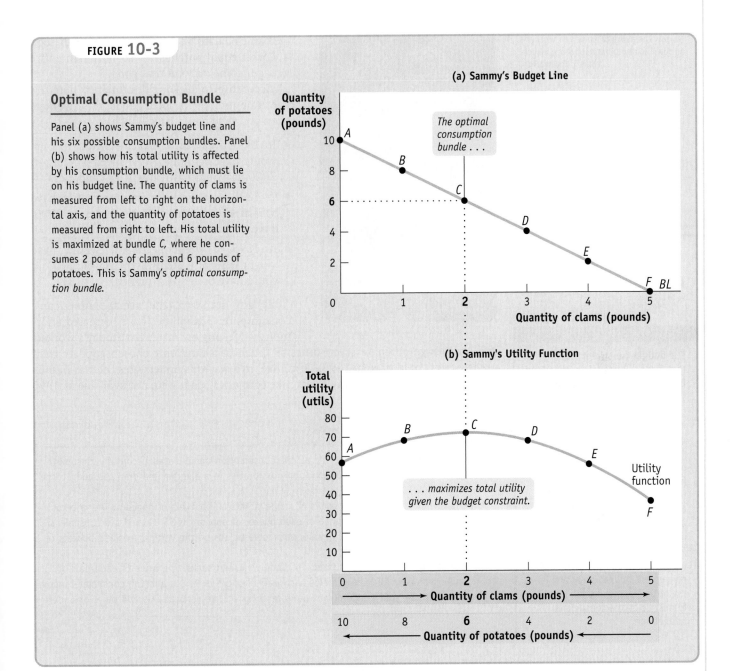

FIGURE 10-3

Optimal Consumption Bundle

Panel (a) shows Sammy's budget line and his six possible consumption bundles. Panel (b) shows how his total utility is affected by his consumption bundle, which must lie on his budget line. The quantity of clams is measured from left to right on the horizontal axis, and the quantity of potatoes is measured from right to left. His total utility is maximized at bundle *C*, where he consumes 2 pounds of clams and 6 pounds of potatoes. This is Sammy's *optimal consumption bundle.*

(a) Sammy's Budget Line

The optimal consumption bundle . . .

(b) Sammy's Utility Function

. . . *maximizes total utility given the budget constraint.*

Utility function

►*ECONOMICS IN ACTION*

The Consumption Possibilities of American Workers, 1895–2000

Over the past century, the consumption possibilities of the average American worker have increased radically as the nation has become vastly richer. A good illustration of this change comes from a comparison made by the economist J. Bradford DeLong.

He compared the cost of a number of items in the 1895 Montgomery Ward catalog to the cost of similar items today by calculating the number of hours an average worker would work to earn enough money to buy them. If we assume that a worker puts in 2,000 hours per year—40 hours per week, with two weeks of vacation—

Today, the average American worker's annual income buys a lot more bicycle than it did in 1895.

RTN Productions/Corbis

we can calculate how many units of each good a worker could purchase by spending an entire year's income only on that good.

According to DeLong's estimates, here are the amounts of various goods that workers then and now could have bought:

- In 1895, an average worker's annual income would have bought 7.7 one-speed bicycles; in 2000, it would have bought 278 bicycles.
- In 1895, the worker's income would have bought 45 full sets of dinner plates; in 2000, it would have bought 556 sets.
- In 1895, a worker's income would have bought 0.83 of a Steinway piano; in 2000, it would have bought 1.8 pianos.

By any standard, the average American's consumption possibilities have increased enormously. DeLong estimates that today's workers can on average purchase seven times as much of a randomly chosen good as their predecessors could have in 1895. Of course, in a way this understates the rise in purchasing power: there are many goods, like computers, that were not available in 1895 at any price. ▲

— < < < < < < < < < < <

> **CHECK YOUR UNDERSTANDING** 10-2

1. In the following two examples, find all the consumption bundles that lie on the consumer's budget line. Illustrate these consumption possibilities in a diagram and draw the budget line through them.
   a. The consumption bundle consists of movie tickets and buckets of popcorn. The price of each ticket is $10.00, the price of each bucket of popcorn is $5.00, and the consumer's income is $20.00. In your diagram, put movie tickets on the vertical axis and buckets of popcorn on the horizontal axis.
   b. The consumption bundle consists of underwear and socks. The price of each pair of underwear is $4.00, the price of each pair of socks is $2.00, and the consumer's income is $12.00. In your diagram, put pairs of socks on the vertical axis and pairs of underwear on the horizontal axis.

Solutions appear at back of book.

Spending the Marginal Dollar

As we've just seen, we can find Sammy's optimal consumption choice by finding the total utility he receives from each consumption bundle on his budget line and then choosing the bundle at which total utility is maximized. But we can use marginal analysis instead, turning Sammy's problem of finding his optimal consumption choice into a "how much" problem. How do we do this? By thinking about choosing an optimal consumption bundle as a problem of *how much to spend on each good.* That is, to find the optimal consumption bundle with marginal analysis we ask the question of whether Sammy can make himself better off by spending a little bit more of his income on clams and less on potatoes, or by doing the opposite—spending a little bit more on potatoes and less on clams. In other words, the marginal decision is a question of how to *spend the marginal dollar*—how to allocate an additional dollar between clams and potatoes in a way that maximizes utility.

Our first step in applying marginal analysis is to ask if Sammy is made better off by spending an additional dollar on either good; and if so, by how much is he better off.

THE RIGHT MARGINAL COMPARISON

Marginal analysis solves "how much" decisions by setting the marginal *benefit* of some activity equal to its marginal *cost*. As we saw in Chapter 9, finding Babette's optimal serving size was a marginal decision: it was found by setting the marginal benefit of increasing her serving size equal to its marginal cost. In production decisions like Babette's, using marginal analysis is particularly simple. If you were to extend the way we solved Babette's problem to Sammy's problem without any change, you would be tempted to say that Sammy's optimal consumption bundle is where the marginal utility of clams is equal to the marginal utility of potatoes. But that would be wrong because in consumption decisions, unlike production decisions, there's a budget constraint. And that budget constraint must be accounted for when doing marginal analysis.

The right answer for marginal decisions involving consumption is that the *marginal utility per dollar* spent on each good must be the same at the optimal consumption bundle. By factoring in prices, this comparison takes into account the fact that a consumer has a limited amount of money to spend. For example, assume you've decided to have pizza for dinner and you have $10 to spend on it. The pizza comes with choices of additional toppings that cost extra. Suppose you really like extra cheese, but you also really like anchovies. If a topping of anchovies costs twice as much as extra cheese, the optimal consumption choice isn't where you gain the same amount of utility from a topping of anchovies as you would from a topping of extra cheese. It's the combination of toppings where a serving of anchovies adds twice as much to utility as a serving of extra cheese. In other words, the marginal utility per dollar has to be the same for anchovies and extra cheese.

To answer this question we must calculate the **marginal utility per dollar** spent on either clams or potatoes—how much additional utility Sammy gets from spending an additional dollar on either good.

> The **marginal utility per dollar** spent on a good or service is the additional utility from spending one more dollar on that good or service.

Marginal Utility per Dollar

We've already introduced the concept of marginal utility, the additional utility a consumer gets from consuming one more unit of a good or service; now let's see how this concept can be used to derive the related measure of marginal utility per dollar.

Table 10-3 shows how to calculate the marginal utility per dollar spent on clams and potatoes, respectively.

TABLE 10-3

Sammy's Marginal Utility per Dollar

(a) Clams (price of clams = $4 per pound)				(b) Potatoes (price of potatoes = $2 per pound)			
Quantity of clams (pounds)	Utility from clams (utils)	Marginal utility per pound of clams (utils)	Marginal utility per dollar (utils)	Quantity of potatoes (pounds)	Utility from potatoes (utils)	Marginal utility per pound of potatoes (utils)	Marginal utility per dollar (utils)
0	0			0	0		
		15	3.75			11.5	5.75
1	15			1	11.5		
		10	2.50			9.9	4.95
2	25			2	21.4		
		6	1.50			8.4	4.20
3	31			3	29.8		
		3	0.75			7.0	3.50
4	34			4	36.8		
		2	0.50			5.7	2.85
5	36			5	42.5		
						4.5	2.25
				6	47.0		
						3.5	1.75
				7	50.5		
						2.7	1.35
				8	53.2		
						2.0	1.00
				9	55.2		
						1.5	0.75
				10	56.7		

In panel (a) of the table, the first column shows different possible amounts of clam consumption. The second column shows the utility Sammy derives from each amount of clam consumption; the third column then shows the marginal utility, the increase in utility Sammy gets from consuming an additional pound of clams. Panel (b) provides the same information for potatoes. The next step is to derive marginal utility *per dollar* for each good. To do this, we must divide the marginal utility of the good by its price in dollars.

To see why we must divide by the price, compare the third and fourth columns of panel (a). Consider what happens if Sammy increases his clam consumption from 2 pounds to 3 pounds. As we can see, this increase in clam consumption raises his total utility by 6 utils. But he must spend $4 for that additional pound, so the increase in his utility per additional dollar spent on clams is 6 utils/$4 = 1.5 utils per dollar. Similarly, if he increases his clam consumption from 3 pounds to 4 pounds, his marginal utility is 3 utils but his marginal utility per dollar is 3 utils/$4 = 0.75 utils per dollar. Notice that because of diminishing marginal utility, Sammy's marginal utility per pound of clams falls as the quantity of clams he consumes rises. As a result, his marginal utility per dollar spent on clams also falls as the quantity of clams he consumes rises.

So the last column of panel (a) shows how Sammy's marginal utility per dollar spent on clams depends on the quantity of clams he consumes. Similarly, the last column of panel (b) shows how his marginal utility per dollar spent on potatoes depends on the quantity of potatoes he consumes. Again, marginal utility per dollar spent on each good declines as the quantity of that good consumed rises, because of diminishing marginal utility.

We will use the symbols MU_C and MU_P to represent the marginal utility per pound of clams and potatoes, respectively. And we will use the symbols P_C and P_P to represent the price of clams (per pound) and the price of potatoes (per pound). Then the marginal utility per dollar spent on clams is MU_C/P_C and the marginal utility per dollar spent on potatoes is MU_P/P_P. In general, the additional utility generated from an additional dollar spent on a good is equal to:

(10-2)   Marginal utility per dollar spent on a good
= Marginal utility of one unit of the good/Price of one unit of the good
= MU_{good}/P_{good}

Now let's see how this concept helps us derive a consumer's optimal consumption using marginal analysis.

Optimal Consumption

Let's consider Figure 10-4. As in Figure 10-3, we can measure both the quantity of clams and the quantity of potatoes on the horizontal axis due to the budget constraint. Along the horizontal axis of Figure 10-4—also as in Figure 10-3—the quantity of clams increases as you move from left to right, and the quantity of potatoes increases as you move from right to left. The curve labeled MU_C/P_C in Figure 10-4 shows Sammy's marginal utility per dollar spent on clams as derived in Table 10-3. Likewise, the curve labeled MU_P/P_P shows his marginal utility per dollar spent on potatoes. Notice that the two curves, MU_C/P_C and MU_P/P_P, cross at the optimal consumption bundle, point C, consisting of 2 pounds of clams and 6 pounds of potatoes. Moreover, Figure 10-4 illustrates an important feature of Sammy's optimal consumption bundle: when Sammy consumes 2 pounds of clams and 6 pounds of potatoes, his marginal utility per dollar spent is the same, 2, for both goods. That is, at the optimal consumption bundle $MU_C/P_C = MU_P/P_P = 2$.

This isn't an accident. Consider another one of Sammy's possible consumption bundles—say, *B* in Figure 10-3, at which he consumes 1 pound of clams and 8 pounds

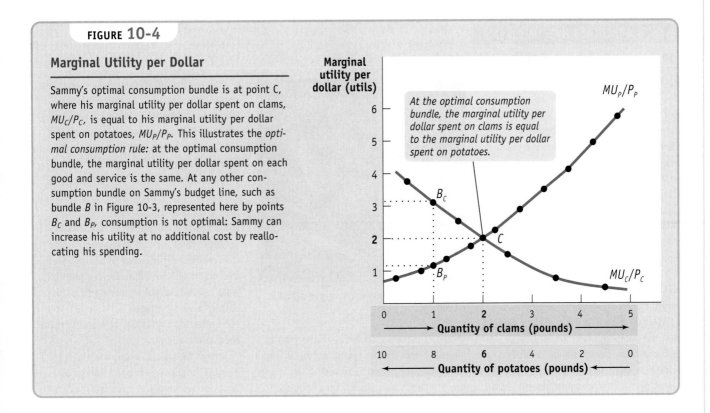

FIGURE 10-4

Marginal Utility per Dollar

Sammy's optimal consumption bundle is at point C, where his marginal utility per dollar spent on clams, MU_C/P_C, is equal to his marginal utility per dollar spent on potatoes, MU_P/P_P. This illustrates the *optimal consumption rule*: at the optimal consumption bundle, the marginal utility per dollar spent on each good and service is the same. At any other consumption bundle on Sammy's budget line, such as bundle B in Figure 10-3, represented here by points B_C and B_P, consumption is not optimal: Sammy can increase his utility at no additional cost by reallocating his spending.

At the optimal consumption bundle, the marginal utility per dollar spent on clams is equal to the marginal utility per dollar spent on potatoes.

of potatoes. The marginal utility per dollar spent on each good is shown by points B_C and B_P in Figure 10-4. At that consumption bundle, Sammy's marginal utility per dollar spent on clams would be approximately 3, but his marginal utility per dollar spent on potatoes would be only approximately 1. This shows that he has made a mistake: he is consuming too many potatoes and not enough clams.

How do we know this? If Sammy's marginal utility per dollar spent on clams is higher than his marginal utility per dollar spent on potatoes, he has a simple way to make himself better off while staying within his budget: spend $1 less on potatoes and $1 more on clams. By spending an additional dollar on clams, he adds about 3 utils to his total utility; meanwhile, by spending $1 less on potatoes, he subtracts only about 1 util from his total utility. Because his marginal utility per dollar spent is higher for clams than for potatoes, reallocating his spending toward clams and away from potatoes would increase his total utility. On the other hand, if his marginal utility per dollar spent on potatoes is higher, he can increase his utility by spending less on clams and more on potatoes. So if Sammy has in fact chosen his optimal consumption bundle, his marginal utility per dollar spent on clams and potatoes must be equal.

This is a general principle, known as the **optimal consumption rule:** when a consumer maximizes utility in the face of a budget constraint, the marginal utility per dollar spent on each good or service in the consumption bundle is the same. That is, for any two goods C and P the optimal consumption rule says that at the optimal consumption bundle

(10-3) $\dfrac{MU_C}{P_C} = \dfrac{MU_P}{P_P}$

It's easiest to understand this rule using examples in which the consumption bundle contains only two goods, but it applies no matter how many goods or services a consumer buys: in the optimal consumption bundle, the marginal utilities per dollar spent for each and every good or service in that bundle are equal.

The **optimal consumption rule** says that when a consumer maximizes utility, the marginal utility per dollar spent must be the same for all goods and services in the consumption bundle.

But Are Consumers Really Rational?

Many companies offer retirement plans that allow their employees to put aside part of their salaries tax-free. Such a plan, called a 401(k), can save a worker thousands of dollars in taxes each year. But the plans sometimes have disadvantages: some companies invest their employees' savings mainly in their own stock, which can be disastrous if the company gets in trouble, leaving the employee with no savings *and* no job. That's what happened to the employees of Enron back in 2001. When the company went under, employees who invested heavily in company stock lost everything. In 2008, many employees of Bear Stearns also lost most of their savings when the company went under.

Clearly, then, people should carefully decide how much of their money to put in an employer-administered retirement plan. They should compare the marginal utility of a dollar spent on current consumption with the marginal utility of a dollar saved for retirement. They should weigh the tax advantages of saving through the employer plan against the risks of letting the employer decide where their savings are invested.

But recent economic research suggests that most people aren't careful at all. For example, some companies have an "opt-in" system for their 401(k); that is, in some companies employees must ask to be enrolled. Other companies have an "opt-out" system; employees are automatically enrolled unless they request otherwise. This

Great new car, but are you saving enough for retirement?

shouldn't make a difference—if the plan is managed well, people should opt in; if it's managed poorly (that is, investing mainly in the company's own stock), they should opt out. Yet when companies switch to automatic enrollment, the number of employees in their 401(k) plans rises dramatically. As the National Bureau of Economic Research puts it, workers seem to follow the path of least resistance, instead of comparing their options and maximizing their utility.

Studies of saving behavior are one example of a growing field known as "behavioral economics." Behavioral economists question the whole concept of the rational consumer. Their research focuses on situations in which people don't seem to be rational—that is, when they behave in ways that can't easily be explained by utility maximization.

One key insight in behavioral economics comes from the work of Herbert Simon, who won the Nobel Prize in economics in 1978. Simon argued that sometimes individuals find that it isn't actually rational to go to great lengths to maximize utility, since searching for the perfect answer is itself a costly activity. Instead, he argued, they engage in *bounded rationality:* individuals save time and effort by making decisions that are "good enough," rather than perfect. In the case of savings plans, this might involve following the path of least resistance: not bothering to participate in a well-managed opt-in plan, and not bothering to opt out of a poorly managed automatic plan.

Today's behavioral economists use insights from psychology to understand behavior seemingly at odds with rationality. The 2002 Nobel Prize went to Daniel Kahneman, a psychologist who, with his late co-author Amos Tversky, laid out a theory of how people make choices in the face of uncertainty. This work and other insights into nonrational behavior are having an important influence on the analysis of financial markets, labor markets, and other economic concerns.

But it's hard to find a behavioral economist who thinks that the insights of this field should replace the analysis of utility maximization. The theory of the rational consumer remains the main way in which economists analyze consumer behavior.

►ECONOMICS IN ACTION

Buying Your Way Out of Temptation

It might seem odd to pay more to get less. But snack food companies have discovered that consumers are indeed willing to pay more for smaller portions, and exploiting this trend is a recipe for success. Over the last few years, sales of 100-calorie packs of crackers, chips, cookies, and candy have passed the $20 million-a-year mark. During 2006, sales of 100-calorie snack packs grew nearly 30%, while the snack industry as a whole grew only 3.5%. A company executive explained why small packages are popular—they help consumers eat less without having to count calories themselves. "The irony," said David Adelman, a food industry analyst, "is if you take Wheat Thins or

Goldfish, buy a large-size box, count out the items and put them in a Ziploc bag, you'd have essentially the same product." He estimates that snack packs are about 20% more profitable for snack makers than larger packages.

It's clear that in this case consumers are making a calculation: the extra utility gained from not having to worry about whether they've eaten too much is worth the extra cost. As one shopper said, "They're pretty expensive, but they're worth it. It's individually packaged for the amount I need, so I don't go overboard." So it's clear that consumers aren't being irrational here. Rather, they're being entirely rational: in addition to their snack, they're buying a little hand-to-mouth restraint. ▲

> > > > > > > > > > > >

> **CHECK YOUR UNDERSTANDING** 10-3

1. In Table 10-3 you can see that marginal utility per dollar spent on clams and marginal utility per dollar spent on potatoes are equal when Sammy increases his consumption of clams from 3 pounds to 4 pounds and his consumption of potatoes from 9 pounds to 10 pounds. Explain why this is not Sammy's optimal consumption bundle. Illustrate your answer using the budget line in Figure 10-3.

2. Explain what is faulty about the following statement, using data from Table 10-3: "In order to maximize utility, Sammy should consume the bundle that gives him the maximum marginal utility per dollar for each good."

Solutions appear at back of book.

From Utility to the Demand Curve

We have now analyzed the optimal consumption choice of a consumer with a given amount of income and who faces one particular set of prices—in our Sammy example, $20 of income per week, $4 per pound of clams, and $2 per pound of potatoes.

But the main reason for studying consumer behavior is to go behind the market demand curve—to understand how the downward slope of the market demand curve is explained by the utility-maximizing behavior of individual consumers.

Marginal Utility, the Substitution Effect, and the Law of Demand

Suppose that the price of fried clams, P_C, rises. This doesn't change the marginal utility a consumer gets from an additional pound of clams, MU_C, at any given level of clam consumption. However, it reduces the marginal utility *per dollar spent* on fried clams, MU_C/P_C. And the decrease in marginal utility per dollar spent on clams gives the consumer an incentive to consume fewer clams when the price of clams rises.

To see why, recall the optimal consumption rule: a utility-maximizing consumer chooses a consumption bundle for which the marginal utility per dollar spent on all goods is the same. If the marginal utility per dollar spent on clams falls because the price of clams rises, the consumer can increase his or her utility by purchasing fewer clams and more of other goods.

The opposite happens if the price of clams falls. In that case the marginal utility per dollar spent on clams, MU_C/P_C, increases at any given level of clam consumption. As a result, a consumer can increase his or her utility by purchasing more clams and less of other goods when the price of clams falls.

So when the price of a good increases, an individual will normally consume less of that good and more of other goods. Correspondingly, when the price of a good decreases, an individual will normally consume more of that good and less of other goods. This explains why the individual demand curve, which relates an individual's consumption of a good to the price of that good, normally slopes downward—that is, it obeys the law of demand. And since—as we learned in Chapter 3—the market

The **substitution effect** of a change in the price of a good is the change in the quantity of that good consumed as the consumer substitutes the good that has become relatively cheaper in place of the good that has become relatively more expensive.

The **income effect** of a change in the price of a good is the change in the quantity of that good consumed that results from a change in the consumer's purchasing power due to the change in the price of the good.

demand curve is the horizontal sum of all the individual demand curves of consumers, it, too, will slope downward.

An alternative way to think about why demand curves slope downward is to focus on opportunity costs. When the price of clams decreases, an individual doesn't have to give up as many units of other goods in order to buy one more unit of clams. So consuming clams becomes more attractive. Conversely, when the price of a good increases, consuming that good becomes a less attractive use of resources, and the consumer buys less.

This effect of a price change on the quantity consumed is always present. It is known as the **substitution effect**—the change in the quantity consumed as the consumer substitutes the good that has become relatively cheaper in place of the good that has become relatively more expensive. When a good absorbs only a small share of the consumer's spending, the substitution effect is essentially the complete explanation of why the individual demand curve of that consumer slopes downward. And, by implication, when a good absorbs only a small share of the typical consumer's spending, the substitution effect is essentially the sole explanation of why the market demand curve slopes downward. However, some goods, such as housing, absorb a large share of a typical consumer's spending. For such goods, the story behind the individual demand curve and the market demand curve becomes slightly more complicated.

The Income Effect

For the vast majority of goods, the substitution effect is pretty much the entire story behind the slopes of the individual and market demand curves. There are, however, some goods, like food or housing, that account for a substantial share of many consumers' spending. In such cases another effect, called the *income effect,* also comes into play.

Consider the case of a family that spends half its income on rental housing. Now suppose that the price of housing increases everywhere. This will have a substitution effect on the family's demand: other things equal, the family will have an incentive to consume less housing—say, by moving to a smaller apartment—and more of other goods. But the family will also, in a real sense, be made poorer by that higher housing price—its income will buy less housing than before. The amount of income adjusted to reflect its true purchasing power is often termed "real income," in contrast to "money income" or "nominal income," which has not been adjusted. And this reduction in a consumer's real income will have an additional effect, beyond the substitution effect, on the family's consumption bundle, including its consumption of housing.

The change in the quantity of a good consumed that results from a change in the overall purchasing power of the consumer due to a change in the price of that good is known as the **income effect** of the price change. In this case, a change in the price of a good effectively changes a consumer's income because it alters the consumer's purchasing power. Along with the substitution effect, the income effect is another means by which changes in prices alter consumption choices.

It's possible to give more precise definitions of the substitution effect and the income effect of a price change, and we do this in Chapter 11. For most purposes, however, there are only two things you need to know about the distinction between these two effects.

First, for the great majority of goods and services, the income effect is not important and has no significant effect on individual consumption. So most market demand curves slope downward solely because of the substitution effect—end of story.

Second, when it matters at all, the income effect usually reinforces the substitution effect. That is, when the price of a good that absorbs a substantial share of

FOR INQUIRING MINDS

Giffen Goods

Back when Ireland was a desperately poor country—not the prosperous "Celtic Tiger" it has lately become—it was claimed that the Irish would eat *more* potatoes when the price of potatoes went up. That is, some observers claimed that Ireland's demand curve for potatoes sloped upward, not downward.

Can this happen? In theory, yes. If Irish demand for potatoes actually sloped upward, it would have been a real-life case of a "Giffen good," named after a nineteenth-century statistician who thought (probably wrongly) that he saw an upward-sloping demand curve in some data he was studying.

Here's the story. Suppose that there is some good that absorbs a large share of consumers' budgets and that this good is also *inferior*—people demand less of it when their income rises. The classic supposed example was, as you might guess, potatoes in Ireland, back when potatoes were an inferior good—they were what poor people ate—and when the Irish were very poor.

Now suppose that the price of potatoes increases. This would, *other things equal,* cause people to substitute other goods for potatoes. But other things are not equal: given the higher price of potatoes, people are poorer. And this *increases* the demand for potatoes, because potatoes are an inferior good.

If this income effect outweighs the substitution effect, a rise in the price of potatoes would increase the quantity demanded; the law of demand would not hold.

In a way the point of this story—which has never been validated in any real situation, nineteenth-century Ireland included—is how unlikely such an event is. The law of demand really is a law, with few exceptions.

income rises, consumers of that good become a bit poorer because their purchasing power falls. And the vast majority of goods are *normal* goods, goods for which demand decreases when income falls. So this effective reduction in income leads to a reduction in the quantity demanded and reinforces the substitution effect.

However, in the case of an *inferior* good, a good for which demand increases when income falls, the income and substitution effects work in opposite directions. Although the substitution effect tends to produce a decrease in the quantity of any good demanded as its price increases, in the case of an inferior good the income effect of a price increase tends to produce an *increase* in the quantity demanded.

As a result, there are hypothetical cases involving inferior goods in which the distinction between income and substitution effects are important (see For Inquiring Minds). As a practical matter, however, it's not a subject we need to worry about when discussing the demand for most goods. Typically, income effects are important only for a very limited number of goods.

►*ECONOMICS IN ACTION*

Mortgage Rates and Consumer Demand

Most people buy houses with mortgages—loans backed by the value of the house. The interest rates on such mortgages change over time; for example, they fell quite a lot over the period from 2000 to 2003. And compared to historical standards, mortgage rates continued to be low through early 2008. When mortgage rates fall, the cost of housing falls for millions of people—even people who have mortgages at high interest rates are often able to "refinance" them at lower rates. The percentage of American households who owned their home increased from 67.1% in 2000 to a historical high of 69.2% in 2004. (Since 2004 it has fallen back slightly, to 67.8% in late 2007, because of turmoil in the financial market for mortgages.)

It's not surprising that the demand for housing goes up when mortgage rates go down. Economists have noticed, however, that the demand for many other goods also rises when mortgage rates fall. Some of these goods are items connected with new or

>> QUICK REVIEW

➤ Most goods absorb only a small fraction of a consumer's spending. For such goods, the **substitution effect** of a price change is the only important effect of the price change on consumption. It causes individual demand curves and the market demand curve to slope downward.

➤ When a good absorbs a large fraction of a consumer's spending, the **income effect** of a price change is present in addition to the substitution effect.

➤ For normal goods, demand rises when a consumer is richer and falls when a consumer is poorer, so that the income effect reinforces the substitution effect. For inferior goods, demand rises when a consumer is poorer and falls when a consumer is richer, so that the income and substitution effects move in opposite directions.

bigger houses, such as furniture. But people also buy new cars, eat more meals in restaurants, and take more vacations. Why?

The answer illustrates the distinction between substitution and income effects. When housing becomes cheaper, there is a *substitution effect:* people have an incentive to substitute housing in place of other goods in their consumption bundle. But housing also happens to be a good that absorbs a large part of consumer spending, with many families spending a quarter or more of their income on mortgage payments. So when the price of housing falls, people are in effect richer—there is a noticeable *income effect.*

The increase in the quantity of housing demanded when mortgage rates fall is the result of both effects: housing becomes a better buy compared with other consumer goods, and people also buy more and bigger houses because they feel richer. And because they feel richer, they also buy more of all other normal goods, such as cars, restaurant meals, and vacations. ▲

◄ ◄ ◄ ◄ ◄ ◄ ◄ ◄ ◄ ◄ ◄ ◄

► CHECK YOUR UNDERSTANDING 10-4

1. In each of the following cases, state whether the income effect, the substitution effect, or both are significant. In which cases do they move in the same direction? In opposite directions? Why?

   a. Orange juice represents a small share of Clare's spending. She buys more lemonade and less orange juice when the price of orange juice goes up. She does not change her spending on other goods.

   b. Apartment rents have risen dramatically this year. Since rent absorbs a major part of her income, Delia moves to a smaller apartment. Assume that rental housing is a normal good.

   c. The cost of a semester-long meal ticket at the student cafeteria rises, representing a significant increase in living costs. As a result, many students have less money to spend on weekend meals at restaurants and eat in the cafeteria instead. Assume that cafeteria meals are an inferior good.

Solutions appear at back of book.

[>> A LOOK AHEAD •••

At this point we have the basic tools to understand consumer behavior and how it gives rise to the market demand curve. Yet there is more to say about consumer choice, and those who want to pursue the subject further should proceed to Chapter 11. Those eager to move on can, however, skip to Chapter 12, where we begin our study of producer behavior and the various types of production costs that producers face. Chapter 13 then focuses on how producers behave in a competitive market. Once you've completed these two chapters, you'll have a good grasp of what underlies both the demand and supply curves.]

SUMMARY

1. Consumers maximize a measure of satisfaction called **utility.** Each consumer has a **utility function** that determines the level of total utility generated by his or her **consumption bundle,** the goods and services that are consumed. We measure utility in hypothetical units called **utils.**

2. A good's or service's **marginal utility** is the additional utility generated by consuming one more unit of the good or service. We usually assume that the **principle of diminishing marginal utility** holds: consumption of another unit of a good or service yields less additional utility than the previous unit. As a result, the **marginal utility curve** slopes downward.

3. A **budget constraint** limits a consumer's spending to no more than his or her income. It defines the consumer's **consumption possibilities,** the set of all affordable consumption bundles. A consumer who spends all of his or her income will choose a consumption bundle on the **budget line.** An individual chooses the consumption bundle that maximizes total utility, the **optimal consumption bundle.**

4. We use marginal analysis to find the optimal consumption bundle by analyzing how to allocate the marginal dollar. The **optimal consumption rule** says that at the optimal consumption bundle the **marginal utility per dollar** spent on each good and service—the marginal utility of a good divided by its price—is the same.

5. Changes in the price of a good affect the quantity consumed in two possible ways: the **substitution effect** and the **income effect.** Most goods absorb only a small share of a consumer's spending; for these goods, only the substitution effect—buying less of the good that has become relatively more expensive and more of the good that has become relatively cheaper—is significant. It causes the individual and the market demand curves to slope downward. When a good absorbs a large fraction of spending, the income effect is also significant: an increase in a good's price makes a consumer poorer, but a decrease in price makes a consumer richer. This change in purchasing power makes consumers demand more or less of a good, depending on whether the good is normal or inferior. For normal goods, the substitution and income effects reinforce each other. For inferior goods, however, they work in opposite directions.

KEY TERMS

Utility, p. 250
Consumption bundle, p. 250
Utility function, p. 250
Util, p. 250
Marginal utility, p. 251
Marginal utility curve, p. 251

Principle of diminishing marginal utility, p. 252
Budget constraint, p. 254
Consumption possibilities, p. 254
Budget line, p. 254
Optimal consumption bundle, p. 255

Marginal utility per dollar, p. 259
Optimal consumption rule, p. 261
Substitution effect, p. 264
Income effect, p. 264

PROBLEMS

1. For each of the following situations, decide whether Al has increasing, constant, or diminishing marginal utility.

   a. The more economics classes Al takes, the more he enjoys the subject. And the more classes he takes, the easier each one gets, making him enjoy each additional class even more than the one before.

   b. Al likes loud music. In fact, according to him, "the louder, the better." Each time he turns the volume up a notch, he adds 5 utils to his total utility.

   c. Al enjoys watching reruns of the old sitcom *Friends*. He claims that these episodes are always funny, but he does admit that the more he sees an episode, the less funny it gets.

   d. Al loves toasted marshmallows. The more he eats, however, the fuller he gets and the less he enjoys each additional marshmallow. And there is a point at which he becomes satiated: beyond that point, more marshmallows actually make him feel worse rather than better.

2. Use the concept of marginal utility to explain the following: Newspaper vending machines are designed so that once you have paid for one paper, you could take more than one paper at a time. But soda vending machines, once you have paid for one soda, dispense only one soda at a time.

3. Brenda likes to have bagels and coffee for breakfast. The accompanying table shows Brenda's total utility from various consumption bundles of bagels and coffee.

Consumption bundle		Total utility (utils)
Quantity of bagels	Quantity of coffee (cups)	
0	0	0
0	2	28
0	4	40
1	2	48
1	3	54
2	0	28
2	2	56
3	1	54
3	2	62
4	0	40
4	2	66

Suppose Brenda knows she will consume 2 cups of coffee for sure. However, she can choose to consume different quantities of bagels: she can choose either 0, 1, 2, 3, or 4 bagels.

a. Calculate Brenda's marginal utility from bagels as she goes from consuming 0 bagel to 1 bagel, from 1 bagel to 2 bagels, from 2 bagels to 3 bagels, and from 3 bagels to 4 bagels.

b. Draw Brenda's marginal utility curve of bagels. Does Brenda have increasing, diminishing, or constant marginal utility of bagels?

4. Brenda, the consumer in Problem 3, now has to make a decision about how many bagels and how much coffee to have for breakfast. She has $8 of income to spend on bagels and coffee. Use the information given in the table in Problem 3 to answer the following questions.

a. Bagels cost $2 each, and coffee costs $2 per cup. Which bundles are on Brenda's budget line? For each of these bundles, calculate the level of utility (in utils) that Brenda enjoys. Which bundle is her optimal bundle?

b. The price of bagels increases to $4, but the price of coffee remains at $2 per cup. Which bundles are now on Brenda's budget line? For each bundle, calculate Brenda's level of utility (in utils). Which bundle is her optimal bundle?

c. What do your answers to parts a and b imply about the slope of Brenda's demand curve for bagels? Describe the substitution effect and the income effect of this increase in the price of bagels, assuming that bagels are a normal good.

5. Bruno can spend his income on two different goods: Beyoncé CDs and notebooks for his class notes. For each of the following three situations, decide if the given consumption bundle is within Bruno's consumption possibilities. Then decide if it lies *on* the budget line or not.

a. CDs cost $10 each, and notebooks cost $2 each. Bruno has income of $60. He is considering a consumption bundle containing 3 CDs and 15 notebooks.

b. CDs cost $10 each, and notebooks cost $5 each. Bruno has income of $110. He is considering a consumption bundle containing 3 CDs and 10 notebooks.

c. CDs cost $20 each, and notebooks cost $10 each. Bruno has income of $50. He is considering a consumption bundle containing 2 CDs and 2 notebooks.

6. Bruno, the consumer in Problem 5, is best friends with Bernie, who shares his love for notebooks and Beyoncé CDs. The accompanying table shows Bernie's utilities from notebooks and Beyoncé CDs.

Quantity of notebooks	Utility from notebooks (utils)	Quantity of CDs	Utility from CDs (utils)
0	0	0	0
2	70	1	80
4	130	2	150
6	180	3	210
8	220	4	260
10	250	5	300

The price of a notebook is $5, the price of a CD is $10, and Bernie has $50 of income to spend.

a. Which consumption bundles of notebooks and CDs can Bernie consume if he spends all his income? Illustrate Bernie's budget line with a diagram, putting notebooks on the horizontal axis and CDs on the vertical axis.

b. Calculate the marginal utility of each notebook and the marginal utility of each CD. Then calculate the marginal utility per dollar spent on notebooks and the marginal utility per dollar spent on CDs.

c. Draw a diagram like Figure 10-4 in which both the marginal utility per dollar spent on notebooks and the marginal utility per dollar spent on CDs are illustrated. Using this diagram and the optimal consumption rule, predict which bundle—from all the bundles on his budget line—Bernie will choose.

7. For each of the following situations, decide whether the bundle Lakshani is considering optimal or not. If it is not optimal, how could Lakshani improve her overall level of utility? That is, determine which good she should spend more on and which good should spend less on.

a. Lakshani has $200 to spend on sneakers and sweaters. Sneakers cost $50 per pair, and sweaters cost $20 each. She is thinking about buying 2 pairs of sneakers and 5 sweaters. She tells her friend that the additional utility she would get from the second pair of sneakers is the same as the additional utility she would get from the fifth sweater.

b. Lakshani has $5 to spend on pens and pencils. Each pen costs $0.50 and each pencil costs $0.10. She is thinking about buying 6 pens and 20 pencils. The last pen would add five times as much to her total utility as the last pencil.

c. Lakshani has $50 per season to spend on tickets to football games and tickets to soccer games. Each football ticket costs $10 and each soccer ticket costs $5. She is thinking about buying 3 football tickets and 2 soccer tickets. Her marginal utility from the third football ticket is twice as much as her marginal utility from the second soccer ticket.

8. Cal "Cool" Cooper has $200 to spend on cell phones and sunglasses.

   a. Each cell phone costs $100 and each pair of sunglasses costs $50. Which bundles lie on Cal's budget line? Draw a diagram like Figure 10-4 in which both the marginal utility per dollar spent on cell phones and the marginal utility per dollar spent on sunglasses are illustrated. Use this diagram and the optimal consumption rule to decide how Cal should allocate his money. That is, from all the bundles on his budget line, which bundle will Cal choose? The accompanying table gives his utility of cell phones and sunglasses.

Quantity of cell phones	Utility from cell phones (utils)	Quantity of sunglasses (pairs)	Utility from sunglasses (utils)
0	0	0	0
1	400	2	600
2	700	4	700

   b. The price of cell phones falls to $50 each, but the price of sunglasses remains at $50 per pair. Which bundles lie on Cal's budget line? Draw a diagram like Figure 10-4 in which both the marginal utility per dollar spent on cell phones and the marginal utility per dollar spent on sunglasses are illustrated. Use this diagram and the optimal consumption rule to decide how Cal should allocate his money. That is, from all the bundles on his budget line, which bundle will Cal choose? The accompanying table gives his utility of cell phones and sunglasses.

Quantity of cell phones	Utility from cell phones (utils)	Quantity of sunglasses (pairs)	Utility from sunglasses (utils)
0	0	0	0
1	400	1	325
2	700	2	600
3	900	3	825
4	1,000	4	700

   c. How does Cal's consumption of cell phones change as the price of cell phones falls? In words, describe the income effect and the substitution effect of this fall in the price of cell phones, assuming that cell phones are a normal good.

9. Damien Matthews is a busy actor. He allocates his free time to watching movies and working out at the gym. The accompanying table shows his utility from the number of times per week he watches a movie or goes to the gym.

Quantity of gym visits per week	Utility from gym visits (utils)	Quantity of movies per week	Utility from movies (utils)
1	100	1	60
2	180	2	110
3	240	3	150
4	280	4	180
5	310	5	190
6	330	6	195
7	340	7	197

Damien has 14 hours per week to spend on watching movies and going to the gym. Each movie takes 2 hours and each gym visit takes 2 hours. (*Hint:* Damien's free time is analogous to income he can spend. The hours needed for each activity are analogous to the price of that activity.)

   a. Which bundles of gym visits and movies can Damien consume per week if he spends all his time either going to the gym or watching movies? Draw Damien's budget line in a diagram with gym visits on the horizontal axis and movies on the vertical axis.

   b. Calculate the marginal utility of each gym visit and the marginal utility of each movie. Then calculate the marginal utility per hour spent at the gym and the marginal utility per hour spent watching movies.

   c. Draw a diagram like Figure 10-4 in which both the marginal utility per hour spent at the gym and the marginal utility per hour spent watching movies are illustrated. Use this diagram and the optimal consumption rule to decide how Damien should allocate his time.

10. Anna Jenniferson is an actress, who currently spends several hours each week watching movies and going to the gym. On the set of a new movie she meets Damien, the consumer in Problem 9. She tells him that she likes watching movies much more than going to the gym. In fact, she says that if she had to give up seeing 1 movie, she would need to go to the gym twice to make up for the loss in utility from not seeing the movie. A movie takes 2 hours, and a gym visit also lasts 2 hours. Damien tells Anna that she is not watching enough movies. Is he right?

11. Sven is a poor student who covers most of his dietary needs by eating cheap breakfast cereal, since it contains most of the important vitamins. As the price of cereal increases, he decides to buy even less of other foods and even more breakfast cereal to maintain his intake of important nutrients. This makes breakfast cereal a Giffen good for Sven. Describe in words the substitution effect and the income effect from this increase in the price of cereal. In which direction does each effect move, and why? What does this imply for the slope of Sven's demand curve for cereal?

12. In each of the following situations, describe the substitution effect and, if it is significant, the income effect. In which direction does each of these effects move? Why?

a. Ed spends a large portion of his income on his children's education. Because tuition fees rise, one of his children has to withdraw from college.

b. Homer spends much of his monthly income on home mortgage payments. The interest on his adjustable-rate mortgage falls, lowering his mortgage payments, and Homer decides to move to a larger house.

c. Pam thinks that Spam is an inferior good. Yet as the price of Spam rises, she decides to buy less of it.

13. Restaurant meals and housing (measured in the number of rooms) are the only two goods that Neha buys. She has income of $1,000. Initially, she buys a consumption bundle such that she spends exactly half her income on restaurant meals and the other half of her income on housing. Then her income increases by 50%, but the price of restaurant meals increases by 100% (it doubles). The price of housing remains the same. After these changes, if she wanted to, could Neha still buy the same consumption bundle as before?

14. Scott finds that the higher the price of orange juice, the more money he spends on orange juice. Does that mean that Scott has discovered a Giffen good?

15. Margo's marginal utility of one dance lesson is 100 utils per lesson. Her marginal utility of a new pair of dance shoes is 300 utils per pair. The price of a dance lesson is $50 per lesson. She currently spends all her income, and she buys her optimal consumption bundle. What is the price of a pair of dance shoes?

16. According to data from the U.S. Department of Energy, the average retail price of regular gasoline rose from $0.93 in 1985 to $1.81 in 2005, a 95% increase.

a. Other things equal, describe the effect of this price increase on the quantity of gasoline demanded. In your explanation, make use of the optimal consumption rule and describe income and substitution effects.

In fact, however, other things were not equal. Over the same time period, the prices of other goods and services rose as well. According to data from the Bureau of Labor Statistics, the overall price of a bundle of goods and services consumed by an average consumer rose by 82%.

b. Taking into account the rise in the price of gasoline and in overall prices, other things equal, describe the effect on the quantity of gasoline demanded.

However, this is not the end of the story. Between 1985 and 2005, the typical consumer's nominal income increased, too: the U.S. Census Bureau reports that U.S. median household nominal income rose from $23,618 in 1985 to $46,326 in 2005, an increase of 96%.

c. Taking into account the rise in the price of gasoline, in overall prices, and in consumers' incomes, describe the effect on the quantity of gasoline demanded.

 www.worthpublishers.com/krugmanwells

chapter: 11

Consumer Preferences and Consumer Choice

A TALE OF TWO CITIES

Do you want to earn a high salary? Maybe you should consider moving to San Jose, California, the metropolitan area that contains much of Silicon Valley, America's leading cluster of high-tech industries. The average family in San Jose has an income far higher than that of the average American family. According to bestplaces.net, a website that compares living conditions in different cities, average household income in San Jose is more than twice as high as that in Cincinnati.

But before you rush to San Jose, there's something else you should know: housing is very expensive there—about four times as expensive per square foot of living space as in Cincinnati. Understandably, the average apartment or house in San Jose is small by American standards.

So is life better or worse in San Jose than in Cincinnati? It depends a lot on what you want. For young people without children, the high wage they can earn in San Jose probably outweighs the high price of housing. They are willing to accept more cramped living quarters in return for the ability to consume greater quantities of other goods such as restaurant meals or clothing. People with large families, however, might prefer midwestern locations like Cincinnati, where the average wage is lower than in San Jose but a dollar buys many more square feet of living space. That is, they would choose to eat fewer restaurant meals but live in more spacious housing.

For individuals whose preferences lie somewhere between those of childless urban professionals and those of proud parents, the choice between San Jose and Cincinnati may not be easy. In fact, some people would be *indifferent* between living in the two locations. That's not to say that they would live the same way in San Jose and in Cincinnati; in San Jose they would live in small apartments and eat out a lot, but in

Spacious house in the suburbs or cozy apartment in the city—how would you choose?

Cincinnati they would be homebodies. And they would find both lifestyles equally good.

Our comparison of San Jose and Cincinnati has several morals. One is that different people have different preferences. But we also see that even given an individual's preferences, there may be different consumption bundles—different combinations of the goods and services an individual consumes—that yield the same total utility. This insight leads to the concept of *indifference curves*, a useful way to represent individual preferences.

The example also shows that an individual's total utility depends not only on income but also on prices—and that both income and prices affect consumer choices. We will apply this more complete analysis of consumer choice to the important distinction between *complements* and *substitutes*. Finally, we will use this insight to examine further the *income* and *substitution effects* we covered briefly in Chapter 10.

But, let's begin with indifference curves.

WHAT YOU WILL LEARN IN THIS CHAPTER:

➤ Why economists use **indifference curves** to illustrate a person's preferences

➤ The importance of the **marginal rate of substitution,** the rate at which a consumer is just willing to substitute one good in place of another

➤ An alternative way of finding a consumer's optimal consumption bundle using indifference curves and the budget line

➤ How the shape of indifference curves helps determine whether goods are substitutes or complements

➤ An in-depth understanding of income and substitution effects

---

Mapping the Utility Function

In Chapter 10 we introduced the concept of a utility function, which determines a consumer's total utility given his or her consumption bundle. In Figure 10-1 we saw how Cassie's total utility changed as we changed the quantity of fried clams consumed, holding fixed the quantities of other items in her bundle. That is, in Figure 10-1 we showed how total utility changed as consumption of only *one* good changed. But we also learned in Chapter 10, from our example of Sammy, that finding the optimal consumption bundle involves the problem of how to allocate the last dollar spent between *two* goods, clams and potatoes. In this chapter we will extend the analysis by learning how to express total utility as a function of consumption of two goods. In this way we will deepen our understanding of the trade-off involved when choosing the optimal consumption bundle and of how the optimal consumption bundle itself changes in response to changes in the prices of goods. In order to do that, we now turn to a different way of representing a consumer's utility function, based on the concept of *indifference curves*.

Indifference Curves

Ingrid is a consumer who buys only two goods: housing, measured in the number of rooms, and restaurant meals. How can we represent her utility function in a way that takes account of her consumption of both goods?

One way is to draw a three-dimensional picture. Figure 11-1 shows a three-dimensional "utility hill." The distance along the horizontal axis measures the quantity of housing Ingrid consumes in terms of numbers of rooms; the distance along the vertical axis measures the number of restaurant meals she consumes. The altitude or height of the hill at each point is indicated by a contour line, along which the height of the hill is constant. For example, point *A,* which corresponds to a consumption bundle of 3 rooms and 30 restaurant meals, lies on the contour line labeled 450. So the total utility Ingrid receives from consuming 3 rooms and 30 restaurant meals is 450 utils.

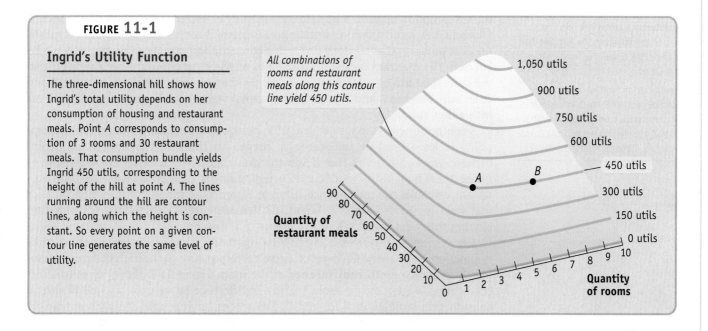

FIGURE 11-1

Ingrid's Utility Function

The three-dimensional hill shows how Ingrid's total utility depends on her consumption of housing and restaurant meals. Point A corresponds to consumption of 3 rooms and 30 restaurant meals. That consumption bundle yields Ingrid 450 utils, corresponding to the height of the hill at point A. The lines running around the hill are contour lines, along which the height is constant. So every point on a given contour line generates the same level of utility.

A three-dimensional picture like Figure 11-1 helps us think about the relationship between consumption bundles and total utility. But anyone who has ever used a topographical map to plan a hiking trip knows that it is possible to represent a three-dimensional surface in only two dimensions. A topographical map doesn't offer a three-dimensional view of the terrain; instead, it conveys information about altitude solely through the use of contour lines.

The same principle can be applied to representing the utility function. In Figure 11-2, Ingrid's consumption of rooms is measured on the horizontal axis and her consumption of restaurant meals on the vertical axis. The curve here corresponds to the contour line in Figure 11-1, drawn at a total utility of 450 utils. This curve shows all

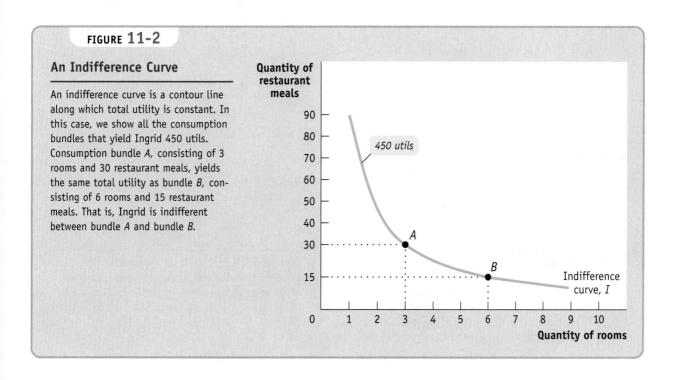

FIGURE 11-2

An Indifference Curve

An indifference curve is a contour line along which total utility is constant. In this case, we show all the consumption bundles that yield Ingrid 450 utils. Consumption bundle A, consisting of 3 rooms and 30 restaurant meals, yields the same total utility as bundle B, consisting of 6 rooms and 15 restaurant meals. That is, Ingrid is indifferent between bundle A and bundle B.

An **indifference curve** is a line that shows all the consumption bundles that yield the same amount of total utility for an individual.

The entire utility function of an individual can be represented by an **indifference curve map**, a collection of indifference curves in which each curve corresponds to a different total utility level.

the consumption bundles that yield a total utility of 450 utils. One point on that contour line is A, a consumption bundle consisting of 3 rooms and 30 restaurant meals. Another point on that contour line is B, a consumption bundle consisting of 6 rooms but only 15 restaurant meals. Because B lies on the same contour line, it yields Ingrid the same total utility—450 utils—as A. We say that Ingrid is *indifferent* between A and B: because bundles A and B yield the same total utility level, Ingrid is equally well off with either bundle.

A contour line that maps consumption bundles yielding the same amount of total utility is known as an **indifference curve.** An individual is always indifferent between any two bundles that lie on the same indifference curve. For a given consumer, there is an indifference curve corresponding to each possible level of total utility. For example, the indifference curve in Figure 11-2 shows consumption bundles that yield Ingrid 450 utils; different indifference curves would show consumption bundles that yield Ingrid 400 utils, 500 utils, and so on.

A collection of indifference curves that represents a given consumer's entire utility function, with each indifference curve corresponding to a different level of total utility, is known as an **indifference curve map.** Figure 11-3 shows three indifference curves—I_1, I_2, and I_3—from Ingrid's indifference curve map, as well as several consumption bundles, A, B, C, and D. The accompanying table lists each bundle, its composition of rooms and restaurant meals, and the total utility it yields. Because bundles A and B generate the same number of utils, 450, they lie on the same indifference curve, I_2. Although Ingrid is indifferent between A and B, she is certainly not indifferent between A and C: as you can see from the table, C generates only 391 utils, a lower total utility than A or B. So Ingrid prefers consumption bundles A and B to bundle C. This is represented by the fact that C is on indifference curve I_1, and I_1 lies

FIGURE 11-3   An Indifference Curve Map

Consumption bundle	Quantity of rooms	Quantity of meals	Total utility (utils)
A	3	30	450
B	6	15	450
C	5	10	391
D	4	45	519

The utility function can be represented in greater detail by increasing the number of indifference curves drawn, each corresponding to a different level of total utility. In this figure bundle C lies on an indifference curve corresponding to a total utility of 391 utils. As in Figure 11-2, bundles A and B lie on an indifference curve corresponding to a total utility of 450 utils. Bundle D lies on an indifference curve corresponding to a total utility of 519 utils. Ingrid prefers any bundle on I_2 to any bundle on I_1, and she prefers any bundle on I_3 to any bundle on I_2.

Are Utils Useful?

In the table that accompanies Figure 11-3, we give the number of utils achieved on each of the indifference curves shown in the figure. But is this information actually needed?

The answer is no. As you will see shortly, the indifference curve map tells us all we need to know in order to find a consumer's optimal consumption bundle. That is, it's important that Ingrid has higher total util-ity along indifference curve I_2 than she does along I_1, but it doesn't matter *how much higher* her total utility is. In other words, we don't have to measure utils in order to understand how consumers make choices.

Economists say that consumer theory requires an "ordinal" measure of utility—one that ranks consumption bundles in terms of desirability—so that we can say that bundle X is better than bundle Y. The theory does not, however, require "cardi-nal" utility, which actually assigns a spe-cific number to the total utility yielded by each bundle.

So why introduce the concept of utils at all? The answer is that it is much easier to understand the basis of rational choice by using the concept of measurable utility.

below I_2. Bundle D, though, generates 519 utils, a higher total utility than A and B. It is on I_3, an indifference curve that lies above I_2. Clearly, Ingrid prefers D to either A or B. And, even more strongly, she prefers D to C.

Properties of Indifference Curves

No two individuals have the same indifference curve map because no two individu-als have the same preferences. But economists believe that, regardless of the person, every indifference curve map has two general properties. These are illustrated in panel (a) of Figure 11-4 on the next page:

- *Indifference curves never cross.* Suppose that we tried to draw an indifference curve map like the one depicted in the left diagram in panel (a), in which two indifference curves cross at A. What is the total utility at A? Is it 100 utils or 200 utils? Indifference curves cannot cross because each consumption bundle must correspond to a unique total utility level—not, as shown at A, two different total utility levels.

- *The farther out an indifference curve lies—the farther it is from the origin—the higher the level of total utility it indicates.* The reason, illustrated in the right diagram in panel (a), is that we assume that more is better—we consider only the consump-tion bundles for which the consumer is not satiated. Bundle B, on the outer indif-ference curve, contains more of both goods than bundle A on the inner indiffer-ence curve. So B, because it generates a higher total utility level (200 utils), lies on a higher indifference curve than A.

  Furthermore, economists believe that, for most goods, consumers' indifference curve maps also have two additional properties. They are illustrated in panel (b) of Figure 11-4:

- *Indifference curves slope downward.* Here, too, the reason is that more is better. The left diagram in panel (b) shows four consumption bundles on the same indiffer-ence curve: W, X, Y, and Z. By definition, these consumption bundles yield the same level of total utility. But as you move along the curve to the right, from W to Z, the quantity of rooms consumed increases. The only way a person can consume more rooms without gaining utility is by giving up some restaurant meals. So the indifference curve must slope downward.

- *Indifference curves have a convex shape.* The right diagram in panel (b) shows that the slope of each indifference curve changes as you move down the curve to the right: the curve gets flatter. If you move up an indifference curve to the left, the curve gets steeper. So the indifference curve is steeper at A than it is at B. When this occurs, we say that an indifference curve has a *convex* shape—it is bowed-in toward the ori-gin. This feature arises from diminishing marginal utility, a principle we discussed in Chapter 10. Recall that when a consumer has diminishing marginal utility, consumption of another unit of a good generates a smaller increase in total utility than the previous unit consumed. In the next section, we will examine in detail how diminishing marginal utility gives rise to convex-shaped indifference curves.

Goods that satisfy all four properties of indifference curve maps are called *ordinary goods*. The vast majority of goods in any consumer's utility function fall into this category. In the next section, we will define ordinary goods and see the key role that diminishing marginal utility plays for them.

FIGURE 11-4   Properties of Indifference Curves

(a) Properties of All Indifference Curves

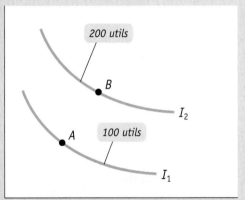

(b) Additional Properties of Indifference Curves for Ordinary Goods

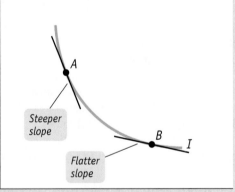

Panel (a) represents two general properties that all indifference curve maps share. The left diagram shows why indifference curves cannot cross: if they did, a consumption bundle such as A would yield both 100 and 200 utils, a contradiction. The right diagram of panel (a) shows that indifference curves that are farther out yield higher total utility: bundle B, which contains more of both goods than bundle A, yields higher total utility. Panel (b) depicts two additional properties of indifference curves for ordinary goods. The left dia-gram of panel (b) shows that indifference curves slope downward: as you move down the curve from bundle W to bundle Z, consumption of rooms increases. To keep total utility constant, this must be offset by a reduction in quantity of restaurant meals. The right diagram of panel (b) shows a convex-shaped indifference curve. The slope of the indifference curve gets flatter as you move down the curve to the right, a feature arising from diminishing marginal utility.

▶ **CHECK YOUR UNDERSTANDING** 11-1

1. The accompanying table shows Samantha's preferences for consumption bundles composed of chocolate kisses and licorice drops.

   a. With chocolate kisses on the horizontal axis and licorice drops on the vertical axis, draw hypothetical indifference curves for Samantha and locate the bundles on the curves. Assume that both items are ordinary goods.

Consumption bundle	Quantity of chocolate kisses	Quantity of licorice drops	Total utility (utils)
A	1	3	6
B	2	3	10
C	3	1	6
D	2	1	4

   b. Suppose you don't know the number of utils provided by each bundle. Assuming that more is better, predict Samantha's ranking of each of the four bundles to the extent possible.

2. On the left diagram in panel (a) of Figure 11-4, draw a point B anywhere on the 200-util indifference curve and a point C anywhere on the 100-util indifference curve (but *not* at the same location as point A). By comparing the utils generated by bundles A and B and those generated by bundles A and C, explain why indifference curves cannot cross.

Solutions appear at back of book.

Indifference Curves and Consumer Choice

At the beginning of the last section, we used indifference curves to represent the preferences of Ingrid, whose consumption bundles consist of rooms and restaurant meals. Our next step is to show how to use Ingrid's indifference curve map to find her utility-maximizing consumption bundle given her budget constraint, the fact that she must choose a consumption bundle that costs no more than her total income.

It's important to understand how our analysis here relates to what we did in Chapter 10. We are not offering a new theory of consumer behavior in this chapter—just as in Chapter 10, consumers are assumed to maximize total utility. In particular, we know that consumers will follow the *optimal consumption rule* from Chapter 10: the optimal consumption bundle lies on the budget line, and the marginal utility per dollar is the same for every good in the bundle.

But as we'll see shortly, we can derive this optimal consumer behavior in a somewhat different way—a way that yields deeper insights into consumer choice.

The Marginal Rate of Substitution

The first element of our approach is a new concept, the *marginal rate of substitution*. The essence of this concept is illustrated in Figure 11-5 on the next page.

Recall from the last section that for most goods, consumers' indifference curves are downward sloping and convex. Figure 11-5 shows such an indifference curve. The points labeled V, W, X, Y, and Z all lie on this indifference curve—that is, they represent consumption bundles that yield Ingrid the same level of total utility. The table accompanying the figure shows the components of each of the bundles. As we move along the indifference curve from V to Z, Ingrid's consumption of housing steadily increases from 2 rooms to 6 rooms, her consumption of restaurant meals steadily decreases from 30 meals to 10 meals, and her total utility is kept constant. As we move down the indifference curve, then, Ingrid is trading more of one good in place of less of the other, with the *terms* of that trade-off—the ratio of additional rooms consumed to restaurant meals sacrificed—chosen to keep her total utility constant.

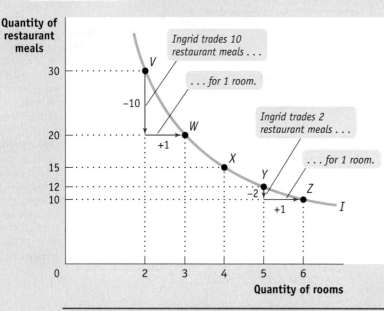

FIGURE 11-5 **The Changing Slope of an Indifference Curve**

Ingrid trades 10 restaurant meals . . .

. . . for 1 room.

Ingrid trades 2 restaurant meals . . .

. . . for 1 room.

Consumption bundle	Quantity of rooms	Quantity of restaurant meals
V	2	30
W	3	20
X	4	15
Y	5	12
Z	6	10

This indifference curve is downward sloping and convex, implying that restaurant meals and rooms are ordinary goods for Ingrid. As Ingrid moves down her indifference curve from V to Z, she trades reduced consumption of restaurant meals for increased consumption of housing. However, the terms of that trade-off change. As she moves from V to W, she is willing to give up 10 restaurant meals in return for 1 more room. As her consumption of rooms rises and her consumption of restaurant meals falls, she is willing to give up fewer restaurant meals in return for each additional room. The flattening of the slope as you move from left to right arises from diminishing marginal utility.

Notice that the quantity of restaurant meals that Ingrid is willing to give up in return for an additional room changes along the indifference curve. As we move from V to W, housing consumption rises from 2 to 3 rooms and restaurant meal consumption falls from 30 to 20—a trade-off of 10 restaurant meals for 1 additional room. But as we move from Y to Z, housing consumption rises from 5 to 6 rooms and restaurant meal consumption falls from 12 to 10, a trade-off of only 2 restaurant meals for an additional room.

To put it in terms of slopes, the slope of the indifference curve between V and W is −10: the change in restaurant meal consumption, −10, divided by the change in housing consumption, 1. Similarly, the slope of the indifference curve between Y and Z is −2. So the indifference curve gets flatter as we move down it to the right—that is, it has a convex shape, one of the four properties of an indifference curve for ordinary goods.

Why does the trade-off change in this way? Let's think about it intuitively, then work through it more carefully. When Ingrid moves down her indifference curve, whether from V to W or from Y to Z, she gains utility from her additional consumption of housing but loses an equal amount of utility from her reduced consumption of restaurant meals. But at each step, the initial position from which Ingrid begins is different. At V, Ingrid consumes only a small quantity of rooms; because of diminishing marginal utility, her marginal utility per room at that point is high. At V, then, an additional room adds a lot to Ingrid's total utility. But at V she already consumes a large quantity of restaurant meals, so her marginal utility of restaurant meals is low at that point. This means that it takes a large reduction in her quantity of restaurant meals consumed to offset the increased utility she gets from the extra room of housing.

At Y, in contrast, Ingrid consumes a much larger quantity of rooms and a much smaller quantity of restaurant meals than at V. This means that an additional room adds fewer utils, and a restaurant meal forgone costs more utils, than at *V*. So Ingrid is willing to give up fewer restaurant meals in return for another room of housing at *Y* (where she gives up 2 meals for 1 room) than she is at *V* (where she gives up 10 meals for 1 room).

Now let's express the same idea—that the trade-off Ingrid is willing to make depends on where she is starting from—by using a little math. We do this by examining how the slope of the indifference curve changes as we move down it. Moving down the indifference curve—reducing restaurant meal consumption and increasing housing consumption—will produce two opposing effects on Ingrid's total utility: lower restaurant meal consumption will reduce her total utility, but higher housing consumption will raise her total utility. And since we are moving down the indifference curve, these two effects must exactly cancel out:

Along the indifference curve:
  (11-1) (Change in total utility due to lower restaurant meal consumption) +
         (Change in total utility due to higher housing consumption) = 0

or, rearranging terms,

Along the indifference curve:
  (11-2) −(Change in total utility due to lower restaurant meal consumption) =
         (Change in total utility due to higher housing consumption)

Let's now focus on what happens as we move only a short distance down the indifference curve, trading off a small increase in housing consumption in place of a small decrease in restaurant meal consumption. Following our notation from Chapter 10, let's use MU_R and MU_M to represent the marginal utility of rooms and restaurant meals, respectively, and ΔQ_R and ΔQ_M to represent the changes in room and meal consumption, respectively. In general, the change in total utility caused by a small change in consumption of a good is equal to the change in consumption multiplied by the *marginal utility* of that good. This means that we can calculate the change in Ingrid's total utility generated by a change in her consumption bundle using the following equations:

  (11-3) Change in total utility due to a change in restaurant meal consumption
         $= MU_M \times \Delta Q_M$

and

  (11-4) Change in total utility due to a change in housing consumption
         $= MU_R \times \Delta Q_R$

So we can write Equation 11-2 in symbols as:

  (11-5) *Along the indifference curve:* $-MU_M \times \Delta Q_M = MU_R \times \Delta Q_R$

Note that the left-hand side of Equation 11-5 has a minus sign; it represents the loss in total utility from decreased restaurant meal consumption. This must equal the gain in total utility from increased room consumption, represented by the right-hand side of the equation.

What we want to know is how this translates into the slope of the indifference curve. To find the slope, we divide both sides of Equation 11-5 by ΔQ_R, and again by $-MU_M$, in order to get the ΔQ_M, ΔQ_R terms on one side and the MU_R, MU_M terms on the other. This results in:

  (11-6) *Along the indifference curve:* $\dfrac{\Delta Q_M}{\Delta Q_R} = -\dfrac{MU_R}{MU_M}$

The **marginal rate of substitution,** or **MRS,** of good R in place of good M is equal to MU_R/MU_M, the ratio of the marginal utility of R to the marginal utility of M.

The principle of **diminishing marginal rate of substitution** states that the more of good R a person consumes in proportion to good M, the less M he or she is willing to substitute for another unit of R.

Two goods, R and M, are **ordinary goods** in a consumer's utility function when (1) the consumer requires additional units of R to compensate for less M, and vice versa; and (2) the consumer experiences a diminishing marginal rate of substitution when substituting one good in place of another.

The left-hand side of Equation 11-6 is the slope of the indifference curve; it is the rate at which Ingrid is willing to trade rooms (the good on the horizontal axis) in place of restaurant meals (the good on the vertical axis) without changing her total utility level. The right-hand side of Equation 11-6 is minus the ratio of the marginal utility of rooms to the marginal utility of restaurant meals—that is, the ratio of what she gains from one more room to what she gains from one more meal.

Putting all this together, we see that Equation 11-6 shows that, along the indifference curve, the quantity of restaurant meals Ingrid is willing to give up in return for a room, $\Delta Q_M/\Delta Q_R$, is exactly equal to minus the ratio of the marginal utility of a room to that of a meal, $-MU_R/MU_M$. Only when this condition is met will her total utility level remain constant as she consumes more rooms and fewer restaurant meals.

Economists have a special name for the ratio of the marginal utilities found in the right-hand side of Equation 11-6: it is called the **marginal rate of substitution,** or **MRS,** of rooms (the good on the horizontal axis) in place of restaurant meals (the good on the vertical axis). That's because as we slide down Ingrid's indifference curve, we are substituting more rooms in place of fewer restaurant meals in her consumption bundle. As we'll see shortly, the marginal rate of substitution plays an important role in finding the optimal consumption bundle.

Recall that indifference curves get flatter as you move down them to the right. The reason, as we've just discussed, is diminishing marginal utility: as Ingrid consumes more housing and fewer restaurant meals, her marginal utility from housing falls and her marginal utility from restaurant meals rises. So her marginal rate of substitution, which is equal to minus the slope of her indifference curve, falls as she moves down the indifference curve.

The flattening of indifference curves as you slide down them to the right—which reflects the same logic as the principle of diminishing marginal utility—is known as the principle of **diminishing marginal rate of substitution.** It says that an individual who consumes only a little bit of good A and a lot of good B will be willing to trade off a lot of B in return for one more unit of A; an individual who already consumes a lot of A and not much B will be less willing to make that trade-off.

We can illustrate this point by referring back to Figure 11-5. At point V, a bundle with a high proportion of restaurant meals to rooms, Ingrid is willing to forgo 10 restaurant meals in return for 1 room. But at point Y, a bundle with a low proportion of restaurant meals to rooms, she is willing to forgo only 2 restaurant meals in return for 1 room.

From this example we can see that, in Ingrid's utility function, rooms and restaurant meals possess the two additional properties that characterize ordinary goods. Ingrid requires additional rooms to compensate her for the loss of a meal, and vice versa; so her indifference curves for these two goods slope downward. And her indifference curves are convex: the slope of her indifference curve—*minus* the marginal rate of substitution—becomes flatter as we move down it. In fact, an indifference curve is convex only when it has diminishing marginal rate of substitution—these two conditions are equivalent.

With this information, we can define **ordinary goods,** which account for the great majority of goods in any consumer's utility function. A pair of goods are ordinary goods in a consumer's utility function if they possess two properties: the consumer requires more of one good to compensate for less of the other, and the consumer experiences a diminishing marginal rate of substitution when substituting one good in place of the other.

Next we will see how to determine Ingrid's optimal consumption bundle using indifference curves.

The Tangency Condition

Now let's put some of Ingrid's indifference curves on the same diagram as her budget line, to illustrate an alternative way of representing her optimal consumption choice. Figure 11-6 shows Ingrid's budget line, BL, when her income is $2,400 per month, housing costs $150 per room each month, and restaurant meals cost $30 each. What is her optimal consumption bundle?

FIGURE 11-6

The Optimal Consumption Bundle

The budget line, *BL,* shows Ingrid's possible consumption bundles given an income of $2,400 per month, when rooms cost $150 per month and restaurant meals cost $30 each. I_1, I_2, and I_3 are indifference curves. Consumption bundles such as *B* and *C* are not optimal because Ingrid can move to a higher indifference curve. The optimal consumption bundle is *A,* where the budget line is just tangent to the highest possible indifference curve.

To answer this question, we show several of Ingrid's indifference curves: I_1, I_2, and I_3. Ingrid would like to achieve the total utility level represented by I_3, the highest of the three curves, but she cannot afford to because she is constrained by her income: no consumption bundle on her budget line yields that much total utility. But she shouldn't settle for the level of total utility generated by *B,* which lies on I_1: there are other bundles on her budget line, such as *A,* that clearly yield higher total utility than *B.*

In fact, *A*—a consumption bundle consisting of 8 rooms and 40 restaurant meals per month—is Ingrid's optimal consumption choice. The reason is that *A* lies on the highest indifference curve Ingrid can reach given her income.

At the optimal consumption bundle *A,* Ingrid's budget line *just touches* the relevant indifference curve—the budget line is *tangent* to the indifference curve. This **tangency condition** between the indifference curve and the budget line applies to the optimal consumption bundle when the indifference curves have the typical convex shape: *at the optimal consumption bundle, the budget line just touches—is tangent to—the indifference curve.*

To see why, let's look more closely at how we know that a consumption bundle that *doesn't* satisfy the tangency condition can't be optimal. Reexamining Figure 11-6, we can see that the consumption bundles *B* and *C* are both affordable because they lie on the budget line. However, neither is optimal. Both of them lie on the indifference curve I_1, which cuts through the budget line at both points. But because I_1 cuts through the budget line, Ingrid can do better: she can move down the budget line from *B* or up the budget line from *C,* as indicated by the arrows. In each case, this allows her to get onto a higher indifference curve, I_2, which increases her total utility.

Ingrid cannot, however, do any better than I_2: any other indifference curve either cuts through her budget line or doesn't touch it at all. And the bundle that allows her to achieve I_2 is, of course, her optimal consumption bundle.

The Slope of the Budget Line

Figure 11-6 shows us how to use a graph of the budget line and the indifference curves to find the optimal consumption bundle, the bundle at which the budget line and the indifference curve are tangent. But rather than rely on drawing graphs, we

The **tangency condition** between the indifference curve and the budget line holds when the indifference curve and the budget line just touch. This condition determines the optimal consumption bundle when the indifference curves have the typical convex shape.

The **relative price** of good R in terms of good M is equal to P_R/P_M, the rate at which R trades for M in the market.

can determine the optimal consumption bundle by using a bit of math. As you can see from Figure 11-6, at A, the optimal consumption bundle, the budget line and the indifference curve have the same slope. Why? Because two curves can only touch each other if they have the same slope at their point of tangency. Otherwise, they would cross each other somewhere. And we know that if we are on an indifference curve that crosses the budget line (like I_1 in Figure 11-6), we can't be on the indifference curve that contains the optimal consumption bundle (like I_2).

So we can use information about the slopes of the budget line and the indifference curve to find the optimal consumption bundle. To do that, we must first analyze the slope of the budget line, a fairly straightforward task. We know that Ingrid will get the highest possible utility by spending all of her income and consuming a bundle on her budget line. So we can represent Ingrid's budget line, the consumption bundles available to her when she spends all of her income, with the equation:

$$(11\text{-}7)\quad (Q_R \times P_R) + (Q_M \times P_M) = N$$

where N stands for Ingrid's income. To find the slope of the budget line, we divide its vertical intercept (where the budget line hits the vertical axis) by its horizontal intercept (where it hits the horizontal axis). The vertical intercept is the point at which Ingrid spends all her income on restaurant meals and none on housing (that is, $Q_R = 0$). In that case the number of restaurant meals she consumes is:

$$(11\text{-}8)\quad Q_M = N/P_M = \$2,400/(\$30 \text{ per meal}) = 80 \text{ meals}$$
$$= \text{Vertical intercept of budget line}$$

At the other extreme, Ingrid spends all her income on housing and none on restaurant meals (so that $Q_M = 0$). This means that at the horizontal intercept of the budget line, the number of rooms she consumes is:

$$(11\text{-}9)\quad Q_R = N/P_R = \$2,400/(\$150 \text{ per room}) = 16 \text{ rooms}$$
$$= \text{Horizontal intercept of budget line}$$

Now we have the information needed to find the slope of the budget line. It is:

$$(11\text{-}10)\quad \text{Slope of budget line} = -(\text{Vertical intercept})/(\text{Horizontal intercept})$$

$$= -\frac{\dfrac{N}{P_M}}{\dfrac{N}{P_R}} = -\frac{P_R}{P_M}$$

Notice the minus sign in Equation 11-10; it's there because the budget line slopes downward. The quantity P_R/P_M is known as the **relative price** of rooms in terms of restaurant meals, to distinguish it from an ordinary price in terms of dollars. Because buying one more room requires Ingrid to give up P_R/P_M quantity of restaurant meals, or 5 meals, we can interpret the relative price P_R/P_M as the rate at which a room trades for restaurant meals in the market; it is the price—in terms of restaurant meals—Ingrid has to "pay" to get one more room.

Looking at this another way, the slope of the budget line—minus the relative price—tells us the opportunity cost of each good in terms of the other. The relative price illustrates the opportunity cost to an individual of consuming one more unit of one good in terms of how much of the other good in his or her consumption bundle must be forgone. This opportunity cost arises from the consumer's limited resources—his or her limited budget. It's useful to note that Equations 11-8, 11-9, and 11-10 give us all the information we need about what happens to the budget line when relative price or income changes. From Equations 11-8 and 11-9 we can see that a change in income, N, leads to a parallel shift of the budget line: both the vertical and horizontal intercepts will shift. That is, how far out the budget line is from the origin depends on the consumer's income. If a consumer's income rises, the budget line moves outward. If the consumer's income shrinks, the budget line shifts inward. In each case, the slope of the budget line stays the same because the relative price of one good in terms of the other does not change.

In contrast, a change in the relative price P_R/P_M will lead to a change in the slope of the budget line. We'll analyze these changes in the budget line and how the optimal consumption bundle changes when the relative price changes or when income changes in greater detail later in the chapter.

> The **relative price rule** says that at the optimal consumption bundle, the marginal rate of substitution between two goods is equal to their relative price.

Prices and the Marginal Rate of Substitution

Now we're ready to bring together the slope of the budget line and the slope of the indifference curve to find the optimal consumption bundle. From Equation 11-6, we know that the slope of the indifference curve at any point is equal to minus the marginal rate of substitution:

(11-11) Slope of indifference curve $= -\dfrac{MU_R}{MU_M}$

As we've already noted, at the optimal consumption bundle the slope of the budget line and the slope of the indifference curve are equal. We can write this formally by putting Equations 11-10 and 11-11 together, which gives us the **relative price rule** for finding the optimal consumption bundle:

(11-12) *At the optimal consumption bundle:* $-\dfrac{MU_R}{MU_M} = -\dfrac{P_R}{P_M}$

or $\dfrac{MU_R}{MU_M} = \dfrac{P_R}{P_M}$

That is, at the optimal consumption bundle, the marginal rate of substitution between any two goods is equal to the ratio of their prices. Or to put it in a more intuitive way, at Ingrid's optimal consumption bundle, the rate at which she would trade a room in exchange for having fewer restaurant meals along her indifference curve, MU_R/MU_M, is equal to the rate at which rooms are traded for restaurant meals in the market, P_R/P_M.

What would happen if this equality did not hold? We can see by examining Figure 11-7 on the next page. There, at point B, the slope of the indifference curve, $-MU_R/MU_M$, is greater in absolute value than the slope of the budget line, $-P_R/P_M$. This means that, at B, Ingrid values an additional room in place of meals *more* than it costs her to buy an additional room and forgo some meals. As a result, Ingrid would be better off moving down her budget line toward A, consuming more rooms and fewer restaurant meals—and because of that, B could not have been her optimal bundle! Likewise, at C, the slope of Ingrid's indifference curve is less than the slope of the budget line. The implication is that, at C, Ingrid values additional meals in place of a room *more* than it costs her to buy additional meals and forgo a room. Again, Ingrid would be better off moving along her budget line—consuming more restaurant meals and fewer rooms—until she reaches A, her optimal consumption bundle.

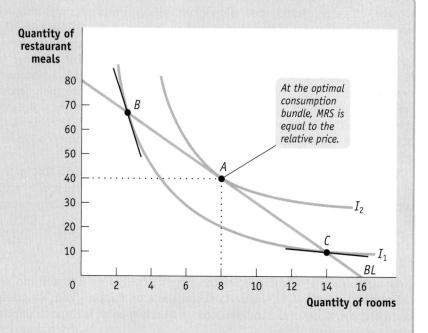

FIGURE 11-7

Understanding the Relative Price Rule

The *relative price* of rooms in terms of restaurant meals is equal to minus the slope of the budget line. The *marginal rate of substitution* of rooms in place of restaurant meals is equal to minus the slope of the indifference curve. The *relative price rule* says that at the optimal consumption bundle, the marginal rate of substitution must equal the relative price. This point can be demonstrated by considering what happens when the marginal rate of substitution is not equal to the relative price. At consumption bundle B, the marginal rate of substitution is larger than the relative price; Ingrid can increase her total utility by moving down her budget line, *BL*. At C, the marginal rate of substitution is smaller than the relative price, and Ingrid can increase her total utility by moving up the budget line. Only at A, where the relative price rule holds, is her total utility maximized given her budget constraint.

At the optimal consumption bundle, MRS is equal to the relative price.

But suppose that we do the following transformation to the last term of Equation 11-12: divide both sides by P_R and multiply both by MU_M. Then the relative price rule becomes (from Chapter 10, Equation 10-3):

(11-13)   *Optimal consumption rule:* $\dfrac{MU_R}{P_R} = \dfrac{MU_M}{P_M}$

So using either the optimal consumption rule (from Chapter 10) or the relative price rule (from this chapter), we find the same optimal consumption bundle.

Preferences and Choices

Now that we have seen how to represent optimal consumption choice in an indifference curve diagram, we can turn briefly to the relationship between consumer preferences and consumer choices.

When we say that two consumers have different preferences, we mean that they have different utility functions. This in turn means that they will have indifference curve maps with different shapes. And those different maps will translate into different consumption choices, even among consumers with the same income and who face the same prices.

To see this, suppose that Ingrid's friend Lars also consumes only housing and restaurant meals. However, Lars has a stronger preference for restaurant meals and a weaker preference for housing. This difference in preferences is shown in Figure 11-8, which shows *two* sets of indifference curves: panel (a) shows Ingrid's preferences and panel (b) shows Lars's preferences. Note the difference in their shapes.

Suppose, as before, that rooms cost $150 per month and restaurant meals cost $30. Let's also assume that both Ingrid and Lars have incomes of $2,400 per month, giving them identical budget lines. Nonetheless, because they have different preferences, they will make different consumption choices, as shown in Figure 11-8. Ingrid will choose 8 rooms and 40 restaurant meals; Lars will choose 4 rooms and 60 restaurant meals.

FIGURE 11-8

Differences in Preferences

Ingrid and Lars have different preferences, reflected in the different shapes of their indifference curve maps. So they will choose different consumption bundles even when they have the same possible choices. Both of them have an income of $2,400 per month and face prices of $30 per meal and $150 per room. Panel (a) shows Ingrid's consumption choice: 8 rooms and 40 restaurant meals. Panel (b) shows Lars's choice: even though he has the same budget line, he consumes fewer rooms and more restaurant meals.

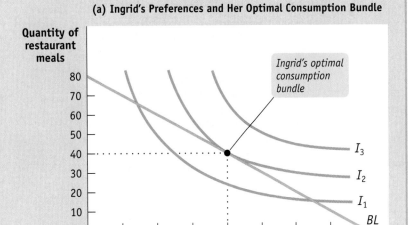

(a) Ingrid's Preferences and Her Optimal Consumption Bundle

(b) Lars's Preferences and His Optimal Consumption Bundle

►ECONOMICS IN ACTION

Rats and Rational Choice

Let's admit it: the theory of consumer choice does not bear much resemblance to the way most of us think about our consumption decisions. The purpose of the theory is, however, to help economists think systematically about how a rational consumer would behave. The practical question is whether consumers actually behave rationally.

One simple test for rationality would look like the one shown in Figure 11-9 on the next page. First, give a consumer the budget line labeled BL_1, and observe what consumption bundle the consumer chooses; the result is indicated in the figure as A. Then change the budget constraint, so that the new budget line is BL_2. Here the consumer is still able to afford the original consumption bundle A but also has some new choices available.

FIGURE 11-9

A Test for Rationality

Suppose that a consumer has the budget line BL_1 and chooses the consumption bundle A. If that consumer is now given a new budget line such as BL_2, it would be irrational to choose a bundle such as B; the consumer could have afforded that bundle before but chose A instead. A rational consumer would always at least stay at A or choose a new consumption bundle that was not affordable before, such as C. It's difficult to test people in this way—but it works for rats!

Would a rational consumer then choose a bundle like B? No. The reason is that B lies *inside* the original budget line—that is, when the budget line was BL_1, the consumer could have afforded it but chose A instead. It would be irrational to choose it now, when A is still available. So the new choice for a rational consumer must be either A or some bundle that has just become available, such as C.

It's hard to perform experiments like this on people—at any rate, it's not ethical (though more indirect experiments do suggest that people behave more or less rationally in their consumption choices). However, there is clear evidence that animals, such as rats, are able to make rational choices!

Economists have conducted experiments in which rats are presented with a "budget constraint"—a limited number of times per hour they can push either of two levers. One of the levers yields small cups of water; the other yields pellets of food. After the rat's choices have been observed, the budget constraint is changed by varying the number of lever pushes required to get each good. Sure enough, the rats satisfy the rule for rational choice.

If rats are rational, can people be far behind? ▲

< < < < < < < < < < < <

▶ CHECK YOUR UNDERSTANDING 11-2

1. Lucinda and Kyle each consume 3 comic books and 6 video games. Lucinda's marginal rate of substitution of books in place of games is 2 and Kyle's is 5.
   a. For each person, find another consumption bundle that yields the same total utility as the current bundle. Who is less willing to trade games for books? In a diagram with books on the horizontal axis and games on the vertical axis, how would this be reflected in differences in the slopes of their indifference curves at their current consumption bundles?
   b. Find the relative price of books in terms of games at which Lucinda's current bundle is optimal. Is Kyle's bundle optimal given this relative price? If not, how should Kyle rearrange his consumption?

Solutions appear at back of book.

Using Indifference Curves: Substitutes and Complements

Now that we've seen how to analyze consumer choice using indifference curves, we can get some payoffs from our new technique. First up is a new insight into the distinction between *substitutes* and *complements.*

Back in Chapter 3, we pointed out that the price of one good often affects the demand for another but that the direction of this effect can go either way: a rise in the price of tea increases the demand for coffee, but a rise in the price of cream reduces the demand for coffee. Tea and coffee are substitutes; cream and coffee are complements.

But what determines whether two goods are substitutes or complements? It depends on the shape of a consumer's indifference curves. This relationship can be illustrated with two extreme cases: the cases of *perfect substitutes* and *perfect complements*.

> Two goods are **perfect substitutes** if the marginal rate of substitution of one good in place of the other good is constant, regardless of how much of each an individual consumes.

Perfect Substitutes

Consider Cokie, who likes cookies. She isn't particular: it doesn't matter to her whether she has 3 peanut butter cookies and 7 chocolate chip cookies, or vice versa. What would her indifference curves between peanut butter and chocolate chip cookies look like?

The answer is that they would be straight lines like I_1 and I_2 in Figure 11-10. For example, I_1 shows that any combination of peanut butter cookies and chocolate chip cookies that adds up to 10 cookies yields Cokie the same utility.

A consumer whose indifference curves are straight lines is always willing to substitute the same amount of one good in place of one unit of the other, regardless of how much of either good he or she consumes. Cokie, for example, is always willing to accept one less peanut butter cookie in exchange for one more chocolate chip cookie, making her marginal rate of substitution *constant*.

When indifference curves are straight lines, we say that goods are **perfect substitutes.** When two goods are perfect substitutes, there is only one relative price at which consumers will be willing to purchase both goods; a slightly higher or lower relative price will cause consumers to buy only one of the two goods.

Figure 11-11 on the next page illustrates this point. The indifference curves are the same as those in Figure 11-10, but now we include Cokie's budget line, *BL*. In each panel we assume that Cokie has $12 to spend. In panel (a) we assume that

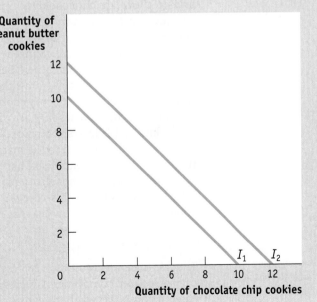

FIGURE 11-10

Perfect Substitutes

Two goods are perfect substitutes when the marginal rate of substitution does not depend on the quantities consumed. In that case, the indifference curves are straight lines.

FIGURE **11-11** | Consumer Choice Between Perfect Substitutes

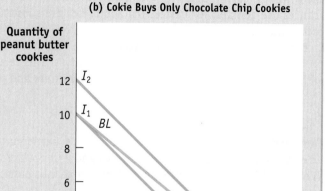

When two goods are perfect substitutes, small price changes lead to large changes in the consumption bundle. In panel (a), the relative price of chocolate chip cookies is slightly higher than the marginal rate of substitution of chocolate chip cookies in place of peanut butter cookies; this is enough to induce Cokie to choose consumption bun-

dle *A*, which consists entirely of peanut butter cookies. In panel (b), the relative price of chocolate chip cookies is slightly lower than the marginal rate of substitution of chocolate chip cookies in place of peanut butter cookies; this induces Cokie to choose bundle *B*, consisting entirely of chocolate chip cookies.

chocolate chip cookies cost $1.20 and peanut butter cookies cost $1.00. Cokie's optimal consumption bundle is then at point *A*: she buys 12 peanut butter cookies and no chocolate chip cookies. In panel (b) the situation is reversed: chocolate chip cookies cost $1.00 and peanut butter cookies cost $1.20. In this case, her optimal consumption is at point *B*, where she consumes only chocolate chip cookies.

Why does such a small change in the price cause Cokie to switch all her consumption from one good to the other? Because her marginal rate of substitution is constant and therefore doesn't depend on the composition of her consumption bundle. If the relative price of chocolate chip cookies is more than the marginal rate of substitution of chocolate chip cookies in place of peanut butter cookies, she buys only peanut butter cookies; if it is less, she buys only chocolate chip. And if the relative price of chocolate chip cookies is equal to the marginal rate of substitution, Cokie can maximize her utility by buying any bundle on her budget line. That is, she will be equally happy with any combination of chocolate chip cookies and peanut butter cookies that she can afford. As a result, in this case we cannot predict which particular bundle she will choose among all the bundles that lie on her budget line.

Perfect Complements

The case of perfect substitutes represents one extreme form of consumer preferences; the case of perfect complements represents the other. Goods are **perfect complements** when a consumer wants to consume two goods in the same ratio, regardless of their relative price.

Two goods are **perfect complements** when a consumer wants to consume the goods in the same ratio regardless of their relative price.

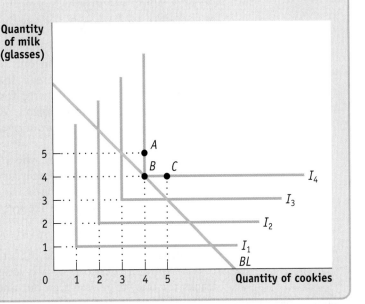

FIGURE 11-12

Perfect Complements

When two goods are perfect complements, a consumer wants to consume the goods in the same ratio regardless of their relative price. Indifference curves take the form of right angles. In this case, Aaron will choose to consume 4 glasses of milk and 4 cookies (bundle B) regardless of the slope of the budget line passing through B. The reason is that neither an additional glass of milk without an additional cookie (bundle A) nor an additional cookie without an additional glass of milk (bundle C) adds to his total utility.

Suppose that Aaron likes cookies and milk—but only together. An extra cookie without an extra glass of milk yields no additional utility; neither does an extra glass of milk without another cookie. In this case, his indifference curves will form right angles, as shown in Figure 11-12.

To see why, consider the three bundles labeled A, B, and C. At B, on I_4, Aaron consumes 4 cookies and 4 glasses of milk. At A, he consumes 4 cookies and 5 glasses of milk; but the extra glass of milk adds nothing to his utility. So A is on the same indifference curve as B, I_4. Similarly, at C he consumes 5 cookies and 4 glasses of milk, but this yields the same total utility as 4 cookies and 4 glasses of milk. So C is also on the same indifference curve, I_4.

Also shown in Figure 11-12 is a budget line that would allow Aaron to choose bundle B. The important point is that the slope of the budget line has no effect on his relative consumption of cookies and milk. This means that he will always consume the two goods in the same proportions regardless of prices—which makes the goods perfect complements.

You may be wondering what happened to the marginal rate of substitution in Figure 11-12. That is, exactly what is Aaron's marginal rate of substitution between cookies and milk, given that he is unwilling to make any substitutions between them? The answer is that in the case of perfect complements, the marginal rate of substitution is *undefined* because an individual's preferences don't allow *any* substitution between goods.

Less Extreme Cases

There are real-world examples of pairs of goods that are very close to being perfect substitutes. For example, the list of ingredients on a package of Bisquick pancake mix says that it contains "soybean and/or cottonseed oil": the producer uses whichever is cheaper, since consumers can't tell the difference. There are other pairs of goods that are very close to being perfect complements—for example, cars and tires.

In most cases, however, the possibilities for substitution lie somewhere between these extremes. In some cases, as illustrated by the following Economics in Action, it isn't easy to be sure whether goods are substitutes or complements.

➤ECONOMICS IN ACTION

Publicity or Piracy?

When the practice of audio file-sharing took off in the late 1990s, a controversy erupted at the same time. On one side were musicians and the music industry, who argued that the widespread sharing of audio files was a modern version of theft. Listeners were not paying for the music they enjoyed, depriving performers of their rightful compensation. Why, they argued, spend years and hundreds of thousands of dollars to produce a CD when file-sharing would rob them of any reward?

On the other side were those who argued that instead of serving as a substitute for buying the CD, file-sharing actually acted as a complement. That is, after hearing one or two tracks from a CD via file-sharing, a listener was more likely to go out and buy the CD. So file-sharing acted like free publicity, allowing an artist to reach a wider audience.

Who was right?

It turns out that the music industry and artists were right. Most people seem to want only the best one or two songs on a CD. Once they've downloaded those tracks for free, they won't go out and buy the CD. So file-sharing and the purchase of a CD are substitutes, not complements. As this pattern became clear, the music industry went to court and in 2001 they forced free file-sharing operations like Napster to close, claiming copyright infringement. The music industry then picked up where Napster left off, creating the for-profit industry of audio file downloads that prevails today. (In 2003, Napster re-opened as a for-payment download service.) ▲

< < < < < < < < < < < <

➤ CHECK YOUR UNDERSTANDING 11-3

1. In each of the following cases, determine whether the two goods are perfect substitutes, perfect complements, or ordinary goods. Explain your answer, paying particular attention to the marginal rate of substitution of one good in place of the other good.
   a. Sanjay cares only about the number of jelly beans he receives and not about whether they are banana-flavored or pineapple-flavored.
   b. Hillary's marginal utility of cherry pie goes up as she has more scoops of vanilla ice cream to go with each slice. But she is willing to consume some cherry pie without any vanilla ice cream.
   c. Despite repeated reductions in price, customers won't buy software programs made by Omnisoft Corporation unless the company also sells the computer operating system that enables a computer to read these software programs.
   d. Darnell works part time at the campus bookstore. The manager has asked him to work additional hours this week. Darnell is willing to do additional work, but he finds that the more hours he has already worked, the less willing he is to work yet another hour. (*Hint:* Think of the goods in question as being income and leisure time.)

Solutions appear at back of book.

Prices, Income, and Demand

Let's return now to Ingrid's consumption choices. In the situation we've considered, her income was $2,400 per month, housing cost $150 per room, and restaurant meals cost $30 each. Her optimal consumption bundle, as seen in Figure 11-7, contained 8 rooms and 40 restaurant meals.

Let's now ask how her consumption choice would change if either the rent per room or her income changed. As we'll see, we can put these pieces together to deepen our understanding of consumer demand.

The Effects of a Price Increase

Suppose that for some reason there is a sharp increase in housing prices. Ingrid must now pay $600 per room instead of $150. Meanwhile, the price of restaurant meals and her income remain unchanged. How does this change affect her consumption choices?

When the price of rooms rises, the relative price of rooms in terms of restaurant meals rises; as a result, Ingrid's budget line changes (for the worse—but we'll get to that). She responds to that change by choosing a new consumption bundle.

Figure 11-13 shows Ingrid's original (BL_1) and new (BL_2) budget lines—again, under the assumption that her income remains constant at $2,400 per month. With housing costing $150 per room and a restaurant meal costing $30, her budget line, BL_1, intersected the horizontal axis at 16 rooms and the vertical axis at 80 restaurant meals. After the price of a room rises to $600 per room, the budget line, BL_2, still hits the vertical axis at 80 restaurant meals, but it hits the horizontal axis at only 4 rooms. That's because we know from Equation (11-9) that the new horizontal intercept of the budget line is now $2,400/$600 = 4. Her budget line has rotated inward and become steeper, reflecting the new, higher relative price of a room in terms of restaurant meals.

Figure 11-14 on the next page shows how Ingrid responds to her new circumstances. Her original optimal consumption bundle consists of 8 rooms and 40 meals. After her budget line rotates in response to the change in relative price, she finds her new optimal consumption bundle by choosing the point on BL_2 that brings her to as high an indifference curve as possible. At the new optimal consumption bundle, she consumes fewer rooms and more restaurant meals than before: 1 room and 60 restaurant meals.

PITFALLS

"OTHER THINGS EQUAL," REVISITED

One of the biggest sources of confusion and error in economics—both in the classroom and in the real world—is failure to keep in mind the principle that all economic relationships are defined "other things equal." You may recall from Chapter 3 that a demand curve shows the effect of a good's price on its quantity demanded, *other things equal*—that is, all other things that influence demand being unchanged. Among those "other things" are the prices of other goods and the incomes of consumers.

To see how important it is to be clear about what is being held constant, let's compare two experiments. First, what happens to Ingrid's budget line if we increase the price of rooms, holding the price of restaurant meals and Ingrid's income constant? Second, what happens to her budget line if we increase the price of housing and *at the same time also increase the price of restaurant meals and Ingrid's income*?

We've just seen the effects of raising the price of rooms from $150 per month to $600. But now imagine that the price of restaurant meals also quadruples from $30 to $120 and that Ingrid's income quadruples from $2,400 to $9,600 per month. How does her budget line change?

The answer (check it yourself) is that quadrupling all three numbers—the price of rooms, the price of restaurant meals, and Ingrid's income—has *no* effect on her budget line. Because the relative price is unchanged, it won't affect her consumption choice. So the law of demand, which says that increasing the price of a good reduces the quantity demanded, is only an "other things equal" proposition; a higher price results in a lower quantity demanded, holding other prices and income constant.

FIGURE 11-13

Effects of a Price Increase on the Budget Line

An increase in the price of rooms, holding the price of restaurant meals constant, increases the relative price of rooms in terms of restaurant meals. As a result, Ingrid's original budget line, BL_1, rotates inward to BL_2. Her maximum possible purchase of restaurant meals is unchanged, but her maximum possible purchase of rooms is reduced.

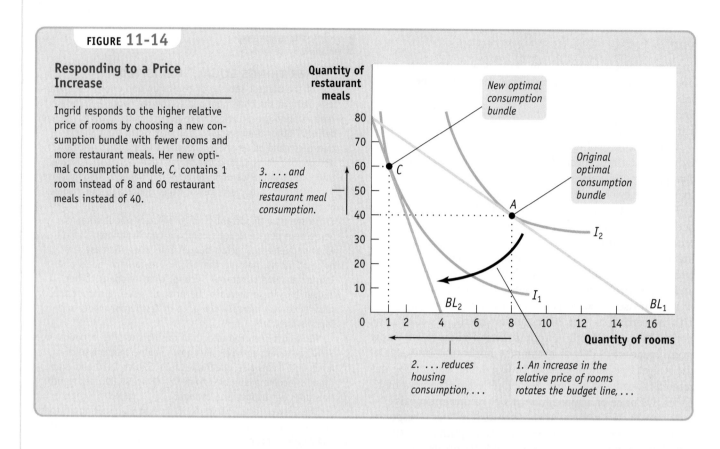

FIGURE 11-14

Responding to a Price Increase

Ingrid responds to the higher relative price of rooms by choosing a new consumption bundle with fewer rooms and more restaurant meals. Her new optimal consumption bundle, *C*, contains 1 room instead of 8 and 60 restaurant meals instead of 40.

3. . . . and increases restaurant meal consumption.

New optimal consumption bundle

Original optimal consumption bundle

2. . . . reduces housing consumption, . . .

1. An increase in the relative price of rooms rotates the budget line, . . .

Why does Ingrid's consumption of rooms fall? Part—but only part—of the reason is that the rise in the price of rooms reduces her purchasing power, making her poorer. That is, the higher relative price of rooms rotates her budget line inward toward the origin, reducing her consumption possibilities and putting her on a lower indifference curve. In a sense, when she faces a higher price of housing, it's as if her income declined.

To understand this effect, and to see why it isn't the whole story, let's consider a different change in Ingrid's circumstances: a change in her income.

Income and Consumption

In Chapter 3 we learned about the individual demand curve, which shows how a consumer's consumption choice will change as the price of one good changes, holding income and the prices of other goods constant. That is, movement along the individual demand curve primarily shows the substitution effect, as we learned in Chapter 10—how quantity consumed changes in response to changes in the *relative price* of the two goods. But we can also ask how the consumption choice will change if *income* changes, holding relative price constant.

Before we proceed, it's important to understand how a change in income, holding relative price constant, affects the budget line. Suppose that Ingrid's income fell from $2,400 to $1,200 and we hold prices constant at $150 per room and $30 per restaurant meal. As a result, the maximum number of rooms she can afford drops from 16 to 8, and the maximum

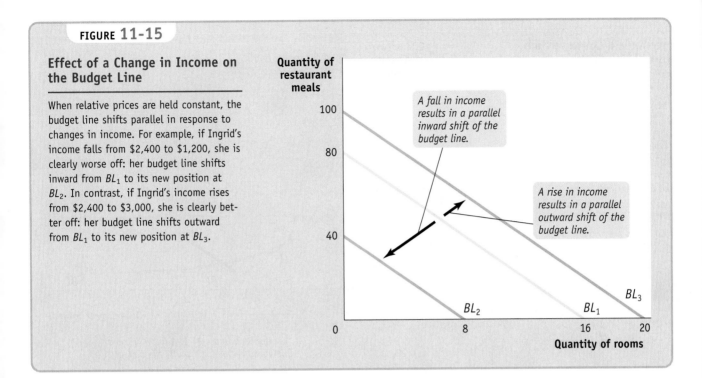

FIGURE 11-15

Effect of a Change in Income on the Budget Line

When relative prices are held constant, the budget line shifts parallel in response to changes in income. For example, if Ingrid's income falls from $2,400 to $1,200, she is clearly worse off: her budget line shifts inward from BL_1 to its new position at BL_2. In contrast, if Ingrid's income rises from $2,400 to $3,000, she is clearly better off: her budget line shifts outward from BL_1 to its new position at BL_3.

A fall in income results in a parallel inward shift of the budget line.

A rise in income results in a parallel outward shift of the budget line.

number of restaurant meals drops from 80 to 40. In other words, Ingrid's consumption possibilities have shrunk, as shown by the parallel inward shift of the budget line in Figure 11-15 from BL_1 to BL_2. It's a parallel shift because the slope of the budget line—the relative price—remains unchanged when income changes. Alternatively, suppose Ingrid's income rises from $2,400 to $3,000. She can now afford a maximum of 20 rooms or 100 meals, leading to a *parallel outward shift* of the budget line—the shift from BL_1 to BL_3 in Figure 11-15. In this case, Ingrid's consumption possibilities have expanded.

Now we are ready to consider how Ingrid responds to a direct change in income—that is, a change in her income level holding relative price constant. Figure 11-16 on the next page compares Ingrid's budget line and optimal consumption choice at an income of $2,400 per month ($BL_1$) with her budget line and optimal consumption choice at an income of $1,200 per month ($BL_2$), keeping prices constant at $150 per room and $30 per restaurant meal. Point A is Ingrid's optimal consumption bundle at an income of $2,400, and point B is her optimal consumption bundle at an income of $1,200. In each case, her optimal consumption bundle is given by the point at which the budget line is tangent to the indifference curve. As you can see, at the lower income her budget line shifts inward compared to her budget line at the higher income but maintains the same slope because relative price has not changed.

This means that she must reduce her consumption of either housing or restaurant meals, or both. As a result, she is at a lower level of total utility, represented by a lower indifference curve.

As it turns out, Ingrid chooses to consume less of both goods when her income falls: as her income goes from $2,400 to $1,200, her consumption of housing falls from 8 to 4 rooms and her consumption of restaurant meals falls from 40 to 20. This is because in her utility function both goods are *normal goods,* as defined in Chapter 3: goods for which demand increases when income rises and for which demand decreases when income falls.

Although most goods are normal goods, we also pointed out in Chapter 6 that some goods are *inferior goods,* goods for which demand moves in the opposite

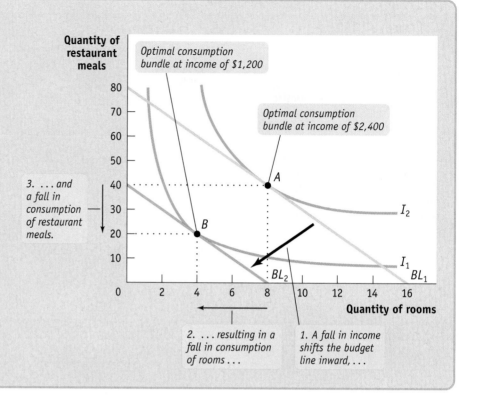

FIGURE 11-16

Income and Consumption: Normal Goods

At a monthly income of $2,400, Ingrid chooses bundle *A*, consisting of 8 rooms and 40 restaurant meals. When relative price remains unchanged, a fall in income shifts her budget line inward to BL_2. At a monthly income of $1,200, she chooses bundle *B*, consisting of 4 rooms and 20 restaurant meals. Since Ingrid's consumption of both restaurant meals and rooms falls when her income falls, both goods are normal goods.

Optimal consumption bundle at income of $1,200

Optimal consumption bundle at income of $2,400

3. ...and a fall in consumption of restaurant meals.

2. ...resulting in a fall in consumption of rooms...

1. A fall in income shifts the budget line inward, ...

direction to the change in income: demand decreases when income rises, and demand increases when income falls. An example might be second-hand furniture. Whether a good is an inferior good depends on the consumer's indifference curve map. Figure 11-17 illustrates such a case, where second-hand furniture is

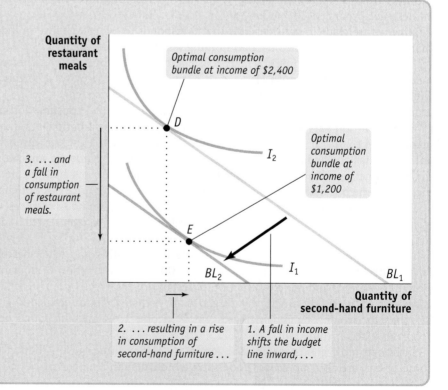

FIGURE 11-17

Income and Consumption: An Inferior Good

When Ingrid's income falls from $2,400 to $1,200, her optimal consumption bundle changes from *D* to *E*. Her consumption of second-hand furniture increases, implying that second-hand furniture is an inferior good. In contrast, her consumption of restaurant meals falls, implying that restaurant meals are a normal good.

Optimal consumption bundle at income of $2,400

Optimal consumption bundle at income of $1,200

3. ...and a fall in consumption of restaurant meals.

2. ...resulting in a rise in consumption of second-hand furniture...

1. A fall in income shifts the budget line inward, ...

measured on the horizontal axis and restaurant meals are measured on the vertical axis. Note that when Ingrid's income falls from $2,400 ($BL_1$) to $1,200 ($BL_2$), and her optimal consumption bundle goes from D to E, her consumption of second-hand furniture increases—implying that second-hand furniture is an inferior good. Simultaneously, her consumption of restaurant meals decreases—implying that restaurant meals are a normal good.

Income and Substitution Effects

Now that we have examined the effects of a change in income, we can return to the issue of a change in price—and show in a more specific way that the effect of a higher price on demand has an income component.

Figure 11-18 shows, once again, Ingrid's original (BL_1) and new (BL_2) budget lines and consumption choices with a monthly income of $2,400. At a housing price of $150 per room, Ingrid chooses the consumption bundle at A; at a housing price of $600 per room, she chooses the consumption bundle at C.

Let's notice again what happens to Ingrid's budget line after the increase in the price of housing. It continues to hit the vertical axis at 80 restaurant meals; that is, if Ingrid were to spend all her income on restaurant meals, the increase in the price of housing would not affect her. But the new budget line hits the horizontal axis at only 4 rooms. So the budget line has rotated, *shifting inward* and *becoming steeper,* as a consequence of the rise in the relative price of rooms.

We already know what happens: Ingrid's consumption of housing falls from 8 rooms to 1 room. But the figure suggests that there are *two* reasons for the fall in Ingrid's housing consumption. One reason she consumes fewer rooms is that, because of the higher relative price of rooms, the opportunity cost of a room measured in restaurant meals—the quantity of restaurant meals she must give up to consume an additional room—has increased. This change in opportunity cost, which is reflected in the steeper slope of the budget line, gives her an incentive to substitute restaurant meals in place of rooms in her consumption.

FIGURE 11-18

Income and Substitution Effects

The movement from Ingrid's original optimal consumption bundle when the price of rooms is $150, A, to her new optimal consumption bundle when the price of rooms is $600, C, can be decomposed into two parts. The movement from A to B—the movement along the original indifference curve, I_2, as relative price changes—is the pure substitution effect. It captures how her consumption would change if she were given a hypothetical increase in income that just compensates her for the increase in the price of rooms so that her total utility is unchanged. The movement from B to C, the change in consumption when we remove that hypothetical income compensation, is the income effect of the price increase—how her consumption changes as a result of the fall in her purchasing power.

But the other reason Ingrid consumes fewer rooms after their price increases is that the rise in the price of rooms makes her *poorer*. True, her money income hasn't changed. But she must pay more for rooms, and as a result her budget line has rotated inward. So she cannot reach the same level of total utility as before, meaning that her real income has fallen. That is why she ends up on a lower indifference curve.

In the real world, these effects—an increase in the price of a good raises its opportunity cost and also makes consumers poorer—usually go together. But in our imagination we can separate them. In Chapter 10 we introduced the distinction between the *substitution effect* of a price change (the change in consumption that arises from the substitution of the good that is now relatively cheaper in place of the good that is now relatively more expensive) and the *income effect* (the change in consumption caused by the change in purchasing power arising from a price change). Now we can show these two effects more clearly.

To isolate the substitution effect, let's temporarily change the story about why Ingrid faces an increase in rent: it's not that housing has become more expensive, it's the fact that she has moved from Cincinnati to San Jose, where rents are higher. But let's consider a hypothetical scenario—let's suppose momentarily that she earns more in San Jose and that the higher income is just enough to *compensate* her for the higher price of housing, so that her total utility is exactly the same as before.

Figure 11-18 shows her situation before and after the move. The bundle labeled *A* represents Ingrid's original consumption choice: 8 rooms and 40 restaurant meals. When she moves to San Jose, she faces a higher price of housing, so her budget line becomes steeper. But we have just assumed that her move increases her income by just enough to compensate for the higher price of housing—that is, just enough to let her reach the original indifference curve. So her new *hypothetical* optimal consumption bundle is at *B*, where the steeper dashed hypothetical budget line (BL_S) is just tangent to the original indifference curve (I_2). By assuming that we have compensated Ingrid for the loss in purchasing power due to the increase in the price of housing, we isolate the *pure substitution effect* of the change in relative price on her consumption.

At *B*, Ingrid's consumption bundle contains 2 rooms and 120 restaurant meals. This costs $4,800 (2 rooms at $600 each, and 120 meals at $30 each). So if Ingrid faces an increase in the price of housing from $150 to $600 per room, but also experiences a rise in her income from $2,400 to $4,800 per month, she ends up with the same level of total utility.

The movement from *A* to *B* is the pure substitution effect of the price change. It is the effect on Ingrid's consumption choice when we change the relative price of housing while keeping her total utility constant.

Now that we have isolated the substitution effect, we can bring back the income effect of the price change. That's easy: we just go back to the original story, in which Ingrid faces an increase in the price of housing *without* any rise in income. We already know that this leads her to C in Figure 11-18. But we can think of the move from *A* to *C* as taking place in two steps. First, Ingrid moves from *A* to *B*, the substitution effect of the change in relative price. Then we take away the extra income needed to keep her on the original indifference curve, causing her to move to *C*. The movement from *B* to *C* is the additional change in Ingrid's demand that results because the increase in housing prices actually reduces her utility. So this is the income effect of the price change.

We can use Figure 11-18 to confirm that rooms are a normal good in Ingrid's preferences. For normal goods, the income effect and the substitution effect work in the same direction: a price increase induces a fall in quantity consumed by the substitution effect (the move from *A* to *B*) and a fall in quantity consumed by the income effect (the move from *B* to *C*). That's why demand curves for normal goods always slope downward.

What would have happened as a result of the increase in the price of housing if, instead of being a normal good, rooms had been an inferior good for Ingrid? First, the movement from *A* to *B* depicted in Figure 11-18, the substitution effect, would remain unchanged. But an income change causes quantity consumed to move in the opposite direction for an inferior good. So the movement from *B* to *C* shown in Figure 11-18, the income effect for a normal good, would no longer hold. Instead, the income effect for an inferior good would cause Ingrid's quantity of rooms consumed to *increase* from *B*—say, to a bundle consisting of 3 rooms and 20 restaurant meals.

In the end, the demand curves for inferior goods normally slope downward: if Ingrid consumes 3 rooms after the increase in the price of housing, it is still 5 fewer rooms than she consumed before. So although the income effect moves in the opposite direction of the substitution effect in the case of an inferior good, in this example the substitution effect is stronger than the income effect.

But what if there existed a type of inferior good in which the income effect is so strong that it dominates the substitution effect? Would a demand curve for that good then slope upward—that is, would quantity demanded increase when price increases? The answer is yes: you have encountered such a good already—it is called a *Giffen good,* and it was described in For Inquiring Minds in Chapter 10. As we noted there, Giffen goods are rare creatures, but they cannot be ruled out.

Is the distinction between income and substitution effects important in practice? For analyzing the demand for goods, the answer is that it usually isn't that important. However, in Chapter 20 we'll discuss how individuals make decisions about how much of their labor to supply to employers. In that case income and substitution effects work in opposite directions, and the distinction between them becomes crucial.

➤ECONOMICS IN ACTION

How Much Housing?

To illustrate the substitution effect, we offered a hypothetical example in which Ingrid moves from Cincinnati to San Jose, gaining a higher income but facing a higher price of housing. We made up the numbers for that example, but the real comparison between the two cities is not that different.

As we mentioned at the beginning of this chapter, the website bestplaces.net reports that household incomes are more than twice as high in San Jose as they are in Cincinnati but that housing is also far more expensive. The website also offers an estimate of the cost of living—that is, an estimate of how much income a family would need to achieve a "typical" level of utility. According to this estimate, the cost of living in San Jose is also about twice that in Cincinnati. So, on average, families live about as well in the two metropolitan areas.

But they don't live the same way because relative prices are different. Houses are typically smaller in San Jose, with fewer rooms and fewer square feet. Most noticeably, the great majority of new homes in the Cincinnati area are single-family houses on big lots; in San Jose, people are much more likely to live in townhouses or apartments. ▲

> > > > > > > > > > > >

➤ CHECK YOUR UNDERSTANDING 11-4

1. Sammy has $60 in weekly income, the current price of clams is $5 per pound, and the current price of potatoes is $1 per pound. Both are normal goods for Sammy. For each of the following situations, construct a diagram that, like Figure 11-18, shows the substitution effect alone and also shows the substitution and income effects together. Put the quantity of clams (in pounds) on the horizontal axis and the quantity of potatoes (in pounds) on the vertical axis.

a. The price of a pound of clams falls from $5 to $2.50, and the price of a pound of potatoes remains at $1.

b. The price of a pound of clams rises from $5 to $10, and the price of a pound of potatoes remains at $1.

Solutions appear at back of book.

[>> A LOOK AHEAD •••

With the end of this chapter, our analysis of consumer behavior and what lies behind the demand curve is complete. Next we turn to the study of producer behavior under perfect competition. In Chapter 12 we learn about the different types of costs that a producer faces and how a producer determines his or her profit-maximizing level of output. Then in Chapter 13 we will examine how competitive industries behave. On completing Chapters 12 and 13, we will have covered both the demand side (in Chapters 10 and 11) and the supply side of the perfectly competitive market model.]

SUMMARY

1. Preferences can be represented by an **indifference curve map,** a series of **indifference curves.** Each curve shows all the consumption bundles that yield a given level of total utility. Indifference curves have two general properties: they never cross, and greater distance from the origin indicates higher total utility levels. The indifference curves of ordinary goods have two additional properties: they slope downward and are convex in shape.

2. The **marginal rate of substitution,** or **MRS,** of R in place of M—the rate at which a consumer is willing to substitute more R for less M—is equal to MU_R/MU_M and is also equal to minus the slope of the indifference curve when R is on the horizontal axis and M is on the vertical axis. Convex indifference curves get flatter as you move to the right along the horizontal axis and steeper as you move upward along the vertical axis because of *diminishing marginal utility:* a consumer requires more and more units of R to substitute for a forgone unit of M as the amount of R consumed rises relative to the amount of M consumed.

3. Most goods are **ordinary goods,** goods for which a consumer requires additional units of some other good as compensation for giving up some of the good and for which there is **diminishing marginal rate of substitution.**

4. A consumer maximizes utility by moving to the highest indifference curve his or her budget constraint allows. Using the **tangency condition,** the consumer chooses the bundle at which the indifference curve just touches the budget line. At this point, the **relative price** of R in terms of M, P_R/P_M (which is equal to minus the slope of the budget line when R is on the horizontal axis and M is on the vertical axis) is equal to the marginal rate of

substitution of R in place of M, MU_R/MU_M (which is equal to minus the slope of the indifference curve). This gives us the **relative price rule:** at the optimal consumption bundle, the relative price is equal to the marginal rate of substitution. Rearranging this equation also gives us the optimal consumption rule of Chapter 10. Two consumers faced with the same prices and income, but with different preferences and so different indifference curve maps, will make different consumption choices.

5. When the marginal rate of substitution is constant, two goods are **perfect substitutes** and indifference curves are straight lines: there is only one relative price at which the consumer is willing to purchase both goods. When a consumer wants to consume the two goods in the same ratio, regardless of the relative price, the goods are **perfect complements.** In this case, the indifference curves form right angles and the marginal rate of substitution is undefined. The relationship between most goods for most people lies between these two extremes.

6. The effect of a change in price on consumer choice can be decomposed into the substitution effect and the income effect. The substitution effect is shown by a movement along the original indifference curve in response to the change in relative price, as the consumer substitutes more of the relatively cheaper good in place of the relatively more expensive good. The income effect is shown by a change to a new indifference curve, reflecting the fact that a change in a good's price alters the purchasing power of a given level of income.

7. The income and substitution effects work in the same direction for normal goods, ensuring that demand curves slope downward.

KEY TERMS

Indifference curve, p. 274
Indifference curve map, p. 274
Marginal rate of substitution (*MRS*), p. 280
Diminishing marginal rate of substitution, p. 280

Ordinary goods, p. 280
Tangency condition, p. 281
Relative price, p. 282

Relative price rule, p. 283
Perfect substitutes, p. 287
Perfect complements, p. 288

PROBLEMS

1. For each of the following situations, draw a diagram containing three of Isabella's indifference curves.

   a. For Isabella, cars and tires are perfect complements, but in a ratio of 1:4; that is, for each car, Isabella wants exactly four tires. Be sure to label and number the axes of your diagram. Place tires on the horizontal axis and cars on the vertical axis.

   b. Isabella gets utility only from her caffeine intake. She can consume Valley Dew or cola, and Valley Dew contains twice as much caffeine as cola. Be sure to label and number the axes of your diagram. Place cola on the horizontal axis and Valley Dew on the vertical axis.

   c. Isabella gets utility from consuming two goods: leisure time and income. Both have diminishing marginal utility. Be sure to label the axes of your diagram. Place leisure on the horizontal axis and income on the vertical axis.

   d. Isabella can consume two goods: skis and bindings. For each ski she wants exactly one binding. Be sure to label and number the axes of your diagram. Place bindings on the horizontal axis and skis on the vertical axis.

   e. Isabella gets utility from consuming soda. But she gets no utility from consuming water: any more, or any less, water leaves her total utility level unchanged. Be sure to label the axes of your diagram. Place water on the horizontal axis and soda on the vertical axis.

2. Use the four properties of indifference curves for ordinary goods illustrated in Figure 11-4 to answer the following questions.

   a. Can you rank the following two bundles? If so, which property of indifference curves helps you rank them?

   Bundle *A:* 2 movie tickets and 3 cafeteria meals

   Bundle *B:* 4 movie tickets and 8 cafeteria meals

   b. Can you rank the following two bundles? If so, which property of indifference curves helps you rank them?

   Bundle *A:* 2 movie tickets and 3 cafeteria meals

   Bundle *B:* 4 movie tickets and 3 cafeteria meals

   c. Can you rank the following two bundles? If so, which property of indifference curves helps you rank them?

   Bundle *A:* 12 videos and 4 bags of chips

   Bundle *B:* 5 videos and 10 bags of chips

   d. Suppose you are indifferent between the following two bundles:

   Bundle *A:* 10 breakfasts and 4 dinners

   Bundle *B:* 4 breakfasts and 10 dinners

   Now compare bundle *A* and the following bundle:

   Bundle *C:* 7 breakfasts and 7 dinners

   Can you rank bundle *A* and bundle *C*? If so, which property of indifference curves helps you rank them? (*Hint:* It may help if you draw this, placing dinners on the horizontal axis and breakfasts on the vertical axis. And remember that breakfasts and dinners are ordinary goods.)

3. The four properties of indifference curves for ordinary goods illustrated in Figure 11-4 rule out certain indifference curves. Determine whether those general properties allow each of the following indifference curves. If not, state which of the general principles rules out the curves.

   a.

   b.

c.

d.

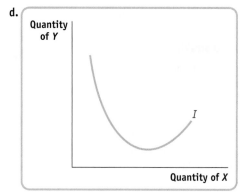

4. Restaurant meals and housing (measured by the number of rooms) are the only two goods that Neha can buy. She has income of $1,000, and the price of each room is $100. The relative price of 1 room in terms of restaurant meals is 5. How many restaurant meals can she buy if she spends all her money on them?

5. Answer the following questions based on two assumptions:
(1) Inflation increases the prices of all goods by 20%.
(2) Ina's income increases from $50,000 to $55,000.

   a. Has Ina's budget line become steeper, less steep, or equally as steep?

   b. Has Ina's budget line shifted outward, inward, or not at all?

6. Kory has an income of $50, which she can spend on two goods: CDs and cups of hot chocolate. Both are normal goods for her. Each CD costs $10, and each cup of hot chocolate costs $2. For each of the following situations, decide whether this is Kory's optimal consumption bundle. If not, what should Kory do to achieve her optimal consumption bundle?

   a. Kory is considering buying 4 CDs and 5 cups of hot chocolate. At that bundle, her marginal rate of substitution of CDs in place of hot chocolate is 1; that is, she would be willing to forgo only 1 cup of hot chocolate to acquire 1 CD.

   b. Kory is considering buying 2 CDs and 15 cups of hot chocolate. Kory's marginal utility of the second CD is 25,

and her marginal utility of the fifteenth cup of hot chocolate is 5.

   c. Kory is considering buying 1 CD and 10 cups of hot chocolate. At that bundle, her marginal rate of substitution of CDs in place of hot chocolate is 5; that is, she would be just willing to exchange 5 cups of hot chocolate for 1 CD.

7. Raul has 4 Cal Ripken and 2 Nolan Ryan baseball cards. The prices of these baseball cards are $24 for Cal and $12 for Nolan. Raul, however, would be willing to exchange 1 Cal card for 1 Nolan card.

   a. What is Raul's marginal rate of substitution of Cal Ripken in place of Nolan Ryan baseball cards?

   b. Can Raul buy and sell baseball cards to make himself better off? How?

   c. Suppose Raul has traded baseball cards and after trading still has some of each kind of card. Also, he now no longer wants to make any more trades. What is his marginal rate of substitution of Cal Ripken in place of Nolan Ryan cards now?

8. Ralph and Lauren are talking about how much they like going to the gym and how much they like eating out at their favorite restaurant and they regularly do some of each. A session at the gym costs the same as a meal at the restaurant. Ralph says that, for his current consumption of gym sessions and restaurant meals, he values 1 more meal twice as much as he values 1 more session at the gym. Lauren is studying economics, and she tells him that his current consumption bundle cannot be optimal.

   a. Is Lauren right? Why or why not? Draw a diagram of Ralph's budget line and the indifference curve that he is on by making his current consumption choice. Place restaurant meals on the horizontal axis and gym sessions on the vertical axis.

   b. How should Ralph adjust his consumption so that it is optimal? Illustrate an optimal choice in your diagram.

9. Sabine can't tell the difference between Coke and Pepsi—the two taste exactly the same to her.

   a. What is Sabine's marginal rate of substitution of Coke in place of Pepsi?

   b. Draw a few of Sabine's indifference curves for Coke and Pepsi. Place Coke on the horizontal axis and Pepsi on the vertical axis.

   c. Sabine has $6 to spend on cola this week. Coke costs $1.50 per six-pack and Pepsi costs $1.00. Draw Sabine's budget line for Coke and Pepsi on the same diagram.

   d. What is Sabine's optimal consumption bundle? Show this on your diagram.

   e. If the price of Coke and Pepsi is the same, what combination of Coke and Pepsi will Sabine buy?

10. For Norma, both nachos and salsa are normal goods. They are also ordinary goods for Norma. The price of nachos rises, but the price of salsa remains unchanged.

    a. Can you determine definitively whether she consumes more or fewer nachos? Explain with a diagram, placing nachos on the horizontal axis and salsa on the vertical axis.

    b. Can you determine definitively whether she consumes more or less salsa? Explain with a diagram, placing nachos on the horizontal axis and salsa on the vertical axis.

11. Tyrone is a utility maximizer. His income is $100, which he can spend on cafeteria meals and on notepads. Each meal costs $5, and each notepad costs $2. At these prices Tyrone chooses to buy 16 cafeteria meals and 10 notepads.

    a. Draw a diagram that shows Tyrone's choice using an indifference curve and his budget line, placing notepads on the vertical axis and cafeteria meals on the horizontal axis. Label the indifference curve I_1 and the budget line BL_1.

    b. The price of notepads falls to $1; the price of cafeteria meals remains the same. On the same diagram, draw Tyrone's budget line with the new prices and label it BL_H.

    c. Lastly, Tyrone's income falls to $90. On the same diagram, draw his budget line with this income and the new prices and label it BL_2. Is he worse off, better off, or equally as well off with these new prices and lower income than compared to the original prices and higher income? (*Hint:* Determine whether Tyrone can afford to buy his original consumption bundle of 16 meals and 10 notepads with the lower income and new prices.) Illustrate your answer using an indifference curve and label it I_2.

    d. Give an intuitive explanation of your answer to part c.

12. Gus spends his income on gas for his car and food. The government raises the tax on gas, thereby raising the price of gas. But the government also lowers the income tax, thereby increasing Gus's income. And this rise in income is just enough to place Gus on the same indifference curve as the one he was on before the price of gas rose. Will Gus buy more, less, or the same amount of gas as before these changes? Illustrate your answer with a diagram, placing gas on the horizontal axis and food on the vertical axis.

13. Pam spends her money on bread and Spam, and her indifference curves obey the four properties of indifference curves for ordinary goods. Suppose that, for Pam, Spam is an inferior, but not a Giffen, good; bread is a normal good. Bread costs $2 per loaf, and Spam costs $2 per can. Pam has $20 to spend.

    a. Draw a diagram of Pam's budget line, placing Spam on the horizontal axis and bread on the vertical axis. Suppose her optimal consumption bundle is 4 cans of Spam and 6 loaves of bread. Illustrate that bundle and draw the indifference curve on which it lies.

    b. The price of Spam falls to $1; the price of bread remains the same. Pam now buys 7 loaves of bread and 6 cans of Spam. Illustrate her new budget line and new optimal consumption bundle in your diagram. Also draw the indifference curve on which this bundle lies.

    c. In your diagram, show the income and substitution effects from this fall in the price of Spam. Remember that Spam is an inferior good for Pam.

14. Katya commutes to work. She can either use public transport or her own car. Her indifference curves obey the four properties of indifference curves for ordinary goods.

    a. Draw Katya's budget line with car travel on the vertical axis and public transport on the horizontal axis. Suppose that Katya consumes some of both goods. Draw an indifference curve that helps you illustrate her optimal consumption bundle.

    b. Now the price of public transport falls. Draw Katya's new budget line.

    c. For Katya, public transport is an inferior, but not a Giffen, good. Draw an indifference curve that illustrates her optimal consumption bundle after the price of public transport has fallen. Is Katya consuming more or less public transport?

    d. Show the income and substitution effects from this fall in the price of public transport.

15. For Crandall, cheese cubes and crackers are perfect complements: he wants to consume exactly 1 cheese cube with each cracker. He has $2.40 to spend on cheese and crackers. One cheese cube costs 20 cents, and 1 cracker costs 10 cents. Draw a diagram, with crackers on the horizontal axis and cheese cubes on the vertical axis, to answer the following questions.

    a. Which bundle will Crandall consume?

    b. The price of crackers rises to 20 cents. How many cheese cubes and how many crackers will Crandall consume?

    c. Show the income and substitution effects from this price rise.

16. Carmen consumes nothing but cafeteria meals and CDs. Her indifference curves exhibit the four general properties of indifference curves. Cafeteria meals cost $5 each, and CDs cost $10. Carmen has $50 to spend.

    a. Draw Carmen's budget line and an indifference curve that illustrates her optimal consumption bundle. Place cafeteria meals on the horizontal axis and CDs on the vertical axis. You do not have enough information to know the specific tangency point, so choose one arbitrarily.

    b. Now Carmen's income rises to $100. Draw her new budget line on the same diagram, as well as an indifference curve that illustrates her optimal consumption bundle. Assume that cafeteria meals are an inferior good.

    c. Can you draw an indifference curve showing that cafeteria meals and CDs are both inferior goods?

17. The Japanese Ministry of Internal Affairs and Communications collects data on the prices of goods and services in the Ku-area of Tokyo, as well as data on the average Japanese household's monthly income. The accompanying table shows some of this data. (¥ denotes the Japanese currency the yen.)

Year	Price of eggs (per pack of 10)	Price of tuna (per 100-gram portion)	Average monthly income
2003	¥187	¥392	¥524,810
2005	231	390	524,585

  www.worthpublishers.com/krugmanwells

a. For each of the two years for which you have data, what is the maximum number of packs of eggs that an average Japanese household could have consumed each month? The maximum number of 100-gram portions of tuna? In one diagram, draw the average Japanese household's budget line in 2003 and in 2005.

b. Calculate the relative price of eggs in terms of tuna for each year. Use the relative price rule to determine how the average household's consumption of eggs and tuna would have changed between 2003 and 2005.

>> # Behind the Supply Curve:
Inputs and Costs

THE FARMER'S MARGIN

"**O**BEAUTIFUL FOR SPACIOUS SKIES, FOR amber waves of grain." So begins the song "America the Beautiful." And those amber waves of grain are for real: though farmers are now only a small minority of America's population, our agricultural industry is immensely productive and feeds much of the world.

If you look at agricultural statistics, however, something may seem a bit surprising: when it comes to yield per acre, U.S. farmers are often nowhere near the top. For example, farmers in western European countries grow about three times as much wheat per acre as their U.S. counterparts. Are the Europeans better at growing wheat than we are?

No: European farmers are very skillful, but no more so than Americans. They produce more wheat per acre because they employ more inputs—more fertilizer and, especially, more labor—per acre. Of course, this means that European farmers have higher costs than their American counterparts. But because of government policies, European farmers receive a much higher price for their wheat than American farmers. This gives them an incentive to use more inputs and to expend more effort at the margin to increase the crop yield per acre.

Notice our use of the phrase "at the margin." Like most decisions that involve a comparison of benefits and costs, decisions about inputs and production involve a comparison of marginal quantities—the marginal cost versus the marginal benefit of producing a bit more from each acre.

In Chapter 9 we used the example of Babette's Cajun Café to illustrate the *principle of marginal analysis,* showing how Babette could use marginal analysis to determine the optimal portion size of a serving in her restaurant—that is, the portion size that generates the maximum total net gain or profit. Like Babette, the producers we will encounter in this chapter also face a production decision: choosing the output level that maximizes profit. In this chapter and in Chapter 13, we will show how marginal analysis can be used to understand these output decisions—decisions that lie behind the supply curve. The first step in this analysis is to show how the relationship between a firm's inputs and its output—its *production function*—determines its *cost curves,* the relationship between cost and quantity of output produced. That is what we do in this chapter. In Chapter 13, we will use our understanding of the firm's cost curves to derive the individual and the market supply curves.

How intensively an acre of land is worked—a decision at the margin—depends on the price of wheat a farmer faces.

The Production Function

A *firm* is an organization that produces goods or services for sale. To do this, it must transform inputs into output. The quantity of output a firm produces depends on the quantity of inputs; this relationship is known as the firm's **production function.** As we'll see, a firm's production function underlies its *cost curves.* As a first step, let's look at the characteristics of a hypothetical production function.

Inputs and Output

To understand the concept of a production function, let's consider a farm that we assume, for the sake of simplicity, produces only one output, wheat, and uses only two inputs, land and labor. This particular farm is owned by a couple named George and Martha. They hire workers to do the actual physical labor on the farm. Moreover, we will assume that all potential workers are of the same quality—they are all equally knowledgeable and capable of performing farmwork.

George and Martha's farm sits on 10 acres of land; no more acres are available to them, and they are currently unable to either increase or decrease the size of their farm by selling, buying, or leasing acreage. Land here is what economists call a **fixed input**—an input whose quantity is fixed for a period of time and cannot be varied. George and Martha are, however, free to decide how many workers to hire. The labor provided by these workers is called a **variable input**—an input whose quantity the firm can vary at any time. (In the example of Babette's Cajun Café in Chapter 9, Babette's fixed inputs were her restaurant equipment and her own labor; her variable inputs were her ingredients and her employees' labor.)

In reality, whether or not the quantity of an input is really fixed depends on the time horizon. In the **long run**—that is, given that a long enough period of time has elapsed—firms can adjust the quantity of any input. So there are no fixed inputs in the long run. In contrast, the **short run** is defined as the time period during which at least one input is fixed. Later in this chapter, we'll look more carefully at the distinction between the short run and the long run. But for now, we will restrict our attention to the short run and assume that at least one input is fixed.

George and Martha know that the quantity of wheat they produce depends on the number of workers they hire. Using modern farming techniques, one worker can cultivate the 10-acre farm, albeit not very intensively. When an additional worker is added, the land is divided equally among all the workers: each worker has 5 acres to cultivate when 2 workers are employed, each cultivates 3⅓ acres when 3 are employed, and so on. So as additional workers are employed, the 10 acres of land are cultivated more intensively and more bushels of wheat are produced. The relationship between the quantity of labor and the quantity of output, for a given amount of the fixed input, constitutes the farm's production function. The production function for George and Martha's farm, where land is the fixed input and labor is a variable input, is shown in the first two columns of the table in Figure 12-1; the diagram there shows the same information graphically. The curve in Figure 12-1 shows how the quantity of output depends on the quantity of the variable input, for a given quantity of the

A **production function** is the relationship between the quantity of inputs a firm uses and the quantity of output it produces.

A **fixed input** is an input whose quantity is fixed for a period of time and cannot be varied.

A **variable input** is an input whose quantity the firm can vary at any time.

The **long run** is the time period in which all inputs can be varied.

The **short run** is the time period in which at least one input is fixed.

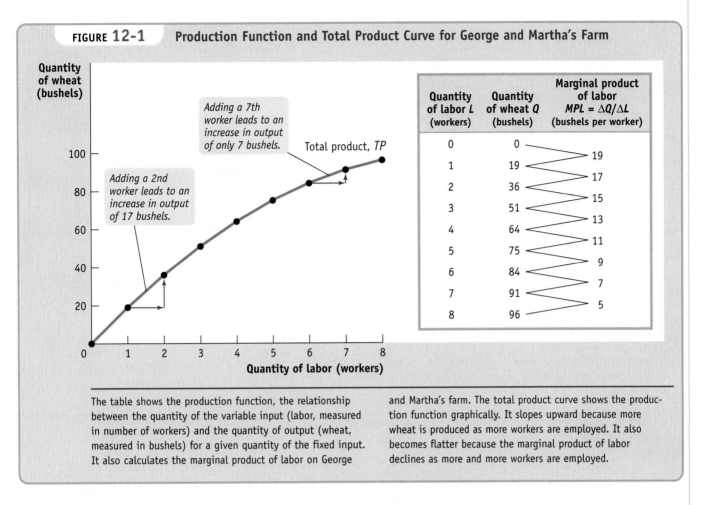

FIGURE 12-1   Production Function and Total Product Curve for George and Martha's Farm

The table shows the production function, the relationship between the quantity of the variable input (labor, measured in number of workers) and the quantity of output (wheat, measured in bushels) for a given quantity of the fixed input. It also calculates the marginal product of labor on George and Martha's farm. The total product curve shows the production function graphically. It slopes upward because more wheat is produced as more workers are employed. It also becomes flatter because the marginal product of labor declines as more and more workers are employed.

fixed input; it is called the farm's **total product curve.** The physical quantity of output, bushels of wheat, is measured on the vertical axis; the quantity of the variable input, labor (that is, the number of workers employed), is measured on the horizontal axis. The total product curve here slopes upward, reflecting the fact that more bushels of wheat are produced as more workers are employed.

Although the total product curve in Figure 12-1 slopes upward along its entire length, the slope isn't constant: as you move up the curve to the right, it flattens out. To understand this changing slope, look at the third column of the table in Figure 12-1, which shows the *change in the quantity of output* that is generated by adding one more worker. That is, it shows the **marginal product** of labor, or *MPL*: the additional quantity of output from using one more unit of labor (that is, one more worker).

In this example, we have data at intervals of 1 worker—that is, we have information on the quantity of output when there are 3 workers, 4 workers, and so on. Sometimes data aren't available in increments of 1 unit—for example, you might have information only on the quantity of output when there are 40 workers and when there are 50 workers. In this case, you can use the following equation to calculate the marginal product of labor:

(12-1) $\text{Marginal product of labor} = \frac{\text{Change in quantity of output produced by one additional unit of labor}}{\text{Change in quantity of labor}} = \frac{\text{Change in quantity of output}}{\text{Change in quantity of labor}}$

or

$$MPL = \frac{\Delta Q}{\Delta L}$$

In this equation, Δ, the Greek uppercase delta, represents the change in a variable.

The **total product curve** shows how the quantity of output depends on the quantity of the variable input, for a given quantity of the fixed input.

The **marginal product** of an input is the additional quantity of output that is produced by using one more unit of that input.

GLOBAL COMPARISON | WHEAT YIELDS AROUND THE WORLD

Wheat yields differ substantially around the world. The disparity between France and the United States that you see in this graph is particularly striking, given that they are both wealthy countries with comparable agricultural technology. Yet the reason for that disparity is straightforward: differing government policies. In the United States, farmers receive payments from the government to supplement their incomes, but European farmers benefit from price floors. Since European farmers face higher prices for their output than American farmers, they employ more variable inputs and produce significantly higher yields. Interestingly, in poor countries like Uganda and Ethiopia, foreign aid can lead to significantly depressed yields. Foreign aid from wealthy countries has often taken the form of surplus food, which depresses local market prices, severely hurting the local agriculture that poor countries normally depend on. Charitable organizations like OXFAM have asked wealthy food-producing countries to modify their aid policies—principally, to give aid in cash rather than in food products except in the case of acute food shortages—to avoid this problem.

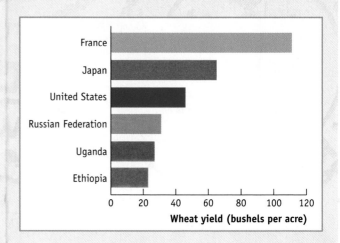

Source: Food and Agriculture Organization of the United Nations. Data are from 2005.

Now we can explain the significance of the slope of the total product curve: it is equal to the marginal product of labor. The slope of a line is equal to "rise" over "run" (see the appendix to Chapter 2). This implies that the slope of the total product curve is the change in the quantity of output (the "rise") divided by the change in the quantity of labor (the "run"). And this, as we can see from Equation 12-1, is simply the marginal product of labor. So in Figure 12-1, the fact that the marginal product of the first worker is 19 also means that the slope of the total product curve in going from 0 to 1 worker is 19. Similarly, the slope of the total product curve in going from 1 to 2 workers is the same as the marginal product of the second worker, 17, and so on.

In this example, the marginal product of labor steadily declines as more workers are hired—that is, each successive worker adds less to output than the previous worker. So as employment increases, the total product curve gets flatter.

Figure 12-2 shows how the marginal product of labor depends on the number of workers employed on the farm. The marginal product of labor, *MPL,* is measured on the vertical axis in units of physical output—bushels of wheat—produced per additional worker, and the number of workers employed is measured on the horizontal axis. You can see from the table in Figure 12-1 that if 5 workers are employed instead of 4, output rises from 64 to 75 bushels; in this case the marginal product of labor is 11 bushels—the same number found in Figure 12-2. To indicate that 11 bushels is the marginal product when employment rises from 4 to 5, we place the point corresponding to that information halfway between 4 and 5 workers.

In this example the marginal product of labor falls as the number of workers increases. That is, there are *diminishing returns to labor* on George and Martha's farm. In general, there are **diminishing returns to an input** when an increase in the quantity of that input, holding the quantity of all other inputs fixed, reduces that input's marginal product. Due to diminishing returns to labor, the *MPL* curve is negatively sloped.

There are **diminishing returns to an input** when an increase in the quantity of that input, holding the levels of all other inputs fixed, leads to a decline in the marginal product of that input.

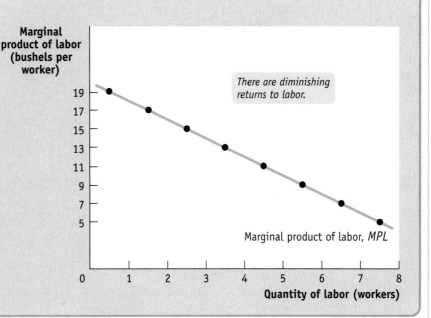

FIGURE 12-2

Marginal Product of Labor Curve for George and Martha's Farm

The marginal product of labor curve plots each worker's marginal product, the increase in the quantity of output generated by each additional worker. The change in the quantity of output is measured on the vertical axis and the number of workers employed on the horizontal axis. The first worker employed generates an increase in output of 19 bushels, the second worker generates an increase of 17 bushels, and so on. The curve slopes downward due to diminishing returns to labor.

To grasp why diminishing returns can occur, think about what happens as George and Martha add more and more workers without increasing the number of acres. As the number of workers increases, the land is farmed more intensively and the number of bushels increases. But each additional worker is working with a smaller share of the 10 acres—the fixed input—than the previous worker. As a result, the additional worker cannot produce as much output as the previous worker. So it's not surprising that the marginal product of the additional worker falls.

The crucial point to emphasize about diminishing returns is that, like many propositions in economics, it is an "other things equal" proposition: each successive unit of an input will raise production by less than the last *if the quantity of all other inputs is held fixed.*

What would happen if the levels of other inputs were allowed to change? You can see the answer illustrated in Figure 12-3 on the next page. Panel (a) shows two total product curves, TP_{10} and TP_{20}. TP_{10} is the farm's total product curve when its total area is 10 acres (the same curve as in Figure 12-1). TP_{20} is the total product curve when the farm has increased to 20 acres. Except when 0 workers are employed, TP_{20} lies everywhere above TP_{10} because with more acres available, any given number of workers produces more output. Panel (b) shows the corresponding marginal product of labor curves. MPL_{10} is the marginal product of labor curve given 10 acres to cultivate (the same curve as in Figure 12-2), and MPL_{20} is the marginal product of labor curve given 20 acres. Both curves slope downward because, in each case, the amount of land is fixed, albeit at different levels. But MPL_{20} lies everywhere above MPL_{10}, reflecting the fact that the marginal product of the same worker is higher when he or she has more of the fixed input to work with.

Figure 12-3 demonstrates a general result: the position of the total product curve depends on the quantities of other inputs. If you change the quantity of the other inputs, both the total product curve and the marginal product curve of the remaining input will shift. The importance of the "other things equal" assumption in discussing diminishing returns is illustrated in the For Inquiring Minds on the next page.

PITFALLS

WHAT'S A UNIT?

The marginal product of labor (or any other input) is defined as the increase in the quantity of output when you increase the quantity of that input by one unit. But what do we mean by a "unit" of labor? Is it an additional hour of labor, an additional week, or a person-year?

The answer is that it doesn't matter, *as long as you are consistent.* One common source of error in economics is getting units confused—say, comparing the output added by an additional *hour* of labor with the cost of employing a worker for a *week*. Whatever units you use, always be careful that you use the same units throughout your analysis of any problem.

FIGURE 12-3   Total Product, Marginal Product, and the Fixed Input

(a) Total Product Curves

(b) Marginal Product Curves

This figure shows how the quantity of output—illustrated by the total product curve—and marginal product depend on the level of the fixed input. Panel (a) shows two total product curves for George and Martha's farm, TP_{10} when their farm is 10 acres and TP_{20} when it is 20 acres. With more land, each worker can produce more wheat. So an increase in the fixed input shifts the total product curve up from TP_{10} to TP_{20}. This also implies that the marginal product of each worker is higher when the farm is 20 acres than when it is 10 acres. As a result, an increase in acreage also shifts the marginal product of labor curve up from MPL_{10} to MPL_{20}. Panel (b) shows the marginal product of labor curves. Note that both marginal product of labor curves still slope downward due to diminishing returns to labor.

FOR INQUIRING MINDS

Was Malthus Right?

In 1798, Thomas Malthus, an English pastor, authored the book *An Essay on the Principle of Population*, which introduced the principle of diminishing returns to an input. Malthus's writings were influential in his own time and continue to provoke heated argument to this day.

Malthus argued that as a country's population grew but its land area remained fixed, it would become increasingly difficult to grow enough food. Though more intensive cultivation of the land could increase yields, each successive farmer would add less to the total than the last as the marginal product of labor declined.

From this argument, Malthus drew a powerful conclusion—that misery was the normal condition of humankind. In a country with a small population and abundant land, he argued, families would be large and the population would grow rapidly (a description of the United States at the time). Ultimately, the pressure of population on the land would

reduce the condition of most people to a level where starvation and disease held the population in check. (Arguments like this led the historian Thomas Carlyle to dub economics the "dismal science.")

Happily, over the long term, Malthus's predictions have turned out to be wrong. World population has increased from about 1 billion when Malthus wrote to more than 6.6 billion in 2008, but in most of the world people eat better now than ever before. So was Malthus completely wrong? And do his incorrect predictions refute the idea of diminishing returns? No, on both counts.

First, the Malthusian story is a pretty accurate description of 57 of the last 59 centuries: peasants in eighteenth-century France probably did not live much better than Egyptian peasants in the age of the pyramids. Yet diminishing returns does not mean that using more labor to grow food on a given amount of land will lead to a decline in the marginal product of labor—*if*

there is also a radical improvement in farming technology. Fortunately, since the eighteenth century, technological progress has been so rapid that it has alleviated much of the limits imposed by diminishing returns. Diminishing returns implies that the marginal product declines when *all* other things—including technology—remain the same. So the happy fact that Malthus's predictions were wrong does not invalidate the concept of diminishing returns.

Typically, however, technological progress relaxes the limits imposed by diminishing returns only over the very long term. This was demonstrated in 2008 when bad weather, an ethanol-driven increase in the demand for corn, and a brisk rise in world income led to soaring world grain prices. As farmers scrambled to plant more acreage, they ran up against limits in the availability of inputs like land and fertilizer. Hopefully, we can prove Malthus wrong again before long.

From the Production Function to Cost Curves

Once George and Martha know their production function, they know the relationship between inputs of labor and land and output of wheat. But if they want to maximize their profits, they need to translate this knowledge into information about the relationship between the quantity of output and cost. Let's see how they can do this.

To translate information about a firm's production function into information about its costs, we need to know how much the firm must pay for its inputs. We will assume that George and Martha face either an explicit or an implicit cost of $400 for the use of the land. As we learned in Chapter 9, it is irrelevant whether George and Martha must rent the land for $400 from someone else or whether they own the land themselves and forgo earning $400 from renting it to someone else. Either way, they pay an opportunity cost of $400 by using the land to grow wheat. Moreover, since the land is a fixed input, the $400 George and Martha pay for it is a **fixed cost,** denoted by *FC*—a cost that does not depend on the quantity of output produced (in the short run). In business, fixed cost is often referred to as "overhead cost."

We also assume that George and Martha must pay each worker $200. Using their production function, George and Martha know that the number of workers they must hire depends on the amount of wheat they intend to produce. So the cost of labor, which is equal to the number of workers multiplied by $200, is a **variable cost,** denoted by *VC*—a cost that depends on the quantity of output produced. Adding the fixed cost and the variable cost of a given quantity of output gives the **total cost,** or *TC*, of that quantity of output. We can express the relationship among fixed cost, variable cost, and total cost as an equation:

(12-2)   Total cost = Fixed cost + Variable cost

or

$$TC = FC + VC$$

The table in Figure 12-4 on the next page shows how total cost is calculated for George and Martha's farm. The second column shows the number of workers employed, *L*. The third column shows the corresponding level of output, *Q*, taken from the table in Figure 12-1. The fourth column shows the variable cost, *VC*, equal to the number of workers multiplied by $200. The fifth column shows the fixed cost, *FC*, which is $400 regardless of how many workers are employed. The sixth column shows the total cost of output, *TC*, which is the variable cost plus the fixed cost.

The first column labels each row of the table with a letter, from *A* to *I*. These labels will be helpful in understanding our next step: drawing the **total cost curve,** a curve that shows how total cost depends on the quantity of output.

George and Martha's total cost curve is shown in the diagram in Figure 12-4, where the horizontal axis measures the quantity of output in bushels of wheat and the vertical axis measures total cost in dollars. Each point on the curve corresponds to one row of the table in Figure 12-4. For example, point *A* shows the situation when 0 workers are employed: output is zero, and total cost is equal to fixed cost, $400. Similarly, point *B* shows the situation when 1 worker is employed: output is 19 bushels, and total cost is $600, equal to the sum of $400 in fixed cost and $200 in variable cost.

Like the total product curve, the total cost curve slopes upward: due to the variable cost, the more output produced, the higher the farm's total cost. But unlike the total product curve, which gets flatter as employment rises, the total cost curve gets *steeper.* That is, the slope of the total cost curve is greater as the amount of output produced increases. As we will soon see, the steepening of the total cost curve is also due to diminishing returns to the variable input. Before we can understand this, we must first look at the relationships among several useful measures of cost.

A **fixed cost** is a cost that does not depend on the quantity of output produced. It is the cost of the fixed input.

A **variable cost** is a cost that depends on the quantity of output produced. It is the cost of the variable input.

The **total cost** of producing a given quantity of output is the sum of the fixed cost and the variable cost of producing that quantity of output.

The **total cost curve** shows how total cost depends on the quantity of output.

FIGURE 12-4

Total Cost Curve for George and Martha's Farm

The table shows the variable cost, fixed cost, and total cost for various output quantities on George and Martha's 10-acre farm. The total cost curve shows how total cost (measured on the vertical axis) depends on the quantity of output (measured on the horizontal axis). The labeled points on the curve correspond to the rows of the table. The total cost curve slopes upward because the number of workers employed, and hence total cost, increases as the quantity of output increases. The curve gets steeper as output increases due to diminishing returns to labor.

Point on graph	Quantity of labor L (workers)	Quantity of wheat Q (bushels)	Variable cost VC	Fixed cost FC	Total cost TC = FC + VC
A	0	0	$0	$400	$400
B	1	19	200	400	600
C	2	36	400	400	800
D	3	51	600	400	1,000
E	4	64	800	400	1,200
F	5	75	1,000	400	1,400
G	6	84	1,200	400	1,600
H	7	91	1,400	400	1,800
I	8	96	1,600	400	2,000

➤ECONOMICS IN ACTION

The Mythical Man-Month

The concept of diminishing returns to an input was first formulated by economists during the late eighteenth century (see the preceding For Inquiring Minds). These economists, notably including Thomas Malthus, drew their inspiration from agricultural examples. Although still valid, examples drawn from agriculture can seem somewhat musty and old-fashioned in our modern economy.

However, the idea of diminishing returns to an input applies with equal force to the most modern of economic activities—such as, say, the design of software. In 1975 Frederick P. Brooks Jr., a project manager at IBM during the days when it dominated the computer business, published a book titled *The Mythical Man-Month* that soon became a classic—so much so that a special anniversary edition was published 20 years later.

The chapter that gave its title to the book is basically about diminishing returns to labor in the writing of software. Brooks observed that multiplying the number of programmers assigned to a project did not produce a proportionate reduction in the time it took to get the program written. A project that could be done by 1 programmer in 12 months could *not* be done by 12 programmers in 1 month—hence the "mythical man-month," the false notion that the number of lines of programming code produced was proportional to the number of code writers employed. In fact, above a certain number, adding another programmer on a project actually *increased* the time to completion.

The argument of *The Mythical Man-Month* is summarized in Figure 12-5. The upper part of the figure shows how the quantity of the project's output, as measured by the number of lines of code produced per month, varies with the number of programmers. Each additional programmer accomplishes less than the previous one, and beyond a certain point an additional programmer is actually counterproductive. The lower part of the figure shows the marginal product of each successive programmer, which falls as more programmers are employed and eventually becomes negative. In other words, programming is subject to diminishing returns so severe that at some point more programmers actually have negative marginal product. The source of the diminishing returns lies in the nature of the production function for a programming project: each programmer must coordinate his or her work with that of all the other programmers on the project, leading to each person spending more and more time communicating with others as the number of programmers increases. In other words, other things equal, there are diminishing returns to labor. It is likely, however, that if fixed inputs devoted to programming projects are increased—say, installing a faster Wiki system—the problem of diminishing returns for additional programmers can be mitigated.

FIGURE 12-5 The Mythical Man-Month

Beyond a certain point, an additional programmer is counterproductive.

Beyond a certain point, adding an additional programmer is counterproductive—output falls and the slope of the total product curve becomes negative. At this point the marginal product of labor curve crosses the horizontal axis—and the marginal product of labor becomes negative.

A reviewer of the reissued edition of *The Mythical Man-Month* summarized the reasons for these diminishing returns: "There is an inescapable overhead to yoking up programmers in parallel. The members of the team must 'waste time' attending meetings, drafting project plans, exchanging e-mail, negotiating interfaces, enduring performance reviews, and so on. . . . At Microsoft, there will be at least one team member that just designs T-shirts for the rest of the team to wear." (See source note on copyright page.) ▲

> > > > > > > > > > > >

▶ CHECK YOUR UNDERSTANDING 12-1

1. Bernie's ice-making company produces ice cubes using a 10-ton machine and electricity. The quantity of output, measured in terms of pounds of ice, is given in the accompanying table.
   a. What is the fixed input? What is the variable input?
   b. Construct a table showing the marginal product of the variable input. Does it show diminishing returns?
   c. Suppose a 50% increase in the size of the fixed input increases output by 100% for any given amount of the variable input. What is the fixed input now? Construct a table showing the quantity of output and marginal product in this case.

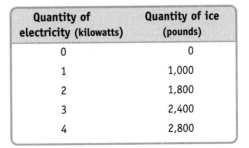

Quantity of electricity (kilowatts)	Quantity of ice (pounds)
0	0
1	1,000
2	1,800
3	2,400
4	2,800

Solutions appear at back of book.

Two Key Concepts: Marginal Cost and Average Cost

We've just learned how to derive a firm's total cost curve from its production function. Our next step is to take a deeper look at total cost by deriving two extremely useful measures: *marginal cost* and *average cost*. As we'll see, these two measures of the cost of production have a somewhat surprising relationship to each other. Moreover, they will prove to be vitally important in Chapter 13, where we will use them to analyze the firm's output decision and the market supply curve.

Marginal Cost

We defined marginal cost in Chapter 9: it is the change in total cost generated by producing one more unit of output. We've already seen that marginal product is easiest to calculate if data on output are available in increments of one unit of input. Similarly, marginal cost is easiest to calculate if data on total cost are available in increments of one unit of output. When the data come in less convenient increments, it's still possible to calculate marginal cost over each interval. But for the sake of simplicity, let's work with an example in which the data come in convenient 1-unit increments.

Selena's Gourmet Salsas produces bottled salsa; Table 12-1 shows how its costs per day depend on the number of cases of salsa it produces per day. The firm has fixed cost of $108 per day, shown in the second column, which represents the daily cost of its food-preparation equipment. The third column shows the variable cost, and the fourth column shows the total cost. Panel (a) of Figure 12-6 plots the total cost curve. Like the total cost curve for George and Martha's farm in Figure 12-4, this curve slopes upward, getting steeper as you move up it to the right.

The significance of the slope of the total cost curve is shown by the fifth column of Table 12-1, which calculates *marginal cost:* the additional cost of each additional unit. The general formula for marginal cost is:

$$\text{(12-3)}\quad \text{Marginal cost} = \frac{\text{Change in total cost generated by one additional unit of output}}{} = \frac{\text{Change in total cost}}{\text{Change in quantity of output}}$$

or

$$MC = \frac{\Delta TC}{\Delta Q}$$

As in the case of marginal product, marginal cost is equal to "rise" (the increase in total cost) divided by "run" (the increase in the quantity of output). So just as marginal product is equal to the slope of the total product curve, marginal cost is equal to the slope of the total cost curve.

Now we can understand why the total cost curve gets steeper as we move up it to the right: as you can see in Table 12-1, marginal cost at Selena's Gourmet Salsas rises as output increases. Panel (b) of Figure 12-6 shows the marginal cost curve corresponding to the data in Table 12-1. Notice that, as in Figure 12-2, we plot the marginal cost for increasing output from 0 to 1 case of salsa halfway between 0 and 1, the marginal cost for increasing output from 1 to 2 cases of salsa halfway between 1 and 2, and so on.

Why does the marginal cost curve slope upward? Because there are diminishing returns to inputs in this example. As output increases, the marginal product of the variable input declines. This implies that more and more of the variable input must be used to produce each additional unit of output as the amount of output already produced rises. And since each unit of the variable input must be paid for, the additional cost per additional unit of output also rises.

TABLE 12-1

Costs at Selena's Gourmet Salsas

Quantity of salsa Q (cases)	Fixed cost FC	Variable cost VC	Total cost TC = FC + VC	Marginal cost of case MC = ΔTC/ΔQ
0	$108	$0	$108	
				$12
1	108	12	120	
				36
2	108	48	156	
				60
3	108	108	216	
				84
4	108	192	300	
				108
5	108	300	408	
				132
6	108	432	540	
				156
7	108	588	696	
				180
8	108	768	876	
				204
9	108	972	1,080	
				228
10	108	1,200	1,308	

In addition, recall that the flattening of the total product curve is also due to diminishing returns: the marginal product of an input falls as more of that input is used if the quantities of other inputs are fixed. The flattening of the total product curve as output increases and the steepening of the total cost curve as output increases are just flip-sides of the same phenomenon. That is, as output increases, the marginal cost of output also increases because the marginal product of the variable input decreases.

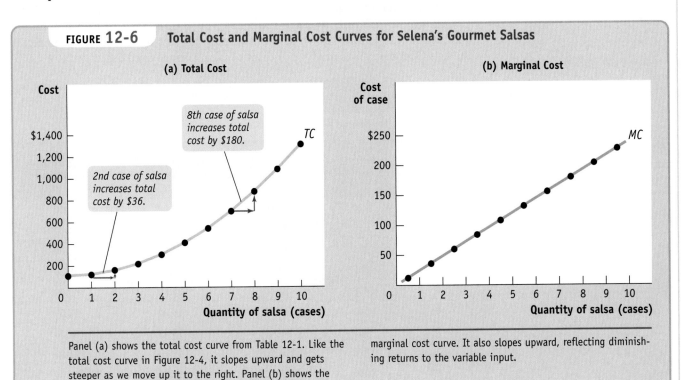

FIGURE 12-6   Total Cost and Marginal Cost Curves for Selena's Gourmet Salsas

Panel (a) shows the total cost curve from Table 12-1. Like the total cost curve in Figure 12-4, it slopes upward and gets steeper as we move up it to the right. Panel (b) shows the marginal cost curve. It also slopes upward, reflecting diminishing returns to the variable input.

We will return to marginal cost in Chapter 13, when we consider the firm's profit-maximizing output decision. Our next step is to introduce another measure of cost: *average cost*.

Average Cost

In addition to total cost and marginal cost, it's useful to calculate another measure, **average total cost,** often simply called **average cost.** The average total cost is total cost divided by the quantity of output produced; that is, it is equal to total cost per unit of output. If we let *ATC* denote average total cost, the equation looks like this:

$$\textbf{(12-4)} \quad ATC = \frac{\text{Total cost}}{\text{Quantity of output}} = \frac{TC}{Q}$$

Average total cost is important because it tells the producer how much the *average* or *typical* unit of output costs to produce. Marginal cost, meanwhile, tells the producer how much *one more* unit of output costs to produce. Although they may look very similar, these two measures of cost typically differ. And confusion between them is a major source of error in economics, both in the classroom and in real life, as illustrated by the upcoming Economics in Action.

Table 12-2 uses data from Selena's Gourmet Salsas to calculate average total cost. For example, the total cost of producing 4 cases of salsa is $300, consisting of $108 in fixed cost and $192 in variable cost (from Table 12-1). So the average total cost of producing 4 cases of salsa is $300/4 = $75. You can see from Table 12-2 that as quantity of output increases, average total cost first falls, then rises.

Figure 12-7 plots that data to yield the *average total cost curve*, which shows how average total cost depends on output. As before, cost in dollars is measured on the vertical axis and quantity of output is measured on the horizontal axis. The average total cost curve has a distinctive U shape that corresponds to how average total cost first falls and then rises as output increases. Economists believe that such **U-shaped average total cost curves** are the norm for producers in many industries.

To help our understanding of why the average total cost curve is U-shaped, Table 12-2 breaks average total cost into its two underlying components, *average fixed cost* and *average variable cost*. **Average fixed cost,** or *AFC,* is fixed cost divided by the quantity of output, also known as the fixed cost per unit of output. For example, if Selena's Gourmet Salsas produces 4 cases of salsa, average fixed cost is $108/4 = $27

TABLE 12-2

Average Costs for Selena's Gourmet Salsas

Quantity of salsa Q (cases)	Total cost TC	Average total cost of case ATC = TC/Q	Average fixed cost of case AFC = FC/Q	Average variable cost of case AVC = VC/Q
1	$120	$120.00	$108.00	$12.00
2	156	78.00	54.00	24.00
3	216	72.00	36.00	36.00
4	300	75.00	27.00	48.00
5	408	81.60	21.60	60.00
6	540	90.00	18.00	72.00
7	696	99.43	15.43	84.00
8	876	109.50	13.50	96.00
9	1,080	120.00	12.00	108.00
10	1,308	130.80	10.80	120.00

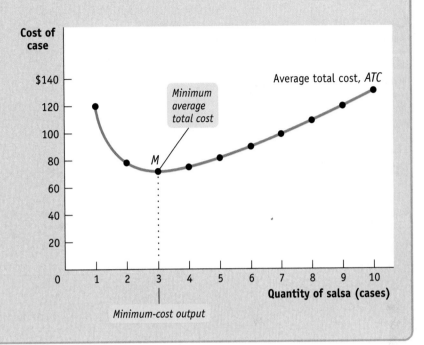

FIGURE 12-7

Average Total Cost Curve for Selena's Gourmet Salsas

The average total cost curve at Selena's Gourmet Salsas is U-shaped. At low levels of output, average total cost falls because the "spreading effect" of falling average fixed cost dominates the "diminishing returns effect" of rising average variable cost. At higher levels of output, the opposite is true and average total cost rises. At point M, corresponding to an output of three cases of salsa per day, average total cost is at its minimum level, the minimum average total cost.

per case. **Average variable cost,** or AVC, is variable cost divided by the quantity of output, also known as variable cost per unit of output. At an output of 4 cases, average variable cost is $192/4 = $48 per case. Writing these in the form of equations:

$$\textbf{(12-5)}\quad AFC = \frac{\text{Fixed cost}}{\text{Quantity of output}} = \frac{FC}{Q}$$

$$AVC = \frac{\text{Variable cost}}{\text{Quantity of output}} = \frac{VC}{Q}$$

Average total cost is the sum of average fixed cost and average variable cost; it has a U shape because these components move in opposite directions as output rises.

Average fixed cost falls as more output is produced because the numerator (the fixed cost) is a fixed number but the denominator (the quantity of output) increases as more is produced. Another way to think about this relationship is that, as more output is produced, the fixed cost is spread over more units of output; the end result is that the fixed cost *per unit of output*—the average fixed cost—falls. You can see this effect in the fourth column of Table 12-2: average fixed cost drops continuously as output increases.

Average variable cost, however, rises as output increases. As we've seen, this reflects diminishing returns to the variable input: each additional unit of output incurs more variable cost to produce than the previous unit. So variable cost rises at a faster rate than the quantity of output increases.

So increasing output has two opposing effects on average total cost—the "spreading effect" and the "diminishing returns effect":

- *The spreading effect.* The larger the output, the greater the quantity of output over which fixed cost is spread, leading to lower average fixed cost.

- *The diminishing returns effect.* The larger the output, the greater the amount of variable input required to produce additional units, leading to higher average variable cost.

At low levels of output, the spreading effect is very powerful because even small increases in output cause large reductions in average fixed cost. So at low levels of output, the spreading effect dominates the diminishing returns effect and causes the average total cost curve to slope downward. But when output is large, average fixed cost is already quite

Average variable cost is the variable cost per unit of output.

FIGURE 12-8

Marginal Cost and Average Cost Curves for Selena's Gourmet Salsas

Here we have the family of cost curves for Selena's Gourmet Salsas: the marginal cost curve (*MC*), the average total cost curve (*ATC*), the average variable cost curve (*AVC*), and the average fixed cost curve (*AFC*). Note that the average total cost curve is U-shaped and the marginal cost curve crosses the average total cost curve at the bottom of the U, point *M*, corresponding to the minimum average total cost from Table 12-2 and Figure 12-7.

small, so increasing output further has only a very small spreading effect. Diminishing returns, however, usually grow increasingly important as output rises. As a result, when output is large, the diminishing returns effect dominates the spreading effect, causing the average total cost curve to slope upward. At the bottom of the U-shaped average total cost curve, point *M* in Figure 12-7, the two effects exactly balance each other. At this point average total cost is at its minimum level, the minimum average total cost.

Figure 12-8 brings together in a single picture four members of the family of cost curves that we have derived from the total cost curve for Selena's Gourmet Salsas: the marginal cost curve (*MC*), the average total cost curve (*ATC*), the average variable cost curve (*AVC*), and the average fixed cost curve (*AFC*). All are based on the information in Tables 12-1 and 12-2. As before, cost is measured on the vertical axis and the quantity of output is measured on the horizontal axis.

Let's take a moment to note some features of the various cost curves. First of all, marginal cost slopes upward—the result of diminishing returns that make an additional unit of output more costly to produce than the one before. Average variable cost also slopes upward—again, due to diminishing returns—but is flatter than the marginal cost curve. This is because the higher cost of an additional unit of output is averaged across all units, not just the additional units, in the average variable cost measure. Meanwhile, average fixed cost slopes downward because of the spreading effect.

Finally, notice that the marginal cost curve intersects the average total cost curve from below, crossing it at its lowest point, point *M* in Figure 12-8. This last feature is our next subject of study.

Minimum Average Total Cost

For a U-shaped average total cost curve, average total cost is at its minimum level at the bottom of the U. Economists call the quantity of output that corresponds to the minimum average total cost the **minimum-cost output.** In the case of Selena's Gourmet Salsas, the minimum-cost output is three cases of salsa per day.

In Figure 12-8, the bottom of the U is at the level of output at which the marginal cost curve crosses the average total cost curve from below. Is this an accident? No—it reflects general principles that are always true about a firm's marginal cost and average total cost curves:

The **minimum-cost output** is the quantity of output at which average total cost is lowest—the bottom of the U-shaped average total cost curve.

- At the minimum-cost output, average total cost *is equal to* marginal cost.

- At output less than the minimum-cost output, marginal cost *is less than* average total cost and average total cost is falling.

- And at output greater than the minimum-cost output, marginal cost *is greater than* average total cost and average total cost is rising.

To understand these principles, think about how your grade in one course—say, a 3.0 in physics—affects your overall grade point average. If your GPA before receiving that grade was more than 3.0, the new grade lowers your average.

Similarly, if marginal cost—the cost of producing one more unit—is less than average total cost, producing that extra unit lowers average total cost. This is shown in Figure 12-9 by the movement from A_1 to A_2. In this case, the marginal cost of producing an additional unit of output is low, as indicated by the point MC_L on the marginal cost curve. When the cost of producing the next unit of output is less than average total cost, increasing production reduces average total cost. So any quantity of output at which marginal cost is less than average total cost must be on the downward-sloping segment of the U.

FIGURE 12-9

The Relationship Between the Average Total Cost and the Marginal Cost Curves

To see why the marginal cost curve (*MC*) must cut through the average total cost curve at the minimum average total cost (point *M*), corresponding to the minimum-cost output, we look at what happens if marginal cost is different from average total cost. If marginal cost is *less* than average total cost, an increase in output must reduce average total cost, as in the movement from A_1 to A_2. If marginal cost is *greater* than average total cost, an increase in output must increase average total cost, as in the movement from B_1 to B_2.

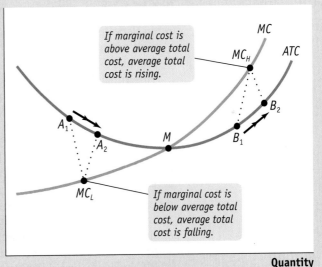

But if your grade in physics is more than the average of your previous grades, this new grade raises your GPA. Similarly, if marginal cost is greater than average total cost, producing that extra unit raises average total cost. This is illustrated by the movement from B_1 to B_2 in Figure 12-9, where the marginal cost, MC_H, is higher than average total cost. So any quantity of output at which marginal cost is greater than average total cost must be on the upward-sloping segment of the U.

Finally, if a new grade is exactly equal to your previous GPA, the additional grade neither raises nor lowers that average—it stays the same. This corresponds to point *M* in Figure 12-9: when marginal cost equals average total cost, we must be at the bottom of the U, because only at that point is average total cost neither falling nor rising.

Does the Marginal Cost Curve Always Slope Upward?

Up to this point, we have emphasized the importance of diminishing returns, which lead to a marginal product curve that always slopes downward and a marginal cost curve that always slopes upward. In practice, however, economists believe that marginal cost curves

FIGURE 12-10

More Realistic Cost Curves

A realistic marginal cost curve has a "swoosh" shape. Starting from a very low output level, marginal cost often falls as the firm increases output. That's because hiring additional workers allows greater specialization of their tasks and leads to increasing returns. Once specialization is achieved, however, diminishing returns to additional workers set in and marginal cost rises. The corresponding average variable cost curve is now U-shaped, like the average total cost curve.

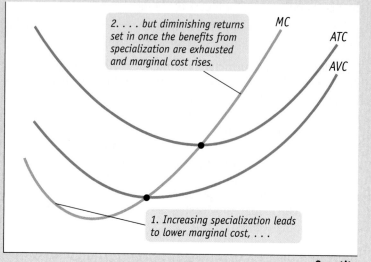

often slope *downward* as a firm increases its production from zero up to some low level, sloping upward only at higher levels of production: they look like the curve *MC* in Figure 12-10.

This initial downward slope occurs because a firm often finds that, when it starts with only a very small number of workers, employing more workers and expanding output allows its workers to specialize in various tasks. This, in turn, lowers the firm's marginal cost as it expands output. For example, one individual producing salsa would have to perform all the tasks involved: selecting and preparing the ingredients, mixing the salsa, bottling and labeling it, packing it into cases, and so on. As more workers are employed, they can divide the tasks, with each worker specializing in one or a few aspects of salsa-making. This specialization leads to *increasing returns* to the hiring of additional workers and results in a marginal cost curve that initially slopes downward. But once there are enough workers to have completely exhausted the benefits of further specialization, diminishing returns to labor set in and the marginal cost curve changes direction and slopes upward. So typical marginal cost curves actually have the "swoosh" shape shown by *MC* in Figure 12-10. For the same reason, average variable cost curves typically look like *AVC* in Figure 12-10: they are U-shaped rather than strictly upward sloping.

However, as Figure 12-10 also shows, the key features we saw from the example of Selena's Gourmet Salsas remain true: the average total cost curve is U-shaped, and the marginal cost curve passes through the point of minimum average total cost.

►ECONOMICS IN ACTION

Don't Put Out the Welcome Mat

Housing developments have traditionally been considered as American as apple pie. With our abundant supply of undeveloped land, real estate developers have long found it profitable to buy big parcels of land, build a large number of homes, and create entire new communities. But what is profitable for developers is not necessarily good for the existing residents.

In the past few years, real estate developers have encountered increasingly stiff resistance from local residents because of the additional costs—the marginal costs—imposed on existing homeowners from new developments. Let's look at why.

In the United States, a large percentage of the funding for local services comes from taxes paid by local homeowners. In a sense, the local township authority uses those taxes to "produce" municipal services for the town. The overall level of property taxes is set to reflect the costs of providing those services. The highest service cost by far, in most communities, is the cost of public education.

The local tax rate that new homeowners pay on their new homes is the same as what existing homeowners pay on their older homes. That tax rate reflects the current total cost of services, and the taxes that an average homeowner pays reflect the average total cost of providing services to a household. The average total cost of providing services is based on the town's use of existing facilities, such as the existing school buildings, the existing number of teachers, the existing fleet of school buses, and so on.

But when a large development of homes is constructed, those facilities are no longer adequate: new schools must be built, new teachers hired, and so on. The quantity of output increases. So the *marginal cost* of providing municipal services per household associated with a new, large-scale development turns out to be much higher than the *average total cost* per household of existing homes. As a result, new developments and facilities cause everyone's local tax rate to go up, just as you would expect from Figure 12-9. A recent study in Massachusetts estimated that a $250,000 new home with one school-age child imposed an additional cost to the community of

New housing developments lead to higher taxes for everyone in the neighborhood.

$5,527 per year over and above the taxes paid by the new homeowners. As a result, in many towns across America, potential new housing developments and newcomers are now facing a distinctly chilly reception. ▲

> > > > > > > > > > > >

> **CHECK YOUR UNDERSTANDING** 12-2

1. Alicia's Apple Pies is a roadside business. Alicia must pay $9.00 in rent each day. In addition, it costs her $1.00 to produce the first pie of the day, and each subsequent pie costs 50% more to produce than the one before. For example, the second pie costs $1.00 × 1.5 = $1.50 to produce, and so on.

   a. Calculate Alicia's marginal cost, variable cost, average total cost, average variable cost, and average fixed cost as her daily pie output rises from 0 to 6. (*Hint:* The variable cost of two pies is just the marginal cost of the first pie, plus the marginal cost of the second, and so on.)

   b. Indicate the range of pies for which the spreading effect dominates and the range for which the diminishing returns effect dominates.

   c. What is Alicia's minimum-cost output? Explain why making one more pie lowers Alicia's average total cost when output is lower than the minimum-cost output. Similarly, explain why making one more pie raises Alicia's average total cost when output is greater than the minimum-cost output.

Solutions appear at back of book.

Short-Run versus Long-Run Costs

Up to this point, we have treated fixed cost as completely outside the control of a firm because we have focused on the short run. But as we noted earlier, all inputs are variable in the long run: this means that in the long run fixed cost may also be varied. *In the long run, in other words, a firm's fixed cost becomes a variable it can choose.* For example, given time, Selena's Gourmet Salsas can acquire additional food-preparation equipment or dispose of some of its existing equipment. In this section, we will examine how a firm's costs behave in the short run and in the long run. We will also see that the firm will choose its fixed cost in the long run based on the level of output it expects to produce.

Let's begin by supposing that Selena's Gourmet Salsas is considering whether to acquire additional food-preparation equipment. Acquiring additional machinery will affect its total cost in two ways. First, the firm will have to either rent or buy the additional equipment; either way, that will mean higher fixed cost in the short run. Second, if the workers have more equipment, they will be more productive: fewer workers will be needed to produce any given output, so variable cost for any given output level will be reduced.

The table in Figure 12-11 shows how acquiring an additional machine affects costs. In our original example, we assumed that Selena's Gourmet Salsas had a fixed cost of $108. The left half of the table shows variable cost as well as total cost and average total cost assuming a fixed cost of $108. The average total cost curve for this level of fixed cost is given by ATC_1 in Figure 12-11. Let's compare that to a situation in which the firm buys additional food-preparation equipment, doubling its fixed cost to $216 but reducing its variable cost at any given level of output. The right half of the table shows the firm's variable cost, total cost, and average total cost with this higher level of fixed cost. The average total cost curve corresponding to $216 in fixed cost is given by ATC_2 in Figure 12-11.

From the figure you can see that when output is small, 4 cases of salsa per day or fewer, average total cost is smaller when Selena forgoes the additional equipment and

FIGURE 12-11

Choosing the Level of Fixed Cost for Selena's Gourmet Salsas

There is a trade-off between higher fixed cost and lower variable cost for any given output level, and vice versa. ATC_1 is the average total cost curve corresponding to a fixed cost of $108; it leads to lower fixed cost and higher variable cost. ATC_2 is the average total cost curve corresponding to a higher fixed cost of $216 but lower variable cost. At low output levels, at 4 or fewer cases of salsa per day, ATC_1 lies below ATC_2: average total cost is lower with only $108 in fixed cost. But as output goes up, average total cost is lower with the higher amount of fixed cost, $216: at more than 4 cases of salsa per day, ATC_2 lies below ATC_1.

At low output levels, low fixed cost yields lower average total cost.

At high output levels, high fixed cost yields lower average total cost.

Low fixed cost · ATC_1

High fixed cost · ATC_2

Quantity of salsa (cases)	Low fixed cost (FC = $108)			High fixed cost (FC = $216)		
	High variable cost	Total cost	Average total cost of case ATC_1	Low variable cost	Total cost	Average total cost of case ATC_2
1	$12	$120	$120.00	$6	$222	$222.00
2	48	156	78.00	24	240	120.00
3	108	216	72.00	54	270	90.00
4	192	300	75.00	96	312	78.00
5	300	408	81.60	150	366	73.20
6	432	540	90.00	216	432	72.00
7	588	696	99.43	294	510	72.86
8	768	876	109.50	384	600	75.00
9	972	1,080	120.00	486	702	78.00
10	1,200	1,308	130.80	600	816	81.60

maintains the lower fixed cost of $108: ATC_1 lies below ATC_2. For example, at 3 cases per day, average total cost is $72 without the additional machinery and $90 with the additional machinery. But as output increases beyond 4 cases per day, the firm's average total cost is lower if it acquires the additional equipment, raising its fixed cost to $216. For example, at 9 cases of salsa per day, average total cost is $120 when fixed cost is $108 but only $78 when fixed cost is $216.

Why does average total cost change like this when fixed cost increases? When output is low, the increase in fixed cost from the additional equipment outweighs the reduction in variable cost from higher worker productivity—that is, there are too few units of output over which to spread the additional fixed cost. So if Selena plans to produce 4 or fewer cases per day, she would be better off choosing the lower level of fixed cost, $108, to achieve a lower average total cost of production. When planned output is high, however, she should acquire the additional machinery.

In general, for each output level there is some choice of fixed cost that minimizes the firm's average total cost for that output level. So when the firm has a desired output level that it expects to maintain over time, it should choose the level of fixed cost optimal for that level—that is, the level of fixed cost that minimizes its average total cost.

Now that we are studying a situation in which fixed cost can change, we need to take time into account when discussing average total cost. All of the average total cost curves we have considered until now are defined for a given level of fixed cost—that is, they are defined for the short run, the period of time over which fixed cost doesn't vary. To reinforce that distinction, for the rest of this chapter we will refer to these average total cost curves as "short-run average total cost curves."

For most firms, it is realistic to assume that there are many possible choices of fixed cost, not just two. The implication: for such a firm, many possible short-run average total cost curves will exist, each corresponding to a different choice of fixed cost and so giving rise to what is called a firm's "family" of short-run average total cost curves.

At any given point in time, a firm will find itself on one of its short-run cost curves, the one corresponding to its current level of fixed cost; a change in output will cause it to move along that curve. If the firm expects that change in output level to be long-standing, then it is likely that the firm's current level of fixed cost is no longer optimal. Given sufficient time, it will want to adjust its fixed cost to a new level that minimizes average total cost for its new output level. For example, if Selena had been producing 2 cases of salsa per day with a fixed cost of $108 but found herself increasing her output to 8 cases per day for the foreseeable future, then in the long run she should purchase more equipment and increase her fixed cost to a level that minimizes average total cost at the 8-cases-per-day output level.

Suppose we do a thought experiment and calculate the lowest possible average total cost that can be achieved for each output level if the firm were to choose its fixed cost for each output level. Economists have given this thought experiment a name: the *long-run average total cost curve*. Specifically, the **long-run average total cost curve,** or *LRATC,* is the relationship between output and average total cost when fixed cost has been chosen to minimize average total cost *for each level of output.* If there are many possible choices of fixed cost, the long-run average total cost curve will have the familiar, smooth U shape, as shown by *LRATC* in Figure 12-12 on the next page.

We can now draw the distinction between the short run and the long run more fully. In the long run, when a producer has had time to choose the fixed cost appropriate for its desired level of output, that producer will be at some point on the long-run average total cost curve. But if the output level is altered, the firm will no longer be on its long-run average total cost curve and will instead be moving along its current short-run average total cost curve. It will not be on its long-run average total cost curve again until it readjusts its fixed cost for its new output level.

Figure 12-12 illustrates this point. The curve ATC_3 shows short-run average total cost if Selena has chosen the level of fixed cost that minimizes average total cost at an output of 3 cases of salsa per day. This is confirmed by the fact that at 3 cases per day, ATC_3 touches *LRATC*, the long-run average total cost curve. Similarly, ATC_6 shows short-run average total cost if Selena has chosen the level of fixed cost that minimizes average total

The **long-run average total cost curve** shows the relationship between output and average total cost when fixed cost has been chosen to minimize average total cost for each level of output.

FIGURE 12-12

Short-Run and Long-Run Average Total Cost Curves

Short-run and long-run average total cost curves differ because a firm can choose its fixed cost in the long run. If Selena has chosen the level of fixed cost that minimizes short-run average total cost at an output of 6 cases, and actually produces 6 cases, then she will be at point C on LRATC and ATC₆. But if she produces only 3 cases, she will move to point B. If she expects to produce only 3 cases for a long time, in the long run she will reduce her fixed cost and move to point A on ATC₃. Likewise, if she produces 9 cases (putting her at point Y) and expects to continue this for a long time, she will increase her fixed cost in the long run and move to point X.

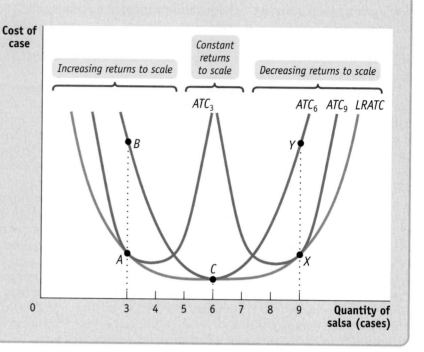

cost if her output is 6 cases per day. It touches *LRATC* at 6 cases per day. And *ATC₉* shows short-run average total cost if Selena has chosen the level of fixed cost that minimizes average total cost if her output is 9 cases per day. It touches *LRATC* at 9 cases per day.

Suppose that Selena initially chose to be on *ATC₆*. If she actually produces 6 cases of salsa per day, her firm will be at point *C* on both its short-run and long-run average total cost curves. Suppose, however, that Selena ends up producing only 3 cases of salsa per day. In the short run, her average total cost is indicated by point *B* on *ATC₆*; it is no longer on *LRATC*. If Selena had known that she would be producing only 3 cases per day, she would have been better off choosing a lower level of fixed cost, the one corresponding to *ATC₃*, thereby achieving a lower average total cost. Then her firm would have found itself at point *A* on the long-run average total cost curve, which lies below point *B*.

Suppose, conversely, that Selena ends up producing 9 cases per day even though she initially chose to be on *ATC₆*. In the short run her average total cost is indicated by point *Y* on *ATC₆*. But she would be better off purchasing more equipment and incurring a higher fixed cost in order to reduce her variable cost and move to *ATC₉*. This would allow her to reach point *X* on the long-run average total cost curve, which lies below *Y*.

The distinction between short-run and long-run average total costs is extremely important in making sense of how real firms operate over time. A company that has to increase output suddenly to meet a surge in demand will typically find that in the short run its average total cost rises sharply because it is hard to get extra production out of existing facilities. But given time to build new factories or add machinery, short-run average total cost falls.

Returns to Scale

What determines the shape of the long-run average total cost curve? The answer is that *scale*, the size of a firm's operations, is often an important determinant of its long-run average total cost of production. Firms that experience scale effects in production find that their long-run average total cost changes substantially depending on the quantity of output they produce. There are **increasing returns to scale** (also known as *economies of scale*) when long-run average total cost declines as output increases. As you can see in Figure 12-12, Selena's Gourmet Salsas experiences increasing returns to scale over out-

There are **increasing returns to scale** when long-run average total cost declines as output increases.

put levels ranging from 0 up to 5 cases of salsa per day—the output levels over which the long-run average total cost curve is declining. In contrast, there are **decreasing returns to scale** (also known as *diseconomies of scale*) when long-run average total cost increases as output increases. For Selena's Gourmet Salsas, decreasing returns to scale occur at output levels greater than 7 cases, the output levels over which its long-run average total cost curve is rising. There is also a third possible relationship between long-run average total cost and scale: firms experience **constant returns to scale** when long-run average total cost is constant as output increases. In this case, the firm's long-run average total cost curve is horizontal over the output levels for which there are constant returns to scale. As you can see in Figure 12-12, Selena's Gourmet Salsas has constant returns to scale when it produces anywhere from 5 to 7 cases of salsa per day.

What explains these scale effects in production? The answer ultimately lies in the firm's technology of production. Increasing returns often arise from the increased *specialization* that larger output levels allow—a larger scale of operation means that individual workers can limit themselves to more specialized tasks, becoming more skilled and efficient at doing them. Another source of increasing returns is very large initial setup cost; in some industries—such as auto manufacturing, electricity generating, or petroleum refining—incurring a high fixed cost in the form of plant and equipment is necessary to produce any output. A third source of increasing returns, found in certain high-tech industries such as software development, is *network externalities,* a topic covered in Chapter 17. As we'll see in Chapter 14, where we study monopoly, increasing returns have very important implications for how firms and industries interact and behave.

Decreasing returns—the opposite scenario—typically arise in large firms due to problems of coordination and communication: as the firm grows in size, it becomes ever more difficult and so more costly to communicate and to organize its activities. Although increasing returns induce firms to get larger, decreasing returns tend to limit their size. And when there are constant returns to scale, scale has no effect on a firm's long-run average total cost: it is the same regardless of whether the firm produces 1 unit or 100,000 units.

> There are **decreasing returns to scale** when long-run average total cost increases as output increases.
>
> There are **constant returns to scale** when long-run average total cost is constant as output increases.

Summing Up Costs: The Short and Long of It

If a firm is to make the best decisions about how much to produce, it has to understand how its costs relate to the quantity of output it chooses to produce. Table 12-3 provides a quick summary of the concepts and measures of cost you have learned about.

TABLE 12-3

Concepts and Measures of Cost

	Measurement	Definition	Mathematical term
Short run	Fixed cost	Cost that does not depend on the quantity of output produced	FC
	Average fixed cost	Fixed cost per unit of output	$AFC = FC/Q$
Short run and long run	Variable cost	Cost that depends on the quantity of output produced	VC
	Average variable cost	Variable cost per unit of output	$AVC = VC/Q$
	Total cost	The sum of fixed cost (short run) and variable cost	$TC = FC$ (short run) $+ VC$
	Average total cost (average cost)	Total cost per unit of output	$ATC = TC/Q$
	Marginal cost	The change in total cost generated by producing one more unit of output	$MC = \Delta TC/\Delta Q$
Long run	Long-run average total cost	Average total cost when fixed cost has been chosen to minimize average total cost for each level of output	$LRATC$

A lesson in returns to scale: cities with higher average annual snowfall maintain larger snowplow fleets.

➤ECONOMICS IN ACTION

There's No Business Like Snow Business

Anyone who has lived both in a snowy city, like Chicago, and in a city that only occasionally experiences significant snowfall, like Washington, D.C., is aware of the differences in total cost that arise from making different choices about fixed cost.

In Washington, even a minor snowfall—say, an inch or two overnight—is enough to create chaos during the next morning's commute. The same snowfall in Chicago has hardly any effect at all. The reason is not that Washingtonians are wimps and Chicagoans are made of sterner stuff; it is that Washington, where it rarely snows, has only a fraction as many snowplows and other snow-clearing equipment as cities where heavy snow is a fact of life.

In this sense Washington and Chicago are like two producers who expect to produce different levels of output, where the "output" is snow removal. Washington, which rarely has significant snow, has chosen a low level of fixed cost in the form of snow-clearing equipment. This makes sense under normal circumstances but leaves the city unprepared when major snow does fall. Chicago, which knows that it will face lots of snow, chooses to accept the higher fixed cost that leaves it in a position to respond effectively. ▲

< < < < < < < < < < < <

➤ CHECK YOUR UNDERSTANDING 12-3

1. The accompanying table shows three possible combinations of fixed cost and average variable cost. Average variable cost is constant in this example (it does not vary with the quantity of output produced).
   a. For each of the three choices, calculate the average total cost of producing 12,000, 22,000, and 30,000 units. For each of these quantities, which choice results in the lowest average total cost?

Choice	Fixed cost	Average variable cost
1	$8,000	$1.00
2	12,000	0.75
3	24,000	0.25

   b. Suppose that the firm, which has historically produced 12,000 units, experiences a sharp, permanent increase in demand that leads it to produce 22,000 units. Explain how its average total cost will change in the short run and in the long run.
   c. Explain what the firm should do instead if it believes the change in demand is temporary.

2. In each of the following cases, explain what kind of scale effects you think the firm will experience and why.
   a. A telemarketing firm in which employees make sales calls using computers and telephones
   b. An interior design firm in which design projects are based on the expertise of the firm's owner
   c. A diamond-mining company

3. Draw a graph like Figure 12-12 and insert a short-run average total cost curve corresponding to a long-run output choice of 5 cases of salsa per day. Use the graph to show why Selena should change her fixed cost if she expects to produce only 4 cases per day for a long period of time.

Solutions appear at back of book.

[➤➤ A LOOK AHEAD •••

We've just learned how to derive the various types of a firm's costs from its production function and from input prices. Our next step is to go from our analysis of costs to an analysis of the supply curve. To understand the supply curve for a particular good, we will need to look both at how a profit-maximizing firm chooses its quantity of output and at how it decides whether to enter or exit the industry producing that good.]

SUMMARY ⋯⋯⋯⋯⋯⋯⋯⋯⋯⋯⋯⋯⋯⋯⋯⋯⋯⋯⋯⋯⋯⋯⋯⋯⋯⋯⋯⋯ ∎

1. The relationship between inputs and output is a producer's **production function.** In the **short run,** the quantity of a **fixed input** cannot be varied but the quantity of a **variable input** can. In the **long run,** the quantities of all inputs can be varied. For a given amount of the fixed input, the **total product curve** shows how the quantity of output changes as the quantity of the variable input changes. We may also calculate the **marginal product** of an input, the increase in output from using one more unit of that input.

2. There are **diminishing returns to an input** when its marginal product declines as more of the input is used, holding the quantity of all other inputs fixed.

3. **Total cost,** represented by the **total cost curve,** is equal to the sum of **fixed cost,** which does not depend on output, and **variable cost,** which does depend on output. Due to diminishing returns, marginal cost, the increase in total cost generated by producing one more unit of output, normally increases as output increases.

4. **Average total cost** (also known as **average cost**), total cost divided by quantity of output, is the cost of the average unit of output, and marginal cost is the cost of one more unit produced. Economists believe that **U-shaped average total cost curves** are typical, because average total cost consists of two parts: **average fixed cost,** which falls when output increases (the spreading effect), and **average variable cost,** which rises with output (the diminishing returns effect).

5. When average total cost is U-shaped, the bottom of the U is the level of output at which average total cost is minimized, the point of **minimum-cost output.** This is also the point at which the marginal cost curve crosses the average total cost curve from below. Due to gains from specialization, the marginal cost curve may slope downward initially before sloping upward, giving it a "swoosh" shape.

6. In the long run, a producer can change its fixed input and its level of fixed cost. By accepting higher fixed cost, a firm can lower its variable cost for any given output level, and vice versa. The **long-run average total cost curve** shows the relationship between output and average total cost when fixed cost has been chosen to minimize average total cost at each level of output. A firm moves along its short-run average total cost curve as it changes the quantity of output, and it returns to a point on both its short-run and long-run average total cost curves once it has adjusted fixed cost to its new output level.

7. As output increases, there are **increasing returns to scale** if long-run average total cost declines; **decreasing returns to scale** if it increases; and **constant returns to scale** if it remains constant. Scale effects depend on the technology of production.

KEY TERMS ⋯⋯⋯⋯⋯⋯⋯⋯⋯⋯⋯⋯⋯⋯⋯⋯⋯⋯⋯⋯⋯⋯⋯⋯⋯⋯⋯⋯ ∎

Production function, p. 304
Fixed input, p. 304
Variable input, p. 304
Long run, p. 304
Short run, p. 304
Total product curve, p. 305
Marginal product, p. 305
Diminishing returns to an input, p. 306

Fixed cost, p. 309
Variable cost, p. 309
Total cost, p. 309
Total cost curve, p. 309
Average total cost, p. 314
Average cost, p. 314
U-shaped average total cost curve, p. 314
Average fixed cost, p. 314

Average variable cost, p. 315
Minimum-cost output, p. 316
Long-run average total cost curve, p. 321
Increasing returns to scale, p. 322
Decreasing returns to scale, p. 323
Constant returns to scale, p. 323

PROBLEMS ⋯⋯⋯⋯⋯⋯⋯⋯⋯⋯⋯⋯⋯⋯⋯⋯⋯⋯⋯⋯⋯⋯⋯⋯⋯⋯⋯⋯ ∎

1. Changes in the prices of key commodities can have a significant impact on a company's bottom line. According to a September 27, 2007, article in the *Wall Street Journal,* "Now, with oil, gas and electricity prices soaring, companies are beginning to realize that saving energy can translate into dramatically lower costs." Another *Wall Street Journal* article, dated September 9, 2007, states, "Higher grain prices are taking an increasing financial toll." Energy is an input into virtually all types of production; corn is an input into the production of beef, chicken, high-fructose corn syrup, and ethanol (the gasoline substitute fuel).

   a. Explain how the cost of energy can be both a fixed cost and a variable cost for a company.

   b. Suppose energy is a fixed cost and energy prices rise. What happens to the company's average total cost curve? What happens to its marginal cost curve? Illustrate your answer with a diagram.

c. Explain why the cost of corn is a variable cost but not a fixed cost for an ethanol producer.

d. When the cost of corn goes up, what happens to the average total cost curve of an ethanol producer? What happens to its marginal cost curve? Illustrate your answer with a diagram.

2. Marty's Frozen Yogurt is a small shop that sells cups of frozen yogurt in a university town. Marty owns three frozen-yogurt machines. His other inputs are refrigerators, frozen-yogurt mix, cups, sprinkle toppings, and, of course, workers. He estimates that his daily production function when he varies the number of workers employed (and at the same time, of course, yogurt mix, cups, and so on) is as shown in the accompanying table.

Quantity of labor (workers)	Quantity of frozen yogurt (cups)
0	0
1	110
2	200
3	270
4	300
5	320
6	330

a. What are the fixed inputs and variable inputs in the production of cups of frozen yogurt?

b. Draw the total product curve. Put the quantity of labor on the horizontal axis and the quantity of frozen yogurt on the vertical axis.

c. What is the marginal product of the first worker? The second worker? The third worker? Why does marginal product decline as the number of workers increases?

3. The production function for Marty's Frozen Yogurt is given in Problem 2. Marty pays each of his workers $80 per day. The cost of his other variable inputs is $0.50 per cup of yogurt. His fixed cost is $100 per day.

a. What is Marty's variable cost and total cost when he produces 110 cups of yogurt? 200 cups? Calculate variable and total cost for every level of output given in Problem 2.

b. Draw Marty's variable cost curve. On the same diagram, draw his total cost curve.

c. What is the marginal cost per cup for the first 110 cups of yogurt? For the next 90 cups? Calculate the marginal cost for all remaining levels of output.

4. The production function for Marty's Frozen Yogurt is given in Problem 2. The costs are given in Problem 3.

a. For each of the given levels of output, calculate the average fixed cost (AFC), average variable cost (AVC), and average total cost (ATC) per cup of frozen yogurt.

b. On one diagram, draw the AFC, AVC, and ATC curves.

c. What principle explains why the AFC declines as output increases? What principle explains why the AVC increases as output increases? Explain your answers.

d. How many cups of frozen yogurt are produced when average total cost is minimized?

5. The accompanying table shows a car manufacturer's total cost of producing cars.

Quantity of cars	TC
0	$500,000
1	540,000
2	560,000
3	570,000
4	590,000
5	620,000
6	660,000
7	720,000
8	800,000
9	920,000
10	1,100,000

a. What is this manufacturer's fixed cost?

b. For each level of output, calculate the variable cost (VC). For each level of output except zero output, calculate the average variable cost (AVC), average total cost (ATC), and average fixed cost (AFC). What is the minimum-cost output?

c. For each level of output, calculate this manufacturer's marginal cost (MC).

d. On one diagram, draw the manufacturer's AVC, ATC, and MC curves.

6. Labor costs represent a large percentage of total costs for many firms. According to a September 1, 2007, Wall Street Journal article, U.S. labor costs were up 0.9% during the preceding three months and 0.8% over the three months preceding those.

a. When labor costs increase, what happens to average total cost and marginal cost? Consider a case in which labor costs are only variable costs and a case in which they are both variable and fixed costs.

An increase in labor productivity means each worker can produce more output. Recent data on productivity show that labor productivity in the U.S. nonfarm business sector grew 2% for each of the years 2005, 2006, and 2007. Annual growth in labor productivity averaged 1.5% from the mid-1970s to mid-1990s, 2.6% in the past decade, and 4% for a couple of years in the early 2000s.

b. When productivity growth is positive, what happens to the total product curve and the marginal product of labor curve? Illustrate your answer with a diagram.

c. When productivity growth is positive, what happens to the marginal cost curve and the average total cost curve? Illustrate your answer with a diagram.

d. If labor costs are rising over time on average, why would a company want to adopt equipment and methods that increase labor productivity?

7. Magnificent Blooms is a florist specializing in floral arrangements for weddings, graduations, and other events. Magnificent Blooms has a fixed cost associated with space and equipment of $100 per day. Each worker is paid $50 per day. The daily production function for Magnificent Blooms is shown in the accompanying table.

Quantity of labor (workers)	Quantity of floral arrangements
0	0
1	5
2	9
3	12
4	14
5	15

a. Calculate the marginal product of each worker. What principle explains why the marginal product per worker declines as the number of workers employed increases?

b. Calculate the marginal cost of each level of output. What principle explains why the marginal cost per floral arrangement increases as the number of arrangements increases?

8. You have the information shown in the accompanying table about a firm's costs. Complete the missing data.

Quantity	TC	MC	ATC	AVC
0	$20		—	—
		$20		
1	?		?	?
		10		
2	?		?	?
		16		
3	?		?	?
		20		
4	?		?	?
		24		
5	?		?	?

9. Evaluate each of the following statements. If a statement is true, explain why; if it is false, identify the mistake and try to correct it.

a. A decreasing marginal product tells us that marginal cost must be rising.

b. An increase in fixed cost increases the minimum-cost output.

c. An increase in fixed cost increases marginal cost.

d. When marginal cost is above average total cost, average total cost must be falling.

10. Mark and Jeff operate a small company that produces souvenir footballs. Their fixed cost is $2,000 per month. They can hire workers for $1,000 per worker per month. Their monthly production function for footballs is as given in the accompanying table.

Quantity of labor (workers)	Quantity of footballs
0	0
1	300
2	800
3	1,200
4	1,400
5	1,500

a. For each quantity of labor, calculate average variable cost (AVC), average fixed cost (AFC), average total cost (ATC), and marginal cost (MC).

b. On one diagram, draw the AVC, ATC, and MC curves.

c. At what level of output is Mark and Jeff's average total cost minimized?

11. You produce widgets. Currently you produce 4 widgets at a total cost of $40.

a. What is your average total cost?

b. Suppose you could produce one more (the fifth) widget at a marginal cost of $5. If you do produce that fifth widget, what will your average total cost be? Has your average total cost increased or decreased? Why?

c. Suppose instead that you could produce one more (the fifth) widget at a marginal cost of $20. If you do produce that fifth widget, what will your average total cost be? Has your average total cost increased or decreased? Why?

12. In your economics class, each homework problem set is graded on the basis of a maximum score of 100. You have completed 9 out of 10 of the problem sets for the term, and your current average grade is 88. What range of grades for your 10th problem set will raise your overall average? What range will lower your overall average? Explain your answer.

13. Don owns a small concrete-mixing company. His fixed cost is the cost of the concrete-batching machinery and his mixer trucks. His variable cost is the cost of the sand, gravel, and other inputs for producing concrete; the gas and maintenance for the machinery and trucks; and his workers. He is trying to decide how many mixer trucks to purchase. He has estimated the costs shown in the accompanying table based on estimates of the number of orders his company will receive per week.

Quantity of trucks	FC	VC 20 orders	VC 40 orders	VC 60 orders
2	$6,000	$2,000	$5,000	$12,000
3	7,000	1,800	3,800	10,800
4	8,000	1,200	3,600	8,400

a. For each level of fixed cost, calculate Don's total cost for producing 20, 40, and 60 orders per week.

b. If Don is producing 20 orders per week, how many trucks should he purchase and what will his average total cost be? Answer the same questions for 40 and 60 orders per week.

14. Consider Don's concrete-mixing business described in Problem 13. Assume that Don purchased 3 trucks, expecting to produce 40 orders per week.

    a. Suppose that, in the short run, business declines to 20 orders per week. What is Don's average total cost per order in the short run? What will his average total cost per order in the short run be if his business booms to 60 orders per week?

    b. What is Don's long-run average total cost for 20 orders per week? Explain why his short-run average total cost of producing 20 orders per week when the number of trucks is fixed at 3 is greater than his long-run average total cost of producing 20 orders per week.

    c. Draw Don's long-run average total cost curve. Draw his short-run average total cost curve if he owns 3 trucks.

15. True or False? Explain your reasoning.

    a. The short-run average total cost can never be less than the long-run average total cost.

    b. The short-run average variable cost can never be less than the long-run average total cost.

www.worthpublishers.com/krugmanwells

c. In the long run, choosing a higher level of fixed cost shifts the long-run average total cost curve upward.

16. Wolfsburg Wagon (WW) is a small automaker. The accompanying table shows WW's long-run average total cost.

Quantity of cars	*LRATC* of car
1	$30,000
2	20,000
3	15,000
4	12,000
5	12,000
6	12,000
7	14,000
8	18,000

a. For which levels of output does WW experience increasing returns to scale?

b. For which levels of output does WW experience decreasing returns to scale?

c. For which levels of output does WW experience constant returns to scale?

>> Perfect Competition and the Supply Curve

DOING WHAT COMES NATURALLY

FOOD CONSUMERS IN THE UNITED STATES ARE concerned about health issues. Demand for natural foods and beverages, such as bottled water and organically grown fruits and vegetables, increased rapidly over the past decade, at an average growth rate of 20% per year. The small group of farmers who had pioneered organic farming techniques prospered thanks to higher prices.

But everyone knew that the high prices of organic produce were unlikely to persist even if the new, higher demand for naturally grown food continued: the supply of organic food, although relatively price-inelastic in the short run, was surely price-elastic in the long run. Over time, farms already producing organically would increase their capacity, and conventional farmers would enter the organic food business. So the increase in the quantity supplied in response to the increase in price would be much larger in the long run than in the short run.

Where does the supply curve come from? Why is there a difference between the short-run and the long-run supply curve? In this chapter

we will use our understanding of costs, developed in Chapter 12, as the basis for an analysis of the supply curve. As we'll see, this will require that we understand the behavior both of individual firms and of an entire industry, composed of these many individual firms.

Our analysis in this chapter assumes that the industry in question is characterized by *perfect competition*. We begin by explaining the concept of perfect competition, providing a brief introduction to the conditions that give rise to a perfectly competitive industry. We then show how a producer under perfect competition decides how much to produce. Finally, we use the cost curves of the individual producers to derive the *industry supply curve* under perfect competition. By analyzing the way a competitive industry evolves over time, we will come to understand the distinction between the short-run and long-run effects of changes in demand on a competitive industry—such as, for example, the effect of America's new taste for organic food on the organic farming industry. We will conclude with a deeper discussion of the conditions necessary for perfect competition.

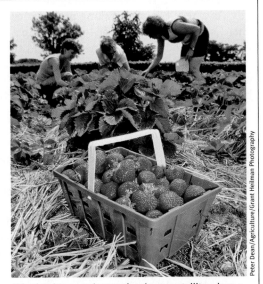

Whether it's organic strawberries or satellites, how a good is produced determines its cost of production.

Perfect Competition

Suppose that Yves and Zoe are neighboring farmers, both of whom grow organic tomatoes. Both sell their output to the same grocery store chains that carry organic foods; so, in a real sense, Yves and Zoe compete with each other.

Does this mean that Yves should try to stop Zoe from growing tomatoes or that Yves and Zoe should form an agreement to grow less? Almost certainly not: there are hundreds or thousands of organic tomato farmers, and Yves and Zoe are competing with all those other growers as well as with each other. Because so many farmers sell organic tomatoes, if any one of them produced more or less, there would be no measurable effect on market prices.

When people talk about business competition, the image they often have in mind is a situation in which two or three rival firms are intensely struggling for advantage. But economists know that when a business focuses on a few main competitors, it's actually a sign that competition is fairly limited. As the example of organic tomatoes suggests, when there is enough competition it doesn't even make sense to identify your rivals: there are so many competitors that you cannot single out any one of them as a rival.

We can put it another way: Yves and Zoe are **price-taking producers.** A producer is a price-taker when its actions cannot affect the market price of the good or service it sells. As a result, a price-taking producer considers the market price as given. When there is enough competition—when competition is what economists call "perfect"—then every producer is a price-taker. And there is a similar definition for consumers: a **price-taking consumer** is a consumer who cannot influence the market price of the good or service by his or her actions. That is, the market price is unaffected by how much or how little of the good the consumer buys.

Defining Perfect Competition

In a **perfectly competitive market,** all market participants, both consumers and producers, are price-takers. That is, neither consumption decisions by individual consumers nor production decisions by individual producers affect the market price of the good.

The supply and demand model, which we introduced in Chapter 3 and have used repeatedly since then, is a model of a perfectly competitive market. It depends fundamentally on the assumption that no individual buyer or seller of a good, such as coffee beans or organic tomatoes, believes that it is possible to individually affect the price at which he or she can buy or sell the good.

As a general rule, consumers are indeed price-takers. Instances in which consumers are able to affect the prices they pay are rare. It is, however, quite common for producers to have a significant ability to affect the prices they receive, a phenomenon we'll address in Chapter 14. So the model of perfect competition is appropriate for some but not all markets. An industry in which producers are price-takers is

---

A **price-taking producer** is a producer whose actions have no effect on the market price of the good or service it sells.

A **price-taking consumer** is a consumer whose actions have no effect on the market price of the good or service he or she buys.

A **perfectly competitive market** is a market in which all market participants are price-takers.

called a **perfectly competitive industry.** Clearly, some industries aren't perfectly competitive; in later chapters we'll learn how to analyze industries that don't fit the perfectly competitive model.

Under what circumstances will all producers be price-takers? In the next section we will find that there are two necessary conditions for a perfectly competitive industry and that a third condition is often present as well.

Two Necessary Conditions for Perfect Competition

The markets for major grains, like wheat and corn, are perfectly competitive: individual wheat and corn farmers, as well as individual buyers of wheat and corn, take market prices as given. In contrast, the markets for some of the food items made from these grains—in particular, breakfast cereals—are by no means perfectly competitive. There is intense competition among cereal brands, but not *perfect* competition. To understand the difference between the market for wheat and the market for shredded wheat cereal is to understand the two necessary conditions for perfect competition.

First, for an industry to be perfectly competitive, it must contain many producers, none of whom have a large **market share.** A producer's market share is the fraction of the total industry output accounted for by that producer's output. The distribution of market share constitutes a major difference between the grain industry and the breakfast cereal industry. There are thousands of wheat farmers, none of whom account for more than a tiny fraction of total wheat sales. The breakfast cereal industry, however, is dominated by four producers: Kellogg's, General Mills, Post, and Quaker Foods. Kellogg's alone accounts for about one-third of all cereal sales. Kellogg's executives know that if they try to sell more corn flakes, they are likely to drive down the market price of corn flakes. That is, they know that their actions influence market prices, simply because they are so large a part of the market that changes in their production will significantly affect the overall quantity supplied. It makes sense to assume that producers are price-takers only when an industry does *not* contain any large players like Kellogg's.

Second, an industry can be perfectly competitive only if consumers regard the products of all producers as equivalent. This clearly isn't true in the breakfast cereal market: consumers don't consider Cap'n Crunch to be a good substitute for Wheaties. As a result, the maker of Wheaties has some ability to increase its price without fear that it will lose all its customers to the maker of Cap'n Crunch. Contrast this with the case of a **standardized product,** which is a product that consumers regard as the same good even when it comes from different producers, sometimes known as a **commodity.** Because wheat is a standardized product, consumers regard the output of one wheat producer as a perfect substitute for that of another producer. Consequently, one farmer cannot increase the price for his or her wheat without losing all sales to other wheat farmers. So the second necessary condition for a competitive industry is that the industry output is a standardized product (see For Inquiring Minds on the next page).

Free Entry and Exit

All perfectly competitive industries have many producers with small market shares, producing a standardized product. Most perfectly competitive industries are also characterized by one more feature: it is easy for new firms to enter the industry or for firms that are currently in the industry to leave. That is, no obstacles in the form of government regulations or limited access to key resources prevent new producers from entering the market. And no additional costs are associated with shutting down a company and leaving the industry. Economists refer to the arrival of new firms into an industry as *entry;* they refer to the departure of firms from an industry as *exit.*

A **perfectly competitive industry** is an industry in which producers are price-takers.

A producer's **market share** is the fraction of the total industry output accounted for by that producer's output.

A good is a **standardized product,** also known as a **commodity,** when consumers regard the products of different producers as the same good.

What's a Standardized Product?

A perfectly competitive industry must produce a standardized product. But is it enough for the products of different firms actually to be the same? No: people must also *think* that they are the same. And producers often go to great lengths to convince consumers that they have a distinctive, or *differentiated,* product, even when they don't.

Consider, for example, champagne—not the superexpensive premium champagnes but the more ordinary stuff. Most people cannot tell the difference between champagne actually produced in the Champagne region of France, where the product originated, and similar products from Spain or California. But the French government has sought and obtained legal protection for the winemakers of Champagne, ensuring that around the world only bubbly wine from that region can be called champagne.

In the end, only kimchi eaters can tell you if there is truly a difference between Korean-produced kimchi and the Japanese-produced variety.

If it's from someplace else, all the seller can do is say that it was produced using the *méthode Champenoise.* This creates a differentiation in the minds of consumers and lets the champagne producers of Champagne charge higher prices.

Similarly, Korean producers of *kimchi,* the spicy fermented cabbage that is the Korean national side dish, are doing their best to convince consumers that the same product packaged by Japanese firms is just not the real thing. The purpose is, of course, to ensure higher prices for Korean *kimchi.*

So is an industry perfectly competitive if it sells products that are indistinguishable except in name but that consumers, for whatever reason, don't think are standardized? No. When it comes to defining the nature of competition, the consumer is always right.

When there are no obstacles to entry into or exit from an industry, we say that the industry has **free entry and exit.**

Free entry and exit is not strictly necessary for perfect competition. In Chapter 5 we described the case of New Jersey clam fishing, where regulations have the effect of limiting the number of fishing boats. Despite this, there are enough boats operating that the fishermen are price-takers. But free entry and exit is a key factor in most competitive industries. It ensures that the number of producers in an industry can adjust to changing market conditions. And, in particular, it ensures that producers in an industry cannot act to keep other firms out.

To sum up, then, perfect competition depends on two necessary conditions. First, the industry must contain many producers, each having a small market share. Second, the industry must produce a standardized product. In addition, perfectly competitive industries are normally characterized by free entry and exit.

How does an industry that meets these three criteria behave? As a first step toward answering that question, let's look at how an individual producer in a perfectly competitive industry maximizes profit.

►ECONOMICS IN ACTION

The Pain of Competition

Sometimes it is possible to see an industry become perfectly competitive. In fact, it happens on a regular basis in the case of pharmaceuticals: the conditions for perfect competition are often met as soon as the patent on a popular drug expires.

When a company develops a new drug, it is usually able to receive a patent—a legal monopoly that gives it the exclusive right to sell that drug for 20 years from the date

An industry has **free entry and exit** when new producers can easily enter into an industry and existing producers can easily leave that industry.

of filing. When the patent expires, the field is open for other companies to sell their own versions of the drug—marketed as "generics" and sold under the medical name of the drug rather than the brand name used by the original producer. Generics are standardized products, much like aspirin, and are often sold by many producers.

A good example came in 1984, when Upjohn's patent on ibuprofen—a painkiller that the company still markets under the brand name Motrin—expired. Most people who use ibuprofen, like most people who use aspirin, now purchase a generic version made by one of many producers.

The shift to perfect competition, not coincidentally, is accompanied by a sharp fall in market price. When its patent expired, Upjohn immediately cut the price of Motrin by 35%, but as more companies started selling the generic drug, the price of ibuprofen eventually fell by another two-thirds.

Ten years later the patent on the painkiller naproxen—sold under the brand name Naprosyn—expired. The generic version of naproxen was soon selling at only one-tenth of the original price of Naprosyn. ▲

> > > > > > > > > > > > >

> **CHECK YOUR UNDERSTANDING** 13-1

1. In each of the following situations, do you think the industry described will be perfectly competitive or not? Explain your answer.
    a. There are two producers of aluminum in the world, a good sold in many places.
    b. The price of natural gas is determined by global supply and demand. A small share of that global supply is produced by a handful of companies located in the North Sea.
    c. Dozens of designers sell high-fashion clothes. Each designer has a distinctive style and a loyal clientele.
    d. There are many baseball teams in the United States, one or two in each major city, and each selling tickets to its home-town events.

Solutions appear at back of book.

Production and Profits

Consider Jennifer and Jason, who run an organic tomato farm. Suppose that the market price of organic tomatoes is $18 per bushel and that Jennifer and Jason are price-takers—they can sell as much as they like at that price. Then we can use the data in Table 13-1 to find their profit-maximizing level of output by direct calculation.

TABLE 13-1

Profit for Jennifer and Jason's Farm When Market Price Is $18

Quantity of tomatoes Q (bushels)	Total revenue TR	Total cost TC	Profit TR − TC
0	$0	$14	−$14
1	18	30	−12
2	36	36	0
3	54	44	10
4	72	56	16
5	90	72	18
6	108	92	16
7	126	116	10

Marginal revenue is the change in total revenue generated by an additional unit of output.

The **optimal output rule** says that profit is maximized by producing the quantity of output at which the marginal revenue of the last unit produced is equal to its marginal cost.

The first column shows the quantity of output in bushels, and the second column shows Jennifer and Jason's total revenue from their output: the market value of their output. Total revenue, *TR*, is equal to the market price multiplied by the quantity of output:

(13-1) $TR = P \times Q$

In this example, total revenue is equal to $18 per bushel times the quantity of output in bushels.

The third column of Table 13-1 shows Jennifer and Jason's total cost. The fourth column of Table 13-1 shows their profit, equal to total revenue minus total cost:

(13-2) $\text{Profit} = TR - TC$

As indicated by the numbers in the table, profit is maximized at an output of 5 bushels, where profit is equal to $18. But we can gain more insight into the profit-maximizing choice of output by viewing it as a problem of marginal analysis, a task we'll do next.

Using Marginal Analysis to Choose the Profit-Maximizing Quantity of Output

Recall from Chapter 9 the *principle of marginal analysis:* the optimal amount of an activity is the level at which marginal benefit is equal to marginal cost. To apply this principle, consider the effect on a producer's profit of increasing output by one unit. The marginal benefit of that unit is the additional revenue generated by selling it; this measure has a name—it is called the **marginal revenue** of that output. The general formula for marginal revenue is:

(13-3) $\text{Marginal revenue} = \dfrac{\text{Change in total revenue generated by one additional unit of output}}{} = \dfrac{\text{Change in total revenue}}{\text{Change in quantity of output}}$

or

$MR = \Delta TR / \Delta Q$

So Jennifer and Jason maximize their profit by producing bushels up to the point at which the marginal revenue is equal to marginal cost. We can summarize this as the producer's **optimal output rule:** profit is maximized by producing the quantity at which the marginal revenue of the last unit produced is equal to its marginal cost. That is, $MR = MC$ at the optimal quantity of output.

We can learn how to apply the optimal output rule with the help of Table 13-2, which provides various short-run cost measures for Jennifer and Jason's farm. The second column contains the farm's variable cost, and the third column shows its total cost of output based on the assumption that the farm incurs a fixed cost of $14. The fourth column shows their marginal cost. Notice that, in this example, the marginal cost initially falls as output rises but then begins to increase, so that the marginal cost curve has the "swoosh" shape described in the Selena's Gourmet Salsas example in Chapter 12. (Shortly it will become clear that this shape has important implications for short-run production decisions.)

The fifth column contains the farm's marginal revenue, which has an important feature: Jennifer and Jason's marginal revenue is constant at $18 for every output level. The sixth and final column shows the calculation of the net gain per bushel of tomatoes, which is equal to marginal revenue minus marginal cost—or, equivalently in this case, market price minus marginal cost. As you can see, it is positive for the

TABLE 13-2

Short-Run Costs for Jennifer and Jason's Farm

Quantity of tomatoes Q (bushels)	Variable cost VC	Total cost TC	Marginal cost of bushel $MC = \Delta TC/\Delta Q$	Marginal revenue of bushel MR	Net gain of bushel = $MR - MC$
0	$0	$14			
			$16	$18	$2
1	16	30			
			6	18	12
2	22	36			
			8	18	10
3	30	44			
			12	18	6
4	42	56			
			16	18	2
5	58	72			
			20	18	−2
6	78	92			
			24	18	−6
7	102	116			

The **price-taking firm's optimal output rule** says that a price-taking firm's profit is maximized by producing the quantity of output at which the market price is equal to the marginal cost of the last unit produced.

The **marginal revenue curve** shows how marginal revenue varies as output varies.

1st through 5th bushels; producing each of these bushels raises Jennifer and Jason's profit. For the 6th and 7th bushels, however, net gain is negative: producing them would decrease, not increase, profit. (You can verify this by examining Table 13-1.) So 5 bushels are Jennifer and Jason's profit-maximizing output; it is the level of output at which marginal cost is equal to the market price, $18.

This example, in fact, illustrates another general rule derived from marginal analysis—the **price-taking firm's optimal output rule,** which says that a price-taking firm's profit is maximized by producing the quantity of output at which the market price is equal to the marginal cost of the last unit produced. That is, $P = MC$ *at the price-taking firm's optimal quantity of output.* In fact, the price-taking firm's optimal output rule is just an application of the optimal output rule to the particular case of a price-taking firm. Why? Because *in the case of a price-taking firm, marginal revenue is equal to the market price.* A price-taking firm cannot influence the market price by its actions. It always takes the market price as given because it cannot lower the market price by selling more or raise the market price by selling less. So, for a price-taking firm, the additional revenue generated by producing one more unit is always the market price. We will need to keep this fact in mind in future chapters, where we will learn that marginal revenue is not equal to the market price if the industry is not perfectly competitive; as a result, firms are not price-takers when an industry is not perfectly competitive.

For the remainder of this chapter, we will assume that the industry in question is like organic tomato farming, perfectly competitive. Figure 13-1 on the next page shows that Jennifer and Jason's profit-maximizing quantity of output is, indeed, the number of bushels at which the marginal cost of production is equal to price. The figure shows the marginal cost curve, *MC,* drawn from the data in the fourth column of Table 13-2. As in Chapter 9, we plot the marginal cost of increasing output from 1 to 2 bushels halfway between 1 and 2, and so on. The horizontal line at $18 is Jennifer and Jason's **marginal revenue curve.** Note that whenever a firm is a price-taker, its marginal revenue curve is a horizontal line at the market price: it can sell as much as it likes at the market price. Regardless of whether it sells more or less, the market price is unaffected. In effect, the individual firm faces a horizontal, perfectly elastic demand curve for its output—an individual demand curve for its output that is equivalent to its marginal revenue curve. The marginal cost curve crosses the marginal revenue curve at point *E.* Sure enough, the quantity of output at *E* is 5 bushels.

PITFALLS

WHAT IF MARGINAL REVENUE AND MARGINAL COST AREN'T EXACTLY EQUAL?

The optimal output rule says that to maximize profit, you should produce the quantity at which marginal revenue is equal to marginal cost. But what do you do if there is no output level at which marginal revenue equals marginal cost? In that case, you produce the largest quantity for which marginal revenue exceeds marginal cost. This is the case in Table 13-2 at an output of 5 bushels. The simpler version of the optimal output rule applies when production involves large numbers, such as hundreds or thousands of units. In such cases marginal cost comes in small increments, and there is always a level of output at which marginal cost almost exactly equals marginal revenue.

FIGURE 13-1

The Price-Taking Firm's Profit-Maximizing Quantity of Output

At the profit-maximizing quantity of output, the market price is equal to marginal cost. It is located at the point where the marginal cost curve crosses the marginal revenue curve, which is a horizontal line at the market price. Here, the profit-maximizing point is at an output of 5 bushels of tomatoes, the output quantity at point *E*.

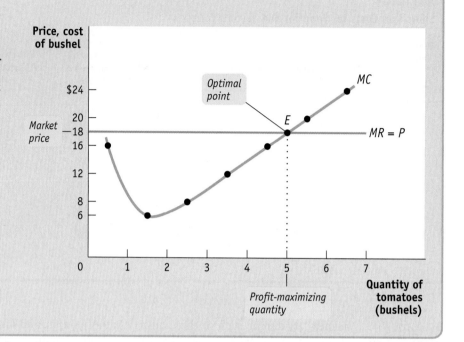

Does this mean that the price-taking firm's production decision can be entirely summed up as "produce up to the point where the marginal cost of production is equal to the price"? No, not quite. Before applying the principle of marginal analysis to determine how much to produce, a potential producer must as a first step answer an "either–or" question: should it produce at all? If the answer to that question is yes, it then proceeds to the second step—a "how much" decision: maximizing profit by choosing the quantity of output at which marginal cost is equal to price.

To understand why the first step in the production decision involves an "either–or" question, we need to ask how we determine whether it is profitable or unprofitable to produce at all.

When Is Production Profitable?

Recall from Chapter 9 that a firm's decision whether or not to stay in a given business depends on its *economic profit*—a measure based on the opportunity cost of resources used in the business. To put it a slightly different way: in the calculation of economic profit, a firm's total cost incorporates the implicit cost—the benefits forgone in the next best use of the firm's resources—as well as the explicit cost in the form of actual cash outlays. In contrast, *accounting profit* is profit calculated using only the explicit costs incurred by the firm. This means that economic profit incorporates the opportunity cost of resources owned by the firm and used in the production of output, while accounting profit does not. As in the example of Babette's Cajun Café in Chapter 9, a firm may make positive accounting profit while making zero or even negative economic profit. It's important to understand clearly that a firm's decision to produce or not, to stay in business or to close down permanently, should be based on economic profit, not accounting profit.

So we will assume, as we always do, that the cost numbers given in Tables 13-1 and 13-2 include all costs, implicit as well as explicit, and that the profit numbers in Table 13-1 are economic profit. So what determines whether Jennifer and Jason's farm

TABLE 13-3

Short-Run Average Costs for Jennifer and Jason's Farm

Quantity of tomatoes Q (bushels)	Variable cost VC	Total cost TC	Short-run average variable cost of bushel AVC = VC/Q	Short-run average total cost of bushel ATC = TC/Q
1	$16.00	$30.00	$16.00	$30.00
2	22.00	36.00	11.00	18.00
3	30.00	44.00	10.00	14.67
4	42.00	56.00	10.50	14.00
5	58.00	72.00	11.60	14.40
6	78.00	92.00	13.00	15.33
7	102.00	116.00	14.57	16.57

earns a profit or generates a loss? The answer is that, given the farm's cost curves, whether or not it is profitable depends on the market price of tomatoes—specifically, *whether the market price is more or less than the farm's minimum average total cost.*

In Table 13-3 we calculate short-run average variable cost and short-run average total cost for Jennifer and Jason's farm. These are short-run values because we take fixed cost as given. (We'll turn to the effects of changing fixed cost shortly.) The short-run average total cost curve, *ATC*, is shown in Figure 13-2, along with the marginal cost curve, *MC*, from Figure 13-1. As you can see, average total cost is minimized at point *C*, corresponding to an output of 4 bushels—the *minimum-cost output*—and an average total cost of $14 per bushel.

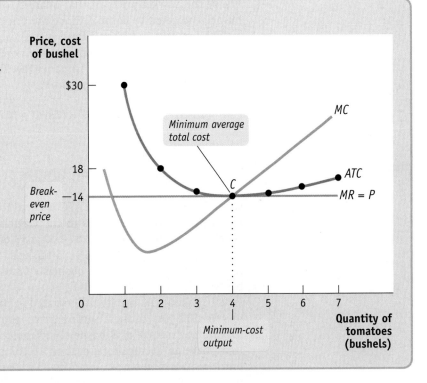

FIGURE 13-2

Costs and Production in the Short Run

This figure shows the marginal cost curve, *MC*, and the short-run average total cost curve, *ATC*. When the market price is $14, output will be 4 bushels of tomatoes (the minimum-cost output), represented by point *C*. The price of $14, equal to the firm's minimum average total cost, is the firm's *break-even price*.

To see how these curves can be used to decide whether production is profitable or unprofitable, recall that profit is equal to total revenue minus total cost, $TR - TC$. This means:

- If the firm produces a quantity at which $TR > TC$, the firm is profitable.
- If the firm produces a quantity at which $TR = TC$, the firm breaks even.
- If the firm produces a quantity at which $TR < TC$, the firm incurs a loss.

We can also express this idea in terms of revenue and cost per unit of output. If we divide profit by the number of units of output, Q, we obtain the following expression for profit per unit of output:

(13-4) $\text{Profit}/Q = TR/Q - TC/Q$

TR/Q is average revenue, which is the market price. TC/Q is average total cost. So a firm is profitable if the market price for its product is more than the average total cost of the quantity the firm produces; a firm loses money if the market price is less than average total cost of the quantity the firm produces. This means:

- If the firm produces a quantity at which $P > ATC$, the firm is profitable.
- If the firm produces a quantity at which $P = ATC$, the firm breaks even.
- If the firm produces a quantity at which $P < ATC$, the firm incurs a loss.

Figure 13-3 illustrates this result, showing how the market price determines whether a firm is profitable. It also shows how profits are depicted graphically. Each panel shows the marginal cost curve, MC, and the short-run average total cost curve, ATC. Average total cost is minimized at point C. Panel (a) shows the case we have already analyzed, in which the market price of tomatoes is $18 per bushel. Panel (b) shows the case in which the market price of tomatoes is lower, $10 per bushel.

In panel (a), we see that at a price of $18 per bushel the profit-maximizing quantity of output is 5 bushels, indicated by point E, where the marginal cost curve, MC, intersects the marginal revenue curve—which for a price-taking firm is a horizontal line at the market price. At that quantity of output, average total cost is $14.40 per bushel, indicated by point Z. Since the price per bushel exceeds average total cost per bushel, Jennifer and Jason's farm is profitable.

Jennifer and Jason's total profit when the market price is $18 is represented by the area of the shaded rectangle in panel (a). To see why, notice that total profit can be expressed in terms of profit per unit:

(13-5) $\text{Profit} = TR - TC = (TR/Q - TC/Q) \times Q$

or, equivalently,

$\text{Profit} = (P - ATC) \times Q$

since P is equal to TR/Q and ATC is equal to TC/Q. The height of the shaded rectangle in panel (a) corresponds to the vertical distance between points E and Z. It is equal to $P - ATC = \$18.00 - \$14.40 = \$3.60$ per bushel. The shaded rectangle has a width equal to the output: $Q = 5$ bushels. So the area of that rectangle is equal to Jennifer and Jason's profit: 5 bushels $\times$ \$3.60 profit per bushel = \$18—the same number we calculated in Table 13-1.

What about the situation illustrated in panel (b)? Here the market price of tomatoes is $10 per bushel. Setting price equal to marginal cost leads to a profit-maximizing output of 3 bushels, indicated by point A. At this output, Jennifer and Jason have an average total cost of $14.67 per bushel, indicated by point Y. At their profit-maximizing output quantity—3 bushels—average total cost exceeds the market price. This means that Jennifer and Jason's farm generates a loss, not a profit.

FIGURE 13-3

Profitability and the Market Price

In panel (a) the market price is $18. The farm is profitable because price exceeds minimum average total cost, the break-even price, $14. The farm's optimal output choice is indicated by point *E*, corresponding to an output of 5 bushels. The average total cost of producing 5 bushels is indicated by point *Z* on the *ATC* curve, corresponding to an amount of $14.40. The vertical distance between *E* and *Z* corresponds to the farm's per-unit profit, $18.00 − $14.40 = $3.60. Total profit is given by the area of the shaded rectangle, 5 × $3.60 = $18.00. In panel (b) the market price is $10; the farm is unprofitable because the price falls below the minimum average total cost, $14. The farm's optimal output choice when producing is indicated by point *A*, corresponding to an output of three bushels. The farm's per-unit loss, $14.67 − $10.00 = $4.67, is represented by the vertical distance between *A* and *Y*. The farm's total loss is represented by the shaded rectangle, 3 × $4.67 = $14.00 (adjusted for rounding error).

(a) Market Price = $18

(b) Market Price = $10

How much do they lose by producing when the market price is $10? On each bushel they lose $ATC − P = \$14.67 − \$10.00 = \$4.67$, an amount corresponding to the vertical distance between points *A* and *Y*. And they would produce 3 bushels, which corresponds to the width of the shaded rectangle. So the total value of the losses is $\$4.67 \times 3 = \$14.00$ (adjusted for rounding error), an amount that corresponds to the area of the shaded rectangle in panel (b).

But how does a producer know, in general, whether or not its business will be profitable? It turns out that the crucial test lies in a comparison of the market price to the producer's *minimum average total cost*. On Jennifer and Jason's farm, minimum average total cost, which is equal to $14, occurs at an output quantity of 4 bushels,

The **break-even price** of a price-taking firm is the market price at which it earns zero profits.

PITFALLS

ECONOMIC PROFIT, AGAIN
Some readers may wonder why firms would enter an industry when they will do little more than break even. Wouldn't people prefer to go into other businesses that yield a better profit?

The answer is that here, as always, when we calculate cost, we mean *opportunity cost*—that is, cost that includes the return a business owner could get by using his or her resources elsewhere. And so the profit that we calculate is *economic profit*; if the market price is above the break-even level, potential business owners can earn more in this industry than they could elsewhere.

indicated by point *C*. Whenever the market price exceeds minimum average total cost, the producer can find some output level for which the average total cost is less than the market price. In other words, the producer can find a level of output at which the firm makes a profit. So Jennifer and Jason's farm will be profitable whenever the market price exceeds $14. And they will achieve the highest possible profit by producing the quantity at which marginal cost equals the market price.

Conversely, if the market price is less than minimum average total cost, there is no output level at which price exceeds average total cost. As a result, the firm will be unprofitable at any quantity of output. As we saw, at a price of $10—an amount less than minimum average total cost—Jennifer and Jason did indeed lose money. By producing the quantity at which marginal cost equals the market price, Jennifer and Jason did the best they could, but the best that they could do was a loss of $14. Any other quantity would have increased the size of their loss.

The minimum average total cost of a price-taking firm is called its **break-even price,** the price at which it earns zero profit. (Recall that's *economic profit.*) A firm will earn positive profit when the market price is above the break-even price, and it will suffer losses when the market price is below the break-even price. Jennifer and Jason's break-even price of $14 is the price at point *C* in Figures 13-2 and 13-3.

So the rule for determining whether a producer of a good is profitable depends on a comparison of the market price of the good to the producer's break-even price—its minimum average total cost:

- Whenever the market price exceeds minimum average total cost, the producer is profitable.

- Whenever the market price equals minimum average total cost, the producer breaks even.

- Whenever the market price is less than minimum average total cost, the producer is unprofitable.

The Short-Run Production Decision

You might be tempted to say that if a firm is unprofitable because the market price is below its minimum average total cost, it shouldn't produce any output. In the short run, however, this conclusion isn't right. In the short run, sometimes the firm should produce even if price falls below minimum average total cost. The reason is that total cost includes *fixed cost*—cost that does not depend on the amount of output produced and can only be altered in the long run. In the short run, fixed cost must still be paid, regardless of whether or not a firm produces. For example, if Jennifer and Jason have rented a tractor for the year, they have to pay the rent on the tractor regardless of whether they produce any tomatoes. *Since it cannot be changed in the short run, their fixed cost is irrelevant to their decision about whether to produce or shut down in the short run.* Although fixed cost should play no role in the decision about whether to produce in the short run, other costs—variable costs—do matter. An example of variable costs is the wages of workers who must be hired to help with planting and harvesting. Variable costs can be saved by *not* producing; so they should play a role in determining whether or not to produce in the short run.

Let's turn to Figure 13-4: it shows both the short-run average total cost curve, *ATC,* and the short-run average variable cost curve, *AVC,* drawn from the information in Table 13-3. Recall that the difference between the two curves—the vertical distance between them—represents average fixed cost, the fixed cost per unit of output, *FC/Q.* Because the marginal cost curve has a "swoosh" shape—falling at first before rising—the short-run average variable cost curve is U-shaped: the initial fall in marginal cost causes average variable cost to fall as well, before rising marginal cost eventually pulls it up again. The short-run average variable cost curve reaches its minimum value of $10 at point *A,* at an output of 3 bushels.

FIGURE 13-4

The Short-Run Individual Supply Curve

When the market price equals or exceeds Jennifer and Jason's *shut-down price* of $10, the minimum average variable cost indicated by point *A*, they will produce the output quantity at which marginal cost is equal to price. So at any price equal to or above the minimum average *variable* cost, the short-run individual supply curve is the firm's marginal cost curve; this corresponds to the upward-sloping segment of the individual supply curve. When market price falls below minimum average variable cost, the firm ceases operation in the short run. This corresponds to the vertical segment of the individual supply curve along the vertical axis.

We are now prepared to fully analyze the optimal production decision in the short run. We need to consider two cases:

- When the market price is below minimum average *variable* cost
- When the market price is greater than or equal to minimum average *variable* cost

When the market price is below minimum average variable cost, the price the firm receives per unit is not covering its variable cost per unit. A firm in this situation should cease production immediately. Why? Because there is no level of output at which the firm's total revenue covers its variable costs—the costs it can avoid by not operating. In this case the firm maximizes its profits by not producing at all—by, in effect, minimizing its losses. It will still incur a fixed cost in the short run, but it will no longer incur any variable cost. This means that the minimum average variable cost is equal to the **shut-down price,** the price at which the firm ceases production in the short run.

When price is greater than minimum average variable cost, however, the firm should produce in the short run. In this case, the firm maximizes profit—or minimizes loss—by choosing the output quantity at which its marginal cost is equal to the market price. For example, if the market price of tomatoes is $18 per bushel, Jennifer and Jason should produce at point *E* in Figure 13-4, corresponding to an output of 5 bushels. Note that point *C* in Figure 13-4 corresponds to the farm's break-even price of $14 per bushel. Since *E* lies above *C*, Jennifer and Jason's farm will be profitable; they will generate a per-bushel profit of $18.00 − $14.40 = $3.60 when the market price is $18.

But what if the market price lies between the shut-down price and the break-even price—that is, between minimum average *variable* cost and minimum average *total* cost? In the case of Jennifer and Jason's farm, this corresponds to prices anywhere between $10 and $14—say, a market price of $12. At $12, Jennifer and Jason's farm is not profitable; since the market price is below minimum average total cost, the farm is losing the difference between price and average total cost per unit produced. Yet even if it isn't covering its total cost per unit, it is covering its variable cost per

A firm will cease production in the short run if the market price falls below the **shut-down price,** which is equal to minimum average variable cost.

The **short-run individual supply curve** shows how an individual producer's profit-maximizing output quantity depends on the market price, taking fixed cost as given.

unit and some—but not all—of the fixed cost per unit. If a firm in this situation shuts down, it would incur no variable cost but would incur the *full* fixed cost. As a result, shutting down generates an even greater loss than continuing to operate.

This means that whenever price falls between minimum average total cost and minimum average variable cost, the firm is better off producing some output in the short run. The reason is that by producing, it can cover its variable cost per unit and at least some of its fixed cost, even though it is incurring a loss. In this case, the firm maximizes profit—that is, minimizes loss—by choosing the quantity of output at which its marginal cost is equal to the market price. So if Jennifer and Jason face a market price of $12 per bushel, their profit-maximizing output is given by point *B* in Figure 13-4, corresponding to an output of 3.5 bushels.

It's worth noting that the decision to produce when the firm is covering its variable costs but not all of its fixed cost is similar to the decision to ignore *sunk costs*, a concept we studied in Chapter 9. You may recall that a sunk cost is a cost that has already been incurred and cannot be recouped; and because it cannot be changed, it should have no effect on any current decision. In the short-run production decision, fixed cost is, in effect, like a sunk cost—it has been spent, and it can't be recovered in the short run. This comparison also illustrates why variable cost does indeed matter in the short run: it can be avoided by not producing.

And what happens if market price is exactly equal to the shut-down price, minimum average variable cost? In this instance, the firm is indifferent between producing 3 units or 0 units. As we'll see shortly, this is an important point when looking at the behavior of an industry as a whole. For the sake of clarity, we'll assume that the firm, although indifferent, does indeed produce output when price is equal to the shut-down price.

Putting everything together, we can now draw the **short-run individual supply curve** of Jennifer and Jason's farm, the red line in Figure 13-4; it shows how the profit-maximizing quantity of output in the short run depends on the price. As you can see, the curve is in two segments. The upward-sloping red segment starting at point *A* shows the short-run profit-maximizing output when market price is equal to or above the shut-down price of $10 per bushel. As long as the market price is equal to or above the shut-down price, Jennifer and Jason produce the quantity of output at which marginal cost is equal to the market price. That is, at market prices equal to or above the shut-down price, the firm's short-run supply curve corresponds to its marginal cost curve. But at any market price below minimum average variable cost—in this case, $10 per bushel—the firm shuts down and output drops to zero in the short run. This corresponds to the vertical segment of the curve that lies on top of the vertical axis.

Do firms really shut down temporarily without going out of business? Yes. In fact, in some businesses temporary shut-downs are routine. The most common examples are industries in which demand is highly seasonal, like outdoor amusement parks in climates with cold winters. Such parks would have to offer very low prices to entice customers during the colder months—prices so low that the owners would not cover their variable costs (principally wages and electricity). The wiser choice economically is to shut down until warm weather brings enough customers who are willing to pay a higher price.

Changing Fixed Cost

Although fixed cost cannot be altered in the short run, in the long run firms can acquire or get rid of machines, buildings, and so on. As we learned in Chapter 12, in the long run the level of fixed cost is a matter of choice. There we saw that a firm will choose the level of fixed cost that minimizes the average total cost for its desired output quantity. Now we will focus on an even bigger question facing a firm when choosing its fixed cost: whether to incur *any* fixed cost at all by remaining in its current business.

In the long run, a producer can always eliminate fixed cost by selling off its plant and equipment. If it does so, of course, it can't ever produce—it has exited the industry. In contrast, a potential producer can take on some fixed cost by acquiring machines and other resources, which puts it in a position to produce—it can enter the industry. In most perfectly competitive industries the set of producers, although fixed in the short run, changes in the long run as firms enter or exit the industry.

Consider Jennifer and Jason's farm once again. In order to simplify our analysis, we will sidestep the problem of choosing among several possible levels of fixed cost. Instead, we will assume from now on that Jennifer and Jason have only one possible choice of fixed cost if they operate, the amount of $14 that was the basis for the calculations in Tables 13-1, 13-2, and 13-3. Alternatively, they can choose a fixed cost of zero if they exit the industry. (With this assumption, Jennifer and Jason's short-run average total cost curve and long-run average total cost curve are one and the same.)

Suppose that the market price of organic tomatoes is consistently less than $14 over an extended period of time. In that case, Jennifer and Jason never fully cover their fixed cost: their business runs at a persistent loss. In the long run, then, they can do better by closing their business and leaving the industry. In other words, *in the long run* firms will exit an industry if the market price is consistently less than their break-even price—their minimum average total cost.

Conversely, suppose that the price of organic tomatoes is consistently above the break-even price, $14, for an extended period of time. Because their farm is profitable, Jennifer and Jason will remain in the industry and continue producing. But things won't stop there. The organic tomato industry meets the criterion of *free entry*: there are many potential organic tomato producers because the necessary inputs are easy to obtain. And the cost curves of those potential producers are likely to be similar to those of Jennifer and Jason, since the technology used by other producers is likely to be very similar to that used by Jennifer and Jason. If the price is high enough to generate profits for existing producers, it will also attract some of these potential producers into the industry. So *in the long run* a price in excess of $14 should lead to entry: new producers will come into the organic tomato industry.

As we will see in the next section, exit and entry lead to an important distinction between the *short-run industry supply curve* and the *long-run industry supply curve*.

Summing Up: The Perfectly Competitive Firm's Profitability and Production Conditions

In this chapter, we've studied where the supply curve for a perfectly competitive, price-taking firm comes from. Every perfectly competitive firm makes its production decisions by maximizing profit, and these decisions determine the supply curve. Table 13-4 summarizes the perfectly competitive firm's profitability and production conditions. It also relates them to entry into and exit from the industry.

TABLE **13-4**

Summary of the Perfectly Competitive Firm's Profitability and Production Conditions

Profitability condition (minimum *ATC* = break-even price)	Result
P > minimum *ATC*	Firm profitable. Entry into industry in the long run.
P = minimum *ATC*	Firm breaks even. No entry into or exit from industry in the long run.
P < minimum *ATC*	Firm unprofitable. Exit from industry in the long run.
Production condition (minimum *AVC* = shut-down price)	**Result**
P > minimum *AVC*	Firm produces in the short run. If *P* < minimum *ATC*, firm covers variable cost and some but not all of fixed cost. If *P* > minimum *ATC*, firm covers all variable cost and fixed cost.
P = minimum *AVC*	Firm indifferent between producing in the short run or not. Just covers variable cost.
P < minimum *AVC*	Firm shuts down in the short run. Does not cover variable cost.

➤*ECONOMICS IN ACTION*

Prices Are Up . . . but So Are Costs

In 2005 Congress passed the Energy Policy Act, mandating that, by the year 2012, 7.5 billion gallons of alternative fuel—mostly corn-based ethanol—be added to the American fuel supply with the goal of reducing gasoline consumption. The unsurprising result of this mandate: the demand for corn skyrocketed, along with its price. In spring 2007, the price of corn was 50% higher than it had been a year earlier.

This development caught the eye of American farmers like Ronnie Gerik, of Aquilla, Texas, who in response to surging corn prices reduced the size of his cotton crop and increased his corn acreage by 40%. He was not alone; within a year, the amount of U.S. acreage planted in corn increased by 15%.

Although this sounds like a sure way to make a profit, Gerik was actually taking a big gamble: even though the price of corn increased, so did the cost of the raw materials needed to grow it—by 20%. Consider the cost of just two inputs: fertilizer and fuel. Corn requires more fertilizer than other crops and, with more farmers planting corn, the increased demand for fertilizer led to a price increase. Corn also has to be transported farther away from the farm than cotton; at the same time that Gerik began shifting to greater corn production, diesel fuel became very expensive. Moreover, corn is much more sensitive to the amount of rainfall than a crop like cotton. So farmers who plant corn in drought-prone places like Texas are increasing their risk of loss. Gerik had to incorporate into his calculations his best guess of what a dry spell would cost him.

Despite all of this, what Gerik did made complete economic sense. By planting more corn, he was moving up his individual short-run supply curve for corn production. And because his individual supply curve is his marginal cost curve, his costs also went up because he has to apply more inputs—inputs that are now more expensive to obtain.

So the moral of this story is that farmers will increase their corn acreage until the marginal cost of producing corn is approximately equal to the market price of corn—which shouldn't come as a surprise because corn production satisfies all the requirements of a perfectly competitive industry. ▲

❮ ❮ ❮ ❮ ❮ ❮ ❮ ❮ ❮ ❮ ❮ ❮ ❮

Although Gerik was taking a big gamble when he cut the size of his cotton crop to plant more corn, his decision made good economic sense.

➤➤ QUICK REVIEW

➤ A producer chooses output according to the **optimal output rule.** For a price-taking firm, **marginal revenue** is equal to price and it chooses output according to the **price-taking firm's optimal output rule.**

➤ A firm is profitable whenever price exceeds its **break-even price,** equal to its minimum average total cost. Below that price it is unprofitable. It breaks even when price is equal to its break-even price.

➤ Fixed cost is irrelevant to the firm's optimal short-run production decision. When price exceeds its **shutdown price,** minimum average variable cost, the price-taking firm produces the quantity of output at which marginal cost equals price. When price is lower than its shutdown price, it ceases production in the short run. This defines the firm's **short-run individual supply curve.**

➤ Over time, fixed cost matters. If price consistently falls below minimum average total cost, a firm will exit the industry. If price exceeds minimum average total cost, the firm is profitable and will remain in the industry; other firms will enter the industry in the long run.

➤ CHECK YOUR UNDERSTANDING 13-2

1. Draw a short-run diagram showing a U-shaped average total cost curve, a U-shaped average variable cost curve, and a "swoosh"-shaped marginal cost curve. On it, indicate the range of output and the range of price for which the following actions are optimal.
   a. The firm shuts down immediately.
   b. The firm operates in the short run despite sustaining a loss.
   c. The firm operates while making a profit.

2. The state of Maine has a very active lobster industry, which harvests lobsters during the summer months. During the rest of the year, lobsters can be obtained from other parts of the world but at a much higher price. Maine is also full of "lobster shacks," roadside restaurants serving lobster dishes that are open only during the summer. Explain why it is optimal for lobster shacks to operate only during the summer.

Solutions appear at back of book.

The Industry Supply Curve

Why will an increase in the demand for organic tomatoes lead to a large price increase at first but a much smaller increase in the long run? The answer lies in the behavior of the **industry supply curve**—the relationship between the price and the total output of an industry as a whole. The industry supply curve is what we referred to in earlier chapters as *the* supply curve or the market supply curve. But here we take some extra care to distinguish between the *individual supply curve* of a single firm and the supply curve of the industry as a whole.

As you might guess from the previous section, the industry supply curve must be analyzed in somewhat different ways for the short run and the long run. Let's start with the short run.

The Short-Run Industry Supply Curve

Recall that in the short run the number of producers in an industry is fixed—there is no entry or exit. And you may also remember from Chapter 3 that the industry supply curve is the horizontal sum of the individual supply curves of all producers—you find it by summing the total output across all suppliers at every given price. We will do that exercise here under the assumption that all the producers are alike—an assumption that makes the derivation particularly simple. So let's assume that there are 100 organic tomato farms, each with the same costs as Jennifer and Jason's farm.

Each of these 100 farms will have an individual short-run supply curve like the one in Figure 13-4. At a price below $10, no farms will produce. At a price of more than $10, each farm will produce the quantity of output at which its marginal cost is equal to the market price. As you can see from Figure 13-4, this will lead each farm to produce 4 bushels if the price is $14 per bushel, 5 bushels if the price is $18, and so on. So if there are 100 organic tomato farms and the price of organic tomatoes is $18 per bushel, the industry as a whole will produce 500 bushels, corresponding to 100 farms × 5 bushels per farm, and so on. The result is the **short-run industry supply curve,** shown as *S* in Figure 13-5. This curve shows the quantity that producers will supply at each price, *taking the number of producers as given.*

The demand curve *D* in Figure 13-5 crosses the short-run industry supply curve at E_{MKT}, corresponding to a price of $18 and a quantity of 500 bushels. Point E_{MKT} is a **short-run market equilibrium:** the quantity supplied equals the quantity demanded, taking the number of producers as given. But the long run may look quite different, because in the long run farms may enter or exit the industry.

> The **industry supply curve** shows the relationship between the price of a good and the total output of the industry as a whole.
>
> The **short-run industry supply curve** shows how the quantity supplied by an industry depends on the market price given a fixed number of producers.
>
> There is a **short-run market equilibrium** when the quantity supplied equals the quantity demanded, taking the number of producers as given.

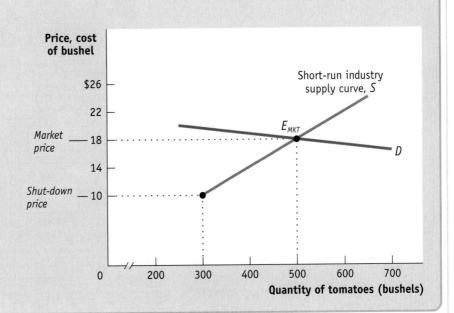

FIGURE 13-5

The Short-Run Market Equilibrium

The short-run industry supply curve, *S*, is the industry supply curve taking the number of producers—here, 100—as given. It is generated by adding together the individual supply curves of the 100 producers. Below the shut-down price of $10, no producer wants to produce in the short run. Above $10, the short-run industry supply curve slopes upward, as each producer increases output as price increases. It intersects the demand curve, *D*, at point E_{MKT}, the point of short-run market equilibrium, corresponding to a market price of $18 and a quantity of 500 bushels.

The Long-Run Industry Supply Curve

Suppose that in addition to the 100 farms currently in the organic tomato business, there are many other potential producers. Suppose also that each of these potential producers would have the same cost curves as existing producers like Jennifer and Jason if it entered the industry.

When will additional producers enter the industry? Whenever existing producers are making a profit—that is, whenever the market price is above the break-even price of $14 per bushel, the minimum average total cost of production. For example, at a price of $18 per bushel, new firms will enter the industry.

What will happen as additional producers enter the industry? Clearly, the quantity supplied at any given price will increase. The short-run industry supply curve will shift to the right. This will, in turn, alter the market equilibrium and result in a lower market price. Existing firms will respond to the lower market price by reducing their output, but the total industry output will increase because of the larger number of firms in the industry.

Figure 13-6 illustrates the effects of this chain of events on an existing firm and on the market; panel (a) shows how the market responds to entry, and panel (b) shows how an individual existing firm responds to entry. (Note that these two graphs have been rescaled in comparison to Figures 13-4 and 13-5 to better illustrate how profit changes in response to price.) In panel (a), S_1 is the initial short-run industry supply curve, based on the existence of 100 producers. The initial short-run market equilibrium is at E_{MKT},

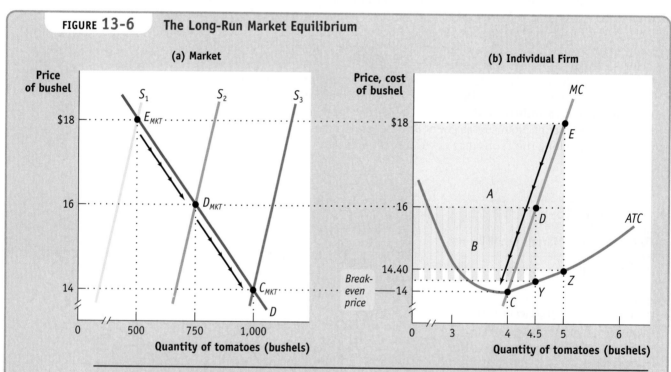

FIGURE 13-6 The Long-Run Market Equilibrium

Point E_{MKT} of panel (a) shows the initial short-run market equilibrium. Each of the 100 existing producers makes an economic profit, illustrated in panel (b) by the green rectangle labeled A, the profit of an existing firm. Profits induce entry by additional producers, shifting the short-run industry supply curve outward from S_1 to S_2 in panel (a), resulting in a new short-run equilibrium at point D_{MKT}, at a lower market price of $16 and higher industry output. Existing firms reduce output and profit falls to the area

given by the striped rectangle labeled B in panel (b). Entry continues to shift out the short-run industry supply curve, as price falls and industry output increases yet again. Entry ceases at point C_{MKT} on supply curve S_3 in panel (a). Here market price is equal to the break-even price; existing producers make zero economic profits and there is no incentive for entry or exit. Therefore C_{MKT} is also a long-run market equilibrium.

with an equilibrium market price of $18 and a quantity of 500 bushels. At this price existing producers are profitable, which is reflected in panel (b): an existing firm makes a total profit represented by the green shaded rectangle labeled A when market price is $18.

These profits will induce new producers to enter the industry, shifting the short-run industry supply curve to the right. For example, the short-run industry supply curve when the number of producers has increased to 167 is S_2. Corresponding to this supply curve is a new short-run market equilibrium labeled D_{MKT}, with a market price of $16 and a quantity of 750 bushels. At $16, each firm produces 4.5 bushels, so that industry output is $167 \times 4.5 = 750$ bushels (rounded). From panel (b) you can see the effect of the entry of 67 new producers on an existing firm: the fall in price causes it to reduce its output, and its profit falls to the area represented by the striped rectangle labeled B.

Although diminished, the profit of existing firms at D_{MKT} means that entry will continue and the number of firms will continue to rise. If the number of producers rises to 250, the short-run industry supply curve shifts out again to S_3, and the market equilibrium is at C_{MKT}, with a quantity supplied and demanded of 1,000 bushels and a market price of $14 per bushel.

Like E_{MKT} and D_{MKT}, C_{MKT} is a short-run equilibrium. But it is also something more. Because the price of $14 is each firm's break-even price, an existing producer makes zero economic profit—neither a profit nor a loss, earning only the opportunity cost of the resources used in production—when producing its profit-maximizing output of 4 bushels. At this price there is no incentive either for potential producers to enter or for existing producers to exit the industry. So C_{MKT} corresponds to a **long-run market equilibrium**—a situation in which quantity supplied equals the quantity demanded given that sufficient time has elapsed for producers to either enter or exit the industry. In a long-run market equilibrium, all existing and potential producers have fully adjusted to their optimal long-run choices; as a result, no producer has an incentive to either enter or exit the industry.

To explore further the significance of the difference between short-run and long-run equilibrium, consider the effect of an increase in demand on an industry with free entry that is initially in long-run equilibrium. Panel (b) in Figure 13-7 on the next page shows the market adjustment; panels (a) and (c) show how an existing individual firm behaves during the process.

In panel (b) of Figure 13-7, D_1 is the initial demand curve and S_1 is the initial short-run industry supply curve. Their intersection at point X_{MKT} is both a short-run and a long-run market equilibrium because the equilibrium price of $14 leads to zero economic profit—and therefore neither entry nor exit. It corresponds to point X in panel (a), where an individual existing firm is operating at the minimum of its average total cost curve.

Now suppose that the demand curve shifts out for some reason to D_2. As shown in panel (b), in the short run, industry output moves along the short-run industry supply curve S_1 to the new short-run market equilibrium at Y_{MKT}, the intersection of S_1 and D_2. The market price rises to $18 per bushel, and industry output increases from Q_X to Q_Y. This corresponds to an existing firm's movement from X to Y in panel (a) as the firm increases its output in response to the rise in the market price.

But we know that Y_{MKT} is not a long-run equilibrium, because $18 is higher than minimum average total cost, so existing producers are making economic profits. This will lead additional firms to enter the industry. Over time entry will cause the short-run industry supply curve to shift to the right. In the long run, the short-run industry supply curve will have shifted out to S_2, and the equilibrium will be at Z_{MKT}—with the price falling back to $14 per bushel and industry output increasing yet again, from Q_Y to Q_Z. Like X_{MKT} before the increase in demand, Z_{MKT} is both a short-run and a long-run market equilibrium.

The effect of entry on an existing firm is illustrated in panel (c), in the movement from Y to Z along the firm's individual supply curve. The firm reduces its output in response to the fall in the market price, ultimately arriving back at its original output

A market is in **long-run market equilibrium** when the quantity supplied equals the quantity demanded, given that sufficient time has elapsed for entry into and exit from the industry to occur.

FIGURE 13-7   The Effect of an Increase in Demand in the Short Run and the Long Run

(a) Existing Firm Response to Increase in Demand

(b) Short-Run and Long-Run Market Response to Increase in Demand

(c) Existing Firm Response to New Entrants

Panel (b) shows how an industry adjusts in the short and long run to an increase in demand; panels (a) and (c) show the corresponding adjustments by an existing firm. Initially the market is at point X_{MKT} in panel (b), a short-run and long-run equilibrium at a price of $14 and industry output of Q_X. An existing firm makes zero economic profit, operating at point X in panel (a) at minimum average total cost. Demand increases as D_1 shifts rightward to D_2, in panel (b), raising the market price to $18. Existing firms increase their output, and industry output moves along the short-run industry supply curve S_1 to a short-run equilibrium at Y_{MKT}. Correspondingly, the existing firm in panel (a) moves from point X to point Y. But at a price of $18 existing firms are profitable. As shown in panel (b), in the

long run new entrants arrive and the short-run industry supply curve shifts rightward, from S_1 to S_2. There is a new equilibrium at point Z_{MKT}, at a lower price of $14 and higher industry output of Q_Z. An existing firm responds by moving from Y to Z in panel (c), returning to its initial output level and zero economic profit. Production by new entrants accounts for the total increase in industry output, $Q_Z - Q_X$. Like X_{MKT}, Z_{MKT} is also a short-run and long-run equilibrium: with existing firms earning zero economic profit, there is no incentive for any firms to enter or exit the industry. The horizontal line passing through X_{MKT} and Z_{MKT}, LRS, is the *long-run industry supply curve*: at the break-even price of $14, producers will produce any amount that consumers demand in the long run.

quantity, corresponding to the minimum of its average total cost curve. In fact, every firm that is now in the industry—the initial set of firms and the new entrants—will operate at the minimum of its average total cost curve, at point *Z*. This means that the entire increase in industry output, from Q_X to Q_Z, comes from production by new entrants.

The line *LRS* that passes through X_{MKT} and Z_{MKT} in panel (b) is the **long-run industry supply curve.** It shows how the quantity supplied by an industry responds to the price given that producers have had time to enter or exit the industry.

In this particular case, the long-run industry supply curve is horizontal at $14. In other words, in this industry supply is *perfectly elastic* in the long run: given time to enter or exit, producers will supply any quantity that consumers demand at a price of $14. Perfectly elastic long-run supply is actually a good assumption for many industries. In this case we speak of there being *constant costs across the industry*: each firm, regardless of whether it is an incumbent or a new entrant, faces the same cost structure (that is, they each have the same cost curves). Industries that satisfy this condition are industries in which there is a perfectly elastic supply of inputs—industries like agriculture or bakeries. In other industries, however, even the long-run industry supply curve slopes upward. The usual reason for this is that producers must use some input that is in limited supply (that is, inelastically supplied). As the industry expands, the price of that input is driven up. Consequently, later entrants in the industry find that they have a

The **long-run industry supply curve** shows how the quantity supplied responds to the price once producers have had time to enter or exit the industry.

FIGURE 13-8

Comparing the Short-Run and Long-Run Industry Supply Curves

The long-run industry supply curve may slope upward, but it is always flatter—more elastic—than the short-run industry supply curve. This is because of entry and exit: a higher price attracts new entrants in the long run, resulting in a rise in industry output and a fall in price; a lower price induces existing producers to exit in the long run, generating a fall in industry output and a rise in price.

Short-run industry supply curve, S

Long-run industry supply curve, LRS

The long-run industry supply curve is always flatter—more elastic—than the short-run industry supply curve.

higher cost structure than early entrants. An example is beachfront resort hotels, which must compete for a limited quantity of prime beachfront property. Industries that behave like this are said to have *increasing costs across the industry.* Finally, it is possible for the long-run industry supply curve to slope downward, a condition that occurs when later entrants have a lower cost structure than earlier entrants. This is usually found in the area of high-tech products, where earlier technological advances—such as in software development—make it cheaper for new entrants to operate. We'll explore the case of *decreasing costs across the industry* in more detail in Chapter 17.

Regardless of whether the long-run industry supply curve is horizontal or upward sloping or even downward sloping, the long-run price elasticity of supply is *higher* than the short-run price elasticity whenever there is free entry and exit. As shown in Figure 13-8, the long-run industry supply curve is always flatter than the short-run industry supply curve. The reason is entry and exit: a high price caused by an increase in demand attracts entry by new producers, resulting in a rise in industry output and an eventual fall in price; a low price caused by a decrease in demand induces existing firms to exit, leading to a fall in industry output and an eventual increase in price.

The distinction between the short-run industry supply curve and the long-run industry supply curve is very important in practice. We often see a sequence of events like that shown in Figure 13-7: an increase in demand initially leads to a large price increase, but prices return to their initial level once new firms have entered the industry. Or we see the sequence in reverse: a fall in demand reduces prices in the short run, but they return to their initial level as producers exit the industry.

The Cost of Production and Efficiency in Long-Run Equilibrium

Our analysis leads us to three conclusions about the cost of production and efficiency in the long-run equilibrium of a perfectly competitive industry. These results will be important in our discussion in Chapter 14 of how monopoly gives rise to inefficiency.

First, in a perfectly competitive industry in equilibrium, the value of marginal cost is the same for all firms. That's because all firms produce the quantity of output at which marginal cost equals the market price, and as price-takers they all face the same market price.

Second, in a perfectly competitive industry with free entry and exit, each firm will have zero economic profit in long-run equilibrium. Each firm produces the quantity of output that minimizes its average total cost—corresponding to point *Z* in panel (c) of Figure 13-7. So the total cost of production of the industry's output is minimized in a perfectly competitive industry. (The exception is an industry with increasing costs across the industry. Given a sufficiently high market price, early entrants make positive economic profits, but the last entrants do not. Costs are minimized for later entrants, but not necessarily for the early ones.)

The third and final conclusion is that the long-run market equilibrium of a perfectly competitive industry is efficient: no mutually beneficial transactions go unexploited. To understand this, we need to recall a fundamental requirement for efficiency from Chapter 4: all consumers who have a willingness to pay greater than or equal to sellers' costs actually get the good. And we also learned that when a market is efficient (except under certain, well-defined conditions), the market price matches all consumers with a willingness to pay greater than or equal to the market price to all sellers who have a cost of producing the good less than or equal to the market price.

So in the long-run equilibrium of a perfectly competitive industry, production is efficient: costs are minimized and no resources are wasted. In addition, the allocation of goods to consumers is efficient: every consumer willing to pay the cost of producing a unit of the good gets it. Indeed, no mutually beneficial transaction is left unexploited. Moreover, this condition tends to persist over time as the environment changes: the force of competition makes producers responsive to changes in consumers' desires and to changes in technology.

►ECONOMICS IN ACTION

A Crushing Reversal

For some reason, starting in the mid-1990s, Americans began drinking a lot more wine. Part of this increase in demand may have reflected a booming economy, but the surge in wine consumption continued even after the economy stumbled in 2001. By 2006, Americans were consuming 59% more wine than they did in 1993—a total of 2.4 gallons of wine per year per U.S. resident.

At first, the increase in wine demand led to sharply higher prices; between 1993 and 2000, the price of red wine grapes rose approximately 50%, and California grape growers earned high profits. As a result, there was a rapid expansion of the industry, both because existing grape growers expanded their capacity and because new growers entered the industry. Between 1994 and 2002, production of red wine grapes almost doubled.

The result was predictable: the price of grapes fell as the supply curve shifted out. As demand growth slowed in 2002, prices plunged by 17%. The effect was to end the California wine industry's expansion. In fact, some grape producers began to exit the industry. By 2004, U.S. grape production had fallen by 20% compared to 2002. ▲

< < < < < < < < < < < <

► CHECK YOUR UNDERSTANDING 13-3

1. Which of the following events will induce firms to enter an industry? Which will induce firms to exit? When will entry or exit cease? Explain your answer.
   a. A technological advance lowers the fixed cost of production of every firm in the industry.
   b. The wages paid to workers in the industry go up for an extended period of time.
   c. A permanent change in consumer tastes increases demand for the good.
   d. The price of a key input rises due to a long-term shortage of that input.

2. Assume that the egg industry is perfectly competitive and is in long-run equilibrium with a perfectly elastic long-run industry supply curve. Health concerns about cholesterol then lead to a decrease in demand. Construct a figure similar to Figure 13-7, showing the short-run behavior of the industry and how long-run equilibrium is reestablished.

Solutions appear at back of book.

[>> A LOOK AHEAD •••

In this chapter, we have seen how the rational decisions of producers in a perfectly competitive industry give rise to that industry's supply curve. But as we have noted, although perfect competition is a useful benchmark, it is not an accurate description of many industries. In fact, outside of the realm of standardized products (commodities), most industries are not perfectly competitive. The next three chapters will address various forms of imperfectly competitive industries: monopoly, oligopoly, and monopolistic competition. Under these different industry structures, we will have to significantly modify the results about firm and industry behavior that we have drawn from studying perfect competition. With them, we will gain a much deeper and more realistic understanding of how actual firms and industries operate.]

SUMMARY

1. In a **perfectly competitive market** all producers are **price-taking producers** and all consumers are **price-taking consumers**—no one's actions can influence the market price. Consumers are normally price-takers, but producers often are not. In a **perfectly competitive industry,** all producers are price-takers.

2. There are two necessary conditions for a perfectly competitive industry: there are many producers, none of whom have a large **market share,** and the industry produces a **standardized product** or **commodity**—goods that consumers regard as equivalent. A third condition is often satisfied as well: **free entry and exit** into and from the industry.

3. A producer chooses output according to the **optimal output rule:** produce the quantity at which **marginal revenue** equals marginal cost. For a price-taking firm, marginal revenue is equal to price and its **marginal revenue curve** is a horizontal line at the market price. It chooses output according to the **price-taking firm's optimal output rule:** produce the quantity at which price equals marginal cost. However, a firm that produces the optimal quantity may not be profitable.

4. A firm is profitable if total revenue exceeds total cost or, equivalently, if the market price exceeds its **break-even price**—minimum average total cost. If market price exceeds the break-even price, the firm is profitable; if it is less, the firm is unprofitable; if it is equal, the firm breaks even. When profitable, the firm's per-unit profit is $P - ATC$; when unprofitable, its per-unit loss is $ATC - P$.

5. Fixed cost is irrelevant to the firm's optimal short-run production decision, which depends on its **shut-down price**—its minimum average variable cost—and the market price. When the market price is equal to or exceeds the shut-down price, the firm produces the output quantity where marginal cost equals the market price. When

the market price falls below the shut-down price, the firm ceases production in the short run. This generates the firm's **short-run individual supply curve.**

6. Fixed cost matters over time. If the market price is below minimum average total cost for an extended period of time, firms will exit the industry in the long run. If above, existing firms are profitable and new firms will enter the industry in the long run.

7. The **industry supply curve** depends on the time period. The **short-run industry supply curve** is the industry supply curve given that the number of firms is fixed. The **short-run market equilibrium** is given by the intersection of the short-run industry supply curve and the demand curve.

8. The **long-run industry supply curve** is the industry supply curve given sufficient time for entry into and exit from the industry. In the **long-run market equilibrium**—given by the intersection of the long-run industry supply curve and the demand curve—no producer has an incentive to enter or exit. The long-run industry supply curve is often horizontal. It may slope upward if there is limited supply of an input, resulting in increasing costs across the industry. It may even slope downward, the case of decreasing costs across the industry. But it is always more elastic than the short-run industry supply curve.

9. In the long-run market equilibrium of a competitive industry, profit maximization leads each firm to produce at the same marginal cost, which is equal to market price. Free entry and exit means that each firm earns zero economic profit—producing the output corresponding to its minimum average total cost. So the total cost of production of an industry's output is minimized. The outcome is efficient because every consumer with a willingness to pay greater than or equal to marginal cost gets the good.

KEY TERMS ....■

Price-taking producer, p. 330
Price-taking consumer, p. 330
Perfectly competitive market, p. 330
Perfectly competitive industry, p. 331
Market share, p. 331
Standardized product, p. 331
Commodity, p. 331

Free entry and exit, p. 332
Marginal revenue, p. 334
Optimal output rule, p. 334
Price-taking firm's optimal output rule, p. 335
Marginal revenue curve, p. 335
Break-even price, p. 340

Shut-down price, p. 341
Short-run individual supply curve, p. 342
Industry supply curve, p. 344
Short-run industry supply curve, p. 345
Short-run market equilibrium, p. 345
Long-run market equilibrium, p. 347
Long-run industry supply curve, p. 348

PROBLEMS ....■

1. For each of the following, is the business a price-taking producer? Explain your answers.

    a. A cappuccino café in a university town where there are dozens of very similar cappuccino cafés

    b. The makers of Pepsi-Cola

    c. One of many sellers of zucchini at a local farmers' market

2. For each of the following, is the industry perfectly competitive? Referring to market share, standardization of the product, and/or free entry and exit, explain your answers.

    a. Aspirin

    b. Alicia Keys concerts

    c. SUVs

3. Kate's Katering provides catered meals, and the catered meals industry is perfectly competitive. Kate's machinery costs $100 per day and is the only fixed input. Her variable cost consists of the wages paid to the cooks and the food ingredients. The variable cost per day associated with each level of output is given in the accompanying table.

Quantity of meals	VC
0	$0
10	200
20	300
30	480
40	700
50	1,000

    a. Calculate the total cost, the average variable cost, the average total cost, and the marginal cost for each quantity of output.

    b. What is the break-even price? What is the shut-down price?

    c. Suppose that the price at which Kate can sell catered meals is $21 per meal. In the short run, will Kate earn a profit? In the short run, should she produce or shut down?

    d. Suppose that the price at which Kate can sell catered meals is $17 per meal. In the short run, will Kate earn a

profit? In the short run, should she produce or shut down?

    e. Suppose that the price at which Kate can sell catered meals is $13 per meal. In the short run, will Kate earn a profit? In the short run, should she produce or shut down?

4. Bob produces DVD movies for sale, which requires a building and a machine that copies the original movie onto a DVD. Bob rents a building for $30,000 per month and rents a machine for $20,000 a month. Those are his fixed costs. His variable cost per month is given in the accompanying table.

Quantity of DVDs	VC
0	$0
1,000	5,000
2,000	8,000
3,000	9,000
4,000	14,000
5,000	20,000
6,000	33,000
7,000	49,000
8,000	72,000
9,000	99,000
10,000	150,000

    a. Calculate Bob's average variable cost, average total cost, and marginal cost for each quantity of output.

    b. There is free entry into the industry, and anyone who enters will face the same costs as Bob. Suppose that currently the price of a DVD is $25. What will Bob's profit be? Is this a long-run equilibrium? If not, what will the price of DVD movies be in the long run?

5. Consider Bob's DVD company described in Problem 4. Assume that DVD production is a perfectly competitive industry. For each of the following questions, explain your answers.

    a. What is Bob's break-even price? What is his shut-down price?

b. Suppose the price of a DVD is $2. What should Bob do in the short run?

c. Suppose the price of a DVD is $7. What is the profit-maximizing quantity of DVDs that Bob should produce? What will his total profit be? Will he produce or shut down in the short run? Will he stay in the industry or exit in the long run?

d. Suppose instead that the price of DVDs is $20. Now what is the profit-maximizing quantity of DVDs that Bob should produce? What will his total profit be now? Will he produce or shut down in the short run? Will he stay in the industry or exit in the long run?

6. Consider again Bob's DVD company described in Problem 4.

a. Draw Bob's marginal cost curve.

b. Over what range of prices will Bob produce no DVDs in the short run?

c. Draw Bob's individual supply curve.

7. a. A profit-maximizing business incurs an economic loss of $10,000 per year. Its fixed cost is $15,000 per year. Should it produce or shut down in the short run? Should it stay in the industry or exit in the long run?

b. Suppose instead that this business has a fixed cost of $6,000 per year. Should it produce or shut down in the short run? Should it stay in the industry or exit in the long run?

8. The first sushi restaurant opens in town. Initially people are very cautious about eating tiny portions of raw fish, as this is a town where large portions of grilled meat have always been popular. Soon, however, an influential health report warns consumers against grilled meat and suggests that they increase their consumption of fish, especially raw fish. The sushi restaurant becomes very popular and its profit increases.

a. What will happen to the short-run profit of the sushi restaurant? What will happen to the number of sushi restaurants in town in the long run? Will the first sushi restaurant be able to sustain its short-run profit over the long run? Explain your answers.

b. Local steakhouses suffer from the popularity of sushi and start incurring losses. What will happen to the number of steakhouses in town in the long run? Explain your answer.

9. A perfectly competitive firm has the following short-run total cost:

Quantity	TC
0	$5
1	10
2	13
3	18
4	25
5	34
6	45

Market demand for the firm's product is given by the following market demand schedule:

Price	Quantity demanded
$12	300
10	500
8	800
6	1,200
4	1,800

a. Calculate this firm's marginal cost and, for all output levels except zero, the firm's average variable cost and average total cost.

b. There are 100 firms in this industry that all have costs identical to those of this firm. Draw the short-run industry supply curve. In the same diagram, draw the market demand curve.

c. What is the market price, and how much profit will each firm make?

10. A new vaccine against a deadly disease has just been discovered. Presently, 55 people die from the disease each year. The new vaccine will save lives, but it is not completely safe. Some recipients of the shots will die from adverse reactions. The projected effects of the inoculation are given in the accompanying table:

Percent of population inoculated	Total deaths due to disease	Total deaths due to inoculation	Marginal benefit of inoculation	Marginal cost of inoculation	"Profit" of inoculation
0	55	0	—	—	—
10	45	0	—	—	—
20	36	1	—	—	—
30	28	3	—	—	—
40	21	6	—	—	—
50	15	10	—	—	—
60	10	15	—	—	—
70	6	20	—	—	—
80	3	25	—	—	—
90	1	30	—	—	—
100	0	35	—	—	—

a. What are the interpretations of "marginal benefit" and "marginal cost" here? Calculate marginal benefit and marginal cost per each 10% increase in the rate of inoculation. Write your answers in the table.

b. What proportion of the population should optimally be inoculated?

c. What is the interpretation of "profit" here? Calculate the profit for all levels of inoculation.

11. Evaluate each of the following statements. If a statement is true, explain why; if it is false, identify the mistake and try to correct it.

a. A profit-maximizing firm in a perfectly competitive industry should select the output level at which the difference between the market price and marginal cost is greatest.

b. An increase in fixed cost lowers the profit-maximizing quantity of output produced in the short run.

12. The production of agricultural products like wheat is one of the few examples of a perfectly competitive industry. In this question, we analyze results from a study released by the U.S. Department of Agriculture about wheat production in the United States in 1998.

a. The average variable cost per acre planted with wheat was $107 per acre. Assuming a yield of 50 bushels per acre, calculate the average variable cost per bushel of wheat.

b. The average price of wheat received by a farmer in 1998 was $2.65 per bushel. Do you think the average farm would have exited the industry in the short run? Explain.

c. With a yield of 50 bushels of wheat per acre, the average total cost per farm was $3.80 per bushel. The harvested acreage for rye (a type of wheat) in the United States fell from 418,000 acres in 1998 to 274,000 in 2006. Using the information on prices and costs here and in parts a and b, explain why this might have happened.

d. Using the above information, do you think the prices of wheat were higher or lower prior to 1998? Why?

13. The accompanying table presents prices for washing and ironing a man's shirt taken from a survey of California dry cleaners in 2004.

Dry Cleaner	City	Price
A-1 Cleaners	Santa Barbara	$1.50
Regal Cleaners	Santa Barbara	1.95
St. Paul Cleaners	Santa Barbara	1.95
Zip Kleen Dry Cleaners	Santa Barbara	1.95
Effie the Tailor	Santa Barbara	2.00
Magnolia Too	Goleta	2.00
Master Cleaners	Santa Barbara	2.00
Santa Barbara Cleaners	Goleta	2.00
Sunny Cleaners	Santa Barbara	2.00
Casitas Cleaners	Carpinteria	2.10
Rockwell Cleaners	Carpinteria	2.10
Norvelle Bass Cleaners	Santa Barbara	2.15
Ablitt's Fine Cleaners	Santa Barbara	2.25
California Cleaners	Goleta	2.25
Justo the Tailor	Santa Barbara	2.25
Pressed 4 Time	Goleta	2.50
King's Cleaners	Goleta	2.50

a. What is the average price per shirt washed and ironed in Goleta? In Santa Barbara?

b. Draw typical marginal cost and average total cost curves for California Cleaners in Goleta, assuming it is a perfectly competitive firm but is making a profit on each shirt in the short run. Mark the short-run equilibrium point and shade the area that corresponds to the profit made by the dry cleaner.

c. Assume $2.25 is the short-run equilibrium price in Goleta. Draw a typical short-run demand and supply curve for the market. Label the equilibrium point.

d. Observing profits in the Goleta area, another dry cleaning service, Diamond Cleaners, enters the market. It charges $1.95 per shirt. What is the new average price of washing and ironing a shirt in Goleta? Illustrate the effect of entry on the average Goleta price by a shift of the short-run supply curve, the demand curve, or both.

e. Assume that California Cleaners now charges the new average price and just breaks even (that is, makes zero economic profit) at this price. Show the likely effect of the entry on your diagram in part b.

f. If the dry cleaning industry is perfectly competitive, what does the average difference in price between Goleta and Santa Barbara imply about costs in the two areas?

 www.worthpublishers.com/krugmanwells

>> Monopoly

EVERYBODY MUST GET STONES

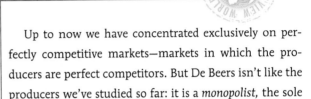

A FEW YEARS AGO DE BEERS, THE WORLD'S main supplier of diamonds, ran an ad urging men to buy their wives diamond jewelry. "She married you for richer, for poorer," read the ad. "Let her know how it's going."

Crass? Yes. Effective? No question. For generations diamonds have been a symbol of luxury, valued not only for their appearance but also for their rarity.

But geologists will tell you that diamonds aren't all that rare. In fact, according to the *Dow Jones-Irwin Guide to Fine Gems and Jewelry,* diamonds are "more common than any other gem-quality colored stone. They only seem rarer . . ."

Why do diamonds seem rarer than other gems? Part of the answer is a brilliant marketing campaign. (We'll talk more about marketing and product differentiation in Chapter 16.) But mainly diamonds seem rare because De Beers *makes* them rare: the company controls most of the world's diamond mines and limits the quantity of diamonds supplied to the market.

"Got stones?"

Up to now we have concentrated exclusively on perfectly competitive markets—markets in which the producers are perfect competitors. But De Beers isn't like the producers we've studied so far: it is a *monopolist,* the sole (or almost sole) producer of a good. Monopolists behave differently from producers in perfectly competitive industries: whereas perfect competitors take the price at which they can sell their output as given, monopolists know that their actions affect market prices and take that effect into account when deciding how much to produce. Before we begin our analysis, let's step back and look at monopoly and perfect competition as parts of a broader system for classifying markets.

Perfect competition and monopoly are particular types of *market structure.* They are particular categories in a system economists use to classify markets and industries according to two main dimensions. This chapter begins with a brief overview of types of market structure. It will help us here and in subsequent chapters to understand on a deeper level why markets differ and why producers in those markets behave quite differently.

355

Types of Market Structure

In the real world, there is a mind-boggling array of different markets. We observe widely different behavior patterns by producers across markets: in some markets producers are extremely competitive; in others, they seem somehow to coordinate their actions to avoid competing with one another; and, as we have just described, some markets are monopolies in which there is no competition at all. In order to develop principles and make predictions about markets and how producers will behave in them, economists have developed four principal models of market structure: *perfect competition, monopoly, oligopoly,* and *monopolistic competition.*

This system of market structures is based on two dimensions:

■ The number of producers in the market (one, few, or many)

■ Whether the goods offered are identical or *differentiated*

Differentiated goods are goods that are different but considered somewhat substitutable by consumers (think Coke versus Pepsi).

Figure 14-1 provides a simple visual summary of the types of market structure classified according to the two dimensions. In *monopoly,* a single producer sells a single, undifferentiated product. In *oligopoly,* a few producers—more than one but not a large number—sell products that may be either identical or differentiated. In *monopolistic competition,* many producers each sell a differentiated product (think of producers of economics textbooks). And finally, as we know, in *perfect competition* many producers each sell an identical product.

You might wonder what determines the number of firms in a market: whether there is one (monopoly), a few (oligopoly), or many (perfect competition and

---

FIGURE 14-1

Types of Market Structure

The behavior of any given firm and the market it occupies are analyzed using one of four models of market structure—monopoly, oligopoly, perfect competition, or monopolistic competition. This system for categorizing market structure is based on two dimensions: (1) whether products are differentiated or identical and (2) the number of producers in the industry—one, a few, or many.

How many producers are there?	Are products differentiated?	
	No	Yes
One	Monopoly	Not applicable
Few	Oligopoly	Oligopoly
Many	Perfect competition	Monopolistic competition

monopolistic competition). We won't answer that question here, because it will be covered in detail later in this chapter and in Chapters 15 and 16, which analyze oligopoly and monopolistic competition. We will just briefly note that in the long run it depends on whether there are conditions that make it difficult for new firms to enter the market, such as government regulations that discourage entry, increasing returns to scale in production, technological superiority, or control of necessary resources or inputs. When these conditions are present, industries tend to be monopolies or oligopolies; when they are not present, industries tend to be perfectly competitive or monopolistically competitive.

You might also wonder why some markets have differentiated products but others have identical ones. The answer is that it depends on the nature of the good and consumers' preferences. Some goods—soft drinks, economics textbooks, breakfast cereals—can readily be made into different varieties in the eyes and tastes of consumers. Other goods—hammers, for example—are much less easy to differentiate.

Although this chapter is devoted to monopoly, important aspects of monopoly carry over to oligopoly and monopolistic competition. In the next section, we will define monopoly and review the conditions that make it possible. These same conditions, in less extreme form, also give rise to oligopoly. We then show how a monopolist can increase profit by limiting the quantity supplied to a market—behavior that also occurs in oligopoly and monopolistic competition. As we'll see, this kind of behavior is good for the producer but bad for consumers; it also causes inefficiency. An important topic of study will be the ways in which public policy tries to limit the damage. Finally, we turn to one of the surprising effects of monopoly—one that is very often present in oligopoly and monopolistic competition as well: the fact that different consumers often pay different prices for the same good.

> A **monopolist** is a firm that is the only producer of a good that has no close substitutes. An industry controlled by a monopolist is known as a **monopoly.**

The Meaning of Monopoly

The De Beers monopoly of South Africa was created in the 1880s by Cecil Rhodes, a British businessman. By 1880 mines in South Africa already dominated the world's supply of diamonds. There were, however, many mining companies, all competing with each other. During the 1880s Rhodes bought the great majority of those mines and consolidated them into a single company, De Beers. By 1889 De Beers controlled almost all of the world's diamond production.

De Beers, in other words, became a **monopolist.** A producer is a monopolist if it is the sole supplier of a good that has no close substitutes. When a firm is a monopolist, the industry is a **monopoly.**

Monopoly: Our First Departure from Perfect Competition

As we saw in the Chapter 13 section "Defining Perfect Competition," the supply and demand model of a market is not universally valid. Instead, it's a model of perfect competition, which is only one of several different types of market structure. Back in Chapter 13 we learned that a market will be perfectly competitive only if there are many producers, all of whom produce the same good. Monopoly is the most extreme departure from perfect competition.

In practice, true monopolies are hard to find in the modern American economy, partly because of legal obstacles. A contemporary entrepreneur who tried to consolidate all the firms in an industry the way that Rhodes did would soon find himself in court, accused of breaking *antitrust* laws, which are intended to prevent monopolies from emerging. Oligopoly, a market structure in which there is a small number of large producers, is much more common. In fact, most of the goods you buy, from autos to airline tickets, are supplied by oligopolies, which we will examine in detail in Chapter 15.

Market power is the ability of a firm to raise prices.

Monopolies do, however, play an important role in some sectors of the economy, such as pharmaceuticals. Furthermore, our analysis of monopoly will provide a foundation for our later analysis of other departures from perfect competition, such as oligopoly and monopolistic competition.

What Monopolists Do

Why did Rhodes want to consolidate South African diamond producers into a single company? What difference did it make to the world diamond market?

Figure 14-2 offers a preliminary view of the effects of monopoly. It shows an industry in which the supply curve under perfect competition intersects the demand curve at C, leading to the price P_C and the output Q_C.

Suppose that this industry is consolidated into a monopoly. The monopolist *moves up the demand curve* by reducing quantity supplied to a point like M, at which the quantity produced, Q_M, is lower and the price, P_M, is higher than under perfect competition.

The ability of a monopolist to raise its price above the competitive level by reducing output is known as **market power.** And market power is what monopoly is all about. A wheat farmer who is one of 100,000 wheat farmers has no market power: he or she must sell wheat at the going market price. Your local water utility company, though, does have market power: it can raise prices and still keep many (though not all) of its customers, because they have nowhere else to go. In short, it's a monopolist.

The reason a monopolist reduces output and raises price compared to the perfectly competitive industry levels is to increase profit. Cecil Rhodes consolidated the diamond producers into De Beers because he realized that the whole would be worth more than the sum of its parts—the monopoly would generate more profit than the sum of the profits of the individual competitive firms. As we saw in Chapter 13, under perfect competition economic profits normally vanish in the long run as competitors enter the market. Under monopoly the profits don't go away—a monopolist is able to continue earning economic profits in the long run.

FIGURE 14-2

What a Monopolist Does

Under perfect competition, the price and quantity are determined by supply and demand. Here, the equilibrium is at C, where the price is P_C and the quantity is Q_C. A monopolist reduces the quantity supplied to Q_M, and moves up the demand curve from C to M, raising the price to P_M.

2. ... and raises price.

1. Compared to perfect competition, a monopolist reduces output . . .

In fact, monopolists are not the only types of firms that possess market power. In the next chapter we will study *oligopolists,* firms that can have market power as well. Under certain conditions, oligopolists can earn positive economic profits in the long run by restricting output like monopolists do.

But why don't profits get competed away? What allows monopolists to be monopolists?

Why Do Monopolies Exist?

A monopolist making profits will not go unnoticed by others. (Recall that this is "economic profit," revenue over and above the opportunity costs of the firm's resources.) But won't other firms crash the party, grab a piece of the action, and drive down prices and profits in the long run? For a profitable monopoly to persist, something must keep others from going into the same business; that "something" is known as a **barrier to entry.** There are four principal types of barriers to entry: control of a scarce resource or input, increasing returns to scale, technological superiority, and government-created barriers.

Control of a Scarce Resource or Input A monopolist that controls a resource or input crucial to an industry can prevent other firms from entering its market. Cecil Rhodes created the De Beers monopoly by establishing control over the mines that produced the great bulk of the world's diamonds.

Increasing Returns to Scale Many Americans have natural gas piped into their homes, for cooking and heating. Invariably, the local gas company is a monopolist. But why don't rival companies compete to provide gas?

In the early nineteenth century, when the gas industry was just starting up, companies did compete for local customers. But this competition didn't last long; soon local gas supply became a monopoly in almost every town because of the large fixed costs involved in providing a town with gas lines. The cost of laying gas lines didn't depend on how much gas a company sold, so a firm with a larger volume of sales had a cost advantage: because it was able to spread the fixed costs over a larger volume, it had lower average total costs than smaller firms.

Local gas supply is an industry in which average total cost falls as output increases. As we learned in Chapter 12, this phenomenon is called *increasing returns to scale.* There we learned that when average total cost falls as output increases, firms tend to grow larger. In an industry characterized by increasing returns to scale, larger companies are more profitable and drive out smaller ones. For the same reason, established companies have a cost advantage over any potential entrant—a potent barrier to entry. So increasing returns to scale can both give rise to and sustain monopoly.

A monopoly created and sustained by increasing returns to scale is called a **natural monopoly.** The defining characteristic of a natural monopoly is that it possesses increasing returns to scale over the range of output that is relevant for the industry. This is illustrated in Figure 14-3 on the next page, showing the firm's average total cost curve and the market demand curve. Here we can see that the natural monopolist's *ATC* curve declines over the output levels at which price is greater than or equal to average total cost. So the natural monopolist has increasing returns to scale over the entire range of output for which any firm would want to remain in the industry—the range of output at which the firm would at least break even in the long run. The source of this condition is large fixed costs: when large fixed costs are required to operate, a given quantity of output is produced at lower average total cost by one large firm than by two or more smaller firms.

The most visible natural monopolies in the modern economy are local utilities—water, gas, electricity, local land-line phone service, and, in most locations, cable television. As we'll see later in this chapter, natural monopolies pose a special challenge to public policy.

To earn economic profits, a monopolist must be protected by a **barrier to entry**—something that prevents other firms from entering the industry.

A **natural monopoly** exists when increasing returns to scale provide a large cost advantage to a single firm that produces all of an industry's output.

FIGURE 14-3

Increasing Returns to Scale Create Natural Monopoly

A natural monopoly can arise when fixed costs required to operate are very high. When this occurs, the firm's *ATC* curve declines over the range of output at which price is greater than or equal to average total cost. This gives the firm increasing returns to scale over the entire range of output at which the firm would at least break even in the long run. As a result, a given quantity of output is produced more cheaply by one large firm than by two or more smaller firms.

Technological Superiority A firm that maintains a consistent technological advantage over potential competitors can establish itself as a monopolist. For example, from the 1970s through the 1990s the chip manufacturer Intel was able to maintain a consistent advantage over potential competitors in both the design and production of microprocessors, the chips that run computers. But technological superiority is typically not a barrier to entry over the longer term: over time competitors will invest in upgrading their technology to match that of the technology leader. In fact, in the last few years Intel found its technological superiority eroded by a competitor, Advanced Micro Devices (also known as AMD), which now produces chips approximately as fast and as powerful as Intel chips.

We should note, however, that in certain high-tech industries, technological superiority is not a guarantee of success against competitors. Some high-tech industries are characterized by *network externalities,* a condition that arises when the value of a good to the consumer rises as the number of people who also use the good rises. In these industries, the firm possessing the largest network—the largest number of consumers currently using its product—has an advantage over its competitors in attracting new customers, an advantage that may allow it to become a monopolist. Microsoft is often cited as an example of a company with a technologically inferior product—its computer operating system—that grew into a monopolist through the phenomenon of network externalities. (You can read more about network externalities in Chapter 17.)

Government-Created Barriers In 1998 the pharmaceutical company Merck introduced Propecia, a drug effective against baldness. Despite the fact that Propecia was very profitable and other drug companies had the know-how to produce it, no other firms challenged Merck's monopoly. That's because the U.S. government had given Merck the sole legal right to produce the drug in the United States. Propecia is an example of a monopoly protected by government-created barriers.

The most important legally created monopolies today arise from *patents* and *copyrights.* A **patent** gives an inventor the sole right to make, use, or sell that invention for a period that in most countries lasts between 16 and 20 years. Patents are given to the creators of new products, such as drugs or devices. Similarly, a **copyright** gives the creator of a literary or artistic work the sole rights to profit from that work, usually for a period equal to the creator's lifetime plus 70 years.

A **patent** gives an inventor a temporary monopoly in the use or sale of an invention.

A **copyright** gives the creator of a literary or artistic work sole rights to profit from that work.

The justification for patents and copyrights is a matter of incentives. If inventors are not protected by patents, they would gain little reward from their efforts: as soon as a valuable invention was made public, others would copy it and sell products based on it. And if inventors could not expect to profit from their inventions, then there would be no incentive to incur the costs of invention in the first place. Likewise for the creators of literary or artistic works. So the law gives a temporary monopoly through imposing temporary property rights that encourage invention and creation. Patents and copyrights are temporary because the law strikes a compromise. The higher price for the good that holds while the legal protection is in effect compensates inventors for the cost of invention; conversely, the lower price that results once the legal protection lapses and competition emerges benefits consumers and increases economic efficiency.

Because the length of the temporary monopoly cannot be tailored to specific cases, this system is imperfect and leads to some missed opportunities. In some cases there can be significant welfare issues. For example, the violation of American drug patents by pharmaceutical companies in poor countries has been a major source of controversy, pitting the needs of poor patients who cannot afford retail drug prices against the interests of drug manufacturers who have incurred high research costs to discover these drugs. To solve this problem, some American drug companies and poor countries have negotiated deals in which the patents are honored but the American companies sell their drugs at deeply discounted prices. (This is an example of *price discrimination*, which we'll learn more about later in this chapter.)

GLOBAL COMPARISON   THE PRICE WE PAY

Although providing cheap patent-protected drugs to patients in poor countries is a new phenomenon, charging different prices to consumers in different countries is not: it's an example of price discrimination. A monopolist will maximize profits by charging a higher price in the country with a lower price elasticity (the rich country) and a lower price in the country with a higher price elasticity (the poor country). Interestingly, however, drug prices can differ substantially even among countries with comparable income levels. How do we explain this?

The answer to that question lies in differences in regulation. This figure uses the Australian price of a given basket of drugs as a standard of comparison. It shows that American consumers pay much more for their drugs than residents of other wealthy countries: over 200% more than Australian consumers, and almost equally as much more than consumers in New Zealand or Spain. The reason: Governments in these other countries more actively regulate drug prices than the United States does to help keep drugs affordable for their citizens.

To save money on medicine, it's not surprising that some Americans travel to countries like Canada and Mexico, where prices are cheaper, or buy less expensive drugs from abroad via the Internet.

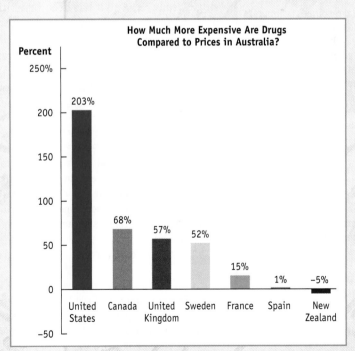

How Much More Expensive Are Drugs Compared to Prices in Australia?

Source: Judith L. Wagner and Elizabeth McCarthy, "International Differences in Drug Prices," *Annual Review of Public Health* 25(2004): 475–495.

➤ECONOMICS IN ACTION

Low Supply and Soaring Demand: A Diamond Producer's Best Friend

When Cecil Rhodes created the De Beers monopoly, it was a particularly opportune moment. The new diamond mines in South Africa dwarfed all previous sources, so almost all of the world's diamond production was concentrated in a few square miles.

Until recently, De Beers was able to extend its control of resources even as new mines opened. De Beers either bought out new producers or entered into agreements with local governments that controlled some of the new mines, effectively making them part of the De Beers monopoly. The most remarkable of these was an agreement with the former Soviet Union, which ensured that Russian diamonds would be marketed through De Beers, preserving its ability to control retail prices. De Beers also went so far as to stockpile a year's supply of diamonds in its London vaults so that when demand dropped, newly mined stones would be stored rather than sold, restricting retail supply until demand and prices recovered.

However, over the past few years the De Beers monopoly has been under assault. Government regulators have forced De Beers to loosen its control of the market. For the first time, De Beers has competition: a number of independent companies have begun mining for diamonds in other African countries. In addition, high-quality, inexpensive synthetic diamonds have become an alternative to real gems, eating into De Beers's profits. So does this mean an end to high diamond prices and De Beers's high profits?

Not really. Although today's De Beers is more of a "near-monopolist" than a true monopolist, it still mines more of the world's supply of diamonds than any other single producer. And it has been benefiting from newly emerging markets. Consumer demand for diamonds has soared in countries like China and India, leading to a 4% to 5% increase in prices during 2007 and 2008. In fact, the demand for diamonds has been rising much more quickly than supply—so quickly, in fact, that De Beers's London stockpile is now gone.

In the end, although a diamond monopoly may not be forever, a near-monopoly with soaring consumer demand may be just as profitable. ▲

‹ ‹ ‹ ‹ ‹ ‹ ‹ ‹ ‹ ‹ ‹ ‹

► CHECK YOUR UNDERSTANDING 14-1

1. Currently, Texas Tea Oil Co. is the only local supplier of home heating oil in Frigid, Alaska. This winter residents were shocked that the price of a gallon of heating oil had doubled and believed that they were the victims of market power. Explain which of the following pieces of evidence support or undermine that conclusion.
   a. There is a national shortage of heating oil, and Texas Tea could procure only a limited amount.
   b. Last year, Texas Tea and several other competing local oil-supply firms merged into a single firm.
   c. The cost to Texas Tea of purchasing heating oil from refineries has gone up significantly.
   d. Recently, some nonlocal firms have begun to offer heating oil to Texas Tea's regular customers at a price much lower than Texas Tea's.
   e. Texas Tea has acquired an exclusive government license to draw oil from the only heating oil pipeline in the state.

2. Suppose the government is considering extending the length of a patent from 20 years to 30 years. How would this change each of the following?
   a. The incentive to invent new products
   b. The length of time during which consumers have to pay higher prices

How a Monopolist Maximizes Profit

As we've suggested, once Cecil Rhodes consolidated the competing diamond producers of South Africa into a single company, the industry's behavior changed: the quantity supplied fell and the market price rose. In this section, we will learn how a monopolist increases its profit by reducing output. And we will see the crucial role that market demand plays in leading a monopolist to behave differently from a perfectly competitive industry. (Remember that profit here is economic profit, not accounting profit.)

The Monopolist's Demand Curve and Marginal Revenue

In Chapter 13 we derived the firm's optimal output rule: a profit-maximizing firm produces the quantity of output at which the marginal cost of producing the last unit of output equals marginal revenue—the change in total revenue generated by that last unit of output. That is, $MR = MC$ at the profit-maximizing quantity of output. Although the optimal output rule holds for *all* firms, we will see shortly that its application leads to different profit-maximizing output levels for a monopolist compared to a firm in a perfectly competitive industry—that is, a price-taking firm. The source of that difference lies in the comparison of the demand curve faced by a monopolist to the demand curve faced by an individual perfectly competitive firm.

In addition to the optimal output rule, we also learned in Chapter 13 that even though the *market* demand curve always slopes downward, each of the firms that make up a perfectly competitive industry faces a horizontal, *perfectly elastic* demand curve, like D_C in panel (a) of Figure 14-4. Any attempt by an individual firm in a perfectly competitive industry to charge more than the going market price will cause it to lose all its sales. It can, however, sell as much as it likes at the market price. As we saw in Chapter 13, the marginal revenue of a perfectly competitive producer is simply the market price.

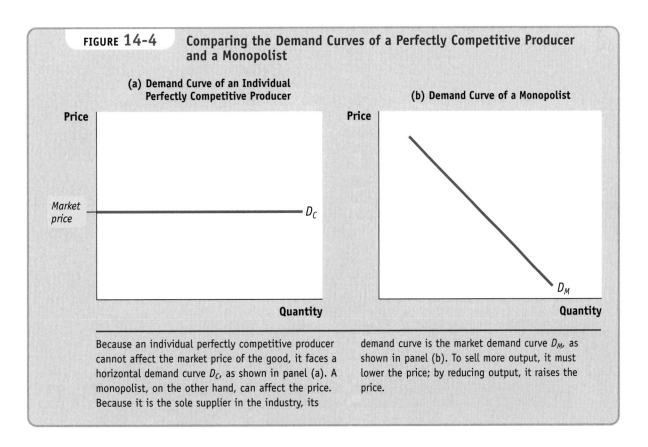

FIGURE 14-4 **Comparing the Demand Curves of a Perfectly Competitive Producer and a Monopolist**

(a) Demand Curve of an Individual Perfectly Competitive Producer

(b) Demand Curve of a Monopolist

Because an individual perfectly competitive producer cannot affect the market price of the good, it faces a horizontal demand curve D_C, as shown in panel (a). A monopolist, on the other hand, can affect the price. Because it is the sole supplier in the industry, its demand curve is the market demand curve D_M, as shown in panel (b). To sell more output, it must lower the price; by reducing output, it raises the price.

As a result, the price-taking firm's optimal output rule is to produce the output level at which the marginal cost of the last unit produced is equal to the market price.

A monopolist, in contrast, is the sole supplier of its good. So its demand curve is simply the market demand curve, which slopes downward, like D_M in panel (b) of Figure 14-4. This downward slope creates a "wedge" between the price of the good and the marginal revenue of the good—the change in revenue generated by producing one more unit.

Table 14-1 shows this wedge between price and marginal revenue for a monopolist, by calculating the monopolist's total revenue and marginal revenue schedules from its demand schedule.

The first two columns of Table 14-1 show a hypothetical demand schedule for De Beers diamonds. For the sake of simplicity, we assume that all diamonds are exactly alike. And to make the arithmetic easy, we suppose that the number of diamonds sold is far smaller than is actually the case. For instance, at a price of $500 per diamond, we assume that only 10 diamonds are sold. The demand curve implied by this schedule is shown in panel (a) of Figure 14-5.

TABLE 14-1

Demand, Total Revenue, and Marginal Revenue for the De Beers Monopoly

Price of diamond P	Quantity of diamonds Q	Total revenue $TR = P \times Q$	Marginal revenue $MR = \Delta TR / \Delta Q$
$1,000	0	$0	
			$950
950	1	950	
			850
900	2	1,800	
			750
850	3	2,550	
			650
800	4	3,200	
			550
750	5	3,750	
			450
700	6	4,200	
			350
650	7	4,550	
			250
600	8	4,800	
			150
550	9	4,950	
			50
500	10	5,000	
			−50
450	11	4,950	
			−150
400	12	4,800	
			−250
350	13	4,550	
			−350
300	14	4,200	
			−450
250	15	3,750	
			−550
200	16	3,200	
			−650
150	17	2,550	
			−750
100	18	1,800	
			−850
50	19	950	
			−950
0	20	0	

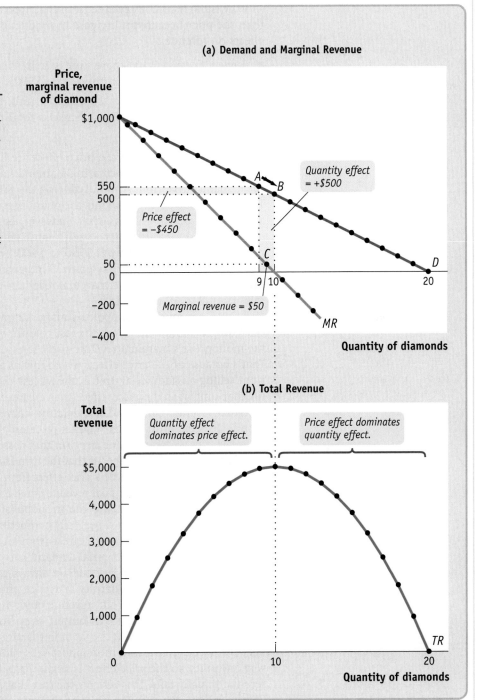

FIGURE 14-5

A Monopolist's Demand, Total Revenue, and Marginal Revenue Curves

Panel (a) shows the monopolist's demand and marginal revenue curves for diamonds from Table 14-1. The marginal revenue curve lies below the demand curve. To see why, consider point *A* on the demand curve, where 9 diamonds are sold at $550 each, generating total revenue of $4,950. To sell a 10th diamond, the price on all 10 diamonds must be cut to $500, as shown by point *B*. As a result, total revenue increases by the green area (the quantity effect: +$500) but decreases by the orange area (the price effect: −$450). So the marginal revenue from the 10th diamond is $50 (the difference between the green and orange areas), which is much lower than its price, $500. Panel (b) shows the monopolist's total revenue curve for diamonds. As output goes from 0 to 10 diamonds, total revenue increases. It reaches its maximum at 10 diamonds—the level at which marginal revenue is equal to 0—and declines thereafter. The quantity effect dominates the price effect when total revenue is rising; the price effect dominates the quantity effect when total revenue is falling.

The third column of Table 14-1 shows De Beers's total revenue from selling each quantity of diamonds—the price per diamond multiplied by the number of diamonds sold. The last column calculates marginal revenue, the change in total revenue from producing and selling another diamond.

Clearly, after the 1st diamond, the marginal revenue a monopolist receives from selling one more unit is less than the price at which that unit is sold. For example, if De Beers sells 10 diamonds, the price at which the 10th diamond is sold is $500. But the marginal revenue—the change in total revenue in going from 9 to 10 diamonds—is only $50.

Why is the marginal revenue from that 10th diamond less than the price? It is less than the price because an increase in production by a monopolist has two opposing effects on revenue:

- *A quantity effect.* One more unit is sold, increasing total revenue by the price at which the unit is sold (in this case, +$500).
- *A price effect.* In order to sell that last unit, the monopolist must cut the market price on *all* units sold. This decreases total revenue (in this case, by $9 \times -\$50 = -\$450$).

The quantity effect and the price effect are illustrated by the two shaded areas in panel (a) of Figure 14-5. Increasing diamond sales from 9 to 10 means moving down the demand curve from A to B, reducing the price per diamond from $550 to $500. The green-shaded area represents the quantity effect: De Beers sells the 10th diamond at a price of $500. This is offset, however, by the price effect, represented by the orange-shaded area. In order to sell that 10th diamond, De Beers must reduce the price on all its diamonds from $550 to $500. So it loses $9 \times \$50 = \$450$ in revenue, the orange-shaded area. So, as point C indicates, the total effect on revenue of selling one more diamond—the marginal revenue—derived from an increase in diamond sales from 9 to 10 is only $50.

Point C lies on the monopolist's marginal revenue curve, labeled *MR* in panel (a) of Figure 14-5 and taken from the last column of Table 14-1. The crucial point about the monopolist's marginal revenue curve is that it is always *below* the demand curve. That's because of the price effect, which means that a monopolist's marginal revenue from selling an additional unit is always less than the price the monopolist receives for that unit. It is the price effect that creates the wedge between the monopolist's marginal revenue curve and the demand curve: in order to sell an additional diamond, De Beers must cut the market price on all units sold.

In fact, this wedge exists for any firm that possesses market power, such as an oligopolist. Having market power means that the firm faces a downward-sloping demand curve. As a result, there will always be a price effect from an increase in its output. So for a firm with market power, the marginal revenue curve always lies below its demand curve.

Take a moment to compare the monopolist's marginal revenue curve with the marginal revenue curve for a perfectly competitive firm, one without market power. For such a firm there is no price effect from an increase in output: its marginal revenue curve is simply its horizontal demand curve. So for a perfectly competitive firm, market price and marginal revenue are always equal.

To emphasize how the quantity and price effects offset each other for a firm with market power, De Beers's total revenue curve is shown in panel (b) of Figure 14-5. Notice that it is hill-shaped: as output rises from 0 to 10 diamonds, total revenue increases. This reflects the fact that *at low levels of output, the quantity effect is stronger than the price effect:* as the monopolist sells more, it has to lower the price on only very few units, so the price effect is small. As output rises beyond 10 diamonds, total revenue actually falls. This reflects the fact that *at high levels of output, the price effect is stronger than the quantity effect:* as the monopolist sells more, it now has to lower the price on many units of output, making the price effect very large. Correspondingly, the marginal revenue curve lies below zero at output levels above 10 diamonds. For example, an increase in diamond production from 11 to 12 yields only $400 for the 12th diamond, simultaneously reducing the revenue from diamonds 1 through 11 by $550. As a result, the marginal revenue of the 12th diamond is −$150.

The Monopolist's Profit-Maximizing Output and Price

To complete the story of how a monopolist maximizes profit, we now bring in the monopolist's marginal cost. Let's assume that there is no fixed cost of production; we'll also assume that the marginal cost of producing an additional diamond is constant at

FIGURE **14-6**

FIGURE **14-6**

The Monopolist's Profit-Maximizing Output and Price

This figure shows the demand, marginal revenue, and marginal cost curves. Marginal cost per diamond is constant at $200, so the marginal cost curve is horizontal at $200. According to the optimal output rule, the profit-maximizing quantity of output for the monopolist is at *MR = MC*, shown by point *A*, where the marginal cost and marginal revenue curves cross at an output of 8 diamonds. The price De Beers can charge per diamond is found by going to the point on the demand curve directly above point *A*, which is point *B* here—a price of $600 per diamond. It makes a profit of $400 × 8 = $3,200. A perfectly competitive industry produces the output level at which *P = MC*, given by point *C*, where the demand curve and marginal cost curves cross. So a competitive industry produces 16 diamonds, sells at a price of $200, and makes zero profit.

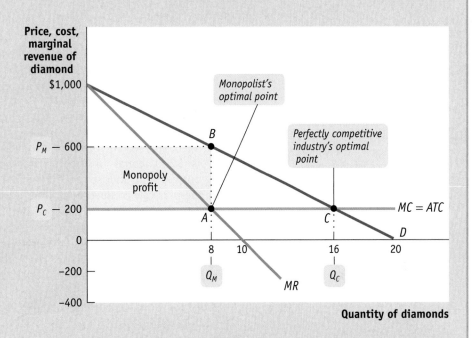

$200, no matter how many diamonds De Beers produces. Then marginal cost will always equal average total cost, and the marginal cost curve (and the average total cost curve) is a horizontal line at $200, as shown in Figure 14-6.

To maximize profit, the monopolist compares marginal cost with marginal revenue. If marginal revenue exceeds marginal cost, De Beers increases profit by producing more; if marginal revenue is less than marginal cost, De Beers increases profit by producing less. So the monopolist maximizes its profit by using the optimal output rule:

(14-1) *MR = MC* at the monopolist's profit-maximizing quantity of output

The monopolist's optimal point is shown in Figure 14-6. At *A*, the marginal cost curve, *MC*, crosses the marginal revenue curve, *MR*. The corresponding output level, 8 diamonds, is the monopolist's profit-maximizing quantity of output, Q_M. The price at which consumers demand 8 diamonds is $600, so the monopolist's price, P_M, is $600—corresponding to point *B*. The average total cost of producing each diamond is $200, so the monopolist earns a profit of $600 − $200 = $400 per diamond, and total profit is 8 × $400 = $3,200, as indicated by the shaded area.

Monopoly versus Perfect Competition

When Cecil Rhodes consolidated many independent diamond producers into De Beers, he converted a perfectly competitive industry into a monopoly. We can now use our analysis to see the effects of such a consolidation.

PITFALLS

FINDING THE MONOPOLY PRICE

In order to find the *profit-maximizing quantity of output* for a monopolist, you look for the point where the marginal revenue curve crosses the marginal cost curve. Point *A* in Figure 14-6 is an example.

However, it's important not to fall into a common error: imagining that point *A* also shows the *price* at which the monopolist sells its output. It doesn't: it shows the *marginal revenue* received by the monopolist, which we know is less than the price.

To find the monopoly price, you have to go up vertically from *A* to the demand curve. There you find the price at which consumers demand the profit-maximizing quantity. So the profit-maximizing price–quantity combination is always a point on the demand curve, like *B* in Figure 14-6.

IS THERE A MONOPOLY SUPPLY CURVE?

Given how a monopolist applies its optimal output rule, you might be tempted to ask what this implies for the supply curve of a monopolist. But this is a meaningless question: *monopolists don't have supply curves.*

Remember that a supply curve shows the quantity that producers are willing to supply for any given market price. A monopolist, however, does not take the price as given; it chooses a profit-maximizing quantity, taking into account its own ability to influence the price.

Let's look again at Figure 14-6 and ask how this same market would work if, instead of being a monopoly, the industry were perfectly competitive. We will continue to assume that there is no fixed cost and that marginal cost is constant, so average total cost and marginal cost are equal.

If the diamond industry consists of many perfectly competitive firms, each of those producers takes the market price as given. That is, each producer acts as if its marginal revenue is equal to the market price. So each firm within the industry uses the price-taking firm's optimal output rule:

(14-2) $P = MC$ at the perfectly competitive firm's profit-maximizing quantity of output

In Figure 14-6, this would correspond to producing at C, where the price per diamond, P_C, is $200, equal to the marginal cost of production. So the profit-maximizing output of an industry under perfect competition, Q_C, is 16 diamonds.

But does the perfectly competitive industry earn any profits at C? No: the price of $200 is equal to the average total cost per diamond. So there are no economic profits for this industry when it produces at the perfectly competitive output level.

We've already seen that once the industry is consolidated into a monopoly, the result is very different. The monopolist's calculation of marginal revenue takes the price effect into account, so that marginal revenue is less than the price. That is,

(14-3) $P > MR = MC$ at the monopolist's profit-maximizing quantity of output

As we've already seen, the monopolist produces less than the competitive industry—8 diamonds rather than 16. The price under monopoly is $600, compared with only $200 under perfect competition. The monopolist earns a positive profit, but the competitive industry does not.

So, just as we suggested earlier, we see that compared with a competitive industry, a monopolist does the following:

- Produces a smaller quantity: $Q_M < Q_C$
- Charges a higher price: $P_M > P_C$
- Earns a profit

FOR INQUIRING MINDS

Monopoly Behavior and the Price Elasticity of Demand

A monopolist faces marginal revenue that is less than the market price. But how much lower? The answer depends on the *price elasticity of demand.*

Remember from Chapter 6 that the price elasticity of demand determines how *total revenue* from sales changes when the price changes. If the price elasticity is greater than 1 (elastic demand), a fall in the price increases total revenue, because the rise in the quantity demanded outweighs the lower price of each unit sold. If the price elasticity is less than 1 (inelastic demand), a lower price reduces total revenue.

When a monopolist increases output by one unit, it must reduce the market price in order to sell that unit. If the price elasticity of demand is less than 1, this will actually reduce revenue—that is, marginal revenue will be negative. The monopolist can increase revenue by producing more only if the price elasticity of demand is greater than 1; the higher the elasticity, the closer the additional revenue is to the initial market price.

What this tells us is that the difference between monopoly behavior and perfectly competitive behavior depends on the price

elasticity of demand. A monopolist that faces highly elastic demand will behave almost like a firm in a perfectly competitive industry.

For example, Amtrak has a monopoly of intercity passenger service in the Northeast Corridor, but it has very little ability to raise prices: potential train travelers will switch to cars and planes. In contrast, a monopolist that faces less elastic demand—like most cable TV companies—will behave very differently from a perfect competitor: it will charge much higher prices and restrict output more.

Monopoly: The General Picture

Figure 14-6 involved specific numbers and assumed that marginal cost was constant, there was no fixed cost, and therefore, that the average total cost curve was a horizontal line. Figure 14-7 shows a more general picture of monopoly in action: *D* is the market demand curve; *MR*, the marginal revenue curve; *MC*, the marginal cost curve; and *ATC*, the average total cost curve. Here we return to the usual assumption that the marginal cost curve has a "swoosh" shape and the average total cost curve is U-shaped.

Applying the optimal output rule, we see that the profit-maximizing level of output is the output at which marginal revenue equals marginal cost, indicated by point *A*. The profit-maximizing quantity of output is Q_M, and the price charged by the monopolist is P_M. At the profit-maximizing level of output, the monopolist's average total cost is ATC_M, shown by point *C*.

Recalling how we calculated profit in Equation 13-5, profit is equal to the difference between total revenue and total cost. So we have

(14-4) Profit = $TR - TC$
$$= (P_M \times Q_M) - (ATC_M \times Q_M)$$
$$= (P_M - ATC_M) \times Q_M$$

Profit is equal to the area of the shaded rectangle in Figure 14-7, with a height of $P_M - ATC_M$ and a width of Q_M.

In Chapter 13 we learned that a perfectly competitive industry can have profits *in the short run but not in the long run.* In the short run, price can exceed average total cost, allowing a perfectly competitive firm to make a profit. But we also know that this cannot persist. In the long run, any profit in a perfectly competitive industry will be competed away as new firms enter the market. In contrast, barriers to entry allow a monopolist to make profits in both the short run and the long run.

> **FIGURE 14-7**   The Monopolist's Profit

In this case, the marginal cost curve has a "swoosh" shape and the average total cost curve is U-shaped. The monopolist maximizes profit by producing the level of output at which *MR = MC*, given by point *A*, generating quantity Q_M. It finds its monopoly price, P_M, from the point on the demand curve directly above point *A*, point *B* here. The average total cost of Q_M is shown by point *C*. Profit is given by the area of the shaded rectangle.

►*ECONOMICS IN ACTION*

California Power Play

The winter of 2000–2001 was a grim time for California, as power shortages gripped the state. One factor involved in the shortages was the soaring price of natural gas, especially in the southern part of the state.

The strange thing was that natural gas prices in California were much higher than in Texas, the source of most of the state's natural gas. That is, the marginal cost of supplying natural gas to California—the cost of buying it in Texas, plus the small expense of shipping it across state lines—was much less than the price of California gas. So why wasn't more gas supplied?

The answer appears to have been that natural gas is transported via interstate pipelines and that the El Paso Corporation, which held a near-monopoly of pipelines supplying southern California, deliberately restricted the quantity of gas available in order to drive up market prices.

The STRUGGLING U.S. Postal Service takes a LESSON from the POWER COMPANIES...

WHOOPS! STAMP SHORTAGE! NOW THEY'RE TWO BUCKS EACH

©Reprinted with special permission of King Feature Syndicate.

Because pipelines tend to be monopolies, they are subject to *price regulation,* discussed later in this chapter. As a result, the price a pipeline company can charge for shipping natural gas is limited. However, El Paso, in addition to running the pipelines, also has an unregulated subsidiary that sells natural gas in California. A judge at the Federal Energy Regulatory Commission concluded that the company used its control of the pipeline to drive up the prices received by its marketing subsidiary. It did this by reducing output—by running pipelines at low pressure and by scheduling nonessential mainte-nance during periods of peak demand. This conclusion was part-ly based on internal memos at El Paso, which seemed to say that the company was "idling large blocks of transport" to widen price spreads between natural gas delivered to Texas and to California. At its peak, the price spread between natural gas in Texas and natural gas delivered to California was more than five times greater than the spread in other parts of the country.

El Paso denied the charges and has never admitted exercising market power. In 2003, however, the company agreed to a settlement in which it paid the state of California $1.7 billion. Many analysts—including the staff at the Federal Energy Regulatory Commission—believe that El Paso's exercise of market power in the natural gas market was part of a broad pattern of market manipulation that played a key role in California's energy crisis during 2000–2001. ▲

< < < < < < < < < < <

> CHECK YOUR UNDERSTANDING 14-2

1. Use the accompanying total revenue schedule of Emerald, Inc., a monopoly producer of 10-carat emeralds, to calculate the answers to parts a–d. Then answer part e.
   a. The demand schedule
   b. The marginal revenue schedule
   c. The quantity effect component of mar-ginal revenue per output level
   d. The price effect component of marginal revenue per output level
   e. What additional information is needed to determine Emerald, Inc.'s profit-maximizing output?

Quantity of emeralds demanded	Total revenue
1	$100
2	186
3	252
4	280
5	250

2. Use Figure 14-6 to show what happens to the following when the marginal cost of diamond production rises from $200 to $400.
   a. Marginal cost curve
   b. Profit-maximizing price and quantity
   c. Profit of the monopolist
   d. Perfectly competitive industry profits

Solutions appear at back of book.

Monopoly and Public Policy

It's good to be a monopolist, but it's not so good to be a monopolist's customer. A monopolist, by reducing output and raising prices, benefits at the expense of con-sumers. But buyers and sellers always have conflicting interests. Is the conflict of interest under monopoly any different than it is under perfect competition?

The answer is yes, because monopoly is a source of inefficiency: the losses to con-sumers from monopoly behavior are larger than the gains to the monopolist. Because monopoly leads to net losses for the economy, governments often try either to pre-vent the emergence of monopolies or to limit their effects. In this section, we will see why monopoly leads to inefficiency and examine the policies governments adopt in an attempt to prevent this inefficiency.

Welfare Effects of Monopoly

By restricting output below the level at which marginal cost is equal to the market price, a monopolist increases its profit but hurts consumers. To assess whether this is a net benefit or loss to society, we must compare the monopolist's gain in profit to the consumer loss. And what we learn is that the consumer loss is larger than the monopolist's gain. Monopoly causes a net loss for society.

To see why, let's return to the case where the marginal cost curve is horizontal, as shown in the two panels of Figure 14-8. Here the marginal cost curve is MC, the demand curve is D, and, in panel (b), the marginal revenue curve is MR.

Panel (a) shows what happens if this industry is perfectly competitive. Equilibrium output is Q_C; the price of the good, P_C, is equal to marginal cost, and marginal cost is also equal to average total cost because there is no fixed cost and marginal cost is constant. Each firm is earning exactly its average total cost per unit of output, so there is no producer surplus in this equilibrium. The consumer surplus generated by the market is equal to the area of the blue-shaded triangle CS_C shown in panel (a). Since there is no producer surplus when the industry is perfectly competitive, CS_C also represents the total surplus.

Panel (b) shows the results for the same market, but this time assuming that the industry is a monopoly. The monopolist produces the level of output, Q_M, at which marginal cost is equal to marginal revenue, and it charges the price P_M. The industry now earns profit—which is also the producer surplus—equal to the area of the green rectangle, PS_M. Note that this profit is surplus that has been captured from consumers as consumer surplus shrinks to the area of the blue triangle, CS_M.

By comparing panels (a) and (b), we see that in addition to the redistribution of surplus from consumers to the monopolist, another important change has occurred: the sum of profit and consumer surplus—total surplus—is *smaller* under monopoly than under perfect competition. That is, the sum of CS_M and PS_M in panel (b) is less than the area CS_C in panel (a). In Chapter 7, we analyzed how taxes generated *deadweight loss* to society. Here we show that monopoly creates a deadweight loss to society equal to the area of the yellow triangle, DL. So monopoly produces a net loss for society.

FIGURE 14-8   Monopoly Causes Inefficiency

(a) Total Surplus with Perfect Competition

(b) Total Surplus with Monopoly

Panel (a) depicts a perfectly competitive industry: output is Q_C, and market price, P_C, is equal to MC. Since price is exactly equal to each producer's average total cost of production per unit, there is no producer surplus. So total surplus is equal to consumer surplus, the entire shaded area. Panel (b) depicts the industry under monopoly: the monopolist decreases output to Q_M and charges P_M. Consumer surplus (blue area) has shrunk: a portion of it has been captured as profit (green area), and a portion of it has been lost to deadweight loss (yellow area), the value of mutually beneficial transactions that do not occur because of monopoly behavior. As a result, total surplus falls.

In **public ownership** of a monopoly, the good is supplied by the government or by a firm owned by the government.

This net loss arises because some mutually beneficial transactions do not occur. There are people for whom an additional unit of the good is worth more than the marginal cost of producing it but who don't consume it because they are not willing to pay P_M.

Those who recall our discussion of the deadweight loss from taxes in Chapter 7 will notice that the deadweight loss from monopoly looks quite similar. Indeed, by driving a wedge between price and marginal cost, monopoly acts much like a tax on consumers and produces the same kind of inefficiency.

So monopoly hurts the welfare of society as a whole and is a source of market failure. Is there anything government policy can do about it?

Preventing Monopoly

Policy toward monopoly depends crucially on whether or not the industry in question is a natural monopoly, one in which increasing returns to scale ensure that a bigger producer has lower average total cost. If the industry is *not* a natural monopoly, the best policy is to prevent monopoly from arising or break it up if it already exists. Let's focus on that case first, then turn to the more difficult problem of dealing with natural monopoly.

The De Beers monopoly on diamonds didn't have to happen. Diamond production is not a natural monopoly: the industry's costs would be no higher if it consisted of a number of independent, competing producers (as is the case, for example, in gold production).

So if the South African government had been worried about how a monopoly would have affected consumers, it could have blocked Cecil Rhodes in his drive to dominate the industry or broken up his monopoly after the fact. Today, governments often try to prevent monopolies from forming and break up existing ones.

De Beers is a rather unique case: for complicated historical reasons, it was allowed to remain a monopoly. But over the last century, most similar monopolies have been broken up. The most celebrated example in the United States is Standard Oil, founded by John D. Rockefeller in 1870. By 1878 Standard Oil controlled almost all U.S. oil refining; but in 1911 a court order broke the company into a number of smaller units, including the companies that later became Exxon and Mobil (and more recently merged to become ExxonMobil).

The government policies used to prevent or eliminate monopolies are known as *antitrust policy,* which we will discuss in the next chapter.

Dealing with Natural Monopoly

Breaking up a monopoly that isn't natural is clearly a good idea: the gains to consumers outweigh the loss to the producer. But it's not so clear whether a natural monopoly, one in which large producers have lower average total costs than small producers, should be broken up, because this would raise average total cost. For example, a town government that tried to prevent a single company from dominating local gas supply—which, as we've discussed, is almost surely a natural monopoly—would raise the cost of providing gas to its residents.

Yet even in the case of a natural monopoly, a profit-maximizing monopolist acts in a way that causes inefficiency—it charges consumers a price that is higher than marginal cost and, by doing so, prevents some potentially beneficial transactions. Also, it can seem unfair that a firm that has managed to establish a monopoly position earns a large profit at the expense of consumers.

What can public policy do about this? There are two common answers.

Public Ownership In many countries, the preferred answer to the problem of natural monopoly has been **public ownership.** Instead of allowing a private monopolist to control an industry, the government establishes a public agency to provide the good and protect consumers' interests. In Britain, for example, telephone service was provided by the state-owned British Telecom before 1984, and airline travel was provided by the state-owned British Airways before 1987. (These companies still exist, but they have been privatized, competing with other firms in their respective industries.)

There are some examples of public ownership in the United States. Passenger rail service is provided by the public company Amtrak; regular mail delivery is provided by the U.S. Postal Service; some cities, including Los Angeles, have publicly owned electric power companies.

The advantage of public ownership, in principle, is that a publicly owned natural monopoly can set prices based on the criterion of efficiency rather than profit maximization. In a perfectly competitive industry, profit-maximizing behavior *is* efficient, because producers set prices equal to marginal cost; that is why there is no economic argument for public ownership of, say, wheat farms.

Experience suggests, however, that public ownership as a solution to the problem of natural monopoly often works badly in practice. One reason is that publicly owned firms are often less eager than private companies to keep costs down or offer high-quality products. Another is that publicly owned companies all too often end up serving political interests—providing contracts or jobs to people with the right connections. For example, Amtrak has notoriously provided train service at a loss to destinations that attract few passengers—but that are located in the districts of influential members of Congress.

Regulation   In the United States, the more common answer has been to leave the industry in private hands but subject it to regulation. In particular, most local utilities like electricity, telephone service, natural gas, and so on are covered by **price regulation** that limits the prices they can charge.

We saw in Chapter 5 that imposing a *price ceiling* on a competitive industry is a recipe for shortages, black markets, and other nasty side effects. Doesn't imposing a limit on the price that, say, a local gas company can charge have the same effects?

Not necessarily: a price ceiling on a monopolist need not create a shortage—in the absence of a price ceiling, a monopolist would charge a price that is higher than its marginal cost of production. So even if forced to charge a lower price—as long as that price is above *MC* and the monopolist at least breaks even on total output—the monopolist still has an incentive to produce the quantity demanded at that price.

Figure 14-9 on the next page shows an example of price regulation of a natural monopoly—a highly simplified version of a local gas company. The company faces a demand curve *D*, with an associated marginal revenue curve *MR*. For simplicity, we assume that the firm's total costs consist of two parts: a fixed cost and variable costs that are incurred at a constant proportion to output. So marginal cost is constant in this case, and the marginal cost curve (which here is also the average variable cost curve) is the horizontal line *MC*. The average total cost curve is the downward-sloping curve *ATC*; it slopes downward because the higher the output, the lower the average fixed cost (the fixed cost per unit of output). Because average total cost slopes downward over the range of output relevant for market demand, this is a natural monopoly.

Panel (a) illustrates a case of natural monopoly without regulation. The unregulated natural monopolist chooses the monopoly output Q_M and charges the price P_M. Since the monopolist receives a price greater than its average total cost, it earns a profit. This profit is exactly equal to the producer surplus in this market, represented by the green-shaded rectangle. Consumer surplus is given by the blue-shaded triangle.

Now suppose that regulators impose a price ceiling on local gas deliveries—one that falls below the monopoly price P_M but above *ATC*, say, at P_R in panel (a). At that price the quantity demanded is Q_R.

FIGURE 14-9   **Unregulated and Regulated Natural Monopoly**

This figure shows the case of a natural monopolist. In panel (a), if the monopolist is allowed to charge P_M, it makes a profit, shown by the green area; consumer surplus is shown by the blue area. If it is regulated and must charge the lower price P_R, output increases from Q_M to Q_R and consumer surplus increases. Panel (b) shows what happens when the monopolist must charge a price equal to average total cost, the price P_R^*. Output expands to Q_R^*, and consumer surplus is now the entire blue area. The monopolist makes zero profit. This is the greatest total surplus possible when the monopolist is allowed to at least break even, making P_R^* the best regulated price.

Does the company have an incentive to produce that quantity? Yes. If the price at which the monopolist can sell its product is fixed by regulators, the firm's output no longer affects the market price—so it ignores the *MR* curve and is willing to expand output to meet the quantity demanded as long as the price it receives for the next unit is greater than marginal cost and the monopolist at least breaks even on total output. So with price regulation, the monopolist produces more, at a lower price.

Of course, the monopolist will not be willing to produce at all if the imposed price means producing at a loss. That is, the price ceiling has to be set high enough to allow the firm to cover its average total cost. Panel (b) shows a situation in which regulators have pushed the price down as far as possible, at the level where the average total cost curve crosses the demand curve. At any lower price the firm loses money. The price here, P_R^*, is the best regulated price: the monopolist is just willing to operate and produces Q_R^*, the quantity demanded at that price. Consumers and society gain as a result.

The welfare effects of this regulation can be seen by comparing the shaded areas in the two panels of Figure 14-9. Consumer surplus is increased by the regulation, with the gains coming from two sources. First, profits are eliminated and added instead to consumer surplus. Second, the larger output and lower price leads to an overall welfare gain—an increase in total surplus. In fact, panel (b) illustrates the largest total surplus possible.

This all looks terrific: consumers are better off, profits are eliminated, and overall welfare increases. Unfortunately, things are rarely that easy in practice. The main problem is that regulators don't have the information required to set the price exactly at the level at which the demand curve crosses the average total cost curve. Sometimes they set it too low, creating shortages; at other times they set it too high. Also, regulated monopolies, like publicly owned firms, tend to exaggerate their costs to regulators and to provide inferior quality to consumers.

Must Monopoly Be Controlled? Sometimes the cure is worse than the disease. Some economists have argued that the best solution, even in the case of natural monopoly, may be to live with it. The case for doing nothing is that attempts to control monopoly will, one way or another, do more harm than good—for example, by the politicization of pricing, which leads to shortages, or by the creation of opportunities for political corruption.

The following Economics in Action describes the case of cable television, a natural monopoly that has been alternately regulated and deregulated as politicians change their minds about the appropriate policy.

➤ECONOMICS IN ACTION

Cable Dilemmas

Most price regulation in the United States goes back a long way: electricity, local phone service, water, and gas have been regulated in most places for generations. But cable television is a relatively new industry. Until the late 1970s, only rural areas too remote to support local broadcast stations were served by cable. After 1972, new technology and looser rules made it profitable to offer cable service to major metropolitan areas; new networks like HBO and CNN emerged to take advantage of the possibilities.

Until recently local cable TV was a natural monopoly: running cable through a town entails large fixed costs that don't depend on how many people actually subscribe. Having more than one cable company would involve a lot of wasteful duplication. But if the local cable company is a monopoly, should its prices be regulated?

At first, most local governments thought so, and cable TV was subject to price regulation. In 1984, however, Congress passed a law prohibiting most local governments from regulating cable prices. (The law was the result both of widespread skepticism about whether price regulation was actually a good idea and of intensive lobbying by the cable companies.)

After the law went into effect, however, cable television rates increased sharply. The resulting consumer backlash led to a new law, in 1992, which once again allowed local governments to set limits on cable prices.

Was the second round of regulation a success? As measured by the prices of "basic" cable service, it was: after rising rapidly during the period of deregulation, the cost of basic service leveled off.

However, price regulation in cable applies only to "basic" service. Cable operators can try to evade the restrictions by charging more for premium channels like HBO or by offering fewer channels in the "basic" package. So some skeptics have questioned whether current regulation has actually been effective.

Yet technological change has begun providing relief to consumers in some areas. Although cable TV is a natural monopoly, there is now another means of delivering video programs to homes: over a high-speed fiber-optic Internet connection. In some locations, fiber-optic Internet providers have begun competing aggressively with traditional cable TV companies. Studies have shown that when a second provider enters a market, prices can drop significantly, as much as 30%. In fact, the United States is currently behind on this front: today 60% of households in Hong Kong watch TV programs delivered over the Internet. What will these changes mean for the cable TV monopolies? Stay tuned. ▲

> > > > > > > > > > > > >

> ➤ **CHECK YOUR UNDERSTANDING** **14-3**

1. What policy should the government adopt in the following cases? Explain.
   a. Internet service in Anytown, OH, is provided by cable. Customers feel they are being overcharged, but the cable company claims it must charge prices that let it recover the costs of laying cable.

A **single-price monopolist** offers its product to all consumers at the same price.

Sellers engage in **price discrimination** when they charge different prices to different consumers for the same good.

b. The only two airlines that currently fly to Alaska need government approval to merge. Other airlines wish to fly to Alaska but need government-allocated landing slots to do so.

2. True or false? Explain your answer.
   a. Society's welfare is lower under monopoly because some consumer surplus is transformed into profit for the monopolist.
   b. A monopolist causes inefficiency because there are consumers who are willing to pay a price greater than or equal to marginal cost but less than the monopoly price.

3. Suppose a monopolist mistakenly believes that its marginal revenue is always equal to the market price. Assuming constant marginal cost and no fixed cost, draw a diagram comparing the level of profit, consumer surplus, total surplus, and deadweight loss for this misguided monopolist compared to a smart monopolist.

Solutions appear at back of book.

Price Discrimination

Up to this point, we have considered only the case of a **single-price monopolist,** one that charges all consumers the same price. As the term suggests, not all monopolists do this. In fact, many if not most monopolists find that they can increase their profits by charging different customers different prices for the same good: they engage in **price discrimination.**

The most striking example of price discrimination most of us encounter regularly involves airline tickets. Although there are a number of airlines, most routes in the United States are serviced by only one or two carriers, which, as a result, have market power and can set prices. So any regular airline passenger quickly becomes aware that the question "How much will it cost me to fly there?" rarely has a simple answer. If you are willing to buy a nonrefundable ticket a month in advance and stay over a Saturday night, the round trip may cost only $150—or less if you are a senior citizen or a student. But if you have to go on a business trip tomorrow, which happens to be Tuesday, and come back on Wednesday, the same round trip might cost $550. Yet the business traveler and the visiting grandparent receive the same product—the same cramped seat, the same awful food.

You might object that airlines are not usually monopolists—that in most flight markets the airline industry is an oligopoly. In fact, price discrimination takes place under oligopoly and monopolistic competition as well as monopoly. But it doesn't happen under perfect competition. And once we've seen why monopolists sometimes price-discriminate, we'll be in a good position to understand why it happens in other cases, too.

The Logic of Price Discrimination

To get a preliminary view of why price discrimination might be more profitable than charging all consumers the same price, imagine that Air Sunshine offers the only nonstop flights between Bismarck, North Dakota, and Ft. Lauderdale, Florida. Assume that there are no capacity problems—the airline can fly as many planes as the number of passengers warrants. Also assume that there is no fixed cost. The marginal cost to the airline of providing a seat is $125, however many passengers it carries.

Further assume that the airline knows there are two kinds of potential passengers. First, there are business travelers, 2,000 of whom want to travel between the destinations each week. Second, there are students, 2,000 of whom also want to travel each week.

Will potential passengers take the flight? It depends on the price. The business travelers, it turns out, really need to fly; they will take the plane as long as the price is no more than $550. Since they are flying purely for business, we assume that cut-

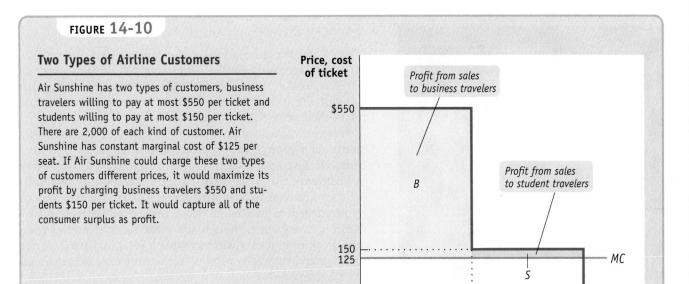

FIGURE 14-10

Two Types of Airline Customers

Air Sunshine has two types of customers, business travelers willing to pay at most $550 per ticket and students willing to pay at most $150 per ticket. There are 2,000 of each kind of customer. Air Sunshine has constant marginal cost of $125 per seat. If Air Sunshine could charge these two types of customers different prices, it would maximize its profit by charging business travelers $550 and students $150 per ticket. It would capture all of the consumer surplus as profit.

ting the price below $550 will not lead to any increase in business travel. The students, however, have less money and more time; if the price goes above $150, they will take the bus. The implied demand curve is shown in Figure 14-10.

So what should the airline do? If it has to charge everyone the same price, its options are limited. It could charge $550; that way it would get as much as possible out of the business travelers but lose the student market. Or it could charge only $150; that way it would get both types of travelers but would make significantly less money from sales to business travelers.

We can quickly calculate the profits from each of these alternatives. If the airline charged $550, it would sell 2,000 tickets to the business travelers, earning total revenue of 2,000 × $550 = $1.1 million and incurring costs of 2,000 × $125 = $250,000; so its profit would be $850,000, illustrated by the shaded area B in Figure 14-10. If the airline charged only $150, it would sell 4,000 tickets, receiving revenue of 4,000 × $150 = $600,000 and incurring costs of 4,000 × $125 = $500,000; so its profit would be $100,000. If the airline must charge everyone the same price, charging the higher price and forgoing sales to students is clearly more profitable.

What the airline would really like to do, however, is charge the business travelers the full $550 but offer $150 tickets to the students. That's a lot less than the price paid by business travelers, but it's still above marginal cost; so if the airline could sell those extra 2,000 tickets to students, it would make an additional $50,000 in profit. That is, it would make a profit equal to the areas B plus S in Figure 14-10.

It would be more realistic to suppose that there is some "give" in the demand of each group: at a price below $550, there would be some increase in business travel; and at a price above $150, some students would still purchase tickets. But this, it turns out, does not do away with the argument for price discrimination. The important point is that the two groups of consumers differ in their *sensitivity to price*—that a high price has a larger effect in discouraging purchases by students than by business travelers. As long as different groups of customers respond differently to the price, a monopolist will find that it can capture more consumer surplus and increase its profit by charging them different prices.

On many airline routes, the fare you pay depends on the type of traveler you are.

Price Discrimination and Elasticity

A more realistic description of the demand that airlines face would not specify particular prices at which different types of travelers would choose to fly. Instead, it would distinguish between the groups on the basis of their sensitivity to the price—their price elasticity of demand.

Suppose that a company sells its product to two easily identifiable groups of people—business travelers and students. It just so happens that business travelers are very insensitive to the price: there is a certain amount of the product they just have to have whatever the price, but they cannot be persuaded to buy much more than that no matter how cheap it is. Students, though, are more flexible: offer a good enough price and they will buy quite a lot, but raise the price too high and they will switch to something else. What should the company do?

The answer is the one already suggested by our simplified example: the company should charge business travelers, with their low price elasticity of demand, a higher price than it charges students, with their high price elasticity of demand.

The actual situation of the airlines is very much like this hypothetical example. Business travelers typically place a high priority on being at the right place at the right time and are not very sensitive to the price. But nonbusiness travelers are fairly sensitive to the price: faced with a high price, they might take the bus, drive to another airport to get a lower fare, or skip the trip altogether.

So why doesn't an airline simply announce different prices for business and nonbusiness customers? First, this would probably be illegal (U.S. law places some limits on the ability of companies to practice open price discrimination). Second, even if it were legal, it would be a hard policy to enforce: business travelers might be willing to wear casual clothing and claim they were visiting family in Ft. Lauderdale in order to save $400.

So what the airlines do—quite successfully—is impose rules that indirectly have the effect of charging business and nonbusiness travelers different fares. Business travelers usually travel during the week and want to be home on the weekend; so the round-trip fare is much higher if you don't stay over a Saturday night. The requirement of a weekend stay for a cheap ticket effectively separates business from nonbusiness travelers. Similarly, business travelers often visit several cities in succession rather than make a simple round trip; so round-trip fares are much lower than twice the one-way fare. Many business trips are scheduled on short notice; so fares are much lower if you book far in advance. Fares are also lower if you travel standby, taking your chances on whether you actually get a seat—business travelers have to make it to that meeting; people visiting their relatives don't. And because customers must show their ID at check-in, airlines make sure there are no resales of tickets between the two groups that would undermine their ability to price-discriminate—students can't buy cheap tickets and resell them to business travelers. Look at the rules that govern ticket-pricing, and you will see an ingenious implementation of profit-maximizing price discrimination.

Perfect Price Discrimination

Let's return to the example of business travelers and students traveling between Bismarck and Ft. Lauderdale, illustrated in Figure 14-10, and ask what would happen if the airline could distinguish between the two groups of customers in order to charge each a different price.

Clearly, the airline would charge each group its willingness to pay—that is, as we learned in Chapter 4, the maximum that each group is willing to pay. For business

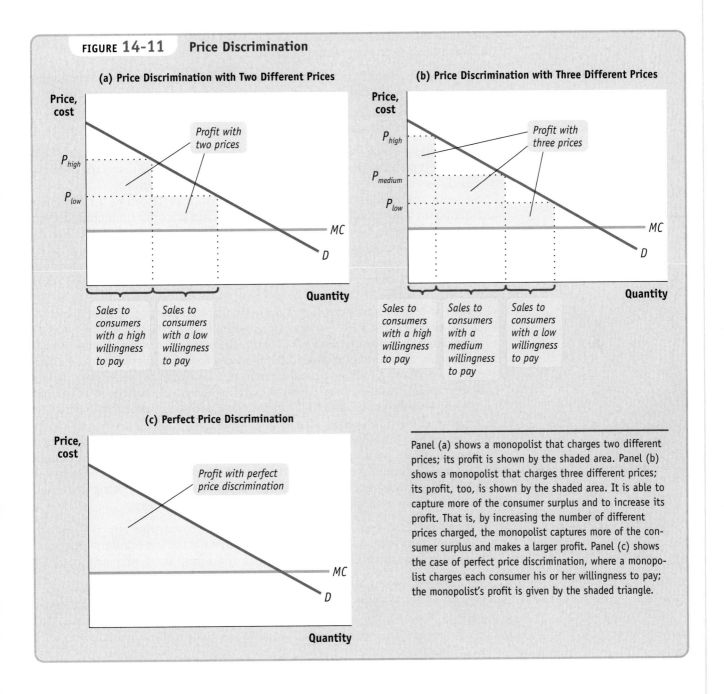

FIGURE **14-11**   **Price Discrimination**

(a) Price Discrimination with Two Different Prices

Price, cost

P_{high}

P_{low}

Profit with two prices

MC

D

Quantity

Sales to consumers with a high willingness to pay

Sales to consumers with a low willingness to pay

(b) Price Discrimination with Three Different Prices

Price, cost

P_{high}

P_{medium}

P_{low}

Profit with three prices

MC

D

Quantity

Sales to consumers with a high willingness to pay

Sales to consumers with a medium willingness to pay

Sales to consumers with a low willingness to pay

(c) Perfect Price Discrimination

Price, cost

Profit with perfect price discrimination

MC

D

Quantity

Panel (a) shows a monopolist that charges two different prices; its profit is shown by the shaded area. Panel (b) shows a monopolist that charges three different prices; its profit, too, is shown by the shaded area. It is able to capture more of the consumer surplus and to increase its profit. That is, by increasing the number of different prices charged, the monopolist captures more of the consumer surplus and makes a larger profit. Panel (c) shows the case of perfect price discrimination, where a monopolist charges each consumer his or her willingness to pay; the monopolist's profit is given by the shaded triangle.

travelers, the willingness to pay is $550; for students, it is $150. As we have assumed, the marginal cost is $125 and does not depend on output, making the marginal cost curve a horizontal line. As we noted earlier, we can easily determine the airline's profit: it is the sum of the areas of the rectangle *B* and the rectangle *S*.

In this case, the consumers do not get any consumer surplus! The entire surplus is captured by the monopolist in the form of profit. When a monopolist is able to capture the entire surplus in this way, we say that it achieves **perfect price discrimination.**

In general, the greater the number of different prices a monopolist is able to charge, the closer it can get to perfect price discrimination. Figure 14-11 shows a monopolist facing a downward-sloping demand curve, a monopolist who we assume is able to charge different prices to different groups of consumers, with the consumers who are willing to pay the most being charged the most. In panel (a) the

Perfect price discrimination takes place when a monopolist charges each consumer his or her willingness to pay—the maximum that the consumer is willing to pay.

monopolist charges two different prices; in panel (b) the monopolist charges three different prices. Two things are apparent:

- The greater the number of prices the monopolist charges, the lower the lowest price—that is, some consumers will pay prices that approach marginal cost.
- The greater the number of prices the monopolist charges, the more money it extracts from consumers.

With a very large number of different prices, the picture would look like panel (c), a case of perfect price discrimination. Here, consumers least willing to buy the good pay marginal cost, and the entire consumer surplus is extracted as profit.

Both our airline example and the example in Figure 14-11 can be used to make another point: a monopolist that can engage in perfect price discrimination doesn't cause any inefficiency! The reason is that the source of inefficiency is eliminated: all potential consumers who are willing to purchase the good at a price equal to or above marginal cost are able to do so. The perfectly price-discriminating monopolist manages to "scoop up" all consumers by offering some of them lower prices than it charges others.

Perfect price discrimination is almost never possible in practice. At a fundamental level, the inability to achieve perfect price discrimination is a problem of prices as economic signals, a phenomenon we noted in Chapter 4. When prices work as economic signals, they convey the information needed to ensure that all mutually beneficial transactions will indeed occur: the market price signals the seller's cost, and a consumer signals willingness to pay by purchasing the good whenever that willingness to pay is at least as high as the market price. The problem in reality, however, is that prices are often not perfect signals: a consumer's true willingness to pay can be disguised, as by a business traveler who claims to be a student when buying a ticket in order to obtain a lower fare. When such disguises work, a monopolist cannot achieve perfect price discrimination. However, monopolists do try to move in the direction of perfect price discrimination through a variety of pricing strategies. Common techniques for price discrimination include the following:

- *Advance purchase restrictions.* Prices are lower for those who purchase well in advance (or in some cases for those who purchase at the last minute). This separates those who are likely to shop for better prices from those who won't.

- *Volume discounts.* Often the price is lower if you buy a large quantity. For a consumer who plans to consume a lot of a good, the cost of the last unit—the marginal cost to the consumer—is considerably less than the average price. This separates those who plan to buy a lot and so are likely to be more sensitive to price from those who don't.

- *Two-part tariffs.* In a discount club like Sam's Club (which is not a monopolist but a monopolistic competitor), you pay an annual fee in addition to the cost of the items you purchase. So the cost of the first item you buy is in effect much higher than that of subsequent items, making the two-part tariff behave like a volume discount.

Our discussion also helps explain why government policies on monopoly typically focus on preventing deadweight losses, not preventing price discrimination—unless it causes serious issues of equity. Compared to a single-price monopolist, price discrimination—even when it is not perfect—can increase the efficiency of the market. If sales to consumers formerly priced out of the market but now able to purchase the good at a lower price generate enough surplus to offset the loss in surplus to those now facing a higher price and no longer buying the good, then total surplus increases when price discrimination is introduced. An example of this might be a drug that is disproportionately prescribed to senior citizens, who are often on fixed incomes and so are very sensitive to price. A policy that allows a drug company to charge senior citizens a low price and everyone else a high price may indeed increase total surplus compared to a situation in which everyone is charged the same price. But price discrimination that creates serious concerns about equity is likely to be prohibited—for example, an ambulance service that charges patients based on the severity of their emergency.

➤ECONOMICS IN ACTION

Sales, Factory Outlets, and Ghost Cities

Have you ever wondered why department stores occasionally hold sales, offering their merchandise for considerably less than the usual prices? Or why, driving along America's highways, you sometimes encounter clusters of "factory outlet" stores, often a couple of hours' drive from the nearest city? These familiar features of the economic landscape are actually rather peculiar if you think about them: why should sheets and towels be suddenly cheaper for a week each winter, or raincoats be offered for less in Freeport, Maine, than in Boston? In each case the answer is that the sellers—who are often oligopolists or monopolistic competitors—are engaged in a subtle form of price discrimination.

Why hold regular sales of sheets and towels? Stores are aware that some consumers buy these goods only when they discover that they need them; they are not likely to put a lot of effort into searching for the best price and so have a relatively low price elasticity of demand. So the store wants to charge high prices for customers who come in on an ordinary day. But shoppers who plan ahead, looking for the lowest price, will wait until there is a sale. So by scheduling such sales only now and then, the store is in effect able to price-discriminate between high-elasticity and low-elasticity customers.

An outlet store serves the same purpose: by offering merchandise for low prices, but only a considerable distance away from downtown, a seller is able to establish a separate market for those customers who are willing to make a significant effort to search out lower prices—and who therefore have a relatively high price elasticity of demand.

Finally, let's return to airline tickets to mention one of the truly odd features of their prices. Often a flight from one major destination to another—say, from Chicago to Los Angeles—is cheaper than a much shorter flight to a smaller city—say, from Chicago to Salt Lake City. Again, the reason is a difference in the price elasticity of demand: customers have a choice of many airlines between Chicago and Los Angeles, so the demand for any one flight is quite elastic; customers have very little choice in flights to a small city, so the demand is much less elastic.

But often there is a flight between two major destinations that makes a stop along the way—say, a flight from Chicago to Los Angeles with a stop in Salt Lake City. In these cases, it is sometimes cheaper to fly to the more distant city than to the city that is a stop along the way. For example, it may be cheaper to purchase a ticket to Los Angeles and get off in Salt Lake City than to purchase a ticket to Salt Lake City! It sounds ridiculous but makes perfect sense given the logic of monopoly pricing.

So why don't passengers simply buy a ticket from Chicago to Los Angeles, but get off at Salt Lake City? Well, some do—but the airlines, understandably, make it difficult for customers to find out about such "ghost cities." In addition, the airline will not allow you to check baggage only part of the way if you have a ticket for the final destination. (And airlines refuse to honor tickets for return flights when a passenger has not completed all the legs of the outbound flight.) All these restrictions are meant to enforce the separation of markets necessary to allow price discrimination. ▲

> > > > > > > > > > > >

➤➤ **QUICK REVIEW**

> Not every monopolist is a **single-price monopolist.** Many monopolists, as well as oligopolists and monopolistic competitors, engage in **price discrimination.**

> Price discrimination is profitable when consumers differ in their sensitivity to the price. A monopolist would like to charge high prices to consumers willing to pay them without driving away others who are willing to pay less.

> It is profit-maximizing to charge higher prices to low-elasticity consumers and lower prices to high-elasticity ones.

> A monopolist able to charge each consumer his or her willingness to pay for the good achieves **perfect price discrimination** and does not cause inefficiency because all mutually beneficial transactions are exploited.

► CHECK YOUR UNDERSTANDING 14-4

1. True or false? Explain your answer.
   a. A single-price monopolist sells to some customers that a price-discriminating monopolist refuses to.
   b. A price-discriminating monopolist creates more inefficiency than a single-price monopolist because it captures more of the consumer surplus.
   c. Under price discrimination, a customer with highly elastic demand will pay a lower price than a customer with inelastic demand.

2. Which of the following are cases of price discrimination and which are not? In the cases of price discrimination, identify the consumers with high and those with low price elasticity of demand.
   a. Damaged merchandise is marked down.
   b. Restaurants have senior citizen discounts.
   c. Food manufacturers place discount coupons for their merchandise in newspapers.
   d. Airline tickets cost more during the summer peak flying season.

Solutions appear at back of book.

[►► A LOOK AHEAD •••

We've now taken one large step away from the world of perfect competition. As we have seen, a monopolized industry behaves quite differently from a perfectly competitive one.

But pure monopoly is actually quite rare in the modern economy. More typical are industries in which there is some competition, but not perfect competition—that is, where there is *imperfect competition*. In the next two chapters, we examine two types of imperfect competition: oligopoly and monopolistic competition.

You might expect an oligopoly to act something like a cross between a monopoly and a perfectly competitive industry, but it turns out that oligopoly raises issues that arise neither in perfect competition nor in monopoly—issues of *strategic interaction* and *collusion* between firms. Likewise, monopolistic competition creates yet another set of issues, such as tastes, product differentiation, and advertising.]

SUMMARY

1. There are four main types of market structure based on the number of firms in the industry and product differentiation: perfect competition, monopoly, oligopoly, and monopolistic competition.

2. A **monopolist** is a producer who is the sole supplier of a good without close substitutes. An industry controlled by a monopolist is a **monopoly.**

3. The key difference between a monopoly and a perfectly competitive industry is that a single perfectly competitive firm faces a horizontal demand curve but a monopolist faces a downward-sloping demand curve. This gives the monopolist **market power,** the ability to raise the market price by reducing output compared to a perfectly competitive firm.

4. To persist, a monopoly must be protected by a **barrier to entry.** This can take the form of control of a natural resource or input, increasing returns to scale that give

rise to **natural monopoly,** technological superiority, or government rules that prevent entry by other firms, such as **patents** or **copyrights.**

5. The marginal revenue of a monopolist is composed of a quantity effect (the price received from the additional unit) and a price effect (the reduction in the price at which all units are sold). Because of the price effect, a monopolist's marginal revenue is always less than the market price, and the marginal revenue curve lies below the demand curve.

6. At the monopolist's profit-maximizing output level, marginal cost equals marginal revenue, which is less than market price. At the perfectly competitive firm's profit-maximizing output level, marginal cost equals the market price. So in comparison to perfectly competitive industries, monopolies produce less, charge higher prices, and earn profits in both the short run and the long run.

7. A monopoly creates deadweight losses by charging a price above marginal cost: the loss in consumer surplus exceeds the monopolist's profit. Thus monopolies are a source of market failure and should be prevented or broken up, except in the case of natural monopolies.

8. Natural monopolies can still cause deadweight losses. To limit these losses, governments sometimes impose **public ownership** and at other times impose **price regulation.** A price ceiling on a monopolist, as opposed to a perfectly competitive industry, need not cause shortages and can increase total surplus.

9. Not all monopolists are **single-price monopolists.** Monopolists, as well as oligopolists and monopolistic competitors, often engage in **price discrimination** to make higher profits, using various techniques to differentiate consumers based on their sensitivity to price and charging those with less elastic demand higher prices. A monopolist that achieves **perfect price discrimination** charges each consumer a price equal to his or her willingness to pay and captures the total surplus in the market. Although perfect price discrimination creates no inefficiency, it is practically impossible to implement.

KEY TERMS ···■

Monopolist, p. 357
Monopoly, p. 357
Market power, p. 358
Barrier to entry, p. 359

Natural monopoly, p. 359
Patent, p. 360
Copyright, p. 360
Public ownership, p. 372

Price regulation, p. 373
Single-price monopolist, p. 376
Price discrimination, p. 376
Perfect price discrimination, p. 379

PROBLEMS ··■

1. Each of the following firms possesses market power. Explain its source.

   a. Merck, the producer of the patented cholesterol-lowering drug Zetia

   b. WaterWorks, a provider of piped water

   c. Chiquita, a supplier of bananas and owner of most banana plantations

   d. The Walt Disney Company, the creators of Mickey Mouse

2. Skyscraper City has a subway system, for which a one-way fare is $1.50. There is pressure on the mayor to reduce the fare by one-third, to $1.00. The mayor is dismayed, thinking that this will mean Skyscraper City is losing one-third of its revenue from sales of subway tickets. The mayor's economic adviser reminds her that she is focusing only on the price effect and ignoring the quantity effect. Explain why the mayor's estimate of a one-third loss of revenue is likely to be an overestimate. Illustrate with a diagram.

3. Consider an industry with the demand curve (D) and marginal cost curve (MC) shown in the accompanying diagram. There is no fixed cost. If the industry is a single-price monopoly, the monopolist's marginal revenue curve would be MR. Answer the following questions by naming the appropriate points or areas.

   a. If the industry is perfectly competitive, what will be the total quantity produced? At what price?

   b. Which area reflects consumer surplus under perfect competition?

   c. If the industry is a single-price monopoly, what quantity will the monopolist produce? Which price will it charge?

   d. Which area reflects the single-price monopolist's profit?

   e. Which area reflects consumer surplus under single-price monopoly?

   f. Which area reflects the deadweight loss to society from single-price monopoly?

   g. If the monopolist can price-discriminate perfectly, what quantity will the perfectly price-discriminating monopolist produce?

4. Bob, Bill, Ben, and Brad Baxter have just made a documentary movie about their basketball team. They are thinking about making the movie available for download on the Internet, and they can act as a single-price monopolist if they choose to. Each time the movie is downloaded, their Internet service provider charges them a fee of $4. The Baxter brothers are arguing about which price to charge customers per download. The accompanying table shows the demand schedule for their film.

Price of download	Quantity of downloads demanded
$10	0
8	1
6	3
4	6
2	10
0	15

a. Calculate the total revenue and the marginal revenue per download.

b. Bob is proud of the film and wants as many people as possible to download it. Which price would he choose? How many downloads would be sold?

c. Bill wants as much total revenue as possible. Which price would he choose? How many downloads would be sold?

d. Ben wants to maximize profit. Which price would he choose? How many downloads would be sold?

e. Brad wants to charge the efficient price. Which price would he choose? How many downloads would be sold?

5. Jimmy has a room that overlooks, from some distance, a major league baseball stadium. He decides to rent a telescope for $50.00 a week and charge his friends and classmates to use it to peep at the game for 30 seconds. He can act as a single-price monopolist for renting out "peeps." For each person who takes a 30-second peep, it costs Jimmy $0.20 to clean the eyepiece. The accompanying table shows the information Jimmy has gathered about the demand for the service in a given week.

Price of peep	Quantity of peeps demanded
$1.20	0
1.00	100
0.90	150
0.80	200
0.70	250
0.60	300
0.50	350
0.40	400
0.30	450
0.20	500
0.10	550

a. For each price in the table, calculate the total revenue from selling peeps and the marginal revenue per peep.

b. At what quantity will Jimmy's profit be maximized? What price will he charge? What will his total profit be?

c. Jimmy's landlady complains about all the visitors coming into the building and tells Jimmy to stop selling peeps. Jimmy discovers, however, that if he gives the landlady $0.20 for every peep he sells, she will stop complaining. What effect does the $0.20-per-peep bribe have on Jimmy's marginal cost per peep? What is the new profit-maximizing quantity of peeps? What effect does the $0.20-per-peep bribe have on Jimmy's total profit?

6. Suppose that De Beers is a single-price monopolist in the market for diamonds. De Beers has five potential customers: Raquel, Jackie, Joan, Mia, and Sophia. Each of these customers will buy at most one diamond—and only if the price is just equal to, or lower than, her willingness to pay. Raquel's willingness to pay is $400; Jackie's, $300; Joan's, $200; Mia's, $100; and Sophia's, $0. De Beers's marginal cost per diamond is $100. This leads to the demand schedule for diamonds shown in the accompanying table.

Price of diamond	Quantity of diamonds demanded
$500	0
400	1
300	2
200	3
100	4
0	5

a. Calculate De Beers's total revenue and its marginal revenue. From your calculation, draw the demand curve and the marginal revenue curve.

b. Explain why De Beers faces a downward-sloping demand curve.

c. Explain why the marginal revenue from an additional diamond sale is less than the price of the diamond.

d. Suppose De Beers currently charges $200 for its diamonds. If it lowers the price to $100, how large is the price effect? How large is the quantity effect?

e. Add the marginal cost curve to your diagram from part a and determine which quantity maximizes De Beers's profit and which price De Beers will charge.

7. Use the demand schedule for diamonds given in Problem 6. The marginal cost of producing diamonds is constant at $100. There is no fixed cost.

a. If De Beers charges the monopoly price, how large is the individual consumer surplus that each buyer experiences? Calculate total consumer surplus by summing the individual consumer surpluses. How large is producer surplus?

Suppose that upstart Russian and Asian producers enter the market and the market becomes perfectly competitive.

b. What is the perfectly competitive price? What quantity will be sold in this perfectly competitive market?

c. At the competitive price and quantity, how large is the consumer surplus that each buyer experiences? How large is total consumer surplus? How large is producer surplus?

d. Compare your answer to part c to your answer to part a. How large is the deadweight loss associated with monopoly in this case?

8. Use the demand schedule for diamonds given in Problem 6. De Beers is a monopolist, but it can now price-discriminate perfectly among all five of its potential customers. De Beers's marginal cost is constant at $100. There is no fixed cost.

a. If De Beers can price-discriminate perfectly, to which customers will it sell diamonds and at what prices?

b. How large is each individual consumer surplus? How large is total consumer surplus? Calculate producer surplus by summing the producer surplus generated by each sale.

9. Download Records decides to release an album by the group Mary and the Little Lamb. It produces the album with no fixed cost, but the total cost of downloading an album to a CD and paying Mary her royalty is $6 per album. Download Records can act as a single-price monopolist. Its marketing division finds that the demand schedule for the album is as shown in the accompanying table.

Price of album	Quantity of albums demanded
$22	0
20	1,000
18	2,000
16	3,000
14	4,000
12	5,000
10	6,000
8	7,000

a. Calculate the total revenue and the marginal revenue per album.

b. The marginal cost of producing each album is constant at $6. To maximize profit, what level of output should Download Records choose, and which price should it charge for each album?

c. Mary renegotiates her contract and now needs to be paid a higher royalty per album. So the marginal cost rises to be constant at $14. To maximize profit, what level of output should Download Records now choose, and which price should it charge for each album?

10. The accompanying diagram illustrates your local electricity company's natural monopoly. The diagram shows the demand curve for kilowatt-hours (kWh) of electricity, the company's

marginal revenue (*MR*) curve, its marginal cost (*MC*) curve, and its average total cost (*ATC*) curve. The government wants to regulate the monopolist by imposing a price ceiling.

a. If the government does not regulate this monopolist, which price will it charge? Illustrate the inefficiency this creates by shading the deadweight loss from monopoly.

b. If the government imposes a price ceiling equal to the marginal cost, $0.30, will the monopolist make profits or lose money? Shade the area of profit (or loss) for the monopolist. If the government does impose this price ceiling, do you think the firm will continue to produce in the long run?

c. If the government imposes a price ceiling of $0.50, will the monopolist make a profit, lose money, or break even?

11. The movie theater in Collegetown serves two kinds of customers: students and professors. There are 900 students and 100 professors in Collegetown. Each student's willingness to pay for a movie ticket is $5. Each professor's willingness to pay for a movie ticket is $10. Each will buy at most one ticket. The movie theater's marginal cost per ticket is constant at $3, and there is no fixed cost.

a. Suppose the movie theater cannot price-discriminate and needs to charge both students and professors the same price per ticket. If the movie theater charges $5, who will buy tickets and what will the movie theater's profit be? How large is consumer surplus?

b. If the movie theater charges $10, who will buy movie tickets and what will the movie theater's profit be? How large is consumer surplus?

c. Now suppose that, if it chooses to, the movie theater can price-discriminate between students and professors by requiring students to show their student ID. If the movie theater charges students $5 and professors $10, how much profit will the movie theater make? How large is consumer surplus?

12. A monopolist knows that in order to expand the quantity of output it produces from 8 to 9 units that it must lower the price of its output from $2 to $1. Calculate the quantity effect and the price effect. Use these results to calculate the monopolist's marginal revenue of producing the 9th unit.

The marginal cost of producing the 9th unit is positive. Is it a good idea for the monopolist to produce the 9th unit?

13. In the United States, the Federal Trade Commission (FTC) is charged with promoting competition and challenging mergers that would likely lead to higher prices. In 1996, Staples and Office Depot, two of the largest office supply superstores, announced their agreement to merge.

   a. Some critics of the merger argued that, in many parts of the country, a merger between the two companies would create a monopoly in the office supply superstore market. Based on the FTC's argument and its mission to challenge mergers that would likely lead to higher prices, do you think it allowed the merger?

   b. Staples and Office Depot argued that, while in some parts of the country they might create a monopoly in the office supply superstore market, the FTC should consider the larger market for all office supplies, which includes many smaller stores that sell office supplies (such as grocery stores and other retailers). In that market, Staples and Office Depot would face competition from many other, smaller stores. If the market for all office supplies is the relevant market that the FTC should consider, would it make the FTC more or less likely to allow the merger?

14. Prior to the late 1990s, the same company that generated your electricity also distributed it to you over high voltage lines. Since then, 16 states and the District of Columbia have begun separating the generation from the distribution of electricity, allowing competition between electricity generators and between electricity distributors.

   a. Assume that the market for electricity distribution was and remains a natural monopoly. Use a graph to illustrate the market for electricity distribution if the government sets price equal to average total cost.

   b. Assume that deregulation of electricity generation creates a perfectly competitive market. Also assume that electricity generation does not exhibit the characteristics of a natural monopoly. Use a graph to illustrate the cost curves in the long-run equilibrium for an individual firm in this industry.

 www.worthpublishers.com/krugmanwells

>> Oligopoly

CAUGHT IN THE ACT

THE AGRICULTURAL PRODUCTS COMPANY ARCHER Daniels Midland (also known as ADM) has often described itself as "supermarket to the world." Its name is familiar to many Americans not only because of its important role in the economy but also because of its advertising and sponsorship of public television programs. But on October 25, 1993, ADM itself was on camera.

On that day executives from ADM and its Japanese competitor Ajinomoto met at the Marriott Hotel in Irvine, California, to discuss the market for lysine, an additive used in animal feed. (How is lysine produced? It's excreted by genetically engineered bacteria.) In this and subsequent meetings, the two companies joined with several other competitors to set targets for the market price of lysine, behavior called *price-fixing*. Each company agreed to limit its production in order to achieve those targets. Agreeing on specific limits would be their biggest challenge—or so they thought.

What the participants in the meeting didn't know was that they had a bigger problem: the FBI had bugged the room and was filming them with a camera hidden in a lamp.

What the companies were doing was illegal. To understand why it was illegal and why the companies were doing it anyway, we need to examine the issues posed by industries that are neither perfectly competitive nor purely monopolistic. In this chapter we focus on *oligopoly*, a type of market structure in which there are only a few producers. As we'll see, oligopoly is a very important reality—much more important, in fact, than monopoly and arguably more typical of modern economies than perfect competition.

Although much that we have learned about both perfect competition and monopoly is relevant to oligopoly, oligopoly also raises some entirely new issues. Among other things, firms in an oligopoly are often tempted to engage in the kind of behavior that got ADM, Ajinomoto, and other lysine producers into trouble with the law. Over the past few years, there have been numerous investigations and some convictions for price-fixing in a variety of industries, from insurance to air cargo to computer chips. For example, in 2007 the European Union, which has anti-price-fixing laws similar to those of the United States, fined five elevator companies $1.3 billion (yes, that's billion) for collusion across several European countries.

We will begin by examining what oligopoly is and why it is so important. Then we'll turn to the behavior of oligopolistic industries. Finally, we'll look at *antitrust policy*, which is primarily concerned with trying to keep oligopolies "well behaved."

The law catches up with a colluding oligopolist.

Bryan Smith/Zuma Press

The Prevalence of Oligopoly

At the time of that elaborately bugged meeting, no one company controlled the world lysine industry, but there were only a few major producers. An industry with only a few sellers is known as an **oligopoly**; a firm in such an industry is known as an **oligopolist.**

Oligopolists obviously compete with each other for sales. But ADM and Ajinomoto weren't like firms in a perfectly competitive industry, which take the price at which they can sell their product as given. Each of these firms knew that its decision about how much to produce would affect the market price. That is, like monopolists, each of the firms had some *market power.* So the competition in this industry wasn't "perfect."

Economists refer to a situation in which firms compete but also possess market power—which enables them to affect market prices—as **imperfect competition.** As we saw in Chapter 14, there are actually two important forms of imperfect competition: oligopoly and *monopolistic competition.* Of these, oligopoly is probably the more important in practice.

Although lysine is a multibillion-dollar business, it is not exactly a product familiar to most consumers. However, many familiar goods and services are supplied by only a few competing sellers, which means the industries in question are oligopolies. For example, most air routes are served by only two or three airlines: in recent years, regularly scheduled shuttle service between New York and either Boston or Washington, D.C., has been provided only by Delta and US Airways. Three firms—Chiquita, Dole, and Del Monte, which own huge banana plantations in Central America—control 65% of world banana exports. Most cola beverages are sold by Coca-Cola and Pepsi. This list could go on for many pages.

It's important to realize that an oligopoly isn't necessarily made up of large firms. What matters isn't size per se; the question is how many competitors there are. When a small town has only two grocery stores, grocery service there is just as much an oligopoly as air shuttle service between New York and Washington.

Why are oligopolies so prevalent? Essentially, oligopoly is the result of the same factors that sometimes produce monopoly, but in somewhat weaker form. Probably the most important source of oligopoly is the existence of *increasing returns to scale,* which give bigger producers a cost advantage over smaller ones. When these effects are very strong, they lead to monopoly; when they are not that strong, they lead to an industry with a small number of firms. For example, larger grocery stores typically have lower costs than smaller stores. But the advantages of large scale taper off once grocery stores are reasonably large, which is why two or three stores often survive in small towns.

If oligopoly is so common, why has most of this book focused on competition in industries where the number of sellers is very large? And why did we study monopoly, which is relatively uncommon, first? The answer has two parts. First, much of what we learn from the study of perfectly competitive markets—about costs, entry and exit, and efficiency—remains valid despite the fact that many industries are not perfectly competitive. Second, the analysis of oligopoly turns out to present some puzzles for which there is no easy solution. It is almost always a good idea—in exams and in life in general—first to deal with the questions you can answer, then to puzzle over

---

An **oligopoly** is an industry with only a small number of producers. A producer in such an industry is known as an **oligopolist.**

When no one firm has a monopoly, but producers nonetheless realize that they can affect market prices, an industry is characterized by **imperfect competition.**

the harder ones. We have simply followed the same strategy, developing the relatively clear-cut theories of perfect competition and monopoly first, and only then turning to the puzzles presented by oligopoly.

►ECONOMICS IN ACTION

Is it an Oligopoly or Not?

In practice, it is not always easy to determine an industry's market structure just by looking at the number of sellers. Many oligopolistic industries contain a number of small "niche" producers, which don't really compete with the major players. For example, the U.S. airline industry includes a number of regional airlines like New Mexico Airlines, which flies propeller planes between Albuquerque and Carlsbad, New Mexico; if you count these carriers, the U.S. airline industry contains nearly one hundred sellers, which doesn't sound like competition among a small group. But there are only a handful of national competitors like American and United, and on many routes, as we've seen, there are only two or three competitors.

To get a better picture of market structure, economists often use a measure called the *Herfindahl-Hirschman Index,* or HHI. The HHI for an industry is the square of each firm's share of market sales summed over the firms in the industry. For example, if an industry contains only 3 firms and their market shares are 60%, 25%, and 15%, then the HHI for the industry is:

$$HHI = 60^2 + 25^2 + 15^2 = 4,450$$

By squaring each market share, the HHI calculation produces numbers that are much larger when a larger share of an industry output is dominated by fewer firms. This is confirmed by the data in Table 15-1. Here, the indices for industries dominated by a small number of firms, like the personal computer operating systems industry or the wide-body aircraft industry are many times larger than the index for the retail grocery industry, which has numerous firms of approximately equal size.

The HHI is used by the U.S. Justice Department and the Federal Trade Commission, which have the job of enforcing *antitrust policy,* a topic we'll investigate in more detail later in this chapter. Their mission is to try to ensure that there is adequate competition in an industry by prosecuting price-fixing, breaking up economically inefficient monopolies, and disallowing mergers between firms when it's believed that the merger will reduce competition. According to Justice Department guidelines, an HHI below 1,000 indicates a strongly competitive market, between 1,000 and 1,800 indicates a somewhat competitive market, and over 1,800 indicates

TABLE 15-1

The HHI for Some Oligopolistic Industries

Industry	HHI	Largest firms
PC operating systems	9,182	Microsoft, Linux
Wide-body aircraft	5,098	Boeing, Airbus
Diamond mining	2,338	De Beers, Alrosa, Rio Tinto
Automobiles	1,432	GM, Ford, Chrysler, Toyota, Honda, Nissan, VW
Movie distributors	1,096	Buena Vista, Sony Pictures, 20th Century Fox, Warner Bros., Universal, Paramount, Lionsgate
Internet service providers	750	SBC, Comcast, AOL, Verizon, Road Runner, Earthlink, Charter, Qwest
Retail grocers	321	Wal-Mart, Kroger, Sears, Target, Costco, Walgreens, Ahold, Albertsons

Sources: Canadian Government; Diamond Facts 2006; www.w3counter.com; Planet retail; Autodata; Reuters; ISP Planet; Swivel. Data cover 2006–2007.

an oligopoly. In an industry with an HHI over 1,000, a merger that results in a significant increase in the HHI will receive special scrutiny and is likely to be disallowed.

However, as recent events have shown, defining an industry can be tricky. In 2007, Whole Foods and Wild Oats, two purveyors of high-end organic foods, proposed a merger. The Justice Department disallowed it, claiming it would substantially reduce competition and defining the industry as consisting of only natural food groceries. However, this was appealed to a federal court, which found the merger allowable since regular supermarkets now carried organic foods as well, arguing that they would provide sufficient competition after the merger. The Justice Department has appealed and, as of the time of writing, the case is still undecided. ▲

< < < < < < < < < < < < <

> CHECK YOUR UNDERSTANDING 15-1

1. Explain why each of the following industries is an oligopoly, not a perfectly competitive industry.
   a. The world oil industry, where a few countries near the Persian Gulf control much of the world's oil reserves
   b. The microprocessor industry, where two firms, Intel and its bitter rival AMD, dominate the technology
   c. The wide-bodied passenger jet industry, composed of the American firm Boeing and the European firm Airbus, where production is characterized by extremely large fixed cost

2. The accompanying table shows the market shares for Internet search engines in 2006.
   a. Calculate the HHI in this industry.
   b. If Yahoo! and MSN were to merge, what would the HHI be?

Search engine	Market share
Google	44%
Yahoo!	29
MSN	13
AOL	6
Ask	5
Other	3

Solutions appear at back of book.

Understanding Oligopoly

How much will a firm produce? Up to this point, we have always answered: the quantity that maximizes its profit. Together with its cost curves, the assumption that a firm maximizes profit is enough to determine its output when it is a perfect competitor or when it's a monopolist.

When it comes to oligopoly, however, we run into some difficulties. Indeed, economists often describe the behavior of oligopolistic firms as a "puzzle."

A Duopoly Example

Let's begin looking at the puzzle of oligopoly with the simplest version, an industry in which there are only two producing firms—a **duopoly**—and each is known as a **duopolist.**

Going back to our opening story, imagine that ADM and Ajinomoto are the only two producers of lysine. To make things even simpler, suppose that once a company has incurred the fixed cost needed to produce lysine, the marginal cost of producing another pound is zero. So the companies are concerned only with the revenue they receive from sales.

Table 15-2 shows a hypothetical demand schedule for lysine and the total revenue of the industry at each price–quantity combination.

If this were a perfectly competitive industry, each firm would have an incentive to produce more as long as the market price was above marginal cost. Since the marginal cost is assumed to be zero, this would mean that at equilibrium lysine would be provided free. Firms would produce until price equals zero, yielding a total output of 120 million pounds and zero revenue for both firms.

An oligopoly consisting of only two firms is a **duopoly**. Each firm is known as a **duopolist.**

TABLE **15-2**

Demand Schedule for Lysine

Price of lysine (per pound)	Quantity of lysine demanded (millions of pounds)	Total revenue (millions)
$12	0	$0
11	10	110
10	20	200
9	30	270
8	40	320
7	50	350
6	60	360
5	70	350
4	80	320
3	90	270
2	100	200
1	110	110
0	120	0

Sellers engage in **collusion** when they cooperate to raise their joint profits. A **cartel** is an agreement among several producers to obey output restrictions in order to increase their joint profits.

However, surely the firms would not be that stupid. With only two firms in the industry, each would realize that by producing more, it would drive down the market price. So each firm would, like a monopolist, realize that profits would be higher if it and its rival limited their production.

So how much will the two firms produce?

One possibility is that the two companies will engage in **collusion**—they will cooperate to raise their joint profits. The strongest form of collusion is a **cartel,** an arrangement between producers that determines how much each is allowed to produce. The world's most famous cartel is the Organization of Petroleum Exporting Countries, described in Economics in Action later in the chapter. As its name indicates, it's actually an agreement among governments rather than firms. There's a reason this most famous of cartels is an agreement among governments: cartels among firms are illegal in the United States and many other jurisdictions. But let's ignore the law for a moment (which is, of course, what ADM and Ajinomoto did in real life—to their own detriment).

So suppose that ADM and Ajinomoto were to form a cartel and that this cartel decided to act as if it were a monopolist, maximizing total industry profits. It's obvious from Table 15-2 that in order to maximize the combined profits of the firms, this cartel should set total industry output at 60 million pounds of lysine, which would sell at a price of $6 per pound, leading to revenue of $360 million, the maximum possible. Then the only question would be how much of that 60 million pounds each firm gets to produce. A "fair" solution might be for each firm to produce 30 million pounds with revenues for each firm of $180 million.

But even if the two firms agreed on such a deal, they might have a problem: each of the firms would have an incentive to break its word and produce more than the agreed-upon quantity.

Collusion and Competition

Suppose that the presidents of ADM and Ajinomoto were to agree that each would produce 30 million pounds of lysine over the next year. Both would understand that this plan maximizes their combined profits. And both would have an incentive to cheat.

When firms ignore the effects of their actions on each others' profits, they engage in **noncooperative behavior.**

To see why, consider what would happen if Ajinomoto honored its agreement, producing only 30 million pounds, but ADM ignored its promise and produced 40 million pounds. This increase in total output would drive the price down from $6 to $5 per pound, the price at which 70 million pounds are demanded. The industry's total revenue would fall from $360 million ($6 × 60 million pounds) to $350 million ($5 × 70 million pounds). However, ADM's revenue would *rise,* from $180 million to $200 million. Since we are assuming a marginal cost of zero, this would mean a $20 million increase in ADM's profits.

But Ajinomoto's president might make exactly the same calculation. And if *both* firms were to produce 40 million pounds of lysine, the price would drop to $4 per pound. So each firm's profits would fall, from $180 million to $160 million.

Why do individual firms have an incentive to produce more than the quantity that maximizes their joint profits? Because neither firm has as strong an incentive to limit its output as a true monopolist would.

Let's go back for a minute to the theory of monopoly. We know that a profit-maximizing monopolist sets marginal cost (which in this case is zero) equal to marginal revenue. But what is marginal revenue? Recall that producing an additional unit of a good has two effects:

1. A positive *quantity* effect: one more unit is sold, increasing total revenue by the price at which that unit is sold.

2. A negative *price* effect: in order to sell one more unit, the monopolist must cut the market price on *all* units sold.

The negative price effect is the reason marginal revenue for a monopolist is less than the market price. But when considering the effect of increasing production, a firm is concerned only with the price effect on its *own* units of output, not those of its fellow oligopolists. Both ADM and Ajinomoto suffer a negative price effect if ADM decides to produce extra lysine and so drives down the price. But ADM cares only about the negative price effect on the units it produces, not about the loss to Ajinomoto.

This tells us that an individual firm in an oligopolistic industry faces a smaller price effect from an additional unit of output than a monopolist; therefore, the marginal revenue that such a firm calculates is higher. So it will seem to be profitable for any one company in an oligopoly to increase production, even if that increase reduces the profits of the industry as a whole. But if everyone thinks that way, the result is that everyone earns a lower profit!

Until now, we have been able to analyze producer behavior by asking what a producer should do to maximize profits. But even if ADM and Ajinomoto are both trying to maximize profits, what does this predict about their behavior? Will they engage in collusion, reaching and holding to an agreement that maximizes their combined profits? Or will they engage in **noncooperative behavior,** with each firm acting in its own self-interest, even though this has the effect of driving down everyone's profits? Both strategies sound like profit maximization. Which will actually describe their behavior?

Now you see why oligopoly presents a puzzle: there are only a small number of players, making collusion a real possibility. If there were dozens or hundreds of firms, it would be safe to assume they would behave noncooperatively. Yet, when there are only a handful of firms in an industry, it's hard to determine whether collusion will actually materialize.

Since collusion is ultimately more profitable than noncooperative behavior, firms have an incentive to collude if they can. One way to do so is to formalize it—sign an agreement (maybe even make a legal contract) or establish some financial incentives for the companies to set their prices high. But in the United States and many other nations, you can't do that—at least not legally. Companies cannot make a legal contract to keep prices high: not only is the contract unenforceable, but writing it is a

GLOBAL COMPARISON · EUROPE LEVELS THE PLAYING FIELD FOR COKE AND PEPSI

Instead of colluding with a rival, your typical oligopolist would most prefer to have no rival at all; the oligopolist wants to behave like a monopolist. But merging with a rival to create a monopoly isn't an option because government regulators in most countries would intervene to stop such an attempt. So many oligopolistic firms have adopted a tactic called *exclusive dealing,* in which a firm makes an agreement with retailers to sell its products exclusively. By preventing rivals' products from appearing on store shelves, these deals lead to greater market power and higher profits for an oligopolist.

Exclusive dealing is largely prohibited in the United States, but European regulators have been slow to act against it. You can see the effect of this policy difference by comparing the national market shares of Coke and Pepsi in the United States and Europe. In the United States, Coke and Pepsi have maintained relatively similar market shares: 44% versus 32% in 2004. In that same year, thanks to the exclusivity deals that Coke regularly signed with shops, bars, and restaurants across Europe, Coke's market shares in Europe were several times Pepsi's, as you can see in the graph—that is, until European regulators finally made their move, also in 2004. Not surprisingly, Pepsi applauded the change in European policy toward exclusive dealing.

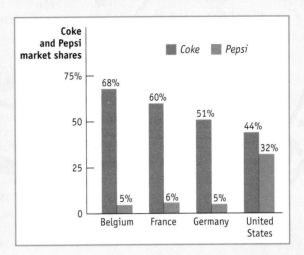

Source: Beverage Digest (reported in *The New York Times,* October 20, 2004).

one-way ticket to jail. Neither can they sign an informal "gentlemen's agreement," which lacks the force of law but perhaps rests on threats of retaliation—that's illegal, too. In fact, executives from rival companies rarely meet without lawyers present, who make sure that the conversation does not stray into inappropriate territory. Even hinting at how nice it would be if prices were higher can bring you an unwelcome interview with the Justice Department or the Federal Trade Commission. For example, in 2003 the Justice Department launched a price-fixing case against Monsanto and other large producers of genetically modified seed. The Justice Department was alerted by a series of meetings held between Monsanto and Pioneer Hi-Bred International, two companies that account for 60% of the U.S. market in maize and soybean seed. The two companies, parties to a licensing agreement involving genetically modified seed, claimed that no illegal discussions of price-fixing occurred in those meetings. But the fact that the two firms discussed prices as part of the licensing agreement was enough to ensure action by the Justice Department.

Sometimes, as we've seen, oligopolistic firms just ignore the rules. But more often they find ways to achieve collusion without a formal agreement. As we'll see in the next section, one important factor in determining how hard it is to achieve collusion without a formal agreement is how easy it is for a firm to increase its output quickly in order to capture sales from its rival.

Competing in Prices versus Competing in Quantities

In our duopoly example, we've assumed that firms choose a quantity of output and sell that output at whatever the market price turns out to be. That's actually a pretty good description of the way the lysine market works. But in other industries, such as automobiles, firms don't choose a level of output; they choose a *price* and sell as much as they can at that price. Does this make any difference?

Yes, it does, at least when we analyze noncooperative behavior. In choosing what to do, an oligopolist must always be concerned about whether a noncooperative rival firm will respond by *undercutting*. In other words, the oligopolist must be concerned that a rival will take some action that allows the rival to steal some sales and capture a larger share of the market. And, it turns out, the answer to whether a rival is willing to engage in undercutting behavior depends on how difficult it is for the rival to increase output to satisfy the additional customers gained by undercutting.

Let's consider a hypothetical example using Airbus and Boeing, duopolists in the large passenger aircraft industry, to gain some intuition. For these firms, deciding their production capacity—how much output they can produce over, say, the next two or three years—is their most important decision. Why? Passenger aircraft are very large and are built in batches, a few planes at a time, in huge hangars. The determining factor in how many planes can be built at any given time is the size of the company's existing production facilities, which can take years to build.

So this means that when Airbus, for example, sets its maximum production capacity at 50 planes per year, Boeing can feel comfortably assured that Airbus won't easily be able to increase this number anytime soon. This, in turn, has important implications for Boeing's actions. If Boeing also sets its production capacity at 50 planes per year, it can safely assume that Airbus's production capacity is *given* and that, as a result, the market will be split 50-50 between the two manufacturers. Airbus won't be able to quickly increase its output and steal some of Boeing's customers by offering them a lower price. The end result is that the total output of the industry is less than the output under perfect competition, and each firm earns a profit. Economists refer to this kind of behavior as *quantity competition* or *Cournot behavior,* after the nineteenth-century French economist who devised the model. The basic insight of the Cournot model is that when firms are restricted in how much they can produce, it is easier for them to avoid excessive competition and to "divvy up" the market, thereby pricing above marginal cost and earning profits. As a result, it is easier for them to achieve an outcome that looks like collusion without a formal agreement.

But how does the behavior of oligopolists change when they are not constrained by limited production capacity? Let's assume that American Airlines and British Airways are duopolists and that they have exclusive rights to fly the Chicago–London route. When the economy is strong and lots of people want to fly between Chicago and London, American Airlines and British Airways are likely to find the number of passengers they can carry constrained by their production capacity—for example, the number of landing slots available. So in this environment they are likely to behave according to the Cournot model and price above marginal cost—say, charging $800 per round trip. But when the business climate is poor, the two airlines are likely to find that they have lots of empty seats at a fare of $800 and that capacity constraints are no longer an issue. What will they do?

Recent history tells us they will engage in a price war by slashing ticket prices. They are no longer able to maintain Cournot behavior because at the ticket price of $800, each has excess capacity. If American Airlines were to try to maintain a price of $800, it would soon find itself undercut by British Airways, which would charge $750 and steal all its customers. In turn, American Airlines would undercut British Airways by charging $700—and so on. As long as each firm finds that it can make additional sales by cutting price, each will continue cutting until price is equal to marginal cost. (Going any lower would cause them to incur an avoidable loss.) This type of behavior is known as *price competition* or *Bertrand behavior,* after another nineteenth-century French economist. The logic behind the Bertrand model is that when firms produce perfect substitutes and have sufficient capacity to satisfy demand when price is equal to marginal cost, then each firm will be compelled to engage in competition by undercutting its rival's price until the price reaches marginal cost—that is, perfect competition.

Oligopolists would, understandably, prefer to avoid Bertrand behavior because it earns them zero profits. Lacking an environment that imposes constraints on their output capacity, firms try other means to avoid direct price competition—such as producing products that are not perfect substitutes but are instead differentiated. We'll examine this strategy in more detail later in this chapter, just noting here that producing differentiated products allows oligopolists to cultivate a loyal set of customers and to charge prices higher than marginal cost.

Even in the absence of limitations on production capacity, firms are often able to maintain collusive behavior (although it may be somewhat harder to do). In the next section, we'll see why such informal collusion often works but sometimes fails.

►ECONOMICS IN ACTION

The Great Vitamin Conspiracy

It was a bitter pill to swallow. In the late 1990s, some of the world's largest drug companies (mainly European and Japanese) agreed to pay billions of dollars in damages to customers after being convicted of a huge conspiracy to rig the world vitamin market.

The conspiracy began in 1989 when the Swiss company Roche and the German company BASF began secret talks about raising prices for vitamins. Soon a French company, Rhone-Poulenc, joined in, followed by several Japanese companies and other companies around the world. The members of the group, which referred to itself as "Vitamins Inc.," met regularly—sometimes at hotels, sometimes at the private homes of executives—to set prices and divide up markets for "bulk" vitamins (like vitamin A, vitamin C, and so on). These bulk vitamins are sold mainly to other companies, such as animal feed makers, food producers, and so on, which include them in their products. Indeed, it was the animal feed companies that grew suspicious about the prices they were being charged, which led to a series of investigations. The case eventually broke open when Rhone-Poulenc made a deal with U.S. officials to provide evidence about the conspiracy. The French company was concerned that rumors about price-fixing would lead U.S. officials to block its planned merger with another company.

This was a huge conspiracy—it makes the lysine case look like, well, chicken feed. How could it have happened?

The main answer probably lies in different national traditions about how to treat oligopolists. The United States has a long tradition of taking tough legal action against price-fixing, as we have just described. European governments, however, have historically been much less stringent. Indeed, in the past some European governments have actually encouraged major companies to form cartels. But European antitrust law has changed recently to become more like U.S. antitrust law. Despite this change, however, the cultural tradition of forming cartels as normal business practice persists within the boardrooms of European companies. ▲

> > > > > > > > > > > >

1. Which of the following factors increase the likelihood that an oligopolist will collude with other firms in the industry? The likelihood that an oligopolist will act noncooperatively and raise output? Explain your answers.
   a. The firm's initial market share is small. (Hint: Think about the price effect.)
   b. The firm has a cost advantage over its rivals.
   c. The firm's customers face additional costs when they switch from the use of one firm's product to another firm's product.
   d. The firm and its rivals are currently operating at maximum production capacity, which cannot be altered in the short run.

Solutions appear at back of book.

When a firm's decision significantly affects the profits of other firms in the industry, the firms are in a situation of **interdependence**.

The study of behavior in situations of interdependence is known as **game theory**.

The reward received by a player in a game, such as the profit earned by an oligopolist, is that player's **payoff**.

A **payoff matrix** shows how the payoff to each of the participants in a two-player game depends on the actions of both. Such a matrix helps us analyze situations of interdependence.

Games Oligopolists Play

In our duopoly example and in real life, each oligopolistic firm realizes both that its profit depends on what its competitor does and that its competitor's profit depends on what it does. That is, the two firms are in a situation of **interdependence,** where each firm's decision significantly affects the profit of the other firm (or firms, in the case of more than two).

In effect, the two firms are playing a "game" in which the profit of each player depends not only on its own actions but on those of the other player (or players). In order to understand more fully how oligopolists behave, economists, along with mathematicians, developed the area of study of such games, known as **game theory.** It has many applications, not just to economics but also to military strategy, politics, and other social sciences.

Let's see how game theory helps us understand oligopoly.

The Prisoners' Dilemma

Game theory deals with any situation in which the reward to any one player—the **payoff**—depends not only on his or her own actions but also on those of other players in the game. In the case of oligopolistic firms, the payoff is simply the firm's profit.

When there are only two players, as in a duopoly, the interdependence between the players can be represented with a **payoff matrix** like that shown in Figure 15-1. Each row corresponds to an action by one player (in this case, ADM); each column corresponds to an action by the other (in this case, Ajinomoto). For simplicity, let's assume that ADM can pick only one of two alternatives: produce 30 million pounds of lysine or produce 40 million pounds. Ajinomoto has the same pair of choices.

The matrix contains four boxes, each divided by a diagonal line. Each box shows the payoff to the two firms that results from a pair of choices; the number below the diagonal shows ADM's profits, the number above the diagonal shows Ajinomoto's profits.

These payoffs show what we concluded from our earlier analysis: the combined profit of the two firms is maximized if they each produce 30 million pounds. Either

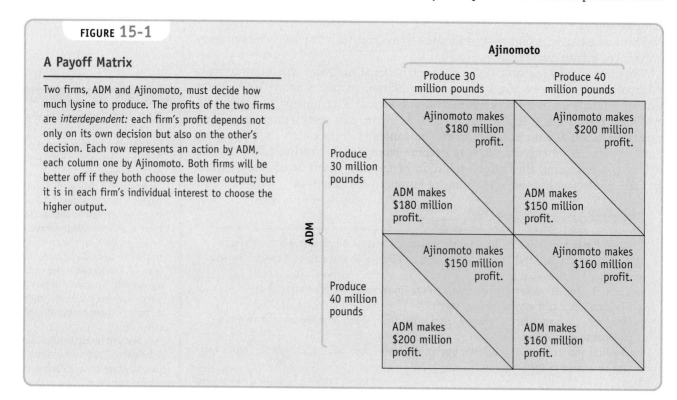

FIGURE 15-1

A Payoff Matrix

Two firms, ADM and Ajinomoto, must decide how much lysine to produce. The profits of the two firms are *interdependent:* each firm's profit depends not only on its own decision but also on the other's decision. Each row represents an action by ADM, each column one by Ajinomoto. Both firms will be better off if they both choose the lower output; but it is in each firm's individual interest to choose the higher output.

firm can, however, increase its own profits by producing 40 million pounds while the other produces only 30 million pounds. But if both produce the larger quantity, both will have lower profits than if they had both held their output down.

The particular situation shown here is a version of a famous—and seemingly paradoxical—case of interdependence that appears in many contexts. Known as the **prisoners' dilemma,** it is a type of game in which the payoff matrix implies the following:

- Each player has an incentive, regardless of what the other player does, to cheat—to take an action that benefits it at the other's expense.

- When both players cheat, both are worse off than they would have been if neither had cheated.

The original illustration of the prisoners' dilemma occurred in a fictional story about two accomplices in crime—let's call them Thelma and Louise—who have been caught by the police. The police have enough evidence to put them behind bars for 5 years. They also know that the pair have committed a more serious crime, one that carries a 20-year sentence; unfortunately, they don't have enough evidence to convict the women on that charge. To do so, they would need each of the prisoners to implicate the other in the second crime.

So the police put the miscreants in separate cells and say the following to each: "Here's the deal: if neither of you confesses, you know that we'll send you to jail for 5 years. If you confess and implicate your partner, and she doesn't do the same, we'll reduce your sentence from 5 years to 2. But if your partner confesses and you don't, you'll get the maximum 20 years. And if both of you confess, we'll give you both 15 years."

Figure 15-2 shows the payoffs that face the prisoners, depending on the decision of each to remain silent or to confess. (Usually the payoff matrix reflects the players' payoffs, and higher payoffs are better than lower payoffs. This case is an exception: a higher number of years in prison is bad, not good!) Let's assume that the prisoners have no way to communicate and that they have not sworn an oath not to harm each other or anything of that sort. So each acts in her own self-interest. What will they do?

> **Prisoners' dilemma** is a game based on two premises: (1) Each player has an incentive to choose an action that benefits itself at the other player's expense; and (2) When both players act in this way, both are worse off than if they had acted cooperatively.

FIGURE 15-2

The Prisoners' Dilemma

Each of two prisoners, held in separate cells, is offered a deal by the police—a light sentence if she confesses and implicates her accomplice but her accomplice does not do the same, a heavy sentence if she does not confess but her accomplice does, and so on. It is in the joint interest of both prisoners not to confess; it is in each one's individual interest to confess.

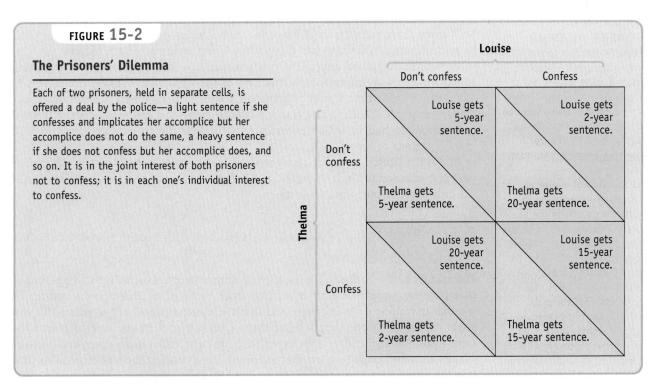

An action is a **dominant strategy** when it is a player's best action regardless of the action taken by the other player.

A **Nash equilibrium**, also known as a **noncooperative equilibrium**, is the result when each player in a game chooses the action that maximizes his or her payoff given the actions of other players, ignoring the effects of his or her action on the payoffs received by those other players.

A firm engages in **strategic behavior** when it attempts to influence the future behavior of other firms.

The answer is clear: both will confess. Look at it first from Thelma's point of view: she is better off confessing, regardless of what Louise does. If Louise doesn't confess, Thelma's confession reduces her own sentence from 5 years to 2. If Louise *does* confess, Thelma's confession reduces her sentence from 20 to 15 years. Either way, it's clearly in Thelma's interest to confess. And because she faces the same incentives, it's clearly in Louise's interest to confess, too. To confess in this situation is a type of action that economists call a *dominant strategy*. An action is a **dominant strategy** when it is the player's best action regardless of the action taken by the other player. It's important to note that not all games have a dominant strategy—it depends on the structure of payoffs in the game. But in the case of Thelma and Louise, it is clearly in the interest of the police to structure the payoffs so that confessing is a dominant strategy for each person. So as long as the two prisoners have no way to make an enforceable agreement that neither will confess (something they can't do if they can't communicate, and the police certainly won't allow them to do so because the police want to compel each one to confess), Thelma and Louise will each act in a way that hurts the other.

So if each prisoner acts rationally in her own interest, both will confess. Yet if neither of them had confessed, both would have received a much lighter sentence! In a prisoners' dilemma, each player has a clear incentive to act in a way that hurts the other player—but when both make that choice, it leaves both of them worse off.

When Thelma and Louise both confess, they reach an *equilibrium* of the game. We have used the concept of equilibrium many times in this book; it is an outcome in which no individual or firm has any incentive to change his or her action. In game theory, this kind of equilibrium, in which each player takes the action that is best for her given the actions taken by other players, and vice versa, is known as a **Nash equilibrium,** after the mathematician and Nobel Laureate John Nash. (Nash's life was chronicled in the best-selling biography *A Beautiful Mind,* which was made into a movie.) Because the players in a Nash equilibrium do not take into account the effect of their actions on others, this is also known as a **noncooperative equilibrium.**

Now look back at Figure 15-1: ADM and Ajinomoto are in the same situation as Thelma and Louise. Each firm is better off producing the higher output, regardless of what the other firm does. Yet if both produce 40 million pounds, both are worse off than if they had followed their agreement and produced only 30 million pounds. In both cases, then, the pursuit of individual self-interest—the effort to maximize profits or to minimize jail time—has the perverse effect of hurting both players.

Prisoners' dilemmas appear in many situations. The upcoming For Inquiring Minds describes an example from the days of the Cold War. Clearly, the players in any prisoners' dilemma would be better off if they had some way of enforcing cooperative behavior—if Thelma and Louise had both sworn to a code of silence, or if ADM and Ajinomoto had signed an enforceable agreement not to produce more than 30 million pounds of lysine.

But in the United States an agreement setting the output levels of two oligopolists isn't just unenforceable, it's illegal. So it seems that a noncooperative equilibrium is the only possible outcome. Or is it?

Overcoming the Prisoners' Dilemma: Repeated Interaction and Tacit Collusion

Thelma and Louise in their cells are playing what is known as a *one-shot* game—that is, they play the game with each other only once. They get to choose once and for all whether to confess or hang tough, and that's it. However, most of the games that oligopolists play aren't one-shot; instead, they expect to play the game repeatedly with the same rivals. An oligopolist usually expects to be in business for many years, and it knows that its decision today about whether to cheat is likely to affect the way other firms treat it in the future. So a smart oligopolist doesn't just decide what to do based on the effect on profit in the short run. Instead, it engages in **strategic behavior,** taking account of the effects of the action it chooses today on the future actions of other players in the game. And under some conditions oligopolists that behave strategically can manage to behave as if they had a formal agreement to collude.

Suppose that ADM and Ajinomoto expect to be in the lysine business for many years and therefore expect to play the game of cheat versus collude shown in Figure 15-1 many times. Would they really betray each other time and again?

Probably not. Suppose that ADM considers two strategies. In one strategy it always cheats, producing 40 million pounds of lysine each year, regardless of what Ajinomoto does. In the other strategy, it starts with good behavior, producing only 30 million pounds in the first year, and watches to see what its rival does. If Ajinomoto also keeps its production down, ADM will stay cooperative, producing 30 million pounds again for the next year. But if Ajinomoto produces 40 million pounds, ADM will take the gloves off and also produce 40 million pounds next year. This latter strategy—start by behaving cooperatively, but thereafter do whatever the other player did in the previous period—is generally known as **tit for tat.**

"Tit for tat" is a form of strategic behavior, which we have just defined as behavior intended to influence the future actions of other players. "Tit for tat" offers a reward to the other player for cooperative behavior—if you behave cooperatively, so will I. It also provides a punishment for cheating—if you cheat, don't expect me to be nice in the future.

The payoff to ADM of each of these strategies would depend on which strategy Ajinomoto chooses. Consider the four possibilities, shown in Figure 15-3:

1. If ADM plays "tit for tat" and so does Ajinomoto, both firms will make a profit of $180 million each year.

2. If ADM plays "always cheat" but Ajinomoto plays "tit for tat," ADM makes a profit of $200 million the first year but only $160 million per year thereafter.

3. If ADM plays "tit for tat" but Ajinomoto plays "always cheat," ADM makes a profit of only $150 million in the first year but $160 million per year thereafter.

4. If ADM plays "always cheat" and Ajinomoto does the same, both firms will make a profit of $160 million each year.

A strategy of **tit for tat** involves playing cooperatively at first, then doing whatever the other player did in the previous period.

FIGURE 15-3

How Repeated Interaction Can Support Collusion

A strategy of "tit for tat" involves playing cooperatively at first, then following the other player's move. This rewards good behavior and punishes bad behavior. If the other player cheats, playing "tit for tat" will lead to only a short-term loss in comparison to playing "always cheat." But if the other player plays "tit for tat," also playing "tit for tat" leads to a long-term gain. So a firm that expects other firms to play "tit for tat" may well choose to do the same, leading to successful tacit collusion.

Ajinomoto

	Tit for tat	Always cheat
Tit for tat	Ajinomoto makes $180 million profit each year. / ADM makes $180 million profit each year.	Ajinomoto makes $200 million profit 1st year, $160 million profit each later year. / ADM makes $150 million profit 1st year, $160 million profit each later year.
Always cheat	Ajinomoto makes $150 million profit 1st year, $160 million profit each later year. / ADM makes $200 million profit 1st year, $160 million profit each later year.	Ajinomoto makes $160 million profit each year. / ADM makes $160 million profit each year.

Prisoners of the Arms Race

Between World War II and the late 1980s, the United States and the Soviet Union were locked in a seemingly endless struggle that never broke out into open war. During this Cold War, both countries spent huge sums on arms, sums that were a significant drain on the U.S. economy and eventually proved a crippling burden for the Soviet Union, whose underlying economic base was much weaker. Yet neither country was ever able to achieve a decisive military advantage.

As many people pointed out, both nations would have been better off if they had both spent less on arms. Yet the arms race continued for 40 years.

Why? As political scientists were quick to notice, one way to explain the arms race was to suppose that the two countries were locked in a classic prisoners' dilemma. Each government would have liked to achieve decisive military superiority, and each feared military inferiority. But both would have preferred a stalemate with low military spending to one with

Caught in the prisoners' dilemma: heavy military spending hastened the collapse of the Soviet Union.

high spending. However, each government rationally chose to engage in high spending. If its rival did not spend heavily, this

would lead to military superiority; not spending heavily would lead to inferiority if the other government continued its arms buildup. So the countries were trapped.

The answer to this trap could have been an agreement not to spend as much; indeed, the two sides tried repeatedly to negotiate limits on some kinds of weapons. But these agreements weren't very effective. In the end the issue was resolved as heavy military spending hastened the collapse of the Soviet Union in 1991.

Unfortunately, the logic of an arms race has not disappeared. A nuclear arms race has developed between Pakistan and India, neighboring countries with a history of mutual antagonism. In 1998 the two countries confirmed the unrelenting logic of the prisoners' dilemma: both publicly tested their nuclear weapons in a tit-for-tat sequence, each seeking to prove to the other that it could inflict just as much damage as its rival.

Which strategy is better? In the first year, ADM does better playing "always cheat," whatever its rival's strategy: it assures itself that it will get either $200 million or $160 million (which of the two payoffs it actually receives depends on whether Ajinomoto plays "tit for tat" or "always cheat"). This is better than what it would get in the first year if it played "tit for tat": either $180 million or $150 million. But by the second year, a strategy of "always cheat" gains ADM only $160 million per year for the second and all subsequent years, regardless of Ajinomoto's actions. Over time, the total amount gained by ADM by playing "always cheat" is less than the amount it would gain by playing "tit for tat": for the second and all subsequent years, it would never get any less than $160 million and would get as much as $180 million if Ajinomoto played "tit for tat" as well. Which strategy, "always cheat" or "tit for tat," is more profitable depends on two things: how many years ADM expects to play the game and what strategy its rival follows.

If ADM expects the lysine business to end in the near future, it is in effect playing a one-shot game. So it might as well cheat and grab what it can. Even if ADM expects to remain in the lysine business for many years (therefore to find itself repeatedly playing this game with Ajinomoto) and, for some reason, expects Ajinomoto always to cheat, it should also always cheat. That is, ADM should follow the old rule "Do unto others before they do unto you."

But if ADM expects to be in the business for a long time and thinks Ajinomoto is likely to play "tit for tat," it will make more profits over the long run by playing "tit for tat," too. It could have made some extra short-term profits by cheating at the beginning, but this would provoke Ajinomoto into cheating, too, and would, in the end, mean lower profits.

The lesson of this story is that when oligopolists expect to compete with each other over an extended period of time, each individual firm will often conclude that it is in its own best interest to be helpful to the other firms in the industry. So it will restrict its output in a way that raises the profits of the other firms, expecting them to return the favor. Despite the fact that firms have no way of making an enforceable agreement to limit output and raise prices (and are in legal jeopardy if they even discuss prices), they manage to act "as if" they had such an agreement. When this happens, we say that firms engage in **tacit collusion.**

> When firms limit production and raise prices in a way that raises each others' profits, even though they have not made any formal agreement, they are engaged in **tacit collusion.**

The Kinked Demand Curve

Once an oligopolistic industry has achieved tacit collusion, individual producers have an incentive to behave carefully—they don't want to do anything to disrupt the collusion. They must behave carefully because under tacit collusion there is no safe communication channel between producers. When a producer changes her output, there is a danger that tacit collusion will collapse. If she increases her output, her rivals may interpret this as cheating, leading them to retaliate and cut prices. But if she reduces her output, she has no assurance that rivals will follow her actions by cutting output and raising their prices. In fact, they may respond by leaving their prices unchanged and stealing some of her sales. As a consequence, the output of an oligopolist may not respond to changes in marginal cost.

Figure 15-4 illustrates this behavior. At the original tacit collusion outcome, the oligopolist produces the quantity Q^* and receives the price P^*, located on her demand curve, D. This demand curve shows how the price she receives for her good varies as she changes her output. As you can see, this demand curve has a special shape—it is *kinked* at the price and quantity combination associated with the tacit collusion outcome, P^* and Q^*.

FIGURE 15-4

The Kinked Demand Curve

This oligopolist believes that her demand curve is kinked at the tacit collusion price and quantity levels, P^* and Q^*. That is, she believes that if she increases her output and lowers her price, her rivals will retaliate, increasing their output and lowering their prices as well, leading to only a small gain in sales. So her demand curve is very steep to the right of Q^*. But the oligopolist believes that if she lowers her output and raises her price, her rivals will refuse to reciprocate and will steal a substantial number of her customers, leading to a large fall in sales. So her demand curve is very flat to the left of Q^*. The kink in the demand curve leads to the break XY in the marginal revenue curve. As shown by the marginal cost curves, MC_1 and MC_2, any marginal cost curve that lies within the break leads the oligopolist to produce the same output level, Q^*. So starting at the tacit collusion outcome, changes in marginal cost within a certain range will leave the firm's output unchanged. But large changes in marginal cost—changes that cause the marginal cost curve to cut the marginal revenue curve in the segment WX or the segment YZ—will lead to changes in output.

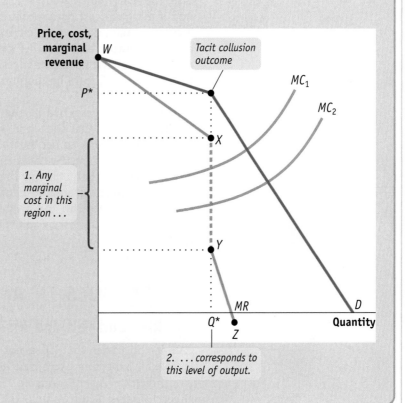

An oligopolist who believes she will lose a substantial number of sales if she reduces output and increases her price but will gain only a few additional sales if she increases output and lowers her price, away from the tacit collusion outcome, faces a **kinked demand curve**—very flat above the kink and very steep below the kink.

On one side, the demand curve slopes steeply downward at output levels greater than $Q*$. The reason is that the oligopolist believes that if she produces more than $Q*$, she will gain very few sales because her rivals will retaliate by also producing more and cutting their prices. On the other side, the demand curve is very flat. If the oligopolist reduces her output below $Q*$, she does not expect rivals to reduce their output as well. Consequently, she will lose a relatively large number of sales if she lowers her output and raises her price as her rivals capture a substantial share of her customers. A demand curve that is very steep on one side and nearly flat on the other is called a **kinked demand curve.** You might ask why the industry can't reestablish tacit collusion at a higher price and lower output after our oligopolist cuts her output and raises her price. It is possible, but by no means assured, that the industry can reestablish tacit collusion. So it is reasonable for an oligopolist to fear that tacit collusion will not be reestablished and to behave as if her demand curve is kinked as in Figure 15-4.

Now that we have explained the source of the oligopolist's kinked demand curve, let's examine how this affects her response to a change in marginal cost. The kink in the demand curve D generates a break in the oligopolist's marginal revenue curve, MR, shown by the gap between the points X and Y. Two marginal cost curves pass through that break in the marginal revenue curve: MC_1 corresponds to a situation of higher marginal cost, and MC_2 corresponds to a situation of lower marginal cost.

Recall that according to the optimal output rule, a firm will maximize profits by producing the output level at which marginal revenue is equal to marginal cost. But given the break between X and Y in the oligopolist's marginal revenue curve, any marginal cost curves that lie within that break—like MC_1 and MC_2—will generate the same output level, $Q*$. To put it in a slightly different way, starting from the tacit collusive output level $Q*$, the oligopolist's output level is unresponsive to changes in marginal cost within a certain range. If marginal cost falls substantially, the oligopolist is more likely to risk a breakdown in collusion and increase her output; in this case, the marginal cost curve cuts the marginal revenue curve in the segment YZ. And if marginal cost rises substantially, shifting the marginal cost curve up so that it cuts the marginal revenue curve in the segment WX, then the oligopolist is likely to reduce output and raise her price despite the risk of losing significant sales to rivals. But if marginal cost changes within a limited range—the range defined by XY— the producer will leave her output level unchanged rather than risk a breakdown in tacit collusion.

The behavior described by the kinked demand curve appears justified when a producer believes that she alone is facing a change in marginal cost—that is, when the change is unique to her. But when the change in marginal cost is clearly shared throughout the industry, this behavior is much less plausible. In that case, each producer knows that a change in a rival's output level and price is just a response to a change in the general level of marginal cost, not a hostile act of noncooperation. Consequently, all the producers in the industry are likely to respond to a change in marginal cost by adjusting their output and prices and thereby maintain tacit collusion.

►*ECONOMICS IN ACTION*

The Rise and Fall and Rise of OPEC

Call it the cartel that does not need to meet in secret. The Organization of Petroleum Exporting Countries, usually referred to as OPEC, includes 13 national governments (Algeria, Angola, Ecuador, Indonesia, Iran, Iraq, Kuwait, Libya, Nigeria, Qatar, Saudi Arabia, the United Arab Emirates, and Venezuela), and it controls 40% of the world's oil exports and 80% of its proven reserves. Two other oil-exporting countries, Norway and Mexico, are not formally part of the cartel but act as if they were. (Russia, also an important oil exporter, has not yet become part of the club.) Unlike corporations, which are often legally prohibited by governments from reaching agreements about production and prices, national governments can talk about whatever they feel like. OPEC members routinely meet to try to set targets for production.

These nations are not particularly friendly with one another. Indeed, OPEC members Iraq and Iran fought a spectacularly bloody war with each other in the 1980s. And, in 1990, Iraq invaded another member, Kuwait. (A mainly American force based in yet another OPEC member, Saudi Arabia, drove the Iraqis out of Kuwait.)

Yet the members of OPEC, like one another or not, are effectively players in a game with repeated interactions. In any given year it is in their combined interest to keep output low and prices high. But it is also in the interest of any one producer to cheat and produce more than the agreed-upon quota—unless that producer believes that this action will bring future retaliation.

So how successful is the cartel? Well, it's had its ups and downs.

Figure 15-5 shows the price of oil in constant dollars (that is, the value of a barrel of oil in terms of other goods) since 1947. OPEC first demonstrated its muscle in 1974: in the aftermath of a war in the Middle East, several OPEC producers limited their output—and they liked the results so much that they decided to continue the practice. Following a second wave of turmoil in the aftermath of Iran's 1979 revolution, prices shot still higher.

By the mid-1980s, however, there was a growing glut of oil on world markets, and cheating by cash-short OPEC members became widespread. The result, in 1985, was that producers who had tried to play by the rules—especially Saudi Arabia, the largest producer—got fed up, and collusion collapsed.

The cartel began to act effectively again at the end of the 1990s, thanks largely to the efforts of Mexico's oil minister to orchestrate output reductions. The cartel's actions helped raise the price of oil from less than $10 a barrel in 1998 to a range of $20 to $30 a barrel in 2003.

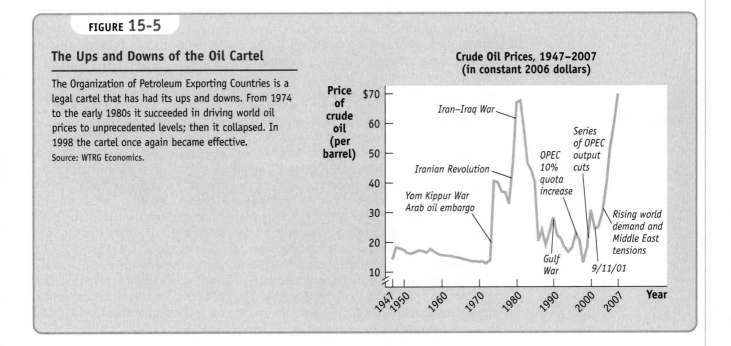

FIGURE 15-5

The Ups and Downs of the Oil Cartel

The Organization of Petroleum Exporting Countries is a legal cartel that has had its ups and downs. From 1974 to the early 1980s it succeeded in driving world oil prices to unprecedented levels; then it collapsed. In 1998 the cartel once again became effective.

Source: WTRG Economics.

Crude Oil Prices, 1947–2007 (in constant 2006 dollars)

In the years after 2003, the cartel became less relevant because it was no longer needed to keep oil prices high. As growing demand, especially from China, pressed against limited capacity, oil prices soared past $100 a barrel. ▲

< < < < < < < < < < < <

► CHECK YOUR UNDERSTANDING 15-3

1. Find the Nash (noncooperative) equilibrium actions for the following payoff matrix. Which actions maximize the total payoff of Nikita and Margaret? Why is it unlikely that they will choose those actions without some communication?

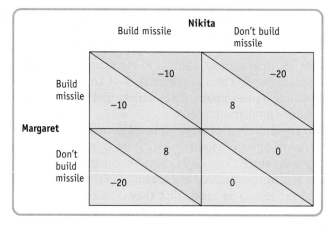

2. Which of the following factors make it more likely that oligopolists will play noncooperatively? Which make it more likely that they will engage in tacit collusion? Explain.
   a. Each oligopolist expects several new firms to enter the market in the future.
   b. It is very difficult for a firm to detect whether another firm has raised output.
   c. The firms have coexisted while maintaining high prices for a long time.

Solutions appear at back of book.

Oligopoly in Practice

In an Economics in Action earlier in the chapter, we described the cartel known as "Vitamins Inc.," which effectively sustained collusion for many years. The conspiratorial dealings of the vitamin makers were not, fortunately, the norm. But how do oligopolies usually work in practice? The answer depends both on the legal framework that limits what firms can do and on the underlying ability of firms in a given industry to cooperate without formal agreements.

The Legal Framework

To understand oligopoly pricing in practice, we must be familiar with the legal constraints under which oligopolistic firms operate. In the United States, oligopoly first became an issue during the second half of the nineteenth century, when the growth of railroads—themselves an oligopolistic industry—created a national market for many goods. Large firms producing oil, steel, and many other products soon emerged. The industrialists quickly realized that profits would be higher if they could limit price competition. So many industries formed cartels—that is, they signed formal agreements to limit production and raise prices. Until 1890, when the first federal legislation against such cartels was passed, this was perfectly legal.

However, although these cartels were legal, they weren't legally *enforceable*—members of a cartel couldn't ask the courts to force a firm that was violating its agreement to reduce its production. And firms often did violate their agreements, for the reason already suggested by our duopoly example: there is always a temptation for each firm in a cartel to produce more than it is supposed to.

In 1881 clever lawyers at John D. Rockefeller's Standard Oil Company came up with a solution—the so-called *trust.* In a trust, shareholders of all the major companies in an industry placed their shares in the hands of a board of trustees who controlled the companies. This, in effect, merged the companies into a single firm that could then engage in monopoly pricing. In this way, the Standard Oil Trust established what was essentially a monopoly of the oil industry, and it was soon followed by trusts in sugar, whiskey, lead, cottonseed oil, and linseed oil.

Eventually there was a public backlash, driven partly by concern about the economic effects of the trust movement, partly by fear that the owners of the trusts were simply becoming too powerful. The result was the Sherman Antitrust Act of 1890, which was intended both to prevent the creation of more monopolies and to break up existing ones. At first this law went largely unenforced. But over the decades that followed, the federal government became increasingly committed to making it difficult for oligopolistic industries either to become monopolies or to behave like them. Such efforts are known to this day as **antitrust policy.**

One of the most striking early actions of antitrust policy was the breakup of Standard Oil in 1911. (Its components formed the nuclei of many of today's large oil companies—Standard Oil of New Jersey became Exxon, Standard Oil of New York became Mobil, and so on.) In the 1980s a long-running case led to the breakup of Bell Telephone, which once had a monopoly of both local and long-distance phone service in the United States. As we mentioned earlier, the Justice Department reviews proposed mergers between companies in the same industry and will bar mergers that it believes will reduce competition.

Among advanced countries, the United States is unique in its long tradition of antitrust policy. Until recently, other advanced countries did not have policies against price-fixing, and some had even supported the creation of cartels, believing that it would help their own firms against foreign rivals. But the situation has changed radically over the past 20 years, as the European Union (EU)—a supranational body tasked with enforcing antitrust policy for its member countries—has converged toward U.S. practices. Today, EU and U.S. regulators often target the same firms because price-fixing has "gone global" as international trade has expanded. During the early 1990s, the United States instituted an amnesty program in which a price-fixer receives a much-reduced penalty if it informs on its co-conspirators. (The Great Vitamin Conspiracy was busted when a French company, Rhone-Poulenc, revealed the cartel in order to get favorable treatment from U.S. regulators.) In addition, Congress substantially increased maximum fines levied upon conviction. These two new policies clearly made informing on your cartel partners a dominant strategy, and it has paid off: in recent years, executives from Belgium, Britain, Canada, France, Germany, Italy, Mexico, the Netherlands, South Korea, and Switzerland, as well as from the United States, have been convicted in U.S. courts of cartel crimes. As one lawyer commented, "you get a race to the courthouse" as each conspirator seeks to be the first to come clean.

Life has gotten much tougher over the past few years if you want to operate a cartel. So what's an oligopolist to do?

Tacit Collusion and Price Wars

If a real industry were as simple as our lysine example, it probably wouldn't be necessary for the company presidents to meet or do anything that could land them in jail. Both firms would realize that it was in their mutual interest to restrict output to 30 million pounds each and that any short-term gains to either firm from producing more would be much less than the later losses as the other firm retaliated. So even without any explicit agreement, the firms would probably achieve the tacit collusion needed to maximize their combined profits.

> **Antitrust policy** are efforts undertaken by the government to prevent oligopolistic industries from becoming or behaving like monopolies.

Real industries are nowhere near that simple; nonetheless, in most oligopolistic industries, most of the time, the sellers do appear to succeed in keeping prices above their noncooperative level. Tacit collusion, in other words, is the normal state of oligopoly.

Although tacit collusion is common, it rarely allows an industry to push prices all the way up to their monopoly level; collusion is usually far from perfect. A variety of factors make it hard for an industry to coordinate on high prices.

Large Numbers Suppose that there were three instead of two firms in the lysine industry and that each was currently producing only 20 million pounds. You can confirm for yourself that in that case any one firm that decided to produce an extra 10 million pounds would gain more in short-term profits—and lose less once another firm responded in kind—than in our original example. The general point is that the more firms there are in an oligopoly, the less is the incentive of any one firm to behave cooperatively, taking into account the impact of its actions on the profits of the other firms. Large numbers of firms in an industry typically are an indication that there are low barriers to entry.

Complex Products and Pricing Schemes In our lysine example the two firms produce only one product. In reality, however, oligopolists often sell thousands or even tens of thousands of different products. Under these circumstances, keeping track of what other firms are producing and what prices they are charging is difficult. This makes it hard to determine whether a firm is cheating on the tacit agreement.

Differences in Interests In the lysine example, a tacit agreement for the firms to split the market equally is a natural outcome, probably acceptable to both firms. In real industries, however, firms often differ both in their perceptions about what is fair and in their real interests.

For example, suppose that Ajinomoto was a long-established lysine producer and ADM a more recent entrant to the industry. Ajinomoto might feel that it deserved to continue producing more than ADM, but ADM might feel that it was entitled to 50% of the business. (A disagreement along these lines was one of the contentious issues in those meetings the FBI was filming.)

Alternatively, suppose that ADM's marginal costs were lower than Ajinomoto's. Even if they could agree on market shares, they would then disagree about the profit-maximizing level of output.

Bargaining Power of Buyers Often oligopolists sell not to individual consumers but to large buyers—other industrial enterprises, nationwide chains of stores, and so on. These large buyers are in a position to bargain for lower prices from the oligopolists: they can ask for a discount from an oligopolist, and warn that they will go to a competitor if they don't get it. An important reason large retailers like Wal-Mart are able to offer lower prices to customers than small retailers is precisely their ability to use their size to extract lower prices from their suppliers.

These difficulties in enforcing tacit collusion have sometimes led companies to defy the law and create illegal cartels. We've already examined the cases of the lysine industry and the bulk vitamin industry. An older, classic example was the U.S. electrical equipment conspiracy of the 1950s, which led to the indictment of and jail sentences for some executives. The industry was one in which tacit collusion was especially difficult because of all the reasons just mentioned. There were many firms—40 companies were indicted. They produced a very complex array of products, often more or less custom-built for particular clients. They differed greatly in size, from giants like General Electric to family firms with only a few dozen employees. And the customers in many cases were large buyers like electrical utilities, which would nor-

The Art of Conspiracy

If you want to sell a valuable work of art, there are really only two places to go: Christie's, the London-based auction house, or Sotheby's, its New York counterpart and competitor. Both are classy operations—literally: many of the employees of Christie's come from Britain's aristocracy, and many of Sotheby's come from blue-blooded American families that might as well have titles. They're not the sort of people you would expect to be seeking plea bargains from prosecutors.

But on October 6, 2000, Diana D. Brooks, the very upper-class former president of Sotheby's, pleaded guilty to a conspiracy. With her counterpart at Christie's, she had engaged in the illegal practice of price-fixing—agreeing on the fees they would charge people who sold artwork through either house. As part of her guilty plea, and in an effort to avoid going to jail, she agreed to help in the investigation of her boss, the former chairman of Sotheby's.

Why would such upper-crust types engage in illegal practices? For the same reasons that respectable electrical equipment industry executives did. By definition, no two works of art are alike; it wasn't easy for the two houses to collude tacitly, because it was too hard to determine what commissions they were charging on any given transaction. To increase profits, then, the companies felt that they needed to reach a detailed agreement. They did, and they got caught.

mally try to force suppliers to compete for their business. Tacit collusion just didn't seem practical—so executives met secretly and illegally to decide who would bid what price for which contract.

The For Inquiring Minds above describes yet another price-fixing conspiracy: the one between the very posh auction houses Sotheby's and Christie's.

Because tacit collusion is often hard to achieve, most oligopolies charge prices that are well below what the same industry would charge if it were controlled by a monopolist—or what they would charge if they were able to collude explicitly. In addition, sometimes collusion breaks down and there is a **price war.** A price war sometimes involves simply a collapse of prices to their noncooperative level. Sometimes they even go *below* that level, as sellers try to put each other out of business or at least punish what they regard as cheating.

Product Differentiation and Price Leadership

Lysine is lysine: there was no question in anyone's mind that ADM and Ajinomoto were producing the same good and that consumers would make their decision about which company's lysine to buy based on the price.

In many oligopolies, however, firms produce products that consumers regard as similar but not identical. A $10 difference in the price won't make many customers switch from a Ford to a Chrysler, or vice versa. Sometimes the differences between products are real, like differences between Froot Loops and Wheaties; sometimes, like differences between brands of vodka (which is *supposed* to be tasteless), they exist mainly in the minds of consumers. Either way, the effect is to reduce the intensity of competition among the firms: consumers will not all rush to buy whichever product is cheapest.

As you might imagine, oligopolists welcome the extra market power that comes when consumers think that their product is different from that of competitors. So in many oligopolistic industries, firms make considerable efforts to create the perception that their product is different—that is, they engage in **product differentiation.**

A firm that tries to differentiate its product may do so by altering what it actually produces, adding "extras," or choosing a different design. It may also use advertising and marketing campaigns to create a differentiation in the minds of consumers, even though its product is more or less identical to the products of rivals.

A classic case of how products may be perceived as different even when they are really pretty much the same is over-the-counter medication. For many years there were only three widely sold pain relievers—aspirin, ibuprofen, and acetaminophen.

A **price war** occurs when tacit collusion breaks down and prices collapse.

Product differentiation is an attempt by a firm to convince buyers that its product is different from the products of other firms in the industry.

In **price leadership,** one firm sets its price first, and other firms then follow.

Firms that have a tacit understanding not to compete on price often engage in intense **nonprice competition,** using advertising and other means to try to increase their sales.

Yet these generic pain relievers were marketed under a number of brand names, each brand using a marketing campaign implying some special superiority (one classic slogan was "contains the pain reliever doctors recommend most"—that is, aspirin).

Whatever the nature of product differentiation, oligopolists producing differentiated products often reach a tacit understanding not to compete on price. For example, during the years when the great majority of cars sold in the United States were produced by the Big Three auto companies (General Motors, Ford, and Chrysler), there was an unwritten rule that none of the three companies would try to gain market share by making its cars noticeably cheaper than those of the other two.

But then who would decide on the overall price of cars? The answer was normally General Motors: as the biggest of the three, it would announce its prices for the year first; and the other companies would match it. This pattern of behavior, in which one company tacitly sets prices for the industry as a whole, is known as **price leadership.**

Interestingly, firms that have a tacit agreement not to compete on price often engage in vigorous **nonprice competition**—adding new features to their products, spending large sums on ads that proclaim the inferiority of their rivals' offerings, and so on.

Perhaps the best way to understand the mix of cooperation and competition in such industries is with a political analogy. During the long Cold War between the United States and the Soviet Union, the two countries engaged in intense rivalry for global influence. They not only provided financial and military aid to their allies; they sometimes supported forces trying to overthrow governments allied with their rival (as the Soviet Union did in Vietnam in the 1960s and early 1970s, and as the United States did in Afghanistan from 1979 until the collapse of the Soviet Union in 1991). They even sent their own soldiers to support allied governments against rebels (as the United States did in Vietnam and the Soviet Union did in Afghanistan). But they did *not* get into direct military confrontations with each other; open warfare between the two superpowers was regarded by both as too dangerous—and tacitly avoided.

Price wars aren't as serious as shooting wars, but the principle is the same.

►*ECONOMICS IN ACTION*

The Price Wars of Christmas

During the last several holiday seasons, the toy aisles of American retailers have been the scene of cutthroat competition: Wal-Mart offers a Furby doll for $10 less than its competitors, Target prices the latest Elmo doll at $3 less than Toys "R" Us, and so on. So extreme is the price-cutting that since 2003 three toy retailers—KB Toys, FAO Schwartz, and Zany Brainy—have been forced into bankruptcy. Due to aggressive price-cutting by Wal-Mart, the market share of Toys "R" Us has fallen from first to third.

What is happening? The turmoil can be traced back to trouble in the toy industry itself as well as to changes in toy retailing. Every year for several years, overall toy sales have fallen a few percentage points as children increasingly turn to video games and the Internet. There have also been new entrants into the toy business—since the 1990s, Wal-Mart and Target have expanded their number of stores and have been aggressive price-cutters. The result is much like a story of tacit collusion sustained by repeated interaction run in reverse: because the overall industry is in a state of decline and there are new entrants, the future payoff from collusion is shrinking. The predictable outcome is a price war.

Since retailers depend on holiday sales for nearly half of their annual sales, the holidays are a time of particularly intense price-cutting. Traditionally, the biggest shopping day of the year was the day after Thanksgiving. But in an effort to expand sales and undercut rivals, retailers—particularly Wal-Mart—have begun their price-cutting earlier in the fall. In 2007, it started in early November, well before Thanksgiving. With other retailers feeling as if they have no choice but to follow this pattern, we have the phenomenon known as "creeping Christmas": the price wars of Christmas arrive earlier each year. ▲

> > > > > > > > > > > >

► CHECK YOUR UNDERSTANDING 15-4

1. Which of the following factors are likely to support the conclusion that there is tacit collusion in this industry? Which are not? Explain.
   a. For many years the price in the industry has changed infrequently, and all the firms in the industry charge the same price. The largest firm publishes a catalog containing a "suggested" retail price. Changes in price coincide with changes in the catalog.
   b. There has been considerable variation in the market shares of the firms in the industry over time.
   c. Firms in the industry build into their products unnecessary features that make it hard for consumers to switch from one company's products to another's.
   d. Firms meet yearly to discuss their annual sales forecasts.
   e. Firms tend to adjust their prices upward at the same times.

Solutions appear at back of book.

QUICK REVIEW

- Oligopolies operate under legal restrictions in the form of **antitrust policy.** But many succeed in achieving tacit collusion.
- Tacit collusion is limited by a number of factors, including large numbers of firms, complex products and pricing, differences in interests among firms, and bargaining power of buyers. When collusion breaks down, there is a **price war.**
- To limit competition, oligopolists often engage in **product differentiation.** When products are differentiated, it is sometimes possible for an industry to achieve tacit collusion through **price leadership.**
- Oligopolists often avoid competing directly on price, engaging in **nonprice competition** through advertising and other means instead.

How Important Is Oligopoly?

We have seen that, across industries, oligopoly is far more common than either perfect competition or monopoly. When we try to analyze oligopoly, the economist's usual way of thinking—asking how self-interested individuals would behave, then analyzing their interaction—does not work as well as we might hope, because we do not know whether rival firms will engage in noncooperative behavior or manage to engage in some kind of collusion. Given the prevalence of oligopoly, then, is the analysis we developed in earlier chapters, which was based on perfect competition, still useful?

The conclusion of the great majority of economists is yes. For one thing, important parts of the economy are fairly well described by perfect competition. And even though many industries are oligopolistic, in many cases the limits to collusion keep prices relatively close to marginal costs—in other words, the industry behaves "almost" as if it were perfectly competitive.

It is also true that predictions from supply and demand analysis are often valid for oligopolies. For example, in Chapter 5 we saw that price controls will produce shortages. Strictly speaking, this conclusion is certain only for perfectly competitive industries. But in the 1970s, when the U.S. government imposed price controls on the definitely oligopolistic oil industry, the result was indeed to produce shortages and lines at the gas pumps.

So how important is it to take account of oligopoly? Most economists adopt a pragmatic approach. As we have seen in this chapter, the analysis of oligopoly is far more difficult and messy than that of perfect competition; so in situations where they do not expect the complications associated with oligopoly to be crucial, economists prefer to adopt the working assumption of perfectly competitive markets. They always keep in mind the possibility that oligopoly might be important; they recognize that there are important issues, from antitrust policies to price wars, where trying to understand oligopolistic behavior is crucial.

We will follow the same approach in the chapters that follow.

[>> A LOOK **AHEAD** •••

We're not yet done with our investigation of market structures other than perfect competition. There are quite a few industries that don't seem to fit either the definition of oligopoly or the definition of perfect competition. Consider, for example, the restaurant business. There are many restaurants, so it's not an oligopoly. But restaurants aren't price-takers, like wheat farmers, so it's not perfectly competitive. What is it?

The answer lies in the next chapter, which turns to the concept of *monopolistic competition.*]

SUMMARY

1. Many industries are **oligopolies:** there are only a few sellers. In particular, a **duopoly** has only two sellers. Oligopolies exist for more or less the same reasons that monopolies exist, but in weaker form. They are characterized by **imperfect competition:** firms compete but possess market power.

2. Predicting the behavior of **oligopolists** poses something of a puzzle. The firms in an oligopoly could maximize their combined profits by acting as a **cartel,** setting output levels for each firm as if they were a single monopolist; to the extent that firms manage to do this, they engage in **collusion.** But each individual firm has an incentive to produce more than it would in such an arrangement—to engage in **noncooperative behavior.** Informal collusion is likely to be easier to achieve in industries in which firms face capacity constraints.

3. The situation of **interdependence,** in which each firm's profit depends noticeably on what other firms do, is the subject of **game theory.** In the case of a game with two players, the **payoff** of each player depends both on its own actions and on the actions of the other; this interdependence can be represented as a **payoff matrix.** Depending on the structure of payoffs in the payoff matrix, a player may have a **dominant strategy**—an action that is always the best regardless of the other player's actions.

4. **Duopolists** face a particular type of game known as a **prisoners' dilemma;** if each acts independently in its own interest, the resulting **Nash equilibrium** or **noncooperative equilibrium** will be bad for both. However, firms that expect to play a game repeatedly tend to engage in **strategic behavior,** trying to influence each other's future actions. A particular strategy that seems to work well in such situations is **tit for tat,** which often leads to **tacit collusion.**

5. The **kinked demand curve** illustrates how an oligopolist that faces unique changes in its marginal cost within a certain range may choose not to adjust its output and price in order to avoid a breakdown in tacit collusion.

6. In order to limit the ability of oligopolists to collude and act like monopolists, most governments pursue an **antitrust policy** designed to make collusion more difficult. In practice, however, tacit collusion is widespread.

7. A variety of factors make tacit collusion difficult: large numbers of firms, complex products and pricing, differences in interests, and bargaining power of buyers. When tacit collusion breaks down, there is a **price war.** Oligopolists try to avoid price wars in various ways, such as through **product differentiation** and through **price leadership,** in which one firm sets prices for the industry. Another is through **nonprice competition,** like advertising.

KEY TERMS

Oligopoly, p. 388
Oligopolist, p. 388
Imperfect competition, p. 388
Duopoly, p. 390
Duopolist, p. 390
Collusion, p. 391
Cartel, p. 391
Noncooperative behavior, p. 392
Interdependence, p. 396

Game theory, p. 396
Payoff, p. 396
Payoff matrix, p. 396
Prisoners' dilemma, p. 397
Dominant strategy, p. 398
Nash equilibrium, p. 398
Noncooperative equilibrium, p. 398
Strategic behavior, p. 398

Tit for tat, p. 399
Tacit collusion, p. 401
Kinked demand curve, p. 402
Antitrust policy, p. 405
Price war, p. 407
Product differentiation, p. 407
Price leadership, p. 408
Nonprice competition, p. 408

PROBLEMS ···■

1. The accompanying table presents market share data for the U.S. breakfast cereal market in 2006.

Company	Market Share
Kellogg	30%
General Mills	26
PepsiCo (Quaker Oats)	14
Kraft	13
Private Label	11
Other	6

Source: Advertising Age

   a. Use the data provided to calculate the Herfindahl–Hirschman Index (HHI) for the market.

   b. Based on this HHI, what type of market structure is the U.S. breakfast cereal market?

2. The accompanying table shows the demand schedule for vitamin D. Suppose that the marginal cost of producing vitamin D is zero.

Price of vitamin D (per ton)	Quantity of vitamin D demanded (tons)
$8	0
7	10
6	20
5	30
4	40
3	50
2	60
1	70

   a. Assume that BASF is the only producer of vitamin D and acts as a monopolist. It currently produces 40 tons of vitamin D at $4 per ton. If BASF were to produce 10 more tons, what would be the price effect for BASF? What would be the quantity effect? Would BASF have an incentive to produce those 10 additional tons?

   b. Now assume that Roche enters the market by also producing vitamin D and the market is now a duopoly. BASF and Roche agree to produce 40 tons of vitamin D in total, 20 tons each. BASF cannot be punished for deviating from the agreement with Roche. If BASF, on its own, were to deviate from that agreement and produce 10 more tons, what would be the price effect for BASF? What would be the quantity effect for BASF? Would BASF have an incentive to produce those 10 additional tons?

3. The market for olive oil in New York City is controlled by two families, the Sopranos and the Contraltos. Both families will ruthlessly eliminate any other family that attempts to enter the New York City olive oil market. The marginal cost of producing olive oil is constant and equal to $40 per gallon. There is no fixed cost. The accompanying table gives the market demand schedule for olive oil.

Price of olive oil (per gallon)	Quantity of olive oil demanded (gallons)
$100	1,000
90	1,500
80	2,000
70	2,500
60	3,000
50	3,500
40	4,000
30	4,500
20	5,000
10	5,500

   a. Suppose the Sopranos and the Contraltos form a cartel. For each of the quantities given in the table, calculate the total revenue for their cartel and the marginal revenue for each additional gallon. How many gallons of olive oil would the cartel sell in total and at what price? The two families share the market equally (each produces half of the total output of the cartel). How much profit does each family make?

   b. Uncle Junior, the head of the Soprano family, breaks the agreement and sells 500 more gallons of olive oil than under the cartel agreement. Assuming the Contraltos maintain the agreement, how does this affect the price for olive oil and the profits earned by each family?

   c. Anthony Contralto, the head of the Contralto family, decides to punish Uncle Junior by increasing his sales by 500 gallons as well. How much profit does each family earn now?

4. In France, the market for bottled water is controlled by two large firms, Perrier and Evian. Each firm has a fixed cost of €1 million and a constant marginal cost of €2 per liter of bottled water (€1 = 1 euro). The following table gives the market demand schedule for bottled water in France.

Price of bottled water (per liter)	Quantity of bottled water demanded (millions of liters)
€10	0
9	1
8	2
7	3
6	4
5	5
4	6
3	7
2	8
1	9

a. Suppose the two firms form a cartel and act as a monopolist. Calculate marginal revenue for the cartel. What will the monopoly price and output be? Assuming the firms divided the output evenly, how much will each produce and what will each firm's profits be?

b. Now suppose Perrier decides to increase production by 1 million liters. Evian doesn't change its production. What will the new market price and output be? What is Perrier's profit? What is Evian's profit?

c. What if Perrier increases production by 3 million liters? Evian doesn't change its production. What would its output and profits be relative to those in part b?

d. What do your results tell you about the likelihood of cheating on such agreements?

5. To preserve the North Atlantic fish stocks, it is decided that only two fishing fleets, one from the United States and the other from the European Union (EU), can fish in those waters. The accompanying table shows the market demand schedule per week for fish from these waters. The only costs are fixed costs, so fishing fleets maximize profit by maximizing revenue.

Price of fish (per pound)	Quantity of fish demanded (pounds)
$17	1,800
16	2,000
15	2,100
14	2,200
12	2,300

a. If both fishing fleets collude, what is the revenue-maximizing output for the North Atlantic fishery? What price will a pound of fish sell for?

b. If both fishing fleets collude and share the output equally, what is the revenue to the EU fleet? To the U.S. fleet?

c. Suppose the EU fleet cheats by expanding its own catch by 100 pounds per week. The U.S. fleet doesn't change its catch. What is the revenue to the U.S. fleet? To the EU fleet?

d. In retaliation for the cheating by the EU fleet, the U.S. fleet also expands its catch by 100 pounds per week. What is the revenue to the U.S. fleet? To the EU fleet?

6. Suppose that the fisheries agreement in Problem 5 breaks down, so that the fleets behave noncooperatively. Assume that the United States and the EU each can send out either one or two fleets. The more fleets in the area, the more fish they catch in total but the lower the catch of each fleet. The accompanying matrix shows the profit (in dollars) per week earned by the two sides.

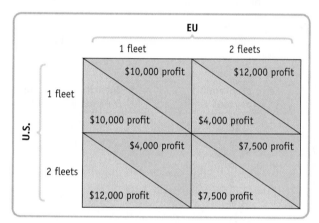

a. What is the noncooperative Nash equilibrium? Will each side choose to send out one or two fleets?

b. Suppose that the fish stocks are being depleted. Each region considers the future and comes to a "tit-for-tat" agreement whereby each side will send only one fleet out as long as the other does the same. If either of them breaks the agreement and sends out a second fleet, the other will also send out two and will continue to do so until its competitor sends out only one fleet. If both play this "tit-for-tat" strategy, how much profit will each make every week?

7. Untied and Air "R" Us are the only two airlines operating flights between Collegeville and Bigtown. That is, they operate in a duopoly. Each airline can charge either a high price or a low price for a ticket. The accompanying matrix shows their payoffs, in profits per seat (in dollars), for any choice that the two airlines can make.

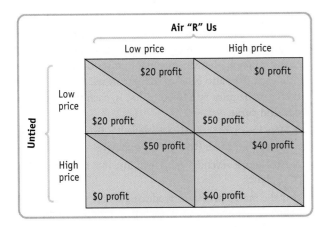

Price of Pepsi (per can)	Quantity of Pepsi demanded (millions of cans)
$0.10	5
0.20	4
0.30	3
0.40	2
0.50	1

a. Suppose the two airlines play a one-shot game—that is, they interact only once and never again. What will be the Nash (noncooperative) equilibrium in this one-shot game?

b. Now suppose the two airlines play this game twice. And suppose each airline can play one of two strategies: it can play either "always charge the low price" or "tit for tat"—that is, it starts off charging the high price in the first period, and then in the second period it does whatever the other airline did in the previous period. Write down the payoffs to Untied from the following four possibilities:

   i. Untied plays "always charge the low price" when Air "R" Us also plays "always charge the low price."

   ii. Untied plays "always charge the low price" when Air "R" Us plays "tit for tat."

   iii. Untied plays "tit for tat" when Air "R" Us plays "always charge the low price."

   iv. Untied plays "tit for tat" when Air "R" Us also plays "tit for tat."

8. Suppose that Coke and Pepsi are the only two producers of cola drinks, making them duopolists. Both companies have zero marginal cost and a fixed cost of $100,000.

a. Assume first that consumers regard Coke and Pepsi as perfect substitutes. Currently both are sold for $0.20 per can, and at that price each company sells 4 million cans per day.

   i. How large is Pepsi's profit?

   ii. If Pepsi were to raise its price to $0.30 cents per can, and Coke does not respond, what would happen to Pepsi's profit?

b. Now suppose that each company advertises to differentiate its product from the other company's. As a result of advertising, Pepsi realizes that if it raises or lowers its price, it will sell less or more of its product, as shown by the demand schedule in the accompanying table.

If Pepsi now were to raise its price to $0.30 per can, what would happen to its profit?

c. Comparing your answer to part a(i) and to part b, what is the maximum amount Pepsi would be willing to spend on advertising?

9. Philip Morris and R.J. Reynolds spend huge sums of money each year to advertise their tobacco products in an attempt to steal customers from each other. Suppose each year Philip Morris and R.J. Reynolds have to decide whether or not they want to spend money on advertising. If neither firm advertises, each will earn a profit of $2 million. If they both advertise, each will earn a profit of $1.5 million. If one firm advertises and the other does not, the firm that advertises will earn a profit of $2.8 million and the other firm will earn $1 million.

a. Use a payoff matrix to depict this problem.

b. Suppose Philip Morris and R.J. Reynolds can write an enforceable contract about what they will do. What is the cooperative solution to this game?

c. What is the Nash equilibrium without an enforceable contract? Explain why this is the likely outcome.

10. Over the last 30 years the Organization of Petroleum Exporting Countries (OPEC) has had varied success in forming and maintaining its cartel agreements. Explain how the following factors may contribute to the difficulty of forming and/or maintaining its price and output agreements.

a. New oil fields are discovered and increased drilling is undertaken in the Gulf of Mexico and the North Sea by nonmembers of OPEC.

b. Crude oil is a product that is differentiated by sulfur content: it costs less to refine low-sulfur crude oil into gasoline. Different OPEC countries possess oil reserves of different sulfur content.

c. Cars powered by hydrogen are developed.

11. Suppose you are an economist working for the Antitrust Division of the Department of Justice. In each of the following cases you are given the task of determining whether the behavior warrants an antitrust investigation for possible illegal acts or is just an example of undesirable, but not illegal, tacit collusion. Explain your reasoning.

a. Two companies dominate the industry for industrial lasers. Several people sit on the boards of directors of both companies.

b. Three banks dominate the market for banking in a given state. Their profits have been going up recently as they add new fees for customer transactions. Advertising among the banks is fierce, and new branches are springing up in many locations.

c. The two oil companies that produce most of the petroleum for the western half of the United States have decided to forgo building their own pipelines and to share a common pipeline, the only means of transporting petroleum products to that market.

d. The two major companies that dominate the market for herbal supplements have each created a subsidiary that sells the same product as the parent company in large quantities but with a generic name.

e. The two largest credit card companies, Passport and OmniCard, have required all banks and retailers who accept their cards to agree to limit their use of rival credit cards.

o··o

▼ **www.worthpublishers.com/krugmanwells**

12. The industry for small, single-engine airplanes is oligopolistic, and it has achieved tacit collusion. Each firm currently sells 10 airplanes at a price of $200,000 each. Each firm believes that it will sell 1 fewer airplane if it raises the price by $5,000. And each firm also believes that it can sell 1 more airplane if it lowers the price by $10,000. That is, each firm has a kinked demand curve.

a. How much additional revenue will a firm generate if it produces 1 more (the 11th) airplane?

b. How much revenue will a firm lose if it produces 1 fewer airplane?

c. If the marginal cost of producing an airplane is $120,000, how many airplanes will each firm produce, and at what price?

d. If the marginal cost of producing an airplane is $140,000, how many airplanes will each firm produce, and at what price?

Monopolistic Competition and Product Differentiation

FAST-FOOD DIFFERENTIATION

A BEST-SELLING BOOK TITLED *FAST FOOD NATION* offered a fascinating if rather negative report on the burgers, pizza, tacos, and fried chicken that make up so much of the modern American diet. According to the book, all fast-food chains produce and deliver their food in pretty much the same way. In particular, a lot of the taste of fast food—whatever kind of fast food it is—comes from food additives manufactured in New Jersey.

But each fast-food provider goes to great lengths to convince you that it has something special to offer. Everyone recognizes Ronald McDonald the clown, a symbol of McDonald's carefully cultivated image as the place kids love. Rival Wendy's took a bite out of McDonald's market share with a little old lady yelling "Where's the beef?", a campaign that emphasized Wendy's somewhat bigger burgers.

So how would you describe the fast-food industry? On the one side, it clearly isn't a monopoly. When you go to a fast-food court, you have a choice among vendors, and there is real competition between the different burger outlets and between the burgers and the fried chicken. On the other side, in a way each vendor *does* possess some aspects of a monopoly: at one point McDonald's had the slogan "Nobody does it like McDonald's."

That was literally true—though McDonald's competitors would claim that they did it *better*. In any case, the point is that each fast-food provider offers a product that is *differentiated* from its rivals' products.

In the fast-food industry, many firms compete to satisfy more or less the same demand—the desire of consumers for something tasty but quick. But each firm offers to satisfy that demand with a distinctive, differentiated product—products that consumers typically view as close but not perfect substitutes. When there are many firms offering competing, differentiated products, as there are in the fast-food industry, economists say that the industry is characterized by *monopolistic competition*. This is the fourth and final market structure that we will discuss, after perfect competition, monopoly, and oligopoly.

We'll start by defining monopolistic competition more carefully and explaining its characteristic features. Then we'll explore how firms differentiate their products; this will allow us to analyze how monopolistic competition works. The chapter concludes with a discussion of some ongoing controversies about product differentiation—in particular, the question of why advertising is effective.

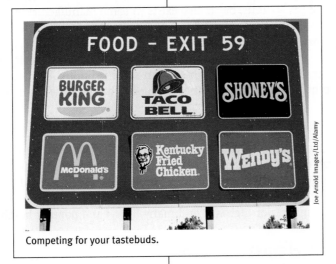

Competing for your tastebuds.

The Meaning of Monopolistic Competition

Leo manages the Wonderful Wok stand in the food court of a big shopping mall. He offers the only Chinese food there, but there are more than a dozen alternatives, from Bodacious Burgers to Pizza Paradise. When deciding what to charge for a meal, Leo knows that he must take those alternatives into account: even people who normally prefer stir-fry won't order a $15 lunch from Leo when they can get a burger, fries, and drink for $4.

But Leo also knows that he won't lose all his business even if his lunches cost a bit more than the alternatives. Chinese food isn't the same thing as burgers or pizza. Some people will really be in the mood for Chinese that day, and they will buy from Leo even if they could have dined more cheaply on burgers. Of course, the reverse is also true: even if Chinese is a bit cheaper, some people will choose burgers instead. In other words, Leo does have some market power: he has *some* ability to set his own price.

So how would you describe Leo's situation? He definitely isn't a price-taker, so he isn't in a situation of perfect competition. But you wouldn't exactly call him a monopolist, either. Although he's the only seller of Chinese food in that food court, he does face competition from other food vendors.

Yet it would also be wrong to call him an oligopolist. Oligopoly, remember, involves competition among a small number of interdependent firms in an industry protected by some—albeit limited—barriers to entry and whose profits are highly interdependent. Because their profits are highly interdependent, oligopolists have an incentive to collude, tacitly or explicitly. But in Leo's case there are *lots* of vendors in the shopping mall, too many to make tacit collusion feasible.

Economists describe Leo's situation as one of **monopolistic competition.** Monopolistic competition is particularly common in service industries like restaurants and gas stations, but it also exists in some manufacturing industries. It involves three conditions: large numbers of competing producers, differentiated products, and free entry into and exit from the industry in the long run. In a monopolistically competitive industry, each producer has some ability to set the price of her differentiated product. But exactly how high she can set it is limited by the competition she faces from other existing and potential producers that produce close, but not identical, products.

Large Numbers

In a monopolistically competitive industry there are many producers. Such an industry does not look either like a monopoly, where the firm faces no competition, or an oligopoly, where each firm has only a few rivals. Instead, each seller has many competitors. For example, there are many vendors in a big food court, many gas stations along a major highway, and many hotels at a popular beach resort.

Differentiated Products

In a monopolistically competitive industry, each producer has a product that consumers view as somewhat distinct from the products of competing firms; at the same time, though, consumers see these competing products as close substitutes. If Leo's food court contained 15 vendors selling exactly the same kind and quality of food,

Monopolistic competition is a market structure in which there are many competing producers in an industry, each producer sells a differentiated product, and there is free entry into and exit from the industry in the long run.

there would be perfect competition: any seller who tried to charge a higher price would have no customers. But suppose that Wonderful Wok is the only Chinese food vendor, Bodacious Burgers is the only hamburger stand, and so on. The result of this differentiation is that each seller has some ability to set his own price: each producer has some—albeit limited—market power.

Free Entry and Exit in the Long Run

In monopolistically competitive industries, new producers, with their own distinct products, can enter the industry freely in the long run. For example, other food vendors would open outlets in the food court if they thought it would be profitable to do so. In addition, firms will exit the industry if they find they are not covering their costs in the long run.

Monopolistic competition, then, differs from the three market structures we have examined so far. It's not the same as perfect competition: firms have some power to set prices. It's not pure monopoly: firms face some competition. And it's not the same as oligopoly: because there are many firms and free entry, the potential for collusion so important in oligopoly no longer exists.

We'll see in a moment how prices, output, and the number of products available are determined in monopolistically competitive industries. But first, let's look a little more closely at what it means to have differentiated products.

Product Differentiation

We pointed out in Chapter 15 that product differentiation often plays an important role in oligopolistic industries. In such industries, product differentiation reduces the intensity of competition between firms when tacit collusion cannot be achieved. Product differentiation plays an even more crucial role in monopolistically competitive industries. Because tacit collusion is virtually impossible when there are many producers, product differentiation is the only way monopolistically competitive firms can acquire some market power.

How do firms in the same industry—such as fast-food vendors, gas stations, or chocolate makers—differentiate their products? Sometimes the difference is mainly in the minds of consumers rather than in the products themselves. We'll discuss the role of advertising and the importance of brand names in achieving this kind of product differentiation later in the chapter. But, in general, firms differentiate their products by—surprise!—actually making them different.

The key to product differentiation is that consumers have different preferences and are willing to pay somewhat more to satisfy those preferences. Each producer can carve out a market niche by producing something that caters to the particular preferences of some group of consumers better than the products of other firms. There are three important forms of product differentiation: differentiation by style or type, differentiation by location, and differentiation by quality.

Differentiation by Style or Type

The sellers in Leo's food court offer different types of fast food: hamburgers, pizza, Chinese food, Mexican food, and so on. Each consumer arrives at the food court with some preference for one or another of these offerings. This preference may depend on the consumer's mood, her diet, or what she has already eaten that day. These preferences will not make consumers indifferent to price: if Wonderful Wok were to charge $15 for an egg roll, everybody would go to Bodacious Burgers or Pizza Paradise instead. But some people will choose a more expensive meal if that type of food is closer to their preference. So the products of the different vendors are substitutes, but they aren't *perfect* substitutes—they are *imperfect substitutes.*

Vendors in a food court aren't the only sellers who differentiate their offerings by type. Clothing stores concentrate on women's or men's clothes, on business attire or sportswear, on trendy or classic styles, and so on. Auto manufacturers offer sedans, minivans, sport-utility vehicles, and sports cars, each type aimed at drivers with different needs and tastes.

Books offer yet another example of differentiation by type and style. Mysteries are differentiated from romances; among mysteries, we can differentiate among hard-boiled detective stories, whodunits, and police procedurals. And no two writers of hard-boiled detective stories are exactly alike: Raymond Chandler and Sue Grafton each have their devoted fans.

In fact, product differentiation is characteristic of most consumer goods. As long as people differ in their tastes, producers find it possible and profitable to produce a range of varieties.

Differentiation by Location

Gas stations along a road offer differentiated products. True, the gas may be exactly the same. But the location of the stations is different, and location matters to consumers: it's more convenient to stop for gas near your home, near your workplace, or near wherever you are when the gas gauge gets low.

In fact, many monopolistically competitive industries supply goods differentiated by location. This is especially true in service industries, from dry cleaners to hairdressers, where customers often choose the seller who is closest rather than cheapest.

Differentiation by Quality

Do you have a craving for chocolate? How much are you willing to spend on it? You see, there's chocolate and then there's chocolate: although ordinary chocolate may not be very expensive, gourmet chocolate can cost several dollars per bite.

With chocolate, as with many goods, there is a range of possible qualities. You can get a usable bicycle for less than $100; you can get a much fancier bicycle for 10 times

---

Can't Buy Love

The American Customer Satisfaction Index (or ACSI) measures customer satisfaction for 200 companies in 40 industries. It's regarded as the definitive measure of how consumers feel about what they buy. And what comes through loud and clear from the index is that low prices can't buy consumers' love for a company. Although it may seem counterintuitive, cheaper and better products do not always translate into sales. As a 2007 *New York Times* article stated, ". . . the harder companies work to make products cheaper and better, the less they seem to impress their customers."

This has happened because customers have come to view falling prices as the norm in many industries, such as airlines, digital gadgets and computers. As products get cheaper year after year, offering great bargains often doesn't win customers' loyalty. According to one analyst, "Price has an effect on whether you buy or not. It

has less of an impact on whether you're satisfied or not." For example, Hewlett-Packard, the computer and printer maker, has offered improved products at lower prices year after year, and it has a relatively low ACSI score.

Not surprisingly, companies that assiduously cater to consumer preferences have higher ACSI scores. Take, for example, Starbucks, which has a relatively high

Sometimes a quick and cheap cup just won't do.

score: you don't visit a Starbucks to grab a cheap cup of coffee; rather, you are there for the experience. After paying several dollars to sip a double-mocha latte, you can settle into a deep chair while that day's Starbucks music selection plays in the background. Perhaps you'll order one of the many delectable desserts on display. Likewise, you might shop for books at amazon.com, another high scorer, rather than at some other online bookseller that might offer better prices, because amazon.com has kept a record of your previous selections and uses that information to suggest new books that suit your particular tastes.

In other words, companies that exploit the strategy of product differentiation have higher ACSI scores. By finding out what consumers enjoy and providing it, even at higher prices, companies like Starbucks and amazon.com make customers happy and improve their own bottom lines.

as much. It all depends on how much the additional quality matters to you and how much you will miss the other things you could have purchased with that money.

Because consumers vary in what they are willing to pay for higher quality, producers can differentiate their products by quality—some offering lower-quality, inexpensive products and others offering higher-quality products at a higher price.

Product differentiation, then, can take several forms. Whatever form it takes, however, there are two important features of industries with differentiated products: *competition among sellers* and *value in diversity.*

Competition among sellers means that even though sellers of differentiated products are not offering identical goods, they are to some extent competing for a limited market. If more businesses enter the market, each will find that it sells less quantity at any given price. For example, if a new gas station opens along a road, each of the existing gas stations will sell a bit less.

Value in diversity refers to the gain to consumers from the proliferation of differentiated products. A food court with eight vendors makes consumers happier than one with only six vendors, even if the prices are the same, because some customers will get a meal that is closer to what they had in mind. A road on which there is a gas station every two miles is more convenient for motorists than a road where gas stations are five miles apart. When a product is available in many different qualities, fewer people are forced to pay for more quality than they need or to settle for lower quality than they want. There are, in other words, benefits to consumers from a greater diversity of available products.

As we'll see next, competition among the sellers of differentiated products is the key to understanding how monopolistic competition works.

►ECONOMICS IN ACTION

Any Color, So Long as It's Black

The early history of the auto industry offers a classic illustration of the power of product differentiation.

The modern automobile industry was created by Henry Ford, who first introduced assembly-line production. This technique made it possible for him to offer the famous Model T at a far lower price than anyone else was charging for a car; by 1920, Ford dominated the automobile business.

Ford's strategy was to offer just one style of car, which maximized his economies of scale in production but made no concessions to differences in consumer's tastes. He supposedly declared that customers could get the Model T in "any color, so long as it's black."

This strategy was challenged by Alfred P. Sloan, who had merged a number of smaller automobile companies into General Motors. Sloan's strategy was to offer a range of car types, differentiated by quality and price. Chevrolets were basic cars that directly challenged the Model T, Buicks were bigger and more expensive, and so on up to Cadillacs. And you could get each model in several different colors.

By the 1930s the verdict was clear: customers preferred a range of styles, and General Motors, not Ford, became the dominant auto manufacturer for the rest of the twentieth century. ▲

> > > > > > > > > > > >

► CHECK YOUR UNDERSTANDING 16-1

1. Each of the following goods and services are differentiated products. Which are differentiated as a result of monopolistic competition and which are not? Explain your answers.
   a. Ladders
   b. Soft drinks
   c. Department stores
   d. Steel

>> QUICK REVIEW

➤ In **monopolistic competition** there are many competing producers, each with a differentiated product, and free entry and exit in the long run.

➤ Product differentiation can occur in oligopolies that fail to achieve tacit collusion as well as in monopolistic competition. It takes three main forms: by style or type, by location, or by quality. The products of competing sellers are considered imperfect substitutes.

➤ Producers compete for the same market, so entry by more producers reduces the quantity each existing producer sells at any given price. In addition, consumers gain from the increased diversity of products.

2. You must determine which of two types of market structure better describes an industry, but you are allowed to ask only one question about the industry. What question should you ask to determine if an industry is:
   a. Perfectly competitive or monopolistically competitive?
   b. A monopoly or monopolistically competitive?

Solutions appear at back of book.

Understanding Monopolistic Competition

Suppose an industry is monopolistically competitive: it consists of many producers, all competing for the same consumers but offering differentiated products. How does such an industry behave?

As the term *monopolistic competition* suggests, this market structure combines some features typical of monopoly with others typical of perfect competition. Because each firm is offering a distinct product, it is in a way like a monopolist: it faces a downward-sloping demand curve and has some market power—the ability within limits to determine the price of its product. However, unlike a pure monopolist, a monopolistically competitive firm does face competition: the amount of its product it can sell depends on the prices and products offered by other firms in the industry.

The same, of course, is true of an oligopoly. In a monopolistically competitive industry, however, there are *many* producers, as opposed to the small number that defines an oligopoly. This means that the "puzzle" of oligopoly—will firms collude or will they behave noncooperatively?—does not arise in the case of monopolistically competitive industries. True, if all the gas stations or all the restaurants in a town could agree—explicitly or tacitly—to raise prices, it would be in their mutual interest to do so. But such collusion is virtually impossible when the number of firms is large and, by implication, there are no barriers to entry. So in situations of monopolistic competition, we can safely assume that firms behave noncooperatively and ignore the potential for collusion.

Monopolistic Competition in the Short Run

We introduced the distinction between short-run and long-run equilibrium back in Chapter 13. The short-run equilibrium of an industry takes the number of firms as given. The long-run equilibrium, by contrast, is reached only after enough time has elapsed for firms to enter or exit the industry. To analyze monopolistic competition, we focus first on the short run and then on how an industry moves from the short run to the long run.

Panels (a) and (b) of Figure 16-1 show two possible situations that a typical firm in a monopolistically competitive industry might face in the short run. In each case, the firm looks like any monopolist: it faces a downward-sloping demand curve, which implies a downward-sloping marginal revenue curve.

We assume that every firm has an upward-sloping marginal cost curve but that it also faces some fixed costs, so that its average total cost curve is U-shaped. This assumption doesn't matter in the short run; but, as we'll see shortly, it is crucial to understanding the long-run equilibrium.

In each case the firm, in order to maximize profit, sets marginal revenue equal to marginal cost. So how do these two figures differ? In panel (a) the firm is profitable; in panel (b) it is unprofitable. (Recall that we are referring always to economic profit and not accounting profit—that is, a profit given that all factors of production are earning their opportunity costs.)

In panel (a) the firm faces the demand curve D_P and the marginal revenue curve MR_P. It produces the profit-maximizing output Q_P, the quantity at which marginal revenue is equal to marginal cost, and sells it at the price P_P. This price is above the average total cost at this output, ATC_P. The firm's profit is indicated by the area of the shaded rectangle.

| **FIGURE 16-1** | **The Monopolistically Competitive Firm in the Short Run** |

(a) A Profitable Firm

(b) An Unprotitable Firm

Profit-maximizing quantity

Loss-minimizing quantity

The firm in panel (a) can be profitable for some output quantities: the quantities for which its average total cost curve, *ATC*, lies below its demand curve, *D_P*. The profit-maximizing output quantity is *Q_P*, the output at which marginal revenue, *MR_P*, is equal to marginal cost, *MC*. The firm charges price *P_P* and earns a profit, represented by the area of the green shaded rectangle. The firm in panel (b), however, can never be profitable because its average total cost curve lies above its demand curve, *D_U*, for every output quantity. The best that it can do if it produces at all is to produce quantity *Q_U* and charge price *P_U*. This generates a loss, indicated by the area of the yellow shaded rectangle. Any other output quantity results in a greater loss.

In panel (b) the firm faces the demand curve D_U and the marginal revenue curve MR_U. It chooses the quantity Q_U at which marginal revenue is equal to marginal cost. However, in this case the price P_U is *below* the average total cost ATC_U; so at this quantity the firm loses money. Its loss is equal to the area of the shaded rectangle. Since Q_U is the profit-maximizing quantity—which means, in this case, the loss-minimizing quantity—there is no way for a firm in this situation to make a profit. We can confirm this by noting that at *any* quantity of output, the average total cost curve in panel (b) lies above the demand curve D_U. Because $ATC > P$ at all quantities of output, this firm always suffers a loss.

As this comparison suggests, the key to whether a firm with market power is profitable or unprofitable in the short run lies in the relationship between its demand curve and its average total cost curve. In panel (a) the demand curve D_P crosses the average total cost curve, meaning that some of the demand curve lies above the average total cost curve. So there are some price–quantity combinations available at which price is higher than average total cost, indicating that the firm can choose a quantity at which it makes positive profit.

In panel (b), by contrast, the demand curve D_U does not cross the average total cost curve—it always lies below it. So the price corresponding to each quantity demanded is always less than the average total cost of producing that quantity. There is no quantity at which the firm can avoid losing money.

These figures, showing firms facing downward-sloping demand curves and their associated marginal revenue curves, look just like ordinary monopoly analysis. The "competition" aspect of monopolistic competition comes into play, however, when we move from the short run to the long run.

In the long run, a monopolistically competitive industry ends up in **zero-profit equilibrium**: each firm makes zero profit at its profit-maximizing quantity.

Monopolistic Competition in the Long Run

Obviously, an industry in which existing firms are losing money, like the one in panel (b) of Figure 16-1, is not in long-run equilibrium. When existing firms are losing money, some firms will *exit* the industry. The industry will not be in long-run equilibrium until the persistent losses have been eliminated by the exit of some firms.

It may be less obvious that an industry in which existing firms are earning profits, like the one in panel (a) of Figure 16-1, is also not in long-run equilibrium. Given there is *free entry* into the industry, persistent profits earned by the existing firms will lead to the entry of additional producers. The industry will not be in long-run equilibrium until the persistent profits have been eliminated by the entry of new producers.

How will entry or exit by other firms affect the profits of a typical existing firm? Because the differentiated products offered by firms in a monopolistically competitive industry compete for the same set of customers, entry or exit by other firms will affect the demand curve facing every existing producer. If new gas stations open along a highway, each of the existing gas stations will no longer be able to sell as much gas as before at any given price. So, as illustrated in panel (a) of Figure 16-2, entry of additional producers into a monopolistically competitive industry will lead to a *leftward* shift of the demand curve and the marginal revenue curve facing a typical existing producer.

Conversely, suppose that some of the gas stations along the highway close. Then each of the remaining stations will be able to sell more gasoline at any given price. So as illustrated in panel (b), exit of firms from an industry leads to a *rightward* shift of the demand curve and marginal revenue curve facing a typical remaining producer.

The industry will be in long-run equilibrium when there is neither entry nor exit. This will occur only when every firm earns zero profit. So in the long run, a monopolistically competitive industry will end up in **zero-profit equilibrium,** in which firms just manage to cover their costs at their profit-maximizing output quantities.

We have seen that a firm facing a downward-sloping demand curve will earn positive profits if any part of that demand curve lies above its average total cost curve; it

---

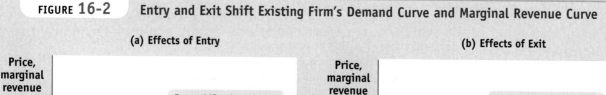

FIGURE 16-2   **Entry and Exit Shift Existing Firm's Demand Curve and Marginal Revenue Curve**

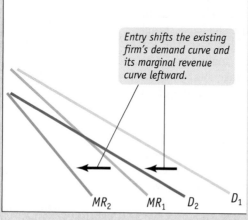

(a) Effects of Entry

Entry shifts the existing firm's demand curve and its marginal revenue curve leftward.

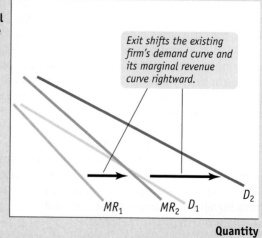

(b) Effects of Exit

Exit shifts the existing firm's demand curve and its marginal revenue curve rightward.

Entry will occur in the long run when existing firms are profitable. In panel (a), entry causes each existing firm's demand curve and marginal revenue curve to shift to the left. The firm receives a lower price for every unit it sells, and its profit falls. Entry will cease when firms make zero profit. Exit will occur in the long run when existing firms are unprofitable. In panel (b), exit from the industry shifts each remaining firm's demand curve and marginal revenue curve to the right. The firm receives a higher price for every unit it sells, and profit rises. Exit will cease when the remaining firms make zero profit.

Hits and Flops

On the face of it, the movie business seems to meet the criteria for monopolistic competition. Movies compete for the same consumers; each movie is different from the others; new companies can and do enter the business. But where's the zero-profit equilibrium? After all, some movies are enormously profitable.

The key is to realize that for every successful blockbuster, there are several flops—and that the movie studios don't know in advance which will be which. (One observer of Hollywood summed up his conclusions as follows: "Nobody knows any-

thing.") And by the time it becomes clear that a movie will be a flop, it's too late to cancel it.

The difference between movie-making and the type of monopolistic competition we model in this chapter is that the fixed costs of making a movie are also *sunk costs*—once they've been incurred, they can't be recovered.

Yet there is still, in a way, a zero-profit equilibrium. If movies on average were highly profitable, more studios would enter the industry and more movies would be made. If movies on average lost money,

fewer movies would be made. In fact, as you might expect, the movie industry on average earns just about enough to cover the cost of production—that is, it earns roughly zero economic profit.

This kind of situation—in which firms earn zero profit on average but have a mixture of highly profitable hits and money-losing flops—can be found in other industries characterized by high up-front sunk costs. A notable example is the pharmaceutical industry, where many research projects lead nowhere but a few lead to highly profitable drugs.

will incur a loss if its demand curve lies everywhere below its average total cost curve. So in zero-profit equilibrium, the firm must be in a borderline position between these two cases; its demand curve must just touch its average total cost curve. That is, it must be just *tangent* to it at the firm's profit-maximizing output quantity—the output quantity at which marginal revenue equals marginal cost.

If this is not the case, the firm operating at its profit-maximizing quantity will find itself making either a profit or loss, as illustrated in the panels of Figure 16-1. But we also know that free entry and exit means that this cannot be a long-run equilibrium. Why? In the case of a profit, new firms will enter the industry, shifting the demand curve of every existing firm leftward until all profits are extinguished. In the case of a loss, some existing firms exit and so shift the demand curve of every remaining firm to the right until all losses are extinguished. All entry and exit ceases only when every existing firm makes zero profit at its profit-maximizing quantity of output.

Figure 16-3 shows a typical monopolistically competitive firm in such a zero-profit equilibrium. The firm produces Q_{MC}, the output at which $MR_{MC} = MC$, and

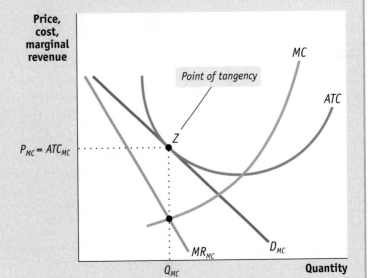

FIGURE 16-3

The Long-Run Zero-Profit Equilibrium

If existing firms are profitable, entry will occur and shift each existing firm's demand curve leftward. If existing firms are unprofitable, each remaining firm's demand curve shifts rightward as some firms exit the industry. Entry and exit will cease when every existing firm makes zero profit at its profit-maximizing quantity. So, in long-run zero-profit equilibrium, the demand curve of each firm is tangent to its average total cost curve at its profit-maximizing quantity: at the profit-maximizing quantity, Q_{MC}, price, P_{MC}, equals average total cost, ATC_{MC}. A monopolistically competitive firm is like a monopolist without monopoly profits.

charges price P_{MC}. At this price and quantity, represented by point Z, the demand curve is just tangent to its average total cost curve. The firm earns zero profit because price, P_{MC}, is equal to average total cost, ATC_{MC}.

The normal long-run condition of a monopolistically competitive industry, then, is that each producer is in the situation shown in Figure 16-3. Each producer acts like a monopolist, facing a downward-sloping demand curve and setting marginal cost equal to marginal revenue so as to maximize profits. But this is just enough to achieve zero economic profit. The producers in the industry are like monopolists without monopoly profits.

►ECONOMICS IN ACTION

The Last Stand of the 6-Percenters?

The vast majority of home sales in the United States are transacted with the use of real estate agents. A homeowner looking to sell hires an agent, who lists the house for sale and shows it to interested buyers. Correspondingly, prospective home buyers hire their own agent to arrange inspections of available houses. Traditionally, agents are paid by the seller: the seller pays a commission equal to 6% of the sales price of the house, which the seller's agent and the buyer's agent split equally. If a house sells for $300,000, for example, the seller's agent and the buyer's agent each receives $9,000 (equal to 3% of $300,000).

The real estate brokerage industry fits the model of monopolistic competition quite well: in any given local market, there are many real estate agents, all competing with one another, but the agents are differentiated by location and personality, as well as by the type of home they sell (some focus on condominiums, others on very expensive homes, and so on). And the industry has free entry: it's relatively easy for someone to become a real estate agent (take a course and then pass a test to obtain a license). But there's one feature that doesn't fit the model of monopolistic competition: the fixed 6% commission that has not changed over time and is unaffected by the ups and downs of the housing market. In some markets such as southern California, where house prices have tripled over the past 15 years, agents receive three times as much compensation as they did 15 years ago even though it's no harder to broker a deal today than it was then.

You may wonder why new agents don't enter the market and drive the commission rate down to the zero-profit level. The answer lies in aggressive action taken by agents to protect the 6% rate. One advantage they have is control of the Multiple Listing Service, or MLS, which lists nearly all the homes for sale in a community. Sellers who don't agree to the 6% commission aren't allowed to list their homes because agents have restricted access to the MLS to only those buyers who agree to the traditional fee structure.

But traditional agents are facing competition and resistance. The excessive profits generated by the current system during the housing boom of 2002 to 2006 led to the appearance of numerous discount real estate agencies that provide their services at much lower cost. They either charge sellers a much lower commission or hand their own commission back to the buyers in the form of a rebate. Traditional agents have fought back, often refusing to work with discount agents. But the Justice Department, the Federal Trade Commission, and several states have been fighting such tactics. The Justice Department sued the National Association of Realtors, the powerful trade group of agents, in 2005. The intensity of the fight indicates that traditional agents know that their system, rigged to avoid reaching the zero-profit equilibrium, is in serious jeopardy. At this point, with government oversight of agents and the housing market bust of 2008, industry observers are predicting that the 6-percenters won't be able to hold out much longer. ▲

< < < < < < < < < < < <

► CHECK YOUR UNDERSTANDING 16-2

1. Currently a monopolistically competitive industry, composed of firms with U-shaped average total cost curves, is in long-run equilibrium. Describe how the industry adjusts, in both the short and long run, in each of the following situations.

►► QUICK REVIEW

➤ Like a monopolist, each firm in a monopolistically competitive industry faces a downward-sloping demand curve and marginal revenue curve. In the short run, it may earn a profit or incur a loss at its profit-maximizing quantity.

➤ If the typical firm earns positive profit, new firms will enter the industry in the long run, shifting each existing firm's demand curve to the left. If the typical firm incurs a loss, some existing firms will exit the industry in the long run, shifting the demand curve of each remaining firm to the right.

➤ The long-run equilibrium of a monopolistically competitive industry is a **zero-profit equilibrium** in which firms just break even. The typical firm's demand curve is tangent to its average total cost curve at its profit-maximizing quantity.

a. A technological change that increases fixed cost for every firm in the industry

b. A technological change that decreases marginal cost for every firm in the industry

2. Why, in the long run, is it impossible for firms in a monopolistically competitive industry to create a monopoly by joining together to form a single firm?

Solutions appear at back of book.

Monopolistic Competition versus Perfect Competition

In a way, long-run equilibrium in a monopolistically competitive industry looks a lot like long-run equilibrium in a perfectly competitive industry. In both cases, there are many firms; in both cases, profits have been competed away; in both cases, the price received by every firm is equal to the average total cost of production.

However, the two versions of long-run equilibrium are different—in ways that are economically significant.

Price, Marginal Cost, and Average Total Cost

Figure 16-4 compares the long-run equilibrium of a typical firm in a perfectly competitive industry with that of a typical firm in a monopolistically competitive industry. Panel (a) shows a perfectly competitive firm facing a market price equal to its minimum average total cost; panel (b) reproduces Figure 16-3. Comparing the panels, we see two important differences.

FIGURE 16-4 **Comparing Long-Run Equilibrium in Perfect Competition and Monopolistic Competition**

Panel (a) shows the situation of the typical firm in long-run equilibrium in a perfectly competitive industry. The firm operates at the minimum-cost output Q_{PC}, sells at the competitive market price P_{PC}, and makes zero profit. It is indifferent to selling another unit of output because P_{PC} is equal to its marginal cost, MC_{PC}. Panel (b) shows the situation of the typical firm in long-run equilibrium in a monopolistically competitive industry. At Q_{MC} it makes zero profit because its price P_{MC} just equals average total cost, ATC_{MC}. At Q_{MC} the firm would like to sell another unit at price P_{MC} since P_{MC} exceeds marginal cost, MC_{MC}. But it is unwilling to lower price to make more sales. It therefore operates to the left of the minimum-cost output level and has excess capacity.

Firms in a monopolistically competitive industry have **excess capacity**: they produce less than the output at which average total cost is minimized.

First, in the case of the perfectly competitive firm shown in panel (a), the price, P_{PC}, received by the firm at the profit-maximizing quantity, Q_{PC}, is equal to the firm's marginal cost of production, MC_{PC}, at that quantity of output. By contrast, at the profit-maximizing quantity chosen by the monopolistically competitive firm in panel (b), Q_{MC}, the price, P_{MC}, is *higher* than the marginal cost of production, MC_{MC}.

This difference translates into a difference in the attitude of firms toward consumers. A wheat farmer, who can sell as much wheat as he likes at the going market price, would not get particularly excited if you offered to buy some more wheat at the market price. Since he has no desire to produce more at that price and can sell the wheat to someone else, you are not doing him a favor.

But if you decide to fill up your tank at Jamil's gas station rather than at Katy's, you are doing Jamil a favor. He is not willing to cut his price to get more customers—he's already made the best of that trade-off. But if he gets a few more customers than he expected at the *posted* price, that's good news: an additional sale at the posted price increases his revenue more than it increases his costs because the posted price exceeds marginal cost.

The fact that monopolistic competitors, unlike perfect competitors, want to sell more at the going price is crucial to understanding why they engage in activities like advertising that help increase sales.

The other difference between monopolistic competition and perfect competition that is visible in Figure 16-4 involves the position of each firm on its average total cost curve. In panel (a), the perfectly competitive firm produces at point Q_{PC}, at the bottom of the U-shaped *ATC* curve. That is, each firm produces the quantity at which average total cost is minimized—the *minimum-cost output*. As a consequence, the total cost of industry output is also minimized.

Under monopolistic competition, in panel (b), the firm produces at Q_{MC}, on the *downward-sloping* part of the U-shaped *ATC* curve: it produces less than the quantity that would minimize average total cost. This failure to produce enough to minimize average total cost is sometimes described as the **excess capacity** issue. The typical vendor in a food court or a gas station along a road is not big enough to take maximum advantage of available cost savings. So the total cost of industry output is not minimized in the case of a monopolistically competitive industry.

Some people have argued that, because every monopolistic competitor has excess capacity, monopolistically competitive industries are inefficient. But the issue of efficiency under monopolistic competition turns out to be a subtle one that does not have a clear answer.

Is Monopolistic Competition Inefficient?

A monopolistic competitor, like a monopolist, charges a price that is above marginal cost. As a result, some people who are willing to pay at least as much for an egg roll at Wonderful Wok as it costs to produce it are deterred from doing so. In monopolistic competition, some mutually beneficial transactions go unexploited.

Furthermore, it is often argued that monopolistic competition is subject to a further kind of inefficiency: that the excess capacity of every monopolistic competitor implies *wasteful duplication* because monopolistically competitive industries offer too many varieties. According to this argument, it would be better if there were only two or three vendors in the food court, not six or seven. If there were fewer vendors, they would each have lower average total costs and so could offer food more cheaply.

Is this argument against monopolistic competition right—that it lowers total surplus by causing inefficiency? Not necessarily. It's true that if there were fewer gas stations along a highway, each gas station would sell more gasoline and so would have lower costs per gallon. But there is a drawback: motorists would be inconvenienced because gas stations would be farther apart. The point is that the diversity of products offered in a monopolistically competitive industry is beneficial to consumers. So the higher price consumers pay because of excess capacity is offset to some extent by the value they receive from greater diversity.

There is, in other words, a trade-off: more producers means higher average total costs but also greater product diversity. Does a monopolistically competitive industry arrive at the socially optimal point on this trade-off? Probably not—but it is hard to say whether there are too many firms or too few! Most economists now believe that duplication of effort and excess capacity in monopolistically competitive industries are not important issues in practice.

> > > > > > > > > > > >

1. True or false? Explain your answers.
   a. Like a firm in a perfectly competitive industry, a firm in a monopolistically competitive industry is willing to sell a good at any price that equals or exceeds marginal cost.
   b. Suppose there is a monopolistically competitive industry in long-run equilibrium that possesses excess capacity. All the firms in the industry would be better off if they merged into a single firm and produced a single product, but whether consumers are made better off by this is ambiguous.
   c. Fads and fashions are more likely to arise in monopolistic competition or oligopoly than in monopoly or perfect competition.

Solutions appear at back of book.

Controversies about Product Differentiation

Up to this point, we have assumed that products are differentiated in a way that corresponds to some real desire of consumers. There is real convenience in having a gas station in your neighborhood; Chinese food and Mexican food are really different from each other.

In the real world, however, some instances of product differentiation can seem puzzling if you think about them. What is the real difference between Crest and Colgate toothpaste? Between Energizer and Duracell batteries? Or a Marriott and a Hilton hotel room? Most people would be hard-pressed to answer any of these questions. Yet the producers of these goods make considerable efforts to convince consumers that their products are different from and better than those of their competitors.

No discussion of product differentiation is complete without spending at least a bit of time on the two related issues—and puzzles—of *advertising* and *brand names*.

The Role of Advertising

Wheat farmers don't advertise their wares on TV, but car dealers do. That's not because farmers are shy and car dealers are outgoing; it's because advertising is worthwhile only in industries in which firms have at least some market power. The purpose of advertisements is to convince people to buy more of a seller's product at the going price. A perfectly competitive firm, which can sell as much as it likes at the going market price, has no incentive to spend money convincing consumers to buy more. Only a firm that has some market power, and which therefore charges a price that is above marginal cost, can gain from advertising. (Industries that are more or less perfectly competitive, like the milk industry, do advertise—but these ads are sponsored by an association on behalf of the industry as a whole, not on behalf of the milk that comes from the cows on a particular farm.)

Given that advertising "works," it's not hard to see why firms with market power would spend money on it. But the big question about advertising is *why* it works. A related question is whether advertising is, from society's point of view, a waste of resources.

Not all advertising poses a puzzle. Much of it is straightforward: it's a way for sellers to inform potential buyers about what they have to offer (or, occasionally, for buyers to inform potential sellers about what they want). Nor is there much controversy about the economic usefulness of ads that provide information: the real estate ad that declares "sunny, charming, 2 br, 1 ba, a/c" tells you things you need to know (even if a few euphemisms are involved—"charming," of course, means "small").

But what information is being conveyed when a TV actress proclaims the virtues of one or another toothpaste or a sports hero declares that some company's batteries are better than those inside that pink mechanical rabbit? Surely nobody believes that the sports star is an expert on batteries—or that he chose the company that he personally believes makes the best batteries, as opposed to the company that offered to pay him the most. Yet companies believe, with good reason, that money spent on such promotions increases their sales—and that they would be in big trouble if they stopped advertising but their competitors continued to do so.

Why are consumers influenced by ads that do not really provide any information about the product? One answer is that consumers are not as rational as economists typically assume. Perhaps consumers' judgments, or even their tastes, can be influenced by things that economists think ought to be irrelevant, such as which company has hired the most charismatic celebrity to endorse its product. And there is surely some truth to this. Consumer rationality is a useful working assumption; it is not an absolute truth.

However, another answer is that consumer response to advertising is not entirely irrational, because ads can serve as indirect "signals" in a world where consumers don't have good information about products. Suppose, to take a common example, that you need to avail yourself of some local service that you don't use regularly—body work on your car, say, or furniture moving. You turn to the Yellow Pages, where you see a number of small listings and several large display ads. You know that those display ads are large because the firms paid extra for them; still, it may be quite rational to call one of the firms with a big display ad. After all, the big ad probably means that it's a relatively large, successful company—otherwise, the company wouldn't have found it worth spending the money for the larger ad.

The same principle may partly explain why ads feature celebrities. You don't really believe that the supermodel prefers that watch; but the fact that the watch manufacturer is willing and able to pay her fee tells you that it is a major company that is likely to stand behind its product. According to this reasoning, an expensive advertisement serves to establish the quality of a firm's products in the eyes of consumers.

The possibility that it is rational for consumers to respond to advertising also has some bearing on the question of whether advertising is a waste of resources. If ads only work by manipulating the weak-minded, the $149 billion U.S. businesses spent on advertising in 2007 would have been an economic waste—except to the extent that ads sometimes provide entertainment. To the extent that advertising conveys important information, however, it is an economically productive activity after all.

Brand Names

You've been driving all day, and you decide that it's time to find a place to sleep. On your right, you see a sign for the Bates Motel; on your left, you see a sign for a Motel 6, or a Best Western, or some other national chain. Which one do you choose?

Unless they were familiar with the area, most people would head for the chain. In fact, most motels in the United States are members of major chains; the same is true of most fast-food restaurants and many, if not most, stores in shopping malls.

Motel chains and fast-food restaurants are only one aspect of a broader phenomenon: the role of **brand names,** names owned by particular companies that differentiate their products in the minds of consumers. In many cases, a company's brand name is the most important asset it possesses: clearly, McDonald's is worth far more than the sum of the deep-fat fryers and hamburger grills the company owns.

> A **brand name** is a name owned by a particular firm that distinguishes its products from those of other firms.

In fact, companies often go to considerable lengths to defend their brand names, suing anyone else who uses them without permission. You may talk about blowing your nose on a kleenex or xeroxing a term paper, but unless the product in question comes from Kleenex or Xerox, legally the seller must describe it as a facial tissue or a photocopier.

As with advertising, with which they are closely linked, the social usefulness of brand names is a source of dispute. Does the preference of consumers for known brands reflect consumer irrationality? Or do brand names convey real information? That is, do brand names create unnecessary market power, or do they serve a real purpose?

As in the case of advertising, the answer is probably some of both. On the one hand, brand names often do create unjustified market power. Consumers often pay more for brand-name goods in the supermarket even though consumer experts assure us that the cheaper store brands are equally good. Similarly, many common medicines, like aspirin, are cheaper—with no loss of quality—in their generic form.

On the other hand, for many products the brand name does convey information. A traveler arriving in a strange town can be sure of what awaits in a Holiday Inn or a McDonald's; a tired and hungry traveler may find this preferable to trying an independent hotel or restaurant that might be better—but might be worse.

In addition, brand names offer some assurance that the seller is engaged in repeated interaction with its customers and so has a reputation to protect. If a traveler eats a bad meal at a restaurant in a tourist trap and vows never to eat there again, the restaurant owner may not care, since the chance is small that the traveler will be in the same area again in the future. But if that traveler eats a bad meal at McDonald's and vows never to eat at a McDonald's again, that matters to the company. This gives McDonald's an incentive to provide consistent quality, thereby assuring travelers that quality controls are in place.

►*ECONOMICS IN ACTION*

Absolut Irrationality

Advertising often serves a useful function. Among other things, it can make consumers aware of a wider range of alternatives, which leads to increased competition and lower prices. Indeed, in some cases the courts have viewed industry agreements *not* to advertise as violations of antitrust law. For example, in 1995 the California Dental Association was convicted of conspiracy to prevent competition by discouraging its members from advertising. It had, according to the judge, "withheld from the public information about prices, quality, superiority of service, guarantees, and the use of procedures to allay patient anxiety."

Conversely, advertising sometimes creates product differentiation and market power where there is no real difference in the product. Consider, in particular, the spectacularly successful advertising campaign of Absolut vodka.

In *Twenty Ads That Shook the World,* James B. Twitchell puts it this way: "The pull of Absolut's magnetic advertising is curious because the product itself is so bland. Vodka is aquavit, and aquavit is the most unsophisticated of alcohols. . . . No taste, no smell. . . . In fact, the Swedes, who make the stuff, rarely drink Absolut. They prefer cheaper brands such as Explorer, Renat Brannwinn, or Skane. That's because Absolut can't advertise in Sweden, where alcohol advertising is against the law."

But here's a metaphysical question: if Absolut doesn't really taste any different from other brands, but advertising convinces consumers that they are getting a distinctive product, who are we to say that they aren't? Isn't distinctiveness in the mind of the beholder? ▲

< < < < < < < < < < < <

➤ CHECK YOUR UNDERSTANDING 16-4

1. In which of the following cases is advertising likely to be economically useful? Economically wasteful? Explain your answer.
   a. Advertisements on the benefits of aspirin
   b. Advertisements for Bayer aspirin
   c. Advertisements on the benefits of drinking orange juice
   d. Advertisements for Tropicana orange juice
   e. Advertisements that state how long a plumber or an electrician has been in business

2. Some industry analysts have stated that a successful brand name is like a barrier to entry. Explain the reasoning behind this statement.

Solutions appear at back of book.

[>> A LOOK AHEAD •••

With the end of this chapter, we complete our analysis of market structure. Having studied first consumer behavior and then producer behavior, we've constructed a detailed picture of how markets work. Although we've analyzed cases that deviate from the competitive market model—cases such as monopoly, colluding oligopolists, and differentiated monopolistic competitors—the framework we have used up until now still rests on assumptions of the competitive market model. That is, we have assumed that as long as no one can exercise market power, all mutually beneficial trades will occur and the market outcome will maximize social welfare.

But, in reality, this often isn't the case. There are indeed situations in which the market outcome *doesn't* maximize social welfare even if the market is perfectly competitive. A market in which pollution is a by-product of production or consumption is an example of this. As we mentioned in the Introduction, this is a case of market failure—situations in which markets, left to themselves, lead to inefficient outcomes. In the next chapter, we'll begin our study of the problem of market failure with the topic of *externalities,* of which pollution is an example. As we'll soon see, one of the key roles of government is to correct market failure.]

SUMMARY ■

1. **Monopolistic competition** is a market structure in which there are many competing producers, each producing a differentiated product, and there is free entry and exit in the long run. Product differentiation takes three main forms: by style or type, by location, or by quality. Products of competing sellers are considered imperfect substitutes, and each firm has its own downward-sloping demand curve and marginal revenue curve.

2. Short-run profits will attract entry of new firms in the long run. This reduces the quantity each existing producer sells at any given price and shifts its demand curve to the left. Short-run losses will induce exit by some firms in the long run. This shifts the demand curve of each remaining firm to the right.

3. In the long run, a monopolistically competitive industry is in **zero-profit equilibrium:** at its profit-maximizing quantity, the demand curve for each existing firm is tangent to its average total cost curve. There are zero profits in the industry and no entry or exit.

4. In long-run equilibrium, firms in a monopolistically competitive industry sell at a price greater than marginal cost. They also have **excess capacity** because they produce less than the minimum-cost output; as a result, they have higher costs than firms in a perfectly competitive industry. Whether or not monopolistic competition is inefficient is ambiguous because consumers value the diversity of products that it creates.

5. A monopolistically competitive firm will always prefer to make an additional sale at the going price, so it will engage in advertising to increase demand for its product and enhance its market power. Advertising and **brand names** that provide useful information to consumers are economically valuable. But they are economically wasteful when their only purpose is to create market power. In reality, advertising and brand names are likely to be some of both: economically valuable and economically wasteful.

KEY TERMS ■

Monopolistic competition, p. 416
Zero-profit equilibrium, p. 422

Excess capacity, p. 426

Brand name, p. 429

PROBLEMS ■

1. Use the three conditions for monopolistic competition discussed in the chapter to decide which of the following firms are likely to be operating as monopolistic competitors. If they are not monopolistically competitive firms, are they monopolists, oligopolists, or perfectly competitive firms?

   a. A local band that plays for weddings, parties, and so on

   b. Minute Maid, a producer of individual-serving juice boxes

   c. Your local dry cleaner

   d. A farmer who produces soybeans

2. You are thinking of setting up a coffee shop. The market structure for coffee shops is monopolistic competition. There are three Starbucks shops, and two other coffee shops very much like Starbucks, in your town already. In order for you to have some degree of market power, you may want to differentiate your coffee shop. Thinking about the three different ways in which products can be differentiated, explain how you would decide whether you should copy Starbucks or whether you should sell coffee in a completely different way.

3. The restaurant business in town is a monopolistically competitive industry in long-run equilibrium. One restaurant owner asks for your advice. She tells you that, each night, not all

tables in her restaurant are full. She also tells you that if she lowered the prices on her menu, she would attract more customers and that doing so would lower her average total cost. Should she lower her prices? Draw a diagram showing the demand curve, marginal revenue curve, marginal cost curve, and average total cost curve for this restaurant to explain your advice. Show in your diagram what would happen to the restaurant owner's profit if she were to lower the price so that she sells the minimum-cost output.

4. The market structure of the local gas station industry is monopolistic competition. Suppose that currently each gas station incurs a loss. Draw a diagram for a typical gas station to show this short-run situation. Then, in a separate diagram, show what will happen to the typical gas station in the long run. Explain your reasoning.

5. The local hairdresser industry has the market structure of monopolistic competition. Your hairdresser boasts that he is making a profit and that if he continues to do so, he will be able to retire in five years. Use a diagram to illustrate your hairdresser's current situation. Do you expect this to last? In a separate diagram, draw what you expect to happen in the long run. Explain your reasoning.

6. Magnificent Blooms is a florist in a monopolistically competitive industry. It is a successful operation, producing the quantity that minimizes its average total cost and making a profit. The owner also says that at its current level of output, its marginal cost is above marginal revenue. Illustrate the current situation of Magnificent Blooms in a diagram. Answer the following questions by illustrating with a diagram.

a. In the short run, could Magnificent Blooms increase its profit?

b. In the long run, could Magnificent Blooms increase its profit?

7. "In the long run, there is no difference between monopolistic competition and perfect competition." Discuss whether this statement is true, false, or ambiguous with respect to the following criteria:

a. The price charged to consumers

b. The average total cost of production

c. The efficiency of the market outcome

d. The typical firm's profit in the long run

8. "In both the short run and in the long run, the typical firm in monopolistic competition and a monopolist each make a profit." Do you agree with this statement? Explain your reasoning.

9. The market for clothes has the structure of monopolistic competition. What impact will fewer firms in this industry have on you as a consumer? Address the following issues:

a. Variety of clothes

b. Differences in quality of service

c. Price

10. For each of the following situations, decide whether advertising is directly informative about the product or simply an indirect signal of its quality. Explain your reasoning.

a. Golf champion Tiger Woods drives a Buick in a TV commercial and claims that he prefers it to any other car.

b. A newspaper ad states, "For sale: 1999 Honda Civic, 160,000 miles, new transmission."

c. McDonald's spends millions of dollars on an advertising campaign that proclaims: "I'm lovin' it."

d. Subway advertises one of its sandwiches by claiming that it contains 6 grams of fat and fewer than 300 calories.

11. In each of the following cases, explain how the advertisement functions as a signal to a potential buyer. Explain what information the buyer lacks that is being supplied by the advertisement and how the information supplied by the advertisement is likely to affect the buyer's willingness to buy the good.

a. "Looking for work. Excellent references from previous employers available."

b. "Electronic equipment for sale. All merchandise carries a one-year, no-questions-asked warranty."

c. "Car for sale by original owner. All repair and maintenance records available."

12. The accompanying table shows the Herfindahl–Hirschman Index (HHI) for the restaurant, cereal, movie, and laundry detergent industries as well as the advertising expenditures of the top 10 firms in each industry in 2006. Use the information in the table to answer the following questions.

Industry	HHI	Advertising expenditures (millions)
Restaurants	179	$1,784
Cereal	2,098	732
Movie studios	918	3,324
Laundry detergent	2,068	132

a. Which market structure—oligopoly or monopolistic competition—best characterizes each of the industries?

b. Based on your answer to part a, which type of market structure has higher advertising expenditures? Use the characteristics of each market structure to explain why this relationship might exist.

13. McDonald's spends millions of dollars each year on legal protection of its brand name, thereby preventing any unauthorized use of it. Explain what information this conveys to you as a consumer about the quality of McDonald's products.

www.worthpublishers.com/krugmanwells

>> Externalities

WHO'LL STOP THE RAIN?

FOR MANY PEOPLE IN THE NORTHEASTERN UNITED States, there is no better way to relax than to fish in one of the region's thousands of lakes. But in the 1960s, avid fishermen noticed something alarming: lakes that had formerly teemed with fish were now almost empty. What had happened?

The answer was acid rain, caused mainly by coal-burning power plants. When coal is burned, it releases sulfur dioxide and nitric oxide into the atmosphere; these gases react with water, producing sulfuric acid and nitric acid. The result in the Northeast, downwind from the nation's industrial heartland, was rain sometimes as acidic as lemon juice. Acid rain didn't just kill fish; it also damaged trees and crops and in time even began to dissolve limestone buildings.

You'll be glad to hear that the acid rain problem today is much less serious than it was in the 1960s. Power plants have reduced their emissions by switching to low-sulfur coal and installing scrubbers in their smokestacks. But they didn't do this out of the goodness of their hearts; they did it in response to government policy. Without such government intervention, power companies would have had no incentive to take the environmental effects of their actions into account.

When individuals impose costs on or provide benefits for others, but don't have an economic incentive to take those costs or benefits into account, economists say that *externalities* are generated. You may recall that we briefly noted this phenomenon in Chapters 1 and 4. There we stated that one of the principal sources of market failure is actions that create *side effects* that are not properly taken into account—that is, externalities. In this chapter, we'll examine the economics of externalities, seeing how they can get in the way of economic efficiency and lead to market failure, why they provide a reason for government intervention in markets, and how economic analysis can be used to guide government policy.

Because externalities arise from the side effects of actions, we need to study them from two slightly different vantage points. First, we consider the situation in which the

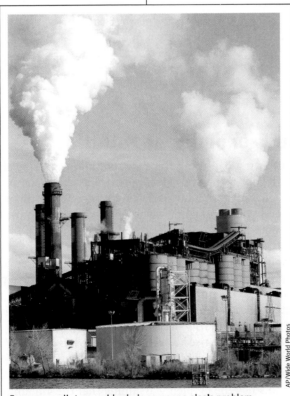

For many polluters, acid rain is someone else's problem.

AP/Wide World Photos

side effect can be directly observed and quantified. Here, we'll study the case of pollution, which generates a *negative externality*—a side effect that imposes costs on others. Whenever a side effect can be directly observed and quantified, it can be regulated: by imposing direct controls on it, by taxing it, or by subsidizing it. As we will see, government intervention in this case should be aimed directly at moving the market to the right quantity of the side effect.

But in many situations, only the original activity, not its side effect, can be observed. For example, we can't observe how many fewer cases of flu there are among your family and friends because you get a flu shot, so the government is unable to implement policies that control the side effect directly. (That is, it can't reward you based on how many fewer people caught the flu due to your decision to get vaccinated.) What it can do is employ policies that affect the *original* activity—getting a flu shot. So in the second part of our analysis, we will consider how governments can indirectly achieve the right quantity of the side effect through influencing the activity that generates it. This method is particularly important in policies directed at *positive externalities,* a side effect that generates benefits for others. In a fundamental way, however, the two approaches—targeting the side effect versus targeting the original activity—are equivalent: each one involves, at the margin, setting the benefit of doing a little bit more of something equal to the cost of doing that little bit more.

Lastly, we'll consider the case of *network externalities,* a type of side effect that's particularly common in high-tech industries. We'll learn about what creates a network externality and why industries that have them are particularly difficult to regulate.

WHAT YOU WILL LEARN IN THIS CHAPTER:

➤ What **externalities** are and why they can lead to inefficiency in a market economy and support for government intervention

➤ The difference among **negative, positive**, and **network externalities**

➤ The importance of the **Coase theorem,** which explains how private individuals can sometimes remedy externalities

➤ Why some government policies to deal with externalities, such as **emissions taxes, tradable emissions permits,** or **Pigouvian subsidies,** are efficient, although others, like **environmental standards,** are inefficient

➤ How positive externalities give rise to arguments for **industrial policy**

➤ Why **network externalities** are an important feature of high-tech industries

The Economics of Pollution

Pollution is a bad thing. Yet most pollution is a side effect of activities that provide us with good things: our air is polluted by power plants generating the electricity that lights our cities, and our rivers are damaged by fertilizer runoff from farms that grow our food. Why shouldn't we accept a certain amount of pollution as the cost of a good life?

Actually, we do. Even highly committed environmentalists don't think that we can or should completely eliminate pollution—even an environmentally conscious society would accept *some* pollution as the cost of producing useful goods and services. What environmentalists argue is that unless there is a strong and effective environmental policy, our society will generate *too much* pollution—too much of a bad thing. And the great majority of economists agree.

To see why, we need a framework that lets us think about how much pollution a society *should* have. We'll then be able to see why a market economy, left to itself, will produce more pollution than it should. We'll start by adopting the simplest framework to study the problem—assuming that the amount of pollution emitted by a polluter is directly observable and controllable.

The **marginal social cost of pollution** is the additional cost imposed on society as a whole by an additional unit of pollution.

The **marginal social benefit of pollution** is the additional gain to society as a whole from an additional unit of pollution.

The **socially optimal quantity of pollution** is the quantity of pollution that society would choose if all the costs and benefits of pollution were fully accounted for.

Costs and Benefits of Pollution

How much pollution should society allow? We learned in Chapter 9 that "how much" decisions always involve comparing the marginal benefit from an additional unit of something with the marginal cost of that additional unit. The same is true of pollution.

The **marginal social cost of pollution** is the additional cost imposed on society as a whole by an additional unit of pollution. For example, acid rain damages fisheries, crops, and forests, and each additional ton of sulfur dioxide released into the atmosphere increases the damage.

The **marginal social benefit of pollution**—the additional benefit to society from an additional unit of pollution—may seem like a confusing concept. What's good about pollution? However, avoiding pollution requires using scarce resources that could have been used to produce other goods and services. For example, to reduce the quantity of sulfur dioxide they emit, power companies must either buy expensive low-sulfur coal or install special scrubbers to remove sulfur from their emissions. The more sulfur dioxide they are allowed to emit, the lower these extra costs. Suppose we could calculate how much money the power industry would save if it were allowed to emit an additional ton of sulfur dioxide. That saving would be the marginal benefit to society of emitting an extra ton of sulfur dioxide.

Using hypothetical numbers, Figure 17-1 shows how we can determine the **socially optimal quantity of pollution**—the quantity of pollution society would choose if all its costs and benefits were fully accounted for. The upward-sloping marginal social cost curve, *MSC*, shows how the marginal cost to society of an additional ton of pollution emissions varies with the quantity of emissions. (An upward slope is likely

PITFALLS

SO HOW DO YOU MEASURE THE MARGINAL SOCIAL COST OF POLLUTION?

It might be confusing to think of marginal *social* cost—after all, we have up to this point always defined marginal cost as being incurred by an individual or a firm, not society as a whole. But it is easily understandable once we link it to the familiar concept of willingness to pay: the marginal social cost of a unit of pollution is equal to the *sum of the willingness to pay among all members of society* to avoid that unit of pollution. (It's the sum because, in general, more than one person is affected by the pollution.) But calculating the true cost to society of pollution—marginal or average—is a difficult matter, requiring a great deal of scientific knowledge, as the upcoming Economics in Action illustrates. As a result, society often underestimates the true marginal social cost of pollution.

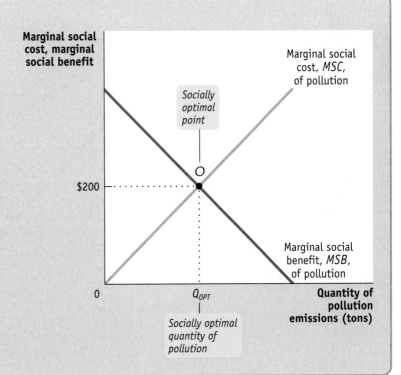

FIGURE 17-1

The Socially Optimal Quantity of Pollution

Pollution yields both costs and benefits. Here the curve *MSC* shows how the marginal cost to society as a whole from emitting one more ton of pollution emissions depends on the quantity of emissions. The curve *MSB* shows how the marginal benefit to society as a whole of emitting an additional ton of pollution emissions depends on the quantity of pollution emissions. The socially optimal quantity of pollution is Q_{OPT}; at that quantity, the marginal social benefit of pollution is equal to the marginal social cost, corresponding to $200.

PITFALLS ⊶- - - - - - - - - - - - - - - - -○

**SO HOW DO YOU MEASURE THE MAR-
GINAL SOCIAL BENEFIT OF POLLUTION?**
Similar to the problem of measuring the marginal
social cost of pollution, the concept of willingness
to pay helps us understand the marginal social
benefit of pollution in contrast to the marginal
benefit to an individual or firm. The marginal
social benefit of a unit of pollution is simply equal
to the highest willingness to pay for the right to
emit that unit measured across all polluters. But
unlike the marginal social cost of pollution, the
value of the marginal social benefit of pollution is
○ a number likely to be known—to polluters, that is.

because nature can often safely handle low levels of pollution but is
increasingly harmed as pollution reaches high levels.) The marginal social
benefit curve, *MSB*, is downward-sloping because it is progressively harder, and therefore more expensive, to achieve a further reduction in pollution as the total amount of pollution falls—increasingly more expensive
technology must be used. As a result, as pollution falls, the cost savings to
a polluter of being allowed to emit one more ton rises.

The socially optimal quantity of pollution in this example isn't zero.
It's Q_{OPT}, the quantity corresponding to point *O*, where *MSB* crosses
MSC. At Q_{OPT}, the marginal social benefit from an additional ton of
emissions and its marginal social cost are equalized at $200.

But will a market economy, left to itself, arrive at the socially optimal
quantity of pollution? No, it won't.

Pollution: An External Cost

Pollution yields both benefits and costs to society. But in a market economy without
government intervention, those who benefit from pollution—like the owners of
power companies—decide how much pollution occurs. They have no incentive to take
into account the costs of pollution that they impose on others.

To see why, remember the nature of the benefits and costs from pollution. For polluters, the benefits take the form of monetary savings: by emitting an extra ton of sulfur dioxide, any given polluter saves the cost of buying expensive, low-sulfur coal or
installing pollution-control equipment. So the benefits of pollution accrue directly to
the polluters.

The costs of pollution, though, fall on people who have no say in the decision
about how much pollution takes place: for example, people who fish in northeastern
lakes do not control the decisions of power plants.

Figure 17-2 shows the result of this asymmetry between who reaps the benefits
and who pays the costs. In a market economy without government intervention to

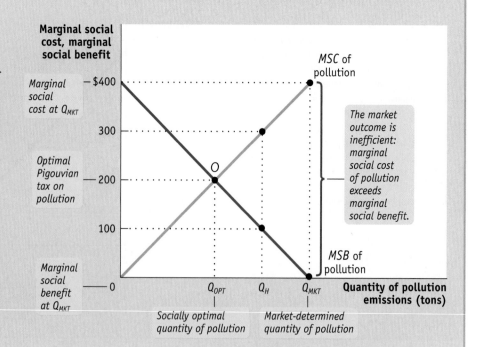

FIGURE 17-2

Why a Market Economy Produces Too Much Pollution

In the absence of government
intervention, the quantity of pollution will be Q_{MKT}, the level at which
the marginal social benefit of pollution is zero. This is an inefficiently
high quantity of pollution: the marginal social cost, $400, greatly
exceeds the marginal social benefit,
$0. An optimal Pigouvian tax of
$200, the value of the marginal
social cost of pollution when it
equals the marginal social benefit
of pollution, can move the market
to the socially optimal quantity of
pollution, Q_{OPT}.

Talking and Driving

Why is that woman in the car in front of us driving so erratically? Is she drunk? No, she's talking on her cell phone.

Traffic safety experts take the risks posed by driving while talking very seriously. Using hands-free, voice-activated phones doesn't seem to help much because the main danger is distraction. As one traffic safety consultant put it, "It's not where your eyes are; it's where your head is." And we're not talking about a trivial problem. One estimate suggests that people who talk on their cell phones while driving may be responsible for 600 or more traffic deaths each year.

The National Safety Council urges people not to use phones while driving. But a

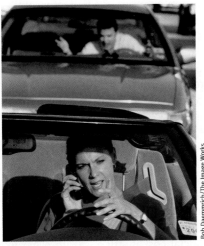

"It's not where your eyes are; it's where your head is."

growing number of people say that voluntary standards aren't enough; they want the use of cell phones while driving made illegal, as it already is in five states and the District of Columbia, as well as in Japan, Israel, and many other countries.

Why not leave the decision up to the driver? Because the risk posed by driving while talking isn't just a risk to the driver; it's also a safety risk to others—especially people in other cars. Even if you decide that the benefit to you of taking that call is worth the cost, you aren't taking into account the cost to other people. Driving while talking, in other words, generates a serious—sometimes fatal—negative externality.

protect the environment, only the benefits of pollution are taken into account in choosing the quantity of pollution. So the quantity of emissions won't be the socially optimal quantity Q_{OPT}; it will be Q_{MKT}, the quantity at which the marginal social benefit of an additional ton of pollution is zero, but the marginal social cost of that additional ton is much larger—$400. The quantity of pollution in a market economy without government intervention will be higher than its socially optimal quantity. (The Pigouvian tax noted in Figure 17-2 will be explained shortly.)

The reason is that in the absence of government intervention, those who derive the benefits from pollution—in this case, the owners of power plants—don't have to compensate those who bear the costs. So the marginal cost of pollution to any given polluter is zero: polluters have no incentive to limit the amount of emissions. For example, before the Clean Air Act of 1970, midwestern power plants used the cheapest type of coal available, despite the fact that cheap coal generated more pollution, and they did nothing to scrub their emissions.

The environmental costs of pollution are the best-known and most important example of an **external cost**—an uncompensated cost that an individual or firm imposes on others. There are many other examples of external costs besides pollution. Another important, and certainly very familiar, external cost is traffic congestion—an individual who chooses to drive during rush hour increases congestion and so increases the travel time of other drivers.

We'll see later in this chapter that there are also important examples of **external benefits,** benefits that individuals or firms confer on others without receiving compensation. External costs and benefits are jointly known as **externalities,** with external costs called **negative externalities** and external benefits called **positive externalities.**

As we've already suggested, externalities can lead to individual decisions that are not optimal for society as a whole. Let's take a closer look at why, focusing on the case of pollution.

The Inefficiency of Excess Pollution

We have just shown that in the absence of government action, the quantity of pollution will be *inefficient*: polluters will pollute up to the point at which the marginal social benefit of pollution is zero, as shown by the pollution quantity, Q_{MKT}, in

An **external cost** is an uncompensated cost that an individual or firm imposes on others.

An **external benefit** is a benefit that an individual or firm confers on others without receiving compensation.

External costs and benefits are known as **externalities.** External costs are **negative externalities,** and external benefits are **positive externalities.**

According to the **Coase theorem,** even in the presence of externalities an economy can always reach an efficient solution as long as **transaction costs**— the costs to individuals of making a deal—are sufficiently low.

When individuals take external costs or benefits into account, they **internalize the externality.**

Figure 17-2. Recall that an outcome is inefficient if some people could be made better off without making others worse off. In Chapter 4 we showed why the market equilibrium quantity in a perfectly competitive market is the efficient quantity of the good, the quantity that maximizes total surplus. Here, we can use a variation of that analysis to show how the presence of a negative externality upsets that result.

Because the marginal social benefit of pollution is zero at Q_{MKT}, reducing the quantity of pollution by one ton would subtract very little from the total social benefit from pollution. In other words, the benefit to polluters from that last unit of pollution is very low—virtually zero. Meanwhile, the marginal social cost imposed on the rest of society of that last ton of pollution at Q_{MKT} is quite high—$400. In other words, by reducing the quantity of pollution at Q_{MKT} by one ton, the total social cost of pollution falls by $400, but total social benefit falls by virtually zero. So total surplus rises by approximately $400 if the quantity of pollution at Q_{MKT} is reduced by one ton.

If the quantity of pollution is reduced further, there will be more gains in total surplus, though they will be smaller. For example, if the quantity of pollution is Q_H in Figure 17-2, the marginal social benefit of a ton of pollution is $100, but the marginal social cost is still $300. In other words, reducing the quantity of pollution by one ton leads to a net gain in total surplus of approximately $300 − $100 = $200. This tells us that Q_H is still an inefficiently high quantity of pollution. Only if the quantity of pollution is reduced to Q_{OPT}, where the marginal social cost and the marginal social benefit of an additional ton of pollution are both $200, is the outcome efficient.

Private Solutions to Externalities

Can the private sector solve the problem of externalities without government intervention? Bear in mind that when an outcome is inefficient, there is potentially a deal that makes people better off. Why don't individuals find a way to make that deal?

In an influential 1960 article, the economist and Nobel laureate Ronald Coase pointed out that in an ideal world the private sector could indeed deal with all externalities. According to the **Coase theorem,** even in the presence of externalities an economy can always reach an efficient solution provided that the costs of making a deal are sufficiently low. The costs of making a deal are known as **transaction costs.**

To get a sense of Coase's argument, imagine two neighbors, Mick and Christina, who both like to barbecue in their backyards on summer afternoons. Mick likes to play golden oldies on his boombox while barbecuing, but this annoys Christina, who can't stand that kind of music.

Who prevails? You might think that it depends on the legal rights involved in the case: if the law says that Mick has the right to play whatever music he wants, Christina just has to suffer; if the law says that Mick needs Christina's consent to play music in his backyard, Mick has to live without his favorite music while barbecuing.

But as Coase pointed out, the outcome need not be determined by legal rights, because Christina and Mick can make a private deal. Even if Mick has the right to play his music, Christina could pay him not to. Even if Mick can't play the music without an OK from Christina, he can offer to pay her to give that OK. These payments allow them to reach an efficient solution, regardless of who has the legal upper hand. If the benefit of the music to Mick exceeds its cost to Christina, the music will go on; if the benefit to Mick is less than the cost to Christina, there will be silence.

The implication of Coase's analysis is that externalities need not lead to inefficiency because individuals have an incentive to make mutually beneficial deals—deals that lead them to take externalities into account when making decisions. When individuals *do* take externalities into account when making decisions, economists say that they **internalize the externality.** If externalities are fully internalized, the outcome is efficient even without government intervention.

Why can't individuals always internalize externalities? Our barbecue example implicity assumes the transaction costs are low enough for Mick and Christina to be able to make a deal. In many situations involving externalities, however, transaction costs prevent individuals from making efficient deals. Examples of transaction costs include the following:

- *The costs of communication among the interested parties.* Such costs may be very high if many people are involved.

- *The costs of making legally binding agreements.* Such costs may be high if expensive legal services are required.

- *Costly delays involved in bargaining.* Even if there is a potentially beneficial deal, both sides may hold out in an effort to extract more favorable terms, leading to increased effort and forgone utility.

In some cases, people do find ways to reduce transaction costs, allowing them to internalize externalities. For example, a house with a junk-filled yard and peeling paint has a negative externality on the neighboring houses, diminishing their value in the eyes of potential house buyers. So many people live in private communities that set rules for home maintenance and behavior, making bargaining between neighbors unnecessary. But in many other cases, transaction costs are too high to make it possible to deal with externalities through private action. For example, tens of millions of people are adversely affected by acid rain. It would be prohibitively expensive to try to make a deal among all those people and all those power companies.

When transaction costs prevent the private sector from dealing with externalities, it is time to look for government solutions. We turn to public policy in the next section.

►*ECONOMICS IN ACTION*
....

Thank You for Not Smoking

New Yorkers call them the "shiver-and-puff people"—the smokers who stand outside their workplaces, even in the depths of winter, to take a cigarette break. Over the past couple of decades, rules against smoking in spaces shared by others have become ever stricter. This is partly a matter of personal dislike—nonsmokers really don't like to smell other people's cigarette smoke—but it also reflects concerns over the health risks of second-hand smoke. As the Surgeon General's warning on many packs says, "Smoking causes lung cancer, heart disease, emphysema, and may complicate pregnancy." And there's no question that being in the same room as someone who smokes exposes you to at least some health risk.

Second-hand smoke, then, is clearly an example of a negative externality. But how important is it? Putting a dollar-and-cents value on it—that is, measuring the marginal social cost of cigarette smoke—requires not only estimating the health effects but putting a value on these effects. Despite the difficulty, economists have tried. A paper published in 1993 in the *Journal of Economic Perspectives* surveyed the research on the external costs of both cigarette smoking and alcohol consumption.

According to this paper, valuing the health costs of cigarettes depends on whether you count the costs imposed on members of smokers' families, including unborn children, in addition to costs borne by smokers. If you don't, the external costs of second-hand smoke have been estimated at about only $0.19 per pack smoked. (Using this method of calculation, $0.19 corresponds to the *average* social cost of smoking per pack at the current level of smoking in society.) A 2005 study raised this estimate to $0.52 per pack smoked. If you include effects on smokers' families, the number rises considerably—family members who live with smokers are exposed to a lot more smoke. (They are also exposed to the risk of

►►QUICK REVIEW

➤ There are costs as well as benefits to reducing pollution, so the optimal quantity of pollution isn't zero. Instead, the **socially optimal quantity of pollution** is the quantity at which the **marginal social cost of pollution** is equal to the **marginal social benefit of pollution.**

➤ Left to itself, a market economy will typically generate too much pollution because polluters have no incentive to take into account the costs they impose on others.

➤ External costs and benefits are known as **externalities.** Pollution is an example of an **external cost,** or **negative externality;** in contrast, some activities can give rise to **external benefits,** or **positive externalities.**

➤ According to the **Coase theorem,** the private sector can sometimes resolve externalities on its own: if **transaction costs** aren't too high, individuals can reach a deal to **internalize the externality.** When transaction costs are too high, government intervention may be warranted.

fires, which alone is estimated at $0.09 per pack.) If you include the effects of smoking by pregnant women on their unborn children's future health, the cost is immense—$4.80 per pack, which is more than twice the wholesale price charged by cigarette manufacturers.

(See source note on copyright page.) ▲

< < < < < < < < < < < <

► **CHECK YOUR UNDERSTANDING** 17-1

1. Wastewater runoff from large poultry farms adversely affects their neighbors. Explain the following:
   a. The nature of the external cost imposed
   b. The outcome in the absence of government intervention or a private deal
   c. The socially optimal outcome

2. According to Yasmin, any student who borrows a book from the university library and fails to return it on time imposes a negative externality on other students. She claims that rather than charging a modest fine for late returns, the library should charge a huge fine, so that borrowers will never return a book late. Is Yasmin's economic reasoning correct?

Solutions appear at back of book.

Policies Toward Pollution

Before 1970, there were no rules governing the amount of sulfur dioxide power plants in the United States could emit—which is why acid rain got to be such a problem. After 1970, the Clean Air Act set rules about sulfur dioxide emissions—and the acidity of rainfall declined significantly. Economists argued, however, that a more flexible system of rules that exploited the effectiveness of markets could achieve lower pollution at less cost. In 1990 this theory was put into effect with a modified version of the Clean Air Act. And guess what? The economists were right!

In this section we'll look at the policies governments use to deal with pollution and at how economic analysis has been used to improve those policies.

Environmental Standards

The most serious external costs in the modern world are surely those associated with actions that damage the environment—air pollution, water pollution, habitat destruction, and so on. Protection of the environment has become a major role of government in all advanced nations. In the United States, the Environmental Protection Agency is the principal enforcer of environmental policies at the national level, supported by the actions of state and local governments.

How does a country protect its environment? At present the main policy tools are **environmental standards,** rules that protect the environment by specifying actions by producers and consumers. A familiar example is the law that requires almost all vehicles to have catalytic converters, which reduce the emission of chemicals that can cause smog and lead to health problems. Other rules require communities to treat their sewage or factories to avoid or limit certain kinds of pollution, and so on.

Environmental standards came into widespread use in the 1960s and 1970s, and they have had considerable success in reducing pollution. For example, since the United States passed the Clean Air Act in 1970, overall emission of pollutants into the air has fallen by more than a third, even though the population has grown by a third and the size of the economy has more than doubled. Even in Los Angeles, still famous for its smog, the air has improved dramatically: in 1988 ozone levels in the South Coast Air Basin exceeded federal standards on 178 days; in 2006, on only 35 days.

Environmental standards are rules that protect the environment by specifying actions by producers and consumers.

GLOBAL COMPARISON · ECONOMIC GROWTH AND GREENHOUSE GASES IN FIVE COUNTRIES

At first glance, a comparison of the per capita greenhouse gas emissions of various countries, shown in panel (a) of this graph, suggests that the United States, Canada, and Australia are the worst offenders. The average American is responsible for 23.7 tonnes of greenhouse gas emissions (measured in CO_2 equivalents)—the pollution that causes global warming—compared to only 3.3 tonnes for the average Chinese and 1.3 tonnes for the average Indian. (A tonne, also called a metric ton, equals 1.10 ton.) Such a conclusion, however, ignores an important factor in determining the level of a country's greenhouse gas emissions: its gross domestic product, or GDP—the total value of a country's domestic output. Output typically cannot be produced without more energy, and more energy usage typically results in more pollution. In fact, some have argued that criticizing a country's level of greenhouse gases without taking account of its level of economic development is misguided. It would be equivalent to faulting a country for being at a more advanced stage of economic development.

A more meaningful way to compare pollution across countries is to measure emissions per $1,000 of a country's GDP, as shown in panel (b). On this basis, the United States, Canada,

and Australia are now "green" countries, but China and India are not. What explains the reversal once GDP is accounted for? The answer: both economics and government behavior. First, there is the issue of economics. Countries that are poor and have begun to industrialize, such as China and India, often view money spent to reduce pollution as better spent on other things. From their perspective, they are still too poor to afford as clean an environment as wealthy advanced countries. They claim that to impose a wealthy country's environmental standards on them would jeopardize their economic growth. Second, there is the issue of government behavior—or more precisely, whether or not a government possesses the tools necessary to effectively control pollution. China is a good illustration of this problem. The Chinese government lacks sufficient regulatory power to enforce its own environmental rules, promote energy conservation, or encourage pollution reduction. To produce $1 of GDP, China spends three times the world average on energy—far more than Indonesia, for example, which is also a poor country. The case of China illustrates just how important government intervention is in improving society's welfare in the presence of externalities.

Despite these successes, economists believe that when regulators can control a polluter's emissions directly, there are more efficient ways than environmental standards to deal with pollution. By using methods grounded in economic analysis, society can achieve a cleaner environment at lower cost. Most current environmental standards are inflexible and don't allow reductions in pollution to be achieved at minimum cost. For example, two power plants—plant A and plant B—might be ordered to reduce pollution by the same percentage, even if their costs of achieving that objective are very different.

How does economic theory suggest that pollution should be directly controlled? There are actually two approaches: taxes and tradable permits. As we'll see, either approach can achieve the efficient outcome at the minimum feasible cost.

An **emissions tax** is a tax that depends on the amount of pollution a firm produces.

Emissions Taxes

One way to deal with pollution directly is to charge polluters an **emissions tax.** Emissions taxes are taxes that depend on the amount of pollution a firm produces. For example, power plants might be charged $200 for every ton of sulfur dioxide they emit.

Look again at Figure 17-2, which shows that the socially optimal quantity of pollution is Q_{OPT}. At that quantity of pollution, the marginal social benefit and marginal social cost of an additional ton of emissions are equal at $200. But in the absence of government intervention, power companies have no incentive to limit pollution to the socially optimal quantity Q_{OPT}; instead, they will push pollution up to the quantity Q_{MKT}, at which marginal social benefit is zero.

It's now easy to see how an emissions tax can solve the problem. If power companies are required to pay a tax of $200 per ton of emissions, they now face a marginal cost of $200 per ton and have an incentive to reduce emissions to Q_{OPT}, the socially optimal quantity. This illustrates a general result: an emissions tax equal to the marginal social cost at the socially optimal quantity of pollution induces polluters to internalize the externality—to take into account the true costs to society of their actions.

Why is an emissions tax an efficient way (that is, a cost-minimizing way) to reduce pollution but environmental standards generally are not? Because an emissions tax ensures that the marginal benefit of pollution is equal for all sources of pollution, but an environmental standard does not. Figure 17-3 shows a hypothetical industry consisting of only two plants, plant A and plant B. We'll assume that plant A uses newer technology than plant B and so has a lower cost of reducing pollution. Reflecting this difference in costs, plant A's marginal benefit of pollution curve, MB_A, lies below plant B's marginal benefit of pollution curve, MB_B. Because it is more costly for plant B to reduce its pollution at any output quantity, an additional ton of pollution is worth more to plant B than to plant A.

In the absence of government action, we know that polluters will pollute until the marginal social benefit of an additional unit of emissions is equal to zero. Recall that the marginal social benefit of pollution is the cost savings, at the margin, to polluters of an additional unit of pollution. As a result, without government intervention each plant will pollute until its own marginal benefit of pollution is equal to zero. This corresponds to an emissions quantity of 600 tons each for plants A and B—the quantity of pollution at which MB_A and MB_B are each equal to zero. So although plant A and plant B value a ton of emissions differently, without government action they will each choose to emit the same amount of pollution.

Now suppose that the government decides that overall pollution from this industry should be cut in half, from 1,200 tons to 600 tons. Panel (a) of Figure 17-3 shows how this might be achieved with an environmental standard that requires each plant to cut its emissions in half, from 600 to 300 tons. The standard has the desired effect of reducing overall emissions from 1,200 to 600 tons but accomplishes it in an inefficient way. As you can see from panel (a), the environmental standard leads plant A to produce at point S_A, where its marginal benefit of pollution is $150, but plant B produces at point S_B, where its marginal benefit of pollution is twice as high, $300.

This difference in marginal benefits between the two plants tells us that the same quantity of pollution can be achieved at lower total cost by allowing plant B to pollute more than 300 tons but inducing plant A to pollute less. In fact, the efficient way to reduce pollution is to ensure that at the industry-wide outcome, the marginal benefit of pollution is the same for all plants. When each plant values a unit of pollution equally, there is no way to rearrange pollution reduction among the various plants that achieves the optimal quantity of pollution at a lower total cost.

| FIGURE 17-3 | Environmental Standards Versus Emissions Taxes |

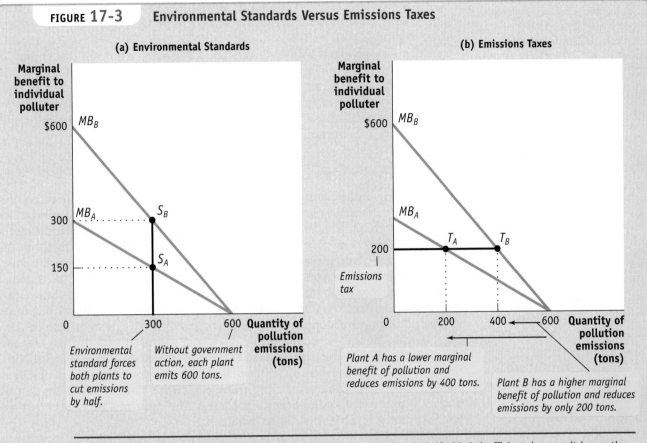

(a) Environmental Standards

Marginal benefit to individual polluter

MB_B

$600

MB_A S_B

300

S_A

150

0   300   600   **Quantity of pollution emissions (tons)**

Environmental standard forces both plants to cut emissions by half.

Without government action, each plant emits 600 tons.

(b) Emissions Taxes

Marginal benefit to individual polluter

MB_B

$600

MB_A

T_A T_B

200

Emissions tax

0   200   400 ◄   600   **Quantity of pollution emissions (tons)**

Plant A has a lower marginal benefit of pollution and reduces emissions by 400 tons.

Plant B has a higher marginal benefit of pollution and reduces emissions by only 200 tons.

In both panels, MB_A shows the marginal benefit of pollution to plant A and MB_B shows the marginal benefit of pollution to plant B. In the absence of government intervention, each plant would emit 600 tons. However, the cost of reducing emissions is lower for plant A, as shown by the fact that MB_A lies below MB_B. Panel (a) shows the result of an environmental standard that requires both plants to cut emissions in half; this is inefficient, because it leaves the marginal benefit of pollution higher for plant B than for plant A. Panel (b) shows that an emissions tax achieves the same quantity of overall pollution efficiently: faced with an emissions tax of $200 per ton, both plants reduce pollution to the point where its marginal benefit is $200.

We can see from panel (b) how an emissions tax achieves exactly that result. Suppose both plant A and plant B pay an emissions tax of $200 per ton, so that the marginal cost of an additional ton of emissions to each plant is now $200 rather than zero. As a result, plant A produces at T_A and plant B produces at T_B. So plant A reduces its pollution more than it would under an inflexible environmental standard, cutting its emissions from 600 to 200 tons; meanwhile, plant B reduces its pollution less, going from 600 to 400 tons. In the end, total pollution—600 tons—is the same as under the environmental standard, but total surplus is higher. That's because the reduction in pollution has been achieved efficiently, allocating most of the reduction to plant A, the plant that can reduce emissions at lower cost.

The term *emissions tax* may convey the misleading impression that taxes are a solution to only one kind of external cost, pollution. In fact, taxes can be used to discourage any activity that generates negative externalities, such as driving during rush hour or operating a noisy bar in a residential area. In general, taxes designed to reduce external costs are known as **Pigouvian taxes,** after the economist A. C. Pigou, who emphasized their usefulness in a classic 1920 book, *The Economics of*

Taxes designed to reduce external costs are known as **Pigouvian taxes.**

Tradable emissions permits are licenses to emit limited quantities of pollutants that can be bought and sold by polluters.

Welfare. In our example, the optimal Pigouvian tax is $200; as you can see from Figure 17-2, this corresponds to the marginal social cost of pollution at the optimal output quantity, Q_{OPT}.

Are there any problems with emissions taxes? The main concern is that in practice government officials usually aren't sure how high the tax should be set. If they set the tax too low, there will be too little improvement in the environment; if they set it too high, emissions will be reduced by more than is efficient. This uncertainty cannot be eliminated, but the nature of the risks can be changed by using an alternative strategy, issuing tradable emissions permits.

Tradable Emissions Permits

Tradable emissions permits are licenses to emit limited quantities of pollutants that can be bought and sold by polluters. They are usually issued to polluting firms according to some formula reflecting their history. For example, each power plant might be issued permits equal to 50% of its emissions before the system went into effect. The more important point, however, is that these permits are *tradable*. Firms with differing costs of reducing pollution can now engage in mutually beneficial transactions: those that find it easier to reduce pollution will sell some of their permits to those that find it more difficult. In other words, firms will use transactions in permits to reallocate pollution reduction among themselves, so that in the end those with the lowest cost will reduce their pollution the most, and those with the highest cost will reduce their pollution the least. Assume that the government issues 300 licenses each to plant A and plant B, where one license allows the emission of one ton of pollution. Under a system of tradable emissions permits, plant A will find it profitable to sell 100 of its 300 government-issued licenses to plant B. The effect of a tradable permit system is to create a market in rights to pollute.

Just like emissions taxes, tradable permits provide polluters with an incentive to take the marginal social cost of pollution into account. To see why, suppose that the market price of a permit to emit one ton of sulfur dioxide is $200. Then every plant has an incentive to limit its emissions of sulfur dioxide to the point where its marginal benefit of emitting another ton of pollution is $200. This is obvious for plants that buy rights to pollute: if a plant must pay $200 for the right to emit an additional ton of sulfur dioxide, it faces the same incentives as a plant facing an emissions tax of $200 per ton. But it's equally true for plants that have more permits than they plan to use: by *not* emitting a ton of sulfur dioxide, a plant frees up a permit that it can sell for $200, so the opportunity cost of a ton of emissions to the plant's owner is $200.

In short, tradable emissions permits have the same cost-minimizing advantage as emissions taxes over environmental standards: either system ensures that those who can reduce pollution most cheaply are the ones who do so. The socially optimal quantity of pollution shown in Figure 17-2 could be efficiently achieved either way: by imposing an emissions tax of $200 per ton of pollution or by issuing tradable permits to emit Q_{OPT} tons of pollution. If regulators choose to issue Q_{OPT} permits, where one permit allows the release of one ton of emissions, then the equilibrium market price of a permit among polluters will indeed be $200. Why? You can see from Figure 17-2 that at Q_{OPT}, only polluters with a marginal benefit of pollution of $200 or more will buy a permit. And the last polluter who buys—who has a marginal benefit of exactly $200—sets the market price.

It's important to realize that emissions taxes and tradable permits do more than induce polluting industries to reduce their output. Unlike rigid environmental standards, emissions taxes and tradable permits provide incentives to create and use technology that emits less pollution—new technology that lowers the socially optimal level of pollution. The main effect of the permit system for sulfur dioxide has been to change *how* electricity is produced rather than to reduce the nation's electricity output. For example, power companies have shifted to the use of alternative fuels such as low-sulfur coal and natural gas; they have also installed scrubbers that take much of the sulfur dioxide out of a power plant's emissions.

The main problem with tradable emissions permits is the flip-side of the problem with emissions taxes: because it is difficult to determine the optimal quantity of pollution, governments can find themselves either issuing too many permits (that is, they don't reduce pollution enough) or issuing too few (that is, they reduce pollution too much).

After first relying on environmental standards, the U.S. government has turned to a system of tradable permits to control acid rain. Current proposals would extend the system to other major sources of pollution. And in 2005 the European Union created the largest emissions-trading scheme, with the purpose of controlling emissions of carbon dioxide, also known as greenhouse gases. The EU scheme is part of a larger global market for the trading of greenhouse gas permits. The Economics in Action that follows describes these two systems in greater detail.

►ECONOMICS IN ACTION

Cap and Trade

The tradable emissions permit systems for both acid rain in the United States and greenhouse gases in the European Union are examples of *cap and trade systems:* the government sets a *cap* (a total amount of pollutant that can be emitted), issues tradable emissions permits, and enforces a yearly rule that a polluter must hold a number of permits equal to the amount of pollutant emitted. The goal is to set the cap low enough to generate environmental benefits and, at the same time, to give polluters flexibility in meeting environmental standards and motivate them to adopt new technologies that will lower the cost of reducing pollution.

In 1994 the United States began a cap and trade system for the sulfur dioxide emissions that cause acid rain by issuing permits to power plants based on their historical consumption of coal. Thanks to the system, it's estimated that by 2010 we will enjoy the benefits of a 50% reduction in acid rain from 1980 levels. Economists who have analyzed the sulfur dioxide cap and trade system point to another reason for its success: it would have been a lot more expensive—80% more to be exact—to reduce emissions by this much using a non-market-based regulatory policy.

The EU cap and trade scheme is the world's only mandatory trading scheme for greenhouse gases and covers all 27 member nations of the European Union. Available data indicate that within the system 321 metric tons of emissions were transacted in 2005 and 1,101 metric tons in 2006, an astonishing increase of 243%. Although it is still too early to evaluate the system's performance, at the time of writing the U.S. Senate was impressed enough with the preliminary results to consider proposing an American cap and trade system for greenhouse gases.

Despite all this good news, however, cap and trade systems are not silver bullets for the world's pollution problems. Although they are appropriate for pollution that's geographically dispersed, like sulfur dioxide and greenhouse gases, they don't work for pollution that's localized, like mercury or lead contamination. In addition, the amount of overall reduction in pollution depends on the level of the cap. Under industry pressure, regulators run the risk of issuing too many permits, effectively eliminating the cap. Finally, there must be vigilant monitoring of compliance if the system is to work. Without oversight of how much a polluter is actually emitting, there is no way to know for sure that the rules are being followed. ▲

> > > > > > > > > > > >

1. Some opponents of tradable emissions permits object to them on the grounds that polluters that sell their permits benefit monetarily from their contribution to polluting the environment. Assess this argument.

2. Explain the following:
   a. Why an emissions tax smaller than or greater than the marginal social cost at Q_{OPT} reduces total surplus compared to the total surplus if the emissions tax had been set optimally.
   b. Why a system of tradable emissions permits that sets the total quantity of allowable pollution higher or lower than Q_{OPT} reduces total surplus compared to the total surplus if the number of permits had been set optimally.

Solutions appear at back of book.

Production, Consumption, and Externalities

Nobody imposes external costs like pollution out of malice. Pollution, traffic congestion, and other harmful externalities are side effects of activities, like electricity generation or driving, that are otherwise desirable. We've just learned how government regulators can move the market to the socially optimal quantity when the side effect can be directly controlled. But as we cautioned earlier, in some cases it's not possible to directly control the side effect; only the original activity can be influenced. As we'll see shortly, government policies in these situations must instead be geared to changing the quantity of the original activity, which in turn changes the quantity of the side effect produced.

This approach, although slightly more complicated, has several advantages. First, for activities that generate external *costs*, it gives us a clear understanding of how the quantity of the original, desirable activity is altered by policies designed to manage its side effects (which will, in fact, typically occur both when the side effect can be directly controlled and when it can't). Second, it helps us think about a phenomenon that is different but related to the problem of external costs: what should be done when an activity generates external *benefits*. It's important to realize that not all externalities are negative. There are, in fact, many positive externalities that we encounter every day; for example, a neighbor's bird-feeder has the side effect of maintaining the local wild bird population for everyone's enjoyment. Using the approach of targeting the original activity, we'll now turn our attention to the topic of positive externalities.

Private versus Social Benefits

At the beginning of the chapter, we pointed out that getting a flu shot has benefits to people beyond the person getting the shot. Under some conditions, getting a flu vaccination reduces the expected number of *other* people who get the flu by as much as 1.5. This prompted one economist to suggest a new T-shirt slogan, one particularly suited for the winter months: "Kiss Me, I'm Vaccinated!" When you get vaccinated against the flu, it's likely that you're conferring a substantial benefit on those around you—a benefit for others that you are not compensated for. In other words, getting a flu shot generates a positive externality.

The government can directly control the external costs of pollution because it can measure emissions. In contrast, it can't observe the reduction in flu cases caused by you getting a flu shot, so it can't directly control the external benefits—say, by rewarding you based on how many fewer people caught the flu because of your actions. So if the government wants to influence the level of external benefits from flu vaccinations, it must target the original activity—getting a flu shot.

From the point of view of society as a whole, a flu shot carries both costs (the price you pay for the shot, which compensates the vaccine maker and your health care provider for the inputs and factors of production necessary to grow the vaccine and deliver it to your bloodstream) and benefits. Those benefits are the private benefit that accrues to you from not getting the flu yourself, but they also include the external benefits that accrue to others from a lower likelihood of catching the flu. However, you have no incentive to take into account the beneficial side effects that are generated by your actions. As a result, in the absence of government intervention, too few people will choose to be vaccinated.

Panel (a) of Figure 17-4 illustrates this point. The market demand curve for flu shots is represented by the curve D; the market, or industry, supply curve is given by the curve S. In the absence of government intervention, market equilibrium will be at point E_{MKT}, yielding the amount produced and consumed (that is, flu shots) Q_{MKT} and the market price P_{MKT}. At that point, the marginal cost to society of another flu shot is equal to the marginal benefit *gained by the individual consumer who purchases that flu shot*, measured by the market price.

However, when there are external benefits, the demand curve does not reflect the true benefit to society of consumption of the good. That's because the demand curve represents the marginal benefit that accrues to *consumers of the good*: each point on the demand curve, D, corresponds to the willingness to pay of the last consumer to purchase the good at the corresponding price. But it does not incorporate the benefits to society as a whole from consuming the good—in this case, the reduction in the number of flu cases.

In order to account for the true benefit to society of another additional unit consumed of the good (that is, another flu shot performed), we must define the

FIGURE 17-4 **Positive Externalities and Consumption**

(a) Positive Externality

(b) Optimal Pigouvian Subsidy

Consumption of flu shots generates external benefits, so the marginal social benefit curve, *MSB*, of flu shots, corresponds to the demand curve, *D*, shifted upward by the marginal external benefit. Panel (a) shows that without government action, the market produces Q_{MKT}. It is lower than the socially optimal quantity of consumption, Q_{OPT}, the quantity at which

MSB crosses the supply curve, *S*. At Q_{MKT}, the marginal social benefit of another flu shot, P_{MSB}, is greater than the marginal benefit to consumers of another flu shot, P_{MKT}. Panel (b) shows how an optimal Pigouvian subsidy to consumers, equal to the marginal external benefit, moves consumption to Q_{OPT} by lowering the price paid by consumers.

The **marginal social benefit of a good or activity** is equal to the marginal benefit that accrues to consumers plus its marginal external benefit.

A **Pigouvian subsidy** is a payment designed to encourage activities that yield external benefits.

A **technology spillover** is an external benefit that results when knowledge spreads among individuals and firms.

An **industrial policy** is a policy that supports industries believed to yield positive externalities.

marginal social benefit of a good or activity—the marginal benefit that accrues to consumers from an additional unit of the good or activity, plus the marginal external benefit to society from an additional unit. As you can see from panel (a) of Figure 17-4, the marginal social benefit curve, MSB, corresponds to the demand curve, D, *shifted upward* by the amount of the marginal external benefit. With the marginal social benefit curve and the supply curve, we can find the socially optimal quantity of a good or activity that generates external benefits: it is the quantity Q_{OPT}, the quantity corresponding to O, the point at which MSB and S cross. Reflecting the proper accounting for the external benefit, Q_{OPT} is greater than Q_{MKT}; it's the quantity at which the marginal cost of production (measured by S) is equal to the marginal social benefit (measured by MSB). So left to its own, a market will result in too little production and consumption of a good or activity that generates external benefits. Correspondingly, without government action, the price to consumers of such a good or activity is too high: at the market output level Q_{MKT}, the unregulated market price is P_{MKT} and the marginal benefit to consumers of an additional flu shot is lower than P_{MSB}, the true marginal benefit to society of an additional flu shot.

How can the economy be induced to produce Q_{OPT}, the socially optimal level of flu shots? The answer is a **Pigouvian subsidy:** a payment designed to encourage activities that yield external benefits. The optimal Pigouvian subsidy, shown in panel (b) of Figure 17-4, is equal to the marginal external benefit of consuming another unit of flu shots. In this example, a Pigouvian subsidy works by lowering the price to consumers of consuming the good: consumers pay a price for a flu shot that is equal to the market price *minus* the subsidy. In 2001, Japan began a program of subsidizing 71% of the cost of flu shots for the elderly in large cities. A 2005 study found that the subsidy significantly reduced the incidence of pneumonia- and influenza-caused mortality, at a net benefit to Japanese society of $1.08 billion dollars.

The most important single source of external benefits in the modern economy is the creation of knowledge. In high-tech industries like semiconductors, software design, and bioengineering, innovations by one firm are quickly emulated and improved upon by rival firms and by firms in other industries. Such spreading of knowledge among individuals and firms is known as **technology spillover.** Such spillovers often take place through face-to-face contact. For example, bars and restaurants in California's Silicon Valley are famed for their technical gossip. Workers in the industry know that the best way to keep up with the latest technological innovations is to hang around in the right places, have a drink, and gossip. Such informal contact helps to spread useful knowledge, which may also explain why so many high-tech firms are clustered close to one another.

The existence of technology spillovers often leads to calls for **industrial policy,** a general term for a policy of supporting industries believed to yield positive externalities. The principal tools of industrial policy are to subsidize production by firms in the industry or to hinder competition from foreign firms by imposing trade restrictions. Although the economic logic behind industrial policy is impeccable, economists are generally less enthusiastic about industrial policies that promote positive externalities than they are about policies that discourage negative externalities. This lack of enthusiasm reflects a mixture of practical and political judgments. First, positive externalities are typically much harder to identify and measure than negative externalities. In addition, producers gain monetarily from industrial policy: they receive a higher price than they otherwise would. So many economists also fear, with some historical justification, that a program intended to promote industries that yield positive externalities will degenerate into a program that promotes industries with political pull.

However, there is one activity that is widely believed to generate positive externalities and is provided with considerable subsidies: education, which we will examine in the Economics in Action at the end of this section.

Private versus Social Costs

Now let's turn briefly to consider a case in which production of a good creates external costs—namely, the livestock industry. Whatever it is—cows, pigs, chicken, sheep, or salmon—livestock farming produces prodigious amounts of what is euphemistically known as "muck." But that's not all: scientists estimate that the amount of methane gas produced by livestock currently rivals the amount caused by the burning of fossil fuels in the creation of greenhouse gases. From the point of view of society as a whole, then, the cost of livestock farming includes both direct production costs (payments for factors of production and inputs) and the external environmental costs imposed as a by-product.

In order to account for the true cost to society of production of an additional unit of livestock, we must define the **marginal social cost of a good or activity,** which is equal to the marginal cost of production plus the marginal external cost generated by an additional unit of the good or activity. Panel (a) in Figure 17-5 shows the marginal social cost curve, *MSC*, of livestock; it corresponds to the industry supply curve, *S, shifted upward* by the amount of the marginal external cost. (Recall that in a competitive industry, the industry supply curve is the horizontal sum of the individual firms' supply curves, which are the same as their marginal cost curves.) In the absence of government intervention, the market equilibrium will be at point E_{MKT}, yielding the amount produced and consumed Q_{MKT}, and the market price P_{MKT}. Q_{MKT} is greater than Q_{OPT}, the socially optimal quantity of livestock, which is the quantity corresponding to O, the point at which *MSC* and *D* cross.

> The **marginal social cost of a good or activity** is equal to the marginal cost of production plus its marginal external cost.

FIGURE 17-5   **Negative Externalities and Production**

(a) Negative Externality

(b) Optimal Pigouvian Tax

Livestock production generates external costs, so the marginal social cost curve, *MSC*, of livestock, corresponds to the supply curve, *S*, shifted upward by the marginal external cost. Panel (a) shows that without government action, the market produces the quantity Q_{MKT}. It is greater than the socially optimal quantity of livestock production, Q_{OPT}, the quantity at which *MSC* crosses the demand curve, *D*. At Q_{MKT}, the market price, P_{MKT}, is less than P_{MSC}, the true marginal cost to society of livestock production. Panel (b) shows how an optimal Pigouvian tax on livestock production, equal to its marginal external cost, moves the production to Q_{OPT}, resulting in lower output and a higher price to consumers.

So left to its own, the market will produce too much of a good that generates an external cost in production, and the price to consumers of such a good is too low: P_{MKT} is less than P_{MSC}, the true marginal cost to society of another unit of livestock. As panel (b) of Figure 17-5 shows, an optimal Pigouvian tax on livestock production, equal to the marginal external cost, moves the market to the socially optimal level of production, Q_{OPT}.

At this point, you might ask whether a regulator would choose a method of control that targets pollution directly, such as a cap and trade system, or control the production of the original good or activity with a Pigouvian tax. Generally, it is a good idea to target the pollution directly whenever feasible. The main reason is that this method creates incentives for the invention and adoption of production methods that create less pollution. An example of this phenomenon is the company AgCert, founded in 2002, which has devised methods for capturing greenhouse gases emitted by industrial agricultural production. The captured gases can then be burnt as biofuel or used as tradable emissions reductions in a cap and trade system.

►ECONOMICS IN ACTION

The Impeccable Economic Logic of Early Childhood Intervention Programs

One of the most vexing problems facing any society is how to break what researchers call the "cycle of poverty": children who grow up with disadvantaged socioeconomic backgrounds are far more likely to remain trapped in poverty as adults, even after we account for differences in ability. They are more likely to be unemployed or underemployed, to engage in crime, and to suffer chronic health problems.

Early childhood intervention has offered some hope of breaking the cycle. A 2006 study by the RAND Corporation found that high-quality early-childhood programs that focus on education and health care lead to significant social, intellectual, and financial advantages for kids who would otherwise be at risk of dropping out of high school and of engaging in criminal behavior. Children in programs like Head Start were less likely to engage in such destructive behaviors and more likely to end up with a job and to earn a high salary later in life. Another study by researchers at the University of Pittsburgh in 2003 looked at early-childhood intervention programs from a dollars-and-cents perspective, finding from $4 to $7 in benefits for every $1 spent on early-childhood intervention programs. The study also pointed to one program whose participants, by age 20, were 26% more likely to have finished high school, 35% less likely to have been charged in juvenile court, and 40% less likely to have repeated a grade compared to individuals of similar socioeconomic background who did not attend preschool. The observed external benefits to society of these programs are so large that the Brookings Institution predicts that providing high-quality preschool education to every American child would result in an increase in GDP, the total value of a country's domestic output, by almost 2%, representing over 3 million more jobs. ▲

< < < < < < < < < < < <

► CHECK YOUR UNDERSTANDING 17-3

1. Explain how the London congestion charge described in Chapter 3, in which cars entering central London during business hours must pay a fee of £8 (about $16), can be an optimal policy to manage inner-city pollution and congestion.

2. In each of the following cases, determine whether an external cost or an external benefit is imposed and what an appropriate policy response would be.
   a. Trees planted in urban areas improve air quality and lower summer temperatures.

b. Water-saving toilets reduce the need to pump water from rivers and aquifers. The cost of a gallon of water to homeowners is virtually zero.

c. Old computer monitors contain toxic materials that pollute the environment when improperly disposed of.

Solutions appear at back of book.

> A good is subject to a **network externality** when the value of the good to an individual is greater when a large number of other people also use the good.

Network Externalities

Suppose you owned the only fax machine in the world. What would it be worth to you? The answer, of course, is nothing. A fax machine derives its value only from the fact that other people also possess fax machines so that you and they can exchange faxes. And, in general, the more people who have fax machines, the more valuable a fax machine is to you.

This phenomenon, in which a good's value to an individual is greater when many other people own or use the same good, is common in technology-driven sectors of the economy. This "fax machine effect" is called a **network externality** because the most obvious versions occur when the goods involved form some kind of communications or transportation network. But the phenomenon is considerably more widespread than that. Unlike the phenomenon of positive and negative externalities, network externalities have no inherently favorable or adverse effect on society. What they share, rather, is the existence of an external effect from one person's actions.

Network externalities play a key role both in the modern economy and in a number of policy controversies. Let's look at where and how network externalities occur and then at some of the issues they raise.

Types of Network Externalities

The most obvious examples of network externalities involve communications. At different points in history the prime examples have been telegraphs, telephones, fax machines, and e-mail accounts. In each case the value of the good is derived entirely from its ability to link many people possessing the same good. As a result, the marginal benefit of the good to any one individual depends on the number of other individuals who use it.

However, network externalities can also arise in less dramatic ways. For example, network externalities can exist when other users are not strictly necessary for the use of a good, as long as they enhance its usefulness. In the early days of railroad development, a railroad from New York to Chicago would have had considerable value all by itself, as would have a railroad from Kansas City to Chicago. However, each line was worth more given the existence of the other, because once both were in place, goods could be shipped via Chicago between New York and Kansas City. In the modern world, a scheduled flight between two airports becomes more valuable if one or both of those airports is a hub with connections to other places.

Even this kind of direct link need not be necessary to create important network externalities. Any way in which other people's consumption of a good increases your own marginal benefit from consumption of that good can give rise to network effects.

Perhaps the classic case of indirect network externalities is that of computer operating systems. The operating system of a computer is the underlying software that runs the machine's basic operations, underpinning and coordinating the various programs—word processors, spreadsheets, e-mail programs, and so on—that the user runs. Most personal computers around the world run on Windows, the system sold by Microsoft, although a significant minority of users own computers produced by Apple, which has its own operating system. And a growing number of computers run on Linux, a system designed by programmers who believe that operating systems should not be corporate property.

A good is subject to **positive feedback** when success breeds greater success and failure breeds failure.

Why is Windows so dominant? Is a personal computer running Windows like a fax machine, which is useful only to the extent that other people possess the same good? Not in a direct sense: a computer can be used to type a term paper, do calculations on a spreadsheet, even send and receive e-mail regardless of how many other people have computers running the same operating system. So there isn't a literal network issue making Windows the preferred system.

Nonetheless, the dominance of Windows turns out to be self-reinforcing, for at least two indirect reasons. First, it is easier for a Windows user to get help and advice from other computer users than for someone using a less popular system. So it's a good idea, if possible, to use the same system that your colleague in the next office uses. Second, because Windows is used so widely, it attracts more attention from software developers. As a result, there are more programs that run on Windows than on any other operating system.

Network externalities in this broad sense occur for many goods. Even your choice of a car is influenced by a form of network externalities. Most people would be reluctant to switch to a car that runs on natural gas because fueling the car would be difficult: very few gas stations offer natural gas. And the reason service stations do not offer natural gas is, of course, that few people drive anything other than gasoline-powered cars. Or to take a less drastic example, people who live in small towns are reluctant to drive an unusual imported vehicle: where would they find a mechanic who knows how to fix it? So the circularity that makes one person choose Windows because everyone else uses Windows also applies to non-high-tech goods like cars.

When a good is subject to a network externality, it exhibits **positive feedback:** if large numbers of people buy the good, other people become more likely to buy it too. If people *don't* buy the good, others become less likely to buy it. So both success and failure tend to be self-reinforcing. This leads to a kind of "chicken-versus-egg problem": if each person places a positive value on a good based on whether another person owns it, how do you get anyone to buy it in the first place? Producers of goods that are subject to network externalities are aware of this problem, understanding that of two competing goods, it's the one with the largest network—not necessarily the one that's the better product—that will win in the end. That is, the product with the largest network will eventually dominate the market, and competing products will eventually disappear.

One way to gain an advantage at the early stages of this kind of market is to sell the product cheaply, perhaps at a loss, in order to increase the size of the network. So we often see companies introducing new high-technology products at a price well below production costs. For example, during the 1990s, the two main competitors in the market for Internet browser software, Netscape Navigator and Microsoft Internet Explorer, both offered their products for free. And even today, many cell phone companies give away free handsets to attract consumers to their wireless network.

Finally, network externalities present special challenges for antitrust regulators because the antitrust laws do not, strictly speaking, forbid monopoly. Rather, they only prohibit "monopolization"—efforts to create a monopoly. If you just happen to end up ruling an industry, that's OK, but if you take actions designed to drive out competition, that's not OK. So we could argue that monopolies in goods with network externalities, because they occur naturally, should not pose legal problems.

Unfortunately, it isn't that simple. Firms investing in new technologies are clearly trying to establish monopoly positions. Furthermore, in the face of positive feedback, firms have an incentive to engage in aggressive strategies to push their goods in order to increase their network size and tip the market in their direction. So what is the dividing line between legal and illegal actions?

At this point, the rules are somewhat in flux. In the Microsoft antitrust case, described in the following Economics in Action, reasonable economists and legal experts disagreed sharply both about whether the company had broken the law by pursuing a monopoly position and about whether the company should be broken up to diminish its ability to tip new markets in its favor.

►ECONOMICS IN ACTION

The Microsoft Case

In 2000 the Justice Department took on Microsoft in one of the most watched antitrust cases in history. By that time, Microsoft had become the world's most valuable corporation, and its founder, Bill Gates, was the world's richest man. What the government sought was nothing less than the breakup of the company.

The case involved almost all of the issues raised by goods with network externalities. Microsoft was, by any reasonable definition, a monopoly: leaving aside the niches of Apple customers and Linux users, just about all personal computers ran the Windows operating system. The key fact sustaining the Windows system was the force of a network externality: people used Windows because other people used Windows.

The government did not, however, challenge the Windows monopoly itself (although some economists urged it to). Most experts agreed that monopoly per se is a natural thing in such industries and should not be prevented. What the government claimed, however, was that Microsoft had used its monopoly position in operating systems to give its other products an advantage over competitors. For example, by including Internet Explorer as part of the Windows system, it was alleged, Microsoft was giving itself an unfair advantage over its rival Netscape in the browser software market.

Why was this considered harmful? The government argued both that monopolies were being created unnecessarily and that Microsoft was discouraging innovation. Potential innovators in software, the government claimed, were unwilling to invest large sums out of fear that Microsoft would use its control of the operating system to take away any market competitors might win: Microsoft would produce a competing product that would then be sold as a bundle with the Windows operating system. For its part, Microsoft argued that by setting the precedent that companies would be punished for success, the government was the real opponent of innovation—innovation that had benefited customers with lower prices and increasingly sophisticated products.

At first the case went against Microsoft, when a judge ordered the company split in two—into an operating-system company and a company selling the firm's other products. But this judgment was overturned on appeal. In November 2001, the government reached a settlement with Microsoft in which the company agreed to provide other companies with the technology to develop products that interacted seamlessly with Microsoft's software, thus removing the company's special advantage acquired through bundling its products.

The Microsoft case involved almost all of the issues raised by goods with network externalities.

Competitors complained bitterly that this settlement had far too many loopholes and that Microsoft's ability to exploit its monopoly position would remain. And by early 2004, the government agreed: antitrust lawyers from the Justice Department reported to the judge who negotiated the original settlement that they were increasingly uneasy about the plan's ability to spur competition. However, in mid-2004 a federal appeals court upheld the 2001 settlement, and in November 2007, Microsoft's obligations under the original settlement expired. ▲

< < < < < < < < < < < <

▶ CHECK YOUR UNDERSTANDING 17-4

1. For each of the following goods, explain the nature of the network externality present.
   a. Appliances using a particular voltage, such as 110 volts versus 220 volts
   b. $8\frac{1}{2}$-by-11-inch paper versus 8-by-$12\frac{1}{2}$-inch paper

2. Suppose there are two competing companies in an industry that has a network externality. Explain why it is likely that the company able to sustain the largest initial losses will eventually dominate the market.

Solutions appear at back of book.

[▶▶ A LOOK AHEAD • • •

Externalities are an important justification for government intervention in the economy. As we've seen, government programs such as emissions taxes or tradable permit systems may be necessary to bring individual incentives in line with social costs or benefits.

In the next chapter, we'll turn to some related justifications for government intervention: the problems of *public goods* like lighthouses, which won't be provided in the absence of government action, and *common resources* like fish in the sea, which will be overused in the absence of government action.]

SUMMARY

1. When pollution can be directly observed and controlled, government policies should be geared directly to producing the **socially optimal quantity of pollution,** the quantity at which the **marginal social cost of pollution** is equal to the **marginal social benefit of pollution.** In the absence of government intervention, a market produces too much pollution because polluters take only their benefit from polluting into account, not the costs imposed on others.

2. The costs to society of pollution are an example of an **external cost;** in some cases, however, economic activities yield **external benefits.** External costs and benefits are jointly known as **externalities,** with external costs called **negative externalities** and external benefits called **positive externalities.**

3. According to the **Coase theorem,** individuals can find a way to **internalize the externality,** making government intervention unnecessary, as long as **transaction costs**—the costs of making a deal—are sufficiently low. However, in many cases transaction costs are too high to permit such deals.

4. Governments often deal with pollution by imposing **environmental standards,** a method, economists argue, that is usually an inefficient way to reduce pollution. Two efficient (cost-minimizing) methods for reducing pollution are **emissions taxes,** a form of **Pigouvian tax,** and **tradable emissions permits.** The optimal Pigouvian tax on pollution is equal to its marginal social cost at the socially optimal quantity of pollution. These methods also provide incentives for the creation and adoption of production technologies that cause less pollution.

5. When a good or activity yields external benefits, such as **technology spillovers,** the **marginal social benefit of the good or activity** is equal to the marginal benefit accruing to consumers plus its marginal external benefit. Without government intervention, the market produces too little of the good or activity. An optimal **Pigouvian subsidy** to producers, equal to the marginal external benefit, moves the market to the socially optimal quantity of production. This yields higher output and a higher price to producers. It is a form of **industrial policy,** a policy to support industries that are believed to generate

positive externalities. Economists are often skeptical of industrial policies because external benefits are hard to measure and they motivate producers to lobby for lucrative benefits.

6. When only the original good or activity can be controlled, government policies are geared to influencing how much of it is produced. When there are external costs from production, the **marginal social cost of a good or activity** exceeds its marginal cost to producers, the difference being the marginal external cost. Without government action, the market produces too much of the good or activity. The optimal Pigouvian tax on production of the good or activity is equal to its marginal external cost, yielding lower output and a higher price to consumers. A system of tradable production permits for the right to produce the good or activity can also achieve efficiency at minimum cost.

7. Communications, transportation, and high-technology goods are frequently subject to **network externalities,** which arise when the value of the good to an individual is greater when a large number of people use the good. Such goods are likely to be subject to **positive feedback:** if large numbers of people buy the good, other people are more likely to buy it too. So success breeds greater success and failure breeds failure: the good with the larger network will eventually dominate, and rival goods will disappear. As a result, producers have an incentive to take aggressive action in the early stages of the market to increase the size of their network. Markets with network externalities tend to be monopolies. They are especially challenging for antitrust regulators because it can be hard to differentiate between the natural progression of the network externality and illegal monopolization efforts by producers.

KEY TERMS

Marginal social cost of pollution, p. 435
Marginal social benefit of pollution, p. 435
Socially optimal quantity of pollution, p. 435
External cost, p. 437
External benefit, p. 437
Externalities, p. 437
Negative externalities, p. 437
Positive externalities, p. 437

Coase theorem, p. 438
Transaction costs, p. 438
Internalize the externality, p. 438
Environmental standards, p. 440
Emissions tax, p. 442
Pigouvian taxes, p. 443
Tradable emissions permits, p. 444
Marginal social benefit of a good or activity, p. 448

Pigouvian subsidy, p. 448
Technology spillover, p. 448
Industrial policy, p. 448
Marginal social cost of a good or activity, p. 449
Network externality, p. 451
Positive feedback, p. 452

PROBLEMS

1. What type of externality (positive or negative) is present in each of the following examples? Is the marginal social benefit of the activity greater than or equal to the marginal benefit to the individual? Is the marginal social cost of the activity greater than or equal to the marginal cost to the individual? Without intervention, will there be too little or too much (relative to what would be socially optimal) of this activity?

   a. Mr. Chau plants lots of colorful flowers in his front yard.

   b. Your next-door neighbor likes to build bonfires in his backyard, and sparks often drift onto your house.

   c. Maija, who lives next to an apple orchard, decides to keep bees to produce honey.

   d. Justine buys a large SUV that consumes a lot of gasoline.

2. The loud music coming from the sorority next to your dorm is a negative externality that can be directly quantified. The accompanying table shows the marginal social benefit and the marginal social cost per decibel (dB, a measure of volume) of music.

Volume of music (dB)	Marginal social benefit of dB	Marginal social cost of dB
90		
	$36	$0
91		
	30	2
92		
	24	4
93		
	18	6
94		
	12	8
95		
	6	10
96		
	0	12
97		

   a. Draw the marginal social benefit curve and the marginal social cost curve. Use your diagram to determine the socially optimal volume of music.

b. Only the members of the sorority benefit from the music and they bear none of the cost. Which volume of music will they choose?

c. The college imposes a Pigouvian tax of $3 per decibel of music played. From your diagram, determine the volume of music the sorority will now choose.

3. Many dairy farmers in California are adopting a new technology that allows them to produce their own electricity from methane gas captured from animal wastes. (One cow can produce up to 2 kilowatts a day.) This practice reduces the amount of methane gas released into the atmosphere. In addition to reducing their own utility bills, the farmers are allowed to sell any electricity they produce at favorable rates.

a. Explain how the ability to earn money from capturing and transforming methane gas behaves like a Pigouvian tax on methane gas pollution and can lead dairy farmers to emit the efficient amount of methane gas pollution.

b. Suppose some dairy farmers have lower costs of transforming methane into electricity than others. Explain how this system leads to an efficient allocation of emissions reduction among farmers.

4. The accompanying table shows the total revenue and the total cost that accrue to steel producers from producing steel. Producing a ton of steel imposes a marginal external cost of $60 per ton.

Quantity of steel (tons)	Total revenue	Total cost to producers
1	$115	$10
2	210	30
3	285	60
4	340	100
5	375	150

a. Calculate the marginal revenue per ton of steel and the marginal cost per ton of steel to steel producers. Then calculate the marginal social cost per ton of steel.

b. What is the market equilibrium quantity of steel production?

c. What is the socially optimal quantity of steel production?

d. What is the optimal Pigouvian tax to remedy the problem created by the negative externality?

5. Voluntary environmental programs were extremely popular in the United States, Europe, and Japan in the 1990s. Part of their popularity stems from the fact that these programs do not require legislative authority, which is often hard to obtain. The 33/50 program started by the Environmental Protection Agency (EPA) is an example of such a program. With this program, the EPA attempted to reduce industrial emissions of 17

toxic chemicals by providing information on relatively inexpensive methods of pollution control. Companies were asked to voluntarily commit to reducing emissions from their 1988 levels by 33% by 1992 and by 50% by 1995. The program actually met its second target by 1994.

a. As in Figure 17-3, draw marginal benefit curves for pollution generated by two plants, A and B, in 1988. Assume that without government intervention, each plant emits the same amount of pollution, but that at all levels of pollution less than this amount, plant A's marginal benefit of polluting is less than that of plant B. Label the vertical axis "Marginal benefit to individual polluter" and the horizontal axis "Quantity of pollution emissions." Mark the quantity of pollution each plant produces without government action.

b. Do you expect the total quantity of pollution before the program was put in place to have been less than or more than the optimal quantity of pollution? Why?

c. Suppose the plants whose marginal benefit curves you depicted in part a were participants in the 33/50 program. In a replica of your graph from part a, mark targeted levels of pollution in 1995 for the two plants. Which plant was required to reduce emissions more? Was this solution necessarily efficient?

d. What kind of environmental policy does the 33/50 program most closely resemble? What is the main shortcoming of such a policy? Compare it to two other types of environmental policy discussed in this chapter.

6. Smoking produces a negative externality because it imposes a health risk on others who inhale second-hand smoke. Cigarette smoking also causes productivity losses to the economy due to the shorter expected life span of a smoker. The U.S. Centers for Disease Control (CDC) has estimated the average social cost of smoking a single pack of cigarettes for different states by taking these negative externalities into account. The accompanying table provides the price of cigarettes and the estimated average social cost of smoking in five states.

State	Cigarette retail price with taxes (per pack)	CDC estimate of smoking cost in 2006 (per pack)
California	$4.40	$15.10
New York	5.82	21.91
Florida	3.80	10.14
Texas	4.76	9.94
Ohio	4.60	9.19

a. At the current level of consumption, what is the optimal retail price of a pack of cigarettes in the different states? Is the current price below or above this optimal price? Does this suggest that the current level of consumption is too high or too low? Explain your answer.

b. In order to deal with negative externalities, state governments currently impose excise taxes on cigarettes. Are current taxes set at the optimal level? Justify your answer.

c. What is the correct size of an additional Pigouvian tax on cigarette sales in the different states if the CDC's estimate for smoking cost does not change with an increase in the retail price of cigarettes?

7. Education is an example of an activity that generates a positive externality: acquiring more education benefits the individual student and having a more highly educated workforce is good for the economy as a whole. The accompanying table illustrates the marginal benefit to Sian per year of education and the marginal cost per year of education. Each year of education has a marginal external benefit to society equal to $8,000. Assume that the marginal social cost is the same as the marginal cost paid by an individual student.

Quantity of education (years)	Sian's marginal benefit per year	Sian's marginal cost per year
9		
	$20,000	$15,000
10		
	19,000	16,000
11		
	18,000	17,000
12		
	17,000	18,000
13		
	16,000	19,000
14		
	15,000	20,000
15		
	14,000	21,000
16		
	13,000	22,000
17		

a. Find Sian's market equilibrium number of years of education.

b. Calculate the marginal social benefit schedule. What is the socially optimal number of years of education?

c. You are in charge of education funding. Would you use a Pigouvian tax or a Pigouvian subsidy to induce Sian to choose the socially optimal amount of education? How high would you set this tax or subsidy per year of education?

8. Planting a tree improves the environment: trees transform greenhouse gases into oxygen, improve water retention in the soil, and improve soil quality. Assume that the value of this environmental improvement to society is $10 for the expected lifetime of the tree. The following table contains a hypothetical demand schedule for trees to be planted.

Price of tree	Quantity of trees demanded (thousands)
$30	0
25	6
20	12
15	18
10	24
5	30
0	36

a. Assume that the marginal cost of producing a tree for planting is constant at $20. Draw a diagram that shows the market equilibrium quantity and price for trees to be planted.

b. What type of externality is generated by planting a tree? Draw a diagram that shows the optimal number of trees planted. How does this differ from the market outcome?

c. On your diagram from part b, indicate the optimal Pigouvian tax/subsidy (as the case may be). Explain how this moves the market to the optimal outcome.

9. According to a report from the U.S. Census Bureau, "the average [lifetime] earnings of a full-time, year round worker with a high school education are about $1.2 million compared with $2.1 million for a college graduate." This indicates that there is a considerable benefit to a graduate from investing in his or her own education. Tuition at most state universities covers only about two-thirds to three-quarters of the cost, so the state applies a Pigouvian subsidy to college education.

If a Pigouvian subsidy is appropriate, is the externality created by a college education a positive or a negative externality? What does this imply about the differences between the costs and benefits to students compared to social costs and benefits? What are some reasons for the differences?

10. Fishing for sablefish has been so intensive that sablefish were threatened with extinction. After several years of banning such fishing, the government is now proposing to introduce tradable vouchers, each of which entitles its holder to a catch of a certain size. Explain how fishing generates a negative externality and how the voucher scheme may overcome the inefficiency created by this externality.

11. The two dry-cleaning companies in Collegetown, College Cleaners and Big Green Cleaners, are a major source of air pollution. Together they currently produce 350 units of air pollution, which the town wants to reduce to 200 units. The accompanying table shows the current pollution level produced by each company and each company's marginal cost of reducing its pollution. The marginal cost is constant.

Companies	Initial pollution level (units)	Marginal cost of reducing pollution (per unit)
College Cleaners	230	$5
Big Green Cleaners	120	$2

a. Suppose that Collegetown passes an environmental standards law that limits each company to 100 units of pollution. What would be the total cost to the two companies of each reducing its pollution emissions to 100 units?

Suppose instead that Collegetown issues 100 pollution vouchers to each company, each entitling the company to one unit of pollution, and that these vouchers can be traded.

b. How much is each pollution voucher worth to College Cleaners? to Big Green Cleaners? (That is, how much would each company, at most, be willing to pay for one more voucher?)

c. Who will sell vouchers and who will buy them? How many vouchers will be traded?

d. What is the total cost to the two companies of the pollution controls under this voucher system?

12. Ronald owns a cattle farm at the source of a long river. His cattle's waste flows into the river and down many miles to where Carla lives. Carla gets her drinking water from the river. By allowing his cattle's waste to flow into the river, Ronald imposes a negative externality on Carla. In each of the two following cases, do you think, that through negotiation, Ronald and Carla can find an efficient solution? What might this solution look like?

a. There are no telephones, and for Carla to talk to Ronald, she has to travel for two days on a rocky road.

b. Carla and Ronald both have e-mail access, making it costless for them to communicate.

13. a. EAuction and EMarketplace are two competing Internet auction sites, where buyers and sellers transact goods. Each auction site earns money by charging sellers for listing their goods. EAuction has decided to eliminate fees for the first transaction for sellers that are new to their site. Explain why this is likely to be a good strategy for EAuction in its competition with EMarketplace.

b. EMarketplace complained to the Justice Department that EAuction's practice of eliminating fees for new sellers was anti-competitive and would lead to monopolization of the Internet auction industry. Is EMarketplace correct? How should the Justice Department respond?

c. EAuction stopped its practice of eliminating fees for new sellers. But since it provided much better technical service than its rival, EMarketplace, buyers and sellers came to prefer EAuction. Eventually, EMarketplace closed down, leaving EAuction as a monopolist. Should the Justice Department intervene to break EAuction into two companies? Explain.

d. EAuction is now a monopolist in the Internet auction industry. It also owns a site that handles payments over the Internet, called PayForIt. It is competing with another Internet payment site, called PayBuddy. EAuction has now stipulated that any transaction on its auction site must use PayForIt, rather than PayBuddy, for the payment. Should the Justice Department intervene? Explain.

14. Which of the following are characterized by network externalities? Which are not? Explain.

a. The choice between installing 110-volt electrical current in structures rather than 220-volt

b. The choice between purchasing a Toyota versus a Ford

c. The choice of a printer, where each printer requires its own specific type of ink cartridge

d. The choice of whether to purchase an iPod or an iPod Nano.

Public Goods and Common Resources

THE GREAT STINK

BY THE MIDDLE OF THE NINETEENTH CENTURY, London had become the world's largest city, with close to 2.5 million inhabitants. Unfortunately, all those people produced a lot of waste—and there was no place for it to go except into the Thames, the river flowing through the city. Nobody with a working nose could ignore the results. And the river didn't just smell bad—it carried dangerous waterborne diseases like cholera and typhoid. London neighborhoods close to the Thames had death rates from cholera more than six times greater than the neighborhoods farthest away. And the great majority of Londoners drew their drinking water from the Thames.

What the city needed, said reformers, was a sewage system that would carry waste away from the river. Yet no private individual was willing to build such a system, and influential people were opposed to the idea that the government should take responsibility for the problem. For example, the magazine *The Economist* weighed in against proposals for a government-built sewage system, declaring that "suffering and evil are nature's admonitions—they cannot be got rid of."

But the hot summer of 1858 brought what came to be known as the Great Stink, which was so bad that one health journal reported "men struck down with the stench." Even the privileged and powerful suffered: Parliament met in a building next to the river. After unsuccessful efforts to stop the smell by covering the windows with chemical-soaked curtains, Parliament finally approved a plan for an immense system of sewers and pumping stations to direct sewage away from the city. The system, opened in 1865, brought dramatic improvement in the city's quality of life; cholera and typhoid epidemics, which had been regular occurrences, completely disappeared. The Thames was turned from the filthiest to the cleanest metropolitan river in the world, and the sewage system's principal engineer, Sir Joseph Bazalgette, was lauded as having "saved more lives

London's River Thames then . . .

. . . and the same river now, thanks to government intervention.

than any single Victorian public official." It was estimated at the time that Bazalgette's sewer system added 20 years to the life span of the average Londoner.

The story of the Great Stink and the policy response that followed illustrate two important reasons for government intervention in the economy. London's new sewage system was a clear example of a *public good*—a good that benefits many people, whether or not they have paid for it, and whose benefits to any one individual do not depend on how many others also benefit. As we will see shortly, public goods differ in important ways from the *private goods* we have studied so far—and these differences mean that public goods cannot be efficiently supplied by the market.

In addition, clean water in the Thames is an example of a *common resource,* a good that many people can consume whether or not they have paid for it but whose consumption by each person reduces the amount available to others. Such goods tend to be overused by individuals in a market system unless the government takes action.

In earlier chapters, we saw that markets sometimes fail to deliver efficient levels of production and consumption of a good or activity. We saw how inefficiency can arise from market power, which allows monopolists and colluding oligopolists to charge prices that are higher than marginal cost, thereby preventing mutually beneficial transactions from occurring. We also saw how inefficiency can arise from positive and negative externalities, which cause a divergence between the costs and benefits of an individual's or industry's actions and the costs and benefits of those actions borne by society as a whole.

In this chapter, we will take a somewhat different approach to the question of why markets sometimes fail. Here we focus on how *the characteristics of goods often determine whether markets can deliver them efficiently.* When goods have the "wrong" characteristics, the resulting market failures resemble those associated with externalities or market power. This alternative way of looking at sources of inefficiency deepens our understanding of why markets sometimes don't work well and how government can take actions that increase society's welfare.

WHAT YOU WILL LEARN IN THIS CHAPTER:

➤ A way to classify goods that predicts whether or not a good is a **private good**—a good that can be efficiently provided by markets

➤ What **public goods** are, and why markets fail to supply them

➤ What **common resources** are, and why they are overused

➤ What **artificially scarce goods** are, and why they are underconsumed

➤ How government intervention in the production and consumption of these types of goods can make society better off

➤ Why finding the right level of government intervention is often difficult

---

Private Goods—And Others

What's the difference between installing a new bathroom in a house and building a municipal sewage system? What's the difference between growing wheat and fishing in the open ocean?

These aren't trick questions. In each case there is a basic difference in the characteristics of the goods involved. Bathroom appliances and wheat have the characteristics necessary to allow markets to work efficiently. Public sewage systems and fish in the sea do not.

Let's look at these crucial characteristics and why they matter.

Characteristics of Goods

Goods like bathroom fixtures or wheat have two characteristics that, as we'll soon see, are essential if a good is to be efficiently provided by a market economy.

- They are **excludable:** suppliers of the good can prevent people who don't pay from consuming it.
- They are **rival in consumption:** the same unit of the good cannot be consumed by more than one person at the same time.

When a good is both excludable and rival in consumption, it is called a **private good.** Wheat is an example of a private good. It is *excludable:* the farmer can sell a bushel to one consumer without having to provide wheat to everyone in the county. And it is *rival in consumption:* if I eat bread baked with a farmer's wheat, that wheat cannot be consumed by someone else.

But not all goods possess these two characteristics. Some goods are **nonexcludable**— the supplier cannot prevent consumption of the good by people who do not pay for it. Fire protection is one example: a fire department that puts out fires before they spread protects the whole city, not just people who have made contributions to the Firemen's Benevolent Association. An improved environment is another: the city of London couldn't have ended the Great Stink for some residents while leaving the River Thames foul for others.

Nor are all goods rival in consumption. Goods are **nonrival in consumption** if more than one person can consume the same unit of the good at the same time. TV programs are nonrival in consumption: your decision to watch a show does not prevent other people from watching the same show.

Because goods can be either excludable or nonexcludable, rival or nonrival in consumption, there are four types of goods, illustrated by the matrix in Figure 18-1:

- *Private goods,* which are excludable and rival in consumption, like wheat
- *Public goods,* which are nonexcludable and nonrival in consumption, like a public sewer system
- *Common resources,* which are nonexcludable but rival in consumption, like clean water in a river
- *Artificially scarce goods,* which are excludable but nonrival in consumption, like pay-per-view movies on cable TV

There are, of course, many other characteristics that distinguish between types of goods—necessities versus luxuries, normal versus inferior, and so on. Why focus on whether goods are excludable and rival in consumption?

A good is **excludable** if the supplier of that good can prevent people who do not pay from consuming it.

A good is **rival in consumption** if the same unit of the good cannot be consumed by more than one person at the same time.

A good that is both excludable and rival in consumption is a **private good.**

When a good is **nonexcludable,** the supplier cannot prevent consumption by people who do not pay for it.

A good is **nonrival in consumption** if more than one person can consume the same unit of the good at the same time.

FIGURE 18-1

Four Types of Goods

There are four types of goods. The type of a good depends on (1) whether or not it is excludable— whether a producer can prevent someone from consuming it; and (2) whether or not it is rival in consumption—whether it is impossible for the same unit of a good to be consumed by more than one person at the same time.

	Rival in consumption	Nonrival in consumption
Excludable	**Private goods** • Wheat • Bathroom fixtures	**Artificially scarce goods** • Pay-per-view movies • Computer software
Non-excludable	**Common resources** • Clean water • Biodiversity	**Public goods** • Public sanitation • National defense

Why Markets Can Supply Only Private Goods Efficiently

As we learned in earlier chapters, markets are typically the best means for a society to deliver goods and services to its members; that is, markets are efficient except in the case of the well-defined problems of market power, externalities, or other

Goods that are nonexcludable suffer from the **free-rider problem:** individuals have no incentive to pay for their own consumption and instead will take a "free ride" on anyone who does pay.

---

instances of market failure. But there is yet another condition that must be met, one rooted in the nature of the good itself: markets cannot supply goods and services efficiently unless they are private goods—excludable and rival in consumption.

To see why excludability is crucial, suppose that a farmer had only two choices: either produce no wheat or provide a bushel of wheat to every resident of the county who wants it, whether or not that resident pays for it. It seems unlikely that anyone would grow wheat under those conditions.

Yet the operator of a municipal sewage system faces pretty much the same problem as our hypothetical farmer. A sewage system makes the whole city cleaner and healthier—but that benefit accrues to all the city's residents, whether or not they pay the system operator. That's why no private entrepreneur came forward with a plan to end London's Great Stink.

The general point is that if a good is nonexcludable, rational consumers won't be willing to pay for it—they will take a "free ride" on anyone who *does* pay. So there is a **free-rider problem.** Examples of the free-rider problem are familiar from daily life. One example you may have encountered happens when students are required to do a group project. There is often a tendency of some group members to shirk, relying on others in the group to get the work done. The shirkers *free-ride* on someone else's effort.

Because of the free-rider problem, the forces of self-interest alone do not lead to an efficient level of production for a nonexcludable good. Even though consumers would benefit from increased production of the good, no one individual is willing to pay for more, and so no producer is willing to supply it. The result is that nonexcludable goods suffer from *inefficiently low production* in a market economy. In fact, in the face of the free-rider problem, self-interest may not ensure that any amount of the good—let alone the efficient quantity—is produced.

Goods that are excludable and nonrival in consumption, like pay-per-view movies, suffer from a different kind of inefficiency. As long as a good is excludable, it is possible to earn a profit by making it available only to those who pay. Therefore, producers are willing to supply an excludable good. But the marginal cost of letting an additional viewer watch a pay-per-view movie is zero because it is nonrival in consumption. So the efficient price to the consumer is also zero—or, to put it another way, individuals should watch TV movies up to the point where their marginal benefit is zero. But if the cable company actually charges viewers $4, viewers will consume the good only up to the point where their marginal benefit is $4. When consumers must pay a price greater than zero for a good that is nonrival in consumption, the price they pay is higher than the marginal cost of allowing them to consume that good, which is zero. So in a market economy goods that are nonrival in consumption suffer from *inefficiently low consumption*.

Now we can see why private goods are the only goods that can be efficiently produced and consumed in a competitive market. (That is, a private good will be efficiently produced and consumed in a market free of market power, externalities, or other instances of market failure.) Because private goods are excludable, producers can charge for them and so have an incentive to produce them. And because they are also rival in consumption, it is efficient for consumers to pay a positive price—a price equal to the marginal cost of production. If one or both of these characteristics are lacking, a market economy will not lead to efficient production and consumption of the good.

Fortunately for the market system, most goods are private goods. Food, clothing, shelter, and most other desirable things in life are excludable and rival in consumption, so markets can provide us with most things. Yet there are crucial goods that don't meet these criteria—and in most cases, that means that the government must step in.

PITFALLS

MARGINAL COST OF WHAT EXACTLY?

In the case of a good that is nonrival in consumption, it's easy to confuse the marginal cost of *producing* a unit of the good with the marginal cost of *allowing* a unit of the good *to be consumed.* For example, your local cable company incurs a marginal cost in making a movie available to its subscribers that is equal to the cost of the resources it uses to produce and broadcast that movie. However, *once that movie is being broadcast,* no marginal cost is incurred by letting an additional family watch it. In other words, no costly resources are "used up" when one more family consumes a movie that has already been produced and is being broadcast.

This complication does not arise, however, when a good is rival in consumption. In that case, the resources used to produce a unit of the good are "used up" by a person's consumption of it—they are no longer available to satisfy someone else's consumption. So when a good is rival in consumption, the marginal cost to society of allowing an individual to consume a unit is equal to the resource cost of producing that unit—that is, equal to the marginal cost of producing it.

►ECONOMICS IN ACTION

A Policeman's Lot

We tend to think of crime prevention as a function of government, yet individuals take their own measures to prevent theft: homeowners put locks on their doors, and many businesses hire their own security guards.

Why, then, do we also have public police departments? Because law enforcement, as opposed to self-protection, is a public good. The benefits of keeping a potential thief off your own property are rival and excludable. But the benefits of tracking down criminals and bringing them to justice, and of policing public areas, accrue to all law-abiding citizens.

The beginning of modern police departments can be traced to two eighteenth-century institutions that concentrated on these clearly public-good aspects of crime prevention: the Bow Street Runners, an early detective agency that concentrated on finding and catching criminals, and the Thames River Police, who patrolled the dock areas. In 1829 Sir Robert Peel, building on the lessons from these institutions, oversaw the creation of a unified London police force, which served as a model for police forces throughout the world. To this day British police officers are known, after Sir Robert, as "bobbies." ▲

> > > > > > > > > > > >

► CHECK YOUR UNDERSTANDING 18-1

1. Classify each of the following goods according to whether they are excludable and whether they are rival in consumption. What kind of good is each?
   a. Use of a public space such as a park
   b. A cheese burrito
   c. Information from a website that is password-protected
   d. Publicly announced information on the path of an incoming hurricane

2. Which of the goods in Question 1 will be provided by a competitive market? Which will not be? Explain your answer.

Solutions appear at back of book.

Public Goods

A **public good** is the exact opposite of a private good: it is a good that is both nonexcludable and nonrival in consumption. A public sewage system is an example of a public good: you can't keep a river clean without making it clean for everyone who lives near its banks, and my protection from great stinks does not come at my neighbor's expense.

Here are some other examples of public goods:

- *Disease prevention.* When doctors act to stamp out the beginnings of an epidemic before it can spread, they protect people around the world.

- *National defense.* A strong military protects all citizens.

- *Scientific research.* More knowledge benefits everyone.

Because these goods are nonexcludable, they suffer from the free-rider problem, so no private firm would be willing to produce them. And because they are nonrival in consumption, it would be inefficient to charge people for consuming them. As a result, society must find nonmarket methods for providing these goods.

Providing Public Goods

Public goods are provided through a variety of means. The government doesn't always get involved—in many cases a nongovernmental solution has been found for the free-rider problem. But these solutions are usually imperfect in some way.

A **public good** is both nonexcludable and nonrival in consumption.

>> **QUICK REVIEW**

➤ Goods can be classified according to two attributes: whether they are **excludable** and whether they are **rival in consumption.**

➤ Goods that are both excludable and rival in consumption are **private goods.** Private goods can be efficiently produced and consumed in a competitive market.

➤ When goods are **nonexcludable,** there is a **free-rider problem:** consumers will not pay producers, leading to inefficiently low production.

➤ When goods are **nonrival in consumption,** the efficient price for consumption is zero. But if a positive price is charged to compensate producers for the cost of production, the result is inefficiently low consumption.

On the prowl: a British TV detection van at work.

Some public goods are supplied through voluntary contributions. For example, private donations support a considerable amount of scientific research. But private donations are insufficient to finance huge, socially important projects like basic medical research.

Some public goods are supplied by self-interested individuals or firms because those who produce them are able to make money in an indirect way. The classic example is broadcast television, which in the United States is supported entirely by advertising. The downside of such indirect funding is that it skews the nature and quantity of the public goods that are supplied, as well as imposing additional costs on consumers. TV stations show the programs that yield the most advertising revenue (that is, programs best suited for selling antacids, hair-loss remedies, antihistamines, and the like to the segment of the population that buys them), which are not necessarily the programs people most want to see. And viewers must also endure many commercials.

Some potentially public goods are deliberately made excludable and therefore subject to charge, like pay-per-view movies. In the United Kingdom, where most television programming is paid for by a yearly license fee assessed on every television owner (£135.50, or about $270 in 2008), television viewing is made artificially excludable by the use of "television detection vans": vans that roam neighborhoods in an attempt to detect televisions in non-licensed households and fine them. However, as noted earlier, when suppliers charge a price greater than zero for a nonrival good, consumers will consume an inefficiently low quantity of that good.

In small communities, a high level of social encouragement or pressure can be brought to bear on people to contribute money or time to provide the efficient level of a public good. Volunteer fire departments, which depend both on the volunteered services of the firefighters themselves and on contributions from local residents, are a good example. But as communities grow larger and more anonymous, social pressure is increasingly difficult to apply, compelling larger towns and cities to tax residents and depend on salaried firefighters for fire protection services.

As this last example suggests, when these other solutions fail, it is up to the government to provide public goods. Indeed, the most important public goods—national defense, the legal system, disease control, fire protection in large cities, and so on—are provided by government and paid for by taxes. Economic theory tells us that the provision of public goods is one of the crucial roles of government.

How Much of a Public Good Should Be Provided?

In some cases, provision of a public good is an "either–or" decision: London would either have a sewage system—or not. But in most cases, governments must decide not only whether to provide a public good but also *how much* of that public good to provide. For example, street cleaning is a public good—but how often should the streets be cleaned? Once a month? Twice a month? Every other day?

Imagine a city in which there are only two residents, Ted and Alice. Assume that the public good in question is street cleaning and that Ted and Alice truthfully tell the government how much they value a unit of the public good, where a unit is equal to one street cleaning per month. Specifically, each of them tells the government *his or her willingness to pay for another unit of the public good supplied*—an amount that corresponds to that *individual's marginal benefit* of another unit of the public good.

Using this information plus information on the cost of providing the good, the government can use marginal analysis to find the efficient level of providing the public good: the level at which the *marginal social benefit* of the public good is equal to the marginal cost of producing it. Recall from Chapter 17 that the marginal social benefit of a good is the benefit that accrues to society as a whole from the consumption of one additional unit of the good.

But what is the marginal social benefit of another unit of a public good—a unit that generates utility for *all* consumers, not just one consumer, because it is nonexcludable and nonrival in consumption? This question leads us to an important principle: *In the special case of a public good, the marginal social benefit of a unit of the good is equal to the sum of the individual marginal benefits that are enjoyed by all consumers of that unit.* Or to consider it from a slightly different angle, if a consumer could be compelled to pay for a unit before consuming it (the good is made excludable), then the marginal social benefit of a unit is equal to the *sum* of each consumer's willingness to pay for that unit. Using this principle, the marginal social benefit of an additional street cleaning per month is equal to Ted's individual marginal benefit from that additional cleaning *plus* Alice's individual marginal benefit.

Why? Because a public good is nonrival in consumption—Ted's benefit from a cleaner street does not diminish Alice's benefit from that same clean street, and vice versa. Because people can all simultaneously consume the same unit of a public good, the marginal social benefit of an additional unit of that good is the *sum* of the individual marginal benefits of all who enjoy the public good. And the efficient quantity of a public good is the quantity at which the marginal social benefit is equal to the marginal cost of providing it.

Figure 18-2 on the next page illustrates the efficient provision of a public good, showing three marginal benefit curves. Panel (a) shows Ted's individual marginal benefit curve from street cleaning, MB_T: he would be willing to pay $25 for the city to clean its streets once a month, an additional $18 to have it done a second time, and so on. Panel (b) shows Alice's individual marginal benefit curve from street cleaning, MB_A. Panel (c) shows the marginal social benefit curve from street cleaning, MSB: it is the vertical sum of Ted's and Alice's individual marginal benefit curves, MB_T and MB_A.

To maximize society's welfare, the government should clean the street up to the level at which the marginal social benefit of an additional cleaning is no longer greater than the marginal cost. Suppose that the marginal cost of street cleaning is $6 per cleaning. Then the city should clean its streets 5 times per month, because the marginal social benefit of going from 4 to 5 cleanings is $8, but going from 5 to 6 cleanings would yield a marginal social benefit of only $2.

Figure 18-2 can help reinforce our understanding of why we cannot rely on individual self-interest to yield provision of an efficient quantity of public goods. Suppose that the city did one fewer street cleaning than the efficient quantity and that either Ted or Alice was asked to pay for the last cleaning. Neither one would be willing to pay for it! Ted would personally gain only the equivalent of $3 in utility from adding one more street cleaning—so he wouldn't be willing to pay the $6 marginal cost of another cleaning. Alice would personally gain the equivalent of $5 in utility—so she wouldn't be willing to pay either. The point is that the marginal social benefit of one more unit of a public good is always greater than the individual marginal benefit to any one individual. That is why no individual is willing to pay for the efficient quantity of the good.

Does this description of the public good problem, in which the marginal social benefit of an additional unit of the public good is greater than any individual's marginal benefit, sound a bit familiar? It should: we encountered a somewhat similar situation in our discussion of *positive externalities*. Remember that in the case of a positive externality, the marginal social benefit accruing to all consumers of another unit of the good is greater than the price that the producer receives for that unit; as a result, the market produces too little of the good. In the case of a public good, the individual marginal benefit of a consumer plays the same role as the price received by the producer plays in the case of positive externalities: both cases create insufficient incentive to provide an efficient amount of the good. So the problem of providing public goods is very similar to the problem of dealing with positive externalities; in both cases there is a market failure that calls for government intervention. One basic rationale for the existence of government is that it provides a way for citizens to tax themselves in order to provide public goods—particularly a vital public good like national defense.

FIGURE 18-2   A Public Good

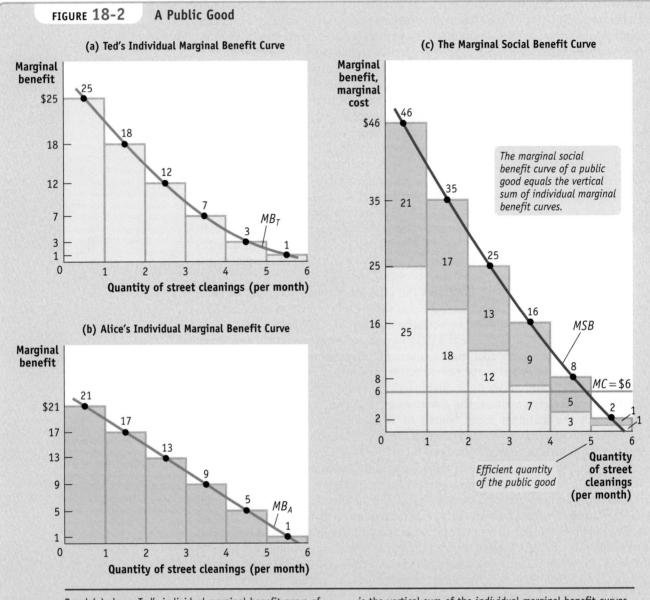

Panel (a) shows Ted's individual marginal benefit curve of street cleanings per month, MB_T, and panel (b) shows Alice's individual marginal benefit curve, MB_A. Panel (c) shows the marginal social benefit of the public good, equal to the *sum* of the individual marginal benefits to all consumers (in this case, Ted and Alice). The marginal social benefit curve, MSB, is the vertical sum of the individual marginal benefit curves MB_T and MB_A. At a constant marginal cost of $6, there should be 5 street cleanings per month, because the marginal social benefit of going from 4 to 5 cleanings is $8 ($3 for Ted plus $5 for Alice), but the marginal social benefit of going from 5 to 6 cleanings is only $2.

Of course, if society really consisted of only two individuals, they would probably manage to strike a deal to provide the good. But imagine a city with a million residents, each of whose individual marginal benefit from provision of the good is only a tiny fraction of the marginal social benefit. It would be impossible for people to reach a voluntary agreement to pay for the efficient level of street cleaning—the potential for free-riding makes it too difficult to make and enforce an agreement among so many people. But they could and would vote to tax themselves to pay for a citywide sanitation department.

Voting as a Public Good

It's a sad fact that many Americans who are eligible to vote don't bother to. As a result, their interests tend to be ignored by politicians. But what's even sadder is that this self-defeating behavior may be completely rational.

As the economist Mancur Olson pointed out in a famous book titled *The Logic of Collective Action,* voting is a public good, one that suffers from severe free-rider problems.

Imagine that you are one of a million people who would stand to gain the equivalent of $100 each if some plan is passed in a statewide referendum—say, a plan to improve public schools. And suppose that the opportunity cost of the time it would take you to vote is $10. Will you be sure to go to the polls and vote for the referendum? If you are rational, the answer is no! The reason is that it is very unlikely that your vote will decide the issue, either way. If the measure passes, you benefit, even if you didn't bother to vote—the benefits are nonexcludable. If the measure doesn't pass, your vote would not have changed the outcome. Either way, by not voting—by free-riding on those who do vote—you save $10.

Of course, many people do vote out of a sense of civic duty. But because political action is a public good, in general people devote too little effort to defending their own interests.

The result, Olson pointed out, is that when a large group of people share a common political interest, they are likely to exert too little effort promoting their cause and so will be ignored. Conversely, small, well-organized interest groups that act on issues narrowly targeted in their favor tend to have disproportionate power.

Is this a reason to distrust democracy? Winston Churchill said it best: "Democracy is the worst form of government, except for all the other forms that have been tried."

GLOBAL COMPARISON

VOTING AS A PUBLIC GOOD: THE GLOBAL PERSPECTIVE

Despite the fact that it can be an entirely rational choice not to vote, many countries consistently achieve astonishingly high turnout rates in their elections by adopting policies that encourage voting. In Italy and Australia, voting is compulsory; eligible voters are penalized if they fail to do their civic duty by casting their ballots. Other countries have policies that reduce the cost of voting; for example, declaring election day a work holiday (giving citizens ample time to cast their ballots), allowing voter registration on election day (eliminating the need for advance planning), and permitting voting by mail (increasing convenience).

This figure indicates turnout rates in several countries, measured as the percentage of eligible voters who cast ballots, averaged over elections held between 1945 and 2008. As you can see, Italy, South Africa, and Australia have the highest voter turnout rates. The United States, however, performs poorly: it has the lowest turnout rate among advanced countries. In general, the past four decades have seen a decline in voter turnout rates in the major democracies, most dramatically among the youngest voters.

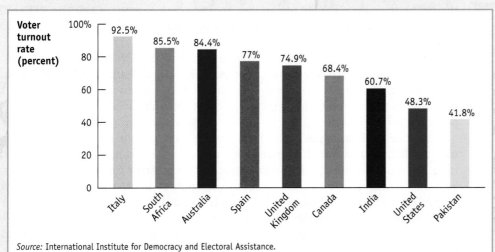

Source: International Institute for Democracy and Electoral Assistance.

Governments engage in **cost-benefit analysis** when they estimate the social costs and social benefits of providing a public good.

Cost-Benefit Analysis

How do governments decide in practice how much of a public good to provide? Sometimes policy makers just guess—or do whatever they think will get them reelected. However, responsible governments try to estimate both the social benefits and the social costs of providing a public good, a process known as **cost-benefit analysis.**

It's straightforward to estimate the cost of supplying a public good. Estimating the benefit is harder. In fact, it is a very difficult problem.

Now you might wonder why governments can't figure out the marginal social benefit of a public good just by asking people their willingness to pay for it (their individual marginal benefit). But it turns out that it's hard to get an honest answer.

This is not a problem with private goods: we can determine how much an individual is willing to pay for one more unit of a private good by looking at his or her actual choices. But because people don't actually pay for public goods, the question of willingness to pay is always hypothetical.

Worse yet, it's a question that people have an incentive not to answer truthfully. People naturally want more rather than less. Because they cannot be made to pay for whatever quantity of the public good they use, people are apt to overstate their true feelings when asked how much they desire a public good. For example, if street cleaning were scheduled according to the stated wishes of homeowners alone, the streets would be cleaned every day—an inefficient level of provision. So governments must be aware that they cannot simply rely on the public's statements when deciding how much of a public good to provide—if they do, they are likely to provide too much. In contrast, as For Inquiring Minds on the previous page explains, relying on the public to indicate how much of the public good they want through voting has problems as well—and is likely to lead to too little of the public good being provided.

➤ECONOMICS IN ACTION

Old Man River

It just keeps rolling along—but now and then it decides to roll in a different direction. In fact, the Mississippi River changes its course every few hundred years. Sediment carried downstream gradually clogs the river's route to the sea, and eventually the river breaches its banks and opens a new channel. Over the millennia the mouth of the Mississippi has swung back and forth along an arc some 200 miles wide.

So when is the Mississippi due to change course again? Oh, about 40 years ago.

The Mississippi currently runs to the sea past New Orleans; but by 1950 it was apparent that the river was about to shift course, taking a new route to the sea. If the Army Corps of Engineers hadn't gotten involved, the shift would probably have happened by 1970.

A shift in the Mississippi would have severely damaged the Louisiana economy. A major industrial area would have lost good access to the ocean, and salt water would have contaminated much of its water supply. So the Army Corps of Engineers has kept the Mississippi in its place with a huge complex of dams, walls, and gates known as the Old River Control Structure. At times the amount of water released by this control structure is five times the flow at Niagara Falls.

The Old River Control Structure is a dramatic example of a public good. No individual would have had an incentive to build it, yet it protects many billions of dollars' worth of private property. The history of the Army Corps of Engineers, which handles water-control projects across the United States, illustrates a persistent problem associated with government provision of public goods. That is, everyone wants a project that benefits his or her own property—if other people are going to pay for it. So there is a systematic tendency for potential beneficiaries of Corps projects to overstate the benefits. And the Corps has become notorious for undertaking expensive projects that cannot be justified with any reasonable cost-benefit analysis.

The flip-side of the problem of overfunding of public projects is chronic underfunding. A tragic illustration of this problem was the devastation of New Orleans by Hurricane Katrina in 2005. Although it was well understood from the time of its founding that New Orleans was at risk for severe flooding because it sits below sea level, very little was done to shore up the crucial system of levees and pumps that protects the city. More than 50 years of inadequate funding for construction and maintenance, coupled with inadequate supervision, left the system weakened and unable to cope with the onslaught from Katrina. The catastrophe was compounded by the failure of local and state government to develop an evacuation plan in the event of a hurricane. In the end, because of this neglect of a public good, 1,464 people in and around New Orleans lost their lives and the city suffered economic losses totaling billions of dollars. ▲

> > > > > > > > > > > >

▶ CHECK YOUR UNDERSTANDING 18-2

1. The town of Centreville, population 16, has two types of residents, Homebodies and Revelers. Using the accompanying table, the town must decide how much to spend on its New Year's Eve party. No individual resident expects to directly bear the cost of the party.

a. Suppose there are 10 Homebodies and 6 Revelers. Determine the marginal social benefit schedule of money spent on the party. What is the efficient level of spending?

b. Suppose there are 6 Homebodies and 10 Revelers. How do your answers to part a change? Explain.

c. Suppose that the individual marginal benefit schedules are known but no one knows the true proportion of Homebodies versus Revelers. Individuals are asked their preferences. What is the likely outcome? Why is it likely to result in an inefficiently high level of spending? Explain.

Money spent on party	Individual marginal benefit of additional $1 spent on party	
	Homebody	Reveler
$0		
	$0.05	$0.13
1		
	0.04	0.11
2		
	0.03	0.09
3		
	0.02	0.07
4		

Solutions appear at back of book.

Common Resources

A **common resource** is a good that is nonexcludable but is rival in consumption. An example is the stock of fish in a limited fishing area, like the fisheries off the coast of New England. Traditionally, anyone who had a boat could go out to sea and catch fish—fish in the sea were a nonexcludable good. Yet because the total number of fish is limited, the fish that one person catches are no longer available to be caught by someone else. So fish in the sea are rival in consumption.

Other examples of common resources are clean air and water as well as the diversity of animal and plant species on the planet (biodiversity). In each of these cases the fact that the good, though rival in consumption, is nonexcludable poses a serious problem.

A **common resource** is nonexcludable and rival in consumption: you can't stop me from consuming the good, and more consumption by me means less of the good available for you.

Common resources left to the market suffer from **overuse**: individuals ignore the fact that their use depletes the amount of the resource remaining for others.

The Problem of Overuse

Because common resources are nonexcludable, individuals cannot be charged for their use. Yet, because they are rival in consumption, an individual who uses a unit depletes the resource by making that unit unavailable to others. As a result, a common resource is subject to **overuse**: an individual will continue to use it until his or her marginal benefit of its use is equal to his or her own individual marginal cost, ignoring the cost that this action inflicts on society as a whole. As we will see shortly, the problem of overuse of a common resource is similar to a problem we studied in Chapter 17: the problem of a good that generates a negative externality, such as pollution-creating electricity generation or livestock farming.

Fishing is a classic example of a common resource. In heavily fished waters, my fishing imposes a cost on others by reducing the fish population and making it harder for others to catch fish. But I have no personal incentive to take this cost into account, since I cannot be charged for fishing. As a result, from society's point of view, I catch too many fish. Traffic congestion is another example of overuse of a common resource. A major highway during rush hour can accommodate only a certain number of vehicles per hour. If I decide to drive to work alone rather than carpool or work at home, I make the commute of many other people a bit longer; but I have no incentive to take these consequences into account.

In the case of a common resource, the *marginal social cost* of my use of that resource is higher than my *individual marginal cost,* the cost to me of using an additional unit of the good.

Figure 18-3 illustrates the point. It shows the demand curve for fish, which measures the marginal benefit of fish—the benefit to consumers when an additional unit of fish is caught and consumed. It also shows the supply curve for fish, which measures the marginal cost of production of the fishing industry. We know from Chapter 13 that the industry supply curve is the horizontal sum of each individual fisherman's supply curve—equivalent to his or her individual marginal cost curve. The fishing industry supplies the quantity where its marginal cost is equal to the price, the quantity Q_{MKT}. But the efficient outcome is to catch the quantity Q_{OPT}, the quantity of output that equates the marginal benefit to the marginal social cost, not to the

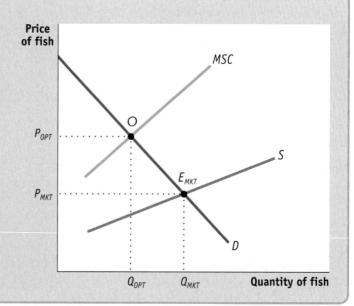

FIGURE 18-3

A Common Resource

The supply curve *S*, which shows the marginal cost of production of the fishing industry, is composed of the individual supply curves of the individual fishermen. But each fisherman's individual marginal cost does not include the cost that his or her actions impose on others: the depletion of the common resource. As a result, the marginal social cost curve, *MSC*, lies above the supply curve; in an unregulated market, the quantity of the common resource used, Q_{MKT}, exceeds the efficient quantity of use, Q_{OPT}.

A Water Fight in Maine

In the eyes of many, Maine is a natural paradise at the forefront of environmentalism. The state has adopted strict guidelines to protect its beautiful ponds, forests, and wildlife. But since 2004, Mainers have been engaged in a fierce battle over one of their natural resources: groundwater.

Maine's groundwater, or natural water, is a valuable commodity as drinking water, long prized for its purity and taste. And bottled water is big business—everyone has encountered Poland Spring Water of Maine, whose bottles can be found in stores across America. In Maine, the principle of "capture" defines the ownership of water: a property owner can pump any amount of groundwater without regard to the effect on the underground aquifer, the naturally occurring underground reservoir of an area's water. This situation presented no problem when water was drawn only to satisfy local demand because there was plenty of water available to satisfy Mainers' needs.

But with big companies like Poland Spring extracting groundwater to satisfy

What do water bottlers owe the citizens of Maine for extracting and selling a valuable common resource?

Carl D. Walsh/Aurora Photos

the demands of millions of customers across the country, some Mainers fear that they can no longer afford this policy. The concerns expressed over commercial water extraction are twofold. One is the problem of managing a common resource. Without oversight, what prevents water bottlers from overdrawing Maine's aquifer, leaving too little water for its residents?

Second, by law the underground aquifer belongs to the people of Maine. Why shouldn't they revoke the principle of capture and receive some compensation from bottlers for the sale of their water? They point to the example of Alaska, with its huge oil reserves, where the state government imposes a 22.5% tax on oil company profits. Tax revenues are distributed to Alaska residents in the form of greater services and lower taxes (and even subsidies). The water bottlers counter that the property taxes and wages that they already pay bring millions of dollars into the Maine economy.

The debate over groundwater came to a head when a statewide referendum regulating groundwater usage and imposing a $0.19 per gallon tax on large water bottlers failed due to technicalities. As of the time of writing, supporters of the referendum vow to continue the fight, and water bottlers vow to leave Maine if new taxes are imposed on them.

fishing industry's marginal cost of production. The market outcome results in overuse of the common resource.

As we noted, there is a close parallel between the problem of managing a common resource and the problem posed by negative externalities. In the case of an activity that generates a negative externality, the marginal social cost of production is greater than the industry's marginal cost of production, the difference being the marginal external cost imposed on society. Here, the loss to society arising from a fisherman's depletion of the common resource plays the same role as the external cost plays when there is a negative externality. In fact, many negative externalities (such as pollution) can be thought of as involving common resources (such as clean air).

The Efficient Use and Maintenance of a Common Resource

Because common resources pose problems similar to those created by negative externalities, the solutions are also similar. To ensure efficient use of a common resource, society must find a way of getting individual users of the resource to take into account the costs they impose on other users. This is basically the same principle as that of getting individuals to internalize a negative externality that arises from their actions.

There are three fundamental ways to induce people who use common resources to internalize the costs they impose on others.

- Tax or otherwise regulate the use of the common resource
- Create a system of tradable licenses for the right to use the common resource
- Make the common resource excludable and assign property rights to some individuals

Like activities that generate negative externalities, use of a common resource can be reduced to the efficient quantity by imposing a Pigouvian tax. For example, some countries have imposed "congestion charges" on those who drive during rush hour, in effect charging them for use of the common resource of highway space. Likewise, visitors to national parks must pay a fee, and the number of visitors to any one park is restricted.

A second way to correct the problem of overuse is to create a system of tradable licenses for the use of the common resource much like the systems designed to address negative externalities. The policy maker issues the number of licenses that corresponds to the efficient level of use of the good. Making the licenses tradable ensures that the right to use the good is allocated efficiently—that is, those who end up using the good (those willing to pay the most for a license) are those who gain the most from its use.

But when it comes to common resources, often the most natural solution is simply to assign property rights. At a fundamental level, common resources are subject to overuse because *nobody owns them*. The essence of ownership of a good—the *property right* over the good—is that you can limit who can and cannot use the good as well as how much of it can be used. When a good is nonexcludable, in a very real sense no one owns it because a property right cannot be enforced—and consequently no one has an incentive to use it efficiently. So one way to correct the problem of overuse is to make the good excludable and assign property rights over it to someone. The good now has an owner who has an incentive to protect the value of the good—to use it efficiently rather than overuse it.

As the upcoming Economics in Action shows, a system of tradable licenses has been a successful strategy in some fisheries.

►*ECONOMICS IN ACTION*

A Tale of Two Fisheries

A few years ago, the *New York Times Magazine* carried a story titled "A Tale of Two Fisheries," which compared the lives of lobstermen in two places: Point Judith, Rhode Island, and Port Lincoln, Australia.

Point Judith used to call itself the "tuna capital of the world," but tuna—along with swordfish, cod, halibut, and other species that used to be plentiful offshore—are now hard to find anywhere in the vicinity. Fishermen in the United States have been free to catch as many fish as they like; as a result of overfishing, the once-great fisheries of New England have largely collapsed. This includes lobsters, except for some areas of Maine where "lobster gangs" have protected the common resource by sabotaging the boats of outsiders. As lobster stocks have plunged, life for the lobstermen of Point Judith has gotten increasingly difficult.

In Australia, however, a different system prevails. To set a lobster trap, you must have a license, and only a limited number of licenses have been issued. A license now sells for about $21,000. At first Australian lobstermen were skeptical of a system that limited their fishing. But they now support the system enthusiastically because it sustains the value of their licenses—and also sustains their livelihood.

The system is popular because it works: an Australian lobster trap typically comes up with more and bigger lobsters than its American counterpart. As a result, the lobstermen of Port Lincoln, Australia, are far more prosperous than those of Point Judith, Rhode Island.

By the way, we don't want to give the impression that establishing property rights over common resources is un-American. The New Jersey clam fishery, which was in serious trouble in the late 1980s, now operates under a license system similar to that of the Australian lobster fishery. And both the clams and the New Jersey clam industry have staged a spectacular comeback. ▲

> > > > > > > > > > > >

> **CHECK YOUR UNDERSTANDING** 18-3

1. Rocky Mountain Forest is a government-owned forest in which private citizens were allowed in the past to harvest as much timber as they wanted free of charge. State in economic terms why this is problematic from society's point of view.

2. You are the new Forest Service Commissioner and have been instructed to come up with ways to preserve the forest for the general public. Name three different methods you could use to maintain the efficient level of tree harvesting and explain how each would work. For each method, what information would you need to know in order to achieve an efficient outcome?

Solutions appear at back of book.

Artificially Scarce Goods

An **artificially scarce good** is a good that is excludable but nonrival in consumption. As we've already seen, pay-per-view movies are a familiar example. The marginal cost to society of allowing an individual to watch the movie is zero, because one person's viewing doesn't interfere with other people's viewing. Yet cable companies prevent an individual from seeing a movie if he or she hasn't paid. Goods like computer software or audio files, which are valued for the information they embody (and are sometimes called "information goods"), are also artificially scarce.

As we've already seen, markets will supply artificially scarce goods: because they are excludable, the producers can charge people for consuming them.

But artificially scarce goods are nonrival in consumption, which means that the marginal cost of an individual's consumption is zero. So the price that the supplier of an artificially scarce good charges exceeds marginal cost. Because the efficient price is equal to the marginal cost of zero, the good is "artificially scarce," and consumption of the good is inefficiently low. However, unless the producer can somehow earn revenue for producing and selling the good, he or she will be unwilling to produce at all—an outcome that leaves society even worse off than it would otherwise be with positive but inefficiently low consumption.

Figure 18-4 on the next page illustrates the loss in total surplus caused by artificial scarcity. The demand curve shows the quantity of pay-per-view movies watched at any given price. The marginal cost of allowing an additional person to watch the movie is zero, so the efficient quantity of movies viewed is Q_{OPT}. The cable company charges a positive price, in this case $4, to unscramble the signal, and as a result only Q_{MKT} pay-per-view movies will be watched. This leads to a deadweight loss equal to the area of the shaded triangle.

Does this look familiar? Like the problems that arise with public goods and common resources, the problem created by artificially scarce goods is similar to something we have already seen: in this case, it is the problem of *natural monopoly*. A natural monopoly, you will recall, is an industry in which average total cost is above

An **artificially scarce good** is excludable but nonrival in consumption.

FIGURE 18-4

An Artificially Scarce Good

An artificially scarce good is excludable and nonrival in consumption. It is made artificially scarce because producers charge a positive price but the marginal cost of allowing one more person to consume the good is zero. In this example, the market price of a pay-per-view movie is $4 and the quantity demanded at that price is Q_{MKT}. But the efficient level of consumption is Q_{OPT}, the quantity demanded when the price is zero. The efficient quantity, Q_{OPT}, exceeds the quantity demanded in an unregulated market, Q_{MKT}. The shaded area represents the loss in total surplus from charging a price of $4.

marginal cost for the relevant output range. In order to be willing to produce output, the producer must charge a price at least as high as average total cost—that is, a price above marginal cost. But a price above marginal cost leads to inefficiently low consumption.

►ECONOMICS IN ACTION

Blacked-Out Games

It's the night of the big game for your local team—a game that is being nationally televised by one of the major networks. So you flip to the local channel that is an affiliate of that network—but the game isn't on. Instead, you get some other show with a message scrolling across the bottom of the screen that this game has been blacked out in your area. What the message probably doesn't say, though you understand quite well, is that this blackout is at the insistence of the team's owners, who don't want people who might have paid for tickets staying home and watching the game on TV instead.

So the good in question—watching the game on TV—has been made artificially scarce. Because the game is being broadcast anyway, no scarce resources would be used to make it available in its immediate locality as well. But it isn't available—which means a loss in welfare to those who would have watched the game on TV but are not willing to pay the price, in time and money, to go to the stadium. ▲

‒ < < < < < < < < < < <

> ## CHECK YOUR UNDERSTANDING 18-4

1. Xena is a software program produced by Xenoid. Each year Xenoid produces an upgrade that costs $300,000 to produce. It costs nothing to allow customers to download it from the company's website. The demand schedule for the upgrade is shown in the accompanying table.

>>QUICK REVIEW

- An **artificially scarce good** is excludable but nonrival in consumption.
- Because the good is nonrival in consumption, the efficient price to consumers is zero. However, because it is excludable, sellers charge a positive price, which leads to inefficiently low consumption.
- The problems of artificially scarce goods are similar to those posed by a natural monopoly.

a. What is the efficient price to a consumer of this upgrade? Explain your answer.

b. What is the lowest price at which Xenoid is willing to produce and sell the upgrade? Draw the demand curve and show the loss of total surplus that occurs when Xenoid charges this price compared to the efficient price.

Price of upgrade	Quantity of upgrades demanded
$180	1,700
150	2,000
120	2,300
90	2,600
0	3,500

Solutions appear at back of book.

>> A LOOK AHEAD •••

In 2007 the various levels of U.S. government—federal, state, and local—spent about $4.4 trillion. Where did the money go?

The answer, in large part, is that it went to provide public goods. National defense and homeland security took a big chunk; so did education, which is widely regarded as a public good. Then there was spending on highways, public health, fire prevention, and so on.

However, not all government spending is on items that can easily be described as public goods. As we'll see in Chapter 19, much spending at the federal level goes for *social insurance,* programs intended to help individuals and families in trouble, as well as for providing medical care for the elderly and poor. Although providing public goods is still a central feature of government budgets, government programs that provide social insurance and health care, collectively known as the *welfare state,* account for an increasing share of government spending in advanced countries like the United States. In the next chapter, we will examine the economic rationale behind the welfare state in general and the structure of the U.S. welfare state in particular.]

SUMMARY .... ■

1. Goods may be classified according to whether or not they are **excludable** and whether or not they are **rival in consumption.**

2. Free markets can deliver efficient levels of production and consumption for **private goods,** which are both excludable and rival in consumption. When goods are nonexcludable, nonrival in consumption, or both, free markets cannot achieve efficient outcomes.

3. When goods are **nonexcludable,** there is a **free-rider problem:** consumers will not pay for the good, leading to inefficiently low production. When goods are **nonrival in consumption,** they should be free, and any positive price leads to inefficiently low consumption.

4. A **public good** is nonexcludable and nonrival in consumption. In most cases a public good must be supplied by the government. The marginal social benefit of a public good is equal to the sum of the individual marginal benefits to each consumer. The efficient quantity of a public good is the quantity at which marginal social benefit equals the marginal cost of providing the good. Like a positive externality, marginal social benefit is greater than any one individual's marginal benefit, so no individual is willing to provide the efficient quantity.

5. One rationale for the presence of government is that it allows citizens to tax themselves in order to provide public goods. Governments use **cost-benefit analysis** to determine the efficient provision of a public good. Such analysis is difficult, however, because individuals have an incentive to overstate the good's value to them.

6. A **common resource** is rival in consumption but nonexcludable. It is subject to **overuse,** because an individual does not take into account the fact that his or her use depletes the amount available for others. This is similar to the problem of a negative externality: the marginal social cost of an individual's use of a common resource is always higher than his or her individual marginal cost. Pigouvian taxes, the creation of a system of tradable licenses, or the assignment of property rights are possible solutions.

7. **Artificially scarce goods** are excludable but nonrival in consumption. Because no marginal cost arises from allowing another individual to consume the good, the efficient price is zero. A positive price compensates the producer for the cost of production but leads to inefficiently low consumption. The problem of an artificially scarce good is similar to that of a natural monopoly.

KEY TERMS ··· ■

Excludable, p. 461
Rival in consumption, p. 461
Private good, p. 461
Nonexcludable, p. 461

Nonrival in consumption, p. 461
Free-rider problem, p. 462
Public good, p. 463
Cost-benefit analysis, p. 468

Common resource, p. 469
Overuse, p. 470
Artificially scarce good, p. 473

PROBLEMS ··· ■

1. The government is involved in providing many goods and services. For each of the goods or services listed, determine whether it is rival or nonrival in consumption and whether it is excludable or nonexcludable. What type of good is it? Without government involvement, would the quantity provided be efficient, inefficiently low, or inefficiently high?

   a. Street signs

   b. Amtrak rail service

   c. Regulations limiting pollution

   d. An interstate highway without tolls

   e. A lighthouse on the coast

2. An economist gives the following advice to a museum director: "You should introduce 'peak pricing': at times when the museum has few visitors, you should admit visitors for free. And at times when the museum has many visitors, you should charge a higher admission fee."

   a. When the museum is quiet, is it rival or nonrival in consumption? Is it excludable or nonexcludable? What type of good is the museum at those times? What would be the efficient price to charge visitors during that time, and why?

   b. When the museum is busy, is it rival or nonrival in consumption? Is it excludable or nonexcludable? What type of good is the museum at those times? What would be the efficient price to charge visitors during that time, and why?

3. In many planned communities, various aspects of community living are subject to regulation by a homeowners' association. These rules can regulate house architecture; require snow removal from sidewalks; exclude outdoor equipment, such as backyard swimming pools; require appropriate conduct in shared spaces such as the community clubhouse; and so on. Suppose there has been some conflict in one such community because some homeowners feel that some of the regulations mentioned above are overly intrusive. You have been called in to mediate. Using what you have learned about public goods and common resources, how would you decide what types of regulations are warranted and what types are not?

4. A residential community has 100 residents who are concerned about security. The accompanying table gives the total cost of hiring a 24-hour security service as well as each individual resident's total benefit.

Quantity of security guards	Total cost	Total individual benefit to each resident
0	$0	$0
1	150	10
2	300	16
3	450	18
4	600	19

   a. Explain why the security service is a public good for the residents of the community.

   b. Calculate the marginal cost, the individual marginal benefit for each resident, and the marginal social benefit.

   c. If an individual resident were to decide about hiring and paying for security guards on his or her own, how many guards would that resident hire?

   d. If the residents act together, how many security guards will they hire?

5. The accompanying table shows Tanisha's and Ari's individual marginal benefit of different amounts of street cleanings per month. Suppose that the marginal cost of street cleanings is constant at $9 each.

Quantity of street cleanings per month	Tanisha's individual marginal benefit	Ari's individual marginal benefit
0		
	$10	$8
1		
	6	4
2		
	2	1
3		

   a. If Tanisha had to pay for street cleaning on her own, how many street cleanings would there be?

   b. Calculate the marginal social benefit of street cleaning. What is the optimal number of street cleanings?

c. Consider the optimal number of street cleanings. The last street cleaning of that number costs $9. Is Tanisha willing to pay for that last cleaning on her own? Is Ari willing to pay for that last cleaning on his own?

6. Anyone with a radio receiver can listen to public radio, which is funded largely by donations.

a. Is public radio excludable or nonexcludable? Is it rival in consumption or nonrival? What type of good is it?

b. Should the government support public radio? Explain your reasoning.

c. In order to finance itself, public radio decides to transmit only to satellite radios, for which users have to pay a fee. What type of good is public radio then? Will the quantity of radio listening be efficient? Why or why not?

7. Your economics professor assigns a group project for the course. Describe the free-rider problem that can lead to a sub-optimal outcome for your group. To combat this problem, the instructor asks you to evaluate the contribution of your peers in a confidential report. Will this evaluation have the desired effects?

8. The village of Upper Bigglesworth has a village "commons," a piece of land on which each villager, by law, is free to graze his or her cows. Use of the commons is measured in units of the number of cows grazing on it. Assume that each resident has a constant marginal cost of sending cows to graze (that is, the marginal cost is the same, whether 1 or 10 cows are grazing). But each additional cow grazed means less grass available for others, and the damage done by overgrazing of the commons increases as the number of cows grazing increases. Finally, assume that the benefit to the villagers of each additional cow grazing on the commons declines as more cows graze, since each additional cow has less grass to eat than the previous one.

a. Is the commons excludable or nonexcludable? Is it rival in consumption or nonrival? What kind of good is the commons?

b. Draw a diagram, with the quantity of cows that graze on the commons on the horizontal axis. How does the quantity of cows grazing in the absence of government intervention compare to the efficient quantity? Show both in your diagram.

c. The villagers hire you to tell them how to achieve an efficient use of the commons. You tell them that there are three possibilities: a Pigouvian tax, the assignment of property rights over the commons, and a system of tradable licenses for the right to graze a cow. Explain how each one of these options would lead to an efficient use of the commons. Draw a diagram that shows the Pigouvian tax.

9. Prior to 2003, the city of London was often one big parking lot. Traffic jams were common, and it could take hours to travel a couple of miles. Each additional commuter contributed to the congestion, which can be measured by the total number of cars on London roads. Although each com-

muter suffered by spending valuable time in traffic, none of them paid for the inconvenience they caused others. The total cost of travel includes the opportunity cost of time spent in traffic and any fees levied by London authorities.

a. Draw a graph illustrating the overuse of London roads, assuming that there is no fee to enter London in a vehicle and that roads are a common resource. Put the cost of travel on the vertical axis and the quantity of cars on the horizontal axis. Draw typical demand, individual marginal cost (MC), and marginal social cost (MSC) curves and label the equilibrium point. (*Hint:* The marginal cost takes into account the opportunity cost of spending time on the road for individual drivers but not the inconvenience they cause to others.)

b. In February 2003, the city of London began charging a £5 congestion fee on all vehicles traveling in London. Illustrate the effects of this congestion charge on your graph and label the new equilibrium point. Assume the new equilibrium point is not optimally set (that is, assume that the £5 charge is too low relative to what would be efficient).

c. The congestion fee was raised to £8 in July 2005. Illustrate the new equilibrium point on your graph, assuming the new charge is now optimally set.

10. The accompanying table shows six consumers' willingness to pay (his or her individual marginal benefit) for one MP3 file copy of a Dr. Dre album. The marginal cost of making the file accessible to one additional consumer is constant, at zero.

Consumer	Individual marginal benefit
Adriana	$2
Bhagesh	15
Chizuko	1
Denzel	10
Emma	5
Frank	4

a. What would be the efficient price to charge for a download of the file?

b. All six consumers are able to download the file for free from a file-sharing service, Pantster. Which consumers will download the file? What will be the total consumer surplus to those consumers?

c. Pantster is shut down for copyright law infringement. In order to download the file, consumers now have to pay $4.99 at a commercial music site. Which consumers will download the file? What will be the total consumer surplus to those consumers? How much producer surplus accrues to the commercial music site? What is the total surplus? What is the deadweight loss from the new pricing policy?

11. Butchart Gardens is a very large garden in Victoria, British Columbia, renowned for its beautiful plants. It is so large that it could hold many times more visitors than currently visit it. The garden charges an admission fee of C$25 (C$1 equals approximately U.S. $1). At this price, 1,000 people visit the garden each day. If admission were free, 2,000 people would visit each day.

a. Are visits to Butchart Gardens excludable or nonexcludable? Are they rival in consumption or nonrival? What type of good is it?

b. In a diagram, illustrate the demand curve for visits to Butchart Gardens. Indicate the situation when Butchart Gardens charges an admission fee of C$25. Also indicate the situation when Butchart Gardens charges no admission fee.

c. Illustrate the deadweight loss from charging a C$25 admission fee. Explain why charging a C$25 admission fee is inefficient.

12. Software has historically been an artificially scarce good—it is nonrival because the cost of replication is negligible once the investment to write the code is made, but software companies make it excludable by charging for user licenses. Recently, however, open-source software has emerged, most of which is free to download and can be modified and maintained by anyone.

a. Discuss the free-rider problem that might exist in the development of open-source software. What effect might this have on quality? Why does this problem not exist for proprietary software, such as the products of a company like Microsoft or Adobe?

b. Some argue that open-source software serves an unsatisfied market demand that proprietary software ignores.

○·······································○

Draw a typical diagram that illustrates how proprietary software may be underproduced. Put the price and marginal cost of software on the vertical axis and the quantity of software on the horizontal axis. Draw a typical demand curve and a marginal cost curve (MC) that is always equal to zero. Assume that the software company charges a positive price, P, for the software. Label the equilibrium point and the efficient point.

13. In developing a vaccine for the SARS virus a pharmaceutical company incurs a very high fixed cost. The marginal cost of delivering the vaccine to patients, however, is negligible (consider it to be equal to zero). The pharmaceutical company holds the exclusive patent to the vaccine. You are a regulator who must decide what price the pharmaceutical company is allowed to charge.

a. Draw a diagram that shows the price for the vaccine that would arise if the company is unregulated, and label it P_M. What is the efficient price for the vaccine? Show the deadweight loss that arises from the price P_M.

b. On another diagram, show the lowest price that the regulator can enforce that would still induce the pharmaceutical company to develop the vaccine. Label it P^*. Show the deadweight loss that arises from this price. How does it compare to the deadweight loss that arises from the price P_M?

c. Suppose you have accurate information about the pharmaceutical company's fixed cost. How could you use price regulation of the pharmaceutical company, combined with a subsidy to the company, to have the efficient quantity of the vaccine provided at the lowest cost to the government?

The Economics of the Welfare State

INSURING CHILDREN'S HEALTH

SENATOR TED KENNEDY OF MASSACHUSETTS, A liberal Democrat, and Senator Orrin Hatch of Utah, a conservative Republican, didn't see eye to eye on much in the 1990s. Yet the two men came together in 1997 to sponsor a bill creating a new government program known as SCHIP (pronounced "ess-chip"), the State Children's Health Insurance Program.

SCHIP, as its name suggests, provides health insurance to children. (The "state" in the title refers to the fact that the federal government provides grants to the states, rather than running the program directly itself.) It wasn't the first child health insurance program: in 1997 there were already almost 15 million American children receiving health coverage from Medicaid, a program designed to help the poor. What SCHIP did was extend coverage to several million more children, those in families with incomes too high to qualify for Medicaid but not, in the judgment of the program's creators, high enough to afford private health insurance.

A decade after its creation, SCHIP would become the object of a tough political fight between Democrats who wanted to expand the program and Republicans who didn't. But it's revealing that the program was originally created through a bipartisan initiative. In modern America, politicians often disagree about how much help lower-income families should receive to pay for their health care, housing, food, and other items, but there is a broad political consensus that they should receive *some* help. And they do.

It's the same around the world. Modern governments, especially in wealthy countries, devote a large chunk of their budgets to health care, income support for the elderly, aid to the poor, and other programs that reduce economic insecurity and, to some degree, income inequality. The collection of government programs devoted to these tasks is known as the *welfare state*.

We start this chapter by discussing the underlying rationale for welfare state programs. Then we'll describe and analyze the two main kinds of programs operating in the United States: income support programs, of which Social Security is by far the largest, and health care programs, dominated by Medicare and Medicaid.

Senators Ted Kennedy ((left) and Orrin Hatch (right) sponsored SCHIP, The State Children's Health Insurance Program, which extended health coverage to children from families with incomes too high to qualify for Medicaid but not high enough to afford private insurance.

Poverty, Inequality, and Public Policy

During World War II a British clergyman gave a speech in which he contrasted the "warfare state" of Nazi Germany, dedicated to conquest, with Britain's "welfare state," dedicated to serving the welfare of its people. Since then, the term **welfare state** has come to refer to the collection of government programs that are designed to alleviate economic hardship. A large share of the government spending of all wealthy countries consists of **government transfers**—payments by the government to individuals and families—that provide financial aid to the poor, assistance to unemployed workers, guaranteed income for the elderly, and assistance in paying medical bills for those with large health care expenses.

The Logic of the Welfare State

Suppose that the Taylor family, which has an income of only $15,000 a year, were to receive a government check for $1,500. This check might allow the Taylors to afford a better place to live, eat a more nutritious diet, or in other ways significantly improve their quality of life. Also suppose that the Fisher family, which has an income of $300,000 a year, were to face an extra tax of $1,500. This probably wouldn't make much difference to their quality of life: at worst, they might have to give up a few minor luxuries.

This hypothetical exchange illustrates one major rationale for the welfare state: *alleviating income inequality.* Because a marginal dollar is worth more to a poor person than a rich one, modest transfers from the rich to the poor will do the rich little harm but benefit the poor a lot. So, according to this argument, a government that plays Robin Hood, taking from the rich to give to the poor, does more good than harm. Programs that are designed to aid the poor are known as **poverty programs.**

There is a second major rationale for the welfare state: *alleviating economic insecurity.* Imagine ten families, each of which can expect an income next year of $50,000 if nothing goes wrong. But suppose the odds are that something *will* go wrong for one of the families, although nobody knows which one. For example, suppose each of the families has a one in ten chance of experiencing a sharp drop in income because one family member is laid off or incurs large medical bills. And assume that this event will produce severe hardship for the family—a family member will have to drop out of school or the family will lose its home. Now suppose there's a government program that provides aid to families in distress, paying for that aid by taxing families that are having a good year. Arguably, this program will make all the families better off, because even those families that don't currently receive aid from the program are likely to need it at some point in the future. Each family will feel safer knowing that the government stands ready to help when disaster strikes. Programs designed to provide protection against unpredictable financial distress are known as **social insurance programs.**

These two rationales for the welfare state are closely related to the *ability-to-pay principle* we learned about in Chapter 7. Recall how the ability-to-pay principle is used to justify progressive taxation: it says that people with low incomes, for whom an additional dollar makes a big difference to economic well-being, should pay a

The **welfare state** is the collection of government programs designed to alleviate economic hardship.

A **government transfer** is a government payment to an individual or a family.

A **poverty program** is a government program designed to aid the poor.

A **social insurance program** is a government program designed to provide protection against unpredictable financial distress.

Justice and the Welfare State

In 1971 the philosopher John Rawls published *A Theory of Justice,* the most famous attempt to date to develop a theory of economic fairness. He asked readers to imagine deciding economic and social policies behind a "veil of ignorance" about their own identity. That is, suppose you knew you would be a human being but did not know whether you would be rich or poor, healthy or sick, and so on. Rawls argued that the policies that would emerge if people had to make decisions behind the veil of ignorance define what we mean by economic justice. It's sort of a generalized version of the Golden Rule: do unto others as you would have them do unto you if you were in their place.

Rawls further argued that people behind the veil of ignorance would choose policies that placed a high value on the well-being of the worst-off members of society: after all, each of us might be one of those unlucky individuals. As a result, Rawlsian theory is often used as an argument for a generous welfare state.

Three years after Rawls published his book, another philosopher, Robert Nozick, published *Anarchy, State, and Utopia,* which is often considered the libertarian response. Nozick argued that justice is a matter of rights, not results, and that the government has no right to force people with high incomes to support others with lower incomes. He argued for a minimal government that enforces the law and provides security—the "night watchman state"—and against the welfare state programs that account for so much government spending.

Philosophers, of course, don't run the world. But real-world political debate often contains arguments that clearly reflect either a Rawls-type or a Nozick-type position.

smaller fraction of their income in taxes than people with higher incomes, for whom an additional dollar makes much less difference. The same principle suggests that those with very low incomes should actually get money back from the tax system.

More broadly, as the above For Inquiring Minds explains, some political philosophers argue that principles of social justice demand that society take care of the poor and unlucky. Others disagree, arguing that welfare state programs go beyond the proper role of government. To an important extent, the difference between those two philosophical positions defines what we mean in politics by "liberalism" and "conservatism."

But before we get carried away, it's important to realize that things aren't quite that cut and dried. Even conservatives who believe in limited government typically support some welfare state programs. And even economists who support the goals of the welfare state are concerned about the effects of large-scale aid to the poor and unlucky on their incentives to work and save. Like taxes, welfare state programs can create substantial deadweight losses, so their true economic costs can be considerably larger than the direct monetary cost. We'll turn to the costs and benefits of the welfare state later in this chapter. First, however, let's examine the problems the welfare state is supposed to address.

The Problem of Poverty

For at least the past 70 years, every U.S. president has promised to do his best to reduce poverty. In 1964 President Lyndon Johnson went so far as to declare a "war on poverty," creating a number of new programs to aid the poor. Antipoverty programs account for a significant part of the U.S. welfare state, although social insurance programs are an even larger part.

But what, exactly, do we mean by poverty? Any definition is somewhat arbitrary. Since 1965, however, the U.S. government has maintained an official definition of the **poverty threshold,** a minimum annual income that is considered adequate to purchase the necessities of life. Families whose incomes fall below the poverty threshold are considered poor. The history of this official definition is described in the upcoming For Inquiring Minds.

The official poverty threshold depends on the size and composition of a family. In 2007 the poverty threshold for an adult living alone was $10,787; for a household consisting of two adults and two children, it was $21,027.

The **poverty threshold** is the annual income below which a family is officially considered poor.

FOR INQUIRING MINDS

Defining Poverty

Who decided how much income an American family needs to escape poverty? Mollie Orshansky! Orshansky, a research analyst at the Social Security Administration, developed initial estimates of the poverty threshold in 1963–1964.

Orshansky started by estimating the cost of buying an inexpensive but nutritionally adequate diet. She then observed that families with children spent about one-third of their income on food; so she argued that any family earning less than three times the cost of purchasing an adequate diet did not have adequate income.

Was this the right measure of poverty? When it was created, Orshansky's calculation made a lot of sense, and it has been the basis for U.S. poverty statistics ever since. But many experts now think that this measure of poverty is badly outdated because the composition of spending by low-income families has changed significantly since the 1960s. On average, the share of income spent on food has fallen to less than 20%, but the share spent on things such as housing, health care, transportation, and child care has risen. Many state governments have recognized this trend and now make families with incomes up to 150% or 200% of the poverty threshold eligible to receive assistance from some poverty programs. Some states offer assistance to families with incomes as high as 275% to 300% of the poverty threshold.

The **poverty rate** is the percentage of the population with incomes below the poverty threshold.

Trends in Poverty Contrary to popular misconceptions, although the official poverty threshold is adjusted each year to reflect changes in the cost of living, it has *not* been adjusted upward over time to reflect the long-term rise in the standard of living of the average American family. As a result, as the economy grows and becomes more prosperous, and average incomes rise, you might expect the percentage of the population living below the poverty threshold to steadily decline.

Somewhat surprisingly, however, this hasn't happened. Figure 19-1 shows the U.S. **poverty rate**—the percentage of the population living below the poverty threshold—from 1959 to 2006. As you can see, the poverty rate fell steeply during the 1960s and early 1970s. Since then, however, it has fluctuated up and down, with no clear trend. In fact, in 2006 the poverty rate was higher than it had been in 1973.

Who Are the Poor? Many Americans probably hold a stereotyped image of poverty: an African-American or Hispanic family with no husband present and the female head of the household unemployed at least part of the time. This picture isn't completely off-base: poverty is disproportionately high among African-Americans and

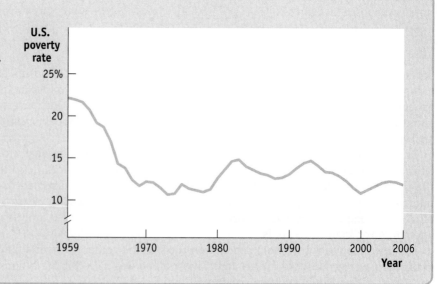

FIGURE 19-1

Trends in the U.S. Poverty Rate, 1959–2006

The poverty rate fell sharply from the 1960s to the early 1970s but has not shown a clear trend since then.

Source: U.S. Census Bureau.

GLOBAL COMPARISON   POOR PEOPLE IN RICH COUNTRIES

How does America's poverty problem compare with the situation in other wealthy countries? The answer depends, in part, on the definition of poverty—although the United States performs relatively poorly regardless of the definition.

The figure shows poverty rates in 2000 in five rich countries, under two definitions. One definition, which is widely used in international comparisons, defines someone as poor if they live in a household with less than half their country's median income, which we define in an upcoming section. This is a *relative* definition of poverty: you're poor if you have a low income compared with other people in your country. As the orange bars in the figure show, by this measure the United States has high poverty compared with other rich nations.

One objection to this comparison is that America is even richer than other rich countries and has a somewhat higher median income than the other countries shown. Does the United States still have high poverty when this is taken into account?

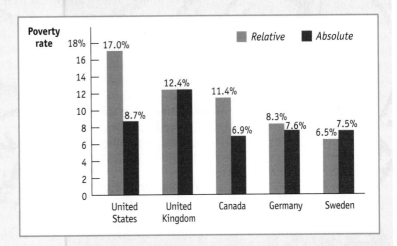

The purple bars use a measure of *absolute* poverty, similar to the official U.S. poverty threshold. The United States is no longer the country with the highest poverty rate by this measure—it is in second place. By either measure, the United States has a high poverty rate compared to other rich countries.

Source: T. Smeeding, "Poor People in Rich Nations: The United States in Comparative Perspective," Syracuse University working paper, 2006.

Hispanics as well as among female-headed households. But a majority of the poor don't fit the stereotype.

In 2006, about 36.5 million Americans were in poverty—12.3% of the population, or about one in eight persons. About one-quarter of the poor were African-American and a roughly equal number, Hispanic. Within these two groups, poverty rates were well above the national average: 24.3% of African-Americans and 20.6% of Hispanics. But there was also widespread poverty among non-Hispanic Whites, who had a poverty rate of 8.2%.

There is also a correlation between family makeup and poverty. Female-headed families with no husband present had a very high poverty rate: 30.5%. Married couples were much less likely to be poor, with a poverty rate of only 4.9%; still, about 38% of poor families were married couples.

What really stands out from the data, however, is the association between poverty and lack of adequate employment. Adults who work full time are very unlikely to be poor: only 2.7% of full-time workers were poor in 2006. Adults who worked part time or not at all during the year made up 88.3% of the poor in 2006. Many industries, particularly in the retail and service sectors, now rely primarily on part-time workers. Part-time work typically lacks benefits such as health plans, paid vacation days, and retirement benefits, and it also usually pays a lower hourly wage than comparable full-time work. As a result, many of the poor are members of what analysts call the *working poor*: workers whose income falls at or below the poverty threshold.

What Causes Poverty?

Poverty is often blamed on lack of education, and educational attainment clearly has a strong positive effect on income level—those with more education earn, on average, higher incomes than those with less education. For example, in 1979 the average hourly wage of men with a college degree was 36% higher than that of men with only a high school diploma; by 2006 the "college premium" had increased to 83%. Lack of proficiency in English is also a barrier to higher income. For example, Mexican-born male workers in the United States—two-thirds of whom have not graduated from high school and many of whom have poor English skills—earn less than half of what native-born men earn. And it's important not to overlook the role of racial and gender discrimination; although less pervasive today than 50 years ago, discrimination still erects formidable barriers to advancement for many Americans. Non-Whites earn less and are less likely to be employed than Whites with comparable levels of education. Studies find that African-American males suffer persistent discrimination by employers in favor of Whites, African-American women, and Hispanic immigrants. Women earn lower incomes than men with similar qualifications.

In addition, one important source of poverty that should not be overlooked is bad luck. Many families find themselves impoverished when a wage-earner loses a job or a family member falls seriously ill.

Consequences of Poverty   The consequences of poverty are often severe, particularly for children. Currently, more than 17.4% of children in the United States live in poverty. Poverty is often associated with lack of access to health care, which can lead to further health problems that erode the ability to attend school and work later in life. Affordable housing is also frequently a problem, leading poor families to move often, disrupting school and work schedules. Recent medical studies have shown that children raised in severe poverty tend to suffer from lifelong learning disabilities. As a result, American children growing up in or near poverty don't have an equal chance at the starting line: they tend to be at a disadvantage throughout their lives. For example, even talented children who come from poor families are unlikely to finish college.

Table 19-1 shows the results of a long-term survey conducted by the U.S. Department of Education, which tracked a group of students who were in eighth grade in 1988. That year, the students took a mathematics test that the study used as an indicator of their innate ability; the study also scored students by the socioeconomic status of their families, a measure that took into account their parents' income and employment. As you can see, the results were disturbing: only 29% of students who were in the highest-scoring 25% on the test but whose parents were of low status finished college. By contrast, the equally talented children of high-status parents had a 74% chance of finishing college—and children of high-status parents had a 30% chance of finishing college even if they had low test scores. What this tells us is that poverty is, to an important degree, self-perpetuating: the children of the poor start at such a disadvantage relative to other Americans that it's very hard for them to achieve a better life.

TABLE 19-1

Percent of Eighth-Graders Finishing College, 1988

	Mathematics test score in bottom quartile	Mathematics test score in top quartile
Parents in bottom quartile	3%	29%
Parents in top quartile	30	74

Source: National Center for Education Statistics, *The Condition of Education 2003,* p. 47.

Economic Inequality

The United States is a rich country. In 2006, the average U.S. household had an income of more than $66,000, far exceeding the poverty threshold. How is it possible, then, that so many Americans still live in poverty? The answer is that income is

TABLE 19-2

U.S. Income Distribution in 2006

Income group	Income range	Average income	Percent of total income
Bottom quintile	Less than $20,032	$11,352	3.4%
Second quintile	$20,032 to $37,771	28,777	8.6
Third quintile	$37,771 to $60,000	48,223	14.5
Fourth quintile	$60,000 to $97,030	76,329	22.9
Top quintile	More than $97,030	168,170	50.5
Top 5%	More than $174,000	297,405	22.3
Mean income = $66,570		**Median income = $48,201**	

Source: U.S. Census Bureau.

unequally distributed, with many households earning much less than the average and others earning much more.

Table 19-2 shows the distribution of pre-tax income among U.S. families in 2006—income before federal income taxes are paid—as estimated by the Census Bureau. Households are grouped into *quintiles,* each containing 20% or one-fifth of the population. The first, or bottom, quintile contains households whose income put them below the 20th percentile in income, the second quintile contains households whose income put them between the 20th and 40th percentiles, and so on. The Census Bureau also provides data on the 5% of families with the highest incomes.

For each group, Table 19-2 shows three numbers. The second column shows the range of incomes that define the group. For example, in 2006, the bottom quintile consisted of households with annual incomes of less than $20,032; the next quintile of households with incomes between $20,032 and $37,771; and so on. The third column shows the average income in each group, ranging from $11,352 for the bottom fifth to $297,405 for the top 5 percent. The fourth column shows the percentage of total U.S. income received by each group.

At the bottom of Table 19-2 are two useful numbers for thinking about the incomes of American households. **Mean household income,** also called average household income, is the total income of all U.S. households divided by the number of households. **Median household income** is the income of a household in the exact middle of the income distribution—the level of income at which half of all households have lower income and half have higher income. It's very important to realize that these two numbers do not measure the same thing. Economists often illustrate the difference by asking people first to imagine a room containing several dozen more or less ordinary wage-earners, then to think about what happens to the mean and median incomes of the people in the room if a Wall Street tycoon, some of whom earn more than a billion dollars a year, walks in. The mean income soars, because the tycoon's income pulls up the average, but median income hardly rises at all. This example helps explain why economists generally regard median income as a better guide to the economic status of typical American families than mean income: mean income is strongly affected by the incomes of a relatively small number of very-high-income Americans, who are not representative of the population as a whole; median income is not.

What we learn from Table 19-2 is that income in the United States is quite unequally distributed. The average income of the poorest fifth of families is less than a quarter of the average income of families in the middle, and the richest fifth have an average income more than three times that of families in the middle. The incomes

Mean household income is the average income across all households.

Median household income is the income of the household lying at the exact middle of the income distribution.

The **Gini coefficient** is a number that summarizes a country's level of income inequality based on how unequally income is distributed across quintiles.

of the richest fifth of the population are, on average, about 15 times as high as those of the poorest fifth. In fact, the distribution of income in America has become more unequal since 1980, rising to a level that has made it a significant political issue. The Economics in Action at the end of this section discusses long-term trends in U.S. income inequality, which declined in the 1930s and 1940s, was stable for more than 30 years after World War II, but began rising again in the late 1970s.

It's often convenient to have a single number that summarizes a country's level of income inequality. The **Gini coefficient,** the most widely used measure of inequality, is based on how disparately income is distributed across the quintiles. A country with a perfectly equal distribution of income—that is, one in which the bottom 20% of the population received 20% of the income, the bottom 40% of the population received 40% of the income, and so on—would have a Gini coefficient of 0. At the other extreme, the highest possible value for the Gini coefficient is 1—the level it would attain if all a country's income went to just one person.

One way to get a sense of what Gini coefficients mean in practice is to look at international comparisons. Figure 19-2 shows the most recent estimates of the Gini coefficient for many of the world's countries. Aside from a few countries in Africa, the highest levels of income inequality are found in Latin America, especially Brazil; countries with a high degree of inequality, such as Brazil, have Gini coefficients close to 0.6. The most equal distributions of income are in Europe, especially in Scandinavia; countries with very equal income distributions, such as Sweden, have Gini coefficients around 0.25. Compared to other wealthy countries, the United States, with a Gini coefficient of 0.470 in 2006, has unusually high inequality, though it isn't as unequal as in Latin America.

Figure 19-2 Income Inequality Around the World
The highest levels of income inequality are found in Africa and Latin America. The most equal distributions of income are in Europe, especially in Scandinavia. Compared to other wealthy countries, the United States, with a Gini coefficient of 0.470 in 2006, has unusually high inequality.

Source: World Bank, *Human Development Report 2007–2008.*

How serious an issue is income inequality? In a direct sense, high income inequality means that some people don't share in a nation's overall prosperity. As we've seen, rising inequality explains how it's possible that the U.S. poverty rate has failed to fall for the past 35 years even though the country as a whole has become considerably

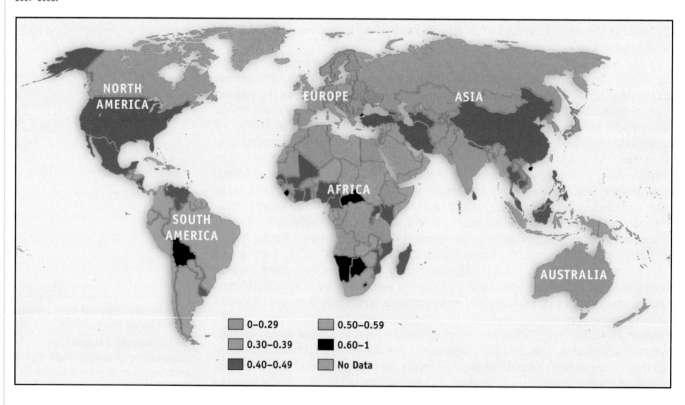

0–0.29	0.50–0.59
0.30–0.39	0.60–1
0.40–0.49	No Data

richer. Also, extreme inequality, as found in Latin America, is often associated with political instability, because of tension between a wealthy minority and the rest of the population.

It's important to realize, however, that the data shown in Table 19-2 overstate the true degree of inequality in America, for several reasons. One is that the data represent a snapshot for a single year, whereas the incomes of many individual families fluctuate over time. That is, many of those near the bottom in any given year are having an unusually bad year and many of those at the top are having an unusually good one. Over time, their incomes will revert to a more normal level. So a table showing average incomes within quintiles over a longer period, such as a decade, would not show as much inequality. Furthermore, a family's income tends to vary over its life cycle: most people earn considerably less in their early working years than they will later in life, then experience a considerable drop in income when they retire. Consequently, the numbers in Table 19-2, which combine young workers, mature workers, and retirees, show more inequality than would a table that compares families of similar ages.

Despite these qualifications, there is a considerable amount of genuine inequality in the United States. Moreover, the fact that families' incomes fluctuate from year to year isn't entirely good news. Measures of inequality in a given year *do* overstate true inequality. But those year-to-year fluctuations are part of a problem that worries even affluent families—economic insecurity.

Economic Insecurity

As we stated earlier, although the rationale for the welfare state rests in part on the social benefits of reducing poverty and inequality, it also rests in part on the benefits of reducing economic insecurity, which afflicts even relatively well-off families.

One form economic insecurity takes is the risk of a sudden loss of income, which usually happens when a family member loses a job and either spends an extended period without work or is forced to take a new job that pays considerably less. In a given year, according to recent estimates, about one in six American families will see their income cut in half from the previous year. Related estimates show that the percentage of people who find themselves below the poverty threshold for at least one year over the course of a decade is several times higher than the percentage of people below the poverty threshold in any given year.

Even if a family doesn't face a loss in income, it can face a surge in expenses. The most common reason for such surges is a medical problem that requires expensive treatment, such as heart disease or cancer. Many Americans have health insurance that covers a large share of their expenses in such cases, but a substantial number either do not have health insurance or rely on insurance provided by the government.

►*ECONOMICS IN ACTION*

Long-Term Trends in Income Inequality in the United States

Does inequality tend to rise, fall, or stay the same over time? The answer is yes—all three. Over the course of the past century, the United States has gone through periods characterized by all three trends: an era of falling inequality during the 1930s and 1940s, an era of stable inequality for about 35 years after World War II, and an era of rising inequality over the past generation.

Detailed U.S. data on income by quintiles, as shown in Table 19-2, are only available starting in 1947. Panel (a) of Figure 19-3 on the next page shows the annual rate of growth of income, adjusted for inflation, for each quintile over two periods: from

FIGURE **19-3**   Trends in U.S. Income Inequality

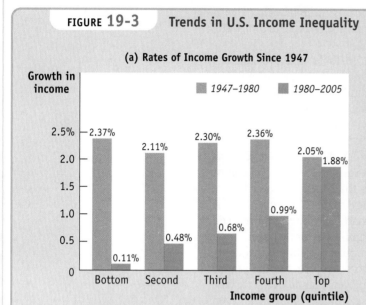

(a) Rates of Income Growth Since 1947

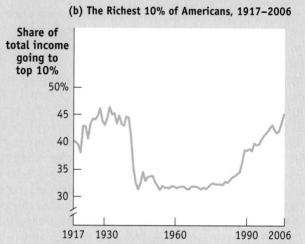

(b) The Richest 10% of Americans, 1917–2006

Panel (a) compares the rates of income growth for quintiles over two periods since World War II. In the earlier period, income grew at about the same rate for all quintiles, so the distribution of income was more or less stable. Since 1980, however, income has grown much more rapidly at the top than in the middle or at the bottom, so inequality has

increased. Panel (b) shows the income share going to the richest 10% of the population since 1917. This shows a sharp fall in inequality between the 1930s and the late 1940s—the Great Compression—and a rise in inequality since 1980.

Sources: U.S. Census Bureau (panel (a)). Emmanuel Saez, "Striking It Richer: The Evolution of Top Incomes in the United States," University of California, Berkeley, discussion paper, 2008 (panel (b)).

1947 to 1980, and from 1980 to 2005. There's a clear difference between the two periods. In the first period, income within each group grew at about the same rate—that is, there wasn't much change in the inequality of income, just growing incomes across the board. After 1980, however, incomes grew much more quickly at the top than in the middle, and more quickly in the middle than at the bottom. So inequality has increased substantially since 1980. Overall, inflation-adjusted income for the top quintile rose 60% between 1980 and 2005, but it rose only 3% for the bottom quintile.

Although detailed data on income distribution aren't available before 1947, economists have instead used other information like income tax data to estimate the share of income going to the top 10% of the population all the way back to 1917. Panel (b) of Figure 19-3 shows this measure from 1917 to 2006. These data, like the more detailed data available since 1947, show that American inequality was more or less stable between 1947 and the late 1970s but has risen substantially since. The longer-term data also show, however, that the relatively equal distribution of 1947 was something new. In the late nineteenth century, often referred to as the Gilded Age, American income was very unequally distributed; this high level of inequality persisted into the 1930s. But inequality declined sharply between the late 1930s and the end of World War II. In a famous paper, Claudia Goldin and Robert Margo, two economic historians, dubbed this narrowing of income inequality "the Great Compression."

The Great Compression roughly coincided with World War II, a period during which the U.S. government imposed special controls on wages and prices. Evidence indicates that these controls were applied in ways that reduced inequality—for example, it was much easier for employers to get approval to increase the wages of their lowest-paid employees than to increase executive salaries. What remains puzzling is that the equality imposed by wartime controls lasted for decades after those controls were lifted in 1946.

Since the 1970s, as we've already seen, inequality has increased substantially. In fact, pre-tax income appears to be as unequally distributed in America today as it was in the 1920s, prompting many commentators to describe the current state of the nation as a new Gilded Age—albeit one in which the effects of inequality are moderated by taxes and the existence of the welfare state. There is intense debate among economists about the causes of this widening inequality. The most popular explanation is rapid technological change, which has increased the demand for highly skilled or talented workers more rapidly than the demand for other workers, leading to a rise in the wage gap between the highly skilled and other workers. Growing international trade may also have contributed by allowing the United States to import labor-intensive products from low-wage countries rather than making them domestically, reducing the demand for less skilled American workers and depressing their wages. Rising immigration may be yet another source. On average, immigrants have lower education levels than native-born workers and increase the supply of low-skilled labor while depressing low-skilled wages.

All these explanations, however, fail to account for one key feature: much of the rise in inequality doesn't reflect a rising gap between highly educated workers and those with less education but rather growing differences among highly educated workers themselves. For example, schoolteachers and top business executives have similarly high levels of education, but executive paychecks have risen dramatically and teachers' salaries have not. For some reason, the economy now pays a few "superstars"—a group that includes literal superstars in the entertainment world but also such groups as Wall Street traders and top corporate executives—much higher incomes than it did a generation ago. It's still unclear what caused the change. ▲

> > > > > > > > > > > >

➤ CHECK YOUR UNDERSTANDING 19-1

1. Indicate whether each of the following programs is a poverty program or a social insurance program.
   a. A pension guarantee program, which provides pensions for retirees if they have lost their employment-based pension due to their employer's bankruptcy
   b. The SCHIP program, which provides health care for children in families that are above the poverty threshold but still have relatively low income
   c. The Section 8 housing program, which provides housing subsidies for low-income households
   d. The federal flood program, which provides financial help to communities hit by major floods

2. Recall that the poverty threshold is not adjusted to reflect changes in the standard of living. As a result, is the poverty threshold a relative or an absolute measure of poverty? That is, does it define poverty according to how poor someone is relative to others or according to some fixed measure that doesn't change over time. Explain.

3. The accompanying table gives the distribution of income for a very small economy.
   a. What is the mean income? What is the median income? Which measure is more representative of the income of the average person in the economy? Why?
   b. What income range defines the first quintile? The third quintile?

	Income
Sephora	$39,000
Kelly	17,500
Raul	900,000
Vijay	15,000
Oskar	28,000

4. Which of the following statements more accurately reflects the principal source of rising inequality in the United States today?
   a. The salary of the manager of the local branch of Sunrise Bank has risen relative to the salary of the neighborhood gas station attendant.
   b. The salary of the CEO of Sunrise Bank has risen relative to the salary of the local branch bank manager, who have similar education levels.

Solutions appear at back of book.

The U.S. Welfare State

The U.S. welfare state consists of three huge programs—Social Security, Medicare, and Medicaid—several other fairly big programs, including Temporary Assistance for Needy Families, food stamps, the Earned Income Tax Credit, and a number of smaller programs. Table 19-3 shows one useful way to categorize these programs, along with the amount spent on each listed program in 2005.

First, the table distinguishes between programs that are **means-tested** and those that are not. In means-tested programs, benefits are available only to families or individuals whose income and/or wealth falls below some minimum. Basically, means-tested programs are poverty programs designed to help only those with low incomes. By contrast, non-means-tested programs provide their benefits to everyone, although, as we'll see, they tend in practice to reduce income inequality.

Second, the table distinguishes between programs that provide monetary transfers that beneficiaries can spend as they choose and those that provide **in-kind benefits,** which are given in the form of goods or services rather than money. As the numbers suggest, in-kind benefits are dominated by Medicare and Medicaid, which pay for health care. We'll discuss health care in the next section of this chapter. For now, let's examine the other major programs.

TABLE 19-3

Major U.S. Welfare State Programs, 2005

	Monetary transfers	In-kind
Means-tested	Temporary Assistance for Needy Families: $8.9 billion	Food stamps: $28.5 billion
	Supplemental Security Income: $37.2 billion	Medicaid: $304.4 billion
	Earned Income Tax Credit: $34.6 billion	
Not means-tested	Social Security: $518.7 billion	Medicare: $332.6 billion
	Unemployment insurance: $31.8 billion	

Means-Tested Programs

When people use the term *welfare,* they're often referring to monetary aid to poor families. The main source of such monetary aid in the United States is Temporary Assistance for Needy Families, or TANF. This program does not aid everyone who is poor; it is available only to poor families with children and only for a limited period of time.

TANF was introduced in the 1990s to replace a highly controversial program known as Aid to Families with Dependent Children, or AFDC. The older program was widely accused of creating perverse incentives for the poor, including encouraging family breakup. Partly as a result of the change in programs, the benefits of modern "welfare" are considerably less generous than those available a generation ago, once the data are adjusted for inflation. Also, TANF contains time limits, so welfare recipients—even single parents—must eventually seek work. As you can see from Table 19-3, TANF is a relatively small part of the modern U.S. welfare state.

Other means-tested programs, though more expensive, are less controversial. The Supplemental Security Income program aids disabled Americans who are unable to work and have no other source of income. The food stamp program helps low-income families and individuals, who can use food stamps to buy food staples but not other items.

Finally, economists use the term **negative income tax** for a program that supplements the earnings of low-income working families. The United States has a program known as the Earned Income Tax Credit (EITC), which provides additional income to millions of workers. It has become more generous as traditional welfare has become less generous. Only workers who earn income are eligible for the EITC; over a certain range of incomes, the more a worker earns, the higher the amount of EITC received. That is, the EITC acts as a negative income tax for low-wage workers. In 2007, married couples with two children earning less than $11,790 per year received EITC payments equal to 40% of their earnings. (Payments were slightly lower for single-parent families or workers without children.) At higher incomes the EITC is phased out, disappearing at an income of $37,783 in 2007.

A **means-tested** program is a program available only to individuals or families whose incomes fall below a certain level.

An **in-kind benefit** is a benefit given in the form of goods or services.

A **negative income tax** is a program that supplements the income of low-income working families.

Social Security and Unemployment Insurance

Social Security, the largest program in the U.S. welfare state, is a non-means-tested program that guarantees retirement income to qualifying older Americans. It also provides benefits to workers who become disabled and "survivor benefits" to family members of workers who die. Social Security is supported by a dedicated tax on wages: the Social Security portion of the payroll tax, which was described in Chapter 7, pays for Social Security benefits. The benefits workers receive on retirement depend on their taxable earnings during their working years: the more you earn up to the maximum amount subject to Social Security taxes ($102,000 in 2008), the more you receive in retirement. Benefits are not, however, strictly proportional to earnings. Instead, they're determined by a formula that gives high earners more than low earners, but with a sliding scale that makes the program relatively more generous for low earners.

Because most seniors don't receive pensions from their former employers, and most don't own enough assets to live off the income from their assets, Social Security benefits are an enormously important source of income for them. Fully 60% of Americans 65 and older rely on Social Security for more than half their income, and 20% have no income at all except for Social Security.

Unemployment insurance, although a much smaller amount of government transfers than Social Security, is another key social insurance program. It provides workers who lose their jobs with about 35% of their previous salary until they find a new job or until 26 weeks have passed. Unemployment insurance is financed by a tax on employers.

The Effects of the Welfare State on Poverty and Inequality

Because the people who receive government transfers tend to be different from those who are taxed to pay for those transfers, the U.S. welfare state has the effect of redistributing income from some people to others. Each year the Census Bureau estimates the effect of this redistribution in a report titled "The Effects of Government Taxes and Transfers on Income and Poverty." The report calculates only the *direct* effect of taxes and transfers, without taking into account changes in behavior that the taxes and transfers might cause. For example, the report doesn't try to estimate how many older Americans who are now retired would still be working if they weren't receiving Social Security checks. As a result, the estimates are only a partial indicator of the true effects of the welfare state. Nonetheless, the results are striking.

Table 19-4 shows how taxes and government transfers affected the poverty threshold for the population as a whole and for different age groups in 2005. It shows two numbers for each group: the percentage of the group that *would have had* incomes below the poverty threshold if the government neither collected taxes nor

TABLE 19-4

Effects of Taxes and Transfers on the Poverty Rate, 2005

Group (by age)	Poverty rate without taxes and transfers	Poverty rate with taxes and transfers
All	18.9%	10.3%
Under 18	20.1	13.0
18 to 64	14.6	9.9
65 and over	38.6	6.7

Source: U.S. Census Bureau.

TABLE **19-5**

Effects of Taxes and Transfers on the Income Distribution, 2005

Quintiles	Share of aggregate income without taxes and transfers	Share of aggregate income with taxes and transfers
Bottom quintile	1.5%	4.4%
Second quintile	7.3	9.9
Third quintile	14.0	15.3
Fourth quintile	23.4	23.1
Top quintile	53.8	47.3

Source: U.S. Census Bureau.

made transfers, and the percentage that actually fell below the poverty threshold once taxes and transfers were taken into account. (For technical reasons, the second number is somewhat lower than the standard measure of the poverty rate.) Overall, the combined effect of taxes and transfers is to cut the U.S. poverty rate nearly in half. The elderly derived the greatest benefits from redistribution, which reduced their potential poverty rate of 38.6% to an actual poverty rate of 6.7%.

Table 19-5 shows the effect of taxes and transfers on the share of aggregate income going to each quintile of the income distribution in 2005. Like Table 19-4, it shows both what the distribution of income *would have been* if there were no taxes or government transfers, and the actual distribution of income taking into account both taxes and transfers. The effect of government programs was to increase the share of income going to the poorest 60% of the population, especially the share going to the poorest 20%, while reducing the share of income going to the richest 20%.

►ECONOMICS IN ACTION

Britain's War on Poverty

Between 1979 and 1997, Britain, like the United States, experienced a substantial increase in inequality. Britain doesn't have any single official definition of poverty, but the measure that most closely approximates the U.S. measurement of the poverty threshold indicates that poverty in Britain fell only slightly between 1979 and the mid-1990s even though average income rose substantially.

In 1997, however, control of Britain's government switched from the Conservative Party, which generally sought to limit the size of Britain's welfare state, to the Labour Party, which promised to reduce poverty and inequality. In its efforts to accomplish this, Britain's Labour government has adopted policies that include child benefits paid to every family with children and a "work benefit" that is similar to the U.S. Earned Income Tax Credit but considerably more generous.

As panel (a) of Figure 19-4 shows, the effects of these policies on British poverty have been impressive: the British poverty measure that corresponds most closely to the U.S. measure shows that the poverty rate was cut in half between 1997 and 2005, though it has since risen again slightly. The British government is frustrated, however, that its policies don't seem to have helped a persistent underclass of the very poor.

The effect of Labour's policy on overall inequality is less clear. Panel (b) of Figure 19-4 shows Britain's Gini coefficient, which rose sharply in the 1980s and has since stabilized but not fallen significantly. Closer examination of the British data reveal that income inequality has actually declined among the bottom 99% of the population; as in the United States, however, the incomes of the top 1% of the population have been rising much faster than everyone else's (though not to the same extent as

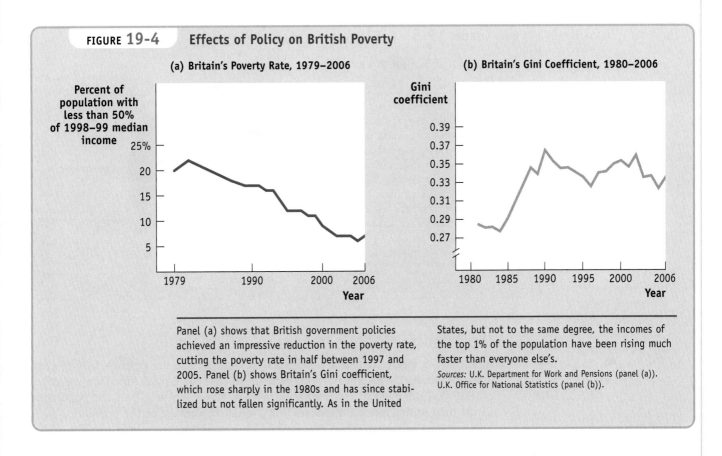

FIGURE 19-4   Effects of Policy on British Poverty

(a) Britain's Poverty Rate, 1979–2006

(b) Britain's Gini Coefficient, 1980–2006

Panel (a) shows that British government policies achieved an impressive reduction in the poverty rate, cutting the poverty rate in half between 1997 and 2005. Panel (b) shows Britain's Gini coefficient, which rose sharply in the 1980s and has since stabilized but not fallen significantly. As in the United States, but not to the same degree, the incomes of the top 1% of the population have been rising much faster than everyone else's.

Sources: U.K. Department for Work and Pensions (panel (a)). U.K. Office for National Statistics (panel (b)).

in the United States). Defenders of the British government's policies argue that even stabilizing inequality represents a partial success. They argue that without the government's equalizing policies, inequality would have continued to rise, as it has on this side of the Atlantic. ▲

> > > > > > > > > > > >

► CHECK YOUR UNDERSTANDING   19-2

1. Explain how the negative income tax avoids the disincentive to work that characterizes poverty programs that simply give benefits based on low income.

2. According to Table 19-4, what effect does the U.S. welfare state have on the overall poverty rate? On the poverty rate for those aged 65 and over?

Solutions appear at back of book.

The Economics of Health Care

A large part of the welfare state, in both the United States and other wealthy countries, is devoted to paying for health care. In most wealthy countries, the government pays between 70% and 80% of all medical costs. The private sector plays a larger role in the U.S. health care system. Yet even in America the government pays almost half of all health care costs; furthermore, it indirectly subsidizes private health insurance through the federal tax code.

Figure 19-5 on the next page shows who paid for U.S. health care in 2006. Only 12% of medical bills were paid "out of pocket"—that is, paid directly by individuals. A much larger share, 46%, was paid by the government, mainly through Medicare and Medicaid. About 34% was paid by private insurance companies, with the remaining 7% coming mainly from charities. To understand this pattern, we need to examine the special economics of health care.

►► QUICK REVIEW

➤ **Means-tested** programs are designed to reduce poverty, but in practice non-means-tested programs do so as well. Programs are classified according to whether they provide monetary or **in-kind benefits.**

➤ "Welfare," now known as TANF, aid to poor families with children, is far less generous today than a generation ago due to concerns about its effect on incentives to work and family breakup. The **negative income tax** addresses these concerns: it supplements the incomes of only low-income working families.

➤ Social Security, the largest program in the U.S. welfare state, is a non-means-tested program that provides retirement income for the elderly. It provides a significant share of the income of most elderly Americans. Unemployment insurance is also a key social insurance program.

➤ The American welfare state is redistributive. It increases the share of income going to the poorest 60% while reducing the share going to the richest 20%.

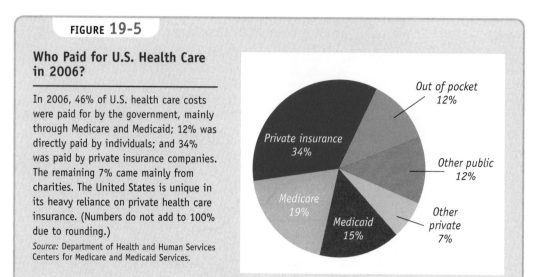

FIGURE 19-5

Who Paid for U.S. Health Care in 2006?

In 2006, 46% of U.S. health care costs were paid for by the government, mainly through Medicare and Medicaid; 12% was directly paid by individuals; and 34% was paid by private insurance companies. The remaining 7% came mainly from charities. The United States is unique in its heavy reliance on private health care insurance. (Numbers do not add to 100% due to rounding.)

Source: Department of Health and Human Services Centers for Medicare and Medicaid Services.

The Need for Health Insurance

In 2006, U.S. personal health care expenses were $7,026 per person—16% of gross domestic product. This did not, however, mean that the typical American spent just over $7,000 on medical treatment. In fact, in any given year half the population incurs only minor medical expenses, but a small percentage of the population faces huge medical bills. In 2002, 20% of the U.S. population accounted for 80% of the medical costs, and 5% of the population accounted for almost half the costs.

Is it possible to predict who will have high medical costs? To a limited extent, yes: there are broad patterns to illness. For example, the elderly are more likely to need expensive surgery and/or drugs than the young. But the fact is that anyone can suddenly find himself or herself needing very expensive medical treatment, costing many thousands of dollars in a very short time—far beyond what most families can easily afford. Yet nobody wants to be unable to afford such treatment if it becomes necessary.

Market economies have an answer to this problem: health insurance. Under **private health insurance,** each member of a large pool of individuals agrees to pay a fixed amount into a common fund that is managed by a private company, which then pays most of the medical expenses of the pool's members. Although members must pay fees even in years in which they don't have large medical expenses, they benefit from the reduction in risk: if they do turn out to have high medical costs, the pool will take care of those expenses.

There are, however, inherent problems with the market for private health insurance. These problems arise from the fact that medical expenses, although unpredictable, aren't *completely* unpredictable. That is, people often have some idea whether or not they are likely to face large medical bills over the next few years. This creates a serious problem for private insurance companies.

Suppose that an insurance company offers a "one-size-fits-all" health care policy, under which customers pay an annual premium equal to the average American's annual medical expenses, plus a bit more to cover the company's operating expenses and a normal rate of profit. In return, the insurance company pays the policyholder's medical bills, whatever they are.

If all potential customers had an equal risk of incurring high medical expenses for the year, this might be a workable business proposition. In reality, however, people often have very different risks of facing high medical expenses—and, crucially, they often know this ahead of time. This reality would quickly undermine any attempt by an insurance company to offer one-size-fits-all insurance. The policy would be a bad deal for healthy

Under **private health insurance,** each member of a large pool of individuals pays a fixed amount to a private company that agrees to pay most of the medical expenses of the pool's members.

people, who don't face a large risk of high medical bills: on average, they would pay much more in insurance premiums than the cost of their actual medical bills. But it would be a very good deal for people with chronic, costly conditions, who would on average pay less in premiums than the cost of their care. As a result, some healthy people would probably decide to take their chances and go without insurance; as a result, the insurance company's customers would be less healthy than the average American, which would raise the company's costs per customer. That is, the insurance company would face a problem called *adverse selection,* which is analyzed in greater detail in Chapter 21. Because of adverse selection, a company that tried to offer health insurance to everyone at a price reflecting average medical costs would find itself losing a lot of money.

The insurance company could respond by charging more—raising its premium to reflect the higher-than-average medical bills of its customers. But this would drive off even more healthy people, leaving the company with an even sicker, higher-cost clientele, forcing it to raise the premium even more, driving off even more healthy people, and so on. This phenomenon is known as the *adverse selection death spiral.*

This description of the problems with health insurance might lead you to believe that private health insurance can't work. In fact, however, most Americans do have private health insurance. Insurance companies are able, to some extent, to overcome the problem of adverse selection by carefully screening people who apply for coverage, charging people who are likely to have high medical expenses higher-than-average premiums—or, in many cases, refusing to cover them at all. For the most part, however, insurance companies overcome adverse selection by selling insurance indirectly, to peoples' employers rather than to individuals. The big advantage of *employment-based health insurance—* insurance that a company provides to its employees—is that these employees are likely to contain a representative mix of healthy and less healthy people, rather than a selected group of people who want insurance because they expect to pay high medical bills. This is especially true if the employer is a large company with thousands or tens of thousands of workers. As long as healthy employees are not allowed to opt out, there are typically enough healthy employees to help subsidize the cost of less-healthy employees.

There's another reason employment-based insurance is widespread in the United States: it gets special, favorable tax treatment. Workers pay taxes on their paychecks, but workers who receive health insurance from their employers don't pay taxes on the value of the benefit. So employment-based health insurance is, in effect, subsidized by the U.S. tax system. Economists estimate the value of this subsidy at about $150 billion each year.

In spite of this subsidy, however, many Americans don't receive employment-based health insurance. Those who aren't covered include most older Americans, because relatively few employers offer workers insurance that continues after they retire; the many workers whose employers don't offer coverage; and the unemployed.

FOR INQUIRING MINDS

A California Death Spiral

At the beginning of 2006, 116,000 workers at more than 6,000 California small businesses received health coverage from PacAdvantage, a "purchasing pool" that offered employees at member businesses a choice of insurance plans. The idea behind PacAdvantage, which was founded in 1992, was that by banding together, small businesses could get better deals on employee health insurance.

But in August 2006 PacAdvantage announced that it was closing up shop because it could no longer find insurance companies willing to offer plans to its members.

What happened? It was the adverse selection death spiral. PacAdvantage offered the same policies to everyone, regardless of their prior health history. But employees didn't have to get insurance from PacAdvantage—they were free, if they chose, to opt out and buy insurance on their own. And sure enough, healthy workers started to find that they could get lower rates by buying insurance directly for themselves, even though that meant giving up the advantages of bulk purchasing. As a result, PacAdvantage began to lose healthy clients, leaving behind an increasingly sick—and expensive—pool of customers. Premiums had to go up, driving out even more healthy workers, and eventually the whole plan had to shut down.

TABLE **19-6**

Number of Americans Covered by Health Insurance, 2006 (thousands)	
Covered by private health insurance	**201,690**
Employment-based	177,152
Direct purchase	27,066
Covered by government	**80,270**
Medicaid	38,281
Medicare	40,343
Military health care	10,547
Not covered	**46,995**

Source: U.S. Census Bureau.

Government Health Insurance

Table 19-6 shows the breakdown of health insurance coverage across the U.S. population in 2006. Most Americans, more than 177 million people, received health insurance through employers. The majority of those who didn't have private insurance were covered by two government programs, Medicare and Medicaid. (The numbers don't add up because some people have more than one form of coverage. For example, many recipients of Medicare also have supplemental coverage either through Medicaid or private policies.)

Medicare is available to all Americans 65 and older, regardless of their income and wealth. It began in 1966 as a program to cover the cost of hospitalization but has since been expanded to cover a number of other medical expenses. You can get an idea of how much difference Medicare makes to the finances of elderly Americans by comparing the median income per person of Americans 65 and older—$15,696—with average annual Medicare payments per recipient, which were more than $8,000 (2006 data). (As with health care spending in general, however, the average can be misleading: in a given year, about 7% of Medicare recipients account for 50% of the costs.)

At the beginning of 2006, there was a major expansion of Medicare, this time to cover the cost of prescription drugs. At the time Medicare was created, drugs played a relatively minor role in medicine and were rarely a major expense for patients. Today, however, many health problems, especially among the elderly, are treated with expensive drugs that must be taken for years on end, placing severe strains on some people's finances. As a result, a new Medicare program, known as "Part D," was created to help pay these expenses.

Unlike Medicare, Medicaid is a means-tested program. There's no simple way to summarize the criteria for eligibility because it is partly paid for by state governments and each state sets its own rules. Of the 38.3 million Americans covered by Medicaid in 2006, 20.1 million were children under 18, and many of the rest were parents of children under 18. (The SCHIP program, which we described in the opening story, is counted in these numbers as part of Medicaid.) Most of the cost of Medicaid, however, is accounted for by a small number of older Americans, especially those needing long-term care.

In addition to the 79 million Americans covered by Medicare and Medicaid, nearly 11 million Americans receive health insurance as a consequence of military service. Unlike Medicare and Medicaid, which pay medical bills but don't deliver health care directly, the Veterans Health Administration, which has 4.4 million clients, runs hospitals and clinics around the country.

The U.S. health care system, then, offers a mix of private insurance, mainly from employers, and public insurance of various forms. Most Americans have health insurance either from private insurance companies or through various forms of government insurance. However, 47 million people in America, 15.8% of the population, have no health insurance at all. What accounts for the uninsured, and how much does the problem of the uninsured matter?

Medicare was expanded in 2006 to cover the cost of prescription drugs.

Jose Luis Pelaez/Getty

The Problem of the Uninsured

The Kaiser Family Foundation, an independent nonpartisan group that studies health care issues, offers a succinct summary of who is uninsured in America: "The uninsured are largely low-income adult workers for whom coverage is unaffordable or unavailable." The reason the uninsured are primarily adults is that Medicaid, supplemented by SCHIP, covers many, though not all, low-income children but is much less likely to provide coverage to adults, especially if they do not have children. Low-income workers tend to be uninsured for two reasons: they are less likely than workers with higher income to have jobs that provide health insurance benefits, and they are less likely to be able to afford to directly purchase heath insurance themselves. Finally, insurance companies frequently refuse to cover people, regardless of their income, if they have a preexisting medical condition or something in their medical history suggesting that they are likely to need expensive medical treatment at some future date. As a result, a significant number of Americans with incomes that most would consider middle class cannot get insurance.

It's important to realize that lack of insurance is not synonymous with poverty. Most people in America without health insurance have incomes above the poverty threshold, and 35% of the uninsured have incomes more than twice the poverty threshold. We should also note that some of the uninsured are relatively healthy people who could afford insurance but prefer to save money and take their chances, although there is dispute about how large the group of voluntarily uninsured is.

Like poverty, lack of health insurance has serious consequences, both medical and financial. On the medical side, the uninsured frequently have limited access to health care. Panel (a) of Figure 19-6 shows one summary of common problems associated with access to care, all of which are much worse for the uninsured than for the insured. On the financial side, those who are uninsured often face serious financial problems when illness strikes. Panel (b) shows a summary of the main financial problems associated with medical care, all of which are much worse for those without health insurance.

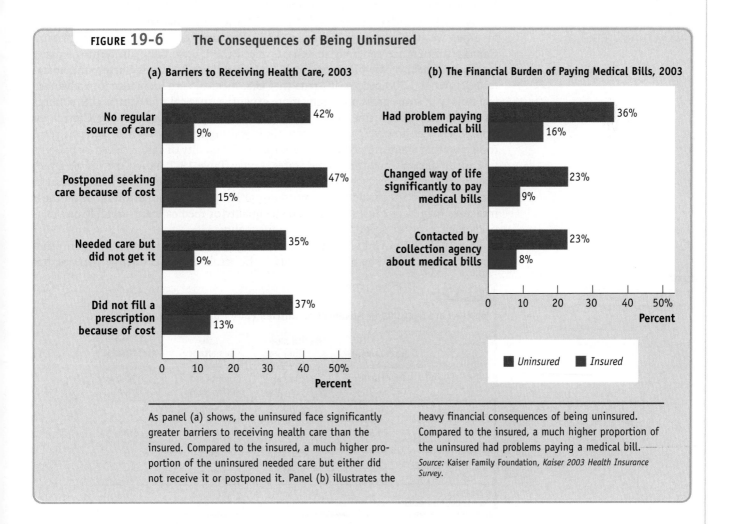

FIGURE 19-6   The Consequences of Being Uninsured

As panel (a) shows, the uninsured face significantly greater barriers to receiving health care than the insured. Compared to the insured, a much higher proportion of the uninsured needed care but either did not receive it or postponed it. Panel (b) illustrates the heavy financial consequences of being uninsured. Compared to the insured, a much higher proportion of the uninsured had problems paying a medical bill.

Source: Kaiser Family Foundation, *Kaiser 2003 Health Insurance Survey.*

A **single-payer system** is a health care system in which the government is the principal payer of medical bills funded through taxes.

Health Care in Other Countries

Health care is one area in which the United States is very different from other wealthy countries, including both European nations and Canada. In fact, we're distinctive in three ways. First, we rely much more on private health insurance than any other wealthy country. Second, we spend much more on health care per person. Third, we're the only wealthy nation in which large numbers of people lack health insurance.

Table 19-7 compares the United States with three other wealthy countries: Canada, France, and Britain. The United States is the only one of the four countries that relies on private health insurance to cover most people; as a result, it's the only one in which private spending on health care is (slightly) larger than public spending on health care. Canada has a **single-payer system:** a health care system in which the government acts as the principal payer of medical bills funded through taxes. For comparison, Medicare is basically a single-payer system for older Americans—and the Canadian system is, in fact, called Medicare. The British system is like the American Veterans Health Administration, extended to everyone: a government agency, the British National Health Service, employs health care workers and runs hospitals and clinics that are available free of charge to the public. France is somewhere in between the Canadian and British systems: the government acts as a single-payer, providing health insurance to everyone, and French citizens can receive treatment from private doctors and hospitals; but they also have the choice of receiving care from a sizable health care system run directly by the French government.

All three non-U.S. systems provide health insurance to all their citizens; the United States does not. Yet all three spend much less on health care per person than we do. Many Americans assume this must mean that foreign health care is inferior in quality. But many health care experts disagree with the claim that the health care systems of other wealthy countries deliver poor-quality care. As they point out, Britain, Canada, and France generally match or exceed the United States in terms of many measures of health care provision, such as the number of doctors, nurses, and hospital beds per 100,000 people. It's true that U.S. medical care includes more advanced technology in some areas and many more expensive surgical procedures. U.S. patients also have shorter waiting times for elective surgery than patients in Canada or Britain. France, however, also has very short waiting times. Surveys of patients seem to suggest that there are no large differences in the quality of care received by patients in Canada, Europe, and the United States. And as Table 19-7 shows, the United States does considerably *worse* than other advanced countries in terms of basic measures such as life expectancy and infant mortality, although our poor performance on these measures may have causes other than the quality of medical care—notably our relatively high levels of poverty and income inequality.

So why does the United States spend so much more on health care than other wealthy countries? Some of the disparity is the result of higher doctors' salaries, but

TABLE 19-7

Health Care Systems in Advanced Countries (2005 data unless indicated)

	Government share of health care spending	Health care spending per capita (US$, purchasing power parity)	Life expectancy (total population at birth, years)	Infant mortality (deaths per 1,000 live births)
United States	45.1%	$6,401	77.8*	6.8*
Canada	70.3	3,326	80.2*	5.3*
France	79.8	3,374	80.3	3.6
Britain	87.1	2,724	79.0	5.1

*2004 data
Source: OECD health data, 2007.

most studies suggest that this is a secondary factor. One possibility is that Americans *are* getting better care than their counterparts abroad, but in ways that don't show up in either surveys of patient experiences or statistics on health performance. Another possibility is that the U.S. system suffers from serious inefficiencies that other countries manage to avoid. Critics of the U.S. system emphasize the fact that our system's reliance on private insurance companies, which expend resources on such activities as marketing and trying to identify and weed out high-risk patients, leads to high operating costs. On average, the operating costs of private health insurers eats up 14% of the premiums clients pay, leaving only 86% to spend on providing health care; by contrast, Medicare spends only 3% of its funds on operating costs, leaving 97% to spend on health care. A study by the McKinsey Global Institute found that the United States spends almost six times as much per person on health care administration as other wealthy countries. The United States also pays higher prices for prescription drugs, because in other countries government agencies bargain with pharmaceutical companies to get lower drug prices.

The Health Care Crisis and Proposals for Reform

Whatever one thinks of the past performance of the U.S. health care system, that system is clearly in trouble today. The root of the problem is the rising cost of health insurance, whether private or public.

For one thing, the cost of private insurance has risen much faster than incomes. For example, between 2001 and 2007 the average premiums for employment-based health insurance rose 78%, but the wages of the average worker rose only 19%. By 2007, the average cost of insurance for a family of four was more than $12,000.

As a result of these rising costs, employment-based health insurance, the centerpiece of the system for Americans under 65, is in decline. Figure 19-7 shows selected changes in the insurance status of Americans between 2000 and 2006. Over that period, the total population rose by 17 million. But the number of people with employment-based health insurance not only failed to keep up with population growth—it declined by more than 2 million. However, more people were covered by government programs, mainly due to an expansion of Medicaid. But this expansion did not keep up with population growth, and more than 8 million people joined the ranks of the uninsured.

Even as private health insurance seems to be faltering and the number of Americans without health insurance is rising, public health insurance is coming under increasing financial strain. Partly this is because Medicaid and other government programs now cover more people than in the past. Mainly, however, it is

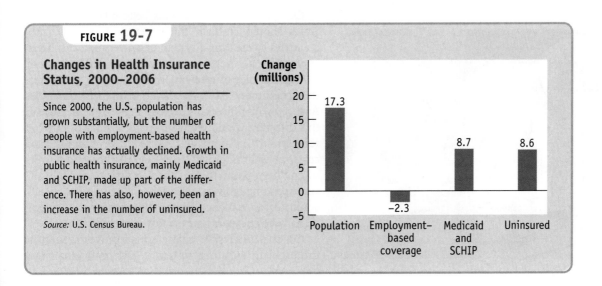

FIGURE 19-7

Changes in Health Insurance Status, 2000–2006

Since 2000, the U.S. population has grown substantially, but the number of people with employment-based health insurance has actually declined. Growth in public health insurance, mainly Medicaid and SCHIP, made up part of the difference. There has also, however, been an increase in the number of uninsured.

Source: U.S. Census Bureau.

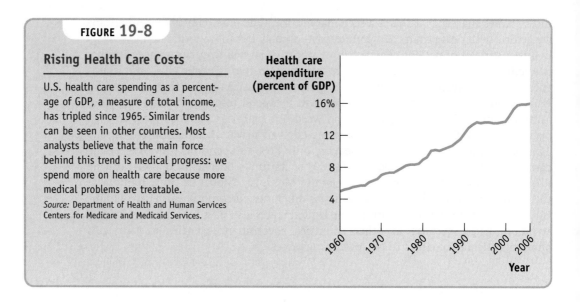

FIGURE 19-8

Rising Health Care Costs

U.S. health care spending as a percentage of GDP, a measure of total income, has tripled since 1965. Similar trends can be seen in other countries. Most analysts believe that the main force behind this trend is medical progress: we spend more on health care because more medical problems are treatable.

Source: Department of Health and Human Services Centers for Medicare and Medicaid Services.

because the cost per beneficiary of government health insurance, like the cost per beneficiary of private insurance, has been rising rapidly.

What's behind these rising costs? Figure 19-8 shows overall U.S. spending on health care as a percentage of GDP, a measure of the nation's total income, since the 1960s. As you can see, health spending has tripled as a share of income since 1965; this increase in spending explains why health insurance has become more expensive. Similar trends can be observed in other countries.

But why is health spending rising? The consensus of health experts is that it's a result of medical progress. As medical science progresses, conditions that could not be treated in the past become treatable—but often only at great expense. The upcoming Economics in Action gives some examples. Both private insurers and government programs feel compelled to cover the new procedures—but this means higher costs, which either have to be passed on in the form of higher insurance premiums or require larger commitments of taxpayer funds.

The combination of a rising number of uninsured and rising costs has led to many calls for health care reform in the United States. There are, however, sharp political divisions over what kind of reform is needed. Broadly speaking, the division is between those who believe that the answer is a further expansion of the welfare state and those who believe that the appropriate response is more reliance on markets and individual incentives.

On one side, many liberals believe that the United States should emulate the systems of other wealthy countries by creating a system of universal health insurance, although most current proposals would offer individuals a choice of receiving that insurance either from the government or from private insurance companies. Advocates of universal coverage argue that a move in this direction would reduce the inefficiency of our current system, in particular by reducing administrative costs, as well as provide coverage to those now uninsured. They point to the striking difference in health care spending between the United States and other rich countries as evidence that a universal system would actually be cheaper than what we have now.

On the other side, many conservatives argue that the problem with our system is that individuals lack much incentive to pay attention to medical costs, because the bills are covered by either public or private insurance. They call for a move to "consumer-directed" health care, in which individuals would pay a larger share of their own health care bills and therefore choose more carefully which medical procedures they want performed and bargain more over prices. They often argue that the market for health insurance is distorted by the subsidy that the tax code creates for employment-based insurance. Proposals for health care reform on the conservative side typically involve limiting the tax deduction for employment-based health insurance but offering comparable tax breaks to those who purchase insurance as individuals. Critics counter, however, that this would not solve the problem faced by individuals who are refused private insurance because of pre-existing medical conditions.

One thing is sure: the debate over health care reform will be an important part of the U.S political scene for many years to come.

►ECONOMICS IN ACTION

The Trouble with Medical Progress

It's widely accepted among health care experts that medical progress leads to higher health care spending. A 2008 report from the Congressional Budget Office (CBO) tried to put numbers to this effect and also offered a number of striking examples of just how the process works. Figure 19-9 shows the growth in expensive treatments for a few major medical problems that, not too long ago, couldn't be treated at all.

■ *Coronary artery disease.* "In the 1950s and much of the 1960s," writes the CBO, "caring for patients with coronary artery disease was inexpensive because physicians could do little to help them." But then came the development of open-heart surgery and other techniques such as angioplasty. The result is that many heart-disease patients who might have died receive a second lease on life—but at huge expense.

■ *Kidney failure.* "Until techniques and devices were developed that could perform the waste-removing functions of the kidneys (renal replacement therapy)," writes the CBO, "patients who suffered severe kidney failure tended to die quickly." Now they can be kept alive for years thanks to dialysis—again, at great expense.

■ *Joint problems.* In the past, joint problems, which can often be crippling, simply had to be suffered. Now, however, it's common to receive hip and knee replacement, a tremendous gain—but again, at great expense.

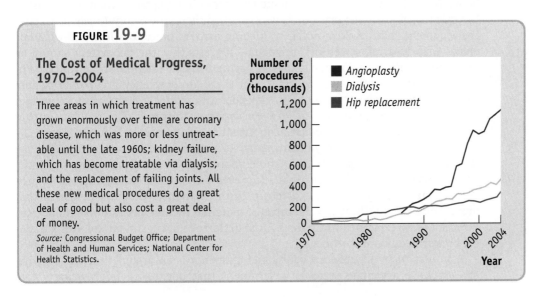

FIGURE 19-9

The Cost of Medical Progress, 1970–2004

Three areas in which treatment has grown enormously over time are coronary disease, which was more or less untreatable until the late 1960s; kidney failure, which has become treatable via dialysis; and the replacement of failing joints. All these new medical procedures do a great deal of good but also cost a great deal of money.

Source: Congressional Budget Office; Department of Health and Human Services; National Center for Health Statistics.

Medical progress is a wonderful thing. But as we've seen, the growing cost of health care is causing severe strains on both private and public health insurance, both in the United States and in the rest of the world. It remains to be seen how the tension between what doctors can do and what society can afford will be resolved. ▲

< < < < < < < < < < < <

▶ CHECK YOUR UNDERSTANDING 19-3

1. If you are enrolled in a four-year degree program, it is likely that you are required to enroll in a health insurance program run by your school.
   a. Explain how you and your parents benefit from this health insurance program even though, given your age, it is unlikely that you will need expensive medical treatment.
   b. Explain how your school's health insurance program avoids the adverse selection death spiral by requiring all students to join and pay premiums.

2. According to its critics, what partly accounts for the higher costs of the U.S. health care system compared to other wealthy countries?

Solutions appear at back of book.

The Debate Over the Welfare State

The goals of the welfare state seem laudable: to help the poor, protect everyone from financial risk, and ensure that people can afford essential health care. But good intentions don't always make for good policy. There is an intense debate about how large the welfare state should be, a debate that partly reflects differences in philosophy but also reflects concern about the possibly counterproductive effects of welfare state programs. Disputes about the size of the welfare state are also one of the defining issues of modern politics.

Problems with the Welfare State

There are two different lines of argument against the welfare state. One, which we described earlier in this chapter, is based on philosophical concerns about the proper role of government. As we learned, some political theorists believe that redistributing income is not a legitimate role of government—that government's role should be limited to maintaining the rule of law, providing public goods, and managing externalities.

The more conventional argument against the welfare state involves the trade-off between efficiency and equity, an issue that arose in Chapter 7 when we discussed the case for progressive taxation. As we explained there, the *ability-to-pay-principle*—the argument that an extra dollar of income matters more to a less well-off individual than to a more well-off individual—suggests that the tax system should be progressive, with high-income taxpayers paying a higher fraction of their income in taxes than those with lower incomes. But there are efficiency arguments against making marginal tax rates too high. Consider an extremely progressive tax system that imposes a marginal rate of 90% on very high incomes. The problem is that such a high marginal rate reduces the incentive to increase a family's income by working hard or making risky investments. As a result, an extremely progressive tax system tends to make society as a whole poorer, which could hurt even those the system was intended to benefit. That's why even economists who strongly favor progressive taxation don't support a return to the extremely progressive system that prevailed in the 1950s, when the top U.S. marginal income tax rate was more than 90%. So, as we explained in Chapter 7, the design of the tax system involves a trade-off between equity and efficiency.

A similar trade-off between equity and efficiency is an argument against having too extensive a welfare state. A government that operates a large welfare state requires more revenue than one that limits itself mainly to provision of public goods such as national defense. So nations that have a large welfare state must have higher tax revenue, and higher marginal tax rates, than countries with a small welfare state. Table 19-8 shows "social expenditure," a measure that roughly corresponds to welfare state spending, as a percentage of

TABLE **19-8**

Social Expenditure and Marginal Tax Rates

	Social expenditure in 2003 (percent of GDP)	Marginal tax rate in 2006
United States	18.6%	33.98%
Britain	22.1	40.60
France	29.4	55.84

Sources: OECD Social Expenditure Database; OECD Taxing Wages Database.

GDP in the United States, Britain, and France; it also compares this with an estimate of the marginal tax rate faced by an average wage-earner, including payroll taxes paid by employers and state and local taxes. As you can see, France's large welfare state goes along with a high marginal rate of taxation. As the upcoming Economics in Action explains, some but not all economists believe that this high rate of taxation is a major reason the French work substantially fewer hours per year than Americans.

The trade-off between a large welfare state and high marginal tax rates seems to suggest that we should try to hold down the cost of the welfare state. One way to do this is to means-test benefits: make them available only to those who need them. But means-testing, it turns out, creates a different kind of trade-off between equity and efficiency. Consider the following example: Suppose there is some means-tested benefit, worth $2,000 per year, that is available only to families with incomes of less than $20,000 per year. Now suppose that a family currently has an income of $19,500 but that one family member is deciding whether to take a new job that will raise the family's income to $20,500. Well, taking that job will actually make the family worse off, because it will gain $1,000 in earnings but lose the $2,000 government benefit.

This situation, in which earning more actually leaves a family worse off through lost benefits, is known as a *notch*. It is a well-known problem with programs that aid the poor and behaves much like a high marginal tax rate on income. Most welfare state programs are designed to avoid creating a notch. This is typically done by setting a sliding scale for benefits such that they fall off gradually as the recipient's income rises rather than come to an abrupt end. Even so, the combined effects of the major means-tested programs shown in Table 19-3, plus additional means-tested programs such as housing aid that are offered by some state and local governments, can be to create very high effective marginal tax rates. For example, one 2005 study found that a family consisting of two adults and two children that raised its income from $20,000 a year—just above the poverty threshold in 2005—to $35,000 would find almost all its increase in after-tax income offset by loss of benefits such as food stamps, the Earned Income Tax Credit, and Medicaid.

The Politics of the Welfare State

In 1791, in the early phase of the French Revolution, France had a sort of congress, the National Assembly, in which representatives were seated according to social class: nobles, who pretty much liked the way things were, sat on the right; commoners, who wanted big changes, sat on the left. Ever since, it has been common in political discourse to talk about politicians as being on the "right" (more conservative) or on the "left" (more liberal).

But what do modern politicians on the left and right disagree about? In the modern United States, they mainly disagree about the appropriate size of the welfare state. For example, as we mentioned in the opening story, SCHIP, which provides children with health insurance, was created in 1997 with bipartisan support. But in 2007 there was a fierce political debate over whether to expand the program.

You might think that saying that political debate is really about just one thing—how big to make the welfare state—is a huge oversimplification. But political scientists have found that once you carefully rank members of Congress from right to left, a congressperson's position in that ranking does a very good job of predicting his or her votes on proposed legislation. Modern politics isn't completely one-dimensional—but it comes pretty close.

The same studies that show a strong left–right spectrum in U.S. politics also show strong polarization between the major parties on this spectrum. Thirty years ago there was a substantial overlap between the parties: some Democrats were to the right of some Republicans, or, if you prefer, some Republicans were to the left of some Democrats. Today, however, the rightmost Democrats appear to be to the left of the leftmost Republicans. There's nothing necessarily wrong with this. Although it's common to decry "partisanship," it's hard to see why members of different political parties shouldn't have different views about policy.

Can economic analysis help resolve this political conflict? Only up to a point.

Some of the political controversy over the welfare state involves differences in opinion about the trade-offs we have just discussed: if you believe that the disincentive effects of generous benefits and high taxes are very large, you're likely to look less favorably on welfare state programs than if you believe they're fairly small. Economic analysis, by improving our knowledge of the facts, can help resolve some of these differences.

To an important extent, however, differences of opinion on the welfare state reflect differences in values and philosophy. And those are differences economics can't resolve.

►*ECONOMICS IN ACTION*

French Family Values

The United States has the smallest welfare state of any major advanced economy. France has one of the largest. As we've already described, France has much higher social spending than America as a percentage of total national income, and French citizens face much higher tax rates than Americans. One argument against a large welfare state is that it has negative effects on efficiency. Does French experience support this argument?

On the face of it, the answer would seem to be a clear yes. French GDP per capita—the total value of the economy's output, divided by the total population—is only 72% of the U.S. level. This reflects the fact that the French work less: French workers and U.S. workers have almost exactly the same productivity per hour, but a smaller fraction of the French population is employed, and the average French employee works substantially fewer hours over the course of a year than his or her American counterpart. Some economists have argued that high tax rates in France explain this difference: the incentives to work are less in France than in the United States, because the government takes away so much of what you earn from an additional hour of work.

A closer examination, however, reveals that the story is more complicated than that. The low level of employment in France is entirely the result of low rates of employment among the young and the old; 80% of French residents of prime working age, 25–54, are employed, exactly the same percentage as in the United States. So high tax rates don't seem to discourage the French from working in the prime of their lives. And young people in France don't work in part because they don't have to: college education is generally free, and students receive financial support, so French students, unlike their American counterparts, rarely work while attending school. The French will tell you that that's a virtue of their system, not a problem.

Shorter working hours also reflect factors besides tax rates. French law requires employers to offer at least a month of vacation, but most U.S. workers take less than two weeks off. Here, too, the French will tell you that their policy is better than ours, because it helps families spend time together.

The aspect of French policy even the French agree is a big problem is that their retirement system allows workers to collect generous pensions even if they retire very early. As a result, only 40% of French residents between the ages of 55 and 64 are employed, compared with more than 60% in America. The cost of supporting all those early retirees is a major burden on the French welfare state—and getting worse as the French population ages. ▲

> > > > > > > > > > > >

➤ CHECK YOUR UNDERSTANDING 19-4

1. Explain how each of the following policies creates a disincentive to work or undertake a risky investment.
   a. A high sales tax on consumer items
   b. The loss of a housing subsidy when yearly income rises above $25,000

2. Over the past 30 years, has the polarization in Congress increased, decreased, or stayed the same?

Solutions appear at back of book.

[➤➤ A LOOK AHEAD •••

The welfare state provides some families with additional income in the form of government transfers. For the most part, however, families receive their income in payment for the resources they supply to the economy—mostly the labor they supply, but also the capital and land they own. But what determines wage rates, land rents, and other sources of income? In the next chapter, we describe how *factor markets*, markets in factors of production rather than in goods and services, operate.]

1. The **welfare state** absorbs a large share of government spending in all wealthy countries. **Government transfers** are the payments made by the government to individuals and families. **Poverty programs** alleviate income inequality by helping the poor; **social insurance programs** alleviate economic insecurity.

2. Despite the fact that the **poverty threshold** is adjusted according to the cost of living but not according to the standard of living, and that the average American income has risen substantially over those 30 years, the **poverty rate,** the percentage of the population with an income below the poverty threshold, is no lower than it was 30 years ago. There are various causes of poverty: lack of education, the legacy of discrimination, and bad luck. The consequences of poverty are particularly harmful for children.

3. **Median household income,** the income of a family at the center of the income distribution, is a better indicator of the income of the typical household than **mean household income** because it is not distorted by the inclusion of a small number of very wealthy households. The **Gini coefficient,** a number that summarizes a country's level of income inequality based on how unequally income is distributed across quintiles, is used to compare income inequality across countries.

4. Both **means-tested** and non-means-tested programs reduce poverty. The major **in-kind benefits** programs are Medicare and Medicaid, which pay for medical care. Due to concerns about the effects on incentives to work and on family cohesion, aid to poor families has become significantly less generous even as the **negative income tax** has become more generous. Social Security, the largest U.S. welfare state program, has significantly reduced poverty among the elderly. Unemployment insurance is also a key social insurance program.

5. Health insurance satisfies an important need because most families cannot afford expensive medical treatment. **Private health insurance,** unless it is employment-based, has the potential to fall into an adverse selection death spiral. Most Americans are covered by employment-based private health insurance; most of the remaining are covered by Medicare (for those over 65) or Medicaid (for those with low incomes).

6. Compared to other countries, the United States relies more heavily on private health insurance and has substantially higher health care costs per person without providing better care. Some countries have a **single-payer system,** a system in which the government pays most medical bills, funded through taxes.

7. Debates over the size of the welfare state are based on philosophical and equity-versus-efficiency considerations. Although high marginal tax rates to finance an extensive welfare state can reduce the incentive to work, means-testing programs in order to reduce the cost of the welfare state also reduce the incentive to work.

8. Politicians on the left tend to favor a bigger welfare state and those on the right oppose it. This left–right distinction is central to today's politics. America's two major political parties have become more polarized in recent decades, with a much clearer distinction than in the past about where their members stand on the left-right spectrum.

Welfare state, p. 480
Government transfer, p. 480
Poverty program, p. 480
Social insurance programs, p. 480
Poverty threshold, p. 481

Poverty rate, p. 482
Mean household income, p. 485
Median household income, p. 485
Gini coefficient, p. 486
Means-tested, p. 490

In-kind benefit, p. 490
Negative income tax, p. 490
Private health insurance, p. 494
Single-payer system, p. 498

1. The accompanying table contains data on the U.S. economy for the years 1983 and 2006. The second column shows the poverty threshold. The third column shows the consumer price index (CPI), a measure of the overall level of prices. And the fourth column shows U.S. gross domestic product (GDP) per capita, a measure of the standard of living.

Year	Poverty threshold	CPI (1982–1984 = 100)	GDP per capita
1983	$5,180	99.6	$15,092
2006	10,488	201.6	44,007

Source: U.S. Census Bureau; Bureau of Labor Statistics; Bureau of Economic Analysis.

a. By what factor has the poverty threshold increased from 1983 to 2006? That is, has it doubled, tripled, and so on?

b. By what factor has the CPI (a measure of the overall price level) increased from 1983 to 2006? That is, has it doubled, tripled, and so on?

c. By what factor has GDP per capita (a measure of the standard of living) increased from 1983 to 2006? That is, has it doubled, tripled, and so on?

d. What do your results tell you about how those people officially classified as "poor" have done economically relative to other U.S. citizens?

2. In the city of Metropolis, there are 100 residents, each of whom lives until age 75. Residents of Metropolis have the following incomes over their lifetime: through age 14, they earn nothing. From age 15 until age 29, they earn 200 metros (the currency of Metropolis) per year. From age 30 to age 49, they earn 400 metros. From age 50 to age 64, they earn 300 metros. Finally, at age 65 they retire and are paid a pension of 100 metros per year until they die at age 75. Each year, everyone consumes whatever their income is that year (that is, there is no saving and no borrowing). Currently, 20 residents are 10 years old, 20 residents are 20 years old, 20 residents are 40 years old, 20 residents are 60 years old, and 20 residents are 70 years old.

a. Study the income distribution among all residents of Metropolis. Split the population into quintiles according to their income. How much income does a resident in the lowest quintile have? In the second, third, fourth, and top quintiles? Which share of total income of all residents goes to the residents in each quintile? Construct a table showing the share of total income that goes to each quintile. Does this income distribution show inequality?

b. Now look only at the 20 residents of Metropolis who are currently 40 years old, and study the income distribution among only those residents. Split those 20 residents into quintiles according to their income. How much income does a resident in the lowest quintile have? In the second, third, fourth, and top quintiles? Which share of total income of all 40-year-olds goes to the residents in each quintile? Does this income distribution show inequality?

c. What is the relevance of these examples for assessing data on the distribution of income in any country?

3. The accompanying table presents data from the U.S. Census Bureau on median and mean income of male workers for the years 1972 and 2005. The income figures are adjusted to eliminate the effect of inflation.

Year	Median income	Mean income
	(in 2005 dollars)	
1972	$42,617	$47,708
2005	42,188	58,779

Source: U.S. Census Bureau.

a. By what percentage has median income changed over this period? By what percentage has mean income changed over this period?

b. Between 1972 and 2005, has the income distribution become less or more unequal? Explain.

4. There are 100 households in the economy of Equalor. Initially, 99 of them have an income of $10,000 each, and one household has an income of $1,010,000.

a. What is the median income in this economy? What is the mean income?

Through its poverty programs, the government of Equalor now redistributes income: it takes $990,000 away from the richest household and distributes it equally among the remaining 99 households.

b. What is the median income in this economy now? What is the mean income? Has the median income changed? Has the mean income changed? Which indicator (mean or median household income) is a better indicator of the typical Equalorian household's income? Explain.

5. The country of Marxland has the following income tax and social insurance system. Each citizen's income is taxed at an average tax rate of 100%. A social insurance system then provides transfers to each citizen such that each citizen's after-tax income is exactly equal. That is, each citizen gets (through a government transfer payment) an equal share of the income tax revenue. What is the incentive for one individual citizen to work and earn income? What will the total tax revenue in Marxland be? What will be the after-tax income (including the transfer payment) for each citizen? Do you think such a tax system that creates perfect equality will work?

6. The tax system in Taxilvania includes a negative income tax. For all incomes below $10,000, individuals pay an income tax of –40% (that is, they receive a payment of 40% of their income). For any income above the $10,000 threshold, the tax rate on that additional income is 10%. For the first three scenarios below, calculate the amount of income tax to be paid and after-tax income.

a. Lowani earns income of $8,000.

b. Midram earns income of $40,000.

c. Hi-Wan earns income of $100,000.

d. Can you find a notch in this tax system? That is, can you find a situation where earning more pre-tax income actually results in *less* after-tax income?

7. In the city of Notchingham, each worker is paid a wage rate of $10 per hour. Notchingham administers its own unemployment benefit, which is structured as follows: if you are unemployed (that is, if you do not work at all), you get unemployment benefits (a transfer from the government) of $50 per day. As soon as you work for only one hour, the unemployment benefit is completely withdrawn. That is, there is a notch in the benefit system.

a. How much income does an unemployed person have per day? How much daily income does an individual have who works four hours per day? How many hours do you need to work to earn just the same as if you were unemployed?

b. Will anyone ever accept a part-time job that requires working four hours per day, rather than being unemployed?

c. Suppose that Notchingham now changes the way in which the unemployment benefit is withdrawn. For each additional dollar an individual earns, $0.50 of the unemployment benefit is withdrawn. How much daily income does an individual who works four hours per day now have? Is there an incentive now to work four hours per day rather than being unemployed?

8. In a private insurance market, there are two different kinds of people: some who are more likely to require expensive medical treatment and some who are less likely to require medical treatment and who, if they do, require less expensive treatment. One health insurance policy is offered, tailored to the average person's health care needs: the premium is equal to the average person's medical expenses (plus the insurer's expenses and normal profit).

a. Explain why such an insurance policy is unlikely to be feasible.

In an effort to avoid the adverse selection death spiral, a private health insurer offers two health insurance policies: one that is intended for those who are more likely to require expensive treatment (and therefore charges a higher premium) and one that is intended for those who are less likely to require treatment (and therefore charges a lower premium).

b. Could this system overcome the problem created by adverse selection?

c. How does the British National Health Service (NHS) avoid these problems?

9. The accompanying table shows data on the total number of people in the United States and the number of all people who were uninsured, for selected years from 1997 to 2005. It also shows data on the total number of poor children in the United States—those under 18 and below the poverty threshold—and the number of poor children who were uninsured.

Year	Total people	Uninsured people	Total poor children	Uninsured poor children
			(millions)	
1997	269.1	43.4	14.1	3.4
1999	276.8	40.2	12.3	2.8
2001	282.1	41.2	11.7	2.5
2003	288.3	45.0	12.9	2.5
2005	293.8	46.6	12.9	2.4

Source: U.S. Census Bureau.

For each year, calculate the percentage of all people who were uninsured and the percentage of poor children who were uninsured. How have these percentages changed over time? What is a possible explanation for the change in the percentage of uninsured poor children?

10. The American National Election Studies conducts periodic research on the opinions of U.S. voters. The accompanying table shows the percentage of people, in selected years from 1952 to 2004, who agreed with the statement "There are important differences in what the Republicans and Democrats stand for."

Year	Agree with statement
1952	50%
1972	46
1992	60
2004	76

Source: American National Election Studies.

What do these data say about the degree of partisanship in U.S. politics over time?

www.worthpublishers.com/krugmanwells

Factor Markets and the Distribution of Income

THE VALUE OF A DEGREE

DOES HIGHER EDUCATION PAY? YES, IT DOES: IN the modern economy, employers are willing to pay a premium for workers with more education. And the size of that premium has increased a lot over the last few decades. Back in 1973 workers with advanced degrees, such as law degrees or MBAs, earned only 76% more than those who had only graduated from high school. By 2006, the premium for an advanced degree had risen to over 170%.

Who decided that the wages of workers with advanced degrees would rise so much compared with those of high school grads? The answer, of course, is that nobody decided it. Wage rates are prices, the prices of different kinds of labor; and they are decided, like other prices, by supply and demand.

Still, there is a qualitative difference between the wage rate of high school grads and the price of used textbooks: the wage rate isn't the price of a *good*, it's the price of a *factor of production*. And although markets for factors of production are in many ways similar to those for goods, there are also some important differences.

In this chapter, we examine *factor markets*, the markets in which the factors of production such as labor, land, and capital are traded. Factor markets, like goods markets, play a crucial role in the economy: they allocate productive resources to producers and help ensure that those resources are used efficiently.

This chapter begins by describing the major factors of production. Then we consider the demand for factors of production, which leads us to a crucial insight: the *marginal productivity theory of income distribution*. We then consider some challenges to the marginal productivity theory. Next, we examine the markets for capital and for land. The chapter concludes with a discussion of the supply of the most important factor, labor.

If you've ever had doubts about attending college, consider this: factory workers with only high school degrees will make much less than college grads. The present discounted value of the difference in lifetime earnings is as much as $300,000.

The Economy's Factors of Production

You may recall that we defined a factor of production in Chapter 2 in the context of the circular-flow diagram; it is any resource that is used by firms to produce goods and services, items that are consumed by households. Factors of production are bought and sold in *factor markets,* and the prices in factor markets are known as *factor prices.*

What are these factors of production, and why do factor prices matter?

The Factors of Production

As we learned in Chapter 2, economists divide factors of production into four principal classes: land, labor, physical capital, and human capital. Land is a resource provided by nature; labor is the work done by human beings.

In Chapter 9 we defined capital; it is the value of the assets that are used by a firm in producing its output. There are two broad types of capital. **Physical capital**—often referred to simply as "capital"—consists of manufactured resources such as equipment, buildings, tools, and machines.

In the modern economy, **human capital,** the improvement in labor created by education and knowledge, and embodied in the workforce, is at least equally significant. The importance of human capital has been greatly increased by the progress of technology, which has made a high level of technical sophistication essential to many jobs—one cause of the increased premium paid for workers with advanced degrees.

Physical capital—often referred to simply as "capital"—consists of manufactured productive resources such as equipment, buildings, tools, and machines.

Human capital is the improvement in labor created by education and knowledge that is embodied in the workforce.

Why Factor Prices Matter: The Allocation of Resources

Factor markets and factor prices play a key role in one of the most important processes that must take place in any economy: the allocation of resources among producers.

Consider the example of Mississippi and Louisiana in the aftermath of Hurricane Katrina, which was the costliest hurricane to hit the U.S. mainland to date. The states had an urgent need for workers in the building trades—carpenters, plumbers, and so on—to repair or replace damaged homes and businesses. What ensured that those needed workers actually came? The factor market: the high demand for workers drove up wages. During 2005, the average U.S. weekly wage grew at a rate of around 6%. But in areas heavily affected by Katrina, the average wage during the fall of 2005 grew by 30% more than the national rate, and some areas saw a rate of increase twice as high. Over time, these higher wages led large numbers of workers with the right skills to move temporarily to these states to do the work. In other words, the market for a factor

PITFALLS

WHAT IS A FACTOR, ANYWAY?
Imagine a business that produces shirts. The business will make use of workers and machines—that is, of labor and capital. But it will also use other inputs, such as electricity and cloth. Are all of these inputs factors of production? No: labor and capital are factors of production, but cloth and electricity are not.

The key distinction is that a factor of production earns income from the selling of its services over and over again but an input cannot. For example, a worker earns income over time from repeatedly selling his or her efforts; the owner of a machine earns income over time from repeatedly selling the use of that machine. So a factor of production, such as labor and capital, represents an enduring source of income. An input like electricity or cloth, however, is used up in the production process. Once exhausted, it cannot be a source of future income for its owner.

of production—construction workers—allocated that factor of production to where it was needed.

In this sense factor markets are similar to goods markets, which allocate goods among consumers. But there are two features that make factor markets special. Unlike in a goods market, demand in a factor market is what we call *derived demand*. That is, demand for the factor is derived from the firm's output choice. The second feature is that factor markets are where most of us get the largest shares of our income (government transfers being the next largest source of income in the economy).

> The **factor distribution of income** is the division of total income among labor, land, and capital.

Factor Incomes and the Distribution of Income

Most American families get most of their income in the form of wages and salaries—that is, they get their income by selling labor. Some people, however, get most of their income from physical capital: when you own stock in a company, what you really own is a share of that company's physical capital. And some people get much of their income from rents earned on land they own.

Obviously, then, the prices of factors of production have a major impact on how the economic "pie" is sliced among different groups. For example, a higher wage rate, other things equal, means that a larger proportion of the total income in the economy goes to people who derive their income from labor, and less goes to those who derive their income from capital or land. Economists refer to how the economic pie is sliced as the "distribution of income." Specifically, factor prices determine the **factor distribution of income**—how the total income of the economy is divided among labor, land, and capital.

As the following Economics in Action explains, the factor distribution of income in the United States has been quite stable over the past few decades. In other times and places, however, large changes have taken place in the factor distribution. One notable example: during the Industrial Revolution, the share of total income earned by landowners fell sharply, while the share earned by capital owners rose. As explained in the following For Inquiring Minds, this shift had a profound effect on society.

FOR INQUIRING MINDS

The Factor Distribution of Income and Social Change in the Industrial Revolution

Have you read any novels by Jane Austen? How about Charles Dickens? If you've read both, you probably noticed that they seem to be describing quite different societies. Austen's novels, set around 1800, describe a world in which the leaders of society are land-owning aristocrats. Dickens, writing about 50 years later, describes a world in which businessmen, especially factory owners, are in control.

This literary shift reflects a dramatic transformation in the factor distribution of income. The Industrial Revolution, which took place between

By altering how people lived and worked, the Industrial Revolution led to huge economic and social changes.

the late eighteenth century and the middle of the nineteenth century, changed England from a mainly agricultural country, in which land earned a fairly substantial share of income, to an urbanized and industrial one, in which land rents were dwarfed by capital income. Recent estimates by the economist Nancy Stokey show that between 1780 and 1850 the share of national income represented by land fell from 20% to 9%, but the share represented by capital rose from 35% to 44%. That shift changed everything—even literature.

►*ECONOMICS IN ACTION*

The Factor Distribution of Income in the United States

When we talk about the factor distribution of income, what are we talking about in practice?

In the United States, as in all advanced economies, payments to labor account for most of the economy's total income. Figure 20-1 shows the factor distribution of income in the United States in 2007: in that year, 70.4% of total income in the economy took the form of "compensation of employees"—a number that includes both wages and benefits such as health insurance. This number has been quite stable over the long run; 35 years earlier, in 1972, compensation of employees was very similar, at 72.2% of total income.

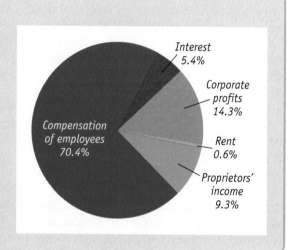

FIGURE 20-1

Factor Distribution of Income in the United States in 2007

In 2007, compensation of employees accounted for most income earned in the United States—about 70% of the total. Most of the remainder—consisting of earnings paid in the form of interest, corporate profits, and rent—went to owners of physical capital. Finally, proprietors' income—9.3% of the total—went to individual owners of businesses as compensation for their labor and capital expended in their businesses.

Source: Bureau of Economic Analysis.

Interest 5.4%

Corporate profits 14.3%

Compensation of employees 70.4%

Rent 0.6%

Proprietors' income 9.3%

However, measured wages and benefits don't capture the full income of "labor" because a significant fraction of total income in the United States (usually between 7% and 10%) is "proprietors' income"—the earnings of people who own their own businesses. Part of that income should be considered wages these business owners pay themselves. So the true share of labor in the economy is probably a few percentage points higher than the reported "compensation of employees" share.

But much of what we call compensation of employees is really a return on human capital. A surgeon isn't just supplying the services of a pair of ordinary hands (at least the patient hopes not!): that individual is also supplying the result of many years and hundreds of thousands of dollars invested in training and experience. We can't directly measure what fraction of wages is really a payment for education and training, but many economists believe that human capital has become *the* most important factor of production in modern economies. ▲

< < < < < < < < < < < <

►► QUICK REVIEW

➤ Economists usually divide the economy's factors of production into four principal categories: labor, land, **physical capital**, and **human capital.**

➤ The demand for a factor is a derived demand. Factor prices, which are set in factor markets, determine the **factor distribution of income.** Labor receives the bulk—approximately 70%—of the income in the modern U.S. economy. Although the exact share is not directly measurable, much of what is called compensation of employees is a return to human capital.

► CHECK YOUR UNDERSTANDING 20-1

1. Suppose that the government places price controls on the market for college professors, imposing a wage that is lower than the market wage. Describe the effect of this policy on the production of college degrees. What sectors of the economy do you think will be adversely affected by this policy? What sectors of the economy might benefit?

Solutions appear at back of book.

Marginal Productivity and Factor Demand

All economic decisions are about comparing costs and benefits—and usually about comparing marginal costs and marginal benefits. This goes both for a consumer, deciding whether to buy another pound of fried clams, and for a producer, deciding whether to hire an additional worker.

Although there are some important exceptions, most factor markets in the modern American economy are perfectly competitive, meaning that buyers and sellers of a given factor are price-takers. And in a competitive labor market, it's clear how to define an employer's marginal cost of a worker: it is simply the worker's wage rate. But what is the marginal benefit of that worker? To answer that question, we return to a concept first introduced in Chapter 12: the production function, which relates inputs to output. And as in Chapter 13, we will assume throughout this chapter that all producers are price-takers in their output markets—that is, they operate in a perfectly competitive industry.

Value of the Marginal Product

Figure 20-2 reproduces Figures 12-1 and 12-2, which showed the production function for wheat on George and Martha's farm. Panel (a) uses the total product curve to show how total wheat production depends on the number of workers employed on the farm; panel (b) shows how the *marginal product* of labor, the increase in output from employing one more worker, depends on the number of workers employed. Table 20-1 on the next page, which reproduces the table in Figure 12-1, shows the numbers behind the figure.

Assume that George and Martha want to maximize their profit, that workers must be paid $200 each, and that wheat sells for $20 per bushel. What is their optimal number of workers? That is, how many workers should they employ to maximize profit?

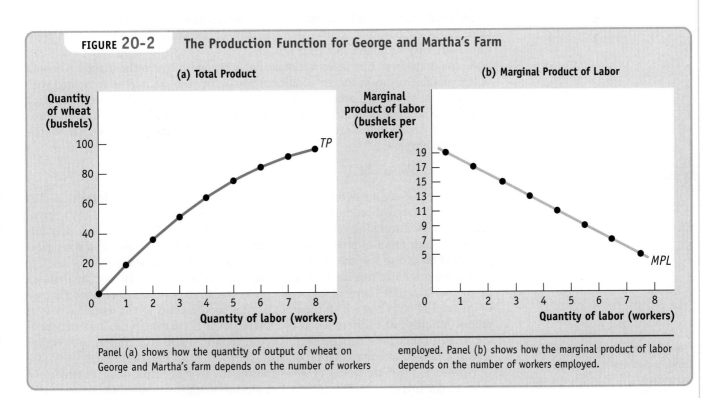

FIGURE 20-2   The Production Function for George and Martha's Farm

Panel (a) shows how the quantity of output of wheat on George and Martha's farm depends on the number of workers employed. Panel (b) shows how the marginal product of labor depends on the number of workers employed.

TABLE 20-1

Employment and Output for George and Martha's Farm

Quantity of labor L (workers)	Quantity of wheat Q (bushels)	Marginal product of labor $MPL = \frac{\Delta Q}{\Delta L}$ (bushels per worker)
0	0	
		19
1	19	
		17
2	36	
		15
3	51	
		13
4	64	
		11
5	75	
		9
6	84	
		7
7	91	
		5
8	96	

In Chapters 12 and 13 we showed how to answer this question in several steps. In Chapter 12 we used information from the producer's production function to derive the firm's total cost and its marginal cost. And in Chapter 13 we derived the *price-taking firm's optimal output rule:* a price-taking firm's profit is maximized by producing the quantity of output at which the marginal cost of the last unit produced is equal to the market price. Having determined the optimal quantity of output, we can go back to the production function and find the optimal number of workers—it is simply the number of workers needed to produce the optimal quantity of output.

There is, however, another way to use marginal analysis to find the number of workers that maximizes a producer's profit. We can go directly to the question of what level of employment maximizes profit. This alternative approach is equivalent to the approach we outlined in the preceding paragraph—it's just a different way of looking at the same thing. But it gives us more insight into the demand for factors as opposed to the supply of goods.

To see how this alternative approach works, let's suppose that George and Martha are considering whether or not to employ an additional worker. The increase in *cost* from employing that additional worker is the wage rate, *W*. The *benefit* to George and Martha from employing that extra worker is the value of the extra output that worker can produce. What is this value? It is the marginal product of labor, *MPL*, multiplied by the price per unit of output, *P*. This amount—the extra value of output that is generated by employing one more unit of labor—is known as the **value of the marginal product** of labor, or *VMPL*:

(20-1) Value of the marginal product of labor $= VMPL = P \times MPL$

So should George and Martha hire that extra worker? The answer is yes, if the value of the extra output is more than the cost of the worker—that is, if *VMPL* > *W*. Otherwise they shouldn't hire that worker.

So the decision to hire labor is a marginal decision, in which the marginal benefit to the producer from hiring an additional worker (*VMPL*) should be compared with the marginal cost to the producer (*W*). And as with any marginal decision, the optimal choice is where marginal benefit is just equal to marginal cost. That is, to maximize profit George and Martha will employ workers up to the point at which, for the last worker employed,

(20-2) $VMPL = W$

This rule doesn't apply only to labor; it applies to any factor of production. The value of the marginal product of any factor is its marginal product times the price of the good it produces. The general rule is that *a profit-maximizing price-taking producer employs each factor of production up to the point at which the value of the marginal product of the last unit of the factor employed is equal to that factor's price.*

It's important to realize that this rule doesn't conflict with our analysis in Chapters 12 and 13. There we saw that a profit-maximizing producer of a good chooses the level of output at which the price of that good is equal to the marginal cost of production. It's just a different way of looking at the same rule. If the level of output is chosen so that price equals marginal cost, then it is also true that at that output level the value of the marginal product of labor will equal the wage rate.

Now let's look more closely at why choosing the level of employment at which the value of the marginal product of the last worker employed is equal to the wage rate works—and at how it helps us understand factor demand.

The **value of the marginal product** of a factor is the value of the additional output generated by employing one more unit of that factor.

Value of the Marginal Product and Factor Demand

Table 20-2 calculates the value of the marginal product of labor on George and Martha's farm, on the assumption that the price of wheat is $20 per bushel. In Figure 20-3 the horizontal axis shows the number of workers employed; the vertical axis measures the value of the marginal product of labor *and* the wage rate. The curve shown is the **value of the marginal product curve** of labor. This curve, like the marginal product of labor curve, slopes downward because of diminishing returns to labor in production. That is, the value of the marginal product of each worker is less than that of the preceding worker, because the marginal product of each worker is less than that of the preceding worker.

TABLE 20-2

Value of the Marginal Product of Labor for George and Martha's Farm

Quantity of labor L (workers)	Marginal product of labor MPL (bushels per worker)	Value of the marginal product of labor VMPL = P × MPL
0		
	19	$380
1		
	17	340
2		
	15	300
3		
	13	260
4		
	11	220
5		
	9	180
6		
	7	140
7		
	5	100
8		

We have just seen that to maximize profit, George and Martha must hire workers up to the point at which the wage rate is equal to the value of the marginal product of the last worker employed. Let's use the example to see how this principle really works.

Assume that George and Martha currently employ 3 workers and that workers must be paid the market wage rate of $200. Should they employ an additional worker?

Looking at Table 20-2, we see that if George and Martha currently employ 3 workers, the value of the marginal product of an additional worker is $260. So if they employ an additional worker, they will increase the value of their production by $260 but increase their cost by only $200, yielding an increased profit of $60. In fact, a producer can

The **value of the marginal product curve** of a factor shows how the value of the marginal product of that factor depends on the quantity of the factor employed.

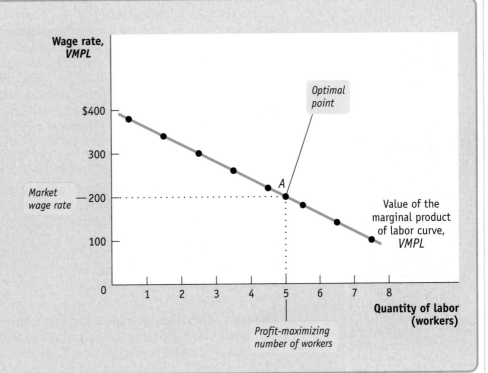

FIGURE 20-3

The Value of the Marginal Product Curve

This curve shows how the value of the marginal product of labor depends on the number of workers employed. It slopes downward because of diminishing returns to labor in production. To maximize profit, George and Martha choose the level of employment at which the value of the marginal product of labor is equal to the market wage rate. For example, at a wage rate of $200 the profit-maximizing level of employment is 5 workers, shown by point A. The value of the marginal product curve of a factor is the producer's individual demand curve for that factor.

always increase profit by employing one more unit of a factor of production as long as the value of the marginal product produced by that unit exceeds its factor price.

Alternatively, suppose that George and Martha employ 8 workers. By reducing the number of workers to 7, they can save $200 in wages. In addition, the value of the marginal product of the last one, the 8th worker, was only $100. So, by reducing employment by one worker, they can increase profit by $200 − $100 = $100. In other words, a producer can always increase profit by employing one less unit of a factor of production as long as the value of the marginal product produced by that unit is less than the factor price.

Using this method, we can see from Table 20-2 that the profit-maximizing employment level is 5 workers given a wage rate of $200. The value of the marginal product of the 5th worker is $220, so adding the 5th worker results in $20 of additional profit. But George and Martha should not hire more than 5 workers: the value of the marginal product of the 6th worker is only $180, $20 less than the cost of that worker. So, to maximize profit, George and Martha should employ workers up to but not beyond the point at which the value of the marginal product of the last worker employed is equal to the wage rate.

Now look again at the value of the marginal product curve in Figure 20-3. To determine the profit-maximizing level of employment, we set the value of the marginal product of labor equal to the price of labor—a wage rate of $200 per worker. This means that the profit-maximizing level of employment is at point A, corresponding to an employment level of 5 workers. If the wage rate were higher, we would simply move up the curve and decrease the number of workers employed: if the wage rate were lower than $200, we move down the curve and increase the number of workers employed.

In this example, George and Martha have a small farm in which the potential employment level varies from 0 to 8 workers, and they hire workers up to the point at which the value of the marginal product of the last worker is no less than the wage rate. Suppose, however, that the firm in question is large and has the potential of hiring many workers. When there are many employees, the value of the marginal product of labor falls only slightly when an additional worker is employed. As a result, there will be some worker whose value of the marginal product almost exactly equals the wage rate. (In keeping with the George and Martha example, this means that some worker generates a value of the marginal product of approximately $200.) In this case, the firm maximizes profit by choosing a level of employment at which the value of the marginal product of the last worker hired *equals* (to a very good approximation) the wage rate.

In the interest of simplicity, we will assume from now on that firms use this rule to determine the profit-maximizing level of employment. *This means that the value of the marginal product of labor curve is the individual producer's labor demand curve.* And in general, a producer's value of the marginal product curve for any factor of production is that producer's individual demand curve for that factor of production.

Shifts of the Factor Demand Curve

As in the case of ordinary demand curves, it is important to distinguish between movements along the factor demand curve and shifts of the factor demand curve. What causes factor demand curves to shift? There are three main causes:

- Changes in prices of goods
- Changes in supply of other factors
- Changes in technology

Changes in Prices of Goods Remember that factor demand is derived demand: if the price of the good that is produced with a factor changes, so will the value of the marginal product of the factor. That is, in the case of labor demand, if P changes, $VMPL = P \times MPL$ will change at any given level of employment.

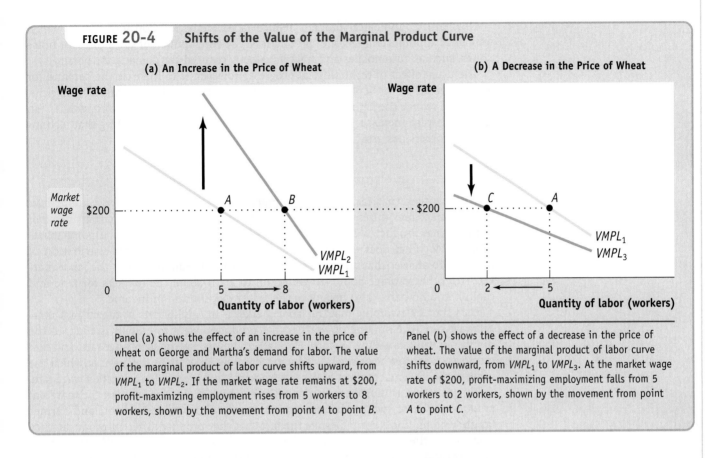

FIGURE 20-4   **Shifts of the Value of the Marginal Product Curve**

Panel (a) shows the effect of an increase in the price of wheat on George and Martha's demand for labor. The value of the marginal product of labor curve shifts upward, from $VMPL_1$ to $VMPL_2$. If the market wage rate remains at $200, profit-maximizing employment rises from 5 workers to 8 workers, shown by the movement from point A to point B.

Panel (b) shows the effect of a decrease in the price of wheat. The value of the marginal product of labor curve shifts downward, from $VMPL_1$ to $VMPL_3$. At the market wage rate of $200, profit-maximizing employment falls from 5 workers to 2 workers, shown by the movement from point A to point C.

Figure 20-4 illustrates the effects of changes in the price of wheat, assuming that $200 is the current wage rate. Panel (a) shows the effect of an *increase* in the price of wheat. This shifts the value of the marginal product of labor curve upward, because *VMPL* rises at any given level of employment. If the wage rate remains unchanged at $200, the optimal point moves from point A to point B: the profit-maximizing level of employment rises.

Panel (b) shows the effect of a *decrease* in the price of wheat. This shifts the value of the marginal product of labor curve downward. If the wage rate remains unchanged at $200, the optimal point moves from point A to point C: the profit-maximizing level of employment falls.

Changes in Supply of Other Factors   Suppose that George and Martha acquire more land to cultivate—say, by clearing a woodland on their property. Each worker now produces more wheat because each one has more land to work with. As a result, the marginal product of labor on the farm rises at any given level of employment. This has the same effect as an increase in the price of wheat, which is illustrated in panel (a) of Figure 20-4: the value of the marginal product of labor curve shifts upward, and at any given wage rate the profit-maximizing level of employment rises. Similarly, suppose George and Martha cultivate less land. This leads to a fall in the marginal product of labor at any given employment level. Each worker produces less wheat because each has less land to work with. As a result, the value of the marginal product of labor curve shifts downward—as in panel (b) of Figure 20-4—and the profit-maximizing level of employment falls.

Changes in Technology   In general, the effect of technological progress on the demand for any given factor can go either way: improved technology can either increase or reduce the demand for a given factor of production.

How can technological progress reduce factor demand? Consider horses, which were once an important factor of production. The development of substitutes for horse power, such as automobiles and tractors, greatly reduced the demand for horses.

The usual effect of technological progress, however, is to increase the demand for a given factor. In particular, although there have been persistent fears that machinery would reduce the demand for labor, over the long run the U.S. economy has seen both large wage increases and large increases in employment, suggesting that technological progress has greatly increased labor demand.

The Marginal Productivity Theory of Income Distribution

We've now seen that each perfectly competitive producer in a perfectly competitive factor market maximizes profit by hiring labor up to the point at which its value of the marginal product is equal to its price—in the case of labor, to the point where $VMPL = W$. What does this tell us about labor's share in the factor distribution of income? To answer that question, we need to examine equilibrium in the labor market. From that vantage point we will go on to learn about the markets for land and capital, and how they also influence the factor distribution of income.

Let's start by assuming that the labor market is in equilibrium: at the current market wage rate, the number of workers that producers want to employ is equal to the number of workers willing to work. Thus, all employers pay the *same* wage rate, and *each* employer, whatever he or she is producing, employs labor up to the point at which the value of the marginal product of the last workers hired is equal to the market wage rate.

This situation is illustrated in Figure 20-5, which shows the value of the marginal product curves of two producers—Farmer Jones, who produces wheat, and Farmer Smith, who produces corn. Despite the fact that they produce different products, they compete for the same workers and so must pay the same wage rate, $200. When both farmers maximize profit, both hire labor up to the point at which its value of the marginal product is equal to the wage rate. In the figure, this corresponds to employment of 5 workers by Jones and 7 by Smith.

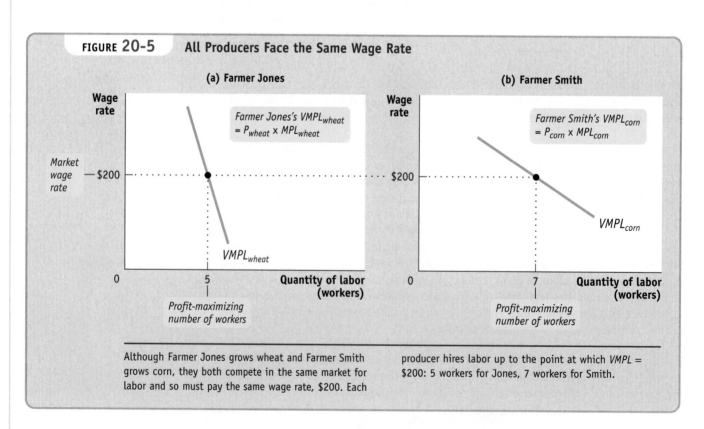

FIGURE 20-5   **All Producers Face the Same Wage Rate**

(a) Farmer Jones

Farmer Jones's $VMPL_{wheat}$ = $P_{wheat} \times MPL_{wheat}$

$VMPL_{wheat}$

Profit-maximizing number of workers

(b) Farmer Smith

Farmer Smith's $VMPL_{corn}$ = $P_{corn} \times MPL_{corn}$

$VMPL_{corn}$

Profit-maximizing number of workers

Although Farmer Jones grows wheat and Farmer Smith grows corn, they both compete in the same market for labor and so must pay the same wage rate, $200. Each producer hires labor up to the point at which $VMPL$ = $200: 5 workers for Jones, 7 workers for Smith.

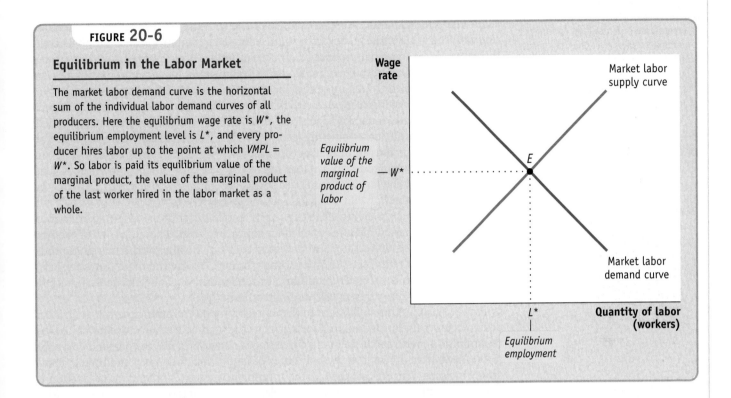

FIGURE 20-6

Equilibrium in the Labor Market

The market labor demand curve is the horizontal sum of the individual labor demand curves of all producers. Here the equilibrium wage rate is W^*, the equilibrium employment level is L^*, and every producer hires labor up to the point at which $VMPL = W^*$. So labor is paid its equilibrium value of the marginal product, the value of the marginal product of the last worker hired in the labor market as a whole.

Figure 20-6 illustrates the labor market as a whole. The *market labor demand curve*, like the market demand curve for a good (shown in Figure 3-5), is the horizontal sum of all the individual labor demand curves of all the producers who hire labor. And recall that each producer's individual labor demand curve is the same as his or her value of the marginal product of labor curve. For now, let's simply assume an upward-sloping labor supply curve; we'll discuss labor supply later in this chapter. Then the equilibrium wage rate is the wage rate at which the quantity of labor supplied is equal to the quantity of labor demanded. In Figure 20-6, this leads to an equilibrium wage rate of W^* and the corresponding equilibrium employment level of L^*. (The equilibrium wage rate is also known as the market wage rate.)

And as we showed in the examples of the farms of George and Martha and of Farmer Jones and Farmer Smith (where the equilibrium wage rate is $200), each farm hires labor up to the point at which the value of the marginal product of labor is equal to the equilibrium wage rate. Therefore, in equilibrium, the value of the marginal product of labor is the same for all employers. So the equilibrium (or market) wage rate is equal to the **equilibrium value of the marginal product** of labor—the additional value produced by the last unit of labor employed in the labor market as a whole. It doesn't matter where that additional unit is employed, since equilibrium *VMPL* is the same for all producers.

What we have just learned, then, is that the market wage rate is equal to the equilibrium value of the marginal product of labor. And the same is true of each factor of production: in a perfectly competitive market economy, the market price of each factor is equal to its equilibrium value of the marginal product. Let's examine the markets for land and (physical) capital now. (From this point on, we'll refer to physical capital as simply "capital.")

The Markets for Land and Capital

If we maintain the assumption that the markets for goods and services are perfectly competitive, the result that we derived for the labor market also applies to other factors of production. Suppose, for example, that a farmer is considering whether to rent an

The **equilibrium value of the marginal product** of a factor is the additional value produced by the last unit of that factor employed in the factor market as a whole.

The **rental rate** of either land or capital is the cost, explicit or implicit, of using a unit of that asset for a given period of time.

additional acre of land for the next year. He or she will compare the cost of renting that acre with the value of the additional output generated by employing an additional acre—the value of the marginal product of an acre of land. To maximize profit, the farmer must employ land up to the point at which the value of the marginal product of an acre of land is equal to the rental rate per acre.

What if the farmer already owns the land? We already saw the answer in Chapter 9, which dealt with economic decisions: even if you own land, there is an implicit cost—the opportunity cost—of using it for a given activity, because it could be used for something else, such as renting it out to other farmers at the market rental rate. So a profit-maximizing producer employs additional acres of land up to the point at which the cost of the last acre employed, explicit or implicit, is equal to the value of the marginal product of that acre.

The same is true for capital. The explicit or implicit cost of using a unit of land or capital for a set period of time is called its **rental rate.** In general, a unit of land or capital is employed up to the point at which that unit's value of the marginal product is equal to its rental rate over that time period. How are the rental rates for land and capital determined? By the equilibria in the land market and the capital market, of course. Figure 20-7 illustrates those outcomes.

Panel (a) shows the equilibrium in the market for land. Summing over the individual demand curves for land of all producers gives us the market demand curve for land. Due to diminishing returns, the demand curve slopes downward, like the demand curve for labor. As we have drawn it, the supply curve of land is relatively steep and therefore relatively inelastic. This reflects the fact that finding new supplies of land for production is typically difficult and expensive—for example, creating new farmland through expensive irrigation. The equilibrium rental rate for land, R^*_{Land}, and the equilibrium quantity of land employed in production, Q^*_{Land}, are given by the intersection of the two curves.

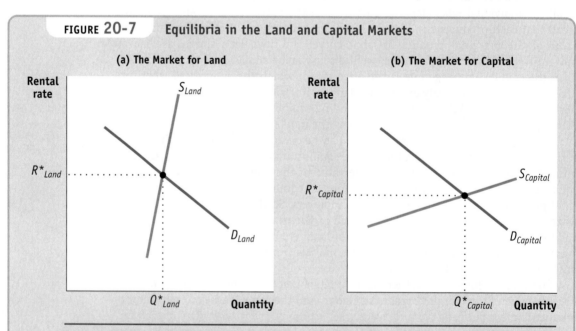

FIGURE 20-7 **Equilibria in the Land and Capital Markets**

(a) The Market for Land

(b) The Market for Capital

Panel (a) illustrates equilibrium in the market for land; panel (b) illustrates equilibrium in the market for capital. The supply curve for land is relatively steep, reflecting the high cost of increasing the quantity of productive land. The supply curve for capital, in contrast, is relatively flat, due to the relatively high responsiveness of savings to changes in the rental rate for capital. The equilibrium rental rates for land and capital, as well as the equilibrium quantities transacted, are given by the intersections of the demand and supply curves. In a competitive land market, each unit of land will be paid the equilibrium value of the marginal product of land, R^*_{Land}. Likewise, in a competitive capital market, each unit of capital will be paid the equilibrium value of the marginal product of capital, $R^*_{Capital}$.

Panel (b) shows the equilibrium in the market for capital. In contrast to the supply curve for land, the supply curve for capital is relatively elastic. That's because the supply of capital is relatively responsive to price: capital comes from the savings of investors, and the amount of savings that investors make available is relatively responsive to the rental rate for capital. The equilibrium rental rate for capital, $R^*_{Capital}$, and the equilibrium quantity of capital employed in production, $Q^*_{Capital}$, are given by the intersection of the two curves.

One small aside—you may have noted that producers frequently purchase land or capital rather than rent it over time. Does this fact mean that our model no longer works? No—it just means that we have to make an adjustment. We have to take into account that a parcel of land or a piece of machinery that has been purchased by a producer generates future revenue as well as current revenue. Using the present value method, which we learned in Chapter 9, we can convert the value of the marginal product stream that the parcel of land or machine generates today and in the future into its present value. Thus, a producer will purchase parcels of land or pieces of machinery up to the point at which the present value of its current and future stream of the value of the marginal product is equal to its factor price. If you examine our analysis of present value in Chapter 9, you'll see that, other things equal, present value increases when the interest rate falls. This leads to an important observation about how markets interact: other things equal, a fall in the interest rate (the *real* interest rate, which is the interest rate adjusted for changes in the purchasing power of money) leads to a rightward shift of the demand curves for land and for capital, with higher equilibrium prices and quantities transacted.

The Marginal Productivity Theory of Income Distribution

So we have learned that when the markets for goods and services and the factor markets are perfectly competitive, a factor of production will be employed up to the point at which its value of the marginal product is equal to its market equilibrium price. That is, it will be paid its equilibrium value of the marginal product. What does this say about the factor distribution of income? It leads us to the **marginal productivity theory of income distribution,** which says that each factor is paid the value of the output generated by the last unit of that factor employed in the factor market as a whole—its equilibrium value of the marginal product.

To understand why the marginal productivity theory of income distribution is important, look back at Figure 20-1, which shows the factor distribution of income in the United States, and ask yourself this question: who or what decided that labor would get 70.4% of total U.S. income? Why not 90% or 50%?

The answer, according to the marginal productivity theory of income distribution, is that the division of income among the economy's factors of production isn't arbitrary: it is determined by each factor's marginal productivity at the economy's equilibrium. The wage rate earned by *all* workers in the economy is equal to the increase in the value of output generated by the last worker employed in the economy-wide labor market.

Here we have assumed that all workers are of the same ability. (Similarly, we've assumed that all units of land and capital are equally productive.) But in reality workers differ considerably in ability. Rather than thinking of one labor market for all workers in the economy, we can instead think of different markets for different types of workers, where workers are of equivalent ability within each market. For example, the market for computer programmers is different from the market for pastry chefs. And in the market for computer programmers, all participants are assumed to have equal ability; likewise for the market for pastry chefs. In this scenario, the marginal productivity theory of income distribution still holds. That is, when the labor market for computer programmers is in equilibrium, the wage rate earned by all computer programmers is equal to the market's equilibrium value of the marginal product—the value of the marginal product of the last computer programmer hired in that market.

According to the **marginal productivity theory of income distribution,** every factor of production is paid its equilibrium value of the marginal product.

PITFALLS

GETTING MARGINAL PRODUCTIVITY THEORY RIGHT
It's important to be careful about what the marginal productivity theory of income distribution says: it says that *all* units of a factor get paid the factor's equilibrium value of the marginal product—the additional value produced by the *last* unit of the factor employed.

The most common source of error is to forget that the relevant value of the marginal product is the equilibrium value, not the value of the marginal products you calculate on the way to equilibrium. In looking at Table 20-2, you might be tempted to think that because the first worker has a value of the marginal product of $380, that worker is paid $380 in equilibrium. Not so: if the equilibrium value of the marginal product in the labor market is equal to $200, then *all* workers receive $200.

The marginal productivity theory of income distribution holds for skilled machinists at Hamill Manufacturing.

►ECONOMICS IN ACTION

Help Wanted!

Hamill Manufacturing of Pennsylvania makes precision components for military helicopters and nuclear submarines. Their highly skilled senior machinists are well paid compared to other workers in manufacturing, earning nearly $70,000 in 2006, excluding benefits. Like most skilled machinists in the United States, Hamill's machinists are very productive: according to the National Mechanists Association, in 2006 each skilled American machinist generated approximately $120,000 in yearly revenue.

But there is a $50,000 difference between the salary paid to Hamill machinists and the revenue they generate. Does this mean that the marginal productivity theory of income distribution doesn't hold? Doesn't the theory imply that machinists should be paid $120,000, the average revenue that each one generates? The answer is no, for two reasons. First, the $120,000 figure is averaged over *all machinists currently employed.* The theory says that machinists will be paid the value of the marginal product of the *last machinist hired,* and due to diminishing returns to labor, that value will be lower than the average over all machinists currently employed. Second, a worker's equilibrium wage rate includes other costs, such as employee benefits, that have to be added to the $70,000 salary. The marginal productivity theory of income distribution says that workers are paid a wage rate, *including all benefits,* equal to the value of the marginal product. You can see all these costs are present at Hamill. There the machinists have good benefits and job security, which add to their salary. Including these benefits, machinists' total compensation will be equal to the value of the marginal product of the last machinist employed.

In Hamill's case, there is yet another factor that explains the $50,000 gap: there are not enough machinists at the current wage rate. Although the company increased the number of employees from 85 in 2004 to 110 in 2006, they would like to hire more. Why doesn't Hamill raise its wages in order to attract more skilled machinists? The problem is that the work they do is so specialized that it is hard to hire from the outside, even when the company raises wages as an inducement. To address this problem, Hamill is now spending a significant amount of money training each new hire. In the end, it does appear that the marginal productivity theory of income distribution holds. ▲

‹ ‹ ‹ ‹ ‹ ‹ ‹ ‹ ‹ ‹ ‹ ‹

► CHECK YOUR UNDERSTANDING 20-2

1. In the following cases, state the direction of the shift of the demand curve for labor and what will happen, other things equal, to the market equilibrium wage rate and quantity of labor employed as a result.
   a. Service industries, such as retailing and banking, experience an increase in demand. These industries use relatively more labor than nonservice industries.
   b. Due to overfishing, there is a fall in the amount of fish caught per day by commercial fishers; this decrease affects their demand for workers.

2. Explain the following statement: "When firms in different industries all compete for the same workers, then the value of the marginal product of the last worker hired will be equal across all firms regardless of whether they are in different industries."

Solutions appear at back of book.

Is the Marginal Productivity Theory of Income Distribution Really True?

Although the marginal productivity theory of income distribution is a well-established part of economic theory, closely linked to the analysis of markets in general, it is a source of some controversy. There are two main objections to it.

First, in the real world we see large disparities in income between factors of production that, in the eyes of some observers, should receive the same payment. Perhaps the most conspicuous examples in the United States are the large differences in the average wages between women and men and among various racial and ethnic groups. Do these wage differences really reflect differences in marginal productivity, or is something else going on?

Second, many people wrongly believe that the marginal productivity theory of income distribution gives a *moral* justification for the distribution of income, implying that the existing distribution is fair and appropriate. This misconception sometimes leads other people, who believe that the current distribution of income is unfair, to reject marginal productivity theory.

To address these controversies, we'll start by looking at income disparities across gender and ethnic groups. Then we'll ask what factors might account for these disparities and whether these explanations are consistent with the marginal productivity theory of income distribution.

Wage Disparities in Practice

Wage rates in the United States cover a very wide range. In 2007, hundreds of thousands of workers received the legal federal minimum of $5.85 per hour. At the other extreme, the chief executives of several companies were paid more than $100 million, which works out to $20,000 per hour even if they worked 100-hour weeks. Even leaving out these extremes, there is a huge range of wage rates. Are people really that different in their marginal productivities?

A particular source of concern is the existence of systematic wage differences across gender and ethnicity. Figure 20-8 compares annual median earnings in 2006 of workers 25 years or older classified by gender and ethnicity. As a group, White males had the highest earnings. Other data show that women (averaging across all ethnicities) earned only about 60% as much; African-American workers (male and female combined) only 64% as much; Hispanic workers only 54% as much.

We are a nation founded on the belief that all men are created equal—and if the Constitution were rewritten today, we would say that *all people* are created equal. So why do they receive such unequal pay? Let's start with the marginal productivity explanations, then look at other influences.

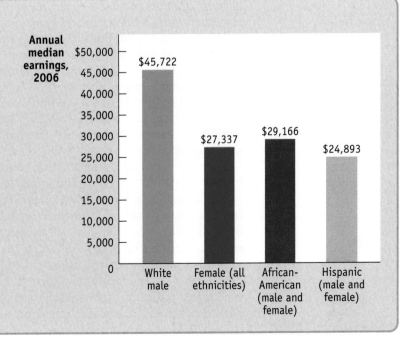

FIGURE 20-8

Median Earnings by Gender and Ethnicity, 2006

The U.S. labor market continues to show large differences across workers according to gender and ethnicity. Women are paid substantially less than men; African-American and Hispanic workers are paid substantially less than White male workers.

Source: Bureau of Labor Statistics.

Compensating differentials are wage differences across jobs that reflect the fact that some jobs are less pleasant than others.

Marginal Productivity and Wage Inequality

A large part of the observed inequality in wages can be explained by considerations that are consistent with the marginal productivity theory of income distribution. In particular, there are three well-understood sources of wage differences across occupations and individuals.

First is the existence of **compensating differentials:** across different types of jobs, wages are often higher or lower depending on how attractive or unattractive the job is. Workers with unpleasant or dangerous jobs demand a higher wage in comparison to workers with jobs that require the same skill and effort but lack the unpleasant or dangerous qualities. For example, truckers who haul hazardous loads are paid more than truckers who haul normal loads. But for any *given* job, the marginal productivity theory of income distribution generally holds true. For example, hazardous-load truckers are paid a wage equal to the equilibrium value of the marginal product of the last person employed in the market for hazardous-load truckers.

A second reason for wage inequality that is clearly consistent with marginal productivity theory is differences in talent. People differ in their abilities: a high-ability person, by producing a better product that commands a higher price compared to a lower-ability person, generates a higher value of the marginal product. And these differences in the value of the marginal product translate into differences in earning potential. We all know that this is true in sports: practice is important, but 99.99% (at least) of the population just doesn't have what it takes to hit golf balls like Tiger Woods or hit tennis balls like Maria Sharapova. The same is true, though less obvious, in other fields of endeavor.

A third, very important reason for wage differences is differences in the quantity of *human capital.* Recall that human capital—education and training—is at least as important in the modern economy as physical capital in the form of buildings and machines. Different people "embody" quite different quantities of human capital, and a person with a higher quantity of human capital typically generates a higher value of the marginal product by producing a product that commands a higher price. So differences in human capital account for substantial differences in wages. People with high levels of human capital, such as skilled surgeons or engineers, generally receive high wages.

The most direct way to see the effect of human capital on wages is to look at the relationship between educational levels and earnings. Figure 20-9 shows earnings differentials by gender, ethnicity, and three educational levels for people 25 years or older in 2006. As you can see, regardless of gender or ethnicity, higher education is associated with higher median earnings. For example, in 2006 White females with 9 to 12 years of schooling but without a high school diploma had median earnings 31% less than those with a high school diploma and 64% less than those with a college degree—and similar patterns exist for the other five groups. Additional data show that surgeons—an occupation that requires steady hands and many years of formal training—earned an average of $184,150 in 2006.

Because even now men typically have had more years of education than women and Whites more years than non-Whites, differences in level of education are part of the explanation for the earnings differences shown in Figure 20-8.

It's also important to realize that formal education is not the only source of human capital; on-the-job training and experience are also very important. This point was highlighted by a 2003 National Science Foundation report on earnings differences between male and female scientists and engineers. The study was motivated by concerns over the male–female earnings gap: the median salary for women in science and engineering is about 24% less than the median salary for men. The study found that women in these occupations are, on average, younger than men and have considerably less experience than their male counterparts. This difference in age and experience, according to the study, explained most of the earnings differential. Differences in job tenure and experience can partly explain one notable aspect of

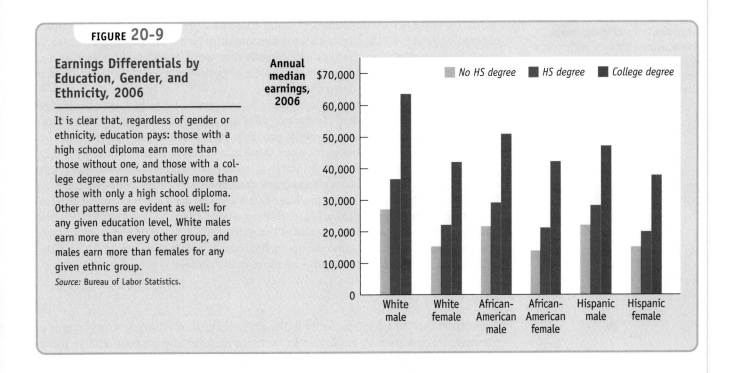

FIGURE 20-9

Earnings Differentials by Education, Gender, and Ethnicity, 2006

It is clear that, regardless of gender or ethnicity, education pays: those with a high school diploma earn more than those without one, and those with a college degree earn substantially more than those with only a high school diploma. Other patterns are evident as well: for any given education level, White males earn more than every other group, and males earn more than females for any given ethnic group.

Source: Bureau of Labor Statistics.

Figure 20-9: that, across all ethnicities, women's median earnings are less than men's median earnings for any given education level.

But it's also important to emphasize that earnings differences arising from differences in human capital are not necessarily "fair." A society in which non-White children typically receive a poor education because they live in underfunded school districts, then go on to earn low wages because they are poorly educated, may have labor markets that are well described by marginal productivity theory (and would be consistent with the earnings differentials across ethnic groups shown in Figure 20-8). Yet many people would still consider the resulting distribution of income unfair.

Still, many observers think that actual wage differentials cannot be entirely explained by compensating differentials, differences in talent, and differences in human capital. They believe that market power, *efficiency wages,* and discrimination also play an important role. We will examine these forces next.

Market Power

The marginal productivity theory of income distribution is based on the assumption that factor markets are perfectly competitive. In such markets we can expect workers to be paid the equilibrium value of their marginal product, regardless of who they are. But how valid is this assumption?

We studied markets that are *not* perfectly competitive in Chapters 14, 15, and 16; now let's touch briefly on the ways in which labor markets may deviate from the competitive assumption.

One undoubted source of differences in wages between otherwise similar workers is the role of **unions**—organizations that try to raise wages and improve working conditions for their members. Labor unions, when they are successful, replace one-on-one wage deals between workers and employers with "collective bargaining," in which the employer must negotiate wages with union representatives. Without question, this leads to higher wages for those workers who are represented by unions. In 2007 the median weekly earnings of union members in the United States were $863, compared with $663 for workers not represented by unions—about a 23% difference.

Unions are organizations of workers that try to raise wages and improve working conditions for their members by bargaining collectively.

According to the **efficiency-wage model,** some employers pay an above-equilibrium wage as an incentive for better performance.

Just as workers can sometimes organize to extract higher wages than they would otherwise receive, employers can sometimes organize to pay *lower* wages than would result from competition. For example, health care workers—doctors, nurses, and so on—sometimes argue that health maintenance organizations (HMOs) are engaged in a collective effort to hold down their wages.

How much does collective action, either by workers or by employers, affect wages in the modern United States? Several decades ago, when around 30% of American workers were union members, unions probably had a significant upward effect on wages. Today, however, most economists think unions exert a fairly minor influence. Union membership in the United States is relatively limited: less than 9% of the employees of private businesses are represented by unions. And although there are fields like health care in which a few large firms account for a sizable share of employment in certain geographical areas, the sheer size of the U.S. labor market is enormous and the ease with which most workers can move in search of higher-paying jobs probably means that concerted efforts to hold wages below the unrestrained market equilibrium level rarely occur and even more rarely succeed.

Efficiency Wages

A second source of wage inequality is the phenomenon of *efficiency wages*—a type of incentive scheme used by employers to motivate workers to work hard and to reduce worker turnover. Suppose a worker performs a job that is extremely important but that the employer can observe how well the job is being performed only at infrequent intervals—say, serving as a caregiver for the employer's child. Then it often makes sense for the employer to pay more than the worker could earn in an alternative job—that is, more than the equilibrium wage. Why? Because earning a premium makes losing this job and having to take the alternative job quite costly for the worker. So a worker who happens to be observed performing poorly and is therefore fired is now worse off for having to accept a lower-paying job. The threat of losing a job that pays a premium motivates the worker to perform well and avoid being fired. Likewise, paying a premium also reduces worker turnover—the frequency with which an employee leaves a job voluntarily. Despite the fact that it may take no more effort and skill to be a child's caregiver than to be an office worker, efficiency wages show why it often makes economic sense for a parent to pay a caregiver more than the equilibrium wage of an office worker.

The **efficiency-wage model** explains why we may observe wages offered above their equilibrium level. Like the price floors we studied in Chapter 5—and, in particular, much like the minimum wage—this phenomenon leads to a surplus of labor in labor markets that are characterized by the efficiency-wage model. This surplus of labor translates into unemployment—some workers are actively searching for a high-paying efficiency-wage job but are unable to get one, and other more fortunate but no more deserving workers are able to acquire one. As a result, two workers with exactly the same profile—the same skills and same job history—may earn unequal wages: the worker who is lucky enough to get an efficiency-wage job earns more than the worker who gets a standard job (or who remains unemployed while searching for a higher-paying job). Efficiency wages are a response to a type of market failure that arises from the fact that some employees don't always perform as well as they should and are able to hide that fact. As a result, employers use nonequilibrium wages in order to motivate their employees, leading to an inefficient outcome.

Discrimination

It is a real and ugly fact that throughout history there has been discrimination against workers who are considered to be of the wrong race, ethnicity, gender, or other characteristics. How does this fit into our economic models?

The main insight economic analysis offers is that discrimination is *not* a natural consequence of market competition. On the contrary, market forces tend to work against discrimination. To see why, consider the incentives that would exist if social convention dictated that women be paid, say, 30% less than men with equivalent qualifications and experience. A company whose management was itself unbiased would then be able to reduce its costs by hiring women rather than men—and such companies would have an advantage over other companies that hired men despite their higher cost. The result would be to create an excess demand for female workers, which would tend to drive up their wages.

But if market competition works against discrimination, how is it that so much discrimination has taken place? The answer is twofold. First, when labor markets don't work well, employers may have the ability to discriminate without hurting their profits. For example, market interferences (such as unions or minimum-wage laws) or market failures (such as efficiency wages) can lead to wages that are above their equilibrium levels. In these cases, there are more job applicants than there are jobs, leaving employers free to discriminate among applicants. In research published in the *American Economic Review,* two economists, Marianne Bertrand and Sendhil Mullainathan, documented discrimination in hiring by sending ficti- tious résumés to prospective employers on a random basis. Applicants with "White-sounding" names such as Emily Walsh were 50% more likely to be con- tacted than applicants with "African-American-sounding" names such as Lakisha Washington. Also, applicants with White-sounding names and good credentials were much more likely to be contacted than those without such credentials. By contrast, potential employers seemed to ignore the credentials of applicants with African-American-sounding names.

Second, discrimination has sometimes been institutionalized in government poli- cy. This institutionalization of discrimination has made it easier to maintain it against market pressure, and historically it is the form that discrimination has typi- cally taken. For example, at one time in the United States, African-Americans were barred from attending "Whites-only" public schools and universities in many parts of the country and forced to attend inferior schools. Although market competition tends to work against *current* discrimination, it is not a remedy for past discrimina- tion, which typically has had an impact on the education and experience of its vic- tims and thereby reduces their income. The following Economics in Action illustrates the way in which government policy enforced discrimination in the world's most famous racist regime, that of the former government of South Africa.

So Does Marginal Productivity Theory Work?

The main conclusion you should draw from this discussion is that the marginal productivity theory of income distribution is not a perfect description of how fac- tor incomes are determined but that it works pretty well. The deviations are important. But, by and large, in a modern economy with well-functioning labor markets, factors of production are paid the equilibrium value of the marginal product—the value of the marginal product of the last unit employed in the mar- ket as a whole.

It's important to emphasize, once again, that this does not mean that the factor distribution of income is morally justified.

►*ECONOMICS IN ACTION*

The Economics of Apartheid

The Republic of South Africa is the richest nation in Africa, but it also has a harsh political history. Until the peaceful transition to majority rule in 1994, the country was controlled by its White minority, Afrikaners, the descendants of European (mainly Dutch) immigrants. This minority imposed an economic system known as apartheid, which overwhelmingly favored White interests over those of native Africans and other groups considered "non-White," such as Asians.

The origins of apartheid go back to the early years of the twentieth century, when large numbers of White farmers began moving into South Africa's growing cities. There they discovered, to their horror, that they did not automatically earn higher wages than other races. But they had the right to vote—and non-Whites did not. And so the South African government instituted "job-reservation" laws designed to ensure that only Whites got jobs that paid well. The government also set about creating jobs for Whites in government-owned industries. As Allister Sparks notes in *The Mind of South Africa* (1990), in its efforts to provide high-paying jobs for Whites, the country "eventually acquired the largest amount of nationalized industry of any country outside the Communist bloc."

In other words, racial discrimination was possible because it was backed by the power of the government, which prevented markets from following their natural course.

A postscript: in 1994, in one of the political miracles of modern times, the White regime ceded power and South Africa became a full-fledged democracy. Apartheid was abolished. Unfortunately, large racial differences in earnings remain. The main reason is that apartheid created huge disparities in human capital, which will persist for many years to come. ▲

< < < < < < < < < < < <

> **CHECK YOUR UNDERSTANDING** 20-3

1. Assess each of the following statements. Do you think they are true, false, or ambiguous? Explain.
   a. The marginal productivity theory of income distribution is inconsistent with the presence of income disparities associated with gender, race, or ethnicity.
   b. Companies that engage in workplace discrimination but whose competitors do not are likely to have lower profits as a result of their actions.
   c. Workers who are paid less because they have less experience are not the victims of discrimination.

Solutions appear at back of book.

QUICK REVIEW

➤ Existing large disparities in wages both among individuals and across groups lead some to question the marginal productivity theory of income distribution.

➤ **Compensating differentials,** as well as differences in the values of the marginal products of workers that arise from differences in talent, job experience, and human capital, account for some wage disparities.

➤ Market power, in the form of **unions** or collective action by employers, as well as the **efficiency-wage model,** also explain how some wage disparities arise.

➤ Discrimination has historically been a major factor in wage disparities. Market competition tends to work against discrimination.

The Supply of Labor

Up to this point we have focused on the demand for factors, which determines the quantities demanded of labor, capital, or land by producers as a function of their factor prices. What about the supply of factors?

In this section we focus exclusively on the supply of labor. We do this for two reasons. First, in the modern U.S. economy, labor is the most important factor of production, accounting for most of factor income. Second, as we'll see, labor supply is the area in which factor markets look most different from markets for goods and services.

Work versus Leisure

In the labor market, the roles of firms and households are the reverse of what they are in markets for goods and services. A good such as wheat is supplied by firms and demanded by households; labor, though, is demanded by firms and supplied by households. How do people decide how much labor to supply?

As a practical matter, most people have limited control over their work hours: either you take a job that involves working a set number of hours per week, or you don't get the job at all. To understand the logic of labor supply, however, it helps to put realism to one side for a bit and imagine an individual who can choose to work as many or as few hours as he or she likes.

Why wouldn't such an individual work as many hours as possible? Because workers are human beings, too, and have other uses for their time. An hour spent on the job is an hour not spent on other, presumably more pleasant, activities. So the decision about how much labor to supply involves making a decision about **time allocation**—how many hours to spend on different activities.

By working, people earn income that they can use to buy goods. The more hours an individual works, the more goods he or she can afford to buy. But this increased purchasing power comes at the expense of a reduction in **leisure,** the time spent not working. (Leisure doesn't necessarily mean time goofing off. It could mean time spent with one's family, pursuing hobbies, exercising, and so on.) And though purchased goods yield utility, so does leisure. Indeed, we can think of leisure itself as a normal good, which most people would like to consume more of as their incomes increase.

How does a rational individual decide how much leisure to consume? By making a marginal comparison, of course. In analyzing consumer choice, we asked how a utility-maximizing consumer uses a marginal *dollar.* In analyzing labor supply, we ask how an individual uses a marginal *hour.*

Consider Clive, an individual who likes both leisure and the goods money can buy. Suppose that his wage rate is $10 per hour. In deciding how many hours he wants to work, he must compare the marginal utility of an additional hour of leisure with the additional utility he gets from $10 worth of goods. If $10 worth of goods adds more to his total utility than an additional hour of leisure, he can increase his total utility by giving up an hour of leisure in order to work an additional hour. If an extra hour of leisure adds more to his total utility than $10 worth of goods, he can increase his total utility by working one fewer hour in order to gain an hour of leisure.

At Clive's optimal labor supply choice, then, his marginal utility of one hour of leisure is equal to the marginal utility he gets from the goods that his hourly wage can purchase. This is very similar to the *optimal consumption rule* we encountered in Chapter 10, except that it is a rule about time rather than money.

Our next step is to ask how Clive's decision about time allocation is affected when his wage rate changes.

Wages and Labor Supply

Suppose that Clive's wage rate doubles, from $10 to $20 per hour. How will he change his time allocation?

You could argue that Clive will work longer hours, because his incentive to work has increased: by giving up an hour of leisure, he can now gain twice as much money as before. But you could equally well argue that he will work less, because he doesn't need to work as many hours to generate the income to pay for the goods he wants.

As these opposing arguments suggest, the quantity of labor Clive supplies can either rise or fall when his wage rate rises. To understand why, let's recall the distinction between *substitution effects* and *income effects* that we learned in Chapters 10 and 11. We saw there that a price change affects consumer choice in two ways: by changing the opportunity cost of a good in terms of other goods (the substitution effect) and by making the consumer richer or poorer (the income effect).

Now think about how a rise in Clive's wage rate affects his demand for leisure. The opportunity cost of leisure—the amount of money he gives up by taking an hour off instead of working—rises. That substitution effect gives him an incentive, other things equal, to consume less leisure and work longer hours. Conversely, a higher wage rate makes Clive richer—and this income effect leads him, other things equal, to want to consume *more* leisure and supply less labor, because leisure is a normal good.

So in the case of labor supply, the substitution effect and the income effect work in opposite directions. If the substitution effect is so powerful that it dominates the

> Decisions about labor supply result from decisions about **time allocation:** how many hours to spend on different activities.
>
> **Leisure** is time available for purposes other than earning money to buy marketed goods.

income effect, an increase in Clive's wage rate leads him to supply *more* hours of labor. If the income effect is so powerful that it dominates the substitution effect, an increase in the wage rate leads him to supply *fewer* hours of labor.

We see, then, that the **individual labor supply curve**—the relationship between the wage rate and the number of hours of labor supplied by an individual worker—does not necessarily slope upward. If the income effect dominates, a higher wage rate will reduce the quantity of labor supplied.

Figure 20-10 illustrates the two possibilities for labor supply. If the substitution effect dominates the income effect, the individual labor supply curve slopes upward; panel (a) shows an increase in the wage rate from $10 to $20 per hour leading to a *rise* in the number of hours worked from 40 to 50. However, if the income effect dominates, the quantity of labor supplied goes down when the wage rate increases. Panel (b) shows the same rise in the wage rate leading to a *fall* in the number of hours worked from 40 to 30. (Economists refer to an individual labor supply curve that contains both upward-sloping and downward-sloping segments as a "backward-bending labor supply curve"—a concept that we analyze in detail in this chapter's appendix.)

Is a negative response of the quantity of labor supplied to the wage rate a real possibility? Yes: many labor economists believe that income effects on the supply of labor may be somewhat stronger than substitution effects. The most compelling piece of evidence for this belief comes from Americans' increasing consumption of leisure over the past century. At the end of the nineteenth century, wages adjusted for inflation were only about one-eighth what they are today; the typical work week was 70 hours, and very few workers retired at age 65. Today the typical work week is less than 40 hours, and most people retire at age 65 or earlier. So it seems that Americans have chosen to take advantage of higher wages in part by consuming more leisure.

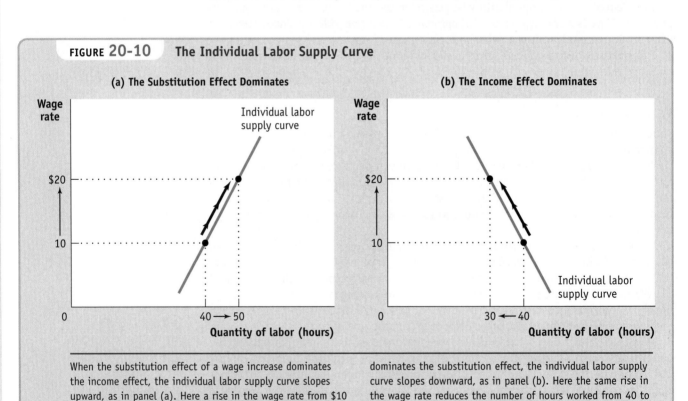

FIGURE 20-10   **The Individual Labor Supply Curve**

When the substitution effect of a wage increase dominates the income effect, the individual labor supply curve slopes upward, as in panel (a). Here a rise in the wage rate from $10 to $20 per hour increases the number of hours worked from 40 to 50. But when the income effect of a wage increase dominates the substitution effect, the individual labor supply curve slopes downward, as in panel (b). Here the same rise in the wage rate reduces the number of hours worked from 40 to 30.

Why You Can't Find a Cab When It's Raining

Everyone says that you can't find a taxi in New York when you really need one—say, when it's raining. That could be because everyone else is trying to get a taxi at the same time. But according to a study published in the *Quarterly Journal of Economics,* it's more than that: cab drivers actually go home early when it's raining.

The reason is that the hourly wage rate of a taxi driver depends on the weather: when it's raining, drivers get more fares

and therefore earn more per hour. And it seems that the income effect of this higher wage rate outweighs the substitution effect.

This behavior leads the authors of the study to question drivers' rationality. They point out that if taxi drivers thought in terms of the long run, they would realize that rainy days and nice days tend to average out and that their high earnings on a rainy day don't really

affect their long-run income very much. Indeed, experienced drivers (who have probably figured this out) are less likely than inexperienced drivers to go home early on a rainy day. But leaving such issues to one side, the study does seem to show clear evidence of a labor supply curve that slopes downward instead of upward, thanks to income effects. (See source note on copyright page.)

Shifts of the Labor Supply Curve

Now that we have examined how income and substitution effects shape the individual labor supply curve, we can turn to the market labor supply curve. In any labor market, the market supply curve is the horizontal sum of the individual labor supply curves of all workers in that market. A change in any factor *other than the wage* that alters workers' willingness to supply labor causes a shift of the labor supply curve. A variety of factors can lead to such shifts, including changes in preferences and social norms, changes in population, changes in opportunities, and changes in wealth.

Changes in Preferences and Social Norms Changes in preferences and social norms can lead workers to increase or decrease their willingness to work at any given wage. A striking example of this phenomenon is the large increase in the number of employed women—particularly married employed women—that has occurred in the United States since the 1960s. Until that time, women who could afford to largely avoided working outside the home. Changes in preferences and norms in post–World War II America (helped along by the invention of labor-saving home appliances such as washing machines, increasing urbanization of the population, and higher female education levels) have induced large numbers of American women to join the workforce—a phenomenon often repeated in other countries that experience similar social and technological forces.

Changes in Population Changes in the population size generally lead to shifts of the labor supply curve. A larger population tends to shift the labor supply curve rightward as more workers are available at any given wage; a smaller population tends to shift the labor supply curve leftward. Currently the size of the U.S. labor force grows by approximately 1% per year, a result of immigration from other countries and, in comparison to other developed countries, a relatively high birth rate. As a result, many labor markets in the United States are experiencing rightward shifts of their labor supply curves.

Changes in Opportunities At one time, teaching was the only occupation considered suitable for well-educated women. However, as opportunities in other professions opened up to women starting in the 1960s, many women left teaching and potential female teachers chose other careers. This generated a leftward shift of the supply curve for teachers, reflecting a fall in the willingness to work at any given wage and forcing school districts to pay more to maintain an adequate teaching staff. These events illustrate a general result: when superior alternatives arise for workers in

THE OVERWORKED AMERICAN?

Americans today may work less than they did 100 years ago, but they still work more than workers in other developed countries. This figure compares average annual hours worked in the United States with average annual hours worked elsewhere. The differences result from a combination of shorter work weeks and longer vacation times. For example, the great majority of full-time American workers work at least 40 hours per week; until recently, however, a government mandate limited most French workers to a 35-hour work week. Americans also take less vacation time than their peers in other countries, and their vacation time is shrinking. About 25% of American workers in the private sector do not get any paid vacation time, and another 33% take only a one-week vacation. A 2006 U.S. survey found that only 40% of respondents planned to take a vacation over the next six months, the lowest percentage recorded in 28 years. In contrast, in many European countries, workers get four to six weeks of annual leave each year. Why do Europeans work less than Americans? Recent economic research suggests that the main reasons for these differences are government regulations that limit the number of hours worked per week as well as a guaranteed minimum amount of vacation time.

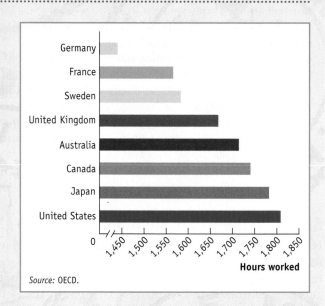

Source: OECD.

another labor market, the supply curve in the original labor market shifts leftward as workers move to the new opportunities. Similarly, when opportunities diminish in one labor market—say, layoffs in the manufacturing industry due to increased foreign competition—the supply in alternative labor markets increases as workers move to these other markets.

Changes in Wealth   A person whose wealth increases will buy more normal goods, including leisure. So when a class of workers experiences a general rise in their wealth levels—say, due to a stock market boom—the income effect from the wealth increase will shift the labor supply curve associated with those workers leftward as workers consume more leisure and work less. Note that *the income effect caused by a change in wealth shifts the labor supply curve,* but *the income effect from a wage rate increase*—as we discussed in the case of the individual labor supply curve—*is a movement along the labor supply curve.* The following Economics in Action illustrates how such a change in the wealth levels of many families during the late 1990s led to a shift of the market labor supply curve associated with their employable children.

►*ECONOMICS IN ACTION*

The Decline of the Summer Job

Come summertime, resort towns along the New Jersey shore find themselves facing a recurring annual problem: a serious shortage of lifeguards. Traditionally, lifeguard positions, together with many other seasonal jobs, have been filled mainly by high school and college students. But in recent years a growing number of young Americans have chosen not to take summer jobs. In 1979, 71% of Americans between the ages of 16 and 19 were in the summer workforce. Twenty years later that number had fallen to 63%; and by 2007, it was 42%. Data show that young men in particular have become much less willing to take summer jobs.

One explanation for the decline in the summer labor supply is that more students feel they should devote their summers to additional study. But an important factor in the decline is increasing household affluence. As a result, many teenagers no longer feel pressured to contribute to household finances by taking a summer job; that is, the income effect leads to a reduced labor supply. Another factor points to the substitution effect: increased competition from immigrants, who are now doing the jobs typically done by teenagers (mowing lawns, delivering pizzas), has led to a decline in wages. So many teenagers forgo summer work and consume leisure instead. ▲

> > > > > > > > > > > >

1. Formerly, Clive was free to work as many or as few hours per week as he wanted. But a new law limits the maximum number of hours he can work per week to 35. Explain under what circumstances, if at all, he is made:
   a. Worse off
   b. Equally as well off
   c. Better off

2. Explain in terms of the income and substitution effects how a fall in Clive's wage rate can induce him to work more hours than before.

Solutions appear at back of book.

[**>> A LOOK** AHEAD •••

The next chapter, the final one in this book, addresses a topic that is everywhere in today's economy: risk. Up until this point, we've limited ourselves to studying an economy in which there are no surprises and the future is perfectly predictable. But in the real world, uncertainty abounds: prices fluctuate, wages change, industries are created and destroyed, and so on. Risk is uncertainty about future outcomes; but more to the point, it is the potential for future economic loss. A substantial and growing part of today's global economy is devoted to managing risk. In this final chapter we'll learn about the markets for managing risk—insurance, including health insurance, as well as the stock market. We'll come to understand why these markets are so important and how the ability of individuals and institutions to trade risk improves society's welfare.]

SUMMARY

1. Just as there are markets for goods and services, there are markets for factors of production, including labor, land, and both **physical capital** and **human capital.** These markets determine the **factor distribution of income.**

2. Profit-maximizing price-taking producers will employ a factor up to the point at which its price is equal to its **value of the marginal product**—the marginal product of the factor multiplied by the price of the output it produces. The **value of the marginal product curve** is therefore the individual price-taking producer's demand curve for a factor.

3. The market demand curve for labor is the horizontal sum of the individual demand curves of producers in that market. It shifts for three main reasons: changes in output price, changes in the supply of other factors, and technological changes.

4. When a competitive labor market is in equilibrium, the market wage is equal to the **equilibrium value of the marginal product** of labor, the additional value produced by the last worker hired in the labor market as a whole. The same principle applies to other factors of production: the **rental rate** of land or capital is equal to the equilibrium value of the marginal products. This insight leads to the **marginal productivity theory of income distribution,** according to which each factor is paid the value of the marginal product of the last unit of that factor employed in the factor market as a whole.

5. Large disparities in wages raise questions about the validity of the marginal productivity theory of income distribution. Many disparities can be explained by **compensating differentials** and by differences in talent, job experience, and human capital across workers. Market interference in the forms of **unions** and collective action by employers also creates wage disparities. The **efficiency-wage model,** which arises from a type of market failure, shows how wage disparities can result from employers' attempts to increase worker performance. Free markets tend to diminish discrimination, but discrimination remains a real source of wage disparity. Discrimination is typically maintained either through problems in labor markets or (historically) through institutionalization in government policies.

6. Labor supply is the result of decisions about **time allocation,** where each worker faces a trade-off between **leisure** and work. An increase in the hourly wage rate tends to increase work hours via the substitution effect but to reduce work hours via the income effect. If the net result is that a worker increases the quantity of labor supplied in response to a higher wage, the **individual labor supply curve** slopes upward. If the net result is that a worker reduces work hours, the individual labor supply curve—unlike supply curves for goods and services—slopes downward.

7. The market labor supply curve is the horizontal sum of the individual labor supply curves of all workers in that market. It shifts for four main reasons: changes in preferences and social norms, changes in population, changes in opportunities, and changes in wealth.

KEY TERMS

Physical capital, p. 510
Human capital, p. 510
Factor distribution of income, p. 511
Value of the marginal product, p. 514
Value of the marginal product curve, p. 515

Equilibrium value of the marginal product, p. 519
Rental rate, p. 520
Marginal productivity theory of income distribution, p. 521
Compensating differentials, p. 524

Unions, p. 525
Efficiency-wage model, p. 526
Time allocation, p. 529
Leisure, p. 529
Individual labor supply curve, p. 530

PROBLEMS

1. In 2007, national income in the United States was $11,186.9 billion. In the same year, 137 million workers were employed, at an average wage of $57,526 per worker per year.

   a. How much compensation of employees was paid in the United States in 2007?

   b. Analyze the factor distribution of income. What percentage of national income was received in the form of compensation to employees in 2007?

   c. Suppose that a huge wave of corporate downsizing leads many terminated employees to open their own businesses. What is the effect on the factor distribution of income?

   d. Suppose the supply of labor rises due to an increase in the retirement age. What happens to the percentage of national income received in the form of compensation of employees?

2. Marty's Frozen Yogurt has the production function per day shown in the accompanying table. The equilibrium wage rate for a worker is $80 per day. Each cup of frozen yogurt sells for $2.

Quantity of labor (workers)	Quantity of frozen yogurt (cups)
0	0
1	110
2	200
3	270
4	300
5	320
6	330

   a. Calculate the marginal product of labor for each worker and the value of the marginal product of labor per worker.

   b. How many workers should Marty employ?

3. Patty's Pizza Parlor has the production function per hour shown in the accompanying table. The hourly wage rate for each worker is $10. Each pizza sells for $2.

Quantity of labor (workers)	Quantity of pizza
0	0
1	9
2	15
3	19
4	22
5	24

   a. Calculate the marginal product of labor for each worker and the value of the marginal product of labor per worker.

   b. Draw the value of the marginal product of labor curve. Use your diagram to determine how many workers Patty should employ.

   c. Now the price of pizza increases to $4. Calculate the value of the marginal product of labor per worker, and draw the new value of the marginal product of labor curve in your diagram. Use your diagram to determine how many workers Patty should employ now.

4. The production function for Patty's Pizza Parlor is given in the table in Problem 3. The price of pizza is $2, but the hourly wage rate rises from $10 to $15. Use a diagram to determine how Patty's demand for workers responds as a result of this wage rate increase.

5. Patty's Pizza Parlor initially had the production function given in the table in Problem 3. A worker's hourly wage rate was $10, and pizza sold for $2. Now Patty buys a new high-tech pizza oven that allows her workers to become twice as productive as before. That is, the first worker now produces 18 pizzas per hour instead of 9, and so on.

   a. Calculate the new marginal product of labor and the new value of the marginal product of labor.

   b. Use a diagram to determine how Patty's hiring decision responds to this increase in the productivity of her workforce.

6. Jameel runs a driver education school. The more driving instructors he hires, the more driving lessons he can sell. But because he owns a limited number of training automobiles, each additional driving instructor adds less to Jameel's output of driving lessons. The accompanying table shows Jameel's production function per day. Each driving lesson can be sold at $35 per hour.

Quantity of labor (driving instructors)	Quantity of driving lessons (hours)
0	0
1	8
2	15
3	21
4	26
5	30
6	33

   Determine Jameel's labor demand schedule (his demand schedule for driving instructors) for each of the following daily wage rates for driving instructors: $160, $180, $200, $220, $240, and $260.

7. Dale and Dana work at a self-service gas station and convenience store. Dale opens up everyday, and Dana arrives later to help stock the store. They are both paid the current market wage of $9.50 per hour. But Dale feels he should be paid much more because the revenue generated from the gas pumps he turns on every morning is much higher than the revenue generated by the items that Dana stocks. Assess this argument.

8. A *New York Times* article published in September 2007 observed that the wage of farmworkers in Mexico is $11 an hour but the wage of immigrant Mexican farmworkers in California is $9 an hour.

   a. Assume that the output sells for the same price in the two countries. Does this imply that the marginal product of labor of farmworkers is higher in Mexico or in California? Explain your answer, and illustrate with a diagram that shows the demand and supply curves for labor in the respective markets. In your diagram, assume that the quantity supplied of labor for any given wage rate is the same for Mexican farmworkers as it is for immigrant Mexican farmworkers in California.

   b. Now suppose that farmwork in Mexico is more arduous and more dangerous than farmwork in California. As a result, the quantity supplied of labor for any given wage rate is not the same for Mexican farmworkers as it is for immigrant Mexican farmworkers in California. How does this change your answer to part a? What concept best accounts for the difference between wage rates between Mexican farmworkers and immigrant Mexican farmworkers in California?

   c. Illustrate your answer to part b with a diagram. In this diagram, assume that the quantity of labor demanded for any given wage rate is the same for Mexican employers as it is for Californian employers.

9. Kendra is the owner of Wholesome Farms, a commercial dairy. Kendra employs labor, land, and capital. In her operations, Kendra can substitute between the amount of labor she employs and the amount of capital she employs. That is, to produce the same quantity of output she can use more labor and less land; similarly, to produce the same quantity of output she can use less labor and more land. However, if she uses more land, she must use more of both labor and capital; if she uses less land, she can use less of both labor and capital. Let w^* represent the annual cost of labor in the market, let r_L^* represent the annual cost of a unit of land in the market, and let r_K^* represent the annual cost of a unit of capital in the market.

   a. Suppose that Kendra can maximize her profits by employing less labor and more capital than she is currently using but the same amount of land. What three conditions must now hold for Kendra's operations (involving her value of the marginal product of labor, land and capital) for this to be true?

   b. Kendra believes that she can increase her profits by renting and using more land. What three conditions must hold (involving her value of the marginal product of labor, land, and capital) for this to be true?

10. For each of the following situations in which similar workers are paid different wages, give the most likely explanation for these wage differences.

    a. Test pilots for new jet aircraft earn higher wages than airline pilots.

    b. College graduates usually have higher earnings in their first year on the job than workers without college degrees have in their first year on the job.

    c. Full professors command higher salaries than assistant professors for teaching the same class.

    d. Unionized workers are generally better paid than non-unionized workers.

11. Research consistently finds that despite nondiscrimination policies, African-American workers on average receive lower wages than White workers do. What are the possible reasons for this? Are these reasons consistent with marginal productivity theory?

12. Greta is an enthusiastic amateur gardener and spends a lot of her free time working in her yard. She also has a demanding and well-paid job as a freelance advertising consultant. Because the advertising business is going through a difficult time, the hourly consulting fee Greta can charge falls. Greta decides to spend more time gardening and less time consulting. Explain her decision in terms of income and substitution effects.

13. Wendy works at a fast-food restaurant. When her wage rate was $5 per hour, she worked 30 hours per week. When her wage rate rose to $6 per hour, she decided to work 40 hours. But when her wage rate rose further to $7, she decided to work only 35 hours.

    a. Draw Wendy's individual labor supply curve.

    b. Is Wendy's behavior irrational, or can you find a rational explanation? Explain your answer.

14. You are the governor's economic policy adviser. The governor wants to put in place policies that encourage employed people to work more hours at their jobs and that encourage unemployed people to find and take jobs. Assess each of the following policies in terms of reaching that goal. Explain your reasoning in terms of income and substitution effects, and indicate when the impact of the policy may be ambiguous.

    a. The state income tax rate is lowered, which has the effect of increasing workers' after-tax wage rate.

    b. The state income tax rate is increased, which has the effect of decreasing workers' after-tax wage rate.

    c. The state property tax rate is increased, which reduces workers' after-tax income.

15. A study by economists at the Federal Reserve Bank of Boston found that between 1965 and 2003 the average American's leisure time increased by between 4 and 8 hours a week. The study claims that this increase is primarily driven by a rise in wage rates.

    a. Use the income and substitution effects to describe the labor supply for the average American. Which effect dominates?

    b. The study also finds an increase in female labor force participation—more women are choosing to hold jobs rather than exclusively perform household tasks. For the average woman who has newly entered the labor force, which effect dominates?

    c. Draw typical individual labor supply curves that illustrate your answers to part a and part b above.

Chapter 20 Appendix: Indifference Curve Analysis of Labor Supply

In the body of this chapter, we explained why the labor supply curve can slope downward instead of upward: the substitution effect of a higher wage rate, which provides an incentive to work longer hours, can be outweighed by the income effect of a higher wage rate, which may lead individuals to consume more leisure. In this appendix we show how this analysis can be carried out using the *indifference curves* introduced in Chapter 11.

> A **time allocation budget line** shows an individual's trade-off between consumption of leisure and the income that allows consumption of marketed goods.

The Time Allocation Budget Line

Let's return to the example of Clive, who likes leisure but also likes having money to spend. We now assume that Clive has a total of 80 hours per week that he could spend either working or enjoying as leisure time. (The remaining hours in his week, we assume, are taken up with necessary activities, mainly sleeping.) Let's also assume, initially, that his hourly wage rate is $10.

His consumption possibilities are defined by the **time allocation budget line** in Figure 20A-1, a budget line that shows Clive's trade-offs between consumption of leisure and income. Hours of leisure per week are measured on the horizontal axis, and the money he earns from working is measured on the vertical axis.

The horizontal intercept, point *X*, is at 80 hours: if Clive didn't work at all, he would have 80 hours of leisure per week but would not earn any money. The vertical intercept, point *Y*, is at $800: if Clive worked all the time, he would earn $800 per week.

Why can we use a budget line to describe Clive's time allocation choice? The budget lines found in Chapters 10 and 11 represented the trade-offs facing consumers deciding how to allocate their income among different goods. Here, instead of asking how

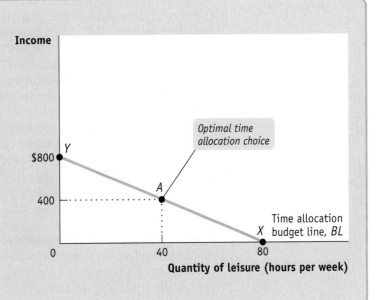

FIGURE 20A-1

The Time Allocation Budget Line

Clive's time allocation budget line shows his trade-off between work, which pays a wage rate of $10 per hour, and leisure. At point *X* he allocates all his time, 80 hours, to leisure but has no income. At point *Y* he allocates all his time to work, earning $800, but consumes no leisure. His hourly wage rate of $10, the opportunity cost of an hour of leisure, is equal to minus the slope of the time allocation budget line. We have assumed that point *A*, at 40 hours of leisure and $400 in income, is Clive's optimal time allocation. It obeys the optimal time allocation rule: the additional utility Clive gets from one more hour of leisure must equal the additional utility he gets from the goods he can purchase with one hour's wages.

The **optimal time allocation rule** says that an individual should allocate time so that the marginal utility gained from the income earned from an additional hour worked is equal to the marginal utility of an additional hour of leisure.

Clive allocates his income, we ask how he allocates his *time*. But the principles underlying the allocation of income and the allocation of time are the same: each involves allocating a fixed amount of a resource (80 hours of time in this case) with a constant trade-off (Clive must forgo $10 for each additional hour of leisure). So using a budget line is just as appropriate for time allocation as it is for income allocation.

As in the case of ordinary budget lines, opportunity cost plays a key role. The opportunity cost of an hour of leisure is what Clive must forgo by working one less hour—$10 in income. This opportunity cost is, of course, Clive's hourly wage rate and is equal to minus the slope of his time allocation budget line. You can verify this by noting that the slope is equal to minus the vertical intercept, point Y, divided by the horizontal intercept, point X—that is, −$800/(80 hours) = −$10 per hour.

To maximize his utility, Clive must choose the optimal point on the time allocation budget line in Figure 20A-1. In Chapter 10 we saw that a consumer who allocates spending to maximize utility finds the point on the budget line that satisfies the *optimal consumption rule:* the marginal utility per dollar spent on two goods must be equal. Although Clive's choice involves allocating time rather than money, the same principles apply.

Since Clive "spends" time rather than money, the counterpart of the optimal consumption rule is the **optimal time allocation rule:** the marginal utility Clive gets from the extra money earned from an additional hour spent working must equal the marginal utility of an additional hour of leisure.

The Effect of a Higher Wage Rate

Depending on his tastes, Clive's utility-maximizing choice of hours of leisure and income could lie anywhere on the time allocation budget line in Figure 20A-1. Let's assume that his optimal choice is point A, at which he consumes 40 hours of leisure and earns $400. Now we are ready to link the analysis of time allocation to labor supply.

When Clive chooses a point like A on his time allocation budget line, he is also choosing the quantity of labor he supplies to the labor market. By choosing to consume 40 of his 80 available hours as leisure, he has also chosen to supply the other 40 hours as labor.

Now suppose that Clive's wage rate doubles, from $10 to $20 per hour. The effect of this increase in his wage rate is shown in Figure 20A-2. His time allocation budget line rotates outward: the vertical intercept, which represents the amount he could earn if he devoted all 80 hours to work, shifts upward from point Y to point Z. As a result of the doubling of his wage, Clive would earn $1,600 instead of $800 if he devoted all 80 hours to working.

But how will Clive's time allocation actually change? As we saw in the chapter, this depends on the *income effect* and *substitution effect* that we learned about in Chapters 10 and 11.

The substitution effect of an increase in the wage rate works as follows. When the wage rate increases, the opportunity cost of an hour of leisure increases; this induces Clive to consume less leisure and work more hours—that is, to substitute hours of work in place of hours of leisure as the wage rate rises. If the substitution effect were the whole story, the individual labor supply curve would look like any ordinary supply curve and would always slope upward—a higher wage rate leads to a greater quantity of labor supplied.

What we learned in our analysis of demand was that for most consumer goods, the income effect isn't very important because most goods account for only a very small share of a consumer's spending. In addition, in the few cases of goods where the income effect is significant—for example, major purchases like housing—it usually reinforces the substitution effect: most goods are normal goods, so when a price increase makes a consumer poorer, he or she buys less of that good.

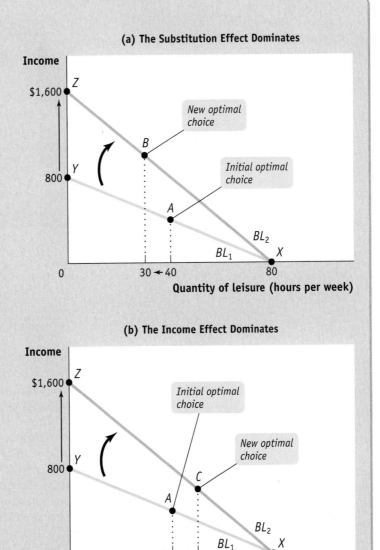

FIGURE 20A-2

An Increase in the Wage Rate

The two panels show Clive's initial optimal choice, point A, on BL_1, the time allocation budget line corresponding to a wage rate of $10. After his wage rate rises to $20, his budget line rotates out to the new budget line, BL_2: if he spends all his time working, the amount of money he earns rises from $800 to $1,600, reflected in the movement from point Y to point Z. This generates two opposing effects: the substitution effect pushes him to consume less leisure and to work more hours; the income effect pushes him to consume more leisure and to work fewer hours. Panel (a) shows the change in time allocation when the substitution effect is stronger: Clive's new optimal choice is point B, representing a decrease in hours of leisure to 30 hours and an increase in hours of labor to 50 hours. In this case the individual labor supply curve slopes upward. Panel (b) shows the change in time allocation when the income effect is stronger: point C is the new optimal choice, representing an increase in hours of leisure to 50 hours and a decrease in hours of labor to 30 hours. Now the individual labor supply curve slopes downward.

In the labor/leisure choice, however, the income effect takes on a new significance, for two reasons. First, most people get the great majority of their income from wages. This means that the income effect of a change in the wage rate is *not* small: an increase in the wage rate will generate a significant increase in income. Second, leisure is a normal good: when income rises, other things equal, people tend to consume more leisure and work fewer hours.

So the income effect of a higher wage rate tends to *reduce* the quantity of labor supplied, working in opposition to the substitution effect, which tends to *increase* the quantity of labor supplied. So the net effect of a higher wage rate on the quantity of labor Clive supplies could go either way—depending on his preferences, he might choose to supply more labor, or he might choose to supply less labor. The two panels of Figure 20A-2 illustrate these two outcomes. In each panel, point A represents Clive's initial consumption choice. Panel (a) shows the case in which Clive works more hours in response to a higher wage rate. An increase in the wage rate induces him to move from point A to point B, where he consumes less leisure than at A and therefore works more hours. Here the substitution effect prevails over the

FIGURE 20A-3

A Backward-Bending Individual Labor Supply Curve

At lower wage rates, the substitution effect dominates the income effect for this individual. This is illustrated by the movement along the individual labor supply curve from point A to point B: a rise in the wage rate from W_1 to W_2 leads the quantity of labor supplied to increase from L_1 to L_2. But at higher wage rates, the income effect dominates the substitution effect, shown by the movement from point B to point C: here, a rise in the wage rate from W_2 to W_3 leads the quantity of labor supplied to decrease from L_2 to L_3.

income effect. Panel (b) shows the case in which Clive works fewer hours in response to a higher wage rate. Here, he moves from point A to point C, where he consumes more leisure and works *fewer* hours than at A. Here the income effect prevails over the substitution effect.

When the income effect of a higher wage rate is stronger than the substitution effect, the individual labor supply curve, which shows how much labor an individual will supply at any given wage rate, slopes the "wrong" way—downward: a higher wage rate leads to a smaller quantity of labor supplied.

Economists believe that the substitution effect usually dominates the income effect in the labor supply decision when an individual's wage rate is low. An individual labor supply curve typically slopes upward for lower wage rates as people work more in response to rising wage rates. But they also believe that many individuals have stronger preferences for leisure and will choose to cut back the number of hours worked as their wage rate continues to rise. For these individuals, the income effect eventually dominates the substitution effect as the wage rate rises, leading their individual labor supply curves to change slope and to "bend backward" at high wage rates. An individual labor supply curve with this feature, called a **backward-bending individual labor supply curve,** is shown in Figure 20A-3. Although an *individual* labor supply curve may bend backward, *market* labor supply curves almost always slope upward over their entire range as higher wage rates draw more new workers into the labor market.

Indifference Curve Analysis

In Chapter 11, we showed that consumer choice can be represented using the concept of *indifference curves,* which provide a "map" of consumer preferences. If you have covered Chapter 11, you may find it interesting to learn that indifference curves are also useful for addressing the issue of labor supply. In fact, this is one place where they are particularly helpful.

Using indifference curves, Figure 20A-4 shows how an increase in the wage rate can lead to a fall in the quantity of labor supplied. Point A is Clive's initial optimal

A **backward-bending individual labor supply curve** is an individual labor supply curve that slopes upward at low to moderate wage rates and slopes downward at higher wage rates.

FIGURE 20A-4

Labor Supply Choice: The Indifference Curve Approach

Point A, on BL_1, is Clive's initial optimal choice. After a wage rate increase his income and utility level increase: his new time allocation budget line is BL_2 and his new optimal choice is point C. This change can be decomposed into the substitution effect—the fall in the hours of leisure from point A to point S, and the income effect—the increase in the number of hours of leisure from point S to point C. As shown here, the income effect dominates the substitution effect: the net result of an increase in the wage rate is an increase in the hours of leisure consumed and a decrease in the hours of labor supplied.

choice, given an hourly wage rate of $10. It is the same as point A in Figure 20A-2; this time, however, we include an indifference curve to show that it is a point at which the budget line is tangent to the highest possible indifference curve.

Now consider the effect of a rise in the wage rate to $20. Imagine, for a moment, that at the same time Clive was offered a higher wage, he was told that he had to start repaying his student loan and that the good-news/bad-news combination left his utility unchanged. Then he would find himself at point S: on the same indifference curve as at A, but tangent to a steeper budget line, the dashed line BL_S in Figure 20A-4, which is parallel to BL_2. The move from point A to point S is the substitution effect of his wage increase: it leads him to consume less leisure and therefore supply more labor.

But now cancel the repayment on the student loan, and Clive is able to move to a higher indifference curve. His new optimum is at point C, which corresponds to C in panel (b) of Figure 20A-2. The move from point S to point C is the income effect of his wage increase. And we see that this income effect can outweigh the substitution effect: at C he consumes more leisure, and therefore supplies less labor, than he did at A.

PROBLEMS

1. Leandro has 16 hours per day that he can allocate to work or leisure. His job pays a wage rate of $20. Leandro decides to consume 8 hours of leisure. His indifference curves have the usual shape: they slope downward, they do not cross, and they have the characteristic convex shape.

   a. Draw Leandro's time allocation budget line for a typical day. Then illustrate the indifference curve at his optimal choice.

   Now Leandro's wage rate falls to $10.

   b. Draw Leandro's new budget line.

   c. Suppose that Leandro now works only 4 hours as a result of his reduced wage rate. Illustrate the indifference curve at his new optimal choice.

   d. Leandro's decision to work less as the wage rate falls is the result of a substitution effect and an income effect. In your diagram, show the income effect and the substitution effect from this reduced wage rate. Which effect is stronger?

2. Florence is a highly paid fashion consultant who earns $100 per hour. She has 16 hours per day that she can allocate to work or leisure, and she decides to work for 12 hours.

   a. Draw Florence's time allocation budget line for a typical day, and illustrate the indifference curve at her optimal choice.

   One of Florence's clients is featured on the front page of *Vague*, an influential fashion magazine. As a result, Florence's consulting fee now rises to $500 per hour. Florence decides to work only 10 hours per day.

b. Draw Florence's new time allocation budget line, and illustrate the indifference curve at her optimal choice.

c. In your diagram, show the income effect and the substitution effect from this increase in the wage rate. Which effect is stronger?

3. Tamara has 80 hours per week that she can allocate to work or leisure. Her job pays a wage rate of $20 per hour, but Tamara is being taxed on her income in the following way. On the first $400 that Tamara makes, she pays no tax. That is, for the first 20 hours she works, her net wage—what she takes home after taxes—is $20 per hour. On all income above $400, Tamara pays a 75% tax. That is, for all hours above the first 20 hours, her net wage rate is only $5 per hour. Tamara decides to work 30 hours. Her indifference curves have the usual shape.

a. Draw Tamara's time allocation budget line for a typical week. Also illustrate the indifference curve at her optimal choice.

The government changes the tax scheme. Now only the first $100 of income is tax-exempt. That is, for the first 5 hours she works, Tamara's net wage rate is $20 per hour. But the government reduces the tax rate on all other income to 50%. That is, for all hours above the first 5 hours, Tamara's net wage rate is now $10. After these changes, Tamara finds herself exactly equally as well off as before. That is, her new optimal choice is on the same indifference curve as her initial optimal choice.

b. Draw Tamara's new time allocation budget line on the same diagram. Also illustrate her optimal choice. Bear in mind that she is equally as well off (on the same indifference curve) as before the tax changes occurred.

c. Will Tamara work more or less than before the changes to the tax scheme? Why?

························○

 www.worthpublishers.com/krugmanwells

Uncertainty, Risk, and Private Information

THE YEAR OF THE HURRICANE

THE NATIONAL WEATHER SERVICE RANKS THE intensity of hurricanes on a scale from 1 to 5, with a category-5 hurricane being the most powerful, producing wind speeds in excess of 155 miles per hour. The destructive capacity of a category-5 hurricane was made clear in August 2005, when Hurricane Katrina slammed into Mississippi and southeastern Louisiana. The widespread devastation was worse than that created by any natural disaster the United States had seen before: over 1,400 dead and entire communities wiped out. The monetary losses were also huge: up to $50 billion in losses to private insurers and $23 billion in losses to the National Flood Insurance Program. And these figures significantly understate the true level of loss because many people were uninsured while others were underinsured, and as a consequence their insurance payments fell far short of their actual losses.

Unbelievably, disaster struck three times that year. One month after Katrina, Hurricane Rita, another category-5 hurricane, blew into Texas and southwestern Louisiana, causing over $11 billion in damage. In October 2005, another category-5 hurricane, Wilma, caused over $29 billion in damage to Florida. (Fortunately, both Rita and Wilma had diminished to category-3 hurricanes by the time of landfall).

Although 2005 was a terribly unlucky year for residents of Louisiana, Mississippi, Florida, and

Texas, and for their insurers, it was consistent with a pattern newly recognized by atmospheric scientists: the incidence of the most destructive hurricanes had doubled over the past 35 years. Not surprisingly, in response to the losses they suffered in 2005 and the potential for future catastrophic losses, in 2006 private insurers began to significantly reduce the number of policies they wrote in coastal areas. For the lucky few homeowners who were able to get insurance, premiums skyrocketed. In Louisiana and Mississippi, the lack of insurance has severely hampered the ability of some communities to rebuild. Mortgage companies typically won't lend money for rebuilding without proof that a homeowner has insurance, and businesses are usually unwilling to invest without insurance for their facilities. To address the pullback of insurers that threatened the state economy, Florida

2005 was a year of catastrophic losses for victims of hurricanes and their insurers.

Ethan Miller/Getty Images

created a state-run insurance program, the Citizens Property Insurance Corporation. In 2008, it had written more than 1.3 million policies.

Anyone who lives in an area threatened by hurricanes or floods knows that uncertainty is an important feature of the real-world. Up to this point, we have largely assumed that people make decisions with knowledge of exactly how the future will unfold. (The exception is health insurance discussed in Chapter 19.) In reality, however, people often make economic decisions—such as whether to build a house in a coastal area—without full knowledge of future events. As the residents of Louisiana, Mississippi, Florida, and Texas know, making decisions when the future is uncertain carries with it the *risk* of loss.

Yet it is often possible for individuals to use markets to reduce the risk they face. For example, hurricane victims who had insurance were able to receive some, if not complete, compensation for their losses. In fact, through insurance and other devices, the modern economy offers many ways for individuals to reduce their exposure to risk.

However, as the retrenchment of the insurers illustrates, a market economy cannot always solve the problems created by uncertainty. Markets for insurance do very well at coping with situations in which two conditions hold: when risk can be reasonably well *diversified* and when the probability of loss is equally well known to everyone. Private insurers cut back their policy-writing in coastal areas due to the failure of the first condition: with deteriorating weather patterns over a huge area of the country, they no longer believed that profits from areas with good weather would be sufficient to offset losses from hurricane-hit areas. (In contrast, state-run insurance programs like the one in Florida can tap tax revenues to cover losses.) But in practice, the second condition is the more limiting one. Markets run into trouble when some people know things that others do not—a situation that involves *private information*. We'll see that private information can cause inefficiency by preventing mutually beneficial transactions.

In this chapter we'll examine the economics of risk and private information. We'll start by looking at why people dislike risk. Then we'll explore how a market economy allows people to reduce risk, at a price. Finally, we'll turn to the special problems created when some people have information that others don't.

The Economics of Risk Aversion

In general, people don't like risk and are willing to pay a price to avoid it. Just ask the U.S. insurance industry, which collects more than $1 trillion in premiums every year. But what exactly is risk? And why don't people like it? To answer these questions, we need to look briefly at the concept of *expected value* and the meaning of uncertainty. Then we can turn to why people dislike *risk*.

Expectations and Uncertainty

The Lee family doesn't know how big its medical bills will be next year. If all goes well, it won't have any medical expenses at all. Let's assume that there's a 50% chance of that happening. But if family members require hospitalization or expensive drugs, they will face medical expenses of $10,000. Let's assume that there's also a 50% chance that these high medical expenses will materialize.

In this example—which is designed to illustrate a point, rather than to be realistic—the Lees' medical expenses for the coming year are a **random variable,** a variable that has an uncertain future value. No one can predict which of its possible values, or outcomes, a random variable will take. But that doesn't mean we can say nothing about the Lees' future medical expenses. On the contrary, an actuary (a person trained in evaluating uncertain future events) could calculate the **expected value** of expenses next year—the weighted average of all possible values, where the weights on each possible value correspond to the probability of that value occurring. In this example, the expected value of the Lees' medical expenses is $(0.5 \times \$0) + (0.5 \times \$10,000) = \$5,000$.

To derive the general formula for the expected value of a random variable, we imagine that there are a number of different **states of the world,** possible future events. Each state is associated with a different realized value—the value that actually occurs—of the random variable. You don't know which state of the world will actually occur, but you can assign probabilities, one for each state of the world. Let's assume that P_1 is the probability of state 1, P_2 the probability of state 2, and so on. And you know the realized value of the random value in each state of the world: S_1 in state 1, S_2 in state 2, and so on. Let's also assume that there are N possible states. Then the expected value of a random variable is:

(21-1) *Expected value of a random variable*
$$EV = (P_1 \times S_1) + (P_2 \times S_2) + \ldots + (P_N \times S_N)$$

In the case of the Lee family, there are only two possible states of the world, each with a probability of 0.5.

Notice, however, that the Lee family doesn't actually expect to pay $5,000 in medical bills next year. That's because in this example there is no state of the world in which the family pays exactly $5,000. Either the family pays nothing, or it pays $10,000. So the Lees face considerable uncertainty about their future medical expenses.

But what if the Lee family can buy health insurance that will cover its medical expenses, whatever they turn out to be? Suppose, in particular, that the family can pay $5,000 up front in return for full coverage of whatever medical expenses actually arise during the coming year. Then the Lees' future medical expenses are no longer uncertain *for them:* in return for $5,000—an amount equal to the expected value of the medical expenses—the insurance company assumes all responsibility for paying those medical expenses. Would this be a good deal from the Lees' point of view?

Yes, it would—or at least most families would think so. Most people prefer, other things equal, to reduce **risk**—uncertainty about future outcomes. (We'll focus here on **financial risk,** in which the uncertainty is about monetary outcomes, as opposed to uncertainty about outcomes that can't be assigned a monetary value.) In fact, most people are willing to pay a substantial price to reduce their risk; that's why we have an insurance industry. But before we study the market for insurance, we need to understand why people feel that risk is a bad thing, an attitude that economists call *risk aversion.* The source of risk aversion lies in a concept we first encountered in our analysis of consumer demand, back in Chapter 10: *diminishing marginal utility.*

The Logic of Risk Aversion

To understand how diminishing marginal utility gives rise to risk aversion, we need to look not only at the Lees' medical costs but also at how those costs affect the income the family has left after medical expenses. Let's assume the family knows that

A **random variable** is a variable with an uncertain future value.

The **expected value** of a random variable is the weighted average of all possible values, where the weights on each possible value correspond to the probability of that value occurring.

A **state of the world** is a possible future event.

Risk is uncertainty about future outcomes. When the uncertainty is about monetary outcomes, it becomes **financial risk.**

Expected utility is the expected value of an individual's total utility given uncertainty about future outcomes.

it will have an income of $30,000 next year. If the family has no medical expenses, it will be left with all of that income. If its medical expenses are $10,000, its income after medical expenses will be only $20,000. Since we have assumed that there is an equal chance of these two outcomes, the expected value of the Lees' income after medical expenses is (0.5 × $30,000) + (0.5 × $20,000) = $25,000. At times we will simply refer to this as expected income.

But as we'll now see, if the family's utility function has the shape typical of most families', its **expected utility**—the expected value of its total utility given uncertainty about future outcomes—is less than it would be if the family didn't face any risk and knew with certainty that its income after medical expenses would be $25,000.

To see why, we need to look at how total utility depends on income. Panel (a) of Figure 21-1 shows a hypothetical utility function for the Lee family, where total utility depends on income—the amount of money the Lees have available for consumption of goods and services (after they have paid any medical bills). The table within the figure shows how the family's total utility varies over the income range of

FIGURE 21-1   **The Utility Function and Marginal Utility Curve of a Risk-Averse Family**

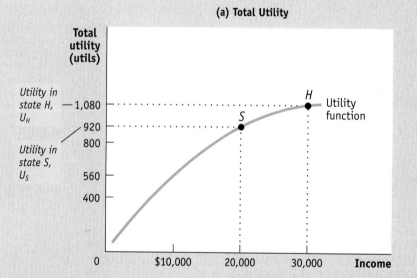

(a) Total Utility

Income	Total utility (utils)
$20,000	920
21,000	945
22,000	968
23,000	989
24,000	1,008
25,000	1,025
26,000	1,040
27,000	1,053
28,000	1,064
29,000	1,073
30,000	1,080

(b) Marginal Utility

Panel (a) shows how the total utility of the Lee family depends on its income available for consumption (that is, its income after medical expenses). The curve slopes upward: more income leads to higher total utility. But it gets flatter as we move up it and to the right, reflecting diminishing marginal utility. Panel (b) reflects the negative relationship between income and marginal utility when there is risk aversion: the marginal utility from each additional $1,000 of income is lower the higher your income. So the marginal utility of income is higher when the family has high medical expenses (point S) than when it has low medical expenses (point H).

$20,000 to $30,000. As usual, the utility function slopes upward, because more income leads to higher total utility. Notice as well that the curve gets flatter as we move up and to the right, which reflects diminishing marginal utility.

In Chapter 10 we applied the principle of diminishing marginal utility to individual goods and services: each successive unit of a good or service that a consumer purchases adds less to his or her total utility. The same principle applies to income used for consumption: each successive dollar of income adds less to total utility than the previous dollar. Panel (b) shows how marginal utility varies with income, confirming that marginal utility of income falls as income rises. As we'll see in a moment, diminishing marginal utility is the key to understanding the desire of individuals to reduce risk.

To analyze how a person's utility is affected by risk, economists start from the assumption that individuals facing uncertainty maximize their *expected* utility. We can use the data in Figure 21-1 to calculate the Lee family's expected utility. We'll first do the calculation assuming that the Lees have no insurance, and then we'll recalculate it assuming that they have purchased insurance.

Without insurance, if the Lees are lucky and don't incur any medical expenses, they will have an income of $30,000, generating total utility of 1,080 utils. But if they have no insurance and are unlucky, incurring $10,000 in medical expenses, they will have just $20,000 of their income to spend on consumption and total utility of only 920 utils. So *without insurance,* the family's expected utility is (0.5 × 1,080) + (0.5 × 920) = 1,000 utils.

Now let's suppose that an insurance company offers to pay whatever medical expenses the family incurs during the next year in return for a **premium**—a payment to the insurance company—of $5,000. Note that the amount of the premium in this case is equal to the expected value of the Lees' medical expenses—the expected value of their future claim against the policy. An insurance policy with this feature, for which the premium is equal to the expected value of the claim, has a special name—a **fair insurance policy.**

If the family purchases this fair insurance policy, the expected value of its income available for consumption is the *same* as it would be without insurance: $25,000—that is, $30,000 minus the $5,000 premium. But the family's risk has been eliminated: the family has an income available for consumption of $25,000 *for sure,* which means that it receives the utility level associated with an income of $25,000. Reading from the table in Figure 21-1, we see that this utility level is 1,025 utils. Or to put it a slightly different way, their expected utility with insurance is 1 × 1,025 = 1,025 utils, because with insurance they will receive a utility of 1,025 utils with a probability of 1. And this is higher than the level of expected utility without insurance—only 1,000 utils. So by eliminating risk through the purchase of a fair insurance policy, the family increases its expected utility even though its expected income hasn't changed.

The calculations for this example are summarized in Table 21-1. This example shows that the Lees, like most people in real life, are **risk-averse:** they will choose to

A **premium** is a payment to an insurance company in return for the insurance company's promise to pay a claim in certain states of the world.

A **fair insurance policy** is an insurance policy for which the premium is equal to the expected value of the claim.

Risk-averse individuals will choose to reduce the risk they face when that reduction leaves the expected value of their income or wealth unchanged.

TABLE 21-1

The Effect of Fair Insurance on the Lee Family's Income Available for Consumption and Expected Utility

	Income in different states of the world		Expected value of income available for consumption	Expected utility
	$0 in medical expenses (0.5 probability)	$10,000 in medical expenses (0.5 probability)		
Without insurance	$30,000	$20,000	(0.5 × $30,000) + (0.5 × $20,000) = $25,000	(0.5 × 1,080 utils) + (0.5 × 920 utils) = 1,000 utils
With fair insurance	$25,000	$25,000	(0.5 × $25,000) + (0.5 × $25,000) = $25,000	(0.5 × 1,025 utils) + (0.5 × 1,025 utils) = 1,025 utils

reduce the risk they face when the cost of that reduction leaves the expected value of their income or wealth unchanged. So the Lees, like most people, will be willing to buy fair insurance.

You might think that this result depends on the specific numbers we have chosen. In fact, however, the proposition that purchase of a fair insurance policy increases expected utility depends on only one assumption: diminishing marginal utility. The reason is that *with diminishing marginal utility, a dollar gained when income is low adds more to utility than a dollar gained when income is high.* That is, having an additional dollar matters more when you are facing hard times than when you are facing good times. And as we will shortly see, a fair insurance policy is desirable because it transfers a dollar from high-income states (where it is valued less) to low-income states (where it is valued more).

But first, let's see how diminishing marginal utility leads to risk aversion by examining expected utility more closely. In the case of the Lee family, there are two states of the world; let's call them H and S, for healthy and sick. In state H the family has no medical expenses; in state S it has $10,000 in medical expenses. Let's use the symbols U_H and U_S to represent the Lee family's total utility in each state. Then the family's expected utility is:

(21-2) Expected utility = (Probability of state H × Total utility in state H) +
                            (Probability of state S × Total utility in state S)
                         = $(0.5 \times U_H) + (0.5 \times U_S)$

The fair insurance policy *reduces* the family's income available for consumption in state H by $5,000, but it *increases* it in state S by the same amount. As we've just seen, we can use the utility function to directly calculate the effects of these changes on expected utility. But as we have also seen in many other contexts, we gain more insight into individual choice by focusing on *marginal* utility.

To use marginal utility to analyze the effects of fair insurance, let's imagine introducing the insurance a bit at a time, say in 5,000 small steps. At each of these steps, we reduce income in state H by $1 and simultaneously increase income in state S by $1. At each of these steps, total utility in state H falls by the marginal utility of income in that state but total utility in state S rises by the marginal utility of income in that state.

Now look again at panel (b) of Figure 21-1, which shows how marginal utility varies with income. Point S shows marginal utility when the Lee family's income is $20,000; point H shows marginal utility when income is $30,000. Clearly, marginal utility is higher when income after medical expenses is low. Because of diminishing marginal utility, an additional dollar of income adds more to total utility when the family has low income (point S) than when it has high income (point H).

This tells us that the gain in expected utility from increasing income in state S is larger than the loss in expected utility from reducing income in state H by the same amount. So at each step of the process of reducing risk, by transferring $1 of income from state H to state S, expected utility increases. This is the same as saying that the family is risk-averse; that is, risk aversion is a result of diminishing marginal utility.

Almost everyone is risk-averse, because almost everyone has diminishing marginal utility. But the degree of risk aversion varies among individuals—some people are more risk-averse than others. To illustrate this point, Figure 21-2 compares two individuals, Danny and Mel. We suppose that each of them earns the same income now but is confronted with the possibility of earning either $1,000 more or $1,000 less. Panel (a) shows how each individual's total utility would be affected by the change in income. Danny would gain very few utils from a rise in income, which moves him from N to H_D, but lose a large number of utils from a fall in income, which moves him from N to L_D. That is, he is highly risk-averse. This is reflected in panel (b) by his steeply declining marginal utility curve. Mel, though, as shown in panel (a), would gain almost as many utils from higher income, which moves him from N to H_M, as he

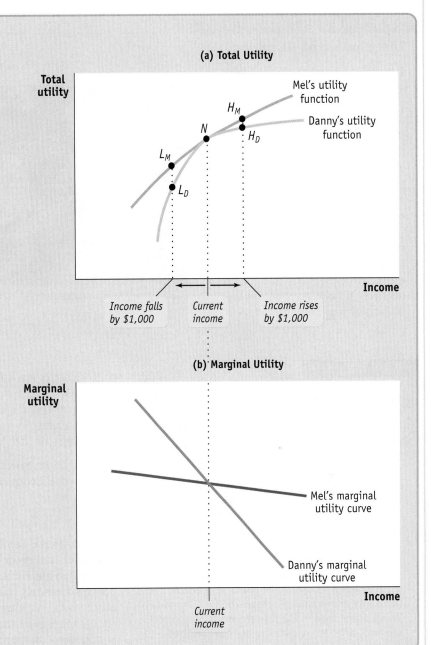

FIGURE 21-2

Differences in Risk Aversion

Danny and Mel have different utility functions. Danny is highly risk-averse: a gain of $1,000 in income, which moves him from *N* to H_D, adds only a few utils to his total utility, but a $1,000 fall in income, which moves him from *N* to L_D, reduces his total utility by a large number of utils. By contrast, Mel gains almost as many utils from a $1,000 rise in income (the movement from *N* to H_M) as he loses from a $1,000 fall in income (the movement from *N* to L_M). This difference—reflected in the differing slopes of the two men's marginal utility curves—means that Danny would be willing to pay much more than Mel for insurance.

(a) Total Utility

(b) Marginal Utility

would lose from lower income, which moves him from *N* to L_M. He is barely risk-averse at all. This is reflected in his marginal utility curve in panel (b), which is almost horizontal. So other things equal, Danny will gain a lot more utility from insurance than Mel will. Someone who is completely insensitive to risk is called **risk-neutral.**

Individuals differ in risk aversion for two main reasons: differences in preferences and differences in initial income or wealth.

- *Differences in preferences.* Other things equal, people simply differ in how much their marginal utility is affected by their level of income. Someone whose marginal utility is relatively unresponsive to changes in income will be much less sensitive to risk. In contrast, someone whose marginal utility depends greatly on changes in income will be much more risk-averse.

A **risk-neutral** person is completely insensitive to risk.

FOR INQUIRING MINDS

The Paradox of Gambling

If most people are risk-averse and risk-averse individuals won't take a fair gamble, how come Las Vegas, Atlantic City, and other places where gambling is legal do so much business?

After all, a casino doesn't even offer gamblers a fair gamble: all the games in any gambling facility are designed so that, on average, the casino makes money. So why would anyone play their games?

You might argue that the gambling industry caters to the minority of people who are actually the opposite of risk-averse: risk-loving. But a glance at the customers of Las Vegas hotels quickly refutes that hypothesis: most of them

Gambling: enjoyment or addiction?

aren't daredevils who also sky-dive and hang-glide. Instead, most of them are ordinary people who have health and life insurance and who wear seat belts. In other words, they are risk-averse like the rest of us.

So why do people gamble? Presumably because they enjoy the experience.

Also, gambling may be one of those areas where the assumption of rational behavior goes awry. Psychologists have concluded that gambling can be addictive in ways that are not that different from the addictive effects of drugs. Taking dangerous drugs is irrational; so is excessive gambling. Alas, both happen all the same.

PITFALLS

BEFORE THE FACT VERSUS AFTER THE FACT

Why is an insurance policy different from a doughnut?

No, it's not a riddle. Although the supply and demand for insurance behave like the supply and demand for any good or service, the payoff is very different. When you buy a doughnut, you know what you're going to get; when you buy insurance, by definition you *don't* know what you're going to get. If you bought car insurance and then didn't have an accident, you got nothing from the policy, except peace of mind, and might wish that you hadn't bothered. But if you did have an accident, you probably would be glad that you bought insurance that covered the cost.

This means we have to be careful in assessing the rationality of insurance purchases (or, for that matter, any decision made in the face of uncertainty). *After the fact*—after the uncertainty has been resolved—such decisions are almost always subject to second-guessing. But that doesn't mean that the decision was wrong *before the fact,* given the information available at the time.

One highly successful Wall Street investor told us that he never looks back—that as long as he believes he made the right decision given what he knew when he made it, he never reproaches himself if things turn out badly. That's the right attitude, and it almost surely contributes to his success.

- *Differences in initial income or wealth.* The possible loss of $1,000 makes a big difference to a family living below the poverty threshold; it makes very little difference to someone who earns $1 million a year. In general, people with high incomes or high wealth will be less risk-averse.

Differences in risk aversion have an important consequence: they affect how much an individual is willing to pay to avoid risk.

Paying to Avoid Risk

The risk-averse Lee family is clearly better off taking out a fair insurance policy—a policy that leaves their expected income unchanged but eliminates their risk. Unfortunately, real insurance policies are rarely fair: because insurance companies have to cover other costs, such as salaries for salespeople and actuaries, they charge more than they expect to pay in claims. Will the Lee family still want to purchase an "unfair" insurance policy—one for which the premium is larger than the expected claim?

It depends on the size of the premium. Look again at Table 21-1. We know that without insurance expected utility is 1,000 utils and that insurance costing $5,000 raises expected utility to 1,025 utils. If the premium were $6,000, the Lees would be left with an income of $24,000, which, as you can see from Figure 21-1, would give them a total utility of 1,008 utils—which is still higher than their expected utility if they had no insurance at all. So the Lees would be willing to buy insurance with a $6,000 premium. But they wouldn't be willing to pay $7,000, which would reduce their income to $23,000 and their total utility to 989 utils.

This example shows that risk-averse individuals are willing to make deals that reduce their expected income but also reduce their risk: they are willing to pay a premium that exceeds their expected claim. The more risk-averse they are, the higher the premium they are willing to pay. That willingness to pay is what makes the insurance industry possible. In contrast, a risk-neutral person is unwilling to pay at all to reduce his or her risk.

➤ECONOMICS IN ACTION

Warranties

Many expensive consumer goods—stereos, major appliances, cars—come with some form of *warranty*. Typically, the manufacturer guarantees to repair or replace the item if something goes wrong with it during some specified period after purchase—usually six months or one year.

Why do manufacturers offer warranties? Part of the answer is that warranties *signal* to consumers that the goods are of high quality (see the discussion of private information later in this chapter). But mainly warranties are a form of consumer insurance. For many people, the cost of repairing or replacing an expensive item like a refrigerator—or, worse yet, a car—would be a serious burden. If they were obliged to come up with the cash, their consumption of other goods would be restricted; as a result, their marginal utility of income would be higher than if they didn't have to pay for repairs.

So a warranty that covers the cost of repair or replacement increases the consumer's expected utility, even if the cost of the warranty is greater than the expected future claim paid by the manufacturer. ▲

> > > > > > > > > > > >

➤ **CHECK YOUR UNDERSTANDING** 21-1

1. Compare two families who own homes near the coast in Florida. Which family is likely to be more risk-averse—(i) a family with income of $2 million per year or (ii) a family with income of $60,000 per year? Would either family be willing to buy an "unfair" insurance policy to cover losses to their Florida home?

2. Karma's income next year is uncertain: there is a 60% probability she will make $22,000 and a 40% probability she will make $35,000. The accompanying table shows some income and utility levels for Karma.

Income	Total utility (utils)
$22,000	850
25,000	1,014
26,000	1,056
35,000	1,260

   a. What is Karma's expected income? Her expected utility?

   b. What certain income level leaves her as well off as her uncertain income? What does this imply about Karma's attitudes toward risk? Explain.

   c. Would Karma be willing to pay some amount of money greater than zero for an insurance policy that guarantees her an income of $26,000? Explain.

   Solutions appear at back of book.

Buying, Selling, and Reducing Risk

Lloyd's of London is the oldest existing commercial insurance company, and it is an institution with an illustrious past. Originally formed in the eighteenth century to help merchants cope with the risks of commerce, it grew in the heyday of the British Empire into a mainstay of imperial trade.

The basic idea of Lloyd's was simple. In the eighteenth century, shipping goods via sailing vessels was risky: the chance that a ship would sink in a storm or be captured by pirates was fairly high. The merchant who owned the ship and its cargo could easily be ruined financially by such an event. Lloyd's matched shipowners seeking insurance with wealthy investors who promised to compensate a merchant if his ship was lost. In return, the merchant paid the investor a fee in advance; if his ship *didn't* sink, the investor still kept the fee. In effect, the merchant paid a price to relieve himself of risk. By matching people who wanted to purchase insurance with people who wanted to provide it, Lloyd's performed the functions of a market. The fact that British merchants could use Lloyd's to reduce their risk made many more people in Britain willing to undertake merchant trade.

The funds that an insurer places at risk when providing insurance is called the insurer's **capital at risk.**

Insurance companies have changed quite a lot from the early days of Lloyd's. They no longer consist of wealthy individuals deciding on insurance deals over port and boiled mutton. But asking why Lloyd's worked to the mutual benefit of merchants and investors is a good way to understand how the market economy as a whole "trades" and thereby transforms risk.

The insurance industry rests on two principles. The first is that trade in risk, like trade in any good or service, can produce mutual gains. In this case, the gains come when people who are less willing to bear risk transfer it to people who are more willing to bear it. The second is that some risk can be made to disappear through *diversification*. Let's consider each principle in turn.

Trading Risk

It may seem a bit strange to talk about "trading" risk. After all, risk is a bad thing—and aren't we supposed to be trading goods and services?

But people often trade away things they don't like to other people who dislike them less. Suppose you have just bought a house for $100,000, the average price for a house in your community. But you have now learned, to your horror, that the building next door is being turned into an all-night disco. You want to sell the house immediately and are willing to accept $95,000 for it. But who will now be willing to buy it? The answer: a person who doesn't really mind late-night noise. Such a person might be willing to pay up to $100,000. So there is an opportunity here for a mutually beneficial deal—you are willing to sell for as little as $95,000, and the other person is willing to pay as much as $100,000, so any price in between will benefit both of you.

The key point is that the two parties have different sensitivities to noise, which enables those who most dislike noise, in effect, to pay other people to make their lives quieter. Trading risk works exactly the same way: people who want to reduce the risk they face can pay other people who are less sensitive to risk to take some of their risk away.

As we saw in the previous section, individual preferences account for some of the variations in people's attitudes toward risk, but differences in income and wealth are probably the principal reason behind different risk sensitivities. Lloyd's made money by matching wealthy investors who were more risk-tolerant with less wealthy and therefore more risk-averse shipowners.

Suppose, staying with our Lloyd's of London story, that a merchant whose ship went down would lose £1,000 and that there was a 10% chance of such a disaster. The expected loss in this case would be $0.10 \times £1,000 = £100$. But the merchant, whose whole livelihood was at stake, might have been willing to pay £150 to be compensated in the amount of £1,000 if the ship sank. Meanwhile, a wealthy investor for whom the loss of £1,000 was no big deal would have been willing to take this risk for a return only slightly better than the expected loss—say, £110. Clearly, there is room for a mutually beneficial deal here: the merchant pays something less than £150 and more than £110—say, £130—in return for compensation if the ship goes down. In effect, he has paid a less risk-averse individual to bear the burden of his risk. Everyone has been made better off by this transaction.

The funds that an insurer places at risk when providing insurance are called the insurer's **capital at risk.** In our example, the wealthy Lloyd's investor places capital of £1,000 at risk in return for a premium of £130. In general, the amount of capital that potential insurers are willing to place at risk depends, other things equal, on the premium offered. If every ship is worth £1,000 and has a 10% chance of going down, nobody would offer insurance for less than a £100 premium, equal to the expected claim. In fact, only an investor who isn't risk-averse at all—that is, who is risk-neutral—would be willing to offer a policy at that price, because accepting a £100 premium would leave the insurer's expected income unchanged while increasing his or her risk. Suppose there is one investor who is risk-neutral; but the next most willing

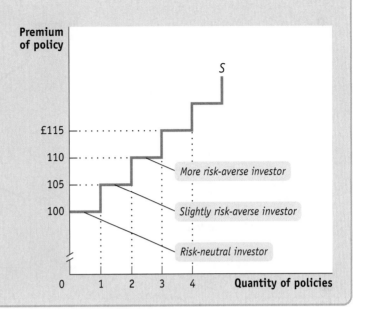

FIGURE 21-3

The Supply of Insurance

This is the supply of insurance policies to provide £1,000 in coverage to a merchant ship that has a 10% chance of being lost. Each investor has £1,000 of capital at risk. The lowest possible premium at which a policy is offered is £100, equal to the expected claim, and only a risk-neutral investor is willing to supply this policy. As the premium increases, investors who are more risk-averse are induced to supply policies to the market, increasing the quantity of policies supplied.

investor is slightly risk-averse and insists on a £105 premium. The next investor, being somewhat more risk-averse, demands a premium of £110, and so on. By varying the premium and asking how many insurers would be willing to provide insurance at that premium, we can trace out a supply curve for insurance, as shown in Figure 21-3. As the premium increases as we move up the supply curve, more risk-averse investors are induced to provide coverage.

Meanwhile, potential buyers will consider their willingness to pay a given premium, defining the demand curve for insurance. In Figure 21-4, the highest premium that any shipowner is willing to pay is £200. Who's willing to pay this? The most risk-averse shipowner, of course. A slightly less risk-averse shipowner might be willing to pay £190, an even slightly less risk-averse shipowner is willing to pay £180, and so on.

FIGURE 21-4

The Demand for Insurance

This is the demand for insurance policies for £1,000 in coverage of a merchant ship that has a 10% chance of being lost. In this example, the highest premium at which anyone demands a policy is £200, which only the most risk-averse shipowner will desire. As the premium falls, shipowners who are less risk-averse are induced to demand policies, increasing the quantity of policies demanded.

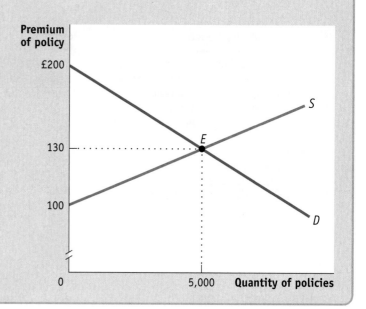

FIGURE 21-5

The Insurance Market

Here we represent the hypothetical market for insuring a merchant ship, where each ship requires £1,000 in coverage. The demand curve is made up of shipowners who wish to buy insurance, and the supply curve is made up of wealthy investors who wish to supply insurance. In this example, at a premium of £200, only the most risk-averse shipowners will purchase insurance; at a premium of £100, only risk-neutral investors are willing to supply insurance. The equilibrium is at a premium of £130 with 5,000 policies bought and sold. In the absence of *private information,* the insurance market leads to an efficient allocation of risk.

Now imagine a market in which there are thousands of shipowners and potential insurers, so that the supply and demand curves for insurance are smooth lines. In this market, as in markets for ordinary goods and services, there will be an equilibrium price and quantity. Figure 21-5 illustrates such a market equilibrium at a premium of £130, with a total quantity of 5,000 policies bought and sold, representing a total capital at risk of £5,000,000.

Notice that in this market risk is transferred from the people who most want to get rid of it (the most risk-averse shipowners) to the people least bothered by risk (the least risk-averse investors). So just as markets for goods and services typically produce an efficient allocation of resources, markets for risk also typically lead to an **efficient allocation of risk**—an allocation of risk in which those who are most willing to bear risk are those who end up bearing it. But as in the case of the markets for goods and services, there is an important qualification to this result: there are well-defined cases in which the market for risk fails to achieve efficiency. These arise from the presence of *private information,* an important topic that we will cover in the next section.

The trading of risk between individuals who differ in their degree of risk aversion plays an extremely important role in the economy, but it is not the only way that markets can help people cope with risk. Under some circumstances, markets can perform a sort of magic trick: they can make some (though rarely all) of the risk that individuals face simply disappear.

Making Risk Disappear: The Power of Diversification

In the early days of Lloyd's, British merchant ships traversed the world, trading spices and silk from Asia, tobacco and rum from the New World, and textiles and wool from Britain, among many other goods. Each of the many routes that British ships took had its own unique risks—pirates in the Caribbean, gales in the North Atlantic, typhoons in the Indian Ocean.

In the face of all these risks, how were merchants able to survive? One important way was by reducing their risks by not putting all their eggs in one basket: by sending different ships to different destinations, they could reduce the probability that all their ships would be lost. A strategy of investing in such a way as to reduce the probability of severe losses is known as *diversification.* As we'll now see, diversification can often make some of the economy's risk disappear.

An **efficient allocation of risk** is an allocation of risk in which those who are most willing to bear risk are those who end up bearing it.

Let's stay with our shipping example. It was all too likely that a pirate might seize a merchant ship in the Caribbean or that a typhoon might sink another ship in the Indian Ocean. But the key point here is that the various threats to shipping didn't have much to do with each other. So it was considerably less likely that a merchant who had one ship in the Caribbean and another ship in the Indian Ocean in a given year would lose them both, one to a pirate and the other to a typhoon. After all, there was no connection: the actions of cutthroats in the Caribbean had no influence on weather in the Indian Ocean, or vice versa.

Statisticians refer to such events—events that have no connection, so that one is no more likely to happen if the other does than if it does not—as **independent events.** Many unpredictable events are independent of each other. If you toss a coin twice, the probability that it will come up heads on the second toss is the same whether it came up heads or tails on the first toss. If your house burns down today, it does not affect the probability that my house will burn down the same day (unless we live next door to each other or employ the services of the same incompetent electrician).

There is a simple rule for calculating the probability that two independent events will both happen: multiply the probability that one event would happen on its own by the probability that the other event would happen on its own. If you toss a coin once, the probability that it will come up heads is 0.5; if you toss the coin twice, the probability that it will come up heads *both* times is 0.5 × 0.5 = 0.25.

But what did it matter to shipowners or Lloyd's investors that ship losses in the Caribbean and ship losses in the Indian Ocean were independent events? The answer is that by spreading their investments across different parts of the world, shipowners or Lloyd's investors could make some of the riskiness of the shipping business simply disappear.

Let's suppose that Joseph Moneypenny, Esq., is wealthy enough to outfit two ships—and let's ignore for a moment the possibility of insuring his ships. Should Mr. Moneypenny equip two ships for the Caribbean trade and send them off together? Or should he send one ship to Barbados and one to Calcutta?

Assume that both voyages will be equally profitable if successful, yielding £1,000 if the voyage is completed. Also assume that there is a 10% chance both that a ship sent to Barbados will run into a pirate and that a ship sent to Calcutta will be sunk by a typhoon. And if two ships travel to the same destination, we will assume that they share the same fate. So if Mr. Moneypenny were to send both his ships to either destination, he would face a probability of 10% of losing all his investment.

But if Mr. Moneypenny were instead to send one ship to Barbados and one to Calcutta, the probability that he would lose both of them would be only 0.1 × 0.1 = 0.01, or just 1%. As we will see shortly, his expected payoff would be the same—but the chance of losing it all would be much less. So by engaging in **diversification**—investing in several different things, where the possible losses are independent events—he could make some of his risk disappear.

Table 21-2 on the next page summarizes Mr. Moneypenny's options and their possible consequences. If he sends both ships to the same destination, he runs a 10% chance of losing them both. If he sends them to different destinations, there are three possible outcomes. Both ships could arrive safely: because there is a 0.9 probability of either one making it, the probability that both will make it is 0.9 × 0.9 = 81%. Both could be lost—but the probability of that happening is only 0.1 × 0.1 = 1%. Finally, there are two ways that only one ship can arrive. The probability that the first ship arrives and the second ship is lost is 0.9 × 0.1 = 9%. The probability that the first ship is lost but the second ship arrives is 0.1 × 0.9 = 9%. So the probability that only one ship makes it is 9% + 9% = 18%.

You might think that diversification is a strategy available only to those with a lot of money to begin with. Can Mr. Moneypenny diversify if he is able to afford only one ship? There are ways for even small investors to diversify. Even if Mr. Moneypenny is only wealthy enough to equip one ship, he can enter a partnership

TABLE **21-2**

How Diversification Reduces Risk

(a) If both ships sent to the same destination

State	Probability	Payoff	Expected payoff
Both ships arrive	0.9 = 90%	£2,000	$(0.9 \times £2,000) + (0.1 \times £0) = £1,800$
Both ships lost	0.1 = 10%	0	

(b) If one ship sent east, one west

State	Probability	Payoff	Expected payoff
Both ships arrive	0.9 × 0.9 = 81%	£2,000	$(0.81 \times £2,000) + (0.01 \times £0) +$
Both ships lost	0.1 × 0.1 = 1%	0	$(0.18 \times £1,000) = £1,800$
One ship arrives	(0.9 × 0.1) + (0.1 × 0.9) = 18%	1,000	

with another merchant. They can jointly outfit two ships, agreeing to share the profits equally, and then send those ships to different destinations. That way each faces less risk than if he equips one ship alone.

In the modern economy, diversification is made much easier for investors by the fact that they can easily buy shares in many companies by using the *stock market*. The owner of a **share** in a company is the owner of part of that company—typically a very small part, one-millionth or less. An individual who put all of his or her wealth in shares of a single company would lose all of that wealth if the company went bankrupt. But most investors hold shares in many companies, which makes the chance of losing all their investment very small.

In fact, Lloyd's of London wasn't just a way to trade risks; it was also a way for investors to diversify. To see how this worked, let's introduce Lady Penelope Smedley-Smythe, a wealthy aristocrat, who decides to increase her income by placing £1,000 of her capital at risk via Lloyd's. She could use that capital to insure just one ship. But more typically she would enter a "syndicate," a group of investors, who would jointly insure a number of ships going to different destinations, agreeing to share the cost if any one of those ships went down. Because it would be much less likely for all the ships insured by the syndicate to sink than for any one of them to go down, Lady Smedley-Smythe would be at much less risk of losing her entire capital.

In some cases, an investor can make risk almost entirely disappear by taking a small share of the risk in many independent events. This strategy is known as **pooling.** Consider the case of a health insurance company, which has millions of policyholders, with thousands of them requiring expensive treatment each year. The insurance company can't know whether any given individual will, say, require a heart bypass operation. But heart problems for two different individuals are pretty much independent events. And when there are many possible independent events, it is possible, using statistical analysis, to predict with great accuracy *how many* events of a given type will happen. For example, if you toss a coin 1,000 times, it will come up heads about 500 times—and it is very unlikely to be more than a percent or two off that figure. So a company offering fire insurance can predict very accurately how many of its clients' homes will burn down in a given year; a company offering health insurance can predict very accurately how many of its clients will need heart surgery in a given year; a life insurance company can predict how many of its clients will . . . Well, you get the idea.

When an insurance company is able to take advantage of the predictability that comes from aggregating a large number of independent events, it is said to engage in *pooling of risks*. And this pooling often means that even though insurance companies protect people from risk, the owners of the insurance companies may not themselves face much risk.

A **share** in a company is a partial ownership of that company.

Pooling is a strong form of diversification in which an investor takes a small share of the risk in many independent events. This produces a payoff with very little total overall risk.

FOR INQUIRING MINDS

Those Pesky Emotions

For a small investor (someone investing less than several hundred thousand dollars), financial economists agree that the best strategy for investing in stocks is to buy an index fund. Why index funds? Because they contain a wide range of stocks that reflect the overall market, they achieve diversification; and they have very low management fees. In addition, financial economists agree that it's a losing strategy to try to "time" the market: to buy when the stock market is low and sell when it's high. Instead, small investors should buy a fixed dollar amount of stocks and other financial assets every year, regardless of the state of the market.

Yet many, if not most, small investors don't follow this advice. Instead, they buy individual stocks or funds that charge high fees. They spend endless hours in Internet chat rooms chasing the latest hot tip or sifting through data trying to discern patterns in stocks' behavior. They try to time

"Your mother called to remind you to diversify."

the market but invariably buy when stocks are high and refuse to sell losers before they lose even more. And they fail to diversify, instead concentrating too much money in a few stocks they think are "winners."

So why are human beings so dense when it comes to investing? According to many experts, the culprit is emotion. In his recent book *Your Money and Your Brain*, Jason Zweig states, "the brain is not an optimal tool for making financial decisions." As he

explains it, the problem is that the human brain evolved to detect and interpret simple patterns. (Is there a lion lurking in that bush?) As a consequence, "when it comes to investing, our incorrigible search for patterns leads us to assume that order exists where it often doesn't." In other words, investors fool themselves into believing that they've discovered a lucrative stock market pattern when, in fact, stock market behavior is largely random. Not surprisingly, how people make financial decisions is a major topic of study in the area of behavioral economics, a new branch of economics that studies why human beings often fail to behave rationally.

So, what's the typical twenty-first-century investor to do? According to Mr. Zweig, there's hope: if you recognize the influence of your emotions, then you can tame them. One test of how well you've evolved from a Cro-Magnon state of mind: are you diversified?

(See source note on copyright page.)

Lloyd's of London wasn't just a way for wealthy individuals to get paid for taking on some of the risks of less wealthy merchants. It was also a vehicle for pooling some of those risks. The effect of that pooling was to shift the supply curve in Figure 21-5 rightward: to make investors willing to accept more risk, at a lower price, than would otherwise have been possible.

The Limits of Diversification

Diversification can reduce risk. In some cases it can eliminate it. But these cases are not typical, because there are important limits to diversification. We can see the most important reason for these limits by returning to Lloyd's one more time.

During the period when Lloyd's was creating its legend, there was one important hazard facing British shipping other than pirates or storms: war. Between 1690 and 1815, Britain fought a series of wars, mainly with France (which, among other things, went to war with Britain in support of the American Revolution). Each time, France would sponsor "privateers"—basically pirates with official backing—to raid British shipping and thus indirectly damage Britain's war effort.

Whenever war broke out between Britain and France, losses of British merchant ships would suddenly increase. Unfortunately, merchants could not protect themselves against this eventuality by sending ships to different ports: the privateers would prey on British ships anywhere in the world. So the loss of a ship to French privateers in the Caribbean and the loss of another ship to French privateers in the Indian Ocean would *not* be independent events. It would be quite likely that they would happen in the same year.

Two events are **positively correlated** if each event is more likely to occur if the other event also occurs.

When an event is more likely to occur if some other event occurs, these two events are said to be **positively correlated.** And like the risk of having a ship seized by French privateers, many financial risks are, alas, positively correlated.

Here are some of the positively correlated financial risks that investors in the modern world face:

- *Severe weather.* Within any given region of the United States, losses due to weather are definitely not independent events. When a hurricane hits Florida, a lot of Florida homes will suffer hurricane damage. To some extent, insurance companies can diversify away this risk by insuring homes in many states. But events like El Niño (a recurrent temperature anomaly in the Pacific Ocean that disrupts weather around the world) can cause simultaneous flooding across the United States. And as we mentioned in our opening story, the positive correlation between the incidence of highly destructive hurricanes in the United States has gone up.

- *Political events.* Modern governments do not, thankfully, license privateers—although submarines served much the same function during World War II. Even today, however, some kinds of political events—say, a war or revolution in a key raw-material-producing area—can damage business around the globe.

- *Business cycles.* The causes of *business cycles,* fluctuations in the output of the economy as a whole, are a subject for macroeconomics. What we can say here is that if one company suffers a decline in business because of a nationwide economic slump, many other companies will also suffer such declines. So these events will be positively correlated.

When events are positively correlated, the risks they pose cannot be diversified away. An investor can protect herself from the risk that any one company will do badly by investing in many companies; she cannot use the same technique to protect against an economic slump in which *all* companies do badly. An insurance company can protect itself against the risk of losses from local flooding by insuring houses in many different places; but a global weather pattern that produces floods in many places will defeat this strategy. Not surprisingly, then, insurers pulled back from writing policies in U.S. coastal areas when it became clear that global weather patterns for hurricanes had become worse. They could no longer be confident that profits from policies written in good weather areas would be sufficient to compensate for losses incurred on policies in hurricane-prone areas.

So institutions like insurance companies and stock markets cannot make risk go away completely. There is always an irreducible core of risk that cannot be diversified. Markets for risk, however, do accomplish two things: First, they enable the economy to eliminate the risk that can be diversified. Second, they allocate the risk that remains to the people most willing to bear it.

►*ECONOMICS IN ACTION*

When Lloyd's Almost Llost It

At the end of the 1980s, the venerable institution of Lloyd's found itself in severe trouble. Investors who had placed their capital at risk, believing that the risks were small and the return on their investments more or less assured, found themselves required to make large payments to satisfy enormous claims. A number of investors, including members of some very old aristocratic families, found themselves pushed into bankruptcy.

What happened? Part of the answer is that ambitious managers at Lloyd's had persuaded investors to take on risks that were much larger than the investors realized. (Or to put it a different way, the premiums the investors accepted were too small for the true level of risk contained in the policies.)

But the biggest single problem was that many of the events against which Lloyd's had become a major insurer were *not* independent. In the 1970s and 1980s, Lloyd's had become a major provider of corporate liability insurance in the United States:

it protected American corporations against the possibility that they might be sued for selling defective or harmful products. Everyone expected such suits to be more or less independent events. Why should one company's legal problems have much to do with another's?

The answer turned out to lie in one word: asbestos. For decades, this fireproofing material had been used in many products, which meant that many companies were responsible for its use. Then it turned out that asbestos can cause severe damage to the lungs, especially in children. The result was a torrent of lawsuits by people who believed they were injured by asbestos and billions of dollars in damage awards—many of them ultimately paid by Lloyd's investors. ▲

> > > > > > > > > > > > >

► CHECK YOUR UNDERSTANDING 21-2

1. Explain how each of the following events would change the equilibrium premium and quantity of insurance in the market, indicating any shifts in the supply and demand curves.
   a. An increase in the number of ships traveling the same trade routes and so facing the same kinds of risks
   b. An increase in the number of trading routes, with the same number of ships traveling a greater variety of routes and so facing different kinds of risk
   c. An increase in the degree of risk aversion among the shipowners in the market
   d. An increase in the degree of risk aversion among the investors in the market
   e. An increase in the risk affecting the economy as a whole
   f. A fall in the wealth levels of investors in the market

Solutions appear at back of book.

Private Information: What You Don't Know Can Hurt You

Markets do very well at dealing with diversifiable risk and with risk due to uncertainty: situations in which nobody knows what is going to happen, whose house will be flooded, or who will get sick. However, markets have much more trouble with situations in which *some people know things that other people don't know*—situations of **private information.** As we will see, private information can distort economic decisions and sometimes prevent mutually beneficial economic transactions from taking place. (Sometimes economists use the term *asymmetric information* rather than *private information,* but they are equivalent.)

Why is some information private? The most important reason is that people generally know more about themselves than other people do. For example, you know whether or not you are a careful driver; but unless you have already been in several accidents, your auto insurance company does not. You are more likely to have a better estimate than your insurance company of whether or not you will need an expensive medical procedure. And if you are selling me your used car, you are more likely to be aware of any problems with it than I am.

But why should such differences in who knows what be a problem? It turns out that there are two distinct sources of trouble: *adverse selection,* which arises from having private information about the way things are, and *moral hazard,* which arises from having private information about what people do.

Adverse Selection: The Economics of Lemons

Suppose that someone offers to sell you an almost brand-new car—purchased just three months ago, with only 2,000 miles on the odometer and no dents or scratches. Will you be willing to pay almost the same for it as for a car direct from the dealer?

Probably not, for one main reason: you cannot help but wonder why this car is being sold. Is it because the owner has discovered that something is wrong with it— that it is a "lemon"? Having driven the car for a while, the owner knows more about it than you do—and people are more likely to sell cars that give them trouble.

Private information is information that some people have that others do not.

Adverse selection occurs when an individual knows more about the way things are than other people do. Private information leads buyers to expect hidden problems in items offered for sale, leading to low prices and the best items being kept off the market.

Adverse selection can be reduced through **screening:** using observable information about people to make inferences about their private information.

You might think that the fact that sellers of used cars know more about them than the buyers do represents an advantage to the sellers. But potential buyers know that potential sellers are likely to offer them lemons—they just don't know exactly which car is a lemon. Because potential buyers of a used car know that potential sellers are more likely to sell lemons than good cars, buyers will offer a lower price than they would if they had a guarantee of the car's quality. Worse yet, this poor opinion of used cars tends to be self-reinforcing, precisely because it depresses the prices that buyers offer. Used cars sell at a discount because buyers expect a disproportionate share of those cars to be lemons. Even a used car that is not a lemon would sell only at a large discount, because buyers don't know whether it's a lemon or not. But potential sellers who have good cars are unwilling to sell them at a deep discount, except under exceptional circumstances. So good used cars are rarely offered for sale, and used cars that are offered for sale have a strong tendency to be lemons. (This is why people who have a compelling reason to sell a car, such as moving overseas, make a point of revealing that information to potential buyers—as if to say "This car is not a lemon!")

The end result, then, is not only that used cars sell for low prices and that there are a large number of used cars with hidden problems. Equally important, many potentially beneficial transactions—sales of good cars by people who would like to get rid of them to people who would like to buy them—end up being frustrated by the inability of potential sellers to convince potential buyers that their cars are actually worth the higher price demanded. So some mutually beneficial trades between those who want to sell used cars and those who want to buy them go unexploited.

Although economists sometimes refer to situations like this as the "lemons problem" (the issue was introduced in a famous 1970 paper by economist and Nobel laureate George Akerlof entitled "The Market for Lemons"), the more formal name of the problem is **adverse selection.** The reason for the name is obvious: because the potential sellers know more about the quality of what they are selling than the potential buyers, they have an incentive to select the worst things to sell.

Adverse selection does not apply only to used cars. It is a problem for many parts of the economy—notably for insurance companies, and most notably for health insurance companies. Suppose that a health insurance company were to offer a standard policy to everyone with the same premium. The premium would reflect the *average* risk of incurring a medical expense. But that would make the policy look very expensive to healthy people, who know that they are less likely than the average person to incur medical expenses. So healthy people would be less likely than less healthy people to buy the policy, leaving the health insurance company with exactly the customers it doesn't want: people with a higher-than-average risk of needing medical care, who would find the premium to be a good deal. In order to cover its expected losses from this sicker customer pool, the health insurance company is compelled to raise premiums, driving away more of the remaining healthier customers, and so on. Because the insurance company can't determine who is healthy and who is not, it must charge everyone the same premium, thereby discouraging healthy people from purchasing policies and encouraging unhealthy people to buy policies.

As we discussed in Chapter 19, adverse selection can lead to a phenomenon called an *adverse selection death spiral* as the market for health insurance collapses: insurance companies refuse to offer policies because there is no premium at which the company can cover its losses. Because of the severe adverse selection problems, governments in many advanced countries assume the role of providing health insurance to their citizens. As we saw in Chapter 19, the U.S. government, through its various health insurance programs like Medicare, Medicaid, and SCHIP, now disburses more than half the total payments for medical care in the United States.

In general, people or firms faced with the problem of adverse selection follow one of several well-established strategies for dealing with it. One strategy is **screening:** using observable information to make inferences about private information. If you apply to purchase health insurance, you'll find that the insurance company will demand documentation of your health status in an attempt to "screen out" sicker applicants—customers they will refuse to insure or will insure only at very high premiums. Auto insurance also provides a very good example. An insurance company may not know whether you are a careful driver, but it has statistical data on the accident rates of people who resemble your profile—and it uses those data in setting premiums. A 19-year-old male who drives a sports car and has already had a fender-bender is likely to pay a very high premium. A 40-year-old female who drives a minivan and has never had an accident is likely to pay much less. In some cases, this may be quite unfair: some adolescent males are very careful drivers, and some mature women drive their minivans as if they were F-16's. But nobody can deny that the insurance companies are right on average.

Another strategy is for people who are good prospects to do something **signaling** their private information—taking some action that wouldn't be worth taking unless they were indeed good prospects. Reputable used-car dealers often offer warranties— promises to repair any problems with the cars they sell that arise within a given amount of time. This isn't just a way of insuring their customers against possible expenses; it's a way of credibly showing that they are not selling lemons. As a result, more sales occur and dealers can command higher prices for their used cars.

Finally, in the face of adverse selection, it can be very valuable to establish a good **reputation:** a used-car dealership will often advertise how long it has been in business to show that it has continued to satisfy its customers. As a result, new customers will be willing to purchase cars and to pay more for that dealer's cars.

Moral Hazard

In the late 1970s, New York and other major cities experienced an epidemic of suspicious fires—fires that appeared to be deliberately set. Some of the fires were probably started by teenagers on a lark, others by gang members struggling over turf. But investigators eventually became aware of patterns in a number of the fires. Particular landlords who owned several buildings seemed to have an unusually large number of their buildings burn down. Although it was difficult to prove, police had few doubts that most of these fire-prone landlords were hiring professional arsonists to torch their own properties.

Why burn your own building? These buildings were typically in declining neighborhoods, where rising crime and middle-class flight had led to a decline in property values. But the insurance policies on the buildings were written to compensate owners based on historical property values, and so would pay the owner of a destroyed building more than the building was worth in the current market. For an unscrupulous landlord who knew the right people, this presented a profitable opportunity.

The arson epidemic became less severe during the 1980s, partly because insurance companies began making it difficult to overinsure properties, and partly because a boom in real estate values made many previously arson-threatened buildings worth more unburned.

The arson episodes make it clear that it is a bad idea for insurance companies to let customers insure buildings for more than their value—it gives the customers some destructive incentives. You might think, however, that the incentive problem would go away as long as the insurance is no more than 100% of the value of what is being insured.

But, unfortunately, anything close to 100% insurance still distorts incentives—it induces policyholders to behave differently than they would in the absence of insurance. The reason is that preventing fires requires effort and cost on the part of a building's owner. Fire alarms and sprinkler systems have to be kept in good repair, fire safety rules have to be strictly enforced, and so on. All of this takes time and money— time and money that the owner may not find worth spending if the insurance policy will provide close to full compensation for any losses.

Adverse selection can be diminished by people **signaling** their private information through actions that credibly reveal what they know.

A long-term **reputation** allows an individual to reassure others that he or she isn't concealing adverse private information.

Moral hazard occurs when an individual knows more about his or her own actions than other people do. This leads to a distortion of incentives to take care or to exert effort when someone else bears the costs of the lack of care or effort.

A **deductible** in an insurance policy is a sum that the insured individual must pay before being compensated for a claim.

Of course, the insurance company could specify in the policy that it won't pay if basic safety precautions have not been taken. But it isn't always easy to tell how careful a building's owner has been—the owner knows, but the insurance company does not.

The point is that the building's owner has private information about his or her own actions, about whether he or she has really taken all appropriate precautions. As a result, the insurance company is likely to face greater claims than if it were able to determine exactly how much effort a building owner exerts to prevent a loss. The problem of distorted incentives arises when an individual has private information about his or her own actions but someone else bears the costs of a lack of care or effort. This is known as **moral hazard.**

To deal with moral hazard, it is necessary to give individuals with private information some personal stake in what happens, a stake that gives them a reason to exert effort even if others cannot verify that they have done so. Moral hazard is the reason salespeople in many stores receive a commission on sales: it's hard for managers to be sure how hard the salespeople are really working, and if they were paid only straight salary, they would not have an incentive to exert effort to make those sales. As described in the following Economics in Action, similar logic explains why many stores and restaurants, even if they are part of national chains, are actually franchises, licensed outlets owned by the people who run them.

Insurance companies deal with moral hazard by requiring a **deductible:** they compensate for losses only above a certain amount, so that coverage is always less than 100%. The insurance on your car, for example, may pay for repairs only after the first $500 in loss. This means that a careless driver who gets into a fender-bender will end up paying $500 for repairs even if he is insured, which provides at least some incentive to be careful and reduces moral hazard.

In addition to reducing moral hazard, deductibles provide a partial solution to the problem of adverse selection. Your insurance premium often drops substantially if you are willing to accept a large deductible. This is an attractive option to people who know they are low-risk customers; it is less attractive to people who know they are high-risk—and so are likely to have an accident and end up paying the deductible. By offering a menu of policies with different premiums and deductibles, insurance companies can screen their customers, inducing them to sort themselves out on the basis of their private information.

As the example of deductibles suggests, moral hazard limits the ability of the economy to allocate risks efficiently. You generally can't get full (100%) insurance on your home or car, even though you would like to buy it, and you bear the risk of large deductibles, even though you would prefer not to. The following Economics in Action illustrates how in some cases moral hazard limits the ability of investors to diversify their investments.

➤ *ECONOMICS IN ACTION*

Franchise Owners Try Harder

When Americans go out for a quick meal, they often end up at one of the fast-food chains—McDonald's, Burger King, and so on. Because these are large corporations, most customers probably imagine that the people who serve them are themselves employees of large corporations. But usually they aren't. Most fast-food restaurants—for example, 85% of McDonald's outlets—are franchises. That is, some individual has paid the parent company for the right to operate a restaurant selling its product; he or she may look like an arm of a giant company but is in fact a small-business owner.

Becoming a franchisee is not a guarantee of success. You must put up a large amount of money, both to buy the license and to set up the restaurant itself (to open a Taco Bell, for example, cost approximately $1.7 million in 2008). And although McDonald's takes care that its franchises are not too close to each other, they often face stiff competition from rival chains and even from a few truly independent restaurants. Becoming a franchise owner, in other words, involves taking on quite a lot of risk.

But why should people be willing to take these risks? Didn't we just learn that it is better to diversify, to spread your wealth among many investments? The logic of diversification would seem to say that it's better for someone with $1.7 million to invest in a wide range of stocks rather than put it all into one Taco Bell. This implies that Taco Bell would find it hard to attract franchisees: nobody would be willing to be a franchisee unless they expected to earn considerably more than they would as a simple hired manager with their wealth invested in a diversified portfolio of stocks. So wouldn't it be more profitable for McDonald's or Taco Bell simply to hire managers to run their restaurants?

It turns out that it isn't, because the success of a restaurant depends a lot on how hard the manager works, on the effort he or she puts into choosing the right employees, on keeping the place clean and attractive to customers, and so on. Could McDonald's get the right level of effort from a salaried manager? Probably not. The problem is moral hazard: the manager knows whether he or she is really putting 100% into the job; but company headquarters, which bears the costs of a poorly run restaurant, does not. So a salaried manager, who gets a salary even without doing everything possible to make the restaurant a success, does not have the incentive to do that extra bit—an incentive the owner does have because he or she has a substantial personal stake in the success of the restaurant.

In other words, there is a moral hazard problem when a salaried manager runs a McDonald's, where the private information is how hard the manager works. Franchising resolves this problem. A franchisee, whose wealth is tied up in the business and who stands to profit personally from its success, has every incentive to work extremely hard.

The result is that fast-food chains rely mainly on franchisees to operate their restaurants, even though the contracts with these owner-managers allow the franchisees on average to make much more than it would have cost the companies to employ store managers. The higher earnings of franchisees compensate them for the risk they accept, and the companies are compensated by higher sales that lead to higher license fees. In addition, franchisees are forbidden by the licensing agreement with the company from reducing their risk by taking actions such as selling shares of the franchise to outside investors and using the proceeds to diversify. It's an illustration of the fact that moral hazard prevents the elimination of risk through diversification. ▲

> > > > > > > > > > > >

> **CHECK YOUR UNDERSTANDING** 21-3

1. Your car insurance premiums are lower if you have had no moving violations for several years. Explain how this feature tends to decrease the potential inefficiency caused by adverse selection.

2. A common feature of home construction contracts is that when it costs more to construct a building than was originally estimated, the contractor must absorb the additional cost. Explain how this feature reduces the problem of moral hazard but also forces the contractor to bear more risk than she would like.

3. True or false? Explain your answer, stating what concept analyzed in this chapter accounts for the feature.
   People with higher deductibles on their auto insurance:
   a. Generally drive more carefully
   b. Pay lower premiums
   c. Generally are wealthier

Solutions appear at back of book.

[>> A LOOK AHEAD•••

With this chapter we've completed our study of microeconomics. We hope that it has illuminated the world around you, helping you to understand the common linkages between events and human behavior. And we hope that it has sparked in you a continuing interest in economics because, in the end, there is always more to learn. Perhaps, soon, you will turn to the study of macroeconomics.]

SUMMARY ∙∙∎

1. The **expected value** of a **random variable** is the weighted average of all possible values, where the weight corresponds to the probability of a given value occurring.

2. **Risk** is uncertainty about future events or **states of the world.** It is **financial risk** when the uncertainty is about monetary outcomes.

3. Under uncertainty, people maximize **expected utility.** A **risk-averse** person will choose to reduce risk when that reduction leaves the expected value of his or her income or wealth unchanged. A **fair insurance policy** has that feature: the **premium** is equal to the expected value of the claim. A **risk-neutral** person is completely insensitive to risk and therefore unwilling to pay any premium to avoid it.

4. Risk aversion arises from diminishing marginal utility: an additional dollar of income generates higher marginal utility in low-income states than in high-income states. A fair insurance policy increases a risk-averse person's utility because it transfers a dollar from a high-income state (a state when no loss occurs) to a low-income state (a state when a loss occurs).

5. Differences in preferences and income or wealth lead to differences in risk aversion. Depending on the size of the premium, a risk-averse person is willing to purchase "unfair" insurance, a policy for which the premium exceeds the expected value of the claim. The greater your risk aversion, the higher the premium you are willing to pay.

6. There are gains from trade in risk, leading to an **efficient allocation of risk:** those who are most willing to bear risk put their **capital at risk** to cover the losses of those least willing to bear risk.

7. Risk can also be reduced through **diversification,** investing in several different things that correspond to **independent events.** The stock market, where **shares** in companies are traded, offers one way to diversify. Insurance companies can engage in **pooling,** insuring many independent events so as to eliminate almost all risk. But when the underlying events are **positively correlated,** all risk cannot be diversified away.

8. **Private information** can cause inefficiency in the allocation of risk. One problem is **adverse selection,** private information about the way things are. It creates the "lemons problem" in used-car markets, where sellers of high-quality cars drop out of the market. Adverse selection can be limited in several ways—through **screening** of individuals, through **signaling** that people use to reveal their private information, and through the building of a **reputation.**

9. A related problem is **moral hazard:** individuals have private information about their actions, which distorts their incentives to exert effort or care when someone else bears the costs of that lack of effort or care. It limits the ability of markets to allocate risk efficiently. Insurance companies try to limit moral hazard by imposing **deductibles,** placing more risk on the insured.

KEY TERMS ∙∙∙∎

Random variable, p. 545
Expected value, p. 545
State of the world, p. 545
Risk, p. 545
Financial risk, p. 545
Expected utility, p. 546
Premium, p. 547
Fair insurance policy, p. 547

Risk-averse, p. 547
Risk-neutral, p. 549
Capital at risk, p. 552
Efficient allocation of risk, p. 554
Independent events, p. 555
Diversification, p. 555
Share, p. 556
Pooling, p. 556

Positively correlated, p. 558
Private information, p. 559
Adverse selection, p. 560
Screening, p. 560
Signaling, p. 561
Reputation, p. 561
Moral hazard, p. 562
Deductible, p. 562

PROBLEMS ∙∙∎

1. For each of the following situations, calculate the expected value.

   a. Tanisha owns one share of IBM stock, which is currently trading at $80. There is a 50% chance that the share price will rise to $100 and a 50% chance that it will fall to $70. What is the expected value of the future share price?

   b. Sharon buys a ticket in a small lottery. There is a probability of 0.7 that she will win nothing, of 0.2 that she will win $10, and of 0.1 that she will win $50. What is the expected value of Sharon's winnings?

   c. Aaron is a farmer whose rice crop depends on the weather. If the weather is favorable, he will make a profit of $100. If the weather is unfavorable, he will make a profit of −$20 (that is, he will lose money). The weather forecast reports that the probability of weather being favorable is 0.9 and the probability of weather being unfavorable is 0.1. What is the expected value of Aaron's profit?

2. Vicky N. Vestor is considering investing some of her money in a startup company. She currently has income of $4,000, and she is considering investing $2,000 of that in the company. There is a 0.5 probability that the company will succeed and will pay out $8,000 to Vicky (her original investment of $2,000 plus $6,000 of the company's profits). And there is a 0.5 probability that the company will fail and Vicky will get nothing (and lose her investment). The accompanying table illustrates Vicky's utility function.

Income	Total utility (utils)
$0	0
1,000	50
2,000	85
3,000	115
4,000	140
5,000	163
6,000	183
7,000	200
8,000	215
9,000	229
10,000	241

a. Calculate Vicky's marginal utility of income for each income level. Is Vicky risk-averse?

b. Calculate the expected value of Vicky's income if she makes this investment.

c. Calculate Vicky's expected utility from making the investment.

d. What is Vicky's utility from not making the investment? Will Vicky therefore invest in the company?

3. Vicky N. Vestor's utility function was given in Problem 2. As in Problem 2, Vicky currently has income of $4,000. She is considering investing in a startup company, but the investment now costs $4,000 to make. If the company fails, Vicky will get nothing from the company. But if the company succeeds, she will get $10,000 from the company (her original investment of $4,000 plus $6,000 of the company's profits). Each event has a 0.5 probability of occurring. Will Vicky invest in the company?

4. You have $1,000 that you can invest. If you buy Ford stock, you face the following returns and probabilities from holding the stock for one year: with a probability of 0.2 you will get $1,500; with a probability of 0.4 you will get $1,100; and with a probability of 0.4 you will get $900. If you put the money into the bank, in one year's time you will get $1,100 for certain.

a. What is the expected value of your earnings from investing in Ford stock?

b. Suppose you are risk-averse. Can we say for sure whether you will invest in Ford stock or put your money into the bank?

5. You have $1,000 that you can invest. If you buy General Motors stock, then, in one year's time: with a probability of 0.4 you will get $1,600; with a probability of 0.4 you will get $1,100; and with a probability of 0.2 you will get $800. If you put the money into the bank, in one year's time you will get $1,100 for certain.

a. What is the expected value of your earnings from investing in General Motors stock?

b. Suppose you prefer putting your money into the bank to investing it in General Motors stock. What does that tell us about your attitude to risk?

6. Wilbur is an airline pilot who currently has income of $60,000. If he gets sick and loses his flight medical certificate, he loses his job and has only $10,000 income. His probability of staying healthy is 0.6, and his probability of getting sick is 0.4. Wilbur's utility function is given in the accompanying table.

Income	Total utility (utils)
$0	0
10,000	60
20,000	110
30,000	150
40,000	180
50,000	200
60,000	210

a. What is the expected value of Wilbur's income?

b. What is Wilbur's expected utility?

Wilbur thinks about buying "loss-of-license" insurance that will compensate him if he loses his flight medical certificate.

c. One insurance company offers Wilbur full compensation for his income loss (that is, the insurance company pays Wilbur $50,000 if he loses his flight medical certificate), and it charges a premium of $40,000. That is, regardless of whether he loses his flight medical certificate, Wilbur's income after insurance will be $20,000. What is Wilbur's utility? Will he buy the insurance?

d. What is the highest premium Wilbur would just be willing to pay for full insurance (insurance that completely compensates him for the income loss)?

7. In 2003, 1 in approximately every 200 cars in the United States was stolen. Beth owns a car worth $20,000 and is considering purchasing an insurance policy to protect herself from car theft. For the following questions, assume that the chance of car theft is the same in all regions and across all car models.

a. What should the premium for a fair insurance policy have been in 2003 for a policy that replaces Beth's car if it is stolen?

b. Suppose an insurance company charges 0.6% of the car's value for a policy that pays for replacing a stolen car. How much will the policy cost Beth?

c. Will Beth purchase the insurance in part b if she is risk-neutral?

d. Discuss a possible moral hazard problem facing Beth's insurance company if she purchases the insurance.

8. Hugh's income is currently $5,000. His utility function is shown in the accompanying table.

Income	Total utility (utils)
$0	0
1,000	100
2,000	140
3,000	166
4,000	185
5,000	200
6,000	212
7,000	222
8,000	230
9,000	236
10,000	240

a. Calculate Hugh's marginal utility of income. What is his attitude toward risk?

b. Hugh is thinking about gambling in a casino. With a probability of 0.5 he will lose $3,000, and with a probability of 0.5 he will win $5,000. What is the expected value of Hugh's income? What is Hugh's expected utility? Will he decide to gamble? (Suppose that he gets no extra utility from going to the casino.)

c. Suppose that the "spread" (how much he can win versus how much he can lose) of the gamble narrows, so that with a probability of 0.5 Hugh will lose $1,000, and with a probability of 0.5 he will win $3,000. What is the expected value of Hugh's income? What is his expected utility? Is this gamble better for him than the gamble in part b? Will he decide to gamble?

9. Eva is risk-averse. Currently she has $50,000 to invest. She faces the following choice: she can invest in the stock of a dot-com company, or she can invest in IBM stock. If she invests in the dot-com company, then with probability 0.5 she will lose $30,000, but with probability 0.5 she will gain $50,000. If she invests in IBM stock, then with probability 0.5 she will lose only $10,000, but with probability 0.5 she will gain only $30,000. Can you tell which investment she will prefer to make?

10. Suppose you have $1,000 that you can invest in Ted and Larry's Ice Cream Parlor and/or Ethel's House of Cocoa. The price of a share of stock in either company is $100. The fortunes of each company are closely linked to the weather. When it is warm, the value of Ted and Larry's stock rises to $150 but the value of Ethel's stock falls to $60. When it is cold, the value of Ethel's stock rises to $150 but the value of Ted and Larry's stock falls to $60. There is an equal chance of the weather being warm or cold.

a. If you invest all your money in Ted and Larry's, what is your expected stock value? What if you invest all your money in Ethel's?

b. Suppose you diversify and invest half of your $1,000 in each company. How much will your total stock be worth if the weather is warm? What if it is cold?

c. Suppose you are risk-averse. Would you prefer to put all your money in Ted and Larry's, as in part a? Or would you prefer to diversify, as in part b? Explain your reasoning.

11. *U.S. Mid Cap Companies* and *International Aggregate* are two portfolios constructed from U.S. and international stocks, respectively. The accompanying table shows historical data from the period 1975–2006, which suggest the expected value of the annual percentage returns associated with these portfolios.

Portfolio	Expected value of return (percent)
U.S. Mid Cap Companies	17.0%
International Aggregate	14.5

a. Which portfolio would a risk-neutral investor prefer?

b. Juan, a risk-averse investor, chooses to invest in the International Aggregate portfolio. What can be inferred about the risk of the two portfolios from Juan's choice of investment? Based on historical performance, would a risk-neutral investor ever choose International Aggregate?

c. Juan is aware that diversification can reduce risk. He considers a portfolio in which half his investment is in U.S. companies and the other half in international companies. What is the expected value of the return for this combined portfolio? Would you expect this combined portfolio to be more risky or less risky than the International Aggregate portfolio? Why or why not?

12. You are considering buying a second-hand Volkswagen. From reading car magazines, you know that half of all Volkswagens have problems of some kind (they are "lemons") and the other half run just fine (they are "plums"). If you knew that you were getting a plum, you would be willing to pay $10,000 for it: this is how much a plum is worth to you. You would also be willing to buy a lemon, but only if its price was no more than $4,000: this is how much a lemon is worth to you. And someone who owns a plum would be willing to sell it at any price above $8,000. Someone who owns a lemon would be willing to sell it for any price above $2,000.

a. For now, suppose that you can immediately tell whether the car that you are being offered is a lemon or a plum. Suppose someone offers you a plum. Will there be trade?

Now suppose that the seller has private information about the car she is selling: the seller knows whether she has a lemon or a plum. But when the seller offers you a Volkswagen, you do not know whether it is a lemon or a plum. So this is a situation of adverse selection.

b. Since you do not know whether you are being offered a plum or a lemon, you base your decision on the expected value to you of a Volkswagen, assuming you are just as likely to buy a lemon as a plum. Calculate this expected value.

c. Suppose, from driving the car, the seller knows she has a plum. However, you don't know whether this particular car is a lemon or a plum, so the most you are willing to pay is your expected value. Will there be trade?

13. You own a company that produces chairs, and you are thinking about hiring one more employee. Each chair produced gives you revenue of $10. There are two potential employees, Fred Ast and Sylvia Low. Fred is a fast worker who produces ten chairs per day, creating revenue for you of $100. Fred knows that he is fast and so will work for you only if you pay him more than $80 per day. Sylvia is a slow worker who produces only five chairs per day, creating revenue for you of $50. Sylvia knows that she is slow and so will work for you if you pay her more than $40 per day. Although Sylvia knows she is slow and Fred knows he is fast, you do not know who is fast and who is slow. So this is a situation of adverse selection.

a. Since you do not know which type of worker you will get, you think about what the expected value of your revenue will be if you hire one of the two. What is that expected value?

b. Suppose you offered to pay a daily wage equal to the expected revenue you calculated in part a. Whom would you be able to hire: Fred, or Sylvia, or both, or neither?

c. If you knew whether a worker is fast or slow, which one would you prefer to hire and why? Can you devise a compensation scheme to guarantee that you employ only the type of worker you prefer?

14. For each of the following situations, do the following: first describe whether it is a situation of moral hazard or of adverse selection. Then explain what inefficiency can arise from this situation and explain how the proposed solution reduces the inefficiency.

a. When you buy a second-hand car, you do not know whether it is a lemon (low quality) or a plum (high quality), but the seller knows. A solution is for sellers to offer a warranty with the car that pays for repair costs.

b. Some people are prone to see doctors unnecessarily for minor complaints like headaches, and health maintenance organizations do not know how urgently you need a doctor. A solution is for insurees to have to make a co-payment of a certain dollar amount (for example, $10) each time they visit a health care provider. All insurees are risk-averse.

c. When airlines sell tickets, they do not know whether a buyer is a business traveler (who is willing to pay a lot for a seat) or a leisure traveler (who has a low willingness to pay). A solution for a profit-maximizing airline is to offer an expensive ticket that is very flexible (it allows date and route changes) and a cheap ticket that is very inflexible (it has to be booked in advance and cannot be changed).

d. A company does not know whether workers on an assembly line work hard or whether they slack off. A solution is to pay the workers "piece rates," that is, pay them according to how much they have produced each day. All workers are risk-averse, but the company is not risk-neutral.

e. When making a decision about hiring you, prospective employers do not know whether you are a productive or unproductive worker. A solution is for productive workers to provide potential employers with references from previous employers.

15. Kory owns a house that is worth $300,000. If the house burns down, she loses all $300,000. If the house does not burn down, she loses nothing. Her house burns down with a probability of 0.02. Kory is risk-averse.

a. What would a fair insurance policy cost?

b. Suppose an insurance company offers to insure her fully against the loss from the house burning down, at a premium of $1,500. Can you say for sure whether Kory will or will not take the insurance?

c. Suppose an insurance company offers to insure her fully against the loss from the house burning down, at a premium of $6,000. Can you say for sure whether Kory will or will not take the insurance?

d. Suppose that an insurance company offers to insure her fully against the loss from the house burning down, at a premium of $9,000. Can you say for sure whether Kory will or will not take the insurance?

 www.worthpublishers.com/krugmanwells

> Macroeconomics: The Big Picture

HOOVERVILLES

TODAY MANY PEOPLE ENJOY WALKING, BIKING, and horseback riding in New York's Central Park. But in 1932 there were also many people living there: Central Park contained one of the "Hoovervilles"—shantytowns—that had sprung up all across America as a result of a catastrophic economic slump that started in 1929, leaving millions of workers out of work, reduced to standing on breadlines or selling apples on street corners. The U.S. economy would stage a partial recovery beginning in 1933, but joblessness stayed high throughout the 1930s. The whole period would come to be known as the Great Depression.

Why Hoovervilles? The shantytowns got their derisive name from Herbert Hoover, who had been elected president in 1928—and who lost his bid for reelection because many Americans blamed him for the Depression. Hoover began his career as an engineer, and until he became president he had a reputation as a can-do, highly competent

manager. But when the Depression struck, neither he nor his economic advisers had any idea what to do.

Hoover's cluelessness was no accident. At the time of the Great Depression, *microeconomics*, which is concerned with the production and consumption decisions of individual consumers and producers and with the allocation of scarce resources among industries, was already a well-developed branch of economics. But *macroeconomics*, which focuses on the behavior of the economy as a whole, was still in its infancy.

What happened between 1929 and 1933, and on a smaller scale on many other occasions (most recently in 2008), was a blow to the economy as a whole. At any given moment there are always some industries laying off workers. For example, the number of independent record stores in America fell almost 30% between 2003 and 2007, as consumers turned to online purchases. But workers who lost their jobs at record stores had a good

During the Great Depression, Hoovervilles sprang up across America, named after the economically clueless President Herbert Hoover.

chance of finding new jobs elsewhere, because other industries were expanding even as record stores shut their doors. In the early 1930s, however, there were no expanding industries: everything was headed downward.

Macroeconomics came into its own as a branch of economics during the Great Depression. Economists realized that they needed to understand the nature of the catastrophe that had overtaken the United States and much of the rest of the world, in order to extricate themselves, as well as to learn how to avoid such catastrophes in the future. To this day, the effort to understand economic slumps and find ways to prevent them is at the core of macroeconomics. Over time, however, macroeconomics has broadened its reach to encompass a number of other subjects, such as *long-run economic growth, inflation,* and *open-economy macroeconomics.*

This chapter offers an overview of macroeconomics. We start with a general description of the difference between macroeconomics and microeconomics, then briefly describe some of the field's major concerns.

WHAT YOU WILL LEARN IN THIS CHAPTER:

➤ What makes macroeconomics different from microeconomics

➤ What a **business cycle** is and why policy makers seek to diminish the severity of business cycles

➤ How **long-run economic growth** determines a country's standard of living

➤ The meaning of **inflation** and **deflation** and why **price stability** is preferred

➤ The importance of **open economy macroeconomics** and how economies interact through **trade deficits** and **trade surpluses**

The Nature of Macroeconomics

What makes macroeconomics different from microeconomics? As we stated earlier, the distinguishing feature of macroeconomics is that it focuses on the behavior of the economy as a whole.

Macroeconomic Questions

Table 22-1 lists some typical questions that involve economics. A microeconomic version of the question appears on the left paired with a similar macroeconomic question on the right. By comparing the questions, you can begin to get a sense of the difference between microeconomics and macroeconomics.

TABLE 22-1

Microeconomic versus Macroeconomic Questions

Microeconomic Questions	Macroeconomic Questions
Should I go to business school or take a job right now?	How many people are employed in the economy as a whole this year?
What determines the salary offered by Citibank to Cherie Camajo, a new MBA?	What determines the overall salary levels paid to workers in a given year?
What determines the cost to a university or college of offering a new course?	What determines the overall level of prices in the economy as a whole?
What government policies should be adopted to make it easier for low-income students to attend college?	What government policies should be adopted to promote employment and growth in the economy as a whole?
What determines whether Citibank opens a new office in Shanghai?	What determines the overall trade in goods, services, and financial assets between the United States and the rest of the world?

As these questions illustrate, microeconomics focuses on how decisions are made by individuals and firms and the consequences of those decisions. For example, we use microeconomics to determine how much it would cost a university or college to offer a new course, which includes the instructor's salary, the cost of class materials, and so on. The school can then decide whether or not to offer the course by weighing the costs and benefits. Macroeconomics, in contrast, examines the *overall* behavior of the economy—how the actions of all the individuals and firms in the economy interact to produce a particular economy-wide level of economic performance. For example, macroeconomics is concerned with the general level of prices in the economy and how high or how low they are relative to prices last year, rather than with the price of one particular good or service.

You might imagine that macroeconomic questions can be answered simply by adding up microeconomic answers. For example, the model of supply and demand we introduced in Chapter 3 tells us how the equilibrium price of an individual good or service is determined in a competitive market. So you might think that applying supply-and-demand analysis to every good and service in the economy, then summing the results, is the way to understand the overall level of prices in the economy as a whole.

But that turns out not to be right: although basic concepts such as supply and demand are as essential to macroeconomics as they are to microeconomics, answering macroeconomic questions requires an additional set of tools and an expanded frame of reference.

Macroeconomics: The Whole Is Greater Than the Sum of Its Parts

If you occasionally drive on a highway, you probably know what a rubber-necking traffic jam is and why it is so annoying. Someone pulls over to the side of the road for something minor, such as changing a flat tire, and, pretty soon, a long traffic jam occurs as drivers slow down to take a look. What makes it so annoying is that the length of the traffic jam is greatly out of proportion to the minor event that precipitated it. Because some drivers hit their brakes in order to rubber-neck, the drivers behind them must also hit their brakes, those behind them must do the same, and so on. The accumulation of all the individual hitting of brakes eventually leads to a long, wasteful traffic jam as each driver slows down a little bit more than the driver in front of him or her. In other words, each person's response leads to an exaggerated response by the next person.

Understanding a rubber-necking traffic jam gives us some insight into one very important way in which macroeconomics is different from microeconomics: many thousands or millions of individual actions compound upon one another to produce an outcome that isn't simply the sum of those individual actions. Consider, for example, what macroeconomists call the *paradox of thrift:* when families and businesses are worried about the possibility of economic hard times, they prepare by cutting their spending. This reduction in spending depresses the economy as consumers spend less and businesses react by laying off workers. As a result, families and businesses may end up worse off than if they hadn't tried to act responsibly by cutting their spending. This is a paradox because seemingly virtuous behavior—preparing for hard times by saving more—ends up harming everyone. And there is a flip-side to this story: when families and businesses are feeling optimistic about the future, they spend more today. This stimulates the economy, leading businesses to hire more workers, which further expands the economy. Seemingly profligate behavior leads to good times for all.

Or consider what happens when something causes the quantity of cash circulating through the economy to rise. An individual with more cash on hand is richer. But if everyone has more cash, the long-run effect is simply to push the overall level of prices higher, taking the purchasing power of the total amount of cash in circulation right back to where it was before.

In a **self-regulating economy**, problems such as unemployment are resolved without government intervention, through the working of the invisible hand.

According to **Keynesian economics**, economic slumps are caused by inadequate spending and they can be mitigated by government intervention.

Monetary policy uses changes in the quantity of money to alter interest rates and affect overall spending.

Fiscal policy uses changes in government spending and taxes to affect overall spending.

A key insight of macroeconomics, then, is that the combined effect of individual decisions can have results that are very different from what any one individual intended, results that are sometimes perverse. The behavior of the macroeconomy is, indeed, greater than the sum of individual actions and market outcomes.

Macroeconomics: Theory and Policy

To a much greater extent than microeconomists, macroeconomists are concerned with questions about *policy,* about what the government can do to make macroeconomic performance better. This policy focus was strongly shaped by history, in particular by the Great Depression of the 1930s.

Before the 1930s, economists tended to regard the economy as **self-regulating:** they believed that problems such as unemployment would be corrected through the working of the invisible hand and that government attempts to improve the economy's performance would be ineffective at best—and would probably make things worse.

The Great Depression changed all that. The sheer scale of the catastrophe, which left a quarter of the U.S. workforce without jobs and threatened the political stability of many countries—the Depression is widely believed to have been a major factor in the Nazi takeover of Germany—created a demand for action. It also led to a major effort on the part of economists to understand economic slumps and find ways to prevent them.

In 1936 the British economist John Maynard Keynes (pronounced "canes") published *The General Theory of Employment, Interest, and Money,* a book that transformed macroeconomics. According to **Keynesian economics,** a depressed economy is the result of inadequate spending. In addition, Keynes argued that government intervention can help a depressed economy through *monetary policy* and *fiscal policy.* **Monetary policy** uses changes in the quantity of money to alter interest rates, which in turn affect the level of overall spending. **Fiscal policy** uses changes in taxes and government spending to affect overall spending. In general, Keynes established the idea that managing the economy is a government responsibility. Keynesian ideas continue to have a strong influence on both economic theory and public policy: in 2007 and 2008, Congress, the White House, and the Federal Reserve (a quasi-governmental agency that manages the U. S. money supply) took steps to fend off an economic slump that were clearly Keynesian in spirit as described in the following Economics in Action.

►*ECONOMICS IN ACTION*

Why George W. Bush Wasn't Herbert Hoover

Herbert Hoover didn't do much to fight the Great Depression—but not because he lacked initiative. At the time, conventional wisdom dictated that the government take a hands-off approach to the economy, even in the face of severe economic distress. Hoover later described the advice he received from Andrew Mellon, Secretary of the U. S. Treasury, who advised him to let the slump run its course: "Liquidate labor, liquidate stocks, liquidate the farmers, liquidate real estate." Mellon even argued that the slump was a good thing: "It will purge the rottenness out of the system. High costs of living and high living will come down. People will work harder, live a more moral life. Values will be adjusted, and enterprising people will pick up the wrecks from less competent people."

Leading economists offered similar advice. Joseph Schumpeter, an Austria-born Harvard professor who is honored today for his pathbreaking work on innovation, warned against "remedial measures which work through money and credit. Policies of this class are particularly apt to produce additional trouble for the future."

Fast-forward 75 years to the administration of President George W. Bush. Like Hoover, Bush was pro-business and an ardent defender of free markets. But the Bush administration didn't share the Hoover administration's view that slumps should be allowed to run their course. The 2004 *Economic Report of the President*, prepared by the White House Council of Economic Advisers, expressed satisfaction with the economy's recovery from a slump earlier in the decade—and gave credit for the recovery to precisely the sort of Keynesian remedial measures econo-

mists had warned against at the beginning of the Great Depression. "Strong fiscal policy actions by this Administration and the Congress, together with the Federal Reserve's stimulative monetary policy," the report declared, "have softened the impact of the recession and have also put the economy on an upward trajectory." The boost to the economy given by fiscal policy and the Federal Reserve's interest rate cuts reduced the severity and duration of the 2001 recession.

As this book goes to press in late 2008, the United States is experiencing widespread financial dislocation and a severe recession, similar to the events of the 1930s. Heeding Keynes's advice, policy makers are rushing to contain the damage. Congress has passed legislation for fiscal stimulation, and it appears that more is on the way. The Federal Reserve and the U.S. Treasury have adopted and used an aggressive range of tactics, from emergency interest rate cuts to recapitalizing banks and other financial institutions suffering from heavy losses.

What changed from Hoover to Bush? The rise of macroeconomics as a discipline. Modern macroeconomic theory, accepted by politicians across much, though not all, of the political spectrum, tells us that slumps can be fought with judicious policy—and modern presidents try to do just that. ▲

> > > > > > > > > > > > >

© 2008 Patrick Corrigan, *The Toronto Star*, and Politicalcartoons.com

>> QUICK REVIEW

➤ Microeconomics focuses on decision-making by individuals and firms and the consequences of the decisions made. Macroeconomics focuses on the overall behavior of the economy.

➤ The combined effect of individual actions can have unintended consequences and lead to worse or better macroeconomic outcomes for everyone.

➤ Before the 1930s, economists tended to regard the economy as **self-regulating.** After the Great Depression, **Keynesian economics** provided the rationale for government intervention through **monetary policy** and **fiscal policy** to help a depressed economy.

➤ CHECK YOUR UNDERSTANDING 22-1

1. Which of the following questions involve microeconomics, and which involve macroeconomics? In each case, explain your answer.
   a. Why did consumers switch to smaller cars in 2008?
   b. Why did overall consumer spending slow down in 2008?
   c. Why did the standard of living rise more rapidly in the first generation after World War II than in the second?
   d. Why have starting salaries for students with geology degrees risen sharply of late?
   e. What determines the choice between rail and road transportation?
   f. Why has salmon gotten cheaper over the past 20 years?
   g. Why did inflation fall in the 1990s?

2. In 2008, problems in the financial sector led to a drying up of credit around the country: homebuyers were unable to get mortgages, students were unable to get student loans, car buyers were unable to get car loans, etc.
   a. Explain how the drying up of credit can lead to compounding effects throughout the economy and result in an economic slump.
   b. If you believed the economy is self-regulating, what would you advocate that policy makers do?
   c. If you believed in Keynesian economics, what would you advocate that policy makers do?

Solutions appear at back of book.

Recessions, or contractions, are periods of economic downturn when output and employment are falling.

Expansions, or recoveries, are periods of economic upturn when output and employment are rising.

The **business cycle** is the short-run alternation between recessions and expansions.

The point at which the economy turns from expansion to recession is a **business-cycle peak.**

The point at which the economy turns from recession to expansion is a **business-cycle trough.**

The Business Cycle

The Great Depression was by far the worst economic crisis in U.S. history. But although the economy has managed to avoid catastrophe over the past 75 years, it has experienced many ups and downs.

It's true that the ups have consistently been bigger than the downs: a chart of any of the major numbers used to track the U.S. economy shows a strong upward trend over time. For example, panel (a) of Figure 22-1 shows total U.S. private-sector employment (the total number of jobs offered by private businesses) measured along the left vertical axis with the actual data from 1988 to 2008 given by the purple line. The graph also shows the index of industrial production (a measure of the total output of U.S. factories) measured along the right vertical axis, with the actual data from 1988 to 2008 given by the red line. Both private-sector employment and industrial production were much higher at the end of these two decades than at the beginning, and in most years both measures rose.

But they didn't rise steadily. As you can see from the figure, there were three periods—in the early 1990s, in the early 2000s, and again beginning in late 2007—when both employment and industrial output stumbled. Panel (b) emphasizes these stumbles by showing the *rate of change* of employment and industrial production over the previous year. For example, the percent change in employment for December 2007 was 0.7, because employment in December 2007 was 0.7% higher than it had been in December 2006. The three big downturns stand out clearly. What's more, a detailed look at the data makes it clear that in each period the stumble wasn't confined to only a few industries: in each downturn, just about every sector of the U.S. economy cut back on production and on the number of people employed.

The economy's forward march, in other words, isn't smooth. And the uneven pace of the economy's progress, its ups and downs, is one of the main preoccupations of macroeconomics.

FIGURE 22-1   Growth, Interrupted, 1988–2008

(a) Private–Sector Employment and Industrial Production Index

(b) Percent Change from Year Earlier

Panel (a) shows two important economic numbers, the industrial production index and total private-sector employment. Both numbers grew substantially from 1988 to 2008—but they didn't grow steadily. Instead, both suffered from three downturns due to *recessions,* which are indicated by the shaded areas in the figure. Panel

(b) emphasizes those downturns by showing the annual rate of change of industrial production and employment, that is, the percentage increase over the past year. The simultaneous downturns in both numbers during the three recessions are clear.

Source: Federal Reserve Bank of St. Louis.

Charting the Business Cycle

Figure 22-2 shows a stylized representation of the way the economy evolves over time. The vertical axis shows either employment or an indicator of how much the economy is producing, such as industrial production or *real gross domestic product (real GDP)*, a measure of the economy's overall output that we'll learn about in Chapter 23. As the data in Figure 22-1 suggest, these two measures tend to move together. Their common movement is the starting point for a major theme of macroeconomics: the economy's alternation between short-run downturns and upturns.

A broad-based downturn, in which output and employment fall in many industries, is called a **recession** (sometimes referred to as a *contraction*). Recessions, as officially declared by the National Bureau of Economic Research (see the upcoming For Inquiring Minds), are indicated by the shaded areas in Figure 22-1. When the economy isn't in a recession, when most economic numbers are following their normal upward trend, the economy is said to be in an **expansion** (sometimes referred to as a *recovery*). The alternation between recessions and expansions is known as the **business cycle.** The point in time at which the economy shifts from expansion to recession is known as a **business-cycle peak;** the point at which the economy shifts from recession to expansion is known as a **business-cycle trough.**

The business cycle is an enduring feature of the economy. Table 22-2 shows the official list of business-cycle peaks and troughs, as declared by the National Bureau of Economic Research. As you can see, there have been recessions and expansions for at least the past 150 years. Whenever there is a prolonged expansion, as there was in the 1960s and again in the 1990s, books and articles come out proclaiming the end of the business cycle. Such proclamations have always proved wrong: The cycle always comes back. But why does it matter?

TABLE 22-2

The History of the Business Cycle

Business-Cycle Peak	Business-Cycle Trough
no prior data available	December 1854
June 1857	December 1858
October 1860	June 1861
April 1865	December 1867
June 1869	December 1870
October 1873	March 1879
March 1882	May 1885
March 1887	April 1888
July 1890	May 1891
January 1893	June 1894
December 1895	June 1897
June 1899	December 1900
September 1902	August 1904
May 1907	June 1908
January 1910	January 1912
January 1913	December 1914
August 1918	March 1919
January 1920	July 1921
May 1923	July 1924
October 1926	November 1927
August 1929	March 1933
May 1937	June 1938
February 1945	October 1945
November 1948	October 1949
July 1953	May 1954
August 1957	April 1958
April 1960	February 1961
December 1969	November 1970
November 1973	March 1975
January 1980	July 1980
July 1981	November 1982
July 1990	March 1991
March 2001	November 2001
December 2007	To be determined

Source: National Bureau of Economic Research.

FIGURE 22-2

The Business Cycle

This is a stylized picture of the business cycle. The vertical axis measures either employment or total output in the economy. Periods when these two variables turn down are *recessions;* periods when they turn up are *expansions.* The point at which the economy turns down is a *business-cycle peak;* the point at which it turns up again is a *business-cycle trough.*

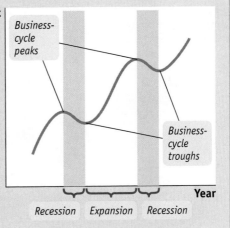

Defining Recessions and Expansions

Some readers may be wondering exactly how recessions and expansions are defined. The answer is that there is no exact definition!

In many countries, economists adopt the rule that a recession is a period of at least two consecutive quarters (a quarter is three months) during which the total output of the economy shrinks. The two-consecutive-quarters requirement is designed to avoid classifying brief hiccups in the economy's performance, with no lasting significance, as recessions.

Sometimes, however, this definition seems too strict. For example, an economy that has three months of sharply declining output, then three months of slightly positive growth, then another three months of rapid decline, should surely be considered to have endured a nine-month recession.

In the United States, we try to avoid such misclassifications by assigning the task of determining when a recession begins and ends to an independent panel of experts at the National Bureau of Economic Research (NBER). This panel looks at a variety of economic indicators, with the main focus on employment and production. But, ultimately, the panel makes a judgment call.

Sometimes this judgment is controversial. In fact, there is lingering controversy over the 2001 recession. According to the NBER, that recession began in March 2001 and ended in November 2001 when output began rising. Some critics argue, however, that the recession really began several months earlier, when industrial production began falling. Other critics argue that the recession didn't really end in 2001 because employment continued to fall and the job market remained weak for another year and a half.

The Pain of Recession

Not many people complain about the business cycle when the economy is expanding. Recessions, however, create a great deal of pain.

The most important effect of a recession is its effect on the ability of workers to find and hold jobs. The most widely used indicator of conditions in the labor market is the *unemployment rate.* We'll explain how that rate is calculated in Chapter 24, but for now it's enough to say that a high unemployment rate tells us that jobs are scarce and a low unemployment rate tells us that jobs are easy to find. Figure 22-3 shows the unemployment rate from 1988 to 2008. As you can see, the U.S. unemployment rate surged during and after each recession but eventually fell during periods of expansion. The rising unemployment rate in 2008 was a sign that a new recession might be under way, which was later confirmed by the NBER to have begun in December 2007.

FIGURE 22-3

The U.S. Unemployment Rate, 1988–2008

The unemployment rate, a measure of joblessness, rises sharply during recessions and usually falls during expansions.

Source: Bureau of Labor Statistics.

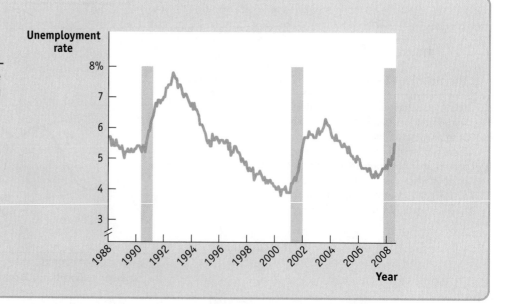

Because recessions cause many people to lose their jobs and also make it hard to find new ones, recessions hurt the standard of living of many families. Recessions are usually associated with a rise in the number of people living below the poverty line, an increase in the number of people who lose their houses because they can't afford the mortgage payments, and a fall in the percentage of Americans with health insurance coverage.

You should not think, however, that workers are the only group that suffers during a recession. Recessions are also bad for firms: like employment and wages, profits suffer during recessions and do well during expansions.

All in all, then, recessions are bad for almost everyone. Can anything be done to reduce their frequency and severity?

Taming the Business Cycle

Modern macroeconomics largely came into being as a response to the worst recession in history—the 43-month downturn that began in 1929 and continued into 1933, ushering in the Great Depression. The havoc wreaked by the 1929–1933 recession spurred economists to search both for understanding and for solutions: they wanted to know how such things could happen and how to prevent them.

As we explained earlier in this chapter, the work of John Maynard Keynes, published during the Great Depression, suggested that monetary and fiscal policies could be used to mitigate the effects of recessions, and to this day governments turn to Keynesian policies when recession strikes. Later work, notably that of another great macroeconomist, Milton Friedman, led to a consensus that it's important to rein in booms as well as to fight slumps. So modern policy makers try to "smooth out" the business cycle. They haven't been completely successful, as a look at Figure 22-3 makes clear. It's widely believed, however, that policy guided by macroeconomic analysis has helped make the economy more stable.

Although the business cycle is one of the main concerns of macroeconomics and historically played a crucial role in fostering the development of the field, macroeconomists are also concerned with other issues. We turn next to the question of long-run growth.

GLOBAL COMPARISON INTERNATIONAL BUSINESS CYCLES

This figure shows the annual rate of growth in employment—the percent change in each year's employment over the previous year—for two economies during 1988 to 2007: the United States and the eurozone, the group of European countries that have adopted the euro as their common currency. Does the eurozone have business cycles similar to those in the United States?

The answer, which is clear from the figure, is yes. Furthermore, the eurozone and U.S. business cycles seem to be roughly synchronized. In the early 1990s, job growth stumbled in the United States, then, slightly later, did the same thing in eurozone. At the beginning of the next decade job growth fell on both sides of the Atlantic, although the fall was steeper in the United States. The business cycle, in other words, is an international phenomenon.

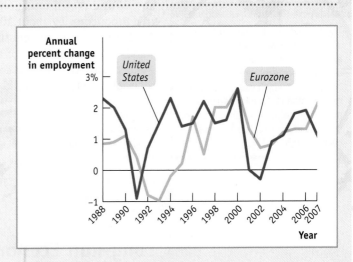

Source: OECD.

►ECONOMICS IN ACTION

Comparing Recessions

The alternation of recessions and expansions seems to be an enduring feature of economic life. However, not all business cycles are created equal. In particular, some recessions have been much worse than others.

Let's compare three historical recessions: the terrible slump of 1929–1933, the 1981–1982 recession—generally considered the worst economic slump since the Great Depression—and the relatively mild 2001 recession. These recessions differed in duration: the first lasted 43 months; the second, 16 months; the third, only 8 months. Even more important, however, they differed greatly in depth.

In Figure 22-4 we compare the depth of the recessions by looking at what happened to industrial production over the months after the recession began. In each case, production is measured as a percentage of its level at the recession's start. Thus the line for the 1929–1933 recession shows that industrial production eventually fell to less than 50% of its initial level.

FIGURE 22-4

Three Recessions

Some recessions are worse than others. This figure shows the path of industrial production in three recessions, in each case measured as a percentage of production at the business-cycle peak just before the recession started. The 2001 recession was relatively brief and mild compared with the recession of 1981–1982. And that recession was nothing compared with the gigantic, prolonged drop that marked the beginning of the Great Depression.

Source: Federal Reserve Bank of St. Louis.

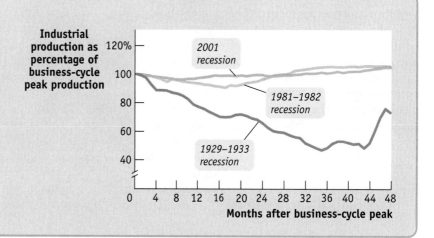

Clearly, the 1929–1933 recession hit the economy vastly harder than either of the post–World War II recessions. The 1981–1982 recession did eventually reduce industrial production by about 10%, although production then staged a rapid recovery. In 2001, the decline in industrial production was very modest. By Great Depression standards, or even those of the 1980s, the 2001 recession was very mild.

Of course, this was no consolation to the millions of American workers who lost their jobs, even in this mild recession. ▲

< < < < < < < < < < < <

> ►►QUICK REVIEW

> ➤ The **business cycle,** the short-run alternation between **recessions** and **expansions,** is a major concern of modern macroeconomics.
> ➤ The point at which expansion shifts to recession is a **business-cycle peak.** The point at which recession shifts to expansion is a **business-cycle trough.**

> ► CHECK YOUR UNDERSTANDING 22-2

1. Why do we talk about business cycles for the economy as a whole, rather than just talking about the ups and downs of particular industries?

2. Describe who gets hurt in a recession, and how.

Solutions appear at back of book.

Long-Run Economic Growth

In 1955, Americans were delighted with the nation's prosperity. The economy was expanding, consumer goods that had been rationed during World War II were available for everyone to buy, and most Americans believed, rightly, that they were better

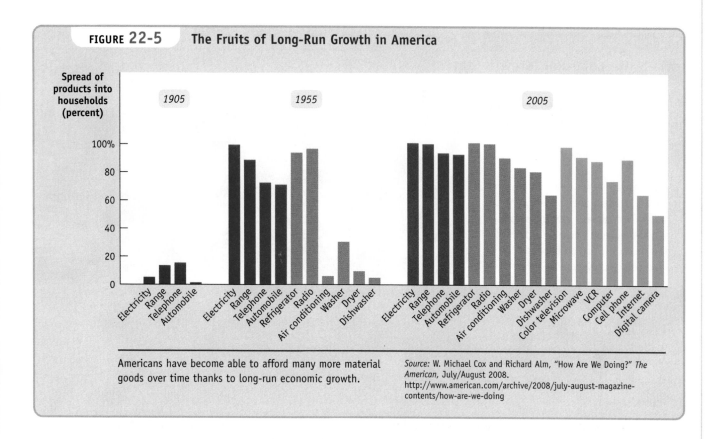

FIGURE 22-5   The Fruits of Long-Run Growth in America

Americans have become able to afford many more material goods over time thanks to long-run economic growth.

Source: W. Michael Cox and Richard Alm, "How Are We Doing?" *The American,* July/August 2008. http://www.american.com/archive/2008/july-august-magazine-contents/how-are-we-doing

off than the citizens of any other nation, past or present. Yet by today's standards, Americans were quite poor in 1955. Figure 22-5 shows the percentage of American homes equipped with a variety of appliances in 1905, 1955, and 2005: in 1955 only 37% of American homes contained washing machines and hardly anyone had air conditioning. And if we turn the clock back another half-century, to 1905, we find that life for many Americans was startlingly primitive by today's standards.

Why are the vast majority of Americans today able to afford conveniences that many Americans lacked in 1955? The answer is **long-run economic growth,** the sustained rise in the quantity of goods and services the economy produces. Figure 22-6 shows the growth since 1900 in real GDP per capita, a measure of total output per person in the economy. The severe recession of 1929–1933 stands out, but business

Long-run economic growth is the sustained upward trend in the economy's output over time.

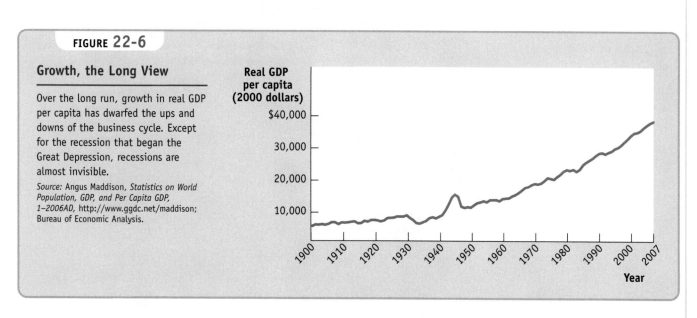

FIGURE 22-6

Growth, the Long View

Over the long run, growth in real GDP per capita has dwarfed the ups and downs of the business cycle. Except for the recession that began the Great Depression, recessions are almost invisible.

Source: Angus Maddison, *Statistics on World Population, GDP, and Per Capita GDP, 1–2006AD,* http://www.ggdc.net/maddison; Bureau of Economic Analysis.

When Did Long-Run Growth Start?

Today, the United States is much richer than it was in 1955; in 1955 it was much richer than it had been in 1905. But how did 1855 compare with 1805? Or 1755? How far back does long-run economic growth go?

The answer is that long-run growth is a relatively modern phenomenon. The U.S. economy was already growing steadily by the mid-nineteenth century—think railroads. But if you go back to the period before 1800, you find a world economy that grew extremely slowly by today's standards. Furthermore, the population grew almost as fast as the economy, so that there was very little increase in output per person. From 1000 to 1800, real aggregate output around the world grew less than 0.2% per year, with population rising at about the same rate. Economic stagnation meant unchanging living standards. For example, information on prices and wages from

Economic stagnation and unchanging living standards prevailed for centuries until the Industrial Revolution in the mid-1800s ushered in a new era of wealth and sustained increases in living standards.

such sources as monastery records shows that workers in England weren't significantly better off in the early eighteenth century than they had been five centuries earlier. And it's a good bet that they weren't much better off than Egyptian peasants in the age of the pharaohs. However, long-run economic growth has increased significantly since 1800. In the last 50 years or so, real GDP per capita has grown about 3.5% per year.

cycles since World War II are almost invisible, dwarfed by the strong upward trend. Part of the long-run increase in output is accounted for by the fact that we have a growing population and workforce. But the economy's overall production has increased by much more than the population. On average, in 2007 the U.S. economy produced almost $40,000 worth of goods and services per person, about three times as much as in 1955 and about eight times as much as in 1900.

Long-run economic growth is fundamental to many of the most pressing economic questions today. Responses to key policy questions, like the country's ability to bear the future costs of government programs such as Social Security and Medicare, depend in part on how fast the U.S. economy grows over the next few decades. More broadly, the public's sense that the country is making progress depends crucially on success in achieving long-run growth. When growth slows, as it did in the 1970s, it can help feed a national mood of pessimism. In particular, *long-run growth per capita*—a sustained upward trend in output per person—is the key to higher wages and a rising standard of living. A major concern of macroeconomics—and the theme of Chapter 25—is trying to understand the forces behind long-run growth.

Long-run growth is an even more urgent concern in poorer, less developed countries. In these countries, which would like to achieve a higher standard of living, the question of how to accelerate long-run growth is the central concern of economic policy.

As we'll see, macroeconomists don't use the same models to think about long-run growth that they use to think about the business cycle. It's always important to keep both sets of models in mind, because what is good in the long run can be bad in the short run, and vice versa. For example, we've already mentioned the paradox of thrift: an attempt by households to increase their savings can cause a recession. But a higher level of savings, as we'll see in Chapter 26, plays a crucial role in encouraging long-run economic growth.

➤ECONOMICS IN ACTION

A Tale of Two Colonies

Many countries have experienced long-run growth, but not all have done equally well. One of the most informative contrasts is between Canada and Argentina, two countries that, at the beginning of the twentieth century, seemed to be in a good economic position.

From today's vantage point, it's surprising to realize that Canada and Argentina looked rather similar before World War I. Both were major exporters of agricultural products; both attracted large numbers of European immigrants; both also attracted large amounts of European investment, especially in the railroads that opened up their agricultural hinterlands. Economic historians believe that the average level of per capita income was about the same in the two countries as late as the 1930s.

After World War II, however, Argentina's economy performed poorly, largely due to political instability and bad macroeconomic policies. (Argentina experienced several periods of extremely high inflation, during which the cost of living soared.) Meanwhile, Canada made steady progress. Thanks to the fact that Canada has achieved sustained long-run growth since 1930, but Argentina has not, Canada today has almost as high a standard of living as the United States—and is about three times as rich as Argentina. ▲

> > > > > > > > > > > >

➤ CHECK YOUR UNDERSTANDING 22-3

1. Many poor countries have high rates of population growth. What does this imply about the long-run growth rates of overall output that they must achieve in order to generate a higher standard of living per person?

2. Argentina used to be as rich as Canada; now it's much poorer. Does this mean that Argentina is poorer than it was in the past? Explain.

Solutions appear at back of book.

Inflation and Deflation

In 1970 the average production worker in the United States was paid $3.40 an hour. By August 2008, the average hourly earnings for such a worker had risen to $18.05 an hour. Three cheers for economic progress!

But wait. American workers were paid much more in 2008, but they also faced a much higher cost of living. In 1970, a dozen eggs cost only about $0.58; by August 2008, that was up to $1.85. The price of a loaf of white bread went from about $0.20 to $1.38. And the price of a gallon of gasoline rose from just $0.33 to $3.84. Figure 22-7

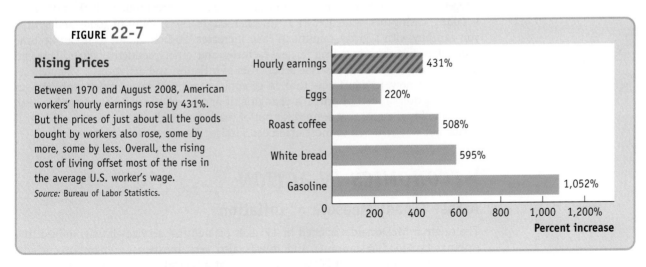

FIGURE 22-7

Rising Prices

Between 1970 and August 2008, American workers' hourly earnings rose by 431%. But the prices of just about all the goods bought by workers also rose, some by more, some by less. Overall, the rising cost of living offset most of the rise in the average U.S. worker's wage.

Source: Bureau of Labor Statistics.

	Percent increase
Hourly earnings	431%
Eggs	220%
Roast coffee	508%
White bread	595%
Gasoline	1,052%

A rising overall level of prices is **inflation.**

A falling overall level of prices is **deflation.**

The economy has **price stability** when the overall level of prices changes slowly or not at all.

compares the percentage increase in hourly earnings between 1970 and August 2008 with the increases in the prices of some standard items: the average worker's paycheck went further in terms of some goods, but less far in terms of others. Overall, the rise in the cost of living wiped out many, if not all, of the wage gains of the typical worker from 1970 to 2008. In other words, once inflation is taken into account, the living standard of the typical U.S. worker has stagnated from 1970 to the present.

The point is that between 1970 and 2008 the economy experienced substantial **inflation:** a rise in the overall level of prices. Understanding the causes of inflation and its opposite, **deflation**—a fall in the overall level of prices—is another main concern of macroeconomics.

The Causes of Inflation and Deflation

You might think that changes in the overall level of prices are just a matter of supply and demand. For example, higher gasoline prices reflect the higher price of crude oil, and higher crude oil prices reflect such factors as the exhaustion of major oil fields, growing demand from China and other emerging economies as more people grow rich enough to buy cars, and so on. Can't we just add up what happens in each of these markets to find out what happens to the overall level of prices?

The answer is no, we can't. Supply and demand can only explain why a particular good or service becomes more expensive *relative to other goods and services.* It can't explain why, for example, the price of chicken has risen over time in spite of the facts that chicken production has become more efficient (you don't want to know) and that chicken has become substantially cheaper compared to other goods.

What causes the overall level of prices to rise or fall? As we'll learn in Chapter 24, in the short run, movements in inflation are closely related to the business cycle. When the economy is depressed and jobs are hard to find, inflation tends to fall; when the economy is booming, inflation tends to rise. For example, prices of most goods and services fell sharply during the terrible recession of 1929–1933.

In the long run, by contrast, the overall level of prices is mainly determined by changes in the *money supply,* the total quantity of assets that can be readily used to make purchases. As we'll see in Chapter 32, *hyperinflation,* in which prices rise by thousands or hundreds of thousands of percent, invariably occurs when governments print money to pay their bills.

The Pain of Inflation and Deflation

Both inflation and deflation can pose problems for the economy. Here are two examples: inflation discourages people from holding onto cash, because cash loses value over time if the overall price level is rising. That is, the amount of goods and services you can buy with a given amount of cash falls. In extreme cases, people stop holding cash altogether and turn to barter. Deflation can cause the reverse problem. If the price level is falling, cash gains value over time. In other words, the amount of goods and sevices you can buy with a given amount of cash increases. So holding on to it can become more attractive than investing in new factories and other productive assets. This can deepen a recession. We'll describe other costs of inflation and deflation in Chapters 24 and 32. For now, let's just note that, in general, economists regard **price stability**—in which the overall level of prices is changing, if at all, only slowly—as a desirable goal. Price stability is a goal that seemed far out of reach for much of the post–World War II period but was achieved to most macroeconomists' satisfaction in the 1990s.

►*ECONOMICS IN ACTION*

A Fast (Food) Measure of Inflation

The original McDonald's opened in 1954. It offered fast service—it was, indeed, the original fast-food restaurant. And it was also very inexpensive: hamburgers cost $0.15, $0.25 with fries. In 2008 a hamburger at a typical McDonald's cost six times as much, about $0.90. Has McDonald's lost touch with its fast-food roots? Have burgers become luxury cuisine?

No—in fact, compared with other consumer goods, a burger is a better bargain today than it was in 1954. Burger prices were about 6 times as high in 2008 as they were in 1954. But the Consumer Price Index, the most widely used measure of the cost of living, was 8.1 times as high in 2008 as it was in 1954. ▲

> > > > > > > > > > > >

► CHECK YOUR UNDERSTANDING 22-4

1. Which of these sound like inflation, which sound like deflation, and which are ambiguous?
   a. Gasoline prices are up 10%, food prices are down 20%, and the prices of most services are up 1–2%.
   b. Gas prices have doubled, food prices are up 50%, and most services seem to be up 5 or 10%.
   c. Gas prices haven't changed, food prices are way down, and services have gotten cheaper, too.

Solutions appear at back of book.

►► QUICK REVIEW

➤ A dollar today doesn't buy what it did in 1970, because the prices of most goods have risen. This rise in the overall price level has wiped out most if not all of the wage increases received by the typical American worker from 1970–2008.

➤ One area of macroeconomic study is in the overall level of prices. Because either **inflation** or **deflation** can cause problems for the economy, economists typically advocate maintaining **price stability.**

International Imbalances

The United States is an **open economy:** an economy that trades goods and services with other countries. There have been times when that trade was more or less balanced—when the United States sold about as much to the rest of the world as it bought. But this isn't one of those times.

In 2007 the United States ran a big **trade deficit**—that is, the value of the goods and services U.S. residents bought from the rest of the world was a lot larger than the value of the goods and services American producers sold to customers abroad. Meanwhile, some other countries were selling much more to foreigners than they were buying: Figure 22-8 shows the exports and imports of goods of several important economies in 2007. As you can see, the United States imported much more than it exported, but Germany, China, and Saudi Arabia did the reverse: they each ran a **trade surplus.** A country runs a trade surplus when the value of the goods and services it buys from the rest of the world is smaller than the value of the goods and services it sells abroad. Was America's trade deficit a sign that something was wrong with our economy—that we weren't able to make things that people in other countries wanted to buy?

No, not really. Trade deficits and their opposite, trade surpluses, are macroeconomic phenomena. They're the result of situations in which the whole is very different from the sum of its parts. You might think that countries with highly

An **open economy** is an economy that trades goods and services with other countries.

A country runs a **trade deficit** when the value of goods and services bought from foreigners is more than the value of goods and services it sells to them. It runs a **trade surplus** when the value of goods and services bought from foreigners is less than the value of the goods and services it sells to them.

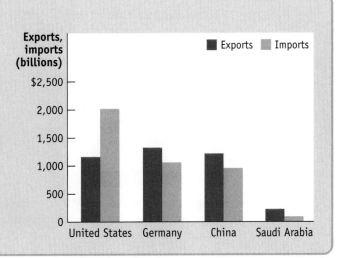

FIGURE 22-8

Unbalanced Trade

In 2007, the goods the United States bought from other countries were worth considerably more than the goods we sold abroad. Germany, China, and Saudi Arabia were in the reverse position. Trade deficits and trade surpluses reflect macroeconomic forces, especially differences in savings and investment spending.

Source: World Trade Organization.

productive workers or widely desired products and services to sell run trade surpluses but countries with unproductive workers or poor-quality products and services run deficits. But the reality is that there's no simple relationship between the success of an economy and whether it runs trade surpluses or deficits.

Microeconomic analysis tells us why countries trade but not why they run trade surpluses or deficits. In Chapter 2 we learned that international trade is the result of comparative advantage: countries export goods they're relatively good at producing and import goods they're not as good at producing. That's why the United States exports wheat and imports coffee. One important thing the concept of comparative advantage doesn't explain, however, is why the value of a country's imports is sometimes much larger than the value of its exports, or vice versa.

So what does determine whether a country runs a trade surplus or a trade deficit? In Chapter 34 we'll learn the surprising answer: the determinants of the overall balance between exports and imports lie in decisions about savings and investment spending—spending on goods like machinery and factories that are in turn used to produce goods and services for consumers. Countries with high investment spending relative to savings run trade deficits; countries with low investment spending relative to savings run trade surpluses.

►*ECONOMICS IN ACTION*

Estonia's Miraculous Trade Deficit

The Soviet Union, once second only to the United States as a world power, broke up into 15 independent countries in 1991. Many of these countries experienced hard economic times in the years that followed. The small nation of Estonia, however, thrived— so much so that economists routinely talk of an Estonian economic "miracle."

You might think that such a successful economy would run a big trade surplus, exporting much more than it imports. In fact, however, Estonia runs trade deficits that are small in dollar terms because it's a small country (just 1.3 million people) but are large compared with the size of the economy. In fact, relative to the size of its economy, Estonia's trade deficit in 2007 was almost three times that of the United States.

Why does Estonia run such large trade deficits? Because it's so successful! The success of the economy has led to high rates of investment, much of it by companies based in other European countries. And as we've just suggested, trade deficits are high when investment spending is high compared with savings. ▲

< < < < < < < < < < < <

► CHECK YOUR UNDERSTANDING 22-5

1. Which of the following reflect comparative advantage, and which reflect macroeconomic forces?
   a. Thanks to the discovery of huge oil sands in Alberta, Canada, it has become an exporter of oil and an importer of manufactured goods.
   b. Like many consumer goods, the Apple iPod is assembled in China, although many of the components are made in other countries.
   c. Since 2002, China has been running huge trade surpluses, exporting much more than it imports.
   d. The United States, which had roughly balanced trade in the early 1990s, began running large trade deficits later in the decade, as the technology boom took off.

Solutions appear at back of book.

[►► A LOOK AHEAD ···

In the chapters ahead, we will examine in depth the issues described so briefly here. Before we begin analyzing macroeconomic issues, however, we need to know how macroeconomists keep track of the economy. What measures do we use to assess macroeconomic performance, and how are they calculated?]

SUMMARY

1. Macroeconomics is the study of the behavior of the economy as a whole, which can be different from the sum of its parts. Macroeconomics differs from microeconomics in the type of questions it tries to answer. Macroeconomics also has a strong policy focus: **Keynesian economics,** which emerged during the Great Depression, advocates the use of **monetary policy** and **fiscal policy** to fight economic slumps. Prior to the Great Depression, the economy was thought to be **self-regulating.**

2. One key concern of macroeconomics is the **business cycle,** the short-run alternation between **recessions,** periods of falling employment and output, and **expansions,** periods of rising employment and output. The point at which expansion turns to recession is a **business-cycle peak.** The point at which recession turns to expansion is a **business-cycle trough.**

3. Another key area of macroeconomic study is **long-run economic growth,** the sustained upward trend in the economy's output over time. Long-run economic growth is the force behind long-term increases in living standards and is important for financing some economic programs. It is especially important for poorer countries.

4. When the prices of most goods and services are rising, so that the overall level of prices is going up, the economy experiences **inflation.** When the overall level of prices is going down, the economy is experiencing **deflation.** In the short run, inflation and deflation are closely related to the business cycle. In the long run, prices tend to reflect changes in the overall quantity of money. Because inflation and deflation can cause problems, economists and policy makers generally aim for **price stability.**

5. Although comparative advantage explains why **open economies** export some things and import others, macroeconomic analysis is needed to explain why countries run **trade surpluses** or **trade deficits.** The determinants of the overall balance between exports and imports lie in decisions about savings and investment spending.

KEY TERMS

Self-regulating economy, p. 572
Keynesian economics, p. 572
Monetary policy, p. 572
Fiscal policy, p. 572
Recession, p. 574
Expansion, p. 574

Business cycle, p. 574
Business-cycle peak, p. 574
Business-cycle trough, p. 574
Long-run economic growth, p. 579
Inflation, p. 582

Deflation, p. 582
Price stability, p. 582
Open economy, p. 583
Trade deficit, p. 583
Trade surplus, p. 583

PROBLEMS

1. Which of the following questions are relevant for the study of macroeconomics and which for microeconomics?

   a. How will Ms. Martin's tips change when a large manufacturing plant near the restaurant where she works closes?

   b. What will happen to spending by consumers when the economy enters a downturn?

   c. How will the price of oranges change when a late frost damages Florida's orange groves?

   d. How will wages at a manufacturing plant change when its workforce is unionized?

   e. What will happen to U.S. exports as the dollar becomes less expensive in terms of other currencies?

   f. What is the relationship between a nation's unemployment rate and its inflation rate?

2. When one person saves, that person's wealth is increased, meaning that he or she can consume more in the future. But when everyone saves, everyone's income falls, meaning that everyone must consume less today. Explain this seeming contradiction.

3. Before the Great Depression, the conventional wisdom among economists and policy makers was that the economy is largely self-regulating.

   a. Was this view consistent or inconsistent with Keynesian economics? Explain.

   b. What effect did the Great Depression have on conventional wisdom?

   c. Contrast the response of policy makers during the 2001 recession to the actions of policy makers during the Great Depression. What would have been the likely outcome of the 2001 recession if policy makers had responded in the same fashion as policy makers during the Great Depression?

4. How do economists in the United States determine when a recession begins and when it ends? How do other countries determine whether or not a recession is occurring?

5. The U.S. Department of Labor reports statistics on employment and earnings that are used as key indicators by many economists to gauge the health of the economy. During a

recession, the weekly claims for unemployment insurance tend to spike. Figure 22-3 in the text plots historical data on the unemployment rate each month. Noticeably, the numbers were high during the recessions in the early 1990s and in 2001.

a. Locate the latest data on the national unemployment rate. (*Hint:* Go to the website of the Bureau of Labor Statistics, www.bls.gov, and locate the latest release of the Employment Situation.)

b. Compare the current numbers with the recessions in the early 1990s and 2001 as well as with the periods of relatively high economic growth just before the recessions. Are the current numbers indicative of a recessionary trend?

6. The accompanying figure shows the annual rate of growth in employment for the United Kingdom and Japan from 1988 to 2005. (The annual growth rate is the percent change in each year's employment over the previous year.)

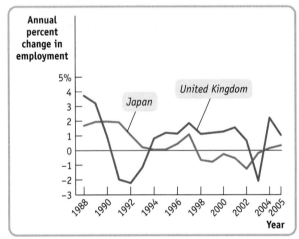

a. Comment on the business cycles of these two economies. Are their business cycles similar or dissimilar?

b. Use the accompanying figure and the figure in the Global Comparison on international business cycles in the chapter to compare the business cycles of each of these two economies with those of the United States and the eurozone.

7 **a.** What three measures of the economy tend to move together during the business cycle? Which way do they move during an upturn? During a downturn?

b. Who in the economy is hurt during a recession? How?

c. How did Milton Friedman alter the consensus that had developed in the aftermath of the Great Depression on how the economy should be managed? What is the current goal of policy makers in managing the economy?

8. Why do we consider a business-cycle expansion different from long-run economic growth? Why do we care about the size of the long-run growth rate of real GDP versus the size of the growth rate of the population?

9. In 1798, Thomas Malthus's *Essay on the Principle of Population* was published. In it, he wrote: "Population, when unchecked,

increases in a geometrical ratio. Subsistence increases only in an arithmetical ratio. . . . This implies a strong and constantly operating check on population from the difficulty of subsistence." Malthus was saying that the growth of the population is limited by the amount of food available to eat; people will live at the subsistence level forever. Why didn't Malthus's description apply to the world after 1800?

10. College tuition has risen significantly in the last few decades. From the 1977–1978 academic year to the 2007–2008 academic year, total tuition, room, and board paid by full-time undergraduate students went from $2,038 to $13,589 at public institutions and from $4,240 to $32,307 at private institutions. This is an average annual tuition increase of 6.5% at public institutions and 7.0% at private institutions. Over the same time, average personal income after taxes rose from $6,517 to $33,705 per year, which is an average annual rate of growth of personal income of 5.6%. Have these tuition increases made it more difficult for the average student to afford college tuition?

11. In May of each year, *The Economist* publishes data on the price of the Big Mac in different countries and exchange rates. The accompanying table shows some data used for the index from 2003 and 2007. Use this information to answer the following questions.

Country	2003		2007	
	Price of Big Mac (in local currency)	Price of Big Mac (in U.S. dollars)	Price of Big Mac (in local currency)	Price of Big Mac (in U.S. dollars)
Argentina	peso4.10	$1.42	peso8.25	$2.65
Canada	C$3.20	$2.21	C$3.63	$3.08
Eurozone	€2.71	$2.98	€2.94	$3.82
Japan	¥262	$2.18	¥280	$2.31
United States	$2.71	$2.71	$3.22	$3.22

a. Where was it cheapest to buy a Big Mac in U.S. dollars in 2003?

b. Where was it cheapest to buy a Big Mac in U.S. dollars in 2007?

c. Using the increase in the local currency price of the Big Mac in each country to measure the percent change in the overall price level from April 2003 to January 2007, which nation experienced the most inflation? Did any of the nations experience deflation?

12. The accompanying figure illustrates the increasing trade deficit of the United States. The United States has been increasingly importing more goods than it has been exporting. One of the countries it runs a trade deficit with is China. Which of the following statements are valid possible explanations of this fact? Explain.

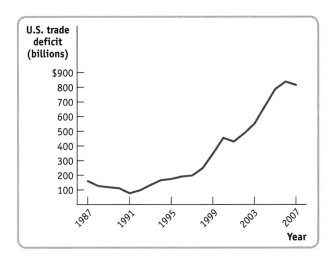

a. Many products, such as televisions, that were formerly manufactured in the United States are now manufactured in China.

b. The wages of the average Chinese worker are far lower than the wages of the average American worker.

c. Investment spending in the United States is high relative to its level of savings, but the level of savings in China is high relative to its investment spending.

www.worthpublishers.com/krugmanwells

chapter: 23

Tracking the Macroeconomy

AFTER THE REVOLUTION

IN DECEMBER 1975 THE GOVERNMENT OF PORTUGAL— a provisional government in the process of establishing a democracy—feared that it was facing an economic crisis. Business owners, alarmed by the rise of leftist political parties, issued dire warnings about plunging production. Newspapers speculated that the economy had shrunk 10 to 15% since the 1974 revolution that had overthrown the country's long-standing dictatorship.

In the face of these reports of economic collapse, some Portuguese were pronouncing democracy itself a failure. Others declared that capitalism was the culprit, demanding that the government seize control of the nation's factories and force them to produce more. But how bad was the situation, really?

To answer this question, Portugal's top monetary official invited his old friend Richard Eckaus, an economist at the Massachusetts Institute of Technology, and two

other MIT economists to look at the country's national accounts, the set of data collected on the country's economic activity. The visiting experts had to engage in a lot of educated guesswork: Portugal's economic data collection had always been somewhat incomplete, and it had been further disrupted by political upheavals. For example, the country's statisticians normally tracked construction with data on the sales of structural steel and concrete. But in the somewhat chaotic situation of 1975, these indicators were moving in opposite directions because many builders were ignoring the construction regulations and using very little steel. (Travel tip: if you find yourself visiting Portugal, try to avoid being in a 1975-vintage building during an earthquake.)

Still, they went to work with the available data, and within a week they were able to make a rough estimate: aggregate output had declined only 3% from 1974 to 1975.

With accurate economic data, Portugal was able to make the transition from revolution in 1975 to a prosperous democracy today.

The economy had indeed suffered a serious setback, but its decline was much less drastic than the calamity being portrayed in the newspapers. (While later revisions pushed the decline up to 4.5%, that was still much less than feared.) The Portuguese government certainly had work to do, but there was no need to abandon either democracy or a market economy. In fact, the economy soon began to recover. Over the past three decades, Portugal has, on the whole, been a success story. A once-backward dictatorship is now a fairly prosperous, solidly democratic member of the European Union.

What's the lesson of this story? It is that economic measurement matters. If the government of Portugal had believed the scare stories some were telling during 1975, it might have made major policy mistakes. Good macroeconomic policy depends on good measurement of what is happening in the economy as a whole.

In this chapter, we explain how macroeconomists measure key aspects of the economy. We first explore ways to measure the economy's total output and total income. We then turn to the problem of how to measure the level of prices and the change in prices in the economy.

WHAT YOU WILL LEARN IN THIS CHAPTER:

- ➤ How economists use aggregate measures to track the performance of the economy

- ➤ What **gross domestic product,** or **GDP,** is and the three ways of calculating it

- ➤ The difference between **real GDP** and **nominal GDP** and why real GDP is the appropriate measure of real economic activity

- ➤ What a **price index** is and how it is used to calculate the **inflation rate**

The National Accounts

Almost all countries calculate a set of numbers known as the *national income and product accounts.* In fact, the accuracy of a country's accounts is a remarkably reliable indicator of its state of economic development—in general, the more reliable the accounts, the more economically advanced the country. When international economic agencies seek to help a less developed country, typically the first order of business is to send a team of experts to audit and improve the country's accounts.

In the United States, these numbers are calculated by the Bureau of Economic Analysis, a division of the U.S. government's Department of Commerce. The **national income and product accounts,** often referred to simply as the **national accounts,** keep track of the spending of consumers, sales of producers, business investment spending, government purchases, and a variety of other flows of money between different sectors of the economy. Let's see how they work.

The Circular-Flow Diagram, Revisited and Expanded

To understand the principles behind the national accounts, it helps to look at Figure 23-1, a revised and expanded *circular-flow diagram* similar to the one we introduced in Chapter 2. Recall that in Figure 2-7 we showed the flows of money, goods and services, and factors of production through the economy. Here we restrict ourselves to flows of money but add extra elements that allow us to show the key concepts behind the national accounts. As in our original version of the circular-flow diagram, the underlying principle is that the inflow of money into each market or sector is equal to the outflow of money coming from that market or sector.

Figure 2-7 showed a simplified world containing only two kinds of "inhabitants," households and firms. And it illustrated the circular flow of money between households and firms, which remains visible in Figure 23-1. In the markets for goods and services, households engage in **consumer spending,** buying goods and services from domestic firms and from firms in the rest of the world. Households also own factors

The **national income and product accounts,** or **national accounts,** keep track of the flows of money between different sectors of the economy.

Consumer spending is household spending on goods and services.

FIGURE 23-1   An Expanded Circular-Flow Diagram: The Flows of Money Through the Economy

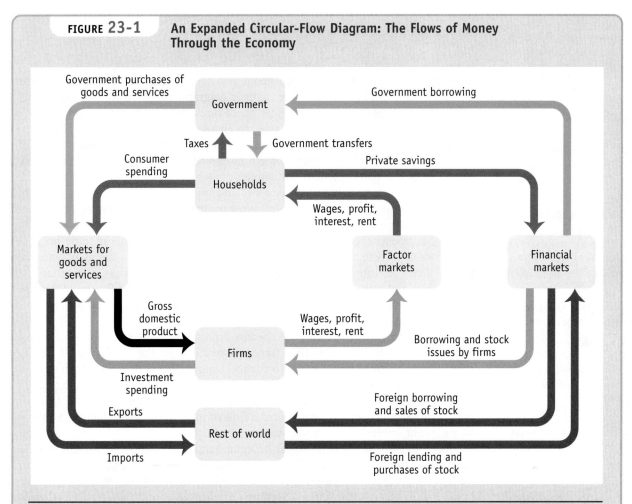

A circular flow of funds connects the four sectors of the economy—households, firms, government, and the rest of the world—via three types of markets: the factor markets, the markets for goods and services, and the *financial markets*. Funds flow from firms to households in the form of wages, profit, interest, and rent through the factor markets. After paying taxes to the government and receiving *government transfers*, households allocate the remaining income—*disposable income*—to private savings and consumer spending. Via the financial markets, *private savings* and funds from the rest of the world are channeled into investment spending by firms, government borrowing, foreign borrowing and lending, and foreign transactions of stocks. In turn, funds flow from the government and households to firms to pay for purchases of goods and services. Finally, exports to the rest of the world generate a flow of funds into the economy and imports lead to a flow of funds out of the economy. If we add up consumer spending on goods and services, investment spending by firms, government purchases of goods and services, and exports, then subtract the value of imports, the total flow of funds represented by this calculation is total spending on final goods and services produced in the United States. Equivalently, it's the value of all the final goods and services produced in the United States—that is, the *gross domestic product* of the economy.

of production—labor, land, physical capital, human capital, and financial capital. They sell the use of these factors of production to firms, receiving wages, profit, interest payments, and rent in return. Firms buy and pay households for the use of those factors of production in the factor markets. Most households derive the bulk of their income from wages earned by selling labor and human capital. But households derive additional income from their indirect ownership of the physical capital used by firms, mainly in the form of **stocks,** shares in the ownership of a company, and **bonds,** borrowing in the form of an IOU that pays interest. So the income households receive from the factor markets includes profit distributed to shareholders and the interest

A **stock** is a share in the ownership of a company held by a shareholder.

A **bond** is borrowing in the form of an IOU that pays interest.

Government transfers are payments by the government to individuals for which no good or service is provided in return.

Disposable income, equal to income plus government transfers minus taxes, is the total amount of household income available to spend on consumption and to save.

Private savings, equal to disposable income minus consumer spending, is disposable income that is not spent on consumption.

The banking, stock, and bond markets, which channel private savings and foreign lending into investment spending, government borrowing, and foreign borrowing, are known as the **financial markets.**

Government borrowing is the amount of funds borrowed by the government in the financial markets.

Government purchases of goods and services are total expenditures on goods and services by federal, state, and local governments.

Goods and services sold to other countries are **exports.** Goods and services purchased from other countries are **imports.**

payments on bonds held by households. Finally, households receive rent in return for allowing firms to use land or structures that they own. So households receive income in the form of wages, profit, interest, and rent via factor markets.

In our original, simplified circular-flow diagram, households spent all the income they received via factor markets on goods and services. Figure 23-1, however, illustrates a more complicated but more realistic diagram. There we see two reasons why goods and services don't in fact absorb all of households' income. First, households don't get to keep all the income they receive via the factor markets. They must pay part of their income to the government in the form of taxes, such as income taxes and sales taxes. In addition, some households receive **government transfers**—payments by the government to individuals for which no good or service is provided in return, such as Social Security benefits and unemployment insurance payments. The total income households have left after paying taxes and receiving government transfers is **disposable income.**

Second, households normally don't spend all their disposable income on goods and services. Instead, a portion of their income is typically set aside as **private savings,** which goes into **financial markets** where individuals, banks, and other institutions buy and sell stocks and bonds as well as make loans. As Figure 23-1 shows, the financial markets also receive funds from the rest of the world and provide funds to the government, to firms, and to the rest of the world.

Before going further, we can use the box representing households to illustrate an important general feature of the circular-flow diagram: the total sum of flows of money out of a given box is equal to the total sum of flows of money into that box. It's simply a matter of accounting: what goes in must come out. So, for example, the total flow of money out of households—the sum of taxes paid, consumer spending, and private savings—must equal the total flow of money into households—the sum of wages, profit, interest, rent, and government transfers.

Now let's look at the other types of inhabitants we've added to the circular-flow diagram, including the government and the rest of the world. The government returns a portion of the money it collects from taxes to households in the form of government transfers. However, it uses much of its tax revenue, plus additional funds borrowed in the financial markets through **government borrowing,** to buy goods and services. **Government purchases of goods and services,** the total purchases by federal, state, and local governments, include everything from military spending on ammunition to your local public school's spending on chalk, erasers, and teacher salaries.

The rest of the world participates in the U.S. economy in three ways. First, some of the goods and services produced in the United States are sold to residents of other countries. For example, more than half of America's annual wheat and cotton crops are sold abroad. Goods and services sold to other countries are known as **exports.** Export sales lead to a flow of funds from the rest of the world into the United States to pay for them. Second, some of the goods and services purchased by residents of the United States are produced abroad. For example, many consumer goods are now made in China. Goods and services purchased from residents of other countries are known as **imports.** Import purchases lead to a flow of funds out of the United States to pay for them. Third, foreigners can participate in U.S. financial markets by making transactions. Foreign lending—lending by foreigners to borrowers in the United States, and purchases by foreigners of shares of stock in American companies—generates a flow of funds into the United States from the rest of the world. Conversely, foreign borrowing—borrowing by foreigners from U.S. lenders and purchases by Americans of stock in foreign companies—leads to a flow of funds out of the United States to the rest of the world.

Finally, let's go back to the markets for goods and services. In Chapter 2 we focused only on purchases of goods and services by households. We now see that there are other types of spending on goods and services, including government purchases, imports, and exports. Notice that firms also buy goods and services in our expanded economy. For example, an automobile company that is building a new factory will buy investment goods—machinery like stamping presses and welding robots—from companies that manufacture these items. It will also accumulate an inventory of finished cars in preparation for shipment to dealers. **Inventories,** then, are stocks of goods and raw materials that firms hold to facilitate their operations. The national accounts count this **investment spending**—spending on productive physical capital, such as machinery and construction of buildings, and on changes to inventories—as part of total spending on goods and services.

You might ask why changes to inventories are included in investment spending—finished cars aren't, after all, used to produce more cars. Changes to inventories of finished goods are counted as investment spending because, like machinery, they change the ability of a firm to make future sales. So spending on additions to inventories is a form of investment spending by a firm. Conversely, a drawing-down of inventories is counted as a fall in investment spending because it leads to lower future sales. It's also important to understand that investment spending includes spending on construction of any structure, regardless of whether it is an assembly plant or a new house. Why include construction of homes? Because, like a plant, a new house produces a future stream of output—housing services for its occupants.

Suppose we add up consumer spending on goods and services, investment spending, government purchases of goods and services, and the value of exports, then subtract the value of imports. This gives us a measure of the overall market value of the goods and services the economy produces. That measure has a name: it's a country's *gross domestic product.* But before we can formally define gross domestic product, or GDP, we have to examine an important distinction between classes of goods and services: the difference between *final goods and services* versus *intermediate goods and services.*

Gross Domestic Product

A consumer's purchase of a new car from a dealer is one example of a sale of **final goods and services:** goods and services sold to the final, or end, user. But an automobile manufacturer's purchase of steel from a steel foundry or glass from a glassmaker is an example of purchasing **intermediate goods and services:** goods and services that are inputs for production of final goods and services. In the case of intermediate goods and services, the purchaser—another firm—is *not* the final user.

Gross domestic product, or **GDP,** is the total value of all *final goods and services* produced in an economy during a given period, usually a year. In 2007 the GDP of the United States was $13,808 billion, or about $46,000 per person. If you are an economist trying to construct a country's national accounts, *one way to calculate GDP is to calculate it directly: survey firms and add up the total value of their production of final goods and services.* We'll explain in detail in the next section why intermediate goods, and some other types of goods as well, are not included in the calculation of GDP.

But adding up the total value of final goods and services produced isn't the only way of calculating GDP. There is another way, based on total spending on final goods and services. Since GDP is equal to the total value of final goods and services produced in the economy, it must also equal the flow of funds received by firms from sales in the goods and services market. If you look again at the circular-flow diagram in Figure 23-1, you will see that the arrow going from markets for goods and services to firms is indeed labeled "Gross domestic product." According to our basic rule of accounting, flows out of any box are equal to flows into the box; so the flow of funds out of the markets for goods and services to firms is equal to the total flow of funds into the markets for goods and services from other sectors. And as you can see from Figure 23-1, the total flow of funds into the markets for goods and services is total or **aggregate spending** on domestically produced final goods and services—the sum of

Inventories are stocks of goods and raw materials held to facilitate business operations.

Investment spending is spending on productive physical capital, such as machinery and construction of structures, and on changes to inventories.

Final goods and services are goods and services sold to the final, or end, user.

Intermediate goods and services are goods and services—bought from one firm by another firm—that are inputs for production of final goods and services.

Gross domestic product, or **GDP,** is the total value of all final goods and services produced in the economy during a given year.

Aggregate spending, the sum of consumer spending, investment spending, government purchases of goods and services, and exports minus imports, is the total spending on domestically produced final goods and services in the economy.

"You wouldn't think there'd be much money in potatoes, chickens, and woodchopping, but it all adds up."

consumer spending, investment spending, government purchases of goods and services, and exports minus imports. *So a second way of calculating GDP is to add up aggregate spending on domestically produced final goods and services in the economy.*

And there is yet another way of calculating GDP, based on total income earned in the economy. Firms, and the factors of production that they employ, are owned by households. So firms must ultimately pay out what they earn to households. The flow from firms to the factor markets is the factor income paid out by firms to households in the form of wages, profit, interest, and rent. Again, by accounting rules, the value of the flow of factor income from firms to households must be equal to the flow of money into firms from the markets for goods and services. And this last value, we know, is the total value of production in the economy—GDP. Why is GDP equal to the total value of factor income paid by firms in the economy to households? Because each sale in the economy must accrue to someone as income—either as wages, profit, interest, or rent. *So a third way of calculating GDP is to sum the total factor income earned by households from firms in the economy.*

Calculating GDP

We've just explained that there are in fact three methods for calculating GDP. Government statisticians use all three methods. To illustrate how these three methods work, we will consider a hypothetical economy, shown in Figure 23-2. This economy consists of three firms—American Motors, Inc., which produces one car per year; American Steel, Inc., which produces the steel that goes into the car; and American Ore, Inc., which mines the iron ore that goes into the steel. So GDP is $21,500, the value of the one car per year the economy produces. Let's look at how the three different methods of calculating GDP yield the same result.

FIGURE 23-2

Calculating GDP

In this hypothetical economy consisting of three firms, GDP can be calculated in three different ways: measuring GDP as the value of production of final goods and services, by summing each firm's value added; measuring GDP as aggregate spending on domestically produced final goods and services; and measuring GDP as factor income earned by households from firms in the economy.

Aggregate spending on domestically produced final goods and services = $21,500

	American Ore, Inc.	American Steel, Inc.	American Motors, Inc.	Total factor income
Value of sales	$4,200 (ore)	$9,000 (steel)	$21,500 (car)	
Intermediate goods	0	4,200 (iron ore)	9,000 (steel)	
Wages	2,000	3,700	10,000	$15,700
Interest payments	1,000	600	1,000	2,600
Rent	200	300	500	1,000
Profit	1,000	200	1,000	2,200
Total expenditure by firm	4,200	9,000	21,500	
Value added per firm = Value of sales – cost of intermediate goods	4,200	4,800	12,500	

Total payments to factors = $21,500

Sum of value added = $21,500

Measuring GDP as the Value of Production of Final Goods and Services

The first method for calculating GDP is to add up the value of all the final goods and services produced in the economy—a calculation that excludes the value of intermediate goods and services. Why are intermediate goods and services excluded? After all, don't they represent a very large and valuable portion of the economy?

To understand why only final goods and services are included in GDP, look at the simplified economy described in Figure 23-2. Should we measure the GDP of this economy by adding up the total sales of the iron ore producer, the steel producer, and the auto producer? If we did, we would in effect be counting the value of the steel twice—once when it is sold by the steel plant to the auto plant, and again when the steel auto body is sold to a consumer as a finished car. And we would be counting the value of the iron ore *three* times—once when it is mined and sold to the steel company, a second time when it is made into steel and sold to the auto producer, and a third time when the steel is made into a car and sold to the consumer. So counting the full value of each producer's sales would cause us to count the same items several times and artificially inflate the calculation of GDP. For example, in Figure 23-2, the total value of all sales, intermediate and final, is $34,700: $21,500 from the sale of the car, plus $9,000 from the sale of the steel, plus $4,200 from the sale of the iron ore. Yet we know that GDP is only $21,500. The way we avoid double-counting is to count only each producer's **value added** in the calculation of GDP: the difference between the value of its sales and the value of the inputs it purchases from other businesses. That is, at each stage of the production process we subtract the cost of inputs—the intermediate goods—at that stage. In this case, the value added of the auto producer is the dollar value of the cars it manufactures *minus* the cost of the steel it buys, or $12,500. The value added of the steel producer is the dollar value of the steel it produces *minus* the cost of the ore it buys, or $4,800. Only the ore producer, which we have assumed doesn't buy any inputs, has value added equal to its total sales, $4,200. The sum of the three producers' value added is $21,500, equal to GDP.

> The **value added** of a producer is the value of its sales minus the value of its purchases of inputs.

Measuring GDP as Spending on Domestically Produced Final Goods and Services

Another way to calculate GDP is by adding up aggregate spending on domestically produced final goods and services. That is, GDP can be measured by the flow of funds into firms. Like the method that estimates GDP as the value of domestic production of final goods and services, this measurement must be carried out in a way that avoids double-counting. In terms of our steel and auto example, we don't want to count both consumer spending on a car (represented in Figure 23-2 by the sales price of the car) and the auto producer's spending on steel (represented in Figure 23-2 by the price of a car's worth of steel). If we counted both, we would be

---

FOR INQUIRING MINDS

Our Imputed Lives

An old line says that when a person marries the household cook, GDP falls. And it's true: when someone provides services for pay, those services are counted as a part of GDP. But the services family members provide to each other are not. Some economists have produced alternative measures that try to "impute" the value of household work—that is, assign an estimate of what the market value of that work would have been if it had been paid for. But the standard measure of GDP doesn't contain that imputation.

GDP estimates do, however, include an imputation for the value of "owner-occupied housing." That is, if you buy the home you were formerly renting, GDP does not go down. It's true that because you no longer pay rent to your landlord, the landlord no longer sells a service to you—namely, use of the house or apartment. But the statisticians make an estimate of what you would have paid if you rented whatever you live in, whether it's an apartment or

a house. For the purposes of the statistics, it's as if you were renting your dwelling from yourself.

If you think about it, this makes a lot of sense. In a homeowning country like the United States, the pleasure we derive from our houses is an important part of the standard of living. So to be accurate, estimates of GDP must take into account the value of housing that is occupied by owners as well as the value of rental housing.

counting the steel embodied in the car twice. We solve this problem by counting only the value of sales to *final buyers,* such as consumers, firms that purchase investment goods, the government, or foreign buyers. In other words, in order to avoid double-counting of spending, we omit sales of inputs from one business to another when estimating GDP using spending data. You can see from Figure 23-2 that aggregate spending on final goods and services—the finished car—is $21,500.

As we've already pointed out, the national accounts *do* include investment spending by firms as a part of final spending. That is, an auto company's purchase of steel to make a car isn't considered a part of final spending, but the company's purchase of new machinery for its factory *is* considered a part of final spending. What's the difference? Steel is an input that is used up in production; machinery will last for a number of years. Since purchases of capital goods that will last for a considerable time aren't closely tied to current production, the national accounts consider such purchases a form of final sales.

In later chapters, we will make use of the proposition that GDP is equal to aggregate spending on domestically produced goods and services by final buyers. We will also develop models of how final buyers decide how much to spend. With that in mind, we'll now examine the types of spending that make up GDP.

Look again at the markets for goods and services in Figure 23-1, and you will see that one component of sales by firms is consumer spending. Let's denote consumer spending with the symbol C. Figure 23-1 also shows three other components of sales: sales of investment goods to other businesses, or investment spending, which we will denote by I; government purchases of goods and services, which we will denote by G; and sales to foreigners—that is, exports—which we will denote by X.

In reality, not all of this final spending goes toward domestically produced goods and services. We must take account of spending on imports, which we will denote by IM. Income spent on imports is income not spent on domestic goods and services—it is income that has "leaked" across national borders. So to accurately value domestic production using spending data, we must subtract out spending on imports. Putting this all together gives us the following equation that breaks GDP down by the four sources of aggregate spending:

(23-1) $GDP = C + I + G + X - IM$

We'll be seeing a lot of Equation 23-1 in later chapters.

PITFALLS

GDP: WHAT'S IN AND WHAT'S OUT

It's easy to confuse what is included and what isn't included in GDP. So let's stop here for a moment and make sure the distinction is clear. The most likely source of confusion is the difference between investment spending and spending on inputs. Investment spending—spending on productive physical capital, construction of structures (residential as well as commercial), and changes to inventories—is included in GDP. But spending on inputs is not. Why the difference? Recall from Chapter 2 that we made a distinction between resources that are *used up* and those that are *not used up* in production. An input, like steel, is used up in production. A metal-stamping machine, an investment good, is not. It will last for many years and will be used repeatedly to make many cars. Since spending on productive physical

capital—investment goods—and construction of structures is not directly tied to current output, economists consider such spending to be spending on final goods. Spending on changes to inventories is considered a part of investment spending, so it is also included in GDP. Why? Because, like a machine, additional inventory is an investment in future sales. And when a good is released for sale from inventories, its value is subtracted from the value of inventories and so from GDP. Used goods are not included in GDP because, as with inputs, to include them would be to double-count: counting them once when sold as new and again when sold as used.

Also, financial assets such as stocks and bonds are not included in GDP because they don't represent either the production or the sale of final goods and services.

Rather, a bond represents a promise to repay with interest, and a stock represents a proof of ownership. And for obvious reasons, foreign-produced goods and services are not included in calculations of GDP.

Here is a summary of what's included and not included in GDP:

Included

- Domestically produced final goods and services, including capital goods, new construction of structures, and changes to inventories

Not Included

- Intermediate goods and services
- Inputs
- Used goods
- Financial assets like stocks and bonds
- Foreign-produced goods and services

Measuring GDP as Factor Income Earned from Firms in the Economy A final way to calculate GDP is to add up all the income earned by factors of production from firms in the economy—the wages earned by labor; the interest earned by those who lend their savings to firms and the government; the rent earned by those who lease their land or structures to firms; and the profit earned by the shareholders, the owners of the firms' physical capital. This is a valid measure because the money firms earn by selling goods and services must go somewhere; whatever isn't paid as wages, interest, or rent is profit. And part of profit is paid out to shareholders as *dividends*.

Figure 23-2 shows how this calculation works for our simplified economy. The shaded column at the far right shows the total wages, interest, and rent paid by all these firms as well as their total profit. Summing up all of these yields total factor income of $21,500—again, equal to GDP.

We won't emphasize factor income as much as the other two methods of calculating GDP. It's important to keep in mind, however, that all the money spent on domestically produced goods and services generates factor income to households—that is, there really is a circular flow.

The Components of GDP Now that we know how GDP is calculated in principle, let's see what it looks like in practice.

Figure 23-3 shows the first two methods of calculating GDP side by side. The height of each bar above the horizontal axis represents the GDP of the U.S. economy in 2007: $13,808 billion. Each bar is divided to show the breakdown of that total in terms of where the value was added and how the money was spent.

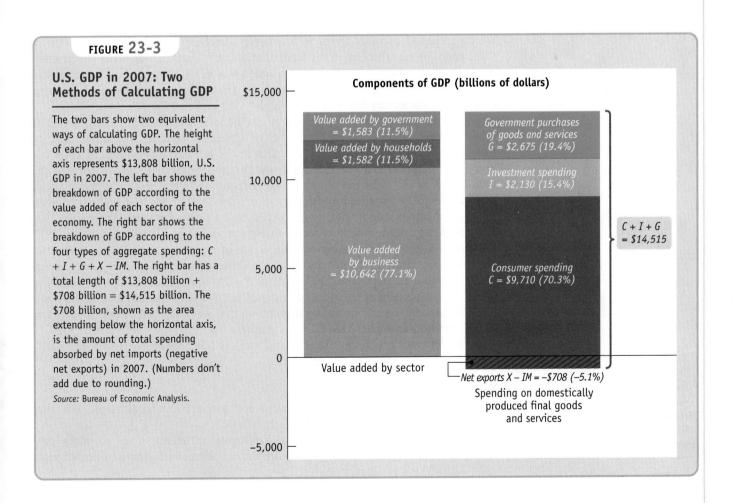

FIGURE 23-3

U.S. GDP in 2007: Two Methods of Calculating GDP

The two bars show two equivalent ways of calculating GDP. The height of each bar above the horizontal axis represents $13,808 billion, U.S. GDP in 2007. The left bar shows the breakdown of GDP according to the value added of each sector of the economy. The right bar shows the breakdown of GDP according to the four types of aggregate spending: $C + I + G + X - IM$. The right bar has a total length of $13,808 billion + $708 billion = $14,515 billion. The $708 billion, shown as the area extending below the horizontal axis, is the amount of total spending absorbed by net imports (negative net exports) in 2007. (Numbers don't add due to rounding.)

Source: Bureau of Economic Analysis.

Components of GDP (billions of dollars)

Value added by government = $1,583 (11.5%)
Value added by households = $1,582 (11.5%)
Value added by business = $10,642 (77.1%)

Government purchases of goods and services $G = $2,675 (19.4%)$
Investment spending $I = $2,130 (15.4%)$
Consumer spending $C = $9,710 (70.3%)$

$C + I + G = $14,515$

Value added by sector

Net exports $X - IM = -$708 (-5.1%)$

Spending on domestically produced final goods and services

Gross What?

Occasionally you may see references not to gross domestic product but to gross *national* product, or GNP. Is this just another name for the same thing? Not quite.

If you look at Figure 23-1 carefully, you may realize that there's a possibility that is missing from the figure. According to the figure, all factor income goes to domestic households. But what happens when profits are paid to foreigners who own stock in General Motors or Microsoft? And where do the profits earned by American companies operating overseas fit in?

To answer these questions, an alternative measure, GNP, was devised. GNP is defined as the total factor income earned by residents of a country. It *excludes* factor income earned by foreigners, like profits

paid to foreign investors who own American stocks and payments to foreigners who work temporarily in the United States. And it *includes* factor income earned abroad by Americans, like the profits of IBM's European operations that accrue to IBM's American shareholders and the wages of Americans who work abroad temporarily.

In the early days of national income accounting, economists usually used GNP rather than GDP as a measure of the economy's size—although the measures were generally very close to each other. They switched to GDP mainly because it's considered a better indicator of short-run movements in production and because data on international flows of factor income are considered somewhat unreliable.

In practice, it doesn't make much difference which measure is used for large economies like that of the United States, where the flows of net factor income to other countries are relatively small. In 2007, America's GNP was about 0.7% larger than its GDP, mainly because of the overseas profit of U.S. companies. For smaller countries, however, GDP and GNP can diverge significantly. For example, much of Ireland's industry is owned by American corporations, whose profit must be deducted from Ireland's GNP. In addition, Ireland has become a host to many temporary workers from poorer regions of Europe, whose wages must also be deducted from Ireland's GNP. As a result, in 2007 Ireland's GNP was only 85% of its GDP.

In the left bar in Figure 23-3, we see the breakdown of GDP by value added according to sector, the first method of calculating GDP. Of the $13,808 billion, $10,642 billion consisted of value added by businesses. Another $1,583 billion consisted of value added by government, in the form of military, education, and other government services. Finally, $1,582 billion of value added was added by households and institutions; a large part of that was the imputed services of owner-occupied housing, described in the earlier For Inquiring Minds "Our Imputed Lives."

The right bar in Figure 23-3 corresponds to the second method of calculating GDP, showing the breakdown by the four types of aggregate spending. The total length of the right bar is longer than the total length of the left bar, a difference of $708 billion (which, as you can see, extends below the horizontal axis). That's because the total length of the right bar represents total spending in the economy, spending on both domestically produced and foreign-produced final goods and services. Within the bar, consumer spending (C), which is 70.3% of GDP, dominates the picture. But some of that spending was absorbed by foreign-produced goods and services. In 2007, **net exports,** the difference between the value of exports and the value of imports ($X - IM$ in Equation 23-1) was negative—the United States was a net importer of foreign goods and services. The 2007 value of $X - IM$ was −$708 billion, or −5.1% of GDP. Thus, a portion of the right bar extends below the horizontal axis by $708 billion to represent the amount of total spending that was absorbed by net imports and so did not lead to higher U.S. GDP. Investment spending (I) constituted 15.4% of GDP; government purchases of goods and services (G) constituted 19.4% of GDP.

What GDP Tells Us

Now we've seen the various ways that gross domestic product is calculated. But what does the measurement of GDP tell us?

The most important use of GDP is as a measure of the size of the economy, providing us a scale against which to measure the economic performance of other years

Net exports are the difference between the value of exports and the value of imports.

or to compare the economic performance of other countries. For example, suppose you want to compare the economies of different nations. A natural approach is to compare their GDPs. In 2007, as we've seen, U.S. GDP was $13,808 billion, Japan's GDP was $4,383 billion, and the combined GDP of the 25 countries that make up the European Union was $16,830 billion. This comparison tells us that Japan, although it has the world's second-largest national economy, carries considerably less economic weight than does the United States. When taken in aggregate, Europe is America's equal or superior.

Still, one must be careful when using GDP numbers, especially when making comparisons over time. That's because part of the increase in the value of GDP over time represents increases in the *prices* of goods and services rather than an increase in output. For example, U.S. GDP was $6,657 billion in 1997 and had more than doubled to $13,808 billion by 2007. But the U.S. economy didn't actually double in size over that period. To measure actual changes in aggregate output, we need a modified version of GDP that is adjusted for price changes, known as *real GDP*. We'll see next how real GDP is calculated.

►ECONOMICS IN ACTION

Creating the National Accounts

The national accounts, like modern macroeconomics, owe their creation to the Great Depression. As the economy plunged into depression, government officials found their ability to respond crippled not only by the lack of adequate economic theories but also by the lack of adequate information. All they had were scattered statistics: railroad freight car loadings, stock prices, and incomplete indexes of industrial production. They could only guess at what was happening to the economy as a whole.

In response to this perceived lack of information, the Department of Commerce commissioned Simon Kuznets, a young Russian-born economist, to develop a set of national income accounts. (Kuznets later won the Nobel Prize in Economics for his work.) The first version of these accounts was presented to Congress in 1937 and in a research report titled *National Income, 1929-35*.

Kuznets's initial estimates fell short of the full modern set of accounts because they focused on income, not production. The push to complete the national accounts came during World War II, when policy makers were in even more need of comprehensive measures of the economy's performance. The federal government began issuing estimates of gross domestic product and gross national product in 1942.

In January 2000, in its publication *Survey of Current Business*, the Department of Commerce ran an article titled "GDP: One of the Great Inventions of the 20th Century." This may seem a bit over the top, but national income accounting, invented in the United States, has since become a tool of economic analysis and policy making around the world. ▲   > > > > > > > > > > > >

► CHECK YOUR UNDERSTANDING 23-1

1. Explain why the three methods of calculating GDP produce the same estimate of GDP.

2. What are the various sectors to which firms make sales? What are the various ways in which households are linked with other sectors of the economy?

3. Consider Figure 23-2 and suppose you mistakenly believed that total value added was $30,500, the sum of the sales price of a car and a car's worth of steel. What items would you be counting twice?

Solutions appear at back of book.

Aggregate output is the economy's total quantity of output of final goods and services.

Real GDP: A Measure of Aggregate Output

In this chapter's opening story we described the economic troubles that afflicted Portugal in 1975. While the economy wasn't in as bad shape as many people thought, output was declining. Strange to say, however, GDP was up. In fact, Portugal's GDP measured in escudos (the national currency at the time, now replaced by the euro) rose 11% between 1974 and 1975.

How was that possible? The answer is that serious inflation was a problem in Portugal at the time. As a result, the escudo value of GDP rose even though output fell.

The moral of this story is that the commonly cited GDP number is an interesting and useful statistic, one that provides a good way to compare the size of different economies, but it's not a good measure of the economy's growth over time. GDP can grow because the economy grows, but it can also grow simply because of inflation. Even if an economy's output doesn't change, GDP will go up if the prices of the goods and services the economy produces have increased. Likewise, GDP can fall either because the economy is producing less or because prices have fallen.

In order to accurately measure the economy's growth, we need a measure of **aggregate output:** the total quantity of final goods and services the economy produces. The measure that is used for this purpose is known as *real GDP*. By tracking real GDP over time, we avoid the problem of changes in prices distorting the value of changes in production of goods and services over time. Let's look first at how real GDP is calculated, then at what it means.

Calculating Real GDP

To understand how real GDP is calculated, imagine an economy in which only two goods, apples and oranges, are produced and in which both goods are sold only to final consumers. The outputs and prices of the two fruits for two consecutive years are shown in Table 23-1.

The first thing we can say about these data is that the value of sales increased from year 1 to year 2. In the first year, the total value of sales was (2,000 billion × $0.25) + (1,000 billion × $0.50) = $1,000 billion; in the second it was (2,200 billion × $0.30) + (1,200 billion × $0.70) = $1,500 billion, which is 50% larger. But it is also clear from the table that this increase in the dollar value of GDP overstates the real growth in the economy. Although the quantities of both apples and oranges increased, the prices of both apples and oranges also rose. So part of the 50% increase in the dollar value of GDP simply reflects higher prices, not higher production of output.

To estimate the true increase in aggregate output produced, we have to ask the following question: how much would GDP have gone up if prices had *not* changed? To answer this question, we need to find the value of output in year 2 expressed in year 1 prices. In year 1 the price of apples was $0.25 each and the price of oranges $0.50

TABLE 23-1

Calculating GDP and Real GDP in a Simple Economy

	Year 1	Year 2
Quantity of apples (billions)	2,000	2,200
Price of apple	$0.25	$0.30
Quantity of oranges (billions)	1,000	1,200
Price of orange	$0.50	$0.70
GDP (billions of dollars)	1,000	1,500
Real GDP (billions of year 1 dollars)	$1,000	$1,150

each. So year 2 output *at year 1 prices* is (2,200 billion × $0.25) + (1,200 billion × $0.50) = $1,150 billion. And output in year 1 at year 1 prices was $1,000 billion. So in this example GDP measured in year 1 prices rose 15%—from $1,000 billion to $1,150 billion.

Now we can define **real GDP:** it is the total value of final goods and services produced in the economy during a year, calculated as if prices had stayed constant at the level of some given base year. A real GDP number always comes with information about what the base year is. A GDP number that has not been adjusted for changes in prices is calculated using the prices in the year in which the output is produced. Economists call this measure **nominal GDP,** GDP at current prices. If we had used nominal GDP to measure the true change in output from year 1 to year 2 in our apples and oranges example, we would have overstated the true growth in output: we would have claimed it to be 50%, when in fact it was only 15%. By comparing output in the two years using a common set of prices—the year 1 prices in this example—we are able to focus solely on changes in the quantity of output by eliminating the influence of changes in prices.

Table 23-2 shows a real-life version of our apples and oranges example. The second column shows nominal GDP in 1993, 2000, and 2007. The third column shows real GDP for each year in 2000 dollars. For 2000 the two numbers are the same. But real GDP in 1993 expressed in 2000 dollars was higher than nominal GDP in 1993, reflecting the fact that prices were in general higher in 2000 than in 1993. Real GDP in 2007 expressed in 2000 dollars, however, was less than nominal GDP in 2007 because prices in 2000 were lower than in 2007.

You might have noticed that there is an alternative way to calculate real GDP using the data in Table 23-1. Why not measure it using the prices of year 2 rather than year 1 as the base-year prices? This procedure seems equally valid. According to that calculation, real GDP in year 1 at year 2 prices is (2,000 billion × $0.30) + (1,000 billion × $0.70) = $1,300 billion; real GDP in year 2 at year 2 prices is $1,500 billion, the same as nominal GDP in year 2. So using year 2 prices as the base year, the growth rate of real GDP is equal to ($1,500 billion − $1,300 billion)/$1,300 billion = 0.154, or 15.4%. This is slightly higher than the figure we got from the previous calculation, in which year 1 prices were the base-year prices. In that calculation, we found that real GDP increased by 15%. Neither answer, 15.4% versus 15%, is more "correct" than the other. In reality, the government economists who put together the U.S. national accounts have adopted a method to measure the change in real GDP known as chain-linking, which uses the average between the GDP growth rate calculated using an early base year and the GDP growth rate calculated using a late base year. As a result, U.S. statistics on real GDP are always expressed in **chained dollars.**

> **Real GDP** is the total value of all final goods and services produced in the economy during a given year, calculated using the prices of a selected base year.
>
> **Nominal GDP** is the value of all final goods and services produced in the economy during a given year, calculated using the prices current in the year in which the output is produced.
>
> **Chained dollars** is the method of calculating changes in real GDP using the average between the growth rate calculated using an early base year and the growth rate calculated using a late base year.
>
> **GDP per capita** is GDP divided by the size of the population; it is equivalent to the average GDP per person.

TABLE 23-2

Nominal versus Real GDP in 1993, 2000, and 2007

	Nominal GDP (billions of current dollars)	Real GDP (billions of 2000 dollars)
1993	$6,657	$7,533
2000	9,817	9,817
2007	13,808	11,524

Source: Bureau of Economic Analysis.

What Real GDP Doesn't Measure

GDP is a measure of a country's aggregate output. Other things equal, a country with a larger population will have higher GDP simply because there are more people working. So if we want to compare GDP across countries but want to eliminate the effect of differences in population size, we use the measure **GDP per capita**—GDP divided by the size of the population, equivalent to the average GDP per person. Correspondingly, real GDP per capita is the average real GDP per person.

Real GDP per capita can be a useful measure in some circumstances, such as in a comparison of labor productivity between countries. However, despite the fact that it is a rough measure of the average real output per person, real GDP per capita has well-known limitations as a measure of a country's living standards. Every once in a while economists are accused of believing that growth in real GDP per capita is the only thing that matters—that is, thinking that increasing real GDP per capita is a goal in itself. In fact, economists rarely make that mistake; the idea that economists care only about real GDP per capita is a sort of urban legend. Let's take a moment to be clear about why a country's real GDP per capita is not a sufficient measure of human welfare in that country and why growth in real GDP per capita is not an appropriate policy goal in itself.

One way to think about this issue is to say that an increase in real GDP means an expansion in the economy's production possibility frontier. Because the economy has increased its productive capacity, there are more things that society can achieve. But whether society actually makes good use of that increased potential to improve living standards is another matter. To put it in a slightly different way, your income may be higher this year than last year, but whether you use that higher income to actually improve your quality of life is your choice.

So let's say it again: real GDP per capita is a measure of an economy's average aggregate output per person—and so of what it *can* do. It is not a sufficient goal in itself because it doesn't address how a country uses that output to affect living standards. A country with a high GDP can afford to be healthy, to be well educated, and in general to have a good quality of life. But there is not a one-to-one match between GDP and the quality of life.

GLOBAL COMPARISON GDP AND THE MEANING OF LIFE

"I've been rich and I've been poor," the actress Mae West famously declared. "Believe me, rich is better." But is the same true for countries?

This figure shows two pieces of information for a number of countries: how rich they are, as measured by GDP per capita, and how satisfied people are with their lives. Life satisfaction was measured by a Gallup world survey that asked people how they feel about their lives on a scale from 0—the worst possible life they could imagine—to 10—the best possible life they could imagine. The figure seems to tell us three things:

1. *Rich is better.* Richer countries on average have higher life satisfaction than poor countries.

2. *Money matters less as you grow richer.* The gain in life satisfaction as you go from GDP per capita of $5,000 to $20,000 is greater than the gain as you go from $20,000 to $35,000.

3. *Money isn't everything.* Danes, though rich by world standards, are poorer than Americans—but they seem more satisfied with their lives. Russia is richer than most Latin American nations, but much more miserable.

These results are consistent with the observation that high GDP per capita makes it easier to achieve a good life but that countries aren't equally successful in taking advantage of that possibility.

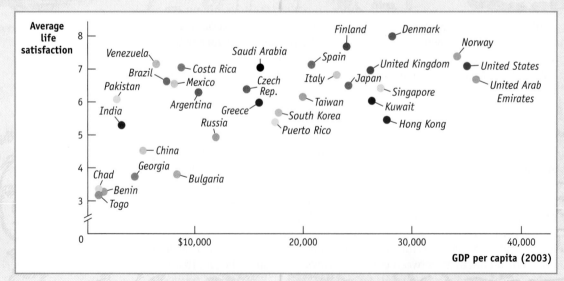

Source: Deaton, A. (2008), "Income, Health, and Well-Being around the World: Evidence from the Gallup World Poll," *Journal of Economic Perspectives*, 22(2), 53–72.

►ECONOMICS IN ACTION

Miracle in Venezuela?

The South American nation of Venezuela has a distinction that may surprise you: in recent years, it has had one of the world's fastest-growing nominal GDPs. Between 1997 and 2007, Venezuelan nominal GDP grew by an average of 28% each year—much faster than nominal GDP in the United States or even in booming economies like China.

So is Venezuela experiencing an economic miracle? No, it's just suffering from unusually high inflation. Figure 23-4 shows Venezuela's nominal and real GDP from

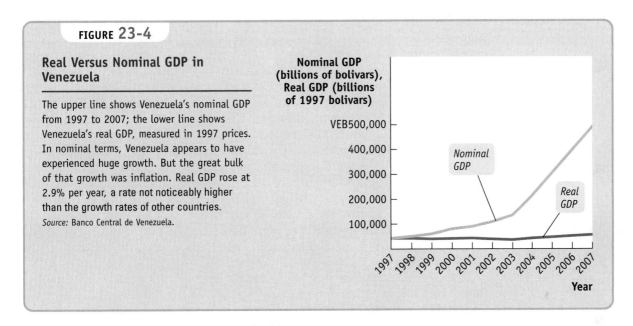

FIGURE 23-4

Real Versus Nominal GDP in Venezuela

The upper line shows Venezuela's nominal GDP from 1997 to 2007; the lower line shows Venezuela's real GDP, measured in 1997 prices. In nominal terms, Venezuela appears to have experienced huge growth. But the great bulk of that growth was inflation. Real GDP rose at 2.9% per year, a rate not noticeably higher than the growth rates of other countries.

Source: Banco Central de Venezuela.

1997 to 2007, with real GDP measured in 1997 prices. Real GDP did grow over the period, but at an annual rate of only 2.9%. That's about the same as the U.S. growth rate over the same period and far short of China's 9% growth. ▲

> > > > > > > > > > >

► CHECK YOUR UNDERSTANDING 23-2

1. Assume there are only two goods in the economy, french fries and onion rings. In 2006, 1,000,000 servings of french fries were sold at $0.40 each and 800,000 servings of onion rings at $0.60 each. From 2006 to 2007, the price of french fries rose by 25% and the servings sold fell by 10%; the price of onion rings fell by 15% and the servings sold rose by 5%.
   a. Calculate nominal GDP in 2006 and 2007. Calculate real GDP in 2007 using 2006 prices.
   b. Why would an assessment of growth using nominal GDP be misguided?

2. From 1990 to 2000, the price of electronic equipment fell dramatically and the price of housing rose dramatically. What are the implications of this in deciding whether to use 1990 or 2000 as the base year in calculating 2007 real GDP?

Solutions appear at back of book.

> **►►QUICK REVIEW**
>
> ➤ To determine the actual growth in **aggregate output,** we calculate **real GDP** using prices from some given base year. In contrast, **nominal GDP** refers to the value of aggregate output calculated with current prices. U.S. statistics on real GDP are always expressed in **chained dollars.**
> ➤ Real **GDP per capita** is a measure of the average aggregate output per person. But it is not a sufficient measure of human welfare, nor is it an appropriate goal in itself, because it does not reflect important aspects of living standards within an economy.

Price Indexes and the Aggregate Price Level

In the summer of 2008, Americans were facing sticker shock at the gas pump: the price of a gallon of regular gasoline had risen from about $3 in late 2007 to more than $4 in most places. Many other prices were also up. Some prices, though, were heading down: some foods, like eggs, were coming down from a run-up earlier in the

The **aggregate price level** is a measure of the overall level of prices in the economy.

A **market basket** is a hypothetical set of consumer purchases of goods and services.

A **price index** measures the cost of purchasing a given market basket in a given year, where that cost is normalized so that it is equal to 100 in the selected base year.

year, and virtually anything involving electronics was getting cheaper as well. Yet, practically everyone felt that the overall cost of living was rising. But how fast?

Clearly, there was a need for a single number summarizing what was happening to consumer prices. Just as macroeconomists find it useful to have a single number representing the overall level of output, they also find it useful to have a single number representing the overall level of prices: the **aggregate price level.** Yet a huge variety of goods and services are produced and consumed in the economy. How can we summarize the prices of all these goods and services with a single number? The answer lies in the concept of a *price index*—a concept best introduced with an example.

Market Baskets and Price Indexes

Suppose that a frost in Florida destroys most of the citrus harvest. As a result, the price of oranges rises from $0.20 each to $0.40 each, the price of grapefruit rises from $0.60 to $1.00, and the price of lemons rises from $0.25 to $0.45. How much has the price of citrus fruit increased?

One way to answer that question is to state three numbers—the changes in prices for oranges, grapefruit, and lemons. But this is a very cumbersome method. Rather than having to recite three numbers in an effort to track changes in the prices of citrus fruit, we would prefer to have some kind of overall measure of the *average* price change.

To measure average price changes for consumer goods and services, economists track changes in the cost of a typical consumer's *consumption bundle*—the typical basket of goods and services purchased before the price changes. A hypothetical consumption bundle, used to measure changes in the overall price level, is known as a **market basket.** Suppose that before the frost a typical consumer bought 200 oranges, 50 grapefruit, and 100 lemons over the course of a year, our market basket for this example.

Table 23-3 shows the pre-frost and post-frost cost of this market basket. Before the frost, it cost $95; after the frost, the same bundle of goods cost $175. Since $175/$95 = 1.842, the post-frost basket costs 1.842 times the cost of the pre-frost basket, a cost increase of 84.2%. In this example, the average price of citrus fruit has increased 84.2% since the base year as a result of the frost, where the base year is the initial year used in the measurement of the price change.

TABLE 23-3

Calculating the Cost of a Market Basket

	Pre-frost	Post-frost
Price of orange	$0.20	$0.40
Price of grapefruit	0.60	1.00
Price of lemon	0.25	0.45
Cost of market basket (200 oranges, 50 grapefruit, 100 lemons)	(200 × $0.20) + (50 × $0.60) + (100 × $0.25) = $95.00	(200 × $0.40) + (50 × $1.00) + (100 × $0.45) = $175.00

Economists use the same method to measure changes in the overall price level: they track changes in the cost of buying a given market basket. In addition, they perform another simplification in order to avoid having to keep track of the information that the market basket cost, for example, $95 in such-and-such a year. They *normalize* the measure of the aggregate price level—that is, they set the cost of the market basket equal to 100 in the chosen base year. Working with a market basket and a base year, and after performing normalization, we obtain what is known as a **price index,** a normalized measure of the overall price level. It is always cited along with the year for which the aggregate price level is being measured and the base year. A price index can be calculated using the following formula:

(23-2) Price index in a given year = $\dfrac{\text{Cost of market basket in a given year}}{\text{Cost of market basket in base year}} \times 100$

In our example, the citrus fruit market basket cost $95 in the base year, the year before the frost. So by Equation 23-2 we define the price index for citrus fruit as (cost of market basket in current year/$95) × 100, yielding an index of 100 for the period before the frost and 184.2 after the frost. You should note that applying Equation 23-2 to calculate the price index for the base year always results in a price index equal to 100. That is, the price index in the base year is equal to: (cost of market basket in base year/cost of market basket in base year) × 100 = 100.

Thus, the price index makes it clear that the average price of citrus has risen 84.2% as a consequence of the frost. Because of its simplicity and intuitive appeal, the method we've just described is used to calculate a variety of price indexes to track average price changes among a variety of different groups of goods and services. For example, the *consumer price index,* which we'll discuss shortly, is the most widely used measure of the aggregate price level, the overall price level of final consumer goods and services across the economy. Price indexes are also the basis for measuring inflation. The **inflation rate** is the annual percent change in an official price index. The inflation rate from year 1 to year 2 is calculated using the following formula, where we assume that year 1 and year 2 are consecutive years.

(23-3) Inflation rate = $\dfrac{\text{Price index in year 2} - \text{Price index in year 1}}{\text{Price index in year 1}} \times 100$

Typically, a news report that cites "the inflation rate" is referring to the annual percent change in the consumer price index.

The Consumer Price Index

The most widely used measure of prices in the United States is the **consumer price index** (often referred to simply as the **CPI**), which is intended to show how the cost of all purchases by a typical urban family has changed over time. It is calculated by surveying market prices for a market basket that is constructed to represent the consumption of a typical family of four living in a typical American city. The base period for the index is currently 1982–1984; that is, the index is calculated so that the average of consumer prices in 1982–1984 is 100.

The market basket used to calculate the CPI is far more complex than the three-fruit market basket we described above. In fact, to calculate the CPI, the Bureau of Labor Statistics sends its employees out to survey supermarkets, gas stations, hardware stores, and so on—some 23,000 retail outlets in 87 cities. Every month it tabulates about 80,000 prices, on everything from romaine lettuce to video rentals. Figure 23-5 shows the weight of major categories in the consumer price index as of December 2007. For example, motor fuel, mainly gasoline, accounted for 7% of the CPI in December 2007. So when gas prices rose by a third, from about $3 a gallon in late 2007 to about $4 a gallon in mid-2008, the effect was to increase the CPI by about a third of 7%—that is, around 2.5%.

Figure 23-6 on the next page shows how the CPI has changed since measurement began in 1913. Since 1940, the CPI has risen steadily, although its annual percent increases in recent years have been much smaller than those of the 1970s and early 1980s. A logarithmic scale is used so that equal percent changes in the CPI appear the same.

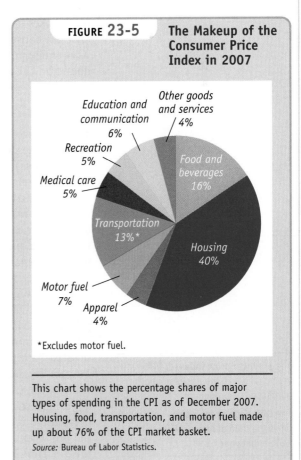

FIGURE 23-5 **The Makeup of the Consumer Price Index in 2007**

Education and communication 6%

Other goods and services 4%

Recreation 5%

Food and beverages 16%

Medical care 5%

Transportation 13%*

Housing 40%

Motor fuel 7%

Apparel 4%

*Excludes motor fuel.

This chart shows the percentage shares of major types of spending in the CPI as of December 2007. Housing, food, transportation, and motor fuel made up about 76% of the CPI market basket.

Source: Bureau of Labor Statistics.

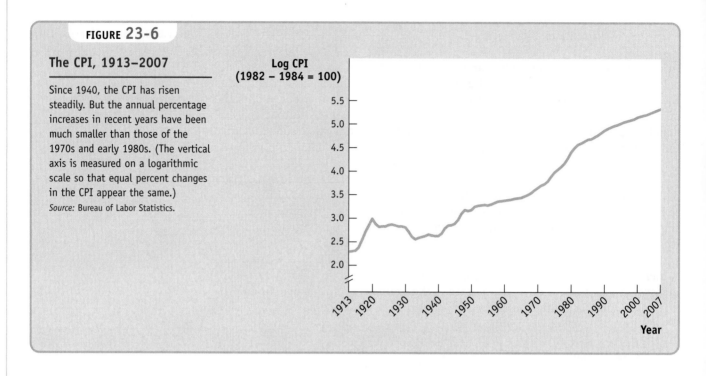

FIGURE 23-6

The CPI, 1913–2007

Since 1940, the CPI has risen steadily. But the annual percentage increases in recent years have been much smaller than those of the 1970s and early 1980s. (The vertical axis is measured on a logarithmic scale so that equal percent changes in the CPI appear the same.)
Source: Bureau of Labor Statistics.

The United States is not the only country that calculates a consumer price index. In fact, nearly every country has one. As you might expect, the market baskets that make up these indexes differ quite a lot from country to country. In poor countries, where people must spend a high proportion of their income just to feed themselves, food makes up a large share of the price index. Among high-income countries, differences in consumption patterns lead to differences in the price indexes: the Japanese price index puts a larger weight on raw fish and a smaller weight on beef than ours does, and the French price index puts a larger weight on wine.

Other Price Measures

There are two other price measures that are also widely used to track economy-wide price changes. One is the **producer price index** (or **PPI,** which used to be known as the *wholesale price index*). As its name suggests, the producer price index measures the cost of a typical basket of goods and services—containing raw commodities such as steel, electricity, coal, and so on—purchased by producers. Because commodity producers are relatively quick to raise prices when they perceive a change in overall demand for their goods, the PPI often responds to inflationary or deflationary pressures more quickly than the CPI. As a result, the PPI is often regarded as an "early warning signal" of changes in the inflation rate.

The other widely used price measure is the *GDP deflator;* it isn't exactly a price index, although it serves the same purpose. Recall how we distinguished between nominal GDP (GDP in current prices) and real GDP (GDP calculated using the prices of a base year). The **GDP deflator** for a given year is equal to 100 times the ratio of nominal GDP for that year to real GDP for that year expressed in prices of a selected base year. Since real GDP is currently expressed in 2000 dollars, the GDP deflator for 2000 is equal to 100. If nominal GDP doubles but real GDP does not change, the GDP deflator indicates that the aggregate price level doubled.

Perhaps the most important point about the different inflation rates generated by these three measures of prices is that they usually move closely together (although the producer price index tends to fluctuate more than either of the other two measures). Figure 23-7 shows the annual percent changes in the three indexes since 1930.

The **producer price index,** or **PPI,** measures changes in the prices of goods purchased by producers.

The **GDP deflator** for a given year is 100 times the ratio of nominal GDP to real GDP in that year.

FIGURE 23-7

The CPI, the PPI, and the GDP Deflator

As the figure shows, these three different measures of inflation usually move closely together. Each reveals a drastic acceleration of inflation during the 1970s and a return to relative price stability in the 1990s.

Sources: Bureau of Labor Statistics; Bureau of Economic Analysis.

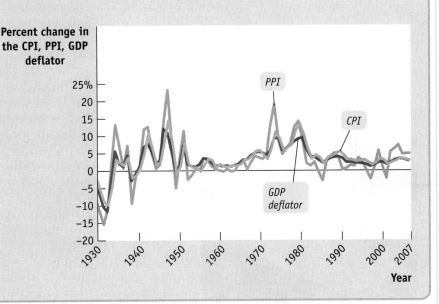

By all three measures, the U.S. economy experienced deflation during the early years of the Great Depression, inflation during World War II, accelerating inflation during the 1970s, and a return to relative price stability in the 1990s. Notice, by the way, the surge in producer prices at the very end of the graph; this reflects a sharp rise in energy and food prices, which play a much bigger role in the PPI than they do in either the CPI or the GDP deflator.

FOR INQUIRING MINDS

Is the CPI Biased?

The U.S. government takes considerable care in measuring consumer prices. Nonetheless, many—but not all—economists believe that the consumer price index systematically overstates the actual rate of inflation. Because many government payments are tied to the CPI, this is an important feature if true.

What do we mean by saying that the CPI overstates inflation? Imagine comparing two families: one in 1985, with an after-tax income of $20,000, and another in 2008, with an after-tax income of $40,000. According to the CPI, prices in 2008 were about twice as high as in 1985, so those two families should have about the same standard of living. Many economists argue, however, that the 2008 family would have a higher standard of living for two reasons.

One reason is the fact that the CPI measures the cost of buying a given market basket. Yet, consumers typically alter the mix of goods and services they buy, reducing purchases of products that have become relatively more expensive and increasing purchases of products that have become relatively cheaper. For example, suppose that the price of hamburgers suddenly doubles. Americans currently eat a lot of burgers, but in the face of such a price rise many of them would switch to other foods. A price index based on a market basket with a lot of hamburgers in it would overstate the true rise in the cost of living.

Actual changes in prices and in the mix of goods and services Americans consume are usually less dramatic than our hypothetical example. But the changing mix of consumption probably leads to some overstatement of inflation by the CPI.

The second reason arises from innovation. In 1985 many goods we now take for granted, especially those using information technology, didn't exist: there was no Internet and there were no iPods. By widening the range of consumer choice, innovation makes a given amount of money worth more. That is, innovation is like a fall in consumer prices.

For both these reasons, many economists believe that the CPI somewhat overstates inflation when we think of inflation as measuring the actual change in the cost of living of a typical urban American family. But there is no consensus on how large the bias is, and for the time being the official CPI remains the basis for most estimates of inflation.

►ECONOMICS IN ACTION

Indexing to the CPI

Although GDP is a very important number for shaping economic policy, official statistics on GDP don't have a direct effect on people's lives. The CPI, by contrast, has a direct and immediate impact on millions of Americans. The reason is that many payments are tied, or "indexed," to the CPI—the amount paid rises or falls when the CPI rises or falls.

A small change in the CPI has large consequences for those dependent on Social Security payments.

The practice of indexing payments to consumer prices goes back to the dawn of the United States as a nation. In 1780 the Massachusetts State Legislature recognized that the pay of its soldiers fighting the British needed to be increased because of inflation that occurred during the Revolutionary War. The legislature adopted a formula that made a soldier's pay proportional to the cost of a market basket, consisting of 5 bushels of corn, 68 4/7 pounds of beef, 10 pounds of sheep's wool, and 16 pounds of sole leather.

Today, 48 million people, most of them old or disabled, receive checks from Social Security, a national retirement program that accounts for almost a quarter of current total federal spending—more than the defense budget. The amount of an individual's check is determined by a formula that reflects his or her previous payments into the system as well as other factors. In addition, all Social Security payments are adjusted each year to offset any increase in consumer prices over the previous year. The CPI is used to calculate the official estimate of the inflation rate used to adjust these payments yearly. So every percentage point added to the official estimate of the rate of inflation adds 1% to the checks received by tens of millions of individuals.

Other government payments are also indexed to the CPI. In addition, income tax brackets, the bands of income levels that determine a taxpayer's income tax rate, are also indexed to the CPI. (An individual in a higher income bracket pays a higher income tax rate in a progressive tax system like ours.) Indexing also extends to the private sector, where many private contracts, including some wage settlements, contain cost-of-living allowances (called COLAs) that adjust payments in proportion to changes in the CPI.

Because the CPI plays such an important and direct role in people's lives, it's a politically sensitive number. The Bureau of Labor Statistics, which calculates the CPI, takes great care in collecting and interpreting price and consumption data. It uses a complex method in which households are surveyed to determine what they buy and where they shop, and a carefully selected sample of stores are surveyed to get representative prices.

As explained in the preceding For Inquiring Minds, however, there is still considerable controversy about whether the CPI accurately measures inflation. ▲

< < < < < < < < < < < <

►►QUICK REVIEW

- ➤ Changes in the **aggregate price level** are measured by the cost of buying a particular **market basket** during different years. A **price index** for a given year is the cost of the market basket in that year normalized so that the price index equals 100 in a selected base year.
- ➤ The **inflation rate** is calculated as the percent change in a price index. The most commonly used price index is the **consumer price index, or CPI,** which tracks the cost of a basket of consumer goods and services. The **producer price index, or PPI,** does the same for goods and services used as inputs by firms. The **GDP deflator** measures the aggregate price level as the ratio of nominal to real GDP times 100. These three measures normally behave quite similarly.

► CHECK YOUR UNDERSTANDING 23-3

1. Consider Table 23-3 but suppose that the market basket is composed of 100 oranges, 50 grapefruit, and 200 lemons. How does this change the pre-frost and post-frost price indexes? Explain. Generalize your explanation to how the construction of the market basket affects the price index.

2. For each of the following events, how would an economist using a 10-year-old market basket create a bias in measuring the change in prices today?
   a. A typical family owns more cars than it would have a decade ago. Over that time, the average price of a car has increased more than the average prices of other goods.

Donald A. Higgs Photography

b. Virtually no households had broadband Internet access a decade ago. Now many households have it, and the price has regularly fallen each year.

3. The consumer price index in the United States (base period 1982–1984) was 201.6 in 2006 and 207.3 in 2007. Calculate the inflation rate from 2006 to 2007.

Solutions appear at back of book.

⟩⟩ A LOOK AHEAD •••

We have now seen how economists put actual numbers to aggregate output and the aggregate price level.

In addition to measures of GDP and inflation, a number of other measures help us track the performance of the economy. One extremely important statistic for economic policy is the unemployment rate because unemployment leads to lost output and lower social welfare. Cases of very high unemployment, such as in a depression, often lead to political unrest.

Inflation also imposes costs on society and can lead to political and social unrest. Governments often must choose whether to fight inflation or unemployment. As a result, these two issues have become an important focus for macroeconomists. In the next chapter, we explore these two issues in detail.]

SUMMARY

1. Economists keep track of the flows of money between sectors with the **national income and product accounts,** or **national accounts.** Households earn income via the factor markets from wages, interest on **bonds,** profit accruing to owners of **stocks,** and rent on land. In addition, they receive **government transfers** from the government. **Disposable income,** total household income minus taxes plus government transfers, is allocated to **consumer spending** (C) and **private savings.** Via the **financial markets,** private savings and foreign lending are channeled to **investment spending** (I), government borrowing, and foreign borrowing. **Government purchases of goods and services** (G) are paid for by tax revenues and any **government borrowing.** **Exports** (X) generate an inflow of funds into the country from the rest of the world, but **imports** (IM) lead to an outflow of funds to the rest of the world. Foreigners can also buy stocks and bonds in the U.S. financial markets.

2. **Gross domestic product,** or **GDP,** measures the value of all **final goods and services** produced in the economy. It does not include the value of **intermediate goods and services,** but it does include **inventories** and **net exports** (X − IM). It can be calculated in three ways: add up the **value added** by all producers; add up all spending on domestically produced final goods and services, leading to the equation GDP = C + I + G + X − IM, also known as **aggregate spending;** or add up all the income paid by

domestic firms to factors of production. These three methods are equivalent because in the economy as a whole, total income paid by domestic firms to factors of production must equal total spending on domestically produced final goods and services.

3. **Real GDP** is the value of the final goods and services produced calculated using the prices of a selected base year. Except in the base year, real GDP is not the same as **nominal GDP,** the value of **aggregate output** calculated using current prices. Analysis of the growth rate of aggregate output must use real GDP because doing so eliminates any change in the value of aggregate output due solely to price changes. Real **GDP per capita** is a measure of average aggregate output per person but is not in itself an appropriate policy goal. U.S. statistics on real GDP are always expressed in **chained dollars.**

4. To measure the **aggregate price level,** economists calculate the cost of purchasing a **market basket.** A **price index** is the ratio of the current cost of that market basket to the cost in a selected base year, multiplied by 100.

5. The **inflation rate** is the yearly percent change in a price index, typically based on the **consumer price index,** or **CPI,** the most common measure of the aggregate price level. A similar index for goods and services purchased by firms is the **producer price index,** or **PPI.** Finally, economists also use the **GDP deflator,** which measures the price level by calculating the ratio of nominal to real GDP times 100.

KEY TERMS

National income and product accounts (national accounts), p. 590
Consumer spending, p. 590
Stock, p. 591
Bond, p. 591
Government transfers, p. 592
Disposable income, p. 592
Private savings, p. 592
Financial markets, p. 592
Government borrowing, p. 592
Government purchases of goods and services, p. 592

Exports, p. 592
Imports, p. 592
Inventories, p. 593
Investment spending, p. 593
Final goods and services, p. 593
Intermediate goods and services, p. 593
Gross domestic product (GDP), p. 593
Aggregate spending, p. 593
Value added, p. 595
Net exports, p. 598
Aggregate output, p. 600
Real GDP, p. 601

Nominal GDP, p. 601
Chained dollars, p. 601
GDP per capita, p. 601
Aggregate price level, p. 604
Market basket, p. 604
Price index, p. 604
Inflation rate, p. 605
Consumer price index (CPI), p. 605
Producer price index (PPI), p. 606
GDP deflator, p. 606

PROBLEMS

1. At right is a simplified circular-flow diagram for the economy of Micronia.

   a. What is the value of GDP in Micronia?

   b. What is the value of net exports?

   c. What is the value of disposable income?

   d. Does the total flow of money out of households—the sum of taxes paid and consumer spending—equal the total flow of money into households?

   e. How does the government of Micronia finance its purchases of goods and services?

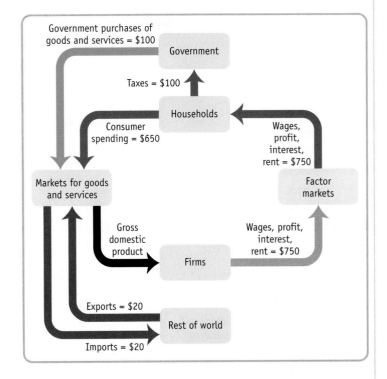

2. A more complex circular-flow diagram for the economy of Macronia is shown at right.

   a. What is the value of GDP in Macronia?

   b. What is the value of net exports?

   c. What is the value of disposable income?

   d. Does the total flow of money out of households—the sum of taxes paid, consumer spending, and private savings—equal the total flow of money into households?

   e. How does the government finance its spending?

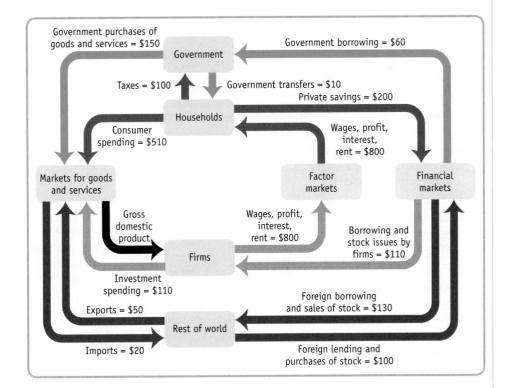

3. The components of GDP in the accompanying table were produced by the Bureau of Economic Analysis.

Category	Components of GDP in 2007 (billions of dollars)
Consumer spending	
Durable goods	$1,082.8
Nondurable goods	2,833.0
Services	5,794.4
Private investment spending	
Fixed investment spending	2,134.0
Nonresidential	1,503.8
Structures	480.3
Equipment and software	1,023.5
Residential	630.2
Change in private inventories	–3.6
Net exports	
Exports	1,662.4
Imports	2,370.2
Government purchases of goods and services and investment spending	
Federal	979.3
National defense	662.2
Nondefense	317.1
State and local	1,695.5

a. Calculate consumer spending.
b. Calculate private investment spending.
c. Calculate net exports.
d. Calculate government purchases of goods and services and investment spending.
e. Calculate gross domestic product.
f. Calculate consumer spending on services as a percentage of total consumer spending.
g. Calculate exports as a percentage of imports.
h. Calculate government purchases on national defense as a percentage of federal government purchases of goods and services.

4. The small economy of Pizzania produces three goods (bread, cheese, and pizza), each produced by a separate company. The bread and cheese companies produce all the inputs they need to make bread and cheese, respectively. The pizza company uses the bread and cheese from the other companies to make its pizzas. All three companies employ labor to help produce their goods, and the difference between the value of goods sold and the sum of labor and input costs is the firm's profit. The accompanying table summarizes the activities of the three

companies when all the bread and cheese produced are sold to the pizza company as inputs in the production of pizzas.

	Bread company	Cheese company	Pizza company
Cost of inputs	$0	$0	$50 (Bread) 35 (Cheese)
Wages	15	20	75
Value of output	50	35	200

a. Calculate GDP as the value added in production.
b. Calculate GDP as spending on final goods and services.
c. Calculate GDP as factor income.

5. In the economy of Pizzania (from Problem 4), bread and cheese produced are sold both to the pizza company for inputs in the production of pizzas and to consumers as final goods. The accompanying table summarizes the activities of the three companies.

	Bread company	Cheese company	Pizza company
Cost of inputs	$0	$0	$50 (Bread) 35 (Cheese)
Wages	25	30	75
Value of output	100	60	200

a. Calculate GDP as the value added in production.
b. Calculate GDP as spending on final goods and services.
c. Calculate GDP as factor income.

6. Which of the following transactions will be included in GDP for the United States?
a. Coca-Cola builds a new bottling plant in the United States.
b. Delta sells one of its existing airplanes to Korean Air.
c. Ms. Moneybags buys an existing share of Disney stock.
d. A California winery produces a bottle of Chardonnay and sells it to a customer in Montreal, Canada.
e. An American buys a bottle of French perfume in Tulsa.
f. A book publisher produces too many copies of a new book; the books don't sell this year, so the publisher adds the surplus books to inventories.

7. The economy of Britannica produces three goods: computers, DVDs, and pizza. The accompanying table shows the prices and output of the three goods for the years 2005, 2006, and 2007.

Year	Computers Price	Computers Quantity	DVDs Price	DVDs Quantity	Pizza Price	Pizza Quantity
2005	$900	10	$10	100	$15	2
2006	1,000	10.5	12	105	16	2
2007	1,050	12	14	110	17	3

a. What is the percent change in production of each of the goods from 2005 to 2006 and from 2006 to 2007?

b. What is the percent change in prices of each of the goods from 2005 to 2006 and from 2006 to 2007?

c. Calculate nominal GDP in Britannica for each of the three years. What is the percent change in nominal GDP from 2005 to 2006 and from 2006 to 2007?

d. Calculate real GDP in Britannica using 2005 prices for each of the three years. What is the percent change in real GDP from 2005 to 2006 and from 2006 to 2007?

8. The accompanying table shows data on nominal GDP (in billions of dollars), real GDP (in billions of 2000 dollars), and population (in thousands) of the United States in 1960, 1970, 1980, 1990, 2000, and 2007, years in which the U.S. price level consistently rose.

Year	Nominal GDP (billions of dollars)	Real GDP (billions of 2000 dollars)	Population (thousands)
1960	$526.4	$2,501.8	180,671
1970	1,038.5	3,771.9	205,052
1980	2,789.5	5,161.7	227,726
1990	5,803.1	7,112.5	250,132
2000	9,817.0	9,817.0	282,388
2007	13,841.3	11,566.8	301,140

a. Why is real GDP greater than nominal GDP for all years before 2000 and lower for 2007? Does nominal GDP have to equal real GDP in 2000?

b. Calculate the percent change in real GDP from 1960 to 1970, 1970 to 1980, 1980 to 1990, and 1990 to 2000. Which period had the highest growth rate?

c. Calculate real GDP per capita for each of the years in the table.

d. Calculate the percent change in real GDP per capita from 1960 to 1970, 1970 to 1980, 1980 to 1990, and 1990 to 2000. Which period had the highest growth rate?

e. How do the percent change in real GDP and the percent change in real GDP per capita compare? Which is larger? Do we expect them to have this relationship?

9. Eastland College is concerned about the rising price of textbooks that students must purchase. To better identify the increase in the price of textbooks, the dean asks you, the Economics Department's star student, to create an index of textbook prices. The average student purchases three English, two math, and four economics textbooks. The prices of these books are given in the accompanying table.

	2005	2006	2007
English textbook	$50	$55	$57
Math textbook	70	72	74
Economics textbook	80	90	100

a. What is the percent change in the price of an English textbook from 2005 to 2007?

b. What is the percent change in the price of a math textbook from 2005 to 2007?

c. What is the percent change in the price of an economics textbook from 2005 to 2007?

d. Using 2005 as a base year, create a price index for these books for all years.

e. What is the percent change in the price index from 2005 to 2007?

10. The consumer price index, or CPI, measures the cost of living for a typical urban household by multiplying the price for each category of expenditure (housing, food, and so on) times a measure of the importance of that expenditure in the average consumer's market basket and summing over all categories. However, using data from the consumer price index, we can see that changes in the cost of living for different types of consumers can vary a great deal. Let's compare the cost of living for a hypothetical retired person and a hypothetical college student. Let's assume that the market basket of a retired person is allocated in the following way: 10% on housing, 15% on food, 5% on transportation, 60% on medical care, 0% on education, and 10% on recreation. The college student's market basket is allocated as follows: 5% on housing, 15% on food, 20% on transportation, 0% on medical care, 40% on education, and 20% on recreation. The accompanying table shows the November 2007 CPI for each of the relevant categories.

	CPI November 2007
Housing	210.7
Food	206.3
Transportation	190.7
Medical care	357.0
Education	121.4
Recreation	118.8

Calculate the overall CPI for the retired person and for the college student by multiplying the CPI for each of the categories by the relative importance of that category to the individual and then summing each of the categories. The CPI for all items in November 2007 was 210.2. How do your calculations for a CPI for the retired person and the college student compare to the overall CPI?

11. Each month the Bureau of Labor Statistics releases the Consumer Price Index Summary for the previous month. Go to www.bls.gov and find the latest report. (On the Bureau of Labor Statistics home page, click on "News Release" under "Latest Numbers—Consumer Price Index" and then choose "Consumer Price Index Summary.") What was the CPI for the previous month? How did it change from the previous month? How does the CPI compare to the same month one year ago?

12. The accompanying table provides the annual real GDP (in billions of 2000 dollars) and nominal GDP (in billions of dollars) for the United States.

	2002	2003	2004	2005	2006
Real GDP (billions of 2000 dollars)	10,048.8	10,301.0	10,675.8	11,003.4	11,319.4
Nominal GDP (billions of dollars)	10,469.6	10,960.8	11,685.9	12,433.9	13,194.7

a. Calculate the GDP deflator for each year.

b. Use the GDP deflator to calculate the inflation rate for all years except 2002.

13. The accompanying table contains two price indexes for the years 2004, 2005, and 2006: the GDP deflator and the CPI. For each price index, calculate the inflation rate from 2004 to 2005 and from 2005 to 2006.

Year	GDP deflator	CPI
2004	109.5	188.9
2005	113.0	195.3
2006	116.6	201.6

14. The cost of a college education in the United States is rising at a rate faster than inflation. The table below shows the average cost of a college education in the United States in 2006 and 2007 for public and private colleges. Assume the costs listed in the table are the only costs experienced by the various college students in a single year.

a. Calculate the cost of living for an average college student in each category for 2006 and 2007.

b. Assume the quantity of goods purchased in each category, i.e., the market basket, is identical for 2006 and 2007. Calculate an inflation rate for each type of college student between 2006 and 2007.

	Cost of college education (averages in 2006 dollars)				
	Tuition and fees	Books and supplies	Room and board	Transportation	Other expenses
Two-year public college: commuter	$ 2,272	$850	$6,299	$1,197	$1,676
Four-year public college: resident	5,836	942	6,690	880	1,739
Four-year public college: commuter	5,836	942	6,917	1,224	2,048
Four-year public college: out-of-state	15,783	942	6,960	880	1,739
Four-year private college: resident	22,218	935	8,149	722	1,277
Four-year private college: commuter	22,218	935	7,211	1,091	1,630
	Cost of college education (averages in 2007 dollars)				
	Tuition and fees	Books and supplies	Room and board	Transportation	Other expenses
Two-year public college: commuter	$ 2,361	$921	$6,875	$1,270	$1,699
Four-year public college: resident	6,185	988	7,404	911	1,848
Four-year public college: commuter	6,185	988	7,419	1,284	2,138
Four-year public college: out-of-state	16,640	988	7,404	911	1,848
Four-year private college: resident	23,712	988	8,595	768	1,311
Four-year private college: commuter	23,712	988	7,499	1,138	1,664

 www.worthpublishers.com/krugmanwells

>> Unemployment and Inflation

DEFEATED INCUMBENTS

IN THE 1992 PRESIDENTIAL CAMPAIGN, BILL CLINTON, the Democratic governor of Arkansas, was running against George H. W. Bush, the incumbent Republican president. Clinton needed a theme for his campaign—a reason for voters to turn out the incumbent. What was that theme? A large sign in the campaign's headquarters read, "It's the economy, stupid."

Clinton sought, in other words, to turn public dissatisfaction with the state of the economy to his advantage. And what really made voters unhappy in 1992 was the lack of jobs: in July 1992 the *unemployment rate* hit 7.8%, up from just 5.2% two years earlier. Sure enough, Clinton defeated Bush that year.

Twelve years earlier, the shoe had been on the other foot: a Republican, Ronald Reagan, was running against the Democratic incumbent president, Jimmy Carter. In that election, too, the state of the economy was the central issue. "Are you better off now than you were four years ago?" Reagan asked. Most people answered no—and Reagan won the election. In 1980 as in 1992, a high rate of unemployment helped stoke public dissatisfaction. In 1980, however, there was also another source of distress: high inflation, with consumer prices in the summer of 1980 more than 14% higher than they had been a year earlier.

Unemployment and inflation are the two great evils of macroeconomics. Therefore, the two principal goals of macroeconomic policy are low unemployment and price stability, usually defined as a low but positive rate of inflation. Unfortunately, those goals sometimes appear to be in conflict with each other: economists often warn that policies intended to fight unemployment run the risk of increasing inflation; conversely, policies intended to bring down inflation can raise unemployment.

The nature of the trade-off between low unemployment and low inflation, along with the policy dilemma it creates, is a topic reserved for later chapters. This chapter provides an overview of the basic facts about unemployment and inflation: how they're measured, how they affect consumers and firms, and how they change over time.

Public dissatisfaction with a high unemployment rate and high inflation helped Ronald Reagan defeat an incumbent to win the presidency in 1980. In 1992, an economy plagued with high unemployment and a lack of jobs helped Bill Clinton do the same.

The Unemployment Rate

As our opening story indicates, a high unemployment rate was a very important issue in the 1992 election—and understandably so. Figure 24-1 shows the U.S. unemployment rate from 1948 to 2008; as you can see, the labor market hit a difficult patch in the early 1990s, with the unemployment rate rising from 5.2% in July 1990 to 7.8% in July 1992, before beginning a gradual decline. What did the rise in the unemployment rate mean and why was it such a big factor in people's lives? To understand why policy makers pay so much attention to employment and unemployment, we need to understand how they are both defined and measured.

Defining and Measuring Unemployment

It's easy to define employment: you're employed if and only if you have a job. **Employment** is the total number of people currently employed, either full time or part time.

Unemployment, however, is a more subtle concept. Just because a person isn't working doesn't mean that we consider that person unemployed. For example, as of July 2007 there were 31 million retired workers in the United States receiving Social Security checks. Most of them were probably happy that they were no longer working, so we wouldn't consider someone who has settled into a comfortable, well-earned retirement to be unemployed. There were also 7 million disabled U.S. workers receiving benefits because they were unable to work. Again, although they weren't working, we wouldn't normally consider them to be unemployed.

Employment is the number of people currently employed in the economy, either full time or part time.

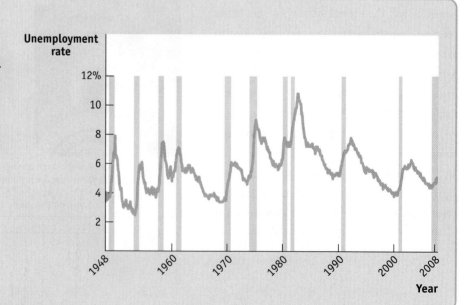

FIGURE 24-1

The U.S. Unemployment Rate, 1948–2008

The unemployment rate has fluctuated widely over time. It always rises during recessions, which are shown by the shaded bars. It usually, but not always, falls during periods of economic expansion.

Source: Bureau of Labor Statistics; National Bureau of Economic Research.

The U.S. Census Bureau, the federal agency tasked with collecting data on unemployment, considers the unemployed to be those who are "jobless, looking for jobs, and available for work." Retired people don't count because they aren't looking for jobs; the disabled don't count because they aren't available for work. More specifically, an individual is considered unemployed if he or she doesn't currently have a job and has been actively seeking a job during the past four weeks. So **unemployment** is defined to be the total number of people who are actively looking for work but aren't currently employed.

A country's **labor force** is the sum of employment and unemployment—that is, of people who are currently working and people who are currently looking for work. The **labor force participation rate,** defined as the share of the working-age population that is in the labor force, is calculated as follows:

$$\textbf{(24-1)} \quad \text{Labor force participation rate} = \frac{\text{Labor force}}{\text{Population age 16 and older}} \times 100$$

The **unemployment rate,** defined as the percentage of the total number of people in the labor force who are unemployed, is calculated as follows:

$$\textbf{(24-2)} \quad \text{Unemployment rate} = \frac{\text{Number of unemployed workers}}{\text{Labor force}} \times 100$$

To estimate the numbers that go into calculating the unemployment rate, the U.S. Census Bureau carries out a monthly survey called the Current Population Survey, which involves interviewing a random sample of 60,000 American families. People are asked whether they are currently employed. If they are not employed, they are asked whether they have been looking for a job during the past four weeks. The results are then scaled up, using estimates of the total population, to estimate the total number of employed and unemployed Americans.

The Significance of the Unemployment Rate

In general, the unemployment rate is a good indicator of how easy or difficult it is to find a job given the current state of the economy. When the unemployment rate is low, nearly everyone who wants a job can find one. In 2000, when the unemployment rate averaged 4%, jobs were so abundant that employers spoke of a "mirror test" for getting a job: if you were breathing (therefore, your breath would fog a mirror), you could find work. By contrast, as this book goes to press late in 2008, the unemployment rate has risen to almost 7%, with many highly qualified workers having lost their jobs and having a hard time finding new ones.

Although the unemployment rate is a good indicator of current labor market conditions, it's not a literal measure of the percentage of people who want a job but can't find one. That's because in some ways the unemployment rate exaggerates the difficulty people have in finding jobs. But in other ways, the opposite is true—a low unemployment rate can conceal deep frustration over the lack of job opportunities.

How the Unemployment Rate Can Overstate the True Level of Unemployment
If you are searching for work, it's normal to take at least a few weeks to find a suitable job. Yet a worker who is quite confident of finding a job, but has not yet accepted a position, is counted as unemployed. As a consequence, the unemployment rate never falls to zero, even in boom times when jobs are plentiful. Even in the buoyant labor market of 2000, when it was easy to find work, the unemployment rate was still 4%. Later in this chapter, we'll discuss in greater depth the reasons that measured unemployment persists even when jobs are abundant.

Unemployment is the number of people who are actively looking for work but aren't currently employed.

The **labor force** is equal to the sum of employment and unemployment.

The **labor force participation rate** is the percentage of the population aged 16 or older that is in the labor force.

The **unemployment rate** is the percentage of the total number of people in the labor force who are unemployed.

Discouraged workers are nonworking people who are capable of working but have given up looking for a job given the state of the job market.

Marginally attached workers would like to be employed and have looked for a job in the recent past but are not currently looking for work.

Underemployment is the number of people who work part time because they cannot find full-time jobs.

How the Unemployment Rate Can Understate the True Level of Unemployment Frequently, people who would like to work but aren't working still don't get counted as unemployed. In particular, an individual who has given up looking for a job for the time being because there are no jobs available—say, a laid-off steelworker in a deeply depressed steel town—isn't counted as unemployed because he or she has not been searching for a job during the previous four weeks. Individuals who want to work but have stated to government researchers that they aren't currently searching because they see little prospect of finding a job given the state of the job market are called **discouraged workers.** Because it does not count discouraged workers, the measured unemployment rate may understate the percentage of people who want to work but are unable to find jobs.

Discouraged workers are part of a larger group, **marginally attached workers.** These are people who say they would like to have a job and have looked for work in the recent past but are not currently looking for work. They also are not included when calculating the unemployment rate.

Finally, another category of workers who are frustrated in their ability to find work but aren't counted as unemployed are the **underemployed:** workers who would like to find full-time jobs but are currently working part time "for economic reasons"—that is, they can't find a full-time job. Again, they aren't counted in the unemployment rate.

The Bureau of Labor Statistics is the federal agency that calculates the official unemployment rate. It also calculates broader "measures of labor underutilization" that include the three categories of frustrated workers. Figure 24-2 shows what happens to the measured unemployment rate once discouraged workers, marginally attached workers, and the underemployed are counted. The broadest measure of un- and underemployment, known as U6, is the sum of these three measures plus the unemployed; it is substantially higher than the rate usually quoted by the news media. But U6 and the unemployment rate move very much in parallel, so changes in the unemployment rate remain a good guide to what's happening in the overall labor market, including frustrated workers.

Finally, it's important to realize that the unemployment rate varies greatly among demographic groups. Other things equal, jobs are generally easier to find for more experienced workers and for workers during their "prime" working years,

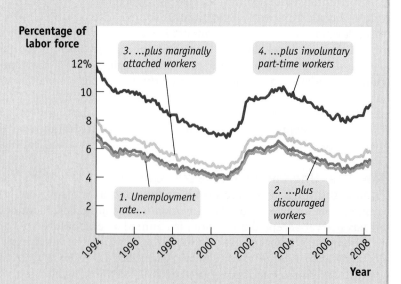

FIGURE 24-2

Alternative Measures of Unemployment, 1994–2008

The unemployment number usually quoted in the news media counts someone as unemployed only if he or she has been looking for work during the past four weeks. Broader measures also count discouraged workers, marginally attached workers, and the underemployed. These broader measures show a higher unemployment rate—but they move closely in parallel with the standard rate.
Source: Bureau of Labor Statistics.

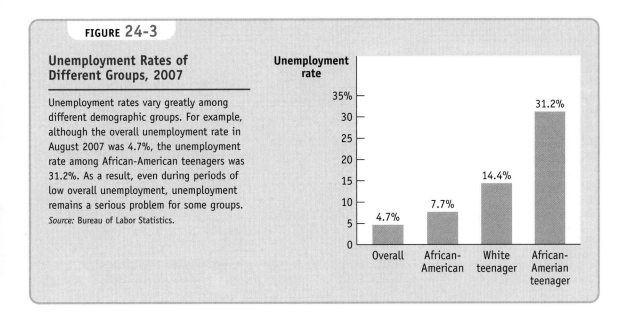

FIGURE 24-3

Unemployment Rates of Different Groups, 2007

Unemployment rates vary greatly among different demographic groups. For example, although the overall unemployment rate in August 2007 was 4.7%, the unemployment rate among African-American teenagers was 31.2%. As a result, even during periods of low overall unemployment, unemployment remains a serious problem for some groups.

Source: Bureau of Labor Statistics.

from ages 25 to 54. For younger workers, as well as workers nearing retirement age, jobs are typically harder to find, other things equal. Figure 24-3 shows unemployment rates for different groups in August 2007, when the overall unemployment rate of 4.7% was low by historical standards. As you can see, in August 2007 the unemployment rate for African-American workers was much higher than the national average; the unemployment rate for White teenagers (ages 16–19) was more than three times the national average; and the unemployment rate for African-American teenagers, at more than 30%, was over six times the national average. (Bear in mind that a teenager isn't considered unemployed, even if he or she isn't working, unless that teenager is looking for work but can't find it.) So even at a time when the overall unemployment rate was relatively low, jobs were hard to find for some groups.

So you should interpret the unemployment rate as an indicator of overall labor market conditions, not as an exact, literal measure of the percentage of people unable to find jobs. The unemployment rate is, however, a very good indicator: the ups and downs of the unemployment rate closely reflect economic changes that have a significant impact on people's lives. Let's turn now to the causes of these fluctuations.

Growth and Unemployment

Compared to Figure 24-1, Figure 24-4 on the next page shows the U.S. unemployment rate over a somewhat shorter period, the 30 years from 1978 to 2008. The shaded bars represent periods of recession. As you can see, during every recession, without exception, the unemployment rate rose. The recession of 1981–1982, the most severe one shown, pushed the unemployment rate into double digits: unemployment peaked in November 1982 at 10.8%.

Correspondingly, during periods of economic expansion the unemployment rate usually falls. The long economic expansion of the 1990s eventually brought the unemployment rate below 4%. However, it's important to recognize that *economic expansions aren't always periods of falling unemployment.* Look at the periods immediately following two recent recessions, those of 1990–1991 and 2001. In each case the unemployment rate continued to rise for more than a year after the recession was officially over. The explanation in both cases is that although the economy was growing, it was not growing fast enough to reduce the unemployment rate.

FIGURE 24-4

Unemployment and Recessions, 1978–2008

This figure shows a close-up of the unemployment rate for the past 30 years, with the shaded bars indicating recessions. It's clear that unemployment always rises during recessions and *usually* falls during expansions. But in both the early 1990s and the early 2000s, unemployment continued to rise for some time after the recession was officially declared over.

Source: Bureau of Labor Statistics; National Bureau of Economic Research.

Figure 24-5 is a scatter diagram showing U.S. data for the period from 1949 to 2007. The horizontal axis measures the annual rate of growth in real GDP—the percent by which each year's real GDP changed compared to the previous year's real GDP. (Notice that there were eight years in which growth was negative—that is, real GDP shrank.) The vertical axis measures the *change* in the unemployment rate over the previous year in percentage points. Each dot represents the observed growth rate of real GDP and change in the unemployment rate for a given year. For example, in 2000 the average

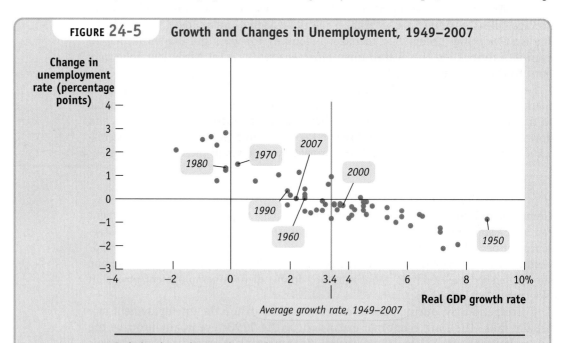

FIGURE 24-5 **Growth and Changes in Unemployment, 1949–2007**

Each dot shows the growth rate of the economy and the change in the unemployment rate for a specific year between 1949 and 2007. For example, in 2000 the economy grew 3.7% and the unemployment rate fell 0.2 percentage points, from 4.2% to 4.0%. In general, the unemployment rate fell when growth was above its average rate of 3.4% a year and rose when growth was below average. Unemployment always rose when real GDP fell.

Source: Bureau of Labor Statistics; Bureau of Economic Analysis.

unemployment rate fell to 4.0% from 4.2% in 1999; this is shown as a value of –0.2 along the vertical axis for the year 2000. Over the same period, real GDP grew by 3.7%; this is the value shown along the horizontal axis for the year 2000.

The downward trend of the scatter points in Figure 24-5 shows that there is a generally strong negative relationship between growth in the economy and the rate of unemployment. Years of high growth in real GDP were also years in which the unemployment rate fell, and years of low or negative growth in real GDP were years in which the unemployment rate rose. The green vertical line in Figure 24-5 at the value of 3.4% indicates the average growth rate of real GDP over the period from 1949 to 2007. Points lying to the right of the vertical line are years of above-average growth. In these years, the value on the vertical axis is usually negative, meaning that the unemployment rate fell. That is, years of above-average growth were usually years in which the unemployment rate was falling. Conversely, points lying to the left of the vertical line were years of below-average growth. In these years, the value on the vertical axis is usually positive, meaning that the unemployment rate rose. That is, years of below-average growth were usually years in which the unemployment rate was rising. Now, there are periods in which GDP is growing, but at a below-average rate; these are periods in which the economy isn't in a recession but unemployment is still rising—sometimes called a "growth recession." But true recessions, periods when real GDP falls, are especially painful for workers. As illustrated by the points to the left of the vertical axis in Figure 24-5, falling real GDP is always associated with a rising rate of unemployment, causing a great deal of hardship to families.

►ECONOMICS IN ACTION

Rocky Mountain Low

In addition to estimating the unemployment rate for the nation as a whole, the U.S. government also estimates unemployment rates for each state. These state unemployment rates often differ considerably—and the differences correspond to real differences in the condition of local labor markets. Figure 24-6 shows how unemployment rates varied across the United States in July 2007.

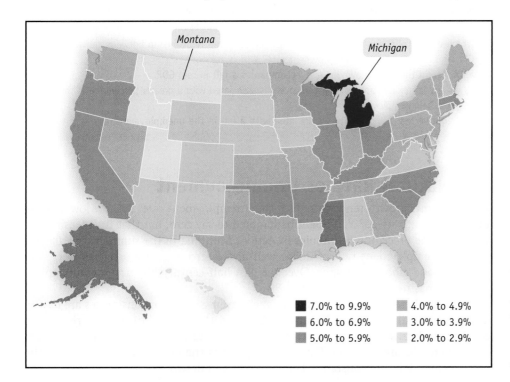

■ 7.0% to 9.9%	■ 4.0% to 4.9%
■ 6.0% to 6.9%	■ 3.0% to 3.9%
■ 5.0% to 5.9%	■ 2.0% to 2.9%

FIGURE 24-6
Unemployment Rates across America, July 2007 At any given time, unemployment rates vary considerably among states. In July 2007 the unemployment rate in Montana, like that in other mountain states, was very low: just 2.7%. Meanwhile, Michigan had a 7.2% unemployment rate.
Source: Bureau of Labor Statistics.

As you can see from Figure 24-6, Montana had one of the lowest unemployment rates in the United States, only 2.7% in July 2007, mainly because the state's booming oil business was creating new jobs even as the state's aging population reduced the size of the labor force. And this low unemployment rate created a seller's market in labor. According to the Associated Press, the owner of the McDonald's franchise in Sidney, Montana, desperate to find workers, "tried advertising in the local newspaper and even offered up to $10 an hour to compete with higher-paying oil field jobs. Yet the only calls were from other business owners upset they would have to raise wages, too."

Michigan was at the opposite extreme. Layoffs by auto manufacturers, the tradi-tional mainstay of Michigan's economy, had given the state the highest unemploy-ment rate in the nation: 7.2% in July 2007. And this high unemployment rate did indeed correspond to a very poor labor market. A poll taken by the *Detroit Free Press* in early 2007 found that 3 in 10 Michigan residents were considering leaving the state, including almost half of the state's young people, because of poor job prospects. These state-to-state comparisons show that the unemployment rate is indeed a good indicator of how easy or hard it is to find a job.

One thing you should know, however, is that differences in state unemployment rates don't tend to persist, in large part because, as that Michigan poll suggested, Americans tend to move to where the jobs are. As recently as 2000, Michigan had an unemployment rate of only 3.7%, well below the national average of 4.0%, while Montana had an unemployment rate of 4.8%, above the national average. ▲

< < < < < < < < < < < <

▶ CHECK YOUR UNDERSTANDING 24-1

1. Suppose that the advent of employment websites enables job-seekers to find suitable jobs more quickly. What effect will this have on the unemployment rate over time? Also suppose that these websites encourage job-seekers who had given up their searches to begin looking again. What effect will this have on the unemployment rate?

2. In which of the following cases is a worker counted as unemployed? Explain.
   a. Rosa, an older worker who has been laid off and who gave up looking for work months ago
   b. Anthony, a schoolteacher who is not working during his three-month summer break
   c. Grace, an investment banker who has been laid off and is currently searching for another position
   d. Sergio, a classically trained musician who can only find work playing for local parties
   e. Natasha, a graduate student who went back to school because jobs were scarce

3. Which of the following are consistent with the observed relationship between growth in real GDP and changes in the unemployment rate? Which are not?
   a. A rise in the unemployment rate accompanies a fall in real GDP.
   b. An exceptionally strong business recovery is associated with a greater percentage of the labor force being employed.
   c. Negative real GDP growth is associated with a fall in the unemployment rate.

Solutions appear at back of book.

The Natural Rate of Unemployment

Fast economic growth tends to reduce the unemployment rate. So how low can the unemployment rate go? You might be tempted to say zero, but that isn't feasible. As we saw in the preceding Economics in Action, Montana in the summer of 2007 still had an unemployment rate of 2.7%, well above zero, even though jobs were very abundant and labor very scarce. Over the past half-century, the national unemploy-ment rate has never dropped below 2.9%.

How can there be so much unemployment even when many businesses are having a hard time finding workers? To answer this question, we need to examine the nature of labor markets and why they normally lead to substantial measured unemployment even when jobs are plentiful. Our starting point is the observation that even in the best of times, jobs are constantly being created and destroyed.

Job Creation and Job Destruction

Even during good times, most Americans know someone who has lost his or her job. The U.S. unemployment rate in July 2007 was only 4.7%, relatively low by historical standards, yet in that month there were 4.5 million "job separations"—terminations of employment that occur because a worker is either fired or quits voluntarily.

There are many reasons for such job loss. One is structural change in the economy: industries rise and fall as new technologies emerge and consumers' tastes change. For example, employment in high-tech industries such as telecommunications surged in the late 1990s but slumped severely after 2000. However, structural change also brings the creation of new jobs: since 2000, the number of jobs in the American health-care sector has surged as new medical technologies and the aging of the population have increased the demand for medical care. Poor management performance or bad luck at individual companies also leads to job loss for their employees. For example, in 2005 General Motors announced plans to eliminate 30,000 jobs after several years of lagging sales, even as Japanese companies such as Toyota announced plans to open new plants in North America to meet growing demand for their cars.

"They just like to remind you about the job market."

This constant churning of the workforce is an inevitable feature of the modern economy. And this churning, in turn, is one source of *frictional unemployment*—one main reason that there is a considerable amount of unemployment even when jobs are abundant.

Frictional Unemployment

When a worker loses a job involuntarily due to job destruction, he or she often doesn't take the first new job offered. For example, suppose a skilled programmer, laid off because her software company's product line was unsuccessful, sees a help-wanted ad for clerical work in the local newspaper. She might respond to the ad and get the job—but that would be foolish. Instead, she should take the time to look for a job that takes advantage of her skills and pays accordingly. In addition, individual workers are constantly leaving jobs voluntarily, typically for personal reasons—family moves, dissatisfaction, and better job prospects elsewhere.

Economists say that workers who spend time looking for employment are engaged in **job search.** If all workers and all jobs were alike, job search wouldn't be necessary; if information about jobs and workers were perfect, job search would be very quick. In practice, however, it's normal for a worker who loses a job, or a young worker seeking a first job, to spend at least a few weeks searching.

Frictional unemployment is unemployment due to the time workers spend in job search. A certain amount of frictional unemployment is inevitable, for two reasons. One is the constant process of job creation and job destruction; the other is the fact that new workers are always entering the labor market. For example, in August 2007, out of 7.1 million workers counted as unemployed, 593,000 were new entrants to the workforce and another 2 million were "re-entrants"—people who had been out of the workforce for a time and had come back.

A limited amount of frictional unemployment is relatively harmless and may even be a good thing. The economy is more productive if workers take the time to find jobs that are well matched to their skills, and workers who are unemployed for a brief period while searching for the right job don't experience great hardship. In fact, when there is a low unemployment rate, periods of unemployment tend to be quite short, suggesting that much of the unemployment is frictional. Figure 24-7 on the next page shows the composition of unemployment in 2000, when the unemployment rate was only 4%. Forty-five percent of the unemployed had been

Workers who spend time looking for employment are engaged in **job search.**

Frictional unemployment is unemployment due to the time workers spend in job search.

FIGURE 24-7

Distribution of the Unemployed by Duration of Unemployment, 2000

In years when the unemployment rate is low, most unemployed workers are unemployed for only a short period. In 2000, a year of low unemployment, 45% of the unemployed had been unemployed for less than 5 weeks and 77% for less than 15 weeks. The short duration of unemployment for most workers suggests that most unemployment in 2000 was frictional.

Source: Bureau of Labor Statistics.

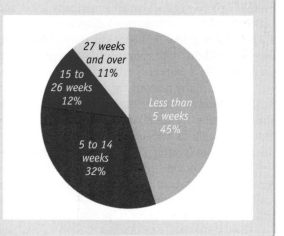

unemployed for less than 5 weeks and only 23% had been unemployed for 15 or more weeks. Just 11% were considered to be "long-term unemployed"—unemployed for 27 or more weeks.

In periods of higher unemployment, however, workers tend to be jobless for longer periods of time, suggesting that a smaller share of unemployment is frictional. By 2003, for instance, the fraction of unemployed workers considered "long-term unemployed" had jumped to 22%.

Structural Unemployment

Frictional unemployment exists even when the number of people seeking jobs is equal to the number of jobs being offered—that is, the existence of frictional unemployment doesn't mean that there is a surplus of labor. Sometimes, however, there is a *persistent surplus* of job-seekers in a particular labor market. For example, there may be more workers with a particular skill than there are jobs available using that skill, or there may be more workers in a particular geographic region than there are jobs available in that region. **Structural unemployment** is unemployment that results when there are more people seeking jobs in a labor market than there are jobs available at the current wage rate.

The supply and demand model tells us that the price of a good, service, or factor of production tends to move toward an equilibrium level that matches the quantity supplied with the quantity demanded. This is equally true, in general, of labor markets. Figure 24-8 shows a typical market for labor. The labor demand curve indicates that when the price of labor—the wage rate—increases, employers demand less labor. The labor supply curve indicates that when the price of labor increases, more workers are willing to supply labor at the prevailing wage rate. These two forces coincide to lead to an equilibrium wage rate for any given type of labor in a particular location. That equilibrium wage rate is shown as W_E.

Even at the equilibrium wage rate W_E, there will still be some frictional unemployment. That's because there will always be some workers engaged in job search even when the number of jobs available is equal to the number of workers seeking jobs. But there wouldn't be any structural unemployment in this labor market. *Structural unemployment occurs when the wage rate is, for some reason, persistently above W_E.* Several factors can lead to a wage rate in excess of W_E, the most important being minimum wages, labor unions, *efficiency wages*, and the side effects of government policies.

Structural unemployment is unemployment that results when there are more people seeking jobs in a labor market than there are jobs available at the current wage rate.

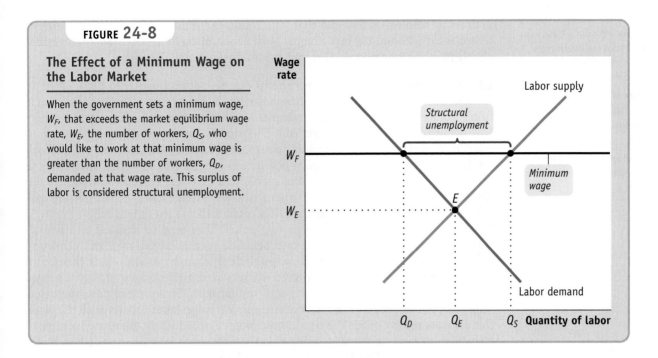

FIGURE 24-8

The Effect of a Minimum Wage on the Labor Market

When the government sets a minimum wage, W_F, that exceeds the market equilibrium wage rate, W_E, the number of workers, Q_S, who would like to work at that minimum wage is greater than the number of workers, Q_D, demanded at that wage rate. This surplus of labor is considered structural unemployment.

Minimum Wages A minimum wage is a government-mandated floor on the price of labor. In the United States, the national minimum wage in 2008 was $6.55 an hour, scheduled to rise to $7.25 an hour in 2009. For many American workers, the minimum wage is irrelevant; the market equilibrium wage for these workers is well above this price floor. But for less skilled workers, the minimum wage may be binding—it affects the wages that people are actually paid and can lead to structural unemployment. Other wealthy countries have higher minimum wages; for example, in 2008 the French minimum wage was €8.63 an hour, or almost $11. In these countries, the range of workers for whom the minimum wage is binding is larger.

Figure 24-8 shows the effect of a binding minimum wage. In this market, there is a legal floor on wages, W_F, which is above the equilibrium wage rate, W_E. This leads to a persistent surplus in the labor market: the quantity of labor supplied, Q_S, is larger than the quantity demanded, Q_D. In other words, more people want to work than can find jobs at the minimum wage, leading to structural unemployment.

Given that minimum wages—that is, binding minimum wages—generally lead to structural unemployment, you might wonder why governments impose them. The rationale is to help ensure that people who work can earn enough income to afford at least a minimally comfortable lifestyle. However, this may come at a cost, because it may eliminate the opportunity to work for some workers who would have willingly worked for lower wages. As illustrated in Figure 24-8, not only are there more sellers of labor than there are buyers, but there are also fewer people working at a minimum wage (Q_D) than there would have been with no minimum wage at all (Q_E).

Although economists broadly agree that a high minimum wage has the employment-reducing effects shown in Figure 24-8, there is some question about whether this is a good description of how the minimum wage actually works in the United States. The minimum wage in the United States is quite low compared with that in other wealthy countries. For three decades, from the 1970s to the mid-2000s, the American minimum wage was so low that it was not binding for the vast majority of workers. In addition, some researchers have produced evidence that increases in the minimum wage actually lead to higher employment when, as was the case in the United States at one time, the minimum wage is low compared to average wages. They argue that firms that employ low-skilled workers sometimes restrict their hiring

Efficiency wages are wages that employers set above the equilibrium wage rate as an incentive for better employee performance.

The **natural rate of unemployment** is the unemployment rate that arises from the effects of frictional plus structural unemployment.

Cyclical unemployment is the deviation of the actual rate of unemployment from the natural rate.

in order to keep wages low and that, as a result, the minimum wage can sometimes be increased without any loss of jobs. Most economists, however, agree that a sufficiently high minimum wage *does* lead to structural unemployment.

Labor Unions The actions of *labor unions* can have effects similar to those of minimum wages, leading to structural unemployment. By bargaining collectively for all of a firm's workers, unions can often win higher wages from employers than workers would have obtained by bargaining individually. This process, known as *collective bargaining,* is intended to tip the scales of bargaining power more to workers and away from employers. Labor unions exercise bargaining power by threatening firms with a *labor strike,* a collective refusal to work. The threat of a strike can have very serious consequences for firms that have difficulty replacing striking workers. In such cases, workers acting collectively can exercise more power than they could if they acted individually.

When workers have greater bargaining power, they tend to demand and receive higher wages. Unions also bargain over benefits, such as health care and pensions, which we can think of as additional wages. Indeed, economists who study the effects of unions on wages find that unionized workers earn higher wages and more generous benefits than non-union workers with similar skills. The result of these increased wages can be the same as the result of a minimum wage: labor unions push the wage that workers receive above the equilibrium wage. Consequently, there are more people willing to work at the wage being paid than there are jobs available. Like a binding minimum wage, this leads to structural unemployment.

Efficiency Wages Actions by firms may also contribute to structural unemployment. Firms may choose to pay **efficiency wages**—wages that employers set above the equilibrium wage rate as an incentive for their workers to deliver better performance.

Employers may feel the need for such incentives for several reasons. For example, employers often have difficulty observing directly how hard an employee works. They can, however, elicit more work effort by paying above-market wages: employees receiving these higher wages are more likely to work harder to ensure that they aren't fired, which would cause them to lose their higher wages.

When many firms pay efficiency wages, the result is a pool of workers who want jobs but can't find them. So the use of efficiency wages by firms leads to structural unemployment.

Side Effects of Public Policy In addition, public policy designed to help workers who lose their jobs can lead to structural unemployment as an unintended side effect. Most economically advanced countries provide benefits to laid-off workers as a way to tide them over until they find a new job. In the United States, these benefits typically replace only a small fraction of a worker's income and expire after 26 weeks. In other countries, particularly in Europe, benefits are more generous and last longer. The drawback to this generosity is that it reduces a worker's incentive to quickly find a new job. Generous unemployment benefits in some European countries are widely believed to be one of the main causes of "Eurosclerosis," the persistent high unemployment that afflicts a number of European economies.

The Natural Rate of Unemployment

Because some frictional unemployment is inevitable and because many economies also suffer from structural unemployment, a certain amount of unemployment is normal, or "natural." Actual unemployment fluctuates around this normal level. The **natural rate of unemployment** is the normal unemployment rate around which the actual unemployment rate fluctuates. It is the rate of unemployment that arises from the effects of frictional plus structural unemployment. **Cyclical unemployment** is the deviation of the actual rate of unemployment from the natural rate; that is, it is the difference between the actual and natural rates of unemployment. As the name suggests, cyclical unemployment is the share of unemployment that arises from the business cycle. We'll see in Chapter 32 that public policy cannot keep the unemployment rate persistently below the natural rate without leading to accelerating inflation.

We can summarize the relationships between the various types of unemployment as follows:

(24-3)   Natural unemployment =
Frictional unemployment + Structural unemployment

(24-4)   Actual unemployment =
Natural unemployment + Cyclical unemployment

Perhaps because of its name, people often imagine that the natural rate of unemployment is a constant that doesn't change over time and can't be affected by policy. Neither proposition is true. Let's take a moment to stress two facts: the natural rate of unemployment changes over time, and it can be affected by economic policies.

GLOBAL COMPARISON   NATURAL UNEMPLOYMENT AROUND THE OECD

The Organization for Economic Cooperation and Development (OECD) is an association of relatively wealthy countries, mainly in Europe and North America but also including Japan, Korea, New Zealand, and Australia. Among other activities, the OECD collects data on unemployment rates in its member nations using the U.S. definition. The figure shows average unemployment, which is a rough estimate of the natural rate of unemployment, for select OECD members, over the period 1996–2006. The purple bar in the middle shows the average across all countries.

The U.S. natural rate of unemployment appears to be somewhat below average; those of many European countries (including the major economies of Germany, Italy, and France) are above average. Many, but not all, economists think that persistently high European unemployment rates are the result of government policies, such as high minimum wages and generous unemployment benefits, which both discourage employers from offering jobs and discourage workers from accepting jobs, leading to high rates of structural unemployment.

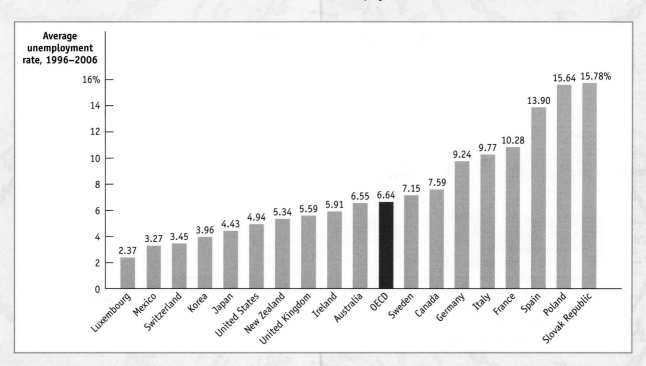

Source: OECD.

Changes in the Natural Rate of Unemployment

Private-sector economists and government agencies need estimates of the natural rate of unemployment both to make forecasts and to conduct policy analyses. Almost all these estimates show that the U.S. natural rate rises and falls over time. For example, the Congressional Budget Office, the independent agency that conducts budget and economic analyses for Congress, believes that the U.S. natural rate of unemployment was 5.3% in 1950, rose to 6.3% by the end of the 1970s, but has fallen to 4.8% today. European countries have experienced even larger swings in their natural rates of unemployment.

What causes the natural rate of unemployment to change? The most important factors are changes in the characteristics of the labor force, changes in labor market institutions, and changes in government policies. Let's look briefly at each factor.

Changes in Labor Force Characteristics

In 2007 the overall rate of unemployment in the United States was 4.6%. Young workers, however, had much higher unemployment rates: 15.7% for teenagers and 8.2% for workers aged 20 to 24. Workers aged 25 to 54 had an unemployment rate of only 3.7%.

In general, unemployment rates tend to be lower for experienced than for inexperienced workers. Because experienced workers tend to stay in a given job longer than do inexperienced ones, they have lower frictional unemployment. Also, because older workers are more likely than young workers to be family breadwinners, they have a stronger incentive to find and keep jobs.

One reason the natural rate of unemployment rose during the 1970s was a large rise in the number of new workers—children of the post–World War II baby boom entered the labor force, as did a rising percentage of married women. As Figure 24-9 shows, both the percentage of the labor force less than 25 years old and the percentage of women in the labor force surged in the 1970s. By the end of the 1990s, however, the share of women in the labor force had leveled off and the percentage of workers under 25 had fallen sharply. As a result, the labor force as a whole is more experienced today than it was in the 1970s, one likely reason that the natural rate of unemployment is lower today than in the 1970s.

Changes in Labor Market Institutions

As we pointed out earlier, unions that negotiate wages above the equilibrium level can be a source of structural unemployment. Some economists believe that strong labor unions are one reason for the high natural rate of unemployment in Europe, discussed in the earlier Global Comparison.

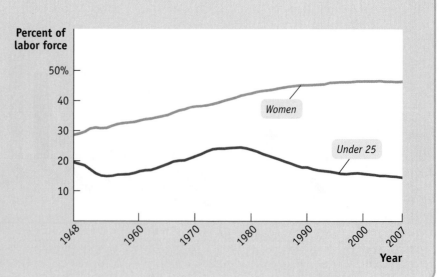

FIGURE 24-9

The Changing Makeup of the U.S. Labor Force, 1948–2007

In the 1970s the percentage of the labor force consisting of women rose rapidly, as did the percentage under age 25. These changes reflected the entry of large numbers of women into the paid labor force for the first time and the fact that baby boomers were reaching working age. The natural rate of unemployment may have risen because many of these workers were relatively inexperienced. Today, the labor force is much more experienced, which is one possible reason the natural rate has fallen since the 1970s.

Source: Bureau of Labor Statistics.

An Unemployment Lockdown?

Most analysts believe that the natural rate of unemployment in the United States has fallen substantially since 1980; the Congressional Budget Office estimate has fallen from 6.2% to 4.8%. As we've seen, the maturing of the workforce is one possible explanation; changes in labor market institutions are another.

But there's one more, less favorable, factor to consider: many of those who would otherwise be counted as unemployed may be behind bars.

Largely owing to changes in law enforcement strategies (which have been successful at greatly reducing the U.S. crime rate), the number of American adults in jail or prison has risen from 503,586 in 1980, or 0.5% of the labor force, to 2.3 million, or 1.5% of the labor force, in 2007. It's likely that those behind bars would, if free, have a high unemployment rate. So part of the decline in the natural rate of unemployment may represent a shift of some Americans from being unemployed—not

working, but looking for work—to being out of the labor force, because they're not free to seek jobs.

How big is the unemployment lockdown? A widely cited 1999 paper by Alan Krueger of Princeton University and Larry Katz of Harvard estimated that the rise in the prison population might have lopped about 0.2 percentage points off the natural rate of unemployment.

In the United States, a sharp fall in union membership after 1980 may have been one reason the natural rate of unemployment fell between the 1970s and the 1990s.

Other institutional changes may also be at work. For example, some labor economists believe that temporary employment agencies, which have proliferated in recent years, have reduced frictional unemployment by helping match workers to jobs. Furthermore, Internet websites such as monster.com may have reduced frictional unemployment.

Technological change, coupled with labor market institutions, can also affect the natural rate of unemployment. Technological change probably leads to an increase in the demand for skilled workers who are familiar with the relevant technology and a reduction in the demand for unskilled workers. Economic theory predicts that wages should increase for skilled workers and decrease for unskilled workers. But if wages for unskilled workers cannot go down—say, due to a binding minimum wage—increased structural unemployment, and therefore a higher natural rate of unemployment, will result.

Changes in Government Policies A high minimum wage can cause structural unemployment. Generous unemployment benefits can increase both structural and frictional unemployment. So government policies intended to help workers can have the undesirable side effect of raising the natural rate of unemployment.

Some government policies, however, may reduce the natural rate. Two examples are job training and employment subsidies. Job-training programs are supposed to provide unemployed workers with skills that widen the range of jobs they can perform. Employment subsidies are payments either to workers or to employers that provide a financial incentive to accept or offer jobs.

➤ ECONOMICS IN ACTION

Structural Unemployment in Eastern Germany

In one of the most dramatic events in world history, a spontaneous popular uprising in 1989 overthrew the communist dictatorship in East Germany. Citizens quickly tore down the wall that had divided Berlin, and in short order East and West Germany became a united, democratic nation.

Then the trouble started.

After reunification, employment in East Germany plunged and the unemployment rate soared. This high unemployment rate has persisted: despite receiving massive aid from the federal German government, the economy of the former East Germany has remained persistently depressed, with an unemployment rate of more than 16% in

2008. Other parts of formerly communist Eastern Europe have done much better. For example, the Czech Republic, which was often cited along with East Germany as a relatively successful communist economy, had an unemployment rate of only 5.5% in July 2007. What went wrong in East Germany?

The answer is that, through nobody's fault, East Germany found itself suffering from severe structural unemployment. When Germany was reunified, it became clear that workers in East Germany were much less productive than their cousins in the west. Yet unions initially demanded wage rates equal to those in West Germany, and these wage rates have been slow to come down, because East German workers don't want to be treated as inferior to their West German counterparts. Meanwhile, productivity in the former East Germany has remained well below West German levels, in part because of decades of misguided investment. The result has been a persistently large mismatch between the number of workers demanded and the number of those seeking jobs. ▲
< < < < < < < < < < < <

► CHECK YOUR UNDERSTANDING 24-2

1. Explain the following.
   a. Frictional unemployment is higher when the pace of technological advance quickens.
   b. Frictional unemployment accounts for a larger share of total unemployment when the unemployment rate is low.

2. Why does collective bargaining have the same general effect on unemployment as a minimum wage? Illustrate your answer with a diagram.

3. Suppose the United States dramatically increases benefits for unemployed workers. Explain what will happen to the natural rate of unemployment.

Solutions appear at back of book.

Inflation and Deflation

As we mentioned in the opening story, in 1980 Americans were dismayed about the state of the economy for two reasons: the unemployment rate was high, and so was inflation. In fact, the high rate of inflation, not the high rate of unemployment, was the principal concern of policy makers at the time—so much so that Paul Volcker, the chairman of the Federal Reserve Board (which controls monetary policy), more or less deliberately created a deep recession in order to bring inflation under control. Only in 1982, after inflation had dropped sharply and the unemployment rate had risen to more than 10%, did fighting unemployment become the chief priority.

Why is inflation something to worry about? Why do policy makers even now get anxious when they see the inflation rate moving upward? The answer is that inflation can impose costs on the economy—but not in the way most people think.

The Level of Prices Doesn't Matter . . .

The most common complaint about inflation, an increase in the price level, is that it makes everyone poorer—after all, a given amount of money buys less. But inflation does not make everyone poorer. To see why, it's helpful to imagine what would happen if the United States did something other countries have done from time to time—replacing the dollar with a new currency.

A recent example of this kind of currency conversion happened in 2002, when France, like a number of other European countries, replaced its national currency, the franc, with the new pan-European currency, the euro. People turned in their franc coins and notes, and received euro coins and notes in exchange, at a rate of precisely 6.55957 francs per euro. At the same time, all contracts were restated in euros at the same rate of exchange. For example, if a French citizen had a home mortgage debt of 500,000 francs, this became a debt of 500,000/6.55957 = 76,224.51 euros. If a worker's contract specified that he or she should be paid 100 francs per hour, it became a contract specifying a wage of 100/6.55957 = 15.2449 euros per hour, and so on.

You could imagine doing the same thing here, replacing the dollar with a "new dollar" at a rate of exchange of, say, 7 to 1. If you owed $140,000 on your home, that would become a debt of 20,000 new dollars. If you had a wage rate of $14 an hour, it would become 2 new dollars an hour, and so on. This would bring the overall U.S. price level back to about what it was when John F. Kennedy was president.

So would everyone be richer as a result, because prices would be only one-seventh as high? Of course not. Prices would be lower, but so would wages and incomes in general. If you cut a worker's wage to one-seventh of its previous value, but also cut all prices to one-seventh of their previous level, the worker's **real wage**—the wage rate divided by the price level—hasn't changed. In fact, bringing the overall price level back to what it was during the Kennedy administration would have no effect on overall purchasing power, because doing so would reduce income exactly as much as it reduced prices. Conversely, the rise in prices that has actually taken place since the early 1960s hasn't made America poorer, because it has also raised incomes by the same amount: **real incomes**—incomes divided by the price level—haven't been affected by the rise in overall prices.

The moral of this story is that the *level* of prices doesn't matter: the United States would be no richer than it is now if the overall level of prices were still as low as it was in 1961; conversely, the rise in prices over the past 45 years hasn't made us poorer.

> The **real wage** is the wage rate divided by the price level.
>
> **Real income** is income divided by the price level.

. . . But The Rate of Change of Prices Does

The conclusion that the level of prices doesn't matter might seem to imply that the inflation rate doesn't matter either. But that's not true.

To see why, it's crucial to distinguish between the *level of prices* and the *inflation rate:* the percent increase in the overall level of prices per year. Recall from Chapter 23 that the inflation rate is defined as follows:

$$\text{Inflation rate} = \frac{\text{Price index in year 2} - \text{Price index in year 1}}{\text{Price index in year 1}} \times 100$$

Figure 24-10 highlights the difference between the price level and the inflation rate in the United States since 1968, with the price level measured along the left vertical axis and the inflation rate measured along the right vertical axis. In the 2000s, the overall level of prices in America was much higher than it had been in 1968—but that,

FIGURE 24-10

The Price Level versus the Inflation Rate, 1968–2008

Over the past 40 years, the consumer price index has continuously gone up. But the *inflation rate*—the rate at which consumer prices are rising—has had both ups and downs.

Source: Bureau of Labor Statistics.

Shoe-leather costs are the increased costs of transactions caused by inflation.

Menu cost is the real cost of changing a listed price.

as we've learned, didn't matter. The inflation rate in the 2000s, however, was much lower than in the 1970s—and that almost certainly made the economy richer than it would have been if high inflation had continued.

Economists believe that high rates of inflation impose significant economic costs. The most important of these costs are *shoe-leather costs, menu costs,* and *unit-of-account costs.* We'll discuss each in turn.

Shoe-Leather Costs People hold money—cash in their wallets and bank deposits on which they can write checks—for convenience in making transactions. A high inflation rate, however, discourages people from holding money, because the purchasing power of the cash in your wallet and the funds in your bank account steadily erodes as the overall level of prices rises. This leads people to search for ways to reduce the amount of money they hold, often at considerable economic cost.

The Economics in Action at the end of this section describes how Israelis spent a lot of time at the bank during the periods of high inflation rates that afflicted Israel in 1984–1985. During the most famous of all inflations, the German *hyperinflation* of 1921–1923, merchants employed runners to take their cash to the bank many times a day to convert it into something that would hold its value, such as a stable foreign currency. In each case, in an effort to avoid having the purchasing power of their money eroded, people used up valuable resources, such as time for Israeli citizens and the labor of those German runners, that could have been used productively elsewhere. During the German hyperinflation, so many banking transactions were taking place that the number of employees at German banks nearly quadrupled—from around 100,000 in 1913 to 375,000 in 1923. More recently, Brazil experienced hyperinflation during the early 1990s; during that episode, the Brazilian banking sector grew so large that it accounted for 15% of GDP, more than twice the size of the financial sector in the United States measured as a share of GDP. The large increase in the Brazilian banking sector needed to cope with the consequences of inflation represented a loss of real resources to its society.

Increased costs of transactions caused by inflation are known as **shoe-leather costs,** an allusion to the wear and tear caused by the extra running around that takes place when people are trying to avoid holding money. Shoe-leather costs are substantial in economies with very high inflation, as anyone who has lived in such an economy—say, one suffering inflation of 100% or more per year—can attest. Most estimates suggest, however, that the shoe-leather costs of inflation at the rates seen in the United States—which in peacetime has never had inflation above 15%—are quite small.

Menu Costs In a modern economy, most of the things we buy have a listed price. There's a price listed under each item on a supermarket shelf, a price printed on the front page of your newspaper, a price listed for each dish on a restaurant's menu. Changing a listed price has a real cost, called a **menu cost.** For example, to change prices in a supermarket requires sending clerks through the store to change the listed price under each item. In the face of inflation, of course, firms are forced to change prices more often than they would if the aggregate price level was more or less stable. This means higher costs for the economy as a whole.

In times of very high inflation, menu costs can be substantial. During the Brazilian inflation of the early 1990s, for instance, supermarket workers reportedly spent half of their time replacing old price stickers with new ones. When inflation is high, merchants may decide to stop listing prices in terms of the local currency and use either an artificial unit—in effect, measuring prices relative to one another—or a more stable currency, such as the U.S. dollar. This is exactly what the Israeli real estate market began doing in the mid-1980s: prices were quoted in U.S. dollars, even though payment was made in Israeli shekels. And this is also what happened in Zimbabwe when, in May 2008, official estimates of the inflation rate reached 1,694,000%.

Menu costs are also present in low-inflation economies, but they are not severe. In low-inflation economies, businesses might update their prices only sporadically—not daily or even more frequently, as is the case in high-inflation or hyperinflation economies. Also, with technological advances, menu costs are becoming less and less important, since prices can be changed electronically and fewer merchants attach price stickers to merchandise.

Unit-of-Account Costs In the Middle Ages, contracts were often specified "in kind": a tenant might, for example, be obliged to provide his landlord with a certain number of cattle each year (the phrase *in kind* actually comes from an ancient word for *cattle*). This may have made sense at the time, but it would be an awkward way to conduct modern business. Instead, we state contracts in monetary terms: a renter owes a certain number of dollars per month, a company that issues a bond promises to pay the bondholder the dollar value of the bond when it comes due, and so on. We also tend to make our economic calculations in dollars: a family planning its budget, or a small business owner trying to figure out how well the business is doing, makes estimates of the amount of money coming in and going out.

This role of the dollar as a basis for contracts and calculation is called the *unit-of-account* role of money. It's an important aspect of the modern economy. Yet it's a role that can be degraded by inflation, which causes the purchasing power of a dollar to change over time—a dollar next year is worth less than a dollar this year. The effect, many economists argue, is to reduce the quality of economic decisions: the economy as a whole makes less efficient use of its resources because of the uncertainty caused by changes in the unit of account, the dollar. The **unit-of-account costs** of inflation are the costs arising from the way inflation makes money a less reliable unit of measurement.

Unit-of-account costs may be particularly important in the tax system, because inflation can distort the measures of income on which taxes are collected. Here's an example: Assume that the inflation rate is 10%, so that the overall level of prices rises 10% each year. Suppose that a business buys an asset, such as a piece of land, for $100,000, then resells it a year later at a price of $110,000. In a fundamental sense, the business didn't make a profit on the deal: in real terms, it got no more for the land than it paid for it. But U.S. tax law would say that the business made a capital gain of $10,000, and it would have to pay taxes on that phantom gain.

During the 1970s, when the United States had relatively high inflation, the distorting effects of inflation on the tax system were a serious problem. Some businesses were discouraged from productive investment spending because they found themselves paying taxes on phantom gains. Meanwhile, some unproductive investments became attractive because they led to phantom losses that reduced tax bills. When inflation fell in the 1980s—and tax rates were reduced—these problems became much less important.

Winners and Losers from Inflation

As we've just learned, a high inflation rate imposes overall costs on the economy. In addition, inflation can produce winners and losers within the economy. The main reason inflation sometimes helps some people while hurting others is that economic transactions often involve contracts that extend over a period of time, such as loans, and these contracts are normally specified in nominal—that is, in dollar—terms. In the case of a loan, the borrower receives a certain amount of funds at the beginning, and the loan contract specifies how much he or she must repay at some future date. But what that dollar repayment is worth in real terms—that is, in terms of purchasing power—depends greatly on the rate of inflation over the intervening years of the loan.

Economists summarize the effect of inflation on borrowers and lenders by distinguishing between the *nominal* interest rate and the *real* interest rate. The **nominal interest rate** is the interest rate in dollar terms—for example, the interest rate on a student loan. The **real interest rate** is the nominal interest rate minus the rate of inflation. For example, if a loan carries an interest rate of 8%, but there is 5% inflation, the real interest rate is 8% − 5% = 3%.

Unit-of-account costs arise from the way inflation makes money a less reliable unit of measurement.

The **nominal interest rate** is the interest rate expressed in dollar terms.

The **real interest rate** is the nominal interest rate minus the rate of inflation.

Disinflation is the process of bringing the inflation rate down.

When a borrower and a lender enter into a loan contract, the contract is normally written in dollar terms—that is, it specifies a nominal interest rate. But each party has an expectation about the future rate of inflation and therefore an expectation about the real interest rate on the loan. If the actual inflation rate is *higher* than expected, borrowers gain at the expense of lenders: borrowers will repay their loans with funds that have a lower real value than had been expected. Conversely, if the inflation rate is *lower* than expected, lenders will gain at the expense of borrowers: borrowers must repay their loans with funds that have a higher real value than had been expected.

Historically, the fact that inflation creates winners and losers has sometimes been a major source of political controversy. In 1896 William Jennings Bryan electrified the Democratic presidential convention with a speech in which he declared, "You shall not crucify mankind on a cross of gold." What he was actually demanding was an inflationary policy. At the time, the U.S. dollar had a fixed value in terms of gold. Bryan wanted to abandon that gold standard and have the U.S. government print more money, which would have raised the level of prices. And the reason he wanted inflation was to help farmers, many of whom were deeply in debt.

In modern America, home mortgages are the most important source of gains and losses from inflation. Americans who took out mortgages in the early 1970s quickly found their real payments reduced by higher-than-expected inflation: by 1983, the purchasing power of a dollar was only 45% of what it had been in 1973. Those who took out mortgages in the early 1990s were not so lucky, because the inflation rate fell to lower-than-expected levels in the following years: in 2003 the purchasing power of a dollar was 78% of what it had been in 1993.

Because gains for some and losses for others result from inflation that is either higher or lower than expected, yet another problem arises: uncertainty about the future inflation rate discourages people from entering into any form of long-term contract. This is an additional cost of high inflation, because high rates of inflation are usually unpredictable, too. In countries with high and uncertain inflation, long-term loans are rare, which makes it difficult in many cases to make long-term investments.

One last point: unexpected *deflation*—a surprise fall in the price level—creates winners and losers, too. Between 1929 and 1933, as the U.S. economy plunged into the Great Depression, the consumer price index fell by 35%. This meant that debtors, including many farmers and homeowners, saw a sharp rise in the real value of their debts, which led to widespread bankruptcy and helped create a banking crisis, as lenders found their customers unable to pay back their loans.

Inflation Is Easy; Disinflation Is Hard

There is not much evidence that a rise in the inflation rate from, say, 2% to 5% would do a great deal of harm to the economy. Still, policy makers generally move forcefully to bring inflation back down when it creeps above 2% or 3%. Why? Because experience shows that bringing the inflation rate down—a process called **disinflation**—is very difficult and costly once a higher rate of inflation has become well established in the economy.

Figure 24-11 shows the inflation rate and the unemployment rate in the United States over a crucial decade, from 1978 to 1988. The decade began with an alarming rise in the inflation rate, but by the end of the period inflation averaged only about 4%. This was considered a major economic achievement—but it came at a high cost. Much of the fall in inflation probably resulted from the very severe recession of 1981–1982, which drove the unemployment rate to 10.7%—its highest level since the Great Depression.

Many economists believe that this period of high unemployment was necessary because they believe that the only way to reduce inflation that has become deeply embedded in the economy is through policies that temporarily depress the economy.

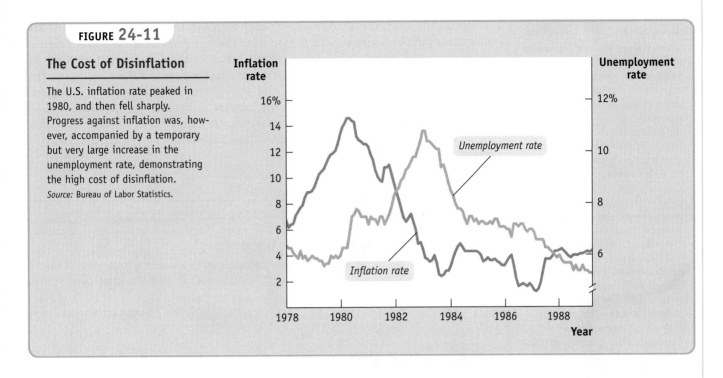

FIGURE 24-11

The Cost of Disinflation

The U.S. inflation rate peaked in 1980, and then fell sharply. Progress against inflation was, however, accompanied by a temporary but very large increase in the unemployment rate, demonstrating the high cost of disinflation.

Source: Bureau of Labor Statistics.

The best way to avoid having to put the economy through a wringer to reduce inflation, however, is to avoid having a serious inflation problem in the first place. So policy makers respond forcefully to signs that inflation may be accelerating as a form of preventive medicine for the economy.

►ECONOMICS IN ACTION

Israel's Experience with Inflation

It's often hard to see the costs of inflation clearly because serious inflation problems are often associated with other problems that disrupt economic life, notably war or political instability (or both). In the mid-1980s, however, Israel experienced a "clean" inflation: there was no war, the government was stable, and there was order in the streets. Yet a series of policy errors led to very high inflation, with prices often rising more than 10% a month.

As it happens, one of the authors spent a month visiting at Tel Aviv University at the height of the inflation, so we can give a first-hand account of the effects.

First, the shoe-leather costs of inflation were substantial. At the time, Israelis spent a lot of time in lines at the bank, moving money in and out of accounts that provided high enough interest rates to offset inflation. People walked around with very little cash in their wallets; they had to go to the bank whenever they needed to make even a moderately large cash payment. Banks responded by opening a lot of branches, a costly business expense.

The shoe-leather costs of inflation in Israel: when the inflation rate hit 500% in 1985, people spent a lot of time in line at banks.

Second, although menu costs weren't that visible to a visitor, what you could see were the efforts businesses made to minimize them. For example, restaurant menus often didn't list prices. Instead, they listed numbers that you had to multiply by another number, written on a chalkboard and changed every day, to figure out the price of a dish.

Finally, it was hard to make decisions because prices changed so much and so often. It was a common experience to walk out of a store because prices were 25% higher than at one's usual shopping destination, only to discover that prices had just been increased 25% there, too. ▲

< < < < < < < < < < < <

► CHECK YOUR UNDERSTANDING 24-3

1. The widespread use of technology has revolutionized the banking industry, making it much easier for customers to access and manage their assets. Does this mean that the shoe-leather costs of inflation are higher or lower than they used to be?

2. Most people in the United States have grown accustomed to a modest inflation rate of around 2-3%. Who would gain and who would lose if inflation came to a complete stop over the next 15 or 20 years?

Solutions appear at back of book.

[>> A LOOK AHEAD •••

From year to year, public concerns about the economy are focused on the twin problems of inflation and unemployment. But these concerns aren't the end of the story. The unemployment rate was lower in 1948 than it was in 2008, yet few Americans would like to go back to the economy of 1948—an economy in which almost everyone had a lower standard of living than most of us have today. The reason for this difference is *long-run economic growth.* In the next chapter, we describe the facts about long-run economic growth and explain why some countries have been much more successful than others in achieving long-run growth.]

SUMMARY ··■

1. Inflation and unemployment are the twin evils of macroeconomics and the main concerns of macroeconomic policy.

2. **Employment** is the number of people employed; **unemployment** is the number of people unemployed and actively looking for work. Their sum is equal to the **labor force,** and the **labor force participation rate** is the percentage of the population age 16 or older that is in the labor force.

3. The **unemployment rate,** the percentage of the labor force that is unemployed and actively looking for work, can both overstate and understate the true level of unemployment. It can overstate because it counts as unemployed those who are continuing to search for a job despite having been offered one (that is, workers who are frictionally unemployed). It can understate because it ignores frustrated workers, such as **discouraged workers, marginally attached workers,** and the

underemployed. In addition, the unemployment rate varies greatly among different groups in the population; it is typically higher for younger workers and for workers near retirement age than for workers in their prime working years.

4. The unemployment rate is affected by the business cycle. The unemployment rate generally falls when the growth rate of real GDP is above average and generally increases when the growth rate of real GDP is below average.

5. Job creation and destruction, as well as voluntary job separations, lead to **job search** and **frictional unemployment.** In addition, a variety of factors such as minimum wages, unions, **efficiency wages,** and government policies designed to help laid-off workers result in a situation in which there is a surplus of labor at the market wage rate, creating **structural unemployment.** As a result, the **natural rate of unemployment,** the sum of frictional and structural employment, is well above zero, even when jobs are plentiful.

6. The actual unemployment rate is equal to the natural rate of unemployment, the share of unemployment that is independent of the business cycle, plus **cyclical unemployment,** the share of unemployment that depends on fluctuations in the business cycle.

7. The natural rate of unemployment changes over time, largely in response to changes in labor force characteristics, labor market institutions, and government policies.

8. Policy makers worry about inflation as well as unemployment; they are sometimes willing to accept high unemployment to bring inflation down.

9. Inflation does not, as many assume, make everyone poorer by raising the level of prices. That's because wages and incomes are adjusted to take into account a rising price level, leaving **real wages** and **real income** unaffected. However, a high inflation rate imposes overall costs on the economy: **shoe-leather costs, menu costs,** and **unit-of-account costs.**

10. Inflation can produce winners and losers within the economy, because long-term contracts are generally written in dollar terms. Loans typically specify a **nominal interest rate,** which differs from the **real interest rate** due to inflation. A higher-than-expected inflation rate is good for borrowers and bad for lenders. A lower-than-expected inflation rate is good for lenders and bad for borrowers.

11. **Disinflation** is very costly, so policy makers try to prevent inflation from becoming excessive in the first place.

KEY TERMS ....■

Employment, p. 616
Unemployment, p. 617
Labor force, p. 617
Labor force participation rate, p. 617
Unemployment rate, p. 617
Discouraged workers, p. 618
Marginally attached workers, p. 618
Underemployment, p. 618

Job search, p. 623
Frictional unemployment, p. 623
Structural unemployment, p. 624
Efficiency wages, p. 626
Natural rate of unemployment, p. 626
Cyclical unemployment, p. 626
Real wage, p. 631

Real income, p. 631
Shoe-leather costs, p. 632
Menu cost, p. 632
Unit-of-account costs, p. 633
Nominal interest rate, p. 633
Real interest rate, p. 633
Disinflation, p. 634

PROBLEMS ....■

1. Each month, usually on the first Friday of the month, the Bureau of Labor Statistics releases the Employment Situation Summary for the previous month. Go to www.bls.gov and find the latest report. (On the Bureau of Labor Statistics home page, on the left side of the page, find "Unemployment" and select "National Unemployment Rate." You will find the Employment Situation under "News Releases.") How does the unemployment rate compare to the rate one month earlier? How does the unemployment rate compare to the rate one year earlier?

2. In general, how do changes in the unemployment rate vary with changes in real GDP? After several quarters of a severe recession, explain why we might observe a decrease in the official unemployment rate. Could we see an increase in the official unemployment rate after several quarters of a strong expansion?

3. In each of the following situations, what type of unemployment is Melanie facing?

  a. After completing a complex programming project, Melanie is laid off. Her prospects for a new job requiring similar skills are good, and she has signed up with a programmer placement service. She has passed up offers for low-paying jobs.

  b. When Melanie and her co-workers refused to accept pay cuts, her employer outsourced their programming tasks to workers in another country. This phenomenon is occurring throughout the programming industry.

  c. Due to the current slump in investment spending, Melanie has been laid off from her programming job. Her employer promises to rehire her when business picks up.

4. Part of the information released in the Employment Situation Summary concerns how long individuals have been unemployed. Go to www.bls.gov to find the latest report. Use the same technique as in Problem 1 to find the Employment Situation Summary. At the end of the Employment Situation, click on the table titled "Unemployed persons by duration of unemployment." Use the seasonally adjusted numbers to answer the following questions.

  a. How many workers were unemployed less than 5 weeks? What percentage of all unemployed workers do these workers represent? How do these numbers compare to the previous month's data?

  b. How many workers were unemployed for 27 or more weeks? What percentage of all unemployed workers do these workers represent? How do these numbers compare to the previous month's data?

c. How long has the average worker been unemployed (average duration, in weeks)? How does this compare to the average for the previous month's data?

d. Comparing the latest month for which there are data with the previous month, has the problem of long-term unemployment improved or deteriorated?

5. There is only one labor market in Profunctia. All workers have the same skills, and all firms hire workers with these skills. Use the accompanying diagram, which shows the supply of and demand for labor, to answer the following questions. Illustrate each answer with a diagram.

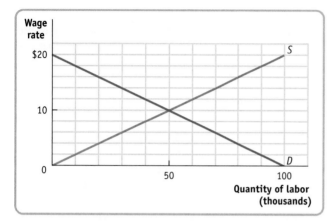

a. What is the equilibrium wage rate in Profunctia? At this wage rate, what are the level of employment, the size of the labor force, and the unemployment rate?

b. If the government of Profunctia sets a minimum wage equal to $12, what will be the level of employment, the size of the labor force, and the unemployment rate?

c. If unions bargain with the firms in Profunctia and set a wage rate equal to $14, what will be the level of employment, the size of the labor force, and the unemployment rate?

d. If the concern for retaining workers and encouraging high-quality work leads firms to set a wage rate equal to $16, what will be the level of employment, the size of the labor force, and the unemployment rate?

6. A country's labor force is the sum of the number of employed and unemployed workers. The accompanying table provides data on the size of the labor force and the number of unemployed workers for different regions of the United States.

Region	Labor force (thousands)		Unemployed (thousands)	
	March 2007	March 2008	March 2007	March 2008
Northeast	27,863.5	28,035.6	1,197.8	1,350.3
South	54,203.8	54,873.9	2,300.9	2,573.8
Midwest	34,824.3	35,048.6	1,718.2	1,870.8
West	35,231.8	35,903.3	1,588.0	1,914.4

Source: Bureau of Labor Statistics.

a. Calculate the number of workers employed in each of the regions in March 2007 and March 2008. Use your answers to calculate the change in the total number of workers employed between March 2007 and March 2008.

b. For each region, calculate the growth in the labor force from March 2007 to March 2008.

c. Compute unemployment rates in the different regions of the country in March 2007 and March 2008.

d. What can you infer about the rise in unemployment rates over this period? Was it caused by a net loss in the number of jobs or by a large increase in the number of people seeking jobs?

7. In which of the following cases is it more likely for efficiency wages to exist? Why?

a. Jane and her boss work as a team selling ice cream.

b. Jane sells ice cream without any direct supervision by her boss.

c. Jane speaks Korean and sells ice cream in a neighborhood in which Korean is the primary language. It is difficult to find another worker who speaks Korean.

8. How will the following changes affect the natural rate of unemployment?

a. The government reduces the time during which an unemployed worker can receive benefits.

b. More teenagers focus on their studies and do not look for jobs until after college.

c. Greater access to the Internet leads both potential employers and potential employees to use the Internet to list and find jobs.

d. Union membership declines.

9. With its tradition of a job for life for most citizens, Japan once had a much lower unemployment rate than that of the United States; from 1960 to 1995, the unemployment rate in Japan exceeded 3% only once. However, since the crash of its stock market in 1989 and slow economic growth in the 1990s, the job-for-life system has broken down and unemployment rose to more than 5% in 2003.

a. Explain the likely effect of the breakdown of the job-for-life system in Japan on the Japanese natural rate of unemployment.

b. As the accompanying diagram shows, the rate of growth of real GDP has picked up in Japan since 2001. Explain the likely effect of this increase in GDP growth on the unemployment rate. Is the likely cause of the change in the unemployment rate during this period a change in the natural rate of unemployment or a change in the cyclical unemployment rate?

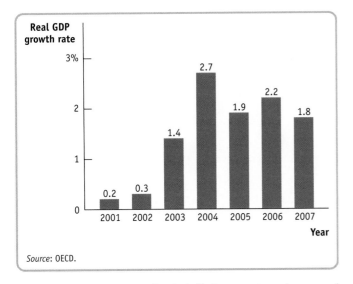

Source: OECD.

10. In the following examples, is inflation creating winners and losers at no net cost to the economy or is inflation imposing a net cost on the economy? If a net cost is being imposed, which type of cost is involved?

  a. When inflation is expected to be high, workers get paid more frequently and make more trips to the bank.

  b. Lanwei is reimbursed by her company for her work-related travel expenses. Sometimes, however, the company takes a long time to reimburse her. So when inflation is high, she is less willing to travel for her job.

  c. Hector Homeowner has a mortgage with a fixed nominal 6% interest rate that he took out five years ago. Over the years, the inflation rate has crept up unexpectedly to its present level of 7%.

  d. In response to unexpectedly high inflation, the manager of Cozy Cottages of Cape Cod must reprint and resend expensive color brochures correcting the price of rentals this season.

11. The accompanying diagram shows mortgage interest rates and inflation during 1990–2005 in the economy of Albernia. When would home mortgages have been especially attractive and why?

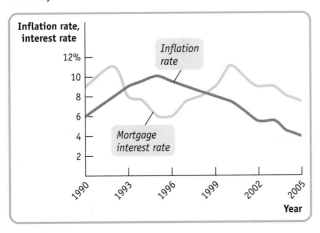

12. The accompanying table provides the inflation rate in the year 2000 and the average inflation rate over the period 2000–2007 for eight different countries.

Country	Inflation rate in 2000	Average inflation rate in 2000–2007
Brazil	7.1%	7.3%
China	0.3	1.6
France	1.7	1.8
Indonesia	3.8	8.8
Japan	−0.7	−0.3
Turkey	56.4	27.8
United States	3.4	2.8
Zimbabwe	55.7	904.1

Source: IMF.

  a. Given the expected relationship between average inflation and menu costs, rank the countries in descending order of menu costs using average inflation over the period 2000–2007.

  b. Rank the countries in order of inflation rates that most favored borrowers with seven-year loans that were taken out in 2000. Assume that the expected inflation rate was the inflation rate in 2000.

  c. Did borrowers who took out seven-year loans in Japan gain or lose overall versus lenders? Explain.

13. The accompanying diagram shows the inflation rate in the United Kingdom from 1980 to 2007.

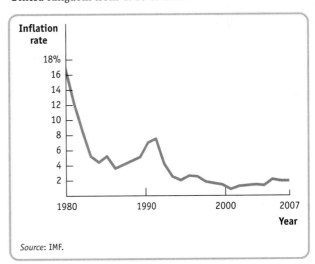

Source: IMF.

  a. What would you predict happened to unemployment between 1980 and 1985?

  b. Policy makers in the United Kingdom react forcefully when the inflation rate rises above a target rate of 2%. Why would it be harmful if inflation rose from 1.9% (the level in 2007) to, say, a level of 5%?

 www.worthpublishers.com/krugmanwells

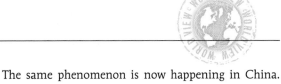

Long-Run Economic Growth

TALL TALES

CHINA IS GROWING—AND SO ARE THE CHINESE. According to official statistics, children in China are almost 2½ inches taller now than they were 30 years ago. The average Chinese citizen is still a lot shorter than the average American, but at the current rate of growth the difference may be largely gone in a couple of generations.

If that does happen, China will be following in Japan's footsteps. Older Americans tend to think of the Japanese as short, but today young Japanese men are more than 5 inches taller on average than they were in 1900, which makes them almost as tall as their American counterparts (and taller, on average, than either author of this book).

There's no mystery about why the Japanese grew taller—it's because they grew richer. In the early twentieth century, Japan was a relatively poor country in which many families couldn't afford to give their children adequate nutrition. As a result, their children grew up to be short adults. However, since World War II, Japan has become an economic powerhouse in which food is ample and young adults are much taller than before.

At 7'6", China's Yao Ming illustrates the positive relationship between a country's rate of long-run economic growth and its average population height.

Bill Baptist/NBAE via Getty Images

The same phenomenon is now happening in China. Although it is still a relatively poor country, China has made great economic strides over the past 30 years. Its recent history is probably the world's most dramatic example of long-run economic growth—a sustained increase in output per capita. Yet despite its impressive performance, China is currently playing catch-up with economically advanced countries like the United States and Japan. It's still a relatively poor country because these other nations began their own processes of long-run economic growth many decades ago—and in the case of the United States and European countries, more than a century ago.

Many economists have argued that long-run economic growth—why it happens and how to achieve it—is the single most important issue in macroeconomics. In this chapter, we present some facts about long-run growth, look at the factors that economists believe determine the pace at which long-run growth takes place, examine how government policies can help or hinder growth, and address questions about the environmental sustainability of long-run growth.

Comparing Economies Across Time and Space

Before we analyze the sources of long-run economic growth, it's useful to have a sense of just how much the U.S. economy has grown over time and how large the gaps are between wealthy countries like the United States and countries that have yet to achieve comparable growth. So let's take a look at the numbers.

Real GDP per Capita

The key statistic used to track economic growth is *real GDP per capita*—real GDP divided by the population size. We focus on GDP because, as we learned in Chapter 23, GDP measures the total value of an economy's production of final goods and services as well as the income earned in that economy in a given year. We use *real* GDP because we want to separate changes in the quantity of goods and services from the effects of a rising price level. We focus on real GDP *per capita* because we want to isolate the effect of changes in the population. For example, other things equal, an increase in the population lowers the standard of living for the average person—there are now more people to share a given amount of real GDP. An increase in real GDP that only matches an increase in population leaves the average standard of living unchanged.

Although we also learned in Chapter 23 that growth in real GDP per capita should not be a policy goal in and of itself, it does serve as a very useful summary measure of a country's economic progress over time. Figure 25-1 shows real GDP per capita for the

---

FIGURE 25-1

Economic Growth in the United States, India, and China over the Past Century

Real GDP per capita from 1907 to 2007, measured in 1990 dollars, is shown for the United States, India, and China. Equal percent changes in real GDP per capita are drawn the same size. India and China currently have a much higher growth rate than the United States. However, China has only just attained the standard of living achieved in the United States in 1907, while India is still poorer than the United States was in 1907.

Source: Angus Maddison, Statistics on World Population, GDP, and Per Capita GDP, 1–2006AD, http://www.ggdc.net/maddison; International Monetary Fund.

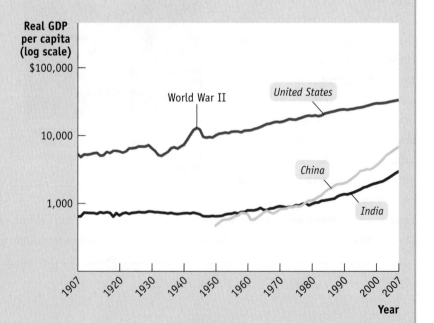

United States, India, and China, measured in 1990 dollars, from 1907 to 2007. (We'll talk about India and China in a moment.) The vertical axis is drawn on a logarithmic scale so that equal percent changes in real GDP per capita across countries are the same size in the graph.

To give a sense of how much the U.S. economy grew during the last century, Table 25-1 shows real GDP per capita at 20-year intervals, expressed two ways: as a percentage of the 1907 level and as a percentage of the 2007 level. In 1927, the U.S. economy already produced 129% as much per person as it did in 1907. In 2007, it produced 620% as much per person as it did in 1907, an over five-fold increase. Alternatively, in 1907 the U.S. economy produced only 16% as much per person as it did in 2007.

The income of the typical family normally grows more or less in proportion to per capita income. For example, a 1% increase in real GDP per capita corresponds, roughly, to a 1% increase in the income of the median or typical family—a family at the center of the income distribution. In 2007, the median American household had an income of about $50,000. Since Table 25-1 tells us that real GDP per capita in 1907 was only 16% of its 2007 level, a typical family in 1907 probably had a purchasing power only 16% as large as the purchasing power of a typical family in 2007. That's around $8,000 in today's dollars, representing a standard of living that we would now consider severe poverty. Today's typical American family, if transported back to the United States of 1907, would feel quite a lot of deprivation.

Yet many people in the world have a standard of living equal to or lower than that of the United States a century ago. That's the message about China and India in Figure 25-1: despite dramatic economic growth in China over the last three decades and the less dramatic acceleration of economic growth in India, China has only just attained the standard of living that the United States enjoyed in 1907, while India is still poorer than the United States was in 1907. And much of the world today is poorer than China or India.

You can get a sense of how poor much of the world remains by looking at Figure 25-2, a map of the world in which countries are classified according to their 2007 levels of

TABLE 25-1

U.S. Real GDP per Capita

Year	Percentage of 1907 real GDP per capita	Percentage of 2007 real GDP per capita
1907	100%	16%
1927	129	21
1947	175	28
1967	283	46
1987	430	69
2007	620	100

Source: Angus Maddison, *Statistics on World Population, GDP, and Per Capita GDP, 1–2006AD,* http://www.ggdc.net/maddison; Bureau of Economic Analysis.

FIGURE 25-2 Incomes Around the World, 2007 Although the countries of Europe and North America—along with a few in the Pacific—have high incomes, much of the world is still very poor. Today, more than 50% of the world's population lives in countries with a lower standard of living than the United States had a century ago.

Source: International Monetary Fund.

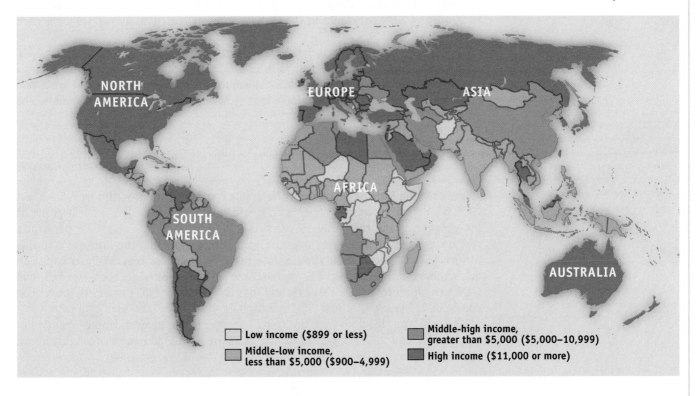

☐ Low income ($899 or less)

◼ Middle-low income, less than $5,000 ($900–4,999)

◼ Middle-high income, greater than $5,000 ($5,000–10,999)

◼ High income ($11,000 or more)

The **Rule of 70** tells us that the time it takes a variable that grows gradually over time to double is approximately 70 divided by that variable's annual growth rate.

GDP per capita, in U.S. dollars. As you can see, large parts of the world have very low incomes. Generally speaking, the countries of Europe and North America, as well as a few in the Pacific, have high incomes. The rest of the world, containing most of its population, is dominated by countries with GDP less than $5,000 per capita—and often much less. In fact, today more than 50% of the world's people live in countries with a lower standard of living than the United States had a century ago.

Growth Rates

How did the United States manage to produce over six times more per person in 2007 than in 1907? A little bit at a time. Long-run economic growth is normally a gradual process in which real GDP per capita grows at most a few percent per year. From 1907 to 2007, real GDP per capita in the United States increased an average of 1.8% each year.

To have a sense of the relationship between the annual growth rate of real GDP per capita and the long-run change in real GDP per capita, it's helpful to keep in mind the **Rule of 70,** a mathematical formula that tells us how long it takes real GDP per capita, or any other variable that grows gradually over time, to double. The approximate answer is:

$$\text{(25-1)} \quad \text{Number of years for variable to double} = \frac{70}{\text{Annual growth rate of variable}}$$

(Note that the Rule of 70 can only be applied to a positive growth rate.) So if real GDP per capita grows at 1% per year, it will take 70 years to double. If it grows at 2% per year, it will take only 35 years to double. In fact, U.S. real GDP per capita rose on average 1.8% per year over the last century. Applying the Rule of 70 to this information implies that it should have taken 39 years for real GDP per capita to double; it would have taken 117 years—three periods of 39 years each—for U.S. real GDP per capita to double three times. That is, the Rule of 70 implies that over the course of 117 years, U.S. real GDP per capita should have increased by a factor of 2 × 2 × 2 = 8. And this does turn out to be a pretty good approximation of reality. Between 1890 and 2007—a period of 117 years—real GDP per capita rose just about eightfold.

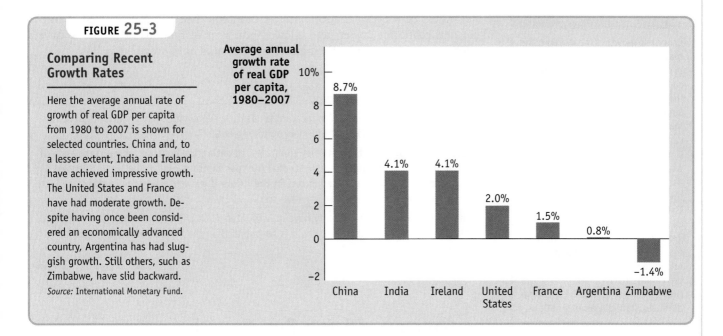

FIGURE 25-3

Comparing Recent Growth Rates

Here the average annual rate of growth of real GDP per capita from 1980 to 2007 is shown for selected countries. China and, to a lesser extent, India and Ireland have achieved impressive growth. The United States and France have had moderate growth. Despite having once been considered an economically advanced country, Argentina has had sluggish growth. Still others, such as Zimbabwe, have slid backward.

Source: International Monetary Fund.

Average annual growth rate of real GDP per capita, 1980–2007

China 8.7%
India 4.1%
Ireland 4.1%
United States 2.0%
France 1.5%
Argentina 0.8%
Zimbabwe −1.4%

Figure 25-3 shows the average annual rate of growth of real GDP per capita for selected countries from 1980 to 2007. Some countries were notable success stories: for example, China, though still quite a poor country, has made spectacular progress. India, although not matching China's performance, has also achieved impressive growth, as discussed in the following Economics in Action.

Some countries, though, have had very disappointing growth. Argentina was once considered a wealthy nation. In the early years of the twentieth century, it was in the same league as the United States and Canada. But since then it has lagged far behind more dynamic economies. And still others, like Zimbabwe, have slid backward.

What explains these differences in growth rates? To answer that question, we need to examine the sources of long-run growth.

►*ECONOMICS IN ACTION*

India Takes Off

India achieved independence from Great Britain in 1947, becoming the world's most populous democracy—a status it has maintained to this day. For more than three decades after independence, however, this happy political story was partly overshadowed by economic disappointment. Despite ambitious economic development plans, India's performance was consistently sluggish. In 1980, India's real GDP per capita was only about 50% higher than it had been in 1947; the gap between Indian living standards and those in wealthy countries like the United States had been growing rather than shrinking.

Since then, however, India has done much better. As Figure 25-3 shows, real GDP per capita has grown at an average rate of 4.1% a year, tripling between 1980 and 2007. India now has a large and rapidly growing middle class. And yes, the well-fed children of that middle class are much taller than their parents.

What went right in India after 1980? Many economists point to policy reforms. For decades after independence, India had a tightly controlled, highly regulated economy. Today, things are very different: a series of reforms opened the economy to international trade and freed up domestic competition. Some economists, however, argue that this can't be the main story, because the big policy reforms weren't adopted until 1991, yet growth accelerated around 1980.

India's high rate of economic growth since 1980 has raised living standards and led to the emergence of a rapidly growing middle class.

Regardless of the explanation, India's economic rise has transformed it into a major new economic power—and allowed hundreds of millions of people to have a much better life, better than their grandparents could have dreamed. ▲

< < < < < < < < < < < <

➤ CHECK YOUR UNDERSTANDING 25-1

1. Why do economists use real GDP per capita to measure economic progress rather than some other measure, such as nominal GDP per capita or real GDP?

2. Apply the Rule of 70 to the data in Figure 25-3 to determine how long it will take each of the countries listed there to double its real GDP per capita. Would India's real GDP per capita exceed that of the United States in the future if growth rates remain the same? Why or why not?

3. Although China and India currently have growth rates much higher than the U.S. growth rate, the typical Chinese or Indian household is far poorer than the typical American household. Explain why.

Solutions appear at back of book.

The Sources of Long-Run Growth

Long-run economic growth depends almost entirely on one ingredient: rising *productivity*. However, a number of factors affect the growth of productivity. Let's look first at why productivity is the key ingredient and then examine what affects it.

The Crucial Importance of Productivity

Sustained economic growth occurs only when the amount of output produced by the average worker increases steadily. The term **labor productivity,** or **productivity** for short, is used to refer either to output per worker or, in some cases, to output per hour (the number of hours worked by an average worker differs to some extent across countries, although this isn't an important factor in the difference between living standards in, say, India and the United States). In this book we'll focus on output per worker. For the economy as a whole, productivity—output per worker—is simply real GDP divided by the number of people working.

You might wonder why we say that higher productivity is the only source of long-run growth. Can't an economy also increase its real GDP per capita by putting more of the population to work? The answer is, yes, but . . . . For short periods of time, an economy can experience a burst of growth in output per capita by putting a higher percentage of the population to work. That happened in the United States during World War II, when millions of women who previously worked only in the home entered the paid workforce. The percentage of adult civilians employed outside the home rose from 50% in 1941 to 58% in 1944, and you can see the resulting bump in real GDP per capita during those years in Figure 25-1.

Over the longer run, however, the rate of employment growth is never very different from the rate of population growth. Over the course of the twentieth century, for example, the population of the United States rose at an average rate of 1.3% per year and employment rose 1.5% per year. Real GDP per capita rose 1.9% per year; of that, 1.7%—that is, almost 90% of the total—was the result of rising productivity. In general, overall real GDP can grow because of population growth, but any large increase in real GDP *per capita* must be the result of increased output *per worker*. That is, it must be due to higher productivity.

So increased productivity is the key to long-run economic growth. But what leads to higher productivity?

Labor productivity, often referred to simply as **productivity,** is output per worker.

Explaining Growth in Productivity

There are three main reasons why the average U.S. worker today produces far more than his or her counterpart a century ago. First, the modern worker has far more *physical capital,* such as machinery and office space, to work with. Second, the modern worker is much better educated and so possesses much more *human capital.* Finally, modern firms have the advantage of a century's accumulation of technical advancements reflecting a great deal of *technological progress.*

Let's look at each of these factors in turn.

Physical Capital Economists define **physical capital** as manufactured resources such as buildings and machines. Physical capital makes workers more productive. For example, a worker operating a backhoe can dig a lot more feet of trench per day than one equipped only with a shovel.

The average U.S. private-sector worker today is backed up by around $130,000 worth of physical capital—far more than a U.S. worker had 100 years ago and far more than the average worker in most other countries has today.

Human Capital It's not enough for a worker to have good equipment—he or she must also know what to do with it. **Human capital** refers to the improvement in labor created by the education and knowledge embodied in the workforce.

The human capital of the United States has increased dramatically over the past century. A century ago, although most Americans were able to read and write, very few had an extensive education. In 1910, only 13.5% of Americans over 25 had graduated from high school and only 3% had four-year college degrees. By 2007, the percentages were 86% and 29%, respectively. It would be impossible to run today's economy with a population as poorly educated as that of a century ago.

Analyses based on *growth accounting,* described later in this chapter, suggest that education—and its effect on productivity—is an even more important determinant of growth than increases in physical capital.

Technology Probably the most important driver of productivity growth is progress in **technology,** which is broadly defined as the technical means for the production of goods and services. We'll see shortly how economists measure the impact of technology on growth.

Workers today are able to produce more than those in the past, even with the same amount of physical and human capital, because technology has advanced over time. It's important to realize that economically important technological progress need not be flashy or rely on cutting-edge science. Historians have noted that past economic growth has been driven not only by major inventions, such as the railroad or the semiconductor chip, but also by thousands of modest innovations, such as the flat-bottomed paper bag, patented in 1870, which made packing groceries and many other goods much easier, and the Post-it® note, introduced in 1981, which has had surprisingly large benefits for office productivity. As the upcoming For Inquiring Minds points out, experts attribute much of the productivity surge that took place in the United States late in the twentieth century to new technology adopted by retail companies like Wal-Mart rather than to high-technology companies.

Physical capital consists of human-made resources such as buildings and machines.

Human capital is the improvement in labor created by the education and knowledge embodied in the workforce.

Technology is the technical means for the production of goods and services.

The **aggregate production function** is a hypothetical function that shows how productivity (real GDP per worker) depends on the quantities of physical capital per worker and human capital per worker as well as the state of technology.

Accounting for Growth: The Aggregate Production Function

Productivity is higher, other things equal, when workers are equipped with more physical capital, more human capital, better technology, or any combination of the three. But can we put numbers to these effects? To do this, economists make use of estimates of the **aggregate production function,** which shows how productivity depends on

An aggregate production function exhibits **diminishing returns to physical
capital** when, holding the amount of
human capital per worker and the state
of technology fixed, each successive increase in the amount of physical capital
per worker leads to a smaller increase
in productivity.

the quantities of physical capital per worker and human capital per worker as well as
the state of technology. In general, all three factors tend to rise over time, as workers
are equipped with more machinery, receive more education, and benefit from technological advances. What the aggregate production function does is allow economists to
disentangle the effects of these three factors on overall productivity.

A recent example of an aggregate production function applied to real data comes
from a comparative study of Chinese and Indian economic growth by the economists
Barry Bosworth and Susan Collins of the Brookings Institution. They used the following aggregate production function:

$$\text{GDP per worker} = T \times (\text{Physical capital per worker})^{0.4} \\ \times (\text{Human capital per worker})^{0.6}$$

where T represented an estimate of the level of technology and they assumed that
each year of education raises workers' human capital by 7%. Using this function, they
tried to explain why China grew faster than India between 1978 and 2004. About half
the difference, they found, was due to China's higher levels of investment spending,
which raised its level of physical capital per worker faster than India's. The other half
was due to faster Chinese technological progress.

In analyzing historical economic growth, economists have discovered a crucial fact
about the estimated aggregate production function: it exhibits **diminishing returns
to physical capital.** That is, when the amount of human capital per worker and the
state of technology are held fixed, each successive increase in the amount of physical
capital per worker leads to a smaller increase in productivity. Table 25-2 gives a hypothetical example of how the level of physical capital per worker might affect the level
of real GDP per worker, holding human capital per worker and the state of technology fixed. In this example, we measure the quantity of physical capital in dollars.

As you can see from the table, there is a big payoff for the first $15,000 of physical
capital: real GDP per worker rises by $30,000. The second $15,000 of physical capital
also raises productivity, but not by as much: real GDP per worker goes up by only
$15,000. The third $15,000 of physical capital raises real GDP per worker by only
$10,000.

To see why the relationship between physical capital per worker and productivity
exhibits diminishing returns, think about how having farm equipment affects the
productivity of farmworkers. A little bit of equipment makes a big difference: a worker
equipped with a tractor can do much more than a worker without one. And a worker
using more expensive equipment will, other things equal, be more productive: a
worker with a $30,000 tractor will normally be able to cultivate more farmland in a
given amount of time than a worker with a $15,000 tractor because the more expen-
sive machine will be more powerful, perform more tasks, or both.

But will a worker with a $30,000 tractor, holding human capital and technology
constant, be twice as productive as a worker with a $15,000 tractor? Probably not:
there's a huge difference between not having a tractor at all and having even an inexpensive tractor; there's much less difference between having an inexpensive tractor

TABLE 25-2

**A Hypothetical Example: How Physical Capital per Worker Affects Productivity,
Holding Human Capital and Technology Fixed**

Physical capital per worker	Real GDP per worker
$0	$0
15,000	30,000
30,000	45,000
45,000	55,000

The Wal-Mart Effect

After 20 years of being sluggish, U.S. pro-ductivity growth accelerated sharply in the late 1990s. That is, starting in the late 1990s productivity grew at a much faster rate. What caused that acceleration? Was it the rise of the Internet?

Not according to analysts at McKinsey and Co., the famous business consulting firm. They found that a major source of pro-ductivity improvement after 1995 was a surge in output per worker in retailing— stores were selling much more merchandise per worker. And why did productivity surge in retailing in the United States? "The rea-son can be explained in just two syllables: Wal-Mart," wrote McKinsey.

Wal-Mart has been a pioneer in using modern technology to improve productiv-ity. For example, it was one of the first companies to use computers to track in-ventory, to use bar-code scanners, to es-tablish direct electronic links with suppliers, and so on. It continued to set the pace in the 1990s, but, increasingly, other companies have imitated Wal-Mart's business practices.

There are two lessons from the "Wal-Mart effect," as McKinsey calls it. One is that how you apply a technology makes all the difference: everyone in the retail business knew about computers, but Wal-Mart figured out what to do with them. The other is that a lot of economic growth comes from everyday improve-ments rather than glamorous new technologies.

and having a better tractor. And we can be sure that a worker with a $150,000 tractor won't be 10 times as productive: a tractor can be improved only so much. Because the same is true of other kinds of equipment, the aggregate production function shows diminishing returns to physical capital.

Diminishing returns to physical capital imply a relationship between physical capital per worker and output per worker like the one shown in Figure 25-4. As the curve illus-trates, more physical capital per worker leads to more output per worker. But each $30,000 increment in physical capital per worker adds less to productivity. By comparing points *A*, *B*, and *C*, you can also see that as physical capital per worker rises, output per worker also rises—but at a diminishing rate. Going from point *A* to point *B*, representing a $30,000 increase in physical capital per worker, leads to an increase of $20,000 in real GDP per worker. Going from point *B* to point *C*, a second $30,000 increase in physical capital per worker, leads to an increase of only $10,000 in real GDP per worker.

FIGURE 25-4

Physical Capital and Productivity

Other things equal, a greater quantity of physical capital per worker leads to higher real GDP per worker but is sub-ject to diminishing returns: each suc-cessive addition to physical capital per worker produces a smaller in-crease in productivity. Starting at point *A*, with $20,000 in physical capital per worker, a $30,000 increase in physical capital per worker leads to an increase of $20,000 in real GDP per worker. At point *B*, with $50,000 in physical capital per worker, a $30,000 increase in physical capital per worker leads to an increase of only $10,000 in real GDP per worker.

Real GDP per worker

Productivity

1. The increase in real GDP per worker becomes smaller . . .

$60,000

50,000

30,000

C

B

A

0    $20,000 ⟶ 50,000 ⟶ 80,000

2. . . . as physical capital per worker rises.

Physical capital per worker (2000 dollars)

PITFALLS

IT MAY BE DIMINISHED . . . BUT IT'S STILL POSITIVE

It's important to understand what diminishing returns to physical capital means and what it doesn't mean. As we've already explained, it's an "other things equal" statement: holding the amount of human capital per worker and the technology fixed, each successive increase in the amount of physical capital per worker results in a smaller increase in real GDP per worker. But this doesn't mean that real GDP per worker eventually falls as more and more physical capital is added. It's just that the *increase* in real GDP per worker gets smaller and smaller, albeit remaining at or above zero. So an increase in physical capital per worker will never reduce productivity. But due to diminishing returns, at some point increasing the amount of physical capital per worker no longer produces an economic payoff: at some point the increase in output is so small that it is not worth the cost of the additional physical capital.

It's important to realize that diminishing returns to physical capital is an "other things equal" phenomenon: additional amounts of physical capital are less productive *when the amount of human capital per worker and the technology are held fixed.* Diminishing returns may disappear if we increase the amount of human capital per worker, or improve the technology, or both at the same time the amount of physical capital per worker is increased. For example, a worker with a $30,000 tractor who has also been trained in the most advanced cultivation techniques may in fact be more than twice as productive as a worker with only a $15,000 tractor and no additional human capital. But diminishing returns to any one input—regardless of whether it is physical capital, human capital, or number of workers—is a pervasive characteristic of production. Typical estimates suggest that in practice a 1% increase in the quantity of physical capital per worker increases output per worker by only one-third of 1%, or 0.33%.

In practice, all the factors contributing to higher productivity rise during the course of economic growth: both physical capital and human capital per worker increase, and technology advances as well. To disentangle the effects of these factors, economists use **growth accounting,** which estimates the contribution of each major factor in the aggregate production function to economic growth. For example, suppose the following are true:

- The amount of physical capital per worker grows 3% a year.
- According to estimates of the aggregate production function, each 1% rise in physical capital per worker, holding human capital and technology constant, raises output per worker by one-third of 1%, or 0.33%.

In that case, we would estimate that growing physical capital per worker is responsible for 3% × 0.33 = 1 percentage point of productivity growth per year. A similar but more complex procedure is used to estimate the effects of growing human capital. The procedure is more complex because there aren't simple dollar measures of the quantity of human capital.

Growth accounting allows us to calculate the effects of greater physical and human capital on economic growth. But how can we estimate the effects of technological progress? We do so by estimating what is left over after the effects of physical and human capital have been taken into account. For example, let's imagine that there was no increase in human capital per worker so that we can focus on changes in physical capital and in technology. In Figure 25-5, the lower curve shows the same hypothetical relationship between physical capital per worker and output per worker shown in Figure 25-4. Let's assume that this was the relationship given the technology available in 1937. The upper curve also shows a relationship between physical capital per worker and productivity, but this time given the technology available in 2007. (We've chosen a 70-year stretch to allow us to use the Rule of 70.) The 2007 curve is shifted up compared to the 1937 curve because technologies developed over the previous 70 years make it possible to produce more output for a given amount of physical capital per worker than was possible with the technology available in 1937. (Note that the two curves are measured in constant dollars.)

Let's assume that between 1937 and 2007 the amount of physical capital per worker rose from $20,000 to $80,000. If this increase in physical capital per worker had taken place without any technological progress, the economy would have moved from *A* to *C*: output per worker would have risen, but only from $30,000 to $60,000, or 1% per year (using the Rule of 70 tells us that a 1% growth rate over 70 years doubles output). In fact, however, the economy moved from *A* to *D*: output rose from $30,000 to $120,000, or 2% per year. There was an increase in both physical capital per worker and technological progress, which shifted the aggregate production function.

Growth accounting estimates the contribution of each major factor in the aggregate production function to economic growth.

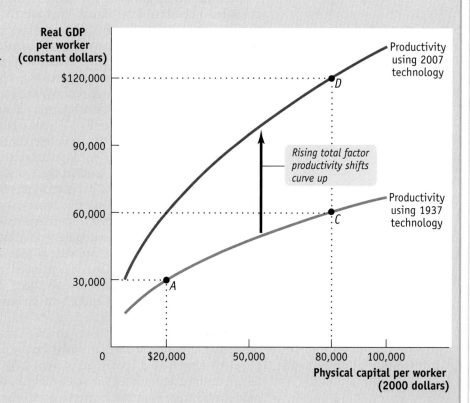

FIGURE 25-5

Technological Progress and Productivity Growth

Technological progress shifts the productivity curve upward. Here we hold human capital per worker fixed. We assume that the lower curve (the same curve as in Figure 25-4) reflects technology in 1937 and the upper curve reflects technology in 2007. Holding technology and human capital fixed, quadrupling physical capital per worker from $20,000 to $80,000 leads to a doubling of real GDP per worker, from $30,000 to $60,000. This is shown by the movement from point A to point C, reflecting an approximately 1% per year rise in real GDP per worker. In reality, technological progress shifted the productivity curve upward and the actual rise in real GDP per worker is shown by the movement from point A to point D. Real GDP per worker grew 2% per year, leading to a quadrupling during the period. The extra 1% in growth of real GDP per worker is due to higher total factor productivity.

In this case, 50% of the annual 2% increase in productivity—that is, 1% in annual productivity growth—is due to higher **total factor productivity,** the amount of output that can be produced with a given amount of factor inputs. So when total factor productivity increases, the economy can produce more output with the same quantity of physical capital, human capital, and labor.

Most estimates find that increases in total factor productivity are central to a country's economic growth. We believe that observed increases in total factor productivity in fact measure the economic effects of technological progress. All of this implies that technological change is crucial to economic growth. The Bureau of Labor Statistics estimates the growth rate of both labor productivity and total factor productivity for nonfarm business in the United States. According to the Bureau's estimates, over the period from 1948 to 2007 American labor productivity rose 2.3% per year. Only 47% of that rise is explained by increases in physical and human capital per worker; the rest is explained by rising total factor productivity—that is, by technological progress.

What About Natural Resources?

In our discussion so far, we haven't mentioned natural resources, which certainly have an effect on productivity. Other things equal, countries that are abundant in valuable natural resources, such as highly fertile land or rich mineral deposits, have higher real GDP per capita than less fortunate countries. The most obvious modern example is the Middle East, where enormous oil deposits have made a few sparsely populated countries very rich. For example, Kuwait has about the same level of real GDP per capita as South Korea, but Kuwait's wealth is based on oil, not manufacturing, the source of South Korea's high output per worker.

Total factor productivity is the amount of output that can be achieved with a given amount of factor inputs.

But other things are often not equal. In the modern world, natural resources are a much less important determinant of productivity than human or physical capital for the great majority of countries. For example, some nations with very high real GDP per capita, such as Japan, have very few natural resources. Some resource-rich nations, such as Nigeria (which has sizable oil deposits), are very poor.

Historically, natural resources played a much more prominent role in determining productivity. In the nineteenth century, the countries with the highest real GDP per capita were those abundant in rich farmland and mineral deposits: the United States, Canada, Argentina, and Australia. As a consequence, natural resources figured prominently in the development of economic thought. In a famous book published in 1798, *An Essay on the Principle of Population,* the English economist Thomas Malthus made the fixed quantity of land in the world the basis of a pessimistic prediction about future productivity. As population grew, he pointed out, the amount of land per worker would decline. And this, other things equal, would cause productivity to fall. His view, in fact, was that improvements in technology or increases in physical capital would lead only to temporary improvements in productivity because they would always be offset by the pressure of rising population and more workers on the supply of land. In the long run, he concluded, the great majority of people were condemned to living on the edge of starvation. Only then would death rates be high enough and birth rates low enough to prevent rapid population growth from outstripping productivity growth.

It hasn't turned out that way, although many historians believe that Malthus's prediction of falling or stagnant productivity was valid for much of human history. Population pressure probably did prevent large productivity increases until the eighteenth century. But in the time since Malthus wrote his book, any negative effects on productivity from population growth have been far outweighed by other, positive factors—advances in technology, increases in human and physical capital, and the opening up of enormous amounts of cultivatable land in the New World.

It remains true, however, that we live on a finite planet, with limited supplies of resources such as oil and limited ability to absorb environmental damage. We address the concerns these limitations pose for economic growth in the final section of this chapter.

➤ECONOMICS IN ACTION

The Information Technology Paradox

From the early 1970s through the mid-1990s, the United States went through a slump in total factor productivity growth. Figure 25-6 shows Bureau of Labor Statistics estimates of annual total factor productivity growth since 1949. As you can see, there was a large fall in the productivity growth rate beginning in the early 1970s. Because higher total factor productivity plays such a key role in long-run growth, the economy's overall growth was also disappointing, leading to a widespread sense that economic progress had ground to a halt.

Many economists were puzzled by the slowdown in total factor productivity growth after 1973, since in other ways the era seemed to be one of rapid technological progress. Modern information technology really began with the development of the first microprocessor—a computer on a chip—in 1971. In the 25 years that followed, a series of inventions that seemed revolutionary became standard equipment in the business world: fax machines, desktop computers, cell phones, and e-mail. Yet the rate of growth of productivity remained stagnant. In a famous remark, MIT economics professor and Nobel laureate Robert Solow, a pioneer in the analysis of economic growth, declared that the information technology revolution could be seen everywhere except in the economic statistics.

FIGURE 25-6

The U.S. Productivity Growth Slowdown and Recovery

These estimates of U.S. total factor productivity growth show that the United States experienced a large fall in its total factor productivity growth rate beginning in the early 1970s and lasting through the mid-1990s. Many economists were puzzled because the fall occurred during a time of rapid technological progress. However, the likely explanation was that growth would accelerate only once people changed their way of doing business in order to take advantage of the new technology—an explanation consistent with the fact that U.S. productivity growth had a significant recovery during the second half of the 1990s.

Source: Bureau of Labor Statistics.

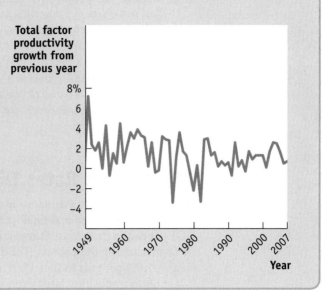

Total factor productivity growth from previous year

Year

Why didn't information technology show large rewards? Paul David, a Stanford University economic historian, offered a theory and a prediction. He pointed out that 100 years earlier another miracle technology—electric power—had spread through the economy, again with surprisingly little impact on productivity growth at first. The reason, he suggested, was that a new technology doesn't yield its full potential if you use it in old ways.

For example, a traditional factory around 1900 was a multistory building, with the machinery tightly crowded together and designed to be powered by a steam engine in the basement. This design had problems: it was very difficult to move people and materials around. Yet owners who electrified their factories initially maintained the multistory, tightly packed layout. Only with the switch to spread-out, one-story factories that took advantage of the flexibility of electric power—most famously Henry Ford's auto assembly line—did productivity take off.

David suggested that the same phenomenon was happening with information technology. Productivity, he predicted, would take off when people really changed their way of doing business to take advantage of the new technology—such as replacing letters and phone calls with e-mail. Sure enough, productivity growth accelerated dramatically in the second half of the 1990s. And, as a For Inquiring Minds earlier in the chapter suggested, a lot of that may have been due to the discovery by companies like Wal-Mart of how to effectively use information technology. ▲

> > > > > > > > > > > > >

► CHECK YOUR UNDERSTANDING 25-2

1. Explain the effect of each of the following events on the growth rate of productivity.
   a. The amounts of physical and human capital per worker are unchanged, but there is significant technological progress.
   b. The amount of physical capital per worker grows, but the level of human capital per worker and technology are unchanged.

2. The economy of Erewhon has grown 3% per year over the past 30 years. The labor force has grown at 1% per year, and the quantity of physical capital has grown at 4% per year. The average education level hasn't changed. Estimates by economists say that each 1% increase in physical capital per worker, other things equal, raises productivity by 0.3%.
   a. How fast has productivity in Erewhon grown?
   b. How fast has physical capital per worker grown?

►► QUICK REVIEW

- ➤ Long-run increases in living standards arise almost entirely from growing **labor productivity,** often simply referred to as **productivity.**
- ➤ An increase in **physical capital** is one source of higher productivity, but it is subject to **diminishing returns to physical capital.**
- ➤ **Human capital** and new **technology** are also sources of increases in productivity.
- ➤ The **aggregate production function** is used to estimate the sources of increases in productivity. **Growth accounting** has shown that rising **total factor productivity,** interpreted as the effect of technological progress, is central to long-run economic growth.
- ➤ Natural resources are less important today than physical and human capital as sources of productivity growth in most economies.

     c. How much has growing physical capital per worker contributed to productivity growth? What percentage of productivity growth is that?

     d. How much has technological progress contributed to productivity growth? What percentage of productivity growth is that?

3. Multinomics, Inc., is a large company with many offices around the country. It has just adopted a new computer system that will affect virtually every function performed within the company. Why might a period of time pass before employees' productivity is improved by the new computer system? Why might there be a temporary decrease in employees' productivity?

Solutions appear at back of book.

Why Growth Rates Differ

In 1820, according to estimates by the economic historian Angus Maddison, Mexico had somewhat higher real GDP per capita than Japan. Today, Japan has higher real GDP per capita than most European nations and Mexico is a poor country, though by no means among the poorest. The difference? Over the long run, real GDP per capita grew at 1.9% per year in Japan but at only 1.2% per year in Mexico.

As this example illustrates, even small differences in growth rates have large consequences over the long run. So why do growth rates differ across countries and across periods of time?

Capital, Technology, and Growth Differences

As one might expect, economies with rapid growth tend to be economies that add physical capital, increase their human capital, or experience rapid technological progress. Striking economic success stories, like Japan in the 1950s and 1960s or China today, tend to be countries that do all three: that rapidly add to their physical capital, upgrade their educational level, and make fast technological progress.

Adding to Physical Capital One reason for differences in growth rates between countries is that some countries are increasing their stock of physical capital much more rapidly than others, through high rates of investment spending. In the 1960s, Japan was the fastest-growing major economy; it also spent a much higher share of its GDP on investment goods than other major economies. Today, China is the fastest-growing major economy, and it similarly spends a very large share of its GDP on investment goods. In 2007, investment spending was 41% of China's GDP, compared with only 15% in the United States.

Where does the money for high investment spending come from? In the next chapter, we'll analyze how financial markets channel savings into investment spending. For now, however, the key point is that investment spending must be paid for either out of savings from domestic households or by an inflow of foreign capital—that is, savings from foreign households. Foreign capital has played an important role in the long-run economic growth of some countries, including the United States, which relied heavily on foreign funds during its early industrialization. For the most part, however, countries that invest a large share of their GDP are able to do so because they have high domestic savings. In fact, China in 2007 saved an even higher percentage of its GDP than it invested at home. The extra savings were invested abroad, largely in the United States.

One reason for differences in growth rates, then, is that countries have different rates of savings and investment spending.

Adding to Human Capital Just as countries differ substantially in the rate at which they add to their physical capital, there have been large differences in the rate at which countries add to their human capital through education.

TABLE 25-3

Human Capital in Latin America and East Asia

	Latin America		East Asia	
	1960	2000	1960	2000
Percentage of population with no schooling	37.9%	14.6%	52.5%	19.8%
Percentage of population with high school or above	5.9	19.5	4.4	26.5

Source: Barro, Robert J. and Lee, Jong-Wha (2001) "International Data on Educational Attainment: Updates and Implications," *Oxford Economic Papers* vol. 53(3), p. 541–563.

A case in point is the comparison between Latin America and East Asia. In both regions the average educational level has risen steadily over time, but it has risen much faster in East Asia. As Table 25-3 shows, East Asia had a significantly less educated population than Latin America in 1960. By 2000, that gap had been closed: East Asia still had a slightly higher fraction of adults with no education—almost all of them elderly— but had moved well past Latin America in terms of secondary and higher education.

Technological Progress The advance of technology is a key force behind economic growth. What drives technology?

Scientific advances make new technologies possible. To take the most spectacular example in today's world, the semiconductor chip—which is the basis for all modern information technology—could not have been developed without the theory of quantum mechanics in physics.

But science alone is not enough: scientific knowledge must be translated into useful products and processes. And that often requires devoting a lot of resources to **research and development,** or **R&D,** spending to create new technologies and prepare them for practical use.

Although some research and development is conducted by governments, much R&D is paid for by the private sector, as discussed below. The United States became the world's leading economy in large part because American businesses were among the first to make systematic research and development a part of their operations. The upcoming For Inquiring Minds describes how Thomas Edison created the first modern industrial research laboratory.

Developing new technology is one thing; applying it is another. There have often been notable differences in the pace at which different countries take advantage of new technologies. As this chapter's Global Comparison shows, America's surge in productivity growth after 1995, as firms learned to make use of information technology, was at least initially not matched in Europe.

> **Research and development,** or **R & D,** is spending to create and implement new technologies.

FOR INQUIRING MINDS

Inventing R&D

Thomas Edison is best known as the inventor of the light bulb and the phonograph. But his biggest invention may surprise you: he invented research and development.

Before Edison's time, there had, of course, been many inventors. Some of them worked in teams. But in 1875 Edison created something new: his Menlo Park, New Jersey, laboratory. It employed 25 men full-time to generate new products and processes for business. In other words, he did not set out to pursue a particular idea and then cash in. He created an organization whose purpose was to create new ideas year after year.

Edison's Menlo Park lab is now a museum. "To name a few of the products that were developed in Menlo Park," says the museum's website, "we can list the following: the carbon button mouthpiece for the telephone, the phonograph, the incandescent light bulb and the electrical distribution system, the electric train, ore separation, the Edison effect bulb, early experiments in wireless, the grasshopper telegraph, and improvements in telegraphic transmission."

You could say that before Edison's lab, technology just sort of happened: people came up with ideas, but businesses didn't plan to make continuous technological progress. Now R&D operations, often much bigger than Edison's original team, are standard practice throughout the business world.

Roads, power lines, ports, information networks, and other underpinnings for economic activity are known as **infrastructure.**

GLOBAL COMPARISON — OLD EUROPE AND NEW TECHNOLOGY

The rate of growth of total factor productivity accelerated dramatically in the United States after 1995, probably because businesses finally figured out how to use modern information technology effectively. But did the rest of the world experience a similar takeoff?

The answer is, not everywhere. This figure shows estimates of total factor productivity growth for three European countries as well as the United States, with the estimates covering both the decade before 1995 and the 11 years that followed. Sweden, like the United States, saw productivity take off after 1995. But in Italy, and to a lesser extent in France, total factor productivity growth actually went into a slump.

There is a lot of dispute both about why much of Europe didn't share in the productivity takeoff and about whether it will soon catch up to the United States. Some economists argue that high levels of government regulation made it hard for European businesses to reorganize themselves to take advantage of new technology. What is clear is that for at least a decade Europe lagged behind.

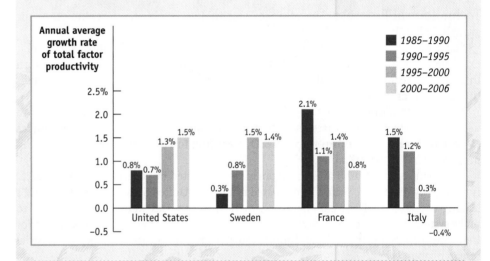

Source: OECD.

The Role of Government in Promoting Economic Growth

Governments can play an important role in promoting—or blocking—all three sources of long-term economic growth: physical capital, human capital, and technological progress.

Governments and Physical Capital Governments play an important direct role in building **infrastructure:** roads, power lines, ports, information networks, and other parts of an economy's physical capital that provide an underpinning, or foundation, for economic activity. Although some infrastructure is provided by private companies, much of it is either provided by the government or requires a great deal of government regulation and support. Ireland, whose economy really took off in the 1990s, is often cited as an example of the importance of government-provided infrastructure: the government invested in an excellent telecommunications infrastructure in the 1980s, and this helped make Ireland a favored location for high-technology companies.

Poor infrastructure—for example, a power grid that often fails, cutting off electricity to homes and businesses—is a major obstacle to economic growth in some countries. To provide good infrastructure, an economy must be able to afford it, but it must also have the political discipline to maintain it and provide for the future.

Perhaps the most crucial infrastructure is something we rarely think about: basic public health measures in the form of a clean water supply and disease control. As we'll see in the next section, poor health infrastructure is a major obstacle to economic growth in poor countries, especially those in Africa.

Governments also play an important indirect role in making high rates of private investment spending possible. Both the amount of savings and the ability of an economy to direct savings into productive investment spending depend on the economy's institutions, notably its financial system. In particular, a well-functioning banking system is very important for economic growth because in most countries it is the principal way in which savings are channeled into business investment spending. If a country's citizens trust their banks, they will place their savings in bank deposits, which the banks will then lend to their business customers. But if people don't trust their banks, they will hoard gold or foreign currency, keeping their savings in safe deposit boxes or under the mattress, where it cannot be turned into productive investment spending. As we'll discuss in a later chapter, a well-functioning financial system requires appropriate government regulation that assures depositors that their funds are protected.

Governments and Human Capital

An economy's physical capital is created mainly through investment spending by individuals and private companies. Much of an economy's human capital, in contrast, is the result of government spending on education. Governments pay for the great bulk of primary and secondary education, although individuals pay a significant share of the costs of higher education.

As a result, differences in the rate at which countries add to their human capital largely reflect government policy. As we saw in Table 25-3, East Asia now has a more educated population than Latin America. This isn't because East Asia is richer than Latin America and so can afford to spend more on education. Until very recently, East Asia was, on average, poorer than Latin America. Instead, it reflects the fact that Asian governments made broad education of the population a higher priority.

Governments and Technology

Technological progress is largely the result of private initiative. But much important R&D is done by government agencies. In the upcoming Economics in Action, we describe Brazil's recent agricultural boom. This boom was made possible by government researchers who discovered that adding crucial nutrients to the soil would allow crops to be grown on previously unusable land, and also developed new varieties of soybeans and breeds of cattle that flourish in Brazil's tropical climate.

Political Stability, Property Rights, and Excessive Government Intervention

There's not much point in investing in a business if rioting mobs are likely to destroy it or saving your money if someone with political connections can steal it. Political stability and protection of property rights are crucial ingredients in long-run economic growth.

Long-run economic growth in successful economies, like that of the United States, has been possible because there are good laws, institutions that enforce those laws, and a stable political system that maintains those institutions. The law must say that your property is really yours so that someone else can't take it away. The courts and the police must be honest so that they can't be bribed to ignore the law. And the political system must be stable so that the law doesn't change capriciously.

Americans take these preconditions for granted, but they are by no means guaranteed. Aside from the disruption caused by war or revolution, many countries find that their economic growth suffers due to corruption among the government officials who should be enforcing the law. For example, until 1991 the Indian government imposed many bureaucratic restrictions on businesses, which often had to bribe government officials to get approval for even routine activities—a tax on business, in effect. Economists have argued that a reduction in this burden of corruption is one reason Indian growth has been much faster in recent years than it was in the first 40 years after India gained independence in 1947.

Even when governments aren't corrupt, excessive government intervention can be a brake on economic growth. If large parts of the economy are supported by government subsidies, protected from imports, or otherwise insulated from competition, productivity tends to suffer because of a lack of incentives. As we'll see in the next section, excessive government intervention is one often-cited explanation for slow growth in Latin America.

►ECONOMICS IN ACTION

The Brazilian Breadbasket

A wry Brazilian joke says that "Brazil is the country of the future—and always will be." The world's fifth most populous country has often been considered as a possible major economic power, yet has never fulfilled that promise.

In recent years, however, Brazil's economy has made a better showing, especially in agriculture. This success depends on exploiting a natural resource, the tropical savanna land known as the *cerrado.* Until a quarter-century ago, the land was considered unsuitable for farming. A combination of three factors changed that: technological progress due to research and development, improved economic policies, and greater physical capital.

The Brazilian Enterprise for Agricultural and Livestock Research, a government-run agency, developed the crucial technologies. It showed that adding lime and phosphorus made *cerrado* land productive, and it developed breeds of cattle and varieties of soybeans suited for the climate. (Now they're working on wheat.) Also, until the 1980s, Brazilian international trade policies discouraged exports, as did an overvalued exchange rate that made the country's goods more expensive to foreigners. After economic reform, investing in Brazilian agriculture became much more profitable and companies began putting in place the farm machinery, buildings, and other forms of physical capital needed to exploit the land.

What still limits Brazil's growth? Infrastructure. According to a report in the *New York Times,* Brazilian farmers are "concerned about the lack of reliable highways, railways and barge routes, which adds to the cost of doing business." Recognizing this, the Brazilian government is investing in infrastructure, and Brazilian agriculture is continuing to expand. The country has already overtaken the United States as the world's largest beef exporter and may not be far behind in soybeans. ▲

‹ ‹ ‹ ‹ ‹ ‹ ‹ ‹ ‹ ‹ ‹ ‹

> ► **CHECK YOUR UNDERSTANDING** 25-3

1. Explain the link between a country's growth rate, its investment spending as a percent of GDP, and its domestic savings.

2. U.S. centers of academic biotechnology research have closer connections with private biotechnology companies than do their European counterparts. What effect might this have on the pace of creation and development of new drugs in the United States versus Europe?

3. During the 1990s in the former U.S.S.R., a lot of property was seized and controlled by those in power. How might this have affected the country's growth rate at that time? Explain.

Solutions appear at back of book.

Success, Disappointment, and Failure

As we've seen, rates of long-run economic growth differ quite a lot around the world. Now let's look at three regions of the world that have had quite different experiences with economic growth over the last few decades.

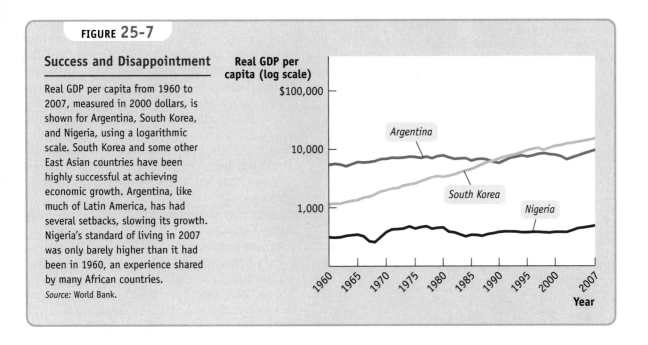

FIGURE 25-7

Success and Disappointment

Real GDP per capita from 1960 to 2007, measured in 2000 dollars, is shown for Argentina, South Korea, and Nigeria, using a logarithmic scale. South Korea and some other East Asian countries have been highly successful at achieving economic growth. Argentina, like much of Latin America, has had several setbacks, slowing its growth. Nigeria's standard of living in 2007 was only barely higher than it had been in 1960, an experience shared by many African countries.

Source: World Bank.

Figure 25-7 shows trends since 1960 in real GDP per capita in 2000 dollars for three countries: Argentina, Nigeria, and South Korea. (As in Figure 25-1, the vertical axis is drawn in logarithmic scale.) We have chosen these countries because each is a particularly striking example of what has happened in its region. South Korea's amazing rise is part of a broad "economic miracle" in East Asia. Argentina's slow progress, interrupted by repeated setbacks, is more or less typical of the disappointment that has characterized Latin America. And Nigeria's unhappy story—real GDP per capita is barely higher now than it was in 1960—is, unfortunately, an experience shared by many African countries.

East Asia's Miracle

In 1960 South Korea was a very poor country. In fact, in 1960 its real GDP per capita was lower than that of India today. But, as you can see from Figure 25-7, beginning in the early 1960s South Korea began an extremely rapid economic ascent: real GDP per capita grew about 7% per year for more than 30 years. Today South Korea, though still somewhat poorer than Europe or the United States, looks very much like an economically advanced country.

South Korea's economic growth is unprecedented in history: it took the country only 35 years to achieve growth that required centuries elsewhere. Yet South Korea is only part of a broader phenomenon, often referred to as the East Asian economic miracle. High growth rates first appeared in South Korea, Taiwan, Hong Kong, and Singapore but then spread across the region, most notably to China. Since 1975, the whole region has increased real GDP per capita by 6% per year, three times America's historical rate of growth.

How have the Asian countries achieved such high growth rates? The answer is that all of the sources of productivity growth have been firing on all cylinders. Very high savings rates, the percentage of GDP that is saved nationally in any given year, have allowed the countries to significantly increase the amount of physical capital per worker. Very good basic education has permitted a rapid improvement in human capital. And these countries have experienced substantial technological progress.

According to the **convergence hypothesis,** international differences in real GDP per capita tend to narrow over time.

Why hasn't any economy achieved this kind of growth in the past? Most economic analysts think that East Asia's growth spurt was possible because of its *relative* backwardness. That is, by the time that East Asian economies began to move into the modern world, they could benefit from adopting the technological advances that had been generated in technologically advanced countries such as the United States. In 1900, the United States could not have moved quickly to a modern level of productivity because much of the technology that powers the modern economy, from jet planes to computers, hadn't been invented yet. In 1970, South Korea probably still had lower labor productivity than the United States had in 1900, but it could rapidly upgrade its productivity by adopting technology that had been developed in the United States, Europe, and Japan over the previous century. This was aided by a huge investment in human capital through widespread schooling.

The East Asian experience demonstrates that economic growth can be especially fast in countries that are playing catch-up to other countries with higher GDP per capita. On this basis, many economists have suggested a general principle known as the **convergence hypothesis.** It says that differences in real GDP per capita among countries tend to narrow over time because countries that start with lower real GDP per capita tend to have higher growth rates. We'll look at the evidence on the convergence hypothesis in the Economics in Action at the end of this section.

Even before we get to that evidence, however, we can say right away that starting with a relatively low level of real GDP per capita is no guarantee of rapid growth, as the examples of Latin America and Africa both demonstrate.

Latin America's Disappointment

In 1900, Latin America was not regarded as an economically backward region. Natural resources, including both minerals and cultivatable land, were abundant. Some countries, notably Argentina, attracted millions of immigrants from Europe in search of a better life. Measures of real GDP per capita in Argentina, Uruguay, and southern Brazil were comparable to those in economically advanced countries.

Since about 1920, however, growth in Latin America has been disappointing. As Figure 25-7 shows in the case of Argentina, it has remained disappointing to this day. The fact that South Korea is now much richer than Argentina would have seemed inconceivable a few generations ago.

Why has Latin America stagnated? Comparisons with East Asian success stories suggest several factors. The rates of savings and investment spending in Latin America have been much lower than in East Asia, partly as a result of irresponsible government policy that has eroded savings through high inflation, bank failures, and other disruptions. Education—especially broad basic education—has been underemphasized: even Latin American nations rich in natural resources often failed to channel that wealth into their educational systems. And political instability, leading to irresponsible economic policies, has taken a toll.

In the 1980s, many economists came to believe that Latin America was suffering from excessive government intervention in markets. They recommended opening the economies to imports, selling off government-owned companies, and, in general, freeing up individual initiative. The hope was that this would produce an East Asian–type economic surge. So far, however, only one Latin American nation, Chile, has achieved really rapid growth. It now seems that pulling off an economic miracle is harder than it looks.

Africa's Troubles

Africa south of the Sahara is home to about 780 million people, more than 2½ times the population of the United States. On average, they are very poor, nowhere close to U.S. living standards 100 or even 200 years ago. And economic progress has been both slow and uneven, as the example of Nigeria, the most populous nation in the region, suggests. In fact, real GDP per capita in sub-Saharan Africa actually fell 13 percent from 1980 to 1994, although it has recovered since then. The consequence of this poor growth performance has been intense and continuing poverty.

This is a very disheartening picture. What explains it?

Several factors are probably crucial. Perhaps first and foremost is the problem of political instability. In the years since 1975, large parts of Africa have experienced savage civil wars (often with outside powers backing rival sides) that have killed millions of people and made productive investment spending impossible. The threat of war and general anarchy has also inhibited other important preconditions for growth, such as education and provision of necessary infrastructure.

Property rights are also a problem. The lack of legal safeguards means that property owners are often subject to extortion because of government corruption, making them averse to owning property or improving it. This is especially damaging in a country that is very poor.

While many economists see political instability and government corruption as the leading causes of underdevelopment in Africa, some—most notably Jeffrey Sachs of Columbia University and the United Nations—believe the opposite. They argue that Africa is politically unstable because Africa is poor. And Africa's poverty, they go on to claim, stems from its extremely unfavorable geographic conditions—much of the continent is landlocked, hot, infested with tropical diseases, and cursed with poor soil.

Sachs, along with economists from the World Health Organization, has highlighted the importance of health problems in Africa. In poor countries, worker productivity is often severely hampered by malnutrition and disease. In particular, tropical diseases such as malaria can only be controlled with an effective public health infrastructure, something that is lacking in much of Africa. At the time of writing, economists are studying certain regions of Africa to determine whether modest amounts of aid given directly to residents for the purposes of increasing crop yields, reducing malaria, and increasing school attendance can produce self-sustaining gains in living standards.

Although the example of African countries represents a warning that long-run economic growth cannot be taken for granted, there are some signs of hope. Mauritius has developed a successful textile industry. Several African countries that are dependent on exporting commodities such as coffee and oil have benefited from the higher prices of those commodities. And Africa's economic performance since the mid-1990s has been generally much better than it was in preceding decades.

➤ *ECONOMICS IN ACTION*

Are Economies Converging?

In the 1950s, much of Europe seemed quaint and backward to American visitors, and Japan seemed very poor. Today, a visitor to Paris or Tokyo sees a city that looks about as rich as New York. Although real GDP per capita is still somewhat higher in the United States, the differences in the standards of living among the United States, Europe, and Japan are relatively small.

Many economists have argued that this convergence in living standards is normal; the convergence hypothesis says that relatively poor countries should have higher rates of growth of real GDP per capita than relatively rich countries. And if we look at today's relatively well-off countries, the convergence hypothesis seems to be true. Panel (a) of Figure 25-8 on the next page shows data for a number of today's wealthy economies measured in 2000 dollars. On the horizontal axis is real GDP per capita in 1955; on the vertical axis is the average annual growth rate of

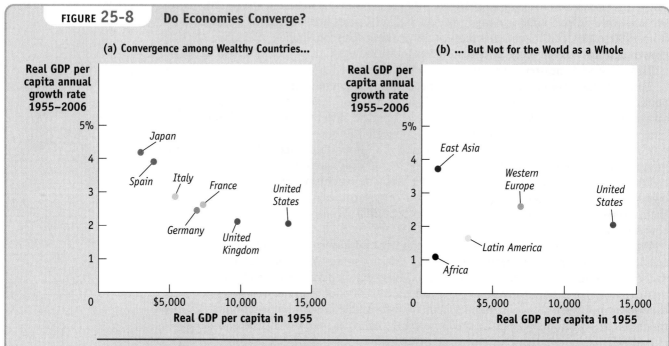

FIGURE 25-8 **Do Economies Converge?**

Data on today's wealthy economies (measured in 2000 dollars) seem to support the convergence hypothesis. In panel (a) we see that among wealthy countries, those that had low levels of real GDP per capita in 1955 have had high growth rates since then, and vice versa. But for the world as a whole, there has been little sign of convergence. Panel (b) shows real GDP per capita in 1955 (also measured in

2000 dollars) and subsequent growth rates in major world regions. Poorer regions did not consistently have higher growth rates than richer regions: poor Africa turned in the worst performance, and relatively wealthy Europe grew faster than Latin America.

Source: Angus Maddison, Statistics on World Population, GDP, and Per Capita GDP, 1–2006AD, http://www.ggdc.net/maddison.

real GDP per capita from 1955 to 2006. There is a clear negative relationship. The United States was the richest country in this group in 1955 and had the slowest rate of growth. Japan and Spain were the poorest countries in 1955 and had the fastest rates of growth. These data suggest that the convergence hypothesis is true.

But economists who looked at similar data realized that these results depend on the countries selected. If you look at successful economies that have a high standard of living today, you find that real GDP per capita has converged. But looking across the world as a whole, including countries that remain poor, there is little evidence of convergence. Panel (b) of Figure 25-8 illustrates this point using data for regions rather than individual countries (other than the United States). In 1955, East Asia and Africa were both very poor regions. Over the next 51 years, the East Asian regional economy grew quickly, as the convergence hypothesis would have predicted, but the African regional economy grew very slowly. In 1955, Western Europe had substantially higher real GDP per capita than Latin America. But, contrary to the convergence hypothesis, the Western European regional economy grew more quickly over the next 51 years, widening the gap between the regions.

So is the convergence hypothesis all wrong? No: economists still believe that countries with relatively low real GDP per capita tend to have higher rates of growth than countries with relatively high real GDP per capita, *other things equal.* But other things—education, infrastructure, rule of law, and so on—are often not equal. Statistical studies find that when you adjust for differences in these other factors, poorer countries do tend to have higher growth rates. This result is known as *conditional convergence.*

Because other factors differ, however, there is no clear tendency toward convergence in the world economy as a whole. Western Europe, North America, and parts of Asia are becoming more similar in real GDP per capita, but the gap between these regions and the rest of the world is growing. ▲

> > > > > > > > > > > >

1. Some economists think the high rates of growth of productivity achieved by many Asian economies cannot be sustained. Why might they be right? What would have to happen for them to be wrong?

2. Which of the following is the better predictor of a future high long-run growth rate: a high standard of living today or high levels of savings and investment spending? Explain your answer.

3. Some economists think the best way to help African countries is for wealthier countries to provide more funds for basic infrastructure. Others think this policy will have no long-run effect unless African countries have the financial and political means to maintain this infrastructure. What policies would you suggest?

Solutions appear at back of book.

Is World Growth Sustainable?

Earlier in this chapter we described the views of Thomas Malthus, the early nineteenth-century economist who warned that the pressure of population growth would tend to limit the standard of living. Malthus was right—about the past: for around 58 centuries, from the origins of civilization until his own time, limited land supplies effectively prevented any large rise in real incomes per capita. Since then, however, technological progress and rapid accumulation of physical and human capital have allowed the world to defy Malthusian pessimism.

But will this always be the case? Some skeptics have expressed doubt about whether long-run economic growth is **sustainable**—whether it can continue in the face of the limited supply of natural resources and the impact of growth on the environment.

Natural Resources and Growth, Revisited

In 1972 a group of scientists called The Club of Rome made a big splash with a book titled *The Limits to Growth,* which argued that long-run economic growth wasn't sustainable due to limited supplies of nonrenewable resources such as oil and natural gas. These "neo-Malthusian" concerns at first seemed to be validated by a sharp rise in resource prices in the 1970s, then came to seem foolish when resource prices fell sharply in the 1980s. After 2005, however, resource prices rose sharply again, leading to renewed concern about resource limitations to growth. Figure 25-9 on the next page shows the real price of oil—the price of oil adjusted for inflation in the rest of the economy. The rise, fall, and rise of concern about resource-based limits to growth have more or less followed the rise, fall, and rise of oil prices shown in the figure.

Differing views about the impact of limited natural resources on long-run economic growth turn on the answers to three questions:

- How large are the supplies of key natural resources?

- How effective will technology be at finding alternatives to natural resources?

- Can long-run economic growth continue in the face of resource scarcity?

It's mainly up to geologists to answer the first question. Unfortunately, there's wide disagreement among the experts, especially about the prospects for future oil

Long-run economic growth is **sustainable** if it can continue in the face of the limited supply of natural resources and the impact of growth on the environment.

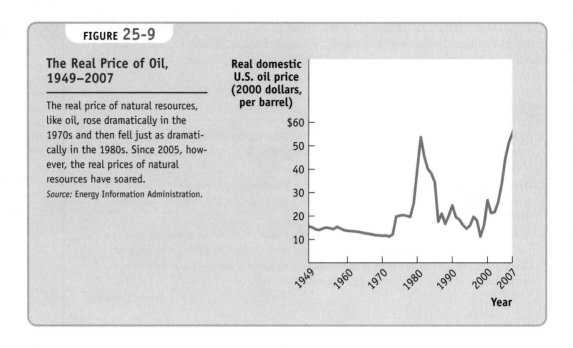

FIGURE 25-9

The Real Price of Oil, 1949–2007

The real price of natural resources, like oil, rose dramatically in the 1970s and then fell just as dramatically in the 1980s. Since 2005, however, the real prices of natural resources have soared.

Source: Energy Information Administration.

production. Some analysts believe that there is enough untapped oil in the ground that world oil production can continue to rise for several decades. Others—including a number of oil company executives—believe that the growing difficulty of finding new oil fields will cause oil production to plateau—that is, stop growing and eventually begin a gradual decline—in the fairly near future. Some analysts believe that we have already reached that plateau.

The answer to the second question, whether there are alternatives to natural resources, has to come from engineers. There's no question that there are many alternatives to the natural resources currently being depleted, some of which are already being exploited. For example, "unconventional" oil extracted from Canadian tar sands is already making a significant contribution to world oil supplies, and electricity generated by wind turbines is rapidly becoming big business—a development highlighted by the fact that T. Boone Pickens, a famous Texas oil man, has become a major investor in wind power.

The third question, whether economies can continue to grow in the face of resource scarcity, is mainly a question for economists. And most, though not all, economists are optimistic: they believe that modern economies can find ways to work around limits on the supply of natural resources. One reason for this optimism is the fact that resource scarcity leads to high resource prices. These high prices in turn provide strong incentives to conserve the scarce resource and to find alternatives.

For example, after the sharp oil price increases of the 1970s, American consumers turned to smaller, more fuel-efficient cars, and U.S. industry also greatly intensified its efforts to reduce energy bills. The result is shown in Figure 25-10, which compares the growth rates of real GDP per capita and oil consumption before and after the 1970s energy crisis. Before 1973, there seemed to be a more or less one-to-one relationship between economic growth and oil consumption, but after 1973 the U.S. economy continued to deliver growth in real GDP per capita even as it substantially reduced use of oil. This move toward conservation paused after 1990, as low real oil prices encouraged consumers to shift back to gas-greedy larger cars and SUVs. But, a sharp rise in oil prices from 2005 to 2008 encouraged renewed shifts toward oil conservation, although these shifts might not persist in the face of prices that were falling again in late 2008.

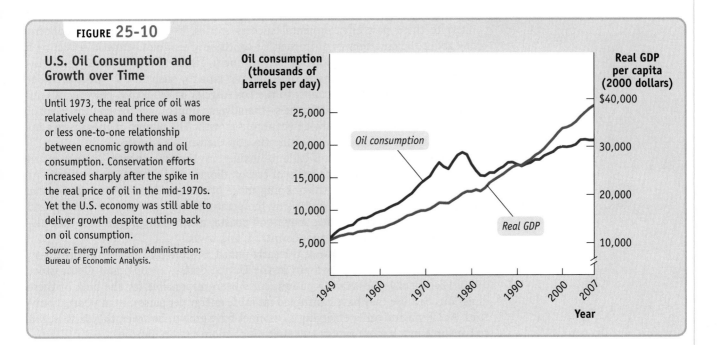

FIGURE 25-10

U.S. Oil Consumption and Growth over Time

Until 1973, the real price of oil was relatively cheap and there was a more or less one-to-one relationship between ecnomic growth and oil consumption. Conservation efforts increased sharply after the spike in the real price of oil in the mid-1970s. Yet the U.S. economy was still able to deliver growth despite cutting back on oil consumption.

Source: Energy Information Administration; Bureau of Economic Analysis.

Given such responses to prices, economists generally tend to see resource scarcity as a problem that modern economies handle fairly well, and so not a fundamental limit to long-run economic growth. Environmental issues, however, pose a more difficult problem because dealing with them requires effective political action.

Economic Growth and the Environment

Economic growth, other things equal, tends to increase the human impact on the environment. For example, China's spectacular economic growth has also brought a spectacular increase in air pollution in that nation's cities. It's important to realize, however, that other things aren't necessarily equal: countries can and do take action to protect their environments. In fact, air and water quality in today's advanced countries is generally much better than it was a few decades ago. London's famous "fog"— actually a form of air pollution, which killed 4,000 people during a two-week episode in 1952—is gone, thanks to regulations that virtually eliminated the use of coal heat. The equally famous smog of Los Angeles, although not extinguished, is far less severe than it was in the 1960s and early 1970s, again thanks to pollution regulations.

FOR INQUIRING MINDS

Coal Comfort on Resources

Those who worry that exhaustion of natural resources will bring an end to economic growth can take some comfort from the story of William Stanley Jevons, a nineteenth-century British economist best known today for his role in the development of marginal analysis. In addition to his work in economic theory, Jevons worked on the real-world economic problems of the day, and in 1865 he published an influential book, *The Coal Question,* that foreshadowed many modern

concerns about resources and growth. But his pessimism was proved wrong.

The Industrial Revolution was launched in Britain, and in 1865 Britain was still the world's richest major economy. But Jevons argued that Britain's economic success had depended on the availability of cheap coal and that the gradual exhaustion of Britain's coal resources, as miners were forced to dig ever deeper, would threaten the nation's long-run prosperity.

He was right about the exhaustion of Britain's coal: production peaked in 1913, and today the British coal industry is a shadow of its former self. But Britain was able to turn to newly developed alternative sources of energy, including imported coal and oil. And economic growth did not collapse: real GDP per capita in Britain today is about seven times its level in 1865.

Despite these past environmental success stories, there is widespread concern today about the environmental impacts of continuing economic growth, reflecting a change in the scale of the problem. Environmental success stories have mainly involved dealing with *local* impacts of economic growth, such as the effect of widespread car ownership on air quality in the Los Angeles basin. Today, however, we are faced with *global* environmental issues—the adverse impacts on the environment of the Earth as a whole by worldwide economic growth. The biggest of these issues involves the impact of fossil-fuel consumption on the world's climate.

Burning coal and oil releases carbon dioxide into the atmosphere. There is broad scientific consensus that rising levels of carbon dioxide and other gases are causing a greenhouse effect on the Earth, trapping more of the sun's energy and raising the planet's overall temperature. And rising temperatures may impose high human and economic costs: rising sea levels may flood coastal areas; changing climate may disrupt agriculture, especially in poor countries; and so on.

The problem of climate change is clearly linked to economic growth. Figure 25-11 shows carbon dioxide emissions from the United States, Europe, and China since 1980. Historically, the wealthy nations have been responsible for the bulk of these emissions because they have consumed far more energy per person than poorer countries. As China and other emerging economies have grown, however, they have begun to consume much more energy and emit much more carbon dioxide.

Is it possible to continue long-run economic growth while curbing the emissions of greenhouse gases? The answer, according to most economists who have studied the issue, is yes. It should be possible to reduce greenhouse gas emissions in a wide variety of ways, ranging from the use of non-fossil-fuel energy sources such as wind, solar, and nuclear power; to preventive measures such as carbon sequestration (capturing the carbon dioxide from power plants and storing it); to simpler things like designing buildings so that they're easier to keep warm in winter and cool in summer. Such measures would impose costs on the economy, but the best available estimates suggest that even a large reduction in greenhouse gas emissions over the next few decades would only modestly dent the long-term rise in real GDP per capita.

The problem is how to make all of this happen. Unlike resource scarcity, environmental problems don't automatically provide incentives for changed behavior. Pollution is

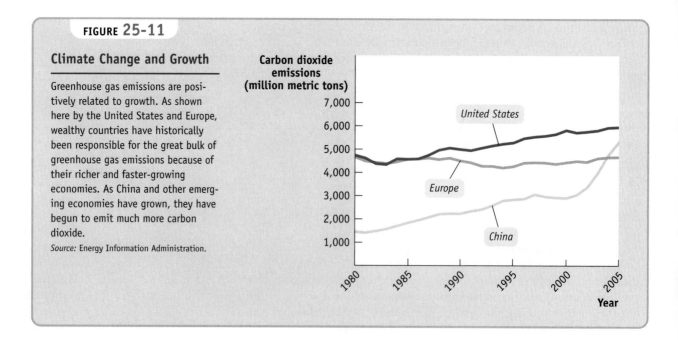

FIGURE 25-11

Climate Change and Growth

Greenhouse gas emissions are positively related to growth. As shown here by the United States and Europe, wealthy countries have historically been responsible for the great bulk of greenhouse gas emissions because of their richer and faster-growing economies. As China and other emerging economies have grown, they have begun to emit much more carbon dioxide.

Source: Energy Information Administration.

Carbon dioxide emissions (million metric tons)

an example of a *negative externality,* a cost that individuals or firms impose on others without having to offer compensation. In the absence of government intervention, individuals and firms have no incentive to reduce negative externalities, which is why it took regulation to reduce air pollution in America's cities. And as Nicholas Stern, the author of an influential report on climate change, put it, greenhouse gas emissions are "the mother of all externalities."

So there is a broad consensus among economists—although there are some dissenters—that government action is needed to deal with climate change. There is also broad consensus that this action should take the form of market-based incentives, either in the form of a carbon tax—a tax per unit of carbon emitted—or a cap and trade system in which the total amount of emissions is capped, and producers must buy licenses to emit greenhouse gases. There is, however, considerable dispute about how much action is appropriate, reflecting both uncertainty about the costs and benefits and scientific uncertainty about the pace and extent of climate change.

There are also several aspects of the climate change problem that make it much more difficult to deal with than, say, smog in Los Angeles. One is the problem of taking the long view. The impact of greenhouse gas emissions on the climate is very gradual: carbon dioxide put into the atmosphere today won't have its full effect on the climate for several generations. As a result, there is the political problem of persuading voters to accept pain today in return for gains that will benefit their children, grandchildren, or even great-grandchildren.

There is also a difficult problem of international burden sharing. As Figure 25-11 shows, today's rich countries have historically been responsible for most greenhouse gas emissions, but newly emerging economies like China are responsible for most of the recent growth. Inevitably, rich countries are reluctant to pay the price of reducing emissions only to have their efforts frustrated by rapidly growing emissions from new players. On the other hand, countries like China, which are still relatively poor, consider it unfair that they should be expected to bear the burden of protecting an environment threatened by the past actions of rich nations.

The general moral of this story is that it is possible to reconcile long-run economic growth with environmental protection. The main question is one of getting political consensus around the necessary policies.

►*ECONOMICS IN ACTION*

The Cost of Climate Protection

At the time of writing, there were a number of bills before the U.S. Congress, some of them with bipartisan sponsorship, calling for ambitious, long-term efforts to reduce U.S. emissions of greenhouse gases. For example, a bill sponsored by Senators Joseph Lieberman and John McCain would use a cap and trade system to gradually reduce emissions over time, eventually—by 2050—reducing them to 60% below their 1990 level. Another bill, sponsored by Senators Barbara Boxer and Bernie Sanders, called for an 80% reduction by 2050.

Would implementing these bills put a stop to long-run economic growth? Not according to a comprehensive study by a team at MIT, which found that reducing emissions would impose significant but not overwhelming costs. Using an elaborate model of the interaction between environmental policy and the economy, the MIT group estimated that the Lieberman–McCain proposal would reduce real GDP per capita in 2050 by 1.11% and the more stringent Sanders–Boxer proposal would reduce real GDP per capita by 1.79%.

These may sound like big numbers—they would amount to between $200 billion and $250 billion today—but they would hardly make a dent in the economy's

➤ There's wide disagreement about whether long-run economic growth is **sustainable**—how scarce natural resources like oil are or how difficult it will be to find alternatives. However, economists generally believe that modern economies can find ways to alleviate limits to growth from natural resource scarcity through the price response that promotes conservation and the creation of alternatives.

➤ The limits to growth arising from environmental degradation, however, are more difficult to overcome because overcoming them requires effective government intervention. The emission of greenhouse gases is clearly linked to growth, and limiting them will require some reduction in growth. However, the best available estimates suggest that a large reduction in emissions would require only a modest reduction in the growth rate.

➤ There is broad consensus that government action to address climate change and greenhouse gases should be in the form of market-based incentives, like a carbon tax or a cap and trade system. It will also require rich and poor countries to come to some agreement on how the cost of emissions reductions will be shared.

long-run growth rate. Remember that over the long run the U.S. economy has on average seen real GDP per capita rise by almost 2% a year. If the MIT group's estimates are correct, even a strong policy to avert climate change would, in effect, require that we give up less than one year's growth over the next four decades. ▲

< < < < < < < < < < < <

▶ CHECK YOUR UNDERSTANDING 25-5

1. Are economists typically more concerned about the limits to growth imposed by environmental degradation or those imposed by resource scarcity? Explain, noting the role of negative externalities in your answer.

2. What is the link between greenhouse gas emissions and growth? What is the expected effect on growth from emissions reduction? Why is international burden sharing of greenhouse gas emissions reduction a contentious problem?

Solutions appear at back of book.

[▶▶ A LOOK AHEAD •••

As we've noted, one of the keys to successful long-run economic growth is the ability of an economy to channel a high level of savings into productive investment spending. How is this accomplished? Through policies, institutions, and financial markets.

The financial system plays a crucial role in an economy's performance in both the long run and the short run. In the next chapter, we examine how that system works.]

SUMMARY

1. Growth is measured as changes in real GDP per capita in order to eliminate the effects of changes in the price level and changes in population size. Levels of real GDP per capita vary greatly around the world: more than half of the world's population lives in countries that are still poorer than the United States was in 1907. Over the course of the twentieth century, real GDP per capita in the United States increased fivefold.

2. Growth rates of real GDP per capita also vary widely. According to the **Rule of 70,** the number of years it takes for real GDP per capita to double is equal to 70 divided by the annual growth rate of real GDP per capita.

3. The key to long-run economic growth is rising **labor productivity,** or just **productivity,** which is output per worker. Increases in productivity arise from increases in **physical capital** per worker and **human capital** per worker as well as advances in **technology.** The **aggregate production function** shows how real GDP per worker depends on these three factors. Other things equal, there are **diminishing returns to physical capital:** holding human capital per worker and technology fixed, each successive addition to physical capital per worker yields a smaller increase in productivity than the one before. Equivalently, more physical capital per worker results in a lower, but still positive, increase in productivity. **Growth accounting,** which estimates the contribution of each factor to a country's economic growth, has shown that rising **total factor productivity,** the amount of output produced from a given amount of factor inputs, is key to long-run growth. It is usually interpreted as the effect of technological progress. In contrast to earlier times, natural resources are a less significant source of productivity growth in most countries today.

4. The large differences in countries' growth rates are largely due to differences in their rates of accumulation of physical and human capital as well as differences in technological progress. A prime factor is differences in savings and investment rates, since most countries that have high investment in physical capital finance it by high domestic savings. Technological progress is largely a result of **research and development,** or **R&D.**

5. Government actions that help growth are the building of **infrastructure,** particularly for public health, the creation and regulation of a well-functioning banking system that channels savings and investment spending, and the financing of both education and R&D. Government actions that retard growth are political instability, the neglect or violation of property rights, corruption, and excessive government intervention.

6. The world economy contains examples of success and failure in the effort to achieve long-run economic growth. East Asian economies have done many things right and achieved very high growth rates. In Latin America, where some important conditions are lacking, growth has generally been disappointing. In Africa, real GDP per capita has declined for several decades, although there are recent signs of progress. The growth rates of economically advanced countries have converged, but not the growth rates of countries across the world. This has led economists to believe that the **convergence hypothesis** fits the data only when factors that affect growth, such as education, infrastructure, and favorable policies and institutions, are held equal across countries.

7. Economists generally believe that environmental degradation poses a greater problem for whether long-run economic growth is **sustainable** than natural resource scarcity. Addressing environmental degradation requires effective governmental intervention, but the problem of natural resource scarcity is often well handled by the market price response.

8. The emission of greenhouse gases is clearly linked to growth, and limiting them will require some reduction in growth. However, the best available estimates suggest that a large reduction in emissions would require only a modest reduction in the growth rate.

9. There is broad consensus that government action to address climate change and greenhouse gases should be in the form of market-based incentives, like a carbon tax or a cap and trade system. It will also require rich and poor countries to come to some agreement on how the cost of emissions reductions will be shared.

KEY TERMS

Rule of 70, p. 644
Labor productivity, p. 646
Productivity, p. 646
Physical capital, p. 647
Human capital, p. 647
Technology, p. 647
Aggregate production function, p. 647
Diminishing returns to physical capital, p. 648
Growth accounting, p. 650
Total factor productivity, p. 651
Research and development (R&D), p. 655
Infrastructure, p. 656
Convergence hypothesis, p. 660
Sustainable, p. 663

PROBLEMS

1. The accompanying table shows data from the Penn World Table, Version 6.2, for real GDP per capita in 2000 U.S. dollars for Argentina, Ghana, South Korea, and the United States for 1960, 1970, 1980, 1990, and 2000.

   a. Complete the table by expressing each year's real GDP per capita as a percentage of its 1960 and 2000 levels.

   b. How does the growth in living standards from 1960 to 2000 compare across these four nations? What might account for these differences?

	Argentina			Ghana			South Korea			United States		
Year	Real GDP per capita (2000 dollars)	Percentage of 1960 real GDP per capita	Percentage of 2000 real GDP per capita	Real GDP per capita (2000 dollars)	Percentage of 1960 real GDP per capita	Percentage of 2000 real GDP per capita	Real GDP per capita (2000 dollars)	Percentage of 1960 real GDP per capita	Percentage of 2000 real GDP per capita	Real GDP per capita (2000 dollars)	Percentage of 1960 real GDP per capita	Percentage of 2000 real GDP per capita
1960	$7,838	?	?	$412	?	?	$1,458	?	?	$12,892	?	?
1970	9,821	?	?	1,052	?	?	2,552	?	?	17,321	?	?
1980	10,921	?	?	1,142	?	?	4,497	?	?	21,606	?	?
1990	8,195	?	?	1,153	?	?	9,593	?	?	27,097	?	?
2000	11,332	?	?	1,392	?	?	15,702	?	?	34,365	?	?

2. The accompanying table shows the average annual growth rate in real GDP per capita for Argentina, Ghana, and South Korea using data from the Penn World Table, Version 6.2, for the past few decades.

	Average annual growth rate of real GDP per capita		
Years	Argentina	Ghana	South Korea
1960–1970	2.53%	15.54%	7.50%
1970–1980	1.12	0.85	7.62
1980–1990	−2.50	0.10	11.33
1990–2000	3.83	2.08	6.37

   a. For each decade and for each country, use the Rule of 70 where possible to calculate how long it would take for that country's real GDP per capita to double.

   b. Suppose that the average annual growth rate that each country achieved over the period 1990–2000 continues indefinitely into the future. Starting from 2000, use the Rule of 70 to calculate, where possible, the year in which a country will have doubled its real GDP per capita.

3. The accompanying table provides approximate statistics on per capita income levels and growth rates for regions defined by income levels. According to the Rule of 70, the high-income countries are projected to double their per capita GDP in approximately 37 years, in 2042. Throughout this question, assume constant growth rates for each of the regions that are fixed at their average value between 2000 and 2005.

Region	GDP per capita (2005)	Average GDP per capita growth (2000–2005)
High-income countries	$28,612	1.9%
Middle-income countries	2,196	5.7
Low-income countries	494	3.6

Source: World Bank.

   a. Calculate the ratio of per capita GDP in 2005 of the following:

   i. Middle-income to high-income countries

   ii. Low-income to high-income countries

   iii. Low-income to middle-income countries

   b. Calculate the number of years it will take the low-income and middle-income countries to double their per capita GDP.

   c. Calculate the per capita GDP of each of the regions in 2042. (*Hint:* How many times does their per capita GDP double in 37 years?)

   d. Repeat part a with the projected per capita GDP in 2042.

   e. Compare your answers to parts a and d. Comment on the change in economic inequality between the regions.

4. You are hired as an economic consultant to the countries of Albernia and Brittania. Each country's current relationship between physical capital per worker and output per worker is given by the curve labeled Productivity$_1$ in the accompanying diagram. Albernia is at point A and Brittania is at point B.

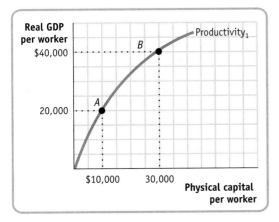

a. In the relationship depicted by the curve Productivity$_1$, what factors are held fixed? Do these countries experience diminishing returns to physical capital per worker?

b. Assuming that the amount of human capital per worker and the technology are held fixed in each country, can you recommend a policy to generate a doubling of real GDP per capita in Albernia?

c. How would your policy recommendation change if the amount of human capital per worker and the technology were not fixed? Draw a curve on the diagram that represents this policy for Albernia.

5. The country of Androde is currently using Method 1 for its production function. By chance, scientists stumble on a technological breakthrough that will enhance Androde's productivity. This technological breakthrough is reflected in another production function, Method 2. The accompanying table shows combinations of physical capital per worker and output per worker for both methods, assuming that human capital per worker is fixed.

Method 1		Method 2	
Physical capital per worker	**Real GDP per worker**	**Physical capital per worker**	**Real GDP per worker**
0	0.00	0	0.00
50	35.36	50	70.71
100	50.00	100	100.00
150	61.24	150	122.47
200	70.71	200	141.42
250	79.06	250	158.11
300	86.60	300	173.21
350	93.54	350	187.08
400	100.00	400	200.00
450	106.07	450	212.13
500	111.80	500	223.61

a. Using the data in the accompanying table, draw the two production functions in one diagram. Androde's current amount of physical capital per worker is 100. In your figure, label that point A.

b. Starting from point A, over a period of 70 years, the amount of physical capital per worker in Androde rises to 400. Assuming Androde still uses Method 1, in your diagram, label the resulting point of production B. Using the Rule of 70, calculate by how many percent per year output per worker has grown.

c. Now assume that, starting from point A, over the same period of 70 years, the amount of physical capital per worker in Androde rises to 400, but that during that time period, Androde switches to Method 2. In your diagram, label the resulting point of production C. Using the Rule of 70, calculate by how many percent per year output per worker has grown now.

d. As the economy of Androde moves from point A to point C, which percentage of the annual productivity growth is due to higher total factor productivity?

6. The Bureau of Labor Statistics regularly releases the "Productivity and Costs" report for the previous month. Go to www.bls.gov and find the latest report. (On the Bureau of Labor Statistics home page, under Latest Numbers, find "Productivity" and click on "News Release.") What were the percent changes in business and nonfarm business productivity for the previous quarter? How does the percent change in that quarter's productivity compare to data from the previous quarter?

7. What roles do physical capital, human capital, technology, and natural resources play in influencing ~~long-run econ~~omic growth of aggregate output per capita?

8. How have U.S. policies and institutions influenced the country's long-run economic growth?

9. Over the next 100 years, real GDP per capita in Groland is expected to grow at an average annual rate of 2.0%. In Sloland, however, growth is expected to be somewhat slower, at an average annual growth rate of 1.5%. If both countries have a real GDP per capita today of $20,000, how will their real GDP per capita differ in 100 years? [Hint: A country that has a real GDP today of $x and grows at y% per year will achieve a real GDP of $x \times (1 + 0.0y)^z$ in z years. We assume that $0 \leq y < 10$.]

10. The accompanying table shows data from the Penn World Table, Version 6.2, for real GDP per capita (2000 U.S. dollars) in France, Japan, the United Kingdom, and the United States in 1950 and 2004. Complete the table. Have these countries converged economically?

	1950		2004	
	Real GDP per capita (2000 dollars)	**Percentage of U.S. real GDP per capita**	**Real GDP per capita (2000 dollars)**	**Percentage of U.S. real GDP per capita**
France	$5,921	?	$26,168	?
Japan	2,188	?	24,661	?
United Kingdom	8,082	?	26,762	?
United States	11,233	?	36,098	?

11. The accompanying table shows data from the Penn World Table, Version 6.2, for real GDP per capita (2000 U.S. dollars) for Argentina, Ghana, South Korea, and the United States in 1960 and 2003. Complete the table. Have these countries converged economically?

	1960		2003	
	Real GDP per capita (2000 dollars)	**Percentage of U.S. real GDP per capita**	**Real GDP per capita (2000 dollars)**	**Percentage of U.S. real GDP per capita**
Argentina	$7,838	?	$10,170	?
Ghana	412	?	1,440	?
South Korea	1,458	?	17,597	?
United States	12,892	?	34,875	?

12. Why would you expect real GDP per capita in California and Pennsylvania to exhibit convergence but not in California and Baja California, a state of Mexico that borders the United States? What changes would allow California and Baja California to converge?

13. According to the *Oil & Gas Journal*, the proven oil reserves of the top 12 oil producers was 1,137 billion barrels of oil in 2007. In that year, the U.S. Energy Information Administration reported that the daily oil production from these nations was 48.2 million barrels a day.

a. At this rate, how many years will the proven oil reserves of the top 12 oil producers last? Discuss the Malthusian view in the context of the number you just calculated.

b. What are some important assumptions implicit in your calculations that challenge the Malthusian view on this issue?

c. Discuss how market forces may affect the amount of time the proven oil reserves will last, assuming that no new oil reserves are discovered and that the demand curve for oil remains unchanged.

14. The accompanying table shows the percent change in verified emissions of carbon dioxide (CO_2) and the percent change in real GDP per capita for selected EU countries.

Country	**Percent change in real GDP per capita 2005–2007**	**Percent change in CO_2 emissions 2005–2007**
Austria	6.30%	−4.90%
Belgium	4.19	−4.60
Cyprus	5.56	6.20
Finland	9.23	28.50
France	2.76	−3.50
Germany	5.79	2.50
Greece	8.09	2
Ireland	6.56	−5.30
Italy	2.28	0.20
Luxembourg	8.55	−1.40
Netherlands	4.61	−0.60
Portugal	2.67	−14.40
Slovenia	11.79	3.80
Spain	4.28	1.60

Sources: European Commission Press Release, May 23, 2008; International Monetary Fund, *World Factbook* 2008.

a. Rank the countries in terms of percentage increase in CO_2 emissions, from highest to lowest. What five countries have the highest percentage increase in emissions? What five countries have the lowest percentage increase in emissions?

b. Now rank the countries in terms of the percentage increase in real GDP per person, from highest to lowest. What five countries have the highest percentage increase? What five countries have the lowest percentage increase?

c. Would you infer from your results that CO_2 emissions are linked to growth in output per person?

d. Do high growth rates necessarily lead to high CO_2 emissions?

> Savings, Investment Spending, and the Financial System

A HOLE IN THE GROUND

Between 1987 and 1994, a large international group of private investors threw $16 billion into a hole in the ground. But this was no ordinary hole: it was the Channel Tunnel, popularly known as the Chunnel. Engineers had dreamed for centuries about linking Britain directly to France so that travelers would no longer have to cross the often-stormy seas of the English Channel. The Chunnel fulfills that dream, allowing passengers to take a comfortable, fast train (and transport their cars, too) underneath the 31-mile-wide strait.

Everyone agrees that the Chunnel is a big improvement on the previously available alternatives. It's much faster than taking a ferry. Even flying from London to Paris can easily be an all-day affair, what with getting to and from the airports and air traffic delays. The *Eurostar,* the express train through the Chunnel, gets you from downtown London to downtown Paris in 2½ hours.

How could such a massive investment be financed? The French and British governments could have built the Chunnel but chose to leave it to private initiative. Yet the size of the required investment was beyond the means of any individual. So how was the money raised?½

The answer: the Eurotunnel Corporation, the company formed to build the Chunnel, was able to turn to the financial markets. It raised $4 billion by selling stock to thousands of people, who then became part-owners of the Chunnel, and an additional $12 billion through bank loans. Raising this much money

was an incredible feat, in a way as incredible as the engineering required in the construction of the Chunnel.

Yet modern economies do this sort of thing all the time. The long-run growth we analyzed in the previous chapter depends crucially on a set of markets and institutions, collectively known as the *financial system,* that channels the funds of savers into productive investment spending. Without this system, businesses would not be able to purchase much of the physical capital that is such an important source of productivity growth. And savers would be forced to accept a lower return on their funds. Historically, financial systems channeled funds into investment projects such as railroads, factories, electrification, and so on. Today, financial systems channel funds into new sources of growth such as telecommunications, advanced technology, and investments in human capital. Without a well-functioning financial system, a country will suffer stunted economic growth.

Due to the savings of millions of people, travelers can now enjoy a quick trip between London and Paris via the Chunnel.

In this chapter, we begin by focusing on the economy as a whole. We examine the relationship between savings and investment spending at the macroeconomic level. Next, we go behind this relationship and analyze the financial system, the means by which savings is transformed into investment spending. We'll see how the financial system works by creating assets, markets, and institutions that increase the welfare of both savers (those with funds to invest) and borrowers (those with investment projects to finance). Finally, we close by examining the behavior of financial markets and why that behavior often resists economists' attempts to explain it.

WHAT YOU WILL LEARN IN THIS CHAPTER:

➤ The relationship between savings and investment spending

➤ Aspects of the **loanable funds market,** which shows how savers are matched with borrowers

➤ The purpose of the five principal types of **financial assets:** stocks, bonds, **loans,** real estate, and **bank deposits**

➤ How **financial intermediaries** help investors achieve **diversification**

➤ Some competing views of what determines stock prices and why stock market fluctuations can be a source of macroeconomic instability

Matching Up Savings and Investment Spending

We learned in the previous chapter that two of the essential ingredients in economic growth are increases in the economy's levels of *human capital* and *physical capital.* Human capital is largely provided by government through public education. (In countries with a large private education sector, like the United States, private post-secondary education is also an important source of human capital.) But physical capital, with the exception of infrastructure, is mainly created through private investment spending—that is, spending by firms rather than by the government.

Who pays for private investment spending? In some cases it's the people or corporations who actually do the spending—for example, a family that owns a business might use its own savings to buy new equipment or a new building, or a corporation might reinvest some of its own profits to build a new factory. In the modern economy, however, individuals and firms who create physical capital often do it with other people's money—money that they borrow or raise by selling stock.

To understand how investment spending is financed, we need to look first at how savings and investment spending are related for the economy as a whole. Then we will examine how savings are allocated among investment projects.

PITFALLS

INVESTMENT VERSUS INVESTMENT SPENDING

When macroeconomists use the term *investment spending,* they almost always mean "spending on new physical capital." This can be confusing, because in ordinary life we often say that someone who buys stocks or purchases an existing building is "investing." The important point to keep in mind is that only spending that adds to the economy's stock of physical capital is "investment spending." In contrast, the act of purchasing an asset such as a share of stock, a bond, or existing real estate is "making an investment."

The Savings–Investment Spending Identity

The most basic point to understand about savings and investment spending is that they are always equal. This is not a theory; it's a fact of accounting called the **savings–investment spending identity.**

To see why the savings–investment spending identity must be true, first imagine a highly simplified economy in which there is no government and no interaction with other countries. The overall income of this simplified economy would, by definition, be equal to total spending in the economy. Why? Because the only way people could earn income would be by selling something to someone else, and every dollar spent in the economy would create income for somebody. So in this simplified economy,

According to the **savings–investment spending identity,** savings and investment spending are always equal for the economy as a whole.

(26-1) Total income = Total spending

Now, what can people do with income? They can either spend it on consumption or save it. So it must be true that

(26-2)   Total income = Consumption spending + Savings

Meanwhile, spending consists of either consumption spending or investment spending:

(26-3)   Total spending = Consumption spending + Investment spending

Putting these together, we get:

(26-4)   Consumption spending + Savings = Consumption spending + Investment spending

Subtract consumption spending from both sides, and we get:

(26-5)   Savings = Investment spending

As we said, then, it's a basic accounting fact that savings equals investment spending for the economy as a whole.

So far, however, we've only looked at a simplified economy in which there is no government and no economic interactions with the rest of the world. Bringing these realistic complications back into the story changes things in two ways.

First, households are not the only parties that can save in an economy. In any given year the government can save, too, if it collects more tax revenue than it spends. When this occurs, the difference is called a **budget surplus** and is equivalent to savings by government. If, alternatively, government spending exceeds tax revenue, there is a **budget deficit**—a negative budget surplus. In this case we often say that the government is "dissaving": by spending more than its tax revenues, the government is engaged in the opposite of saving. We'll define the term **budget balance** to refer to both cases, with the understanding that the budget balance can be positive (a budget surplus) or negative (a budget deficit). **National savings** is equal to the sum of private savings and the budget balance, where private savings is disposable income (income after taxes) minus consumption.

Second, the fact that any one country is part of a wider world economy means that savings need not be spent on physical capital located in the same country in which the savings are generated. That's because the savings of people who live in any one country can be used to finance investment spending that takes place in other countries. So any given country can receive *inflows* of funds—foreign savings that finance investment spending in the country. Any given country can also generate *outflows* of funds—domestic savings that finance investment spending in another country.

The net effect of international inflows and outflows of funds on the total savings available for investment spending in any given country is known as the **capital inflow** into that country, equal to the total inflow of foreign funds minus the total outflow of domestic funds to other countries. Like the budget balance, a capital inflow can be negative—that is, more capital can flow out of a country than flows into it. In recent years the United States has experienced a consistent net inflow of capital from foreigners, who view our economy as an attractive place to put their savings. In 2007, for example, capital inflows into the United States were $720 billion.

It's important to note that, from a national perspective, a dollar generated by national savings and a dollar generated by capital inflow are not equivalent. Yes, they can both finance the same dollar's worth of investment spending. But any dollar borrowed from a saver must eventually be repaid with interest. A dollar that comes from national savings is repaid with interest to someone domestically—either a private party or the government. But a dollar that comes as capital inflow must be repaid with interest to a foreigner. So a dollar of investment spending financed by a capital inflow comes at a higher *national* cost—the interest that must eventually be paid to a foreigner—than a dollar of investment spending financed by national savings.

The **budget surplus** is the difference between tax revenue and government spending when tax revenue exceeds government spending.

The **budget deficit** is the difference between tax revenue and government spending when government spending exceeds tax revenue.

The **budget balance** is the difference between tax revenue and government spending.

National savings, the sum of private savings and the budget balance, is the total amount of savings generated within the economy.

Capital inflow is the net inflow of funds into a country.

PITFALLS

THE DIFFERENT KINDS OF CAPITAL

It's important to understand clearly the three different kinds of capital: physical capital, human capital, and financial capital. As we explained in the previous chapter, physical capital consists of manufactured resources such as buildings and machines. Human capital is the improvement in the labor force generated by education and knowledge. Financial capital is funds from savings that are available for investment spending. So a country that has a positive capital inflow is experiencing a flow of funds into the country from abroad that can be used for investment spending.

So the application of the savings–investment spending identity to an economy that is open to inflows or outflows of capital means that investment spending is equal to savings, where savings is equal to national savings *plus* capital inflow. That is, in an economy with a positive capital inflow, some investment spending is funded by the savings of foreigners. And in an economy with a negative capital inflow (a net outflow), some portion of national savings is funding investment spending in other countries. In the United States in 2007, investment spending totaled $2,593 billion. Private savings (and we include all depreciation here) were $2,173 billion, offset by a budget deficit of $219 billion and supplemented by capital inflows of $720 billion. Notice that these numbers don't quite add up; because data collection isn't perfect, there is a "statistical discrepancy" of $81 billion. But we know that this is an error in the data, not in the theory, because the savings–investment spending identity must hold in reality.

Figure 26-1 shows what this identity actually looked like in 2007 for two of the world's largest economies, those of the United States and Japan. To make the two

FIGURE 26-1   The Savings–Investment Spending Identity in Open Economies: the United States and Japan, 2007

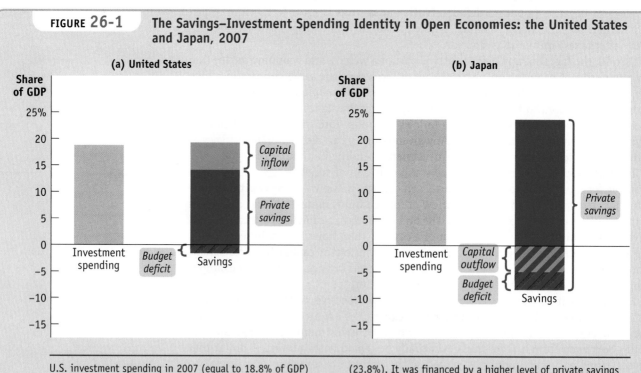

U.S. investment spending in 2007 (equal to 18.8% of GDP) was financed by a combination of private savings (15.7% of GDP) and capital inflows (5.2% of GDP), which were partially offset by a budget deficit (−1.6% of GDP). Japanese investment spending in 2007 was higher as a percentage of GDP (23.8%). It was financed by a higher level of private savings as a percentage of GDP (32.1%), which was offset by both a capital outflow (−4.9% of GDP) and a relatively high budget deficit (−3.4% of GDP).

Source: Bureau of Economic Analysis; OECD.

GLOBAL COMPARISON | AMERICA'S LOW SAVINGS

This figure shows national savings as a percentage of GDP for seven wealthy economies in 2007. The United States had the lowest savings rate, although Britain's savings were only slightly higher.

In this respect, 2007 wasn't unusual. The United States has had consistently low savings compared with other wealthy countries since the 1980s. The main source of these international differences in national savings lies in low U.S. private savings rather than in large budget deficits.

Why does America save so little? The short answer is that economists aren't sure, although there are a number of theories. One is that consumers have easier access to credit in the United States than elsewhere. For example, Japanese lenders have traditionally demanded large down payments from home-buyers; but, until the recent housing bust, it was possible for Americans to buy homes with little or no money down.

It's also argued that the U.S. Social Security system, by guaranteeing income in retirement, may reduce the incentive for private saving. In any case, the United States has been able to maintain high levels of investment spending in spite of its low savings rate because it receives large capital inflows.

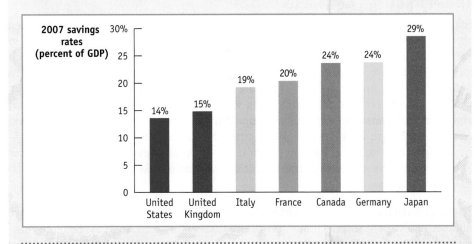

Source: International Monetary Fund.
Note: IMF data differs slightly from other data sources.

economies easier to compare, we've measured savings and investment spending as percentages of GDP. In each panel the bars on the left show total investment spending and those on the right show the components of savings. U.S. investment spending was 18.8% of GDP, financed by a combination of private savings (15.7% of GDP) and capital inflows (5.2% of GDP) and partly offset by a government budget deficit (−1.6% of GDP). (These numbers sum to more than 18.8% due to statistical discrepancy.) Japanese investment spending was higher as a percentage of GDP, at 23.8%. It was financed by a higher level of private savings as a percentage of GDP (32.1%) and was offset by both a capital outflow (−4.9% of GDP) and a budget deficit (−3.4% of GDP).

The economy's savings, then, finance its investment spending. But how are these funds that are available for investment spending allocated among various projects? That is, what determines which projects get financed (such as the Chunnel) and which don't (such as a new jetliner that would fly close to the speed of sound, which Boeing recently declined to fully develop and produce)? We'll see shortly that funds get allocated to investment projects using a familiar method: by the market, via supply and demand.

Who Enforces the Accounting?

The savings–investment spending identity is a fact of accounting. By definition, savings equals investment spending for the economy as a whole. But who enforces the arithmetic? For example, what happens if the amount that businesses want to invest in capital equipment is less than the amount households want to save?

The short answer is that actual and *desired* investment spending aren't always equal. Suppose that households suddenly decide to save more by spending less—say, by putting off the purchase of new cars. The immediate effect will be that unsold goods pile up—in this case, in the form of cars sitting in dealers' lots. And this increase in inventory counts as investment spending, albeit unintended. So the savings–investment spending identity still holds, because auto dealers end up engaging in more investment spending than they intended to. Similarly, if households suddenly decide to save less and spend more, inventories will drop—and this will be counted as *negative* investment spending.

A real-world example occurred in 2001. Savings and investment spending, measured at an annual rate, both fell by $126 billion between the second and the fourth quarter of 2001. But on the investment spending side, $71 billion of that fall took the form of negative inventory investment spending. In particular, car dealers sold many of the vehicles that had been sitting on their lots.

Of course, businesses respond to changes in their inventories by changing their production. The inventory reduction in late 2001 prepared the ground for a spurt in output in early 2002. We'll examine the special role of inventories in economic fluctuations in Chapter 27.

The Market for Loanable Funds

For the economy as a whole, savings always equals investment spending. In a closed economy, savings is equal to national savings. In an open economy, savings is equal to national savings plus capital inflow. At any given time, however, savers, the people with funds to lend, are usually not the same as borrowers, the people who want to borrow to finance their investment spending. How are savers and borrowers brought together?

Savers and borrowers are matched up with one another in much the same way producers and consumers are matched up: through markets governed by supply and demand. In Figure 23-1, the expanded circular-flow diagram, we noted that the *financial markets* channel the savings of households to businesses that want to borrow in order to purchase capital equipment. It's now time to take a look at how those financial markets work.

The Equilibrium Interest Rate As we noted in Chapter 23, there are a large number of different financial markets in the financial system, such as the bond market and the stock market. However, economists often work with a simplified model in which they assume that there is just one market that brings together those who want to lend money (savers) and those who want to borrow (firms with investment spending projects). This hypothetical market is known as the **loanable funds market.** The price that is determined in the loanable funds market is the **interest rate,** denoted by r. It is the return a lender receives for allowing borrowers the use of a dollar for one year, calculated as a percentage of the amount borrowed.

We should note at this point that there are, in reality, many different kinds of interest rates because there are many different kinds of loans—short-term loans, long-term loans, loans made to corporate borrowers, loans made to governments, and so on. In the interest of simplicity, we'll ignore those differences and assume that there is only one type of loan. Figure 26-2 illustrates the hypothetical demand for loanable funds. On the horizontal axis we show the quantity of loanable funds demanded. On the vertical axis we show the interest rate, which is the "price" of borrowing. To see why the demand curve for loanable funds, D, slopes downward, imagine that there are many businesses, each of which has one potential investment project. How does a given business decide whether or not to borrow money to finance its project? The decision depends on the interest rate the business faces and the **rate of return** on its project—the profit earned on the project expressed as a percentage of its cost. This can be expressed in a formula as:

The **loanable funds market** is a hypothetical market that illustrates the market outcome of the demand for funds generated by borrowers and the supply of funds provided by lenders.

The **interest rate** is the price, calculated as a percentage of the amount borrowed, charged by lenders to borrowers for the use of their savings for one year.

The **rate of return** on a project is the profit earned on the project expressed as a percentage of its cost.

(26-6) Rate of return $= \dfrac{\text{Revenue from project} - \text{Cost of project}}{\text{Cost of project}} \times 100$

A business will want a loan when the rate of return on its project is greater than or equal to the interest rate. So, for example, at an interest rate of 12%, only businesses with projects that yield a rate of return greater than or equal to 12% will want a loan. The demand curve in Figure 26-2 shows that if the interest rate is 12%, businesses will want to borrow $150 billion (point A); if the interest rate is only 4%, businesses will want to borrow a larger amount, $450 billion (point B). That's a consequence of our assumption that the demand curve slopes downward: the lower the interest rate, the larger the total quantity of loanable funds demanded. Why do we make that assumption? Because, in reality, the number of potential investment projects that yield at least 4% is always greater than the number that yield at least 12%.

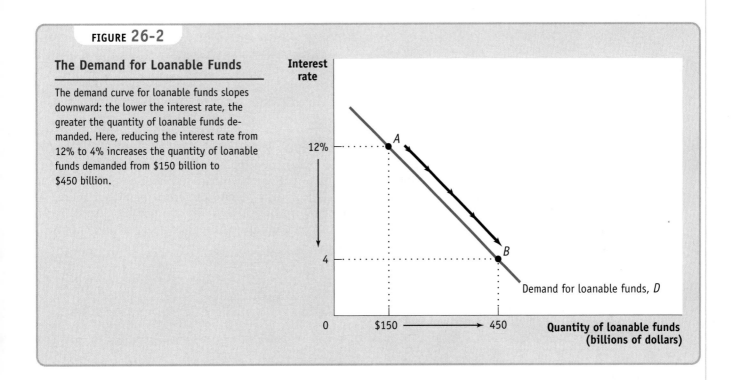

FIGURE 26-2

The Demand for Loanable Funds

The demand curve for loanable funds slopes downward: the lower the interest rate, the greater the quantity of loanable funds demanded. Here, reducing the interest rate from 12% to 4% increases the quantity of loanable funds demanded from $150 billion to $450 billion.

Figure 26-3 on the next page shows the hypothetical supply of loanable funds. Again, the interest rate plays the same role that the price plays in ordinary supply and demand analysis. Savers incur an opportunity cost when they lend to a business; the funds could instead be spent on consumption—say, a nice vacation. Whether a given saver becomes a lender by making funds available to borrowers depends on the interest rate received in return. By saving your money today and earning interest on it, you are rewarded with higher consumption in the future when your loan is repaid with interest. So it is a good assumption that more people are willing to forgo current consumption and make a loan when the interest rate is higher. As a result, our hypothetical supply curve of loanable funds slopes upward. In Figure 26-3, lenders will supply $150 billion to the loanable funds market at an interest rate of 4% (point X); if the interest rate rises to 12%, the quantity of loanable funds supplied will rise to $450 billion (point Y).

The equilibrium interest rate is the interest rate at which the quantity of loanable funds supplied equals the quantity of loanable funds demanded. As you can see in

FIGURE 26-3

The Supply of Loanable Funds

The supply curve for loanable funds slopes upward: the higher the interest rate, the greater the quantity of loanable funds supplied. Here, increasing the interest rate from 4% to 12% increases the quantity of loanable funds supplied from $150 billion to $450 billion.

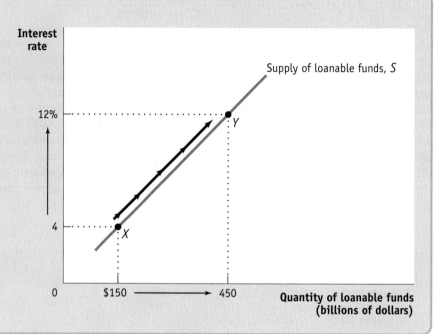

Figure 26-4, the equilibrium interest rate, r^*, and the total quantity of lending, Q^*, are determined by the intersection of the supply and demand curves, at point E. Here, the equilibrium interest rate is 8%, at which $300 billion is lent and borrowed. Investment spending projects with a rate of return of 8% or more are funded; projects with a rate of return of less than 8% are not. Correspondingly, only lenders who are willing to accept an interest rate of 8% or less will have their offers to lend funds accepted.

FIGURE 26-4

Equilibrium in the Loanable Funds Market

At the equilibrium interest rate, the quantity of loanable funds supplied equals the quantity of loanable funds demanded. Here, the equilibrium interest rate is 8%, with $300 billion of funds lent and borrowed. Investment spending projects with a rate of return of 8% or higher receive funding; those with a lower rate of return do not. Lenders who demand an interest rate of 8% or lower have their offers of loans accepted; those who demand a higher interest rate do not.

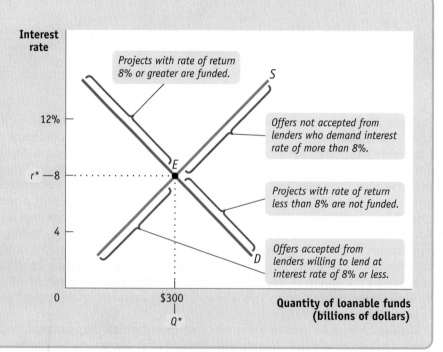

Figure 26-4 shows how the market for loanable funds matches up desired savings with desired investment spending: in equilibrium, the quantity of funds that savers want to lend is equal to the quantity of funds that firms want to borrow. The figure also shows that this match-up is efficient, in two senses. First, the right investments get made: the investment spending projects that are actually financed have higher rates of return than those that do not get financed. Second, the right people do the saving: the potential savers who actually lend funds are willing to lend for lower interest rates than those who do not. The insight that the loanable funds market leads to an efficient use of savings, although drawn from a highly simplified model, has important implications for real life. As we'll see shortly, it is the reason that a well-functioning financial system increases an economy's long-run economic growth rate.

Before we get to that, however, let's look at how the market for loanable funds responds to shifts of demand and supply.

Shifts of the Demand for Loanable Funds

The equilibrium interest rate changes when there are shifts of the demand curve for loanable funds, the supply curve for loanable funds, or both. Let's start by looking at the causes and effects of changes in demand.

The factors that can cause the demand curve for loanable funds to shift include the following:

- *Changes in perceived business opportunities:* A change in beliefs about the rate of return on investment spending can increase or reduce the amount of desired spending at any given interest rate. For example, during the 1990s there was great excitement over the business possibilities created by the Internet, which had just begun to be widely used. As a result, businesses rushed to buy computer equipment, put fiber-optic cables in the ground, and so on. This shifted the demand for loanable funds to the right. By 2001, the failure of many dot-com businesses led to disillusionment with technology-related investment; this shifted the demand for loanable funds back to the left.

- *Changes in the government's borrowing:* Governments that run budget deficits are major sources of the demand for loanable funds. As a result, changes in the budget deficit can shift the demand curve for loanable funds. For example, between 2000 and 2003, as the U.S. federal government went from a budget surplus to a budget deficit, net federal borrowing went from *minus* $189 billion—that is, in 2000 the federal government was actually providing loanable funds to the market, because it was paying off some of its debt—to *plus* $416 billion, because in 2003 the government had to borrow large sums to pay its bills. This change in the federal budget position had the effect, other things equal, of shifting the demand curve for loanable funds to the right.

Figure 26-5 on the next page shows the effects of an increase in the demand for loanable funds. S is the supply of loanable funds, and D_1 is the initial demand curve. The initial equilibrium interest rate is r_1. An increase in the demand for loanable funds means that the quantity of funds demanded rises at any given interest rate, so the demand curve shifts rightward to D_2. As a result, the equilibrium interest rate rises to r_2.

The fact that an increase in the demand for loanable funds leads, other things equal, to a rise in the interest rate has one especially important implication: it tells us one reason to be concerned about persistent government budget deficits. As we've already seen, an increase in the government's deficit shifts the demand curve for loanable funds to the right, which leads to a higher interest rate. If the interest rate rises, businesses will cut back on their investment spending. So a rise in the government budget deficit tends to reduce overall investment spending. Economists call the negative effect of government budget deficits on investment spending **crowding out.** Concerns about crowding out are one key reason to worry about persistent budget deficits.

Crowding out occurs when a government deficit drives up the interest rate and leads to reduced investment spending.

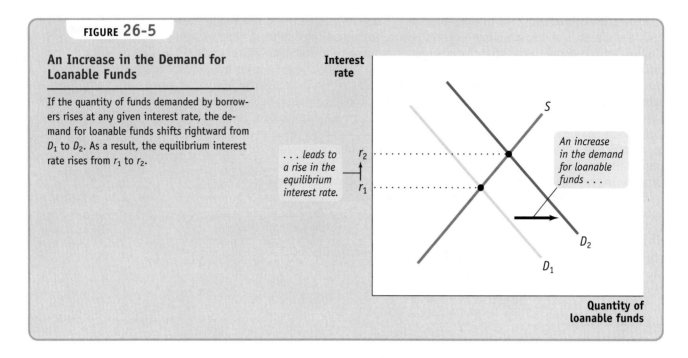

FIGURE 26-5

An Increase in the Demand for Loanable Funds

If the quantity of funds demanded by borrowers rises at any given interest rate, the demand for loanable funds shifts rightward from D_1 to D_2. As a result, the equilibrium interest rate rises from r_1 to r_2.

Shifts of the Supply of Loanable Funds Like the demand for loanable funds, the supply of loanable funds can shift. Among the factors that can cause the supply of loanable funds to shift are the following:

- *Changes in private savings behavior:* A number of factors can cause the level of private savings to change at any given rate of interest. For example, between 2000 and 2006 rising home prices in the United States made many homeowners feel richer, making them willing to spend more and save less. This had the effect of shifting the supply of loanable funds to the left.

- *Changes in capital inflows:* Capital flows into a country can change as investors' perceptions of that country change. For example, Argentina experienced large capital inflows during much of the 1990s because international investors believed that economic reforms early in the decade had made it a safe place to put their funds. By the late 1990s, however, there were signs of economic trouble, and investors lost confidence, causing the inflow of funds to dry up. As we've already seen, the United States has received large capital inflows in recent years, with much of the money coming from China and the Middle East. Those inflows helped fuel a big increase in residential investment spending—newly constructed homes—from 2003 to 2006. As a result of the worldwide slump, those inflows began to trail off in 2008.

Figure 26-6 shows the effects of an increase in the supply of loanable funds. *D* is the demand for loanable funds, and S_1 is the initial supply curve. The initial equilibrium interest rate is r_1. An increase in the supply of loanable funds means that the quantity of funds supplied rises at any given interest rate, so the supply curve shifts rightward to S_2. As a result, the equilibrium interest rate falls to r_2.

Inflation and Interest Rates Anything that shifts either the supply of loanable funds curve or the demand for loanable funds curve changes the interest rate. Historically, major changes in interest rates have been driven by many factors, including changes in government policy and technological innovations that created new investment opportunities. However, arguably the most important factor affecting interest rates over time—the reason, for example, that interest rates today are much lower than they were in the late 1970s and early 1980s—is changing expectations about future inflation, which shift both the supply and the demand for loanable funds.

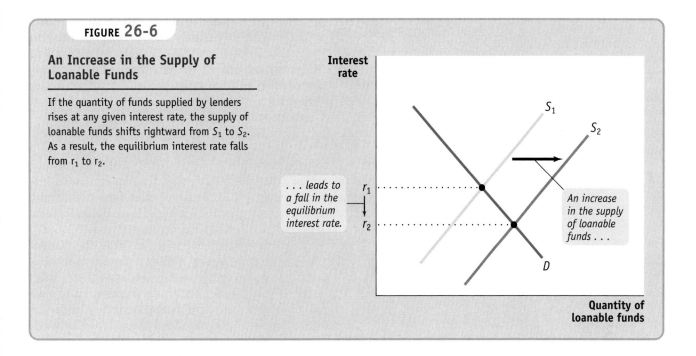

FIGURE 26-6

An Increase in the Supply of Loanable Funds

If the quantity of funds supplied by lenders rises at any given interest rate, the supply of loanable funds shifts rightward from S_1 to S_2. As a result, the equilibrium interest rate falls from r_1 to r_2.

. . . leads to a fall in the equilibrium interest rate.

An increase in the supply of loanable funds . . .

To understand the effect of expected inflation on interest rates, recall our discussion in Chapter 24 of the way inflation creates winners and losers—for example, the way that high U.S. inflation in the 1970s and 1980s reduced the real value of homeowners' mortgages, which was good for the homeowners but bad for the banks. In Chapter 24 we learned that economists summarize the effect of inflation on borrowers and lenders by distinguishing between the *nominal interest rate* and the *real interest rate,* where the difference is as follows:

Real interest rate = Nominal interest rate − Inflation rate

The true cost of borrowing is the real interest rate, not the nominal interest rate. To see why, suppose a firm borrows $10,000 for one year at a 10% nominal interest rate. At the end of the year, it must repay $11,000—the amount borrowed plus the interest. But suppose that over the course of the year the average level of prices increases by 10%, so that the real interest rate is zero. Then the $11,000 repayment has the same purchasing power as the original $10,000 loan. In effect, the borrower has received a zero-interest loan.

Similarly, the true payoff to lending is the real interest rate, not the nominal rate. Suppose that a bank makes a $10,000 loan for one year at a 10% nominal interest rate. At the end of the year, the bank receives an $11,000 repayment. But if the average level of prices rises by 10% per year, the purchasing power of the money the bank gets back is no more than that of the money it lent out. In effect, the bank has made a zero-interest loan.

Now we can add an important detail to our analysis of the loanable funds market. Figures 26-5 and 26-6 are drawn with the vertical axis measuring the *nominal interest rate for a given expected future inflation rate.* Why do we use the nominal interest rate rather than the real interest rate? Because in the real world neither borrowers nor lenders know what the future inflation rate will be when they make a deal. Actual loan contracts therefore specify a nominal interest rate rather than a real interest rate. Because we are holding the expected future inflation rate fixed in Figures 26-5 and 26-6, however, changes in the nominal interest rate also lead to changes in the real interest rate.

According to the **Fisher effect**, an increase in expected future inflation drives up the nominal interest rate, leaving the expected real interest rate unchanged.

The expectations of borrowers and lenders about future inflation rates are normally based on recent experience. In the late 1970s, after a decade of high inflation, borrowers and lenders expected future inflation to be high. By the late 1990s, after a decade of fairly low inflation, borrowers and lenders expected future inflation to be low. And these changing expectations about future inflation had a strong effect on the nominal interest rate, largely explaining why interest rates were much lower in the early years of the twenty-first century than they were in the early 1980s.

Let's look at how changes in the expected future rate of inflation are reflected in the loanable funds model.

In Figure 26-7, the curves S_0 and D_0 show the supply and demand for loanable funds given that the expected future rate of inflation is 0%. In that case, equilibrium is at E_0 and the equilibrium nominal interest rate is 4%. Because expected future inflation is 0%, the equilibrium expected real interest rate over the life of the loan, the real interest rate expected by borrowers and lenders when the loan is contracted, is also 4%.

Now suppose that the expected future inflation rate rises to 10%. The demand curve for funds shifts upward to D_{10}: borrowers are now willing to borrow as much at a nominal interest rate of 14% as they were previously willing to borrow at 4%. That's because with a 10% inflation rate, a 14% nominal interest rate corresponds to a 4% real interest rate. Similarly, the supply curve of funds shifts upward to S_{10}: lenders require a nominal interest rate of 14% to persuade them to lend as much as they would previously have lent at 4%. The new equilibrium is at E_{10}: the result of an expected future inflation rate of 10% is that the equilibrium nominal interest rate rises from 4% to 14%.

This situation can be summarized as a general principle, known as the **Fisher effect** (after the American economist Irving Fisher, who proposed it in 1930): *the expected real interest rate is unaffected by the change in expected future inflation.* According to the Fisher effect, an increase in expected future inflation drives up nominal interest rates, where each additional percentage point of expected future inflation drives up the nominal interest rate by 1 percentage point. The central point is that both lenders and borrowers base their decisions on the expected real interest rate. As long as the level of inflation is expected, it does not affect the equilibrium quantity of loanable funds or the expected real interest rate; all it affects is the equilibrium nominal interest rate.

FIGURE 26-7

The Fisher Effect

D_0 and S_0 are the demand and supply curves for loanable funds when the expected future inflation rate is 0%. At an expected inflation rate of 0%, the equilibrium nominal interest rate is 4%. An increase in expected future inflation pushes both the demand and supply curves upward by 1 percentage point for every percentage point increase in expected future inflation. D_{10} and S_{10} are the demand and supply curves for loanable funds when the expected future inflation rate is 10%. The 10 percentage point increase in expected future inflation raises the equilibrium nominal interest rate to 14%. The expected real interest rate remains at 4%, and the equilibrium quantity of loanable funds also remains unchanged.

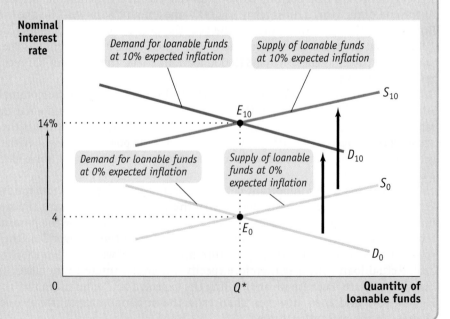

►ECONOMICS IN ACTION

Fifty Years of U.S. Interest Rates

There have been some large movements in U.S. interest rates over the past half-century. These movements clearly show how both changes in expected future inflation and changes in the expected rate of return on investment spending move interest rates.

Panel (a) of Figure 26-8 illustrates the first effect. It shows the average interest rate on bonds issued by the U.S. government—specifically, bonds for which the government promises to repay the full amount after 10 years—from 1958 to 2008, along with the rate of consumer price inflation over the same period. As you can see, the big story about interest rates is the way they soared in the 1970s, before coming back down in the 1980s. It's not hard to see why that happened: inflation shot up during the 1970s, leading to widespread expectations that high inflation would continue. And as we've seen, expected inflation raises the equilibrium interest rate. As inflation came down in the 1980s, so did expectations of future inflation, and this brought interest rates down as well.

Panel (b) illustrates the second effect, how changes in the expected rate of return on investment spending move interest rates, depicting a "close-up" of interest rates from 1998 to 2008. Notice the rise in interest rates during the late 1990s, followed by a sharp drop. We know from other evidence (such as surveys of investor opinion) that expected inflation didn't change much over those years. What happened, instead, was the boom and bust in high-technology investment spending: interest rates rose sharply as businesses rushed to invest in technology, pushing the demand for loanable funds to the right, then fell as the technology boom collapsed, shifting the demand for loanable funds back to the left.

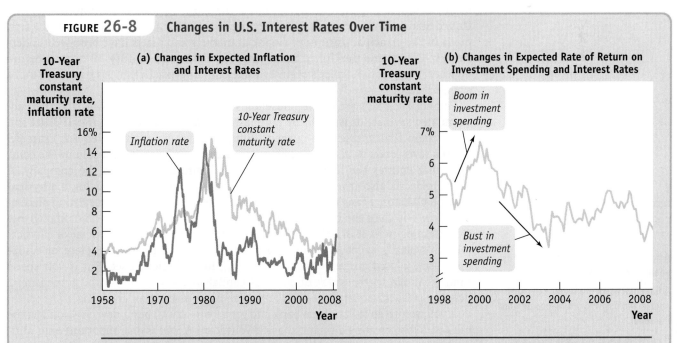

FIGURE 26-8 Changes in U.S. Interest Rates Over Time

As panel (a) shows, high current inflation leads to expectations of high future inflation, which results in a rise in the interest rate. Panel (b) shows the effect of changes in the expected return on investment spending on interest rates. During 1998–2008, expectations of future inflation were relatively constant, but the interest rate first rose and then fell sharply. The rise and eventual decline were driven mainly by the boom and then bust in high-technology investment spending.

Source: Federal Reserve Bank of St. Louis; Bureau of Labor Statistics.

➤ According to the **savings–investment spending identity,** savings is equal to investment spending for the economy as a whole.

➤ The government is a source of savings when it runs a positive **budget balance,** also known as a **budget surplus.** It is a source of dissavings when it runs a **budget deficit.**

➤ Savings is equal to **national savings** plus **capital inflow,** which may be either positive or negative.

➤ The hypothetical **loanable funds market** matches savers to borrowers. In equilibrium, only investment spending projects with a **rate of return** greater than or equal to the equilibrium **interest rate** are funded.

➤ Because the government competes with private borrowers in the loanable funds market, a government deficit can cause **crowding out.**

➤ Higher expected future inflation raises nominal interest rates through the **Fisher effect.**

Throughout this whole process, total savings were equal to total investment spending; and the rise and fall of the interest rate played a key role in matching lenders with borrowers. ▲

< < < < < < < < < < < <

► CHECK YOUR UNDERSTANDING 26-1

1. Use a diagram of the loanable funds market to illustrate the effect of the following events on the equilibrium interest rate and investment spending.
   a. An economy is opened to international movements of capital, and a capital inflow occurs.
   b. Retired people generally save less than working people at any interest rate. The proportion of retired people in the population goes up.

2. Explain what is wrong with the following statement: "Savings and investment spending may not be equal in the economy as a whole because when the interest rate rises, households will want to save more money than businesses will want to invest."

3. Suppose that expected inflation rises from 3% to 6%.
   a. How will the real interest rate be affected by this change?
   b. How will the nominal interest rate be affected by this change?
   c. What will happen to the equilibrium quantity of loanable funds?

Solutions appear at back of book.

The Financial System

A well-functioning financial system that brought together the funds of British, French, and other international investors made the Chunnel possible. But to think that this is an exclusively modern phenomenon is misguided. Financial markets raised the funds that were used to develop colonial markets in India, to build canals across Europe, and to finance the Napoleonic wars in the eighteenth and early nineteenth century. Capital inflows financed the early economic development of the United States, funding investment spending in mining, railroads, and canals. In fact, many of the principal features of financial markets and assets have been well understood in Europe and the United States since the eighteenth century. These features are no less relevant today. So let's begin by understanding exactly what is traded in financial markets.

Financial markets are where households invest their current savings and their accumulated savings, or **wealth,** by purchasing *financial assets.* A **financial asset** is a paper claim that entitles the buyer to future income from the seller. For example, when a saver lends funds to a company, the loan is a financial asset sold by the company that entitles the lender (the buyer) to future income from the company. A household can also invest its current savings or wealth by purchasing a **physical asset,** a claim on a tangible object, such as a preexisting house or preexisting piece of equipment. It gives the owner the right to dispose of the object as he or she wishes (for example, rent it or sell it). Recall that the purchase of a financial or physical asset is typically called investing. So if you purchase a preexisting piece of equipment—say, a used airliner—you are investing in a physical asset. But if you spend funds that *add* to the stock of physical capital in the economy—say, purchasing a newly manufactured airplane—you are engaging in investment spending.

If you were to go to your local bank and get a loan—say, to buy a new car—you and the bank would be creating a financial asset: your loan. A *loan* is one important kind of financial asset in the real world, one that is owned by the lender—in this case, your local bank. In creating that loan, you and the bank would also be creating a **liability,** a requirement to pay income in the future. So although your loan is a financial asset from the bank's point of view, it is a liability from your point of view: a requirement that you repay the loan, including any interest. In addition to loans, there are three other important kinds of financial assets: stocks, bonds, and *bank deposits.* Because a financial asset

---

A household's **wealth** is the value of its accumulated savings.

A **financial asset** is a paper claim that entitles the buyer to future income from the seller.

A **physical asset** is a claim on a tangible object that gives the owner the right to dispose of the object as he or she wishes.

A **liability** is a requirement to pay income in the future.

is a claim to future income that someone has to pay, it is also someone else's liability. We'll explain in detail shortly who bears the liability for each type of financial asset.

These four types of financial assets exist because the economy has developed a set of specialized markets, like the stock market and the bond market, and specialized institutions, like banks, that facilitate the flow of funds from lenders to borrowers. In Chapter 23, in the context of the circular-flow diagram, we defined the financial markets and institutions that make up the financial system. A well-functioning financial system is a critical ingredient in achieving long-run growth because it encourages greater savings and investment spending. It also ensures that savings and investment spending are undertaken efficiently. To understand how this occurs, we first need to know what tasks the financial system needs to accomplish. Then we can see how the job gets done.

> **Transaction costs** are the expenses of negotiating and executing a deal.
>
> **Financial risk** is uncertainty about future outcomes that involve financial losses and gains.

Three Tasks of a Financial System

Our earlier analysis of the loanable funds market ignored three important problems facing borrowers and lenders: *transaction costs, risk,* and the desire for *liquidity*. The three tasks of a financial system are to reduce these problems in a cost-effective way. Doing so enhances the efficiency of financial markets: it makes it more likely that lenders and borrowers will make mutually beneficial trades—trades that make society as a whole richer. We'll turn now to examining how financial assets are designed and how institutions are developed to cope with these problems.

Reducing Transaction Costs **Transaction costs** are the expenses of actually putting together and executing a deal. For example, arranging a loan requires spending time and money negotiating the terms of the deal, verifying the borrower's ability to pay, drawing up and executing legal documents, and so on. Suppose a large business decided that it wanted to raise $1 billion for investment spending. No individual would be willing to lend that much. And negotiating individual loans from thousands of different people, each willing to lend a modest amount, would impose very large total costs because each individual transaction would incur a cost. Total costs would be so large that the entire deal would probably be unprofitable for the business.

Fortunately, that's not necessary: when large businesses want to borrow money, they either go to a bank or sell bonds in the bond market. Obtaining a loan from a bank avoids large transaction costs because it involves only a single borrower and a single lender. We'll explain more about how bonds work in the next section. For now, it is enough to know that the principal reason there is a bond market is that it allows companies to borrow large sums of money without incurring large transaction costs.

Reducing Risk A second problem that real-world borrowers and lenders face is **financial risk,** uncertainty about future outcomes that involve financial losses or gains. Financial risk (which from now on we'll simply call "risk") is a problem because the future is uncertain, typically containing the potential for losses as well as gains. For example, owning and driving a car entails the financial risk of a costly accident. Most people view potential losses and gains in an *asymmetrical* way: the total loss in individual welfare from losing a given amount of money is considered larger than the total gain in welfare from gaining the same amount of money. A person who values potential losses and gains in this asymmetrical way is called *risk-averse*. This attitude toward risk is illustrated in panel (a) of Figure 26-9 on the next page. Here, we show an example of a typical risk-averse person who is faced with the prospect of losing $1,000 or gaining $1,000. The bar on the left, which represents the loss in welfare from losing $1,000, is longer than the bar on the right, which represents the gain in welfare from gaining $1,000. The difference in the lengths of these two bars illustrates risk aversion: a person experiences a $1,000 loss as a significant hardship (equivalent to a $2,000 loss in welfare) and a $1,000 gain as a much less significant benefit (equivalent to a $1,000

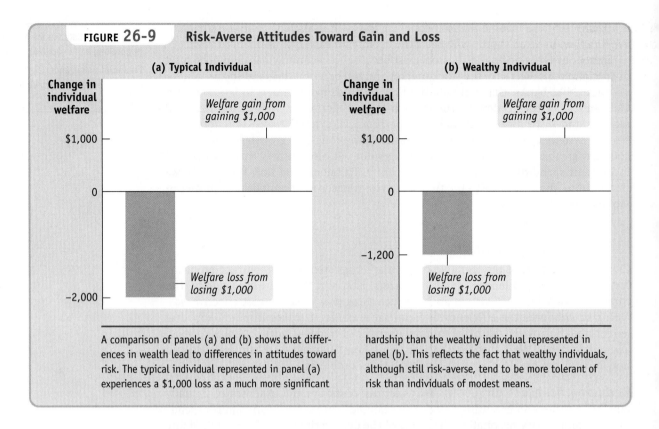

FIGURE 26-9 **Risk-Averse Attitudes Toward Gain and Loss**

(a) Typical Individual

Change in individual welfare

$1,000

0

−2,000

Welfare gain from gaining $1,000

Welfare loss from losing $1,000

(b) Wealthy Individual

Change in individual welfare

$1,000

0

−1,200

Welfare gain from gaining $1,000

Welfare loss from losing $1,000

A comparison of panels (a) and (b) shows that differences in wealth lead to differences in attitudes toward risk. The typical individual represented in panel (a) experiences a $1,000 loss as a much more significant hardship than the wealthy individual represented in panel (b). This reflects the fact that wealthy individuals, although still risk-averse, tend to be more tolerant of risk than individuals of modest means.

gain in welfare). To put it a slightly different way, if you are risk-averse, you are willing to expend more resources to avoid losing $1,000 (say, by buying an auto insurance policy) than you are willing to expend to gain $1,000 (say, by hunting around to find the cheapest mechanic when your car needs a major repair).

Most people are risk-averse, although to differing degrees. For example, people who are wealthy are typically less risk-averse than those who are not so well-off. As panel (b) shows, a wealthy person—although still risk-averse—would consider the loss of $1,000 a lot less of a hardship than would a person of modest means. Such a loss would be experienced as only a $1,200 loss in welfare by a wealthy individual, compared to a $2,000 loss in welfare by a typical individual.

A well-functioning financial system helps people reduce their exposure to risk, which risk-averse people would like to do. Suppose the owner of a business expects to make a greater profit if she buys additional capital equipment, but isn't completely sure that this will indeed happen. She could pay for the equipment by using her savings or selling her house. But if the profit is significantly less than expected, she will have lost her savings, or her house, or both. That is, she would be exposing herself to a lot of risk due to uncertainty about how well or poorly the business performs. (This is why business owners, who typically have a significant portion of their own personal wealth tied up in their businesses, are usually people who are more tolerant of risk than the average person.) So, being risk-averse, this business owner wants to share the risk of purchasing new capital equipment with someone even if that requires sharing some of the profit if all goes well. How can she do this? By selling shares of her company to other people and using the money she receives from selling shares, rather than money from the sale of her other assets, to finance the equipment purchase. By selling shares in her company, she reduces her personal losses if the profit is less than expected: she won't have lost her other assets. But if things go well, the shareholders earn a share of the profit as a return on their investment.

By selling a share of her business, the owner has achieved *diversification*: she has been able to invest in several things in a way that lowers her total risk. She has maintained her investment in her bank account, a financial asset; in ownership of her house, a physical asset; and in ownership of the unsold portion of her business, also a physical asset. These investments are likely to carry some risk of their own; for example, her bank may fail or her house may burn down (though in the modern United States it is likely that she is partly protected against these risks by insurance). But even in the absence of insurance, she is better off having maintained investments in these different assets because their different risks are *unrelated,* or *independent, events.* This means, for example, that her house is no more likely to burn down if her business does poorly, and that her bank is no more likely to fail if her house burns down. To put it another way, if one asset performs poorly, it is very likely that her other assets will be unaffected and, as a result, her total risk of loss has been reduced. But if she had invested all her wealth in her business, she would have faced the prospect of losing everything if the business had performed poorly. By engaging in **diversification**—investing in several assets with unrelated, or independent, risks—our business owner has lowered her total risk of loss.

The desire of individuals to reduce their total risk by engaging in diversification is why we have stocks and a stock market. In the next section, we'll explain in more detail how certain features of the stock market increase the ability of individuals to manage and reduce risk.

Providing Liquidity The third and final task of the financial system is to provide investors with *liquidity,* a concern that—like risk—arises because the future is uncertain. Suppose that, having made a loan, a lender suddenly finds himself in need of cash—say, to meet a medical emergency. Unfortunately, if that loan was made to a business that used it to buy new equipment, the business cannot repay the loan on short notice to satisfy the lender's need to recover his money. Knowing this in advance—that there is a danger of needing to get his money back before the term of the loan is up—our lender might be reluctant to lock up his money by lending it to a business.

An asset is **liquid** if it can be quickly converted into cash without much loss of value, **illiquid** if it cannot. As we'll see, stocks and bonds are a partial answer to the problem of liquidity. Banks provide a further way for individuals to hold liquid assets and still finance illiquid investments.

To help lenders and borrowers make mutually beneficial deals, then, the economy needs ways to reduce transaction costs, to reduce and manage risk through diversification, and to provide liquidity. How does it achieve these tasks?

Types of Financial Assets

In the modern economy there are four main types of financial assets: *loans,* bonds, stocks, and *bank deposits.* In addition, financial innovation has allowed the creation of a wide range of *loan-backed securities.* Each serves a somewhat different purpose. We'll examine loans, bonds, stocks, and loan-backed securities now, reserving our discussion of bank deposits until the following section.

Loans A **loan** is a lending agreement between an individual lender and an individual borrower. Most people encounter loans in the form of bank loans to finance the purchase of a car or a house. And small businesses usually use bank loans to buy new equipment.

The good aspect of loans is that a given loan is usually tailored to the needs of the borrower. Before a small business can get a loan, it usually has to discuss its business plans, its profits, and so on with the lender. This results in a loan that meets the borrower's needs and ability to pay.

The bad aspect of loans is that making a loan to an individual person or a business typically involves a lot of transaction costs, such as the cost of negotiating the terms of the loan, investigating the borrower's credit history and ability to repay, and so on. To minimize these costs, large borrowers such as major corporations and governments often take a more streamlined approach: they sell (or issue) bonds.

> An individual can engage in **diversification** by investing in several different things so that the possible losses are independent events.
>
> An asset is **liquid** if it can be quickly converted into cash without much loss of value.
>
> An asset is **illiquid** if it cannot be quickly converted into cash without much loss of value.
>
> A **loan** is a lending agreement between an individual lender and an individual borrower.

A **default** occurs when a borrower fails to make payments as specified by the loan or bond contract.

A **loan-backed security** is an asset created by pooling individual loans and selling shares in that pool.

Bonds As we learned in Chapter 23, a bond is an IOU issued by the borrower. Normally, the seller of the bond promises to pay a fixed sum of interest each year and to repay the principal—the value stated on the face of the bond—to the owner of the bond on a particular date. So a bond is a financial asset from its owner's point of view and a liability from its issuer's point of view. A bond issuer sells a number of bonds with a given interest rate and maturity date to whoever is willing to buy them, a process that avoids costly negotiation of the terms of a loan with many individual lenders.

Bond purchasers can acquire information free of charge on the quality of the bond issuer, such as the bond issuer's credit history, from *bond-rating agencies* rather than having to incur the expense of investigating it themselves. A particular concern for investors is the possibility of **default,** the risk that the bond issuer fails to make payments as specified by the bond contract. Once a bond's risk of default has been rated, it can be sold on the bond market as a more or less standardized product—a product with clearly defined terms and quality. In general, bonds with a higher default risk must pay a higher interest rate to attract investors.

Another important advantage of bonds is that they are easy to resell. This provides liquidity to bond purchasers. Indeed, a bond will often pass through many hands before it finally comes due. Loans, in contrast, are much more difficult to resell because, unlike bonds, they are not standardized: they differ in size, quality, terms, and so on. This makes them a lot less liquid than bonds.

Loan-Backed Securities

Loan-backed securities, assets created by pooling individual loans and selling shares in that pool (a process called *securitization*), have become extremely popular over the past two decades. While mortgage-backed securities, in which thousands of individual home mortgages are pooled and shares sold to investors, are the best-known example, securitization has also been widely applied to student loans, credit card loans and auto loans. These loan-backed securities trade on financial markets like bonds, and are preferred by investors because they provide more diversification and liquidity than individual loans. However, with so many loans packaged together, it can be difficult to assess the true quality of the asset. That difficulty came to haunt investors during the financial crisis of 2007–2008, when the bursting of the housing bubble led to widespread defaults on mortgages and large losses for holders of "supposedly safe" mortgage-backed securities, pain that spread throughout the entire financial system.

Stocks

As we learned in Chapter 23, a stock is a share in the ownership of a company. A share of stock is a financial asset from its owner's point of view and a liability from the company's point of view. Not all companies sell shares of their stock; "privately held" companies are owned by an individual or a few partners, who get to keep all of the company's profit. Most large companies, however, do sell stock. For example, Microsoft has nearly 11 billion shares outstanding; if you buy one of those shares, you are entitled to one-eleven billionth of the company's profit, as well as 1 of 11 billion votes on company decisions.

Why does Microsoft, historically a very profitable company, allow you to buy a share in its ownership? Why don't Bill Gates and Paul Allen, the two founders of Microsoft, keep complete ownership for themselves and just sell bonds for their investment spending needs? The reason, as we have just learned, is risk: few individuals are risk-tolerant enough to face the risk involved in being the sole owner of a large company.

Reducing the risk that business owners face, however, is not the only way in which the existence of stocks improves society's welfare: it also improves the welfare of investors who buy stocks. Shareowners are able to enjoy the higher returns over time that stocks generally offer in comparison to bonds. Over the past century, stocks have typically yielded about 7% after adjusting for inflation; bonds have yielded only about 2%. But as investment companies warn you, "past performance is no guarantee of future performance." And there is a downside: owning the stock of a given company is riskier than owning a bond issued by the same company. Why? Loosely speaking, a bond is a promise while a stock is a hope: by law, a company must pay what it owes its lenders before it distributes any profit to its shareholders. And if the company should fail (that is, be unable to pay its interest obligations and declare bankruptcy), its physical and financial assets go to its bondholders—its lenders—while its shareholders generally receive nothing. So although a stock generally provides a higher return to an investor than a bond, it also carries higher risk.

But the financial system has devised ways to help investors as well as business owners simultaneously manage risk and enjoy somewhat higher returns. It does that through the services of institutions known as *financial intermediaries*.

Financial Intermediaries

A **financial intermediary** is an institution that transforms funds gathered from many individuals into financial assets. The most important types of financial intermediaries are *mutual funds, pension funds, life insurance companies,* and *banks*. About three-quarters of the financial assets Americans own are held through these intermediaries rather than directly.

Mutual Funds As we've explained, owning shares of a company entails risk in return for a higher potential reward. But it should come as no surprise that stock investors can lower their total risk by engaging in diversification. By owning a *diversified portfolio* of stocks—a group of stocks in which risks are unrelated to, or offset, one another—rather than concentrating investment in the shares of a single company or a group of related companies, investors can reduce their risk. In addition, financial advisers, aware that most people are risk-averse, almost always advise their clients to diversify not only their stock portfolio but also their entire wealth by holding other assets in addition to stock—assets such as bonds, real estate, and cash. (And, for good measure, to have plenty of insurance in case of accidental losses!)

However, for individuals who don't have a large amount of money to invest—say $1 million or more—building a diversified stock portfolio can incur high transaction costs (particularly fees paid to stockbrokers) because they are buying a few shares of a lot of companies. Fortunately for such investors, mutual funds help solve the problem of achieving diversification without high transaction costs. A **mutual fund** is a financial intermediary that creates a stock portfolio by buying and holding shares in companies and then selling *shares of the stock portfolio* to individual investors. By buying these shares, investors with a relatively small amount of money to invest can indirectly hold a diversified portfolio, achieving a better return for any given level of risk than they could otherwise achieve. Table 26-1 shows an example of a diversified mutual fund, the Fidelity Spartan S&P 500 Index Fund. It shows the percentage of investors' money invested in the stocks of the largest companies in the mutual fund's portfolio.

Many mutual funds also perform *market research* on the companies they invest in. This is important because there are thousands of stock-issuing U.S. companies (not to mention foreign companies), each differing in terms of its likely profitability, dividend payments, and so on. It would be extremely time-consuming and costly for an individual investor to do adequate research on even a small number of companies. Mutual funds save transaction costs by doing this research for their customers.

The mutual fund industry represents a huge portion of the modern U.S. economy, not just of the U.S. financial system. In total, U.S mutual funds had assets of $10.6 trillion in late 2008. The largest mutual fund company at the end of 2008 was Fidelity Investments, which managed $1.4 trillion in funds.

We should mention, by the way, that mutual funds charge fees for their services. These fees are quite small for mutual funds that simply hold a diversified portfolio of stocks, without trying to pick winners. But the fees charged by mutual funds that claim to have special expertise in investing your money can be quite high.

A **financial intermediary** is an institution that transforms the funds it gathers from many individuals into financial assets.

A **mutual fund** is a financial intermediary that creates a stock portfolio and then resells shares of this portfolio to individual investors.

TABLE 26-1

Fidelity Spartan S&P 500 Index Fund, Top Holdings (as of September 2008)

Company	Percent of mutual fund assets invested in a company
Exxon Mobil	3.96%
General Electric	2.49
Procter & Gamble	2.08
Microsoft	2.06
Johnson & Johnson	1.90
JPMorgan Chase	1.69
Chevron	1.66
AT&T	1.62
Bank of America	1.57
IBM	1.56

Source: Fidelity Investments.

A **pension fund** is a type of mutual fund that holds assets in order to provide retirement income to its members.

A **life insurance company** sells policies that guarantee a payment to a policyholder's beneficiaries when the policyholder dies.

A **bank deposit** is a claim on a bank that obliges the bank to give the depositor his or her cash when demanded.

A **bank** is a financial intermediary that provides liquid assets in the form of bank deposits to lenders and uses those funds to finance the illiquid investment spending needs of borrowers.

Pension Funds and Life Insurance Companies In addition to mutual funds, many Americans have holdings in **pension funds,** nonprofit institutions that collect the savings of their members and invest those funds in a wide variety of assets, providing their members with income when they retire. Although pension funds are subject to some special rules and receive special treatment for tax purposes, they function much like mutual funds. They invest in a diverse array of financial assets, allowing their members to achieve more cost-effective diversification and market research than they would be able to achieve individually. At the end of 2008, pension funds in the United States held more than $9 trillion in assets.

Americans also have substantial holdings in the policies of **life insurance companies,** which guarantee a payment to the policyholder's beneficiaries (typically, the family) when the policyholder dies. By enabling policyholders to cushion their beneficiaries from financial hardship arising from their death, life insurance companies also improve welfare by reducing risk.

Banks Recall the problem of liquidity: other things equal, people want assets that can be readily converted into cash. Bonds and stocks are much more liquid than physical assets or loans, yet the transaction cost of selling bonds or stocks to meet a sudden expense can be large. Furthermore, for many small and moderate-size companies, the cost of issuing bonds and stocks is too large given the modest amount of money they seek to raise. A *bank* is an institution that helps resolve the conflict between lenders' needs for liquidity and the financing needs of borrowers who don't want to use the stock or bond markets.

A bank works by first accepting funds from *depositors:* when you put your money in a bank, you are essentially becoming a lender by lending the bank your money. In return, you receive credit for a **bank deposit**—a claim on the bank, which is obliged to give you your cash if and when you demand it. So a bank deposit is a financial asset owned by the depositor and a liability of the bank that holds it.

A bank, however, keeps only a fraction of its customers' deposits in the form of ready cash. Most of its deposits are lent out to businesses, buyers of new homes, and other borrowers. These loans come with a long-term commitment by the bank to the borrower: as long as the borrower makes his or her payments on time, the loan cannot be recalled by the bank and converted into cash. So a bank enables those who wish to borrow for long lengths of time to use the funds of those who wish to lend but simultaneously want to maintain the ability to get their cash back on demand. More formally, a **bank** is a financial intermediary that provides liquid financial assets in the form of deposits to lenders and uses their funds to finance the illiquid investment spending needs of borrowers.

In essence, a bank is engaging in a kind of mismatch: lending for long periods of time but also subject to the condition that its depositors could demand their funds back at any time. How can it manage that?

The bank counts on the fact that, on average, only a small fraction of its depositors will want their cash at the same time. On any given day, some people will make withdrawals and others will make new deposits; these will roughly cancel each other out. So the bank needs to keep only a limited amount of cash on hand to satisfy its depositors. In addition, if a bank becomes financially incapable of paying its depositors, individual bank deposits are guaranteed to depositors up to $250,000 by the Federal Deposit Insurance Corporation, or FDIC, a federal agency. This reduces the risk to a depositor of holding a bank deposit, in turn reducing the incentive to withdraw funds if concerns about the financial state of the bank should arise. So, under normal conditions, banks need hold only a fraction of their depositors' cash.

By reconciling the needs of savers for liquid assets with the needs of borrowers for long-term financing, banks play a key economic role. As the following Economics in Action explains, the creation of a well-functioning banking system was a key turning point in South Korea's economic success.

➤ECONOMICS IN ACTION

Banks and the South Korean Miracle

South Korea is one of the great success stories of economic growth. In the early 1960s, it was a very poor nation. Then it experienced spectacularly high rates of economic growth. South Korean banks had a lot to do with it.

In the early 1960s, South Korea's banking system was a mess. Interest rates on deposits were very low at a time when the country was experiencing high inflation. So savers didn't want to save by putting money in a bank, fearing that much of their purchasing power would be eroded by rising prices. Instead, they engaged in current consumption by spending their money on goods and services or used their wealth to buy physical assets such as real estate and gold. Because savers refused to make bank deposits, businesses found it very hard to borrow money to finance investment spending.

In 1965 the South Korean government reformed the country's banks and increased interest rates to a level that was attractive to savers. Over the next five years the value of bank deposits increased 600%, and the national savings rate—the percentage of GDP going into national savings—more than doubled. The rejuvenated banking system made it possible for South Korean businesses to launch a great investment boom, a key element in the country's growth surge.

Many other factors besides banking were involved in South Korea's success, but the country's experience does show how important a good financial system is to economic growth. ▲

> > > > > > > > > > > >

➤ CHECK YOUR UNDERSTANDING 26-2

1. Rank the following assets in terms of (i) level of transaction costs, (ii) level of risk, (iii) level of liquidity.
   a. A bank deposit with a guaranteed interest rate
   b. A share of a highly diversified mutual fund, which can be quickly sold
   c. A share of the family business, which can be sold only if you find a buyer and all other family members agree to the sale
2. What relationship would you expect to find between the level of development of a country's financial system and its level of economic development? Explain in terms of the country's level of savings and level of investment spending.

Solutions appear at back of book.

>> QUICK REVIEW

➤ Households can invest their current savings or their **wealth** by purchasing either **financial assets** or **physical assets.** A financial asset is a **liability** from the point of view of its seller.
➤ A well-functioning financial system reduces **transaction costs,** reduces **financial risk** by enabling **diversification,** and provides **liquid** assets, allowing investors to easily convert their holdings to cash, which investors prefer to **illiquid** assets.
➤ The four main types of financial assets are **loans,** bonds, stocks, and **bank deposits.** A recent innovation is **loan-backed securities,** which are more liquid and more diversified than individual loans. Bonds with a higher **default** risk typically must pay a higher interest rate.
➤ The most important types of **financial intermediaries** are **mutual funds, pension funds, life insurance companies,** and **banks.**
➤ A bank accepts bank deposits, which obliges it to return depositors' cash on demand, and lends those funds to borrowers for long lengths of time.

Financial Fluctuations

We've learned that the financial system is an essential part of the economy; without stock markets, bond markets, and banks, long-run economic growth would be hard to achieve. Yet the news isn't entirely good: the financial system sometimes doesn't function well and instead is a source of instability in the short run. In fact, the financial consequences of a sharp fall in housing prices became a major problem for economic policy makers starting in the summer of 2007. By the fall of 2008, it was clear that the U.S. economy was facing a severe slump as it adjusted to the consequences of greatly reduced home values.

We could easily write a whole book on asset market fluctuations. In fact, many people have. Here, we briefly discuss the causes of asset price fluctuations.

The Demand for Stocks and Other Assets

Once a company issues shares of stock to investors, those shares can then be resold to other investors in the stock market. And these days, thanks to cable TV and the Internet, you can easily spend all day watching stock market fluctuations—the movement up and down of the prices of individual stocks as well as summary measures of stock prices

How Now, Dow Jones?

Financial news reports often lead with the day's stock market action, as measured by changes in the Dow Jones Industrial Average, the S&P 500, and the NASDAQ. What are these numbers, and what do they tell us?

All three are stock market indices. Like the consumer price index, they are numbers constructed as a summary of average prices—in this case, prices of stocks. The Dow, created by the financial analysis company Dow Jones, is an index of the prices of stock in 30 leading companies, such as Microsoft, Wal-Mart, and General Electric. The S&P 500 is an index of 500 companies, created by Standard and Poor's, another financial company. The NASDAQ is compiled by the National Association of Securities Dealers, which trades the stocks of smaller new companies, like the satellite radio company Sirius XM Radio or the computer manufacturer Dell.

Because these indices contain different groups of stocks, they track somewhat different things. The Dow, because it contains only 30 of the largest companies, tends to reflect the "old economy," traditional business powerhouses like Exxon Mobil. The NASDAQ is

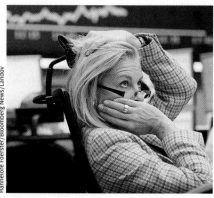

In fall 2008, dramatic fluctuations (often downward) in the Dow, NASDAQ, S&P 500, and stock market indices around the globe confirmed that the world was facing a major economic crisis. The expressions on the faces of these stockbrokers were another indicator.

heavily influenced by technology stocks. The S&P 500, a broad measure, is in between.

Why are these indices important? Because the movement in an index gives investors a quick, snapshot view of how stocks from certain sectors of the economy are doing. As we'll explain shortly, the price of a stock at a given point in time embodies investors' expectations about the future prospects of the underlying company. By implication, an index composed of stocks

drawn from companies in a particular sector embodies investors' expectations of the future prospects of that sector of the economy. So a day on which the NASDAQ moves up but the Dow moves down implies that, on that day, prospects appear brighter for the high-tech sector than for the old-economy sector. The movement in the indices reflects the fact that investors are acting on their beliefs by selling stocks in the Dow and buying stocks in the NASDAQ.

like the Dow Jones Industrial Average. These fluctuations reflect changes in supply and demand by investors. But what causes the supply and demand for stocks to shift?

Remember that stocks are financial assets: they are shares in the ownership of a company. Unlike a good or service, whose value to its owner comes from its consumption, the value of an asset comes from its ability to generate higher future consumption of goods or services. A financial asset allows higher future consumption in two ways. First, many financial assets provide regular income to their owners in the form of interest payments or dividends. But, many companies don't pay dividends; instead, they retain their earnings to finance future investment spending. Investors purchase non-dividend-paying stocks in the belief that they will earn income from selling the stock in the future at a profit, the second way of generating higher future income. Even in the cases of a bond or a dividend-paying stock, investors will not want to purchase an asset that they believe will sell for less in the future than today because such an asset will reduce their wealth when they sell it.

So the value of a financial asset today depends on investors' beliefs about the *future value* or *price* of the asset. If investors believe that it will be worth more in the future, they will demand more of the asset today at any given price; consequently, today's equilibrium price of the asset will rise. Conversely, if investors believe the asset will be worth less in the future, they will demand less today at any given price; consequently, today's equilibrium price of the asset will fall. Today's stock prices will change according to changes in investors' expectations about future stock prices.

Suppose an event occurs that leads to a rise in the expected future price of a company's shares—say, for example, Apple announces that it expects higher profitability due to torrential sales of its iPhones. Demand for Apple shares will increase. At the same time, existing shareholders will be less willing to supply their shares to the market at any given price, leading to a decrease in the supply of Apple shares. And as we know, an increase in demand or a decrease in supply (or both) leads to a rise in price. Alternatively, suppose that an event occurs that leads to a fall in the expected future price of a company's shares—say, Home Depot announces that it expects lower profitability because the slump in home sales has depressed the demand for home improvements. Demand for Home Depot shares will decrease. At the same time, supply will increase because existing shareholders will be more willing to supply their Home Depot shares to the market. Both changes lead to a fall in the stock price. So stock prices are determined by the supply and demand for shares—which, in turn, depend on investors' expectations about the future stock price.

Stock prices are also affected by changes in the attractiveness of substitute assets, like bonds. As we learned early on, the demand for a particular good decreases when purchasing a substitute good becomes more attractive—say, due to a fall in its price. The same lesson holds true for stocks: when purchasing bonds becomes more attractive due to a rise in interest rates, stock prices will fall. And when purchasing bonds becomes less attractive due to a fall in interest rates, stock prices will rise.

Everything we've just said about stocks applies to other assets as well, including physical assets. Consider the demand for commercial real estate—office buildings, shopping malls, and other structures that provide space for business activities. An investor who buys an office building does so for two reasons. First, because space in the building can be rented out, the owner of the building receives income in the form of rents. Second, investors may expect the building to rise in value, meaning that it can be sold at a higher price at some future date. As in the case of stocks, the demand for commercial real estate also depends on the attractiveness of substitute assets, especially bonds. When interest rates rise, the demand for commercial real estate falls; when interest rates fall, the demand for commercial real estate rises.

Most Americans don't own commercial real estate. Only half of the population owns any stock, even indirectly through mutual funds, and for most of those people stock ownership is well under $50,000. However, in 2008 about 70% of American households owned another kind of asset: their own homes. What determines housing prices?

You might wonder whether home prices can be analyzed the same way we analyze stock prices or the price of commercial real estate. After all, stocks pay dividends, commercial real estate yields rents, but when a family lives in its own home, no money changes hands.

In economic terms, however, that doesn't matter very much. To a large extent, the benefit of owning your own home is the fact that you don't have to pay rent to someone else—or, to put it differently, it's as if you were paying rent to yourself. In fact, the U.S. government includes "implicit rent"—an estimate of the amount that homeowners, in effect, pay to themselves—in its estimates of GDP. The amount people are willing to pay for a house depends in part on the implicit rent they expect to receive from that house. The demand for housing, like the demand for other assets, also depends on what people expect to happen to future prices: they're willing to pay more for a house if they believe they can sell it at a higher price sometime in the future. Last but not least, the demand for houses depends on interest rates: a rise in the interest rate increases the cost of a mortgage and leads to a reduction in housing demand; a fall in the interest rate reduces the cost of a mortgage and causes an increase in housing demand.

All asset prices, then, are determined by a similar set of factors. But we haven't yet fully answered the question of what determines asset prices because we haven't explained what determines investors' *expectations* about future asset prices.

Asset Price Expectations

There are two principal competing views about how asset price expectations are determined. One view, which comes from traditional economic analysis, emphasizes the rational reasons why expectations *should* change. The other, widely held by market participants and also supported by some economists, emphasizes the irrationality of market participants.

According to the **efficient markets hypothesis,** asset prices embody all publicly available information.

A **random walk** is the movement over time of an unpredictable variable.

The Efficient Markets Hypothesis Suppose you were trying to assess what Home Depot's stock is really worth. To do this, you would look at the *fundamentals,* the underlying determinants of the company's future profits. These would include factors like the changing shopping habits of the American public and the prospects for home remodeling. You would also want to compare the earnings you could expect to receive from Home Depot with the likely returns on other financial assets, such as bonds.

According to one view of asset prices, the value you would come up with after a careful study of this kind would, in fact, turn out to be the price at which Home Depot stock is already selling in the market. Why? Because all publicly available information about Home Depot's fundamentals is already embodied in its stock price. Any difference between the market price and the value suggested by a careful analysis of the underlying fundamentals indicates a profit opportunity to smart investors, who then sell Home Depot stock if it looks overpriced and buy it if it looks underpriced. The **efficient markets hypothesis** is the general form of this view; it means that asset prices always embody all publicly available information. An implication of the efficient markets hypothesis is that at any point in time stock prices are fairly valued: they reflect all currently available information about fundamentals. So they are neither overpriced nor underpriced.

One implication of the efficient markets hypothesis is that the prices of stocks and other assets should change only in response to new information about the underlying fundamentals. Since new information is by definition unpredictable—if it were predictable, it wouldn't be new information—movements in asset prices are also unpredictable. As a result, the movement of, say, stock prices will follow a **random walk**—the general term for the movement over time of an unpredictable variable.

The efficient markets hypothesis plays an important role in understanding how financial markets work. Most investment professionals and many economists, however, regard it as an oversimplification. Investors, they claim, aren't that rational.

Irrational Markets? Many people who actually trade in the markets, such as individual investors and professional money managers, are skeptical of the efficient markets hypothesis. They believe that markets often behave irrationally and that a smart investor can engage in successful "market timing"—buying stocks when they are underpriced and selling them when they are overpriced.

Although economists are generally skeptical about claims that there are surefire ways to outsmart the market, many have also challenged the efficient markets hypothesis. It's important to understand, however, that finding particular examples where the market got it wrong does not disprove the efficient markets hypothesis. If the price of Home Depot stock plunges from $40 to $10 because of a sudden change in buying patterns, this doesn't mean that the market was inefficient in originally pricing the stock at $40. The fact that buying patterns were about to change wasn't publicly available information, so it wasn't embodied in the earlier stock price.

Serious challenges to the efficient markets hypothesis focus instead either on evidence of systematic misbehavior of market prices or on evidence that individual investors don't behave in the way the theory suggests. For example, some economists believe they have found strong evidence that stock prices fluctuate more than can be explained by news about fundamentals. Others believe they have strong evidence that individual investors behave in systematically irrational ways. For example, people seem to expect that a stock that has risen in the past will keep on rising, even though the efficient markets hypothesis tells us there is no reason to expect this. The same appears to be true of other assets, especially housing: the great housing bubble of the mid-2000s, described in the Economics in Action that follows this section, arose in large part because home-buyers assumed that the rising prices of the early years of the decade would continue in the future.

Asset Prices and Macroeconomics

How should macroeconomists and policy makers deal with the fact that asset prices fluctuate a lot and that these fluctuations can have important economic effects? This question has become one of the major problems facing macroeconomic policy. On one side, policy makers are reluctant to assume that the market is wrong—that asset prices are either too high or too low. In part, this reflects the efficient markets hypothesis, which says that any information that is publicly available is already accounted for in asset prices. More generally, it's hard to make the general case that government officials are better judges of appropriate prices than private investors who are putting their own money on the line.

On the other side, the past 15 years were marked by not one but two huge asset bubbles, each of which created major macroeconomic problems when it burst. In the late 1990s the prices of technology stocks, including but not limited to "dot-com" Internet firms, soared to hard-to-justify heights. When the bubble burst these stocks lost, on average, two-thirds of their value in a short time, helping to cause the 2001 recession and an extended period of high unemployment. A few years later there was a major bubble in housing prices, described in the upcoming Economics in Action. The collapse of this bubble triggered a severe financial crisis that was still ongoing as this book went to press.

These events have led to a fierce debate among economists over whether policy makers should try to pop asset bubbles before they get too big. We'll describe that debate in Chapter 33.

►ECONOMICS IN ACTION

The Great American Housing Bubble

Between 2000 and 2006, there was a huge increase in the price of houses in America. By the summer of 2006, home prices were well over twice as high as they had been in January 2000 in a number of major U.S. metropolitan areas, including Los Angeles, San Diego, San Francisco, Washington, Miami, Las Vegas, and New York. By 2004, as the increase in home prices accelerated, a number of economists (including the authors of this textbook) argued that this price increase was excessive—that it was a "bubble," a rise in asset prices driven by unrealistic expectations about future prices.

It was certainly true that home prices rose much more than the cost of renting a comparable place to live. Panel (a) of Figure 26-10 compares a widely used index of

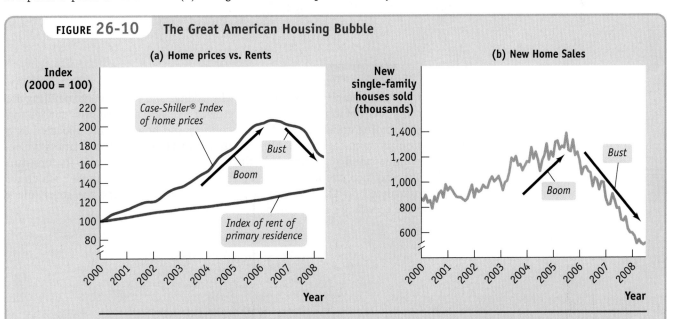

FIGURE 26-10   The Great American Housing Bubble

Panel (a) shows the average prices of U.S. houses compared with an estimate of average rents, both expressed as index numbers with January 2000 = 100. There was a large run-up in home prices after 2000, which some economists argued was not justified by fundamentals. Others disagreed, but by 2007 it was clear that there had indeed been a bubble driven by unrealistic expectations about

future prices. When expectations of rising prices turned into expectations of falling prices, the demand for homes slumped. Panel (b) shows new sales of single-family homes, which reached record levels during the mid-2000s, then fell steeply.

Source: Panel (a): Standard and Poor's; Bureau of Labor Statistics; Panel (b): Federal Reserve Bank of St. Louis.

U.S. housing prices with the U.S. government's index of the cost of renting, both shown as index numbers with January 2000 = 100. Home prices shot up, even though rental rates grew only gradually.

Yet there were also a number of economists who argued that the rise in housing prices was completely justified. They pointed, in particular, to the fact that interest rates were unusually low in the years of rapid price increases, and they argued that low interest rates combined with other factors, such as growing population, explained the surge in prices. Alan Greenspan, the chairman of the Federal Reserve, conceded in 2005 that there might be some "froth" in the markets but denied that there was any national bubble.

Unfortunately, it turned out that the skeptics were right. Greenspan himself would later concede that there had, in fact, been a huge national bubble. In 2006, as home prices began to level off, it became apparent that many buyers had held unrealistic expectations about future prices. Home prices began falling, and the demand for housing fell drastically, as illustrated by panel (b) of Figure 26-10.

The implosion in housing, in turn, created numerous economic difficulties, including severe stress on the banking system, which we will examine in Chapter 30. ▲

< < < < < < < < < < < <

► CHECK YOUR UNDERSTANDING 26-3

1. What is the likely effect of each of the following events on the stock price of a company? Explain your answers.
   a. The company announces that although profits are low this year, it has discovered a new line of business that will generate high profits next year.
   b. The company announces that although it had high profits this year, those profits will be less than had been previously announced.
   c. Other companies in the same industry announce that sales are unexpectedly slow this year.
   d. The company announces that it is on track to meet its previously forecast profit target.

2. Assess the following statement: "Although many investors may be irrational, it is unlikely that over time they will behave irrationally in exactly the same way—such as always buying stocks the day after the Dow has risen by 1%."

Solutions appear at back of book.

[>> A LOOK AHEAD •••

At this point we've completed our study of why savings and investment spending are a critical component of long-run economic growth. We've examined how savings and investment spending are generated in the economy and how they are allocated by a well-functioning financial system. Now it's time for us to turn to the business cycle—that is, to understand the short-run fluctuations around the trend in long-run growth. Our next step, then, is to develop the income–expenditure model, which we will use to analyze how the behavior of producers, consumers, and the government influences the economy's short-run performance.]

SUMMARY

1. Investment in physical capital is necessary for long-run economic growth. So in order for an economy to grow, it must channel savings into investment spending.

2. According to the **savings–investment spending identity,** savings and investment spending are always equal for the economy as a whole. The government is a source of savings when it runs a positive **budget balance,** also known as a **budget surplus;** it is a source of dissavings when it runs a negative budget balance, also known as a **budget deficit.** In a closed economy, savings is equal to **national savings,** the sum of private savings plus the budget balance. In an open economy, savings is equal to national savings plus **capital inflow** of foreign savings. When a capital outflow, or negative capital inflow, occurs, some portion of national savings is funding investment spending in other countries.

3. The hypothetical **loanable funds market** shows how loans from savers are allocated among borrowers with investment spending projects. In equilibrium, only those projects with a **rate of return** greater than or equal to the equilibrium **interest rate** will be funded. By showing how gains from trade between lenders and borrowers are maximized, the loanable funds market shows why a well-functioning financial system leads to greater long-run economic growth. Government budget deficits can raise the interest rate and can lead to **crowding out** of investment spending. Changes in perceived business opportunities and in government borrowing shift the demand curve for loanable funds; changes in private savings and capital inflows shift the supply curve.

4. Because neither borrowers nor lenders can know the future inflation rate, loans specify a nominal interest rate rather than a real interest rate. For a given expected future inflation rate, shifts of the demand and supply curves of loanable funds result in changes in the underlying real interest rate, leading to changes in the nominal interest rate. According to the **Fisher effect,** an increase in expected future inflation raises the nominal interest rate one-to-one so that the expected real interest rate remains unchanged.

5. Households invest their current savings or **wealth**—their accumulated savings—by purchasing assets. Assets come in the form of either a **financial asset,** a paper claim that entitles the buyer to future income from the seller, or a **physical asset,** a claim on a tangible object that gives the owner the right to dispose of it as desired. A financial asset is also a **liability** from the point of view of its seller. There are four main types of financial assets: **loans,** bonds, stocks, and **bank deposits.** Each of them serves a different purpose in addressing the three fundamental tasks of a financial system: reducing **transaction costs**—the cost of making a deal; reducing **financial risk**—uncertainty about future outcomes that involves financial gains and losses; and providing **liquid** assets—assets that can be quickly converted into cash without much loss of value (in contrast to **illiquid** assets, which are not easily converted).

6. Although many small and moderate-size borrowers use bank loans to fund investment spending, larger companies typically issue bonds. Bonds with a higher risk of **default** must typically pay a higher interest rate. Business owners reduce their risk by selling stock. Although stocks usually generate a higher return than bonds, investors typically wish to reduce their risk by engaging in **diversification,** owning a wide range of assets whose returns are based on unrelated, or independent, events. Most people are risk-averse, viewing the loss of a given amount of money as a significant hardship but viewing the gain of an equal amount of money as a much less significant benefit. **Loan-backed securities,** a recent innovation, are assets created by pooling individual loans and selling shares of that pool to investors. Because they are more diversified and more liquid than individual loans, trading on financial markets like bonds, they are preferred by investors. It can be difficult, however, to assess their quality.

7. **Financial intermediaries**—institutions such as **mutual funds, pension funds, life insurance companies,** and **banks**—are critical components of the financial system. Mutual funds and pension funds allow small investors to diversify, and life insurance companies reduce risk.

8. A bank allows individuals to hold liquid bank deposits that are then used to finance illiquid loans. Banks can perform this mismatch because on average only a small fraction of depositors withdraw their savings at any one time. Banks are a key ingredient of long-run economic growth.

9. Asset market fluctuations can be a source of short-run macroeconomic instability. Asset prices are determined by supply and demand as well as by the desirability of competing assets, like bonds: when the interest rate rises, prices of stocks and physical assets such as real estate generally fall, and vice versa. Expectations drive the supply of and demand for assets: expectations of higher future prices push today's asset prices higher, and expectations of lower future prices drive them lower. One view of how expectations are formed is the **efficient markets hypothesis,** which holds that the prices of assets embody all publicly available information. It implies that fluctuations are inherently unpredictable—they follow a **random walk.**

10. Many market participants and economists believe that, based on actual evidence, financial markets are not as rational as the efficient markets hypothesis claims. Such evidence includes the fact that stock price fluctuations are too great to be driven by fundamentals alone. Policy makers assume neither that markets always behave rationally nor that they can outsmart them.

KEY TERMS

Savings–investment spending identity, p. 674
Budget surplus, p. 675
Budget deficit, p. 675
Budget balance, p. 675
National savings, p. 675
Capital inflow, p. 675
Loanable funds market, p. 678
Interest rate, p. 678
Rate of return, p. 678
Crowding out, p. 681

Fisher effect, p. 684
Wealth, p. 686
Financial asset, p. 686
Physical asset, p. 686
Liability, p. 686
Transaction costs, p. 687
Financial risk, p. 687
Diversification, p. 689
Liquid, p. 689
Illiquid, p. 689
Loan, p. 689

Default, p. 690
Loan-backed securities, p. 690
Financial intermediary, p. 691
Mutual fund, p. 691
Pension fund, p. 692
Life insurance company, p. 692
Bank deposit, p. 692
Bank, p. 692
Efficient markets hypothesis, p. 696
Random walk, p. 696

PROBLEMS

1. Given the following information about the closed economy of Brittania, what is the level of investment spending and private savings, and what is the budget balance? What is the relationship among the three? Is national savings equal to investment spending? There are no government transfers.

   GDP = $1,000 million   T = $50 million
   C = $850 million   G = $100 million

2. Given the following information about the open economy of Regalia, what is the level of investment spending and private savings, and what are the budget balance and capital inflow? What is the relationship among the four? There are no government transfers. (*Hint:* capital inflow = the value of imports (*IM*) minus the value of exports (*X*).)

   GDP = $1,000 million   G = $100 million
   C = $850 million   X = $100 million
   T = $50 million   IM = $125 million

3. The accompanying table shows the percentage of GDP accounted for by private savings, investment spending, and capital inflow in the economies of Capsland and Marsalia. Capsland is currently experiencing a net capital inflow and Marsalia, a net capital outflow. What is the budget balance (as a percentage of GDP) in both countries? Are Capsland and Marsalia running a budget deficit or surplus?

	Capsland	Marsalia
Investment spending as a percentage of GDP	20%	20%
Private savings as a percentage of GDP	10	25
Capital inflow as a percentage of GDP	5	−2

4. Assume the economy is open to capital inflows and that capital inflows equals imports (*IM*) minus exports (*X*). Answer each of the following questions.

   a. X = $125 million
   IM = $80 million
   Budget balance = −$200 million
   I = $350 million
   Calculate private savings.

   b. X = $85 million
   IM = $135 million
   Budget balance = $100 million
   Private savings = $250 million
   Calculate *I*.

   c. X = $60 million
   IM = $95 million
   Private savings = $325 million
   I = $300 million
   Calculate the budget balance

   d. Private savings = $325 million
   I = $400 million
   Budget balance = $10 million
   Calculate *IM − X*.

5. The accompanying table, taken from the National Income and Product Accounts Tables, shows the various components of U.S. GDP in 2006 and 2007 in billions of dollars.

Year	Gross domestic product	Private consumption	Gross domestic investment	Government purchases of goods and services	Government savings (budget balance)	Net government taxes after transfers
			(billions of dollars)			
2006	$13,194.7	$9,224.5	$2,643.0	$2,089.3	−$195.4	?
2007	13,841.3	9,734.2	2,593.3	2,221.9	?	$1,989.5

a. Complete the table by filling in the missing figures.

b. Calculate taxes (after transfers) as a percentage of GDP.

c. Calculate national savings and private savings.

6. Use the market for loanable funds shown in the accompanying diagram to explain what happens to private savings, private investment spending, and the rate of interest if the following events occur. Assume that there are no capital inflows or outflows.

a. The government reduces the size of its deficit to zero.

b. At any given interest rate, consumers decide to save more. Assume the budget balance is zero.

c. At any given interest rate, businesses become very optimistic about the future profitability of investment spending. Assume the budget balance is zero.

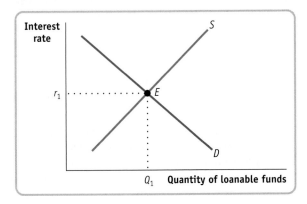

7. The government is running a budget balance of zero when it decides to increase education spending by $200 billion and finance the spending by selling bonds. The accompanying diagram shows the market for loanable funds before the government sells the bonds. Assume that there are no capital inflows or outflows. How will the equilibrium interest rate and the equilibrium quantity of loanable funds change? Is there any crowding out in the market?

8. In 2006, Congress estimated that the cost of the Iraq War was approximately $100 billion a year. Since the U.S. government was running a budget deficit at the time, assume that the war was financed by government borrowing, which increases the demand for loanable funds without affecting supply. This question considers the likely effect of this government expenditure on the interest rate.

a. Draw typical demand (D_1) and supply (S_1) curves for loanable funds without the cost of the war accounted for. Label the vertical axis "Interest rate" and the horizontal axis "Quantity of loanable funds." Label the equilibrium point (E_1) and the equilibrium interest rate (r_1).

b. Now consider a new diagram with the cost of the war included in the analysis. Shift the demand curve in the appropriate direction. Label the new equilibrium point (E_2) and the new equilibrium interest rate (r_2).

c. How does the equilibrium interest rate change in response to government expenditure on the war? Explain.

9. Explain why equilibrium in the loanable funds market maximizes efficiency.

10. How would you respond to a friend who claims that the government should eliminate all purchases that are financed by borrowing because such borrowing crowds out private investment spending?

11. Boris Borrower and Lynn Lender agree that Lynn will lend Boris $10,000 and that Boris will repay the $10,000 with interest in one year. They agree to a nominal interest rate of 8%, reflecting a real interest rate of 3% on the loan and a commonly shared expected inflation rate of 5% over the next year.

    a. If the inflation rate is actually 4% over the next year, how does that lower-than-expected inflation rate affect Boris and Lynn? Who is better off?

    b. If the actual inflation rate is 7% over the next year, how does that affect Boris and Lynn? Who is better off?

12. Using the accompanying diagram, explain what will happen to the market for loanable funds when there is a fall of 2 percentage points in the expected future inflation rate. How will the change in the expected future inflation rate affect the equilibrium quantity of loanable funds?

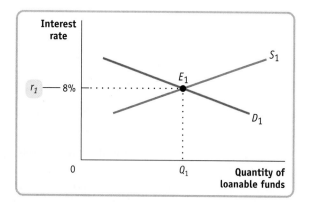

13. The accompanying diagram shows data for the interest rate on 10-year eurozone government bonds as reported by the European Central Bank and inflation for the eurozone for 1996 through mid-2008. How would you describe the relationship between the two? How does the pattern compare to that of the United States in Figure 26-8?

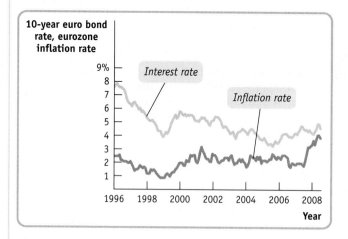

14. Which of the following are examples of investment spending, investing in financial assets, or investing in physical assets?

    a. Rupert Moneybucks buys 100 shares of existing Coca-Cola stock.

    b. Rhonda Moviestar spends $10 million to buy a mansion built in the 1970s.

    c. Ronald Basketballstar spends $10 million to build a new mansion with a view of the Pacific Ocean.

    d. Rawlings builds a new plant to make catcher's mitts.

    e. Russia buys $100 million in U.S. government bonds.

15. Explain how a well-functioning financial system increases savings and investment spending, holding the budget balance and any capital flows fixed.

16. What are the important types of financial intermediaries in the U.S. economy? What are the primary assets of these intermediaries, and how do they facilitate investment spending and saving?

17. Explain the effect on a company's stock price today of the following events, other things held constant.

    a. The interest rate on bonds falls.

    b. Several companies in the same sector announce surprisingly slow sales.

    c. A change in the tax law passed last year reduces this year's profit.

    d. The company unexpectedly announces that due to an accounting error, it must amend last year's accounting statement and reduce last year's reported profit by $5 million. It also announces that this change has no implications for future profits.

18. Sallie Mae is a quasi-governmental agency that packages individual student loans into pools of loans and sells shares of these pools to investors as Sallie Mae bonds.

    a. What is this process called? What effect will it have on investors compared to the situations in which they could only buy and sell individual student loans?

    b. What effect do you think Sallie Mae's actions will have on the ability of students to get loans?

    c. Suppose that a very severe recession hits and, as a consequence, many graduating students cannot get jobs and default on their student loans. What effect will this have on Sallie Mae bonds? Why is it likely that investors now believe Sallie Mae bonds to be riskier than expected? What will be the effect on the availability of student loans?

> Income and Expenditure

FROM BOOM TO BUST

F T. MYERS, FLORIDA, WAS A BOOM TOWN IN 2003, 2004, and most of 2005. Jobs were plentiful: by 2005 the unemployment rate in the Ft. Myers–Cape Coral metropolitan area was less than 3%. The shopping malls were humming, and new stores were opening everywhere.

But then the boom went bust. Jobs became scarce, and by October 2008 the unemployment rate had reached 9.5%. Stores had few customers, and many were closing. One new business was flourishing, however. As the local economy plunged, Marc Joseph, a real estate agent, began offering "foreclosure tours": visits to homes that had been seized by banks after the owners were unable to make mortgage payments—and were available at bargain prices.

What happened? Ft. Myers boomed from 2003 to 2005 because of a surge in home construction, fueled in part by speculators who bought houses not to live in, but because they believed they could resell those houses at much higher prices. Home construction gave jobs to construction workers, electricians, roofers, real estate agents, and others. And these workers, in turn, spent money locally, creating jobs for sales workers in stores, waiters in restaurants, gardeners, pool cleaners, and more. These workers, in turn, also spent money locally, creating further expansion, and so on.

The boom turned into a bust when home construction suddenly came to a virtual halt. It turned out that speculation had been feeding on itself: people were buying houses as investments, then selling them to other people who were also buying houses as investments, and the prices had risen to levels far beyond what people who actually wanted to live in houses were willing to pay. Eventually there was a "Wile E. Coyote moment"—named after the cartoon character who has a habit of running off the edge of cliffs but doesn't fall until he looks down and realizes that nothing is supporting him. Sometime in 2005 people looked down—and suddenly realized that home prices had lost touch with reality. And when they did, the housing market collapsed.

The abrupt collapse of the housing market pulled the local economy down with it, as the process that had created the earlier boom operated in reverse. The jobs created by housing went away, leading to a fall in local spending, leading to a loss of other local jobs, leading to further declines in spending, and so on.

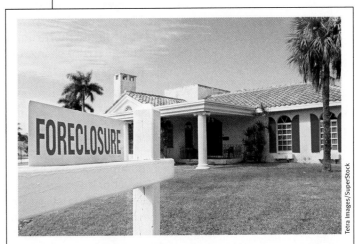

The foreclosure-tour business flourished in Ft. Myers after its housing market went from boom to bust.

The boom and bust in Ft. Myers illustrates, on a relatively small scale, the way booms and busts often happen for the economy as a whole. The business cycle is often driven by ups or downs in investment spending—either residential investment spending (that is, home construction) or nonresidential investment spending (such as the construction of office buildings, factories, and shopping malls). Changes in investment spending, in turn, indirectly lead to changes in consumer spending, which magnify—or, as economists usually say, *multiply*—the effect of the investment spending changes on the economy as a whole.

In this chapter we'll study how this process works, showing how *multiplier* analysis helps us understand the business cycle. As a first step, we introduce the concept of the multiplier informally.

WHAT YOU WILL LEARN IN THIS CHAPTER:

➤ The nature of the **multiplier,** which shows how initial changes in spending lead to further changes

➤ The meaning of the **aggregate consumption function,** which shows how current disposable income affects consumer spending

➤ How expected future income and aggregate wealth affect consumer spending

➤ The determinants of investment spending and the distinction between **planned investment spending** and **unplanned inventory investment**

➤ How the inventory adjustment process moves the economy to a new equilibrium after a change in demand

➤ Why investment spending is considered a leading indicator of the future state of the economy

The Multiplier: An Informal Introduction

The story of the boom and bust in Ft. Myers involves a sort of chain reaction in which an initial rise or fall in spending leads to changes in income, which lead to further changes in spending, and so on. Let's examine that chain reaction more closely, this time thinking through the effects of changes in spending in the economy as a whole.

For the sake of this analysis, we'll make four simplifying assumptions that will have to be reconsidered in later chapters.

1. We assume that *producers are willing to supply additional output at a fixed price.* That is, if consumers or businesses buying investment goods decide to spend an additional $1 billion, that will translate into the production of $1 billion worth of additional goods and services without driving up the overall level of prices. As a result, *changes in overall spending translate into changes in aggregate output,* as measured by real GDP. As we'll learn in the next chapter, this assumption isn't too unrealistic in the short run, but it needs to be changed when we think about the long-run effects of changes in demand.

2. We take the interest rate as given.

3. We assume that there is no government spending and no taxes.

4. We assume that exports and imports are zero.

Given these simplifying assumptions, consider what happens if there is a change in investment spending. Specifically, imagine that for some reason home builders decide to spend an extra $100 billion on home construction over the next year.

The direct effect of this increase in investment spending will be to increase income and the value of aggregate output by the same amount. That's because each dollar spent on home construction translates into a dollar's worth of income for construction workers, suppliers of building materials, electricians, and so on. If the process stopped there, the increase in housing investment spending would raise overall income by exactly $100 billion.

But the process doesn't stop there. The increase in aggregate output leads to an increase in disposable income that flows to households in the form of profits and wages. The increase in households' disposable income leads to a rise in consumer spending, which, in turn, induces firms to increase output yet again. This generates another rise in disposable income, which leads to another round of consumer spending increases, and so on. So there are multiple rounds of increases in aggregate output.

How large is the total effect on aggregate output if we sum the effect from all these rounds of spending increases? To answer this question, we need to introduce the concept of the **marginal propensity to consume,** or **MPC:** the increase in consumer spending when disposable income rises by $1. When consumer spending changes because of a rise or fall in disposable income, *MPC* is the change in consumer spending divided by the change in disposable income:

(27-1) $MPC = \dfrac{\Delta \text{ Consumer spending}}{\Delta \text{ Disposable income}}$

where the symbol Δ (delta) means "change in." For example, if consumer spending goes up by $6 billion when disposable income goes up by $10 billion, *MPC* is $6 billion/$10 billion = 0.6.

Because consumers normally spend part but not all of an additional dollar of disposable income, *MPC* is a number between 0 and 1. The additional disposable income that consumers don't spend is saved; the **marginal propensity to save,** or **MPS,** is the fraction of an additional dollar of disposable income that is saved. *MPS* is equal to $1 - MPC$.

Because we assumed that there are no taxes and no international trade, each $1 increase in spending raises both real GDP and disposable income by $1. So the $100 billion increase in investment spending initially raises real GDP by $100 billion. This leads to a second-round increase in consumer spending, which raises real GDP by a further *MPC* × $100 billion. It is followed by a third-round increase in consumer spending of *MPC* × *MPC* × $100 billion, and so on. After an infinite number of rounds, the total effect on real GDP is:

Increase in investment spending	=	$100 billion
+ Second-round increase in consumer spending	= MPC	× $100 billion
+ Third-round increase in consumer spending	= MPC^2	× $100 billion
+ Fourth-round increase in consumer spending	= MPC^3	× $100 billion
$\vdots$	$\vdots$	

Total increase in real GDP = $(1 + MPC + MPC^2 + MPC^3 + \ldots) \times \$100$ billion

So the $100 billion increase in investment spending sets off a chain reaction in the economy. The net result of this chain reaction is that a $100 billion increase in investment spending leads to a change in real GDP that is a *multiple* of the size of that initial change in spending.

How large is this multiple? It's a mathematical fact that an infinite series of the form $1 + x + x^2 + x^3 + \ldots$, where x is between 0 and 1, is equal to $1/(1 - x)$. So the total effect of a $100 billion increase in investment spending, I, taking into account all the subsequent increases in consumer spending (and assuming no taxes and no international trade), is given by:

(27-2) Total increase in real GDP from $100 billion rise in I

$= \dfrac{1}{1 - MPC} \times \$100$ billion

The **marginal propensity to consume,** or **MPC,** is the increase in consumer spending when disposable income rises by $1.

The **marginal propensity to save,** or **MPS,** is the increase in household savings when disposable income rises by $1.

TABLE 27-1

Rounds of Increases of Real GDP When *MPC* = 0.6

	Increase in real GDP ($ billions)	Total increase in real GDP ($ billions)
First round	100	100
Second round	60	160
Third round	36	196
Fourth round	21.6	217.6
...	...	...
Final round	0	250

Let's consider a numerical example in which *MPC* = 0.6: each $1 in additional disposable income causes a $0.60 rise in consumer spending. In that case, a $100 billion increase in investment spending raises real GDP by $100 billion in the first round. The second-round increase in consumer spending raises real GDP by another 0.6 × $100 billion, or $60 billion. The third-round increase in consumer spending raises real GDP by another 0.6 × $60 billion, or $36 billion. Table 27-1 shows the successive stages of increases, where ". . ." means the process goes on an infinite number of times. In the end, real GDP rises by $250 billion as a consequence of the initial $100 billion rise in investment spending:

$$\frac{1}{1 - 0.6} \times \$100 \text{ billion} = 2.5 \times \$100 \text{ billion} = \$250 \text{ billion}$$

Notice that even though there are an infinite number of rounds of expansion of real GDP, the total rise in real GDP is limited to $250 billion. The reason is that at each stage some of the rise in disposable income "leaks out" because it is saved. How much of an additional dollar of disposable income is saved depends on *MPS*, the marginal propensity to save.

We've described the effects of a change in investment spending, but the same analysis can be applied to any other change in spending. The important thing is to distinguish between the initial change in aggregate spending, before real GDP rises, and the additional change in aggregate spending caused by the change in real GDP as the chain reaction unfolds. For example, suppose that a boom in housing prices makes consumers feel richer and that, as a result, they become willing to spend more at any given level of disposable income. This will lead to an initial rise in consumer spending, before real GDP rises. But it will also lead to second and later rounds of higher consumer spending as real GDP rises.

An initial rise or fall in aggregate spending at a given level of real GDP is called an **autonomous change in aggregate spending.** It's autonomous—which means "self-governing"—because it's the cause, not the result, of the chain reaction we've just described. Formally, the **multiplier** is the ratio of the total change in real GDP caused by an autonomous change in aggregate spending to the size of that autonomous change. If we let Δ*AAS* stand for autonomous change in aggregate spending and Δ*Y* stand for the change in real GDP, then the multiplier is equal to Δ*Y*/Δ*AAS*. And we've already seen how to find the value of the multiplier. Assuming no taxes and no trade, the change in real GDP caused by an autonomous change in spending is:

$$\textbf{(27-3)} \quad \Delta Y = \frac{1}{1 - MPC} \times \Delta AAS$$

So the multiplier is:

$$\textbf{(27-4)} \quad \text{Multiplier} = \frac{\Delta Y}{\Delta AAS} = \frac{1}{1 - MPC}$$

An **autonomous change in aggregate spending** is an initial change in the desired level of spending by firms, households, or government at a given level of real GDP.

The **multiplier** is the ratio of the total change in real GDP caused by an autonomous change in aggregate spending to the size of that autonomous change.

Notice that the size of the multiplier depends on *MPC*. If the marginal propensity to consume is high, so is the multiplier. This is true because the size of *MPC* determines how large each round of expansion is compared with the previous round. To put it another way, the higher *MPC* is, the less disposable income "leaks out" into savings at each round of expansion.

In later chapters we'll use the concept of the multiplier to analyze the effects of fiscal and monetary policies. We'll also see that the formula for the multiplier changes when we introduce various complications, including taxes and foreign trade. First, however, we need to look more deeply at what determines consumer spending.

►ECONOMICS IN ACTION

The Multiplier and the Great Depression

The concept of the multiplier was originally devised by economists trying to understand the greatest economic disaster in history, the collapse of output and employment from 1929 to 1933, which began the Great Depression. Most economists believe that the slump from 1929 to 1933 was driven by a collapse in investment spending. But as the economy shrank, consumer spending also fell sharply, multiplying the effect on real GDP.

Table 27-2 shows what happened to investment spending, consumer spending, and GDP during those four terrible years. All data are in 2000 dollars. What we see is that investment spending imploded, falling by more than 80%. But consumer spending also fell drastically and actually accounted for more of the fall in real GDP. (The total fall in real GDP was larger than the combined fall in consumer and investment spending, mainly because of technical accounting issues.)

The numbers in Table 27-2 suggest that at the time of the Great Depression, the multiplier was around 3. Most current estimates put the size of the multiplier considerably lower—but there's a reason for that change. In 1929, government in the United States was very small by modern standards: taxes were low and major government programs like Social Security and Medicare had not yet come into being. In the modern U.S. economy, taxes are much higher, and so is government spending. Why does this matter? Because taxes and some government programs act as *automatic stabilizers,* reducing the size of the multiplier. The appendix to Chapter 29 explains how taxes change the multiplier. ▲

TABLE 27-2

Investment Spending, Consumer Spending, and Real GDP in the Great Depression (billions of 2000 dollars)

	1929	1933	Change
Investment spending	$91.3	$17.0	−$74.3
Consumer spending	661.4	541.0	−120.4
Real GDP	865.2	635.5	−229.7

Source: Bureau of Economic Analysis.

> > > > > > > > > > >

► CHECK YOUR UNDERSTANDING 27-1

1. Explain why a decline in investment spending caused by a change in business expectations leads to a fall in consumer spending.

2. What is the multiplier if the marginal propensity to consume is 0.5? What is it if *MPC* is 0.8?

3. As a percentage of GDP, savings accounts for a larger share of the economy in the country of Scania compared to the country of Amerigo. Which country is likely to have the larger multiplier? Explain.

Solutions appear at back of book.

>> **QUICK REVIEW**

➤ A change in investment spending arising from a change in expectations starts a chain reaction in which the initial change in real GDP leads to changes in consumer spending, leading to further changes in real GDP, and so on. The total change in aggregate output is a multiple of the initial change in investment spending.

➤ Any **autonomous change in aggregate spending,** a change in spending that is not caused by a change in real GDP, generates the same chain reaction. The total size of the change in real GDP depends on the size of the **multiplier.** Assuming that there are no taxes and no trade, the multiplier is equal to $1/(1 - MPC)$, where **MPC** is the **marginal propensity to consume.** The total change in real GDP, ΔY, is equal to $1/(1 - MPC) \times \Delta AAS$.

Consumer Spending

Should you splurge on a restaurant meal or save money by eating at home? Should you buy a new car and, if so, how expensive a model? Should you redo that bathroom or live with it for another year? In the real world, households are constantly confronted with such choices—not just about the consumption mix but also about how much to spend in total. These choices, in turn, have a powerful effect on the economy: consumer spending normally accounts for two-thirds of total spending on final goods and services. In particular, as we've just seen, the decision about how much of an additional dollar in income to spend—the marginal propensity to consume—determines the size of the multiplier, which determines the ultimate effect on the economy of autonomous changes in spending.

But what determines how much consumers spend?

The **consumption function** is an equation showing how an individual household's consumer spending varies with the household's current disposable income.

Current Disposable Income and Consumer Spending

The most important factor affecting a family's consumer spending is its current disposable income—income after taxes are paid and government transfers are received. It's obvious from daily life that people with high disposable incomes on average drive more expensive cars, live in more expensive houses, and spend more on meals and clothing than people with lower disposable incomes. And the relationship between current disposable income and spending is clear in the data.

The Bureau of Labor Statistics (BLS) collects annual data on family income and spending. Families are grouped by levels of before-tax income, and after-tax income for each group is also reported. Since the income figures include transfers from the government, what the BLS calls a household's after-tax income is equivalent to its current disposable income.

Figure 27-1 is a scatter diagram illustrating the relationship between household current disposable income and household consumer spending for American households by income group in 2006. For example, point A shows that in 2006 the middle fifth of the population had an average current disposable income of $43,799 and average spending of $41,431. The pattern of the dots slopes upward from left to right, making it clear that households with higher current disposable income had higher consumer spending.

It's very useful to represent the relationship between an individual household's current disposable income and its consumer spending with an equation. The **consumption function** is an equation showing how an individual household's consumer spending varies with the household's current disposable income. The simplest version of a consumption function is a linear equation:

$$\textbf{(27-5)} \quad c = a + MPC \times yd$$

where lowercase letters indicate variables measured for an individual household.

In this equation, c is individual household consumer spending and yd is individual household current disposable income. Recall that MPC, the marginal propensity to consume, is the amount by which consumer spending rises if current disposable income rises by $1. Finally, a is a constant term—individual household *autonomous consumer spending*, the amount of spending a household would do if it had zero disposable income. We assume that a is greater than zero because a household with zero disposable income is able to fund some consumption by borrowing or using its savings. Notice, by the way, that we're using y for income. That's standard practice in macroeconomics, even

FIGURE 27-1

Current Disposable Income and Consumer Spending for American Households in 2006

For each income group of households, average current disposable income in 2006 is plotted versus average consumer spending in 2006. For example, the middle income group, with an annual income of $35,095 to $56,221, is represented by point A, indicating a household average current disposable income of $43,799 and average household consumer spending of $41,431. The data clearly show a positive relationship between current disposable income and consumer spending: families with higher current disposable income have higher consumer spending.

Source: Bureau of Labor Statistics.

though *income* isn't actually spelled "yncome." The reason is that *I* is reserved for invest-ment spending.

Recall that we expressed *MPC* as the ratio of a change in consumer spending to the change in current disposable income. We've rewritten it for an individual household as Equation 27-6:

(27-6) $MPC = \Delta c / \Delta yd$

Multiplying both sides of Equation 27-6 by Δyd, we get:

(27-7) $MPC \times \Delta yd = \Delta c$

Equation 27-7 tells us that when *yd* goes up by $1, *c* goes up by $MPC \times \$1$.

Figure 27-2 shows what Equation 27-5 looks like graphically, plotting *yd* on the horizontal axis and *c* on the vertical axis. Individual household autonomous con-sumer spending, *a,* is the value of *c* when *yd* is zero—it is the vertical *intercept* of the consumption function, *cf.* *MPC* is the *slope* of the line, measured by rise over run. If current disposable income rises by Δyd, household consumer spending, *c*, rises by Δc. Since *MPC* is defined as $\Delta c / \Delta yd$, the slope of the consumption function is:

(27-8) Slope of consumption function
        = Rise over run
        = $\Delta c / \Delta yd$
        = *MPC*

In reality, actual data never fit Equation 27-5 perfectly, but the fit can be pretty good. Figure 27-3 on the next page shows the data from Figure 27-1 again, together with a line drawn to fit the data as closely as possible. According to the data on households' consumer spending and current disposable income, the best estimate of *a* is $16,017 and of *MPC* is 0.557. So the consumption function fitted to the data is:

$$c = \$16,017 + 0.557 \times yd$$

That is, the data suggest a marginal propensity to consume of approximately 0.56. This implies that the marginal propensity to save (*MPS*)—the amount of an addition-al $1 of disposable income that is saved—is approximately 0.44, and the multiplier is approximately $1/0.44 = 2.27$.

FIGURE 27-2

The Consumption Function

The consumption function relates a house-hold's current disposable income to its consumer spending. The vertical intercept, *a,* is individual household autonomous consumer spending: the amount of a household's consumer spending if its current disposable income is zero. The slope of the consumption function line, *cf,* is the marginal propensity to consume, or *MPC*: of every additional $1 of current disposable income, $MPC \times \$1$ is spent.

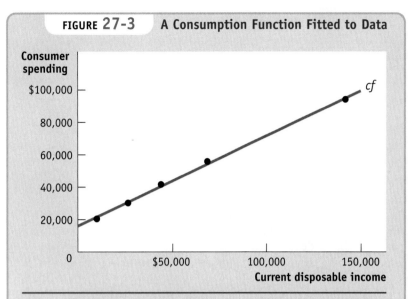

FIGURE **27-3** **A Consumption Function Fitted to Data**

The data from Figure 27-1 are reproduced here, along with a line drawn to fit the data as closely as possible. For American households in 2006, the best estimate of the average household's autonomous consumer spending, *a*, is $16,017 and the best estimate of *MPC* is 0.557, or approximately 0.56.

Source: Bureau of Labor Statistics.

It's important to realize that Figure 27-3 shows a *microeconomic* relationship between the current disposable income of individual households and their spending on goods and services. However, macroeconomists assume that a similar relationship holds *for the economy as a whole*: that there is a relationship, called the **aggregate consumption function,** between aggregate current disposable income and aggregate consumer spending. We'll assume that it has the same form as the household-level consumption function:

$$(27\text{-}9) \quad C = A + MPC \times YD$$

Here, *C* is aggregate consumer spending (called just "consumer spending"); *YD* is aggregate current disposable income (called, for simplicity, just "disposable income"); and *A* is aggregate autonomous consumer spending, the amount of consumer spending when *YD* equals zero. This is the relationship represented in Figure 27-4 by *CF*, analogous to *cf* in Figure 27-3.

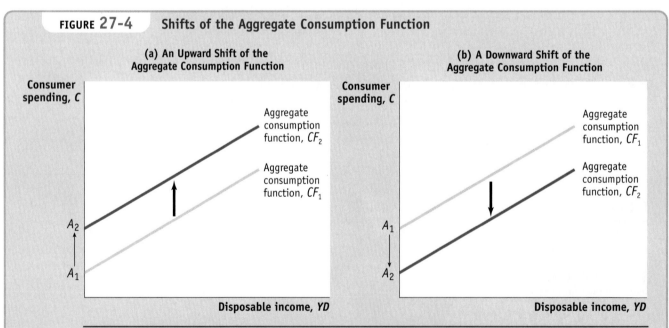

FIGURE **27-4** **Shifts of the Aggregate Consumption Function**

(a) An Upward Shift of the Aggregate Consumption Function

(b) A Downward Shift of the Aggregate Consumption Function

Panel (a) illustrates the effect of an increase in expected aggregate future disposable income. Consumers will spend more at every given level of aggregate current disposable income, *YD*. As a result, the initial aggregate consumption function *CF*₁, with aggregate autonomous consumer spending *A*₁, shifts up to a new position at *CF*₂ and aggregate autonomous consumer spending *A*₂. An increase in aggregate wealth will also shift the aggregate consumption function up.

Panel (b), in contrast, illustrates the effect of a reduction in expected aggregate future disposable income. Consumers will spend less at every given level of aggregate current disposable income, *YD*. Consequently, the initial aggregate consumption function *CF*₁, with aggregate autonomous consumer spending *A*₁, shifts down to a new position at *CF*₂ and aggregate autonomous consumer spending *A*₂. A reduction in aggregate wealth will have the same effect.

Shifts of the Aggregate Consumption Function

The aggregate consumption function shows the relationship between disposable income and consumer spending for the economy as a whole, other things equal. When things other than disposable income change, the aggregate consumption function shifts. There are two principal causes of shifts of the aggregate consumption function: changes in expected future disposable income and changes in aggregate wealth.

Changes in Expected Future Disposable Income Suppose you land a really good, well-paying job on graduating from college in May—but the job, and the pay-checks, won't start until September. So your disposable income hasn't risen yet. Even so, it's likely that you will start spending more on final goods and services right away—maybe buying nicer work clothes than you originally planned—because you know that higher income is coming.

Conversely, suppose you have a good job but learn that the company is planning to downsize your division, raising the possibility that you may lose your job and have to take a lower-paying one somewhere else. Even though your disposable income hasn't gone down yet, you might well cut back on spending even while still employed, to save for a rainy day.

Both of these examples show how expectations about future disposable income can affect consumer spending. The two panels of Figure 27-4, which plot disposable income against consumer spending, show how changes in expected future disposable income affect the aggregate consumption function. In both panels, CF_1 is the initial aggregate consumption function. Panel (a) shows the effect of good news: information that leads consumers to expect higher disposable income in the future than they did before. Consumers will now spend more at any given level of current disposable income YD, corresponding to an increase in A, aggregate autonomous consumer spending, from A_1 to A_2. The effect is to shift the aggregate consumption function up, from CF_1 to CF_2. Panel (b) shows the effect of bad news: information that leads consumers to expect lower disposable income in the future than they did before. Consumers will now spend less at any given level of current disposable income YD, corresponding to a fall in A from A_1 to A_2. The effect is to shift the aggregate consumption function down, from CF_1 to CF_2.

In a famous 1956 book, *A Theory of the Consumption Function*, Milton Friedman showed that taking the effects of expected future income into account explains an otherwise puzzling fact about consumer behavior. If we look at consumer spending during any given year, we find that people with high current income save a larger fraction of their income than those with low current income. (This is obvious from the data in Figure 27-3: people in the highest income group spend considerably less than their income; those in the lowest income group spend more than their income.) You might think this implies that the overall savings rate will rise as the economy grows and average current incomes rise; in fact, however, this hasn't happened.

Friedman pointed out that when we look at individual incomes in a given year, there are systematic differences between current and expected future income that create a positive relationship between current income and the savings rate. On one side, people with low current incomes are often having an unusually bad year. For example, they may be workers who have been laid off but will probably find new jobs eventually. They are people whose expected future income is higher than their current income, so it makes sense for them to have low or even negative savings. On the other side, people with high current incomes in a given year are often having an unusually good year. For example, they may have investments that happened to do extremely well. They are people whose expected future income is lower than their current income, so it makes sense for them to save most of their windfall.

When the economy grows, by contrast, current and expected future incomes rise together. Higher current income tends to lead to higher savings today, but higher expected future income tends to lead to less savings today. As a result, there's a weaker relationship between current income and the savings rate.

The **aggregate consumption function** is the relationship for the economy as a whole between aggregate current disposable income and aggregate consumer spending.

Friedman argued that consumer spending ultimately depends mainly on the income people expect to have over the long term rather than on their current income. This argument is known as the *permanent income hypothesis*.

Changes in Aggregate Wealth   Imagine two individuals, Maria and Mark, both of whom expect to earn $30,000 this year. Suppose, however, that they have different histories. Maria has been working steadily for the past 10 years, owns her own home, and has $200,000 in the bank. Mark is the same age as Maria, but he has been in and out of work, hasn't managed to buy a house, and has very little in savings. In this case, Maria has something that Mark doesn't have: wealth. Even though they have the same disposable income, other things equal, you'd expect Maria to spend more on consumption than Mark. That is, *wealth* has an effect on consumer spending.

The effect of wealth on spending is emphasized by an influential economic model of how consumers make choices about spending versus saving called the *life-cycle hypothesis*. According to this hypothesis, consumers plan their spending over a lifetime, not just in response to their current disposable income. As a result, people try to *smooth* their consumption over their lifetimes—they save some of their current disposable income during their years of peak earnings (typically occurring during a worker's 40s and 50s) and during their retirement live off the wealth they accumulated while working. We won't go into the details of this hypothesis but will simply point out that it implies an important role for wealth in determining consumer spending. For example, a middle-aged couple who have accumulated a lot of wealth—who have paid off the mortgage on their house and already own plenty of stocks and bonds—will, other things equal, spend more on goods and services than a couple who have the same current disposable income but still need to save for their retirement.

Because wealth affects household consumer spending, changes in wealth across the economy can shift the aggregate consumption function. A rise in aggregate wealth—say, because of a booming stock market—increases the vertical intercept A, aggregate autonomous consumer spending. This, in turn, shifts the aggregate consumption function up in the same way as does an expected increase in future disposable income. A decline in aggregate wealth—say, because of a fall in housing prices as occurred in 2008—reduces A and shifts the aggregate consumption function down.

➤*ECONOMICS IN ACTION*

Famous First Forecasting Failures

The Great Depression created modern macroeconomics. It also gave birth to the modern field of econometrics—the use of statistical techniques to fit economic models to empirical data. The aggregate consumption function was one of the first things econometricians studied. And, sure enough, they quickly experienced one of the first major failures of economic forecasting: consumer spending after World War II was much higher than estimates of the aggregate consumption function based on prewar data would have predicted.

Figure 27-5 tells the story. Panel (a) shows aggregate data on disposable income and consumer spending from 1929 to 1941. A simple linear consumption function, CF_1, seems to fit the data very well. And many economists thought this relationship would continue to hold in the future. But panel (b) shows what actually happened in later years. The points in the circle at the left are the data from the Great Depression shown in panel (a). The points in the circle at the right are data from 1946 to 1960. (Data from 1942 to 1945 aren't included because rationing during World War II prevented consumers from spending normally.) The solid line in the figure, CF_1, is the consumption function fitted to 1929–1941 data. As you can see, post–World War II consumer spending was much higher than the relationship from the Depression years would have predicted. For example, in 1960 consumer spending was 13.5% higher than the level predicted by CF_1.

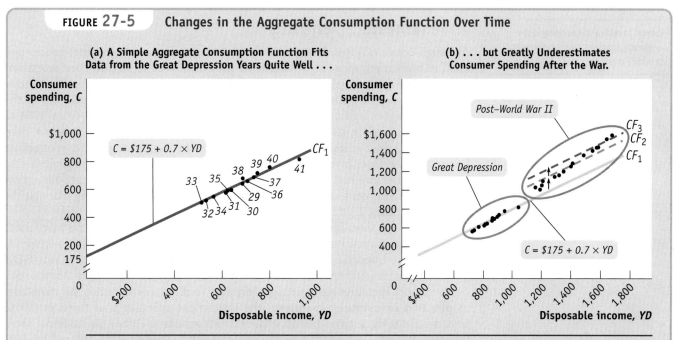

FIGURE 27-5 Changes in the Aggregate Consumption Function Over Time

(a) A Simple Aggregate Consumption Function Fits Data from the Great Depression Years Quite Well ...

$C = \$175 + 0.7 \times YD$

CF_1

(b) ... but Greatly Underestimates Consumer Spending After the War.

Post–World War II

Great Depression

CF_3
CF_2
CF_1

$C = \$175 + 0.7 \times YD$

Panel (a) is a scatter diagram of observations of American households' annual disposable income measured in billions of 2000 dollars versus annual consumer spending, also in billions of 2000 dollars, during the period 1929–1941. A simple consumption function, CF_1 of the form $C = \$175 + 0.7 \times YD$, fits the data quite well and suggests that during the Great Depression the marginal propensity to consume was 0.7. Panel (b) contains the same data as panel (a) and the same consumption function, as well as observations from the post–World War II period. CF_1 lies below the post-war observations and does not fit the data from those years well. In fact, the consumption function shifted up over time, as shown in the figure by the dashed lines, CF_2 and CF_3.

Why was extrapolating from the earlier relationship so misleading? The answer is that from 1946 onward, both expected future disposable income and aggregate wealth were steadily rising. Consumers grew increasingly confident that the Great Depression wouldn't reemerge and that the post–World War II economic boom would continue. At the same time, wealth was steadily increasing. As indicated by the dashed lines in panel (b), CF_2 and CF_3, the increases in expected future disposable income and in aggregate wealth shifted the aggregate consumption function up a number of times.

In macroeconomics, failure—whether of economic policy or of economic prediction—often leads to intellectual progress. The embarrassing failure of early estimates of the aggregate consumption function to predict post–World War II consumer spending led to important progress in our understanding of consumer behavior. ▲

> > > > > > > > > > > >

▶ CHECK YOUR UNDERSTANDING 27-2

1. Suppose the economy consists of three people: Angelina, Felicia, and Marina. The table shows how their consumer spending varies as their current disposable income rises by $10,000.
   a. Derive each individual's consumption function, where *MPC* is calculated for a $10,000 change in current disposable income.
   b. Derive the aggregate consumption function.

2. Suppose that problems in the capital markets make consumers unable either to borrow or to put money aside for future use. What implication does this have for the effects of expected future disposable income on consumer spending?

Current disposable income	Consumer spending		
	Angelina	Felicia	Marina
$0	$8,000	$6,500	$7,250
10,000	12,000	14,500	14,250

▶▶ QUICK REVIEW

➤ The **consumption function** shows the relationship between an individual household's current disposable income and its consumer spending.
➤ The **aggregate consumption function** shows the relationship between disposable income and consumer spending across the economy. It can shift due to changes in expected future disposable income and changes in aggregate wealth.

Solutions appear at back of book.

> **Planned investment spending** is the investment spending that businesses intend to undertake during a given period.

Investment Spending

Although consumer spending is much larger than investment spending, booms and busts in investment spending tend to drive the business cycle. In fact, most recessions originate as a fall in investment spending. Figure 27-6 illustrates this point; it shows the annual percent change of investment spending and consumer spending in the United States, both measured in 2000 dollars, during five recessions from 1973 to 2001. As you can see, swings in investment spending are much more dramatic than those in consumer spending. In addition, due to the multiplier process, economists believe that declines in consumer spending are usually the result of a process that begins with a slump in investment spending. Soon we'll examine in more detail how a slump in investment spending generates a fall in consumer spending through the multiplier process.

Before we do that, however, let's analyze the factors that determine investment spending, which are somewhat different from those that determine consumer spending. The most important ones are the interest rate and expected future real GDP. We'll also revisit a fact that we noted in For Inquiring Minds in Chapter 26: the level of investment spending businesses *actually* carry out is sometimes not the same level as **planned investment spending,** the investment spending that firms *intend* to undertake during a given period. Planned investment spending depends on three principal factors: the interest rate, the expected future level of real GDP, and the current level of production capacity. First, we'll analyze the effect of the interest rate.

The Interest Rate and Investment Spending

Interest rates have their clearest effect on one particular form of investment spending: spending on residential construction—that is, on the construction of homes. The reason is straightforward: home builders only build houses they think they can sell, and houses are more affordable—and so more likely to sell—when the interest rate is low. Consider a potential home-buying family that needs to borrow $150,000 to buy a house. At an interest rate of 7.5%, a 30-year home mortgage will mean payments of $1,048 per month. At an interest rate of 5.5%, those payments would be only $851 per month, making houses significantly more affordable. As described in the upcoming Economics in Action, interest rates actually did drop from roughly 7.5% to 5.5% between the late 1990s and 2003, helping set off the great housing boom described in this chapter's opening story.

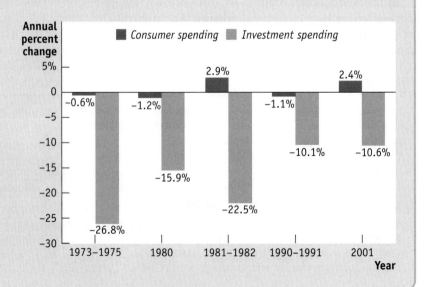

FIGURE 27-6

Fluctuations in Investment Spending and Consumer Spending

The bars illustrate the annual percent change in investment spending and consumer spending during five recent recessions. As the lengths of the bars show, swings in investment spending were much larger in percentage terms than those in consumer spending. This pattern has led economists to believe that recessions typically originate as a slump in investment spending.

Interest rates also affect other forms of investment spending. Firms with investment spending projects will only go ahead with a project if they expect a rate of return higher than the cost of the funds they would have to borrow to finance that project. If the interest rate rises, fewer projects will pass that test, and as a result investment spending will be lower.

You might think that the trade-off a firm faces is different if it can fund its investment project with its past profits rather than through borrowing. Past profits used to finance investment spending are called *retained earnings*. But even if a firm pays for investment spending out of retained earnings, the trade-off it must make in deciding whether or not to fund a project remains the same because it must take into account the opportunity cost of its funds. For example, instead of purchasing new equipment, the firm could lend out the funds and earn interest. The forgone interest earned is the opportunity cost of using retained earnings to fund an investment project. So the trade-off the firm faces when comparing a project's rate of return to the market interest rate has not changed when it uses retained earnings rather than borrowed funds, which means that regardless of whether a firm funds investment spending through borrowing or retained earnings, a rise in the market interest rate makes any given investment project less profitable. Conversely, a fall in the interest rate makes some investment projects that were unprofitable before profitable at the now lower interest rate. So some projects that had been unfunded before will be funded now.

So planned investment spending—spending on investment projects that firms voluntarily decide whether or not to undertake—is negatively related to the interest rate. Other things equal, a higher interest rate leads to a lower level of planned investment spending.

Expected Future Real GDP, Production Capacity, and Investment Spending

Suppose a firm has enough capacity to continue to produce the amount it is currently selling but doesn't expect its sales to grow in the future. Then it will engage in investment spending only to replace existing equipment and structures that wear out or are rendered obsolete by new technologies. But if, instead, the firm expects its sales to grow rapidly in the future, it will find its existing production capacity insufficient for its future production needs. So the firm will undertake investment spending to meet those needs. This implies that, other things equal, firms will undertake more investment spending when they expect their sales to grow.

Now suppose that the firm currently has considerably more capacity than necessary to meet current production needs. Even if it expects sales to grow, it won't have to undertake investment spending for a while—not until the growth in sales catches up with its excess capacity. This illustrates the fact that, other things equal, the current level of productive capacity has a negative effect on investment spending: other things equal, the higher the current capacity, the lower is investment spending.

If we put together the effects on investment spending of growth in expected future sales and the size of current production capacity, we can see one situation in which we can be reasonably sure that firms will undertake high levels of investment spending: when they expect sales to grow rapidly. In that case, even excess production capacity will soon be used up, leading firms to resume investment spending.

What is an indicator of high expected growth of future sales? It's a high expected future growth rate of real GDP. A higher expected future growth rate of real GDP results in a higher level of planned investment spending, but a lower expected future growth rate of real GDP leads to lower planned investment spending. This relationship is summarized in a proposition known as the **accelerator principle.** As we explain in the upcoming Economics in Action, the effects of the accelerator principle play an important role in *investment spending slumps,* periods of low investment spending.

According to the **accelerator principle**, a higher growth rate of real GDP leads to higher planned investment spending, but a lower growth rate of real GDP leads to lower planned investment spending.

Inventories are stocks of goods held to satisfy future sales.

Inventory investment is the value of the change in total inventories held in the economy during a given period.

Unplanned inventory investment occurs when actual sales are more or less than businesses expected, leading to unplanned changes in inventories.

Actual investment spending is the sum of planned investment spending and unplanned inventory investment.

Inventories and Unplanned Investment Spending

Most firms maintain **inventories,** stocks of goods held to satisfy future sales. Firms hold inventories so they can quickly satisfy buyers—a consumer can purchase an item off the shelf rather than waiting for it to be manufactured. In addition, businesses often hold inventories of their inputs to be sure they have a steady supply of necessary materials and spare parts. At the end of the second quarter of 2008, the overall value of inventories in the U.S. economy was estimated at $2.3 trillion, almost 16% of GDP.

As we explained in Chapter 23, a firm that increases its inventories is engaging in a form of investment spending. Suppose, for example, that the U.S. auto industry produces 800,000 cars per month but sells only 700,000. The remaining 100,000 cars are added to the inventory at auto company warehouses or car dealerships, ready to be sold in the future. **Inventory investment** is the value of the change in total inventories held in the economy during a given period. Unlike other forms of investment spending, inventory investment can actually be negative. If, for example, the auto industry reduces its inventory over the course of a month, we say that it has engaged in negative inventory investment.

To understand inventory investment, think about a manager stocking the canned goods section of a supermarket. The manager tries to keep the store fully stocked so that shoppers can almost always find what they're looking for. But the manager does not want the shelves too heavily stocked because shelf space is limited and products can spoil. Similar considerations apply to many firms and typically lead them to manage their inventories carefully. However, sales fluctuate. And because firms cannot always accurately predict sales, they often find themselves holding more or less inventories than they had intended. These unintended swings in inventories due to unforeseen changes in sales are called **unplanned inventory investment.** They represent investment spending, positive or negative, that occurred but was unplanned.

So in any given period, **actual investment spending** is equal to planned investment spending plus unplanned inventory investment. If we let $I_{Unplanned}$ represent unplanned inventory investment, $I_{Planned}$ represent planned investment spending, and I represent actual investment spending, then the relationship among all three can be represented as:

(27-10) $I = I_{Unplanned} + I_{Planned}$

To see how unplanned inventory investment can occur, let's continue to focus on the auto industry and make the following assumptions. First, let's assume that the industry must determine each month's production volume in advance, before it knows the volume of actual sales. Second, let's assume that it anticipates selling 800,000 cars next month and that it plans neither to add to nor subtract from existing inventories. In that case, it will produce 800,000 cars to match anticipated sales.

Now imagine that next month's actual sales are less than expected, only 700,000 cars. As a result, the value of 100,000 cars will be added to investment spending as unplanned inventory investment.

The auto industry will, of course, eventually adjust to this slowdown in sales and the resulting unplanned inventory investment. It is likely that it will cut next month's production volume in order to reduce inventories. In fact, economists who study macroeconomic variables in an attempt to determine the future path of the economy pay careful attention to changes in inventory levels. Rising inventories typically indicate positive unplanned inventory investment and

In 2008, vehicles sat unsold on car dealership lots when the economy slumped and consumer spending plunged.

Fabrizio Costantini/The New York Times/Redux

a slowing economy, as sales are less than had been forecast. Falling inventories typically indicate negative unplanned inventory investment and a growing economy, as sales are greater than forecast. In the next section, we will see how production adjustments in response to fluctuations in sales and inventories ensure that the value of final goods and services actually produced is equal to desired purchases of those final goods and services.

➤ECONOMICS IN ACTION

Interest Rates and the U.S. Housing Boom

The housing boom in the Ft. Myers metropolitan area, described at the beginning of this chapter, was part of a broader housing boom in the country as a whole. There is little question that this housing boom was caused, in the first instance, by low interest rates.

Figure 27-7 shows the interest rate on 30-year home mortgages—the traditional way to borrow money for a home purchase—and the number of housing starts, the number of homes for which construction is started per month, from 1995 to the middle of 2008, in the United States. Panel (a), which shows the mortgage rate, gives you an idea of how much interest rates fell. In the second half of the 1990s, mortgage rates generally fluctuated between 7% and 8%; by 2003, they were down to between 5% and 6%. These lower rates were largely the result of Federal Reserve policy: the Fed cut rates in response to the 2001 recession and continued cutting them into 2003 out of concern that the economy's recovery was too weak to generate sustained job growth.

The low interest rates led to a large increase in residential investment spending, reflected in a surge of housing starts, shown in panel (b). This rise in investment spending drove an overall economic expansion, both through its direct effects and through the multiplier process.

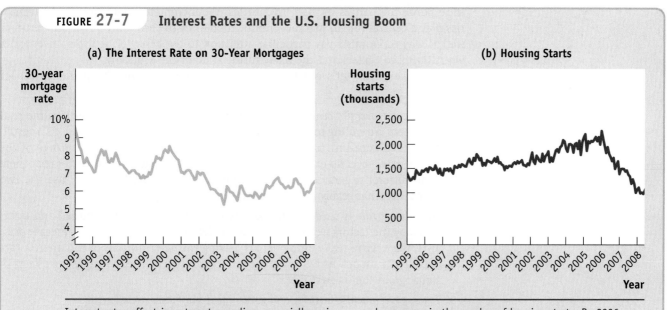

FIGURE 27-7 Interest Rates and the U.S. Housing Boom

Interest rates affect investment spending, especially residential construction spending. Panel (a) shows the interest rate on 30-year mortgages, the standard way of paying for a home purchase. That interest rate fell from about 7.5% in the late 1990s to 5.5% in 2003. Panel (b) shows the result: a huge surge in the number of housing starts. By 2006, however, it became clear that the U.S. housing market was experiencing a bubble, and starts began to fall.

Source: Federal Reserve Bank of St. Louis.

Unfortunately, the housing boom eventually turned into too much of a good thing. By 2006, it was clear that the U.S. housing market was experiencing a bubble: people were buying housing based on unrealistic expectations about future price increases. When the bubble burst, housing—and the U.S. economy—took a fall. ▲

‹ ‹ ‹ ‹ ‹ ‹ ‹ ‹ ‹ ‹ ‹ ‹

▸ CHECK YOUR UNDERSTANDING 27-3

1. For each event, explain whether planned investment spending or unplanned inventory investment will change and in what direction.
   a. An unexpected increase in consumer spending
   b. A sharp rise in the cost of business borrowing
   c. A sharp increase in the economy's growth rate of real GDP
   d. An unanticipated fall in sales

2. Historically, investment spending has experienced more extreme upward and downward swings than consumer spending. Why do you think this is so? (*Hint:* Consider the marginal propensity to consume and the accelerator principle.)

3. Consumer spending was sluggish in late 2007, and economists worried that an *inventory overhang*—a high level of unplanned inventory investment throughout the economy—would make it difficult for the economy to recover anytime soon. Explain why an inventory overhang might, like the existence of too much production capacity, depress current economic activity.

Solutions appear at back of book.

The Income–Expenditure Model

Earlier in this chapter, we described how autonomous changes in spending—such as a fall in investment spending when a housing bubble bursts—lead to a multistage process through the actions of the multiplier that magnifies the effect of these changes on real GDP. In this section, we will examine this multistage process more closely. We'll see that the multiple rounds of changes in real GDP are accomplished through changes in the amount of output produced by firms—changes that they make in response to changes in their inventories. We'll come to understand why inventories play a central role in macroeconomic models of the economy in the short run as well as why economists pay particular attention to the behavior of firms' inventories when trying to understand the likely future state of the economy.

Before we begin, let's quickly recap the assumptions underlying the multiplier process.

1. *Changes in overall spending lead to changes in aggregate output.* We assume that producers are willing to supply additional output at a fixed price level. As a result, changes in spending translate into changes in output rather than moves of the overall price level up or down. A fixed aggregate price level also implies that there is no difference between nominal GDP and real GDP. So we can use the two terms interchangeably in this chapter.

2. *The interest rate is fixed.* We'll take the interest rate as predetermined and unaffected by the factors we analyze in the model. As in the case of the aggregate price level, what we're really doing here is leaving the determinants of the interest rate outside the model. As we'll see, the model can still be used to study the effects of a change in the interest rate.

3. *Taxes, government transfers, and government purchases are all zero.*

4. *Exports and imports are both zero.*

In all subsequent chapters, we will drop the assumption that the aggregate price level is fixed. The Chapter 29 appendix addresses how taxes affect the multiplier process. We'll explain how the interest rate is determined in Chapter 31 and bring foreign trade back into the picture in Chapter 34.

Planned Aggregate Spending and Real GDP

In an economy with no government and no foreign trade, there are only two sources of aggregate spending: consumer spending, C, and investment spending, I. And since we assume that there are no taxes or transfers, aggregate disposable income is equal to GDP (which, since the aggregate price level is fixed, is the same as real GDP): the total value of final sales of goods and services ultimately accrues to households as income. So in this highly simplified economy, there are two basic equations of national income accounting:

(27-11) $GDP = C + I$

(27-12) $YD = GDP$

As we learned earlier in this chapter, the aggregate consumption function shows the relationship between disposable income and consumer spending. Let's continue to assume that the aggregate consumption function is of the same form as in Equation 27-9:

(27-13) $C = A + MPC \times YD$

In our simplified model, we will also assume planned investment spending, $I_{Planned}$, is fixed.

We need one more concept before putting the model together: **planned aggregate spending,** the total amount of planned spending in the economy. Unlike firms, households don't take unintended actions like unplanned inventory investment. So planned aggregate spending is equal to the sum of consumer spending and planned investment spending. We denote planned aggregate spending by $AE_{Planned}$, so:

(27-14) $AE_{Planned} = C + I_{Planned}$

The level of planned aggregate spending in a given year depends on the level of real GDP in that year. To see why, let's look at a specific example, shown in Table 27-3. We assume that the aggregate consumption function is:

(27-15) $C = 300 + 0.6 \times YD$

Real GDP, YD, C, $I_{Planned}$, and $AE_{Planned}$ are all measured in billions of dollars, and we assume that the level of planned investment, $I_{Planned}$, is fixed at $500 billion per year. The first column shows possible levels of real GDP. The second column shows disposable income, YD, which in our simplified model is equal to real GDP. The third column shows consumer spending, C, equal to $300 billion plus 0.6 times disposable income, YD. The fourth column shows planned investment spending, $I_{Planned}$, which we have assumed is $500 billion regardless of the level of real GDP. Finally, the last column shows planned aggregate spending, $AE_{Planned}$, the sum of aggregate consumer spending, C, and planned investment spending, $I_{Planned}$. (To economize on notation, we'll assume that it is understood from now on that all the variables in Table 27-3 are measured in billions of dollars per year.) As you can see, a higher level of real GDP leads to a higher level of disposable income: every 500 increase in real GDP raises YD by 500, which in turn raises C by $500 \times 0.6 = 300$ and $AE_{Planned}$ by 300.

Figure 27-8 on the next page illustrates the information in Table 27-3 graphically. Real GDP is measured on the horizontal axis. CF is the aggregate consumption function; it shows how consumer spending depends on real GDP. $AE_{Planned}$, the planned aggregate spending line, corresponds to the aggregate consumption function shifted up by 500 (the amount of $I_{Planned}$).

Planned aggregate spending is the total amount of planned spending in the economy.

TABLE 27-3

Real GDP	YD	C	$I_{Planned}$	$AE_{Planned}$
(billions of dollars)				
$0	$0	$300	$500	$800
500	500	600	500	1,100
1,000	1,000	900	500	1,400
1,500	1,500	1,200	500	1,700
2,000	2,000	1,500	500	2,000
2,500	2,500	1,800	500	2,300
3,000	3,000	2,100	500	2,600
3,500	3,500	2,400	500	2,900

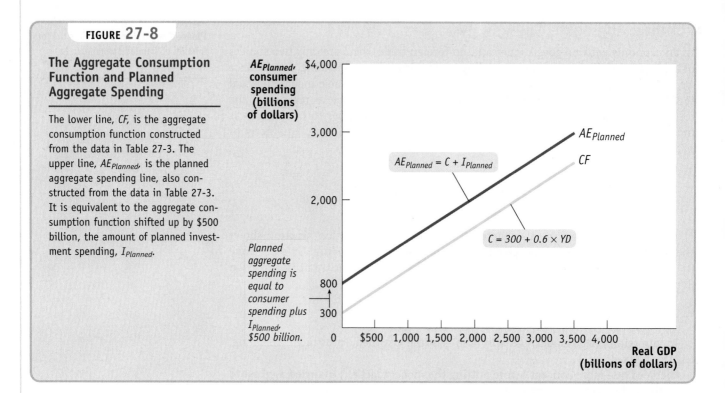

FIGURE 27-8

The Aggregate Consumption Function and Planned Aggregate Spending

The lower line, *CF*, is the aggregate consumption function constructed from the data in Table 27-3. The upper line, $AE_{Planned}$, is the planned aggregate spending line, also constructed from the data in Table 27-3. It is equivalent to the aggregate consumption function shifted up by $500 billion, the amount of planned investment spending, $I_{Planned}$.

It shows how planned aggregate spending depends on real GDP. Both lines have a slope of 0.6, equal to *MPC*, the marginal propensity to consume.

But this isn't the end of the story. Table 27-3 reveals that real GDP equals planned aggregate spending, $AE_{Planned}$, only when the level of real GDP is at 2,000. Real GDP does not equal $AE_{Planned}$ at any other level. Is that possible? Didn't we learn in Chapter 23, with the circular-flow diagram, that total spending on final goods and services in the economy is equal to the total value of output of final goods and services? The answer is that for *brief* periods of time, planned aggregate spending can differ from real GDP because of the role of *unplanned* aggregate spending—$I_{Unplanned}$, unplanned inventory investment. But as we'll see in the next section, the economy moves over time to a situation in which there is no unplanned inventory investment, a situation called *income–expenditure equilibrium*. And when the economy is in income–expenditure equilibrium, planned aggregate spending on final goods and services equals aggregate output.

Income–Expenditure Equilibrium

TABLE 27-4

Real GDP	$AE_{Planned}$	$I_{Unplanned}$
(billions of dollars)		
$0	$800	−$800
500	1,100	−600
1,000	1,400	−400
1,500	1,700	−200
2,000	2,000	0
2,500	2,300	200
3,000	2,600	400
3,500	2,900	600

For all but one value of real GDP shown in Table 27-3, real GDP is either more or less than $AE_{Planned}$, the sum of consumer spending and *planned* investment spending. For example, when real GDP is 1,000, consumer spending, *C*, is 900 and planned investment spending is 500, making planned aggregate spending 1,400. This is 400 *more* than the corresponding level of real GDP. Now consider what happens when real GDP is 2,500; consumer spending, *C*, is 1,800 and planned investment spending is 500, making planned aggregate spending only 2,300, 200 *less* than real GDP.

As we've just explained, planned aggregate spending can be different from real GDP only if there is unplanned inventory investment, $I_{Unplanned}$, in the economy. Let's examine Table 27-4, which includes the numbers for real GDP and for planned aggregate spending from Table 27-3. It also includes the levels of unplanned inventory investment, $I_{Unplanned}$, that each combination of real GDP and planned aggregate spending implies. For example, if real GDP is 2,500, planned aggregate spending is only 2,300. This 200 excess of real GDP over $AE_{Planned}$ must consist of positive unplanned inventory investment. This can happen only if firms have overestimated sales and produced too much, leading to unintended additions to inventories. More generally, any level of real GDP in excess of 2,000 corresponds to a situation in which firms are producing more than consumers and other firms want to purchase, creating an unintended increase in inventories.

Conversely, a level of real GDP below 2,000 implies that planned aggregate spending is *greater* than real GDP. For example, when real GDP is 1,000, planned aggregate spending is much larger, at 1,400. The 400 excess of $AE_{Planned}$ over real GDP corresponds to negative unplanned inventory investment equal to −400. More generally, any level of real GDP below 2,000 implies that firms have underestimated sales, leading to a negative level of unplanned inventory investment in the economy.

By putting together Equations 27-10, 27-11, and 27-14, we can summarize the general relationships between real GDP, planned aggregate spending, and unplanned inventory investment as follows:

(27-16) $GDP = C + I$
$$= C + I_{Planned} + I_{Unplanned}$$
$$= AE_{Planned} + I_{Unplanned}$$

> The economy is in **income–expenditure equilibrium** when aggregate output, measured by real GDP, is equal to planned aggregate spending.
>
> **Income–expenditure equilibrium GDP** is the level of real GDP at which real GDP equals planned aggregate spending.

So whenever real GDP exceeds $AE_{Planned}$, $I_{Unplanned}$ is positive; whenever real GDP is less than $AE_{Planned}$, $I_{Unplanned}$ is negative.

But firms will act to correct their mistakes. We've assumed that they don't change their prices, but they *can* adjust their output. Specifically, they will reduce production if they have experienced an unintended rise in inventories or increase production if they have experienced an unintended fall in inventories. And these responses will eventually eliminate the unanticipated changes in inventories and move the economy to a point at which real GDP is equal to planned aggregate spending. Staying with our example, if real GDP is 1,000, negative unplanned inventory investment will lead firms to increase production, leading to a rise in real GDP. In fact, this will happen whenever real GDP is less than 2,000—that is, whenever real GDP is less than planned aggregate spending. Conversely, if real GDP is 2,500, positive unplanned inventory investment will lead firms to reduce production, leading to a fall in real GDP. This will happen whenever real GDP is greater than planned aggregate spending.

The only situation in which firms won't have an incentive to change output in the next period is when aggregate output, measured by real GDP, is equal to planned aggregate spending in the current period, an outcome known as **income–expenditure equilibrium.** In Table 27-4, income–expenditure equilibrium is achieved when real GDP is 2,000, the only level of real GDP at which unplanned inventory investment is zero. From now on, we'll denote the real GDP level at which income–expenditure equilibrium occurs as Y* and call it the **income-expenditure equilibrium GDP.**

Figure 27-9 on the next page illustrates the concept of income-expenditure equilibrium graphically. Real GDP is on the horizontal axis and planned aggregate spending, $AE_{Planned}$, is on the vertical axis. There are two lines in the figure. The solid line is the planned aggregate spending line. It shows how $AE_{Planned}$, equal to $C + I_{Planned}$, depends on real GDP; it has a slope of 0.6, equal to the marginal propensity to consume, *MPC*, and a vertical intercept equal to $A + I_{Planned}$ (300 + 500 = 800). The dashed line, which goes through the origin with a slope of 1 (often called a 45-degree line), shows all the possible points at which planned aggregate spending is equal to real GDP. This line allows us to easily spot the point of income-expenditure equilibrium, which must lie on both the 45-degree line and the planned aggregate spending line. So the point of income-expenditure equilibrium is at *E*, where the two lines cross. And the income-expenditure equilibrium GDP, Y*, is 2,000—the same outcome we derived in Table 27-4.

Now consider what happens if the economy isn't in income-expenditure equilibrium. We can see from Figure 27-9 that whenever real GDP is less than Y*, the

Income–Expenditure Equilibrium

Income–expenditure equilibrium occurs at E, the point where the planned aggregate spending line, $AE_{Planned}$, crosses the 45-degree line. At E, the economy produces real GDP of $2,000 billion per year, the only point at which real GDP equals planned aggregate spending, $AE_{Planned}$, and unplanned inventory investment, $I_{Unplanned}$, is zero. This is the level of income–expenditure equilibrium GDP, Y^*. At any level of real GDP less than Y^*, $AE_{Planned}$ exceeds real GDP. As a result, unplanned inventory investment, $I_{Unplanned}$, is negative and firms respond by increasing production. At any level of real GDP greater than Y^*, real GDP exceeds $AE_{Planned}$. Unplanned inventory investment, $I_{Unplanned}$, is positive and firms respond by reducing production.

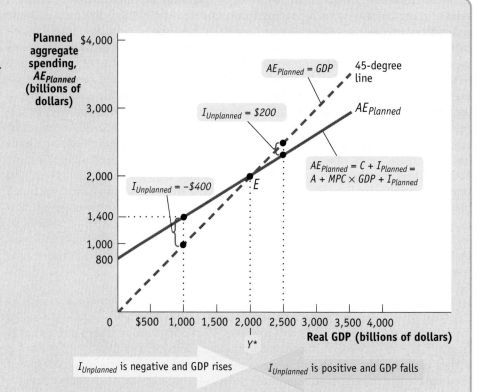

planned aggregate spending line lies above the 45-degree line and $AE_{Planned}$ exceeds real GDP. In this situation, $I_{Unplanned}$ is negative: as shown in the figure, at a real GDP of 1,000, $I_{Unplanned}$ is −400. As a consequence, real GDP will rise. In contrast, whenever real GDP is greater than Y^*, the planned aggregate expenditure line lies below the 45-degree line. Here, $I_{Unplanned}$ is positive: as shown, at a real GDP of 2,500, $I_{Unplanned}$ is 200. The unanticipated accumulation of inventory leads to a fall in real GDP.

The type of diagram shown in Figure 27-9, which identifies income–expenditure equilibrium as the point at which the planned aggregate spending line crosses the 45-degree line, has a special place in the history of economic thought. Known as the **Keynesian cross,** it was developed by Paul Samuelson, one of the greatest economists of the twentieth century (as well as a Nobel Prize winner), to explain the ideas of John Maynard Keynes, the founder of macroeconomics as we know it.

The Multiplier Process and Inventory Adjustment

We've just learned about a very important feature of the macroeconomy: when planned spending by households and firms does not equal the current aggregate output by firms, this difference shows up in changes in inventories. The response of firms to those inventory changes moves real GDP over time to the point at which real GDP and planned aggregate spending are equal. That's why, as we mentioned earlier, changes in inventories are considered a leading indicator of future economic activity.

Now that we understand how real GDP moves to achieve income–expenditure equilibrium for a given level of planned aggregate spending, let's turn to understanding what happens when there is *a shift of the planned aggregate spending line.* How does

The **Keynesian cross** diagram identifies income–expenditure equilibrium as the point where the planned aggregate spending line crosses the 45-degree line.

the economy move from the initial point of income-expenditure equilibrium to a new point of income-expenditure equilibrium? And what are the possible sources of changes in planned aggregate spending?

In our simple model there are only two possible sources of a shift of the planned aggregate spending line: a change in planned investment spending, $I_{Planned}$, or a shift of the aggregate consumption function, CF. For example, a change in $I_{Planned}$ can occur because of a change in the interest rate. (Remember, we're assuming that the interest rate is fixed by factors that are outside the model. But we can still ask what happens when the interest rate changes.) A shift of the aggregate consumption function (that is, a change in its vertical intercept, A) can occur because of a change in aggregate wealth—say, due to a rise in house prices. When the planned aggregate spending line shifts—when there is a change in the level of planned aggregate spending at any given level of real GDP—there is an autonomous change in planned aggregate spending. Recall from earlier in this chapter that an autonomous change in planned aggregate spending is a change in the desired level of spending by firms, households, and government at any given level of real GDP (although we've assumed away the government for the time being). How does an autonomous change in planned aggregate spending affect real GDP in income-expenditure equilibrium?

Table 27-5 and Figure 27-10 on the next page start from the same numerical example we used in Table 27-4 and Figure 27-9. They also show the effect of an autonomous increase in planned aggregate spending of 400—what happens when planned aggregate spending is 400 higher at each level of real GDP. Look first at Table 27-5. Before the autonomous increase in planned aggregate spending, the level of real GDP at which planned aggregate spending is equal to real GDP, Y^*, is 2,000. After the autonomous change, Y^* has risen to 3,000. The same result is visible in Figure 27-10. The initial income-expenditure equilibrium is at E_1, where Y_1^* is 2,000. The autonomous rise in planned aggregate spending shifts the planned aggregate spending line up, leading to a new income-expenditure equilibrium at E_2, where Y_2^* is 3,000.

The fact that the rise in income-expenditure equilibrium GDP, from 2,000 to 3,000, is much larger than the autonomous increase in aggregate spending, which is only 400, has a familiar explanation: the multiplier process. In the specific example we have just described, an autonomous increase in planned aggregate spending of 400 leads to an increase in Y^* from 2,000 to 3,000, a rise of 1,000. So the multiplier in this example is $1,000/400 = 2.5$.

TABLE 27-5

Real GDP	$AE_{Planned}$ before autonomous change	$AE_{Planned}$ after autonomous change
	(billions of dollars)	
$0	$800	$1,200
500	1,100	1,500
1,000	1,400	1,800
1,500	1,700	2,100
2,000	2,000	2,400
2,500	2,300	2,700
3,000	2,600	3,000
3,500	2,900	3,300
4,000	3,200	3,600

FIGURE 27-10

The Multiplier

This figure illustrates the change in Y^* caused by an autonomous increase in planned aggregate spending. The economy is initially at equilibrium point E_1 with an income–expenditure equilibrium GDP, Y_1^*, equal to 2,000. An autonomous increase in $AE_{Planned}$ of 400 shifts the planned aggregate spending line upward by 400. The economy is no longer in income–expenditure equilibrium: real GDP is equal to 2,000 but $AE_{Planned}$ is now 2,400, represented by point X. The vertical distance between the two planned aggregate spending lines, equal to 400, represents $I_{Unplanned} = -400$—the negative inventory investment that the economy now experiences. Firms respond by increasing production, and the economy eventually reaches a new income–expenditure equilibrium at E_2 with a higher level of income–expenditure equilibrium GDP, Y_2^*, equal to 3,000.

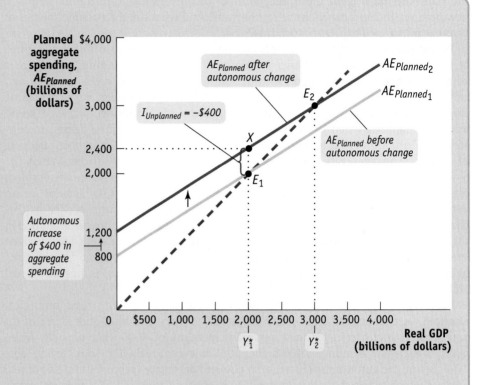

We can examine in detail what underlies the multistage multiplier process by looking more closely at Figure 27-10. First, starting from E_1, the autonomous increase in planned aggregate spending leads to a gap between planned aggregate spending and real GDP. This is represented by the vertical distance between X, at 2,400, and E_1, at 2,000. This gap illustrates an unplanned fall in inventory investment: $I_{Unplanned} = -400$. Firms respond by increasing production, leading to a rise in real GDP from Y_1^*. The rise in real GDP translates into an increase in disposable income, YD. That's the first stage in the chain reaction. But it doesn't stop there— the increase in YD leads to a rise in consumer spending, C, which sets off a second-round rise in real GDP. This in turn leads to a further rise in disposable income and consumer spending, and so on. And we could play this process in reverse: an autonomous fall in aggregate spending will lead to a chain reaction of reductions in real GDP and consumer spending.

We can summarize these results in an equation, where $\Delta AAE_{Planned}$ represents the autonomous change in $AE_{Planned}$, and $\Delta Y^* = Y_2^* - Y_1^*$, the subsequent change in income–expenditure equilibrium GDP:

(27-17) $\Delta Y^* = \text{Multiplier} \times \Delta AAE_{Planned} = \dfrac{1}{1 - MPC} \times \Delta AAE_{Planned}$

Recalling that the multiplier, $1/(1 - MPC)$, is greater than 1, Equation 27-17 tells us that the change in income–expenditure equilibrium GDP, ΔY^*, is several times as large as the autonomous change in planned aggregate spending, $\Delta AAE_{Planned}$. It also helps us recall an important point: because the marginal propensity to consume is less than 1, each increase in disposable income and each corresponding increase in consumer spending is smaller than in the previous round. That's because at each round some of the increase in disposable income leaks out into savings. As a result, although real GDP grows at each round, the increase in real GDP diminishes from each round to the next. At some point the increase in real GDP is negligible, and the economy converges to a new income–expenditure equilibrium GDP at Y_2^*.

The Paradox of Thrift You may recall that in Chapter 22 we mentioned the paradox of thrift to illustrate the fact that in macroeconomics the outcome of many individual actions can generate a result that is different from and worse than the simple sum of those individual actions. In the paradox of thrift, households and firms cut their spending in anticipation of future tough economic times. These actions depress the economy, leaving households and firms worse off than if they hadn't acted virtuously to prepare for tough times. It is called a paradox because what's usually "good" (saving to provide for your family in hard times) is "bad" (because it can make everyone worse off).

Using the multiplier, we can now see exactly how this scenario unfolds. Suppose that there is a slump in consumer spending or investment spending, or both, which causes a fall in income–expenditure equilibrium GDP that is several times larger than the original fall in spending. The fall in real GDP leaves consumers and producers worse off than they would have been if they hadn't cut their spending. Conversely, prodigal behavior is rewarded: if consumers or producers increase their spending, the resulting multiplier process makes the increase in income–expenditure equilibrium GDP several times larger than the original increase in spending. So prodigal spending makes consumers and producers better off than if they had been cautious spenders.

It's important to realize that our result that the multiplier is equal to $1/(1 - MPC)$ depends on the simplifying assumption that there are no taxes or transfers, so that disposable income is equal to real GDP. In the appendix to Chapter 29, we'll bring taxes into the picture, which makes the expression for the multiplier more complicated and the multiplier itself smaller. But the general principle we have just learned—an autonomous change in planned aggregate spending leads to a change in income–expenditure equilibrium GDP, both directly and through an induced change in consumer spending—remains valid.

As we noted earlier in this chapter, declines in planned investment spending are usually the major factor causing recessions, because historically they have been the most common source of autonomous reductions in aggregate spending. The tendency of the consumption function to shift upward over time, which we pointed out earlier in Economics in Action, "Famous First Forecasting Failures," means that autonomous changes in both planned investment spending and consumer spending play important roles in expansions. But regardless of the source, there are multiplier effects in the economy that magnify the size of the initial change in aggregate spending.

►*ECONOMICS IN ACTION*

Inventories and the End of a Recession

A very clear example of the role of inventories in the multiplier process took place in late 2001, as that year's recession came to an end. The driving force behind the recession was a slump in business investment spending. It took several years before investment spending bounced back in the form of a housing boom. Still, the economy did start to recover in late 2001, largely because of an increase in consumer spending—especially on durable goods such as automobiles.

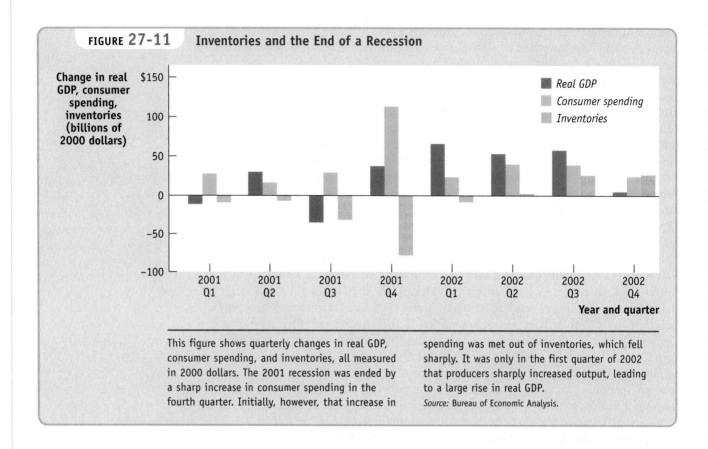

FIGURE 27-11 Inventories and the End of a Recession

Change in real GDP, consumer spending, inventories (billions of 2000 dollars)

This figure shows quarterly changes in real GDP, consumer spending, and inventories, all measured in 2000 dollars. The 2001 recession was ended by a sharp increase in consumer spending in the fourth quarter. Initially, however, that increase in spending was met out of inventories, which fell sharply. It was only in the first quarter of 2002 that producers sharply increased output, leading to a large rise in real GDP.

Source: Bureau of Economic Analysis.

Initially, this increase in consumer spending caught manufacturers by surprise. Figure 27-11 shows changes in real GDP, real consumer spending, and real inventories in each quarter of 2001 and 2002. Notice the surge in consumer spending in the fourth quarter of 2001. It didn't lead to a lot of GDP growth because it was offset by a plunge in inventories. But in the first quarter of 2002 producers greatly increased their production, leading to a jump in real GDP. ▲

< < < < < < < < < < < <

➤ CHECK YOUR UNDERSTANDING 27-4

1. Although economists believe that recessions typically begin as slumps in investment spending, they also believe that consumer spending eventually slumps during a recession. Explain why.

2. a. Use a diagram like Figure 27-10 to show what happens when there is an autonomous fall in planned aggregate spending. Describe how the economy adjusts to a new income–expenditure equilibrium.

   b. Suppose Y^* is originally $500 billion, the autonomous reduction in planned aggregate spending is $300 million ($0.3 billion), and $MPC = 0.5$. Calculate Y^* after such a change.

Solutions appear at back of book.

[►► A LOOK AHEAD •••

In this chapter we studied the inventory adjustment process that underlies the multiplier. But we used a very simplified model that leaves out many important issues. In particular, we took prices as given. In the next chapter we develop a more complete model, the *AD-AS model,* that shows how the aggregate price level and the level of real GDP are simultaneously determined. As we'll see, the *AD-AS* model is at the heart of modern macroeconomics.]

SUMMARY

1. An **autonomous change in aggregate spending** leads to a chain reaction in which the total change in real GDP is equal to the **multiplier** times the initial change in aggregate spending. The size of the multiplier, $1/(1 - MPC)$, depends on the **marginal propensity to consume, MPC,** the fraction of an additional dollar of disposable income spent on consumption. The larger the MPC, the larger the multiplier and the larger the change in real GDP for any given autonomous change in aggregate spending. The **marginal propensity to save, MPS,** is equal to $1 - MPC$.

2. The **consumption function** shows how an individual household's consumer spending is determined by its current disposable income. The **aggregate consumption function** shows the relationship for the entire economy. According to the life-cycle hypothesis, households try to smooth their consumption over their lifetimes. As a result, the aggregate consumption function shifts in response to changes in expected future disposable income and changes in aggregate wealth.

3. **Planned investment spending** depends negatively on the interest rate and on existing production capacity; it depends positively on expected future real GDP. The **accelerator principle** says that investment spending is greatly influenced by the expected growth rate of real GDP.

4. Firms hold **inventories** of goods so that they can satisfy consumer demand quickly. **Inventory investment** is positive when firms add to their inventories, negative when they reduce them. Often, however, changes in inventories are not a deliberate decision but the result of mistakes in forecasts about sales. The result is **unplanned inventory investment,** which can be either positive or negative. **Actual investment spending** is the sum of planned investment spending and unplanned inventory investment.

5. In **income–expenditure equilibrium, planned aggregate spending,** which in a simplified model with no government and no trade is the sum of consumer spending and planned investment spending, is equal to real GDP. At the **income–expenditure equilibrium GDP,** or Y^*, unplanned inventory investment is zero. When planned aggregate spending is larger than Y^*, unplanned inventory investment is negative; there is an unanticipated reduction in inventories and firms increase production. When planned aggregate spending is less than Y^*, unplanned inventory investment is positive; there is an unanticipated increase in inventories and firms reduce production. The **Keynesian cross** shows how the economy self-adjusts to income–expenditure equilibrium through inventory adjustments.

6. After an autonomous change in planned aggregate spending, the inventory adjustment process moves the economy to a new income-expenditure equilibrium. The change in income-expenditure equilibrium GDP arising from an autonomous change in spending is equal to $(1/(1 - MPC)) \times \Delta AAE_{Planned}$.

KEY TERMS

Marginal propensity to consume (*MPC*), p. 705
Marginal propensity to save (*MPS*), p. 705
Autonomous change in aggregate spending, p. 706
Multiplier, p. 706
Consumption function, p. 708

Aggregate consumption function, p. 710
Planned investment spending, p. 714
Accelerator principle, p. 715
Inventories, p. 716
Inventory investment, p. 716
Unplanned inventory investment, p. 716

Actual investment spending, p. 716
Planned aggregate spending, p. 719
Income–expenditure equilibrium, p. 721
Income–expenditure equilibrium GDP, p. 721
Keynesian cross, p. 722

PROBLEMS

1. Due to an increase in consumer wealth, there is a $40 billion autonomous increase in consumer spending in the economies of Westlandia and Eastlandia. Assuming that the aggregate price level is constant, the interest rate is fixed in both countries, and there are no taxes and no foreign trade, complete the accompanying tables to show the various rounds of increased spending that will occur in both economies if the marginal propensity to consume is 0.5 in Westlandia and 0.75 in Eastlandia. What do your results indicate about the relationship between the size of the marginal propensity to consume and the multiplier?

	Westlandia	
Rounds	**Incremental change in GDP**	**Total change in GDP**
1	$\Delta C = \$40$ billion	?
2	$MPC \times \Delta C =$?	?
3	$MPC \times MPC \times \Delta C =$?	?
4	$MPC \times MPC \times MPC \times \Delta C =$?	?
. . .	. . .	. . .
Total change in GDP	$(1/(1 - MPC)) \times \Delta C =$?	

Rounds	Eastlandia		Total change in GDP
	Incremental change in GDP		
1	$\Delta C = \$40$ billion		?
2	$MPC \times \Delta C =$	?	?
3	$MPC \times MPC \times \Delta C =$	?	?
4	$MPC \times MPC \times MPC \times \Delta C =$	?	?
. . .	. . .	. . .	
Total change in GDP	$(1/(1 - MPC)) \times \Delta C =$		?

2. Assuming that the aggregate price level is constant, the interest rate is fixed, and there are no taxes and no foreign trade, what will be the change in GDP if the following events occur?

   a. There is an autonomous increase in consumer spending of $25 billion; the marginal propensity to consume is 2/3.

   b. Firms reduce investment spending by $40 billion; the marginal propensity to consume is 0.8.

   c. The government increases its purchases of military equipment by $60 billion; the marginal propensity to consume is 0.6.

3. Economists observed the only five residents of a very small economy and estimated each one's consumer spending at various levels of current disposable income. The accompanying table shows each resident's consumer spending at three income levels.

Individual consumer spending by	Individual current disposable income		
	$0	$20,000	$40,000
Andre	1,000	$15,000	29,000
Barbara	2,500	12,500	22,500
Casey	2,000	20,000	38,000
Declan	5,000	17,000	29,000
Elena	4,000	19,000	34,000

   a. What is each resident's consumption function? What is the marginal propensity to consume for each resident?

   b. What is the economy's aggregate consumption function? What is the marginal propensity to consume for the economy?

4. From 2003 to 2008, Eastlandia experienced large fluctuations in both aggregate consumer spending and disposable income, but wealth, the interest rate, and expected future disposable income did not change. The accompanying table shows the level of aggregate consumer spending and disposable income in millions of dollars for each of these years. Use this information to answer the following questions.

Year	Disposable income (millions of dollars)	Consumer spending (millions of dollars)
2003	$100	$180
2004	350	380
2005	300	340
2006	400	420
2007	375	400
2008	500	500

   a. Plot the aggregate consumption function for Eastlandia.

   b. What is the marginal propensity to consume? What is the marginal propensity to save?

   c. What is the aggregate consumption function?

5. The Bureau of Economic Analysis reported that overall consumer spending decreased by $102.8 billion during October of 2008.

   a. If the marginal propensity to consume is 0.56, by how much will real GDP change in response?

   b. If there are no other changes to autonomous spending other than the decline in consumer spending in part (a), and unplanned inventory investment, $I_{Unplanned}$, increased by $100 billion, what is the change in real GDP?

   c. GDP at the end of September 2008 was $14,420.5 billion. If GDP were to drop by the amount calculated in part (b), what would be the percent fall in GDP?

6. From the end of 1995 to March 2000, the Standard and Poor's 500 (S&P 500) stock index, a broad measure of stock market prices, rose almost 150%, from 615.93 to a high of 1,527.46. From that time to September 10, 2001, the index fell 28.5% to 1,092.54. How do you think the movements in the stock index influenced both the growth in real GDP in the late 1990s and the concern about maintaining consumer spending after the terrorist attacks on September 11, 2001?

7. How will planned investment spending change as the following events occur?

   a. The interest rate falls as a result of Federal Reserve policy.

   b. The U.S. Environmental Protection Agency decrees that corporations must upgrade or replace their machinery in order to reduce their emissions of sulfur dioxide.

   c. Baby boomers begin to retire in large numbers and reduce their savings, resulting in higher interest rates

8. Explain how each of the following actions will affect the level of planned investment spending and unplanned inventory investment. Assume the economy is initially in income–expenditure equilibrium.

   a. The Federal Reserve raises the interest rate.

   b. There is a rise in the expected growth rate of real GDP.

   c. A sizable inflow of foreign funds into the country lowers the interest rate.

9. a. The accompanying table shows gross domestic product (GDP), disposable income (YD), consumer spending (C), and planned investment spending ($I_{Planned}$) in an economy. Assume there is no government or foreign sector in this economy. Complete the table by calculating planned aggregate spending ($AE_{Planned}$) and unplanned inventory investment ($I_{Unplanned}$).

GDP	YD	C	$I_{Planned}$	$AE_{Planned}$	$I_{Unplanned}$
		(billions of dollars)			
$0	$0	$100	$300	?	?
400	400	400	300	?	?
800	800	700	300	?	?
1,200	1,200	1,000	300	?	?
1,600	1,600	1,300	300	?	?
2,000	2,000	1,600	300	?	?
2,400	2,400	1,900	300	?	?
2,800	2,800	2,200	300	?	?
3,200	3,200	2,500	300	?	?

b. What is the aggregate consumption function?

c. What is Y*, income–expenditure equilibrium GDP?

d. What is the value of the multiplier?

e. If planned investment spending falls to $200 billion, what will be the new Y*?

f. If autonomous consumer spending rises to $200 billion, what will be the new Y*?

10. In an economy with no government and no foreign sectors, autonomous consumer spending is $250 billion, planned investment spending is $350 billion, and the marginal propensity to consume is 2/3.

a. Plot the aggregate consumption function and planned aggregate spending.

b. What is unplanned inventory investment when real GDP equals $600 billion?

c. What is Y*, income–expenditure equilibrium GDP?

d. What is the value of the multiplier?

e. If planned investment spending rises to $450 billion, what will be the new Y*?

11. An economy has a marginal propensity to consume of 0.5, and Y*, income–expenditure equilibrium GDP, equals $500 billion. Given an autonomous increase in planned investment of $10 billion, show the rounds of increased spending that take place by completing the accompanying table. The first and second rows are filled in for you. In the first row, the increase of planned investment spending of $10 billion raises real GDP and YD by $10 billion, leading to an increase in consumer spending of $5 billion (MPC × change in disposable income) in row 2, raising real GDP and YD by a further $5 billion.

Rounds	Change in $I_{Planned}$ or C	Change in real GDP	Change in YD
		(billions of dollars)	
1	$\Delta I_{Planned}$ = $10.00	$10.00	$10.00
2	ΔC = $ 5.00	$ 5.00	$ 5.00
3	ΔC = ?	?	?
4	ΔC = ?	?	?
5	ΔC = ?	?	?
6	ΔC = ?	?	?
7	ΔC = ?	?	?
8	ΔC = ?	?	?
9	ΔC = ?	?	?
10	ΔC = ?	?	?

a. What is the total change in real GDP after the 10 rounds? What is the value of the multiplier? What would you expect the total change in Y* to be based on the multiplier formula? How do your answers to the first and third questions compare?

b. Redo the table starting from round 2, assuming the marginal propensity to consume is 0.75. What is the total change in real GDP after 10 rounds? What is the value of the multiplier? As the marginal propensity to consume increases, what happens to the value of the multiplier?

12. Although the United States is one of the richest nations in the world, it is also the world's largest debtor nation. We often hear that the problem is the nation's low savings rate. Suppose policy makers attempt to rectify this by encouraging greater savings in the economy. What effect will their successful attempts have on real GDP?

13. The United States economy slowed significantly during the beginning of 2008 and policy makers were extremely concerned about growth. To boost the economy, Congress passed an economic relief package that would deliver about $145 billion in direct payments to American families. (The payments were made as rebates to households on their previously paid taxes.) Their objective was to boost the economy by increasing the disposable income of American consumers.

a. Calculate the initial change in aggregate consumer spending as a consequence of this policy measure if the marginal propensity to consume (MPC) in the United States is 0.7. Then calculate the resulting change in real GDP arising from the $145 billion in payments.

b. Illustrate the effect on real GDP with the use of a graph depicting the income-expenditure equilibrium. Label the vertical axis "Planned aggregate spending ($AE_{Planned}$)" and the horizontal axis "Real GDP." Draw two planned aggregate expenditure curves ($AE_{Planned1}$ and $AE_{Planned2}$) and a 45-degree line to show the effect of the autonomous policy change on the equilibrium.

Chapter 27 Appendix: Deriving the Multiplier Algebraically

This appendix shows how to derive the multiplier algebraically. First, recall that in this chapter planned aggregate spending, $AE_{Planned}$, is the sum of consumer spending, C, which is determined by the consumption function, and planned investment spending, $I_{Planned}$. That is, $AE_{Planned} = C + I_{Planned}$. Rewriting this equation to express all its terms fully, we have:

(27A-1) $\quad AE_{Planned} = A + MPC \times YD + I_{Planned}$

Because there are no taxes or government transfers in this model, disposable income is equal to GDP, so Equation 27A-1 becomes:

(27A-2) $\quad AE_{Planned} = A + MPC \times GDP + I_{Planned}$

The income–expenditure equilibrium GDP, Y^*, is equal to planned aggregate spending:

(27A-3) $\quad Y^* = AE_{Planned}$
$$= A + MPC \times Y^* + I_{Planned}$$
in income–expenditure equilibrium

Just two more steps. Subtract $MPC \times Y^*$ from both sides of Equation 27A-3:

(27A-4) $\quad Y^* - MPC \times Y^* = Y^* \times (1 - MPC) = A + I_{Planned}$

Finally, divide both sides by $(1 - MPC)$:

(27A-5) $\quad Y^* = \dfrac{A + I_{Planned}}{1 - MPC}$

Equation 27A-5 tells us that a \$1 autonomous change in planned aggregate spending—a change in either A or $I_{Planned}$—causes a $\$1/(1 - MPC)$ change in income–expenditure equilibrium GDP, Y^*. The multiplier in our simple model is therefore:

(27A-6) $\quad$ Multiplier $= 1/(1 - MPC)$

PROBLEMS

1. In an economy without government purchases, transfers, or taxes, and without imports or exports, aggregate autonomous consumer spending is \$500 billion, planned investment spending is \$250 billion, and the marginal propensity to consume is 0.5.

   a. Write the expression for planned aggregate spending as in Equation 27A-1.

   b. Solve for Y^* algebraically.

   c. What is the value of the multiplier?

   d. How will Y^* change if autonomous consumer spending falls to \$450 billion?

2. Complete the following table by calculating the value of the multiplier and identifying the change in Y^* due to the change in autonomous spending. How does the value of the multiplier change with the marginal propensity to consume?

MPC	Value of multiplier	Change in spending	Change in Y*
0.5	?	$\Delta C = +\$50$ million	?
0.6	?	$\Delta I = -\$10$ million	?
0.75	?	$\Delta C = -\$25$ million	?
0.8	?	$\Delta I = +\$20$ million	?
0.9	?	$\Delta C = -\$2.5$ million	?

>> # Aggregate Demand and Aggregate Supply

SHOCKS TO THE SYSTEM

SOMETIMES IT'S NOT EASY BEING BEN.

In 2008 Ben Bernanke, a distinguished former Princeton economics professor, was the chairman of the Federal Reserve—the institution that sets U.S. *monetary policy,* along with regulating the financial sector. The Federal Reserve's job is to help the economy avoid the twin evils of high inflation and high unemployment. It normally does this, loosely speaking, either by pumping cash into the economy to fight unemployment or by pulling cash out of the economy to fight inflation.

When the U.S. economy went into a recession in 2001, the Fed rushed cash into the system. It was an easy choice: unemployment was rising, and inflation was low and falling. In fact, for much of 2002 the Fed was actually worried about the possibility of *deflation.*

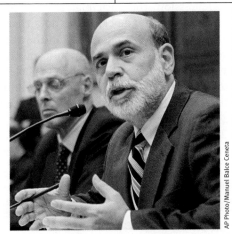

In 2008, *stagflation* made for difficult policy choices for Federal Reserve Chairman Ben Bernanke.

For much of 2008, however, Bernanke faced a much more difficult problem. In fact, he faced the problem people in his position dread most: a combination of unacceptably high inflation and rising unemployment, often referred to as *stagflation.* Stagflation was the scourge of the 1970s: the recessions of 1973–1975 and 1979–1982, the two deepest slumps since the Great Depression, were both accompanied by soaring inflation. And in the first half of 2008, the threat of stagflation seemed to have raised its head yet again.

Why did the economic difficulties of early 2008 look so different from those of 2001? Because the difficulties had a different cause. The lesson of stagflation in the 1970s was that recessions can have different causes and that the appropriate policy response depends on the cause. Many recessions, from the great slump of 1929–1933 to the much milder recession of 2001, have been caused by a fall in investment and consumer spending. In these recessions high inflation isn't a threat. In fact, the 1929–1933 slump was accompanied by a sharp fall in the aggregate price level. And because inflation isn't a problem in such recessions, policy makers unambiguously know what they should do: they should pump cash in, to fight rising unemployment.

The recessions of the 1970s, however, were largely caused by events in the Middle East that led to sharp cuts in world oil production and soaring prices for oil and other fuels. Not coincidentally, soaring oil prices also contributed to the economic difficulties of early 2008. In both periods, high energy prices led to a combination of unemployment and high inflation. They also created a dilemma: should the Fed fight the slump by pumping cash *into* the economy, or should it fight inflation by pulling cash *out* of the economy?

In the previous chapter we developed the *income–expenditure model,* which focuses on the determinants of aggregate spending. This model is extremely useful for understanding events like the recession of 2001 and the recovery that followed. However, the income–expenditure model takes the price level as given,

731

and therefore, it's much less helpful for understanding the problems policy makers faced in 2008.

In this chapter, we'll develop a model that goes beyond the income–expenditure model and shows us how to distinguish between different types of short-run economic fluctuations—*demand shocks*, like those of the Great Depression and the 2001 recession, and *supply shocks*, like those of the 1970s and 2008.

To develop this model, we'll proceed in three steps. First, we'll develop the concept of *aggregate demand*. Then we'll turn to the parallel concept of *aggregate supply*. Finally, we'll put them together in the *AD-AS model*.

WHAT YOU WILL LEARN IN THIS CHAPTER:

➤ How the **aggregate demand curve** illustrates the relationship between the aggregate price level and the quantity of aggregate output demanded in the economy

➤ How the **aggregate supply curve** illustrates the relationship between the aggregate price level and the quantity of aggregate output supplied in the economy

➤ Why the aggregate supply curve is different in the short run compared to the long run

➤ How the *AD–AS* model is used to analyze economic fluctuations

➤ How monetary policy and fiscal policy can stabilize the economy

Aggregate Demand

The Great Depression, the great majority of economists agree, was the result of a massive negative demand shock. What does that mean? In Chapter 3 we explained that when economists talk about a fall in the demand for a particular good or service, they're referring to a leftward shift of the demand curve. Similarly, when economists talk about a negative demand shock to the economy as a whole, they're referring to a leftward shift of the **aggregate demand curve,** a curve that shows the relationship between the aggregate price level and the quantity of aggregate output demanded by households, firms, the government, and the rest of the world.

Figure 28-1 shows what the aggregate demand curve may have looked like in 1933, at the end of the 1929–1933 recession. The horizontal axis shows the total quantity

> The **aggregate demand curve** shows the relationship between the aggregate price level and the quantity of aggregate output demanded by households, businesses, the government, and the rest of the world.

FIGURE 28-1

The Aggregate Demand Curve

The aggregate demand curve shows the relationship between the aggregate price level and the quantity of aggregate output demanded. The curve is downward sloping due to the wealth effect of a change in the aggregate price level and the interest rate effect of a change in the aggregate price level. Corresponding to the actual 1933 data, here the total quantity of goods and services demanded at an aggregate price level of 8.9 is $636 billion in 2000 dollars. According to our hypothetical curve, however, if the aggregate price level had been only 5.0, the quantity of aggregate output demanded would have risen to $950 billion.

A movement down the AD curve leads to a lower aggregate price level and higher aggregate output.

of domestic goods and services demanded, measured in 2000 dollars. We use real GDP to measure aggregate output and will often use the two terms interchangeably. The vertical axis shows the aggregate price level, measured by the GDP deflator. With these variables on the axes, we can draw a curve, *AD*, showing how much aggregate output would have been demanded at any given aggregate price level. Since *AD* is meant to illustrate aggregate demand in 1933, one point on the curve corresponds to actual data for 1933, when the aggregate price level was 8.9 and the total quantity of domestic final goods and services purchased was $636 billion in 2000 dollars.

As drawn in Figure 28-1, the aggregate demand curve is downward sloping, indicating a negative relationship between the aggregate price level and the quantity of aggregate output demanded. A higher aggregate price level, other things equal, reduces the quantity of aggregate output demanded; a lower aggregate price level, other things equal, increases the quantity of aggregate output demanded. According to Figure 28-1, if the price level in 1933 had been 5.0 instead of 8.9, the total quantity of domestic final goods and services demanded would have been $950 billion in 2000 dollars instead of $636 billion.

The first key question about the aggregate demand curve is: why should the curve be downward sloping?

Why Is the Aggregate Demand Curve Downward Sloping?

In Figure 28-1, the curve *AD* is downward sloping. Why? Recall the basic equation of national income accounting:

(28-1) $GDP = C + I + G + X - IM$

where C is consumer spending, I is investment spending, G is government purchases of goods and services, X is exports to other countries, and IM is imports. If we measure these variables in constant dollars—that is, in prices of a base year—then $C + I + G + X - IM$ is the quantity of domestically produced final goods and services demanded during a given period. G is decided by the government, but the other variables are private-sector decisions. To understand why the aggregate demand curve slopes downward, we need to understand why a rise in the aggregate price level reduces C, I, and $X - IM$.

You might think that the downward slope of the aggregate demand curve is a natural consequence of the *law of demand* we defined back in Chapter 3. That is, since the demand curve for any one good is downward sloping, isn't it natural that the demand curve for aggregate output is also downward sloping? This turns out, however, to be a misleading parallel. The demand curve for any individual good shows how the quantity demanded depends on the price of that good, *holding the prices of other goods and services constant*. The main reason the quantity of a good demanded falls when the price of that good rises—that is, the quantity of a good demanded falls as we move up the demand curve—is that people switch their consumption to other goods and services.

But when we consider movements up or down the aggregate demand curve, we're considering *a simultaneous change in the prices of all final goods and services*. Furthermore, changes in the composition of goods and services in consumer spending aren't relevant to the aggregate demand curve: if consumers decide to buy fewer clothes but more cars, this doesn't necessarily change the total quantity of final goods and services they demand.

Why, then, does a rise in the aggregate price level lead to a fall in the quantity of all domestically produced final goods and services demanded? There are two main reasons: the *wealth effect* and the *interest rate effect* of a change in the aggregate price level.

The Wealth Effect An increase in the aggregate price level, other things equal, reduces the purchasing power of many assets. Consider, for example, someone who has $5,000 in a bank account. If the aggregate price level were to rise by 25%, that

The **wealth effect of a change in the aggregate price level** is the effect on consumer spending caused by the effect of a change in the aggregate price level on the purchasing power of consumers' assets.

The **interest rate effect of a change in the aggregate price level** is the effect on consumer spending and investment spending caused by the effect of a change in the aggregate price level on the purchasing power of consumers' and firms' money holdings.

$5,000 would buy only as much as $4,000 would have bought previously. With the loss in purchasing power, the owner of that bank account would probably scale back his or her consumption plans. Millions of other people would respond the same way, leading to a fall in spending on final goods and services, because a rise in the aggregate price level reduces the purchasing power of everyone's bank account. Correspondingly, a fall in the aggregate price level increases the purchasing power of consumers' assets and leads to more consumer demand. The **wealth effect of a change in the aggregate price level** is the effect on consumer spending caused by the effect of a change in the aggregate price level on the purchasing power of consumers' assets. Because of the wealth effect, consumer spending, C, falls when the aggregate price level rises, leading to a downward-sloping aggregate demand curve.

The Interest Rate Effect Economists use the term *money* in its narrowest sense to refer to cash and bank deposits on which people can write checks. People and firms hold money because it reduces the cost and inconvenience of making transactions. An increase in the aggregate price level, other things equal, reduces the purchasing power of a given amount of money holdings. To purchase the same basket of goods and services as before, people and firms now need to hold more money. So, in response to an increase in the aggregate price level, the public tries to increase its money holdings, either by borrowing more or by selling assets such as bonds. This reduces the funds available for lending to other borrowers and drives interest rates up. In Chapter 26 we learned that a rise in the interest rate reduces investment spending because it makes the cost of borrowing higher. It also reduces consumer spending because households save more of their disposable income. So a rise in the aggregate price level depresses investment spending, I, and consumer spending, C, through its effect on the purchasing power of money holdings, an effect known as the **interest rate effect of a change in the aggregate price level.** This also leads to a downward-sloping aggregate demand curve.

We'll have a lot more to say about money and interest rates in Chapter 31 on monetary policy. We'll also see, in Chapter 34, which covers open-economy macroeconomics, that a higher interest rate indirectly tends to reduce exports (X) and increase imports (IM). For now, the important point is that the aggregate demand curve is downward sloping due to both the wealth effect and the interest rate effect of a change in the aggregate price level.

The Aggregate Demand Curve and the Income–Expenditure Model

In the preceding chapter we introduced the *income-expenditure model,* which shows how the economy arrives at *income-expenditure equilibrium.* Now we've introduced the aggregate demand curve, which relates the overall demand for goods and services to the overall price level. How do these concepts fit together?

Recall that one of the assumptions of the income-expenditure model is that the aggregate price level is fixed. We now drop that assumption. We can still use the income-expenditure model, however, to ask what aggregate spending would be *at any given aggregate price level,* which is precisely what the aggregate demand curve shows. So the *AD* curve is actually derived from the income-expenditure model. Economists sometimes say that the income-expenditure model is "embedded" in the *AD-AS* model.

Figure 28-2 shows, once again, how income-expenditure equilibrium is determined. Real GDP is on the horizontal axis; real planned aggregate spending is on the vertical axis. Other things equal, planned aggregate spending, equal to consumer spending plus planned investment spending, rises with real GDP. This is illustrated by the upward-sloping lines $AE_{Planned_1}$ and $AE_{Planned_2}$.

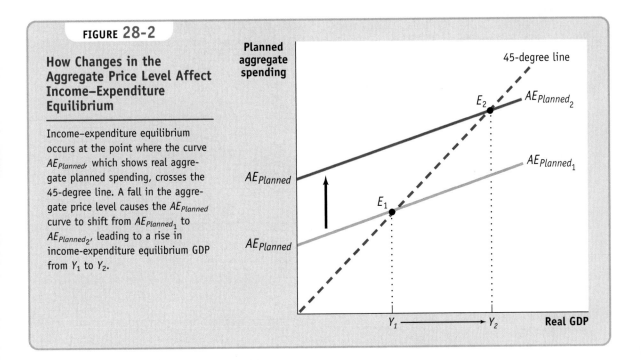

FIGURE 28-2

How Changes in the Aggregate Price Level Affect Income–Expenditure Equilibrium

Income–expenditure equilibrium occurs at the point where the curve $AE_{Planned}$, which shows real aggregate planned spending, crosses the 45-degree line. A fall in the aggregate price level causes the $AE_{Planned}$ curve to shift from $AE_{Planned_1}$ to $AE_{Planned_2}$, leading to a rise in income-expenditure equilibrium GDP from Y_1 to Y_2.

Income–expenditure equilibrium, as we learned in Chapter 27, is at the point where the line representing planned aggregate spending crosses the 45-degree line. For example, if $AE_{Planned_1}$ is the relationship between real GDP and planned aggregate spending, then income–expenditure equilibrium is at point E_1, corresponding to a level of real GDP equal to Y_1.

We've just seen, however, that changes in the aggregate price level change the level of planned aggregate spending *at any given level of real GDP*. This means that when the aggregate price level changes, the $AE_{Planned}$ curve shifts. For example, suppose that the aggregate price level falls. As a result of both the wealth effect and the interest rate effect, the fall in the aggregate price level will lead to higher planned aggregate spending at any given level of real GDP. So the $AE_{Planned}$ curve will shift up, as illustrated in Figure 28-2 by the shift from $AE_{Planned_1}$ to $AE_{Planned_2}$. The increase in planned aggregate spending leads to a multiplier process that moves the income-expenditure equilibrium from point E_1 to point E_2, raising real GDP from Y_1 to Y_2.

Figure 28-3 on the next page shows how the income-expenditure model can be used to derive the aggregate demand curve. Panel (a) is the same as Figure 28-2. It shows how a fall in the aggregate price level, by increasing planned aggregate spending at any given level of real GDP, increases real GDP and planned aggregate spending. Panel (b) shows how the aggregate demand curve is related to income-expenditure equilibrium. The fall in the aggregate price level from P_1 to P_2 generates a movement down the aggregate demand curve from Y_1 to Y_2. At both combinations of aggregate price level and real GDP given by the aggregate demand curve, the quantity of aggregate output demanded is equal to the level of planned aggregate spending and real GDP derived from the income-expenditure model.

So the aggregate demand curve doesn't replace the income-expenditure model. Instead, it's a way to summarize what the income-expenditure model says about the effects of changes in the aggregate price level.

In practice, economists often use the income-expenditure model to analyze short-run economic fluctuations, even though strictly speaking it should be seen as a component of a more complete model. In the short run, in particular, this is usually a reasonable shortcut.

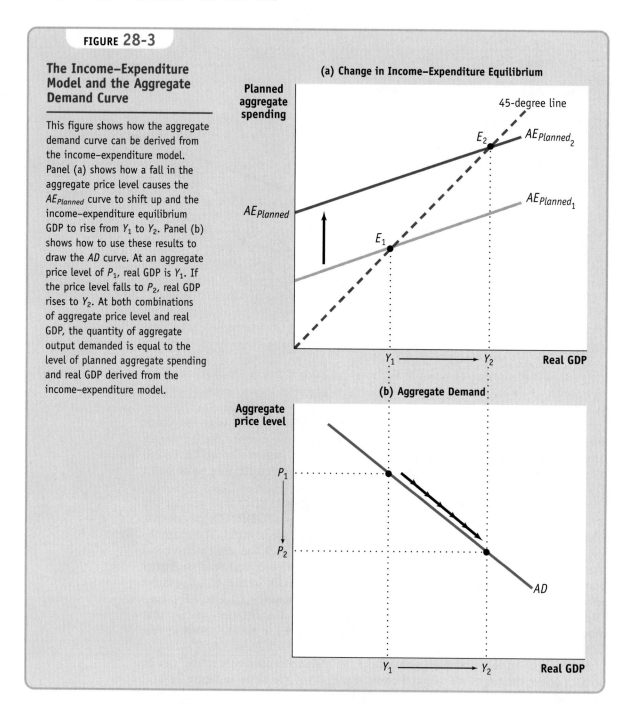

FIGURE 28-3

The Income–Expenditure Model and the Aggregate Demand Curve

This figure shows how the aggregate demand curve can be derived from the income–expenditure model. Panel (a) shows how a fall in the aggregate price level causes the $AE_{Planned}$ curve to shift up and the income–expenditure equilibrium GDP to rise from Y_1 to Y_2. Panel (b) shows how to use these results to draw the AD curve. At an aggregate price level of P_1, real GDP is Y_1. If the price level falls to P_2, real GDP rises to Y_2. At both combinations of aggregate price level and real GDP, the quantity of aggregate output demanded is equal to the level of planned aggregate spending and real GDP derived from the income–expenditure model.

(a) Change in Income–Expenditure Equilibrium

(b) Aggregate Demand

Shifts of the Aggregate Demand Curve

In Chapter 3, where we introduced the analysis of supply and demand in the market for an individual good, we stressed the importance of the distinction between *movements along* the demand curve and *shifts of* the demand curve. The same distinction applies to the aggregate demand curve. Figure 28-1 shows a *movement along* the aggregate demand curve, a change in the aggregate quantity of goods and services demanded as the aggregate price level changes. But there can also be *shifts of* the aggregate demand curve, changes in the quantity of goods and services demanded at any given price level, as shown in Figure 28-4. When we talk about an increase in aggregate demand, we mean a shift of the aggregate demand curve to the right, as shown in panel (a) by the shift from AD_1 to AD_2. A rightward shift occurs when the quantity of aggregate output demanded increases at any given aggregate price level. A decrease in aggregate demand means that the AD curve shifts to the left, as in panel (b). A leftward shift implies that the quantity of aggregate output demanded falls at any given aggregate price level.

FIGURE 28-4   **Shifts of the Aggregate Demand Curve**

Panel (a) shows the effect of events that increase the quantity of aggregate output demanded at any given aggregate price level, such as improvements in business and consumer expectations or increased government spending. Such changes shift the aggregate demand curve to the right, from AD_1 to AD_2. Panel (b) shows the effect of events that decrease the quantity of aggregate output demanded at any given aggregate price level, such as a fall in wealth caused by a stock market decline. This shifts the aggregate demand curve leftward from AD_1 to AD_2.

A number of factors can shift the aggregate demand curve. Among the most important factors are changes in expectations, changes in wealth, and the size of the existing stock of physical capital. In addition, both fiscal and monetary policy can shift the aggregate demand curve. All five factors set the multiplier process in motion. By causing an initial rise or fall in real GDP, they change disposable income, which leads to additional changes in aggregate spending, which lead to further changes in real GDP, and so on. For an overview of factors that shift the aggregate demand curve, see Table 28-1.

TABLE 28-1

Factors That Shift the Aggregate Demand Curve

Changes in expectations	
If consumers and firms become more optimistic, . . .	. . . aggregate demand increases.
If consumers and firms become more pessimistic, . . .	. . . aggregate demand decreases.
Changes in wealth	
If the real value of household assets rises, . . .	. . . aggregate demand increases.
If the real value of household assets falls, . . .	. . . aggregate demand decreases.
Size of the existing stock of physical capital	
If the existing stock of physical capital is relatively small, . . .	. . . aggregate demand increases.
If the existing stock of physical capital is relatively large, . . .	. . . aggregate demand decreases.
Fiscal policy	
If the government increases spending or cuts taxes, . . .	. . . aggregate demand increases.
If the government reduces spending or raises taxes, . . .	. . . aggregate demand decreases.
Monetary policy	
If the central bank increases the quantity of money, . . .	. . . aggregate demand increases.
If the central bank reduces the quantity of money, . . .	. . . aggregate demand decreases.

"CONSUMER CONFIDENCE CRISIS IN AISLE THREE!"

Jim Borgman

Changes in Expectations As explained in Chapter 27, both consumer spending and planned investment spending depend in part on people's expectations about the future. Consumers base their spending not only on the income they have now but also on the income they expect to have in the future. Firms base their planned investment spending not only on current conditions but also on the sales they expect to make in the future. As a result, changes in expectations can push consumer spending and planned investment spending up or down. If consumers and firms become more optimistic, aggregate spending rises; if they become more pessimistic, aggregate spending falls. In fact, short-run economic forecasters pay careful attention to surveys of consumer and business sentiment. In particular, forecasters watch the Consumer Confidence Index, a monthly measure calculated by the Conference Board, and the Michigan Consumer Sentiment Index, a similar measure calculated by the University of Michigan.

Changes in Wealth Consumer spending depends in part on the value of household assets. When the real value of these assets rises, the purchasing power they embody also rises, leading to an increase in aggregate spending. For example, in the 1990s there was a significant rise in the stock market that increased aggregate demand. And when the real value of household assets falls—for example, because of a stock market crash—the purchasing power they embody is reduced and aggregate demand also falls. The stock market crash of 1929 was a significant factor leading to the Great Depression. Similarly, a sharp decline in real estate values was a major factor depressing consumer spending in 2008.

Size of the Existing Stock of Physical Capital Firms engage in planned investment spending to add to their stock of physical capital. Their incentive to spend depends in part on how much physical capital they already have: the more they have, the less they will feel a need to add more, other things equal. The same applies to other types of investment spending—for example, if a large number of houses have been built in recent years, this will depress the demand for new houses and as a result also tend to reduce residential investment spending. In fact, that's part of the reason for the deep slump in residential investment spending that began in 2006. The housing boom of the previous few years had created an oversupply of houses: by spring 2008, the inventory of unsold houses on the market was equal to more than 11 months of sales, and prices had fallen more than 20% from their peak. This gave the construction industry little incentive to build even more homes.

Government Policies and Aggregate Demand

One of the key insights of macroeconomics is that the government can have a powerful influence on aggregate demand and that, in some circumstances, this influence can be used to improve economic performance.

The two main ways the government can influence the aggregate demand curve are through fiscal policy and monetary policy. We'll

---

PITFALLS

CHANGES IN WEALTH: A MOVEMENT ALONG VERSUS A SHIFT OF THE AGGREGATE DEMAND CURVE

In the last section we explained that one reason the *AD* curve is downward sloping is due to the wealth effect of a change in the aggregate price level: a higher aggregate price level reduces the purchasing power of households' assets and leads to a fall in consumer spending, *C*. But in this section we've just explained that changes in wealth lead to a shift of the *AD* curve. Aren't those two explanations contradictory? Which one is it—does a change in wealth move the economy along the *AD* curve or does it shift the *AD* curve? The answer is both: it depends on the *source* of the change in wealth. A movement along the *AD* curve occurs when a change in the aggregate price level changes the purchasing power of consumers' existing wealth (the real value of their assets). This is the *wealth effect of a change in the aggregate price level*—a change in the aggregate price level is the source of the change in wealth. For example, a fall in the aggregate price level increases the purchasing power of consumers' assets and leads to a movement down the *AD* curve. In contrast, a change in wealth *independent of a change in the aggregate price level* shifts the *AD* curve. For example, a rise in the stock market or a rise in real estate values leads to an increase in the real value of consumers' assets at any given aggregate price level. In this case, the source of the change in wealth is a change in the values of assets without any change in the aggregate price level—that is, a change in asset values holding the prices of all final goods and services constant.

briefly discuss their influence on aggregate demand, leaving a full-length discussion for upcoming chapters.

Fiscal Policy As we learned in Chapter 22, fiscal policy is the use of either government spending—government purchases of final goods and services and government transfers—or tax policy to stabilize the economy. In practice, governments often respond to recessions by increasing spending, cutting taxes, or both. They often respond to inflation by reducing spending or increasing taxes.

The effect of government purchases of final goods and services, G, on the aggregate demand curve is *direct* because government purchases are themselves a component of aggregate demand. So an increase in government purchases shifts the aggregate demand curve to the right and a decrease shifts it to the left. History's most dramatic example of how increased government purchases affect aggregate demand was the effect of wartime government spending during World War II. Because of the war, U.S. federal purchases surged 400%. This increase in purchases is usually credited with ending the Great Depression. In the 1990s Japan used large public works projects—such as government-financed construction of roads, bridges, and dams—in an effort to increase aggregate demand in the face of a slumping economy.

In contrast, changes in either tax rates or government transfers influence the economy *indirectly* through their effect on disposable income. A lower tax rate means that consumers get to keep more of what they earn, increasing their disposable income. An increase in government transfers also increases consumers' disposable income. In either case, this increases consumer spending and shifts the aggregate demand curve to the right. A higher tax rate or a reduction in transfers reduces the amount of disposable income received by consumers. This reduces consumer spending and shifts the aggregate demand curve to the left.

Monetary Policy We opened this chapter by talking about the problems faced by the Federal Reserve, which controls monetary policy—the use of changes in the quantity of money or the interest rate to stabilize the economy. We've just discussed how a rise in the aggregate price level, by reducing the purchasing power of money holdings, causes a rise in the interest rate. That, in turn, reduces both investment spending and consumer spending.

But what happens if the quantity of money in the hands of households and firms changes? In modern economies, the quantity of money in circulation is largely determined by the decisions of a *central bank* created by the government. As we'll learn in Chapter 30, the Federal Reserve, the U.S. central bank, is a special institution that is neither exactly part of the government nor exactly a private institution. When the central bank increases the quantity of money in circulation, households and firms have more money, which they are willing to lend out. The effect is to drive the interest rate down at any given aggregate price level, leading to higher investment spending and higher consumer spending. That is, increasing the quantity of money shifts the aggregate demand curve to the right. Reducing the quantity of money has the opposite effect: households and firms have less money holdings than before, leading them to borrow more and lend less. This raises the interest rate, reduces investment spending and consumer spending, and shifts the aggregate demand curve to the left.

➤ECONOMICS IN ACTION

Moving Along the Aggregate Demand Curve, 1979–1980

When looking at data, it's often hard to distinguish between changes in spending that represent *movements along* the aggregate demand curve and *shifts of* the aggregate demand curve. One telling exception, however, is what happened right after the oil crisis of 1979, which we mentioned in this chapter's opening story. Faced with a sharp increase in the aggregate price level—the rate of consumer price inflation reached

14.8% in March of 1980—the Federal Reserve stuck to a policy of increasing the quantity of money slowly. The aggregate price level was rising steeply, but the quantity of money circulating in the economy was growing slowly. The net result was that the purchasing power of the quantity of money in circulation fell.

This led to an increase in the demand for borrowing and a surge in interest rates. The *prime rate,* which is the interest rate banks charge their best customers, climbed above 20%. High interest rates, in turn, caused both consumer spending and investment spending to fall: in 1980 purchases of durable consumer goods like cars fell by 5.3% and real investment spending fell by 8.9%.

In other words, in 1979–1980 the economy responded just as we'd expect if it were moving upward along the aggregate demand curve from right to left: due to the wealth effect and the interest rate effect of a change in the aggregate price level, the quantity of aggregate output demanded fell as the aggregate price level rose. This does not explain, of course, why the aggregate price level rose. But as we'll see in the section "The *AD-AS* Model," the answer to that question lies in the behavior of the *short-run aggregate supply curve.* ▲

< < < < < < < < < < < <

► CHECK YOUR UNDERSTANDING 28-1

1. Determine the effect on aggregate demand of each of the following events. Explain whether it represents a movement along the aggregate demand curve (up or down) or a shift of the curve (leftward or rightward).
   a. A rise in the interest rate caused by a change in monetary policy
   b. A fall in the real value of money in the economy due to a higher aggregate price level
   c. News of a worse-than-expected job market next year
   d. A fall in tax rates
   e. A rise in the real value of assets in the economy due to a lower aggregate price level
   f. A rise in the real value of assets in the economy due to a surge in real estate values

Solutions appear at back of book.

Aggregate Supply

Between 1929 and 1933, there was a sharp fall in aggregate demand—a reduction in the quantity of goods and services demanded at any given price level. One consequence of the economy-wide decline in demand was a fall in the prices of most goods and services. By 1933, the GDP deflator (one of the price indexes we defined in Chapter 23) was 26% below its 1929 level, and other indexes were down by similar amounts. A second consequence was a decline in the output of most goods and services: by 1933, real GDP was 27% below its 1929 level. A third consequence, closely tied to the fall in real GDP, was a surge in the unemployment rate from 3% to 25%.

The association between the plunge in real GDP and the plunge in prices wasn't an accident. Between 1929 and 1933, the U.S. economy was moving down its **aggregate supply curve,** which shows the relationship between the economy's aggregate price level (the overall price level of final goods and services in the economy) and the total quantity of final goods and services, or aggregate output, producers are willing to supply. (As you will recall, we use real GDP to measure aggregate output. So we'll often use the two terms interchangeably.) More specifically, between 1929 and 1933 the U.S. economy moved down its *short-run aggregate supply curve.*

The Short-Run Aggregate Supply Curve

The period from 1929 to 1933 demonstrated that there is a positive relationship in the short run between the aggregate price level and the quantity of aggregate output supplied. That is, a rise in the aggregate price level is associated with a rise in the quantity of aggregate output supplied, other things equal; a fall in the aggregate price level is associated with a fall in the quantity of aggregate output supplied, other things equal. To

The **aggregate supply curve** shows the relationship between the aggregate price level and the quantity of aggregate output supplied in the economy.

understand why this positive relationship exists, consider the most basic question facing a producer: is producing a unit of output profitable or not? Let's define profit per unit:

(28-2)   Profit per unit of output =
Price per unit of output – Production cost per unit of output

Thus, the answer to the question depends on whether the price the producer receives for a unit of output is greater or less than the cost of producing that unit of output. At any given point in time, many of the costs producers face are fixed per unit of output and can't be changed for an extended period of time. Typically, the largest source of inflexible production cost is the wages paid to workers. *Wages* here refers to all forms of worker compensation, such as employer-paid health care and retirement benefits in addition to earnings. Wages are typically an inflexible production cost because the dollar amount of any given wage paid, called the **nominal wage,** is often determined by contracts that were signed some time ago. And even when there are no formal contracts, there are often informal agreements between management and workers, making companies reluctant to change wages in response to economic conditions. For example, companies usually will not reduce wages during poor economic times—unless the downturn has been particularly long and severe—for fear of generating worker resentment. Correspondingly, they typically won't raise wages during better economic times—until they are at risk of losing workers to competitors—because they don't want to encourage workers to routinely demand higher wages. As a result of both formal and informal agreements, then, the economy is characterized by **sticky wages:** nominal wages that are slow to fall even in the face of high unemployment and slow to rise even in the face of labor shortages. It's important to note, however, that nominal wages cannot be sticky forever: ultimately, formal contracts and informal agreements will be renegotiated to take into account changed economic circumstances. As the Pitfalls at the end of this section explains, how long it takes for nominal wages to become flexible is an integral component of what distinguishes the short run from the long run.

To understand how the fact that many costs are fixed in nominal terms gives rise to an upward-sloping short-run aggregate supply curve, it's helpful to know that prices are set somewhat differently in different kinds of markets. In *perfectly competitive markets,* producers take prices as given; in *imperfectly competitive markets,* producers have some ability to choose the prices they charge. In both kinds of markets, there is a short-run positive relationship between prices and output, but for slightly different reasons.

Let's start with the behavior of producers in perfectly competitive markets; remember, they take the price as given. Imagine that, for some reason, the aggregate price level falls, which means that the price received by the typical producer of a final good or service falls. Because many production costs are fixed in the short run, production cost per unit of output doesn't fall by the same proportion as the fall in the price of output. So the profit per unit of output declines, leading perfectly competitive producers to reduce the quantity supplied in the short run.

On the other hand, suppose that for some reason the aggregate price level rises. As a result, the typical producer receives a higher price for its final good or service. Again, many production costs are fixed in the short run, so production cost per unit of output doesn't rise by the same proportion as the rise in the price of a unit. And since the typical perfectly competitive producer takes the price as given, profit per unit of output rises and output increases.

Now consider an imperfectly competitive producer that is able to set its own price. If there is a rise in the demand for this producer's product, it will be able to sell more at any given price. Given stronger demand for its products, it will probably choose to increase its prices as well as its output, as a way of increasing profit per unit of output. In fact, industry analysts often talk about variations in an industry's "pricing power": when demand is strong, firms with pricing power are able to raise prices—and they do.

Conversely, if there is a fall in demand, firms will normally try to limit the fall in their sales by cutting prices.

The **nominal wage** is the dollar amount of the wage paid.

Sticky wages are nominal wages that are slow to fall even in the face of high unemployment and slow to rise even in the face of labor shortages.

What's Truly Flexible, What's Truly Sticky

Most macroeconomists agree that the basic picture shown in Figure 28-5 is correct: there is, other things equal, a positive short-run relationship between the aggregate price level and aggregate output. But many would argue that the details are a bit more complicated.

So far we've stressed a difference in the behavior of the aggregate price level and the behavior of nominal wages. That is, we've said that the aggregate price level is flexible but nominal wages are sticky in the short run. Although this assumption is a good way to explain why the short-run aggregate supply curve is upward sloping, empirical data on wages and prices don't wholly support a sharp distinction between flexible prices of final goods and services and sticky nominal wages. On one side, some nominal wages are in fact flexible even in the short run because some workers are not covered by a contract or informal agreement with their employers. Since some nominal wages are sticky but others are flexible, we observe that the *average nominal wage*—the nominal wage averaged over all workers in the economy—falls when there is a steep rise in unemployment. For example, nominal wages fell substantially in the early years of the Great Depression. On the other side, some prices of final goods and services are sticky rather than flexible. For example, some firms, particularly the makers of luxury or name-

brand goods, are reluctant to cut prices even when demand falls. Instead they prefer to cut output even if their profit per unit hasn't declined.

These complications, as we've said, don't change the basic picture. When the aggregate price level falls, some producers cut output because the nominal wages they pay are sticky. And some producers don't cut their prices in the face of a falling aggregate price level, preferring instead to reduce their output. In both cases, the positive relationship between the aggregate price level and aggregate output is maintained. So, in the end, the short-run aggregate supply curve is still upward sloping.

The **short-run aggregate supply curve** shows the relationship between the aggregate price level and the quantity of aggregate output supplied that exists in the short run, the time period when many production costs can be taken as fixed.

Both the responses of firms in perfectly competitive industries and those of firms in imperfectly competitive industries lead to an upward-sloping relationship between aggregate output and the aggregate price level. The positive relationship between the aggregate price level and the quantity of aggregate output producers are willing to supply during the time period when many production costs, particularly nominal wages, can be taken as fixed is illustrated by the **short-run aggregate supply curve.** The positive relationship between the aggregate price level and aggregate output in the short run gives the short-run aggregate supply curve its upward slope. Figure 28-5

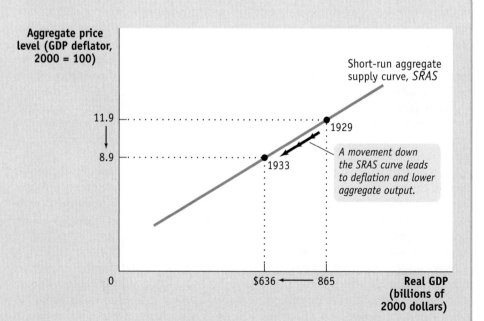

FIGURE 28-5

The Short-Run Aggregate Supply Curve

The short-run aggregate supply curve shows the relationship between the aggregate price level and the quantity of aggregate output supplied in the short run, the period in which many production costs such as nominal wages are fixed. It is upward sloping because a higher aggregate price level leads to higher profit per unit of output and higher aggregate output given fixed nominal wages. Here we show numbers corresponding to the Great Depression, from 1929 to 1933: when deflation occurred and the aggregate price level fell from 11.9 (in 1929) to 8.9 (in 1933), firms responded by reducing the quantity of aggregate output supplied from $865 billion to $636 billion measured in 2000 dollars.

shows a hypothetical short-run aggregate supply curve, *SRAS*, which matches actual U.S. data for 1929 and 1933. On the horizontal axis is aggregate output (or, equivalently, real GDP)—the total quantity of final goods and services supplied in the economy—measured in 2000 dollars. On the vertical axis is the aggregate price level as measured by the GDP deflator, with the value for the year 2000 equal to 100. In 1929, the aggregate price level was 11.9 and real GDP was $865 billion. In 1933, the aggregate price level was 8.9 and real GDP was only $636 billion. The movement down the *SRAS* curve corresponds to the deflation and fall in aggregate output experienced over those years.

Shifts of the Short-Run Aggregate Supply Curve

Figure 28-5 shows a *movement along* the short-run aggregate supply curve, as the aggregate price level and aggregate output fell from 1929 to 1933. But there can also be *shifts of* the short-run aggregate supply curve, as shown in Figure 28-6. Panel (a) shows a *decrease in short-run aggregate supply*—a leftward shift of the short-run aggregate supply curve. Aggregate supply decreases when producers reduce the quantity of aggregate output they are willing to supply at any given aggregate price level. Panel (b) shows an *increase in short-run aggregate supply*—a rightward shift of the short-run aggregate supply curve. Aggregate supply increases when producers increase the quantity of aggregate output they are willing to supply at any given aggregate price level.

To understand why the short-run aggregate supply curve can shift, it's important to recall that producers make output decisions based on their profit per unit of output. The short-run aggregate supply curve illustrates the relationship between the aggregate price level and aggregate output: because some production costs are fixed in the short run, a change in the aggregate price level leads to a change in producers' profit per unit of output and, in turn, leads to a change in aggregate output. But other factors besides the aggregate price level can affect profit per unit and, in turn, aggregate output. It is changes in these other factors that will shift the short-run aggregate supply curve.

FIGURE 28-6   Shifts of the Short-Run Aggregate Supply Curve

(a) Leftward Shift

Aggregate price level

$SRAS_2$ $SRAS_1$

Decrease in Short-Run Aggregate Supply

Real GDP

(b) Rightward Shift

Aggregate price level

$SRAS_1$ $SRAS_2$

Increase in Short-Run Aggregate Supply

Real GDP

Panel (a) shows a decrease in short-run aggregate supply: the short-run aggregate supply curve shifts leftward from $SRAS_1$ to $SRAS_2$, and the quantity of aggregate output supplied at any given aggregate price level falls. Panel (b) shows an increase in short-run aggregate supply: the short-run aggregate supply curve shifts rightward from $SRAS_1$ to $SRAS_2$, and the quantity of aggregate output supplied at any given aggregate price level rises.

To develop some intuition, suppose that something happens that raises production costs—say, an increase in the price of oil. At any given price of output, a producer now earns a smaller profit per unit of output. As a result, producers reduce the quantity supplied at any given aggregate price level, and the short-run aggregate supply curve shifts to the left. If, in contrast, something happens that lowers production costs—say, a fall in the nominal wage—a producer now earns a higher profit per unit of output at any given price of output. This leads producers to increase the quantity of aggregate output supplied at any given aggregate price level, and the short-run aggregate supply curve shifts to the right.

Now we'll discuss some of the important factors that affect producers' profit per unit and so can lead to shifts of the short-run aggregate supply curve.

Changes in Commodity Prices In this chapter's opening story, we described how a surge in the price of oil caused problems for the U.S. economy in the 1970s and in early 2008. Oil is a commodity, a standardized input bought and sold in bulk quantities. An increase in the price of a commodity—oil—raised production costs across the economy and reduced the quantity of aggregate output supplied at any given aggregate price level, shifting the short-run aggregate supply curve to the left. Conversely, a decline in commodity prices reduces production costs, leading to an increase in the quantity supplied at any given aggregate price level and a rightward shift of the short-run aggregate supply curve.

Why isn't the influence of commodity prices already captured by the short-run aggregate supply curve? Because commodities—unlike, say, soft drinks—are not a final good, their prices are not included in the calculation of the aggregate price level. Further, commodities represent a significant cost of production to most suppliers, just like nominal wages do. So changes in commodity prices have large impacts on production costs. And in contrast to noncommodities, the prices of commodities can sometimes change drastically due to industry-specific shocks to supply—such as wars in the Middle East or rising Chinese demand that leaves less oil for the United States.

Changes in Nominal Wages At any given point in time, the dollar wages of many workers are fixed because they are set by contracts or informal agreements made in the past. Nominal wages can change, however, once enough time has passed for contracts and informal agreements to be renegotiated. Suppose, for example, that there is an economy-wide rise in the cost of health care insurance premiums paid by employers as part of employees' wages. From the employers' perspective, this is equivalent to a rise in nominal wages because it is an increase in employer-paid compensation. So this rise in nominal wages increases production costs and shifts the short-run aggregate supply curve to the left. Conversely, suppose there is an economy-wide fall in the cost of such premiums. This is equivalent to a fall in nominal wages from the point of view of employers; it reduces production costs and shifts the short-run aggregate supply curve to the right.

An important historical fact is that during the 1970s the surge in the price of oil had the indirect effect of also raising nominal wages. This "knock-on" effect occurred because many wage contracts included *cost-of-living allowances* that automatically raised the nominal wage when consumer prices increased. Through this channel, the surge in the price of oil—which led to an increase in overall consumer prices—ultimately caused a rise in nominal wages. So the economy, in the end, experienced two leftward shifts of the aggregate supply curve: the first generated by the initial surge in the price of oil, the second generated by the induced increase in nominal wages. The negative effect on the economy of rising oil prices was greatly magnified through the cost-of-living allowances in wage contracts. Today, cost-of-living allowances in wage contracts are rare.

Changes in Productivity An increase in productivity means that a worker can produce more units of output with the same quantity of inputs. For example, the introduction of bar-code scanners in retail stores greatly increased the ability of a single worker to stock, inventory, and resupply store shelves. As a result, the cost to a store of "producing" a dollar of sales fell and profit rose. And, correspondingly, the quantity supplied increased. (Think of Wal-Mart and the increase in the number of its stores as an increase in aggregate supply.) So a rise in productivity, whatever the source, increases producers' profits and shifts the short-run aggregate supply curve to the right. Conversely, a fall in productivity—say, due to new regulations that require workers to spend more time filling out forms—reduces the number of units of output a worker can produce with the same quantity of inputs. Consequently, the cost per unit of output rises, profit falls, and quantity supplied falls. This shifts the short-run aggregate supply curve to the left.

For a summary of the factors that shift the short-run aggregate supply curve, see Table 28-2.

TABLE 28-2

Factors that Shift the Short-Run Aggregate Supply Curve		
Changes in commodity prices		
	If commodity prices fall, . . .	. . . short-run aggregate supply increases.
	If commodity prices rise, . . .	. . . short-run aggregate supply decreases.
Changes in nominal wages		
	If nominal wages fall, . . .	. . . short-run aggregate supply increases.
	If nominal wages rise, . . .	. . . short-run aggregate supply decreases.
Changes in productivity		
	If workers become more productive, . . .	. . . short-run aggregate supply increases.
	If workers become less productive, . . .	. . . short-run aggregate supply decreases.

The Long-Run Aggregate Supply Curve

We've just seen that in the short run a fall in the aggregate price level leads to a decline in the quantity of aggregate output supplied because nominal wages are sticky in the short run. But, as we mentioned earlier, contracts and informal agreements are renegotiated in the long run. So in the long run, nominal wages—like the aggregate price level—are flexible, not sticky. This fact greatly alters the long-run relationship between the aggregate price level and aggregate supply. In fact, in the long run the aggregate price level has *no* effect on the quantity of aggregate output supplied.

To see why, let's conduct a thought experiment. Imagine that you could wave a magic wand—or maybe a magic bar-code scanner—and cut *all prices* in the economy in half at the same time. By "all prices" we mean the prices of all inputs, including nominal wages, as well as the prices of final goods and services. What would happen to aggregate output, given that the aggregate price level has been halved and all input prices, including nominal wages, have been halved?

The answer is: nothing. Consider Equation 28-2 again: each producer would receive a lower price for its product, but costs would fall by the same proportion. As a result, every unit of output profitable to produce before the change in prices would still be profitable to produce after the change in prices. So a halving of *all* prices in the economy has no effect on the economy's aggregate output. In other words, changes in the aggregate price level now have no effect on the quantity of aggregate output supplied.

In reality, of course, no one can change all prices by the same proportion at the same time. But now, we'll consider the *long run, the period of time over which all prices are fully flexible.* In the long run, inflation or deflation has the same effect as someone changing all prices by the same proportion. *As a result, changes in the aggregate price level do not change the quantity of aggregate output supplied in the long run.* That's because changes in

The **long-run aggregate supply curve** shows the relationship between the aggregate price level and the quantity of aggregate output supplied that would exist if all prices, including nominal wages, were fully flexible.

Potential output is the level of real GDP the economy would produce if all prices, including nominal wages, were fully flexible.

the aggregate price level will, in the long run, be accompanied by equal proportional changes in *all* input prices, including nominal wages.

The **long-run aggregate supply curve,** illustrated in Figure 28-7 by the curve *LRAS*, shows the relationship between the aggregate price level and the quantity of aggregate output supplied that would exist if all prices, including nominal wages, were fully flexible. The long-run aggregate supply curve is vertical because changes in the aggregate price level have *no* effect on aggregate output in the long run. At an aggregate price level of 15.0, the quantity of aggregate output supplied is $800 billion in 2000 dollars. If the aggregate price level falls by 50% to 7.5, the quantity of aggregate output supplied is unchanged in the long run at $800 billion in 2000 dollars.

It's important to understand not only that the *LRAS* curve is vertical but also that its position along the horizontal axis represents a significant measure. The horizontal intercept in Figure 28-7, where *LRAS* touches the horizontal axis ($800 billion in 2000 dollars), is the economy's **potential output,** Y_P: the level of real GDP the economy would produce if all prices, including nominal wages, were fully flexible.

In reality, the actual level of real GDP is almost always either above or below potential output. We'll see why later in this chapter, when we discuss the *AD–AS* model. Still, an economy's potential output is an important number because it defines the trend around which actual aggregate output fluctuates from year to year.

In the United States, the Congressional Budget Office, or CBO, estimates annual potential output for the purpose of federal budget analysis. In Figure 28-8, the CBO's estimates of U.S. potential output from 1989 to 2007 are represented by the black line and the actual values of U.S. real GDP over the same period are represented by the blue line. Years shaded purple on the horizontal axis correspond to periods in which actual aggregate output fell short of potential output, years shaded green to periods in which actual aggregate output exceeded potential output.

As you can see, U.S. potential output has risen steadily over time—implying a series of rightward shifts of the *LRAS* curve. What has caused these rightward shifts? The answer lies in the factors related to long-run growth that we discussed in Chapter 25, such as increases in physical capital and human capital as well as technological progress. Over the long run, as the size of the labor force and the productivity of labor both rise, the level of real GDP that the economy is capable of producing also rises.

FIGURE 28-7

The Long-Run Aggregate Supply Curve

The long-run aggregate supply curve shows the quantity of aggregate output supplied when all prices, including nominal wages, are flexible. It is vertical at potential output, Y_P, because in the long run a change in the aggregate price level has no effect on the quantity of aggregate output supplied.

Aggregate price level (GDP deflator, 2000 = 100)

Long-run aggregate supply curve, *LRAS*

15.0

A fall in the aggregate price level...

...*leaves the quantity of aggregate output supplied unchanged in the long run.*

7.5

0

Potential output, Y_P — $800

Real GDP (billions of 2000 dollars)

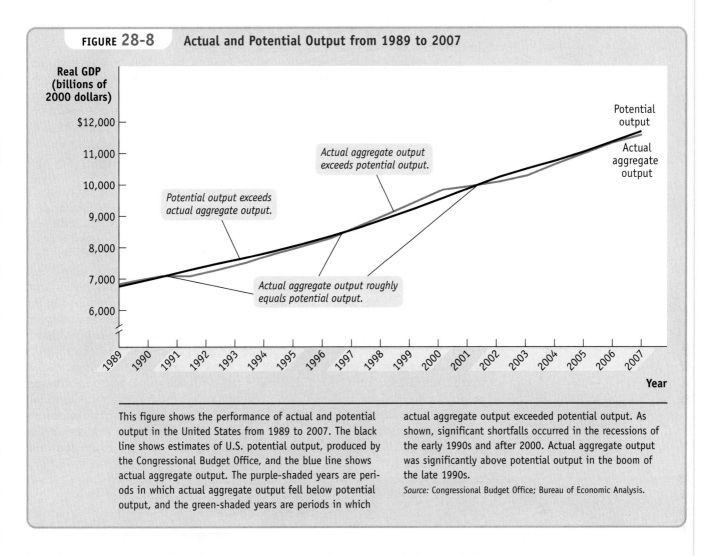

FIGURE 28-8   **Actual and Potential Output from 1989 to 2007**

This figure shows the performance of actual and potential output in the United States from 1989 to 2007. The black line shows estimates of U.S. potential output, produced by the Congressional Budget Office, and the blue line shows actual aggregate output. The purple-shaded years are periods in which actual aggregate output fell below potential output, and the green-shaded years are periods in which actual aggregate output exceeded potential output. As shown, significant shortfalls occurred in the recessions of the early 1990s and after 2000. Actual aggregate output was significantly above potential output in the boom of the late 1990s.

Source: Congressional Budget Office; Bureau of Economic Analysis.

Indeed, one way to think about long-run economic growth is that it is the growth in the economy's potential output. We generally think of the long-run aggregate supply curve as shifting to the right over time as an economy experiences long-run growth.

From the Short Run to the Long Run

As you can see in Figure 28-8, the economy normally produces more or less than potential output: actual aggregate output was below potential output in the early 1990s, above potential output in the late 1990s, below potential output for most of the 2000s. So the economy is normally on its short-run aggregate supply curve—but not on its long-run aggregate supply curve. So why is the long-run curve relevant? Does the economy ever move from the short run to the long run? And if so, how?

The first step to answering these questions is to understand that the economy is always in one of only two states with respect to the short-run and long-run aggregate supply curves. It can be on both curves simultaneously by being at a point where the curves cross (as in the few years in Figure 28-8 in which actual aggregate output and potential output roughly coincided). Or it can be on the short-run aggregate supply curve but not the long-run aggregate supply curve (as in the years in which actual aggregate output and potential output *did not* coincide). But that is not the end of the story. If the economy is on the short-run but not the long-run aggregate supply curve, the short-run aggregate supply curve will shift over time until the economy is at a point where both curves cross—a point where actual aggregate output is equal to potential output.

PITFALLS

ARE WE THERE YET? WHAT THE LONG RUN REALLY MEANS

We've used the term *long run* in two different contexts. In an earlier chapter we focused on *long-run economic growth:* growth that takes place over decades. In this chapter we introduced the *long-run aggregate supply curve,* which depicts the economy's potential output: the level of aggregate output that the economy would produce if all prices, including nominal wages, were fully flexible. It might seem that we're using the same term, *long run,* for two different concepts. But we aren't: these two concepts are really the same thing.

Because the economy always tends to return to potential output in the long run, actual aggregate output *fluctuates around potential output,* rarely getting too far from it. As a result, the economy's rate of growth over long periods of time—say, decades—is very close to the rate of growth of potential output. And potential output growth is determined by the factors we analyzed in the chapter on long-run economic growth. So that means that the "long run" of long-run growth and the "long run" of the long-run aggregate supply curve coincide.

Figure 28-9 illustrates how this process works. In both panels *LRAS* is the long-run aggregate supply curve, *SRAS*$_1$ is the initial short-run aggregate supply curve, and the aggregate price level is at P_1. In panel (a) the economy starts at the initial production point, A_1, which corresponds to a quantity of aggregate output supplied, Y_1, that is higher than potential output, Y_P. Producing an aggregate output level (such as Y_1) that is higher than potential output (Y_P) is possible only because nominal wages haven't yet fully adjusted upward. Until this upward adjustment in nominal wages occurs, producers are earning high profits and producing a high level of output. But a level of aggregate output higher than potential output means a low level of unemployment. Because jobs are abundant and workers are scarce, nominal wages will rise over time, gradually shifting the short-run aggregate supply curve leftward.

FIGURE 28-9   **From the Short Run to the Long Run**

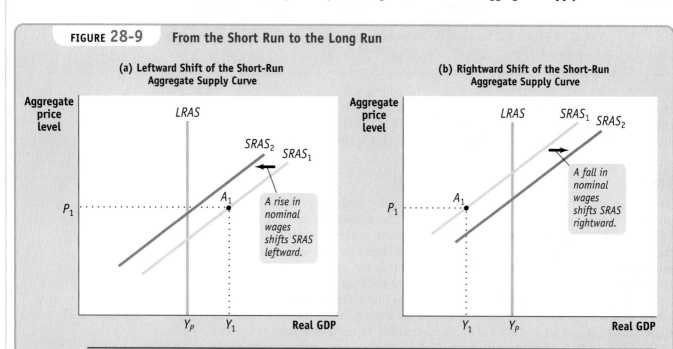

In panel (a), the initial short-run aggregate supply curve is *SRAS*$_1$. At the aggregate price level, P_1, the quantity of aggregate output supplied, Y_1, exceeds potential output, Y_P. Eventually, low unemployment will cause nominal wages to rise, leading to a leftward shift of the short-run aggregate supply curve from *SRAS*$_1$ to *SRAS*$_2$. In panel (b), the reverse happens: at the aggregate price level, P_1, the quantity of aggregate output supplied is less than potential output. High unemployment eventually leads to a fall in nominal wages over time and a rightward shift of the short-run aggregate supply curve.

Eventually it will be in a new position, such as $SRAS_2$. (Later in this chapter, we'll show where the short-run aggregate supply curve ends up. As we'll see, that depends on the aggregate demand curve as well.)

In panel (b), the initial production point, A_1, corresponds to an aggregate output level, Y_1, that is lower than potential output, Y_P. Producing an aggregate output level (such as Y_1) that is lower than potential output (Y_P) is possible only because nominal wages haven't yet fully adjusted downward. Until this downward adjustment occurs, producers are earning low (or negative) profits and producing a low level of output. An aggregate output level lower than potential output means high unemployment. Because workers are abundant and jobs are scarce, nominal wages will fall over time, shifting the short-run aggregate supply curve gradually to the right. Eventually it will be in a new position, such as $SRAS_2$.

We'll see shortly that these shifts of the short-run aggregate supply curve will return the economy to potential output in the long run.

►*ECONOMICS IN ACTION*

Prices and Output During the Great Depression

Figure 28-10 shows the actual track of the aggregate price level, as measured by the GDP deflator, and real GDP, from 1929 to 1942. As you can see, aggregate output and the aggregate price level fell together from 1929 to 1933 and rose together from 1933 to 1937. This is what we'd expect to see if the economy was moving down the short-run aggregate supply curve from 1929 to 1933 and moving up it (with a brief reversal in 1937–1938) thereafter.

But even in 1942 the aggregate price level was still lower than it was in 1929; yet real GDP was much higher. What happened?

The answer is that the short-run aggregate supply curve shifted to the right over time. This shift partly reflected rising productivity—a rightward shift of the underlying long-run aggregate supply curve. But since the U.S. economy was producing

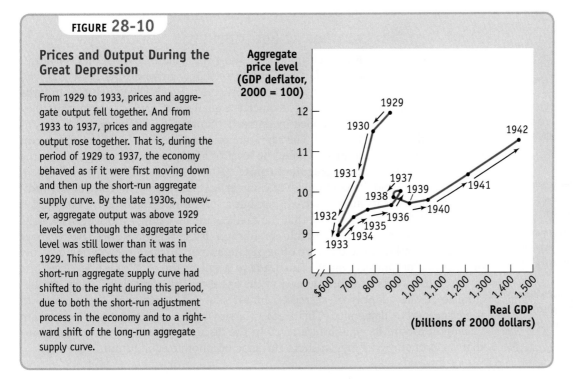

FIGURE 28-10

Prices and Output During the Great Depression

From 1929 to 1933, prices and aggregate output fell together. And from 1933 to 1937, prices and aggregate output rose together. That is, during the period of 1929 to 1937, the economy behaved as if it were first moving down and then up the short-run aggregate supply curve. By the late 1930s, however, aggregate output was above 1929 levels even though the aggregate price level was still lower than it was in 1929. This reflects the fact that the short-run aggregate supply curve had shifted to the right during this period, due to both the short-run adjustment process in the economy and to a rightward shift of the long-run aggregate supply curve.

➤ The **aggregate supply curve** illustrates the relationship between the aggregate price level and the quantity of aggregate output supplied.

➤ The **short-run aggregate supply curve** is upward sloping: a higher aggregate price level leads to higher aggregate output given that **nominal wages** are **sticky.**

➤ Changes in commodity prices, nominal wages, and productivity shift the short-run aggregate supply curve.

➤ In the long run, all prices are flexible, and changes in the aggregate price level have no effect on aggregate output. The **long-run aggregate supply curve** is vertical at **potential output.**

➤ If actual aggregate output exceeds potential output, nominal wages eventually rise and the short-run aggregate supply curve shifts leftward. If potential output exceeds actual aggregate output, nominal wages eventually fall and the short-run aggregate supply curve shifts rightward.

below potential output and had high unemployment during this period, the rightward shift of the short-run aggregate supply curve also reflected the adjustment process shown in panel (b) of Figure 28-9. So the movement of aggregate output from 1929 to 1942 reflected both movements along and shifts of the short-run aggregate supply curve. ▲

< < < < < < < < < < < <

> CHECK YOUR UNDERSTANDING 28-2

1. Determine the effect on short-run aggregate supply of each of the following events. Explain whether it represents a movement along the *SRAS* curve or a shift of the *SRAS* curve.
   a. A rise in the consumer price index (CPI) leads producers to increase output.
   b. A fall in the price of oil leads producers to increase output.
   c. A rise in legally mandated retirement benefits paid to workers leads producers to reduce output.

2. Suppose the economy is initially at potential output and the quantity of aggregate output supplied increases. What information would you need to determine whether this was due to a movement along the *SRAS* curve or a shift of the *LRAS* curve?

Solutions appear at back of book.

The *AD–AS* Model

From 1929 to 1933, the U.S. economy moved down the short-run aggregate supply curve as the aggregate price level fell. In contrast, from 1979 to 1980 the U.S. economy moved up the aggregate demand curve as the aggregate price level rose. In each case, the cause of the movement along the curve was a shift of the other curve. In 1929–1933, it was a leftward shift of the aggregate demand curve—a major fall in consumer spending. In 1979–1980, it was a leftward shift of the short-run aggregate supply curve—a dramatic fall in short-run aggregate supply caused by the oil price shock.

So to understand the behavior of the economy, we must put the aggregate supply curve and the aggregate demand curve together. The result is the **AD–AS model,** the basic model we use to understand economic fluctuations.

Short-Run Macroeconomic Equilibrium

We'll begin our analysis by focusing on the short run. Figure 28-11 shows the aggregate demand curve and the short-run aggregate supply curve on the same diagram. The point at which the *AD* and *SRAS* curves intersect, E_{SR}, is the **short-run macroeconomic equilibrium:** the point at which the quantity of aggregate output supplied is equal to the quantity demanded by domestic households, businesses, the government, and the rest of the world. The aggregate price level at E_{SR}, P_E, is the **short-run equilibrium aggregate price level.** The level of aggregate output at E_{SR}, Y_E, is the **short-run equilibrium aggregate output.**

In the supply and demand model of Chapter 3 we saw that a shortage of any individual good causes its market price to rise but a surplus of the good causes its market price to fall. These forces ensure that the market reaches equilibrium. The same logic applies to short-run macroeconomic equilibrium. If the aggregate price level is above its equilibrium level, the quantity of aggregate output supplied exceeds the quantity of aggregate output demanded. This leads to a fall in the aggregate price level and pushes it toward its equilibrium level. If the aggregate price level is below its equilibrium level, the quantity of aggregate output supplied is less than the quantity of aggregate output demanded. This leads to a rise in the aggregate price level, again pushing it toward its equilibrium level. In the discussion that follows, we'll assume that the economy is always in short-run macroeconomic equilibrium.

In the *AD–AS* **model,** the aggregate supply curve and the aggregate demand curve are used together to analyze economic fluctuations.

The economy is in **short-run macroeconomic equilibrium** when the quantity of aggregate output supplied is equal to the quantity demanded.

The **short-run equilibrium aggregate price level** is the aggregate price level in the short-run macroeconomic equilibrium.

Short-run equilibrium aggregate output is the quantity of aggregate output produced in the short-run macroeconomic equilibrium.

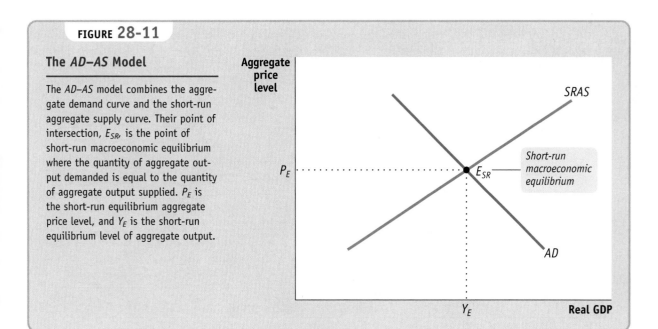

FIGURE 28-11

The *AD–AS* Model

The *AD–AS* model combines the aggregate demand curve and the short-run aggregate supply curve. Their point of intersection, E_{SR}, is the point of short-run macroeconomic equilibrium where the quantity of aggregate output demanded is equal to the quantity of aggregate output supplied. P_E is the short-run equilibrium aggregate price level, and Y_E is the short-run equilibrium level of aggregate output.

We'll also make another important simplification based on the observation that in reality there is a long-term upward trend in both aggregate output and the aggregate price level. We'll assume that a fall in either variable really means a fall compared to the long-run trend. For example, if the aggregate price level normally rises 4% per year, a year in which the aggregate price level rises only 3% would count, for our purposes, as a 1% decline. In fact, since the Great Depression there have been very few years in which the aggregate price level of any major nation actually declined—Japan's period of deflation from 1995 to 2005 is one of the few exceptions. We'll explain why in Chapter 32. There have, however, been many cases in which the aggregate price level fell relative to the long-run trend.

Short-run equilibrium aggregate output and the short-run equilibrium aggregate price level can change either because of shifts of the *AD* curve or because of shifts of the *SRAS* curve. Let's look at each case in turn.

Shifts of Aggregate Demand: Short-Run Effects

An event that shifts the aggregate demand curve, such as a change in expectations or wealth, the effect of the size of the existing stock of physical capital, or the use of fiscal or monetary policy, is known as a **demand shock.** The Great Depression was caused by a negative demand shock, the collapse of wealth and of business and consumer confidence that followed the stock market crash of 1929 and the banking crisis of 1930–1931. The Depression was ended by a positive demand shock—the huge increase in government purchases during World War II. In 2008 the U.S. economy experienced another significant negative demand shock as the housing market turned from boom to bust, leading consumers and firms to scale back their spending.

Figure 28-12 on the next page shows the short-run effects of negative and positive demand shocks. A negative demand shock shifts the aggregate demand curve, *AD,* to the left, from AD_1 to AD_2, as shown in panel (a). The economy moves down along the *SRAS* curve from E_1 to E_2, leading to lower short-run equilibrium aggregate output and a lower short-run equilibrium aggregate price level. A positive demand shock shifts the aggregate demand curve, *AD,* to the right, as shown in panel (b). Here, the economy moves up along the *SRAS* curve, from E_1 to E_2. This leads to higher short-run equilibrium aggregate output and a higher short-run equilibrium aggregate price level. Demand shocks cause aggregate output and the aggregate price level to move in the same direction.

An event that shifts the aggregate demand curve is a **demand shock.**

FIGURE 28-12 **Demand Shocks**

(a) A Negative Demand Shock

A negative demand shock...

SRAS

...leads to a lower aggregate price level and lower aggregate output.

P_1
↓
P_2

E_1

E_2

AD_1

AD_2

$Y_2 \longleftarrow Y_1$ **Real GDP**

Aggregate price level

(b) A Positive Demand Shock

A positive demand shock...

SRAS

...leads to a higher aggregate price level and higher aggregate output.

P_2
↑
P_1

E_2

E_1

AD_1

AD_2

$Y_1 \longrightarrow Y_2$ **Real GDP**

Aggregate price level

A demand shock shifts the aggregate demand curve, moving the aggregate price level and aggregate output in the same direction. In panel (a), a negative demand shock shifts the aggregate demand curve leftward from AD_1 to AD_2, reducing the aggregate price level from P_1 to P_2 and aggregate output from Y_1 to Y_2. In panel (b), a positive demand shock shifts the aggregate demand curve rightward, increasing the aggregate price level from P_1 to P_2 and aggregate output from Y_1 to Y_2.

Shifts of the *SRAS* Curve

An event that shifts the short-run aggregate supply curve, such as a change in commodity prices, nominal wages, or productivity, is known as a **supply shock.** A *negative* supply shock raises production costs and reduces the quantity producers are willing to supply at any given aggregate price level, leading to a leftward shift of the short-run aggregate supply curve. The U.S. economy experienced severe negative supply shocks following disruptions to world oil supplies in 1973 and 1979. In contrast, a *positive* supply shock reduces production costs and increases the quantity supplied at any given aggregate price level, leading to a rightward shift of the short-run aggregate supply curve. The United States experienced a positive supply shock between 1995 and 2000, when the increasing use of the Internet and other information technologies caused productivity growth to surge.

The effects of a negative supply shock are shown in panel (a) of Figure 28-13. The initial equilibrium is at E_1, with aggregate price level P_1 and aggregate output Y_1. The disruption in the oil supply causes the short-run aggregate supply curve to shift to the left, from $SRAS_1$ to $SRAS_2$. As a consequence, aggregate output falls and the aggregate price level rises, an upward movement along the AD curve. At the new equilibrium, E_2, the short-run equilibrium aggregate price level, P_2, is higher, and the short-run equilibrium aggregate output level, Y_2, is lower than before.

The combination of inflation and falling aggregate output shown in panel (a) has a special name: **stagflation,** for "stagnation plus inflation." When an economy experiences stagflation, it's very unpleasant: falling aggregate output leads to rising unemployment, and people feel that their purchasing power is squeezed by rising prices. Stagflation in the 1970s led to a mood of national pessimism. It also, as we'll see shortly, poses a dilemma for policy makers.

A positive supply shock, shown in panel (b), has exactly the opposite effects. A rightward shift of the *SRAS* curve from $SRAS_1$ to $SRAS_2$ results in a rise in aggregate output and a fall in the aggregate price level, a downward movement along the AD curve. The

An event that shifts the short-run aggregate supply curve is a **supply shock.**

Stagflation is the combination of inflation and falling aggregate output.

FIGURE 28-13   Supply Shocks

(a) A Negative Supply Shock

Aggregate price level (vertical axis) / Real GDP (horizontal axis)

A negative supply shock...

$SRAS_2$ $SRAS_1$

E_2

P_2
P_1

...leads to lower aggregate output and a higher aggregate price level.

E_1

AD

$Y_2 \leftarrow Y_1$ Real GDP

(b) A Positive Supply Shock

Aggregate price level (vertical axis) / Real GDP (horizontal axis)

A positive supply shock...

$SRAS_1$
$SRAS_2$

E_1

P_1
P_2

...leads to higher aggregate output and a lower aggregate price level.

E_2

AD

$Y_1 \rightarrow Y_2$ Real GDP

A supply shock shifts the short-run aggregate supply curve, moving the aggregate price level and aggregate output in opposite directions. Panel (a) shows a negative supply shock, which shifts the short-run aggregate supply curve leftward and causes stagflation—lower aggregate output and a higher aggregate price level. Here the short-run aggregate supply curve shifts from $SRAS_1$ to $SRAS_2$, and the economy moves from E_1 to E_2. The aggregate price level rises from P_1 to P_2, and aggregate output falls from Y_1 to Y_2. Panel (b) shows a positive supply shock, which shifts the short-run aggregate supply curve rightward, generating higher aggregate output and a lower aggregate price level. The short-run aggregate supply curve shifts from $SRAS_1$ to $SRAS_2$, and the economy moves from E_1 to E_2. The aggregate price level falls from P_1 to P_2, and aggregate output rises from Y_1 to Y_2.

---

favorable supply shocks of the late 1990s led to a combination of full employment and declining inflation. That is, the aggregate price level fell compared with the long-run trend. This combination produced, for a time, a great wave of national optimism.

The distinctive feature of supply shocks, both negative and positive, is that, unlike demand shocks, they cause the aggregate price level and aggregate output to move in *opposite* directions.

There's another important contrast between supply shocks and demand shocks. As we've seen, monetary policy and fiscal policy enable the government to shift the *AD* curve, meaning that governments are in a position to create the kinds of shocks shown in Figure 28-12. It's much harder for governments to shift the *AS* curve. Are

Pessimism prevails during stagflation as unemployment and prices rise.

GLOBAL COMPARISON

THE SUPPLY SHOCK OF 2007–2008

In the summer of 2007, for reasons that are still a matter of dispute, the prices of many raw materials sold on world markets began shooting up. By the middle of 2008, the price of oil had doubled, the price of rice had tripled, and there had been major increases in the prices of many other commodities, from wheat to iron ore.

The surge in raw-material prices amounted to a global neg-

ative supply shock, affecting all economies. This figure shows the rate of inflation, as measured by the percentage increase in the consumer price index over the previous year, for five major economies from May 2007 to May 2008. The countries started from very different initial positions, ranging from 2.7% inflation in the United States to zero inflation in Japan. Yet all of the countries experienced a substantial jump in prices.

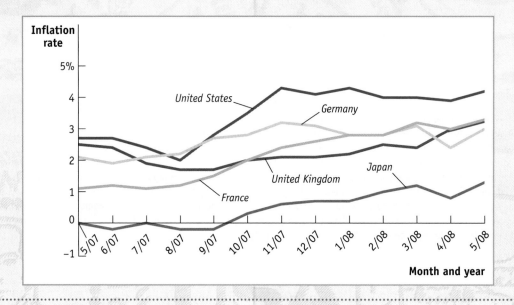

Source: OECD.

there good policy reasons to shift the *AD* curve? We'll turn to that question soon. First, however, let's look at the difference between short-run macroeconomic equilibrium and long-run macroeconomic equilibrium.

Long-Run Macroeconomic Equilibrium

Figure 28-14 combines the aggregate demand curve with both the short-run and long-run aggregate supply curves. The aggregate demand curve, *AD*, crosses the short-run aggregate supply curve, *SRAS*, at E_{LR}. Here we assume that enough time has elapsed that the economy is also on the long-run aggregate supply curve, *LRAS*. As a result, E_{LR} is at the intersection of all three curves—*SRAS*, *LRAS*, and *AD*. So short-run equilibrium aggregate output is equal to potential output, Y_P. Such a situation, in which the point of short-run macroeconomic equilibrium is on the long-run aggregate supply curve, is known as **long-run macroeconomic equilibrium.**

To see the significance of long-run macroeconomic equilibrium, let's consider what happens if a demand shock moves the economy away from long-run macroeconomic equilibrium. In Figure 28-15, we assume that the initial aggregate demand curve is AD_1 and the initial short-run aggregate supply curve is $SRAS_1$. So the initial macroeconomic equilibrium is at E_1, which lies on the long-run aggregate supply curve, *LRAS*. The economy, then, starts from a point of short-run and long-run macroeconomic equilibrium, and short-run equilibrium aggregate output equals potential output at Y_1.

Now suppose that for some reason—such as a sudden worsening of business and consumer expectations—aggregate demand falls and the aggregate demand curve

The economy is in **long-run macroeconomic equilibrium** when the point of short-run macroeconomic equilibrium is on the long-run aggregate supply curve.

FIGURE 28-14

Long-Run Macroeconomic Equilibrium

Here the point of short-run macroeconomic equilibrium also lies on the long-run aggregate supply curve, *LRAS*. As a result, short-run equilibrium aggregate output is equal to potential output, Y_P. The economy is in long-run macroeconomic equilibrium at E_{LR}.

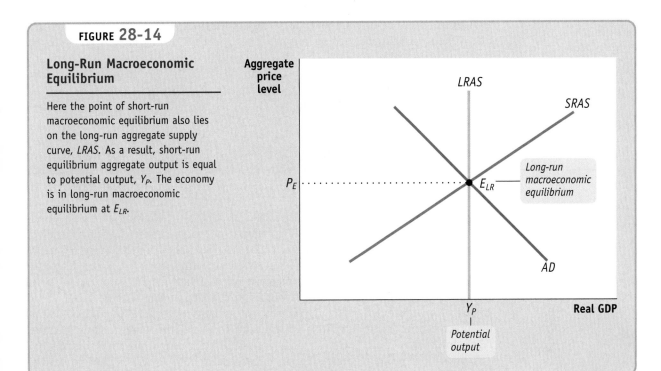

shifts leftward to AD_2. This results in a lower equilibrium aggregate price level at P_2 and a lower equilibrium aggregate output level at Y_2 as the economy settles in the short run at E_2. The short-run effect of such a fall in aggregate demand is what the U.S. economy experienced in 1929–1933: a falling aggregate price level and falling aggregate output.

FIGURE 28-15

Short-Run versus Long-Run Effects of a Negative Demand Shock

In the long run the economy is self-correcting: demand shocks have only a short-run effect on aggregate output. Starting at E_1, a negative demand shock shifts AD_1 leftward to AD_2. In the short run the economy moves to E_2 and a recessionary gap arises: the aggregate price level declines from P_1 to P_2, aggregate output declines from Y_1 to Y_2, and unemployment rises. But in the long run nominal wages fall in response to high unemployment at Y_2, and $SRAS_1$ shifts rightward to $SRAS_2$. Aggregate output rises from Y_2 to Y_1, and the aggregate price level declines again, from P_2 to P_3. Long-run macroeconomic equilibrium is eventually restored at E_3.

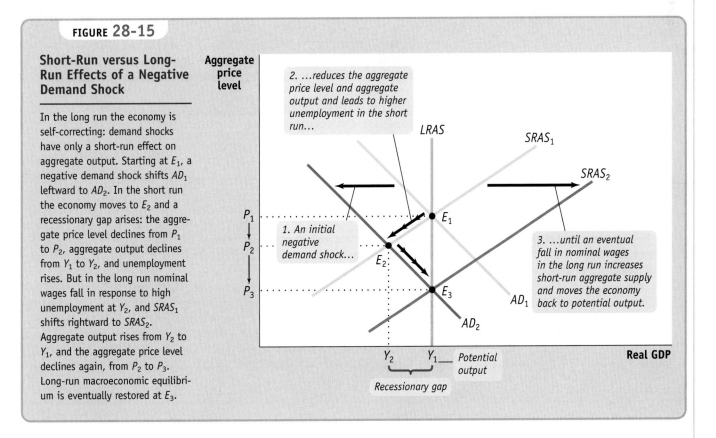

There is a **recessionary gap** when aggregate output is below potential output.

There is an **inflationary gap** when aggregate output is above potential output.

The **output gap** is the percentage difference between actual aggregate output and potential output.

Aggregate output in this new short-run equilibrium, E_2, is below potential output. When this happens, the economy faces a **recessionary gap.** A recessionary gap inflicts a great deal of pain because it corresponds to high unemployment. The large recessionary gap that had opened up in the United States by 1933 caused intense social and political turmoil. And the devastating recessionary gap that opened up in Germany at the same time played an important role in Hitler's rise to power.

But this isn't the end of the story. In the face of high unemployment, nominal wages eventually fall, as do any other sticky prices, ultimately leading producers to increase output. As a result, a recessionary gap causes the short-run aggregate supply curve to gradually shift to the right over time. This process continues until $SRAS_1$ reaches its new position at $SRAS_2$, bringing the economy to equilibrium at E_3, where AD_2, $SRAS_2$, and $LRAS$ all intersect. At E_3, the economy is back in long-run macroeconomic equilibrium; it is back at potential output Y_1 but at a lower aggregate price level, P_3, reflecting a long-run fall in the aggregate price level. In the end, the economy is *self-correcting* in the long run.

What if, instead, there was an increase in aggregate demand? The results are shown in Figure 28-16, where we again assume that the initial aggregate demand curve is AD_1 and the initial short-run aggregate supply curve is $SRAS_1$, so that the initial macroeconomic equilibrium, at E_1, lies on the long-run aggregate supply curve, $LRAS$. Initially, then, the economy is in long-run macroeconomic equilibrium.

Now suppose that aggregate demand rises, and the AD curve shifts rightward to AD_2. This results in a higher aggregate price level, at P_2, and a higher aggregate output level, at Y_2, as the economy settles in the short run at E_2. Aggregate output in this new short-run equilibrium is above potential output, and unemployment is low in order to produce this higher level of aggregate output. When this happens, the economy experiences an **inflationary gap.** As in the case of a recessionary gap, this isn't the end of the story. In the face of low unemployment, nominal wages will rise, as will other sticky prices. An inflationary gap causes the short-run aggregate supply curve to shift gradually to the left as producers reduce output in the face of rising nominal wages. This process continues until $SRAS_1$ reaches its new position at $SRAS_2$, bringing the economy to equilibrium at E_3, where AD_2, $SRAS_2$, and $LRAS$ all intersect. At E_3, the economy is back in long-run macroeconomic equilibrium. It is back at potential output, but at a higher price level, P_3, reflecting a long-run rise in the aggregate price level. Again, the economy is self-correcting in the long run.

To summarize the analysis of how the economy responds to recessionary and inflationary gaps, we can focus on the **output gap,** the percentage difference

FOR INQUIRING MINDS

Where's the Deflation?

The *AD–AS* model says that either a negative demand shock or a positive supply shock should lead to a fall in the aggregate price level—that is, deflation. In fact, however, the United States hasn't experienced an actual fall in the aggregate price level since 1949. Neither have most other countries; Japan, which experienced sustained mild deflation in the late 1990s and the early part of the next decade, is the big (and much discussed) exception. What happened to the deflation?

The basic answer is that since World War II economic fluctuations have taken place around a long-run inflationary trend. Before the war, it was common for prices to fall during recessions, but since then negative demand shocks have been reflected in a *decline in the rate of inflation* rather than an actual fall in prices. For example, the rate of consumer price inflation fell from more than 3% at the beginning of the 2001 recession to 1.1% a year later, but it never went below zero.

A very severe negative demand shock could still bring deflation, which is what happened in Japan. This has not happened in the United States, although there were renewed deflation concerns in the wake of the 2008 financial crisis.

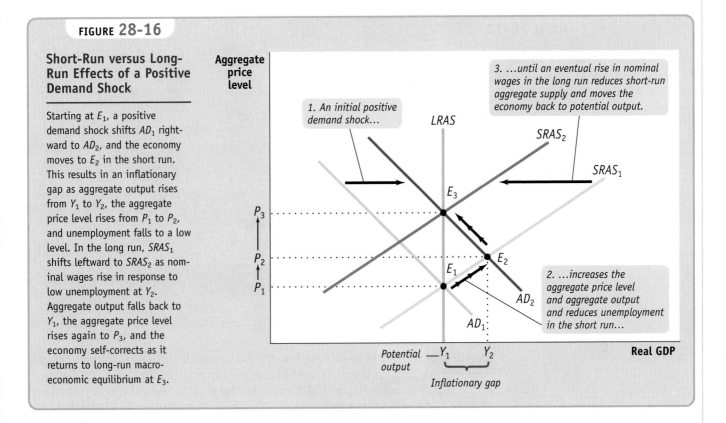

FIGURE 28-16

Short-Run versus Long-Run Effects of a Positive Demand Shock

Starting at E_1, a positive demand shock shifts AD_1 rightward to AD_2, and the economy moves to E_2 in the short run. This results in an inflationary gap as aggregate output rises from Y_1 to Y_2, the aggregate price level rises from P_1 to P_2, and unemployment falls to a low level. In the long run, $SRAS_1$ shifts leftward to $SRAS_2$ as nominal wages rise in response to low unemployment at Y_2. Aggregate output falls back to Y_1, the aggregate price level rises again to P_3, and the economy self-corrects as it returns to long-run macroeconomic equilibrium at E_3.

Aggregate price level

1. An initial positive demand shock...

3. ...until an eventual rise in nominal wages in the long run reduces short-run aggregate supply and moves the economy back to potential output.

LRAS

SRAS₂

SRAS₁

E_3

P_3

P_2

E_1

P_1

E_2

2. ...increases the aggregate price level and aggregate output and reduces unemployment in the short run...

AD_2

AD_1

Potential output — Y_1 Y_2 **Real GDP**

Inflationary gap

between actual aggregate output and potential output. The output gap is calculated as follows:

(28-3) Output gap = $\dfrac{\text{Actual aggregate output} - \text{Potential output}}{\text{Potential output}} \times 100$

Our analysis says that the output gap always tends toward zero.

If there is a recessionary gap, so that the output gap is negative, nominal wages eventually fall, moving the economy back to potential output and bringing the output gap back to zero. If there is an inflationary gap, so that the output gap is positive, nominal wages eventually rise, also moving the economy back to potential output and again bringing the output gap back to zero. So in the long run the economy is **self-correcting:** shocks to aggregate demand affect aggregate output in the short run but not in the long run.

►*ECONOMICS IN ACTION*

Supply Shocks versus Demand Shocks in Practice

How often do supply shocks and demand shocks, respectively, cause recessions? The verdict of most, though not all, macroeconomists is that recessions are mainly caused by demand shocks. But when a negative supply shock does happen, the resulting recession tends to be particularly severe.

Let's get specific. Officially there have been twelve recessions in the United States since World War II. However, two of these, in 1979–1980 and 1981–1982, are often treated as a single "double-dip" recession, bringing the total number down to 11. Of these 11 recessions, only two—the recession of 1973–1975 and the double-dip

The economy is **self-correcting** when shocks to aggregate demand affect aggregate output in the short run, but not in the long run.

FIGURE 28-17

Negative Supply Shocks Are Relatively Rare but Nasty

Only two of eleven postwar recessions seem to fit the profile of a recession caused by a negative supply shock: the recession that followed the increase in oil prices after the 1973 Arab–Israeli war and the recession that followed another surge in oil prices after the Iranian revolution. These two recessions were, however, the worst in terms of unemployment. A third recession that began in December 2007 was at least partially casued by a spike in oil prices.

Source: Bureau of Labor Statistics.

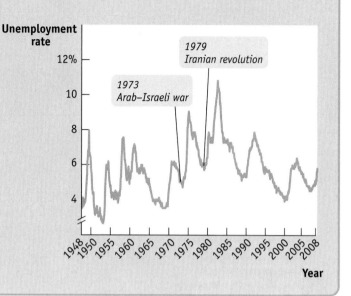

recession of 1979–1982—showed the distinctive combination of falling aggregate output and a surge in the price level that we call stagflation. In each case, the cause of the supply shock was political turmoil in the Middle East—the Arab–Israeli war of 1973 and the Iranian revolution of 1979—that disrupted world oil supplies and sent oil prices skyrocketing. In fact, economists sometimes refer to the two slumps as "OPEC I" and "OPEC II," after the Organization of Petroleum Exporting Countries, the world oil cartel. A third recession that began in December 2007, and that was getting deeper as this book went to press a year later, was at least partially caused by a spike in oil prices.

So eight of eleven postwar recessions were purely the result of demand shocks, not supply shocks. The few supply-shock recessions, however, were the worst as measured by the unemployment rate. Figure 28-17 shows the U.S. unemployment rate since 1948, with the dates of the 1973 Arab–Israeli war and the 1979 Iranian revolution marked on the graph. The two highest unemployment rates since World War II came after these big negative supply shocks.

There's a reason the aftermath of a supply shock tends to be particularly severe for the economy: macroeconomic policy has a much harder time dealing with supply shocks than with demand shocks. Indeed, the reason the Federal Reserve was having a hard time in 2008, as described in the opening story, was the fact that in early 2008 the U.S. economy was in a recession partially caused by a supply shock (although it was also facing a demand shock). We'll see in a moment why supply shocks present such a problem. ▲

< < < < < < < < < < < <

►► QUICK REVIEW

➤ The **AD–AS model** is used to study economic fluctuations.

➤ **Short-run macroeconomic equilibrium** occurs at the intersection of the short-run aggregate supply and aggregate demand curves. This determines the **short-run equilibrium aggregate price level** and the level of **short-run equilibrium aggregate output**.

➤ A **demand shock,** a shift of the *AD* curve, causes the aggregate price level and aggregate output to move in the same direction. A **supply shock,** a shift of the *SRAS* curve, causes them to move in opposite directions. **Stagflation** is the consequence of a negative supply shock.

➤ A fall in nominal wages occurs in response to a **recessionary gap,** and a rise in nominal wages occurs in response to an **inflationary gap.** Both move the economy to **long-run macroeconomic equilibrium,** where the *AD*, *SRAS*, and *LRAS* curves intersect.

➤ The **output gap** always tends toward zero because the economy is **self-correcting** in the long run.

► CHECK YOUR UNDERSTANDING 28-3

1. Describe the short-run effects of each of the following shocks on the aggregate price level and on aggregate output.
   a. The government sharply increases the minimum wage, raising the wages of many workers.
   b. Solar energy firms launch a major program of investment spending.
   c. Congress raises taxes and cuts spending.
   d. Severe weather destroys crops around the world.

2. A rise in productivity increases potential output, but some worry that demand for the additional output will be insufficient even in the long run. How would you respond?

Solutions appear at back of book.

Macroeconomic Policy

We've just seen that the economy is self-correcting in the long run: it will eventually trend back to potential output. Most macroeconomists believe, however, that the process of self-correction typically takes a decade or more. In particular, if aggregate output is below potential output, the economy can suffer an extended period of depressed aggregate output and high unemployment before it returns to normal.

This belief is the background to one of the most famous quotations in economics: John Maynard Keynes's declaration, "In the long run we are all dead." We explain the context in which he made this remark in the accompanying For Inquiring Minds.

Economists usually interpret Keynes as having recommended that governments not wait for the economy to correct itself. Instead, it is argued by many economists, but not all, that the government should use monetary and fiscal policy to get the economy back to potential output in the aftermath of a shift of the aggregate demand curve. This is the rationale for an active **stabilization policy,** which is the use of government policy to reduce the severity of recessions and rein in excessively strong expansions.

> **Stabilization policy** is the use of government policy to reduce the severity of recessions and rein in excessively strong expansions.

FOR INQUIRING MINDS

Keynes and the Long Run

The British economist Sir John Maynard Keynes (1883–1946), probably more than any other single economist, created the modern field of macroeconomics. We'll look at his role, and the controversies that still swirl around some aspects of his thought, in a later chapter on macroeconomic events and ideas. But for now let's just look at his most famous quote.

In 1923 Keynes published *A Tract on Monetary Reform,* a small book on the economic problems of Europe after World War I. In it he decried the tendency of many of his colleagues to focus on how things work out in the long run—as in the long-run macroeconomic equilibrium we have just analyzed—while ignoring the often very painful and possibly disastrous

things that can happen along the way. Here's a fuller version of the quote:

> This *long run* is a misleading guide to current affairs. *In the long run* we are all dead. Economists set themselves too easy, too useless a task if in tempestuous seasons they can only tell us that when the storm is long past the sea is flat again.

Can stabilization policy improve the economy's performance? If we reexamine Figure 28-8, the answer certainly appears to be yes. Under active stabilization policy, the U.S. economy returned to potential output in 1996 after an approximately five-year recessionary gap. Likewise, in 2001 it also returned to potential output after an approximately four-year inflationary gap. These periods are much shorter than the decade or more that economists believe it would take for the economy to self-correct in the absence of active stabilization policy. However, as we'll see shortly, the ability to improve the economy's performance is not always guaranteed. It depends on the kinds of shocks the economy faces.

Policy in the Face of Demand Shocks

Imagine that the economy experiences a negative demand shock, like the one shown in Figure 28-15. As we've discussed in this chapter, monetary and fiscal policy shift the aggregate demand curve. If policy makers react quickly to the fall in aggregate demand, they can use monetary or fiscal policy to shift the aggregate demand curve back to the right. And if policy were able to perfectly anticipate shifts of the aggregate demand curve, it could short-circuit the whole process shown in Figure 28-15. Instead of going through a period of low aggregate output and falling prices, the government could manage the economy so that it would stay at E_1.

Why might a policy that short-circuits the adjustment shown in Figure 28-15 and maintains the economy at its original equilibrium be desirable? For two reasons. First, the temporary fall in aggregate output that would happen without policy intervention is a bad thing, particularly because such a decline is associated with high unemployment. Second, as we explained in Chapter 24, *price stability* is generally regarded as a desirable goal. So preventing deflation—a fall in the aggregate price level—is a good thing.

Does this mean that policy makers should always act to offset declines in aggregate demand? Not necessarily. As we'll see in later chapters, some policy measures to increase aggregate demand, especially those that increase budget deficits, may have long-term costs in terms of lower long-run growth. Furthermore, in the real world policy makers aren't perfectly informed, and the effects of their policies aren't perfectly predictable. This creates the danger that stabilization policy will do more harm than good; that is, attempts to stabilize the economy may end up creating more instability. We'll describe the long-running debate over macroeconomic policy in Chapter 33. Despite these qualifications, most economists believe that a good case can be made for using macroeconomic policy to offset major negative shocks to the *AD* curve.

Should policy makers also try to offset positive shocks to aggregate demand? It may not seem obvious that they should. After all, even though inflation may be a bad thing, isn't more output and lower unemployment a good thing? Not necessarily. Most economists now believe that any short-run gains from an inflationary gap must be paid back later. So policy makers today usually try to offset positive as well as negative demand shocks. For reasons we'll explain in Chapter 33, attempts to eliminate recessionary gaps and inflationary gaps usually rely on monetary rather than fiscal policy. In 2007 and 2008 the Federal Reserve sharply cut interest rates in an attempt to head off a rising recessionary gap; earlier in the decade, when the U.S. economy seemed headed for an inflationary gap, it raised interest rates to generate the opposite effect.

But how should macroeconomic policy respond to supply shocks?

Responding to Supply Shocks

We've now come full circle to the story that began this chapter. We can now explain why people in Ben Bernanke's position dread stagflation.

Back in panel (a) of Figure 28-13 we showed the effects of a negative supply shock: in the short run such a shock leads to lower aggregate output but a higher aggregate price level. As we've noted, policy makers can respond to a negative *demand* shock by using monetary and fiscal policy to return aggregate demand to its original level. But what can or should they do about a negative *supply* shock?

In contrast to the aggregate demand curve, there are no easy policies that shift the short-run aggregate supply curve. That is, there is no government policy that can easily affect producers' profitability and so compensate for shifts of the short-run aggregate supply curve. So the policy response to a negative supply shock cannot aim to simply push the curve that shifted back to its original position.

And if you consider using monetary or fiscal policy to shift the aggregate demand curve in response to a supply shock, the right response isn't obvious. Two bad things are happening simultaneously: a fall in aggregate output, leading to a rise in unemployment, *and* a rise in the aggregate price level. Any policy that shifts the aggregate demand curve helps one problem only by making the other worse. If the government acts to increase aggregate demand and limit the rise in unemployment, it reduces the decline in output but causes even more inflation. If it acts to reduce aggregate demand, it curbs inflation but causes a further rise in unemployment.

It's a trade-off with no good answer. In the end, the United States and other economically advanced nations suffering from the supply shocks of the 1970s eventually chose to stabilize prices even at the cost of higher unemployment. But being an economic policy maker in the 1970s, or in early 2008, meant facing even harder choices than usual.

►ECONOMICS IN ACTION

Is Stabilization Policy Stabilizing?

We've described the theoretical rationale for stabilization policy as a way of responding to demand shocks. But does stabilization policy actually stabilize the economy? One way we might try to answer this question is to look at the long-term historical record. Before World War II, the U.S. government didn't really have a stabilization policy, largely because macroeconomics as we know it didn't exist, and there was no consensus about what to do. Since World War II, and especially since 1960, active stabilization policy has become standard practice.

So here's the question: has the economy actually become more stable since the government began trying to stabilize it? The answer is a qualified yes. It's qualified because data from the pre–World War II era are less reliable than more modern data. But there still seems to be a clear reduction in the size of economic fluctuations.

FIGURE 28-18

Has Stabilization Policy Been Stabilizing?

The nonfarm unemployment rate—the number of unemployed as a percentage of the nonfarm labor force—has fluctuated considerably less since World War II than it did before. This suggests that stabilization policy, which didn't begin until the postwar period and especially after 1960, has in fact been stabilizing. It's also worth noting that the two peaks of postwar unemployment, in 1975 and 1982, both came as a result of supply shocks—the kind of shock that stabilization policy has a hard time handling.

Source: C. Romer, "Spurious Volatility in Historical Unemployment Data." *Journal of Political Economy* 94, no. 1 (1986): 1–37 (years 1890–1928); Bureau of Labor Statistics (years 1929–2007).

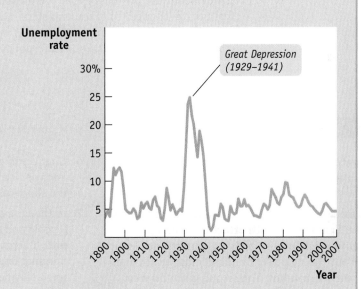

Figure 28-18 shows the number of unemployed as a percentage of the nonfarm labor force since 1890. (We focus on nonfarm workers because farmers, though they often suffer economic hardship, are rarely reported as unemployed.) Even ignoring the huge spike in unemployment during the Great Depression, unemployment seems to have varied a lot more before World War II than after. It's also worth noticing that the two peaks in postwar unemployment, in 1975 and 1982, both corresponded to major supply shocks—the kind of shock for which stabilization policy has no good answer.

It's possible that the greater stability of the economy reflects good luck rather than policy. But on the face of it, the evidence suggests that stabilization policy is indeed stabilizing. ▲   > > > > > > > > > > > > >

► CHECK YOUR UNDERSTANDING 28-4

1. Suppose someone says, "Using monetary or fiscal policy to pump up the economy is counterproductive—you get a brief high, but then you have the pain of inflation."
   a. Explain what this means in terms of the *AD–AS* model.
   b. Is this a valid argument against stabilization policy? Why or why not?

>> QUICK REVIEW

➤ **Stabilization policy** is the use of fiscal or monetary policy to offset demand shocks. There can be drawbacks, however. Such policies may lead to a long-term rise in the budget deficit and lower long-run growth because of crowding out. And, due to incorrect predictions, a misguided policy can increase economic instability.

➤ Negative supply shocks pose a policy dilemma because fighting the slump in aggregate output worsens inflation and fighting inflation worsens the slump.

2. In 2008, in the aftermath of the collapse of the housing bubble and a sharp rise in the price of commodities, particularly oil, there was much internal disagreement within the Fed about how to respond, with some advocating lowering interest rates and others contending that this would set off a rise in inflation. Explain the reasoning behind each one of these views in terms of the *AD–AS* model.

Solutions appear at back of book.

[>> A LOOK AHEAD•••

The *AD–AS* model is a powerful tool for understanding both economic fluctuations and the ways in which economic policy can sometimes fight adverse shocks. But in order to present the basic idea, we've been somewhat sketchy about the details.

In the next three chapters we'll put some flesh on these economic bones. We'll begin by filling in some details about how taxes, transfers, and government purchases fit into the model. As we'll see, putting the government in leads us immediately to one of the key insights of macroeconomics: sometimes the government can do something about the business cycle. We'll explore the potential and the difficulties of fiscal policy—changes in taxes, transfers, and government purchases designed to affect macroeconomic outcomes. And finally, we'll turn to an even more important tool in the government's hands, monetary policy.]

SUMMARY

1. The **aggregate demand curve** shows the relationship between the aggregate price level and the quantity of aggregate output demanded.

2. The aggregate demand curve is downward sloping for two reasons. The first is the **wealth effect of a change in the aggregate price level**—a higher aggregate price level reduces the purchasing power of households' wealth and reduces consumer spending. The second is the **interest rate effect of a change in the aggregate price level**—a higher aggregate price level reduces the purchasing power of households' and firms' money holdings, leading to a rise in interest rates and a fall in investment spending and consumer spending.

3. The aggregate demand curve shifts because of changes in expectations, changes in wealth not due to changes in the aggregate price level, and the effect of the size of the existing stock of physical capital. Policy makers can use fiscal policy and monetary policy to shift the aggregate demand curve.

4. The **aggregate supply curve** shows the relationship between the aggregate price level and the quantity of aggregate output supplied.

5. The **short-run aggregate supply curve** is upward sloping because **nominal wages** are **sticky** in the short run: a higher aggregate price level leads to higher profit per unit of output and increased aggregate output in the short run.

6. Changes in commodity prices, nominal wages, and productivity lead to changes in producers' profits and shift the short-run aggregate supply curve.

7. In the long run, all prices, including nominal wages, are flexible and the economy produces at its **potential output.** If actual aggregate output exceeds potential output, nominal wages will eventually rise in response to low unemployment and aggregate output will fall. If potential output exceeds actual aggregate output, nominal wages will eventually fall in response to high unemployment and aggregate output will rise. So the **long-run aggregate supply curve** is vertical at potential output.

8. In the *AD–AS model,* the intersection of the short-run aggregate supply curve and the aggregate demand curve is the point of **short-run macroeconomic equilibrium.** It determines the **short-run equilibrium aggregate price level** and the level of **short-run equilibrium aggregate output.**

9. Economic fluctuations occur because of a shift of the aggregate demand curve (a *demand shock*) or the short-run aggregate supply curve (a *supply shock*). A **demand shock** causes the aggregate price level and aggregate output to move in the same direction as the economy moves along the short-run aggregate supply curve. A **supply shock** causes them to move in opposite directions as the economy moves along the aggregate demand curve. A particularly nasty occurrence is **stagflation**—inflation

and falling aggregate output—which is caused by a negative supply shock.

10. Demand shocks have only short-run effects on aggregate output because the economy is **self-correcting** in the long run. In a **recessionary gap,** an eventual fall in nominal wages moves the economy to **long-run macroeconomic equilibrium,** where aggregate output is equal to potential output. In an **inflationary gap,** an eventual rise in nominal wages moves the economy to long-run macroeconomic equilibrium. We can use the **output gap,** the percentage difference between actual aggregate output and potential output, to summarize how the economy responds to recessionary and inflationary gaps. Because the economy tends to be self-correcting in the long run, the output gap always tends toward zero.

11. The high cost—in terms of unemployment—of a recessionary gap and the future adverse consequences of an inflationary gap lead many economists to advocate active **stabilization policy:** using fiscal or monetary policy to offset demand shocks. There can be drawbacks, however, because such policies may contribute to a long-term rise in the budget deficit and crowding out of private investment, leading to lower long-run growth. Also, poorly timed policies can increase economic instability.

12. Negative supply shocks pose a policy dilemma: a policy that counteracts the fall in aggregate output by increasing aggregate demand will lead to higher inflation, but a policy that counteracts inflation by reducing aggregate demand will deepen the output slump.

KEY TERMS ∎

Aggregate demand curve, p. 733
Wealth effect of a change in the aggregate price level, p. 734
Interest rate effect of a change in the aggregate price level, p. 734
Aggregate supply curve, p. 740
Nominal wage, p. 741
Sticky wages, p. 741
Short-run aggregate supply curve, p. 742

Long-run aggregate supply curve, p. 746
Potential output, p. 746
AD-AS model, p. 750
Short-run macroeconomic equilibrium, p. 750
Short-run equilibrium aggregate price level, p. 750
Short-run equilibrium aggregate output, p. 750
Demand shock, p. 751

Supply shock, p. 752
Stagflation, p. 752
Long-run macroeconomic equilibrium, p. 754
Recessionary gap, p. 756
Inflationary gap, p. 756
Output gap, p. 756
Self-correcting, p. 757
Stabilization policy, p. 759

PROBLEMS ∎

1. A fall in the value of the dollar against other currencies makes U.S. final goods and services cheaper to foreigners even though the U.S. aggregate price level stays the same. As a result, foreigners demand more American aggregate output. Your study partner says that this represents a movement down the aggregate demand curve because foreigners are demanding more in response to a lower price. You, however, insist that this represents a rightward shift of the aggregate demand curve. Who is right? Explain.

2. Your study partner is confused by the upward-sloping short-run aggregate supply curve and the vertical long-run aggregate supply curve. How would you explain this?

3. Suppose that in Wageland all workers sign annual wage contracts each year on January 1. No matter what happens to prices of final goods and services during the year, all workers earn the wage specified in their annual contract. This year, prices of final goods and services fall unexpectedly after the contracts are signed. Answer the following questions using a diagram and assume that the economy starts at potential output.

   a. In the short run, how will the quantity of aggregate output supplied respond to the fall in prices?

   b. What will happen when firms and workers renegotiate their wages?

4. In each of the following cases, in the short run, determine whether the events cause a shift of a curve or a movement along a curve. Determine which curve is involved and the direction of the change.

   a. As a result of an increase in the value of the dollar in relation to other currencies, American producers now pay less in dollar terms for foreign steel, a major commodity used in production.

   b. An increase in the quantity of money by the Federal Reserve increases the quantity of money that people wish to lend, lowering interest rates.

   c. Greater union activity leads to higher nominal wages.

   d. A fall in the aggregate price level increases the purchasing power of households' and firms' money holdings. As a result, they borrow less and lend more.

5. The economy is at point *A* in the accompanying diagram. Suppose that the aggregate price level rises from P_1 to P_2. How will aggregate supply adjust in the short run and in the long run to the increase in the aggregate price level? Illustrate with a diagram.

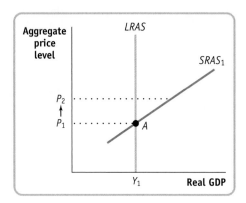

6. Suppose that all households hold all their wealth in assets that automatically rise in value when the aggregate price level rises (an example of this is what is called an "inflation-indexed bond"—a bond whose interest rate, among other things, changes one-for-one with the inflation rate). What happens to the wealth effect of a change in the aggregate price level as a result of this allocation of assets? What happens to the slope of the aggregate demand curve? Will it still slope downward? Explain.

7. Suppose that the economy is currently at potential output. Also suppose that you are an economic policy maker and that a college economics student asks you to rank, if possible, your most preferred to least preferred type of shock: positive demand shock, negative demand shock, positive supply shock, negative supply shock. How would you rank them and why?

8. Explain whether the following government policies affect the aggregate demand curve or the short-run aggregate supply curve and how.

   a. The government reduces the minimum nominal wage.

   b. The government increases Temporary Assistance to Needy Families (TANF) payments, government transfers to families with dependent children.

   c. To reduce the budget deficit, the government announces that households will pay much higher taxes beginning next year.

   d. The government reduces military spending.

9. In Wageland, all workers sign an annual wage contract each year on January 1. In late January, a new computer operating system is introduced that increases labor productivity dramatically. Explain how Wageland will move from one short-run macroeconomic equilibrium to another. Illustrate with a diagram.

10. The Conference Board publishes the Consumer Confidence Index (CCI) every month based on a survey of 5,000 representative U.S. households. It is used by many economists to track the state of the economy. A press release by the Board on April 29, 2008 stated: "The Conference Board Consumer Confidence Index, which had declined sharply in March, fell further in April. The Index now stands at 62.3 (1985 = 100), down from 65.9 in March."

    a. As an economist, is this news encouraging for economic growth?

    b. Explain your answer to part a with the help of the *AD–AS* model. Draw a typical diagram showing two equilibrium points (E_1) and (E_2). Label the vertical axis "Aggregate price level" and the horizontal axis "Real GDP." Assume that all other major macroeconomic factors remain unchanged.

    c. How should the government respond to this news? What are some policy measures that could be used to help neutralize the effect of falling consumer confidence?

11. There were two major shocks to the U.S. economy in 2007, leading to a severe economic slowdown. One shock was related to oil prices; the other was the slump in the housing market. This question analyzes the effect of these two shocks on GDP using the *AD–AS* framework.

    a. Draw typical aggregate demand and short-run aggregate supply curves. Label the horizontal axis "Real GDP" and the vertical axis "Aggregate price level." Label the equilibrium point E_1, the equilibrium quantity Y_1, and equilibrium price P_1.

    b. Data taken from the Department of Energy indicate that the average price of crude oil in the world increased from $54.63 per barrel on January 5, 2007, to $92.93 on December 28, 2007. Would an increase in oil prices cause a demand shock or a supply shock? Redraw the diagram from part a to illustrate the effect of this shock by shifting the appropriate curve.

    c. The Housing Price Index, published by the Office of Federal Housing Enterprise Oversight, calculates that U.S. home prices fell by an average of 3.0% in the 12 months between January 2007 and January 2008. Would the fall in home prices cause a supply shock or demand shock? Redraw the diagram from part b to illustrate the effect of this shock by shifting the appropriate curve. Label the new equilibrium point E_2, the equilibrium quantity Y_2, and equilibrium price P_2.

    d. Compare the equilibrium points E_1 and E_2 in your diagram for part c. What was the effect of the two shocks on real GDP and the aggregate price level (increase, decrease, or indeterminate)?

12. Using aggregate demand, short-run aggregate supply, and long-run aggregate supply curves, explain the process by which each of the following economic events will move the economy from one long-run macroeconomic equilibrium to another. Illustrate with diagrams. In each case, what are the short-run and long-run effects on the aggregate price level and aggregate output?

    a. There is a decrease in households' wealth due to a decline in the stock market.

b. The government lowers taxes, leaving households with more disposable income, with no corresponding reduction in government purchases.

13. Using aggregate demand, short-run aggregate supply, and long-run aggregate supply curves, explain the process by which each of the following government policies will move the economy from one long-run macroeconomic equilibrium to another. Illustrate with diagrams. In each case, what are the short-run and long-run effects on the aggregate price level and aggregate output?

a. There is an increase in taxes on households.

b. There is an increase in the quantity of money.

c. There is an increase in government spending.

14. The economy is in short-run macroeconomic equilibrium at point E_1 in the accompanying diagram. Based on the diagram, answer the following questions.

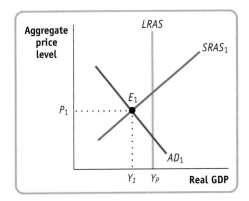

a. Is the economy facing an inflationary or a recessionary gap?

b. What policies can the government implement that might bring the economy back to long-run macroeconomic equilibrium? Illustrate with a diagram.

c. If the government did not intervene to close this gap, would the economy return to long-run macroeconomic equilibrium? Explain and illustrate with a diagram.

d. What are the advantages and disadvantages of the government implementing policies to close the gap?

15. In the accompanying diagram, the economy is in long-run macroeconomic equilibrium at point E_1 when an oil shock shifts the short-run aggregate supply curve to $SRAS_2$. Based on the diagram, answer the following questions.

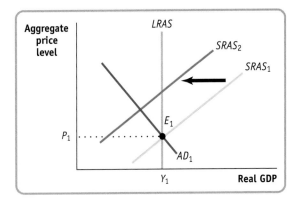

a. How do the aggregate price level and aggregate output change in the short run as a result of the oil shock? What is this phenomenon known as?

b. What fiscal or monetary policies can the government use to address the effects of the supply shock? Use a diagram that shows the effect of policies chosen to address the change in real GDP. Use another diagram to show the effect of policies chosen to address the change in the aggregate price level.

c. Why do supply shocks present a dilemma for government policy makers?

16. The late 1990s in the United States were characterized by substantial economic growth with low inflation; that is, real GDP increased with little, if any, increase in the aggregate price level. Explain this experience using aggregate demand and aggregate supply curves. Illustrate with a diagram.

○···○

 www.worthpublishers.com/krugmanwells

29

Fiscal Policy

JUMPSTARTING THE ECONOMY?

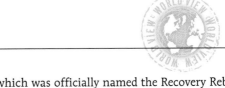

ON FEBRUARY 7, 2008, BIPARTISAN MAJORITIES IN both houses of Congress passed a bill that would send checks to 130 million American families and offer tax breaks to businesses as well, at a total projected cost of $168 billion. At the time, Congress was sharply divided about national priorities, and getting things done was usually a slow and painful process. So both the speed with which the bill was passed and the bipartisan agreement were unusual.

But both sides of the political divide agreed that something needed to be done, fast, about an economy they feared was quickly sliding into recession in the wake of the housing bust and the ensuing financial crisis. And the bill—which was officially named the Recovery Rebate and Stimulus for the American People Act, but which was commonly referred to as the "stimulus package"—was the result of a compromise that everyone hoped would "jumpstart our slowing economy" (as Nancy Pelosi, the Speaker of the House, put it).

The 2008 stimulus package was an example of *discretionary fiscal policy*—the deliberate use of government spending or taxation to manage aggregate demand. It was the latest of many attempts by the U.S. government to fight off an economic slump with tax cuts and/or spending increases, dating back to the 1930s. Many other countries have also tried to manage their economies with discretionary fiscal policy—in some cases on a heroic scale. In particular, during the 1990s Japan began applying massive fiscal stimulus in an attempt to support its ailing economy, ultimately spending more than a trillion dollars.

In this chapter, we will learn how discretionary fiscal policy fits into the models of short-run fluctuations we developed in Chapters 27 and 28. We'll see how deliberate changes in government spending and tax policy affect real GDP. We'll also see how changes in tax revenue caused by short-run fluctuations in GDP—an automatic response that occurs without deliberate changes in policy—help stabilize the economy. Finally, we'll examine long-run consequences of government debt and budget deficits.

WHAT YOU WILL LEARN IN THIS CHAPTER:

➤ What fiscal policy is and why it is an important tool in managing economic fluctuations

➤ Which policies constitute an **expansionary fiscal policy** and which constitute a **contractionary fiscal policy**

➤ Why fiscal policy has a multiplier effect and how this effect is influenced by **automatic stabilizers**

➤ Why governments calculate the **cyclically adjusted budget balance**

➤ Why a large **public debt** may be a cause for concern

➤ Why **implicit liabilities** of the government are also a cause for concern

Fiscal Policy: The Basics

Let's begin with the obvious: modern governments spend a great deal of money and collect a lot in taxes. Figure 29-1 shows government spending and tax revenue as percentages of GDP for a selection of high-income countries in 2006. As you can see, the Swedish government sector is relatively large, accounting for more than half of the Swedish economy. The government of the United States plays a smaller role in the economy than those of Canada or most European countries. But that role is still sizable, with the U.S. government playing a major role in the U.S. economy. As a result, changes in the federal budget—changes in government spending or in taxation—can have large effects on the American economy.

To analyze these effects, we begin by showing how taxes and government spending affect the economy's flow of income. Then we can see how changes in spending and tax policy affect aggregate demand.

Social insurance programs are government programs intended to protect families against economic hardship.

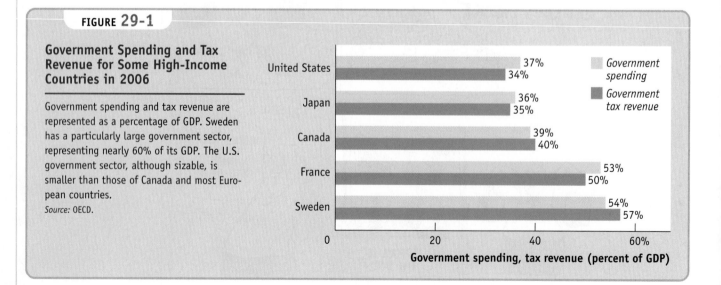

FIGURE **29-1**

Government Spending and Tax Revenue for Some High-Income Countries in 2006

Government spending and tax revenue are represented as a percentage of GDP. Sweden has a particularly large government sector, representing nearly 60% of its GDP. The U.S. government sector, although sizable, is smaller than those of Canada and most European countries.
Source: OECD.

United States — Government spending 37%, Government tax revenue 34%
Japan — Government spending 36%, Government tax revenue 35%
Canada — Government spending 39%, Government tax revenue 40%
France — Government spending 53%, Government tax revenue 50%
Sweden — Government spending 54%, Government tax revenue 57%

Government spending, tax revenue (percent of GDP)

Taxes, Purchases of Goods and Services, Government Transfers, and Borrowing

In Figure 23-1 we showed the circular flow of income and spending in the economy as a whole. One of the sectors represented in that figure was the government. Funds flow *into* the government in the form of taxes and government borrowing; funds flow *out* in the form of government purchases of goods and services and government transfers to households.

What kinds of taxes do Americans pay, and where does the money go? Figure 29-2 shows the composition of U.S. tax revenue in 2007. Taxes, of course, are required payments to the government. In the United States, taxes are collected at the national level by the federal government; at the state level by each state government; and at local levels by counties, cities, and towns. At the federal level, the main taxes are income taxes on both personal income and corporate profits as well as *social insurance* taxes, which we'll explain shortly. At the state and local levels, the picture is more complex: these governments rely on a mix of sales taxes, property taxes, income taxes, and fees of various kinds. Overall, taxes on personal income and corporate profits accounted for 48% of total government revenue in 2007; social insurance taxes accounted for 25%; and a variety of other taxes, collected mainly at the state and local levels, accounted for the rest.

Figure 29-3 shows the composition of total U.S. government spending in 2007, which takes two forms. One form is purchases of goods and services. This includes everything from ammunition for the military to the salaries of public schoolteachers (who are treated in the national accounts as providers of a service—education). The big items here are national defense and education. The large category labeled "Other goods and services" consists mainly of state and local spending on a variety of services, from police and firefighters to highway construction and maintenance.

The other form of government spending is government transfers, which are payments by the government to households for which no good or service is provided in return. In the modern United States, as well as in Canada and Europe, government transfers represent a very large proportion of the budget. Most U.S. government spending on transfer payments is accounted for by three big programs:

- Social Security, which provides guaranteed income to older Americans, disabled Americans, and the surviving spouses and dependent children of deceased beneficiaries

- Medicare, which covers much of the cost of health care for Americans over age 65

- Medicaid, which covers much of the cost of health care for Americans with low incomes

The term **social insurance** is used to describe government programs that are intended to protect families against economic hardship. These include Social Security, Medicare, and Medicaid, as well as smaller programs such as unemployment insurance and food stamps. In the United States, social insurance programs are largely paid for with special, dedicated taxes on wages—the social insurance taxes we mentioned earlier.

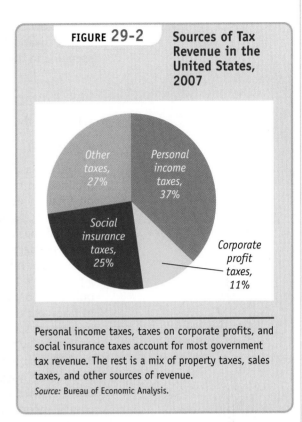

FIGURE 29-2 Sources of Tax Revenue in the United States, 2007

Personal income taxes, taxes on corporate profits, and social insurance taxes account for most government tax revenue. The rest is a mix of property taxes, sales taxes, and other sources of revenue.

Source: Bureau of Economic Analysis.

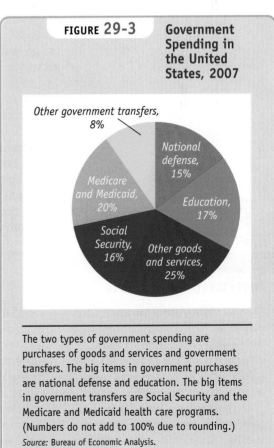

FIGURE 29-3 Government Spending in the United States, 2007

The two types of government spending are purchases of goods and services and government transfers. The big items in government purchases are national defense and education. The big items in government transfers are Social Security and the Medicare and Medicaid health care programs. (Numbers do not add to 100% due to rounding.)

Source: Bureau of Economic Analysis.

But how do tax policy and government spending affect the economy? The answer is that taxation and government spending have a strong effect on total aggregate spending in the economy.

The Government Budget and Total Spending

Let's recall the basic equation of national income accounting:

(29-1) $GDP = C + I + G + X - IM$

The left-hand side of this equation is GDP, the value of all final goods and services produced in the economy. The right-hand side is aggregate spending, total spending on final goods and services produced in the economy. It is the sum of consumer spending (C), investment spending (I), government purchases of goods and services (G), and the value of exports (X) minus the value of imports (IM). It includes all the sources of aggregate demand.

The government directly controls one of the variables on the right-hand side of Equation 29-1: government purchases of goods and services (G). But that's not the only effect fiscal policy has on aggregate spending in the economy. Through changes in taxes and transfers, it also influences consumer spending (C) and, in some cases, investment spending (I).

To see why the budget affects consumer spending, recall that *disposable income,* the total income households have available to spend, is equal to the total income they receive from wages, dividends, interest, and rent, *minus* taxes, *plus* government transfers. So either an increase in taxes or a decrease in government transfers *reduces* disposable income. And a fall in disposable income, other things equal, leads to a fall in consumer spending. Conversely, either a decrease in taxes or an increase in government transfers *increases* disposable income. And a rise in disposable income, other things equal, leads to a rise in consumer spending.

The government's ability to affect investment spending is a more complex story, which we won't discuss in detail (but see the For Inquiring Minds below). The important point is that the government taxes profits, and changes in the rules that determine how much a business owes can increase or reduce the incentive to spend on investment goods.

Because the government itself is one source of spending in the economy, and because taxes and transfers can affect spending by consumers and firms, the government can use changes in taxes or government spending to *shift the aggregate demand curve.* And as we saw in Chapter 28, there are sometimes good reasons to shift the aggregate demand curve. In early 2008, as this chapter's opening story explained, there was bipartisan agreement that the U.S. government should act to prevent a fall in aggregate demand—that is, to move the aggregate demand curve to the right of where it would otherwise be.

FOR INQUIRING MINDS

Investment Tax Credits

When we discuss changes in taxes in this chapter, we focus mainly on the effects of these changes on consumer spending. However, there is one tool of fiscal policy that is designed to affect investment spending—*investment tax credits.*

An investment tax credit is a tax break given to firms based on their investment spending. For example, a firm might be allowed to deduct $1 from its tax bill for every $10 it spends on investment goods. This increases the incentive for investment spending.

One more thing about investment tax credits: they're often temporary, applying only to investment spending within a specific period. For example, Congress introduced an investment tax credit in 2002 that only applied to investment spending over the next two years. Like department store sales that encourage shoppers to spend a lot while the sale is on, temporary investment tax credits tend to generate a lot of investment spending when they're in effect. Even if a firm doesn't think it will need a new computer server or lathe for another year or so, it may make sense to buy it while the tax credit is available, rather than wait.

The 2008 stimulus package was a classic example of *fiscal policy*: the use of taxes, government transfers, or government purchases of goods and services to stabilize the economy by shifting the aggregate demand curve.

Expansionary fiscal policy increases aggregate demand.

Expansionary and Contractionary Fiscal Policy

Why would the government want to shift the aggregate demand curve? Because it wants to close either a recessionary gap, created when aggregate output falls below potential output, or an inflationary gap, created when aggregate output exceeds potential output.

Figure 29-4 shows the case of an economy facing a recessionary gap. *SRAS* is the short-run aggregate supply curve, *LRAS* is the long-run aggregate supply curve, and AD_1 is the initial aggregate demand curve. At the initial short-run macroeconomic equilibrium, E_1, aggregate output is Y_1, below potential output, Y_P. What the government would like to do is increase aggregate demand, shifting the aggregate demand curve rightward to AD_2. This would increase aggregate output, making it equal to potential output. Fiscal policy that increases aggregate demand, called **expansionary fiscal policy,** normally takes one of three forms:

- An increase in government purchases of goods and services
- A cut in taxes
- An increase in government transfers

The fiscal stimulus Japan launched in the 1990s consisted mainly of an increase in government purchases of goods and services, taking the form of massive construction projects—bridges, roads, and so on. The U.S. fiscal stimulus described in the opening story was a mixture of tax cuts and transfer payments.

Figure 29-5 on the next page shows the opposite case—an economy facing an inflationary gap. Again, *SRAS* is the short-run aggregate supply curve, *LRAS* is the long-run aggregate supply curve, and AD_1 is the initial aggregate demand curve. At the initial equilibrium, E_1, aggregate output is Y_1, above potential output, Y_P. As we'll

---

FIGURE 29-4

Expansionary Fiscal Policy Can Close a Recessionary Gap

At E_1 the economy is in short-run macroeconomic equilibrium where the aggregate demand curve, AD_1, intersects the *SRAS* curve. At E_1, there is a recessionary gap of $Y_P - Y_1$. An expansionary fiscal policy—an increase in government purchases of goods and services, a reduction in taxes, or an increase in government transfers—shifts the aggregate demand curve rightward. It can close the recessionary gap by shifting AD_1 to AD_2, moving the economy to a new short-run macroeconomic equilibrium, E_2, which is also a long-run macroeconomic equilibrium.

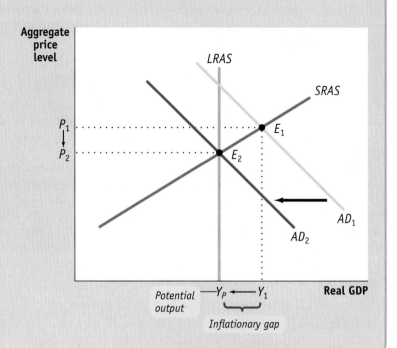

FIGURE 29-5

Contractionary Fiscal Policy Can Close an Inflationary Gap

At E_1 the economy is in short-run macroeconomic equilibrium where the aggregate demand curve, AD_1, intersects the $SRAS$ curve. At E_1, there is an inflationary gap of $Y_1 - Y_P$. A contractionary fiscal policy—such as reduced government purchases of goods and services, an increase in taxes, or a reduction in government transfers—shifts the aggregate demand curve leftward. It closes the inflationary gap by shifting AD_1 to AD_2, moving the economy to a new short-run macroeconomic equilibrium, E_2, which is also a long-run macroeconomic equilibrium.

explain in later chapters, policy makers often try to head off inflation by eliminating inflationary gaps. To eliminate the inflationary gap shown in Figure 29-5, fiscal policy must reduce aggregate demand and shift the aggregate demand curve leftward to AD_2. This reduces aggregate output and makes it equal to potential output. Fiscal policy that reduces aggregate demand, called **contractionary fiscal policy,** is the opposite of expansionary fiscal policy. It is implemented by:

- A reduction in government purchases of goods and services
- An increase in taxes
- A reduction in government transfers

A classic example of contractionary fiscal policy occurred in 1968, when U.S. policy makers grew worried about rising inflation. President Lyndon Johnson imposed a temporary 10% surcharge on income taxes—everyone's income taxes were increased by 10%. He also tried to scale back government purchases of goods and services, which had risen dramatically because of the cost of the Vietnam War.

A Cautionary Note: Lags in Fiscal Policy

Looking at Figures 29-4 and 29-5, it may seem obvious that the government should actively use fiscal policy—always adopting an expansionary fiscal policy when the economy faces a recessionary gap and always adopting a contractionary fiscal policy when the economy faces an inflationary gap. But many economists caution against an extremely active stabilization policy, arguing that a government that tries too hard to stabilize the economy—through either fiscal policy or monetary policy—can end up making the economy less stable.

We'll leave discussion of the warnings associated with monetary policy to Chapter 33. In the case of fiscal policy, one key reason for caution is that there are important *time lags* in its use. To understand the nature of these lags, think about what has to happen before the government increases spending to fight a recessionary gap. First, the government has to realize that the recessionary gap exists: economic data take time to collect and analyze, and recessions are often recognized only months after they have begun. Second, the government has to develop a spending plan, which can itself

Contractionary fiscal policy reduces aggregate demand.

take months, particularly if politicians take time debating how the money should be spent and passing legislation. Finally, it takes time to spend money. For example, a road construction project begins with activities such as surveying that don't involve spending large sums. It may be quite some time before the big spending begins.

Because of these lags, an attempt to increase spending to fight a recessionary gap may take so long to get going that the economy has already recovered on its own. In fact, the recessionary gap may have turned into an inflationary gap by the time the fiscal policy takes effect. In that case, the fiscal policy will make things worse instead of better.

This doesn't mean that fiscal policy should never be actively used. In early 2008 there was good reason to believe that the U.S. economy had begun a lengthy slowdown caused by turmoil in the financial markets, so that a fiscal stimulus designed to arrive within a few months would almost surely push aggregate demand in the right direction. But the problem of lags makes the actual use of both fiscal and monetary policy harder than you might think from a simple analysis like the one we have just given.

►ECONOMICS IN ACTION

Expansionary Fiscal Policy in Japan

"In what may be the biggest public works bonanza since the pharaohs, Japan has spent something like $1.4 trillion trying to pave and build its way back to economic health," began one newspaper report on Japan's efforts during the 1990s to prop up its economy with fiscal policy.

Japan turned to expansionary fiscal policy in the early 1990s. In the 1980s the country's economy boomed, driven in part by soaring prices of stocks and real estate, which boosted consumer spending through the wealth effect and also encouraged investment spending. Japanese economists now refer to this period as the "bubble economy," because the subsequent plunge in stock and land prices confirmed that speculation had driven prices to unreasonably high levels. (The United States experienced a similar bubble in housing prices in the mid-2000s, which began to deflate in 2006—setting the stage for an economic slump and the 2008 stimulus package.) At the end of the 1980s Japan's bubble burst—stock and land values plunged, and the economy slid into recession as consumer and investment spending fell. During the years that followed, Japan relied on large-scale government purchases of goods and services, mainly in the form of construction spending on infrastructure, to prop up aggregate demand. This spending was scaled back after 2000, but at its peak it was truly impressive. In 1996 Japan spent about $300 billion on infrastructure, compared with only $180 billion spent in the United States, even though Japan has less than half America's population and considerably less than half its GDP. Superb roads run through sparsely populated regions, ferries to small islands have been replaced by bridges, and many of the country's riverbeds have been paved, so that they resemble concrete aqueducts.

Was this policy a success? Yes and no. Many economists believe that without all that government spending, the Japanese economy would have slid into a 1930s-type depression after the bursting of the bubble economy. Instead, the economy suffered a slowdown but not a severe slump: growth was sluggish and unemployment rose, but no depression developed.

Furthermore, alternative policies weren't readily available. The alternative to using fiscal policy to prop up a slumping economy is using monetary policy, in which the central bank expands the money supply and drives down interest rates. Japan did that, too; by 1998, short-term interest rates had been cut to approximately zero! Since interest rates can't go below zero, there was no room for further interest rate cuts. Yet the economy remained sluggish. Expansionary fiscal policy became the only obvious way to increase aggregate demand.

Despite all of that spending, expansionary fiscal policy was not able to jump-start the Japanese economy and it remained depressed for a long time. The years of deficit spending led to a high level of government debt that to this day concerns many financial experts. In fact, when Japan was threatened with a new recession in 2008, the burden of debt from the 1990s proved a major problem: as an August 2008 report in the *Financial Times* put it, "Japan's high public sector debt"—a legacy from the 1990s—"limits the government's scope for fiscal measures." ▲

< < < < < < < < < < < <

> CHECK YOUR UNDERSTANDING 29-1

1. In each of the following cases, determine whether the policy is an expansionary or contractionary fiscal policy.
   a. Several military bases around the country, which together employ tens of thousands of people, are closed.
   b. The number of weeks an unemployed person is eligible for unemployment benefits is increased.
   c. The federal tax on gasoline is increased.

2. Explain why federal disaster relief, which quickly disburses funds to victims of natural disasters such as hurricanes, floods, and large-scale crop failures, will stabilize the economy more effectively after a disaster than relief that must be legislated.

Solutions appear at back of book.

Fiscal Policy and the Multiplier

An expansionary fiscal policy, like the 2008 U.S. stimulus package, pushes the aggregate demand curve to the right. A contractionary fiscal policy, like Lyndon Johnson's tax surcharge, pushes the aggregate demand curve to the left. For policy makers, however, knowing the direction of the shift isn't enough: they need estimates of *how much* the aggregate demand curve is shifted by a given policy. To get these estimates, they use the concept of the multiplier, which we learned about in Chapter 27.

Multiplier Effects of an Increase in Government Purchases of Goods and Services

Suppose that a government decides to spend $50 billion building bridges and roads. The government's purchases of goods and services will directly increase total spending on final goods and services by $50 billion. But as we learned in Chapter 27, there will also be an indirect effect because the government's purchases will start a chain reaction throughout the economy. The firms producing the goods and services purchased by the government will earn revenues that flow to households in the form of wages, profit, interest, and rent. This increase in disposable income will lead to a rise in consumer spending. The rise in consumer spending, in turn, will induce firms to increase output, leading to a further rise in disposable income, which will lead to another round of consumer spending increases, and so on.

In Chapter 27 we learned about the concept of the *multiplier:* the ratio of the change in real GDP caused by an autonomous change in aggregate spending to the size of that autonomous change. An increase in government purchases of goods and services is an example of an autonomous increase in aggregate spending. Its effect is illustrated in Figure 29-6, which makes use of the *income–expenditure model* developed in Chapter 27. In Figure 29-6, the line $AE_{Planned_1}$ shows the initial relationship between real GDP, which determines the level of income, and real planned aggregate spending. The economy tends to move to a point of income–expenditure equilibrium, where real planned aggregate spending is equal to real GDP. In this case, the initial equilibrium level of real GDP is Y_1, the level at which $AE_{Planned_1}$ crosses the 45-degree line.

An increase in government spending shifts $AE_{Planned}$ up by the amount of the increase in G, as shown by the upward shift from $AE_{Planned_1}$ to $AE_{Planned_2}$. Real GDP,

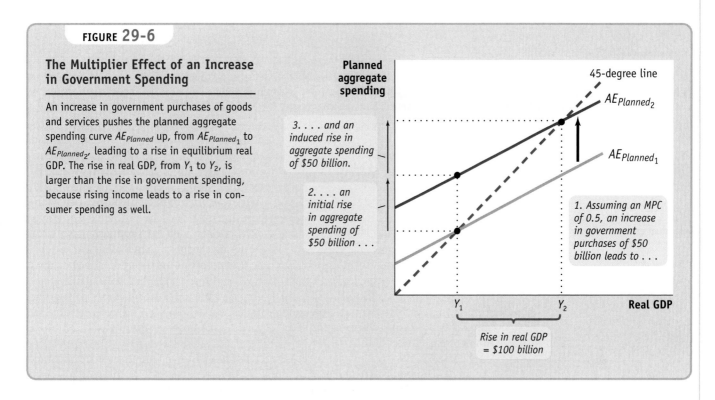

FIGURE 29-6

The Multiplier Effect of an Increase in Government Spending

An increase in government purchases of goods and services pushes the planned aggregate spending curve $AE_{Planned}$ up, from $AE_{Planned_1}$ to $AE_{Planned_2}$, leading to a rise in equilibrium real GDP. The rise in real GDP, from Y_1 to Y_2, is larger than the rise in government spending, because rising income leads to a rise in consumer spending as well.

Planned aggregate spending

45-degree line

$AE_{Planned_2}$

$AE_{Planned_1}$

3. . . . and an induced rise in aggregate spending of $50 billion.

2. . . . an initial rise in aggregate spending of $50 billion . . .

1. Assuming an MPC of 0.5, an increase in government purchases of $50 billion leads to . . .

Y_1 Y_2 Real GDP

Rise in real GDP = $100 billion

however, rises by more than this, because rising income leads to a further rise in consumer spending. The economy finally settles at a new equilibrium, with an increase in real GDP, from Y_1 to Y_2, that is larger than the initial rise in G.

In Chapter 27 we considered a simple case in which there are no taxes or international trade, so that any change in GDP accrues entirely to households. We also assumed that the aggregate price level is fixed, so that any increase in nominal GDP is also a rise in real GDP, and we assumed that the interest rate is fixed. In that case the multiplier is $1/(1 - MPC)$. Recall that MPC is the *marginal propensity to consume,* the fraction of an additional dollar in disposable income that is spent. For example, if the marginal propensity to consume is 0.5, the multiplier is $1/(1 - 0.5) = 1/0.5 = 2$. Given a multiplier of 2, a $50 billion increase in government purchases of goods and services would increase real GDP by $100 billion. Of that $100 billion, $50 billion is the initial effect from the increase in G, and the remaining $50 billion is the subsequent effect arising from the increase in consumer spending.

What happens if government purchases of goods and services are instead reduced? The math is exactly the same, except that there's a minus sign in front: if government purchases of goods and services fall by $50 billion and the marginal propensity to consume is 0.5, real GDP falls by $100 billion.

Multiplier Effects of Changes in Government Transfers and Taxes

Expansionary or contractionary fiscal policy need not take the form of changes in government purchases of goods and services. Governments can also change transfer payments or taxes. In general, however, a change in government transfers or taxes shifts the aggregate demand curve by *less* than an equal-sized change in government purchases, resulting in a smaller effect on real GDP.

To see why, imagine that instead of spending $50 billion on building bridges, the government simply hands out $50 billion in the form of government transfers. In this case, there is no direct effect on aggregate demand as there was with government purchases of goods and services. Real GDP goes up only because households spend some of that $50 billion—and they probably won't spend it all.

TABLE **29-1**

Hypothetical Effects of a Fiscal Policy with Multiplier of 2

Effect on real GDP	$50 billion rise in government purchases of goods and services	$50 billion rise in government transfer payments
First round	$50 billion	$25 billion
Second round	$25 billion	$12.5 billion
Third round	$12.5 billion	$6.25 billion
.	.	.
.	.	.
.	.	.
Eventual effect	$100 billion	$50 billion

Table 29-1 shows a hypothetical comparison of two expansionary fiscal policies assuming an *MPC* equal to 0.5 and a multiplier equal to 2: one in which the government directly purchases $50 billion in goods and services and one in which the government makes transfer payments instead, sending out $50 billion in checks to consumers. In each case there is a first-round effect on real GDP, either from purchases by the government or from purchases by the consumers who received the checks, followed by a series of additional rounds as rising real GDP raises disposable income.

However, the first-round effect of the transfer program is smaller; because we have assumed that the *MPC* is 0.5, only $25 billion of the $50 billion is spent, with the other $25 billion saved. And as a result, all the further rounds are smaller, too. In the end, the transfer payment increases real GDP by only $50 billion. In comparison, a $50 billion increase in government purchases produces a $100 billion increase in real GDP.

Figure 29-7 illustrates the effect of increased transfer payments in the income-expenditure model. An increase in transfers shifts $AE_{Planned}$ up, from $AE_{Planned_1}$ to $AE_{Planned_2}$. Unlike the effect of an increase in government purchases of goods and services, $AE_{Planned}$ shifts up by *less* than the increase in government outlays, because consumers will spend only part of their windfall, saving the rest. However, there will still be a further rise in consumer spending as the economy expands.

Overall, when expansionary fiscal policy takes the form of a rise in transfer payments, real GDP may rise by either more or less than the initial government outlay— that is, the multiplier may be either more or less than 1. In Table 29-1, a $50 billion rise in transfer payments increases real GDP by $50 billion, so that the multiplier is exactly 1. This is the case illustrated in Figure 29-7. If a smaller share of the initial transfer had been spent, the multiplier on that transfer would have been *less* than 1. If a larger share of the initial transfer had been spent, the multiplier would have been *more* than 1.

FIGURE 29-7

The Multiplier Effect of an Increase in Transfers

An increase in transfers leads to an initial rise in consumer spending, shifting the $AE_{Planned}$ curve up, from $AE_{Planned_1}$ to $AE_{Planned_2}$. However, this initial rise in spending is less than the size of the transfer, because consumers will save some of their additional disposable income. The initial rise in consumer spending leads to a rise in real GDP, which further increases consumer spending. The eventual rise in real GDP may be either more or less than the transfer. That is, the multiplier may be either more or less than 1. In the case shown here, the multiplier is exactly 1.

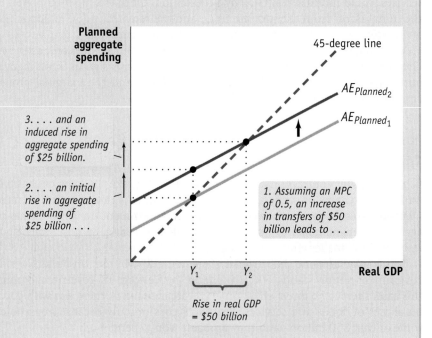

3. . . . and an induced rise in aggregate spending of $25 billion.

2. . . . an initial rise in aggregate spending of $25 billion . . .

1. Assuming an MPC of 0.5, an increase in transfers of $50 billion leads to . . .

Rise in real GDP = $50 billion

A tax cut has an effect similar to the effect of a transfer. It increases disposable income, leading to a series of increases in consumer spending. But the overall effect is smaller than that of an equal-sized increase in government purchases of goods and services: the autonomous increase in aggregate spending is smaller because households save part of the amount of the tax cut.

We should also note that taxes introduce a further complication: they typically change the size of the multiplier. That's because in the real world governments rarely impose **lump-sum taxes,** in which the amount of tax a household owes is independent of its income. Instead, the great majority of tax revenue is raised via taxes that depend positively on the level of real GDP. As we'll discuss shortly, and analyze in detail in the appendix to this chapter, taxes that depend positively on real GDP reduce the size of the multiplier.

In practice, economists often argue that it also matters *who* among the population gets tax cuts or increases in government transfers. For example, compare the effects of an increase in unemployment benefits with a cut in taxes on profits distributed to shareholders as dividends. Consumer surveys suggest that the average unemployed worker will spend a higher share of any increase in his or her disposable income than would the average recipient of dividend income. That is, people who are unemployed tend to have a higher *MPC* than people who own a lot of stocks because the latter tend to be wealthier and tend to save more of any increase in disposable income. If that's true, a dollar spent on unemployment benefits increases aggregate demand more than a dollar's worth of dividend tax cuts. As the Economics in Action at the end of this section explains, such arguments played an important role in the final provisions of the 2008 stimulus package.

How Taxes Affect the Multiplier

When we introduced the analysis of the multiplier in Chapter 27, we simplified matters by assuming that a $1 increase in real GDP raises disposable income by $1. In fact, however, government taxes capture some part of the increase in real GDP that occurs in each round of the multiplier process, since most government taxes depend positively on real GDP. As a result, disposable income increases by considerably less than $1 once we include taxes in the model.

The increase in government tax revenue when real GDP rises isn't the result of a deliberate decision or action by the government. It's a consequence of the way the tax laws are written, which causes most sources of government revenue to increase *automatically* when real GDP goes up. For example, income tax receipts increase when real GDP rises because the amount each individual owes in taxes depends positively on his or her income, and households' taxable income rises when real GDP rises. Sales tax receipts increase when real GDP rises because people with more income spend more on goods and services. And corporate profit tax receipts increase when real GDP rises because profits increase when the economy expands.

The effect of these automatic increases in tax revenue is to reduce the size of the multiplier. Remember, the multiplier is the result of a chain reaction in which higher real GDP leads to higher disposable income, which leads to higher consumer spending, which leads to further increases in real GDP. The fact that the government siphons off some of any increase in real GDP means that at each stage of this process, the increase in consumer spending is smaller than it would be if taxes weren't part of the picture. The result is to reduce the multiplier. The appendix to this chapter shows how to derive the multiplier when taxes that depend positively on real GDP are taken into account.

Many macroeconomists believe it's a good thing that in real life taxes reduce the multiplier. In Chapter 28 we argued that most, though not all, recessions are the result of negative demand shocks. The same mechanism that causes tax revenue to increase when the economy expands causes it to decrease when the economy contracts. Since tax receipts decrease when real GDP falls, the effects of these negative demand shocks are smaller than they would be if there were no taxes. The decrease in tax revenue reduces the adverse effect of the initial fall in aggregate demand. The automatic

Lump-sum taxes are taxes that don't depend on the taxpayer's income.

decrease in government tax revenue generated by a fall in real GDP—caused by a decrease in the amount of taxes households pay—acts like an automatic expansionary fiscal policy implemented in the face of a recession. Similarly, when the economy expands, the government finds itself automatically pursuing a contractionary fiscal policy—a tax increase. Government spending and taxation rules that cause fiscal policy to be automatically expansionary when the economy contracts and automatically contractionary when the economy expands, without requiring any deliberate action by policy makers, are called **automatic stabilizers.**

The rules that govern tax collection aren't the only automatic stabilizers, although they are the most important ones. Some types of government transfers also play a stabilizing role. For example, more people receive unemployment insurance when the economy is depressed than when it is booming. The same is true of Medicaid and food stamps. So transfer payments tend to rise when the economy is contracting and fall when the economy is expanding. Like changes in tax revenue, these automatic changes in transfers tend to reduce the size of the multiplier because the total change in disposable income that results from a given rise or fall in real GDP is smaller.

A historical example of discretionary fiscal policy was the Works Progress Administration (WPA), a relief measure established during the Great Depression that put the unemployed to work building bridges, roads, buildings, and parks.

As in the case of government tax revenue, many macroeconomists believe that it's a good thing that government transfers reduce the multiplier. Expansionary and contractionary fiscal policies that are the result of automatic stabilizers are widely considered helpful to macroeconomic stabilization, because they blunt the extremes of the business cycle. But what about fiscal policy that *isn't* the result of automatic stabilizers? **Discretionary fiscal policy** is fiscal policy that is the direct result of deliberate actions by policy makers rather than automatic adjustment. For example, during a recession, the government may pass legislation that cuts taxes and increases government spending in order to stimulate the economy. In general, economists tend to support the use of discretionary fiscal policy only in special circumstances, such as an especially severe recession. We'll explain why, and describe the debates among macroeconomists on the appropriate role of fiscal policy, in Chapter 33.

➤ECONOMICS IN ACTION

About That Stimulus Package . . .

In early 2008 there was broad bipartisan agreement that the U.S. economy needed a fiscal stimulus. There was, however, sharp partisan disagreement about what form that stimulus should take. The eventual bill was a compromise that left both sides unhappy and arguably made the stimulus less effective than it could have been.

There was never much support for an increase in government purchases of goods and services—that is, neither party wanted to build bridges and roads to stimulate the economy. The reason was time: both parties believed that the economy needed a quick boost, and ramping up spending would take too long. But there was a fierce debate over whether the stimulus should take the form of a tax cut, which would deliver its biggest benefits to those who paid the most taxes, or an increase in transfer payments targeted at Americans most in economic distress.

Republicans favored tax cuts on general political principles: they believed that those who pay the most taxes should get the biggest breaks. Democrats, by contrast, preferred transfer payments, especially increased unemployment benefits and expanded food stamp aid. This was partly a matter of helping the needy, but they also argued that Americans in economic distress would be more likely to spend their checks than the relatively affluent families who pay most taxes. That is, they argued that the multiplier would be higher if the stimulus package was focused on the needy, making it more likely that the stimulus would revive the economy.

Automatic stabilizers are government spending and taxation rules that cause fiscal policy to be automatically expansionary when the economy contracts and automatically contractionary when the economy expands.

Discretionary fiscal policy is fiscal policy that is the result of deliberate actions by policy makers rather than rules.

The eventual compromise gave most taxpayers a flat $600 rebate, $1,200 for married couples. Very-high-income taxpayers were not entitled to a rebate; low earners who didn't make enough to pay income taxes, but did pay other taxes, received $300. In effect, the plan was a combination of tax cuts for most Americans and transfer payments to Americans with low incomes.

How well designed was the stimulus plan? Many economists believed that only a fraction of the rebate checks would actually be spent, so that the eventual multiplier would be fairly low. White House economists appeared to agree: they estimated that the stimulus would raise employment by half a million jobs above what it would have been otherwise, the same number offered by independent economists who believed that the multiplier on the plan would be around 0.75. (Remember, the multiplier on changes in taxes or transfers can be less than 1.) Some economists were critical, arguing that Congress should have insisted on a plan that yielded more bang for the buck.

Both Democratic and Republican economists working for Congress defended the plan, arguing that the perfect is the enemy of the good—that it was the best that could be negotiated on short notice and was likely to be of real help in fighting the economy's weakness. But by the late summer of 2008, with the U.S. economy still in the doldrums, there was widespread agreement that the plan's results had been disappointing. And by late 2008, with the economy shrinking further, the incoming Obama administration was working on a new, much larger stimulus plan that relied more heavily on government purchases. ▲

> > > > > > > > > > > >

▶ CHECK YOUR UNDERSTANDING 29-2

1. Explain why a $500 million increase in government purchases of goods and services will generate a larger rise in real GDP than a $500 million increase in government transfers.

2. Explain why a $500 million reduction in government purchases of goods and services will generate a larger fall in real GDP than a $500 million reduction in government transfers.

3. The country of Boldovia has no unemployment insurance benefits and a tax system using only lump-sum taxes. The neighboring country of Moldovia has generous unemployment benefits and a tax system in which residents must pay a percentage of their income. Which country will experience greater variation in real GDP in response to demand shocks, positive and negative? Explain.

Solutions appear at back of book.

> ▶▶QUICK REVIEW
>
> ➤ The amount by which changes in government purchases raise real GDP is determined by the multiplier.
> ➤ Changes in taxes and government transfers also move real GDP, but by less than equal-sized changes in government purchases.
> ➤ Taxes reduce the size of the multiplier unless they are **lump-sum taxes**.
> ➤ Taxes and some government transfers act as **automatic stabilizers** as tax revenue responds positively to changes in real GDP and some government transfers respond negatively to changes in real GDP. Many economists believe that it is a good thing that they reduce the size of the multiplier. In contrast, the use of **discretionary fiscal policy** is more controversial.

The Budget Balance

Headlines about the government's budget tend to focus on just one point: whether the government is running a surplus or a deficit and, in either case, how big. People usually think of surpluses as good: when the federal government ran a record surplus in 2000, many people regarded it as a cause for celebration. Conversely, people usually think of deficits as bad: when the Congressional Budget Office projected a record federal deficit for 2008, many people regarded it as a cause for concern.

How do surpluses and deficits fit into the analysis of fiscal policy? Are deficits ever a good thing and surpluses a bad thing? To answer those questions, let's look at the causes and consequences of surpluses and deficits.

The Budget Balance as a Measure of Fiscal Policy

What do we mean by surpluses and deficits? The budget balance, which we defined in Chapter 26, is the difference between the government's revenue, in the form of tax revenue, and its spending, both on goods and services and on government transfers, in a given year. That is, the budget balance—savings by government—is defined by Equation 29-2:

(29-2) $S_{Government} = T - G - TR$

where T is the value of tax revenues, G is government purchases of goods and services, and TR is the value of government transfers. As we learned in Chapter 26, a budget surplus is a positive budget balance and a budget deficit is a negative budget balance.

Patrick O'Connor

Other things equal, expansionary fiscal policies—increased government purchases of goods and services, higher government transfers, or lower taxes—reduce the budget balance for that year. That is, expansionary fiscal policies make a budget surplus smaller or a budget deficit bigger. Conversely, contractionary fiscal policies—reduced government purchases of goods and services, lower government transfers, or higher taxes—increase the budget balance for that year, making a budget surplus bigger or a budget deficit smaller.

You might think this means that changes in the budget balance can be used to measure fiscal policy. In fact, economists often do just that: they use changes in the budget balance as a "quick-and-dirty" way to assess whether current fiscal policy is expansionary or contractionary. But they always keep in mind two reasons this quick-and-dirty approach is sometimes misleading:

- Two different changes in fiscal policy that have equal-size effects on the budget balance may have quite unequal effects on the economy. As we have already seen, changes in government purchases of goods and services have a larger effect on real GDP than equal-size changes in taxes and government transfers.

- Often, changes in the budget balance are themselves the result, not the cause, of fluctuations in the economy.

To understand the second point, we need to examine the effects of the business cycle on the budget.

The Business Cycle and the Cyclically Adjusted Budget Balance

Historically there has been a strong relationship between the federal government's budget balance and the business cycle. The budget tends to move into deficit when the economy experiences a recession, but deficits tend to get smaller or even turn into surpluses when the economy is expanding. Figure 29-8 shows the federal budget deficit as a percentage of GDP from 1970 to 2008. Shaded areas indicate recessions; unshaded areas indicate expansions. As you can see, the federal budget deficit increased around the time of each recession and usually declined during expansions. In fact, in the late stages of the long expansion from 1991 to 2000 the deficit actually became negative—the budget deficit became a budget surplus.

The relationship between the business cycle and the budget balance is even clearer if we compare the budget deficit as a percentage of GDP with the unemployment rate, as we do in Figure 29-9. The budget deficit almost always rises when the unemployment rate rises and falls when the unemployment rate falls.

Is this relationship between the business cycle and the budget balance evidence that policy makers engage in discretionary fiscal policy, using expansionary fiscal policy during recessions and contractionary fiscal policy during expansions? Not necessarily. To a large extent the relationship in Figure 29-9 reflects automatic stabilizers at work. As we learned in the discussion of automatic stabilizers, government tax revenue tends to rise and some government transfers, like unemployment benefit payments, tend to fall when the economy expands. Conversely, government tax revenue tends to fall and some government transfers tend to rise when the economy contracts. So the budget tends to move toward surplus during expansions and toward deficit during recessions even without any deliberate action on the part of policy makers.

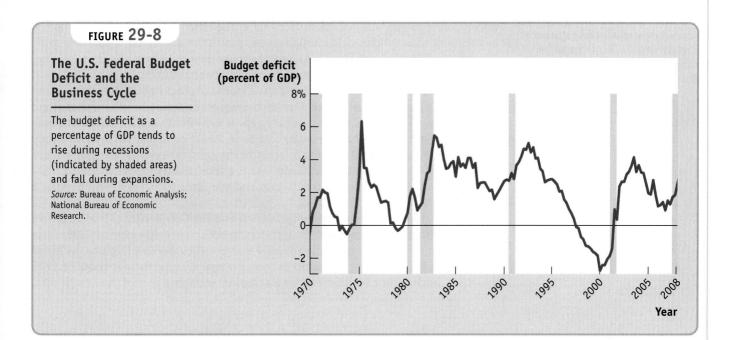

FIGURE 29-8

The U.S. Federal Budget Deficit and the Business Cycle

The budget deficit as a percentage of GDP tends to rise during recessions (indicated by shaded areas) and fall during expansions.

Source: Bureau of Economic Analysis; National Bureau of Economic Research.

In assessing budget policy, it's often useful to separate movements in the budget balance due to the business cycle from movements due to discretionary fiscal policy changes. The former are affected by automatic stabilizers and the latter by deliberate changes in government purchases, government transfers, or taxes. It's important to realize that business-cycle effects on the budget balance are temporary: both recessionary gaps (in which real GDP is below potential output) and inflationary gaps (in which real GDP is above potential output) tend to be eliminated in the long run. Removing their effects on the budget balance sheds light on whether the government's

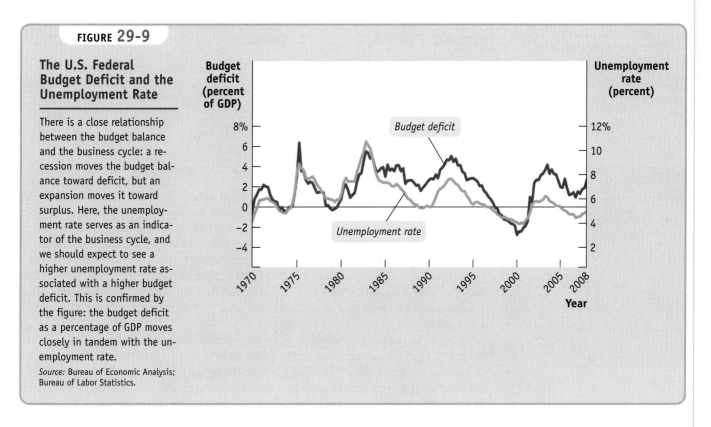

FIGURE 29-9

The U.S. Federal Budget Deficit and the Unemployment Rate

There is a close relationship between the budget balance and the business cycle: a recession moves the budget balance toward deficit, but an expansion moves it toward surplus. Here, the unemployment rate serves as an indicator of the business cycle, and we should expect to see a higher unemployment rate associated with a higher budget deficit. This is confirmed by the figure: the budget deficit as a percentage of GDP moves closely in tandem with the unemployment rate.

Source: Bureau of Economic Analysis; Bureau of Labor Statistics.

The **cyclically adjusted budget balance** is an estimate of what the budget balance would be if real GDP were exactly equal to potential output.

taxing and spending policies are sustainable in the long run. In other words, do the government's tax policies yield enough revenue to fund its spending in the long run? As we'll learn shortly, this is a fundamentally more important question than whether the government runs a budget surplus or deficit in the current year.

To separate the effect of the business cycle from the effects of other factors, many governments produce an estimate of what the budget balance would be if there were neither a recessionary nor an inflationary gap. The **cyclically adjusted budget balance** is an estimate of what the budget balance would be if real GDP were exactly equal to potential output. It takes into account the extra tax revenue the government would collect and the transfers it would save if a recessionary gap were eliminated—or the revenue the government would lose and the extra transfers it would make if an inflationary gap were eliminated.

Figure 29-10 shows the actual budget deficit and the Congressional Budget Office estimate of the cyclically adjusted budget deficit, both as a percentage of GDP, since 1970. As you can see, the cyclically adjusted budget deficit doesn't fluctuate as much as the actual budget deficit. In particular, large actual deficits, such as those of 1975 and 1983, are usually caused in part by a depressed economy.

FIGURE 29-10

The Actual Budget Deficit versus the Cyclically Adjusted Budget Deficit

The cyclically adjusted budget deficit is an estimate of what the budget deficit would be if the economy were at potential output. It fluctuates less than the actual budget deficit, because years of large budget deficits also tend to be years when the economy has a large recessionary gap.

Source: Congressional Budget Office.

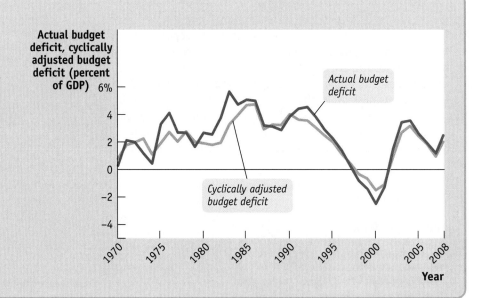

Should the Budget Be Balanced?

As we'll see in the next section, persistent budget deficits can cause problems for both the government and the economy. Yet politicians are always tempted to run deficits because this allows them to cater to voters by cutting taxes without cutting spending or by increasing spending without increasing taxes. As a result, there are occasional attempts by policy makers to force fiscal discipline by introducing legislation—even a constitutional amendment—forbidding the government from running budget deficits. This is usually stated as a requirement that the budget be "balanced"—that revenues at least equal spending each fiscal year. Would it be a good idea to require a balanced budget annually?

Most economists don't think so. They believe that the government should only balance its budget on average—that it should be allowed to run deficits in bad years, offset by surpluses in good years. They don't believe the government should be forced to run a balanced budget *every year* because this would undermine the role of taxes and transfers as automatic stabilizers. As we learned earlier in this chapter, the tendency of tax revenue to fall and transfers to rise when the economy contracts helps to limit the size of recessions. But falling tax revenue and rising transfer payments push the budget toward deficit. If constrained by a balanced-budget rule, the government would have to respond to this deficit with contractionary fiscal policies that would tend to deepen a recession.

Yet policy makers concerned about excessive deficits sometimes feel that rigid rules prohibiting—or at least setting an upper limit on—deficits are necessary. As the following Economics in Action explains, Europe has had a lot of trouble reconciling rules to enforce fiscal responsibility with the challenges of short-run fiscal policy.

►ECONOMICS IN ACTION

Stability Pact—or Stupidity Pact?

In 1999 a group of European nations took a momentous step when they adopted a common currency, the euro, to replace their national currencies, such as the French franc, the German mark, and the Italian lira. Along with the introduction of the euro came the creation of the European Central Bank, which sets monetary policy for the whole region.

As part of the agreement creating the new currency, governments of member countries signed on to the European "stability pact." This agreement required each government to keep its budget deficit—its actual deficit, not a cyclically adjusted number—below 3% of the country's GDP or face fines. The pact was intended to prevent irresponsible deficit spending arising from political pressure that might eventually undermine the new currency. The stability pact, however, had a serious downside: it limited a country's ability to use fiscal policy.

In fact, the stability pact quickly became a problem for the two largest economies in the eurozone. In 2002 both France and Germany were experiencing rising unemployment and also running budget deficits in excess of 3% of GDP. Moreover, it seemed likely that both countries' deficits would go up in 2003, which they did. Under the rules of the stability pact, France and Germany were supposed to lower their budget deficits by raising taxes or cutting spending. Yet contractionary fiscal policy would have led to even higher unemployment.

In October 2002, reacting to these economic problems, one top European official described the stability pact as "stupid." Journalists promptly had a field day, renaming it the "stupidity pact." In fact, when push came to shove, the pact proved unenforceable. Germany and France both had enough political clout to prevent the imposition of penalties. Indeed, in March 2005 the stability pact was rewritten to allow "small and temporary" breaches of the 3% limit, with a special clause allowing Germany to describe aid to the former East Germany as a temporary expense.

Before patting themselves on the back over the superiority of their own fiscal rules, Americans should note that the United States has its own version of the stupidity pact. The federal government's budget acts as an automatic stabilizer, but 49 of the 50 states are required by their state constitutions to balance their budgets every year. When recession struck in 2001, most states were forced to—guess what?—slash spending and raise taxes in the face of a recession, exactly the wrong thing from a macroeconomic point of view. Not surprisingly, some states, like some European countries, found ways to cheat. ▲

> > > > > > > > > > > > >

► CHECK YOUR UNDERSTANDING 29-3

1. Why is the cyclically adjusted budget balance a better measure of the long-run sustainability of government policies than the actual budget balance?

2. Explain why states required by their constitutions to balance their budgets are likely to experience more severe economic fluctuations than states not held to that requirement.

Solutions appear at back of book.

A **fiscal year** runs from October 1 to September 30 and is labeled according to the calendar year in which it ends.

Public debt is government debt held by individuals and institutions outside the government.

Long-Run Implications of Fiscal Policy

During the 1990s the Japanese government engaged in massive deficit spending in an effort to increase aggregate demand. As we saw in Economics in Action, "Expansionary Fiscal Policy in Japan," that policy was partly successful: although Japan's economy was sluggish during the 1990s, it avoided a severe slump comparable to what happened to many countries in the 1930s. Yet the fact that Japan was running large deficits year after year made many observers uneasy, as Japan's debt climbed to alarming levels.

No discussion of fiscal policy is complete if it doesn't take into account the long-run implications of government budget surpluses and deficits. We now turn to those long-run implications.

Deficits, Surpluses, and Debt

When a family spends more than it earns over the course of a year, it has to raise the extra funds either by selling assets or by borrowing. And if a family borrows year after year, it will eventually end up with a lot of debt.

The same is true for governments. With a few exceptions, governments don't raise large sums by selling assets such as national parkland. Instead, when a government spends more than the tax revenue it receives—when it runs a budget deficit—it almost always borrows the extra funds. And governments that run persistent budget deficits end up with substantial debts.

To interpret the numbers that follow, you need to know a slightly peculiar feature of federal government accounting. For historical reasons, the U.S. government does not keep books by calendar years. Instead, budget totals are kept by **fiscal years,** which run from October 1 to September 30 and are labeled by the calendar year in which they end. For example, fiscal 2008 began on October 1, 2007, and ended on September 30, 2008.

At the end of fiscal 2008, the U.S. federal government had total debt equal to $10 trillion. However, part of that debt represented special accounting rules specifying that the federal government as a whole owes funds to certain government programs, especially Social Security. We'll explain those rules shortly. For now, however, let's focus on **public debt:** government debt held by individuals and institutions outside the government. At the end of fiscal 2008, the federal government's public debt was "only" $5.8 trillion, or 40% of GDP. If we include the debts of state and local governments, total government public debt was approximately 48% of GDP. The accompanying Global Comparison contrasts U.S. public debt with the public debt of other wealthy countries.

U.S. federal government public debt at the end of fiscal 2008 was larger than it was at the end of fiscal 2007 because the federal government ran a budget deficit during fiscal 2008. A government that runs persistent budget deficits will experience a rising level of public debt. Why is this a problem?

Problems Posed by Rising Government Debt

There are two reasons to be concerned when a government runs persistent budget deficits. We described one reason in Chapter 26: when the government borrows funds in the financial markets, it is competing with firms that plan to borrow funds for investment spending. As a result, the government's borrowing may "crowd out" private investment spending, increasing interest rates and reducing the economy's long-run rate of growth.

But there's also a second reason: today's deficits, by increasing the government's debt, place financial pressure on future budgets. The impact of

PITFALLS

DEFICITS VERSUS DEBT

One common mistake—it happens all the time in newspaper reports—is to confuse *deficits* with *debt*. Let's review the difference.

A *deficit* is the difference between the amount of money a government spends and the amount it receives in taxes over a given period—usually, though not always, a year. Deficit numbers always come with a statement about the time period to which they apply, as in "the U.S. budget deficit *in fiscal 2008* was $410 billion."

A *debt* is the sum of money a government owes at a particular point in time. Debt numbers usually come with a specific date, as in "U.S. public debt *at the end of fiscal 2008* was $5.8 trillion."

Deficits and debt are linked, because government debt grows when governments run deficits. But they aren't the same thing, and they can even tell different stories. For example, at the end of fiscal 2008, U.S. *debt* as a percentage of GDP was fairly low by historical standards, but the *deficit* during fiscal 2008 was considered quite high.

GLOBAL COMPARISON THE AMERICAN WAY OF DEBT

How does the public debt of the United States stack up internationally? In dollar terms, we're number one—but this isn't very informative, since the U.S. economy and so the government's tax base are much larger than those of any other nation. A more informative comparison is the ratio of public debt to GDP, which the following figure shows for a number of rich countries at the end of 2008. The United States was more or less in the middle of the pack, basically in the same league as France, Britain, and Germany. The real debt champions were Italy, Japan, and Belgium. Italy and Belgium have historically had weak, divided governments that have a hard time acting responsibly. Japan ran up large debts during the 1990s, when it used massive government spending to prop up its economy.

In contrast to the other countries, Norway has a large *negative* public debt. What's going on in Norway? In a word, oil. Norway is the world's third-largest oil exporter, thanks to large offshore deposits in the North Sea. Instead of spending its oil revenues immediately, the government of Norway has used them to build up an investment fund for future needs. As a result, Norway has huge government assets rather than a large government debt.

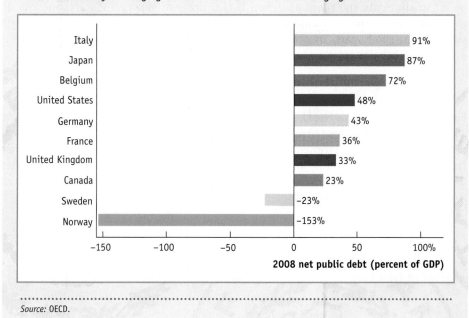

Source: OECD.

current deficits on future budgets is straightforward. Like individuals, governments must pay their bills, including interest payments on their accumulated debt. When a government is deeply in debt, those interest payments can be substantial. In fiscal 2008, the U.S. federal government paid 2.3% of GDP—$343 billion—in interest on its debt. The most heavily indebted government shown in this chapter's Global Comparison, Italy, paid interest of 4.7% of GDP in 2008.

Other things equal, a government paying large sums in interest must raise more revenue from taxes or spend less than it would otherwise be able to afford—or it must borrow even more to cover the gap. And a government that borrows to pay interest on its outstanding debt pushes itself even deeper into debt. This process can eventually push a government to the point where lenders question its ability to repay. Like a consumer who has maxed out his or her credit cards, it will find that lenders are unwilling to lend any more funds. The result can be that the government defaults on its debt—it stops paying what it owes. Default is often followed by deep financial and economic turmoil.

The idea of a government defaulting sounds far-fetched, but it is not impossible. In the 1990s Argentina, a relatively high-income developing country, was widely praised for its economic policies—and it was able to borrow large sums from foreign lenders. By 2001, however, Argentina's interest payments were spiraling out of control, and the country stopped paying the sums that were due. We describe that default in the Economics in Action at the end of this section.

Default creates havoc in a country's financial markets and badly shakes public confidence in both the government and the economy. Argentina's debt default was accompanied by a crisis in the country's banking system and a very severe recession. And even if a highly indebted government avoids default, a heavy debt burden typically forces it to slash spending or raise taxes, politically unpopular measures that can also damage the economy.

One question some people ask is: can't a government that has trouble borrowing just print money to pay its bills? Yes, it can, but this leads to another problem: inflation. In fact, budget problems are the main cause of very severe inflation, as we'll see in Chapter 32. The point for now is that governments do not want to find themselves in a position where the choice is between defaulting on their debts and inflating those debts away.

Concerns about the long-run effects of deficits need not rule out the use of fiscal policy to stimulate the economy when it is depressed. However, these concerns do mean that governments should try to offset budget deficits in bad years with budget surpluses in good years. In other words, governments should run a budget that is approximately balanced over time. Have they actually done so?

Deficits and Debt in Practice

Figure 29-11 shows how the U.S. federal government's budget deficit and its debt have evolved since 1940. Panel (a) shows the federal deficit as a percentage of GDP. As you can see, the federal government ran huge deficits during World War II. It briefly ran surpluses after the war, but it has normally run deficits ever since, especially after 1980. This seems inconsistent with the advice that governments should offset deficits in bad times with surpluses in good times.

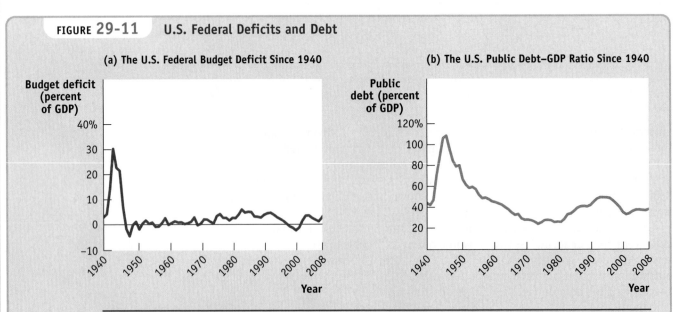

FIGURE 29-11   **U.S. Federal Deficits and Debt**

(a) The U.S. Federal Budget Deficit Since 1940

(b) The U.S. Public Debt–GDP Ratio Since 1940

Panel (a) shows the U.S. federal budget deficit as a percentage of GDP since 1940. The U.S. government ran huge deficits during World War II and has usually run smaller deficits ever since. Panel (b) shows the U.S. debt–GDP ratio. Comparing panels (a) and (b), you can see that in many years the debt–GDP ratio has declined in spite of government deficits. This seeming paradox reflects the fact that the debt–GDP ratio can fall, even when debt is rising, as long as GDP grows faster than debt.

Source: Office of Management and Budget.

FOR INQUIRING MINDS

What Happened to the Debt from World War II?

As you can see from Figure 29-11, the government paid for World War II by borrowing on a huge scale. By the war's end, the public debt was more than 100% of GDP, and many people worried about how it could ever be paid off.

The truth is that it never was paid off. In 1946 public debt was $242 billion; that number dipped slightly in the next few years, as the United States ran postwar budget surpluses, but the government budget went back into deficit in 1950 with the start of the Korean War. By 1962 the public debt was back up to $248 billion.

But by that time nobody was worried about the fiscal health of the U.S. government because the debt–GDP ratio had fallen by more than half. The reason? Vigorous economic growth, plus mild inflation, had led to a rapid rise in GDP. The experience was a clear lesson in the peculiar fact that modern governments can run deficits forever, as long as they aren't too large.

However, panel (b) of Figure 29-11 shows that these deficits have not led to runaway debt. To assess the ability of governments to pay their debt, we often use the **debt–GDP ratio,** the government's debt as a percentage of GDP. We use this measure, rather than simply looking at the size of the debt, because GDP, which measures the size of the economy as a whole, is a good indicator of the potential taxes the government can collect. If the government's debt grows more slowly than GDP, the burden of paying that debt is actually falling compared with the government's potential tax revenue.

What we see from panel (b) is that although the federal debt has grown in almost every year, the debt–GDP ratio fell for 30 years after the end of World War II. This shows that the debt–GDP ratio can fall, even when debt is rising, as long as GDP grows faster than debt. For Inquiring Minds, which focuses on the large debt the U.S. government ran up during World War II, explains how growth and inflation sometimes allow a government that runs persistent budget deficits to nevertheless have a declining debt–GDP ratio.

Still, a government that runs persistent *large* deficits will have a rising debt–GDP ratio when debt grows faster than GDP. Panel (a) of Figure 29-12 shows Japan's

The **debt–GDP ratio** is the government's debt as a percentage of GDP.

FIGURE 29-12   Japanese Deficits and Debt

Panel (a) shows the budget deficit of Japan since 1990 and panel (b) shows its debt–GDP ratio, both expressed as percentages of GDP. The large deficits that the Japanese government began running in the early 1990s have led to a rapid rise in its debt–GDP ratio as debt has grown more quickly than GDP. This has led some analysts to express concern about the long-run fiscal health of the Japanese economy.
Source: OECD.

Implicit liabilities are spending promises made by governments that are effectively a debt despite the fact that they are not included in the usual debt statistics.

budget deficit as a percentage of GDP and panel (b) shows Japan's debt–GDP ratio, both since 1990. As we have already mentioned, Japan began running large deficits in the early 1990s, a by-product of its effort to prop up aggregate demand with government spending. This has led to a rapid rise in the debt–GDP ratio. For this reason, some economic analysts are concerned about the long-run fiscal health of the Japanese economy.

Implicit Liabilities

Looking at Figure 29-11, you might be tempted to conclude that the U.S. federal budget is in fairly decent shape: the return to budget deficits after 2001 caused the debt–GDP ratio to rise a bit, but that ratio is still low compared with both historical experience and some other wealthy countries. In fact, however, experts on long-run budget issues view the situation of the United States (and other countries such as Japan and Italy) with alarm. The reason is the problem of *implicit liabilities*. **Implicit liabilities** are spending promises made by governments that are effectively a debt despite the fact that they are not included in the usual debt statistics.

The largest implicit liabilities of the U.S. government arise from two transfer programs that principally benefit older Americans: Social Security and Medicare. The third-largest implicit liability, Medicaid, benefits low-income families. In each of these cases, the government has promised to provide transfer payments to future as well as current beneficiaries. So these programs represent a future debt that must be honored, even though the debt does not currently show up in the usual statistics. Together, these three programs currently account for almost 40% of federal spending.

The implicit liabilities created by these transfer programs worry fiscal experts. Figure 29-13 shows why. It shows actual spending on Social Security and on Medicare and Medicaid as percentages of GDP from 1962 to 2007, together with Congressional Budget Office projections of spending through 2082. According to these projections, spending on Social Security will rise substantially over the next few decades and spending on the two health care programs will soar. Why?

In the case of Social Security, the answer is demography. Social Security is a "pay-as-you-go" system: current workers pay payroll taxes that fund the benefits of current retirees. So demography—specifically, the ratio of the number of retirees drawing benefits to the number of workers paying into Social Security—has a major

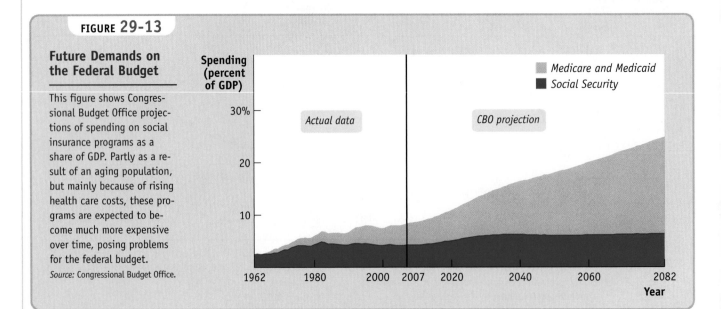

FIGURE 29-13

Future Demands on the Federal Budget

This figure shows Congressional Budget Office projections of spending on social insurance programs as a share of GDP. Partly as a result of an aging population, but mainly because of rising health care costs, these programs are expected to become much more expensive over time, posing problems for the federal budget.

Source: Congressional Budget Office.

impact on Social Security's finances. There was a huge surge in the U.S. birth rate between 1946 and 1964, the years of the baby boom. Baby boomers are currently of working age—which means they are paying taxes, not collecting benefits. As the baby boomers retire, they will stop earning income that is taxed and start collecting benefits. As a result, the ratio of retirees receiving benefits to workers paying into the Social Security system will rise. In 2007 there were 30 retirees receiving benefits for every 100 workers paying into the system. By 2030, according to the Social Security Administration, that number will rise to 45; by 2050, it will rise to 47; and by 2080 that number will be 50. This will raise benefit payments relative to the size of the economy.

The aging of the baby boomers, by itself, poses only a moderately sized long-run fiscal problem. The projected rise in Medicare and Medicaid spending is a much more serious concern. The main story behind projections of higher Medicare and Medicaid spending is the long-run tendency of health care spending to rise faster than overall spending, both for government-funded and for private-funded health care.

To some extent, the implicit liabilities of the U.S. government are already reflected in debt statistics. We mentioned earlier that the government had a total debt of $10 trillion at the end of fiscal 2008, but that only $5.8 trillion of that total was owed to the public. The main explanation for that discrepancy is that both Social Security and part of Medicare (the hospital insurance program) are supported by *dedicated taxes:* their expenses are paid out of special taxes on wages. At times, these dedicated taxes yield more revenue than is needed to pay current benefits. In particular, since the mid-1980s the Social Security system has been taking in more revenue than it currently needs in order to prepare for the retirement of the baby boomers. This surplus in the Social Security system has been used to accumulate a *Social Security trust fund,* which was $2.4 trillion at the end of fiscal 2008.

The money in the trust fund is held in the form of U.S. government bonds, which are included in the $10 trillion in total debt. You could say that there's something funny about counting bonds in the Social Security trust fund as part of government debt. After all, these bonds are owed by one part of the government (the government outside the Social Security system) to another part of the government (the Social Security system itself). But the debt corresponds to a real, if implicit, liability: promises by the government to pay future retirement benefits. So many economists argue that the gross debt of $10 trillion, the sum of public debt and government debt held by Social Security and other trust funds, is a more accurate indication of the government's fiscal health than the smaller amount owed to the public alone.

➤ECONOMICS IN ACTION

Argentina's Creditors Take a Haircut

As we mentioned earlier, the idea that a government's debt can reach a level at which the government can't pay its creditors can seem far-fetched. In the United States, government debt is usually regarded as the safest asset there is.

But countries *do* default on their debts—they fail to repay the money they borrowed. In 1998 Russia defaulted on its bonds, triggering a worldwide panic in financial markets. In 2001, in the biggest default of modern times, the government of Argentina stopped making payments on $81 billion in debt.

How did the Argentine default happen? During much of the 1990s, the country was experiencing an economic boom and the government was easily able to borrow money from abroad. Although deficit spending led to rising government debt, few considered this a problem. In 1998, however, the country slid into an economic slump that reduced tax revenues, leading to much larger deficits. Foreign lenders, increasingly nervous about the country's ability to repay, became unwilling to lend more except at very high interest rates. By 2001, the country was caught in a vicious circle: to cover its deficits and pay off old loans as they came due, it was forced to borrow at much higher interest rates, and the escalating interest rates on new borrowing made the deficits even bigger.

Argentine officials tried to reassure lenders by raising taxes and cutting government spending. But they were never able to balance the budget due to the continuing recession and the negative multiplier impact of their contractionary fiscal policies. These strongly contractionary fiscal policies drove the country deeper into recession. Late in 2001, facing popular protests, the Argentine government collapsed, and the country defaulted on its debt.

Creditors can take individuals who fail to pay debts to court. The court, in turn, can seize the debtors' assets and force them to pay part of future earnings to their creditors. But when a country defaults, it's different. Its creditors can't send in the police to seize the country's assets. They must negotiate a deal with the country for partial repayment. The only leverage creditors have in these negotiations is the defaulting government's fear that if it fails to reach a settlement, its reputation will suffer and it will be unable to borrow in the future. (A report by Reuters, the news agency, on Argentina's debt negotiations was headlined "Argentina to unhappy bondholders: so sue.") It took three years for Argentina to reach an agreement with its creditors because the new Argentine government was determined to strike a hard bargain. And it did. Here's how Reuters described the settlement reached in March 2005: "The deal, which exchanged new paper valued at around 32 cents for every dollar in default, was the biggest 'haircut,' or loss on principal, for investors of any sovereign bond restructuring in modern times." Let's put this into English: Argentina forced its creditors to trade their "sovereign bonds"—debts of a sovereign nation, that is, Argentina—for new bonds worth only 32% as much. Such a reduction in the value of debt is known as a "haircut."

It's important to avoid two misconceptions about this "haircut." First, you might be tempted to think that because Argentina ended up paying only a fraction of the sums it owed, it paid little price for default. In fact, Argentina's default accompanied one of the worst economic slumps of modern times, a period of mass unemployment, soaring poverty, and widespread unrest. Second, it's tempting to dismiss the Argentine story as being of little relevance to countries like the United States. After all, aren't we more responsible than that? But Argentina wouldn't have been able to borrow so much in the first place if its government hadn't been well regarded by international lenders. In fact, as late as 1998 Argentina was widely admired for its economic management. What Argentina's slide into default shows is that concerns about the long-run effects of budget deficits are not at all academic. Due to its large and growing debt–GDP ratio, one recession pushed Argentina over the edge into economic collapse. ▲

< < < < < < < < < < < <

► CHECK YOUR UNDERSTANDING 29-4

1. Explain how each of the following events would affect the public debt or implicit liabilities of the U.S. government, other things equal. Would the public debt or implicit liabilities be greater or smaller?
   a. A higher growth rate of real GDP
   b. Retirees live longer
   c. A decrease in tax revenue
   d. Government borrowing to pay interest on its current public debt

2. Suppose the economy is in a slump and the current public debt is quite large. Explain the trade-off of short-run versus long-run objectives that policy makers face when deciding whether or not to engage in deficit spending.

Solutions appear at back of book.

[>> A LOOK AHEAD •••

Fiscal policy isn't the only way governments can stimulate aggregate demand when the economy is slumping or reduce aggregate demand when it is too high. In fact, although most economists believe that automatic stabilizers play a useful role, many are skeptical about the usefulness of discretionary fiscal policy due to the time lags in its formulation and implementation.

But there's an important alternative: monetary policy. In the next two chapters we'll learn about monetary institutions and see how monetary policy works.]

SUMMARY

1. The government plays a large role in the economy, collecting a large share of GDP in taxes and spending a large share both to purchase goods and services and to make transfer payments, largely for **social insurance.** *Fiscal policy* is the use of taxes, government transfers, or government purchases of goods and services to shift the aggregate demand curve. But many economists caution that a very active fiscal policy may in fact make the economy less stable due to time lags in policy formulation and implementation.

2. Government purchases of goods and services directly affect aggregate demand, and changes in taxes and government transfers affect aggregate demand indirectly by changing households' disposable income. **Expansionary fiscal policy** shifts the aggregate demand curve rightward; **contractionary fiscal policy** shifts the aggregate demand curve leftward.

3. Fiscal policy has a multiplier effect on the economy, the size of which depends upon the fiscal policy. Except in the case of lump-sum taxes, taxes reduce the size of the multiplier. Expansionary fiscal policy leads to an increase in real GDP, while contractionary fiscal policy leads to a reduction in real GDP. Because part of any change in taxes or transfers is absorbed by savings in the first round of spending, changes in government purchases of goods and services have a more powerful effect on the economy than equal-size changes in taxes or transfers.

4. Rules governing taxes—with the exception of **lump-sum taxes**—and some transfers act as **automatic stabilizers,** reducing the size of the multiplier and automatically reducing the size of fluctuations in the business cycle. In contrast, **discretionary fiscal policy** arises from deliberate actions by policy makers rather than from the business cycle.

5. Some of the fluctuations in the budget balance are due to the effects of the business cycle. In order to separate the effects of the business cycle from the effects of discretionary fiscal policy, governments estimate the **cyclically adjusted budget balance,** an estimate of the budget balance if the economy were at potential output.

6. U.S. government budget accounting is calculated on the basis of **fiscal years.** Persistent budget deficits have long-run consequences because they lead to an increase in **public debt.** This can be a problem for two reasons. Public debt may crowd out investment spending, which reduces long-run economic growth. And in extreme cases, rising debt may lead to government default, resulting in economic and financial turmoil.

7. A widely used measure of fiscal health is the **debt–GDP ratio.** This number can remain stable or fall even in the face of moderate budget deficits if GDP rises over time. However, a stable debt–GDP ratio may give a misleading impression that all is well because modern governments often have large **implicit liabilities.** The largest implicit liabilities of the U.S. government come from Social Security, Medicare, and Medicaid, the costs of which are increasing due to the aging of the population and rising medical costs.

KEY TERMS

PROBLEMS ....■

1. The accompanying diagram shows the current macroeconomic situation for the economy of Albernia. You have been hired as an economic consultant to help the economy move to potential output, Y_P.

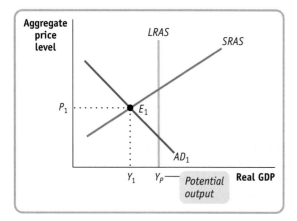

a. Is Albernia facing a recessionary or inflationary gap?

b. Which type of fiscal policy—expansionary or contractionary—would move the economy of Albernia to potential output, Y_P? What are some examples of such policies?

c. Illustrate the macroeconomic situation in Albernia with a diagram after the successful fiscal policy has been implemented.

2. The accompanying diagram shows the current macroeconomic situation for the economy of Brittania; real GDP is Y_1, and the aggregate price level is P_1. You have been hired as an economic consultant to help the economy move to potential output, Y_P.

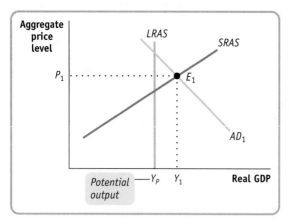

a. Is Brittania facing a recessionary or inflationary gap?

b. Which type of fiscal policy—expansionary or contractionary—would move the economy of Brittania to potential output, Y_P? What are some examples of such policies?

c. Illustrate the macroeconomic situation in Brittania with a diagram after the successful fiscal policy has been implemented.

3. An economy is in long-run macroeconomic equilibrium when each of the following aggregate demand shocks occurs. What kind of gap—inflationary or recessionary—will the economy face after the shock, and what type of fiscal policies would help move the economy back to potential output? How would your recommended fiscal policy shift the aggregate demand curve?

a. A stock market boom increases the value of stocks held by households.

b. Firms come to believe that a recession in the near future is likely.

c. Anticipating the possibility of war, the government increases its purchases of military equipment.

d. The quantity of money in the economy declines and interest rates increase.

4. During an interview on May 16, 2008, the German Finance Minister Peer Steinbrueck said, "We have to watch out that in Europe and beyond, nothing like a combination of downward economic [growth] and high inflation rates emerges—something that experts call stagflation." Such a situation can be depicted by the movement of the short-run aggregate supply curve from its original position $SRAS_1$ to its new position $SRAS_2$, with the new equilibrium point E_2 in the accompanying figure. In this question, we try to understand why stagflation is particularly hard to fix using fiscal policy.

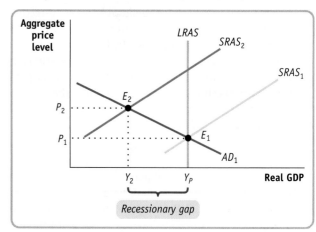

a. What would be the appropriate fiscal policy response to this situation if the primary concern of the government was to maintain economic growth? Illustrate the effect of the policy on the equilibrium point and the aggregate price level using the diagram.

b. What would be the appropriate fiscal policy response to this situation if the primary concern of the government was to maintain price stability? Illustrate the effect of the policy on the equilibrium point and the aggregate price level using the diagram.

c. Discuss the effectiveness of the policies in parts a and b in fighting stagflation.

5. Show why a $10 billion reduction in government purchases of goods and services will have a larger effect on real GDP than a $10 billion reduction in government transfers by completing the accompanying table for an economy with a marginal

propensity to consume (*MPC*) of 0.6. The first and second rows of the table are filled in for you: on the left side of the table, in the first row, the $10 billion reduction in government purchases decreases real GDP and disposable income, *YD*, by $10 billion, leading to a reduction in consumer spending of $6

| Rounds | Decrease in *G* = −$10 billion | | | Decrease in *TR* = −$10 billion | | |
| | Billions of dollars | | | Billions of dollars | | |
	Change in *G* or *C*	Change in real GDP	Change in *YD*	Change in *TR* or *C*	Change in real GDP	Change in *YD*
1	$\Delta G =$ −$10.00	−$10.00	−$10.00	$\Delta TR =$ −$10.00	$0.00	−$10.00
2	$\Delta C =$ −6.00	−6.00	−6.00	$\Delta C =$ −6.00	−6.00	−6.00
3	$\Delta C =$?	?	?	$\Delta C =$?	?	?
4	$\Delta C =$?	?	?	$\Delta C =$?	?	?
5	$\Delta C =$?	?	?	$\Delta C =$?	?	?
6	$\Delta C =$?	?	?	$\Delta C =$?	?	?
7	$\Delta C =$?	?	?	$\Delta C =$?	?	?
8	$\Delta C =$?	?	?	$\Delta C =$?	?	?
9	$\Delta C =$?	?	?	$\Delta C =$?	?	?
10	$\Delta C =$?	?	?	$\Delta C =$?	?	?

billion (*MPC* × change in disposable income) in row 2. However, on the right side of the table, the $10 billion reduction in transfers has no effect on real GDP in round 1 but does lower *YD* by $10 billion, resulting in a decrease in consumer spending of $6 billion in round 2.

a. When government purchases decrease by $10 billion, what is the sum of the changes in real GDP after the 10 rounds?

b. When the government reduces transfers by $10 billion, what is the sum of the changes in real GDP after the 10 rounds?

c. Using the formula for the multiplier for changes in government purchases and for changes in transfers, calculate the total change in real GDP due to the $10 billion decrease in government purchases and the $10 billion reduction in transfers. What explains the difference? (Hint: the multiplier for government purchases of goods and services is $1/(1 − MPC)$. But since each $1 change in government transfers only leads to an initial change in real GDP of $MPC × \$1$, the multiplier for government transfers is $MPC/(1 − MPC)$.)

6. In each of the following cases, either a recessionary or inflationary gap exists. Assume that the aggregate supply curve is horizontal, so that the change in real GDP arising from a shift of the aggregate demand curve equals the size of the shift of the curve. Calculate both the change in government purchases of goods and services and the change in government transfers necessary to close the gap.

a. Real GDP equals $100 billion, potential output equals $160 billion, and the marginal propensity to consume is 0.75.

b. Real GDP equals $250 billion, potential output equals $200 billion, and the marginal propensity to consume is 0.5.

c. Real GDP equals $180 billion, potential output equals $100 billion, and the marginal propensity to consume is 0.8.

7. Most macroeconomists believe it is a good thing that taxes act as automatic stabilizers and lower the size of the multiplier. However, a smaller multiplier means that the change in government purchases of goods and services, government transfers, or taxes necessary to close an inflationary or recessionary gap is larger. How can you explain this apparent inconsistency?

8. The accompanying table shows how consumers' marginal propensities to consume in a particular economy are related to their level of income.

Income range	Marginal propensity to consume
$0–$20,000	0.9
$20,001–$40,000	0.8
$40,001–$60,000	0.7
$60,001–$80,000	0.6
Above $80,000	0.5

a. Suppose the government engages in increased purchases of goods and services. For each of the income groups in the accompanying table, what is the value of the multiplier—that is, what is the "bang for the buck" from each dollar the government spends on government purchases of goods and services in each income group?

b. If the government needed to close a recessionary or inflationary gap, at which group should it primarily aim its fiscal policy of changes in government purchases of goods and services?

9. The government's budget surplus in Macroland has risen consistently over the past five years. Two government policy makers disagree as to why this has happened. One argues that a rising budget surplus indicates a growing economy; the other argues that it shows that the government is using contractionary fiscal policy. Can you determine which policy maker is correct? If not, why not?

10. Figure 29-10 shows the actual budget deficit and the cyclically adjusted budget deficit as a percentage of GDP in the United States since 1970. Assuming that potential output was unchanged, use this figure to determine in which years since 1990 the government used expansionary fiscal policy and in which years it used contractionary fiscal policy.

11. You are an economic adviser to a candidate for national office. She asks you for a summary of the economic consequences of a balanced-budget rule for the federal government and for your recommendation on whether she should support such a rule. How do you respond?

12. In 2008, the policy makers of the economy of Eastlandia projected the debt–GDP ratio and the ratio of the budget deficit to GDP for the economy for the next 10 years under different scenarios for growth in the government's deficit. Real GDP is currently $1,000 billion per year and is expected to grow by 3% per year, the public debt is $300 billion at the beginning of the year, and the deficit is $30 billion in 2008.

Year	Real GDP (billions of dollars)	Debt (billions of dollars)	Budget deficit (billions of dollars)	Debt (percent of real GDP)	Budget deficit (percent of real GDP)
2008	$1,000	$300	$30	?	?
2009	1,030	?	?	?	?
2010	1,061	?	?	?	?
2011	1,093	?	?	?	?
2012	1,126	?	?	?	?
2013	1,159	?	?	?	?
2014	1,194	?	?	?	?
2015	1,230	?	?	?	?
2016	1,267	?	?	?	?
2017	1,305	?	?	?	?
2018	1,344	?	?	?	?

a. Complete the accompanying table to show the debt–GDP ratio and the ratio of the budget deficit to GDP for the economy if the government's budget deficit remains constant at $30 billion over the next 10 years. (Remember that the government's debt will grow by the previous year's deficit.)

b. Redo the table to show the debt–GDP ratio and the ratio of the budget deficit to GDP for the economy if the government's budget deficit grows by 3% per year over the next 10 years.

c. Redo the table again to show the debt–GDP ratio and the ratio of the budget deficit to GDP for the economy if the government's budget deficit grows by 20% per year over the next 10 years.

d. What happens to the debt–GDP ratio and the ratio of the budget deficit to GDP for the economy over time under the three different scenarios?

13. Your study partner argues that the distinction between the government's budget deficit and debt is similar to the distinction between consumer savings and wealth. He also argues that if you have large budget deficits, you must have a large debt. In what ways is your study partner correct and in what ways is he incorrect?

14. In which of the following cases does the size of the government's debt and the size of the budget deficit indicate potential problems for the economy?

a. The government's debt is relatively low, but the government is running a large budget deficit as it builds a high-speed rail system to connect the major cities of the nation.

b. The government's debt is relatively high due to a recently ended deficit-financed war, but the government is now running only a small budget deficit.

c. The government's debt is relatively low, but the government is running a budget deficit to finance the interest payments on the debt.

15. How did or would the following affect the current public debt and implicit liabilities of the U.S. government?

a. In 2003, Congress passed and President Bush signed the Medicare Modernization Act, which provides seniors and individuals with disabilities with a prescription drug benefit. Some of the benefits under this law took effect immediately, but others will not begin until sometime in the future.

b. The age at which retired persons can receive full Social Security benefits is raised to age 70 for future retirees.

c. For future retirees, Social Security benefits are limited to those with low incomes.

d. Because the cost of health care is increasing faster than the overall inflation rate, annual increases in Social Security benefits are increased by the annual increase in health care costs rather than the overall inflation rate.

16. Unlike households, governments are often able to sustain large debts. For example, in September 2007, the U.S. government's total debt reached $9 trillion, approximately 64% of GDP. At the time, according to the U.S. Treasury, the average interest rate paid by the government on its debt was 5.0%. However, running budget deficits becomes hard when very large debts are outstanding.

a. Calculate the dollar cost of the annual interest on the government's total debt assuming the interest rate and debt figures cited above.

b. If the government operates on a balanced budget before interest payments are taken into account, at what rate must GDP grow in order for the debt–GDP ratio to remain unchanged?

c. Calculate the total increase in national debt if the government incurs a deficit of $200 billion in 2008. Assume that the only other change to the government's total debt arises from interest payments on the current debt of $9 trillion.

d. At what rate must GDP grow in order for the debt–GDP ratio to remain unchanged when the deficit in 2008 is $200 billion?

e. Why is the debt–GDP ratio the preferred measure of a country's debt rather than the dollar value of the debt? Why is it important for a government to keep this number under control?

Chapter 29 Appendix: Taxes and the Multiplier

In the chapter, we described how taxes that depend positively on real GDP reduce the size of the multiplier and act as an automatic stabilizer for the economy. Let's look a little more closely at the mathematics of how this works.

Specifically, let's assume that the government "captures" a fraction t of any increase in real GDP in the form of taxes, where t, the tax rate, is a fraction between 0 and 1. And let's repeat the exercise we carried out in Chapter 27, where we consider the effects of a $100 billion increase in investment spending. The same analysis holds for *any* autonomous increase in aggregate spending—in particular, it is also true for increases in government purchases of goods and services.

The $100 billion increase in investment spending initially raises real GDP by $100 billion (the first round). In the absence of taxes, disposable income would rise by $100 billion. But because part of the rise in real GDP is collected in the form of taxes, disposable income only rises by $(1 - t) \times \$100$ billion. The second-round increase in consumer spending, which is equal to the marginal propensity to consume *(MPC)* multiplied by the rise in disposable income, is $(MPC \times (1 - t)) \times \$100$ billion. This leads to a third-round increase in consumer spending of $(MPC \times (1 - t)) \times (MPC \times (1 - t)) \times \$100$ billion, and so on. So the total effect on real GDP is

Increase in investment spending	$=$	$\$100$ billion
+ Second-round increase in consumer spending	$= (MPC \times (1 - t))$	$\times \$100$ billion
+ Third-round increase in consumer spending	$= (MPC \times (1 - t))^2$	$\times \$100$ billion
+ Fourth-round increase in consumer spending	$= (MPC \times (1 - t))^3$	$\times \$100$ billion

$$\cdots \qquad \cdots$$

Total increase in real GDP $= [1 + (MPC \times (1 - t)) + (MPC \times (1 - t))^2$
$+ (MPC \times (1 - t))^3 + \ldots] \times \$100$ billion

As we pointed out in Chapter 27, an infinite series of the form $1 + x + x^2 + \ldots$, with $0 < x < 1$, is equal to $1/(1 - x)$. In this example, $x = (MPC \times (1 - t))$. So the total effect of a $100 billion increase in investment spending, taking into account all the subsequent increases in consumer spending, is to raise real GDP by:

$$\frac{1}{1 - (MPC \times (1 - t))} \times \$100 \text{ billion}$$

When we calculated the multiplier assuming away the effect of taxes, we found that it was $1/(1 - MPC)$. But when we assume that a fraction t of any change in real GDP is collected in the form of taxes, the multiplier is:

$$\text{Multiplier} = \frac{1}{1 - (MPC \times (1 - t))}$$

This is always a smaller number than $1/(1 - MPC)$, and its size diminishes as t grows. Suppose, for example, that $MPC = 0.6$. In the absence of taxes, this implies a multiplier of $1/(1 - 0.6) = 1/0.4 = 2.5$. But now let's assume that $t = 1/3$, that is, that 1/3 of any increase in real GDP is collected by the government. Then the multiplier is:

$$\frac{1}{1 - (0.6 \times (1 - 1/3))} = \frac{1}{1 - (0.6 \times 2/3)} = \frac{1}{1 - 0.4} = \frac{1}{0.6} = 1.667$$

PROBLEMS ···■

1. An economy has a marginal propensity to consume of 0.6, real GDP equals $500 billion, and the government collects 20% of GDP in taxes. If government purchases increase by $10 billion, show the rounds of increased spending that take place by completing the accompanying table. The first and second rows are filled in for you. In the first row, the increase in government purchases of $10 billion raises real GDP by $10 billion, taxes increase by $2 billion, and *YD* increases by $8 billion; in the second row, the increase in *YD* of $8 billion increases consumer spending by $4.80 billion (*MPC* × change in disposable income).

Rounds	Change in *G* or *C*	Change in real GDP	Change in taxes	Change in *YD*
	(billions of dollars)			
1	Δ*G* = $10.00	$10.00	$2.00	$8.00
2	Δ*C* = 4.80	4.80	0.96	3.84
3	Δ*C* = ?	?	?	?
4	Δ*C* = ?	?	?	?
5	Δ*C* = ?	?	?	?
6	Δ*C* = ?	?	?	?
7	Δ*C* = ?	?	?	?
8	Δ*C* = ?	?	?	?
9	Δ*C* = ?	?	?	?
10	Δ*C* = ?	?	?	?

 www.worthpublishers.com/krugmanwells

a. What is the total change in real GDP after the 10 rounds? What is the value of the multiplier? What would you expect the total change in real GDP to be, based on the multiplier formula? How do your two answers compare?

b. Redo the accompanying table, assuming the marginal propensity to consume is 0.75 and the government collects 10% of the rise in real GDP in taxes. What is the total change in real GDP after 10 rounds? What is the value of the multiplier? How do your two answers compare?

2. Calculate the change in government purchases of goods and services necessary to close the recessionary or inflationary gaps in the following cases. Assume that the short-run aggregate supply curve is horizontal so that the change in real GDP arising from a shift of the aggregate demand curve equals the size of the shift of the curve.

a. Real GDP equals $100 billion, potential output equals $160 billion, the government collects 20% of any change in real GDP in the form of taxes, and the marginal propensity to consume is 0.75.

b. Real GDP equals $250 billion, potential output equals $200 billion, the government collects 10% of any change in real GDP in the form of taxes, and the marginal propensity to consume is 0.5.

c. Real GDP equals $180 billion, potential output equals $100 billion, the government collects 25% of any change in real GDP in the form of taxes, and the marginal propensity to consume is 0.8.

Money, Banking, and the Federal Reserve System

FUNNY MONEY

ON OCTOBER 2, 2004, FBI AND SECRET SERVICE agents seized a shipping container that had just arrived in Newark, New Jersey, on a ship from China. Inside the container, under cardboard boxes containing plastic toys, they found what they were looking for: more than $300,000 in counterfeit $100 bills. Two months later, another shipment with $3 million in counterfeit bills was intercepted. Government and law enforcement officials began alleging publicly that these bills—which were high-quality fakes, very hard to tell from the real thing—were being produced by the government of North Korea.

The funny thing is that elaborately decorated pieces of paper have little or no intrinsic value. Indeed, a $100 bill printed with blue or orange ink literally wouldn't be worth the paper it was printed on. But if the ink on that decorated piece of paper is just the right shade of green, people will think that it's *money* and will accept it as payment for very real goods and services. Why? Because they believe, correctly, that they can do the same thing: exchange that piece of green paper for real goods and services.

In fact, here's a riddle: if a fake $100 bill from North Korea enters the United States, and nobody ever realizes it's fake, who gets hurt? Accepting a fake $100 bill isn't like buying a car that turns out to be a lemon, or a meal that turns out to be inedible; as long as the bill's counterfeit nature remains undiscovered, it will pass from hand to hand just like a real $100 bill. The answer to the riddle, as we'll

learn later in this chapter, is that the real victims of North Korean counterfeiting are U.S. taxpayers, because counterfeit dollars reduce the revenues available to pay for the operations of the U.S. government. Accordingly, the Secret Service diligently monitors the integrity of U.S. currency, promptly investigating any reports of counterfeit dollars.

Money is the essential channel that links the various parts of the modern economy.

The efforts of the Secret Service attest to the fact that money isn't like ordinary goods and services; it plays a unique role in the economy; it is the essential channel that links the various parts of the modern economy. In this chapter, we'll look at the role money plays, then look at how a modern monetary system works and at the institutions that sustain and regulate it. This topic is important in itself, and it's also essential background for the understanding of *monetary policy,* which we will examine in the next chapter.

WHAT YOU WILL LEARN IN THIS CHAPTER:

➤ The various roles **money** plays and the many forms it takes in the economy

➤ How the actions of private banks and the Federal Reserve determine the **money supply**

➤ How the Federal Reserve uses **open-market operations** to change the **monetary base**

The Meaning of Money

In everyday conversation, people often use the word *money* to mean "wealth." If you ask, "How much money does Bill Gates have?" the answer will be something like, "Oh, $40 billion or so, but who's counting?" That is, the number will include the value of the stocks, bonds, real estate, and other assets he owns.

But the economist's definition of money doesn't include all forms of wealth. The dollar bills in your wallet are money; other forms of wealth—such as cars, houses, and stock certificates—aren't money. What, according to economists, distinguishes money from other forms of wealth?

What Is Money?

Money is defined in terms of what it does: **money** is any asset that can easily be used to purchase goods and services. In Chapter 26 we defined an asset as *liquid* if it can easily be converted into cash. Money consists of cash itself, which is liquid by definition, as well as other assets that are highly liquid.

You can see the distinction between money and other assets by asking yourself how you pay for groceries. The person at the cash register will accept dollar bills in return for milk and frozen pizza—but he or she won't accept stock certificates or a collection of vintage baseball cards. If you want to convert stock certificates or vintage baseball cards into groceries, you have to sell them—trade them for money—and then use the money to buy groceries.

Of course, many stores allow you to write a check on your bank account in payment for goods (or to pay with a debit card that is linked to your bank account). Does that make your bank account money, even if you haven't converted it into cash? Yes. **Currency in circulation**—actual cash in the hands of the public—is considered money. So are **checkable bank deposits**—bank accounts on which people can write checks.

Are currency and checkable bank deposits the only assets that are considered money? It depends. As we'll see later, there are two widely used definitions of the **money supply,** the total value of financial assets in the economy that are considered money. The narrower definition considers only the most liquid assets to be money: currency in circulation, traveler's checks, and checkable bank deposits. The broader definition includes these three categories plus other assets that are "almost" checkable, such as savings account deposits that can be transferred into a checking account with a phone call. Both definitions of the money supply, however, make a distinction between those assets that can easily be used to purchase goods and services, and those that can't.

Money plays a crucial role in generating *gains from trade,* because it makes indirect exchange possible. Think of what happens when a cardiac surgeon buys a new refrigerator. The surgeon has valuable services to offer—namely, heart operations. The owner of the store has valuable goods to offer: refrigerators and other appliances. It would be extremely difficult for both parties if, instead of using money, they had to directly barter the goods and services they sell. In a barter system, a cardiac surgeon and an appliance store owner could trade only if the store owner happened to want a heart operation *and*

Money is any asset that can easily be used to purchase goods and services.

Currency in circulation is cash held by the public.

Checkable bank deposits are bank accounts on which people can write checks.

The **money supply** is the total value of financial assets in the economy that are considered money.

the surgeon happened to want a new refrigerator. This is known as the problem of finding a "double coincidence of wants": in a barter system, two parties can trade only when each wants what the other has to offer. Money solves this problem: individuals can trade what they have to offer for money and trade money for what they want.

Because the ability to make transactions with money rather than relying on bartering makes it easier to achieve gains from trade, the existence of money increases welfare, even though money does not directly produce anything. As Adam Smith put it, money "may very properly be compared to a highway, which, while it circulates and carries to market all the grass and corn of the country, produces itself not a single pile of either."

Let's take a closer look at the roles money plays in the economy.

> A **medium of exchange** is an asset that individuals acquire for the purpose of trading goods and services rather than for their own consumption.
>
> A **store of value** is a means of holding purchasing power over time.
>
> A **unit of account** is a measure used to set prices and make economic calculations.

Roles of Money

Money plays three main roles in any modern economy: it is a *medium of exchange,* a *store of value,* and a *unit of account.*

Medium of Exchange Our cardiac surgeon/refrigerator example illustrates the role of money as a **medium of exchange**—an asset that individuals use to trade for goods and services rather than for consumption. People can't eat dollar bills; rather, they use dollar bills to trade for edible goods and their accompanying services.

In normal times, the official money of a given country—the dollar in the United States, the peso in Mexico, and so on—is also the medium of exchange in virtually all transactions in that country. During troubled economic times, however, other goods or assets often play that role instead. For example, during economic turmoil people often turn to other countries' moneys as the medium of exchange: U.S. dollars have played this role in troubled Latin American countries, as have euros in troubled Eastern European countries. In a famous example, cigarettes functioned as the medium of exchange in World War II prisoner-of-war camps. Even nonsmokers traded goods and services for cigarettes, because the cigarettes could in turn be easily traded for other items. During the extreme German inflation of 1923, goods such as eggs and lumps of coal became, briefly, mediums of exchange.

Store of Value In order to act as a medium of exchange, money must also be a **store of value**—a means of holding purchasing power over time. To see why this is necessary, imagine trying to operate an economy in which ice-cream cones were the medium of exchange. Such an economy would quickly suffer from, well, monetary meltdown: your medium of exchange would often turn into a sticky puddle before you could use it to buy something else. (As we'll see in Chapter 32, one of the problems caused by high inflation is that, in effect, it causes the value of money to "melt.") Of course, money is by no means the only store of value. Any asset that holds its purchasing power over time is a store of value. So the store-of-value role is a necessary but not distinctive feature of money.

Unit of Account Finally, money normally serves as the **unit of account**—the commonly accepted measure individuals use to set prices and make economic calculations. To understand the importance of this role, consider a historical fact: during the Middle Ages, peasants typically were required to provide landowners with goods and labor rather than money. A peasant might, for example, be required to work on the lord's land one day a week and also hand over one-fifth of his harvest. Today, rents, like other prices, are almost always specified in money terms. That makes things much clearer: imagine how hard it would be to decide which apartment to rent if modern landlords followed medieval practice. Suppose, for example, that Mr. Smith says he'll let you have a place if you clean his house twice a week and bring him a pound of steak every day, whereas Ms. Jones wants you to clean her house just once a week but wants four pounds of chicken every day. Who's offering the better deal? It's hard to say. If, on the other hand, Smith wants $600 a month and Jones wants $700, the comparison is easy. In other words, without a commonly accepted measure, the terms of a transaction are harder to determine, making it more difficult to make transactions and achieve gains from trade.

Commodity money is a good used as a medium of exchange that has intrinsic value in other uses.

Commodity-backed money is a medium of exchange with no intrinsic value whose ultimate value is guaranteed by a promise that it can be converted into valuable goods.

GLOBAL COMPARISON   THE BIG MONEYS

Americans tend to think of the dollar as the world's leading currency—and it does remain the currency most likely to be accepted in payment around the globe. But there are other important currencies, too. One simple measure of a currency's importance is the value of the quantity of that currency in circulation. This figure shows the value, in billions of dollars, of the quantity of four major currencies in circulation at the end of 2006. The value of euros in circulation roughly matched the value of dollars in circulation. This reflected the fact that the U.S. economy and the combined economies of the nations using the euro, the eurozone, are of roughly equal size. Japan's economy is much smaller, but the Japanese rely much more heavily on cash to make transactions than do Europeans and Americans, who rely more heavily on credit cards. So the value of yen in circulation was a close third. And the yuan is rapidly closing in on the rest, thanks to the rising demand for cash in China's rapidly growing economy.

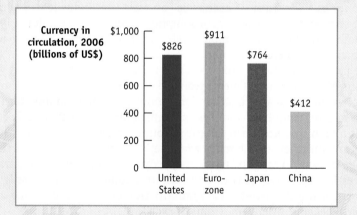

Sources: Federal Reserve Bank of St. Louis; European Central Bank; Bank of Japan; The People's Bank of China.

Types of Money

In some form or another, money has been in use for thousands of years. For most of that period, people used **commodity money:** the medium of exchange was a good, normally gold or silver, that had intrinsic value in other uses. These alternative uses gave commodity money value independent of its role as a medium of exchange. For example, cigarettes, which served as money in World War II POW camps, were also valuable because many prisoners smoked. Gold was valuable because it was used for jewelry and ornamentation, aside from the fact that it was minted into coins.

By 1776, the year in which the United States declared independence and Adam Smith published *The Wealth of Nations,* there was widespread use of paper money in addition to gold or silver coins. Unlike modern dollar bills, however, this paper money consisted of notes issued by private banks, which promised to exchange their notes for gold or silver coins on demand. So the paper currency that initially replaced commodity money was **commodity-backed money,** a medium of exchange with no intrinsic value whose ultimate value was guaranteed by a promise that it could always be converted into valuable goods on demand.

The big advantage of commodity-backed money over simple commodity money, like gold and silver coins, was that it tied up fewer valuable resources. Although a note-issuing bank still had to keep some gold and silver on hand, it had to keep only enough to satisfy demands for redemption of its notes. And it could rely on the fact that on a normal day only a fraction of its paper notes would be redeemed. So the bank needed to keep only a portion of the total value of its notes in circulation in the form of gold and silver in its vaults. It could lend out the remaining gold and silver to those who wished to use it. This allowed society to use the remaining gold and silver for other purposes, all with no loss in the ability to achieve gains from trade.

In a famous passage in *The Wealth of Nations,* Adam Smith described paper money as a "waggon-way through the air." Smith was making an analogy between money and an imaginary highway that did not absorb valuable land beneath it. An actual highway provides a useful service but at a cost: land that could be used to grow crops is instead paved over. If the highway could be built through the air, it wouldn't destroy useful land. As Smith understood, when banks replaced gold and silver money with paper notes, they accomplished a similar feat: they reduced the amount of real resources used by society to provide the functions of money.

At this point you may ask, why make any use at all of gold and silver in the monetary system, even to back paper money? In fact, today's monetary system goes even further than the system Smith admired, having eliminated any role for gold and silver. A U.S. dollar bill isn't commodity money, and it isn't even commodity-backed. Rather, its value arises entirely from the fact that it is generally accepted as a means of payment, a role that is ultimately decreed by the U.S. government. Money whose value derives entirely from its official status as a means of exchange is known as **fiat money** because it exists by government *fiat,* a historical term for a policy declared by a ruler.

Fiat money has two major advantages over commodity-backed money. First, it is even more of a "waggon-way through the air"—it doesn't tie up any real resources, except for the paper it's printed on. Second, the money supply can be managed based on the needs of the economy, instead of being determined by the amount of gold and silver prospectors happen to discover.

On the other hand, fiat money poses some risks. In this chapter's opening story, we described one such risk—counterfeiting. (Counterfeiters usurp a privilege of the U.S. government, which has the sole legal right to print dollar bills. And the benefit that counterfeiters get by exchanging fake bills for real goods and services comes at the expense of the U.S. federal government, which covers a small but nontrivial part of its own expenses by issuing new currency to meet growing demand for money.)

The larger risk is that governments that can create money whenever they feel like it will be tempted to abuse the privilege. In Chapter 32 we'll learn how governments sometimes rely too heavily on printing money to pay their bills, leading to high inflation. In this chapter, however, we'll stay focused on the question of what money is and how it is managed.

Fiat money is a medium of exchange whose value derives entirely from its official status as a means of payment.

A **monetary aggregate** is an overall measure of the money supply.

Near-moneys are financial assets that can't be directly used as a medium of exchange but can be readily converted into cash or checkable bank deposits.

Measuring the Money Supply

The Federal Reserve (an institution we'll talk about shortly) calculates the size of two **monetary aggregates,** overall measures of the money supply, which differ in how strictly money is defined. The two aggregates are known, rather cryptically, as M1 and M2. (There used to be a third aggregate named—you guessed it—M3, but in 2006 the Federal Reserve concluded that measuring it was no longer useful.) M1, the narrowest definition, contains only currency in circulation (also known as cash), traveler's checks, and checkable bank deposits. M2 adds several other kinds of assets, often referred to as **near-moneys**—financial assets that aren't directly usable as a medium of exchange but can be readily converted into cash or checkable bank deposits, such as savings accounts. Examples are time deposits such as small denomination CDs, which

PITFALLS

WHAT'S NOT IN THE MONEY SUPPLY

Are financial assets like stocks and bonds part of the money supply? No, not under any definition, because they're not liquid enough.

M1 consists, roughly speaking, of assets you can use to buy groceries: currency, traveler's checks, and checkable deposits (which work as long as your grocery store accepts either checks or debit cards). M2 is broader, because it includes things like savings accounts that can easily and quickly be converted into M1. Normally, for example, you can switch funds between your savings and checking accounts with a click of a mouse or a call to an automated phone service.

By contrast, converting a stock or a bond into cash requires selling the stock or bond—something that usually takes some time and also involves paying a broker's fee. That makes these assets much less liquid than bank deposits. So stocks and bonds, unlike bank deposits, aren't considered money.

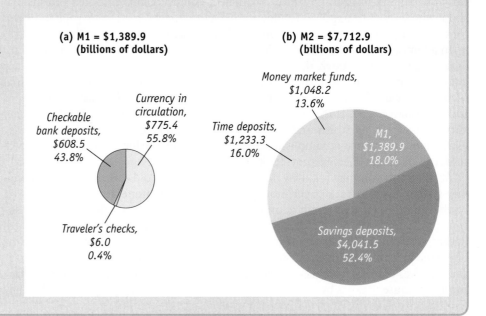

FIGURE 30-1

Monetary Aggregates, August 2008

The Federal Reserve uses two definitions of the money supply, M1 and M2. As panel (a) shows, more than half of M1 consists of currency in circulation, with checkable bank deposits making up almost all of the rest. M2, as panel (b) shows, has a much broader definition: it includes M1, plus a range of other deposits and deposit-like assets, making it more than five times as large.

Source: Federal Reserve Bank of St. Louis.

aren't checkable but can be withdrawn at any time before their maturity date by paying a penalty. Because currency and checkable deposits are directly usable as a medium of exchange, M1 is the most liquid measure of money.

Figure 30-1 shows the actual composition of M1 and M2 in August 2008, in billions of dollars. M1 is valued at $1,389.9 billion, with approximately 56% accounted for by currency in circulation, approximately 44% accounted for by checkable bank deposits, and a tiny slice accounted for by traveler's checks. In turn, M1 made up 18% of M2, valued at $7,712.9 billion. M2 consists of M1 plus other types of assets: two types of bank deposits, known as savings deposits and time deposits, both of which are considered noncheckable, plus money market funds, which are mutual funds that invest only in liquid assets and bear a close resemblance to bank deposits. These near-moneys pay interest while cash (currency in circulation) does not, and they typically pay higher interest rates than any offered on checkable bank deposits.

FOR INQUIRING MINDS

What's with All the Currency?

Alert readers may be a bit startled at one of the numbers in the money supply: $775.4 billion of currency in circulation. That's $2,570 in cash for every man, woman, and child in the United States. How many people do you know who carry $2,570 in their wallets? Not many. So where is all that cash?

Part of the answer is that it isn't in individuals' wallets: it's in cash registers. Businesses as well as individuals need to hold cash.

Economists also believe that cash plays an important role in transactions that people want to keep hidden. Small businesses and the self-employed sometimes prefer to be paid in cash so they can avoid paying taxes by hiding income from the Internal Revenue Service. Also, drug dealers and other criminals obviously don't want bank records of their dealings. In fact, some analysts have tried to infer the amount of illegal activity in the economy

from the total amount of cash holdings held by the public.

The most important reason for those huge currency holdings, however, is foreign use of dollars. The Federal Reserve estimates that 60% of U.S. currency is actually held outside the United States—largely in countries in which residents are so distrustful of their national currencies that the U.S. dollar has become a widely accepted medium of exchange.

➤*ECONOMICS IN ACTION*

The History of the Dollar

U.S. dollar bills are pure fiat money: they have no intrinsic value, and they are not backed by anything that does. But American money wasn't always like that. In the early days of European settlement, the colonies that would become the United States used commodity money, partly consisting of gold and silver coins minted in Europe. But such coins were scarce on this side of the Atlantic, so the colonists relied on a variety of other forms of commodity money. For example, settlers in Virginia used tobacco as money and settlers in the Northeast used "wampum," a type of clamshell.

Later in American history, commodity-backed paper money came into widespread use. But this wasn't paper money as we now know it, issued by the U.S. government and bearing the signature of the Secretary of the Treasury. Before the Civil War, the U.S. government didn't issue any paper money. Instead, dollar bills were issued by private banks, which promised that their bills could be redeemed for silver coins on demand. These promises weren't always credible because banks sometimes failed, leaving holders of their bills with worthless pieces of paper. Understandably, people were reluctant to accept currency from any bank rumored to be in financial trouble. In other words, in this private money system, some dollars were less valuable than others.

A curious legacy of that time was notes issued by the Citizens' Bank of Louisiana, based in New Orleans, that became among the most widely used bank notes in the southern states. These notes were printed in English on one side and French on the other. (At the time, many people in New Orleans, originally a colony of France, spoke French.) Thus, the $10 bill read *Ten* on one side and *Dix*, the French word for "ten," on the other. These $10 bills became known as "dixies," probably the source of the nickname of the U.S. South.

The U.S. government began issuing official paper money, called "greenbacks," during the Civil War, as a way to help pay for the war. At first greenbacks had no fixed value in terms of commodities. After 1873, the U.S. government guaranteed the value of a dollar in terms of gold, effectively turning dollars into commodity-backed money.

In 1933, when President Franklin D. Roosevelt broke the link between dollars and gold, his own federal budget director—who feared that the public would lose confidence in the dollar if it wasn't ultimately backed by gold—declared ominously, "This will be the end of Western civilization." It wasn't. The link between the dollar and gold was restored a few years later, then dropped again—seemingly for good—in August 1971. Despite the warnings of doom, the U.S. dollar is still the world's most widely used currency. ▲   > > > > > > > > > > > >

➤ CHECK YOUR UNDERSTANDING 30-1

1. Suppose you hold a gift certificate, good for certain products at participating stores. Is this gift certificate money? Why or why not?

2. Although most bank accounts pay some interest, depositors can get a higher interest rate by buying a certificate of deposit, or CD. The difference between a CD and a checking account is that the depositor pays a penalty for withdrawing the money before the CD comes due—a period of months or even years. Small CDs are counted in M2, but not in M1. Explain why they are not part of M1.

3. Explain why a system of commodity-backed money uses resources more efficiently than a system of commodity money.

Solutions appear at back of book.

The Monetary Role of Banks

More than half of M1, the narrowest definition of the money supply, consists of currency in circulation—$1 bills, $5 bills, and so on. It's obvious where currency comes from: it's printed by the U.S. Treasury. But the rest of M1 consists of bank deposits, and deposits account for the great bulk of M2, the broader definition of the money supply. By either measure, then, bank deposits are a major component of the money supply. And this fact brings us to our next topic: the monetary role of banks.

What Banks Do

As we learned in Chapter 26, a bank is a *financial intermediary* that uses liquid assets in the form of bank deposits to finance the illiquid investments of borrowers. Banks can create liquidity because it isn't necessary for a bank to keep all of the funds deposited with it in the form of highly liquid assets. Except in the case of a *bank run*—which we'll get to shortly—all of a bank's depositors won't want to withdraw their funds at the same time. So a bank can provide its depositors with liquid assets yet still invest much of the depositors' funds in illiquid assets, such as mortgages and business loans.

Banks can't, however, lend out all the funds placed in their hands by depositors because they have to satisfy any depositor who wants to withdraw his or her funds. In order to meet these demands, a bank must keep substantial quantities of liquid assets on hand. In the modern U.S. banking system, these assets take the form either of currency in the bank's vault or deposits held in the bank's own account at the Federal Reserve. As we'll see shortly, the latter can be converted into currency more or less instantly. Currency in bank vaults and bank deposits held at the Federal Reserve are called **bank reserves.** Because bank reserves are in bank vaults and at the Federal Reserve, not held by the public, they are not part of currency in circulation.

To understand the role of banks in determining the money supply, we start by introducing a simple tool for analyzing a bank's financial position: a **T-account.** A business's T-account summarizes its financial position by showing, in a single table, the business's assets and liabilities, with assets on the left and liabilities on the right. Figure 30-2 shows the T-account for a hypothetical business that *isn't* a bank— Samantha's Smoothies. According to Figure 30-2, Samantha's Smoothies owns a building worth $30,000 and has $15,000 worth of smoothie-making equipment. These are assets, so they're on the left side of the table. To finance its opening, the business borrowed $20,000 from a local bank. That's a liability, so the loan is on the right side of the table. By looking at the T-account, you can immediately see what Samantha's Smoothies owns and what it owes. Oh, and it's called a T-account because the lines in the table make a T-shape.

Samantha's Smoothies is an ordinary, nonbank business. Now let's look at the T-account for a hypothetical bank, First Street Bank, which is the repository of $1 million in bank deposits.

FIGURE 30-2

A T-Account for Samantha's Smoothies

A T-account summarizes a business's financial position. Its assets, in this case consisting of a building and some smoothie-making machinery, are on the left side. Its liabilities, consisting of the money it owes to a local bank, are on the right side.

Assets		Liabilities	
Building	$30,000	Loan from bank	$20,000
Smoothie-making machines	$15,000		

FIGURE 30-3

Assets and Liabilities of First Street Bank

First Street Bank's assets consist of $1,000,000 in loans and $100,000 in reserves. Its liabilities consist of $1,000,000 in deposits—money owed to people who have placed funds in First Street's hands.

Assets		Liabilities	
Loans	$1,000,000	Deposits	$1,000,000
Reserves	$100,000		

Figure 30-3 shows First Street's financial position. The loans First Street has made are on the left side, because they're assets: they represent funds that those who have borrowed from the bank are expected to repay. The bank's only other assets, in this simplified example, are its reserves, which, as we've learned, can take the form either of cash in the bank's vault or deposits at the Federal Reserve. On the right side we show the bank's liabilities, which in this example consist entirely of deposits made by customers at First Street. These are liabilities because they represent funds that must ultimately be repaid to depositors. Notice, by the way, that in this example First Street's assets are larger than its liabilities. That's the way it's supposed to be! In fact, as we'll see shortly, banks are required by law to maintain assets larger by a specific percentage than their liabilities.

In this example, First Street Bank holds reserves equal to 10% of its customers' bank deposits. The fraction of bank deposits that a bank holds as reserves is its **reserve ratio.** In the modern American system, the Federal Reserve—which, among other things, regulates banks operating in the United States—sets a minimum required reserve ratio that banks are required to maintain. To understand why banks are regulated, let's consider a problem banks can face: *bank runs.*

The Problem of Bank Runs

A bank can lend out most of the funds deposited in its care because in normal times only a small fraction of its depositors want to withdraw their funds on any given day. But what would happen if, for some reason, all or at least a large fraction of its depositors *did* try to withdraw their funds during a short period of time, such as a couple of days?

The answer is that if a significant share of its depositors demand their money back at the same time, the bank wouldn't be able to raise enough cash to meet those demands. The reason is that banks convert most of their depositors' funds into loans made to borrowers; that's how banks earn revenue—by charging interest on loans. Bank loans, however, are illiquid: they can't easily be converted into cash on short notice. To see why, imagine that First Street Bank has lent $100,000 to Drive-A-Peach Used Cars, a local dealership. To raise cash to meet demands for withdrawals, First Street can sell its loan to Drive-A-Peach to someone else—another bank or an individual investor. But if First Street tries to sell the loan quickly, potential buyers will be wary: they will suspect that First Street wants to sell the loan because there is something wrong and the loan might not be repaid. As a result, First Street Bank can sell the loan quickly only by offering it for sale at a deep discount—say, a discount of 50%, or $50,000.

The upshot is that if a significant number of First Street's depositors suddenly decided to withdraw their funds, the bank's efforts to raise the necessary cash quickly would force it to sell off its assets very cheaply. Inevitably, this leads to a *bank failure:* the bank would be unable to pay off its depositors in full.

The **reserve ratio** is the fraction of bank deposits that a bank holds as reserves.

A **bank run** is a phenomenon in which many of a bank's depositors try to withdraw their funds due to fears of a bank failure.

Deposit insurance guarantees that a bank's depositors will be paid even if the bank can't come up with the funds, up to a maximum amount per account.

Reserve requirements are rules set by the Federal Reserve that determine the minimum reserve ratio for banks.

What might start this whole process? That is, what might lead First Street's depositors to rush to pull their money out? A plausible answer is a spreading rumor that the bank is in financial trouble. Even if depositors aren't sure the rumor is true, they are likely to play it safe and get their money out while they still can. And it gets worse: a depositor who simply thinks that *other* depositors are going to panic and try to get their money out will realize that this could "break the bank." So he or she joins the rush. In other words, fear about a bank's financial condition can be a self-fulfilling prophecy: depositors who believe that other depositors will rush to the exit will rush to the exit themselves.

A **bank run** is a phenomenon in which many of a bank's depositors try to withdraw their funds due to fears of a bank failure. Moreover, bank runs aren't bad only for the bank in question and its depositors. Historically, they have often proved contagious, with a run on one bank leading to a loss of faith in other banks, causing additional bank runs. The upcoming Economics in Action describes an actual case of just such a contagion, the wave of bank runs that swept across the United States in the early 1930s. In response to that experience and similar experiences in other countries, the United States and most other modern governments have established a system of bank regulations that protects depositors and prevents most bank runs.

Bank Regulation

Should you worry about losing money in the United States due to a bank run? No. After the banking crises of the 1930s, the United States and most other countries put into place a system designed to protect depositors and the economy as a whole against bank runs. This system has three main features: *deposit insurance, capital requirements,* and *reserve requirements.* In addition, banks have access to the *discount window,* a source of cash when it's needed.

Deposit Insurance Almost all banks in the United States advertise themselves as a "member of the FDIC"—the Federal Deposit Insurance Corporation. As we learned in Chapter 26, the FDIC provides **deposit insurance,** a guarantee that depositors will be paid even if the bank can't come up with the funds, up to a maximum amount per account. The FDIC currently guarantees the first $250,000 of each account.

It's important to realize that deposit insurance doesn't just protect depositors if a bank actually fails. The insurance also eliminates the main reason for bank runs: since depositors know their funds are safe even if a bank fails, they have no incentive to rush to pull them out because of a rumor that the bank is in trouble.

Capital Requirements Deposit insurance, although it protects the banking system against bank runs, creates a well-known incentive problem. Because depositors are protected from loss, they have no incentive to monitor their bank's financial health, allowing risky behavior by the bank to go undetected. At the same time, the owners of banks have an incentive to engage in overly risky investment behavior, such as making questionable loans at high interest rates. That's because if all goes well, the owners profit; and if things go badly, the government covers the losses through federal deposit insurance.

To reduce the incentive for excessive risk-taking, regulators require that the owners of banks hold substantially more assets than the value of bank deposits. That way, the bank will still have assets larger than its deposits even if some of its loans go bad, and losses will accrue against the bank owners' assets, not the government. The excess of a bank's assets over its bank deposits and other liabilities is called the *bank's capital.* For example, First State Street Bank has capital of $100,000, equal to 9% of the total value of its assets. In practice, banks' capital is required to equal at least 7% of the value of their assets.

Reserve Requirements Another regulation used to reduce the risk of bank runs is **reserve requirements,** rules set by the Federal Reserve that set the minimum reserve ratio for banks. For example, in the United States, the minimum reserve ratio for checkable bank deposits is 10%.

The Discount Window One final protection against bank runs is the fact that the Federal Reserve, which we'll discuss more thoroughly later in this chapter, stands ready to lend money to banks in trouble, an arrangement known as the **discount window.** The ability to borrow money means a bank can avoid being forced to sell its assets at fire-sale prices in order to satisfy the demands of a sudden rush of depositors demanding cash. Instead, it can turn to the Fed and borrow the funds it needs to pay off depositors.

> The **discount window** is an arrange-ment in which the Federal Reserve stands ready to lend money to banks in trouble.

►ECONOMICS IN ACTION

It's a Wonderful Banking System

Next Christmas time, it's a sure thing that at least one TV channel will show the 1946 film *It's a Wonderful Life,* featuring Jimmy Stewart as George Bailey, a small-town banker whose life is saved by an angel. The movie's climactic scene is a run on Bailey's bank, as fearful depositors rush to take their funds out.

When the movie was made, such scenes were still fresh in Americans' memories. There was a wave of bank runs in late 1930, a second wave in the spring of 1931, and a third wave in early 1933. By the end, more than a third of the nation's banks had failed. To bring the panic to an end, on March 6, 1933, the newly inaugurated president, Franklin Delano Roosevelt, declared a national "bank holiday," closing all banks for a week to give bank regulators time to close unhealthy banks and certify healthy ones.

Since then, regulation has protected the United States and other wealthy countries against most bank runs. In fact, the scene in *It's a Wonderful Life* was already out of date when the movie was made. But the last decade has seen several waves

In July 2008, panicky IndyMac depositors lined up to pull their money out of the troubled California bank.

of bank runs in developing countries. For example, bank runs played a role in an economic crisis that swept Southeast Asia in 1997–1998, and in the severe economic crisis in Argentina which began in late 2001.

Notice that we said "most bank runs." There are some limits on deposit insurance; in particular, currently only the first $250,000 of any bank account is insured. As a result, there can still be a rush out of a bank perceived as troubled. In fact, that's exactly what happened to IndyMac, a Pasadena-based lender that had made a large number of questionable home loans, in July 2008. As questions about IndyMac's financial soundness were raised, depositors began pulling out funds, forcing federal regulators to step in and close the bank. Unlike in the bank runs of the 1930s, however, most depositors got all their funds back—and the panic at IndyMac did not spread to other institutions. ▲

> > > > > > > > > > > >

> **QUICK REVIEW**
>
> ➤ A **T-account** is used to analyze a bank's financial position. A bank holds **bank reserves**—currency in its vaults plus deposits held in its account at the Federal Reserve. The **reserve ratio** is the ratio of bank reserves to customers' bank deposits.
> ➤ Because bank loans are illiquid, but a bank is obligated to return depositors' funds on demand, **bank runs** are a potential problem. Although they took place on a massive scale in the United States during the 1930s, they have been largely eliminated through bank regulation in the form of **deposit insurance,** capital requirements, and **reserve requirements,** as well as through the availability of the **discount window.**

► CHECK YOUR UNDERSTANDING 30-2

1. Suppose you are a depositor at First Street Bank. You hear a rumor that the bank has suffered serious losses on its loans. Every depositor knows that the rumor isn't true, but each thinks that most other depositors believe the rumor. Why, in the absence of deposit insurance, could this lead to a bank run? How does deposit insurance change the situation?

2. A con artist has a great idea: he'll open a bank without investing any capital and lend all the deposits at high interest rates to real estate developers. If the real estate market booms, the loans will be repaid and he'll make high profits. If the real estate market goes bust, the loans won't be repaid and the bank will fail—but he will not lose any of his own wealth. How would modern bank regulation frustrate his scheme?

Solutions appear at back of book.

Determining the Money Supply

Without banks, there would be no checkable deposits, and so the quantity of currency in circulation would equal the money supply. In that case, the money supply would be solely determined by whoever controls government minting and printing presses. But banks do exist, and through their creation of checkable bank deposits they affect the money supply in two ways. First, banks remove some currency from circulation: dollar bills that are sitting in bank vaults, as opposed to sitting in people's wallets, aren't part of the money supply. Second, and much more importantly, banks create money by accepting deposits and making loans—that is, they make the money supply larger than just the value of currency in circulation. Our next topic is how banks create money and what determines the amount of money they create.

How Banks Create Money

To see how banks create money, let's examine what happens when someone decides to deposit currency in a bank. Consider the example of Silas, a miser, who keeps a shoebox full of cash under his bed. Suppose Silas realizes that it would be safer, as well as more convenient, to deposit that cash in the bank and to use his debit card when shopping. Assume that he deposits $1,000 into a checkable account at First Street Bank. What effect will Silas's actions have on the money supply?

Panel (a) of Figure 30-4 shows the initial effect of his deposit. First Street Bank credits Silas with $1,000 in his account, so the economy's checkable bank deposits rise by $1,000. Meanwhile, Silas's cash goes into the vault, raising First Street's reserves by $1,000 as well.

This initial transaction has no effect on the money supply. Currency in circulation, part of the money supply, falls by $1,000; checkable bank deposits, also part of the money supply, rise by the same amount.

But this is not the end of the story, because First Street Bank can now lend out part of Silas's deposit. Assume that it holds 10% of Silas's deposit—$100—in reserves and lends the rest out in cash to Silas's neighbor, Mary. The effect of this second stage is shown in panel (b). First Street's deposits remain unchanged, and so does the value of its assets. But the composition of its assets changes: by making the loan, it reduces its reserves by $900, so that they are only $100 larger than they were before Silas made his deposit. In

---

FIGURE 30-4 **Effect on the Money Supply of Turning Cash into a Checkable Deposit at First Street Bank**

(a) Initial Effect Before Bank Makes a New Loan

Assets		Liabilities	
Loans	No change	Checkable deposits	+$1,000
Reserves	+$1,000		

(b) Effect When Bank Makes a New Loan

Assets		Liabilities
Loans	+$900	No change
Reserves	−$900	

When Silas deposits $1,000 (which had been stashed under his bed) into a checkable bank account, there is initially no effect on the money supply: currency in circulation falls by $1,000, but checkable bank deposits rise by $1,000. The corresponding entries on the bank's T-account, depicted in panel (a), show deposits initially rising by $1,000 and the bank's reserves initially rising by $1,000. In the second stage, depicted in panel (b), the bank holds 10% of Silas's deposit ($100) as reserves and lends out the rest ($900) to Mary. As a result, its reserves fall by $900 and its loans increase by $900. Its liabilities, including Silas's $1,000 deposit, are unchanged. The money supply, the sum of checkable bank deposits and currency in circulation, has now increased by $900—the $900 now held by Mary.

the place of the $900 reduction in reserves, the bank has acquired an IOU, its $900 cash loan to Mary. So by putting $900 of Silas's cash back into circulation by lending it to Mary, First Street Bank has, in fact, increased the money supply. That is, the sum of currency in circulation and checkable bank deposits has risen by $900 compared to what it had been when Silas's cash was still under his bed. Although Silas is still the owner of $1,000, now in the form of a checkable deposit, Mary has the use of $900 in cash from her borrowings.

And this may not be the end of the story. Suppose that Mary uses her cash to buy a television and a DVD player from Acme Merchandise. What does Anne Acme, the store's owner, do with the cash? If she holds on to it, the money supply doesn't increase any further. But suppose she deposits the $900 into a checkable bank deposit—say, at Second Street Bank. Second Street Bank, in turn, will keep only part of that deposit in reserves, lending out the rest, creating still more money.

Assume that Second Street Bank, like First Street Bank, keeps 10% of any bank deposit in reserves and lends out the rest. Then it will keep $90 in reserves and lend out $810 of Anne's deposit to another borrower, further increasing the money supply.

Table 30-1 shows the process of money creation we have described so far. At first the money supply consists only of Silas's $1,000. After he deposits the cash into a checkable bank deposit and the bank makes a loan, the money supply rises to $1,900. After the second deposit and the second loan, the money supply rises to $2,710. And the process will, of course, continue from there. (Although we have considered the case in which Silas places his cash in a checkable bank deposit, the results would be the same if he put it into any type of near-money.)

This process of money creation may sound familiar. In Chapter 27 we described the *multiplier process:* an initial increase in real GDP leads to a rise in consumer spending, which leads to a further rise in real GDP, which leads to a further rise in consumer spending, and so on. What we have here is another kind of multiplier—the *money multiplier.* Next, we'll learn what determines the size of this multiplier.

Reserves, Bank Deposits, and the Money Multiplier

In tracing out the effect of Silas's deposit in Table 30-1, we assumed that the funds a bank lends out always end up being deposited either in the same bank or in another bank—so funds disbursed as loans come back to the banking system, even if not to the lending bank itself. In reality, some of these loaned funds may be held by borrowers in their wallets and not deposited in a bank, meaning that some of the loaned amount "leaks" out of the banking system. Such leaks reduce the size of the money multiplier, just as leaks of real income into savings reduce the size of the real GDP multiplier. (Bear in mind, however, that the "leak" here comes from the fact that borrowers keep some of their funds in currency, rather than the fact that consumers save some of their income.) But let's set that complication aside for a moment and consider how the money supply is determined in a "checkable-deposits-only" monetary system, where funds are always deposited in bank accounts and none are held in wallets as currency. That is, in our checkable-deposits-only monetary system, any and all funds borrowed from a bank are immediately deposited into a checkable bank account. We'll assume that banks are required to satisfy a minimum reserve ratio of 10% and that every bank lends out all of its **excess reserves,** reserves over and above the amount needed to satisfy the minimum reserve ratio.

TABLE 30-1

How Banks Create Money

	Currency in circulation	Checkable bank deposits	Money supply
First stage: Silas keeps his cash under his bed.	$1,000	$0	$1,000
Second stage: Silas deposits cash in First Street Bank, which lends out $900 to Mary, who then pays it to Anne Acme.	900	1,000	1,900
Third stage: Anne Acme deposits $900 in Second Street Bank, which lends out $810 to another borrower.	810	1,900	2,710

Excess reserves are a bank's reserves over and above its required reserves.

The **monetary base** is the sum of currency in circulation and bank reserves.

Now suppose that for some reason a bank suddenly finds itself with $1,000 in excess reserves. What happens? The answer is that the bank will lend out that $1,000, which will end up as a checkable bank deposit somewhere in the banking system, launching a money multiplier process very similar to the process shown in Table 30-1. In the first stage, the bank lends out its excess reserves of $1,000, which becomes a checkable bank deposit somewhere. The bank that receives the $1,000 deposit keeps 10%, or $100, as reserves and lends out the remaining 90%, or $900, which again becomes a checkable bank deposit somewhere. The bank receiving this $900 deposit again keeps 10%, which is $90, as reserves and lends out the remaining $810. The bank receiving this $810 keeps $81 in reserves and lends out the remaining $729, and so on. As a result of this process, the total increase in checkable bank deposits is equal to a sum that looks like:

$$\$1,000 + \$900 + \$810 + \$729 + \ldots$$

We'll use the symbol rr for the reserve ratio. More generally, the total increase in checkable bank deposits that is generated when a bank lends out $1,000 in excess reserves is:

(30-1) Increase in checkable bank deposits from $1,000 in excess reserves = $\$1,000 + \$1,000 \times (1 - rr) + \$1,000 \times (1 - rr)^2 + \$1,000 \times (1 - rr)^3 + \ldots$

As we saw in Chapter 27, an infinite series of this form can be simplified to:

(30-2) Increase in checkable bank deposits from $1,000 in excess reserves = $\$1,000/rr$

Given a reserve ratio of 10%, or 0.1, a $1,000 increase in excess reserves will increase the total value of checkable bank deposits by $1,000/0.1 = $10,000. In fact, in a checkable-deposits-only monetary system, the total value of checkable bank deposits will be equal to the value of bank reserves divided by the reserve ratio. Or to put it a different way, if the reserve ratio is 10%, each $1 of reserves held by a bank supports $1/rr = $1/0.1 = $10 of checkable bank deposits.

The Money Multiplier in Reality

In reality, the determination of the money supply is more complicated than our simple model suggests, because it depends not only on the ratio of reserves to bank deposits but also on the fraction of the money supply that individuals choose to hold in the form of currency. In fact, we already saw this in our example of Silas depositing the cash under his bed: when he chose to hold a checkable bank deposit instead of currency, he set in motion an increase in the money supply.

To define the money multiplier in practice, it's important to recognize that the Federal Reserve controls the *sum* of bank reserves and currency in circulation, called the *monetary base,* but it does not control the allocation of that sum between bank reserves and currency in circulation. Consider Silas and his deposit one more time: by taking the cash from under his bed and depositing it in a bank, he reduced the quantity of currency in circulation but increased bank reserves by an equal amount—leaving the *monetary base,* or net, unchanged. The **monetary base,** which is the quantity the monetary authorities control, is the sum of currency in circulation and reserves held by banks.

The monetary base is different from the money supply in two ways. First, bank reserves, which are part of the monetary base, aren't considered part of the money supply. A $1 bill in someone's wallet is considered money because it's available for an individual to spend, but a $1 bill held as bank reserves in a bank vault or deposited at the Federal Reserve isn't considered part of the money supply because it's not available for spending. Second, checkable bank deposits, which are part of the money supply because they are available for spending, aren't part of the monetary base.

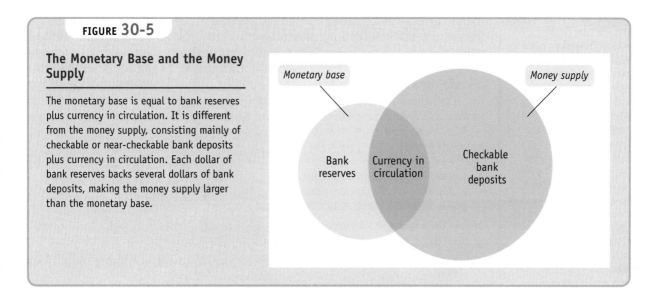

FIGURE 30-5

The Monetary Base and the Money Supply

The monetary base is equal to bank reserves plus currency in circulation. It is different from the money supply, consisting mainly of checkable or near-checkable bank deposits plus currency in circulation. Each dollar of bank reserves backs several dollars of bank deposits, making the money supply larger than the monetary base.

Monetary base

Money supply

Bank reserves

Currency in circulation

Checkable bank deposits

Figure 30-5 shows the two concepts schematically. The circle on the left represents the monetary base, consisting of bank reserves plus currency in circulation. The circle on the right represents the money supply, consisting mainly of currency in circulation plus checkable or near-checkable bank deposits. As the figure indicates, currency in circulation is part of both the monetary base and the money supply. But bank reserves aren't part of the money supply, and checkable or near-checkable bank deposits aren't part of the monetary base. In practice, most of the monetary base actually consists of currency in circulation, which also makes up about half of the money supply.

Now we can formally define the **money multiplier:** it's the ratio of the money supply to the monetary base. The actual money multiplier in the United States, using M1 as our measure of money, is about 1.9. That's a lot smaller than $1/0.1 = 10$, the money multiplier in a checkable-deposits-only system with a reserve ratio of 10% (the minimum required ratio for most checkable deposits in the United States). The reason the actual money multiplier is so small arises from the fact that people hold significant amounts of cash, and a dollar of currency in circulation, unlike a dollar in reserves, doesn't support multiple dollars of the money supply. In fact, currency in circulation normally accounts for more than 90% of the monetary base. In August 2008, currency in circulation was $831 billion, compared with a monetary base of $840 billion.

The **money multiplier** is the ratio of the money supply to the monetary base.

➤ECONOMICS IN ACTION

Multiplying Money Down

In our hypothetical example illustrating how banks create money, we described Silas the miser taking the currency from under his bed and turning it into a checkable bank deposit. This led to an increase in the money supply, as banks engaged in successive waves of lending backed by Silas's funds. It follows that if something happened to make Silas revert to old habits, taking his money out of the bank and putting it back under his bed, the result would be less lending and, ultimately, a decline in the money supply. That's exactly what happened as a result of the bank runs of the 1930s.

Table 30-2 shows what happened between 1929 and 1933, as bank failures shook the public's confidence in the banking system. The second column shows the public's holdings of currency. This increased sharply, as many Americans decided that money under the bed was safer than money

TABLE 30-2

The Effects of Bank Runs, 1929–1933

	Currency in circulation	Checkable bank deposits	M1
	(billions of dollars)		
1929	$3.90	$22.74	$26.64
1933	5.09	14.82	19.91
Percent change	+31%	−35%	−25%

Source: U.S. Census Bureau (1975), *Historical Statistics of the United States.*

in the bank after all. The third column shows the value of checkable bank deposits. This fell sharply, through the multiplier process we have just analyzed, when individuals pulled their cash out of banks. Loans also fell because banks that survived the waves of bank runs increased their excess reserves, just in case another wave began. The fourth column shows the value of M1, the first of the monetary aggregates we described earlier. It fell sharply, because the total reduction in checkable or near-checkable bank deposits was much larger than the increase in currency in circulation. ▲

< < < < < < < < < < < <

> CHECK YOUR UNDERSTANDING 30-3

1. Assume that total reserves are equal to $200 and total checkable bank deposits are equal to $1,000. Also assume that the public does not hold any currency. Now suppose that the required reserve ratio falls from 20% to 10%. Trace out how this leads to an expansion in bank deposits.

2. Take the example of Silas depositing his $1,000 in cash into First Street Bank and assume that the required reserve ratio is 10%. But now assume that each time someone receives a bank loan, he or she keeps half the loan in cash. Trace out the resulting expansion in the money supply.

Solutions appear at back of book.

The Federal Reserve System

Who's in charge of ensuring that banks maintain enough reserves? Who decides how large the monetary base will be? The answer, in the United States, is an institution known as the Federal Reserve (or, informally, as "the Fed"). The Federal Reserve is a **central bank**—an institution that oversees and regulates the banking system, and controls the monetary base. Other central banks include the Bank of England, the Bank of Japan, and the European Central Bank, or ECB. The ECB acts as a common central bank for 15 European countries: Austria, Belgium, Finland, France, Germany, Greece, Ireland, Italy, Luxembourg, the Netherlands, Portugal, Spain, Slovenia, Cyprus, and Malta. The world's oldest central bank, by the way, is Sweden's Sveriges Rijksbank, which awards the Nobel Prize in economics.

The Structure of the Fed

The legal status of the Fed, which was created in 1913, is unusual: it is not exactly part of the U.S. government, but it is not really a private institution either. Strictly speaking, the Federal Reserve System consists of two parts: the Board of Governors and the 12 regional Federal Reserve Banks.

The Board of Governors, which oversees the entire system from its offices in Washington, D.C., is constituted like a government agency: its seven members are appointed by the president and must be approved by the Senate. However, they are appointed for 14-year terms, to insulate them from political pressure in their conduct of monetary policy. (Why this is a potential problem will become clear in Chapter 32, when we discuss inflation.) Although the chairman is appointed more frequently— every four years—it's traditional for chairmen to be reappointed and serve much longer terms. For example, William McChesney Martin was chairman of the Fed from 1951 until 1970. Alan Greenspan, appointed in 1987, served as the Fed's chairman until 2006.

The 12 Federal Reserve Banks each serve a region of the country, providing various banking and supervisory services. One of their jobs, for example, is to audit the books of private-sector banks to ensure their financial health. Each regional bank is run by a board of directors chosen from the local banking and business community. The Federal Reserve Bank of New York plays a special role: it carries out *open-market operations,* usually the main tool of monetary policy. Figure 30-6 shows the 12 Federal Reserve districts and the city in which each regional Federal Reserve Bank is located.

A **central bank** is an institution that oversees and regulates the banking system and controls the monetary base.

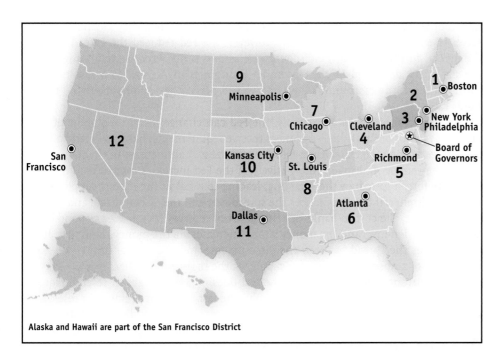

FIGURE 30-6 The Federal Reserve System The Federal Reserve System consists of the Board of Governors in Washington, D.C., plus 12 regional Federal Reserve Banks. This map shows each of the 12 Federal Reserve districts.

Source: Board of Governors of the Federal Reserve System.

Decisions about monetary policy are made by the Federal Open Market Committee, which consists of the Board of Governors plus five of the regional bank presidents. The president of the Federal Reserve Bank of New York is always on the committee, and the other four seats rotate among the 11 other regional bank presidents. The chairman of the Board of Governors normally also serves as the chairman of the Open Market Committee.

The effect of this complex structure is to create an institution that is ultimately accountable to the voting public, because the Board of Governors is chosen by the president and confirmed by the Senate, all of whom are themselves elected officials. But the long terms served by board members, as well as the indirectness of their appointment process, largely insulate them from short-term political pressures.

What the Fed Does: Reserve Requirements and the Discount Rate

The Fed has three main policy tools at its disposal: *reserve requirements,* the *discount rate,* and, most importantly, *open-market operations.*

In our discussion of bank runs, we noted that the Fed sets a minimum reserve ratio requirement, currently equal to 10% for checkable bank deposits. Banks that fail to maintain at least the required reserve ratio on average over a two-week period face penalties.

What does a bank do if it looks as if it has insufficient reserves to meet the Fed's reserve requirement? Normally, it borrows additional reserves from other banks via the **federal funds market,** a financial market that allows banks that fall short of the reserve requirement to borrow reserves (usually just overnight) from banks that are holding excess reserves. The interest rate in this market is determined by supply and demand—but the supply and demand for bank reserves are both strongly affected by Federal Reserve actions. As we'll see in the next chapter, the **federal funds rate,** the interest rate at which funds are borrowed and lent in the federal funds market, plays a key role in modern monetary policy.

Alternatively, banks in need of reserves can borrow from the Fed itself via the *discount window.* The **discount rate** is the rate of interest the Fed charges on those loans. Normally, the discount rate is set 1 percentage point above the federal funds

The **federal funds market** allows banks that fall short of the reserve requirement to borrow funds from banks with excess reserves.

The **federal funds rate** is the interest rate determined in the federal funds market.

The **discount rate** is the rate of interest the Fed charges on loans to banks.

An **open-market operation** is a purchase or sale of government debt by the Fed.

rate in order to discourage banks from turning to the Fed when they are in need of reserves. Beginning in the fall of 2007, however, the Fed reduced the spread between the federal funds rate and the discount rate as part of its response to an ongoing financial crisis, described in the upcoming Economics in Action. As a result, by the spring of 2008 the discount rate was only 0.25 percentage points above the federal funds rate.

In order to alter the money supply, the Fed can change reserve requirements, the discount rate, or both. If the Fed reduces reserve requirements, banks will lend a larger percentage of their deposits, leading to more loans and an increase in the money supply via the money multiplier. Alternatively, if the Fed increases reserve requirements, banks are forced to reduce their lending, leading to a fall in the money supply via the money multiplier. If the Fed reduces the spread between the discount rate and the federal funds rate, the cost to banks of being short of reserves falls; banks respond by increasing their lending, and the money supply increases via the money multiplier. If the Fed increases the spread between the discount rate and the federal funds rate, bank lending falls—and so will the money supply via the money multiplier.

Under current practice, however, the Fed doesn't use changes in reserve requirements to actively manage the money supply. The last significant change in reserve requirements was in 1992. The Fed normally doesn't use the discount rate either, although, as we mentioned earlier, there was a temporary surge in lending through the discount window in 2007 in response to a financial crisis. Today, normal monetary policy is conducted almost exclusively using the Fed's third policy tool: open-market operations.

Open-Market Operations

Like the banks it oversees, the Federal Reserve has assets and liabilities. The Fed's assets consist of its holdings of debt issued by the U.S. government, mainly short-term U.S. government bonds with a maturity of less than one year, known as U.S. Treasury bills. Remember, the Fed isn't exactly part of the U.S. government, so U.S. Treasury bills held by the Fed are a liability of the government but an asset of the Fed. The Fed's liabilities consist of currency in circulation and bank reserves. Figure 30-7 summarizes the normal assets and liabilities of the Fed in the form of a T-account.

In an **open-market operation** the Federal Reserve buys or sells U.S. Treasury bills, normally through a transaction with *commercial banks*—banks that mainly make business loans, as opposed to home loans. The Fed never buys U.S. Treasury bills directly from the federal government. There's a good reason for this: when a central bank buys government debt directly from the government, it is lending directly to the government—in effect, the central bank is printing money to finance the government's budget deficit. As we'll see later in the book, this has historically been a formula for disastrous levels of inflation.

The two panels of Figure 30-8 show the changes in the financial position of both the Fed and commercial banks that result from open-market operations. When the Fed buys

---

FIGURE 30-7

The Federal Reserve's Assets and Liabilities

The Federal Reserve holds its assets mostly in short-term government bonds called U.S. Treasury bills. Its liabilities are the monetary base—currency in circulation plus bank reserves.

Assets	Liabilities
Government debt (Treasury bills)	Monetary base (Currency in circulation + bank reserves)

FIGURE 30-8	Open-Market Operations by the Federal Reserve

(a) An Open-Market Purchase of $100 Million

	Assets		**Liabilities**	
Federal Reserve	Treasury bills	+$100 million	Monetary base	+$100 million

	Assets		**Liabilities**
Commercial banks	Treasury bills	−$100 million	No change
	Reserves	+$100 million	

(b) An Open-Market Sale of $100 Million

	Assets		**Liabilities**	
Federal Reserve	Treasury bills	−$100 million	Monetary base	−$100 million

	Assets		**Liabilities**
Commercial banks	Treasury bills	+$100 million	No change
	Reserves	−$100 million	

In panel (a), the Federal Reserve increases the monetary base by purchasing U.S. Treasury bills from private commercial banks in an open-market operation. Here, a $100 million purchase of U.S. Treasury bills by the Federal Reserve is paid for by a $100 million addition to private bank reserves, generating a $100 million increase in the monetary base. This will ultimately lead to an increase in the money supply via the money multiplier as banks lend out some of these new reserves. In panel (b), the Federal Reserve reduces the monetary base by selling U.S. Treasury bills to private commercial banks in an open-market operation. Here, a $100 million sale of U.S. Treasury bills leads to a $100 million reduction in private bank reserves, resulting in a $100 million decrease in the monetary base. This will ultimately lead to a fall in the money supply via the money multiplier as banks reduce their loans in response to a fall in their reserves.

U.S. Treasury bills from a commercial bank, it pays by crediting the bank's reserve account by an amount equal to the value of the Treasury bills. This is illustrated in panel (a): the Fed buys $100 million of U.S. Treasury bills from commercial banks, which increases the monetary base by $100 million because it increases bank reserves by $100 million. When the Fed sells U.S. Treasury bills to commercial banks, it debits the banks' accounts, reducing their reserves. This is shown in panel (b), where the Fed sells $100 million of U.S. Treasury bills. Here, bank reserves and the monetary base decrease.

You might wonder where the Fed gets the funds to purchase U.S. Treasury bills from banks. The answer is that it simply creates them with a stroke of the pen—or, these days, a click of the mouse—that credits the banks' accounts with extra reserves. (The Fed prints money to pay for Treasury bills only when banks want the additional reserves in the form of currency.) Remember, the modern dollar is fiat money, which isn't backed by anything. So the Fed can create additional monetary base at its own discretion.

The change in bank reserves caused by an open-market operation doesn't directly affect the money supply. Instead, it starts the money multiplier in motion. After the $100 million increase in reserves shown in panel (a), commercial banks would lend out their additional reserves, immediately increasing the money supply by $100 million. Some of those loans would be deposited back into the banking system, increasing reserves again and permitting a further round of loans, and so on, leading to a rise in the money supply. An open-market sale has the reverse effect: bank reserves fall, requiring banks to reduce their loans, leading to a fall in the money supply.

Economists often say, loosely, that the Fed controls the money supply—checkable deposits plus currency in circulation. In fact, it controls only the monetary base—bank reserves plus currency in circulation. But by increasing or reducing the monetary base, the Fed can exert a powerful influence on both the money supply and interest rates. This influence is the basis of monetary policy, the subject of our next chapter.

Who Gets the Interest on the Fed's Assets?

As we've just learned, the Fed owns a lot of assets—Treasury bills—which it bought from commercial banks in exchange for monetary base in the form of credits to banks' reserve accounts. These assets pay interest. Yet the Fed's liabilities consist mainly of the monetary base, liabilities on which the Fed *doesn't* pay interest. So the Fed is, in effect, an institution that has the privilege of borrowing funds at a zero interest rate and lending them out at a positive interest rate. That sounds like a pretty profitable business. Who gets the profits?

The answer is, you do—or rather, U.S. taxpayers do. The Fed keeps some of the interest it receives to finance its opera-

tions, but turns most of it over to the U.S. Treasury. For example, in 2007 the Federal Reserve system received $40.3 billion in interest on its holdings of Treasury bills, of which $34.6 billion was returned to the Treasury.

We can now finish the story of the impact of those forged $100 bills allegedly printed in North Korea. When a fake $100 bill enters circulation, it has the same economic effect as a real $100 bill printed by the U.S. government. That is, as long as nobody catches the forgery, the fake bill serves, for all practical purposes, as part of the monetary base. Meanwhile, the Fed decides on the size of the monetary

base based on economic considerations— in particular, the Fed doesn't let the monetary base get too large, because that can cause inflation. So every fake $100 bill that enters circulation basically means that the Fed prints one less real $100 bill. When the Fed prints a $100 bill legally, however, it gets Treasury bills in return—and the interest on those bills helps pay for the U.S. government's expenses. So a counterfeit $100 bill reduces the amount of Treasury bills the Fed can acquire and thereby reduces the interest payments going to the Fed and the U.S. Treasury. So taxpayers bear the real cost of counterfeiting.

The European Central Bank

As we noted earlier, the Fed is only one of a number of central banks around the world, and it's much younger than Sweden's Rijksbank and Britain's Bank of England. In general, other central banks operate in much the same way as the Fed. That's especially true of the only other central bank that rivals the Fed in terms of importance to the world economy: the European Central Bank.

The European Central Bank, known as the ECB, was created in January 1999 when 11 European nations adopted the euro as their common currency and placed their joint monetary policy in the ECB's hands. (Four more countries have joined since 1999.) The ECB instantly became an extremely important institution: although no single European nation has an economy anywhere near as large as that of the United States, the combined economies of the eurozone, the group of countries that have adopted the euro as their currency, are roughly as big as the U.S. economy. As a result, the ECB and the Fed are the two giants of the monetary world.

Like the Fed, the ECB has a special status: it's not a private institution, but it's not exactly a government agency either. In fact, it can't be a government agency, because there is no pan-European government! Luckily for puzzled Americans, there are strong analogies between European central banking and the Federal Reserve system.

First of all, the ECB, which is located in the German city of Frankfurt, isn't really the counterpart of the whole Federal Reserve system: it's the equivalent of the Board of Governors in Washington. The European counterparts of the regional Federal Reserve Banks are Europe's national central banks: the Bank of France, the Bank of Italy, and so on. Until 1999, each of these national banks was the equivalent of the Fed. For example, the Bank of France controlled the French monetary base. Today these national banks, like regional Feds, provide various financial services to local banks and businesses and conduct open-market operations, but monetary policy making has moved upstream to the ECB. Still, the various European national central banks aren't small institutions: in total, they employ more than 50,000 people, while the ECB employs fewer than 1,300.

In the eurozone, each country chooses who runs its own national central bank. The ECB's Executive Board is the counterpart of the Fed's Board of Governors; its members are chosen by unanimous consent of the eurozone national governments. The counterpart of the Federal Open Market Committee is the ECB's Governing Board. Just as the Fed's Open Market Committee consists of the Board of Governors plus a rotating group of regional Fed presidents, the ECB's Governing Board consists of the Executive Board plus a rotating group of national central bank heads. But there's a special twist: the frequency with which any country's central bank gets a seat at the table is determined by a formula that reflects the size of the country's economy. In other words, Germany, which had a GDP of $3.3 trillion in 2007, gets a seat on the board a lot more often than Greece, which had a GDP of only $313 billion.

In the end, the details probably don't matter much. Like the Fed, the ECB is ultimately answerable to voters but is highly insulated from short-term political pressures.

➤ECONOMICS IN ACTION

The Fed's Balance Sheet, Normal and Abnormal

Figure 30-7 showed a simplified version of the Fed's balance sheet in which the Fed's liabilities consisted entirely of the monetary base and its assets consisted entirely of Treasury bills. That's an oversimplification, because the Fed's operations are complicated in detail, and the Fed's balance sheet includes a numbers of additional items. In normal times, however, Figure 30-7 isn't too bad an approximation: the monetary base typically accounts for about 90% of the Fed's liabilities, and claims on the U.S. Treasury account for about 90% of its assets. The pie chart at left in Figure 30-9 shows the composition of the Fed's assets as of September 5, 2007, which was a more or less normal day.

Lately, however, the Fed has been living in interesting times and, correspondingly, its balance sheet has become more complicated. As described in Chapter 26, there was a huge bust in the housing market beginning in 2006, and this led to large losses for

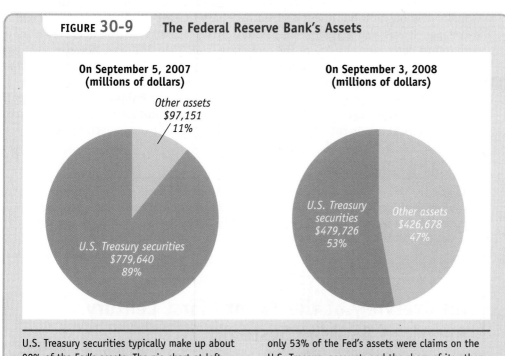

FIGURE 30-9   The Federal Reserve Bank's Assets

On September 5, 2007
(millions of dollars)

Other assets
$97,151
11%

U.S. Treasury securities
$779,640
89%

On September 3, 2008
(millions of dollars)

U.S. Treasury securities
$479,726
53%

Other assets
$426,678
47%

U.S. Treasury securities typically make up about 90% of the Fed's assets. The pie chart at left shows this typical composition on September 5, 2007. Only one year later, as shown in the pie chart at right, the composition of the Fed's assets had changed dramatically: on September 3, 2008, only 53% of the Fed's assets were claims on the U.S. Treasury account, and the share of its other assets—largely loans such as those made to rescue Bear Stearns—had increased to 47%.

Source: Board of Governors of the Federal Reserve System.

financial institutions that had made housing-related loans. It also led to a broad loss of confidence in the financial system, especially in financial institutions that had made housing-related loans. The institutions in trouble included a number of banks, but the housing bust also created big problems at so-called nondepository financial institutions. As the term implies, nondepository financial institutions don't accept bank deposits, but they are nonetheless vulnerable to events that strongly resemble a bank run, because they have liabilities that can be recalled by their creditors on demand, but their assets are illiquid. For example, in 2008 many investors became worried about the health of Bear Stearns, a Wall Street financial institution that engaged in complex financial deals, buying and selling financial assets with borrowed funds. When confidence in Bear Stearns dried up in mid-2008, Bear Stearns found itself unable to raise the funds it needed to deliver on its end of these deals, and the firm quickly spiraled into collapse.

The Fed responded to the financial crisis by expanding its discount window lending—greatly increasing the amount it stood ready to lend to banks, but also opening up lending to nondepository financial institutions such as Wall Street financial firms. As these firms took advantage of the ability to borrow from the Fed, they pledged as collateral their assets on hand—a motley collection of real estate loans, housing loans, business loans, and so on. So in this attempt to prevent financial meltdown, the Fed accumulated large quantities of assets other than Treasury bills, as shown in the pie chart at right in Figure 30-9, which shows the Fed's assets on September 3, 2008. The "other" category included something called the Temporary Auction Facility, an enlarged version of the ordinary discount window. It also included another arrangement called the Temporary Securities Lending Facility, which acted like the discount window but involved loans to nondepository institutions. And as of September 2008, the Fed had a $29 billion loan outstanding to Maiden Lane LLC, a company specially created to let the Fed and U.S. Treasury keep Bear Stearns afloat until it could be merged with J. P. Morgan, another Wall Street financial institution.

The whole episode was very unusual, a major departure from the way the Fed normally does business but one it deemed necessary to stave off financial and economic collapse. It was also a graphic illustration of the fact that the Fed does much more than just determine the size of the monetary base. The odds were, however, that the Fed's balance sheet would return to normal as soon as the crisis ended. Fed officials were very, very unhappy at the prospect of holding on to assets other than U.S. government debt. Not surprisingly, as this book goes to press, the Fed is exploring whether it should expand its regulation to nondepository financial institutions like Bear Stearns (now defunct) to prevent another such near-catastrophe from happening. ▲

< < < < < < < < < < < <

> **CHECK YOUR UNDERSTANDING** 30-4

1. Assume that any money lent by a bank is always deposited back in the banking system as a checkable deposit and that the reserve ratio is 10%. Trace out the effects of a $100 million open-market purchase of U.S. Treasury bills by the Fed on the value of checkable bank deposits. What is the size of the money multiplier?

Solution appears at back of book.

An Overview of the Twenty-First Century American Banking System

Under normal circumstances, banking is a rather staid and unexciting business. Fortunately, bankers and their customers like it that way. However, there have been repeated episodes in which "sheer panic" would be the best description of banking conditions—the panic induced by a bank run and the specter of a collapse of a bank or multiple banks, leaving depositors penniless, bank shareholders wiped out, and borrowers unable to get credit. In this section, we'll give an overview of the behavior and regulation of the American banking system over the last century. Here we will discuss the historical origins of the regulations you learned about earlier in this chapter—regulations designed to strengthen the banking sector and to eliminate bank panics. In fact, the creation of the Federal Reserve system in 1913 was largely a response to lessons learned in the Panic of 1907.

As this book goes to press, the United States finds itself in the midst of a financial crisis that in many ways mirrors the Panic of 1907, which occurred almost exactly 100 years earlier. What are the origins of these financial crises? Was the creation of the Federal Reserve system effective in heading off financial crisis? If so, why has the system failed to head off the current crisis? How have technological advances and financial innovation affected the nature of these crises? And how should the Fed adjust its oversight and regulations to prevent another panic?

Crisis in American Banking at the Turn of the Twentieth Century

The creation of the Federal Reserve system in 1913 marked the beginning of the modern era of American banking. From 1864 until 1913, American banking was dominated by a federally regulated system of national banks. They alone were allowed to issue currency, and the currency notes they issued were printed by the federal government with uniform size and design. How much currency a national bank could issue depended on its capital. Although this system was an improvement on the earlier period in which banks issued their own notes with no uniformity and virtually no regulation, the national banking regime still suffered numerous bank failures and major financial crises—at least one and often two per decade.

The main problem afflicting the system was that the money supply was not sufficiently responsive: it was difficult to shift currency around the country to respond quickly to local economic changes. (In particular, there was often a tug-of-war between New York City banks and rural banks for adequate amounts of currency.) Rumors that a bank had insufficient currency to satisfy demands for withdrawals would quickly lead to a bank run. A bank run would then spark a contagion, setting off runs at other nearby banks, sowing widespread panic and devastation in the local economy. In response, bankers in some locations pooled their resources to create local clearinghouses that would jointly guarantee a member's liabilities in the event of a panic, and some state governments began offering deposit insurance on their banks' deposits.

However, the cause of the Panic of 1907 was different from those of previous crises; in fact, its cause was eerily similar to the roots of the 2008 crisis. Ground zero of the 1907 panic was New York City, but the consequences devastated the entire country, leading to a deep four-year recession. The crisis originated in institutions in New York known as trusts, bank-like institutions that accepted deposits but that were originally intended to manage only inheritances and estates for wealthy clients. Because these trusts were supposed to engage only in low-risk activities, they were less regulated, had lower reserve requirements, and had lower cash reserves than national banks. However, as the American economy boomed during the first decade of the twentieth century, trusts began speculating in real estate and the stock market, areas of speculation forbidden to national banks. Less regulated than national banks, trusts were able to pay their depositors higher returns. Yet trusts took a free ride on national banks' reputation for soundness, with depositors considering them equally safe. As a result, trusts grew rapidly: by 1907, the total assets of trusts in New York City were as large as those of national banks. Meanwhile, the trusts declined to join the New York Clearinghouse, a consortium of New York City national banks that guaranteed one anothers' soundness; that would have required the trusts to hold higher cash reserves, reducing their profits. The Panic of 1907 began with the failure of the Knickerbocker Trust, a large New York City trust that failed when it suffered massive losses in unsuccessful stock market speculation. Quickly, other

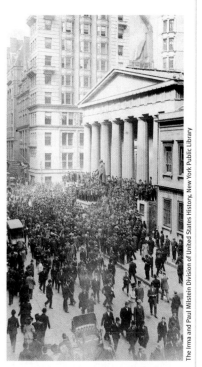

In both the Panic of 1907 and the financial crisis of 2008, large losses from risky speculation destabilized the banking system.

New York trusts came under pressure, and frightened depositors began queuing in long lines to withdraw their funds. The New York Clearinghouse declined to step in and lend to the trusts, and even healthy trusts came under serious assault. Within two days, a dozen major trusts had gone under. Credit markets froze, and the stock market fell dramatically as stock traders were unable to get credit to finance their trades and business confidence evaporated.

Fortunately, New York City's wealthiest man, the banker J. P. Morgan, quickly stepped in to stop the panic. Understanding that the crisis was spreading and would soon engulf healthy institutions, trusts and banks alike, he worked with other bankers, wealthy men such as John D. Rockefeller, and the U.S. Secretary of the Treasury to shore up the reserves of banks and trusts so they could withstand the onslaught of withdrawals. Once people were assured that they could withdraw their money, the panic ceased. Although the panic itself lasted little more than a week, it and the stock market collapse decimated the economy. A four-year recession ensued, with production falling 11% and unemployment rising from 3% to 8%.

Responding to Banking Crises: The Creation of the Federal Reserve

Concerns over the frequency of banking crises and the unprecedented role of J. P. Morgan in saving the financial system prompted the federal government to initiate banking reform. In 1913 the national banking system was eliminated and the Federal Reserve System was created as a way to compel all deposit-taking institutions to hold adequate reserves and to open their accounts to inspection by regulators. The Panic of 1907 convinced many that the time for centralized control of bank reserves had come. In addition, the Federal Reserve was given the sole right to issue currency in order to make the money supply sufficiently responsive to satisfy economic conditions around the country.

Although the new regime standardized and centralized the holding of bank reserves, it did not eliminate the potential for bank runs because banks' reserves were still less than the total value of their deposits. The potential for more bank runs became a reality during the Great Depression. Plunging commodity prices hit American farmers particularly hard, precipitating a series of bank runs in 1930, 1931, and 1933, each of which started at midwestern banks and then spread throughout the country. After the failure of a particularly large bank in 1930, federal officials realized that the economy-wide effects compelled them to take a less hands-off approach and to intervene more vigorously. In 1932, the Reconstruction Finance Corporation (RFC) was established and given the authority to make loans to banks in order to stabilize the banking sector. Also, the Glass-Steagall Act of 1932, which created federal deposit insurance and increased the ability of banks to borrow from the Federal Reserve System, was passed. A loan to a leading Chicago bank from the Federal Reserve appears to have stopped a major banking crisis in 1932. However, the beast had not yet been tamed. Banks became fearful of borrowing from the RFC, because doing so signaled weakness to the public. During the midst of the catastrophic bank run of 1933, the new president, Franklin Delano Roosevelt, was inaugurated. He immediately declared a "bank holiday," closing all banks until regulators could get a handle on the problem. In March 1933, emergency measures were adopted that gave the RFC extraordinary powers to stabilize and restructure the banking industry by providing

Like FDR, Barack Obama, shown here with his team of economic advisors, was faced with a major financial crisis upon taking office.

Brian Kersey-Pool/Getty Images

capital to banks either by loans or by outright purchases of bank shares. With the new regulations, regulators closed nonviable banks and recapitalized viable ones by allowing the RFC to buy preferred shares in banks (shares that gave the U.S. government more rights than regular shareholders) and by greatly expanding banks' ability to borrow from the Federal Reserve. By 1933, the RFC had invested over $16 billion (2008 dollars) in bank capital—one-third of the total capital of all banks in the United States at that time—and purchased shares in almost one-half of all banks. The RFC loaned more than $32 billion (2008 dollars) to banks during this period. Economic historians uniformly agree that the banking crises of the early 1930s greatly exacerbated the severity of the Great Depression, rendering monetary policy ineffective as the banking sector broke down and currency, withdrawn from banks and stashed under beds, reduced the money supply.

Although the powerful actions of the RFC stabilized the banking industry, new legislation was needed to prevent future banking crises. The Glass-Steagall Act of 1933 separated banks into two categories, **commercial banks,** depository banks that accepted deposits and were covered by deposit insurance, and **investment banks,** which engaged in creating and trading financial assets such as stocks and corporate bonds but were not covered by deposit insurance because their activities were considered more risky. Regulation Q prevented commercial banks from paying interest on checking accounts, in the belief that this would promote unhealthy competition between banks. In addition, investment banks were much more lightly regulated than commercial banks. The most important measure for the prevention of bank runs, however, was the adoption of federal deposit insurance (with an original limit of $2,500 per deposit).

These measures were clearly successful, and the United States enjoyed a long period of financial and banking stability. As memories of the bad old days dimmed, Depression-era bank regulations were lifted. In 1980 Regulation Q was eliminated, and by 1999, the Glass-Steagall Act had been so weakened that offering services like trading financial assets were no longer off-limits to commercial banks.

The Savings and Loan Crisis of the 1980s

Along with banks, the banking industry also included **savings and loans** (also called S&Ls or **thrifts**), institutions designed to accept savings and turn them into long-term mortgages for home-buyers. S&Ls were covered by federal deposit insurance and were tightly regulated for safety. However, trouble hit in the 1970s, as high inflation led savers to withdraw their funds from low-interest-paying S&L accounts and put them into higher-paying money market accounts. In addition, the high inflation rate severely eroded the value of the S&Ls' assets, the long-term mortgages they held on their books. In order to improve S&Ls' competitive position versus banks, Congress eased regulations to allow S&Ls to undertake much more risky investments in addition to long-term home mortgages. However, the new freedom did not bring with it increased oversight, leaving S&Ls with less oversight than banks. Not surprisingly, during the real estate boom of the 1970s and 1980s, S&Ls engaged in overly risky real estate lending. Also, corruption occurred as some S&L executives used their institutions as private piggy banks. Unfortunately, during the late 1970s and early 1980s, political interference from Congress kept insolvent S&Ls open when a bank in a comparable situation would have been quickly shut down by bank regulators. By the early 1980s, a large number of S&Ls had failed. Because accounts were covered by federal deposit insurance, the liabilities of a failed S&L were now liabilities of the federal government, and depositors had to be paid from taxpayer funds. From 1986 through 1995, the federal government closed over 1,000 failed S&Ls, costing U.S. taxpayers over $124 billion dollars.

In a classic case of shutting the barn door after the horse has escaped, in 1989 Congress put in place comprehensive oversight of S&L activities. It also empowered

A **commercial bank** accepts deposits and is covered by deposit insurance.

An **investment bank** trades in financial assets and is not covered by deposit insurance.

A **savings and loan (thrift)** is another type of deposit-taking bank, usually specialized in issuing home loans.

A financial institution engages in **leverage** when it finances its investments with borrowed funds.

The **balance sheet effect** is the reduction in a firm's net worth from falling asset prices.

A **vicious cycle of deleveraging** takes place when asset sales to cover losses produce negative balance sheet effects on other firms and force creditors to call in their loans, forcing sales of more assets and causing further declines in asset prices.

Fannie Mae and Freddie Mac to take over much of the home mortgage lending previously done by S&Ls. Fannie Mae and Freddie Mac are quasi-governmental agencies created during the Great Depression to make homeownership more affordable for low- and moderate-income households. It has been calculated that the S&L crisis helped cause a steep slowdown in the finance and real estate industries, leading to the recession of the early 1990s.

Back to the Future: The Financial Crisis of 2008

The financial crisis of 2008 shared features of previous crises. Like the Panic of 1907 and the S&L crisis, it involved institutions that were not as strictly regulated as deposit-taking banks as well as excessive speculation. Like the crises of the early 1930s, it involved a U.S. government that was reluctant to take aggressive action until the scale of the devastation became clear. In addition, by the late 1990s, advances in technology and financial innovation had created yet another systemic weakness that played a central role in 2008. The story of Long-Term Capital Management, or LTCM, highlights these problems.

Long-Term Capital (Mis)Management Created in 1994, LTCM was a hedge fund, a private investment partnership open only to wealthy individuals and institutions. Hedge funds are virtually unregulated, allowing them to make much riskier investments than mutual funds, which are open to the average investor. Using vast amounts of **leverage**—that is, borrowed money—in order to increase its returns, LTCM used sophisticated computer models to make money by taking advantage of small differences in asset prices in global financial markets to buy at a lower price and sell at a higher price. In one year, LTCM made a return as high as 40%. LTCM was also heavily involved in derivatives, complex financial instruments that are constructed—derived—from the obligations of more basic financial assets. Derivatives are popular investment tools because they are cheaper to trade than basic financial assets and can be constructed to suit a buyer's or seller's particular needs. Yet their complexity can make it extremely hard to measure their value. LTCM believed that its computer models allowed it to accurately gauge the risk in the huge bets that it was undertaking in derivatives using borrowed money.

However, LTCM's computer models hadn't factored in a series of financial crises in Asia and in Russia during 1997 and 1998. Through its large borrowing, LTCM had become such a big player in global financial markets that attempts to sell its assets depressed the prices of what it was trying to sell. As the markets fell around the world and LTCM's panic-stricken investors demanded the return on their funds, LTCM's losses mounted as it tried to sell assets to satisfy those demands. Quickly, its operations collapsed because it could no longer borrow money and other parties refused to trade with it. Financial markets around the world froze in panic. The Federal Reserve realized that allowing LTCM's remaining assets to be sold at panic-stricken prices presented a grave risk to the entire financial system through the **balance sheet effect:** as sales of assets by LTCM depressed asset prices all over the world, other firms would see the value of their balance sheets fall as assets held on these balance sheets declined in value. Moreover, falling asset prices meant the value of assets held by borrowers on their balance sheet would fall below a critical threshold, leading to a default on the terms of their credit contracts and forcing creditors to call in their loans. This in turn would lead to more sales of assets as borrowers tried to raise cash to repay their loans, more credit defaults, and more loans called in, creating a **vicious cycle of deleveraging.** The Federal Reserve Bank of New York arranged a $3.625 billion bailout of LTCM in 1998, in which other private institutions took on shares of LTCM's assets and obligations, liquidated them in an orderly manner, and eventually turned a small profit. Quick action by the Federal Reserve Bank of New York prevented LTCM from sparking a contagion, yet virtually all of LTCM's investors were wiped out.

Subprime Lending and the Housing Bubble After the LTCM crisis, U.S. financial markets stabilized. They remained more or less stable even as stock prices fell sharply from 2000 to 2002 and the U.S. economy went into recession. During the recovery from the 2001 recession, however, the seeds for another financial crisis were planted.

The story begins with low interest rates: by 2003, U.S. interest rates were at historically low levels, partly because of Federal Reserve policy and partly because of large inflows of capital from other countries, especially China. These low interest rates helped cause a boom in housing, which in turn led the U.S. economy out of recession. As housing boomed, however, financial institutions began taking on growing risks—risks that were not well understood.

Traditionally, people were only able to borrow money to buy homes if they could show that they had sufficient income to meet the mortgage payments. Home loans to people who don't meet the usual criteria for borrowing, called **subprime lending,** were only a minor part of overall lending. But in the booming housing market of 2003–2006, subprime lending started to seem like a safe bet. Since housing prices kept rising, borrowers who couldn't make their mortgage payments could always pay off their mortgages, if necessary, by selling their homes. As a result, subprime lending exploded. Who was making these subprime loans? For the most part, it wasn't traditional banks lending out depositors' money. Instead, most of the loans were made by "loan originators," who quickly sold mortgages to other investors. These sales were made possible by a process known as **securitization:** financial institutions assembled pools of loans and sold shares in the income from these pools. These shares were considered relatively safe investments, since it was considered unlikely that large numbers of home-buyers would default on their payments at the same time.

But that's exactly what happened. The housing boom turned out to be a bubble, and when home prices started falling in late 2006, many subprime borrowers were unable either to meet their mortgage payments or sell their houses for enough to pay off their mortgages. As a result, investors in securities backed by subprime mortgages started taking heavy losses. Many of the mortgage-backed assets were held by financial institutions, including banks and other institutions playing bank-like roles. Like the trusts that played a key role in the Panic of 1907, these "nonbank banks" were less regulated than commercial banks, which allowed them to offer higher returns to investors but left them extremely vulnerable in a crisis. Mortgage-related losses, in turn, led to a collapse of trust in the financial system. Figure 30-10 shows one measure of this loss of trust: the TED spread, which is

> **Subprime lending** is lending to home-buyers who don't meet the usual criteria for being able to afford their payments.
>
> In **securitization,** a pool of loans is assembled and shares of that pool are sold to investors.

"Honey, we're homeless."

FIGURE 30-10

The TED Spread

The TED spread is the difference between the interest rate at which banks lend to each other and the interest rate on U.S. government debt. It's widely used as a measure of financial stress. The TED spread soared as a result of the financial crisis of 2007–2008.

Source: British Bankers' Association; Federal Reserve Bank of St. Louis.

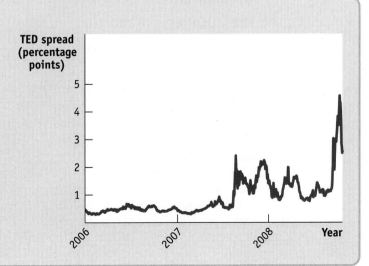

the difference between the interest rate on three-month loans that banks make to each other and the interest rate the federal government pays on three-month bonds. Since government bonds are considered extremely safe, the TED spread shows how much risk banks think they're taking on when lending to each other. Normally the spread is around a quarter of a percentage point, but it shot up in August 2007 and surged to an unprecedented 4.58 percentage points in October 2008.

Crisis and Response The collapse of trust in the financial system, combined with the large losses suffered by financial firms, led to a severe cycle of deleveraging and a credit crunch for the economy as a whole. Firms found it difficult to borrow, even for short-term operations; individuals found home loans unavailable and credit card limits reduced. Overall, the negative economic effect of the financial crisis bore a distinct and troubling resemblance to the effects of the banking crisis of the early 1930s, which helped cause the Great Depression. Policy makers noticed the resemblance and tried to prevent a repeat performance. Beginning in August 2007, the Federal Reserve engaged in a series of efforts to provide cash to the financial system, lending funds to a widening range of institutions and buying private-sector debt. The Fed and the Treasury Department also stepped in to rescue individual firms that were deemed too crucial to be allowed to fail, such as the investment bank Bear Stearns and the insurance company AIG.

In September 2008, however, policy makers decided that one major investment bank, Lehman Brothers, could be allowed to fail. They quickly regretted the decision. Within days of Lehman's failure, widespread panic gripped the financial markets, as illustrated by the late surge in the TED spread shown in Figure 30-10. In response to the intensified crisis, the U.S. government intervened further to support the financial system, as the U.S. Treasury began "injecting" capital into banks. Injecting capital, in practice, meant that the U.S. government would supply cash to banks in return for shares—in effect, partially nationalizing the financial system. This new rescue plan was still in its early stages when this book went to press, and it was too early to judge its success.

It is widely expected that the crisis of 2008 will lead to major changes in the financial system, probably the largest changes since the 1930s. Historically, it was considered enough to insure deposits and regulate commercial banks. The 2008 crisis suggested that both a much wider safety net and much broader regulation were needed. Like the crises preceeding it, the financial crisis of 2008 is exerting a powerful negative effect on the rest of the economy as this book goes to press.

➤ECONOMICS IN ACTION

The 2008 Crisis and the Fed

In Figure 30-7 we saw that the Federal Reserve's financial position is *normally* quite simple: basically, it holds Treasury bills equal in value to the monetary base. The crisis of 2007–2008 was not, however, a normal time. As credit markets froze, the Fed created a series of "lending facilities" designed to keep the markets functioning. These facilities were obscurely named: the TAF (term auction facility), the TSLF (term securities lending facility), and so on. But they all served the same purpose: they made funds available to financial institutions that were unable to raise cash through normal channels.

Figure 30-11, which shows the changing composition of the Fed's assets between January and November 2008, gives you an idea of the extent of the departure from normal operating procedure. Holdings of Treasury bills, the Fed's normal asset, fell sharply; meanwhile an alphabet soup of other assets increased dramatically. By the way, Maiden Lane LLC is a special fund created as part of the bailout of Bear Stearns, and Commercial Paper Funding Facility LLC is the special fund created to inject liquidity into credit markets.

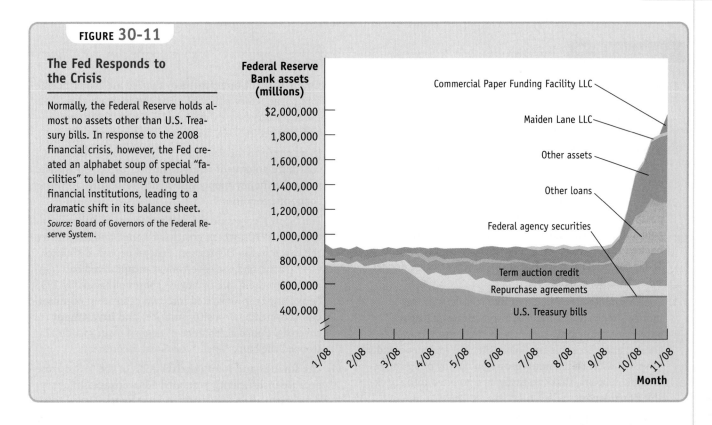

FIGURE 30-11

The Fed Responds to the Crisis

Normally, the Federal Reserve holds almost no assets other than U.S. Treasury bills. In response to the 2008 financial crisis, however, the Fed created an alphabet soup of special "facilities" to lend money to troubled financial institutions, leading to a dramatic shift in its balance sheet.

Source: Board of Governors of the Federal Reserve System.

Fed officials believed that this change in standard operating procedure was necessary to stave off an even more severe financial crisis. At the same time, however, the Fed's new role made them uncomfortable. Why? Because by lending so much money to the private sector, the Fed was taking on a considerable amount of risk. Normally the Fed invests only in U.S. government debt, which is considered a very safe asset; the same could not be said of many of the loans made during 2008.

If and when the crisis ends, the Fed will try to get back to normal procedure as soon as possible. When it does, the simple description in Figure 30-7 will once again be valid. ▲

> > > > > > > > > > > >

► CHECK YOUR UNDERSTANDING 30-5

1. What are the similarities between the Panic of 1907, the S&L crisis, and the crisis of 2008?

2. Why did the creation of the Federal Reserve fail to prevent the bank runs of the Great Depression? What measures did stop the bank runs?

3. Describe the balance sheet effect. Describe the vicious cycle of deleveraging. Why is it necessary for the government to step in to halt a vicious cycle of deleveraging?

Solutions appear at back of book.

[▶▶ A LOOK AHEAD •••

We've just learned how the monetary system is organized. As we've seen, the Fed plays a crucial role in that organization, both by regulating banks and through the money-creation channel of banks, determining the money supply. In the next chapter, we'll discover why the money supply is so important: because changes in it affect interest rates, which in turn have powerful effects on real GDP and the aggregate price level.]

SUMMARY

1. **Money** is any asset that can easily be used to purchase goods and services. **Currency in circulation** and **checkable bank deposits** are both considered part of the **money supply.** Money plays three roles: it is a **medium of exchange** used for transactions, a **store of value** that holds purchasing power over time, and a **unit of account** in which prices are stated.

2. Over time, **commodity money,** which consists of goods possessing value aside from their role as money, such as gold and silver coins, was replaced by **commodity-backed money,** such as paper currency backed by gold. Today the dollar is pure **fiat money,** whose value derives solely from its official role.

3. The Federal Reserve calculates two measures of the money supply. M1 is the narrowest **monetary aggregate,** containing only currency in circulation, traveler's checks, and checkable bank deposits. M2 includes a wider range of assets called **near-moneys,** mainly other forms of bank deposits, that can easily be converted into checkable bank deposits.

4. Banks allow depositors immediate access to their funds, but they also lend out most of the funds deposited in their care. To meet demands for cash, they maintain **bank reserves** composed of both currency held in vaults and deposits at the Federal Reserve. The **reserve ratio** is the ratio of bank reserves to bank deposits. A **T-account** summarizes a bank's financial position, with loans and reserves counted as assets, and deposits counted as liabilities.

5. Banks have sometimes been subject to **bank runs,** most notably in the early 1930s. To avert this danger, depositors are now protected by **deposit insurance,** bank owners face capital requirements that reduce the incentive to make overly risky loans with depositors' funds, and banks must satisfy **reserve requirements.**

6. When currency is deposited in a bank, it starts a multiplier process in which banks lend out **excess reserves,** leading to an increase in the money supply—so banks create money. If the entire money supply consisted of checkable bank deposits, the money supply would be equal to the value of reserves divided by the reserve ratio. In reality, much of the **monetary base** consists of currency in circulation, and the **money multiplier** is the ratio of the money supply to the monetary base.

7. The monetary base is controlled by the Federal Reserve, the **central bank** of the United States. The Fed regulates banks and sets reserve requirements. To meet those requirements, banks borrow and lend reserves in the **federal funds market** at the **federal funds rate.** Through the **discount window** facility, banks can borrow from the Fed at the **discount rate.**

8. **Open-market operations** by the Fed are the principal tool of monetary policy: the Fed can increase or reduce the monetary base by buying U.S. Treasury bills from banks or selling U.S. Treasury bills to banks.

9. In response to the Panic of 1907, the Fed was created to centralize holding of reserves, inspect banks' books, and make the money supply sufficiently responsive to varying economic conditions.

10. The Great Depression sparked widespread bank runs in the early 1930s, which greatly worsened and lengthened the depth of the Depression. Federal deposit insurance was created, and the government recapitalized banks by lending to them and by buying shares of banks. By 1933, banks had been separated into two categories: **commercial** (covered by deposit insurance) and **investment** (not covered). Public acceptance of deposit insurance finally stopped the bank runs of the Great Depression.

11. The **savings and loan (thrift)** crisis of the 1980s arose because insufficiently regulated S&Ls engaged in overly risky speculation and incurred huge losses. Depositors in failed S&Ls were compensated with taxpayer funds because they were covered by deposit insurance. The crisis caused steep losses in the financial and real estate sectors, resulting in a recession in the early 1990s.

12. During the mid-1990s, the hedge fund LTCM used huge amounts of **leverage** to speculate in global financial markets, incurred massive losses, and collapsed. LTCM was so large that, in selling assets to cover its losses, it caused **balance sheet effects** for firms around the world, leading to the prospect of a **vicious cycle of deleveraging.** As a result, credit markets around the world froze. The New York Fed coordinated a private bailout of LTCM and revived world credit markets.

13. **Subprime lending** during the U.S. housing bubble of the mid-2000s spread through the financial system via **securitization.** When the bubble burst, massive losses by banks and nonbank financial institutions led to widespread collapse in the financial system. To prevent another Great Depression, the Fed and the U.S. Treasury expanded lending to bank and nonbank institutions, provided capital through the purchase of bank shares, and purchased private debt. Because much of the crisis originated in nontraditional bank institutions, the crisis of 2008 indicated that a wider safety net and broader regulation are needed in the financial sector.

KEY TERMS

Money, p. 798
Currency in circulation, p. 798
Checkable bank deposits, p. 798
Money supply, p. 798
Medium of exchange, p. 799
Store of value, p. 799
Unit of account, p. 799
Commodity money, p. 800
Commodity-backed money, p. 800
Fiat money, p. 801
Monetary aggregate, p. 801
Near-moneys, p. 801

Bank reserves, p. 804
T-account, p. 804
Reserve ratio, p. 805
Bank run, p. 806
Deposit insurance, p. 806
Reserve requirements, p. 806
Discount window, p. 807
Excess reserves, p. 809
Monetary base, p. 810
Money multiplier, p. 811
Central bank, p. 812
Federal funds market, p. 813

Federal funds rate, p. 813
Discount rate, p. 813
Open-market operation, p. 814
Commercial bank, p. 821
Investment bank, p. 821
Savings and loan (thrift), p. 821
Leverage, p. 822
Balance sheet effect, p. 822
Vicious cycle of deleveraging, p. 822
Subprime lending, p. 823
Securitization, p. 823

PROBLEMS

1. For each of the following transactions, what is the initial effect (increase or decrease) on M1? or M2?

   a. You sell a few shares of stock and put the proceeds into your savings account.

   b. You sell a few shares of stock and put the proceeds into your checking account.

   c. You transfer money from your savings account to your checking account.

   d. You discover $0.25 under the floor mat in your car and deposit it in your checking account.

   e. You discover $0.25 under the floor mat in your car and deposit it in your savings account.

2. There are three types of money: commodity money, commodity-backed money, and fiat money. Which type of money is used in each of the following situations?

   a. Bottles of rum were used to pay for goods in colonial Australia.

   b. Salt was used in many European countries as a medium of exchange.

   c. For a brief time, Germany used paper money (the "Rye Mark") that could be redeemed for a certain amount of rye, a type of grain.

   d. The town of Ithaca, New York, prints its own currency, the Ithaca HOURS, which can be used to purchase local goods and services.

3. The table below shows the components of M1 and M2 in billions of dollars for the month of December in the years 1998 to 2007 as published in the 2008 Economic Report of the President. Complete the table by calculating M1, M2, currency in circulation as a percentage of M1, and currency in circulation as a percentage of M2. What trends or patterns about M1, M2, currency in circulation as a percentage of M1, and currency in circulation as a percentage of M2 do you see? What might account for these trends?

Year	Currency in circulation	Traveler's checks	Checkable deposits	Money market funds	Time deposits smaller than $100,000	Savings deposits	M1	M2	Currency in circulation as a percentage of M1	Currency in circulation as a percentage of M2
					(billions of dollars)					
1998	$460.5	$8.5	$626.5	$728.9	$952.4	$1,605.0	?	?	?	?
1999	517.8	8.6	596.2	819.7	956.8	1,740.3	?	?	?	?
2000	531.2	8.3	548.0	908.0	1,047.6	1,878.8	?	?	?	?
2001	581.2	8.0	592.6	962.3	976.5	2,312.8	?	?	?	?
2002	626.3	7.8	585.6	885.3	896.0	2,778.2	?	?	?	?
2003	662.5	7.7	635.9	777.4	818.7	3,169.1	?	?	?	?
2004	697.6	7.5	671.2	697.1	829.9	3,518.3	?	?	?	?
2005	723.9	7.2	643.4	699.9	995.8	3,621.4	?	?	?	?
2006	748.9	6.7	611.4	799.4	1,170.4	3,698.6	?	?	?	?
2007	759.0	6.3	599.2	976.1	1,216.8	3,889.8	?	?	?	?

Source: 2008 Economic Report of the President.

4. Indicate whether each of the following is part of M1, M2, or neither:

   a. $95 on your campus meal card

   b. $0.55 in the change cup of your car

   c. $1,663 in your savings account

   d. $459 in your checking account

   e. 100 shares of stock worth $4,000

   f. A $1,000 line of credit on your Sears credit card

5. Tracy Williams deposits $500 that was in her sock drawer into a checking account at the local bank.

   a. How does the deposit initially change the T-account of the local bank? How does it change the money supply?

   b. If the bank maintains a reserve ratio of 10%, how will it respond to the new deposit?

   c. If every time the bank makes a loan, the loan results in a new checkable bank deposit in a different bank equal to the amount of the loan, by how much could the total money supply in the economy expand in response to Tracy's initial cash deposit of $500?

   d. If every time the bank makes a loan, the loan results in a new checkable bank deposit in a different bank equal to the amount of the loan and the bank maintains a reserve ratio of 5%, by how much could the money supply expand in response to an initial cash deposit of $500?

6. Ryan Cozzens withdraws $400 from his checking account at the local bank and keeps it in his wallet.

   a. How will the withdrawal change the T-account of the local bank and the money supply?

   b. If the bank maintains a reserve ratio of 10%, how will the bank respond to the withdrawal? Assume that the bank responds to insufficient reserves by reducing the amount of deposits it holds until its level of reserves satisfies its required reserve ratio. The bank reduces its deposits by calling in some of its loans, forcing borrowers to pay back these loans by taking cash from their checking deposits (at the same bank) to make repayment.

   c. If every time the bank decreases its loans, checkable bank deposits fall by the amount of the loan, by how much will the money supply in the economy contract in response to Ryan's withdrawal of $400?

   d. If every time the bank decreases its loans, checkable bank deposits fall by the amount of the loan and the bank maintains a reserve ratio of 20%, by how much will the money supply contract in response to a withdrawal of $400?

7. The government of Eastlandia uses measures of monetary aggregates similar to those used by the United States, and the central bank of Eastlandia imposes a required reserve ratio of 10%. Given the following information, answer the questions below.
   Bank deposits at the central bank = $200 million
   Currency held by public = $150 million
   Currency in bank vaults = $100 million
   Checkable bank deposits = $500 million
   Traveler's checks = $10 million

   a. What is M1?

   b. What is the monetary base?

   c. Are the commercial banks holding excess reserves?

   d. Can the commercial banks increase checkable bank deposits? If yes, by how much can checkable bank deposits increase?

8. In Westlandia, the public holds 50% of M1 in the form of currency, and the required reserve ratio is 20%. Estimate how much the money supply will increase in response to a new cash deposit of $500 by completing the accompanying table. (*Hint:* The first row shows that the bank must hold $100 in minimum reserves—20% of the $500 deposit—against this deposit, leaving $400 in excess reserves that can be loaned out. However, since the public wants to hold 50% of the loan in currency, only $400 × 0.5 = $200 of the loan will be deposited in round 2 from the loan granted in round 1.) How does your answer compare to an economy in which the total amount of the loan is deposited in the banking system and the public doesn't hold any of the loan in currency? What does this imply about the relationship between the public's desire for holding currency and the money multiplier?

Round	Deposits	Required reserves	Excess reserves	Loans	Held as currency
1	$500.00	$100.00	$400.00	$400.00	$200.00
2	200.00	?	?	?	?
3	?	?	?	?	?
4	?	?	?	?	?
5	?	?	?	?	?
6	?	?	?	?	?
7	?	?	?	?	?
8	?	?	?	?	?
9	?	?	?	?	?
10	?	?	?	?	?
Total after 10 rounds	?	?	?	?	?

9. What will happen to the money supply under the following circumstances in a checkable-deposits-only system?

   a. The required reserve ratio is 25%, and a depositor withdraws $700 from his checkable bank deposit.

   b. The required reserve ratio is 5%, and a depositor withdraws $700 from his checkable bank deposit.

   c. The required reserve ratio is 20%, and a customer deposits $750 to her checkable bank deposit.

   d. The required reserve ratio is 10%, and a customer deposits $600 to her checkable bank deposit.

10. Although the U.S. Federal Reserve doesn't use changes in reserve requirements to manage the money supply, the central bank of Albernia does. The commercial banks of Albernia have $100 million in reserves and $1,000 million in check-

able deposits; the initial required reserve ratio is 10%. The commercial banks follow a policy of holding no excess reserves. The public holds no currency, only checkable deposits in the banking system.

a. How will the money supply change if the required reserve ratio falls to 5%?

b. How will the money supply change if the required reserve ratio rises to 25%?

11. Using Figure 30-6, find the Federal Reserve district in which you live. Go to http://www.federalreserve.gov/bios/pres.htm and click on your district to identify the president of the Federal Reserve Bank in your district. Go to http://www.federalreserve.gov/fomc/ and determine if the president of the Fed is currently a voting member of the Federal Open Market Committee (FOMC).

12. Show the changes to the T-accounts for the Federal Reserve and for commercial banks when the Federal Reserve buys $50 million in U.S. Treasury bills. If the public holds a fixed amount of currency (so that all loans create an equal amount of deposits in the banking system), the minimum reserve ratio is 10%, and banks hold no excess reserves, by how much will deposits in the commercial banks change? By how much will the money supply change? Show the final changes to the T-account for commercial banks when the money supply changes by this amount.

13. Show the changes to the T-accounts for the Federal Reserve and for commercial banks when the Federal Reserve sells $30 million in U.S. Treasury bills. If the public holds a fixed amount of currency (so that all new loans create an equal amount of checkable bank deposits in the banking system) and the minimum reserve ratio is 5%, by how much will checkable bank deposits in the commercial banks change? By how much will the money supply change? Show the final changes to the T-account for the commercial banks when the money supply changes by this amount.

14. The Congressional Research Service estimates that at least $45 million of counterfeit U.S. $100 notes produced by the North Korean government are in circulation.

a. Why do U.S. taxpayers lose because of North Korea's counterfeiting?

b. As of September 2008, the interest rate earned on one-year U.S. Treasury bills was 2.2%. At a 2.2% rate of interest, what is the amount of money U.S. taxpayers are losing per year because of these $45 million in counterfeit notes?

15. As shown in Figure 30-9, on September 5, 2007, about 90% of the Federal Reserve's assets were made up of U.S. Treasury

bills. However, on September 3, 2008, only 53% of the Federal Reserve's assets were made up of U.S. Treasury bills. Go to www.federalreserve.gov. Under "Recent Statistical Releases," click on "All Statistical Releases." Under the heading "Money Stock and Reserve Balances," click on "Factors Affecting Reserve Balances." Click on the date of the current release.

a. Under "5. Statement of Condition of Each Federal Reserve Bank," look in the "Total" column. What is the amount displayed next to "Assets"? What is the amount displayed next to "U.S. Treasury"? What percentage of the Federal Reserve's total assets are currently made up of U.S. Treasury bills?

b. Do the Federal Reserve's assets consist primarily of U.S. Treasury securities, as on September 5, 2007, which was a fairly typical day, or does the Fed still own a large number of other assets, as it did on September 3, 2008, when it was responding to a crisis on Wall Street?

16. The accompanying figure shows new U.S. housing starts, in thousands of units per month, between January 1980 and September 2008. The graph shows a large drop in new housing starts in 1984–1991 and 2006–2008. New housing starts are related to the availability of mortgages.

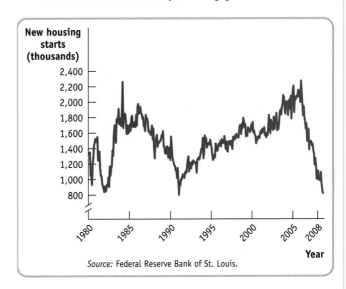

Source: Federal Reserve Bank of St. Louis.

a. What caused the drop in new housing starts in 1984–1991?

b. What caused the drop in new housing starts in 2006–2008?

c. How could better regulation of financial institutions have prevented these two instances?

Monetary Policy

THE FED IS ASLEEP!

J IM CRAMER'S *MAD MONEY* IS ONE OF THE MOST popular shows on CNBC, a cable TV network that specializes in business and financial news. Cramer, who mostly offers investment advice, is known for his sense of showmanship. But few viewers were prepared for his outburst on August 3, 2007, when he began screaming about what he saw as inadequate action from the Federal Reserve:

"Bernanke is being an academic! It is no time to be an academic. . . . **He has no idea how bad it is out there. He has no idea! He has no idea!** . . . And Bill Poole? Has no idea what it's like out there! . . . They're nuts! **They know nothing!** . . . The Fed is asleep! Bill Poole is a shame! He's shameful!!"

Who are Bernanke and Bill Poole? In the previous chapter we described the role of the Federal Reserve System, America's central bank. At the time of Cramer's tirade, Ben Bernanke, a former Princeton professor of economics, was the chairman of the Fed's Board of Governors, and William Poole, also a former economics professor, was the president of the Federal Reserve Bank of St. Louis. Both men, because of their positions, are members of the Federal Open Market Committee, which meets eight times a year to set monetary policy. In August 2007, Cramer was crying out for the Fed to change monetary policy in order to address what he perceived to be a growing financial crisis.

Why was Cramer screaming at the Federal Reserve rather than, say, the U.S. Treasury—or, for that matter, the president? The answer is that the Fed's control of monetary policy makes it the first line of response to macroeconomic difficulties—very much including the financial crisis that had Cramer so upset. Indeed, within a few weeks the Fed swung into action with a dramatic reversal of its previous policies.

In August 2007, an agitated Jim Cramer demanded that the Fed do something to address the growing financial crisis.

In this chapter we'll learn how monetary policy works—how actions by the Federal Reserve can have a powerful effect on the economy. We'll start by looking at the *demand for money* from households and firms. Then we'll see how the Fed's ability to change the *supply of money* allows it to move interest rates in the short run and thereby affect real GDP. We'll look at U.S. monetary policy in practice and compare it to the monetary policy of other central banks. We'll conclude by examining the long-run effects of monetary policy.

The Demand for Money

In Chapter 30 we saw that M1, the most commonly used definition of the money supply, consists of currency in circulation (cash), plus checkable bank deposits, plus traveler's checks. M2, a broader definition of the money supply, consists of M1 plus deposits that can easily be transferred into checkable deposits. We also learned why people hold money—to make it easier to purchase goods and services. Now we'll go deeper, examining what determines *how much* money individuals and firms want to hold at any given time.

The Opportunity Cost of Holding Money

Most economic decisions involve trade-offs at the margin. That is, individuals decide how much of a good to consume by determining whether the benefit they'd gain from consuming a bit more of any given good is worth the cost. The same decision process is used when deciding how much money to hold.

Individuals and firms find it useful to hold some of their assets in the form of money because of the convenience money provides: money can be used to make purchases directly, but other assets can't. But there is a price to be paid for that convenience: money normally yields a lower rate of return than nonmonetary assets.

As an example of how convenience makes it worth incurring some opportunity costs, consider the fact that even today—with the prevalence of credit cards, debit cards, and ATMs—people continue to keep cash in their wallets rather than leave the funds in an interest-bearing account. They do this because they don't want to have to go to an ATM to withdraw money every time they want to buy lunch from a place that doesn't accept credit cards or won't accept them for small amounts because of the processing fee. In other words, the convenience of keeping some cash in your wallet is more valuable than the interest you would earn by keeping that money in the bank.

Even holding money in a checking account involves a trade-off between convenience and earning interest. That's because you can earn a higher interest rate by putting your money in assets other than a checking account. For example, many banks offer certificates of deposit, or CDs, which pay a higher interest rate than ordinary bank accounts. But CDs also carry a penalty if you withdraw the funds before a certain amount of time—say, six months—has elapsed. An individual who keeps funds in a checking account is forgoing the higher interest rate those funds would have earned if placed in a CD in return for the convenience of having cash readily available when needed.

Table 31-1 illustrates the opportunity cost of holding money in a specific month, June 2007. The first row shows the interest rate on one-month certificates of deposit—that is, the interest rate individuals could get if they were willing to tie their funds up for one month. In June 2007, one-month CDs yielded 5.30%. The second row shows the interest rate on interest-bearing bank accounts (specifically, those included in M1). Funds in these accounts were more accessible than those in CDs, but the price of that convenience was a much lower interest rate, only 2.478%. Finally, the last row shows the interest rate on currency—cash in your wallet—which was, of course, zero.

TABLE 31-1

Selected Interest Rates, June 2007	
One-month CDs	5.30%
Interest-bearing demand deposits	2.478
Currency	0

Source: Federal Reserve Bank of St. Louis.

Table 31-1 shows the opportunity cost of holding money at one point in time, but the opportunity cost of holding money changes when the overall level of interest rates changes. Specifically, when the overall level of interest rates falls, the opportunity cost of holding money falls, too.

Table 31-2 illustrates this point by showing how selected interest rates changed between June 2007 and June 2008, a period when the Federal Reserve was slashing rates in an effort to fight off recession. Between June 2007 and June 2008, the federal funds rate, which is the rate the Fed controls most directly, fell by 3.25 percentage points. The interest rate on one-month CDs fell almost as much, 2.8 percentage points. That's not an accident: all **short-term interest rates**—rates on financial assets that come due, or mature, within less than a year—tend to move together, with rare exceptions. (As it happens, one of those exceptional periods occurred in late 2007 and into 2008. This episode is discussed in the upcoming For Inquiring Minds.) The reason short-term interest rates tend to move together is that CDs and other short-term assets (like one-month and three-month U.S. Treasury bills) are in effect competing for the same business. Any short-term asset that offers a lower-than-average interest rate will be sold by investors, who will move their wealth into a higher-yielding short-term asset. The selling of the asset, in turn, forces its interest rate up, because investors must be rewarded with a higher rate in order to induce them to buy it. Conversely, investors will move their wealth into any short-term financial asset that offers an above-average interest rate. The purchase of the asset drives its interest rate down when sellers find they can lower the rate of return on the asset and still find willing buyers. So interest rates on short-term financial assets tend to be roughly the same because no asset will consistently offer a higher-than-average or a lower-than-average interest rate.

But as short-term interest rates fell between June 2007 and June 2008, the interest rates on money didn't fall by the same amount. The interest rate on currency, of course, remained at zero. The interest rate paid on demand deposits did fall, but by much less than short-term interest rates. As a result, the opportunity cost of holding money fell. The last two rows of Table 31-2 show the differences between the interest rates on demand deposits and currency and the interest rate on CDs. These

TABLE 31-2

Interest Rates and the Opportunity Cost of Holding Money

	June 2007	June 2008
Federal funds rate	5.25%	2.00%
One-month certificates of deposit (CD)	5.30	2.50
Interest-bearing demand deposits	2.773	1.353
Currency	0	0
CDs minus interest-bearing demand deposits	**2.527**	**1.147**
CDs minus currency	**5.30**	**2.50**

Source: Federal Reserve Bank of St. Louis.

Short-term interest rates are the interest rates on financial assets that mature within less than a year.

FOR INQUIRING MINDS

Fear and Interest Rates

One important type of short-term bond is Treasury bills issued by the U.S. government. Treasury bills generally pay a slightly lower interest rate than other short-term assets because they're considered especially safe, making investors willing to buy them despite their lower return. In normal times, however, the difference is small. For example, in November 2006, one-month Treasury bills paid 5.13% interest, compared with 5.29% on one-month CDs. 2008, however, wasn't a normal time. In the third week of October 2008, one-month CDs were paying

4.04% interest, but one-month Treasury bills were paying only 0.26%.

What was going on? Fear. A sharp plunge in housing prices had led to big losses at a number of financial institutions, leaving investors nervous about the safety of many non-government assets. There was a "flight to safety" as investors piled into the security of Treasury bills, driving up their price. Because the interest rate earned on any bond falls as its price rises, this drove the interest rate on Treasury bills to very low levels. On December 10, 2008, in fact,

three-month Treasury bills paid 0% interest for a brief period.

It wasn't the first time something like this had happened: every once in a while, fear makes the normal relationships among interest rates disappear. In fact, there had been a similar episode in 1998, when Russia defaulted on its debt and a major hedge fund, LTCM, failed. But such episodes tend to be brief. Infrequent events like these are the exceptions that prove the rule: normally, all short-term interest rates move together.

Long-term interest rates are interest rates on financial assets that mature a number of years in the future.

The **money demand curve** shows the relationship between the quantity of money demanded and the interest rate.

differences declined sharply between June 2007 and June 2008. This reflects a general result: the higher the short-term interest rate, the higher the opportunity cost of holding money; the lower the short-term interest rate, the lower the opportunity cost of holding money.

Table 31-2 contains only short-term interest rates. At any given moment, **long-term interest rates**—rates of interest on financial assets that mature, or come due, a number of years into the future—may be different from short-term interest rates. The difference between short-term and long-term interest rates is sometimes important as a practical matter. Moreover, it's short-term rates rather than long-term rates that affect money demand, because the decision to hold money involves trading off the convenience of holding cash versus the payoff from holding assets that mature in the short-term—a year or less. For our current purposes, however, it's useful to ignore the distinction between short-term and long-term rates and assume that there is only one interest rate.

The Money Demand Curve

Because the overall level of interest rates affects the opportunity cost of holding money, the quantity of money individuals and firms want to hold is, other things equal, negatively related to the interest rate. In Figure 31-1, the horizontal axis shows the quantity of money demanded and the vertical axis shows the interest rate, r, which you can think of as a representative short-term interest rate such as the rate on one-month CDs. The relationship between the interest rate and the quantity of money demanded by the public is illustrated by the **money demand curve**, MD, in Figure 31-1. The money demand curve slopes downward because, other things equal, a higher interest rate increases the opportunity cost of holding money, leading the public to reduce the quantity of money it demands. For example, if the interest rate is very low—say, 1%—the interest forgone by holding money is relatively small. As a result, individuals and firms will tend to hold relatively large amounts of money to avoid the cost and nuisance of converting other assets into money when making purchases. By contrast, if the interest rate is relatively high—say, 15%, a level it reached in the United States in the early 1980s—the opportunity cost of holding money is high. People will respond by keeping only small amounts in cash and deposits, converting assets into money only when needed. (As we discussed in Chapter 26, it is the nominal interest rate, not the real interest rate, that

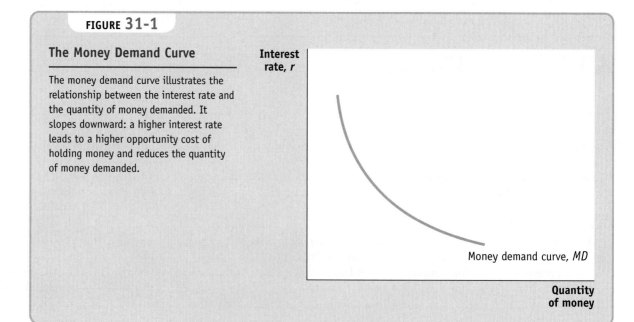

FIGURE 31-1

The Money Demand Curve

The money demand curve illustrates the relationship between the interest rate and the quantity of money demanded. It slopes downward: a higher interest rate leads to a higher opportunity cost of holding money and reduces the quantity of money demanded.

Interest rate, r

Money demand curve, MD

Quantity of money

influences people's money allocation decisions. Hence, *r* in Figure 31-1 and all subsequent figures is the nominal interest rate.)

You might ask why we draw the money demand curve with the interest rate—as opposed to rates of return on other assets, such as stocks or real estate—on the vertical axis. The answer is that for most people the relevant question in deciding how much money to hold is whether to put the funds in the form of other assets that can be turned fairly quickly and easily into money. Stocks don't fit that definition because there are significant broker's fees when you sell stock (which is why stock market investors are advised not to buy and sell too often); selling real estate involves even larger fees and can take a long time as well. So the relevant comparison is with assets that are "close to" money—fairly liquid assets like CDs. And as we've already seen, the interest rates on all these assets normally move closely together.

Shifts of the Money Demand Curve

Like the demand curve for an ordinary good, the money demand curve can be shifted by a number of factors. Figure 31-2 shows shifts of the money demand curve: an increase in the demand for money corresponds to a rightward shift of the *MD* curve, raising the quantity of money demanded at any given interest rate; a fall in the demand for money corresponds to a leftward shift of the *MD* curve, reducing the quantity of money demanded at any given interest rate. The most important factors causing the money demand curve to shift are changes in the aggregate price level, changes in real GDP, changes in banking technology, and changes in banking institutions.

Changes in the Aggregate Price Level Americans keep a lot more cash in their wallets and funds in their checking accounts today than they did in the 1950s. One reason is that they have to if they want to be able to buy anything: almost everything costs more now than it did when you could get a burger, fries, and a drink at McDonald's for 45 cents and a gallon of gasoline for 29 cents. So higher prices increase the demand for money (a rightward shift of the *MD* curve), and lower prices reduce the demand for money (a leftward shift of the *MD* curve).

We can actually be more specific than this: other things equal, the demand for money is *proportional* to the price level. That is, if the aggregate price level rises by 20%, the quantity of money demanded at any given interest rate, such as r_1 in Figure 31-2,

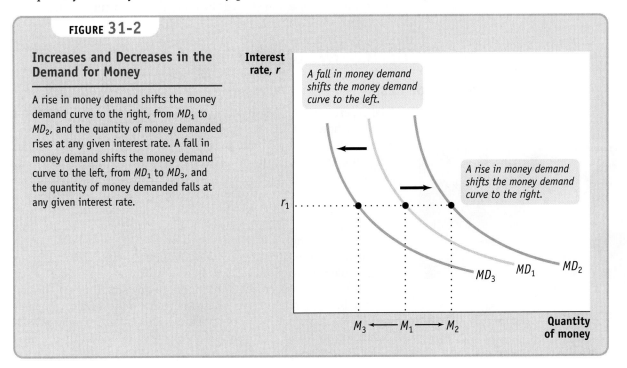

FIGURE 31-2

Increases and Decreases in the Demand for Money

A rise in money demand shifts the money demand curve to the right, from MD_1 to MD_2, and the quantity of money demanded rises at any given interest rate. A fall in money demand shifts the money demand curve to the left, from MD_1 to MD_3, and the quantity of money demanded falls at any given interest rate.

A fall in money demand shifts the money demand curve to the left.

A rise in money demand shifts the money demand curve to the right.

also rises by 20%—the movement from M_1 to M_2. Why? Because if the price of everything rises by 20%, it takes 20% more money to buy the same basket of goods and services. And if the aggregate price level falls by 20%, at any given interest rate the quantity of money demanded falls by 20%—shown by the movement from M_1 to M_3 at the interest rate r_1. As we'll see later, the fact that money demand is proportional to the price level has important implications for the long-run effects of monetary policy.

Changes in Real GDP Households and firms hold money as a way to facilitate purchases of goods and services. The larger the quantity of goods and services they buy, the larger the quantity of money they will want to hold at any given interest rate. So an increase in real GDP—the total quantity of goods and services produced and sold in the economy—shifts the money demand curve rightward. A fall in real GDP shifts the money demand curve leftward.

Changes in Technology There was a time, not so long ago, when withdrawing cash from a bank account required a visit during the bank's hours of operation. And since most people tried to do their banking during lunch hour, they often found themselves standing in line. So people limited the number of times they needed to withdraw funds by keeping substantial amounts of cash on hand. Not surprisingly, this tendency diminished greatly with the advent of ATMs in the 1970s. As a result, the demand for money fell and the money demand curve shifted leftward.

These events illustrate how changes in technology can affect the demand for money. In general, advances in information technology have tended to reduce the demand for money by making it easier for the public to make purchases without holding significant sums of money. ATM machines are only one example of how changes in technology have altered the demand for money. The ability of stores to process credit card and debit card transactions via the Internet has widened their acceptance and similarly reduced the demand for cash.

Changes in Institutions Changes in institutions can increase or decrease the demand for money. For example, until Regulation Q was eliminated in 1980, U.S. banks weren't allowed to offer interest on checking accounts. So the interest you would forgo by holding funds in a checking account instead of an interest-bearing asset made the opportunity cost of holding funds in checking accounts very high. When banking regulations changed, allowing banks to pay interest on checking account funds, the demand for money rose and shifted the money demand curve to the right.

►*ECONOMICS IN ACTION*

A Yen for Cash

Japan, say financial experts, is still a "cash society." Visitors from the United States or Europe are surprised at how little use the Japanese make of credit cards and how much cash they carry around in their wallets. Yet Japan is an economically and technologically advanced country and, according to some measures, ahead of the United States in the use of telecommunications and information technology. So why do the citizens of this economic powerhouse still do business the way Americans and Europeans did a generation ago? The answer highlights the factors affecting the demand for money.

One reason the Japanese use cash so much is that their institutions never made the switch to heavy reliance on plastic. For complex reasons, Japan's retail sector is still dominated by small mom-and-pop stores, which are reluctant to invest in credit card technology. Japan's banks have also been slow about pushing transaction technology; visitors are often surprised to find that ATMs close early in the evening rather than staying open all night.

Regardless of what they are shopping for, Japanese consumers tend to pay with cash rather than plastic.

But there's another reason the Japanese hold so much cash: there's little opportunity cost to doing so. Short-term interest rates in Japan have been below 1% since the mid-1990s. It also helps that the Japanese crime rate is quite low, so you are unlikely to have your wallet full of cash stolen. So why not hold cash? ▲

> > > > > > > > > > > > >

> ► CHECK YOUR UNDERSTANDING 31-1

1. Explain how each of the following would affect the quantity of money demanded. Does the change cause a movement along the money demand curve or a shift of the money demand curve?
   a. Short-term interest rates rise from 5% to 30%.
   b. All prices fall by 10%.
   c. New wireless technology automatically charges supermarket purchases to credit cards, eliminating the need to stop at the cash register.
   d. In order to avoid paying taxes, a vast underground economy develops in which workers are paid their wages in cash rather than with checks.

2. Which of the following will increase the opportunity cost of holding cash? Reduce it? Have no effect? Explain.
   a. Merchants charge a 1% fee on debit/credit card transactions for purchases of less than $50.
   b. To attract more deposits, banks raise the interest paid on six-month CDs.
   c. Real estate prices fall significantly.
   d. The cost of food rises significantly.

Solutions appear at back of book.

Money and Interest Rates

The Federal Open Market Committee decided today to lower its target for the federal funds rate 75 basis points to 2¼ percent.

Recent information indicates that the outlook for economic activity has weakened further. Growth in consumer spending has slowed and labor markets have softened. Financial markets remain under considerable stress, and the tightening of credit conditions and the deepening of the housing contraction are likely to weigh on economic growth over the next few quarters.

So read the beginning of a press release from the Federal Reserve issued on March 18, 2008. (A basis point is equal to 0.01 percentage point. So the statement implies that the Fed lowered the target from 3% to 2.25%.) We learned about the federal funds rate in Chapter 30: it's the rate at which banks lend reserves to each other to meet the required reserve ratio. As the statement implies, at each of its eight-times-a-year meetings, a group called the Federal Open Market Committee sets a target value for the federal funds rate. It's then up to Fed officials to achieve that target. This is done by the Open Market Desk at the Federal Reserve Bank of New York, which buys and sells short-term U.S. government debt, known as Treasury bills, to achieve that target.

As we've already seen, other short-term interest rates, such as the rates on CDs, move with the federal funds rate. So when the Fed reduced its target for the federal funds rate from 3% to 2.25% in March 2008, many other short-term interest rates also fell by about three-quarters of a percentage point.

How does the Fed go about achieving a *target federal funds rate*? And more to the point, how is the Fed able to affect interest rates at all?

The Equilibrium Interest Rate

Recall that, for simplicity, we've assumed that there is only one interest rate paid on nonmonetary financial assets, both in the short run and in the long run. To understand how the interest rate is determined, consider Figure 31-3 on the next page, which illustrates the **liquidity preference model of the interest rate;** this model

According to the **liquidity preference model of the interest rate,** the interest rate is determined by the supply and demand for money.

Equilibrium in the Money Market

The money supply curve, *MS,* is vertical at the money supply chosen by the Federal Reserve, $\overline{M}$. The money market is in equilibrium at the interest rate r_E: the quantity of money demanded by the public is equal to $\overline{M}$, the quantity of money supplied. At a point such as *L,* the interest rate, r_L, is below r_E and the corresponding quantity of money demanded, M_L, exceeds the money supply, $\overline{M}$. In an attempt to shift their wealth out of nonmoney interest-bearing financial assets and raise their money holdings, investors drive the interest rate up to r_E. At a point such as *H,* the interest rate r_H is above r_E and the corresponding quantity of money demanded, M_H, is less than the money supply, $\overline{M}$. In an attempt to shift out of money holdings into non-money interest-bearing financial assets, investors drive the interest rate down to r_E.

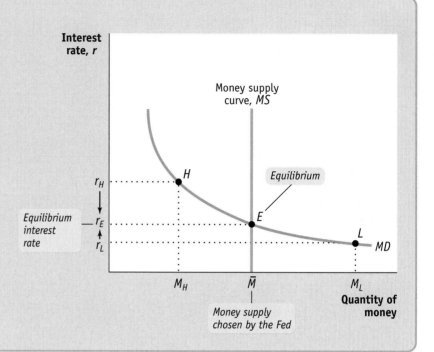

says that the interest rate is determined by the supply and demand for money in the market for money. Figure 31-3 combines the money demand curve, *MD,* with the **money supply curve,** *MS,* which shows how the quantity of money supplied by the Federal Reserve varies with the interest rate.

In Chapter 30 we learned how the Federal Reserve can increase or decrease the money supply: it usually does this through *open-market operations,* buying or selling Treasury bills, but it can also lend via the *discount window* or change *reserve requirements.* Let's assume for simplicity that the Fed, using one or more of these methods, simply chooses the level of the money supply that it believes will achieve its interest rate target. Then the money supply curve is a vertical line, *MS* in Figure 31-3, with a horizontal intercept corresponding to the money supply chosen by the Fed, $\overline{M}$. The money market equilibrium is at *E,* where *MS* and *MD* cross. At this point the quantity of money demanded equals the money supply, $\overline{M}$, leading to an equilibrium interest rate of r_E.

To understand why r_E is the equilibrium interest rate, consider what happens if the money market is at a point like *L,* where the interest rate, r_L, is below r_E. At r_L the public wants to hold the quantity of money M_L, an amount larger than the actual money supply, $\overline{M}$. This means that at point *L,* the public wants to shift some of its wealth out of interest-bearing assets such as high-denomination CDs (which aren't money) into money. This has two implications. One is that the quantity of money demanded is *more* than the quantity of money supplied. The other is that the quantity of interest-bearing nonmoney assets demanded is *less* than the quantity supplied. So those trying to sell nonmoney assets will find that they have to offer a higher interest rate to attract buyers. As a result, the interest rate will be driven up from r_L until the public wants to hold the quantity of money that is actually available, $\overline{M}$. That is, the interest rate will rise until it is equal to r_E.

Now consider what happens if the money market is at a point such as *H* in Figure 31-3, where the interest rate r_H is above r_E. In that case the quantity of money demanded, M_H, is less than the quantity of money supplied, $\overline{M}$. Correspondingly, the quantity of interest-bearing nonmoney assets demanded is greater than the quantity supplied. Those trying to sell interest-bearing nonmoney assets will find that they can offer a lower interest rate and still find willing buyers. This leads to a fall in the interest rate from r_H. It falls until the public wants to hold the quantity of money that is actually available, $\overline{M}$. Again, the interest rate will end up at r_E.

The **money supply curve** shows how the quantity of money supplied varies with the interest rate.

Two Models of Interest Rates?

You might have noticed that this is the second time we have discussed the determination of the interest rate. In Chapter 26 we studied the *loanable funds model* of the interest rate; according to that model, the interest rate is determined by the equalization of the supply of funds from lenders and the demand for funds by borrowers in the market for loanable funds. But here we have described a seemingly different model in which the interest rate is determined by the equalization of the supply and demand for money in the money market. Which of these models is correct?

The answer is both. We explain how the models are consistent with each other in the appendix to this chapter. For now, let's put the loanable funds model to one side and concentrate on the liquidity preference model of the interest rate. The most important insight from this model is that it shows us how monetary policy—actions by the Federal Reserve and other central banks—works.

Monetary Policy and the Interest Rate

Let's examine how the Federal Reserve can use changes in the money supply to change the interest rate. Figure 31-4 shows what happens when the Fed increases the money supply from $\overline{M}_1$ to $\overline{M}_2$. The economy is originally in equilibrium at E_1, with an equilibrium interest rate of r_1 and money supply $\overline{M}_1$. An increase in the money supply by the Fed to $\overline{M}_2$ shifts the money supply curve to the right, from MS_1 to MS_2, and leads to a fall in the equilibrium interest rate to r_2. Why? Because r_2 is the only interest rate at which the public is willing to hold the quantity of money actually supplied, $\overline{M}_2$. So an increase in the money supply drives the interest rate down. Similarly, a reduction in the money supply drives the interest rate up. By adjusting the money supply up or down, the Fed can set the interest rate.

In practice, at each meeting the Federal Open Market Committee decides on the interest rate to prevail for the next six weeks, until its next meeting. The Fed sets a **target federal funds rate,** a desired level for the federal funds rate. This target is then enforced by the Open Market Desk of the Federal Reserve Bank of New York, which adjusts the money supply through the purchase and sale of Treasury bills until the actual federal funds rate

The **target federal funds rate** is the Federal Reserve's desired federal funds rate.

FIGURE 31-4

The Effect of an Increase in the Money Supply on the Interest Rate

The Federal Reserve can lower the interest rate by increasing the money supply. Here, the equilibrium interest rate falls from r_1 to r_2 in response to an increase in the money supply from $\overline{M}_1$ to $\overline{M}_2$. In order to induce people to hold the larger quantity of money, the interest rate must fall from r_1 to r_2.

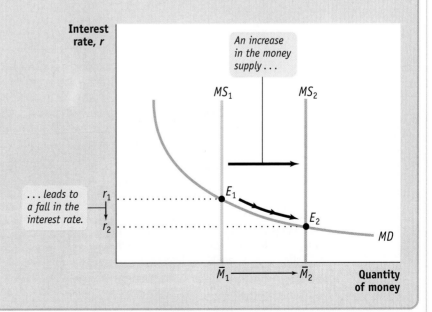

FOR INQUIRING MINDS

Long-Term Interest Rates

Earlier in this chapter we mentioned that *long-term interest rates*—rates on bonds or loans that mature in several years—don't necessarily move with short-term interest rates. How is that possible?

Consider the case of Millie, who has already decided to place $1,000 in CDs for the next two years. However, she hasn't decided whether to put the money in a one-year CD, at a 4% rate of interest, or a two-year CD, at a 5% rate of interest.

You might think that the two-year CD is a clearly better deal—but it may not be. Suppose that Millie expects the rate of in-

terest on one-year CDs to rise sharply next year. If she puts her funds in a one-year CD this year, she will be able to reinvest the money at a much higher rate next year. And this could give her a two-year rate of return that is higher than if she put her funds into the two-year CD. For example, if the rate of interest on one-year CDs rises from 4% this year to 8% next year, putting her funds in a one-year CD will give her an annual rate of return over the next two years of about 6%, better than the 5% rate on two-year CDs.

The same considerations apply to investors deciding between short-term and

long-term bonds. If they expect short-term interest rates to rise, investors may buy short-term bonds even if long-term bonds offer a higher interest rate. If they expect short-term interest rates to fall, investors may buy long-term bonds even if short-term bonds offer a higher interest rate.

In practice, long-term interest rates reflect the average expectation in the market about what's going to happen to short-term rates in the future. When long-term rates are higher than short-term rates, as they were in 2008, the market is signaling that it expects short-term rates to rise in the future.

equals the target rate. The other tools of monetary policy, lending through the discount window and changes in reserve requirements, aren't used on a regular basis (although the Fed used discount window lending in its efforts to address the 2008 financial crisis).

Figure 31-5 shows how this works. In both panels, r_T is the target federal funds rate. In panel (a), the initial money supply curve is MS_1 with money supply $\overline{M}_1$, and the equilibrium interest rate, r_1, is above the target rate. To lower the interest rate to r_T, the Fed makes an open-market purchase of Treasury bills. As we learned in Chapter 30, an open-market purchase of Treasury bills leads to an increase in the money supply via the money multiplier. This is illustrated in panel (a) by the rightward shift of the money supply curve from MS_1 to MS_2 and an increase in the money supply to $\overline{M}_2$. This drives the equilibrium interest rate *down* to the target rate, r_T.

FIGURE 31-5 **Setting the Federal Funds Rate**

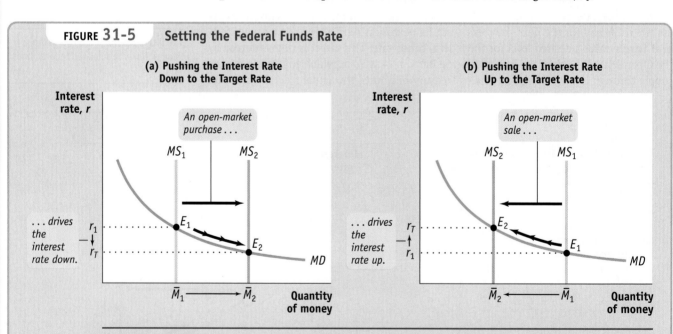

The Federal Reserve sets a target for the federal funds rate and uses open-market operations to achieve that target. In both panels the target rate is r_T. In panel (a) the initial equilibrium interest rate, r_1, is above the target rate. The Fed increases the money supply by making an open-market purchase of Treasury bills, pushing the money supply curve

rightward, from MS_1 to MS_2, and driving the interest rate down to r_T. In panel (b) the initial equilibrium interest rate, r_1, is below the target rate. The Fed reduces the money supply by making an open-market sale of Treasury bills, pushing the money supply curve leftward, from MS_1 to MS_2, and driving the interest rate up to r_T.

Panel (b) shows the opposite case. Again, the initial money supply curve is MS_1 with money supply $\overline{M}_1$. But this time the equilibrium interest rate, r_1, is below the target federal funds rate, r_T. In this case, the Fed will make an open-market sale of Treasury bills, leading to a fall in the money supply to $\overline{M}_2$ via the money multiplier. The money supply curve shifts leftward from MS_1 to MS_2, driving the equilibrium interest rate *up* to the target federal funds rate, r_T.

►ECONOMICS IN ACTION

The Fed Reverses Course

We opened this chapter with Jim Cramer's tirade against the Federal Reserve. Cramer wasn't alone in calling for a change in policy during the summer of 2007, but the Fed was, at first, unmoved. On August 7, 2007, four days after Cramer's outburst, the Federal Open Market Committee decided to stand pat, making no change in its interest rate policy. The official statement did, however, concede that "financial markets have been volatile in recent weeks" and that "credit conditions have become tighter for some households and businesses."

Just three days later, the Fed issued a special statement basically assuring market players that it was paying attention, and on August 17 it issued another statement declaring that it was "monitoring the situation," which is Fed-speak for "we're getting nervous." And on September 18, the Fed did what Cramer wanted: it cut the target federal funds rate "to help forestall some of the adverse effects on the broader economy that might otherwise arise from the disruptions in financial markets." In effect, it conceded that Cramer's worries were at least partly right.

It was the beginning of a major change in monetary policy. Figure 31-6 shows two interest rates from the beginning of 2004 to late 2008: the target federal funds rate decided by the Federal Open Market Committee, which dropped in a series of steps starting in September 2007, and the average effective rate that prevailed in the market each day. The figure shows that the interest rate cut six weeks after Cramer's diatribe was only the first of several cuts. As you can see, this was a reversal of previous policy: previously the Fed had generally been raising rates, not reducing them, out of concern that inflation might become a problem (more on that later in this chapter). But starting in September 2007, fighting the financial crisis took priority.

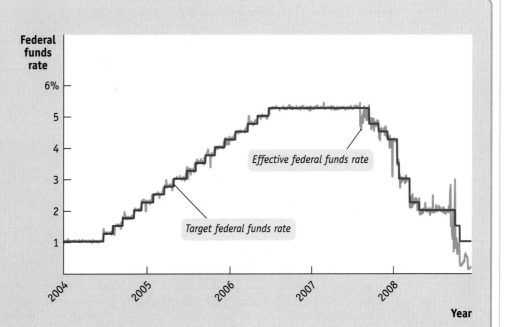

FIGURE 31-6

The Fed Reverses Course

In September 2007, the Fed, worried about the emerging financial crisis, began cutting the target federal funds rate. This was a reversal of its previous policy, which had involved a series of rate increases intended to control inflation. The actual federal funds rate fluctuated to some extent—that is, the Fed didn't always succeed in hitting its target. Overall, however, the Fed achieved a large reduction in the rate at which banks lend to each other.

Source: Federal Reserve Bank of St. Louis.

Figure 31-6 also shows that that the Fed doesn't always hit its target. There were a number of days, especially in 2008, when the actual federal funds rate was significantly above or below the target rate. But these episodes didn't last long, and overall the Fed got what it wanted, at least as far as short-term interest rates were concerned. ▲

< < < < < < < < < < < <

▶ CHECK YOUR UNDERSTANDING 31-2

1. Assume that there is an increase in the demand for money at every interest rate. Using a diagram, show what effect this will have on the equilibrium interest rate for a given money supply.

2. Now assume that the Fed is following a policy of targeting the federal funds rate. What will the Fed do in the situation described in Question 1 to keep the federal funds rate unchanged? Illustrate with a diagram.

Solutions appear at back of book.

Monetary Policy and Aggregate Demand

In Chapter 29 we saw how fiscal policy can be used to stabilize the economy. Now we will see how monetary policy—changes in the money supply or the interest rate, or both—can play the same role.

"I told you the Fed should have tightened."

Robert Mankoff/Cartoonbank.com

Expansionary and Contractionary Monetary Policy

In Chapter 28 we said that monetary policy shifts the aggregate demand curve. We can now explain how that works: through the effect of monetary policy on the interest rate.

Suppose that the Federal Reserve expands the money supply. As we've seen, this leads to a lower interest rate. A lower interest rate, in turn, will lead, other things equal, to more investment spending, which will lead to higher real GDP, which will lead to higher consumer spending, and so on through the multiplier process. So the total quantity of goods and services demanded at any given aggregate price level rises when the quantity of money increases, and the AD curve shifts to the right. Monetary policy that shifts the AD curve to the right, as illustrated in panel (a) of Figure 31-7, is known as **expansionary monetary policy.**

FIGURE 31-7   Monetary Policy and Aggregate Demand

An *expansionary monetary policy,* shown in panel (a), shifts the aggregate demand curve to the right from AD_1 to AD_2.

A *contractionary monetary policy,* shown in panel (b), shifts the aggregate demand curve to the left, from AD_1 to AD_3.

Suppose, alternatively, that the Federal Reserve contracts the money supply. This leads to a higher interest rate. The higher interest rate leads to lower investment spending, which leads to lower real GDP, which leads to lower consumer spending, and so on. So the total quantity of goods and services demanded falls when the money supply is reduced, and the AD curve shifts to the left. Monetary policy that shifts the AD curve to the left, as illustrated in panel (b) of Figure 31-7, is called **contractionary monetary policy.**

> **Expansionary monetary policy** is monetary policy that increases aggregate demand.
>
> **Contractionary monetary policy** is monetary policy that reduces aggregate demand.

Monetary Policy, Income, and Expenditure

In Chapter 27 we learned that the level of output in the short run is determined by *income–expenditure equilibrium*: output moves to the level at which the value of output is equal to planned aggregate spending. How can we think about monetary policy in terms of the income–expenditure framework? As we have just seen, the Fed moves the interest rate down or up by increasing or decreasing the money supply. Changes in the interest rate, in turn, change planned aggregate spending at any given level of output. And this changes the income–expenditure equilibrium.

Figure 31-8 illustrates the effect of monetary policy in terms of the income–expenditure model from Chapter 27. In both panels, the lines labeled AE show how the level of planned aggregate spending depends on the level of real GDP. Income–expenditure equilibrium is always at the point at which the planned aggregate spending line crosses the 45-degree line, so that real GDP is equal to planned aggregate spending.

Panel (a) of Figure 31-8 shows how income–expenditure equilibrium is affected by expansionary monetary policy and a reduction in the interest rate. The initial relationship between real GDP and planned aggregate spending is AE_1, and the initial equilibrium level of real GDP is Y_1. Other things equal, a lower interest rate leads to higher planned investment spending. So a reduction in the interest rate shifts AE_1 upward to AE_2. So the equilibrium level of real GDP rises to Y_2. This expansion reflects both the direct effect of a lower interest rate on investment spending and the indirect effect of rising real GDP on consumer spending, as the rise in investment spending has a multiplier effect on the economy.

Panel (b) of Figure 31-8 shows the opposite case, contractionary monetary policy and an increase in the interest rate. The initial relationship between real GDP and planned aggregate spending is AE_1, and the initial equilibrium level of real GDP is Y_1.

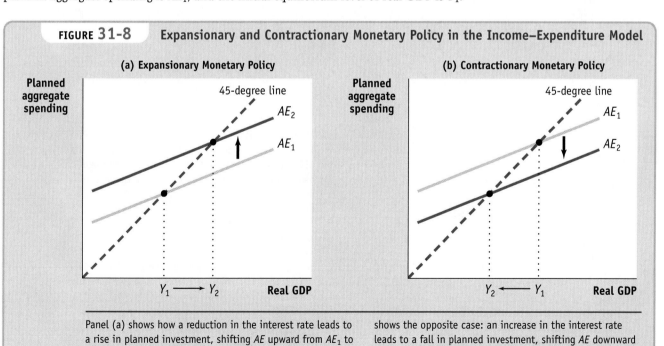

FIGURE 31-8   **Expansionary and Contractionary Monetary Policy in the Income–Expenditure Model**

Panel (a) shows how a reduction in the interest rate leads to a rise in planned investment, shifting AE upward from AE_1 to AE_2. Equilibrium real GDP rises from Y_1 to Y_2. Panel (b) shows the opposite case: an increase in the interest rate leads to a fall in planned investment, shifting AE downward from AE_1 to AE_2. Equilibrium real GDP falls from Y_1 to Y_2.

Other things equal, a higher interest rate leads to lower planned investment spending. So a reduction in the interest rate shifts AE_1 downward to AE_2. So the equilibrium level of real GDP falls to Y_2.

Monetary Policy in Practice

In Chapter 22 we learned that policy makers try to fight recessions. They also try to ensure *price stability*: low (though usually not zero) inflation. Actual monetary policy reflects a combination of these goals.

In general, the Federal Reserve and other central banks tend to engage in expansionary monetary policy when actual real GDP is below potential output. Panel (a) of Figure 31-9 shows the U.S. output gap, which we defined in Chapter 28 as the percentage difference between actual real GDP and potential output, versus the federal funds rate since 1985. (Recall that the output gap is positive when actual real GDP exceeds potential output.) As you can see, the Fed has tended to raise interest rates when the output gap is rising—that is, when the economy is developing an inflationary gap—and cut rates when the output gap is falling. The big exception was the late 1990s, when the Fed left rates steady for several years even as the economy developed a positive output gap (which went along with a low unemployment rate).

One reason the Fed was willing to keep interest rates low in the late 1990s was that inflation was low. Panel (b) of Figure 31-9 compares the inflation rate, measured as

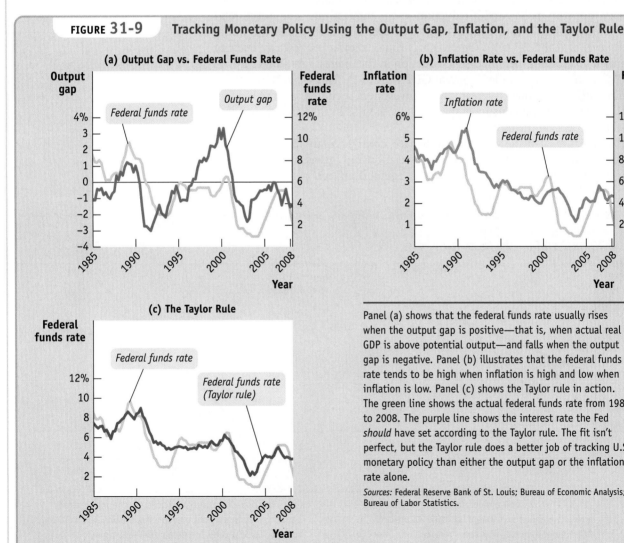

FIGURE 31-9 Tracking Monetary Policy Using the Output Gap, Inflation, and the Taylor Rule

Panel (a) shows that the federal funds rate usually rises when the output gap is positive—that is, when actual real GDP is above potential output—and falls when the output gap is negative. Panel (b) illustrates that the federal funds rate tends to be high when inflation is high and low when inflation is low. Panel (c) shows the Taylor rule in action. The green line shows the actual federal funds rate from 1985 to 2008. The purple line shows the interest rate the Fed *should* have set according to the Taylor rule. The fit isn't perfect, but the Taylor rule does a better job of tracking U.S. monetary policy than either the output gap or the inflation rate alone.

Sources: Federal Reserve Bank of St. Louis; Bureau of Economic Analysis; Bureau of Labor Statistics.

the rate of change in consumer prices excluding food and energy, with the federal funds rate. You can see how low inflation during the mid-1990s and early 2000s helped encourage loose monetary policy both in the late 1990s and in 2002–2003.

In 1993 Stanford economist John Taylor suggested that monetary policy should follow a simple rule that takes into account concerns about both the business cycle and inflation. He also suggested that actual monetary policy often looks as if the Federal Reserve was, in fact, more or less following the proposed rule. The **Taylor rule for monetary policy** is a rule for setting the federal funds rate that takes into account both the inflation rate and the output gap.

The rule Taylor originally suggested was as follows:

$$\text{Federal funds rate} = 1 + (1.5 \times \text{inflation rate}) + (0.5 \times \text{output gap})$$

Panel (c) of Figure 31-9 compares the federal funds rate specified by the Taylor rule with the actual federal funds rate from 1985 to 2008. The Taylor rule doesn't fit the Fed's actual behavior exactly, but it does better than looking at either the output gap alone or the inflation rate alone. Furthermore, the direction of changes in interest rates predicted by an application of the Taylor rule to monetary policy and the direction of changes in actual interest rates have always been the same—further evidence that the Fed is using some form of the Taylor rule to set monetary policy.

Notice, by the way, that the federal funds rate fell substantially more in 2007–2008 than the Taylor rule would have suggested. Why was the Fed so aggressive about cutting rates? The answer goes back to this chapter's opening story: a crisis in the financial markets, which prompted Jim Cramer's screaming. It worried the Fed too, which responded with extra-expansionary monetary policy.

Monetary policy, rather than fiscal policy, is the main tool of stabilization policy. Like fiscal policy, it is subject to lags: it takes time for the Fed to recognize economic problems, and time for monetary policy to affect the economy. However, since the Fed moves much more quickly than Congress, monetary policy is typically the preferred tool.

Inflation Targeting

The Federal Reserve tries to keep inflation low but positive. The Fed does not, however, explicitly commit itself to achieving any particular rate of inflation, although it is widely believed to prefer inflation at around 2% per year.

By contrast, a number of other central banks *do* have explicit inflation targets. So rather than using the Taylor rule to set monetary policy, they instead announce the inflation rate that they want to achieve—the *inflation target*—and set policy in an attempt to hit that target. This method of setting monetary policy, called **inflation targeting,** involves having the central bank announce the inflation rate it is trying to achieve and set policy in an attempt to hit that target. The central bank of New Zealand, which was the first country to adopt inflation targeting, specified a range for that target of 1% to 3%. Other central banks commit themselves to achieving a specific number. For example, the Bank of England is supposed to keep inflation at 2%. In practice, there doesn't seem to be much difference between these versions: central banks with a target range for inflation seem to aim for the middle of that range, and central banks with a fixed target tend to give themselves considerable wiggle room.

One major difference between inflation targeting and the Taylor rule is that inflation targeting is forward-looking rather than backward-looking. That is, the Taylor rule adjusts monetary policy in response to *past* inflation, but inflation targeting is based on a forecast of *future* inflation.

Advocates of inflation targeting argue that it has two key advantages, *transparency* and *accountability*. First, economic uncertainty is reduced because the public knows the objective of an inflation-targeting central bank. Second, the central bank's success can be judged by seeing how closely actual inflation rates have matched the inflation target, making central bankers accountable.

The **Taylor rule for monetary policy** says that the federal funds rate should be set on the basis of inflation and the output gap.

Inflation targeting occurs when the central bank sets an explicit target for the inflation rate and sets monetary policy in order to hit that target.

GLOBAL COMPARISON INFLATION TARGETS

This figure shows the target inflation rates of five central banks that have adopted inflation targeting. The central bank of New Zealand introduced inflation targeting in 1990. It has an inflation target range of from 1% to 3%. The central banks of Canada and Sweden have the same target range but also specify 2% as the precise target. The central banks of Britain and Norway have specific targets for inflation, 2% and 2.5%, respectively. Neither states by how much they're prepared to miss those targets.

In practice, these differences in detail don't seem to lead to any significant difference in results. New Zealand aims for the middle of its range, at 2% inflation; Britain and Norway allow themselves considerable wiggle room around their target inflation rates.

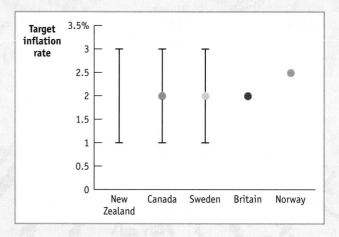

Critics of inflation targeting argue that it's too restrictive because there are times when other concerns—like the stability of the financial system—should take priority over achieving any particular inflation rate. Indeed, in late 2007 and early 2008 the Fed cut interest rates much more than either a Taylor rule or inflation targeting would have dictated because it feared that turmoil in the financial markets would lead to a major recession (which it did, in fact).

Many American macroeconomists have had positive things to say about inflation targeting—including Ben Bernanke, the current chairman of the Federal Reserve. At the time of writing, however, there were no moves to have the Fed adopt an explicit inflation target, and during normal times it still appears to set monetary policy by applying a loosely defined version of the Taylor rule.

►ECONOMICS IN ACTION

What the Fed Wants, the Fed Gets

What's the evidence that the Fed can actually cause an economic contraction or expansion? You might think that finding such evidence is just a matter of looking at what happens to the economy when interest rates go up or down. But it turns out that there's a big problem with that approach: the Fed usually changes interest rates in an attempt to tame the business cycle, raising rates if the economy is expanding and reducing rates if the economy is slumping. So in the actual data, it often looks as if low interest rates go along with a weak economy and high rates go along with a strong economy.

In a famous 1994 paper titled "Monetary Policy Matters," the macroeconomists Christina Romer and David Romer solved this problem by focusing on episodes in which monetary policy *wasn't* a reaction to the business cycle. Specifically, they used

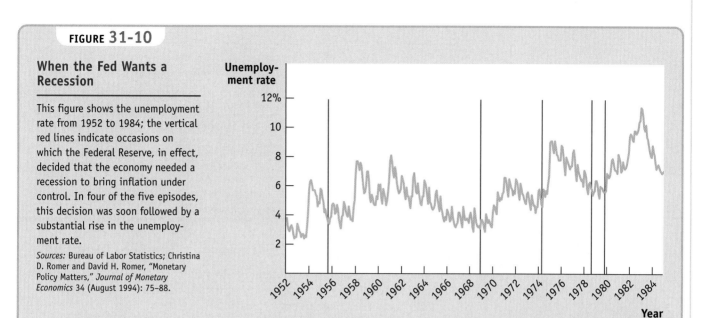

FIGURE 31-10

When the Fed Wants a Recession

This figure shows the unemployment rate from 1952 to 1984; the vertical red lines indicate occasions on which the Federal Reserve, in effect, decided that the economy needed a recession to bring inflation under control. In four of the five episodes, this decision was soon followed by a substantial rise in the unemployment rate.

Sources: Bureau of Labor Statistics; Christina D. Romer and David H. Romer, "Monetary Policy Matters," *Journal of Monetary Economics* 34 (August 1994): 75–88.

minutes from the Federal Open Market Committee and other sources to identify episodes "in which the Federal Reserve in effect decided to attempt to create a recession to reduce inflation." As we'll learn in Chapter 32, contractionary monetary policy is sometimes used to eliminate inflation that has become *embedded* in the economy, rather than just as a tool of macroeconomic stabilization. In this case, the Fed needs to create a recessionary gap—not just eliminate an inflationary gap—to wring embedded inflation out of the economy.

Figure 31-10 shows the unemployment rate between 1952 and 1984 (orange) and also identifies five dates on which, according to Romer and Romer, the Fed decided that it wanted a recession (vertical red lines). In four out of the five cases, the decision to contract the economy was followed, after a modest lag, by a rise in the unemployment rate. On average, Romer and Romer found, the unemployment rate rises by 2 percentage points after the Fed decides that unemployment needs to go up.

So yes, the Fed gets what it wants. ▲

> > > > > > > > > > > > >

► CHECK YOUR UNDERSTANDING 31-3

1. Suppose the economy is currently suffering from a recessionary gap and the Federal Reserve uses an expansionary monetary policy to close that gap. Describe the short-run effect of this policy on the following.
   a. The money supply curve
   b. The equilibrium interest rate
   c. Investment spending
   d. Consumer spending
   e. Aggregate output

2. What is the evidence that the Fed applies a version of the Taylor rule in setting monetary policy? In setting monetary policy, which central bank, the Fed or the Bank of England, is likely to respond more directly to a financial crisis? Explain.

Solutions appear at back of book.

►► QUICK REVIEW

> The Federal Reserve can use **expansionary monetary policy** to increase aggregate demand and **contractionary monetary policy** to reduce aggregate demand. The Federal Reserve and other central banks generally try to tame the business cycle while keeping the inflation rate low but positive.

> The **Taylor rule for monetary policy** says that the target federal funds rate should rise when there is a positive output gap, high inflation, or both and fall when there is a negative output gap, low or negative inflation, or both.

> In contrast, some central banks set monetary policy by **inflation targeting,** a forward-looking policy rule, rather than by using the Taylor rule, a backward-looking policy rule. Although inflation targeting has the benefits of transparency and accountability, some think it is too restrictive. In practice, the Fed appears to follow a loosely defined Taylor rule.

> Because it is subject to fewer lags than fiscal policy, monetary policy is the main tool for macroeconomic stabilization.

Money, Output, and Prices in the Long Run

Through its expansionary and contractionary effects, monetary policy is generally the policy tool of choice to help stabilize the economy. However, not all actions by central banks are productive. In particular, as we'll see in the next chapter, central banks sometimes print money not to fight a recessionary gap but to help the government pay its bills, an action that typically destabilizes the economy.

What happens when a change in the money supply pushes the economy away from, rather than toward, long-run equilibrium? We learned in Chapter 28 that the economy is self-correcting in the long run: a demand shock has only a temporary effect on aggregate output. If the demand shock is the result of a change in the money supply, we can make a stronger statement: in the long run, changes in the quantity of money affect the aggregate price level, but they do not change real aggregate output or the interest rate. To see why, let's look at what happens if the central bank permanently increases the money supply.

Short-Run and Long-Run Effects of an Increase in the Money Supply

To analyze the long-run effects of monetary policy, it's helpful to think of the central bank as choosing a target for the money supply rather than the interest rate. In assessing the effects of an increase in the money supply, we return to the analysis of the long-run effects of an increase in aggregate demand, first introduced in Chapter 28.

Figure 31-11 shows the short-run and long-run effects of an increase in the money supply when the economy begins at potential output, Y_1. The initial short-run aggregate supply curve is $SRAS_1$, the long-run aggregate supply curve is $LRAS$, and the initial aggregate demand curve is AD_1. The economy's initial equilibrium is at E_1, a point of both short-run and long-run macroeconomic equilibrium because it is on both the short-run and the long-run aggregate supply curves. Real GDP is at potential output, Y_1.

Now suppose there is an increase in the money supply. Other things equal, an increase in the money supply reduces the interest rate, which increases investment spending, which leads to a further rise in consumer spending, and so on. So an in-

---

FIGURE 31-11

The Short-Run and Long-Run Effects of an Increase in the Money Supply

An increase in the money supply generates a positive short-run effect, but no long-run effect, on real GDP. Here, the economy begins at E_1, a point of short-run and long-run macroeconomic equilibrium. An increase in the money supply shifts the AD curve rightward, and the economy moves to a new short-run equilibrium at E_2 and a new real GDP of Y_2. But E_2 is not a long-run equilibrium: Y_2 exceeds potential output, Y_1, leading over time to an increase in nominal wages. In the long run, the increase in nominal wages shifts the short-run aggregate supply curve leftward, to a new position at $SRAS_2$. The economy reaches a new short-run and long-run macroeconomic equilibrium at E_3 on the $LRAS$ curve, and output falls back to potential output, Y_1. The only long-run effect of an increase in the money supply is an increase in the aggregate price level from P_1 to P_3.

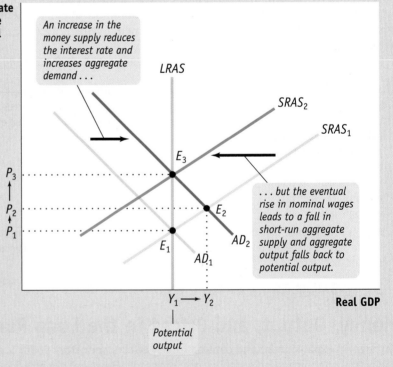

An increase in the money supply reduces the interest rate and increases aggregate demand . . .

. . . but the eventual rise in nominal wages leads to a fall in short-run aggregate supply and aggregate output falls back to potential output.

crease in the money supply increases the quantity of goods and services demanded, shifting the AD curve rightward, to AD_2. In the short run, the economy moves to a new short-run macroeconomic equilibrium at E_2. The price level rises from P_1 to P_2, and real GDP rises from Y_1 to Y_2. That is, both the aggregate price level and aggregate output increase in the short run.

But the aggregate output level Y_2 is above potential output. As a result, nominal wages will rise over time, causing the short-run aggregate supply curve to shift leftward. This process stops only when the $SRAS$ curve ends up at $SRAS_2$ and the economy ends up at point E_3, a point of both short-run and long-run macroeconomic equilibrium. The long-run effect of an increase in the money supply, then, is that the aggregate price level has increased from P_1 to P_3, but aggregate output is back at potential output, Y_1. In the long run, a monetary expansion raises the aggregate price level but has no effect on real GDP.

We won't describe the effects of a monetary contraction in detail, but the same logic applies. In the short run, a fall in the money supply leads to a fall in aggregate output as the economy moves down the short-run aggregate supply curve. In the long run, however, the monetary contraction reduces only the aggregate price level, and real GDP returns to potential output.

> According to the concept of **monetary neutrality,** changes in the money supply have no real effects on the economy.

Monetary Neutrality

How much does a change in the money supply change the aggregate price level in the long run? The answer is that a change in the money supply leads to an equal proportional change in the aggregate price level in the long run. For example, if the money supply falls 25%, the aggregate price level falls 25% in the long run; if the money supply rises 50%, the aggregate price level rises 50% in the long run.

How do we know this? Consider the following thought experiment: suppose all prices in the economy—prices of final goods and services and also factor prices, such as nominal wage rates—double. And suppose the money supply doubles at the same time. What difference does this make to the economy in real terms? The answer is none. All real variables in the economy—such as real GDP and the real value of the money supply (the amount of goods and services it can buy)—are unchanged. So there is no reason for anyone to behave any differently.

We can state this argument in reverse: if the economy starts out in long-run macroeconomic equilibrium and the money supply changes, restoring long-run macroeconomic equilibrium requires restoring all real values to their original values. This includes restoring the real value of the money supply to its original level. So if the money supply falls 25%, the aggregate price level must fall 25%; if the money supply rises 50%, the price level must rise 50%; and so on.

This analysis demonstrates the concept known as **monetary neutrality,** in which changes in the money supply have no real effects on the economy. In the long run, the only effect of an increase in the money supply is to raise the aggregate price level by an equal percentage. Economists argue that *money is neutral in the long run.*

This is, however, a good time to recall the dictum of John Maynard Keynes: "In the long run we are all dead." In the long run, changes in the money supply don't have any effect on real GDP, interest rates, or anything else except the price level. But it would be foolish to conclude from this that the Fed is irrelevant. Monetary policy does have powerful real effects on the economy in the short run, often making the difference between recession and expansion. And that matters a lot for society's welfare.

Changes in the Money Supply and the Interest Rate in the Long Run

In the short run, an increase in the money supply leads to a fall in the interest rate, and a decrease in the money supply leads to a rise in the interest rate. In the long run, however, changes in the money supply don't affect the interest rate.

FIGURE 31-12

The Long-Run Determination of the Interest Rate

In the short run, an increase in the money supply from $\overline{M}_1$ to $\overline{M}_2$ pushes the interest rate down from r_1 to r_2 and the economy moves to E_2, a short-run equilibrium. In the long run, however, the aggregate price level rises in proportion to the increase in the money supply, leading to an increase in money demand at any given interest rate in proportion to the increase in the aggregate price level, as shown by the shift from MD_1 to MD_2. The result is that the quantity of money demanded at any given interest rate rises by the same amount as the quantity of money supplied. The economy moves to long-run equilibrium at E_3 and the interest rate returns to r_1.

Figure 31-12 shows why. It shows the money supply curve and the money demand curve before and after the Fed increases the money supply. We assume that the economy is initially at E_1, in long-run macroeconomic equilibrium at potential output, and with money supply $\overline{M}_1$. The initial equilibrium interest rate, determined by the intersection of the money demand curve MD_1 and the money supply curve MS_1, is r_1.

Now suppose the money supply increases from $\overline{M}_1$ to $\overline{M}_2$. In the short run, the economy moves from E_1 to E_2 and the interest rate falls from r_1 to r_2. Over time, however, the aggregate price level rises, and this raises money demand, shifting the money demand curve rightward from MD_1 to MD_2. The economy moves to a new long-run equilibrium at E_3, and the interest rate rises to its original level at r_1.

And it turns out that the long-run equilibrium interest rate is the original interest rate, r_1. We know this for two reasons. First, due to monetary neutrality, in the long run the aggregate price level rises by the same proportion as the money supply; so if the money supply rises by, say, 50%, the price level will also rise by 50%. Second, the demand for money is, other things equal, proportional to the aggregate price level. So a 50% increase in the money supply raises the aggregate price level by 50%, which increases the quantity of money demanded at any given interest rate by 50%. As a result, the quantity of money demanded at the initial interest rate, r_1, rises exactly as much as the money supply—so that r_1 is still the equilibrium interest rate. In the long run, then, changes in the money supply do not affect the interest rate.

►ECONOMICS IN ACTION

International Evidence of Monetary Neutrality

These days monetary policy is quite similar among wealthy countries. Each major nation (or, in the case of the euro, the eurozone) has a central bank that is insulated from political pressure. All of these central banks try to keep the aggregate price level roughly stable, which usually means inflation of at most 2% to 3% per year.

But if we look at a longer period and a wider group of countries, we see large differences in the growth of the money supply. Between 1970 and the present, the money supply rose only a few percent per year in some countries, such as Switzerland and the United States, but rose much more rapidly in some poorer countries,

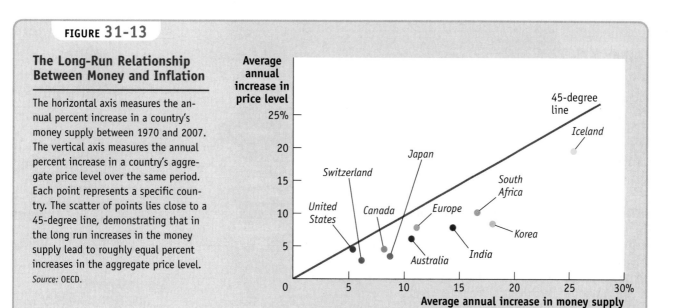

FIGURE 31-13

The Long-Run Relationship Between Money and Inflation

The horizontal axis measures the annual percent increase in a country's money supply between 1970 and 2007. The vertical axis measures the annual percent increase in a country's aggregate price level over the same period. Each point represents a specific country. The scatter of points lies close to a 45-degree line, demonstrating that in the long run increases in the money supply lead to roughly equal percent increases in the aggregate price level.

Source: OECD.

such as South Africa. These differences allow us to see whether it is really true that increases in the money supply lead, in the long run, to equal percent rises in the aggregate price level.

Figure 31-13 shows the annual percentage increases in the money supply and average annual increases in the aggregate price level—that is, the average rate of inflation—for a sample of countries during the period 1970–2007, with each point representing a country. If the relationship between increases in the money supply and changes in the aggregate price level were exact, the points would lie precisely on a 45-degree line. In fact, the relationship isn't exact, because other factors besides money affect the aggregate price level. But the scatter of points clearly lies close to a 45-degree line, showing a more or less proportional relationship between money and the aggregate price level. That is, the data support the concept of monetary neutrality in the long run. ▲

> > > > > > > > > > > > >

▶ CHECK YOUR UNDERSTANDING 31-4

1. Assume the central bank increases the quantity of money by 25%, even though the economy is initially in both short-run and long-run macroeconomic equilibrium. Describe the effects, in the short run and in the long run (giving numbers where possible), on the following:
   a. Aggregate output
   b. Aggregate price level
   c. Real value of the money supply (purchasing power for goods and services)
   d. Interest rate

2. Why does monetary policy affect the economy in the short run but not in the long run?

Solutions appear at back of book.

[▶▶ A LOOK AHEAD •••

Independent of the business cycle, managing the inflation rate plays a major role in shaping monetary policy. In the next chapter, we'll discover why inflation is a concern for policy makers. The problems of excessively high inflation (*hyperinflation*) as well as negative inflation (*deflation*) will be discussed. We'll learn how countries find themselves in these situations and the difficulties they must endure to get out.]

SUMMARY ....■

1. The **money demand curve** arises from a trade-off between the opportunity cost of holding money and the liquidity that money provides. The opportunity cost of holding money depends on **short-term interest rates,** not **long-term interest rates.** Changes in the aggregate price level, real GDP, technology, and institutions shift the money demand curve.

2. According to the **liquidity preference model of the interest rate,** the interest rate is determined in the money market by the money demand curve and the **money supply curve.** The Federal Reserve can change the interest rate in the short run by shifting the money supply curve. In practice, the Fed uses open-market operations to achieve a **target federal funds rate,** which other short-term interest rates generally track.

3. **Expansionary monetary policy** reduces the interest rate by increasing the money supply. This increases investment spending and consumer spending, which in turn increases aggregate demand and real GDP in the short run. **Contractionary monetary policy** raises the interest rate by reducing the money supply. This reduces investment

spending and consumer spending, which in turn reduces aggregate demand and real GDP in the short run.

4. The Federal Reserve and other central banks try to stabilize the economy, limiting fluctuations of actual output around potential output, while also keeping inflation low but positive. Under the **Taylor rule for monetary policy,** the target interest rate rises when there is inflation, or a positive output gap, or both; the target interest rate falls when inflation is low or negative, or when the output gap is negative, or both. Some central banks engage in **inflation targeting,** which is a forward-looking policy rule, whereas the Taylor rule is a backward-looking policy rule. In practice, the Fed appears to operate on a loosely defined version of the Taylor rule. Because monetary policy is subject to fewer implementation lags than fiscal policy, it is the preferred policy tool for stabilizing the economy.

5. In the long run, changes in the money supply affect the aggregate price level but not real GDP or the interest rate. Data show that the concept of **monetary neutrality** holds: changes in the money supply have no real effect on the economy in the long run.

KEY TERMS ....■

Short-term interest rates, p. 833
Long-term interest rates, p. 834
Money demand curve, p. 834
Liquidity preference model of the interest rate, p. 837

Money supply curve, p. 838
Target federal funds rate, p. 839
Expansionary monetary policy, p. 842
Contractionary monetary policy, p. 843

Taylor rule for monetary policy, p. 845
Inflation targeting, p. 845
Monetary neutrality, p. 849

PROBLEMS ....■

1. Go to the FOMC page of the Federal Reserve Board's website (http://www.federalreserve.gov/FOMC/) to find the statement issued after the most recent FOMC meeting. (Click on "Meeting calendars, statements, and minutes" and then click on the most recent statement listed in the calendar.)

   a. What is the target federal funds rate?

   b. Is the target federal funds rate different from the target federal funds rate in the previous FOMC statement? If yes, by how much does it differ?

   c. Does the statement comment on current macroeconomic conditions in the United States? How does it describe the U.S. economy?

2. How will the following events affect the demand for money? In each case, specify whether there is a shift of the demand curve or a movement along the demand curve and its direction.

   a. There is a fall in the interest rate from 12% to 10%.

   b. Thanksgiving arrives and, with it, the beginning of the holiday shopping season.

   c. McDonald's and other fast-food restaurants begin to accept credit cards.

   d. The Fed engages in an open-market purchase of U.S. Treasury bills.

3. a. Go to www.treasurydirect.gov. Under "Quick Links for Individuals," go to "Learn about Treasury Bills, Notes, Bonds, and TIPS." Click on "Treasury bills." Under "at a glance," click on "rates in recent auctions." What is the investment rate for the most recently issued 26-week T-bills?

   b. Go to the website of your favorite bank. What is the interest rate for six-month CDs?

   c. Why are the rates for six-month CDs higher than for 26-week Treasury bills?

4. Go to www.treasurydirect.gov. Under "Quick Links for Individuals," go to "Learn about Treasury Bills, Notes, Bonds, and TIPS." Click on "Treasury notes." Under "at a glance," click on "rates in recent auctions." Then click on "Recent Note, Bond, TIPS Auction Results:"

   a. What are the interest rates on 2-year and 10-year notes?

   b. How do the interest rates on the 2-year and 10-year notes relate to each other? Why is the interest rate on the 10-year note higher (or lower) than the interest rate on the 2-year note?

5. An economy is facing the recessionary gap shown in the accompanying diagram. To eliminate the gap, should the central bank use expansionary or contractionary monetary policy? How will the interest rate, investment spending, consumer spending, real GDP, and the aggregate price level change as monetary policy closes the recessionary gap?

6. An economy is facing the inflationary gap shown in the accompanying diagram. To eliminate the gap, should the central bank use expansionary or contractionary monetary policy? How will the interest rate, investment spending, consumer spending, real GDP, and the aggregate price level change as monetary policy closes the inflationary gap?

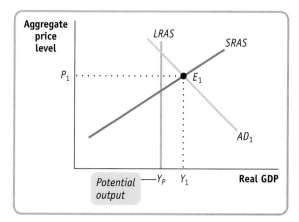

7. In the economy of Eastlandia, the money market is initially in equilibrium when the economy begins to slide into a recession.

   a. Using the accompanying diagram, explain what will happen to the interest rate if the central bank of Eastlandia keeps the money supply constant at $\overline{M}_1$.

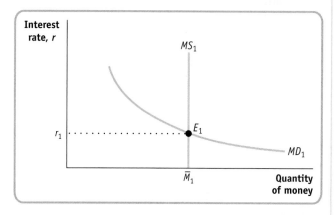

   b. If the central bank is instead committed to maintaining an interest rate target of r_1, then as the economy slides into recession, how should the central bank react? Using your diagram from part a, demonstrate the central bank's reaction.

8. Continuing from the previous problem, now suppose that in the economy of Eastlandia the central bank decides to decrease the money supply.

   a. Using the diagram in problem 7, explain what will happen to the interest rate in the short run.

   b. What will happen to the interest rate in the long run?

9. An economy is in long-run macroeconomic equilibrium with an unemployment rate of 5% when the government passes a law requiring the central bank to use monetary policy to lower the unemployment rate to 3% and keep it there. How could the central bank achieve this goal in the short run? What would happen in the long run? Illustrate with a diagram.

10. According to the European Central Bank website, the treaty establishing the European Community "makes clear that ensuring price stability is the most important contribution that monetary policy can make to achieve a favourable economic environment and a high level of employment." If price stability is the only goal of monetary policy, explain how monetary policy would be conducted during recessions. Analyze both the case of a recession that is the result of a demand shock and the case of a recession that is the result of a supply shock.

11. The effectiveness of monetary policy depends on how easy it is for changes in the money supply to change interest rates. By changing interest rates, monetary policy affects investment spending and the aggregate demand curve. The economies of Albernia and Brittania have very different money demand curves, as shown in the accompanying diagram. In which economy will changes in the money supply be a more effective policy tool? Why?

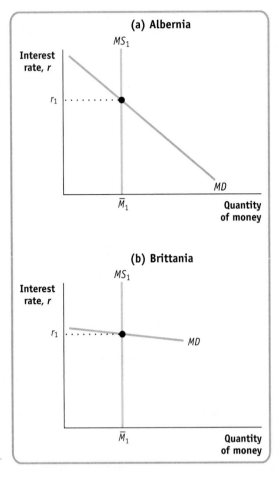

(a) Albernia

Interest rate, r

MS_1

r_1

MD

$\bar{M}_1$ Quantity of money

(b) Brittania

Interest rate, r

MS_1

r_1

MD

$\bar{M}_1$ Quantity of money

idea was to provide a boost to the economy by increasing aggregate demand.

a. Use the liquidity preference model to explain how the Federal Reserve Bank lowers the interest rate in the short run. Draw a typical graph that illustrates the mechanism. Label the vertical axis "Interest rate" and the horizontal axis "Quantity of money." Your graph should show two interest rates, r_1 and r_2.

b. Explain why the reduction in the interest rate causes aggregate demand to increase in the short run.

c. Demonstrate the effect of the policy measure on the *AD* curve. Use the *LRAS* curve to show that the effect of this policy measure on the *AD* curve, other things equal, causes the aggregate price level to rise in the long run. Label the vertical axis "Aggregate price level" and the horizontal axis "Real GDP."

12. During the Great Depression, business people in the United States were very pessimistic about the future of economic growth and reluctant to increase investment spending even when interest rates fell. How did this limit the potential for monetary policy to help alleviate the Depression?

13. Because of an economic slowdown, the Federal Reserve Bank of the United States lowered the federal funds rate from 4.25% on January 1, 2008, to 2.00% on May 1, 2008. The

 www.worthpublishers.com/krugmanwells

Chapter 31 Appendix:
Reconciling the Two Models of the Interest Rate

In the main text of this chapter we developed the liquidity preference model of the interest rate. In this model, the equilibrium interest rate is the rate at which the quantity of money demanded equals the quantity of money supplied. We promised to explain how this is consistent with the loanable funds model of the interest rate we developed in Chapter 26. In that model, the equilibrium interest rate matches the quantity of loanable funds supplied by savers with the quantity of loanable funds demanded for investment spending. We will do this in two steps, focusing first on the short run, then on the long run.

The Interest Rate in the Short Run

As we explained in the main text, a fall in the interest rate leads to a rise in investment spending, I, which then leads to a rise in both real GDP and consumer spending, C. The rise in real GDP doesn't lead only to a rise in consumer spending, however. It also leads to a rise in savings: at each stage of the multiplier process, part of the increase in disposable income is saved. How much do savings rise? In Chapter 26 we introduced the *savings–investment spending identity:* total savings in the economy is always equal to investment spending. This tells us that when a fall in the interest rate leads to higher investment spending, the resulting increase in real GDP generates exactly enough additional savings to match the rise in investment spending. To put it another way, after a fall in the interest rate, the quantity of savings supplied rises exactly enough to match the quantity of savings demanded.

Figure 31A-1 on the next page shows how our two models of the interest rate are reconciled in the short run by the links among changes in the interest rate, changes in real GDP, and changes in savings. Panel (a) represents the liquidity preference model of the interest rate. MS_1 and MD_1 are the initial supply and demand curves for money. According to the liquidity preference model, the equilibrium interest rate in the economy is the rate at which the quantity of money supplied is equal to the quantity of money demanded in the money market. Panel (b) represents the loanable funds model of the interest rate. S_1 is the initial supply curve and D is the demand curve for loanable funds. According to the loanable funds model, the equilibrium interest rate in the economy is the rate at which the quantity of loanable funds supplied is equal to the quantity of loanable funds demanded in the market for loanable funds.

In Figure 31A-1 both the money market and the market for loanable funds are initially in equilibrium at E_1 with the same interest rate, r_1. You might think that this would only happen by accident, but in fact it will always be true. To see why, let's look at what happens when the Fed increases the money supply from $\overline{M}_1$ to $\overline{M}_2$, pushing the money supply curve rightward, to MS_2, causing the equilibrium interest rate in the market for money to fall to r_2, and the economy moves to a short-run equilibrium at E_2. What happens in panel (b), in the market for loanable funds? In the short run, the fall in the interest rate due to the increase in the money supply leads to a rise in real GDP, which generates a rise in savings through the multiplier process. This rise in savings shifts the supply curve for loanable funds rightward, from S_1 to S_2, moving the equilibrium in the loanable funds market from E_1 to E_2 and also reducing

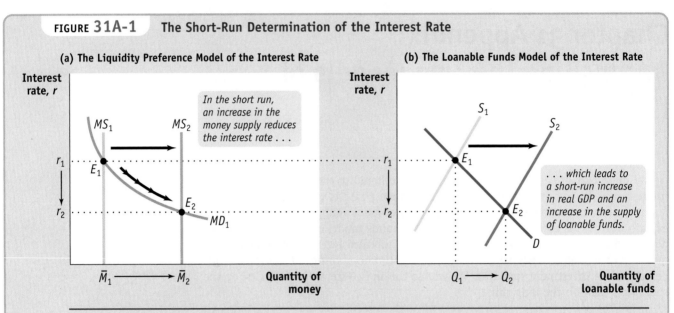

FIGURE 31A-1   The Short-Run Determination of the Interest Rate

Panel (a) shows the liquidity preference model of the interest rate: the equilibrium interest rate matches the money supply to the quantity of money demanded. In the short run, the interest rate is determined in the money market, where an increase in the money supply, from $\bar{M}_1$ to $\bar{M}_2$, pushes the equilibrium interest rate down, from r_1 to r_2. Panel (b) shows the loanable funds model of the interest rate. The fall in the interest rate in the money market leads, through the multiplier effect, to an increase in real GDP and savings; to a rightward shift of the supply curve of loanable funds, from S_1 to S_2; and to a fall in the interest rate, from r_1 to r_2. As a result, the new equilibrium interest rate in the loanable funds market matches the new equilibrium interest rate in the money market at r_2.

the equilibrium interest rate in the loanable funds market. And we know that savings rise by exactly enough to match the rise in investment spending. This tells us that the equilibrium rate in the loanable funds market falls to r_2, the same as the new equilibrium interest rate in the money market.

In the short run, then, the supply and demand for money determine the interest rate, and the loanable funds market follows the lead of the money market. When a change in the supply of money leads to a change in the interest rate, the resulting change in real GDP causes the supply of loanable funds to change as well. As a result, the equilibrium interest rate in the loanable funds market is the same as the equilibrium interest rate in the money market.

Notice our use of the phrase "in the short run." Changes in aggregate demand affect aggregate output only in the short run. In the long run, aggregate output is equal to potential output. So our story about how a fall in the interest rate leads to a rise in aggregate output, which leads to a rise in savings, applies only to the short run. In the long run, as we'll see next, the determination of the interest rate is quite different, because the roles of the two markets are reversed. In the long run, the loanable funds market determines the equilibrium interest rate, and it is the market for money that follows the lead of the loanable funds market.

The Interest Rate in the Long Run

In the short run an increase in the money supply leads to a fall in the interest rate, and a decrease in the money supply leads to a rise in the interest rate. In the long run, however, changes in the money supply don't affect the interest rate.

Figure 31A-2 shows why. As in Figure 31A-1, panel (a) shows the liquidity preference model of the interest rate and panel (b) shows the supply and demand for loanable funds. We assume that in both panels the economy is initially at E_1, in long-run

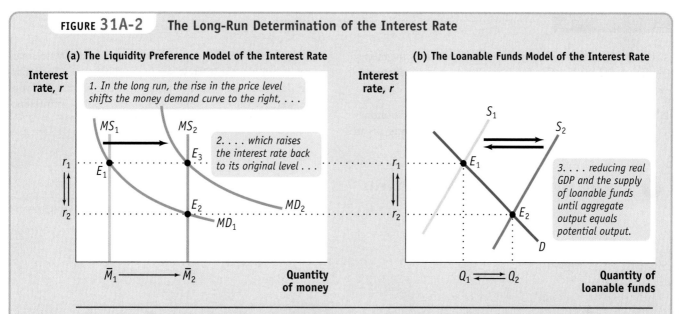

FIGURE 31A-2   The Long-Run Determination of the Interest Rate

(a) The Liquidity Preference Model of the Interest Rate

1. In the long run, the rise in the price level shifts the money demand curve to the right, . . .

2. . . . which raises the interest rate back to its original level . . .

(b) The Loanable Funds Model of the Interest Rate

3. . . . reducing real GDP and the supply of loanable funds until aggregate output equals potential output.

Panel (a) shows the liquidity preference model long-run adjustment to an increase in the money supply from $\bar{M}_1$ to $\bar{M}_2$; panel (b) shows the corresponding long-run adjustment in the loanable funds market. As we discussed in Figure 31A-1, the increase in the money supply reduces the interest rate from r_1 to r_2, increases real GDP, and increases savings in the short run. This is shown in panel (a) and panel (b) as the movement from E_1 to E_2. In the long run, however, the increase in the money supply raises wages and other nominal prices; this shifts the money demand curve in panel (a) from MD_1 to MD_2, leading to an increase in the interest rate from r_1 to r_2 as the economy moves from E_2 to E_3. The rise in the interest rate causes a fall in real GDP and a fall in savings, shifting the loanable funds supply curve back to S_1 from S_2 and moving the loanable funds market from E_2 back to E_1. In the long run, the equilibrium interest rate is determined by matching the supply and demand for loanable funds that arises when real GDP equals potential output.

macroeconomic equilibrium at potential output with the money supply equal to $\bar{M}_1$. The demand curve for loanable funds is D, and the initial supply curve for loanable funds is S_1. The initial equilibrium interest rate in both markets is r_1.

Now suppose the money supply rises from $\bar{M}_1$ to $\bar{M}_2$. As we saw in Figure 31A-1, this initially reduces the interest rate to r_2. We already know, however, from the neutrality of money, that in the long run the aggregate price level rises by the same proportion as the increase in the money supply. We also know that a rise in the aggregate price level increases money demand in the same proportion. So in the long run the money demand curve shifts out to MD_2, and the equilibrium interest rate rises back to its original level, r_1.

Panel (b) of Figure 31A-2 shows what happens in the market for loanable funds. We saw earlier that an increase in the money supply leads to a short-run rise in real GDP and that this shifts the supply of loanable funds rightward from S_1 to S_2. In the long run, however, real GDP falls back to its original level as wages and other nominal prices rise. As a result, the supply of loanable funds, S, which initially shifted from S_1 to S_2, shifts back to S_1.

In the long run, then, changes in the money supply do not affect the interest rate. So what determines the interest rate in the long run—that is, what determines r_1 in Figure 31A-2? The answer is the supply and demand for loanable funds. More specifically, in the long run the equilibrium interest rate matches the supply and demand for loanable funds that arise at potential output.

PROBLEMS ···■

1. Using a figure similar to Figure 31A-1, explain how the money market and the loanable funds market react to a reduction in the money supply in the short run.

2. Contrast the short-run effects of an increase in the money supply on the interest rate to the long-run effects of an increase in the money supply on the interest rate. Which market determines the interest rate in the short run? Which market does so in the long run? What are the implications of your answers for the effectiveness of monetary policy in influencing real GDP in the short run and the long run?

www.worthpublishers.com/krugmanwells

>> Inflation, Disinflation, and Deflation

BRINGING A SUITCASE TO THE BANK

BY THE SUMMER OF 2008, THE AFRICAN NATION of Zimbabwe had achieved an unenviable distinction: in June 2008 it had the world's highest inflation rate, 11 million percent a year. Although the government kept introducing ever-larger denominations of its currency, the Zimbabwe dollar—for example, in May 2008 it introduced a half-billion dollar bill—it still took a lot of currency to pay for the necessities of life: a stack of Zimbabwean cash worth $100 U.S. dollars weighed about 40 pounds. Zimbabwean currency was worth so little that some people withdrawing funds from banks brought suitcases along, in order to be able to walk away with enough cash to pay for ordinary living expenses.

Zimbabwe's experience was shocking, but not unprecedented. In 1994 the inflation rate in Armenia hit 27,000%. In 1991 Nicaraguan inflation exceeded 60,000%. And even Zimbabwe's inflation was mild compared with history's most famous example of extreme inflation, which took place in Germany in 1922–1923. Toward the end of the German hyperinflation, prices were rising 16% a *day*, which—through compounding—meant an increase of approximately 500 billion percent over the course of five months. People became so reluctant to hold paper money, which lost value by the hour, that eggs and lumps of coal began to circulate as currency. German firms would pay their workers several times a day so that they could spend their earnings before they lost value (lending new meaning to the term *hourly wage*). Legend has it that men sitting down at a bar would order two beers at a time, out of fear that the price of a beer would rise before they could order a second round!

The United States has never experienced that kind of inflation. The worst inflation the U.S. has seen in modern times took place at the end of the 1970s, when consumer prices were rising at an annual rate of 13%. Yet inflation at even that rate was profoundly troubling to the American public, and the policies the Federal Reserve pursued in order to get U.S. inflation back down to an acceptable rate led to the deepest recession since the Great Depression.

What causes inflation to rise and fall? In this chapter, we'll look at the underlying reasons for inflation. We'll see that the underlying causes of very high inflation, the type of inflation suffered by Zimbabwe, are quite different from the causes of more moderate inflation. We'll also learn why *disinflation*, a reduction in the inflation rate, is often very difficult. Finally, we'll discuss the special problems associated with a falling price level, or deflation.

Phillimon Bulawayo/epa/Corbis

In 2008, the Zimbabwe dollar was so devalued by extreme inflation that this much currency was needed to pay for a single loaf of bread.

Money and Inflation

As we'll see later in this chapter, moderate levels of inflation such as those experienced in the United States—even the double-digit inflation of the late 1970s—can have complex causes. But very high inflation is always associated with rapid increases in the money supply.

To understand why, we need to revisit the effect of changes in the money supply on the overall price level. Then we'll turn to the reasons governments sometimes increase the money supply very rapidly.

The Classical Model of Money and Prices

In Chapter 31, we learned that in the short run an increase in the money supply increases real GDP by lowering the interest rate and stimulating investment spending and consumer spending. However, in the long run, as nominal wages and other sticky prices rise, real GDP falls back to its original level. So in the long run, an increase in the money supply does not change real GDP. Instead, other things equal, it leads to an equal percent rise in the overall price level; that is, the prices of all goods and services in the economy, including nominal wages and the prices of intermediate goods, rise by the same percentage as the money supply. And when the overall price level rises, the aggregate price level—the prices of all final goods and services—rises as well. As a result, a change in the *nominal* money supply, *M,* leads in the long run to a change in the aggregate price level that leaves the *real* quantity of money, *M/P,* at its original level. As a result, there is no long-run effect on aggregate demand or real GDP. For example, when Turkey dropped six zeros from its currency, the Turkish lira, in January 2005, Turkish real GDP did not change. The only thing that changed was the number of zeros in prices: instead of something costing 2,000,000 lira, it cost 2 lira.

This is, to repeat, what happens in the long run. When analyzing large changes in the aggregate price level, however, macroeconomists often find it useful to ignore the distinction between the short run and the long run. Instead, they work with a simplified model in which the effect of a change in the money supply on the aggregate price level takes place instantaneously rather than over a long period of time. You might be concerned about this assumption given that in previous chapters we've emphasized the difference between the short run and the long run. However, for reasons we'll explain shortly, this is a reasonable assumption to make in the case of high inflation.

A simplified model in which the real quantity of money, *M/P,* is always at its long-run equilibrium level is known as the **classical model of the price level,** because it was commonly used by "classical" economists who wrote before the work of John Maynard Keynes. To understand the classical model and why it is useful in the context of high inflation, let's revisit the *AD-AS* model and what it says about the effects of an increase in the money supply. (Unless otherwise noted, we will always be referring to changes in the *nominal* supply of money.)

According to the **classical model of the price level,** the real quantity of money is always at its long-run equilibrium level.

Figure 32-1 reviews the effects of an increase in the money supply according to the AD-AS model. The economy starts at E_1, a point of short-run and long-run macroeconomic equilibrium. It lies at the intersection of the aggregate demand curve, AD_1, and the short-run aggregate supply curve, $SRAS_1$. It also lies on the long-run aggregate supply curve, $LRAS$. At E_1, the equilibrium aggregate price level is P_1.

Now suppose there is an increase in the money supply. This is an expansionary monetary policy, which shifts the aggregate demand curve to the right, to AD_2, and moves the economy to a new short-run macroeconomic equilibrium at E_2. Over time, however, nominal wages adjust upward in response to the rise in the aggregate price level, and the $SRAS$ curve shifts to the left, to $SRAS_2$. The new long-run macroeconomic equilibrium is at E_3, and real GDP returns to its initial level. As we learned in Chapter 31, the long-run increase in the aggregate price level from P_1 to P_3 is proportional to the increase in the money supply. As a result, in the long run changes in the money supply have no effect on the real quantity of money, M/P, or on real GDP. In the long run, money—as we learned—is *neutral*.

The classical model of the price level ignores the short-run movement from E_1 to E_2, assuming that the economy moves directly from one long-run equilibrium to another long-run equilibrium. In other words, it assumes that the economy moves directly from E_1 to E_3 and that real GDP never changes in response to a change in the money supply. In effect, in the classical model the effects of money supply changes are analyzed as if the short-run as well as the long-run aggregate supply curves were vertical.

In reality, this is a poor assumption during periods of low inflation. With a low inflation rate, it may take a while for workers and firms to react to a monetary expansion by raising wages and prices. In this scenario, some nominal wages and the prices of some goods are sticky in the short run. As a result, under low inflation there is an upward-sloping $SRAS$ curve, and changes in the money supply can indeed change real GDP in the short run.

But what about periods of high inflation? In the face of high inflation, economists have observed that the short-run stickiness of nominal wages and prices tends to vanish. Workers and businesses, sensitized to inflation, are quick to raise their wages and prices in response to changes in the money supply. This implies that under high inflation there is a quicker adjustment of wages and prices of intermediate goods than occurs in the case of low inflation. So the short-run aggregate supply curve shifts leftward more quickly and there is a more rapid return to long-run equilibrium

---

FIGURE 32-1

The Classical Model of the Price Level

Starting at E_1, an increase in the money supply shifts the aggregate demand curve rightward, as shown by the movement from AD_1 to AD_2. There is a new short-run macroeconomic equilibrium at E_2 and a higher price level at P_2. In the long run, nominal wages adjust upward and push the $SRAS$ curve leftward to $SRAS_2$. The total percent increase in the price level from P_1 to P_3 is equal to the percent increase in the money supply. In the *classical model of the price level*, we ignore the transition period and think of the price level as rising to P_3 immediately. This is a good approximation under conditions of high inflation.

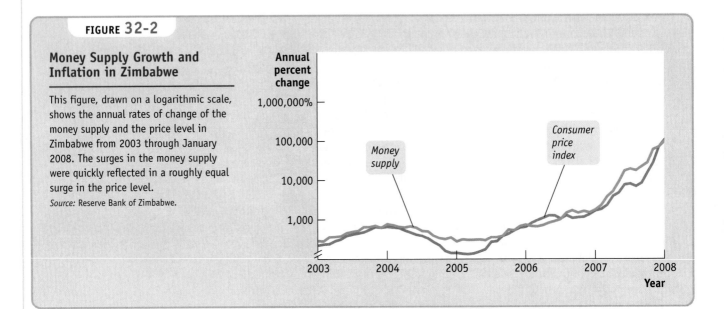

FIGURE 32-2

Money Supply Growth and Inflation in Zimbabwe

This figure, drawn on a logarithmic scale, shows the annual rates of change of the money supply and the price level in Zimbabwe from 2003 through January 2008. The surges in the money supply were quickly reflected in a roughly equal surge in the price level.

Source: Reserve Bank of Zimbabwe.

under high inflation. As a result, the classical model of the price level is much more likely to be a good approximation of reality for economies experiencing persistently high inflation. The following For Inquiring Minds explains this point further.

The consequence of this rapid adjustment of all prices in the economy is that in countries with persistently high inflation, changes in the money supply are quickly translated into changes in the inflation rate. Let's look at Zimbabwe. Figure 32-2 shows the annual rate of growth in the money supply and the annual rate of change of consumer prices from 2003 through January 2008. As you can see, the surge in the growth rate of the money supply coincided closely with a roughly equal surge in the inflation rate. Note that to fit these very large percentage increases—several thousands of percent—onto the figure, we have drawn the vertical axis using a logarithmic scale.

What leads a country to increase its money supply so much that the result is an inflation rate in the millions of percent?

The Inflation Tax

Modern economies use fiat money—pieces of paper that have no intrinsic value but are accepted as a medium of exchange. In the United States and most other wealthy countries, the decision about how many pieces of paper to issue is placed in the hands of a central bank that is somewhat independent of the political process. However, this independence can always be taken away if politicians decide to seize control of monetary policy.

So what is to prevent a government from paying for some of its expenses not by raising taxes or borrowing but simply by printing money? Nothing. In fact, governments, including the U.S. government, do it all the time. How can the U.S. government do this, given that the Federal Reserve issues money, not the U.S. Treasury? The answer is that the Treasury and the Federal Reserve work in concert. The Treasury issues debt to finance the government's purchases of goods and services, and the Fed *monetizes* the debt by creating money and buying the debt back from the public through open-market purchases of Treasury bills. In effect, the U.S. government can and does raise revenue by printing money.

For example, in August 2007 the U.S. monetary base—bank reserves plus currency in circulation—was $20 billion larger than it had been a year earlier. This occurred because, over the course of that year, the Federal Reserve had issued $20 billion in money or its electronic equivalent and put it into circulation through open-market operations. To put it another way, the Fed created money out of thin air and used it to

FOR INQUIRING MINDS

Indexing to Inflation

When an economy experiences high inflation year after year, people try to protect themselves from future inflation. The most common way of achieving such protection is through *indexation*—contracts are written so that the terms of the contract automatically adjust for inflation. When indexation spreads through the economy, prices become much more highly sensitive to changes in the money supply, even in the short run. Even in an economy without indexation, an increase in the money supply quickly pushes up the prices of some types of goods, such as raw materials. In a highly indexed economy, these higher prices feed rapidly into changes in the consumer price index. That, in turn, quickly leads to increases in wages, further leading to increases in other prices, which feed back into wages, and so on. The result is that the long run, the period in which an increase in the money supply raises the overall price level by the same percentage, arrives very quickly—typically in a matter of months. Under indexation, the prospect

that a one-time increase in prices can spark a persistent rise in inflation poses a much greater risk.

To evaluate the effects of indexation on wage contracts, we can compare the recent history of U.S. wages versus wages in the eurozone, the set of European countries that use the euro as their common currency. Nearly one-third of eurozone firms index their workers' wages to inflation, either formally or informally. In Spain, for example, the wages of nearly 70% of private-sector employees rise with the inflation rate. In contrast, less than 1% of American workers have wages indexed to inflation. Most economists believe the reason behind this disparity lies in the fact that organized labor plays a much greater role in the eurozone than in the United States. With powerful unions, eurozone workers are able to negotiate inflation-indexed wage contracts, with contracts for non-unionized workers often following the same pattern.

Figure 32-3 shows the recent history of the inflation rate and percentage changes in

wages in the eurozone and in the United States. As you can see, inflation and wage growth in the eurozone tend to track one another; in contrast, the U.S. shows little linkage between inflation and wage growth. In fact, except for a brief period in 2007, since 2004 U.S. wage growth has lagged behind the inflation rate, leading to a lower real standard of living for many American workers.

So although both Spain and the United States saw their economies sharply slow in 2007 and 2008 in response to bursting housing bubbles, Spanish real wages rose but American real wages fell.

Because indexation tends to magnify price increases, transforming them into sustained inflation, the European Central Bank generally keeps a tighter leash on its economy and maintains a more hawkish stance toward inflation than the Federal Reserve. Indeed, during mid-2008, with both the U.S. and the eurozone clearly moving into recession, the European short-term interest rate stood at 4.25%, but the Fed funds rate stood at only 2%.

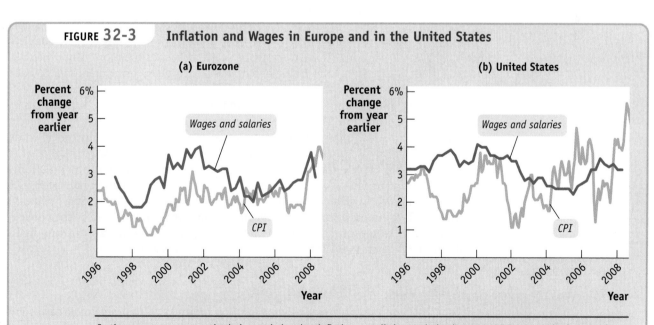

FIGURE 32-3   Inflation and Wages in Europe and in the United States

(a) Eurozone

Percent change from year earlier — *Wages and salaries*, *CPI*

(b) United States

Percent change from year earlier — *Wages and salaries*, *CPI*

In the eurozone, wages and salaries are indexed to inflation to a much greater degree than in the United States. As a result, as panel (a) shows, eurozone wages and salaries track inflation closely. By contrast, as shown in panel (b), there is

little correlation between U.S. wages and salaries and inflation. Since 2004, in most years the growth in U.S. wages has lagged behind the inflation rate.

Sources: European Central Bank; Eurostat; Bureau of Labor Statistics.

STUCKFLATION

©Nate Beeler

buy valuable government securities from the private sector. It's true that the U.S. government pays interest on debt owned by the Federal Reserve—but the Fed, by law, hands the interest payments it receives on government debt back to the Treasury, keeping only enough to fund its own operations. In effect, then, the Federal Reserve's actions enabled the government to pay off $20 billion in outstanding government debt by printing money.

An alternative way to look at this is to say that the right to print money is itself a source of revenue. Economists refer to the revenue generated by the government's right to print money as *seignorage,* an archaic term that goes back to the Middle Ages. It refers to the right to stamp gold and silver into coins, and charge a fee for doing so, that medieval lords—seigneurs, in France—reserved for themselves.

Seignorage accounts for only a tiny fraction (less than 1%) of the U.S. government's budget. Furthermore, concerns about seignorage don't have any influence on the Federal Reserve's decisions about how much money to print; the Fed is worried about inflation and unemployment, not revenue. But this hasn't always been true, even in America: both sides relied on seignorage to help cover budget deficits during the Civil War. And there have been many occasions in history when governments turned to their printing presses as a crucial source of revenue. According to the usual scenario, a government finds itself running a large budget deficit—and lacks either the competence or the political will to eliminate this deficit by raising taxes or cutting spending. Furthermore, the government can't borrow to cover the gap because potential lenders won't extend loans given the fear that the government's weakness will continue and leave it unable to repay its debts.

In such a situation, governments end up printing money to cover the budget deficit. But by printing money to pay its bills, a government increases the quantity of money in circulation. And as we've just seen, increases in the money supply translate into equally large increases in the aggregate price level. So printing money to cover a budget deficit leads to inflation.

Who ends up paying for the goods and services the government purchases with newly printed money? The people who currently hold money pay. They pay because inflation erodes the purchasing power of their money holdings. In other words, a government imposes an **inflation tax,** the reduction in the value of the money held by the public, by printing money to cover its budget deficit and creating inflation.

It's helpful to think about what this tax represents. If the inflation rate is 5%, then a year from now $1 will buy goods and services worth only $0.95 today. So a 5% inflation rate in effect imposes a tax rate of 5% on the value of all money held by the public.

But why would any government push the inflation tax to rates of hundreds or thousands of percent? We turn next to the logic of hyperinflation.

The Logic of Hyperinflation

Inflation imposes a tax on individuals who hold money. And, like most taxes, it will lead people to change their behavior. In particular, when inflation is high, people will try to avoid holding money and will instead substitute real goods as well as interest-bearing assets for money. In this chapter's opening story, we described how, during the German hyperinflation, people began using eggs or lumps of coal as a medium of exchange. They did this because lumps of coal maintained their real value over time but money didn't. Indeed, during the peak of German hyperinflation, people often burned paper money, which was less valuable than wood. Moreover, people don't just

The **inflation tax** is the reduction in the value of money held by the public caused by inflation.

reduce their nominal money holdings—they reduce their *real* money holdings, cutting the amount of money they hold so much that it actually has less purchasing power than the amount of money they would hold if inflation were low. Why? Because the more real money holdings they have, the greater the real amount of resources the government captures from them through the inflation tax.

We are now prepared to understand how countries can get themselves into situations of extreme inflation. High inflation arises when the government must print a large quantity of money, imposing a large inflation tax, to cover a large budget deficit.

Now, the seignorage collected by the government over a short period—say, one month—is equal to the change in the money supply over that period. Let's use M to represent the money supply and use the symbol Δ to mean "monthly change in." Then:

In the 1920s, hyperinflation made German currency worth so little that children made kites from banknotes.

(32-1) Seignorage $= \Delta M$

The money value of seignorage, however, isn't very informative by itself. After all, the whole point of inflation is that a given amount of money buys less and less over time. So it's more useful to look at *real* seignorage, the revenue created by printing money divided by the price level, P:

(32-2) Real seignorage $= \Delta M/P$

Equation 32-2 can be rewritten by dividing and multiplying by the current level of the money supply, M, giving us:

(32-3) Real seignorage $= (\Delta M/M) \times (M/P)$

or

Real seignorage $=$ Rate of growth of the money supply $\times$ Real money supply

But as we've just explained, in the face of high inflation the public reduces the real amount of money it holds, so that the far right-hand term in Equation 32-3, M/P, gets smaller. Suppose that the government needs to print enough money to pay for a given quantity of goods and services—that is, it needs to collect a given *real* amount of seignorage. Then, as the real money supply, M/P, falls as people hold smaller amounts of real money, the government has to respond by accelerating the rate of growth of the money supply, $\Delta M/M$. This will lead to an even higher rate of inflation. And people will respond to this new higher rate of inflation by reducing their real money holdings, M/P, yet again. As the process becomes self-reinforcing, it can easily spiral out of control. Although the amount of real seignorage that the government must ultimately collect to pay off its deficit does not change, the inflation rate the government needs to impose to collect that amount rises. So the government is forced to increase the money supply more rapidly, leading to an even higher rate of inflation, and so on.

Here's an analogy: imagine a city government that tries to raise a lot of money with a special fee on taxi rides. The fee will raise the cost of taxi rides, and this will cause people to turn to easily available substitutes, such as walking or taking the bus. As taxi use declines, the government finds that its tax revenue declines and it must impose a higher fee to raise the same amount of revenue as before. You can imagine the ensuing vicious circle: the government imposes fees on taxi rides, which leads to less taxi use, which causes the government to raise the fee on taxi rides, which leads to even less taxi use, and so on.

Substitute the real money supply for taxi rides and the inflation rate for the increase in the fee on taxi rides, and you have the story of hyperinflation. A race develops between the government printing presses and the public: the presses churn out money at a faster and faster rate, to try to compensate for the fact that the public is reducing its real money holdings. At some point the inflation rate explodes into hyperinflation, and people are unwilling to hold any money at all (and resort to trading in eggs and lumps of coal). The government is then forced to abandon its use of the inflation tax and shut down the printing presses.

➤*ECONOMICS IN ACTION*

Zimbabwe's Inflation

As we noted in this chapter's opening story, Zimbabwe offers a recent example of a country experiencing very high inflation. Figure 32-2 showed that surges in Zimbabwe's money supply growth were matched by almost simultaneous surges in its inflation rate. But looking at rates of change doesn't give a true feel for just how much prices went up.

Figure 32-4 shows Zimbabwe's consumer price index from 1999 to June 2008, with the 2000 level set equal to 100. As in Figure 32-2, we also use a logarithmic scale, which lets us draw equal-sized percent changes as the same size. Over the course of just over nine years, consumer prices rose by approximately 4.5 trillion percent.

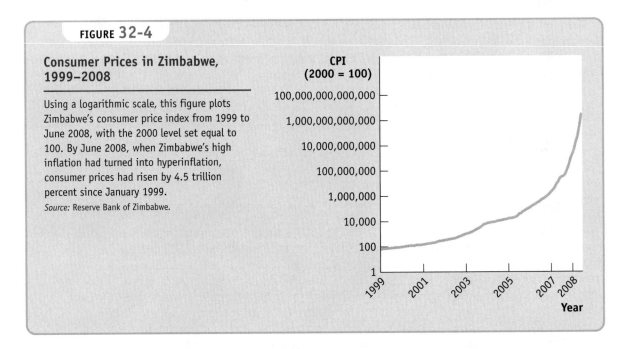

FIGURE 32-4

Consumer Prices in Zimbabwe, 1999–2008

Using a logarithmic scale, this figure plots Zimbabwe's consumer price index from 1999 to June 2008, with the 2000 level set equal to 100. By June 2008, when Zimbabwe's high inflation had turned into hyperinflation, consumer prices had risen by 4.5 trillion percent since January 1999.

Source: Reserve Bank of Zimbabwe.

Why did Zimbabwe's government pursue policies that led to runaway inflation? The reason boils down to political instability, which in turn had its roots in Zimbabwe's history. Until the 1970s, Zimbabwe had been ruled by its small white minority; even after the shift to majority rule, many of the country's farms remained in the hands of whites. Eventually Robert Mugabe, Zimbabwe's president, tried to solidify his position by seizing these farms and turning them over to his political supporters. But because this seizure disrupted production, the result was to undermine the country's economy and its tax base. It became impossible for the country's government to balance its budget either by raising taxes or by cutting spending. At the same time, the regime's instability left Zimbabwe unable to borrow money in world markets. Like many others before it, Zimbabwe's government turned to the printing press to cover the gap—leading to massive inflation. ▲

< < < < < < < < < < < <

➤ CHECK YOUR UNDERSTANDING 32-1

1. Suppose there is a large increase in the money supply in an economy that previously had low inflation. As a consequence, aggregate output expands in the short run. What does this say about situations in which the classical model of the price level applies?

2. Suppose that all wages and prices in an economy are indexed to inflation. Can there still be an inflation tax?

Solutions appear at back of book.

Moderate Inflation and Disinflation

The governments of wealthy, politically stable countries like the United States and Britain don't find themselves forced to print money to pay their bills. Yet over the past 40 years both countries, along with a number of other nations, have experienced uncomfortable episodes of inflation. In the United States, the inflation rate peaked at 13% at the beginning of the 1980s. In Britain, the inflation rate reached 26% in 1975. Why did policy makers allow this to happen?

The answer, in brief, is that in the short run, policies that produce a booming economy also tend to lead to higher inflation, and policies that reduce inflation tend to depress the economy. This creates both temptations and dilemmas for governments.

First, imagine yourself as a politician facing an election in a year or two, and suppose that inflation is fairly low at the moment. You might well be tempted to pursue expansionary policies that will push the unemployment rate down, as a way to please voters, even if your economic advisers warn that this will eventually lead to higher inflation. You might also be tempted to find different economic advisers, who tell you not to worry: in politics, as in ordinary life, wishful thinking often prevails over realistic analysis.

Conversely, imagine yourself as a politician in an economy suffering from inflation. Your economic advisers will probably tell you that the only way to bring inflation down is to push the economy into a recession, which will lead to temporarily higher unemployment. Are you willing to pay that price? Maybe not.

This political asymmetry—inflationary policies often produce short-term political gains, but policies to bring inflation down carry short-term political costs—explains how countries with no need to impose an inflation tax sometimes end up with serious inflation problems. For example, that 26% rate of inflation in Britain was largely the result of the British government's decision in 1971 to pursue highly expansionary monetary and fiscal policies. Politicians disregarded warnings that these policies would be inflationary and were extremely reluctant to reverse course even when it became clear that the warnings had been correct.

But why do expansionary policies lead to inflation? To answer that question, we need to look first at the relationship between output and unemployment.

The Output Gap and the Unemployment Rate

In Chapter 28 we introduced the concept of *potential output,* the level of real GDP that the economy would produce once all prices had fully adjusted. Potential output typically grows steadily over time, reflecting long-run growth. However, as we learned from the aggregate demand–aggregate supply model, actual aggregate output fluctuates around potential output in the short run: a recessionary gap arises when actual aggregate output falls short of potential output; an inflationary gap arises when actual aggregate output exceeds potential output. Recall from Chapter 28 that the percentage difference between the actual level of real GDP and potential output is called the *output gap.* A positive or negative output gap occurs when an economy is producing more than or less than what would be "expected" because all prices have not yet adjusted. And wages, as we've learned, are the prices in the labor market.

Meanwhile, we learned in Chapter 24 that the unemployment rate is composed of cyclical unemployment and natural unemployment, the portion of the unemployment rate unaffected by the business cycle. So there is a relationship between the unemployment rate and the output gap. This relationship is defined by two rules:

- When actual aggregate output is equal to potential output, the actual unemployment rate is equal to the natural rate of unemployment.

- When the output gap is positive (an inflationary gap), the unemployment rate is *below* the natural rate. When the output gap is negative (a recessionary gap), the unemployment rate is *above* the natural rate.

In other words, fluctuations of aggregate output around the long-run trend of potential output correspond to fluctuations of the unemployment rate around the natural rate.

This makes sense. When the economy is producing less than potential output—when the output gap is negative—it is not making full use of its productive resources. Among the resources that are not fully utilized is labor, the economy's most important resource. So we would expect a negative output gap to be associated with unusually high unemployment. Conversely, when the economy is producing more than potential output, it is temporarily using resources at higher-than-normal rates. With this positive output gap, we would expect to see lower-than-normal unemployment.

Figure 32-5 confirms this rule. Panel (a) shows the actual and natural rates of unemployment, as estimated by the Congressional Budget Office (CBO). Panel (b) shows two series. One is cyclical unemployment: the difference between the actual unemployment rate and the CBO estimate of the natural rate of unemployment, measured on the left. The other is the CBO estimate of the output gap, measured on the right. To make the relationship clearer, the output gap series is inverted—shown upside down—so that the line goes down if actual output rises above potential output and up if actual output falls below potential output. As you can see, the two series move together quite closely, showing the strong relationship between the output gap

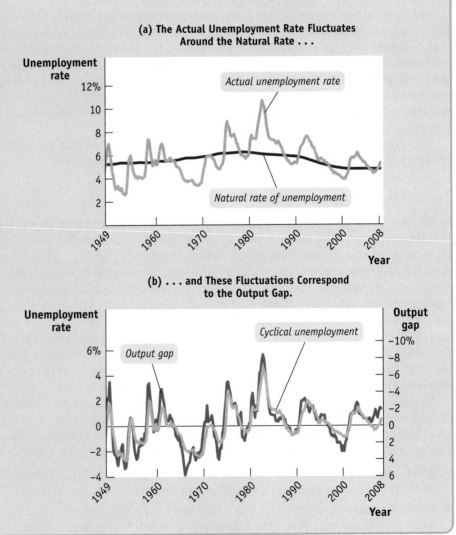

FIGURE 32-5

Cyclical Unemployment and the Output Gap

Panel (a) shows the actual U.S. unemployment rate from 1949 to 2008, together with the Congressional Budget Office estimate of the natural rate of unemployment. The actual rate fluctuates around the natural rate, often for extended periods. Panel (b) shows cyclical unemployment—the difference between the actual unemployment rate and the natural rate of unemployment—and the output gap, also estimated by the CBO. The unemployment rate is measured on the left vertical axis, and the output gap is measured with an inverted scale on the right vertical axis. With an inverted scale, it moves in the same direction as the unemployment rate: when the output gap is positive, the actual unemployment rate is below its natural rate; when the output gap is negative, the actual unemployment rate is above its natural rate. The two series track one another closely, showing the strong relationship between the output gap and cyclical unemployment.

Source: Congressional Budget Office; Bureau of Labor Statistics; Bureau of Economic Analysis.

(a) The Actual Unemployment Rate Fluctuates Around the Natural Rate . . .

Actual unemployment rate

Natural rate of unemployment

(b) . . . and These Fluctuations Correspond to the Output Gap.

Output gap

Cyclical unemployment

Okun's Law

Although cyclical unemployment and the output gap move together, cyclical unemployment seems to move *less* than the output gap. For example, the output gap reached −8% in 1982, but the cyclical unemployment rate reached only 4%. This observation is the basis of an important relationship originally discovered by Arthur Okun, John F. Kennedy's chief economic adviser.

Modern estimates of **Okun's law**—the negative relationship between the output gap and the unemployment rate— typically find that a rise in the output gap of 1 percentage point reduces the unemployment rate by about $\frac{1}{2}$ of a percentage point.

For example, suppose that the natural rate of unemployment is 5.2% and that the economy is currently producing at only 98% of potential output. In that case, the output gap is −2%, and Okun's law predicts an unemployment rate of $5.2\% - \frac{1}{2} \times (-2\%) = 6.2\%$.

The fact that a 1% rise in output reduces the unemployment rate by only $\frac{1}{2}$ of 1% may seem puzzling: you might have expected to see a one-to-one relationship between the output gap and unemployment. Doesn't a 1% rise in aggregate output require a 1% increase in employment? And shouldn't that take 1% off the unemployment rate?

The answer is no: there are several well-understood reasons why the relationship isn't one-to-one. For one thing, companies often meet changes in demand in part by changing the number of hours their existing employees work. For example, a company that experiences a sudden increase in demand for its products may cope by asking (or requiring) its workers to put in longer hours, rather than by hiring more workers. Conversely, a company that sees sales drop will often reduce workers' hours rather than lay off employees. This behavior dampens the effect of output fluctuations on the number of workers employed.

Also, the number of workers looking for jobs is affected by the availability of jobs. Suppose that the number of jobs falls by 1 million. Measured unemployment will rise by less than 1 million because some unemployed workers become discouraged and give up actively looking for work. (Recall from Chapter 24 that workers aren't counted as unemployed unless they are actively seeking work.) Conversely, if the economy adds 1 million jobs, some people who haven't been actively looking for work will begin doing so. As a result, measured unemployment will fall by less than 1 million.

Finally, the rate of growth of labor productivity generally accelerates during booms and slows down or even turns negative during busts. The reasons for this phenomenon are the subject of some dispute among economists. The consequence, however, is that the effects of booms and busts on the unemployment rate are dampened.

and cyclical unemployment. Years of high cyclical unemployment, like 1982 or 1992, were also years of a strongly negative output gap. Years of low cyclical unemployment, like the late 1960s or 2000, were also years of a strongly positive output gap.

The Short-Run Phillips Curve

We've just seen that expansionary policies lead to a lower unemployment rate. Our next step in understanding the temptations and dilemmas facing governments is to show that there is a short-run trade-off between unemployment and inflation—lower unemployment tends to lead to higher inflation, and vice versa. The key concept is that of the *Phillips curve.*

The origins of this concept lie in a famous 1958 paper by the New Zealand–born economist A.W.H. Phillips. Looking at historical data for Britain, he found that when the unemployment rate was high, the wage rate tended to fall, and when the unemployment rate was low, the wage rate tended to rise. Using data from Britain, the United States, and elsewhere, other economists soon found a similar apparent relationship between the unemployment rate and the rate of inflation—that is, the rate of change in the aggregate price level. For example, Figure 32-6 on the next page shows the U.S. unemployment rate and the rate of consumer price inflation over each subsequent year from 1955 to 1968, with each dot representing one year's data.

Looking at evidence like Figure 32-6, many economists concluded that there is a negative short-run relationship between the unemployment rate and the inflation rate, which is called the **short-run Phillips curve,** or *SRPC.* (We'll explain the difference between the short-run and the long-run Phillips curve soon.) Figure 32-7 on the next page shows a hypothetical short-run Phillips curve.

Early estimates of the short-run Phillips curve for the United States were very simple: they showed a negative relationship between the unemployment rate and

Okun's law is the negative relationship between the output gap and cyclical unemployment.

The **short-run Phillips curve** is the negative short-run relationship between the unemployment rate and the inflation rate.

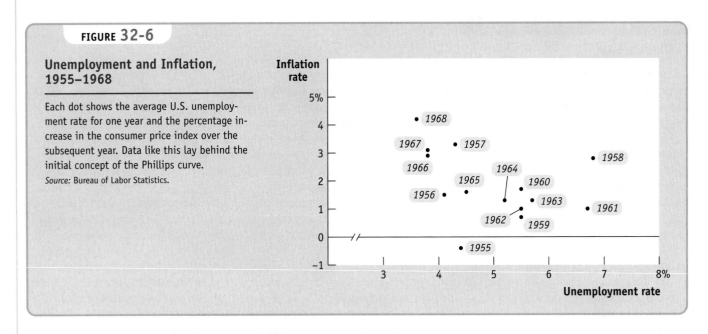

FIGURE 32-6

Unemployment and Inflation, 1955–1968

Each dot shows the average U.S. unemployment rate for one year and the percentage increase in the consumer price index over the subsequent year. Data like this lay behind the initial concept of the Phillips curve.

Source: Bureau of Labor Statistics.

the inflation rate, without taking account of any other variables. During the 1950s and 1960s this simple approach seemed, for a while, to be adequate. And this simple relationship is clear in the data in Figure 32-6.

Even at the time, however, some economists argued that a more accurate short-run Phillips curve would include other factors. In Chapter 28 we discussed the effect of *supply shocks,* such as sudden changes in the price of oil, which shift the short-run aggregate supply curve. Such shocks also shift the short-run Phillips curve: surging oil prices were an important factor in the inflation of the 1970s and also played an important role in the acceleration of inflation in 2007–2008. In general, a negative supply shock shifts *SRPC* up, as the inflation rate increases for every level of the unemployment rate, and a positive supply shock shifts it down as the inflation rate falls for every level of the unemployment rate. Both outcomes are shown in Figure 32-9.

But supply shocks are not the only factors that can change the inflation rate. In the early 1960s, Americans had little experience with inflation as inflation rates had been low for decades. But by the late 1960s, after inflation had been steadily increasing for a

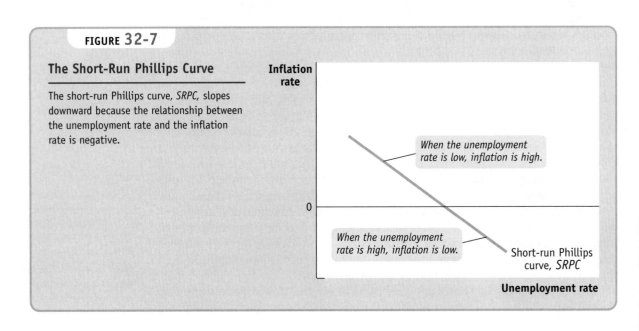

FIGURE 32-7

The Short-Run Phillips Curve

The short-run Phillips curve, *SRPC,* slopes downward because the relationship between the unemployment rate and the inflation rate is negative.

The Aggregate Supply Curve and the Short-Run Phillips Curve

In earlier chapters we made extensive use of the *AD–AS* model, in which the short-run aggregate supply curve—a relationship between real GDP and the aggregate price level—plays a central role. Now we've introduced the concept of the short-run Phillips curve, a relationship between the unemployment rate and the rate of inflation. How do these two concepts fit together?

We can get a partial answer to this question by looking at panel (a) of Figure 32-8, which shows how changes in the aggregate price level and the output gap depend on changes in aggregate demand. Assume that in year 1 the aggregate demand curve is AD_1, the long-run aggregate supply curve is *LRAS,* and the short-run aggregate supply curve is *SRAS.* The initial macroeconomic equilibrium is at E_1, where the price level is 100 and real GDP is \$10 trillion. Notice that at E_1 real GDP is equal to potential output, so the output gap is zero.

Now consider two possible paths for the economy over the next year. One is that aggregate demand remains unchanged and the economy stays at E_1. The other is that aggregate demand shifts rightward to AD_2 and the economy moves to E_2.

At E_2, real GDP is \$10.4 trillion, \$0.4 trillion more than potential output—a 4% output gap. Meanwhile, at E_2 the aggregate price level is 102—a 2% increase. So panel (a) tells us that in this example a zero output gap is associated with zero inflation and a 4% output gap is associated with 2% inflation.

Panel (b) shows what this implies for the relationship between unemployment and inflation. Assume that the natural rate of unemployment is 6% and that a rise of 1 percentage point in the output gap causes a fall of $1/2$ percentage point in the unemployment rate per Okun's law, described in the previous For Inquiring Minds. In that case, the two cases shown in panel (a)—aggregate demand either staying put or

rising—correspond to the two points in panel (b). At E_1, the unemployment rate is 6% and the inflation rate is 0%. At E_2, the unemployment rate is 4%, because an output gap of 4% reduces the unemployment rate by 4% × 0.5 = 2% below its natural rate of 6%—and the inflation rate is 2%. So there is a negative relationship between unemployment and inflation.

So does the short-run aggregate supply curve say exactly the same thing as the short-run Phillips curve? Not quite. The short-run aggregate supply curve seems to imply a relationship between the *change* in the unemployment rate and the inflation rate, but the short-run Phillips curve shows a relationship between the *level* of the unemployment rate and the inflation rate. Reconciling these views completely would go beyond the scope of this book. The important point is that the short-run Phillips curve is a concept that is closely related, though not identical, to the short-run aggregate supply curve.

FIGURE 32-8   **The *AD–AS* Model and the Short-Run Phillips Curve**

(a) An Increase in Aggregate Demand . . .

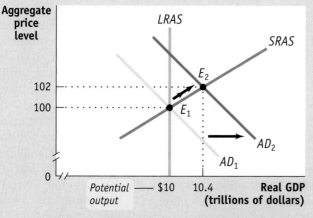

(b) . . . Leads to Both Inflation and a Fall in the Unemployment Rate.

The short-run Phillips curve is closely related to the short-run aggregate supply curve. In panel (a), the economy is initially in equilibrium at E_1, with the aggregate price level at 100 and aggregate output at \$10 trillion, which we assume is potential output. Now consider two possibilities. If the aggregate demand curve remains at AD_1, there is an output gap of zero and 0% inflation. If the aggregate demand curve

shifts out to AD_2, there is an output gap of 4%—reducing unemployment to 4%—and 2% inflation. Assuming that the natural rate of unemployment is 6%, the implications for unemployment and inflation are as follows, shown in panel (b): if aggregate demand does not increase, 6% unemployment and 0% inflation will result; if aggregate demand does increase, 4% unemployment and 2% inflation will result.

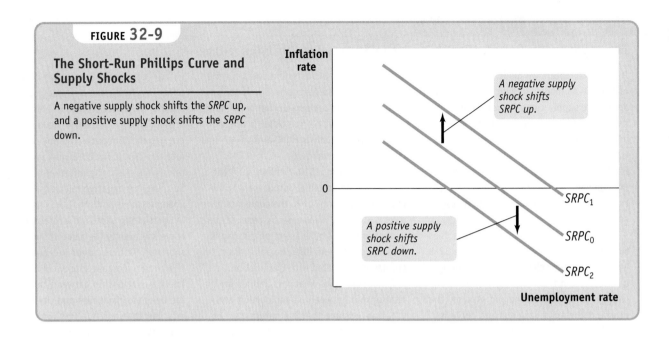

FIGURE 32-9

The Short-Run Phillips Curve and Supply Shocks

A negative supply shock shifts the *SRPC* up, and a positive supply shock shifts the *SRPC* down.

A negative supply shock shifts SRPC up.

A positive supply shock shifts SRPC down.

$SRPC_1$

$SRPC_0$

$SRPC_2$

Inflation rate

Unemployment rate

number of years, Americans had come to expect future inflation. In 1968 two economists—Milton Friedman of the University of Chicago and Edmund Phelps of Columbia University—independently set forth a crucial hypothesis: that expectations about future inflation directly affect the present inflation rate. Today most economists accept that the *expected inflation rate*—the rate of inflation that employers and workers expect in the near future—is the most important factor, other than the unemployment rate, affecting inflation.

Inflation Expectations and the Short-Run Phillips Curve

The expected rate of inflation is the rate of inflation that employers and workers expect in the near future. One of the crucial discoveries of modern macroeconomics is that changes in the expected rate of inflation affect the short-run trade-off between unemployment and inflation and shift the short-run Phillips curve.

Why do changes in expected inflation affect the short-run Phillips curve? Put yourself in the position of a worker or employer about to sign a contract setting the worker's wages over the next year. For a number of reasons, the wage rate they agree to will be higher if everyone expects high inflation (including rising wages) than if everyone expects prices to be stable. The worker will want a wage rate that takes into account future declines in the purchasing power of earnings. He or she will also want a wage rate that won't fall behind the wages of other workers. And the employer will be more willing to agree to a wage increase now if hiring workers later will be even more expensive. Also, rising prices will make paying a higher wage rate more affordable for the employer because the employer's output will sell for more.

For these reasons, an increase in expected inflation shifts the short-run Phillips curve upward: the actual rate of inflation at any given unemployment rate is higher when the expected inflation rate is higher. In fact, macroeconomists believe that the relationship between changes in expected inflation and changes in actual inflation is one-to-one. That is, when the expected inflation rate increases, the actual inflation rate at any given unemployment rate will increase by the same amount. When the expected inflation rate falls, the actual inflation rate at any given level of unemployment will fall by the same amount.

Figure 32-10 shows how the expected rate of inflation affects the short-run Phillips curve. First, suppose that the expected rate of inflation is 0%. $SRPC_0$ is the short-run Phillips curve when the public expects 0% inflation. According to $SRPC_0$,

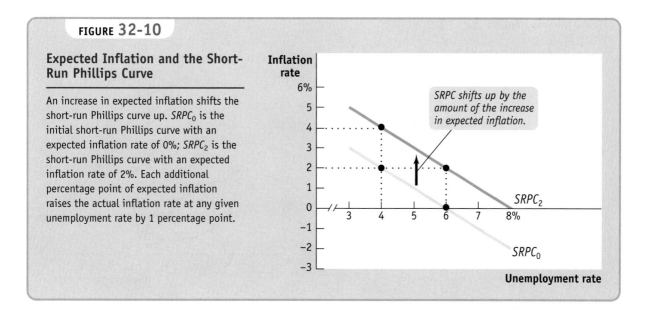

FIGURE 32-10

Expected Inflation and the Short-Run Phillips Curve

An increase in expected inflation shifts the short-run Phillips curve up. $SRPC_0$ is the initial short-run Phillips curve with an expected inflation rate of 0%; $SRPC_2$ is the short-run Phillips curve with an expected inflation rate of 2%. Each additional percentage point of expected inflation raises the actual inflation rate at any given unemployment rate by 1 percentage point.

SRPC shifts up by the amount of the increase in expected inflation.

the actual inflation rate will be 0% if the unemployment rate is 6%; it will be 2% if the unemployment rate is 4%.

Alternatively, suppose the expected rate of inflation is 2%. In that case, employers and workers will build this expectation into wages and prices: at any given unemployment rate, the actual inflation rate will be 2 percentage points higher than it would be if people expected 0% inflation. $SRPC_2$, which shows the Phillips curve when the expected inflation rate is 2%, is $SRPC_0$ shifted upward by 2 percentage points at every level of unemployment. According to $SRPC_2$, the actual inflation rate will be 2% if the unemployment rate is 6%; it will be 4% if the unemployment rate is 4%.

What determines the expected rate of inflation? In general, people base their expectations about inflation on experience. If the inflation rate has hovered around 0% in the last few years, people will expect it to be around 0% in the near future. But if the inflation rate has averaged around 5% lately, people will expect inflation to be around 5% in the near future.

Since expected inflation is an important part of the modern discussion about the short-run Phillips curve, you might wonder why it was not in the original formulation of the Phillips curve. The answer lies in history. Think back to what we said about the early 1960s: at that time, people were accustomed to low inflation rates and reasonably expected that future inflation rates would also be low. It was only after 1965 that persistent inflation became a fact of life. So only then did it become clear that expected inflation would play an important role in price-setting.

►*ECONOMICS IN ACTION*

From the Scary Seventies to the Nifty Nineties

Figure 32-6 showed that the American experience during the 1950s and 1960s supported the belief in the existence of a short-run Phillips curve for the U.S. economy, with a short-run trade-off between unemployment and inflation.

After 1969, however, that relationship appeared to fall apart according to the data. Figure 32-11 on the next page plots the track of U.S. unemployment and inflation rates from 1961 to 1990. As you can see, the track looks more like a tangled piece of yarn than like a smooth curve.

Through much of the 1970s and early 1980s, the economy suffered from a combination of above-average unemployment rates coupled with inflation rates unprecedented

FIGURE 32-11

Unemployment and Inflation, 1961–1990

During the 1970s, the short-run Phillips curve relationship that seemed to hold during the 1950s and 1960s broke down as the U.S. economy experienced a combination of high unemployment and high inflation. Economists believe this was the result both of negative supply shocks and the cumulative effect of several years of higher expected inflation. Inflation came down during the 1980s, and the 1990s were a time of both low unemployment and low inflation.

Source: Bureau of Labor Statistics.

in modern American history. This condition came to be known as *stagflation*—for stagnation combined with high inflation. In the late 1990s, by contrast, the economy was experiencing a blissful combination of low unemployment and low inflation. What explains these developments?

Part of the answer can be attributed to a series of negative supply shocks that the U.S. economy suffered during the 1970s. The price of oil, in particular, soared as wars and revolutions in the Middle East led to a reduction in oil supplies and as oil-exporting countries deliberately curbed production to drive up prices. Compounding the oil price shocks, there was also a slowdown in labor productivity growth. Both of these factors shifted the short-run Phillips curve upward. During the 1990s, by contrast, supply shocks were positive. Prices of oil and other raw materials were generally falling, and productivity growth accelerated. As a result, the short-run Phillips curve shifted downward.

Equally important, however, was the role of expected inflation. As mentioned earlier in the chapter, inflation accelerated during the 1960s. During the 1970s the public came to expect high inflation, and this also shifted the short-run Phillips curve up. It took a sustained and costly effort during the 1980s to get inflation back down. The result, however, was that expected inflation was very low by the late 1990s, allowing actual inflation to be low even with low rates of unemployment. ▲

< < < < < < < < < < <

► CHECK YOUR UNDERSTANDING 32-2

1. Explain how the short-run Phillips curve illustrates the negative relationship between cyclical unemployment and the actual inflation rate for a given level of the expected inflation rate.

2. Which way does the short-run Phillips curve move in response to a fall in commodities prices? To a surge in commodities prices? Explain.

Solutions appear at back of book.

Inflation and Unemployment in the Long Run

The short-run Phillips curve says that at any given point in time there is a trade-off between unemployment and inflation. According to this view, policy makers have a choice: they can choose to accept the price of high inflation in order to achieve low unemployment. In fact, during the 1960s many economists believed that this trade-off represented a real choice.

However, this view was greatly altered by the later recognition that expected inflation affects the short-run Phillips curve. In the short run, expectations often diverge from reality. In the long run, however, any consistent rate of inflation will be reflected in expectations. If inflation is consistently high, as it was in the 1970s, people will come to expect more of the same; if inflation is consistently low, as it has been in recent years, that, too, will become part of expectations.

So what does the trade-off between inflation and unemployment look like in the long run, when actual inflation is incorporated into expectations? Most macroeconomists believe that there is, in fact, no long-run trade-off. That is, it is not possible to achieve lower unemployment in the long run by accepting higher inflation. To see why, we need to introduce another concept: the *long-run Phillips curve*.

The Long-Run Phillips Curve

Figure 32-12 reproduces the two short-run Phillips curves from Figure 32-10, $SRPC_0$ and $SRPC_2$. It also adds an additional short-run Phillips curve, $SRPC_4$, representing a 4% expected rate of inflation. In a moment, we'll explain the significance of the vertical long-run Phillips curve, $LRPC$.

Suppose that the economy has, in the past, had a 0% inflation rate. In that case, the current short-run Phillips curve will be $SRPC_0$, reflecting a 0% expected inflation rate. If the unemployment rate is 6%, the actual inflation rate will be 0%.

Also suppose that policy makers decide to trade off lower unemployment for a higher rate of inflation. They use monetary policy, fiscal policy, or both to drive the unemployment rate down to 4%. This puts the economy at point A on $SRPC_0$, leading to an actual inflation rate of 2%.

Over time, the public will come to expect a 2% inflation rate. *This increase in inflationary expectations will shift the short-run Phillips curve upward to $SRPC_2$*. Now, when the unemployment rate is 6%, the actual inflation rate will be 2%. Given this new short-run Phillips curve, policies adopted to keep the unemployment rate at 4% will lead to a 4% actual inflation rate—point B on $SRPC_2$—rather than point A with a 2% actual inflation rate.

Eventually, the 4% actual inflation rate gets built into expectations about the future inflation rate, and the short-run Phillips curve shifts upward yet again to $SRPC_4$. To keep the unemployment rate at 4% would now require accepting a 6% actual inflation rate, point C on $SRPC_4$, and so on. In short, a persistent attempt to trade off lower unemployment for higher inflation leads to *accelerating* inflation over time.

FIGURE 32-12

The NAIRU and the Long-Run Phillips Curve

$SRPC_0$ is the short-run Phillips curve when the expected inflation rate is 0%. At a 4% unemployment rate, the economy is at point A with an actual inflation rate of 2%. The higher inflation rate will be incorporated into expectations, and the $SRPC$ will shift upward to $SRPC_2$. If policy makers act to keep the unemployment rate at 4%, the economy will be at B and the actual inflation rate will rise to 4%. Inflationary expectations will be revised upward again, and $SRPC$ will shift to $SRPC_4$. At a 4% unemployment rate, the economy will be at C and the actual inflation rate will rise to 6%. Here, an unemployment rate of 6% is the NAIRU, or nonaccelerating inflation rate of unemployment. As long as unemployment is at the NAIRU, the actual inflation rate will match expectations and remain constant. An unemployment rate below 6% requires ever-accelerating inflation. The long-run Phillips curve, $LRPC$, which passes through E_0, E_2, and E_4, is vertical: no long-run trade-off between unemployment and inflation exists.

The **nonaccelerating inflation rate of unemployment,** or **NAIRU,** is the unemployment rate at which inflation does not change over time.

The **long-run Phillips curve** shows the relationship between unemployment and inflation after expectations of inflation have had time to adjust to experience.

Disinflation is the process of bringing down inflation that is embedded in expectations.

To avoid accelerating inflation over time, the unemployment rate must be high enough that the actual rate of inflation matches the expected rate of inflation. This is the situation at E_0 on $SRPC_0$: when the expected inflation rate is 0% and the unemployment rate is 6%, the actual inflation rate is 0%. It is also the situation at E_2 on $SRPC_2$: when the expected inflation rate is 2% and the unemployment rate is 6%, the actual inflation rate is 2%. And it is the situation at E_4 on $SRPC_4$: when the expected inflation rate is 4% and the unemployment rate is 6%, the actual inflation rate is 4%. As we'll learn in the next chapter, this relationship between accelerating inflation and the unemployment rate is known as the *natural rate hypothesis.*

The unemployment rate at which inflation does not change over time—6% in Figure 32-12—is known as the **nonaccelerating inflation rate of unemployment,** or **NAIRU** for short. Keeping the unemployment rate below the NAIRU leads to ever-accelerating inflation and cannot be maintained. Most macroeconomists believe that there is a NAIRU and that there is no long-run trade-off between unemployment and inflation.

We can now explain the significance of the vertical line *LRPC.* It is the **long-run Phillips curve,** the relationship between unemployment and inflation in the long run, after expectations of inflation have had time to adjust to experience. It is vertical because any unemployment rate below the NAIRU leads to ever-accelerating inflation. In other words, the long-run Phillips curve shows that there are limits to expansionary policies because an unemployment rate below the NAIRU cannot be maintained in the long run. Moreover there is a corresponding point we have not yet emphasized: any unemployment rate above the NAIRU leads to decelerating inflation.

The Natural Rate of Unemployment, Revisited

Recall the concept of the natural rate of unemployment, the portion of the unemployment rate unaffected by the swings of the business cycle. Now we have introduced the concept of the *NAIRU.* How do these two concepts relate to each other?

The answer is that the NAIRU is another name for the natural rate. The level of unemployment the economy "needs" in order to avoid accelerating inflation is equal to the natural rate of unemployment.

In fact, economists estimate the natural rate of unemployment by looking for evidence about the NAIRU from the behavior of the inflation rate and the unemployment rate over the course of the business cycle. For example, the way major European countries learned, to their dismay, that their natural rates of unemployment were 9% or more was through unpleasant experience. In the late 1980s, and again in the late 1990s, European inflation began to accelerate as European unemployment rates, which had been above 9%, began to fall, approaching 8%.

In Figure 32-5 we cited Congressional Budget Office estimates of the U.S. natural rate of unemployment. The CBO has a model that predicts changes in the inflation rate based on the deviation of the actual unemployment rate from the natural rate. Given data on actual unemployment and inflation, this model can be used to deduce estimates of the natural rate—and that's where the CBO numbers come from.

The Costs of Disinflation

Through experience, policy makers have found that bringing inflation down is a much harder task than increasing it. The reason is that once the public has come to expect continuing inflation, bringing inflation down is painful.

A persistent attempt to keep unemployment below the natural rate leads to accelerating inflation that becomes incorporated into expectations. To reduce inflationary expectations, policy makers need to run the process in reverse, adopting contractionary policies that keep the unemployment rate above the natural rate for an extended period of time. The process of bringing down inflation that has become embedded in expectations is known as **disinflation.**

GLOBAL COMPARISON DISINFLATION AROUND THE WORLD

The great disinflation of the 1980s wasn't unique to the United States. A number of other advanced countries also experienced high inflation during the 1970s, then brought inflation down during the 1980s at the cost of a severe recession. This figure shows the annual rate of inflation in Britain, Italy, and the United States from 1970 to 2007. All three nations experienced high inflation rates following the two oil shocks of 1973 and 1979, with the U.S. inflation rate the least severe of the three. All three nations then weathered severe recessions in order to bring inflation down. Since the 1980s, inflation has remained low and stable in all wealthy nations.

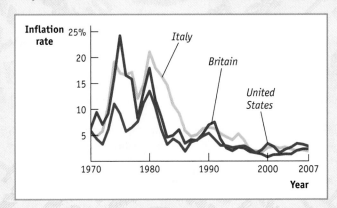

Source: OECD.

Disinflation can be very expensive. As the following Economics in Action documents, the U.S. retreat from high inflation at the beginning of the 1980s appears to have cost the equivalent of about 18% of a year's real GDP, the equivalent of roughly $2.6 trillion today. The justification for paying these costs is that they lead to a permanent gain. Although the economy does not recover the short-term production losses caused by disinflation, it no longer suffers from the costs associated with persistently high inflation. In fact, the United States, Britain, and other wealthy countries that experienced inflation in the 1970s eventually decided that the benefit of bringing inflation down was worth the required suffering—the large reduction in real GDP in the short term.

Some economists argue that the costs of disinflation can be reduced if policy makers explicitly state their determination to reduce inflation. A clearly announced, credible policy of disinflation, they contend, can reduce expectations of future inflation and so shift the short-run Phillips curve downward. Some economists believe that the clear determination of the Federal Reserve to combat the inflation of the 1970s was credible enough that the costs of disinflation, huge though they were, were lower than they might otherwise have been.

►ECONOMICS IN ACTION

The Great Disinflation of the 1980s

As we've mentioned several times in this chapter, the United States ended the 1970s with a high rate of inflation, at least by its own peacetime historical standards—13% in 1980. Part of this inflation was the result of one-time events, especially a world oil crisis. But expectations of future inflation at 10% or more per year appeared to be firmly embedded in the economy.

FIGURE 32-13   The Great Disinflation

(a) The Core Inflation Rate in the United States Came Down in the 1980s . . .

(b) . . . but Only at the Expense of a Huge Sacrifice of Output and High Unemployment.

Panel (a) shows the U.S. *core inflation rate,* which excludes food and energy. It shows the sharp fall in inflation during the 1980s. Panel (b) shows that disinflation came at a heavy cost: the economy developed a huge output gap, and actual aggregate output didn't return to potential output until 1987.

If you add up the output gaps over the period, you find that the economy sacrificed about 18% of a year's real GDP. If we had to do that today, it would mean giving up roughly $2.6 trillion in goods and services.

Sources: Bureau of Labor Statistics; Congressional Budget Office.

By the mid-1980s, however, inflation was running at about 4% per year. Panel (a) of Figure 32-13 shows the annual rate of change in the "core" consumer price index (CPI)—also called the *core inflation rate.* This index, which excludes volatile energy and food prices, is widely regarded as a better indicator of underlying inflation trends than the overall CPI. By this measure, inflation fell from about 12% at the end of the 1970s to about 4% by the mid-1980s.

How was this disinflation achieved? At great cost. Beginning in late 1979, the Federal Reserve imposed strongly contractionary monetary policies, which pushed the economy into its worst recession since the Great Depression. Panel (b) shows the Congressional Budget Office estimate of the U.S. output gap from 1979 to 1989: by 1982, actual output was 7% below potential output, corresponding to an unemployment rate of more than 9%. Aggregate output didn't get back to potential output until 1987.

Our analysis of the Phillips curve tells us that a temporary rise in unemployment, like that of the 1980s, is needed to break the cycle of inflationary expectations. Once expectations of inflation are reduced, the economy can return to the natural rate of unemployment at a lower inflation rate. And that's just what happened.

But the cost was huge. If you add up the output gap over 1980–1987, you find that the economy sacrificed approximately 18% of an average year's output over the period. If we had to do the same thing today, that would mean giving up roughly $2.6 trillion worth of goods and services. ▲

< < < < < < < < < < <

▶ **CHECK YOUR UNDERSTANDING** 32-3

1. Why is there no long-run trade-off between unemployment and inflation?

2. British economists believe that the natural rate of unemployment in that country rose sharply during the 1970s, from around 3% to as much as 10%. During that period, Britain experienced a sharp acceleration of inflation, which for a time went above 20%. How might these facts be related?

3. Why is disinflation so costly for an economy? Are there ways to reduce these costs?

Solutions appear at back of book.

Deflation

Before World War II, *deflation*—a falling aggregate price level—was almost as common as inflation. In fact, the U.S. consumer price index on the eve of World War II was 30% lower than it had been in 1920. After World War II, inflation became the norm in all countries. But in the 1990s, deflation reappeared in Japan and proved difficult to reverse. Concerns about potential deflation played a crucial role in U.S. monetary policy in the early 2000s and again in late 2008.

Why is deflation a problem? And why is it hard to end?

Debt Deflation

Deflation, like inflation, produces both winners and losers—but in the opposite direction. Due to the falling price level, a dollar in the future has a higher real value than a dollar today. So lenders, who are owed money, gain under deflation because the real value of borrowers' payments increases. Borrowers lose because the real burden of their debt rises.

In a famous analysis at the beginning of the Great Depression, Irving Fisher (who first analyzed the *Fisher effect* of expected inflation on interest rates, described in Chapter 26) claimed that the effects of deflation on borrowers and lenders can worsen an economic slump. Deflation, in effect, takes real resources away from borrowers and redistributes them to lenders. Fisher argued that borrowers, who lose from deflation, are typically short of cash and will be forced to cut their spending sharply when their debt burden rises. Lenders, however, are less likely to increase spending sharply when the values of the loans they own rise. The overall effect, said Fisher, is that deflation reduces aggregate demand, deepening an economic slump, which, in a vicious circle, may lead to further deflation. The effect of deflation in reducing aggregate demand, known as **debt deflation,** probably played a significant role in the Great Depression.

Effects of Expected Deflation

Like expected inflation, expected deflation affects the nominal interest rate. Look back at Figure 26-7, which demonstrated how expected inflation affects the equilibrium interest rate. In Figure 26-7, the equilibrium nominal interest rate is 4% if the expected inflation rate is 0%. Clearly, if the expected inflation rate is −3%—if the public expects deflation at 3% per year—the equilibrium nominal interest rate will be 1%.

But what would happen if the expected rate of inflation is −5%? Would the nominal interest rate fall to −1%, in which lenders are paying borrowers 1% on their debt? No. Nobody would lend money at a negative nominal rate of interest because they could do better by simply holding cash. This illustrates what economists call the **zero bound** on the nominal interest rate: it cannot go below zero.

This zero bound can limit the effectiveness of monetary policy. Suppose the economy is depressed, with output below potential output and the unemployment rate above the natural rate. Normally the central bank can respond by cutting interest rates so as to increase aggregate demand. If the nominal interest rate is already zero, however, the central bank cannot push it down any further. Banks refuse to lend and consumers and firms refuse to spend because, with a negative inflation rate and a 0% nominal interest rate, holding cash yields a positive real interest rate. Any further increases in the monetary base will either be held in bank vaults or held as cash by individuals and firms, without being spent.

A situation in which conventional monetary policy to fight a slump—cutting interest rates—can't be used because nominal interest rates are up against the zero bound is known as a **liquidity trap.** A liquidity trap can occur whenever there is a sharp reduction in demand for loanable funds—which is exactly what happened during the Great Depression. Figure 32-14 on the next page shows the interest rate on short-term U.S.

Debt deflation is the reduction in aggregate demand arising from the increase in the real burden of outstanding debt caused by deflation.

There is a **zero bound** on the nominal interest rate: it cannot go below zero.

A **liquidity trap** is a situation in which conventional monetary policy is ineffective because nominal interest rates are up against the zero bound.

FIGURE **32-14**

The Zero Bound in U.S. History

This figure shows U.S. short-term interest rates, specifically the interest rate on three-month Treasury bills, since 1920. As shown by the shaded area at left, for much of the 1930s, interest rates were very close to zero, leaving little room for expansionary monetary policy. After World War II, persistent inflation generally kept rates well above zero. However, in late 2008, in the wake of the housing bubble bursting and the financial crisis, the interest rate on three-month Treasury bills was again virtually zero.

Source: Federal Reserve Bank of St. Louis.

government debt from 1920 to December 2008. As you can see, from 1933 until World War II brought a full economic recovery, the U.S. economy was either close to or up against the zero bound. After World War II, when inflation became the norm around the world, the zero bound largely vanished as a problem as the public came to expect inflation rather than deflation.

However, the recent history of the Japanese economy, shown in Figure 32-15, provides a modern illustration of the problem of deflation and the liquidity trap. Japan experienced a huge boom in the prices of both stocks and real estate in the late 1980s, then saw both bubbles burst. The result was a prolonged period of economic stagnation, the so-called Lost Decade, which gradually reduced the inflation rate and eventually led to persistent deflation. In an effort to fight the weakness of the economy, the Bank of Japan—the equivalent of the Federal

FIGURE **32-15**

Japan's Lost Decade

A prolonged economic slump in Japan led to deflation from the late 1990s on. The Bank of Japan responded by cutting interest rates—but eventually ran up against the zero bound.

Source: OECD.

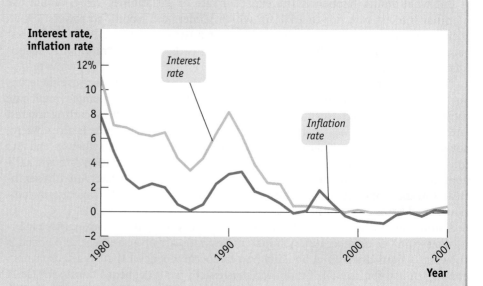

Reserve—repeatedly cut interest rates. Eventually, it arrived at the ZIRP: the zero interest rate policy. The call money rate, the equivalent of the U.S. federal funds rate, was literally set equal to zero. Because the economy was still depressed, it would have been desirable to cut interest rates even further. But that wasn't possible: Japan was up against the zero bound.

As this book goes to press, the Federal Reserve also finds itself up against the zero bound. In the aftermath of the bursting of the housing bubble and the ensuing financial crisis, in late 2008 the interest on short-term U.S. government debt had fallen to virtually zero. As we discuss in the following Economics in Action, the Fed has turned to unconventional monetary policy as conventional policy has been rendered ineffective.

➤ECONOMICS IN ACTION

Turning Unconventional

In 2004, in response to fears of an overheating economy, the Federal Reserve began raising the target federal funds rate. As you can see in Figure 32-16, the rate went from 1% in mid-2004 to 5.25% by mid-2006. As intended, the increases slowed the economy and eventually pricked the housing bubble, the unsustainably high level of house prices that had developed when interest rates were low.

From mid-2006 to mid-2007, believing that troubles in the housing market would stay contained there, the Fed kept monetary policy unchanged. In mid-2007, however, a sharp increase in mortgage defaults led to massive losses in the banking industry and a financial meltdown. At first the Fed was slow to react; but by September 2007, stung by criticism that it was at risk of "getting behind the curve" in rescuing the economy, it began lowering the federal funds rate aggressively.

Why the sharp about-face by the Federal Reserve? Part of the answer lies in the background of Ben Bernanke, Chairman of the Fed. Bernanke, an authority on monetary policy and the Great Depression, understood the threat of deflation arising

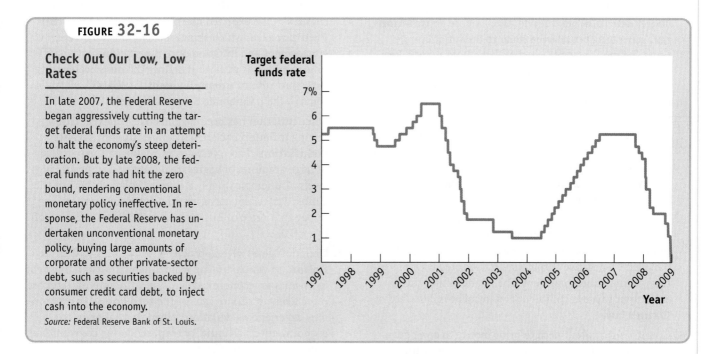

FIGURE 32-16

Check Out Our Low, Low Rates

In late 2007, the Federal Reserve began aggressively cutting the target federal funds rate in an attempt to halt the economy's steep deterioration. But by late 2008, the federal funds rate had hit the zero bound, rendering conventional monetary policy ineffective. In response, the Federal Reserve has undertaken unconventional monetary policy, buying large amounts of corporate and other private-sector debt, such as securities backed by consumer credit card debt, to inject cash into the economy.

Source: Federal Reserve Bank of St. Louis.

from a severe slump and how it could lead to a liquidity trap. Through repeated interest rate cuts, the Fed attempted to get back "ahead of the curve" to stabilize the economy and prevent deflationary expectations that could lead to a liquidity trap.

By the time this book went to press in December 2008, the federal funds rate had been cut to 0%, reaching the zero bound. The economy continued to deteriorate, although it's not yet clear that the economy is experiencing deflation. Understanding the limits of conventional monetary policy, Bernanke has engaged in "unconventional" monetary policy, such as buying large amounts of corporate debt to inject more cash into the economy. Understanding the urgency of the situation, the Fed has turned from conventional central bank to unconventional lender of last resort. ▲

< < < < < < < < < < < <

> CHECK YOUR UNDERSTANDING 32-4

1. Why won't anyone lend money at a negative nominal rate of interest? How can this pose problems for monetary policy?

Solution appears at back of book.

[>> A LOOK AHEAD •••

As we saw in this chapter, the breakdown of the simple Phillips curve in the 1970s led to a major change in economists' understanding of the relationship between inflation and unemployment. This was a prime example of how real-world experience combines with developments in theory to drive the evolution of macroeconomic thought. In the next chapter, we'll look at how events and ideas have interacted to drive the evolution of macroeconomics over the past 70 years.]

SUMMARY ....■

1. In analyzing high inflation, economists use the **classical model of the price level,** which says that changes in the money supply lead to proportional changes in the aggregate price level even in the short run.

2. Governments sometimes print money in order to finance budget deficits. When they do, they impose an **inflation tax,** generating tax revenue equal to the inflation rate times the money supply, on those who hold money. Revenue from the real inflation tax, the inflation rate times the real money supply, is the real value of resources captured by the government. In order to avoid paying the inflation tax, people reduce their real money holdings and force the government to increase inflation to capture the same amount of real inflation tax revenue. In some cases, this leads to a vicious circle of a shrinking real money supply and a rising rate of inflation, leading to hyperinflation and a fiscal crisis.

3. The output gap is the percentage difference between the actual level of real GDP and potential output. A positive output gap is associated with lower-than-normal unemployment; a negative output gap is associated with higher-than-normal unemployment. The relationship between the output gap and cyclical unemployment is described by **Okun's law.**

4. Countries that don't need to print money to cover government deficits can still stumble into moderate infla-

tion, either because of political opportunism or because of wishful thinking.

5. At a given point in time, there is a downward-sloping relationship between unemployment and inflation known as the **short-run Phillips curve.** This curve is shifted by changes in the expected rate of inflation. The **long-run Phillips curve,** which shows the relationship between unemployment and inflation once expectations have had time to adjust, is vertical. It defines the **nonaccelerating inflation rate of unemployment,** or **NAIRU,** which is equal to the natural rate of unemployment.

6. Once inflation has become embedded in expectations, getting inflation back down can be difficult because **disinflation** can be very costly, requiring the sacrifice of large amounts of aggregate output and imposing high levels of unemployment. However, policy makers in the United States and other wealthy countries were willing to pay that price of bringing down the high inflation of the 1970s.

7. Deflation poses several problems. It can lead to **debt deflation,** in which a rising real burden of outstanding debt intensifies an economic downturn. Also, interest rates are more likely to run up against the **zero bound** in an economy experiencing deflation. When this happens, the economy enters a **liquidity trap,** rendering conventional monetary policy ineffective.

KEY TERMS ■

Classical model of the price level, p. 860
Inflation tax, p. 864
Okun's law, p. 869
Short-run Phillips curve, p. 869

Nonaccelerating inflation rate of
    unemployment (NAIRU), p. 876
Long-run Phillips curve, p. 876
Disinflation, p. 876

Debt deflation, p. 879
Zero bound, p. 879
Liquidity trap, p. 879

PROBLEMS ■

1. In the economy of Scottopia, policy makers want to lower the unemployment rate and raise real GDP by using monetary policy. Using the accompanying diagram, show why this policy will ultimately result in a higher aggregate price level but no change in real GDP.

2. In the following examples, would the classical model of the price level be relevant?

a. There is a great deal of unemployment in the economy and no history of inflation.

b. The economy has just experienced five years of hyperinflation.

c. Although the economy experienced inflation in the 10% to 20% range three years ago, prices have recently been stable and the unemployment rate has approximated the natural rate of unemployment.

3. The Federal Reserve regularly releases data on the U.S. monetary base. You can access that data at various websites, including the website for the Federal Reserve Bank of St. Louis. Go to http://research.stlouisfed.org/fred2/ and click on "Reserves and Monetary Base," then on "Monetary Base," and then on "Board of Governors Monetary Base, Adjusted for Changes in Reserve Requirements" for the latest report. Use the Seasonally Adjusted (SA) series.

a. How much did the monetary base grow in the last month?

b. How did this help in the government's efforts to finance its deficit?

c. Why is it important for the central bank to be independent from the part of the government responsible for spending?

4. Answer the following questions about the (real) inflation tax, assuming that the price level starts at 1.

a. Maria Moneybags keeps $1,000 in her sock drawer for a year. Over the year, the inflation rate is 10%. What is the real inflation tax paid by Maria for this year?

b. Maria continues to keep the $1,000 in her drawer for a second year. What is the real value of this $1,000 at the beginning of the second year? Over the year, the inflation rate is again 10%. What is the real inflation tax paid by Maria for the second year?

c. For a third year, Maria keeps the $1,000 in the drawer. What is the real value of this $1,000 at the beginning of the third year? Over the year, the inflation rate is again 10%. What is the real inflation tax paid by Maria for the third year?

d. After three years, what is the cumulative real inflation tax paid?

e. Redo parts a through d with an inflation rate of 25%. Why is hyperinflation such a problem?

5. The inflation tax is often used as a significant source of revenue in developing countries where the tax collection and reporting system is not well developed and tax evasion may be high.

a. Use the numbers in the accompanying table to calculate the inflation tax in the United States and India (Rp = rupees).

	Inflation in 2006	Money supply in 2006 (billions)	Total government receipts in 2006 (billions)
India	5.79%	Rp8,070	Rp3,480
United States	3.23	$1,380	$2,200

Sources: IMF statistics and the budget offices of India and the United States.

b. How large is the inflation tax for the two countries when calculated as a percentage of government receipts?

6. Concerned about the crowding-out effects of government borrowing on private investment spending, a candidate for president argues that the United States should just print money to cover the government's budget deficit. What are the advantages and disadvantages of such a plan?

7. The accompanying scatter diagram shows the relationship between the unemployment rate and the output gap in the United States from 1990 to 2004. Draw a straight line through the scatter of dots in the figure. Assume that this line represents Okun's law:

Unemployment rate = $b - (m \times$ Output gap)
where b is the vertical intercept and $-m$ is the slope

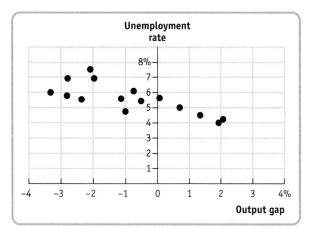

What is the unemployment rate when aggregate output equals potential output? What would the unemployment rate be if the output gap was 2%? What if the output gap was −3%? What do these results tell us about the coefficient m in Okun's law?

8. After experiencing a recession for the past two years, the residents of Albernia were looking forward to a decrease in the unemployment rate. Yet after six months of strong positive economic growth, the unemployment rate has fallen only slightly below what it was at the end of the recession. How can you explain why the unemployment rate did not fall as much although the economy was experiencing strong economic growth?

9. Due to historical differences, countries often differ in how quickly a change in actual inflation is incorporated into a change in expected inflation. In a country such as Japan, which has had very little inflation in recent memory, it will take longer for a change in the actual inflation rate to be reflected in a corresponding change in the expected inflation rate. In contrast, in a country such as Zimbabwe, which has recently had very high inflation, a change in the actual inflation rate will immediately be reflected in a corresponding change in the expected inflation rate. What does this imply about the short-run and long-run Phillips curves in these two types of countries? What does this imply about the effectiveness of monetary and fiscal policy to reduce the unemployment rate?

10. The accompanying table shows data for the average annual rates of unemployment and inflation for the economy of Brittania from 1998 to 2007. Use it to construct a scatter plot similar to Figure 32-6.

Year	Unemployment rate	Inflation rate
1998	4.0%	2.5%
1999	2.0	5.0
2000	10.0	1.0
2001	8.0	1.3
2002	5.0	2.0
2003	2.5	4.0
2004	6.0	1.7
2005	1.0	10.0
2006	3.0	3.0
2007	7.0	1.5

Are the data consistent with a short-run Phillips curve? If the government pursues expansionary monetary policies in the future to keep the unemployment rate below the natural rate of unemployment, how effective will such a policy be?

11. The accompanying table provides data from the United States on the average annual rates of unemployment and inflation. Use the numbers to construct a scatter plot similar to Figure 32-6. Discuss why, in the short run, the unemployment rate rises when inflation falls.

Year	Unemployment rate	Inflation rate
2000	4.0%	3.4%
2001	4.7	2.8
2002	5.8	1.6
2003	6.0	2.3
2004	5.5	2.7
2005	5.1	3.4
2006	4.6	3.2
2007	4.6	2.9

Source: IMF.

12. The economy of Brittania has been suffering from high inflation with an unemployment rate equal to its natural rate. Policy makers would like to disinflate the economy with the lowest economic cost possible. Assume that the state of the economy is not the result of a negative supply shock. How can they try to minimize the unemployment cost of disinflation? Is it possible for there to be no cost of disinflation?

13. Who are the winners and losers when a mortgage company lends $100,000 to the Miller family to buy a house worth $105,000 and during the first year prices unexpectedly fall by 10%? What would you expect to happen if the deflation continued over the next few years? How would continuing deflation affect borrowers and lenders throughout the economy as a whole?

>> # Macroeconomics: Events and Ideas

ALL AVAILABLE TOOLS

"AGGRESSIVE MONETARY POLICY," DEclared the 2004 Economic Report of the President, "can reduce the depth of a recession." Few modern macroeconomists would disagree. There are many public arguments about macroeconomic policy—arguments that can play a central role in political campaigns. But there is a broad consensus among macroeconomists about how the economy works. The view that expansionary monetary policy can be effective in fighting recessions is part of that consensus. And that consensus is reflected in actual policy: as the two panels of the accompanying figure show, monetary policy responded very aggressively to the 2001 recession.

Nor is the Federal Reserve, which controls U.S. monetary policy, shy about taking responsibility for managing the economy. Late in 2008, the National Bureau of Economic Research officially confirmed what most economists already suspected, namely, that the United States had been in a recession since December 2007. Shortly after this report, the Fed, faced with falling real GDP, sharply rising unemployment, and new fears of possible deflation, cut its target interest rate all the way to zero—and declared its willingness to do even more, if necessary. "The Federal Reserve," said the official statement, "will employ all available tools to promote the resumption of sustainable economic growth and to preserve price stability." Most macroeconomists cheered this declaration: faced with a troubled economy, they believed, it was only prudent for the Fed to do whatever it takes to turn things around.

Yet today's consensus about monetary policy didn't always exist. Indeed, there was a time when many economists

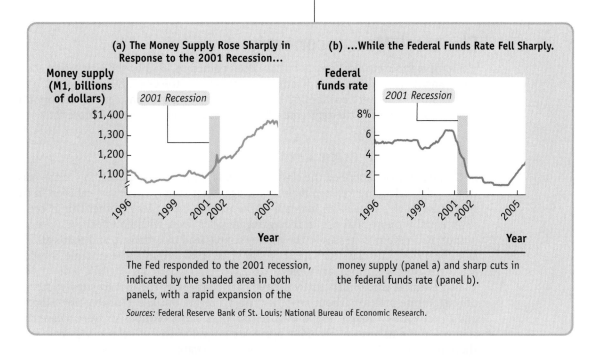

(a) The Money Supply Rose Sharply in Response to the 2001 Recession...

Money supply (M1, billions of dollars)

2001 Recession

(b) ...While the Federal Funds Rate Fell Sharply.

Federal funds rate

2001 Recession

The Fed responded to the 2001 recession, indicated by the shaded area in both panels, with a rapid expansion of the money supply (panel a) and sharp cuts in the federal funds rate (panel b).

Sources: Federal Reserve Bank of St. Louis; National Bureau of Economic Research.

opposed any effort to fight recessions. In Chapter 22 we described how, at the beginning of the Great Depression, Herbert Hoover's secretary of the Treasury actually argued that the slump would be good for the economy in the long run, and how his position was supported by many eminent economists of the day.

When Franklin Roosevelt, Hoover's successor, took office, there was an intense debate among his advisers about whether to pursue expansionary monetary and fiscal policies or to do the opposite. When the expansionists won the debate and the United States went off the gold standard in order to permit monetary expansion, Roosevelt's budget director declared, "This is the end of Western civilization." As far as we can tell, Western civilization is still standing.

How did we get from there to here? How did modern macroeconomics evolve? In preceding chapters we've developed a framework for understanding growth, the

President Franklin Delano Roosevelt used expansionary fiscal and monetary policy to battle the Great Depression.

business cycle, and inflation. In this chapter, we'll look at how this framework was created—how events and ideas interacted in the making of modern macroeconomics.

WHAT YOU WILL LEARN IN THIS CHAPTER:

➤ Why classical macroeconomics wasn't adequate for the problems posed by the Great Depression

➤ How Keynes and the experience of the Great Depression legitimized **macroeconomic policy activism**

➤ What **monetarism** is and its views about the limits of **discretionary monetary policy**

➤ How challenges led to a revision of Keynesian ideas and the emergence of the **new classical macroeconomics**

➤ The elements of the modern consensus and the main remaining disputes

---

Classical Macroeconomics

The term *macroeconomics* appears to have been coined in 1933 by the Norwegian economist Ragnar Frisch. The date, during the worst year of the Great Depression, is no accident. Still, there were economists analyzing what we now consider macroeconomic issues—the behavior of the aggregate price level and aggregate output—before then.

Money and the Price Level

In Chapter 32, we described the *classical model of the price level.* According to the classical model, prices are flexible, making the aggregate supply curve vertical even in the short run. In this model, an increase in the money supply leads, other things equal, to an equal proportional rise in the aggregate price level, with no effect on aggregate output. As a result, increases in the money supply lead to inflation, and that's all. Before the 1930s, the classical model of the price level dominated economic thinking about the effects of monetary policy.

Did classical economists really believe that changes in the money supply affected only aggregate prices, without any effect on aggregate output? Probably not. Historians of economic thought argue that before 1930 most economists were aware that changes in the money supply affect aggregate output as well as aggregate prices in the short run—or, to use modern terms, they were aware that the short-run aggregate supply curve slopes upward. But they regarded such short-run effects as unimportant, stressing the long run instead. It was this attitude that led John Maynard Keynes to scoff at the focus on the long run, in which, as he said, "we are all dead."

The Business Cycle

Classical economists were, of course, also aware that the economy did not grow smoothly. The American economist Wesley Mitchell pioneered the quantitative study of business cycles. In 1920 he founded the National Bureau of Economic Research, an independent, nonprofit organization that to this day has the official role of declaring the beginnings of recessions and expansions. Thanks to Mitchell's work, the *measurement* of business cycles was well advanced by 1930. But there was no widely accepted *theory* of business cycles.

In the absence of any clear theory, views about how policy makers should respond to a recession were conflicting. Some economists favored expansionary monetary and fiscal policies to fight a recession. Others believed that such policies would worsen the slump or merely postpone the inevitable. For example, in 1934 Harvard's Joseph Schumpeter, now famous for his early recognition of the importance of technological change, warned that any attempt to alleviate the Great Depression with expansionary monetary policy "would, in the end, lead to a collapse worse than the one it was called in to remedy." When the Great Depression hit, policy was paralyzed by this lack of consensus. In many cases, economists now believe, policy moved in the wrong direction.

Necessity was, however, the mother of invention. As we'll explain next, the Great Depression provided a strong incentive for economists to develop theories that could serve as a guide to policy—and economists responded.

➤ ECONOMICS IN ACTION

When Did the Business Cycle Begin?

The official chronology of past U.S. business cycles maintained by the National Bureau of Economic Research goes back only to 1854. There are two reasons for this. One is that the farther back in time you go, the less economic data are available. The other is that business cycles, in the modern sense, may have not occurred in the United States before 1854.

In the first half of the nineteenth century the United States had an overwhelmingly rural, agricultural economy. Figure 33-1 shows estimates of the changing percentages

---

FIGURE 33-1

The Changing Character of the Nineteenth-Century Economy

In the first half of the nineteenth century, the United States had an overwhelmingly agricultural economy and probably didn't experience modern business cycles. By the late nineteenth century, however, the economy was mainly industrial, and the modern business cycle had emerged.

Source: Robert E. Gallman, "Economic Growth and Structural Change in the Long Nineteenth Century," in Stanley L. Engerman and Robert E. Gallman, editors. *The Cambridge Economic History of the United States, vol. II: The Long Nineteenth Century* (Cambridge, UK: Cambridge University Press, 2000).

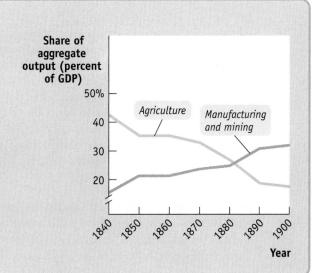

of GDP coming from agriculture and from manufacturing and mining over the period from 1840 to 1900. The figure shows that agriculture dwarfed manufacturing in 1840 and that manufacturing didn't overtake agriculture in economic importance until the 1880s.

Why does this matter? Fluctuations in aggregate output in agricultural economies are very different from the business cycles we know today. That's because prices of agricultural goods tend to be highly flexible. As a result, the short-run aggregate supply curve of a mainly agricultural economy is probably close to vertical, so demand shocks don't cause output fluctuations. Instead, fluctuations on the farm are driven mainly by weather, making shifts of the short-run aggregate supply curve the primary source of fluctuations. In contrast, modern business cycles are largely the result of shifts in the aggregate demand curve.

The modern business cycle probably originated in Britain—home of the Industrial Revolution—which was already a largely industrial and urban society by 1820. The British recession of 1846–1847 had a particularly modern feel: it followed a bout of overoptimism in which firms spent heavily on an exciting new technology—railroads— and then realized they had overdone it. ▲

< < < < < < < < < < < <

► CHECK YOUR UNDERSTANDING 33-1

1. Panel (a) of the figure on the first page of this chapter shows the behavior of M1 before, during, and after the 2001 recession.
   a. How do these data tie in with the quotation from the 2004 Economic Report of the President that opens this chapter?
   b. What would a classical economist have said about the Fed's policy?

Solutions appear at back of book.

> **►► QUICK REVIEW**
>
> ➤ Classical macroeconomists focused on the long-run effects of monetary policy on the aggregate price level, ignoring any short-run effects on aggregate output.
> ➤ By the time of the Great Depression, the measurement of business cycles was well advanced, but there was no widely accepted theory about why they happened.

The Great Depression and the Keynesian Revolution

The Great Depression demonstrated, once and for all, that economists cannot safely ignore the short run. Not only was the economic pain severe; it threatened to destabilize societies and political systems. In particular, the economic plunge helped Adolf Hitler rise to power in Germany.

The whole world wanted to know how this economic disaster could be happening and what should be done about it. But because there was no widely accepted theory of the business cycle, economists gave conflicting and, we now believe, often harmful advice. Some believed that only a huge change in the economic system—such as having the government take over much of private industry and replace markets with a command economy—could end the slump. Others argued that slumps were natural— even beneficial—and that nothing should be done.

Some economists, however, argued that the slump both could and should be cured—without giving up on the basic idea of a market economy. In 1930 the British economist John Maynard Keynes compared the problems of the U.S. and British economies to those of a car with a defective alternator. Getting the economy running, he argued, would require only a modest repair, not a complete overhaul.

Nice metaphor. But what was the nature of the trouble?

Keynes's Theory

In 1936 Keynes presented his analysis of the Great Depression—his explanation of what was wrong with the economy's alternator—in a book titled *The General Theory of Employment, Interest, and Money*. In 1946 the great American economist Paul Samuelson wrote that "it is a badly written book, poorly organized. . . . Flashes of insight and intuition intersperse tedious algebra. . . . We find its analysis to be obvious and at the same time new. In short, it is a work of genius." *The General Theory* isn't easy reading, but it stands with Adam Smith's *The Wealth of Nations* as one of the most influential books on economics ever written.

As Samuelson's description suggests, Keynes's book is a vast stew of ideas. Keynesian economics mainly reflected two innovations. First, Keynes emphasized the short-run effects of shifts in aggregate demand on aggregate output, rather than the long-run determination of the aggregate price level. As Keynes's famous remark about being dead in the long run suggests, until his book appeared most economists had treated short-run macroeconomics as a minor issue. Keynes focused the attention of economists on situations in which the short-run aggregate supply curve slopes upward and shifts in the aggregate demand curve affect aggregate output and employment as well as aggregate prices.

Figure 33-2 illustrates the difference between Keynesian and classical macroeconomics. Both panels of the figure show the short-run aggregate supply curve, *SRAS*; in both it is assumed that for some reason the aggregate demand curve shifts leftward from AD_1 to AD_2—let's say in response to a fall in stock market prices that leads households to reduce consumer spending.

Panel (a) shows the classical view: the short-run aggregate supply curve is vertical. The decline in aggregate demand leads to a fall in the aggregate price level, from P_1 to P_2, but no change in aggregate output. Panel (b) shows the Keynesian view: the short-run aggregate supply curve slopes upward, so the decline in aggregate demand leads to both a fall in the aggregate price level, from P_1 to P_2, and a fall in aggregate output, from Y_1 to Y_2. As we've already explained, many classical macroeconomists would have agreed that panel (b) was an accurate story in the short run—but they regarded the short run as unimportant. Keynes disagreed. (Just to be clear, there isn't any diagram that looks like panel (b) of Figure 33-2 in Keynes's *General Theory*. But Keynes's discussion of aggregate supply, translated into modern terminology, clearly implies an upward-sloping *SRAS* curve.)

Second, classical economists emphasized the role of changes in the money supply in shifting the aggregate demand curve, paying little attention to other factors. Keynes, however, argued that other factors, especially changes in "animal spirits"—

FIGURE 33-2   Classical versus Keynesian Macroeconomics

(a) The Classical View

(b) The Keynesian View

One important difference between classical and Keynesian economics involves the short-run aggregate supply curve. Panel (a) shows the classical view: the *SRAS* curve is vertical, so shifts in aggregate demand affect the aggregate price level but not aggregate output. Panel (b) shows the Keynesian view: in the short run the *SRAS* curve slopes upward, so shifts in aggregate demand affect aggregate output as well as aggregate prices.

The Politics of Keynes

The term *Keynesian economics* is sometimes used as a synonym for *left-wing economics:* authors seem to believe that because Keynes offered a rationale for some kinds of government activism, he was a leftist of some kind, maybe even a socialist. But the truth is more complicated.

As we explain in the text, Keynesian ideas have actually been accepted across a broad part of the political spectrum. In 2004 the president was a conservative, as was his top economist, N. Gregory Mankiw; but Mankiw is also the editor of a collection of readings titled *New Keynesian Economics.*

And Keynes himself was no socialist—and not much of a leftist. At the time *The General Theory* was published, many intellectuals in Britain believed that the Great Depression was the final crisis of the capitalist economic system and that only a

Some people use *Keynesian economics* as a synonym for *left-wing economics*—but the truth is that the ideas of John Maynard Keynes have been accepted across a broad part of the political spectrum.

government takeover of industry could save the economy. Keynes, in contrast, argued that all the system needed was a narrow technical fix. In that sense, his ideas were pro-capitalist and politically conservative.

What is true is that the rise of Keynesian economics in the 1940s, 1950s, and 1960s went along with a general enlargement of the role of government in the economy, and those who favored a larger role for government tended to be enthusiastic Keynesians. Conversely, a swing of the pendulum back toward free-market policies in the 1970s and 1980s was accompanied by a series of challenges to Keynesian ideas, which we describe later in this chapter. But it's perfectly possible to have conservative political preferences while respecting Keynes's contribution and equally possible to be very liberal while questioning Keynes's ideas.

these days usually referred to with the bland term *business confidence*—are mainly responsible for business cycles. Before Keynes, economists often argued that a decline in business confidence would have no effect on either the aggregate price level or aggregate output, as long as the money supply stayed constant. Keynes offered a very different picture.

Keynes's ideas have penetrated deeply into the public consciousness, to the extent that many people who have never heard of Keynes, or have heard of him but think they disagree with his theory, use Keynesian ideas all the time. For example, suppose that a business commentator says something like this: "Because of a decline in business confidence, investment spending slumped, causing a recession." Whether the commentator knows it or not, that statement is pure Keynesian economics.

Keynes himself more or less predicted that his ideas would become part of what "everyone knows." In another famous passage, this from the end of *The General Theory*, he wrote: "Practical men, who believe themselves to be quite exempt from any intellectual influences, are usually the slaves of some defunct economist."

Policy to Fight Recessions

The main practical consequence of Keynes's work was that it legitimized **macroeconomic policy activism**—the use of monetary and fiscal policy to smooth out the business cycle.

Macroeconomic policy activism wasn't something completely new. Before Keynes, many economists had argued for using monetary expansion to fight economic downturns—though others were fiercely opposed. Some economists had even argued that temporary budget deficits were a good thing in times of recession—though others disagreed strongly. In practice, during the 1930s many governments followed policies that we would now call Keynesian. In the United States, the administration of Franklin Roosevelt engaged in modest deficit spending in an effort to create jobs.

Macroeconomic policy activism is the use of monetary and fiscal policy to smooth out the business cycle.

But these efforts were half-hearted. As we saw in the opening story, Roosevelt's advisers were deeply divided over the appropriate policies to take. In fact, in 1937 Roosevelt gave in to advice from non-Keynesian economists who urged him to balance the budget and raise interest rates, even though the economy was still depressed. The result was a renewed slump.

Today, by contrast, there is broad consensus about the useful role monetary and fiscal policy can play in fighting recessions. The 2004 Economic Report of the President, quoted at the beginning of this chapter, was issued by a conservative Republican administration that was generally opposed to government intervention in the economy. Yet its view on economic policy in the face of recession was far more like that of Keynes than like that of most economists before 1936.

It would be wrong, however, to suggest that Keynes's ideas have been fully accepted by modern macroeconomists. In the decades that followed the publication of *The General Theory*, Keynesian economics faced a series of challenges, some of which succeeded in modifying the macroeconomic consensus in important ways.

➤ECONOMICS IN ACTION

The End of the Great Depression

It would make a good story if Keynes's ideas had led to a change in economic policy that brought the Great Depression to an end. Unfortunately, that's not what happened. Still, the way the Depression ended did a lot to convince economists that Keynes was right.

The basic message many of the young economists who adopted Keynes's ideas in the 1930s took from his work was that economic recovery requires aggressive fiscal expansion—deficit spending on a large scale to create jobs. And that is what they eventually got, but it wasn't because politicians were persuaded. Instead, what happened was a very large and expensive war, World War II.

Figure 33-3 shows the U.S. unemployment rate and the federal budget deficit as a share of GDP from 1930 to 1947. As you can see, deficit spending during the 1930s was on a modest scale. In 1940, as the risk of war grew larger, the United States began a large military buildup, and the budget moved deep into deficit. After the attack on

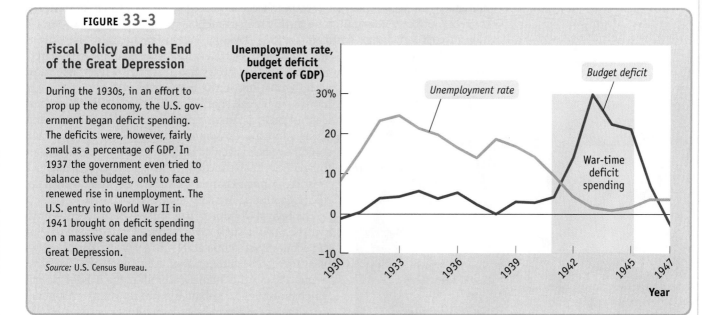

FIGURE 33-3

Fiscal Policy and the End of the Great Depression

During the 1930s, in an effort to prop up the economy, the U.S. government began deficit spending. The deficits were, however, fairly small as a percentage of GDP. In 1937 the government even tried to balance the budget, only to face a renewed rise in unemployment. The U.S. entry into World War II in 1941 brought on deficit spending on a massive scale and ended the Great Depression.

Source: U.S. Census Bureau.

Pearl Harbor on December 7, 1941, the country began deficit spending on an enormous scale: in fiscal 1943, which began in July 1942, the deficit was 30% of GDP. Today that would be a deficit of $4.3 trillion.

And the economy recovered. World War II wasn't intended as a Keynesian fiscal policy, but it demonstrated that expansionary fiscal policy can, in fact, create jobs in the short run. ▲

< < < < < < < < < < < <

> CHECK YOUR UNDERSTANDING 33-2

1. In addition to praising aggressive monetary policy, the 2004 Economic Report of the President says that "tax cuts can boost economic activity by raising after-tax income and enhancing incentives to work, save, and invest." Which part is a Keynesian statement and which part is not? Explain your answer.

Solution appears at back of book.

Challenges to Keynesian Economics

Keynes's ideas fundamentally changed the way economists think about business cycles. They did not, however, go unquestioned. In the decades that followed the publication of *The General Theory*, Keynesian economics faced a series of challenges. As a result, the consensus of macroeconomists retreated somewhat from the strong version of Keynesianism that prevailed in the 1950s. In particular, economists became much more aware of the limits to macroeconomic policy activism.

The Revival of Monetary Policy

Keynes's *General Theory* suggested that monetary policy wouldn't be very effective in depression conditions. Many modern macroeconomists agree: in Chapter 32 we introduced the concept of a *liquidity trap,* a situation in which monetary policy is ineffective because the interest rate is down against the zero bound. In the 1930s, when Keynes wrote, interest rates were, in fact, very close to 0%. (The term *liquidity trap* was first introduced by the British economist John Hicks in a 1937 paper, "Mr. Keynes and The Classics: A Suggested Interpretation," that summarized Keynes's ideas.)

But even when the era of near-0% interest rates came to an end after World War II, many economists continued to emphasize fiscal policy and downplay the usefulness of monetary policy. Eventually, however, macroeconomists reassessed the importance of monetary policy. A key milestone in this reassessment was the 1963 publication of *A Monetary History of the United States, 1867–1960* by Milton Friedman, of the University of Chicago, and Anna Schwartz, of the National Bureau of Economic Research. Friedman and Schwartz showed that business cycles had historically been associated with fluctuations in the money supply. In particular, the money supply fell sharply during the onset of the Great Depression. Friedman and Schwartz persuaded many, though not all, economists that the Great Depression could have been avoided if the Federal Reserve had acted to prevent that monetary contraction. They persuaded most economists that monetary policy should play a key role in economic management.

The revival of interest in monetary policy was significant because it suggested that the burden of managing the economy could be shifted away from fiscal policy—meaning that economic management could largely be taken out of the hands of politicians. Fiscal policy, which must involve changing tax rates or government spending, necessarily involves political choices. If the

Milton Friedman and his co-author Anna Schwartz played a key role in convincing macroeconomists of the importance of monetary policy.

Roger Ressmeyer/Corbis

David Shankbone

government tries to stimulate the economy by cutting taxes, it must decide whose taxes will be cut. If it tries to stimulate the economy with government spending, it must decide what to spend the money on.

Monetary policy, in contrast, does not involve such choices: when the central bank cuts interest rates to fight a recession, it cuts everyone's interest rate at the same time. So a shift from relying on fiscal policy to relying on monetary policy makes macroeconomics a more technical, less political issue. In fact, as we learned in Chapter 30, monetary policy in most major economies is set by an independent central bank that is insulated from the political process.

Monetarism

After the publication of *A Monetary History,* Milton Friedman led a movement that sought to eliminate macroeconomic policy activism while maintaining the importance of monetary policy. **Monetarism** asserted that GDP will grow steadily if the money supply grows steadily. The monetarist policy prescription was to have the central bank target a constant rate of growth of the money supply, such as 3% per year, and maintain that target regardless of any fluctuations in the economy.

It's important to realize that monetarism retained many Keynesian ideas. Like Keynes, Friedman asserted that the short run is important and that short-run changes in aggregate demand affect aggregate output as well as aggregate prices. Like Keynes, he argued that policy should have been much more expansionary during the Great Depression.

Monetarists argued, however, that most of the efforts of policy makers to smooth out the business cycle actually make things worse. In Chapter 29 we discussed concerns over the usefulness of *discretionary fiscal policy*—changes in taxes or government spending, or both, in response to the state of the economy. As we explained, government perceptions about the economy often lag behind reality, and there are further lags in changing fiscal policy and in its effects on the economy. As a result, discretionary fiscal policies intended to fight a recession often end up feeding a boom, and vice versa. According to monetarists, **discretionary monetary policy,** changes in the interest rate or the money supply by the central bank in order to stabilize the economy, faces the same problem of lags as fiscal policy, but to a lesser extent.

Friedman also argued that if the central bank followed his advice and refused to change the money supply in response to fluctuations in the economy, fiscal policy would be much less effective than Keynesians believed. In Chapter 26 we analyzed the phenomenon of *crowding out,* in which government deficits drive up interest rates and lead to reduced investment spending. Friedman and others pointed out that if the money supply is held fixed while the government pursues an expansionary fiscal policy, crowding out will limit the effect of the fiscal expansion on aggregate demand.

Figure 33-4 on the next page illustrates this argument. Panel (a) shows aggregate output and the aggregate price level. AD_1 is the initial aggregate demand curve and *SRAS* is the short-run aggregate supply curve. At the initial equilibrium, E_1, the level of aggregate output is Y_1 and the aggregate price level is P_1. Panel (b) shows the money market. *MS* is the money supply curve and MD_1 is the initial money demand curve, so the initial interest rate is r_1.

Now suppose the government increases purchases of goods and services. We know that this will shift the *AD* curve rightward, as illustrated by the shift from AD_1 to AD_2, and that aggregate output will rise, from Y_1 to Y_2, and the aggregate price level will rise, from P_1 to P_2. Both the rise in aggregate output and the rise in the aggregate price level will, however, increase the demand for money, shifting the money demand curve rightward from MD_1 to MD_2. This drives up the equilibrium interest rate to r_2. Friedman's point was that this rise in the interest rate reduces investment spending, partially offsetting the initial rise in government spending. As a result, the rightward shift of the *AD* curve is smaller than the multiplier analysis in Chapter 29 indicated. And Friedman argued that with a constant money supply, the multiplier is so small that there's not much point in using fiscal policy.

Monetarism asserted that GDP will grow steadily if the money supply grows steadily.

Discretionary monetary policy is the use of changes in the interest rate or the money supply to stabilize the economy.

FIGURE 33-4   Fiscal Policy with a Fixed Money Supply

(a) The Increase in Aggregate Demand from an Expansionary Fiscal Policy Is Limited When the Money Supply Is Fixed...

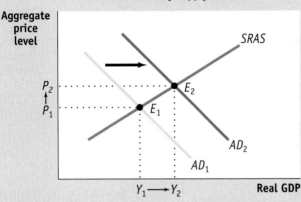

(b) ...Because the Increase in Money Demand Drives up the Interest Rate, Crowding out Some Investment Spending.

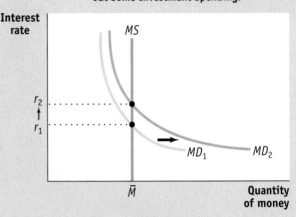

In panel (a) an expansionary fiscal policy shifts the *AD* curve rightward, driving up both the aggregate price level and aggregate output. However, this leads to an increase in the demand for money. If the money supply is held fixed, as in panel (b), the increase in money demand drives up the interest rate, reducing investment spending and offsetting part of the fiscal expansion. So the shift of the *AD* curve is less than it would otherwise be: fiscal policy becomes less effective when the money supply is held fixed.

But Friedman didn't favor activist monetary policy either. He argued that the problems of time lags that limit the ability of discretionary fiscal policy to stabilize the economy also apply to discretionary monetary policy. Friedman's solution was to put monetary policy on "autopilot." The central bank, he argued, should follow a **monetary policy rule,** a formula that determines its actions and left it relatively little discretion. During the 1960s and 1970s, most monetarists favored a monetary policy rule of slow, steady growth in the money supply. Underlying this view was the concept of the **velocity of money,** the ratio of nominal GDP to the money supply. Velocity is a measure of the number of times the average dollar bill in the economy turns over per year between buyers and sellers (e.g., I tip the Starbucks barista a dollar, she uses it to buy lunch, and so on). This concept gives rise to the *velocity equation:*

(33-1) $M \times V = P \times Y$

Where M is the money supply, V is velocity, P is the aggregate price level, and Y is real GDP.

Monetarists believed, with considerable historical justification, that the velocity of money was stable in the short run and changes only slowly in the long run. As a result, they claimed, steady growth in the money supply by the central bank would ensure steady growth in spending, and therefore in GDP.

Monetarism strongly influenced actual monetary policy in the late 1970s and early 1980s. It quickly became clear, however, that steady growth in the money supply didn't ensure steady growth in the economy: the velocity of money wasn't stable enough for such a simple policy rule to work. Figure 33-5 shows how events eventually undermined the monetarists' view. The figure shows the velocity of money, as measured by the ratio of nominal GDP to M1, from 1960 to the middle of 2008. As you can see, until 1980 velocity followed a fairly smooth, seemingly predictable trend. After the Fed began to adopt monetarist ideas in the late 1970s and early 1980s, however, the velocity of money began moving erratically—probably due to financial market innovations.

A **monetary policy rule** is a formula that determines the central bank's actions.

The **velocity of money** is the ratio of nominal GDP to the money supply.

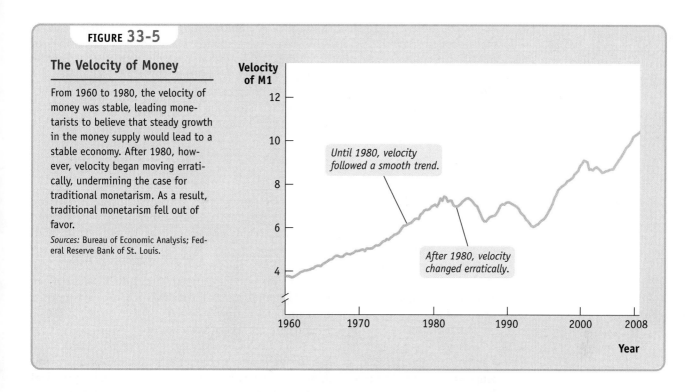

FIGURE 33-5

The Velocity of Money

From 1960 to 1980, the velocity of money was stable, leading monetarists to believe that steady growth in the money supply would lead to a stable economy. After 1980, however, velocity began moving erratically, undermining the case for traditional monetarism. As a result, traditional monetarism fell out of favor.

Sources: Bureau of Economic Analysis; Federal Reserve Bank of St. Louis.

Until 1980, velocity followed a smooth trend.

After 1980, velocity changed erratically.

Traditional monetarists are hard to find among today's macroeconomists. As we'll see later in the chapter, however, the concern that originally motivated the monetarists—that too much discretionary monetary policy can actually destabilize the economy—has become widely accepted.

Inflation and the Natural Rate of Unemployment

At the same time that monetarists were challenging Keynesian views about how macroeconomic policy should be conducted, other economists—some, but not all of them, monetarists—were emphasizing the limits to what activist macroeconomic policy could achieve.

In the 1940s and 1950s, many Keynesian economists believed that expansionary fiscal policy could be used to achieve full employment on a permanent basis. In the 1960s, however, many economists realized that expansionary policies could cause problems with inflation, but they still believed policy makers could choose to trade off low unemployment for higher inflation even in the long run.

In 1968, however, Milton Friedman and Edmund Phelps of Columbia University, working independently, proposed the concept of the natural rate of unemployment, which we discussed in Chapter 24. And in Chapter 32 we showed that the natural rate of unemployment is also the nonaccelerating inflation rate of unemployment, or NAIRU. According to the **natural rate hypothesis,** because inflation is eventually embedded into expectations, to avoid accelerating inflation over time, the unemployment rate must be high enough that the actual inflation rate equals the expected rate of inflation. Attempts to keep the unemployment rate below the natural rate will lead to an ever-rising inflation rate.

The natural rate hypothesis limits the role of activist macroeconomic policy compared to earlier theories. Because the government can't keep unemployment below the natural rate, its task is not to keep unemployment low but to keep it *stable*—to prevent large fluctuations in unemployment in either direction.

The Friedman–Phelps hypothesis made a strong prediction: that the apparent trade-off between unemployment and inflation would not survive an extended period of rising prices. Once inflation was embedded into the public's expectations, inflation

According to the **natural rate hypothesis**, because inflation is eventually embedded into expectations, to avoid accelerating inflation over time the unemployment rate must be high enough that the actual inflation rate equals the expected inflation rate.

A **political business cycle** results when politicians use macroeconomic policy to serve political ends.

would continue even in the face of high unemployment. Sure enough, that's exactly what happened in the 1970s. This accurate prediction was one of the triumphs of macroeconomic analysis, and it convinced the great majority of economists that the natural rate hypothesis was correct. In contrast to traditional monetarism, which declined in influence as more evidence accumulated, the natural rate hypothesis has become almost universally accepted among macroeconomists, with a few qualifications. (Some macroeconomists believe that at very low or negative rates of inflation the hypothesis doesn't work.)

The Political Business Cycle

One final challenge to Keynesian economics focused not on the validity of the economic analysis but on its political consequences. A number of economists and political scientists pointed out that activist macroeconomic policy lends itself to political manipulation.

Statistical evidence suggests that election results tend to be determined by the state of the economy in the months just before the election. In the United States, if the economy is growing rapidly and the unemployment rate is falling in the six months or so before Election Day, the incumbent party tends to be re-elected even if the economy performed poorly in the preceding three years.

This creates an obvious temptation to abuse activist macroeconomic policy: pump up the economy in an election year, and pay the price in higher inflation and/or higher unemployment later. The result can be unnecessary instability in the economy, a **political business cycle** caused by the use of macroeconomic policy to serve political ends.

An often-cited example is the combination of expansionary fiscal and monetary policy that led to rapid growth in the U.S. economy just before the 1972 election and a sharp acceleration in inflation after the election. Kenneth Rogoff, a respected macroeconomist who served as chief economist at the International Monetary Fund, has proclaimed Richard Nixon, the president at the time, "the all-time hero of political business cycles."

As we learned in Chapter 30, one way to avoid a political business cycle is to place monetary policy in the hands of an independent central bank, insulated from political pressure. The political business cycle is also a reason to limit the use of discretionary fiscal policy to extreme circumstances.

►ECONOMICS IN ACTION

The Fed's Flirtation with Monetarism

In the late 1970s and early 1980s the Federal Reserve flirted with monetarism. For most of its prior existence, the Fed had targeted interest rates, adjusting its target based on the state of the economy. In the late 1970s, however, the Fed adopted a monetary policy rule and began announcing target ranges for several measures of the money supply. It also stopped setting targets for interest rates. Most people interpreted these changes as a strong move toward monetarism.

In 1982, however, the Fed turned its back on monetarism. Since 1982 the Fed has pursued a discretionary monetary policy, which has led to large swings in the money supply. At the end of the 1980s, the Fed returned to conducting monetary policy by setting target levels for the interest rate.

Why did the Fed flirt with monetarism, then abandon it? The turn to monetarism largely reflected the events of the 1970s, when a sharp rise in inflation broke the perceived trade-off between inflation and unemployment and discredited traditional Keynesianism. The accuracy of Friedman's prediction of a worsening trade-off between inflation and unemployment increased his prestige and that of his followers. As a result, policy makers adopted Friedman's proposals.

The turn away from monetarism also reflected events: as we saw in Figure 33-5, the velocity of money, which had followed a smooth trend before 1980, became erratic after 1980. This made monetarism seem like a much less good idea. ▲

> > > > > > > > > > > >

1. What would panel (a) of the figure on the first page of this chapter have looked like if the Fed had been following a monetarist policy since 1996?

2. Now look at Figure 33-5. What problems do you think the United States would have had since 1996 if the Fed had followed a monetarist policy?

3. What are the limits of macroeconomic policy activism?

Solutions appear at back of book.

Rational Expectations, Real Business Cycles, and New Classical Macroeconomics

As we have seen, one key difference between classical economics and Keynesian economics is that classical economists believed that the short-run aggregate supply curve is vertical, but Keynes emphasized the idea that the aggregate supply curve slopes upward in the short run. As a result, Keynes argued that demand shocks— shifts in the aggregate demand curve—can cause fluctuations in aggregate output.

The challenges to Keynesian economics that arose in the 1950s and 1960s—the renewed emphasis on monetary policy and the natural rate hypothesis—didn't question the view that an increase in aggregate demand leads to a rise in aggregate output in the short run and that a decrease in aggregate demand leads to a fall in aggregate output in the short run. In the 1970s and 1980s, however, some economists developed an approach to the business cycle known as **new classical macroeconomics,** which returned to the classical view that shifts in the aggregate demand curve affect only the aggregate price level, not aggregate output. The new approach evolved in two steps. First, some economists challenged traditional arguments about the slope of the short-run aggregate supply curve based on the concept of *rational expectations.* Second, some economists suggested that changes in productivity cause economic fluctuations, a view known as *real business cycle theory.*

Rational Expectations

In the 1970s a concept known as *rational expectations* had a powerful impact on macroeconomics. **Rational expectations,** a theory originally introduced by John Muth in 1961, is the view that individuals and firms make decisions optimally, using all available information.

For example, workers and employers bargaining over long-term wage contracts need to estimate the inflation rate they expect over the life of that contract. Rational expectations says that in making estimates of future inflation, they won't just look at past rates of inflation; they will also take into account available information about monetary and fiscal policy. Suppose that prices didn't rise last year, but that the monetary and fiscal policies announced by policy makers make it clear to economic analysts that there will be substantial inflation over the next few years. According to rational expectations, long-term wage contracts will be adjusted today to reflect this future inflation, even though prices didn't rise in the past.

Rational expectations can make a major difference to the effects of government policy. According to the original version of the natural rate hypothesis, a government attempt to trade off higher inflation for lower unemployment would work in the short run but would eventually fail because higher inflation would get built

New classical macroeconomics is an approach to the business cycle that returns to the classical view that shifts in the aggregate demand curve affect only the aggregate price level, not aggregate output.

Rational expectations is the view that individuals and firms make decisions optimally, using all available information.

According to **new Keynesian economics,** market imperfections can lead to price stickiness for the economy as a whole.

Real business cycle theory claims that fluctuations in the rate of growth of total factor productivity cause the business cycle.

into expectations. According to rational expectations, we should remove the word *eventually:* if it's clear that the government intends to trade off higher inflation for lower unemployment, the public will understand this, and expected inflation will immediately rise.

In the 1970s Robert Lucas of the University of Chicago, in a series of highly influential papers, used this logic to argue that monetary policy can change the level of unemployment only if it comes as a surprise to the public. If his analysis was right, monetary policy isn't useful in stabilizing the economy after all. In 1995 Lucas won the Nobel Prize in economics for this work, which remains widely admired. However, many—perhaps most—macroeconomists, especially those advising policy makers, now believe that his conclusions were overstated. The Federal Reserve certainly thinks that it can play a useful role in economic stabilization, a view affirmed by the quote from the 2004 Economic Report of the President that opened this chapter.

Why, in the view of many macroeconomists, doesn't the rational expectations hypothesis accurately describe how the economy behaves? **New Keynesian economics,** a set of ideas that became influential in the 1990s, provides an explanation. It argues that market imperfections interact to make many prices in the economy temporarily sticky. For example, one new Keynesian argument points out that monopolists don't have to be too careful about setting prices exactly "right": if they set a price a bit too high, they'll lose some sales but make more profit on each sale; if they set the price too low, they'll reduce the profit per sale but sell more. As a result, even small costs to changing prices can lead to substantial price stickiness and make the economy as a whole behave in a Keynesian fashion.

Over time, new Keynesian ideas combined with actual experience have reduced the practical influence of the rational expectations concept. Nonetheless, the idea of rational expectations served as a useful caution for macroeconomists who had become excessively optimistic about their ability to manage the economy.

Real Business Cycles

In Chapter 25 we introduced the concept of *total factor productivity,* the amount of output that can be generated with a given level of factor inputs. Total factor productivity grows over time, but that growth isn't smooth. In the 1980s a number of economists argued that slowdowns in productivity growth, which they attributed to pauses in technological progress, are the main cause of recessions. **Real business cycle theory** claims that fluctuations in the rate of growth of total factor productivity cause the business cycle. Believing that the aggregate supply curve is vertical, real business cycle theorists attribute the source of business cycles to shifts of the aggregate supply curve: a recession occurs when a slowdown in productivity growth shifts the aggregate supply curve leftward, and a recovery occurs when a pickup in productivity growth shifts the aggregate supply curve rightward. In the early days of real business cycle theory, the theory's proponents denied that changes in aggregate demand have any effect on aggregate output.

This theory was strongly influential, as shown by the fact that two of the founders of real business cycle theory, Finn Kydland of Carnegie Mellon University and Edward Prescott of the Federal Reserve Bank of Minneapolis, won the 2004 Nobel Prize in economics. The current status of real business cycle theory, however, is somewhat similar to that of rational expectations. The theory is widely recognized as having made valuable contributions to our understanding of the economy, and it serves as a useful caution against too much emphasis on aggregate demand. But many of the real business cycle theorists themselves now acknowledge that their models need an upward-sloping aggregate supply curve to fit the economic data—and that this gives aggregate demand a potential role in determining aggregate output. And as we have seen, policy makers strongly believe that aggregate demand policy has an important role to play in fighting recessions.

Supply-Side Economics

During the 1970s a group of economic writers began propounding a view of economic policy that came to be known as "supply-side economics." The core of this view was the belief that reducing tax rates, and so increasing the incentives to work and invest, would have a powerful positive effect on the growth rate of potential output. The supply-siders urged the government to cut taxes without worrying about matching spending cuts: economic growth, they argued, would offset any negative effects from budget deficits. Some supply-siders even argued that a cut in tax *rates* would have such a miraculous effect on economic growth that tax *revenues*—the total amount taxpayers pay to the government—would actually rise. That is, some supply-siders argued that the

United States was on the wrong side of the *Laffer curve,* a hypothetical relationship between tax rates and total tax revenue that slopes upward at low tax rates but turns downward when tax rates are very high.

In the 1970s supply-side economics was enthusiastically supported by the editors of the *Wall Street Journal* and other figures in the media, and it became popular with politicians. In 1980 Ronald Reagan made supply-side economics the basis of his presidential campaign.

Because supply-side economics emphasizes supply rather than demand, and because the supply-siders themselves are harshly critical of Keynesian economics, it might seem as if supply-side theory belongs in our discussion of new classical

macroeconomics. But unlike rational expectations and real business cycle theory, supply-side economics is generally dismissed by economic researchers.

The main reason for this dismissal is lack of evidence. Almost all economists agree that tax cuts increase incentives to work and invest, but attempts to estimate these incentive effects indicate that at current U.S. tax levels they aren't nearly strong enough to support the strong claims made by supply-siders. In particular, the supply-side doctrine implies that large tax cuts, such as those implemented by Ronald Reagan in the early 1980s, should sharply raise potential output. Yet estimates of potential output by the Congressional Budget Office and others show no sign of an acceleration in growth after the Reagan tax cuts.

➤ ECONOMICS IN ACTION

Total Factor Productivity and the Business Cycle

Real business cycle theory argues that fluctuations in the rate of growth of total factor productivity are the principal cause of business cycles. Although many macroeconomists dispute that claim, the theory did draw attention to the fact that there is a strong correlation between the rate of total factor productivity growth and the business cycle. Figure 33-6 on the next page shows the annual rate of total factor productivity growth estimated by the Bureau of Labor Statistics. The shaded areas represent recessions. Clearly, recessions tend also to be periods in which the growth of total factor productivity slows sharply or even turns negative. And real business cycle theorists deserve a lot of credit for drawing economists' attention to this fact.

There are, however, disputes about how to interpret this correlation. In the early days of real business cycle theory, proponents argued that productivity fluctuations are entirely the result of uneven technological progress. Critics pointed out, however, that in really severe recessions, like those of 1974–1975 or the early 1980s, total factor productivity actually declines. If real business cycle theorists were correct, then technology actually moved backward during those periods—something that is hard to believe.

So what accounts for declining total factor productivity during recessions? Some economists argue that it is a result, not a cause, of economic downturns. An example may be helpful. Suppose we measure productivity at the local post office by the number of pieces of mail handled, divided by the number of postal workers. Since the post office doesn't lay off workers whenever there's a slow mail day, days on which not much mail comes in will seem to be days on which the workers are especially unproductive. But the slump in business is causing the apparent decline in productivity, not the other way around.

FIGURE 33-6

Total Factor Productivity and the Business Cycle

There is a clear correlation between declines in the rate of total factor productivity growth and recessions (indicated by the shaded areas). Real business cycle theory says that fluctuations in productivity growth are the main cause of business cycles. Other economists argue, however, that business cycles cause productivity fluctuations, not the other way around.

Sources: Bureau of Labor Statistics; National Bureau of Economic Research.

>> QUICK REVIEW

➤ **New classical macroeconomics** argues that the short-run aggregate supply curve may be vertical after all. It developed two branches: *rational expectations* and *real business cycle theory*.

➤ **Rational expectations** claims that because workers and firms take all information into account, only unexpected changes in the money supply affect aggregate output.

➤ **New Keynesian economics** argues that market imperfections can lead to price stickiness, so that changes in aggregate demand do affect aggregate output.

➤ **Real business cycle theory** argues that fluctuations in the rate of productivity growth cause the business cycle.

➤ New Keynesianism and actual events have diminished the impact of the rational expectations model. Real business cycle theory is undermined by its implication that technology moves backward during deep recessions. It is now generally believed that the aggregate supply curve is upward sloping.

It's now widely accepted that some of the correlation between total factor productivity and the business cycle is the result of the effect of the business cycle on productivity, rather than the reverse. But the main direction of causation is a subject of continuing research. ▲

< < < < < < < < < < <

➤ CHECK YOUR UNDERSTANDING 33-4

1. In early 2001, as it became clear that the United States was experiencing a recession, the Fed stated that it would fight the recession with an aggressive monetary policy. By 2004, most observers concluded that this aggressive monetary expansion should be given credit for ending the recession.
   a. What would rational expectations theorists say about this conclusion?
   b. What would real business cycle theorists say?

Solutions appear at back of book.

The Modern Consensus

As we've seen, there were intense debates about macroeconomics in the 1960s, 1970s, and 1980s. More recently, however, things have settled down. The age of macroeconomic controversy is by no means over, but there is now a broad consensus about several crucial macroeconomic issues.

To understand the modern consensus, where it came from, and what still remains in dispute, we'll look at how macroeconomists have changed their answers to five key questions about macroeconomic policy. The five questions, and the answers given by macroeconomists over the past 70 years, are summarized in Table 33-1. (In the table, new classical economics is subsumed under classical economics, and new Keynesian economics is subsumed under the modern consensus.) Notice that classical macroeconomics said no to each question; basically, classical macroeconomists didn't think macroeconomic policy could accomplish very much. But let's go through the questions one by one.

Is Expansionary Monetary Policy Helpful in Fighting Recessions?

As we've seen, classical macroeconomists generally believed that expansionary monetary policy was ineffective or even harmful in fighting recessions. In the early years of Keynesian economics, macroeconomists weren't against monetary expansion during

TABLE 33-1

Five Key Questions About Macroeconomic Policy

	Classical macroeconomics	Keynesian macroeconomics	Monetarism	Modern consensus
Is expansionary monetary policy helpful in fighting recessions?	No	Not very	Yes	Yes, except in special circumstances
Is expansionary fiscal policy effective in fighting recessions?	No	Yes	No	Yes
Can monetary and/or fiscal policy reduce unemployment in the long run?	No	Yes	No	No
Should fiscal policy be used in a discretionary way?	No	Yes	No	No, except in special circumstances
Should monetary policy be used in a discretionary way?	No	Yes	No	Still in dispute

recessions, but they tended to believe that it was of doubtful effectiveness. Milton Friedman and his followers convinced economists that monetary policy is effective after all.

Nearly all macroeconomists now agree that monetary policy can be used to shift the aggregate demand curve and to reduce economic instability. The classical view that changes in the money supply affect only aggregate prices, not aggregate output, has few supporters today. The view once held by some Keynesian economists—that changes in the money supply have little effect—has equally few supporters. Now, it is generally agreed that monetary policy is ineffective only in the case of a liquidity trap.

Is Expansionary Fiscal Policy Effective in Fighting Recessions?

Classical macroeconomists were, if anything, even more opposed to fiscal expansion than monetary expansion. Keynesian economists, on the other hand, gave fiscal policy a central role in fighting recessions. Monetarists argued that fiscal policy was ineffective as long as the money supply was held constant. But that strong view has become relatively rare.

Most macroeconomists now agree that fiscal policy, like monetary policy, can shift the aggregate demand curve. Most macroeconomists also agree that the government should not seek to balance the budget regardless of the state of the economy: they agree that the role of the budget as an automatic stabilizer helps keep the economy on an even keel.

Can Monetary and/or Fiscal Policy Reduce Unemployment in the Long Run?

Classical macroeconomists didn't believe the government could do anything about unemployment. Some Keynesian economists moved to the opposite extreme, arguing that expansionary policies could be used to achieve a permanently low unemployment rate, perhaps at the cost of some inflation. Monetarists believed that unemployment could not be kept below the natural rate.

Almost all macroeconomists now accept the natural rate hypothesis. This hypothesis leads them to accept sharp limits to what monetary and fiscal policy can accomplish. Effective monetary and fiscal policy, most macroeconomists believe, can limit the size of fluctuations of the actual unemployment rate around the natural rate, but they can't be used to keep unemployment below the natural rate.

Should Fiscal Policy Be Used in a Discretionary Way?

As we've already seen, views about the effectiveness of fiscal policy have gone back and forth, from rejection by classical macroeconomists, to a positive view by Keynesian economists, to a negative view once again by monetarists. Today most macroeconomists believe that tax cuts and spending increases are at least somewhat effective in increasing aggregate demand.

Many, but not all, macroeconomists, however, believe that *discretionary fiscal policy* is usually counterproductive, for the reasons discussed in Chapter 29: the lags in adjusting fiscal policy mean that, all too often, policies intended to fight a slump end up intensifying a boom.

As a result, the macroeconomic consensus gives monetary policy the lead role in economic stabilization. Discretionary fiscal policy plays the leading role only in special circumstances when monetary policy is ineffective, such as those facing Japan during the 1990s when interest rates were at or near the zero bound and the economy was in a liquidity trap. As this book went to press, the United States similarly found itself at the zero bound, and most macroeconomists supported a large discretionary fiscal expansion.

Should Monetary Policy Be Used in a Discretionary Way?

Classical macroeconomists didn't think that monetary policy should be used to fight recessions; Keynesian economists didn't oppose discretionary monetary policy, but they were skeptical about its effectiveness. Monetarists argued that discretionary monetary policy was doing more harm than good. Where are we today? This remains an area of dispute. Today there is a broad consensus among macroeconomists on these points:

- Monetary policy should play the main role in stabilization policy.
- The central bank should be independent, insulated from political pressures, in order to avoid a political business cycle.
- Discretionary fiscal policy should be used sparingly, both because of policy lags and because of the risks of a political business cycle.

There are, however, debates over how the central bank should set its policy. Should the central bank be given a simple, clearly defined target for its policies, or should it be given discretion to manage the economy as it sees fit? Should the central bank consider the management of asset prices, such as stock prices and real estate prices, part of its responsibility? And what actions should the central bank undertake when interest rates have hit the zero bound and conventional monetary policy has reached its limits?

Central Bank Targets It may sound funny to say this, but it's often not clear exactly what the Federal Reserve, the central bank of the United States, is trying to achieve. Clearly it wants a stable economy with price stability, but there isn't any document setting out the Fed's official view about exactly how stable the economy should be or what the inflation rate should be.

This is not necessarily a bad thing. Experienced staff at the Fed generally believe that the absence of specific guidelines gives the central bank flexibility in coping with economic events and that history proves the Fed uses that flexibility well. In practice, chairmen of the Fed tend to stay in office for a long time—William McChesney Martin was chairman from 1951 to 1970, and Alan Greenspan, appointed in 1987, served as chairman until 2006. These long-serving chairmen acquire personal credibility that reassures the public that the central bank's power will be used well.

As we discussed in Chapter 31, central banks in some other countries have adopted formal guidelines. Some American economists—including some members of the Federal Reserve Board of Governors—believe that the United States should follow suit. The best-known example of a central bank using formal guidelines is the Bank of England. Until 1997, the Bank of England was simply an arm of the British Treasury Department, with no independence. When it became an independent organization like the Federal Reserve, it was given a mandate to achieve an inflation target of 2.5% (in 2003, that target was changed to 2%).

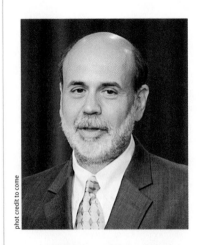

In 2008, Ben Bernanke, the chairman of the Federal Reserve Board of Governors, took a series of unconventional monetary policy actions in response to the deepening recession and financial crisis.

While inflation targeting is now advocated by many macroeconomists, others believe that such a rule can limit the ability of the central bank to respond to events, such as a stock market crash or a world financial crisis.

Unlike the Bank of England, the Fed doesn't have an explicit inflation target. However, it is widely believed to want an inflation rate of about 2%. Once the economy has moved past the current recession and financial crisis, there is likely to be renewed debate about whether the Fed should adopt an explicit inflation target.

Asset Prices During the 1990s many economists warned that the U.S. stock market was losing touch with reality—share prices were much higher than could be justified given realistic forecasts of companies' future profits. Among these economists was Alan Greenspan, the chairman of the Federal Reserve, who warned about "irrational exuberance" in a famous speech. In 2000 the stock market headed downward, taking the economy with it. Americans who had invested in the stock market suddenly felt poorer and so cut back on spending, helping push the economy into a recession.

Just a few years later the same thing happened in the housing market, as home prices climbed above levels that were justified by the incomes of home buyers and the cost of renting rather than buying. This time, however, Alan Greenspan dismissed concerns about a bubble as "most unlikely." But it turned out that there was indeed a bubble, which popped in 2006, leading to the financial crisis we described in Chapter 30, and which pushed the economy into yet another recession.

These events highlighted a long-standing debate over monetary policy: should the central bank restrict its concerns to inflation and possibly unemployment, or should it also try to prevent extreme movements in asset prices, such as the average price of stocks or the average price of houses?

One view is that the central bank shouldn't try to second-guess the value investors place on assets like stocks or houses, even if it suspects that those prices are getting out of line. That is, the central bank shouldn't raise interest rates to curb stock prices or housing prices if overall consumer price inflation remains low. If an overvalued stock market eventually falls and depresses aggregate demand, the central bank can deal with that by cutting interest rates.

The alternative view warns that after a bubble bursts—after overvalued asset prices fall to earth—it may be difficult for monetary and fiscal policy to offset the effects on aggregate demand. After having seen the Japanese economy struggle for years with deflation in the aftermath of the collapse of its bubble economy, proponents of this view argue that the central bank should act to rein in irrational exuberance when it is happening, even if consumer price inflation isn't a problem.

As we explain in the Economics in Action that follows, the 2001 recession and its aftermath gave ammunition to both sides in this debate, which shows no sign of ending.

Unconventional Monetary Policies In 2008, responding to a growing financial crisis, the Federal Reserve began engaging in highly unconventional monetary policy. As we learned in Chapter 31, the Fed normally conducts monetary policy through open-market operations in which it buys short-term U.S. government debt in order to influence interest rates. We also saw in Chapters 30 and 31 that in 2008, faced with severe problems in the financial markets, the Fed vastly expanded its operations. It lent huge sums to a wide variety of financial institutions, and it began large-scale purchases of private assets, including commercial paper (short-term business debts) and assets backed by home mortgages.

These actions and similar actions by other central banks, such as the Bank of Japan, were controversial. Supporters of the moves argued that extraordinary action was necessary to deal with the financial crisis and to cope with the liquidity trap that the economy had fallen into. But skeptics questioned both the effectiveness of the moves and whether the Fed was taking on dangerous risks. However, with interest rates up against the zero bound, it's not clear that the Fed had any other alternative but to turn unconventional. Future attitudes toward unconventional monetary policy will probably depend on how the Fed's efforts play out.

The Clean Little Secret of Macroeconomics

It's important to keep the debates we have just described in perspective. Macroeconomics has always been a contentious field, much more so than microeconomics. There will always be debates about appropriate policies. But the striking thing about current debates is how modest the differences among macroeconomists really are. The clean little secret of modern macroeconomics is how much consensus economists have reached over the past 70 years.

➤ECONOMICS IN ACTION

After the Bubble

During the 1990s, many economists worried that stock prices were irrationally high, and these worries proved justified. Starting in 2000, the NASDAQ, an index made up largely of technology stocks, began declining, ultimately losing two-thirds of its peak value. And in 2001 the plunge in stock prices helped push the United States into recession.

The Fed responded with large, rapid interest rate cuts. But should it have tried to burst the stock bubble when it was happening?

In fall 2008, Alan Greenspan admitted that he had failed to anticipate the looming housing and mortgage-lending crisis.

Many economists expected the aftermath of the 1990s stock market bubble to settle, once and for all, the question of whether central banks should concern themselves about asset prices. But the test results came out ambiguous, failing to settle the issue.

If the Fed had been unable to engineer a recovery—if the U.S. economy had slid into a liquidity trap like that of Japan—critics of the Fed's previous inaction would have had a very strong case. But the recession was, in fact, short: the National Bureau of Economic Research says that the recession began in March 2001 and ended in November 2001.

Furthermore, if the Fed had been able to produce a quick, strong recovery, its inaction during the 1990s would have been strongly vindicated. Unfortunately, that didn't happen either. Although the economy began recovering in late 2001, the recovery was initially weak—so weak that employment continued to drop until the summer of 2003. Also, the fact that the Fed had to cut the federal funds rate to only 1%—uncomfortably close to 0%—suggested that the U.S. economy had come dangerously close to a liquidity trap.

In other words, the events of 2001–2003 probably intensified the debate over monetary policy and asset prices, rather than resolving it.

The bursting of the housing bubble after 2006 offered another test. At the time of writing, it appeared that the post-bubble recession would be both deep and long, strengthening the case for worrying about asset prices and bubbles. But the case of the housing bubble also highlighted the problem of identifying bubbles as they inflate. Even as house prices were souring in late 2004, Alan Greenspan, then Fed Chairman, pronounced a "severe distortion" in housing prices "most unlikely." However, in fall 2008, almost three years after stepping down as Fed chairman, a contrite Alan Greenspan admitted to a Congressional committee that he had failed to anticipate the looming housing and mortgage-lending crisis. It seems safe to predict that, in the future, the Fed will be more inclined to take asset prices into account when setting monetary policy. ▲

< < < < < < < < < < <

> **QUICK REVIEW**

➤ There is a broad consensus that monetary policy is effective but that it can only stabilize the economy, not reduce unemployment below the natural rate.

➤ There is also a broad consensus that discretionary fiscal policy should be avoided except in exceptional cases.

➤ There is a broad consensus that central banks should be independent, but there are disagreements about whether they should have formal inflation targets and how to deal with asset price bubbles.

➤ The Fed undertook unconventional monetary policy in 2008 as the economy fell into a liquidity trap, a controversial move.

> ➤ **CHECK YOUR UNDERSTANDING** 33-5

1. What debates has the modern consensus resolved? What debates has it not resolved?

Solution appears at back of book.

[>> A LOOK AHEAD•••

We have now given a comprehensive overview of the state of modern macroeconomics, with one major exception: we haven't looked at the implications of international trade and international movements of capital. These have become increasingly important in the modern world economy. In the next chapter we will turn to *open-economy macro-economics,* the issues raised by the fact that modern economies are "open" to the world.]

SUMMARY

1. Classical macroeconomics asserted that monetary policy affected only the aggregate price level, not aggregate output, and that the short run was unimportant. By the 1930s, measurement of business cycles was a well-established subject, but there was no widely accepted theory of business cycles.

2. **Keynesian economics** attributed the business cycle to shifts of the aggregate demand curve, often the result of changes in business confidence. Keynesian economics also offered a rationale for **macroeconomic policy activism.**

3. In the decades that followed Keynes's work, economists came to agree that monetary policy as well as fiscal policy is effective under certain conditions. **Monetarism,** a doctrine that called for a **monetary policy rule** as opposed to **discretionary monetary policy,** and which argued—based on a belief that the **velocity of money** was stable—that GDP would grow steadily if the money supply grew steadily, was influential for a time but was eventually rejected by many macroeconomists.

4. The **natural rate hypothesis** became almost universally accepted, limiting the role of macroeconomic policy to stabilizing the economy rather than seeking a permanently lower unemployment rate. Fears of a **political business cycle** led to a consensus that monetary policy should be insulated from politics.

5. **Rational expectations** suggests that even in the short run there might not be a trade-off between inflation and unemployment because expected inflation would change immediately in the face of expected changes in policy. **Real business cycle theory** claims that changes in the rate of growth of total factor productivity are the main cause of business cycles. Both of these versions of **new classical macroeconomics** received wide attention and respect, but policy makers and many economists haven't accepted the conclusion that monetary and fiscal policy are ineffective in changing aggregate output.

6. **New Keynesian economics** argues that market imperfections can lead to price stickiness, so that changes in aggregate demand have effects on aggregate output after all.

7. The modern consensus is that monetary and fiscal policy are both effective in the short run but that neither can reduce the unemployment rate in the long run. Discretionary fiscal policy is considered generally unadvisable, except in special circumstances.

8. There are continuing debates about the appropriate role of monetary policy. Some economists advocate the explicit use of an inflation target, but others oppose it. There's also a debate about whether monetary policy should take steps to manage asset prices and what kind of unconventional monetary policy, if any, should be adopted to address a liquidity trap.

KEY TERMS

Macroeconomic policy activism, p. 890
Monetarism, p. 893
Discretionary monetary policy, p. 893
Monetary policy rule, p. 894

Velocity of money, p. 894
Natural rate hypothesis, p. 895
Political business cycle, p. 896
New classical macroeconomics, p. 897

Rational expectations, p. 897
New Keynesian economics, p. 898
Real business cycle theory, p. 898

PROBLEMS ·· ■

1. Since the crash of its stock market in 1989, the Japanese economy has seen little economic growth and some deflation. The accompanying table from the Organization for Economic Cooperation and Development (OECD) shows some key macroeconomic data for Japan for 1991 (a "normal" year) and 1995–2003.

Year	Real GDP annual growth rate	Short-term interest rate	Government debt (percent of GDP)	Government budget deficit (percent of GDP)
1991	3.4%	7.38%	64.8%	−1.81%
1995	1.9	1.23	87.1	4.71
1996	3.4	0.59	93.9	5.07
1997	1.9	0.60	100.3	3.79
1998	−1.1	0.72	112.2	5.51
1999	0.1	0.25	125.7	7.23
2000	2.8	0.25	134.1	7.48
2001	0.4	0.12	142.3	6.13
2002	−0.3	0.06	149.3	7.88
2003	2.5	0.04	157.5	7.67

a. From the data, determine the type of policies Japan's policy makers undertook at that time to promote growth.

b. We can safely consider a short-term interest rate that is less than 0.1% to effectively be a 0% interest rate. What is this situation called? What does it imply about the effectiveness of monetary policy? Of fiscal policy?

2. The National Bureau of Economic Research (NBER) maintains the official chronology of past U.S. business cycles. Go to its website at http://www.nber.org/cycles/cyclesmain.html to answer the following questions.

a. How many business cycles have occurred since the end of World War II in 1945?

b. What was the average duration of a business cycle when measured from the end of one expansion (its peak) to the end of the next? That is, what was the average duration of a business cycle in the period from 1945 to 2001?

c. When and what was the last announcement by the NBER's Business Cycle Dating Committee, and what was it?

3. The fall of America's military rival, the Soviet Union, in 1989 allowed the U.S. to significantly reduce its defense spending in subsequent years. Using the data in the following table from the Economic Report of the President, replicate Figure 33-3 for the 1990–2000 period. Given the strong economic growth in the U.S. during the late 1990s, why would a Keynesian see the reduction in defense spending during the 1990s as a good thing?

Year	Budget deficit (percent of GDP)	Unemployment rate
1990	3.9%	5.6%
1991	4.5	6.8
1992	4.7	7.5
1993	3.9	6.9
1994	2.9	6.1
1995	2.2	5.6
1996	1.4	5.4
1997	0.3	4.9
1998	−0.8	4.5
1999	−1.4	4.2
2000	−2.4	4.0

4. In the modern world, central banks are free to increase or reduce the money supply as they see fit. However, some people harken back to the "good old days" of the gold standard. Under the gold standard, the money supply could expand only when the amount of available gold increased.

a. Under the gold standard, if the velocity of money was stable when the economy was expanding, what would have had to happen to keep prices stable?

b. Why would modern macroeconomists consider the gold standard a bad idea?

5. Monetarists believed for a period of time that the velocity of money was stable within a country. However, with financial innovation, the velocity began shifting around erratically after 1980. As would be expected, the velocity of money is different across countries depending upon the sophistication of their financial systems—velocity of money tends to be higher in countries with developed financial systems. The accompanying table provides money supply and GDP information in 2005 for six countries.

Country	National currency	M1 (billions in national currency)	Nominal GDP (billions in national currency)
Egypt	Egyptian pounds	101	539
South Korea	Korean won	77,274	806,622
Thailand	Thai baht	863	7,103
United States	U.S. dollars	1,369	12,456
Kenya	Kenyan pounds	231	1,415
India	Indian rupees	7,213	35,314

Source: Datastream.

a. Calculate the velocity of money for each of the countries. The accompanying table shows GDP per capita for each of these countries in 2005 in U.S. dollars.

Country	Nominal GDP per capita (U.S. dollars)
Egypt	$1,270
South Korea	16,444
Thailand	2,707
United States	41,886
Kenya	572
India	710

Source: IMF.

b. Rank the countries in descending order of per capita income and velocity of money. Do wealthy countries or poor countries tend to "turn over" their money more times per year? Would you expect that wealthy countries have more sophisticated financial systems?

6. The chapter explains that Kenneth Rogoff proclaimed Richard Nixon "the all-time hero of political business cycles." Using the table of data below from the Economic Report of the President, explain why Nixon may have earned that title. (*Note:* Nixon entered office in January 1969 and was reelected in November 1972. He resigned in August 1974.)

Year	Government receipts (billions of dollars)	Government spending (billions of dollars)	Government budget balance (billions of dollars)	M1 growth	M2 growth	3-month Treasury bill rate
1969	$186.9	$183.6	$3.2	3.3%	3.7%	6.68%
1970	192.8	195.6	−2.8	5.1	6.6	6.46
1971	187.1	210.2	−23.0	6.5	13.4	4.35
1972	207.3	230.7	−23.4	9.2	13.0	4.07
1973	230.8	245.7	−14.9	5.5	6.6	7.04

7. The economy of Albernia is facing a recessionary gap, and the leader of that nation calls together five of its best economists representing the classical, Keynesian, monetarist, real business cycle, and modern consensus views of the macroeconomy. Explain what policies each economist would recommend and why.

8. Which of the following policy recommendations are consistent with the classical, Keynesian, monetarist, and/or modern consensus views of the macroeconomy?

a. Since the long-run growth of GDP is 2%, the money supply should grow at 2%.

b. Decrease government spending in order to decrease inflationary pressure.

c. Increase the money supply in order to alleviate a recessionary gap.

d. Always maintain a balanced budget.

e. Decrease the budget deficit as a percent of GDP when facing a recessionary gap.

9. Using a graph like Figure 33-4, show how a monetarist can argue that a contractionary fiscal policy need not lead to a fall in real GDP given a fixed money supply. Explain.

Open-Economy Macroeconomics

HAPPY TOURISTS, SAD TOURISTS

"YOU SHOULD SEE, WHEN THEY COME IN the door, the shopping bags they hand off to the coat check. I mean, they're just spending. It's Monopoly money to them." So declared a New York restaurant manager, describing the European tourists who, in the summer of 2008, accounted for a large share of her business. Meanwhile, American tourists in Europe were suffering sticker shock. One American, whose family of four was visiting Paris, explained his changing vacation plans: "We might not stay as long. We might eat cheese sandwiches."

It was quite a change from 2000, when an article in the *New York Times* bore the headline: "Dollar makes the good life a tourist bargain in Europe." What happened? The answer is that there was a large shift in the relative values of the euro, the currency used by much of Europe, and the U.S. dollar. At its low point in 2000, a euro was worth only about 85 cents. By mid-2008, it was worth more than $1.50.

What causes the relative value of the dollar and the euro to change? What are the effects of such changes? These are among the questions addressed by *open-economy macroeconomics*, the branch of macroeconomics that deals with the relationships between national economies. In this chapter we'll learn about some of the key issues in open-economy macroeconomics: the determinants of a country's *balance of payments*, the factors affecting *exchange rates*, the different forms of *exchange rate policy* adopted by various countries, and the relationship between exchange rates and macroeconomic policy.

The value of the dollar was so low and the euro so high in 2008 that European tourists flocked to the United States to sightsee and shop.

Capital Flows and the Balance of Payments

In 2007 people living in the United States sold about $4.5 trillion worth of stuff to people living in other countries and bought about $4.5 trillion worth of stuff in return. What kind of stuff? All kinds. Residents of the United States (including firms operating in the United States) sold airplanes, bonds, wheat, and many other items to residents of other countries. Residents of the United States bought cars, stocks, oil, and many other items from residents of other countries.

How can we keep track of these transactions? In Chapter 23 we learned that economists keep track of the domestic economy using the national income and product accounts. Economists keep track of international transactions using a different but related set of numbers, the *balance of payments accounts.*

Balance of Payments Accounts

A country's **balance of payments accounts** are a summary of the country's transactions with other countries.

To understand the basic idea behind the balance of payments accounts, let's consider a small-scale example: not a country, but a family farm. Let's say that we know the following about how last year went financially for the Costas, who own a small artichoke farm in California:

- They made $100,000 by selling artichokes.

- They spent $70,000 on running the farm, including purchases of new farm machinery, and another $40,000 buying food, paying utility bills, replacing their worn-out car, and so on.

- They received $500 in interest on their bank account but paid $10,000 in interest on their mortgage.

- They took out a new $25,000 loan to help pay for farm improvements but didn't use all the money immediately. So they put the extra in the bank.

How could we summarize the Costas' year? One way would be with a table like Table 34-1, which shows sources of cash coming in and money going out, characterized under a few broad headings. The first row of Table 34-1 shows sales and purchases of goods and services: sales of artichokes; purchases of groceries, heating oil, that new car, and so on. The second row shows interest payments: the interest the Costas received from their bank account and the interest they paid on their mortgage. The third row shows cash coming in from new borrowing versus money deposited in the bank.

In each row we show the net inflow of cash from that type of transaction. So the net in the first row is –$10,000, because the Costas spent $10,000 more than they earned. The net in the second row is –$9,500, the difference between the interest the Costas received on their bank account and the interest they paid on the mortgage. The net in the third row is $19,500: the Costas brought in $25,000 with their new loan but put only $5,500 of that sum in the bank.

A country's **balance of payments accounts** are a summary of the country's transactions with other countries.

TABLE 34-1

The Costas' Financial Year

	Sources of cash	Uses of cash	Net
Purchases or sales of goods and services	Artichoke sales: $100,000	Farm operation and living expenses: $110,000	−$10,000
Interest payments	Interest received on bank account: $500	Interest paid on mortgage: $10,000	−$9,500
Loans and deposits	Funds received from new loan: $25,000	Funds deposited in bank: $5,500	+$19,500
Total	**$125,500**	**$125,500**	**$0**

The last row shows the sum of cash coming in from all sources and the sum of all cash used. These sums are equal, by definition: every dollar has a source, and every dollar received gets used somewhere. (What if the Costas hid money under the mattress? Then that would be counted as another "use" of cash.)

A country's balance of payments accounts summarize its transactions with the world with a table basically similar to the way we just summarized the Costas' financial year.

Table 34-2 shows a simplified version of the U.S. balance of payments accounts for 2007. Where the Costa family's accounts show sources and uses of cash, the balance of payments accounts show payments from foreigners—in effect, sources of cash for the United States as a whole—and payments to foreigners.

Row 1 of Table 34-2 shows payments that arise from sales and purchases of goods and services. For example, the value of U.S. wheat exports and the fees foreigners pay to U.S. consulting companies appear in the second column; the value of U.S. oil imports and the fees American companies pay to Indian call centers—the people who often answer your 1-800 calls—appear in the third column.

Row 2 shows *factor income*—the income countries pay for the use of factors of production owned by residents of other countries. Mostly this means investment income: interest paid on loans from overseas, the profits of foreign-owned corporations, and so on. For example, the profits earned by Disneyland Paris, which is owned by the U.S.-based Walt Disney Company, appear in the second column; the profits

TABLE 34-2

The U.S. Balance of Payments in 2007 (billions of dollars)

	Payments from foreigners	Payments to foreigners	Net
1 **Sales and purchases of goods and services**	$1,646	$2,346	−$700
2 **Factor income**	818	736	82
3 **Transfers**	—	—	−113
Current account (1 + 2 + 3)			**−731**
4 **Official asset sales and purchases**	411	22	389
5 **Private sales and purchases of assets**	1,653	1,267	386
Financial account (4 + 5)			**775**
Total	—	—	**44**

Source: Bureau of Economic Analysis.

A country's **balance of payments on current account,** or **current account,** is its balance of payments on goods and services plus net international transfer payments and factor income.

A country's **balance of payments on goods and services** is the difference between its exports and its imports during a given period.

The **merchandise trade balance,** or **trade balance,** is the difference between a country's exports and imports of goods.

A country's **balance of payments on financial account,** or simply its **financial account,** is the difference between its sales of assets to foreigners and its purchases of assets from foreigners during a given period.

earned by the U.S. operations of Japanese auto companies appear in the third column. This category also includes some labor income. For example, the wages of an American engineer who works temporarily on a construction site in Dubai are counted in the second column.

Row 3 shows *international transfers*—funds sent by residents of one country to residents of another. The main element here is the remittances that immigrants, such as the millions of Mexican-born workers employed in the United States, send to their families in their country of origin. Notice that Table 34-2 only shows the net value of transfers. That's because the U.S. government only provides an estimate of the net, not a breakdown between payments to foreigners and payments from foreigners.

The next two rows of Table 34-2 show payments resulting from sales and purchases of assets, broken down by who is doing the buying and selling. Row 4 shows transactions that involve governments or government agencies, mainly central banks. As we'll learn later, in 2007 most of the U.S. sales in this category involved the accumulation of *foreign exchange reserves* by the central bank of China and oil-exporting countries. Row 5 shows private sales and purchases of assets. For example, the 2008 purchase of Budweiser, an American brewing company, by the Belgian corporation InBev would show up in the second column of row 5; purchases of European stocks by U.S. investors show up in the third column.

In laying out Table 34-2, we have separated rows 1, 2, and 3 into one group and rows 4 and 5 into another. This reflects a fundamental difference in how these two groups of transactions affect the future.

When a U.S. resident sells a good such as wheat to a foreigner, that's the end of the transaction. But a financial asset, such as a bond, is different. Remember, a bond is a promise to pay interest and principal in the future. So when a U.S. resident sells a bond to a foreigner, that sale creates a liability: the U.S. resident will have to pay interest and repay principal in the future. The balance of payments accounts distinguish between transactions that don't create liabilities and those that do.

Transactions that don't create liabilities are considered part of the **balance of payments on current account,** often referred to simply as the **current account:** the balance of payments on goods and services plus net international transfer payments and factor income. The balance of row 1 of Table 34-2, –$700 billion, corresponds to the most important part of the current account: the **balance of payments on goods and services,** the difference between the value of exports and the value of imports during a given period.

By the way, if you read news reports on the economy, you may well see references to another measure, the **merchandise trade balance,** sometimes referred to as the **trade balance** for short. This is the difference between a country's exports and imports of goods alone—not including services. Economists sometimes focus on the merchandise trade balance, even though it's an incomplete measure, because data on international trade in services aren't as accurate as data on trade in physical goods, and they are also slower to arrive.

The current account, as we've just learned, consists of international transactions that don't create liabilities. Transactions that involve the sale or purchase of assets, and therefore do create future liabilities, are considered part of the **balance of payments on financial account,** or the **financial account** for short. (Until a few years ago, economists often referred to the financial account as the *capital account.* We'll use the modern term, but you may run across the older term.)

So how does it all add up? The shaded rows of Table 34-2 show the bottom lines: the overall U.S. current account and financial account for 2007. As you can see, in 2007 the United States ran a current account deficit: the amount it paid to foreigners for goods, services, factors, and transfers was more than the amount it received. Simultaneously, it ran a financial account surplus: the value of the assets it sold to foreigners was more than the value of the assets it bought from foreigners.

In the official data, the U.S. current account deficit and financial account surplus almost, but not quite, offset each other: the financial account surplus was

$44 billion larger than the current account deficit. But that's just a statistical error, reflecting the imperfection of official data. (And a $44 billion error when you're measuring inflows and outflows of $4.5 trillion isn't bad!) In fact, it's a basic rule of balance of payments accounting that the current account and the financial account must sum to zero:

(34-1) Current account (*CA*) + Financial account (*FA*) = 0

or

$$CA = -FA$$

Why must Equation 34-1 be true? We already saw the fundamental explanation in Table 34-1, which showed the accounts of the Costa family: in total, the sources of cash must equal the uses of cash. The same applies to balance of payments accounts. Figure 34-1, a variant on the circular-flow diagram we have found useful in discussing domestic macroeconomics, may help you visualize how this adding up works. Instead of showing the flow of money *within* a national economy, Figure 34-1 shows the flow of money *between* national economies. Money flows into the United States from the rest of the world as payment for U.S. exports of goods and services, as payment for the use of U.S.-owned factors of production, and as transfer payments. These flows (indicated by the lower green arrow) are the positive components of the U.S. current account. Money also flows into the United States from foreigners who purchase U.S. assets (as shown by the lower red arrow)—the positive component of the U.S. financial account.

At the same time, money flows from the United States to the rest of the world as payment for U.S. imports of goods and services, as payment for the use of foreign-owned factors of production, and as transfer payments. These flows, indicated by the upper green arrow, are the negative components of the U.S. current account. Money also flows from the United States to purchase foreign assets, as shown by the upper red arrow—the negative component of the U.S. financial account. As in all circular-flow diagrams, the flow into a box and the flow out of a box are equal. This means that the sum of the red and green arrows going into

FIGURE 34-1

The Balance of Payments

The green arrows represent payments that are counted in the current account. The red arrows represent payments that are counted in the financial account. Because the total flow into the United States must equal the total flow out of the United States, the sum of the current account plus the financial account is zero.

Payments to the rest of the world for assets

Payments to the rest of the world for goods and services, factor income, and transfers

United States

Rest of world

Payments to the United States for goods and services, factor income, and transfers

Payments to the United States for assets

FOR INQUIRING MINDS

GDP, GNP, and the Current Account

When we discussed national income accounting in Chapter 23, we derived the basic equation relating GDP to the components of spending:

$$Y = C + I + G + X - IM$$

where X and IM are exports and imports, respectively, of goods and services. But as we've learned, the balance of payments on goods and services is only one component of the current account balance. Why doesn't the national income equation use the current account as a whole?

The answer is that gross domestic product, which is the value of goods and serv-ices produced in a country, doesn't include two sources of income that are included in calculating the current account balance: international factor income and international transfers. The profits of Ford Motors U.K. aren't included in America's GDP, and the funds Latin American immigrants send home to their families aren't subtracted from GDP.

Shouldn't we have a broader measure that does include these sources of income? Actually, gross *national* product—GNP—does include international factor income. Estimates of U.S. GNP differ slightly from estimates of GDP because GNP adds in items such as the earnings of U.S. compa-nies abroad and subtracts items such as the interest payments on bonds owned by residents of China and Japan. There isn't, however, any regularly calculated measure that includes transfer payments.

Why do economists use GDP rather than a broader measure? Two reasons. First, the original purpose of the national accounts was to track production rather than income. Second, data on international factor income and transfer payments are generally considered somewhat unreliable. So if you're trying to keep track of movements in the economy, it makes sense to focus on GDP, which doesn't rely on these unreliable data.

---

the United States is equal to the sum of the red and green arrows going out of the United States. That is,

(34-2) Positive entries on current account (lower green arrow) + Positive entries on financial account (lower red arrow) = Negative entries on current account (upper green arrow) + Negative entries on financial account (upper red arrow)

Equation 34-2 can be rearranged as follows:

(34-3) Positive entries on current account – Negative entries on current account + Positive entries on financial account – Negative entries on financial account = 0

Equation 34-3 is equivalent to Equation 34-1: the current account plus the financial account—both equal to positive entries minus negative entries—is equal to zero.

But what determines the current account and the financial account?

Modeling the Financial Account

A country's financial account measures its net sales of assets to foreigners. There is, however, another way to think about the financial account: it's a measure of *capital inflows*, of foreign savings that are available to finance domestic investment spending.

What determines these capital inflows?

Part of our explanation will have to wait for a little while, because some international capital flows are carried out by governments and central banks, which sometimes act very differently from private investors. But we can gain insight into the motivations for capital flows that are the result of private decisions by using

GLOBAL COMPARISON CURRENT ACCOUNT SURPLUSES AND DEFICITS

This figure shows the current account balances, in billions of dollars, of six big players in the global economy in two years, 1996 and 2007. Three of the players—the United States, China, and Japan—are individual countries. The other three are groups of countries: the European Union, "newly industrialized Asia" (South Korea, Taiwan, Hong Kong, and Singapore, which have achieved high levels of GDP per capita), and the oil producers of the Middle East.

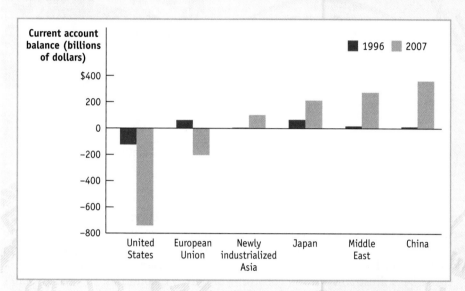

You can see that the huge U.S. current account deficit of 2007 was much smaller 11 years earlier. Although the United States was moving deep into current account deficit, other major players were moving in the opposite direction. China only ran small surpluses before 2002 but began running ever more gigantic surpluses thereafter. Middle Eastern countries, which mainly export oil, also began running huge surpluses after 2002, as oil prices rose. Meanwhile, Japan ran substantial surpluses throughout, and Europe had a nearly balanced current account until 2007.

Overall, the big picture seems to be one of massive surpluses in China and the Middle East, channeled into financing a huge deficit on the part of the United States. In describing the huge surpluses in countries like China, some economists have called it a "global savings glut."

Source: World Bank.

the *loanable funds model* we developed in Chapter 26. In using this model, we make two important simplifications:

■ We simplify the reality of international capital flows by assuming that all flows are in the form of loans. In reality, capital flows take many forms, including purchases of shares of stock in foreign companies and foreign real estate as well as *direct foreign investment*, in which companies build factories or acquire other productive assets abroad.

■ We also ignore the effects of expected changes in *exchange rates*, the relative values of different national currencies. We analyze the determination of exchange rates later in the chapter.

Figure 34-2 on the next page recaps the loanable funds model for a closed economy. Equilibrium corresponds to point *E*, at an interest rate of 4%, where the supply of loanable

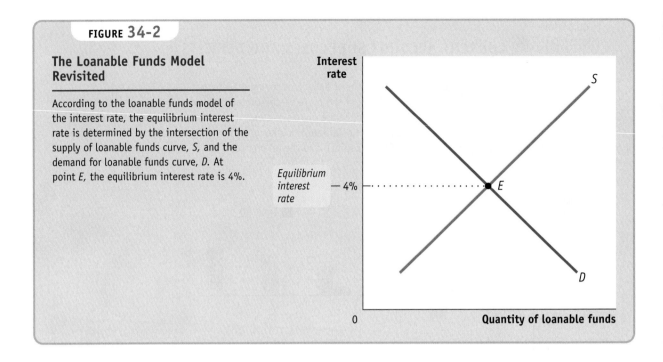

FIGURE 34-2

The Loanable Funds Model Revisited

According to the loanable funds model of the interest rate, the equilibrium interest rate is determined by the intersection of the supply of loanable funds curve, S, and the demand for loanable funds curve, D. At point E, the equilibrium interest rate is 4%.

funds curve, S intersects, the demand for loanable funds, curve D. But if international capital flows are possible, this diagram changes and E may no longer be the equilibrium. We can analyze the causes and effects of international capital flows using Figure 34-3, which places the loanable funds market diagrams for two countries side by side.

Figure 34-3 illustrates a world consisting of only two countries, the United States and Britain. Panel (a) shows the loanable funds market in the United States, where the equilibrium in the absence of international capital flows is at point E_{US} with an interest rate of 6%. Panel (b) shows the loanable funds market in Britain, where the equilibrium in the absence of international capital flows is at point E_B with an interest rate of 2%.

FIGURE 34-3 **Loanable Funds Markets in Two Countries**

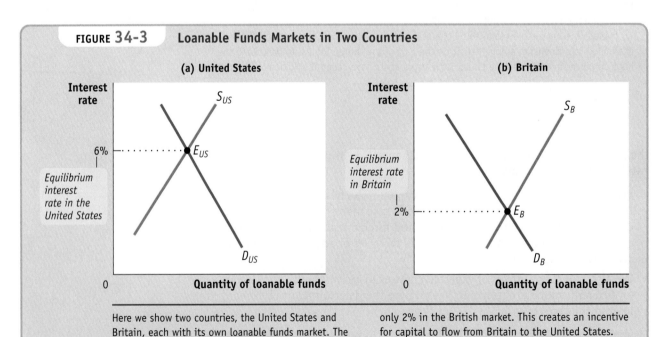

Here we show two countries, the United States and Britain, each with its own loanable funds market. The equilibrium interest rate is 6% in the U.S. market but only 2% in the British market. This creates an incentive for capital to flow from Britain to the United States.

Will the actual interest rate in the United States remain at 6% and that in Britain at 2%? Not if it is easy for British residents to make loans to Americans. In that case, British lenders, attracted by high American interest rates, will send some of their loanable funds to the United States. This capital inflow will increase the quantity of loanable funds supplied to American borrowers, pushing the U.S. interest rate down. At the same time, it will reduce the quantity of loanable funds supplied to British borrowers, pushing the British interest rate up. So international capital flows will narrow the gap between U.S. and British interest rates.

Let's further suppose that British lenders regard a loan to an American as being just as good as a loan to one of their own compatriots, and American borrowers regard a debt to a British lender as no more costly than a debt to an American lender. In that case, the flow of funds from Britain to the United States will continue until the gap between their interest rates is eliminated. In other words, when residents of the two countries believe that a foreign asset is as good as a domestic one and that a foreign liability is as good as a domestic one, then international capital flows will equalize the interest rates in the two countries. Figure 34-4 shows an international equilibrium in the loanable funds markets where the equilibrium interest rate is 4% in both the United States and Britain. At this interest rate, the quantity of loanable funds demanded by American borrowers exceeds the quantity of loanable funds supplied by American lenders. This gap is filled by "imported" funds—a capital inflow from Britain. At the same time, the quantity of loanable funds supplied by British lenders is greater than the quantity of loanable funds demanded by British borrowers. This excess is "exported" in the form of a capital outflow to the United States. And the two markets are in equilibrium at a common interest rate of 4%—at that interest rate, the total quantity of loans demanded by borrowers across the two markets is equal to the total quantity of loans supplied by lenders across the two markets.

In short, international flows of capital are like international flows of goods and services. Capital moves from places where it would be cheap in the absence of international capital flows to places where it would be expensive in the absence of such flows.

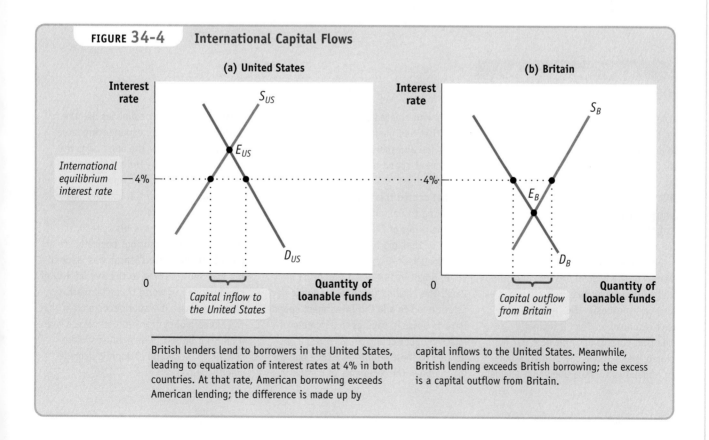

FIGURE 34-4 **International Capital Flows**

British lenders lend to borrowers in the United States, leading to equalization of interest rates at 4% in both countries. At that rate, American borrowing exceeds American lending; the difference is made up by capital inflows to the United States. Meanwhile, British lending exceeds British borrowing; the excess is a capital outflow from Britain.

Underlying Determinants of International Capital Flows

The open-economy version of the loanable funds model helps us understand international capital flows in terms of the supply and demand for funds. But what underlies differences across countries in the supply and demand for funds? Why, in the absence of international capital flows, would interest rates differ internationally, creating an incentive for international capital flows?

International differences in the demand for funds reflect underlying differences in investment opportunities. In particular, a country with a rapidly growing economy, other things equal, tends to offer more investment opportunities than a country with a slowly growing economy. So a rapidly growing economy typically—though not always—has a higher demand for capital and offers higher returns to investors than a slowly growing economy in the absence of capital flows. As a result, capital tends to flow from slowly growing to rapidly growing economies.

The classic example, described in the upcoming Economics in Action, is the flow of capital from Britain to the United States, among other countries, between 1870 and 1914. During that era, the U.S. economy was growing rapidly as the population increased and spread westward and as the nation industrialized. This created a demand for investment spending on railroads, factories, and so on. Meanwhile, Britain had a much more slowly growing population, was already industrialized, and already had a railroad network covering the country. This left Britain with savings to spare, much of which were lent out to the United States and other New World economies.

International differences in the supply of funds reflect differences in savings across countries. These may be the result of differences in private savings rates, which vary widely among countries. For example, in 2006 private savings were 26.5% of Japan's GDP but only 14.8% of U.S. GDP. They may also reflect differences in savings by governments. In particular, government budget deficits, which reduce overall national savings, can lead to capital inflows.

FOR INQUIRING MINDS

A Global Savings Glut?

In the early years of the twenty-first century, the United States moved into massive deficit on current account, which meant that it became the recipient of huge capital inflows from the rest of the world, (especially China), other Asian countries, and the Middle East. Why did that happen?

In an influential speech early in 2005, Ben Bernanke—who was at that time a governor of the Federal Reserve and who would soon become the Fed's chairman—offered a hypothesis: the United States wasn't responsible. The "principal causes of the U.S. current account deficit," he declared, lie "outside the country's borders." Specifically, he argued that special

factors had created a "global savings glut" that had pushed down interest rates worldwide and thereby led to an excess of investment spending over savings in the United States.

What caused this global savings glut? According to Bernanke, the main cause was the series of financial crises that began in Thailand in 1997; ricocheted across much of Asia; then hit Russia in 1998, Brazil in 1999, and Argentina in 2002. The ensuing fear and economic devastation led to a fall in investment spending and a rise in savings in a number of relatively poor countries. As a result, a number of these countries, which had previously been the recipients of capital in-

flows from advanced countries like the United States, began experiencing large capital outflows. For the most part, the capital flowed to the United States, perhaps because "the depth and sophistication of the country's financial markets" made it an attractive destination.

When Bernanke gave his speech, it was viewed as reassuring: basically, he argued that the United States was responding in a sensible way to the availability of cheap money in world financial markets. Later, however, it would become clear that the cheap money from abroad helped fuel a housing bubble, which caused widespread financial and economic damage when it burst.

Two-Way Capital Flows

The loanable funds model helps us understand the direction of *net* capital flows—the excess of inflows into a country over outflows, or vice versa. As we saw in Table 34-2, however, *gross* flows take place in both directions: for example, the United States both sells assets to foreigners and buys assets from foreigners. Why does capital move in both directions?

The answer to this question is that in the real world, as opposed to the simple model we've just learned, there are other motives for international capital flows besides seeking a higher rate of interest. Individual investors often seek to diversify against risk by buying stocks in a number of countries. Stocks in Europe may do well when stocks in the United States do badly, or vice versa, so investors in Europe try to reduce their risk by buying some U.S. stocks, even as investors in the United States try to reduce their risk by buying some European stocks. The result is capital flows in both directions. Meanwhile, corporations often engage in international investment as part of their business strategy—for example, auto companies may find that they can compete better in a national market if they assemble some of their cars locally. Such business investments can also lead to two-way capital flows, as, say, European car makers build plants in the United States even as U.S. computer companies open facilities in Europe. Finally, some countries, including the United States, are international banking centers: people from all over the world put money in U.S. financial institutions, which then invest many of those funds overseas.

The result of these two-way flows is that modern economies are typically both debtors (countries that owe money to the rest of the world) and creditors (countries to which the rest of the world owes money). Due to years of both capital inflows and outflows, at the end of 2007, the United States had accumulated foreign assets worth $17.6 trillion, and foreigners had accumulated assets in the United States worth $20.1 trillion.

►ECONOMICS IN ACTION

The Golden Age of Capital Flows

Technology, it's often said, shrinks the world. Jet planes have put most of the world's cities within a few hours of one another; modern telecommunications transmit information instantly around the globe. So you might think that international capital flows must now be larger than ever.

But if capital flows are measured as a share of world savings and investment, that belief turns out not to be true. The golden age of capital flows actually preceded World War I—from 1870 to 1914.

These capital flows went mainly from European countries, especially Britain, to what were then known as "zones of recent settlement," countries that were attracting large numbers of European immigrants. Among the big recipients of capital inflows were Australia, Argentina, Canada, and the United States.

The large capital flows reflected differences in investment opportunities. Britain, a mature industrial economy with limited natural resources and a slowly growing population, offered relatively limited opportunities for new investment. The zones of recent settlement, with rapidly growing populations and abundant natural resources, offered investors a higher return and attracted capital inflows. Estimates suggest that over this period Britain sent about 40% of its savings abroad, largely to finance railroads and other large projects. No country has matched that record in modern times.

Why can't we match the capital flows of our great-great-grandfathers? Economists aren't completely sure, but they have pointed to two causes: migration restrictions and political risks.

During the golden age of capital flows, capital movements were complementary to population movements: the big recipients of capital from Europe were also places to which large numbers of Europeans were moving. These large-scale population movements were possible before World War I because there were few legal restrictions on immigration. In today's world, by contrast, migration is limited by extensive legal barriers, as anyone considering a move to the United States or Europe can tell you.

The other factor that has changed is political risk. Modern governments often limit foreign investment because they fear it will diminish their national autonomy. And due to political or security concerns, governments sometimes seize foreign property, a risk that deters investors from sending more than a relatively modest share of their wealth abroad. In the nineteenth century such actions were rare, partly because some major destinations of investment were still European colonies, partly because in those days governments had a habit of sending troops and gunboats to enforce the claims of their investors. ▲

< < < < < < < < < < < <

> CHECK YOUR UNDERSTANDING 34-1

1. Which of the balance of payments accounts do the following events affect?
   a. Boeing, a U.S.-based company, sells a newly built airplane to China.
   b. Chinese investors buy stock in Boeing from Americans.
   c. A Chinese company buys a used airplane from American Airlines and ships it to China.
   d. A Chinese investor who owns property in the United States buys a corporate jet, which he will keep in the United States so he can travel around America.

2. Suppose China decides that it needs a huge program of infrastructure spending, which it will finance by borrowing. How would this program affect the U.S. balance of payments?

Solutions appear at back of book.

The Role of the Exchange Rate

We've just seen how differences in the supply of loanable funds from savings and the demand for loanable funds for investment spending lead to international capital flows. We've also learned that a country's balance of payments on current account plus its balance of payments on financial account add to zero: a country that receives net capital inflows must run a matching current account deficit, and a country that generates net capital outflows must run a matching current account surplus.

The behavior of the financial account—reflecting inflows or outflows of capital—is best described by equilibrium in the international loanable funds market. At the same time, the balance of payments on goods and services, the main component of the current account, is determined by decisions in the international markets for goods and services. So given that the financial account reflects the movement of capital and the current account reflects the movement of goods and services, what ensures that the balance of payments really does balance? That is, what ensures that the two accounts actually offset each other?

The answer lies in the role of the *exchange rate,* which is determined in the *foreign exchange market.*

Understanding Exchange Rates

In general, goods, services, and assets produced in a country must be paid for in that country's currency. American products must be paid for in dollars; European products must be paid for in euros; Japanese products must be paid for in yen. Occasionally, sellers will accept payment in foreign currency, but they will then exchange that currency for domestic money.

International transactions, then, require a market—the **foreign exchange market**—in which currencies can be exchanged for each other. This market determines

Currencies are traded in the **foreign exchange market.**

The prices at which currencies trade are known as **exchange rates.**

When a currency becomes more valuable in terms of other currencies, it **appreciates.**

When a currency becomes less valuable in terms of other currencies, it **depreciates.**

exchange rates, the prices at which currencies trade. (The foreign exchange market is, in fact, not located in any one geographic spot. Rather, it is a global electronic market that traders around the world use to buy and sell currencies.)

Table 34-3 shows exchange rates among the world's three most important currencies as of 3:49 P.M., EST, on September 13, 2008. Each entry shows the price of the "row" currency in terms of the "column" currency. For example, at that time US$1 exchanged for €0.7034, so it took €0.7034 to buy US$1. Similarly, it took US$1.4217 to buy €1. These two numbers reflect the same rate of exchange between the euro and the U.S. dollar: 1/1.4127 = 0.7034.

There are two ways to write any given exchange rate. In this case, there were €0.7034 to US$1 and US$1.4217 to €1. Which is the correct way to write it? The answer is that there is no fixed rule. In most countries, people tend to express the exchange rate as the price of a dollar in domestic currency. However, this rule isn't universal, and the U.S. dollar–euro rate is commonly quoted both ways. The important thing is to be sure you know which one you are using! See the Pitfalls below.

When discussing movements in exchange rates, economists use specialized terms to avoid confusion. When a currency becomes more valuable in terms of other currencies, economists say that the currency **appreciates.** When a currency becomes less valuable in terms of other currencies, it **depreciates.** Suppose, for example, that the value of €1 went from $1 to $1.25, which means that the value of US$1 went from €1 to €0.80 (because 1/1.25 = 0.80). In this case, we would say that the euro appreciated and the U.S. dollar depreciated.

Movements in exchange rates, other things equal, affect the relative prices of goods, services, and assets in different countries. Suppose, for example, that the price of an American hotel room is US$100 and the price of a French hotel room is €100. If the exchange rate is €1 = US$1, these hotel rooms have the same price. If the exchange rate is €1.25 = US$1, the French hotel room is 20% cheaper than the American hotel room. If the exchange rate is €0.80 = US$1, the French hotel room is 25% more expensive than the American hotel room.

But what determines exchange rates? Supply and demand in the foreign exchange market.

The Equilibrium Exchange Rate

Imagine, for the sake of simplicity, that there are only two currencies in the world: U.S. dollars and euros. Europeans wanting to purchase American goods, services, and assets come to the foreign exchange market, wanting to exchange euros for U.S. dollars. That is, Europeans demand U.S. dollars from the foreign exchange market and, correspondingly, supply euros to that market. Americans wanting to buy European goods, services, and assets come to the foreign exchange market to exchange U.S. dollars for euros. That is, Americans supply U.S. dollars to the foreign exchange market and, correspondingly, demand euros from that market. (International transfers and payments of factor income also enter into the foreign exchange market, but to make things simple we'll ignore these.)

Figure 34-5 on the next page shows how the foreign exchange market works. The quantity of dollars demanded and supplied at any given euro–U.S. dollar exchange rate is shown on the horizontal axis, and the euro–U.S. dollar exchange rate is shown on the vertical axis. The exchange rate plays the same role as the price of a good or service in an ordinary supply and demand diagram.

TABLE 34-3

Exchange Rates, September 13, 2008, 3:49 P.M.

	U.S. dollars	Yen	Euros
One U.S. dollar exchanged for	1	107.94	0.7034
One yen exchanged for	0.009264	1	0.006516
One euro exchanged for	1.4217	153.46	1

PITFALLS

WHICH WAY IS UP?

Suppose someone says, "The U.S. exchange rate is up." What does that person mean?

It isn't clear. Sometimes the exchange rate is measured as the price of a dollar in terms of foreign currency, sometimes as the price of foreign currency in terms of dollars. So the statement could mean either that the dollar appreciated or that it depreciated!

You have to be particularly careful when using published statistics. Most countries other than the United States state their exchange rates in terms of the price of a dollar in their domestic currency—for example, Mexican officials will say that the exchange rate is 10, meaning 10 pesos per dollar. But Britain, for historical reasons, usually states its exchange rate the other way. At 3:49 P.M. on September 13, 2008, US$1 was worth £0.55878, and £1 was worth US$1.7896. More often than not, this number is reported as an exchange rate of 1.7896. In fact, on occasion, professional economists and consultants embarrass themselves by getting the direction in which the pound is moving wrong!

By the way, Americans generally follow other countries' lead: we usually say that the exchange rate against Mexico is 10 pesos per dollar but that the exchange rate against Britain is 1.8 dollars per pound. But this rule isn't reliable; exchange rates against the euro are often stated both ways.

So it's always important to check before using exchange rate data: which way is the exchange rate being measured?

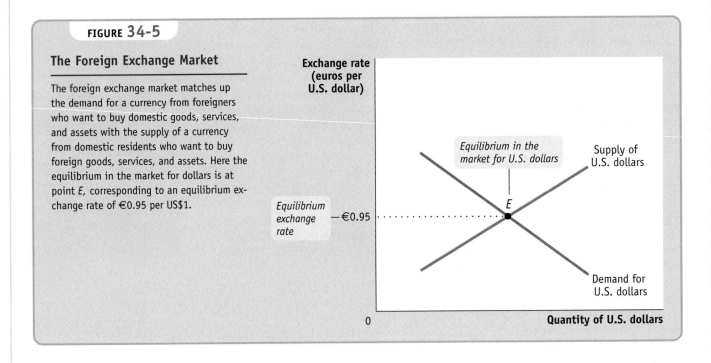

FIGURE 34-5

The Foreign Exchange Market

The foreign exchange market matches up the demand for a currency from foreigners who want to buy domestic goods, services, and assets with the supply of a currency from domestic residents who want to buy foreign goods, services, and assets. Here the equilibrium in the market for dollars is at point *E*, corresponding to an equilibrium exchange rate of €0.95 per US$1.

The **equilibrium exchange rate** is the exchange rate at which the quantity of a currency demanded in the foreign exchange market is equal to the quantity supplied.

The figure shows two curves, the demand curve for U.S. dollars and the supply curve for U.S. dollars. The key to understanding the slopes of these curves is that the level of the exchange rate affects exports and imports. When a country's currency appreciates (becomes more valuable), exports fall and imports rise. When a country's currency depreciates (becomes less valuable), exports rise and imports fall. To understand why the demand curve for U.S. dollars slopes downward, recall that the exchange rate, other things equal, determines the prices of American goods, services, and assets relative to those of European goods, services, and assets. If the U.S. dollar rises against the euro (the dollar appreciates), American products will become more expensive to Europeans relative to European products. So Europeans will buy less from the United States and will acquire fewer dollars in the foreign exchange market: the quantity of U.S. dollars demanded falls as the number of euros needed to buy a U.S. dollar rises. If the U.S. dollar falls against the euro (the dollar depreciates), American products will become relatively cheaper for Europeans. Europeans will respond by buying more from the United States and acquiring more dollars in the foreign exchange market: the quantity of U.S. dollars demanded rises as the number of euros needed to buy a U.S. dollar falls.

A similar argument explains why the supply curve of U.S. dollars in Figure 34-5 slopes upward: the more euros required to buy a U.S. dollar, the more dollars Americans will supply. Again, the reason is the effect of the exchange rate on relative prices. If the U.S. dollar rises against the euro, European products look cheaper to Americans—who will demand more of them. This will require Americans to convert more dollars into euros.

The **equilibrium exchange rate** is the exchange rate at which the quantity of U.S. dollars demanded in the foreign exchange market is equal to the quantity of U.S. dollars supplied. In Figure 34-5, the equilibrium is at point *E*, and the equilibrium exchange rate is 0.95. That is, at an exchange rate of €0.95 per US$1, the quantity of U.S. dollars supplied to the foreign exchange market is equal to the quantity of U.S. dollars demanded.

To understand the significance of the equilibrium exchange rate, it's helpful to consider a numerical example of what equilibrium in the foreign exchange market looks like. Such an example is shown in Table 34-4. (This is a hypothetical table that isn't

TABLE 34-4

Equilibrium in the Foreign Exchange Market: A Hypothetical Example

European purchases of U.S. dollars (trillions of U.S. dollars)	To buy U.S. goods and services: 1.0	To buy U.S. assets: 1.0	Total purchases of U.S. dollars: 2.0
U.S. sales of U.S. dollars (trillions of U.S. dollars)	To buy European goods and services: 1.5	To buy European assets: 0.5	Total sales of U.S. dollars: 2.0
	U.S. balance of payments on current account: −0.5	U.S. balance of payments on financial account: +0.5	

intended to match real numbers.) The first row shows European purchases of U.S. dollars, either to buy U.S. goods and services or to buy U.S. assets. The second row shows U.S. sales of U.S. dollars, either to buy European goods and services or to buy European assets. At the equilibrium exchange rate, the total quantity of U.S. dollars Europeans want to buy is equal to the total quantity of U.S. dollars Americans want to sell.

Remember that the balance of payments accounts divide international transactions into two types. Purchases and sales of goods and services are counted in the current account. (Again, we're leaving out transfers and factor income to keep things simple.) Purchases and sales of assets are counted in the financial account. At the equilibrium exchange rate, then, we have the situation shown in Table 34-4: the sum of the balance of payments on current account plus the balance of payments on financial account is zero.

Now let's briefly consider how a shift in the demand for U.S. dollars affects equilibrium in the foreign exchange market. Suppose that for some reason capital flows from Europe to the United States increase—say, due to a change in the preferences of European investors. The effects are shown in Figure 34-6. The demand for U.S. dollars in the foreign exchange market increases as European investors convert euros into dollars to fund their new investments in the United States. This is shown by the shift of the demand curve from D_1 to D_2. As a result, the U.S. dollar appreciates: the number of euros per U.S. dollar at the equilibrium exchange rate rises from XR_1 to XR_2.

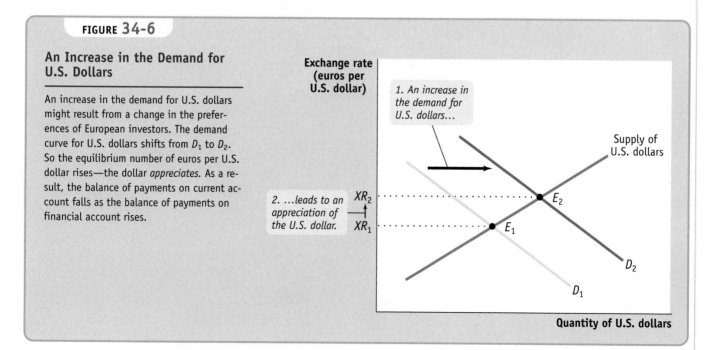

FIGURE 34-6

An Increase in the Demand for U.S. Dollars

An increase in the demand for U.S. dollars might result from a change in the preferences of European investors. The demand curve for U.S. dollars shifts from D_1 to D_2. So the equilibrium number of euros per U.S. dollar rises—the dollar *appreciates*. As a result, the balance of payments on current account falls as the balance of payments on financial account rises.

Exchange rate (euros per U.S. dollar)

1. An increase in the demand for U.S. dollars...

2. ...leads to an appreciation of the U.S. dollar.

XR_2

XR_1

E_2

E_1

Supply of U.S. dollars

D_2

D_1

Quantity of U.S. dollars

Real exchange rates are exchange rates adjusted for international differences in aggregate price levels.

What are the consequences of this increased capital inflow for the balance of payments? The total quantity of U.S. dollars supplied to the foreign exchange market still must equal the total quantity of U.S. dollars demanded. So the increased capital inflow to the United States—an increase in the balance of payments on financial account—must be matched by a decline in the balance of payments on current account. What causes the balance of payments on current account to decline? The appreciation of the U.S. dollar. A rise in the number of euros per U.S. dollar leads Americans to buy more European goods and services and Europeans to buy fewer American goods and services.

Table 34-5 shows how this might work. Europeans are buying more U.S. assets, increasing the balance of payments on financial account from 0.5 to 1.0. This is offset by a reduction in European purchases of U.S. goods and services and a rise in U.S. purchases of European goods and services, both the result of the dollar's appreciation. *So any change in the U.S. balance of payments on financial account generates an equal and opposite reaction in the balance of payments on current account.* Movements in the exchange rate ensure that changes in the financial account and in the current account offset each other.

Let's briefly run this process in reverse. Suppose there is a reduction in capital flows from Europe to the United States—again due to a change in the preferences of European investors. The demand for U.S. dollars in the foreign exchange market falls, and the dollar depreciates: the number of euros per U.S. dollar at the equilibrium exchange rate falls. This leads Americans to buy fewer European products and Europeans to buy more American products. Ultimately, this generates an increase in the U.S. balance of payments on current account. So a fall in capital flows into the United States leads to a weaker dollar, which in turn generates an increase in U.S. net exports.

TABLE 34-5

Effects of Increased Capital Inflows

European purchases of U.S. dollars (trillions of U.S. dollars)	To buy U.S. goods and services: 0.75 (down 0.25)	To buy U.S. assets: 1.5 (up 0.5)	Total purchases of U.S. dollars: 2.25
U.S. sales of U.S. dollars (trillions of U.S. dollars)	To buy European goods and services: 1.75 (up 0.25)	To buy European assets: 0.5 (no change)	Total sales of U.S. dollars: 2.25
	U.S. balance of payments on current account: −1.0 (down 0.5)	U.S. balance of payments on financial account: +1.0 (up 0.5)	

Inflation and Real Exchange Rates

In 1990 one U.S. dollar exchanged, on average, for 2.8 Mexican pesos. By 2007, the peso had fallen against the dollar by almost 75%, with an average exchange rate in 2007 of 10.9 pesos per dollar. Did Mexican products also become much cheaper relative to U.S. products over that 17-year period? Did the price of Mexican products expressed in terms of U.S. dollars also fall by almost 75%? The answer is no, because Mexico had much higher inflation than the United States over that period. In fact, the relative price of U.S. and Mexican products changed little between 1990 and 2007, although the exchange rate changed a lot.

To take account of the effects of differences in inflation rates, economists calculate **real exchange rates,** exchange rates adjusted for international differences in aggregate price levels. Suppose that the exchange rate we are looking at is the number of Mexican pesos per U.S. dollar. Let P_{US} and P_{Mex} be indexes of the aggregate price levels in the United States and Mexico, respectively. Then the real exchange rate between the Mexican peso and the U.S. dollar is defined as:

$$\text{(34-4)} \quad \text{Real exchange rate} = \text{Mexican pesos per U.S. dollar} \times \frac{P_{US}}{P_{Mex}}$$

To distinguish it from the real exchange rate, the exchange rate unadjusted for aggregate price levels is sometimes called the *nominal* exchange rate.

To understand the significance of the difference between the real and nominal exchange rates, let's consider the following example. Suppose that the Mexican peso depreciates against the U.S. dollar, with the exchange rate going from 10 pesos per U.S. dollar to 15 pesos per U.S. dollar, a 50% change. But suppose that at the same time the price of everything in Mexico, measured in pesos, increases by 50%, so that the Mexican price index rises from 100 to 150. At the same time, suppose that there is no change in U.S. prices, so that the U.S. price index remains at 100. Then the initial real exchange rate is:

$$\text{Pesos per dollar} \times \frac{P_{US}}{P_{Mex}} = 10 \times \frac{100}{100} = 10$$

After the peso depreciates and the Mexican price level increases, the real exchange rate is:

$$\text{Pesos per dollar} \times \frac{P_{US}}{P_{Mex}} = 15 \times \frac{100}{150} = 10$$

In this example, the peso has depreciated substantially in terms of the U.S. dollar, but the *real* exchange rate between the peso and the U.S. dollar hasn't changed at all. And because the real peso–U.S. dollar exchange rate hasn't changed, the nominal depreciation of the peso against the U.S. dollar will have no effect either on the quantity of goods and services exported by Mexico to the United States or on the quantity of goods and services imported by Mexico from the United States. To see why, consider again the example of a hotel room. Suppose that this room initially costs 1,000 pesos per night, which is $100 at an exchange rate of 10 pesos per dollar. After both Mexican prices and the number of pesos per dollar rise by 50%, the hotel room costs 1,500 pesos per night—but 1,500 pesos divided by 15 pesos per dollar is $100, so the Mexican hotel room still costs $100. As a result, a U.S. tourist considering a trip to Mexico will have no reason to change plans.

The same is true for all goods and services that enter into trade: *the current account responds only to changes in the real exchange rate, not the nominal exchange rate.* A country's products become cheaper to foreigners only when that country's currency depreciates in real terms, and those products become more expensive to foreigners only when the currency appreciates in real terms. As a consequence, economists who analyze movements in exports and imports of goods and services focus on the real exchange rate, not the nominal exchange rate.

Figure 34-7 illustrates just how important it can be to distinguish between nominal and real exchange rates. The line labeled "Nominal exchange rate" shows the

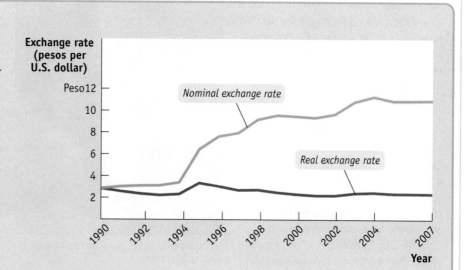

FIGURE 34-7

Real versus Nominal Exchange Rates, 1990–2007

Between 1990 and 2007, the price of a dollar in Mexican pesos increased dramatically. But because Mexico had higher inflation than the United States, the real exchange rate, which measures the relative price of Mexican goods and services, ended up roughly where it started.

Source: OECD.

The **purchasing power parity** between two countries' currencies is the nominal exchange rate at which a given basket of goods and services would cost the same amount in each country.

number of pesos it took to buy a U.S. dollar from 1990 to 2007. As you can see, the peso depreciated massively over that period. But the line labeled "Real exchange rate" shows the real exchange rate: it was calculated using Equation 34-4, with price indexes for both Mexico and the United States set so that 1990 = 100. In real terms, the peso depreciated between 1994 and 1995, but not by nearly as much as the nominal depreciation. By 2007, the real peso–U.S. dollar exchange rate was just about back where it started.

Purchasing Power Parity

A useful tool for analyzing exchange rates, closely connected to the concept of the real exchange rate, is known as *purchasing power parity*. The **purchasing power parity** between two countries' currencies is the nominal exchange rate at which a given basket of goods and services would cost the same amount in each country. Suppose, for example, that a basket of goods and services that costs $100 in the United States costs 1,000 pesos in Mexico. Then the purchasing power parity is 10 pesos per U.S. dollar: at that exchange rate, 1,000 pesos = $100, so the market basket costs the same amount in both countries.

Calculations of purchasing power parities are usually made by estimating the cost of buying broad market baskets containing many goods and services—everything from automobiles and groceries to housing and telephone calls. But as the accompanying For Inquiring Minds explains, once a year the magazine *The Economist* publishes a list of purchasing power parities based on the cost of buying a market basket that contains only one item—a McDonald's Big Mac.

Nominal exchange rates almost always differ from purchasing power parities. Some of these differences are systematic: in general, aggregate price levels are lower in poor countries than in rich countries because services tend to be cheaper in poor countries. But even among countries at roughly the same level of economic development, nominal exchange rates vary quite a lot from purchasing power parity. Figure 34-8 shows the

FOR INQUIRING MINDS

Burgernomics

For a number of years the British magazine *The Economist* has produced an annual comparison of the cost in different countries of one particular consumption item that is found around the world—a McDonald's Big Mac. The magazine finds the price of a Big Mac in local currency, then computes two numbers: the price of a Big Mac in U.S. dollars using the prevailing exchange rate, and the exchange rate at which the price of a Big Mac would equal the U.S. price. If purchasing power parity held for Big Macs, the dollar price of a Big Mac would be the same everywhere. If purchasing power parity is a good theory for the long run, the exchange rate at which a Big Mac's price matches the U.S. price should offer some guidance about where the exchange rate will eventually end up.

In the July 2008 version of the Big Mac index, there were some wide variations in

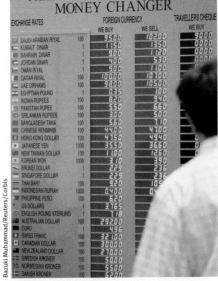

But how much money do I need to exchange if I want to buy lunch?

the dollar price of a Big Mac. In the U.S., the price was $3.57. In China, converting at the official exchange rate, a Big Mac cost only $1.83. In Switzerland, though, the price was $6.36.

The Big Mac index suggested that the euro would eventually fall against the dollar: a Big Mac on average cost €3.37, so that the purchasing power parity was $1.06 per €1 versus an actual market exchange rate of $1.59 per €1.

Serious economic studies of purchasing power parity require data on the prices of many goods and services. It turns out, however, that estimates of purchasing power parity based on the Big Mac index usually aren't that different from more elaborate measures. Fast food seems to make for pretty good fast research.

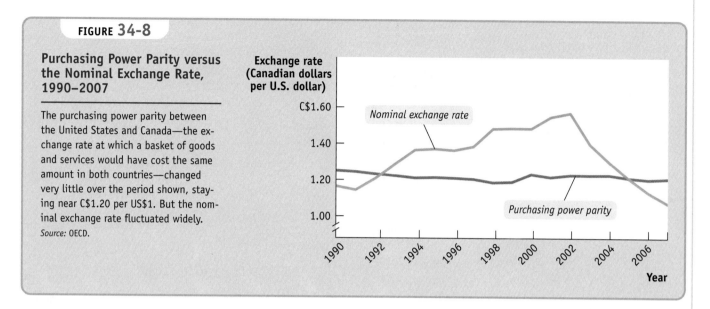

FIGURE 34-8

Purchasing Power Parity versus the Nominal Exchange Rate, 1990–2007

The purchasing power parity between the United States and Canada—the exchange rate at which a basket of goods and services would have cost the same amount in both countries—changed very little over the period shown, staying near C$1.20 per US$1. But the nominal exchange rate fluctuated widely.

Source: OECD.

Exchange rate (Canadian dollars per U.S. dollar)

nominal exchange rate between the Canadian dollar and the U.S. dollar, measured as the number of Canadian dollars per U.S. dollar, from 1990 to 2007, together with an estimate of the purchasing power parity exchange rate between the United States and Canada over the same period. The purchasing power parity didn't change much over the whole period because the United States and Canada had about the same rate of inflation. But at the beginning of the period the nominal exchange rate was below purchasing power parity, so a given market basket was more expensive in Canada than in the United States. By 2002 the nominal exchange rate was far above the purchasing power parity, so a market basket was much cheaper in Canada than in the United States.

Over the long run, however, purchasing power parities are pretty good at predicting actual changes in nominal exchange rates. In particular, nominal exchange rates between countries at similar levels of economic development tend to fluctuate around levels that lead to similar costs for a given market basket. In fact, by July 2005 the nominal exchange rate between the United States and Canada was C$1.22 per US$1—just about the purchasing power parity. And by 2007 the cost of living was once again higher in Canada than in the United States.

►*ECONOMICS IN ACTION*

Low-Cost America

Does the exchange rate matter for business decisions? And how. Consider what European auto manufacturers were doing in 2008. One report from the University of Iowa summarized the situation as follows:

> While luxury German carmakers BMW and Mercedes have maintained plants in the American South since the 1990s, BMW aims to expand U.S. manufacturing in South Carolina by 50% during the next 5 years. Volvo of Sweden is in negotiations to build a plant in New Mexico. Analysts at Italian carmaker Fiat determined that it needs to build a North American factory to profit from the upcoming re-launch of its Alfa Romeo model. Tennessee recently closed a deal with Volkswagen to build a $1 billion factory by offering $577 million in incentives.

Why were European automakers flocking to America? To some extent because they were being offered special incentives, as the case of Volkswagen in Tennessee illustrates. But the big factor was the exchange rate. In the early 2000s one euro was, on average, worth less than a dollar; by the summer of 2008 the exchange rate was

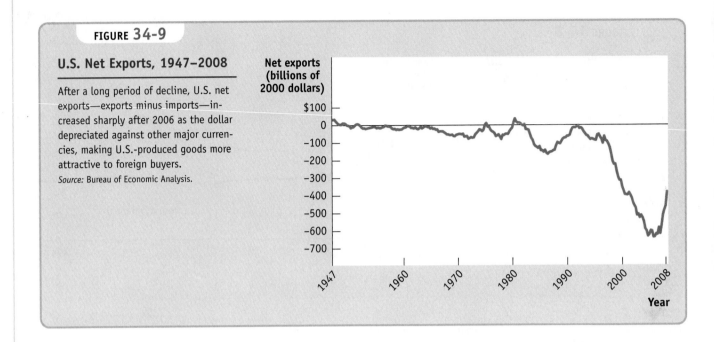

FIGURE 34-9

U.S. Net Exports, 1947–2008

After a long period of decline, U.S. net exports—exports minus imports—increased sharply after 2006 as the dollar depreciated against other major currencies, making U.S.-produced goods more attractive to foreign buyers.

Source: Bureau of Economic Analysis.

around €1 = $1.50. This change in the exchange rate made it substantially cheaper for European car manufacturers to produce in the United States than at home—especially if the cars were intended for the U.S. market.

Automobile manufacturing wasn't the only U.S. industry benefiting from the weak dollar; across the board, U.S. exports surged after 2006 while import growth fell off. Figure 34-9 shows one measure of U.S. trade performance, real net exports of goods and services: exports minus imports, both measured in 2000 dollars. As you can see, this balance, after a long slide, turned sharply upward in 2006.

The positive effects of the weak dollar on net exports were good news for the U.S. economy. The collapse of the housing bubble after 2006 was a big drag on aggregate demand; rising net exports were a welcome offsetting boost. ▲

Source: http://uicifd.blogspot.com/2008/09/did-uncle-sam-trade-in-his-chevy-for.html.

< < < < < < < < < < < <

> CHECK YOUR UNDERSTANDING 34-2

1. Mexico discovers huge reserves of oil and starts exporting oil to the United States. Describe how this would affect the following:
   a. The nominal peso–U.S. dollar exchange rate
   b. Mexican exports of other goods and services
   c. Mexican imports of goods and services

2. A basket of goods and services that costs $100 in the United States costs 800 pesos in Mexico, and the current nominal exchange rate is 10 pesos per U.S. dollar. Over the next five years, the cost of that market basket rises to $120 in the United States and to 1,200 pesos in Mexico, although the nominal exchange rate remains at 10 pesos per U.S. dollar. Calculate the following:
   a. The real exchange rate now and five years from now, if today's price index in both countries is 100
   b. Purchasing power parity today and five years from now

Solutions appear at back of book.

Exchange Rate Policy

The nominal exchange rate, like other prices, is determined by supply and demand. Unlike the price of wheat or oil, however, the exchange rate is the price of a country's money (in terms of another country's money). Money isn't a good or service produced by the private sector; it's an asset whose quantity is determined by government policy. As a result, governments have much more power to influence nominal exchange rates than they have to influence ordinary prices.

The nominal exchange rate is a very important price for many countries: the exchange rate determines the price of imports; it determines the price of exports; in economies where exports and imports are large percentages of GDP, movements in the exchange rate can have major effects on aggregate output and the aggregate price level. What do governments do with their power to influence this important price?

The answer is, it depends. At different times and in different places, governments have adopted a variety of *exchange rate regimes*. Let's talk about these regimes, how they are enforced, and how governments choose a regime. (From now on, we'll adopt the convention that we mean the nominal exchange rate when we refer to the exchange rate.)

Exchange Rate Regimes

An **exchange rate regime** is a rule governing policy toward the exchange rate. There are two main kinds of exchange rate regimes. A country has a **fixed exchange rate** when the government keeps the exchange rate against some other currency at or near a particular target. For example, Hong Kong has an official policy of setting an exchange rate of HK$7.80 per US$1. A country has a **floating exchange rate** when the government lets the exchange rate go wherever the market takes it. This is the policy followed by Britain, Canada, and the United States.

Fixed exchange rates and floating exchange rates aren't the only possibilities. At various times, countries have adopted compromise policies that lie somewhere between fixed and floating exchange rates. These include exchange rates that are fixed at any given time but are adjusted frequently, exchange rates that aren't fixed but are "managed" by the government to avoid wide swings, and exchange rates that float within a "target zone" but are prevented from leaving that zone. In this book, however, we'll focus on the two main exchange rate regimes.

The immediate question about a fixed exchange rate is how it is possible for governments to fix the exchange rate when the exchange rate is determined by supply and demand.

How Can an Exchange Rate Be Held Fixed?

To understand how it is possible for a country to fix its exchange rate, let's consider a hypothetical country, Genovia, which for some reason has decided to fix the value of its currency, the geno, at US$1.50.

The obvious problem is that $1.50 may not be the equilibrium exchange rate in the foreign exchange market: the equilibrium rate may be either higher or lower than the target exchange rate. Figure 34-10 on the next page shows the foreign exchange market for genos, with the quantities of genos supplied and demanded on the horizontal axis and the exchange rate of the geno, measured in U.S. dollars per geno, on the vertical axis. Panel (a) shows the case in which the equilibrium value of the geno is *below* the target exchange rate. Panel (b) shows the case in which the equilibrium value of the geno is *above* the target exchange rate.

Consider first the case in which the equilibrium value of the geno is below the target exchange rate. As panel (a) shows, at the target exchange rate there is a surplus of genos in the foreign exchange market, which would normally push the value of the geno down. How can the Genovian government support the value of the geno to keep the rate where it wants? There are three possible answers, all of which have been used by governments at some point.

One way the Genovian government can support the geno is to "soak up" the surplus of genos by buying its own currency in the foreign exchange market. Government purchases or sales of currency in the foreign exchange market are called **exchange market intervention.** To buy genos in the foreign exchange market, of

An **exchange rate regime** is a rule governing policy toward the exchange rate.

A country has a **fixed exchange rate** when the government keeps the exchange rate against some other currency at or near a particular target.

A country has a **floating exchange rate** when the government lets the exchange rate go wherever the market takes it.

Government purchases or sales of currency in the foreign exchange market are **exchange market intervention.**

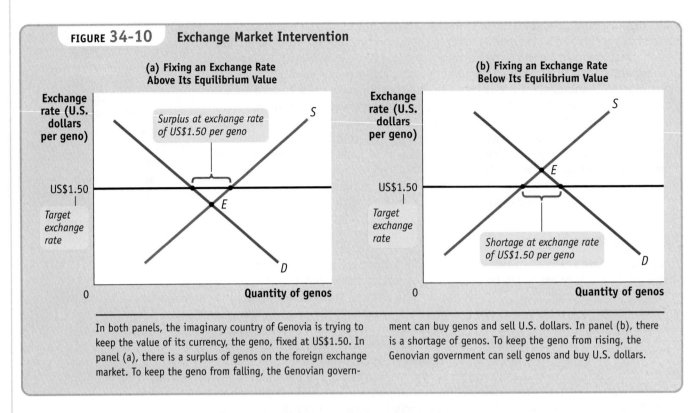

FIGURE 34-10 **Exchange Market Intervention**

(a) Fixing an Exchange Rate Above Its Equilibrium Value

Exchange rate (U.S. dollars per geno)

Surplus at exchange rate of US$1.50 per geno

S

US$1.50

E

Target exchange rate

D

0

Quantity of genos

(b) Fixing an Exchange Rate Below Its Equilibrium Value

Exchange rate (U.S. dollars per geno)

S

E

US$1.50

Target exchange rate

Shortage at exchange rate of US$1.50 per geno

D

0

Quantity of genos

In both panels, the imaginary country of Genovia is trying to keep the value of its currency, the geno, fixed at US$1.50. In panel (a), there is a surplus of genos on the foreign exchange market. To keep the geno from falling, the Genovian govern- ment can buy genos and sell U.S. dollars. In panel (b), there is a shortage of genos. To keep the geno from rising, the Genovian government can sell genos and buy U.S. dollars.

course, the Genovian government must have U.S. dollars to exchange for genos. In fact, most countries maintain **foreign exchange reserves,** stocks of foreign cur- rency (usually U.S. dollars or euros) that they can use to buy their own currency to support its price.

We mentioned earlier in the chapter that an important part of international capi- tal flows is the result of purchases and sales of foreign assets by governments and central banks. Now we can see why governments sell foreign assets: they are support- ing their currency through exchange market intervention. As we'll see in a moment, governments that keep the value of their currency *down* through exchange market in- tervention must *buy* foreign assets. First, however, let's talk about the other ways gov- ernments fix exchange rates.

A second way for the Genovian government to support the geno is to try to shift the supply and demand curves for the geno in the foreign exchange market. Governments usually do this by changing monetary policy. For example, to support the geno the Gen- ovian central bank can raise the Genovian interest rate. This will increase capital flows into Genovia, increasing the demand for genos, at the same time that it reduces capital flows out of Genovia, reducing the supply of genos. So, other things equal, an increase in a country's interest rate will increase the value of its currency.

Third, the Genovian government can support the geno by reducing the supply of genos to the foreign exchange market. It can do this by requiring domestic residents who want to buy foreign currency to get a license and giving these licenses only to people engaging in approved transactions (such as the purchase of imported goods the Genovian government thinks are essential). Licensing systems that limit the right of individuals to buy foreign currency are called **foreign exchange controls.** Other things equal, foreign exchange controls increase the value of a country's currency.

So far we've been discussing a situation in which the government is trying to prevent a depreciation of the geno. Suppose, instead, that the situation is as shown in panel (b) of Figure 34-10, where the equilibrium value of the geno is *above* the target exchange rate and there is a shortage of genos. To maintain the target exchange rate, the Genov- ian government can apply the same three basic options in the reverse direction. It can intervene in the foreign exchange market, in this case *selling* genos and acquiring U.S.

Foreign exchange reserves are stocks of foreign currency that governments maintain to buy their own currency on the foreign exchange market.

Foreign exchange controls are licensing systems that limit the right of individuals to buy foreign currency.

dollars, which it can add to its foreign exchange reserves. It can *reduce* interest rates to increase the supply of genos and reduce the demand. Or it can impose foreign exchange controls that limit the ability of foreigners to buy genos. All of these actions, other things equal, will reduce the value of the geno.

As we said, all three techniques have been used to manage fixed exchange rates. But we haven't said whether fixing the exchange rate is a good idea. In fact, the choice of exchange rate regime poses a dilemma for policy makers, because fixed and floating exchange rates each have both advantages and disadvantages.

The Exchange Rate Regime Dilemma

Few questions in macroeconomics produce as many arguments as that of whether a country should adopt a fixed or a floating exchange rate. The reason there are so many arguments is that both sides have a case.

To understand the case for a fixed exchange rate, consider for a moment how easy it is to conduct business across state lines in the United States. There are a number of things that make interstate commerce trouble-free, but one of them is the absence of any uncertainty about the value of money: a dollar is a dollar, in both New York City and Los Angeles.

By contrast, a dollar isn't a dollar in transactions between New York City and Toronto. The exchange rate between the Canadian dollar and the U.S. dollar fluctuates, sometimes widely. If a U.S. firm promises to pay a Canadian firm a given number of U.S. dollars a year from now, the value of that promise in Canadian currency can vary by 10% or more. This uncertainty has the effect of deterring trade between the two countries. So one benefit of a fixed exchange rate is certainty about the future value of a currency.

There is also, in some cases, an additional benefit to adopting a fixed exchange rate: by committing itself to a fixed rate, a country is also committing itself not to engage in inflationary policies. For example, in 1991 Argentina, which has a long history of irresponsible policies leading to severe inflation, adopted a fixed exchange rate of US$1 per Argentine peso in an attempt to commit itself to non-inflationary policies in the future. (Argentina's fixed exchange rate regime collapsed disastrously in late 2001. But that's another story.)

The point is that there is some economic value in having a stable exchange rate. Indeed, as the upcoming For Inquiring Minds explains, the presumed benefits of stable exchange rates motivated the international system of fixed exchange rates created after World War II. It was also a major reason for the creation of the euro.

However, there are also costs to fixing the exchange rate. To stabilize an exchange rate through intervention, a country must keep large quantities of foreign currency on hand—usually a low-return investment. Furthermore, even large reserves can be quickly exhausted when there are large capital flows out of a country. If a country chooses to stabilize an exchange rate by adjusting monetary policy rather than through intervention, it must divert monetary policy from other goals, notably stabilizing the economy and managing the inflation rate. Finally, foreign exchange controls, like import quotas and tariffs, distort incentives for importing and exporting goods and services. They can also create substantial costs in terms of red tape and corruption.

So there's a dilemma. Should a country let its currency float, which leaves monetary policy available for macroeconomic stabilization but creates uncertainty for business? Or should it fix the exchange rate, which eliminates the uncertainty but means giving up monetary policy, adopting exchange controls, or both? Different countries reach different conclusions at different times. Most European countries, except for Britain, have long believed that exchange rates among major European economies, which do most of their international trade with each other, should be fixed. But Canada seems happy with a floating exchange rate with the United States, even though the United States accounts for most of Canada's trade.

Luckily, we don't have to resolve this dilemma. For the rest of the chapter, we'll take exchange rate regimes as given and ask how they affect macroeconomic policy.

From Bretton Woods to the Euro

In 1944, while World War II was still raging, representatives of Allied nations met in Bretton Woods, New Hampshire, to establish a postwar international monetary system of fixed exchange rates among major currencies. The system was highly successful at first, but it broke down in 1971. After a confusing interval during which policy makers tried unsuccessfully to establish a new fixed exchange rate system, by 1973 most economically advanced countries had moved to floating exchange rates.

In Europe, however, many policy makers were unhappy with floating exchange rates, which they believed created too much uncertainty for business. From the late 1970s on-

ward they tried several times to create a system of more or less fixed exchange rates in Europe, culminating in an arrangement known as the Exchange Rate Mechanism. (The Exchange Rate Mechanism was, strictly speaking, a "target zone" system—exchange rates were free to move within a narrow band, but not outside it.) And in 1991 they agreed to move to the ultimate in fixed exchange rates: a common European currency, the euro. To the surprise of many analysts, they pulled it off: today most of Europe has abandoned national currencies for euros.

Figure 34-11 illustrates the history of European exchange rate arrangements. It shows the exchange rate between the French franc

and the German mark, measured as francs per mark, since 1971. The exchange rate fluctuated widely at first. The "plateaus" you can see in the data—eras when the exchange rate fluctuated only modestly—are periods when attempts to restore fixed exchange rates were in process. The Exchange Rate Mechanism, after a couple of false starts, became effective in 1987, stabilizing the exchange rate at about 3.4 francs per mark. (The wobbles in the early 1990s reflect two *currency crises*—episodes in which widespread expectations of imminent devaluations led to large but temporary capital flows.)

In 1999 the exchange rate was "locked"—no further fluctuations were allowed as the countries prepared to switch from francs and marks to euros. At the end of 2001, the franc and the mark ceased to exist.

The transition to the euro has not been without costs. With most of Europe sharing the same currency, it must also share the same monetary policy. Yet economic conditions in the different countries aren't always the same. Indeed, as this book went to press, there were serious stresses within the eurozone because the world financial crisis was hitting some countries, such as Spain and Ireland, much more severely than it was hitting others, notably Germany.

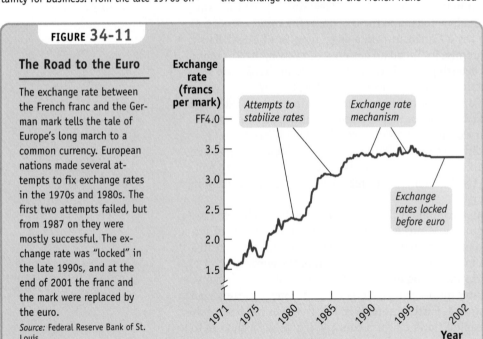

FIGURE 34-11

The Road to the Euro

The exchange rate between the French franc and the German mark tells the tale of Europe's long march to a common currency. European nations made several attempts to fix exchange rates in the 1970s and 1980s. The first two attempts failed, but from 1987 on they were mostly successful. The exchange rate was "locked" in the late 1990s, and at the end of 2001 the franc and the mark were replaced by the euro.

Source: Federal Reserve Bank of St. Louis.

►ECONOMICS IN ACTION

China Pegs the Yuan

In the early years of the twenty-first century, China provided a striking example of the lengths to which countries sometimes go to maintain a fixed exchange rate. Here's the background: China's spectacular success as an exporter led to a rising surplus on current account. At the same time, non-Chinese private investors became increasingly eager to shift funds into China, to take advantage of its growing domestic economy. These capital flows were somewhat limited by foreign exchange controls—but kept coming in anyway. As a result of the current account surplus and private capital inflows, China found itself in the position described by panel (b) of Figure 34-10: at the target exchange rate, the demand for yuan exceeded the supply. Yet the Chinese government was determined to keep the exchange rate fixed (although it began allowing gradual appreciation in 2005).

To keep the rate fixed, China had to engage in large-scale exchange market intervention, selling yuan, buying up other countries' currencies (mainly U.S. dollars) on the foreign exchange market, and adding them to its reserves. During 2007, China added $477 billion to its foreign exchange reserves, bringing the year-end total to $1.5 trillion.

To get a sense of how big these totals are, you have to know that in 2007 China's nominal GDP, converted into U.S. dollars at the prevailing exchange rate, was $3.25 trillion. So in 2007 China bought U.S. dollars and other currencies equal to about 15% of its GDP. That's as if the U.S. government had bought $2 trillion worth of yen and euros in just a single year—and was continuing to buy yen and euros even though it was already sitting on a $7 trillion pile of foreign currencies. Economists expected China to buy even more foreign currency in 2008 and 2009. ▲

> **► CHECK YOUR UNDERSTANDING 34-3** > > > > > > > > > > > >

1. Draw a diagram, similar to Figure 34-10, representing the foreign exchange situation of China when it kept the exchange rate fixed. (*Hint:* Express the exchange rate as U.S. dollars per yuan.) Then show with a diagram how each of the following policy changes might eliminate the disequilibrium in the market.
   a. An appreciation of the yuan
   b. Placing restrictions on foreigners who want to invest in China
   c. Removing restrictions on Chinese who want to invest abroad
   d. Imposing taxes on Chinese exports, such as shipments of clothing, that are causing a political backlash in the importing countries

Solutions appear at back of book.

Exchange Rates and Macroeconomic Policy

When the euro was created in 1999, there were celebrations across the nations of Europe—with a few notable exceptions. You see, some countries chose not to adopt the new currency. The most important of these was Britain, but other European countries, such as Sweden, also decided that the euro was not for them.

Why did Britain say no? Part of the answer was national pride: if Britain gave up the pound, it would also have to give up currency that bears the portrait of the Queen. But there were also serious economic concerns about giving up the pound in favor of the euro. British economists who favored adoption of the euro argued that if Britain used the same currency as its neighbors, the country's international trade would expand and its economy would become more productive. But other economists pointed out that adopting the euro would take away Britain's ability to have an independent monetary policy and might lead to macroeconomic problems.

As this discussion suggests, the fact that modern economies are open to international trade and capital flows adds a new level of complication to our analysis of macroeconomic policy. Let's look at three policy issues raised by open-economy macroeconomics.

Devaluation and Revaluation of Fixed Exchange Rates

Historically, fixed exchange rates haven't been permanent commitments. Sometimes countries with a fixed exchange rate switch to a floating rate, as Argentina did in 2001. In other cases, they retain a fixed rate but change the target exchange rate. Such adjustments in the target were common during the Bretton Woods era described in For Inquiring Minds on the previous page. For example, in 1967 Britain changed the exchange rate of the pound against the U.S. dollar from US$2.80 per £1 to US$2.40 per £1. A modern example is Argentina, which maintained a fixed exchange rate against the dollar from 1991 to 2001, but switched to a floating exchange rate at the end of 2001.

A **devaluation** is a reduction in the value of a currency that is set under a fixed exchange rate regime.

A **revaluation** is an increase in the value of a currency that is set under a fixed exchange rate regime.

A reduction in the value of a currency that is set under a fixed exchange rate regime is called a **devaluation.** As we've already learned, a *depreciation* is a downward move in a currency. A devaluation is a depreciation that is due to a revision in a fixed exchange rate target. An increase in the value of a currency that is set under a fixed exchange rate regime is called a **revaluation.**

A devaluation, like any depreciation, makes domestic goods cheaper in terms of foreign currency, which leads to higher exports. At the same time, it makes foreign goods more expensive in terms of domestic currency, which reduces imports. The effect is to increase the balance of payments on current account. Similarly, a revaluation makes domestic goods more expensive in terms of foreign currency, which reduces exports, and makes foreign goods cheaper in domestic currency, which increases imports. So a revaluation reduces the balance of payments on current account.

Devaluations and revaluations serve two purposes under fixed exchange rates. First, they can be used to eliminate shortages or surpluses in the foreign exchange market. For example, in 2008 some economists were urging China to revalue the yuan so that it would not have to buy up so many U.S. dollars on the foreign exchange market.

Second, devaluation and revaluation can be used as tools of macroeconomic policy. A devaluation, by increasing exports and reducing imports, increases aggregate demand. So a devaluation can be used to reduce or eliminate a recessionary gap. A revaluation has the opposite effect, reducing aggregate demand. So a revaluation can be used to reduce or eliminate an inflationary gap.

Monetary Policy Under Floating Exchange Rates

Under a floating exchange rate regime, a country's central bank retains its ability to pursue independent monetary policy: it can increase aggregate demand by cutting the interest rate or decrease aggregate demand by raising the interest rate. But the exchange rate adds another dimension to the effects of monetary policy. To see why, let's return to the hypothetical country of Genovia and ask what happens if the central bank cuts the interest rate.

Just as in a closed economy, a lower interest rate leads to higher investment spending and higher consumer spending. But the decline in the interest rate also affects the foreign exchange market. Foreigners have less incentive to move funds into Genovia, because they will receive a lower rate of return on their loans. As a result, they have less need to exchange U.S. dollars for genos, so the demand for genos falls. At the same time, Genovians have *more* incentive to move funds abroad because the rate of return on loans at home has fallen, making investments outside the country more attractive. As a result, they need to exchange more genos for U.S. dollars, so the supply of genos rises.

Figure 34-12 shows the effect of an interest rate reduction on the foreign exchange market. The demand curve for genos shifts leftward, from D_1 to D_2, and the supply curve shifts rightward, from S_1 to S_2. The equilibrium exchange rate, as measured in U.S. dollars per geno, falls from XR_1 to XR_2. That is, a reduction in the Genovian interest rate causes the geno to *depreciate*.

The depreciation of the geno, in turn, affects aggregate demand. We've already seen that a devaluation—a depreciation that is the result of a change in a fixed exchange rate—increases exports and reduces imports, thereby increasing aggregate demand. A depreciation that results from an interest rate cut has the same effect: it increases exports and reduces imports, increasing aggregate demand.

In other words, monetary policy under floating rates has effects beyond those we've described in looking at closed economies. In a closed economy, a reduction in the interest rate leads to a rise in aggregate demand because it leads to more investment spending and consumer spending. In an open economy with a floating exchange rate, the interest rate reduction leads to increased investment spending and consumer spending, but it also increases aggregate demand in another way: it leads to a currency depreciation, which increases exports and reduces imports, and further increasing aggregate demand.

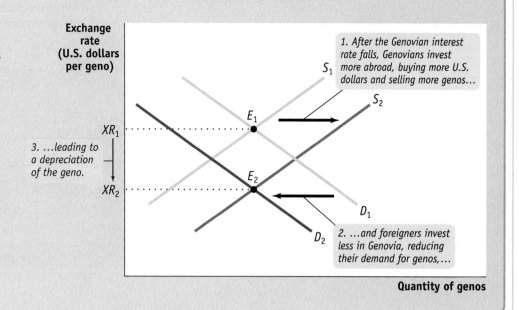

FIGURE 34-12

Monetary Policy and the Exchange Rate

Here we show what happens in the foreign exchange market if Genovia cuts its interest rate. Residents of Genovia have a reduced incentive to keep their funds at home, so they invest more abroad. As a result, the supply of genos shifts rightward, from S_1 to S_2. Meanwhile, foreigners have less incentive to put funds into Genovia, so the demand for genos shifts leftward, from D_1 to D_2. The geno depreciates: the equilibrium exchange rate falls from XR_1 to XR_2.

Exchange rate (U.S. dollars per geno)

1. After the Genovian interest rate falls, Genovians invest more abroad, buying more U.S. dollars and selling more genos...

3. ...leading to a depreciation of the geno.

2. ...and foreigners invest less in Genovia, reducing their demand for genos,...

Quantity of genos

International Business Cycles

Up to this point, we have discussed macroeconomics, even in an open economy, as if all demand shocks originate from the domestic economy. In reality, however, economies sometimes face shocks coming from abroad. For example, recessions in the United States have historically led to recessions in Mexico.

The key point is that changes in aggregate demand affect the demand for goods and services produced abroad as well as at home: other things equal, a recession leads to a fall in imports and an expansion leads to a rise in imports. And one country's imports are another country's exports. This link between aggregate demand in different national economies is one reason business cycles in different countries sometimes—but not always—seem to be synchronized. The prime example is the Great Depression, which affected countries around the world.

The extent of this link depends, however, on the exchange rate regime. To see why, think about what happens if a recession abroad reduces the demand for Genovia's exports. A reduction in foreign demand for Genovian goods and services is also a reduction in demand for genos on the foreign exchange market. If Genovia has a fixed exchange rate, it responds to this decline with exchange market intervention. But if Genovia has a floating exchange rate, the geno depreciates. Because Genovian goods and services become cheaper to foreigners when the demand for exports falls, the quantity of goods and services exported doesn't fall by as much as it would under a fixed rate. At the same time, the fall in the geno makes imports more expensive to Genovians, leading to a fall in imports. Both effects limit the decline in Genovia's aggregate demand compared to what it would have been under a fixed exchange rate.

One of the virtues of a floating exchange rate, according to advocates of such exchange rates, is that they help insulate countries from recessions originating abroad. This theory looked pretty good in the early 2000s: Britain, with a floating exchange rate, managed to stay out of a recession that affected the rest of Europe, and Canada, which also has a floating rate, suffered a less severe recession than the United States.

In 2008, however, a financial crisis that began in the United States seemed to be producing a recession in virtually every country. In this case, it appears that the international linkages between financial markets were much stronger than any insulation from overseas disturbances provided by floating exchange rates.

►ECONOMICS IN ACTION

The Joy of a Devalued Pound

Earlier in the chapter, we mentioned the Exchange Rate Mechanism, the system of European fixed exchange rates that paved the way for the creation of the euro in 1999. Britain joined that system in 1990 but dropped out in 1992. The story of Britain's exit from the Exchange Rate Mechanism is a classic example of open-economy macroeconomic policy.

Britain originally fixed its exchange rate for both the reasons we described earlier in the chapter: British leaders believed that a fixed exchange rate would help promote international trade, and they also hoped that it would help fight inflation. But by 1992 Britain was suffering from high unemployment: the unemployment rate in September 1992 was over 10%. And as long as the country had a fixed exchange rate, there wasn't much the government could do. In particular, the government wasn't able to cut interest rates because it was using high interest rates to help support the value of the pound.

In the summer of 1992, investors began speculating against the pound—selling pounds in the expectation that the currency would drop in value. As its foreign reserves dwindled, this speculation forced the British government's hand. On September 16, 1992, Britain abandoned its fixed exchange rate. The pound promptly dropped 20% against the German mark, the most important European currency at the time.

At first, the devaluation of the pound greatly damaged the prestige of the British government. But the Chancellor of the Exchequer—the equivalent of the U.S. Treasury Secretary—claimed to be happy about it. "My wife has never before heard me singing in the bath," he told reporters. There were several reasons for his joy. One was that the British government would no longer have to engage in large-scale exchange market intervention to support the pound's value. Another was that devaluation increases aggregate demand, so the pound's fall would help reduce British unemployment. Finally, because Britain no longer had a fixed exchange rate, it was free to pursue an expansionary monetary policy to fight its slump.

Indeed, events made it clear that the chancellor's joy was well founded. British unemployment fell over the next two years, even as the unemployment rate rose in France and Germany. One person who did not share in the improving employment picture, however, was the Chancellor himself. Soon after his remark about singing in the bath, he was fired. ▲

‹ ‹ ‹ ‹ ‹ ‹ ‹ ‹ ‹ ‹ ‹ ‹

> **CHECK YOUR UNDERSTANDING** 34-4

1. Look at the data in Figure 34-11. Where do you see devaluations and revaluations of the franc against the mark?

2. In the late 1980s Canadian economists argued that the high interest rate policies of the Bank of Canada weren't just causing high unemployment—they were also making it hard for Canadian manufacturers to compete with the United States. Explain this complaint, using our analysis of how monetary policy works under floating exchange rates.

Solutions appear at back of book.

■ If your interest was sparked by references in this chapter to speculation and currency crises, you can find a supplemental chapter online that explains how expectations can move exchange rates and the balance of payments—sometimes violently. To see the chapter, go to www.worthpublishers.com/krugmanwells.

>> **QUICK REVIEW**

➤ Countries can change fixed exchange rates. **Devaluation** or **revaluation** can help reduce surpluses or shortages in the foreign exchange market and can increase or reduce aggregate demand.

➤ In an open economy with a floating exchange rate, interest rates also affect the exchange rate, and so monetary policy affects aggregate demand through the effects of the exchange rate on imports and exports.

➤ Because one country's imports are another country's exports, business cycles are sometimes synchronized across countries. However, floating exchange rates may reduce this link.

SUMMARY

1. A country's **balance of payments accounts** summarize its transactions with the rest of the world. The **balance of payments on current account,** or **current account,** includes the **balance of payments on goods and services** together with balances on factor income and transfers. The **merchandise trade balance,** or **trade balance,** is a frequently cited component of the balance of payments on goods and services. The **balance of payments on financial account,** or **financial account,** measures capital flows. By definition, the balance of payments on current account plus the balance of payments on financial account is zero.

2. Capital flows respond to international differences in interest rates and other rates of return; they can be usefully analyzed using an international version of the loanable funds model, which shows how a country where the interest rate would be low in the absence of capital flows sends funds to a country where the interest rate would be high in the absence of capital flows. The underlying determinants of capital flows are international differences in savings and opportunities for investment spending.

3. Currencies are traded in the **foreign exchange market;** the prices at which they are traded are **exchange rates.** When a currency rises against another currency, it **appreciates;** when it falls, it **depreciates.** The **equilibrium exchange rate** matches the quantity of that currency supplied to the foreign exchange market to the quantity demanded.

4. To correct for international differences in inflation rates, economists calculate **real exchange rates,** which multiply the exchange rate between two countries' currencies by the ratio of the countries' price levels. The current account responds only to changes in the real exchange rate, not the nominal exchange rate. **Purchasing power parity** is the exchange rate that makes the cost of a basket of goods and services equal in two countries. While purchasing power parity and the nominal exchange rate almost always differ, purchasing power parity is a good predictor of actual changes in the nominal exchange rate.

5. Countries adopt different **exchange rate regimes,** rules governing exchange rate policy. The main types are **fixed exchange rates,** where the government takes action to keep the exchange rate at a target level, and **floating exchange rates,** where the exchange rate is free to fluctuate. Countries can fix exchange rates using **exchange market intervention,** which requires them to hold **foreign exchange reserves** that they use to buy any surplus of their currency. Alternatively, they can change domestic policies, especially monetary policy, to shift the demand and supply curves in the foreign exchange market. Finally, they can use **foreign exchange controls.**

6. Exchange rate policy poses a dilemma: there are economic payoffs to stable exchange rates, but the policies used to fix the exchange rate have costs. Exchange market intervention requires large reserves, and exchange controls distort incentives. If monetary policy is used to help fix the exchange rate, it isn't available to use for domestic policy.

7. Fixed exchange rates aren't always permanent commitments: countries with a fixed exchange rate sometimes engage in **devaluations** or **revaluations.** In addition to helping eliminate a surplus of domestic currency on the foreign exchange market, a devaluation increases aggregate demand. Similarly, a revaluation reduces shortages of domestic currency and reduces aggregate demand.

8. Under floating exchange rates, expansionary monetary policy works in part through the exchange rate: cutting domestic interest rates leads to a depreciation, and through that to higher exports and lower imports, which increases aggregate demand. Contractionary monetary policy has the reverse effect.

9. The fact that one country's imports are another country's exports creates a link between the business cycle in different countries. Floating exchange rates, however, may reduce the strength of that link.

KEY TERMS

PROBLEMS ....■

1. How would the following transactions be categorized in the U.S. balance of payments accounts? Would they be entered in the current account (as a payment to or from a foreigner) or the financial account (as a sale to or purchase of assets from a foreigner)? How will the balance of payments on the current and financial accounts change?

   a. A French importer buys a case of California wine for $500.

   b. An American who works for a French company deposits her paycheck, drawn on a Paris bank, into her San Francisco bank.

   c. An American buys a bond from a Japanese company for $10,000.

   d. An American charity sends $100,000 to Africa to help local residents buy food after a harvest shortfall.

2. The accompanying diagram shows the assets of the rest of the world that are in the United States and U.S. assets abroad, both as a percentage of rest-of-the-world GDP. As you can see from the diagram, both have increased nearly fivefold since 1980.

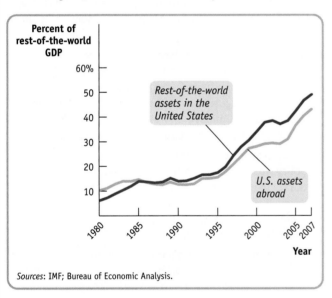

Sources: IMF; Bureau of Economic Analysis.

   a. As U.S. assets abroad have increased as a percentage of rest-of-the-world GDP, does this mean that the United States, over the period, has experienced net capital outflows?

   b. Does this diagram indicate that world economies were more tightly linked in 2007 than they were in 1980?

3. In the economy of Scottopia in 2008, exports equaled $400 billion of goods and $300 billion of services, imports equaled $500 billion of goods and $350 billion of services, and the rest of the world purchased $250 billion of Scottopia's assets. What was the merchandise trade balance for Scottopia? What was the balance of payments on the current account in Scottopia? What was the balance of payments on financial account? What was the value of Scottopia's purchases of assets from the rest of the world?

4. In the economy of Popania in 2008, total Popanian purchases of assets in the rest of the world equaled $300 billion, purchases of Popanian assets by the rest of the world equaled $400 billion, and Popania exported goods and services equal to $350 billion. What was Popania's balance of payments on financial account in 2008? What was its balance of payments on current account? What was the value of its imports?

5. Suppose that Northlandia and Southlandia are the only two trading countries in the world, that each nation runs a balance of payments on both current and financial accounts equal to zero, and that each nation sees the other's assets as identical to its own. Using the accompanying diagrams, explain how the demand and supply of loanable funds, the interest rate, and the balance of payments on current and financial accounts will change in each country if international capital flows are possible.

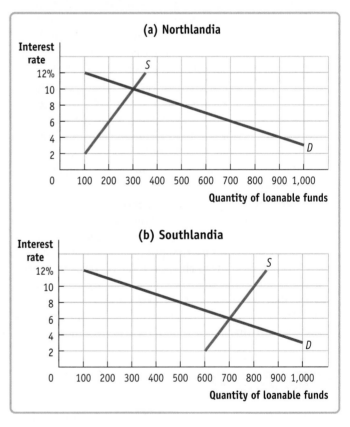

6. Based on the exchange rates for the first trading days of 2007 and 2008 shown in the accompanying table, did the U.S. dollar appreciate or depreciate during 2007? Did the movement in the value of the U.S. dollar make American goods and services more or less attractive to foreigners?

January 2, 2007	January 2, 2008
US$1.97 to buy 1 British pound sterling	US$1.98 to buy 1 British pound sterling
32.38 Taiwan dollars to buy US$1	32.43 Taiwan dollars to buy US$1
US$0.86 to buy 1 Canadian dollar	US$1.01 to buy 1 Canadian dollar
118.82 Japanese yen to buy US$1	109.72 Japanese yen to buy US$1
US$1.33 to buy 1 euro	US$1.47 to buy 1 euro
1.21 Swiss francs to buy US$1	1.12 Swiss francs to buy US$1

7. Go to http://fx.sauder.ubc.ca. Using the table labeled "The Most Recent Cross-Rates of Major Currencies," determine whether the British pound (GBP), the Canadian dollar (CAD), the Japanese yen (JPY), the euro (EUR), and the Swiss franc (CHF) have appreciated or depreciated against the U.S. dollar (USD) since January 2, 2008. The exchange rates on January 2, 2008, are listed in the table in Problem 6 above.

8. Suppose the United States and Japan are the only two trading countries in the world. What will happen to the value of the U.S. dollar if the following occur, other things equal?

   a. Japan relaxes some of its import restrictions.

   b. The United States imposes some import tariffs on Japanese goods.

   c. Interest rates in the United States rise dramatically.

   d. A report indicates that Japanese cars last much longer than previously thought, especially compared with American cars.

9. From January 1, 2001, to June 2003, the U.S. federal funds rate decreased from 6.5% to 1%. During the same period, the marginal lending facility rate at the European Central Bank decreased from 5.75% to 3%.

   a. Considering the change in interest rates over the period and using the loanable funds model, would you have expected funds to flow from the United States to Europe or from Europe to the United States over this period?

   b. The accompanying diagram shows the exchange rate between the euro and the U.S. dollar from January 1, 2001, through September 2008. Is the movement of the exchange rate over the period January 2001 to June 2003 consistent with the movement in funds predicted in part a?

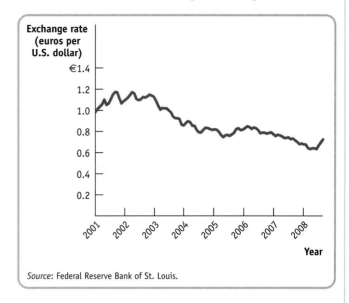

Source: Federal Reserve Bank of St. Louis.

10. In each of the following scenarios, suppose that the two nations are the only trading nations in the world. Given inflation and the change in the nominal exchange rate, which nation's goods become more attractive?

   a. Inflation is 10% in the United States and 5% in Japan; the U.S. dollar–Japanese yen exchange rate remains the same.

   b. Inflation is 3% in the United States and 8% in Mexico; the price of the U.S. dollar falls from 12.50 to 10.25 Mexican pesos.

   c. Inflation is 5% in the United States and 3% in the eurozone; the price of the euro falls from $1.30 to $1.20.

   d. Inflation is 8% in the United States and 4% in Canada; the price of the Canadian dollar rises from US$0.60 to US$0.75.

11. Starting from a position of equilibrium in the foreign exchange market under a fixed exchange rate regime, how must a government react to an increase in the demand for the nation's goods and services by the rest of the world to keep the exchange rate at its fixed value?

12. Suppose that Albernia's central bank has fixed the value of its currency, the bern, to the U.S. dollar (at a rate of US$1.50 to 1 bern) and is committed to that exchange rate. Initially, the foreign exchange market for the bern is also in equilibrium, as shown in the accompanying diagram. However, both Albernians and Americans begin to believe that there are big risks in holding Albernian assets; as a result, they become unwilling

to hold Albernian assets unless they receive a higher rate of return on them than they do on U.S. assets. How would this affect the diagram? If the Albernian central bank tries to keep the exchange rate fixed using monetary policy, how will this affect the Albernian economy?

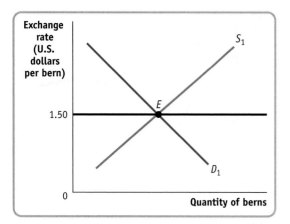

13. Your study partner asks you, "If central banks lose the ability to use discretionary monetary policy under fixed exchange rates, why would nations agree to a fixed exchange rate system?" How do you respond?

 www.worthpublishers.com/krugmanwells

Table I.
MACROECONOMIC DATA FOR THE UNITED STATES 1929–2007[1]

	1929	1933	1939	1945	1950	1955	1960	1965
Nominal GDP and Its Components								
1. + Consumer spending (C)	77.4	45.9	67.2	120.0	192.2	258.8	331.7	443.8
2. + Investment spending (I)	16.5	1.7	9.3	10.8	54.1	69.0	78.9	118.2
3. + Government purchases of goods and services (G)	9.4	8.7	14.8	93.0	46.8	86.5	111.6	151.5
4. + Exports (X)	5.9	2.0	4.0	6.8	12.4	17.7	27.0	37.1
5. − Imports (IM)	5.6	1.9	3.1	7.5	11.6	17.2	22.8	31.5
6. = Gross domestic product (GDP)	103.6	56.4	92.2	223.1	293.8	414.8	526.4	719.1
7. + Income from abroad earned by Americans	1.1	0.4	0.7	0.8	2.2	3.5	4.9	7.9
8. − Income paid to foreigners	0.4	0.1	0.3	0.5	0.7	1.1	1.8	2.6
9. = Gross national product	104.4	56.7	92.5	223.4	295.2	417.2	529.5	724.4
10. National income	94.2	48.9	82.2	198.4	264.4	372.7	474.9	653.4
11. Government transfers	1.2	1.7	2.5	5.6	14.0	15.7	25.7	36.2
12. Taxes	1.7	0.8	1.5	19.4	18.9	32.9	46.1	57.7
13. Disposable income	83.4	46.1	71.4	152.2	210.1	283.3	365.4	498.1
14. Private savings	3.8	-0.7	3.2	31.1	15.1	19.7	26.7	43.0
Real GDP and Growth Measures								
15. Real GDP (billions of 2000 dollars)	865.2	635.5	950.7	1,786.3	1,777.3	2,212.8	2,501.8	3,191.1
16. Real GDP growth (percent change from previous year)	-	-1.3%	8.1%	-1.1%	8.7%	7.1%	2.5%	6.4%
17. Real GDP per capita (2000 dollars)	7,099	5,056	7,256	12,766	11,717	13,389	13,840	16,420
18. Real GDP per capita growth (percent change from previous year)	-	-1.9%	7.2%	-2.2%	6.9%	5.3%	0.4%	5.1%
Prices and Inflation								
19. Consumer Price Index (1982 − 1984 = 100)	17.1	13.0	13.9	18.0	24.1	26.8	29.6	31.5
20. CPI inflation rate	-	-5.1%	-1.4%	2.3%	1.3%	-0.4%	1.7%	1.6%
21. Producer Price Index (all commodities, 1982 = 100)	16.4	11.4	13.3	18.2	27.3	29.3	31.7	32.3
22. PPI inflation rate	-	1.8%	-1.5%	1.7%	3.8%	0.0%	0.0%	2.2%
23. GDP deflator (2000 = 100)	11.9	8.9	9.7	12.5	16.5	18.7	21.0	22.5
24. GDP deflator inflation rate	-	-2.6%	-1.2%	2.6%	0.8%	1.5%	1.4%	1.8%
Population and Employment								
25. Population (thousands)	121,878	125,690	131,028	139,928	151,684	165,275	180,760	194,347
26. Labor force (thousands)[2]	49,180	51,590	55,230	53,860	62,208	65,023	69,628	74,455
27. Unemployed (thousands)[2]	1,550	12,830	9,480	1,040	3,288	2,852	3,852	3,366
28. Unemployment rate	3.2%	24.9%	17.2%	1.9%	5.3%	4.4%	5.5%	4.5%
Government Finance and Money								
29. Government (federal, state and local) budget balance	2.6	-0.5	-0.1	-27.4	6.8	9.2	11.5	9.9
30. Budget balance (percent of GDP)	2.5%	-0.9%	-0.1%	-12.3%	2.3%	2.2%	2.2%	1.4%
31. M1	-	-	-	-	-	-	140.3	163.4
32. M2	-	-	-	-	-	-	304.3	442.5
33. Federal funds rate (yearly average)	-	-	-	-	-	1.8%	3.2%	4.1%
International Trade								
34. Current account balance	-	-	-	-	-	-	2.8	5.4

Source: Bureau of Economic Analysis, Bureau of Labor Statistics, Federal Reserve Bank of St. Louis.

1. Data in billions of current dollars unless otherwise stated. Only select dates shown for 1929 through 1965; annual data supplied for 1965 through 2007.
2. Until 1947, includes workers 14 years and older; 1948 and after, includes workers 16 years and older.

(continued on next page)

	1966	1967	1968	1969	1970	1971	1972	1973	1974
Nominal GDP and Its Components									
1. + Consumer spending (C)	480.9	507.8	558.0	605.2	648.5	701.9	770.6	852.4	933.4
2. + Investment spending (I)	131.3	128.6	141.2	156.4	152.4	178.2	207.6	244.5	249.4
3. + Government purchases of goods and services (G)	171.8	192.7	209.4	221.5	233.8	246.5	263.5	281.7	317.9
4. + Exports (X)	40.9	43.5	47.9	51.9	59.7	63.0	70.8	95.3	126.7
5. − Imports (IM)	37.1	39.9	46.6	50.5	55.8	62.3	74.2	91.2	127.5
6. = **Gross domestic product (GDP)**	**787.8**	**832.6**	**910.0**	**984.6**	**1,038.5**	**1,127.1**	**1,238.3**	**1,382.7**	**1,500.0**
7. + Income from abroad earned by Americans	8.1	8.7	10.1	11.8	12.8	14.0	16.3	23.5	29.8
8. − Income paid to foreigners	3.0	3.3	4.0	5.7	6.4	6.4	7.7	10.9	14.3
9. = **Gross national product**	**792.9**	**838.0**	**916.1**	**990.7**	**1,044.9**	**1,134.7**	**1,246.8**	**1,395.3**	**1,515.5**
10. National income	711.0	751.9	823.2	889.7	930.9	1,008.1	1,111.2	1,247.4	1,342.1
11. Government transfers	39.6	48.0	56.1	62.3	74.7	88.1	97.9	112.6	133.3
12. Taxes	66.4	73.0	87.0	104.5	103.1	101.7	123.6	132.4	151.0
13. Disposable income	537.5	575.3	625.0	674.0	735.7	801.8	869.1	978.3	1,071.6
14. Private savings	44.4	54.4	52.8	52.5	69.5	80.6	77.2	102.7	113.6
Real GDP and Growth Measures									
15. Real GDP (billions of 2000 dollars)	3,399.1	3,484.6	3,652.7	3,765.4	3,771.9	3,898.6	4,105.0	4,341.5	4,319.6
16. Real GDP growth (percent change from previous year)	6.5%	2.5%	4.8%	3.1%	0.2%	3.4%	5.3%	5.8%	-0.5%
17. Real GDP per capita (2000 dollars)	17,290	17,533	18,196	18,573	18,391	18,771	19,555	20,484	20,195
18. Real GDP per capita growth (percent change from previous year)	5.3%	1.4%	3.8%	2.1%	-1.0%	2.1%	4.2%	4.8%	-1.4%
Prices and Inflation									
19. Consumer Price Index (1982 – 1984 = 100)	32.4	33.4	34.8	36.7	38.8	40.5	41.8	44.4	49.3
20. CPI inflation rate	2.9%	3.1%	4.2%	5.5%	5.7%	4.4%	3.2%	6.2%	11.0%
21. Producer Price Index (all commodities, 1982 = 100)	33.3	33.4	34.2	35.6	36.9	38.1	39.8	45.0	53.5
22. PPI inflation rate	3.1%	0.3%	2.4%	4.1%	3.7%	3.3%	4.5%	13.1%	18.9%
23. GDP deflator (2000 = 100)	23.2	23.9	24.9	26.2	27.5	28.9	30.2	31.9	34.7
24. GDP deflator inflation rate	2.8%	3.1%	4.3%	5.0%	5.3%	5.0%	4.3%	5.6%	9.0%
Population and Employment									
25. Population (thousands)	196,599	198,752	200,745	202,736	205,089	207,692	209,924	211,939	213,898
26. Labor force (thousands)[2]	75,770	77,347	78,737	80,734	82,771	84,382	87,034	89,429	91,949
27. Unemployed (thousands)[2]	2,875	2,975	2,817	2,832	4,093	5,016	4,882	4,365	5,156
28. Unemployment rate	3.8%	3.8%	3.6%	3.5%	4.9%	5.9%	5.6%	4.9%	5.6%
Government Finance and Money									
29. Government (federal, state and local) budget balance	10	-2.4	5.2	16.7	-8.1	-21.9	-8.8	4.4	-4.4
30. Budget balance (percent of GDP)	1.3%	-0.3%	0.6%	1.7%	-0.8%	-1.9%	-0.7%	0.3%	-0.3%
31. M1	171.0	177.7	190.1	201.4	209.1	223.1	239.0	256.3	269.1
32. M2	471.4	503.6	545.3	578.7	601.5	674.4	758.2	831.8	880.6
33. Federal funds rate (yearly average)	5.1%	4.2%	5.7%	8.2%	7.2%	4.7%	4.4%	8.7%	10.5%
International Trade									
34. Current account balance	-	3.0	2.6	0.6	0.4	2.3	-1.4	-5.8	7.1	2.0

Source: Bureau of Economic Analysis, Bureau of Labor Statistics, Federal Reserve Bank of St. Louis.

1. Data in billions of current dollars unless otherwise stated. Only select dates shown for 1929 through 1965; annual data supplied for 1965 through 2007.
2. Until 1947, includes workers 14 years and older; 1948 and after, includes workers 16 years and older.

1975	1976	1977	1978	1979	1980	1981	1982	1983	1984	1985	1986	1987
1,034.4	1,151.9	1,278.6	1,428.5	1,592.2	1,757.1	1,941.1	2,077.3	2,290.6	2,503.3	2,720.3	2,899.7	3,100.2
230.2	292.0	361.3	438.0	492.9	479.3	572.4	517.2	564.3	735.6	736.2	746.5	785.0
357.7	383.0	414.1	453.6	500.8	566.2	627.5	680.5	733.5	797.0	879.0	949.3	999.5
138.7	149.5	159.4	186.9	230.1	280.8	305.2	283.2	277.0	302.4	302.0	320.5	363.9
122.7	151.1	182.4	212.3	252.7	293.8	317.8	303.2	328.6	405.1	417.2	453.3	509.1
1,638.3	**1,825.3**	**2,030.9**	**2,294.7**	**2,563.3**	**2,789.5**	**3,128.4**	**3,255.0**	**3,536.7**	**3,933.2**	**4,220.3**	**4,462.8**	**4,739.5**
28.0	32.4	37.2	46.3	68.3	79.1	92.0	101.0	101.9	121.9	112.4	111.4	123.2
15.0	15.5	16.9	24.7	36.4	44.9	59.1	64.5	64.8	85.6	85.9	93.6	105.3
1,651.3	**1,842.1**	**2,051.2**	**2,316.3**	**2,595.3**	**2,823.7**	**3,161.4**	**3,291.5**	**3,573.8**	**3,969.5**	**4,246.8**	**4,480.6**	**4,757.4**
1,445.9	1,611.8	1,798.9	2,027.4	2,249.1	2,439.3	2,742.4	2,864.3	3,084.2	3,482.3	3,723.4	3,902.3	4,173.7
170.0	184.0	194.2	209.6	235.3	279.5	318.4	354.8	383.7	400.1	424.9	451.0	467.6
147.6	172.3	197.5	229.4	268.7	298.9	345.2	354.1	352.3	377.4	417.4	437.3	489.1
1,187.4	1,302.5	1,435.7	1,608.3	1,793.5	2,009.0	2,246.1	2,421.2	2,608.4	2,912.0	3,109.3	3,285.1	3,458.3
125.6	122.3	125.3	142.5	159.1	201.4	244.3	270.8	233.6	314.8	280.0	268.4	241.4
4,311.2	4,540.9	4,750.5	5,015.0	5,173.4	5,161.7	5,291.7	5,189.3	5,423.8	5,813.6	6,053.7	6,263.6	6,475.1
-0.2%	5.3%	4.6%	5.6%	3.2%	-0.2%	2.5%	-1.9%	4.5%	7.2%	4.1%	3.5%	3.4%
19,961	20,822	21,565	22,526	22,982	22,666	23,007	22,346	23,146	24,593	25,382	26,024	26,664
-1.2%	4.3%	3.6%	4.5%	2.0%	-1.4%	1.5%	-2.9%	3.6%	6.3%	3.2%	2.5%	2.5%
53.8	56.9	60.6	65.2	72.6	82.4	90.9	96.5	99.6	103.9	107.6	109.6	113.6
9.1%	5.8%	6.5%	7.6%	11.3%	13.5%	10.3%	6.2%	3.2%	4.3%	3.6%	1.9%	3.6%
58.4	61.1	64.9	69.9	78.7	89.8	98.0	100.0	101.3	103.7	103.2	100.2	102.8
9.2%	4.6%	6.2%	7.7%	12.6%	14.1%	9.1%	2.0%	1.3%	2.4%	-0.5%	-2.9%	2.6%
38.0	40.2	42.8	45.8	49.6	54.1	59.1	62.7	65.2	67.7	69.7	71.3	73.2
9.5%	5.8%	6.4%	7.0%	8.3%	9.1%	9.4%	6.1%	3.9%	3.8%	3.0%	2.2%	2.7%
215,981	218,086	220,289	222,629	225,106	227,726	230,008	232,218	234,333	236,394	238,506	240,683	242,843
93,775	96,158	99,009	102,251	104,962	106,940	108,670	110,204	111,550	113,544	115,461	117,834	119,865
7,929	7,406	6,991	6,202	6,137	7,637	8,273	10,678	10,717	8,539	8,312	8,237	7,425
8.5%	7.7%	7.1%	6.1%	5.8%	7.1%	7.6%	9.7%	9.6%	7.5%	7.2%	7.0%	6.2%
-66.6	-44.4	-31	-7.8	1.7	-44.8	-45.7	-134.1	-168.1	-144.1	-152.6	-169.9	-132.6
-4.1%	-2.4%	-1.5%	-0.3%	0.1%	-1.6%	-1.5%	-4.1%	-4.8%	-3.7%	-3.6%	-3.8%	-2.8%
281.3	297.2	319.9	346.2	372.6	395.7	425.0	453.0	503.2	538.6	586.9	666.3	743.6
963.5	1,086.5	1,221.2	1,322.2	1,425.7	1,540.2	1,679.3	1,833.0	2,057.5	2,222.1	2,419.9	2,616.4	2,786.5
5.8%	5.0%	5.5%	7.9%	11.2%	13.4%	16.4%	12.3%	9.1%	10.2%	8.1%	6.8%	6.7%
18.1	4.3	-14.3	-15.1	-0.3	2.3	5.0	-5.5	-38.7	-94.3	-118.2	-147.2	-160.7

(continued on next page)

	1988	1989	1990	1991	1992	1993	1994	1995	1996
Nominal GDP and Its Components									
1. + Consumer spending (C)	3,353.6	3,598.5	3,839.9	3,986.1	4,235.3	4,477.9	4,743.3	4,975.8	5,256.8
2. + Investment spending (I)	821.6	874.9	861.0	802.9	864.8	953.4	1,097.1	1,144.0	1,240.3
3. + Government purchases of goods and services (G)	1,039.0	1,099.1	1,180.2	1,234.4	1,271.0	1,291.2	1,325.5	1,369.2	1,416.0
4. + Exports (X)	444.1	503.3	552.4	596.8	635.3	655.8	720.9	812.2	868.6
5. – Imports (IM)	554.5	591.5	630.3	624.3	668.6	720.9	814.5	903.6	964.8
6. = Gross domestic product (GDP)	**5,103.8**	**5,484.4**	**5,803.1**	**5,995.9**	**6,337.7**	**6,657.4**	**7,072.2**	**7,397.7**	**7,816.9**
7. + Income from abroad earned by Americans	152.1	177.7	189.1	168.9	152.7	156.2	186.4	233.9	248.7
8. – Income paid to foreigners	128.5	151.5	154.3	138.5	123.0	124.3	160.2	198.1	213.7
9. = Gross national product	**5,127.4**	**5,510.6**	**5,837.9**	**6,026.3**	**6,367.4**	**6,689.3**	**7,098.4**	**7,433.4**	**7,851.9**
10. National income	4,549.4	4,826.6	5,089.1	5,227.9	5,512.8	5,773.4	6,122.3	6,453.9	6,840.1
11. Government transfers	496.6	543.4	595.2	666.4	749.4	790.1	827.3	877.4	925.0
12. Taxes	505.0	566.1	592.8	586.7	610.6	646.6	690.7	744.1	832.1
13. Disposable income	3,748.7	4,021.7	4,285.8	4,464.3	4,751.4	4,911.9	5,151.8	5,408.2	5,688.5
14. Private savings	272.9	287.1	299.4	324.2	366.0	284.0	249.5	250.9	228.4
Real GDP and Growth Measures									
15. Real GDP (billions of 2000 dollars)	6,742.7	6,981.4	7,112.5	7,100.5	7,336.6	7,532.7	7,835.5	8,031.7	8,328.9
16. Real GDP growth (percent change from previous year)	4.1%	3.5%	1.9%	-0.2%	3.3%	2.7%	4.0%	2.5%	3.7%
17. Real GDP per capita (2000 dollars)	27,514	28,221	28,429	28,007	28,556	28,940	29,741	30,128	30,881
18. Real GDP per capita growth (percent change from previous year)	3.2%	2.6%	0.7%	-1.5%	2.0%	1.3%	2.8%	1.3%	2.5%
Prices and Inflation									
19. Consumer Price Index (1982 – 1984 = 100)	118.3	124.0	130.7	136.2	140.3	144.5	148.2	152.4	156.9
20. CPI inflation rate	4.1%	4.8%	5.4%	4.2%	3.0%	3.0%	2.6%	2.8%	3.0%
21. Producer Price Index (all commodities, 1982 = 100)	106.9	112.2	116.3	116.5	117.2	118.9	120.4	124.7	127.7
22. PPI inflation rate	4.0%	5.0%	3.7%	0.2%	0.6%	1.5%	1.3%	3.6%	2.4%
23. GDP deflator (2000 = 100)	75.7	78.6	81.6	84.5	86.4	88.4	90.3	92.1	93.9
24. GDP deflator inflation rate	3.4%	3.8%	3.9%	3.5%	2.3%	2.3%	2.1%	2.0%	1.9%
Population and Employment									
25. Population (thousands)	245,061	247,387	250,181	253,530	256,922	260,282	263,455	266,588	269,714
26. Labor force (thousands)[2]	121,669	123,869	125,840	126,346	128,105	129,200	131,056	132,304	133,943
27. Unemployed (thousands)[2]	6,701	6,528	7,047	8,628	9,613	8,940	7,996	7,404	7,236
28. Unemployment rate	5.5%	5.3%	5.6%	6.8%	7.5%	6.9%	6.1%	5.6%	5.4%
Government Finance and Money									
29. Government (federal, state and local) budget balance	-116.6	-109.3	-164.8	-217.9	-296.7	-272.6	-201.9	-184.9	-116
30. Budget balance (percent of GDP)	-2.3%	-2.0%	-2.8%	-3.6%	-4.7%	-4.1%	-2.9%	-2.5%	-1.5%
31. M1	774.8	782.2	810.6	859.0	965.9	1,078.4	1,145.2	1,143.0	1,106.8
32. M2	2,936.6	3,059.9	3,228.2	3,349.0	3,411.5	3,448.2	3,496.4	3,569.3	3,741.5
33. Federal funds rate (yearly average)	7.6%	9.2%	8.1%	5.7%	3.5%	3.0%	4.2%	5.8%	5.3%
International Trade									
34. Current account balance	-121.2	-99.5	-79.0	2.9	-50.1	-84.8	-121.6	-113.6	-124.8

Source: Bureau of Economic Analysis, Bureau of Labor Statistics, Federal Reserve Bank of St. Louis.

1. Data in billions of current dollars unless otherwise stated. Only select dates shown for 1929 through 1965; annual data supplied for 1965 through 2007.
2. Until 1947, includes workers 14 years and older; 1948 and after, includes workers 16 years and older.

1997	1998	1999	2000	2001	2002	2003	2004	2005	2006	2007
5,547.4	5,879.5	6,282.5	6,739.4	7,055.0	7,350.7	7,703.6	8,195.9	8,694.1	9,207.2	9,710.2
1,389.8	1,509.1	1,625.7	1,735.5	1,614.3	1,582.1	1,664.1	1,888.6	2,086.1	2,220.4	2,130.4
1,468.7	1,518.3	1,620.8	1,721.6	1,825.6	1,961.1	2,092.5	2,216.8	2,355.3	2,508.1	2,674.8
955.3	955.9	991.2	1,096.3	1,032.8	1,005.9	1,040.8	1,182.4	1,311.5	1,480.8	1,662.4
1,056.9	1,115.9	1,251.7	1,475.8	1,399.8	1,430.3	1,540.2	1,797.8	2,025.1	2,238.1	2,370.2
8,304.3	**8,747.0**	**9,268.4**	**9,817.0**	**10,128.0**	**10,469.6**	**10,960.8**	**11,685.9**	**12,421.9**	**13,178.4**	**13,807.5**
286.7	287.1	320.8	382.7	322.4	305.7	336.8	437.5	573.5	725.4	861.7
253.7	265.8	287.0	343.7	278.8	275.0	280.0	361.3	480.5	647.1	759.3
8,337.3	**8,768.3**	**9,302.2**	**9,855.9**	**10,171.6**	**10,500.2**	**11,017.6**	**11,762.1**	**12,514.9**	**13,256.6**	**13,910**
7,292.2	7,752.8	8,236.7	8,795.2	8,979.8	9,229.3	9,632.3	10,306.8	10,974.0	11,795.7	12,270.9
951.2	978.6	1,022.1	1,084.0	1,193.9	1,286.2	1,351.0	1,422.5	1,520.7	1,603.0	1,713.3
926.3	1,027.0	1,107.5	1,235.7	1,237.3	1,051.8	1,001.1	1,046.3	1,207.8	1,353.2	1,492.8
5,988.8	6,395.9	6,695.0	7,194.0	7,486.8	7,830.1	8,162.5	8,680.9	9,062.0	9,640.7	10,170.5
218.3	276.8	158.6	168.5	132.3	184.7	174.9	181.7	32.5	70.7	57.4
8,703.5	9,066.9	9,470.3	9,817.0	9,890.7	10,048.8	10,301.0	10,675.8	10,989.5	11,294.8	11,523.9
4.5%	4.2%	4.4%	3.7%	0.8%	1.6%	2.5%	3.6%	2.9%	2.8%	2.0%
31,886	32,833	33,904	34,755	34,645	34,837	35,403	36,356	37,08	37,750	38,148
3.3%	3.0%	3.3%	2.5%	-0.3%	0.6%	1.5%	2.7%	2.0%	1.8%	1.1%
160.5	163.0	166.6	172.2	177.1	179.9	184.0	188.9	195.3	201.6	207.3
2.3%	1.6%	2.2%	3.4%	2.8%	1.6%	2.3%	2.7%	3.4%	3.2%	2.8%
127.6	124.4	125.5	132.7	134.2	131.1	138.1	146.7	157.4	164.7	172.6
-0.1%	-2.5%	0.9%	5.7%	1.1%	-2.3%	5.3%	6.2%	7.3%	4.6%	4.8%
95.4	96.5	97.9	100.0	102.4	104.2	106.4	109.5	113.0	116.7	119.816
1.7%	1.1%	1.4%	2.2%	2.4%	1.7%	2.1%	2.9%	3.3%	3.2%	2.7%
272,958	276,154	279,328	282,459	285,490	288,451	291,311	294,096	296,972	299,833	301,140
136,297	137,673	139,368	142,583	143,734	144,863	146,510	147,401	149,320	151,428	153,124
6,739	6,210	5,880	5,692	6,801	8,378	8,774	8,149	7,591	7,001	7,078
4.9%	4.5%	4.2%	4.0%	4.7%	5.8%	6.0%	5.5%	5.1%	4.6%	4.6%
-16.7	90.8	154	239.4	51.5	-282.1	-392.5	-369.1	-262.2	-155	-218.9
-0.2%	1.0%	1.7%	2.4%	0.5%	-2.7%	-3.6%	-3.2%	-2.1%	-1.2%	-1.6%
1,070.2	1,080.7	1,102.3	1,103.6	1,140.3	1,196.2	1,273.5	1,344.4	1,371.7	1,374.9	1,369.1
3,928.5	4,211.6	4,524.7	4,793.2	5,209.8	5,598.8	5,988.5	6,268.5	6,540.9	6,851.5	7,264.4
5.5%	5.4%	5.0%	6.2%	3.9%	1.7%	1.1%	1.3%	3.2%	5.0%	5.0
-140.7	-215.1	-301.6	-417.4	-384.7	-461.3	-523.4	-625.0	-729.0	-788.1	-731.2

Table II.
MACROECONOMIC DATA FOR SELECT COUNTRIES
GDP (Billions of U.S. Dollars)

	1985	1986	1987	1988	1989	1990	1991	1992	1993	1994
Argentina	88.187	106.045	108.725	127.35	81.706	141.337	189.594	228.776	236.505	257.44
Australia	172.099	178.606	210.332	266.962	302.726	317.958	319.982	313.419	304.865	347.392
Austria	68.026	96.526	120.71	132.185	131.697	165.396	173.382	195.107	189.709	203.972
Bangladesh	21.337	22.37	24.679	26.637	29.344	30.497	31.432	31.439	32.954	35.802
Belgium	83.434	115.661	143.786	156.114	158.05	197.798	202.874	225.507	216.231	236.043
Brazil	253.078	293.579	319.545	356.976	490.05	507.783	445.242	426.519	478.621	596.762
Bulgaria	27.391	24.242	28.101	45.922	46.77	20.621	2.02	8.2	4.45	7.824
Canada	355.766	368.883	421.583	498.368	555.565	582.805	598.239	579.978	563.94	564.608
Chile	16.486	17.723	20.902	24.641	28.385	31.559	36.425	44.468	47.694	55.155
China	305.259	295.477	321.391	401.072	449.104	387.772	406.09	483.047	613.223	559.225
Colombia	40.642	40.69	42.364	45.672	46.054	46.908	49.519	57.373	65.021	81.707
Cyprus	3.058	3.544	3.904	4.559	4.897	5.614	5.892	6.969	6.656	7.48
Czech Republic	45.329	53.178	59.643	58.933	57.482	52.128	27.18	31.898	36.651	42.538
Denmark	61.633	86.613	107.489	113.448	110.191	136.174	137.189	150.54	140.835	153.901
Dominican Republic	5.065	6.152	6.475	5.93	6.697	6.234	7.637	8.988	9.722	10.739
Ecuador	16.166	11.862	11.084	10.541	10.345	10.505	11.788	12.889	15.057	18.573
Egypt	46.45	51.429	73.571	88	109.714	91.383	46.06	42.006	47.101	51.879
Estonia	n/a	n/a	n/a	n/a	n/a	n/a	n/a	n/a	1.726	2.413
Finland	55.465	72.623	90.506	107.771	117.513	139.83	126.422	110.81	87.421	100.714
France	547.815	761.37	923.289	1,004.33	1,009.81	1,248.45	1,249.07	1,374.29	1,291.99	1,365.88
Germany	639.695	913.641	1,136.93	1,225.73	1,216.80	1,547.03	1,815.06	2,066.73	2,005.56	2,151.03
Ghana	6.647	6.04	5.113	5.509	5.577	6.614	7.328	6.757	5.966	5.44
Greece	45.132	53.102	61.784	71.95	74.562	92.195	99.422	109.556	102.608	109.824
Guatemala	10.385	7.846	6.58	7.285	7.719	7.068	8.7	9.597	10.461	11.839
Hungary	20.624	23.756	26.109	28.571	29.168	33.056	33.429	37.254	38.596	41.506
Iceland	2.94	3.931	5.442	6.067	5.625	6.384	6.82	6.99	6.143	6.3
India	219.901	242.06	267.136	293.121	291.958	313.731	278.533	280.933	274.651	311.813
Ireland	20.996	28.153	33.377	36.565	37.713	47.791	48.439	54.458	50.461	55.371
Israel	27.87	31.332	37.428	46.371	47.256	55.677	63.369	70.688	70.955	80.948
Italy	437.103	619.077	777.009	860.861	895.337	1,135.54	1,198.99	1,271.91	1,022.66	1,054.90
Jamaica	2.212	2.629	2.965	3.534	4.097	5.175	4.858	4.055	5.58	6.784
Japan	1,366.35	2,021.60	2,443.70	2,961.83	2,967.75	3,053.14	3,478.87	3,797.03	4,367.92	4,767.16
Kenya	8.746	10.387	11.387	11.806	11.705	12.18	11.501	11.327	7.869	9.422
Korea	96.676	111.314	140.11	187.732	230.485	263.839	308.274	329.928	362.16	423.455
Latvia	n/a	n/a	n/a	n/a	n/a	n/a	n/a	1.532	2.436	4.095

Source: IMF.

1995	1996	1997	1998	1999	2000	2001	2002	2003	2004	2005	2006	2007
258.032	272.15	292.859	298.948	283.523	284.204	268.697	97.732	127.643	151.958	181.549	212.71	259.999
371.078	417.353	417.988	373.154	401.805	389.983	368.21	412.871	527.852	640.509	713.166	755.946	908.826
239.797	236.473	209	214.146	213.39	194.407	193.345	208.566	255.765	293.605	305.621	323.828	373.943
39.58	41.516	43.388	44.757	46.529	47.048	47.194	49.56	54.476	59.12	61.127	64.854	72.424
277.066	275.623	249.596	255.572	253.866	232.856	231.898	252.579	310.492	359.474	376.166	398.141	453.636
769.74	840.052	871.523	844.126	586.922	644.283	554.411	505.712	552.239	663.552	881.754	1,072.36	1,313.59
13.106	9.901	10.366	12.845	12.977	12.639	13.749	15.646	20.021	24.679	27.26	31.69	39.609
590.65	613.808	637.671	617.434	661.345	725.158	715.632	734.773	868.319	993.938	1,135.45	1,275.28	1,432.14
71.349	75.771	82.807	79.368	72.989	75.2	68.556	67.252	73.99	95.819	118.976	145.845	163.792
727.946	856.002	952.649	1,019.48	1,083.29	1,198.48	1,324.81	1,453.83	1,640.96	1,931.64	2,243.69	2,644.64	3,250.83
92.496	97.147	106.66	98.444	86.186	83.786	81.99	81.122	79.459	98.059	122.9	136.132	171.607
9.254	9.351	8.902	9.556	9.78	9.317	9.678	10.559	13.324	15.824	16.996	18.372	21.303
55.256	62.011	57.135	61.847	60.192	56.717	61.843	75.276	91.358	109.525	124.71	143.018	175.309
182.179	184.481	170.642	173.902	174.172	160.533	160.583	174.42	212.981	244.983	258.58	276.283	311.905
12.102	13.547	15.157	16.034	17.601	20.059	21.943	21.625	16.459	18.435	29.092	31.722	36.396
20.196	21.268	23.636	23.255	16.674	15.934	21.25	24.899	28.636	32.642	37.187	41.402	44.184
60.163	67.632	75.865	84.821	89.942	99.155	95.399	87.506	81.384	78.802	89.794	107.375	127.93
3.767	4.712	5.034	5.572	5.687	5.627	6.192	7.306	9.816	11.903	13.938	16.611	21.278
130.75	128.525	123.428	130.466	130.948	122.222	125.269	135.972	165.031	189.411	196.001	209.745	245.013
1,572.15	1,574.55	1,425.85	1,474.28	1,458.58	1,333.17	1,341.24	1,463.65	1,804.59	2,061.14	2,137.46	2,252.11	2,560.26
2,524.95	2,439.35	2,163.23	2,187.48	2,146.43	1,905.80	1,892.60	2,024.06	2,446.89	2,749.19	2,796.22	2,915.87	3,322.15
6.457	6.926	6.884	7.474	7.71	4.977	5.309	6.16	7.624	8.872	10.72	12.715	14.863
128.895	136.273	133.128	133.869	137.829	127.604	130.994	148.827	193.663	230.291	247.418	268.69	314.615
13.315	14.201	16.089	17.305	16.49	17.187	18.759	20.781	21.93	23.96	27.329	30.206	33.694
44.669	45.163	45.724	47.049	48.044	47.943	53.301	66.621	84.441	102.183	110.506	112.92	138.388
7.021	7.331	7.425	8.294	8.746	8.734	7.97	8.952	10.98	13.264	16.304	16.677	20.003
353.964	363.748	408.504	411.577	440.597	461.914	473.05	494.997	573.167	669.442	783.141	877.224	1,098.95
67.112	74.117	81.357	88.337	96.715	96.671	104.733	122.977	157.653	184.633	201.187	219.368	258.574
94.017	102.861	105.919	107.619	107.717	120.907	118.938	109.39	115.875	123.645	131.33	142.25	161.935
1,126.63	1,259.95	1,193.62	1,218.67	1,202.40	1,100.56	1,118.32	1,223.24	1,510.06	1,730.10	1,779.41	1,858.34	2,104.67
5.145	6.948	7.26	7.638	7.316	7.467	7.894	8.08	7.814	8.801	9.398	10.39	11.206
5,277.87	4,638.43	4,263.85	3,871.96	4,384.27	4,668.79	4,097.96	3,925.11	4,234.92	4,608.14	4,560.67	4,377.05	4,383.76
11.944	12.046	13.281	13.767	12.883	12.316	13.059	13.191	15.036	16.249	19.132	22.819	29.299
517.206	558.031	527.262	348.465	445.557	511.961	481.979	547.856	608.337	681.227	791.572	888.443	957.053
4.891	5.585	6.134	6.617	7.289	7.833	8.313	9.315	11.186	13.762	16.042	20.101	27.341

(continued on next page)

Table II, continued
MACROECONOMIC DATA FOR SELECT COUNTRIES
GDP (Billions of U.S. Dollars)

	1985	1986	1987	1988	1989	1990	1991	1992	1993	1994
Lithuania	n/a	n/a	n/a	n/a	n/a	n/a	n/a	1.968	2.778	4.35
Luxembourg	4.571	6.651	8.261	9.358	9.963	12.705	13.766	15.421	15.81	17.594
Malaysia	31.772	28.243	32.182	35.272	38.845	44.025	49.876	60.045	67.904	75.606
Mexico	195.569	135.406	148.491	183.191	222.956	262.71	314.507	363.661	403.243	420.773
Netherlands	133.171	185.595	226.443	241.381	238.181	295.46	303.462	334.654	324.39	348.911
New Zealand	22.429	27.252	36.044	44.225	42.702	44.044	42.267	40.164	43.466	51.204
Nigeria	25.966	20.563	21.912	24.311	23.487	31.48	28.337	25.522	15.79	18.086
Norway	64.575	77.234	92.544	100.191	100.829	117.865	120.068	128.591	118.284	124.737
Peru	17.209	25.819	42.637	33.734	41.632	28.975	34.545	35.891	34.805	44.859
Philippines	30.734	29.868	33.196	37.885	42.647	44.164	45.321	52.982	54.368	64.084
Poland	70.775	73.677	63.714	68.612	66.895	62.084	80.451	88.713	90.366	103.683
Portugal	26.041	36.214	45.316	53.012	57.192	75.967	85.975	103.394	90.982	95.335
Romania	47.686	51.915	58.061	60.027	53.614	38.248	29.625	19.578	26.357	30.073
Russia	n/a	n/a	n/a	n/a	n/a	n/a	n/a	85.572	183.826	276.901
Saudi Arabia	103.894	86.954	85.696	88.256	95.344	116.778	131.336	136.304	132.151	134.327
Singapore	17.742	18.007	20.571	25.421	30.117	36.842	43.165	49.715	58.158	70.678
South Africa	57.273	65.424	85.792	92.235	95.979	111.998	120.243	130.532	130.448	135.82
Spain	176.69	244.481	309.745	363.913	401.389	520.709	560.796	613.016	514.949	516.718
Sweden	105.948	139.737	170.306	192.457	202.822	242.848	256.344	266.224	202.589	217.844
Switzerland	100.454	143.401	178.957	193.739	186.724	239.332	241.971	251.791	244.198	270.913
Thailand	38.9	43.097	50.535	61.667	72.251	85.64	96.188	109.426	121.796	144.308
Turkey	90.219	101.485	115.987	119.93	142.934	200.558	198.62	209.935	237.937	172.183
Ukraine	n/a	n/a	n/a	n/a	n/a	n/a	n/a	20.784	29.655	36.478
United Arab Emirates	27.349	21.674	23.799	24.19	27.922	35.985	33.193	33.488	36.721	37.439
United Kingdom	461.559	561.595	690.894	838.572	847.85	1,001.02	1,043.47	1,085.40	969.554	1,047.72
United States	4,220.25	4,462.83	4,739.48	5,103.75	5,484.35	5,803.08	5,995.93	6,337.75	6,657.40	7,072.23
Vietnam	14.999	33.873	42.045	23.234	6.293	6.472	7.642	9.867	13.181	16.279

Source: IMF.

1995	1996	1997	1998	1999	2000	2001	2002	2003	2004	2005	2006	2007
6.392	8.072	9.844	11.094	10.84	11.418	12.146	14.134	18.558	22.508	25.732	29.76	38.345
20.696	20.588	18.54	19.38	21.216	20.329	20.216	22.659	29.091	34.115	37.413	42.507	50.16
90.173	102.376	101.682	73.265	80.344	93.789	92.784	100.845	110.202	124.749	137.232	156.091	186.482
286.184	332.337	400.87	421.026	480.593	580.791	621.859	648.629	638.745	683.486	767.69	840.012	893.365
419.348	418.106	387.013	403.202	411.997	386.204	400.998	439.357	539.343	610.691	634.044	670.923	768.704
60.344	66.946	66.839	54.97	56.963	52.403	51.395	60.017	79.705	98.14	109.048	105.344	128.141
36.945	46.02	35.386	32.749	35.943	46.138	43.847	58.331	66.808	86.949	112.248	146.889	166.778
149.007	160.173	158.55	151.156	159.093	168.671	170.982	193.175	225.307	258.986	302.175	337.426	391.498
53.607	55.838	59.093	56.752	51.553	53.323	53.935	56.756	61.342	69.735	79.485	93.027	109.069
75.525	84.371	83.736	66.596	76.157	75.912	71.216	76.814	79.634	86.93	98.718	117.562	144.129
139.095	156.661	157.082	171.996	167.763	171.268	190.405	198.211	216.797	253.021	303.976	341.724	420.284
113.017	117.658	112.134	118.711	121.823	112.98	115.812	127.906	156.712	179.195	185.771	194.974	223.303
35.478	35.315	35.154	42.092	35.729	37.06	40.188	45.825	59.506	75.516	98.861	122.653	165.983
313.451	391.775	404.946	271.038	195.907	259.702	306.583	345.486	431.429	591.861	764.227	988.671	1,289.58
142.457	157.743	164.994	145.967	161.172	188.693	183.257	188.803	214.859	250.673	315.758	349.138	376.029
84.29	92.552	95.865	82.399	82.611	92.717	85.615	88.266	93.152	109.162	119.788	136.566	161.349
151.117	143.831	148.836	134.215	133.105	132.964	118.563	111.13	166.655	216.34	242.219	257.279	282.63
597.278	622.65	573.376	601.625	618.691	582.377	609.631	688.676	885.358	1,045.67	1,131.71	1,231.73	1,438.96
254.105	276.23	252.614	253.154	257.225	246.372	225.546	249.378	311.763	357.721	367.162	393.606	455.319
316.418	305.054	264.703	273.103	268.572	250.195	255.217	279.515	325.27	363.428	372.988	387.982	423.938
168.019	181.948	150.891	111.86	122.63	122.725	115.536	126.877	142.64	161.34	176.42	206.703	245.659
223.74	239.358	250.112	265.605	245.482	265.177	192.672	231.03	304.141	392.886	482.782	528.686	663.419
37.023	44.597	50.149	41.892	31.569	31.262	38.009	42.393	50.133	64.883	86.137	106.469	140.484
40.726	48.006	51.216	48.514	55.181	70.221	68.677	75.285	88.579	103.784	133	163.296	192.603
1,141.36	1,200.83	1,336.16	1,433.97	1,475.73	1,453.84	1,444.71	1,585.02	1,827.63	2,169.39	2,246.33	2,402.00	2,772.57
7,397.65	7,816.83	8,304.33	8,746.98	9,268.43	9,816.98	10,127.95	10,469.60	10,960.75	11,685.93	12,433.93	13,194.70	13,843.83
20.737	24.657	26.823	27.142	28.683	31.196	32.504	35.148	39.63	45.548	53.053	60.995	70.022

Table III.
MACROECONOMIC DATA FOR SELECT COUNTRIES
GDP PER PERSON (U.S. dollars)

	1985	1986	1987	1988	1989	1990	1991	1992	1993	1994
Argentina	2,905.68	3,449.73	3,497.09	4,046.71	2,564.52	4,344.82	5,750.51	6,845.48	6,972.96	7,493.95
Australia	10,881.09	11,129.23	12,905.48	16,105.43	17,969.32	18,604.46	18,482.35	17,891.07	17,227.58	19,424.66
Austria	9,000.85	12,758.60	15,933.79	17,426.48	17,284.04	21,541.98	22,357.74	24,883.82	23,996.95	25,701.69
Bangladesh	212.24	217.23	234.04	246.76	265.615	269.77	271.76	265.73	272.39	289.55
Belgium	8,455.14	11,716.25	14,553.47	15,720.03	15,887.67	19,825.51	20,257.01	22,427.28	21,421.53	23,310.37
Brazil	1,902.85	2,161.62	2,305.75	2,526.14	3,403.19	3,463.91	2,986.31	2,814.44	3,108.22	3,814.86
Bulgaria	3,056.86	2,711.70	3,156.34	5,187.98	5,321.33	2,365.24	233.86	958.73	525.83	934.04
Canada	13,782.06	14,150.50	15,967.70	18,624.35	20,410.35	21,086.64	21,374.96	20,479.82	19,684.99	19,497.28
Chile	1,368.47	1,447.21	1,678.64	1,945.73	2,203.77	2,409.14	2,734.64	3,283.03	3,463.35	3,941.21
China	288.39	274.84	294.05	361.24	398.48	339.16	350.61	412.26	517.41	466.60
Colombia	1,283.76	1,259.56	1,285.18	1,357.44	1,342.15	1,341.39	1,387.63	1,575.90	1,751.30	2,158.76
Cyprus	5,651.31	6,473.94	7,052.50	8,151.62	8,628.75	9,689.01	9,904.03	11,413.24	10,635.82	11,705.40
Czech Republic	4,399.24	5,162.16	5,790.53	5,721.57	5,579.81	5,058.64	2,636.30	3,090.94	3,551.50	4,117.90
Denmark	12,058.85	16,929.76	20,973.49	22,118.89	21,479.65	26,518.75	26,659.38	29,163.19	27,183.00	29,613.34
Dominican Republic	826.41	979.75	1,006.35	900.13	994.61	907.73	1,093.08	1,266.92	1,351.45	1,472.91
Ecuador	1,776.73	1,271.43	1,159.23	1,076.18	1,031.52	1,023.48	1,122.49	1,200.01	1,371.16	1,655.19
Egypt	997.95	1,077.02	1,507.61	1,767.07	2,155.49	1,760.39	869.27	776.71	853.26	920.76
Estonia	n/a	n/a	n/a	n/a	n/a	n/a	n/a	n/a	1,141.95	1,633.85
Finland	11,314.27	14,766.41	18,350.26	21,787.47	23,671.35	28,042.04	25,215.14	21,977.51	17,254.83	19,793.10
France	9,909.06	13,706.89	16,539.30	17,896.73	17,896.95	22,015.08	21,922.95	24,009.25	22,482.17	23,688.97
Germany	8,397.52	11,985.47	14,911.94	15,979.31	15,705.94	19,592.74	22,692.80	25,523.16	24,657.05	26,380.45
Ghana	527.12	467.06	385.50	404.99	399.79	462.29	499.44	449.06	386.61	343.78
Greece	4,566.87	5,352.49	6,205.64	7,199.26	7,424.45	9,121.34	9,755.55	10,645.50	9,866.22	10,453.31
Guatemala	1,432.21	1,055.05	862.85	931.64	963.12	860.71	1,034.67	1,112.81	1,181.69	1,302.34
Hungary	1,945.92	2,249.73	2,484.48	2,730.46	2,798.89	3,186.14	3,222.63	3,591.26	3,723.68	4,010.26
Iceland	12,138.77	16,101.21	21,981.58	24,082.22	22,165.46	24,952.17	26,258.08	26,639.23	23,176.57	23,598.69
India	297.57	320.61	346.48	371.98	362.68	379.13	332.38	329.83	316.42	351.54
Ireland	5,930.97	7,951.40	9,411.26	10,356.18	10,746.04	13,632.02	13,738.79	15,320.99	14,118.58	15,441.31
Israel	6,793.33	7,518.95	8,844.04	10,771.07	10,747.82	12,335.20	13,600.46	14,636.12	14,149.57	15,567.99
Italy	7,724.27	10,938.19	13,729.40	15,207.03	15,804.94	20,029.19	21,129.68	22,403.30	17,997.61	18,557.95
Jamaica	960.55	1,131.60	1,267.01	1,501.19	1,737.21	2,156.20	2,023.97	1,689.70	2,325.14	2,743.19
Japan	11,310.79	16,646.17	20,025.33	24,168.74	24,122.50	24,734.11	28,071.61	30,530.83	35,007.88	38,101.79
Kenya	440.14	504.64	534.26	535.29	513.26	517.14	473.71	453.39	306.68	358.16
Korea	2,369.19	2,700.89	3,366.27	4,466.50	5,429.70	6,154.49	7,120.20	7,541.57	8,194.66	9,485.67
Latvia	n/a	n/a	n/a	n/a	n/a	n/a	n/a	572.46	912.94	1,558.48

Source: IMF.

1995	1996	1997	1998	1999	2000	2001	2002	2003	2004	2005	2006	2007
7,419.16	7,732.50	8,225.37	8,302.88	7,789.40	7,726.32	7,231.55	2,605.11	3,370.59	3,975.25	4,704.30	5,458.22	6,606.27
20,497.09	22,757.17	22,541.17	19,911.11	21,195.07	20,325.17	18,935.69	20,973.02	26,485.52	31,758.08	34,887.75	36,442.40	43,312.32
30,169.60	29,711.30	26,229.84	26,846.10	26,699.40	24,265.76	24,038.81	25,800.53	31,506.86	35,916.12	37,120.15	39,190.19	45,181.12
313.39	322.03	329.89	333.69	340.23	337.42	331.96	341.92	368.72	392.75	398.79	415.42	455.48
27,315.94	27,101.56	24,489.39	25,021.69	24,794.00	22,688.91	22,492.57	24,392.01	29,866.53	34,412.60	35,787.81	37,613.70	42,556.92
4,844.94	5,207.26	5,321.31	5,077.38	3,477.99	3,761.58	3,189.53	2,867.00	3,085.39	3,654.20	4,787.35	5,741.58	6,937.91
1,579.64	1,203.66	1,269.92	1,584.72	1,609.45	1,579.41	1,730.28	1,982.09	2,552.41	3,166.10	3,519.82	4,119.56	5,186.43
20,184.45	20,757.38	21,349.12	20,495.23	21,776.56	23,658.83	23,103.94	23,457.94	27,449.23	31,107.46	35,186.97	39,114.78	43,484.94
5,020.86	5,254.98	5,663.01	5,354.82	4,860.15	4,943.71	4,451.12	4,314.00	4,698.20	5,991.99	7,350.79	8,903.35	9,879.09
601.01	699.41	770.59	817.15	861.21	945.59	1,038.04	1,131.80	1,269.83	1,486.02	1,715.93	2,011.93	2,460.79
2,399.89	2,472.21	2,662.22	2,411.25	2,072.33	1,979.75	1,903.62	1,850.67	1,782.24	2,163.46	2,669.48	2,910.53	3,611.47
14,217.16	14,139.62	13,271.07	14,071.15	14,242.61	13,424.88	13,796.81	14,865.03	18,433.99	21,388.90	22,427.99	23,778.82	27,326.66
5,348.65	6,011.54	5,545.14	6,033.68	5,880.87	5,548.48	6,077.48	7,401.06	8,974.90	10,742.47	12,191.18	13,932.59	17,069.74
34,926.98	35,132.48	32,349.17	32,842.63	32,776.11	30,118.82	30,021.17	32,492.60	39,558.04	45,384.04	47,787.80	50,903.86	57,260.95
1,637.37	1,807.34	1,993.47	2,078.76	2,249.21	2,526.76	2,724.76	2,647.00	1,985.98	2,192.89	3,411.35	3,666.77	4,147.29
1,762.25	1,818.02	1,980.06	1,910.14	1,343.50	1,259.98	1,747.99	1,966.67	2,229.76	2,505.76	2,813.98	3,057.74	3,218.16
1,046.14	1,151.09	1,262.73	1,382.78	1,435.87	1,549.90	1,460.98	1,313.35	1,197.25	1,136.62	1,269.77	1,488.61	1,738.81
2,601.06	3,306.47	3,580.66	3,999.93	4,123.35	4,101.46	4,529.52	5,367.44	7,238.45	8,809.96	10,343.49	12,352.93	15,850.71
25,598.21	25,080.17	24,014.02	25,315.98	25,350.70	23,612.30	24,145.89	26,145.42	31,657.45	36,228.95	37,361.28	39,827.97	46,601.87
27,179.05	27,135.27	24,495.92	25,245.53	24,859.40	22,577.26	22,559.04	24,449.86	29,944.71	33,987.90	35,042.72	36,706.45	41,511.15
30,860.75	29,743.72	26,362.45	26,664.60	26,123.92	23,168.07	22,957.16	24,523.16	29,647.83	33,323.22	33,919.09	35,432.74	40,415.41
397.88	416.09	403.29	426.94	429.44	270.34	281.16	318.07	383.89	435.57	513.21	593.53	676.48
12,096.48	12,688.90	12,311.98	12,308.92	12,610.95	11,627.20	11,896.60	13,482.68	17,510.59	20,785.83	22,290.45	24,157.31	28,273.30
1,426.10	1,481.22	1,634.38	1,712.17	1,588.87	1,612.81	1,714.45	1,849.30	1,876.49	1,971.34	2,151.78	2,326.54	2,531.85
4,321.38	4,375.71	4,438.65	4,576.90	4,685.68	4,690.37	5,225.41	6,547.59	8,325.60	10,100.35	10,943.86	11,206.18	13,762.24
26,203.46	27,165.42	27,258.52	30,083.62	31,343.29	30,823.56	27,812.31	31,031.08	37,786.18	45,179.81	54,366.87	54,205.22	63,830.08
390.90	393.88	433.89	428.95	450.39	458.70	461.29	475.16	541.75	622.88	717.33	791.72	977.74
18,635.63	20,439.78	22,225.13	23,854.79	25,848.65	25,510.34	27,223.27	31,394.15	39,622.15	45,658.24	48,705.22	51,800.07	59,924.42
16,970.53	18,093.37	18,174.17	18,026.59	17,586.42	19,225.13	18,471.56	16,649.88	17,323.22	18,159.09	18,950.92	20,177.26	22,475.07
19,819.03	22,164.10	20,985.09	21,433.70	21,129.55	19,293.40	19,541.11	21,317.51	26,308.26	30,118.99	30,638.87	31,801.63	35,872.42
2,055.21	2,748.85	2,843.44	2,964.70	2,833.97	2,875.14	3,021.81	3,082.04	2,964.84	3,323.31	3,532.04	3,886.78	4,172.20
42,076.09	36,897.51	33,837.14	30,645.05	34,634.41	36,810.99	32,233.80	30,809.29	33,180.06	36,075.92	35,699.41	34,263.65	34,312.14
443.68	437.42	471.61	478.82	438.03	409.18	423.09	418.53	467.47	495.26	572.03	670.24	845.49
11,469.77	12,257.77	11,473.81	7,528.45	9,557.89	10,890.91	10,177.49	11,504.22	12,710.94	14,180.58	16,443.77	18,395.34	19,750.81
1,955.96	2,261.68	2,508.93	2,733.39	3,037.84	3,294.86	3,516.14	3,970.87	4,798.02	5,933.78	6,955.26	8,760.12	11,984.76

(continued on next page)

MACROECONOMIC DATA FOR SELECT COUNTRIES
GDP PER PERSON (U.S. dollars)

	1985	1986	1987	1988	1989	1990	1991	1992	1993	1994
Lithuania	n/a	n/a	n/a	n/a	n/a	n/a	n/a	524.97	734.99	1,154.11
Luxembourg	12,469.15	18,059.15	22,284.20	25,026.75	26,386.38	33,267.96	35,561.42	39,298.54	39,723.15	43,570.22
Malaysia	2,026.29	1,753.14	1,946.87	2,082.17	2,238.90	2,431.97	2,721.34	3,200.32	3,470.94	3,759.35
Mexico	2,591.52	1,758.14	1,890.02	2,286.59	2,730.02	3,156.58	3,709.11	4,210.54	4,584.72	4,698.98
Netherlands	9,189.30	12,736.41	15,441.07	16,353.76	16,040.23	19,760.56	20,136.83	22,119.79	21,286.59	22,742.86
New Zealand	6,907.54	8,317.14	10,903.07	13,255.59	12,668.18	12,913.22	12,073.08	11,353.79	12,143.52	14,113.93
Nigeria	331.052	254.85	263.86	284.38	266.90	347.63	304.17	266.615	160.53	178.95
Norway	15,533.50	18,507.34	22,080.63	23,780.28	23,829.65	27,763.99	28,143.58	29,965.60	27,404.02	28,732.29
Peru	881.80	1,293.36	2,088.50	1,616.59	1,953.21	1,331.98	1,557.51	1,588.30	1,512.64	1,951.30
Philippines	562.18	533.36	578.33	645.41	709.60	718.11	719.38	822.69	825.01	949.21
Poland	1,895.37	1,960.94	1,687.17	1,815.14	1,767.95	1,625.24	2,100.56	2,310.23	2,346.24	2,686.41
Portugal	2,627.71	3,654.34	4,572.71	5,325.13	5,765.51	7,690.95	8,715.27	10,512.64	9,206.79	9,608.35
Romania	2,098.40	2,272.50	2,527.17	2,599.08	2,313.02	1,648.14	1,278.50	848.18	1,148.14	1,318.04
Russia	n/a	n/a	n/a	n/a	n/a	n/a	n/a	576.24	1,237.05	1,865.91
Saudi Arabia	8,732.75	6,960.55	6,532.88	6,407.38	6,592.09	7,689.19	8,235.57	8,042.29	7,648.99	7,588.63
Singapore	6,484.74	6,587.94	7,413.51	8,931.88	10,275.64	12,090.98	13,765.27	15,381.61	17,541.82	20,659.42
South Africa	1,735.62	1,937.54	2,485.04	2,614.36	2,662.24	3,039.44	3,192.05	3,389.85	3,315.64	3,382.24
Spain	4,600.34	6,347.03	8,022.62	9,405.61	10,353.62	13,407.90	14,401.90	15,691.09	13,140.00	13,149.72
Sweden	12,676.02	16,672.02	20,240.56	22,752.00	23,785.74	28,268.90	29,655.26	30,628.56	23,166.01	24,709.03
Switzerland	15,490.58	21,982.48	27,251.86	29,265.80	27,978.41	35,452.95	35,361.64	36,449.46	35,042.82	38,597.06
Thailand	750.97	813.60	938.09	1,122.03	1,306.77	1,518.17	1,686.61	1,899.10	2,084.11	2,441.76
Turkey	1,834.69	2,018.65	2,257.87	2,373.47	2,788.89	3,824.84	3,711.47	3,848.83	4,279.90	3,044.82
Ukraine	n/a	n/a	n/a	n/a	n/a	n/a	n/a	399.27	567.62	702.85
United Arab Emirates	19,818.48	15,051.53	15,865.98	13,513.74	15,011.58	19,514.64	17,220.53	16,652.45	17,628.87	16,788.85
United Kingdom	8,161.38	9,907.47	12,162.77	14,733.50	14,854.75	17,489.08	18,166.49	18,848.69	16,799.28	18,107.23
United States	17,701.24	18,549.30	19,524.04	20,834.40	22,178.17	23,207.90	23,662.66	24,681.91	25,590.97	26,857.44
Vietnam	251.20	556.02	674.88	365.89	97.16	98.03	113.65	144.15	189.26	229.85

Source: IMF.

1995	1996	1997	1998	1999	2000	2001	2002	2003	2004	2005	2006	2007
1,720.68	2,241.35	2,753.61	3,125.76	3,075.80	3,251.18	3,483.27	4,074.34	5,372.64	6,551.52	7,536.45	8,768.05	11,354.35
50,515.36	49,539.13	44,037.74	45,439.25	49,053.28	46,360.39	45,789.99	50,781.69	64,403.84	74,471.23	80,422.70	89,923.23	104,673.28
4,358.45	4,836.12	4,693.25	3,303.27	3,537.53	3,991.91	3,863.93	4,111.69	4,409.42	4,898.40	5,288.05	5,914.23	6,947.64
3,139.88	3,590.09	4,267.92	4,420.17	4,975.88	5,928.50	6,281.78	6,486.14	6,322.91	6,697.57	7,446.86	8,059.88	8,478.68
27,187.80	26,985.21	24,860.92	25,756.79	26,141.54	24,250.65	24,990.27	27,206.57	33,240.83	37,520.24	38,871.29	41,046.19	46,260.69
16,384.04	17,896.12	17,646.71	14,393.33	14,833.72	13,565.82	13,204.35	15,154.46	19,745.23	23,964.31	26,328.34	25,128.65	30,255.58
355.76	431.26	322.73	290.68	310.48	387.87	358.73	464.45	517.69	655.714	823.82	1,049.18	1,159.36
34,149.81	36,521.51	35,955.94	34,075.58	35,619.37	37,520.08	37,840.31	42,525.73	49,316.72	56,344.18	65,604.60	72,768.13	83,922.50
2,296.30	2,355.42	2,454.75	2,321.59	2,076.81	2,115.37	2,107.06	2,183.50	2,323.97	2,601.68	2,920.21	3,365.66	3,885.86
1,104.99	1,206.14	1,170.32	910.44	1,018.88	994.29	913.90	966.18	982.15	1,040.33	1,157.84	1,351.72	1,624.69
3,603.96	4,056.01	4,064.24	4,448.53	4,339.42	4,453.87	4,978.16	5,184.64	5,674.63	6,626.67	7,964.68	8,959.43	11,041.22
11,336.17	11,732.11	11,123.64	11,735.45	11,995.13	11,064.36	11,261.22	12,349.37	15,017.51	17,060.01	17,586.82	18,418.27	21,018.83
1,564.20	1,565.73	1,566.91	1,885.61	1,608.21	1,675.65	1,824.63	2,088.42	2,721.46	3,465.67	4,552.82	5,668.12	7,697.21
2,112.20	2,641.77	2,736.12	1,833.82	1,328.18	1,767.88	2,095.58	2,379.38	2,975.37	4,104.44	5,325.63	6,923.46	9,075.05
7,855.13	8,489.58	8,667.04	7,483.87	8,065.43	9,216.39	8,736.41	8,785.13	9,758.02	11,126.52	13,657.95	14,733.46	15,481.23
23,907.88	25,215.76	25,269.60	21,009.33	20,909.36	23,077.09	20,723.91	21,160.21	22,638.26	26,198.57	28,081.01	31,027.89	35,162.93
3,684.84	3,439.25	3,495.07	3,100.05	3,029.06	2,986.45	2,632.83	2,440.23	3,622.15	4,656.40	5,165.87	5,418.46	5,906.49
15,164.36	15,772.03	14,485.63	15,146.23	15,495.85	14,464.24	14,971.13	16,669.31	21,077.65	24,493.52	26,077.27	27,950.59	32,066.96
28,753.02	31,231.81	28,551.60	28,590.99	29,027.48	27,735.91	25,316.30	27,892.13	34,734.21	39,696.58	40,580.52	43,190.45	49,654.87
44,803.52	43,078.48	37,300.71	38,338.08	37,486.74	34,802.00	35,392.68	38,659.00	44,886.22	50,051.87	51,276.77	53,244.79	58,083.57
2,825.74	3,037.52	2,496.14	1,828.67	1,984.94	1,966.75	1,835.78	1,999.30	2,228.54	2,479.01	2,709.55	3,166.40	3,736.82
3,890.75	4,092.68	4,304.89	4,500.78	4,097.50	4,225.11	3,019.24	3,562.29	4,616.16	5,872.37	7,109.89	7,759.61	9,629.14
718.89	872.74	991.09	834.50	632.64	642.41	787.89	886.45	1,056.72	1,377.55	1,842.53	2,291.33	3,046.13
16,891.58	19,650.32	19,850.98	17,118.62	18,193.68	23,446.15	21,685.14	22,479.73	24,944.77	27,594.83	32,391.58	38,613.42	42,934.13
19,670.10	20,645.59	22,913.27	24,522.82	25,147.08	24,689.06	24,439.83	26,718.89	30,688.62	36,256.87	37,303.31	39,680.88	45,574.74
27,762.90	28,996.24	30,438.61	31,689.37	33,196.97	34,773.78	35,505.43	36,340.28	37,685.03	39,811.63	41,969.76	44,118.01	45,845.48
288.03	337.05	360.98	359.70	374.47	401.82	413.09	440.85	489.87	555.24	637.54	722.68	818.08

Solutions to "Check Your Understanding" Questions

This section offers suggested answers to the "Check Your Understanding" questions found within chapters.

Chapter One

Check Your Understanding
1-1

1.
   a. This illustrates the concept of opportunity cost. Given that a person can only eat so much at one sitting, having a slice of chocolate cake requires that you forgo eating something else, such as a slice of coconut cream pie.
   b. This illustrates the concept that resources are scarce. Even if there were more resources in the world, the total amount of those resources would be limited. As a result, scarcity would still arise. For there to be no scarcity, there would have to be unlimited amounts of everything (including unlimited time in a human life), which is clearly impossible.
   c. This illustrates the concept that people usually exploit opportunities to make themselves better off. Students will seek to make themselves better off by signing up for the tutorials of teaching assistants with good reputations and avoiding those teaching assistants with poor reputations. It also illustrates the concept that resources are scarce. If there were unlimited spaces in tutorials with good teaching assistants, they would not fill up.
   d. This illustrates the concept of marginal analysis. Your decision about allocating your time is a "how much" decision: how much time spent exercising versus how much time spent studying. You make your decision by comparing the benefit of an additional hour of exercising to its cost, the effect on your grades of one fewer hour spent studying.

2.
   a. Yes. The increased time spent commuting is a cost you will incur if you accept the new job. That additional time spent commuting—or equivalently, the benefit you would get from spending that time doing something else—is an opportunity cost of the new job.
   b. Yes. One of the benefits of the new job is that you will be making $50,000. But if you take the new job, you will have to give up your current job; that is, you have to give up your current salary of $45,000. So $45,000 is one of the opportunity costs of taking the new job.
   c. No. A more spacious office is an additional benefit of your new job and does not involve forgoing something else. So it is not an opportunity cost.

Check Your Understanding
1-2

1.
   a. This illustrates the concept that markets usually lead to efficiency. Any seller who wants to sell a book for at least $30 does indeed sell to someone who is willing to buy a book for $30. As a result, there is no way to change how used textbooks are distributed among buyers and sellers in a way that would make one person better off without making someone else worse off.

b. This illustrates the concept that there are gains from trade. Students trade tutoring services based on their different abilities in academic subjects.
c. This illustrates the concept that when markets don't achieve efficiency, government intervention can improve society's welfare. In this case the market, left alone, will permit bars and nightclubs to impose costs on their neighbors in the form of loud music, costs that the bars and nightclubs have no incentive to take into account. This is an inefficient outcome because society as a whole can be made better off if bars and nightclubs are induced to reduce their noise.
d. This illustrates the concept that resources should be used as efficiently as possible to achieve society's goals. By closing neighborhood clinics and shifting funds to the main hospital, better health care can be provided at a lower cost.
e. This illustrates the concept that markets move toward equilibrium. Here, because books with the same amount of wear and tear sell for about the same price, no buyer or seller can be made better off by engaging in a different trade than he or she undertook. This means that the market for used textbooks has moved to an equilibrium.

2.
   a. This does not describe an equilibrium situation. Many students should want to change their behavior and switch to eating at the restaurants. Therefore, the situation described is not an equilibrium. An equilibrium will be established when students are equally as well off eating at the restaurants as eating at the dining hall—which would happen if, say, prices at the restaurants were higher than at the dining hall.
   b. This does describe an equilibrium situation. By changing your behavior and riding the bus, you would not be made better off. Therefore, you have no incentive to change your behavior.

Check Your Understanding
1-3

1.
   a. This illustrates the principle that government policies can change spending. The tax cut would increase people's after-tax incomes, leading to higher consumer spending.
   b. This illustrates the principle that one person's spending is another person's income. As oil companies increase their spending on labor by hiring more workers, or pay existing workers higher wages, those workers' incomes rise. In turn, these workers increase their consumer spending, which becomes income to restaurants and other consumer businesses.
   c. This illustrates the principle that overall spending sometimes gets out of line with the economy's productive capacity. In this case, spending on housing was too high relative to the economy's capacity to create new housing. This first led to a rise in house prices, and then—as a result—to a rise in overall prices, or *inflation*.

Chapter Two

Check Your Understanding
2-1

1. **a.** False. An increase in the resources available to Tom for use in producing coconuts and fish changes his production possibility frontier by shifting it outward. This is because he can now produce more fish and coconuts than before. In the accompanying figure, the line labeled "Tom's original *PPF*" represents Tom's original production possibility frontier, and the line labeled "Tom's new *PPF*" represents the new production possibility frontier that results from an increase in resources available to Tom.

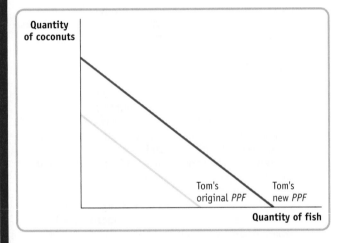

b. True. A technological change that allows Tom to catch more fish for any amount of coconuts gathered results in a change in his production possibility frontier. This is illustrated in the accompanying figure: the new production possibility frontier is represented by the line labeled "Tom's new *PPF*," and the original production frontier is represented by the line labeled "Tom's original *PPF*." Since the maximum quantity of coconuts that Tom can gather is the same as before, the new production possibility frontier intersects the vertical axis at the same point as the old frontier. But since the maximum possible quantity of fish is now greater than before, the new frontier intersects the horizontal axis to the right of the old frontier.

c. False. The production possibility frontier illustrates how much of one good an economy must give up to get more of another good only when resources are used efficiently in production. If an economy is producing inefficiently—that is, inside the frontier—then it does not have to give up a unit of one good in order to get another unit of the other good. Instead, by becoming more efficient in production, this economy can have more of both goods.

2. **a.** The United States has an absolute advantage in automobile production because it takes fewer Americans (6) to produce a car in one day than Italians (8). The United States also has an absolute advantage in washing machine production because it takes fewer Americans (2) to produce a washing machine in one day than Italians (3).

b. In Italy the opportunity cost of a washing machine in terms of an automobile is $\frac{3}{8}$: $\frac{3}{8}$ of a car can be produced with the same number of workers and in the same time it takes to produce 1 washing machine. In the United States the opportunity cost of a washing machine in terms of an automobile is $\frac{2}{6} = \frac{1}{3}$: $\frac{1}{3}$ of a car can be produced with the same number of workers and in the same time it takes to produce 1 washing machine. Since $\frac{1}{3} < \frac{3}{8}$, the United States has a comparative advantage in the production of washing machines: to produce a washing machine, only $\frac{1}{3}$ of a car must be given up in the United States but $\frac{3}{8}$ of a car must be given up in Italy. This means that Italy has a comparative advantage in automobiles. This can be checked as follows. The opportunity cost of an automobile in terms of a washing machine in Italy is $\frac{8}{3}$, equal to $2\frac{2}{3}$: $2\frac{2}{3}$ washing machines can be produced with the same number of workers and in the time it takes to produce 1 car in Italy. And the opportunity cost of an automobile in terms of a washing machine in the United States is $\frac{6}{2}$, equal to 3: 3 washing machines can be produced with the same number of workers and in the time it takes to produce 1 car in the United States.

c. The greatest gains are realized when each country specializes in producing the good for which it has a comparative advantage. Therefore, the United States should specialize in washing machines and Italy should specialize in automobiles.

3. At a trade of 1 fish for 1.5 coconuts, Hank gives up less for a fish than he would if he were producing fish himself—that is, he gives up less than 2 coconuts for 1 fish. Likewise, Tom gives up less for a coconut than he would if he were producing coconuts himself—with trade, a coconut costs $\frac{1}{1.5} = \frac{2}{3}$ of a fish, less than the $\frac{4}{3}$ of a fish he must give up if he does not trade.

4. An increase in the amount of money spent by households results in an increase in the flow of goods to households. This, in turn, generates an increase in demand for factors of production by firms. Therefore, there is an increase in the number of jobs in the economy.

Check Your Understanding
2-2

1. **a.** This is a normative statement because it stipulates what should be done. In addition, it may have no "right" answer. That is, should people be prevented from all dangerous personal behavior if they enjoy that behavior—like skydiving? Your answer will depend on your point of view.

b. This is a positive statement because it is a description of fact.

2. a. True. Economists often have different value judgments about the desirability of a particular social goal. But despite those differences in value judgments, they will tend to agree that society, once it has decided to pursue a given social goal, should adopt the most efficient policy to achieve that goal. Therefore economists are likely to agree on adopting policy choice B.

   b. False. Disagreements between economists are more likely to arise because they base their conclusions on different models or because they have different value judgments about the desirability of the policy.

   c. False. Deciding which goals a society should try to achieve is a matter of value judgments, not a question of economic analysis.

Chapter Three

Check Your Understanding
3-1

1. a. The quantity of umbrellas demanded is higher at any given price on a rainy day than on a dry day. This is a rightward *shift of* the demand curve, since at any given price the quantity demanded rises. This implies that any specific quantity can now be sold at a higher price.

   b. The quantity of weekend calls demanded rises in response to a price reduction. This is a *movement along* the demand curve for weekend calls.

   c. The demand for roses increases the week of Valentine's Day. This is a rightward *shift of* the demand curve.

   d. The quantity of gasoline demanded falls in response to a rise in price. This is a *movement along* the demand curve.

Check Your Understanding
3-2

1. a. The quantity of houses supplied rises as a result of an increase in prices. This is a *movement along* the supply curve.

   b. The quantity of strawberries supplied is higher at any given price. This is a rightward *shift of* the supply curve.

   c. The quantity of labor supplied is lower at any given wage. This is a leftward *shift of* the supply curve compared to the supply curve during school vacation. So, in order to attract workers, fast-food chains have to offer higher wages.

   d. The quantity of labor supplied rises in response to a rise in wages. This is a *movement along* the supply curve.

   e. The quantity of cabins supplied is higher at any given price. This is a rightward *shift of* the supply curve.

Check Your Understanding
3-3

1. a. The supply curve shifts rightward. At the original equilibrium price of the year before, the quantity of grapes supplied exceeds the quantity demanded. This is a case of surplus. The price of grapes will fall.

   b. The demand curve shifts leftward. At the original equilibrium price, the quantity of hotel rooms supplied exceeds the quantity demanded. This is a case of surplus. The rates for hotel rooms will fall.

   c. The demand curve for secondhand snowblowers shifts rightward. At the original equilibrium price, the quantity of secondhand snowblowers demanded exceeds the quantity supplied. This is a case of shortage. The equilibrium price of secondhand snowblowers will rise.

Check Your Understanding
3-4

1. a. The market for large cars: this is a rightward shift in demand caused by a decrease in the price of a complement, gasoline. As a result of the shift, the equilibrium price of large cars will rise and the equilibrium quantity of large cars bought and sold will also rise.

   b. The market for fresh paper made from recycled stock: this is a rightward shift in supply due to a technological innovation. As a result of this shift, the equilibrium price of fresh paper made from recycled stock will fall and the equilibrium quantity bought and sold will rise.

   c. The market for movies at a local movie theater: this is a leftward shift in demand caused by a fall in the price of a substitute, pay-per-view movies. As a result of this shift, the equilibrium price of movie tickets will fall and the equilibrium number of people who go to the movies will also fall.

2. Upon the announcement of the new chip, the demand curve for computers using the earlier chip shifts leftward, as demand decreases, and the supply curve for these computers shifts rightward, as supply increases.

   a. If demand decreases relatively more than supply increases, then the equilibrium quantity falls, as shown here:

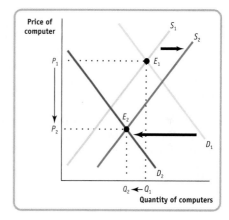

   b. If supply increases relatively more than demand decreases, then the equilibrium quantity rises, as shown here:

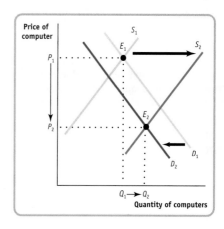

In both cases, the equilibrium price falls.

Chapter Four

Check Your Understanding 4-1

1. A consumer buys each pepper if the price is less than (or just equal to) the consumer's willingness to pay for that pepper. The demand schedule is constructed by asking how many peppers will be demanded at any given price. The accompanying table illustrates the demand schedule.

Price of pepper	Quantity of peppers demanded	Quantity of peppers demanded by Casey	Quantity of peppers demanded by Josey
$0.90	1	1	0
0.80	2	1	1
0.70	3	2	1
0.60	4	2	2
0.50	5	3	2
0.40	6	3	3
0.30	8	4	4
0.20	8	4	4
0.10	8	4	4
0.00	8	4	4

When the price is $0.40, Casey's consumer surplus from the first pepper is $0.50, from his second pepper $0.30, from his third pepper $0.10, and he does not buy any more peppers. Casey's individual consumer surplus is therefore $0.90. Josey's consumer surplus from her first pepper is $0.40, from her second pepper $0.20, from her third pepper $0.00 (since the price is exactly equal to her willingness to pay, she buys the third pepper but receives no consumer surplus from it), and she does not buy any more peppers. Josey's individual consumer surplus is therefore $0.60. Total consumer surplus at a price of $0.40 is therefore $0.90 + $0.60 = $1.50.

Check Your Understanding 4-2

1. A producer supplies each pepper if the price is greater than (or just equal to) the producer's cost of producing that pepper. The supply schedule is constructed by asking how many peppers will be supplied at any price. The accompanying table illustrates the supply schedule.

Price of pepper	Quantity of peppers supplied	Quantity of peppers supplied by Cara	Quantity of peppers supplied by Jamie
$0.90	8	4	4
0.80	7	4	3
0.70	7	4	3
0.60	6	4	2
0.50	5	3	2
0.40	4	3	1
0.30	3	2	1
0.20	2	2	0
0.10	2	2	0
0.00	0	0	0

When the price is $0.70, Cara's producer surplus from the first pepper is $0.60, from her second pepper $0.60, from her third pepper $0.30, from her fourth pepper $0.10, and she does not supply any more peppers. Cara's individual producer surplus is therefore $1.60. Jamie's producer surplus from his first pepper is $0.40, from his second pepper $0.20, from his third pepper $0.00 (since the price is exactly equal to his cost, he sells the third pepper but receives no producer surplus from it), and he does not supply any more peppers. Jamie's individual producer surplus is therefore $0.60. Total producer surplus at a price of $0.70 is therefore $1.60 + $0.60 = $2.20.

Check Your Understanding 4-3

1. The quantity demanded equals the quantity supplied at a price of $0.50, the equilibrium price. At that price, a total quantity of five peppers will be bought and sold. Casey will buy three peppers and receive consumer surplus of $0.40 on his first, $0.20 on his second, and $0.00 on his third pepper. Josey will buy two peppers and receive consumer surplus of $0.30 on her first and $0.10 on her second pepper. Total consumer surplus is therefore $1.00. Cara will supply three peppers and receive producer surplus of $0.40 on her first, $0.40 on her second, and $0.10 on her third pepper. Jamie will supply two peppers and receive producer surplus of $0.20 on his first and $0.00 on his second pepper. Total producer surplus is therefore $1.10. Total surplus in this market is therefore $1.00 + $1.10 = $2.10.

2. a. If Josey consumes one less pepper, she loses $0.60 (her willingness to pay for her second pepper); if Casey consumes one more pepper, he gains $0.30 (his willingness to pay for his fourth pepper). This results in an overall loss of consumer surplus of $0.60 − $0.30 = $0.30.

b. Cara's cost of the last pepper she supplied (the third pepper) is $0.40, and Jamie's cost of producing one more (his third pepper) is $0.70. Total producer surplus therefore falls by $0.70 − $0.40 = $0.30.

c. Josey's willingness to pay for her second pepper is $0.60; this is what she would lose if she were to consume one less pepper. Cara's cost of producing her third pepper is $0.40; this is what she would save if she were to produce one less pepper. If we therefore reduced quantity by one pepper, we would lose $0.60 − $0.40 = $0.20 of total surplus.

3. The new guideline is likely to reduce the total life span of kidney recipients because older recipients (those with small children) are more likely to get a kidney compared to the original guideline. As a result, total surplus is likely to fall. However, this new policy can be justified as an acceptable sacrifice of efficiency for fairness because it's a desirable goal to reduce the chance of a small child losing a parent.

Check Your Understanding 4-4

1. When these rights are separated, someone who owns both the above-ground and the mineral rights can sell each of these separately in the market for above-ground rights and the market for mineral rights. And each of these markets will achieve efficiency: if the market price for above-ground rights is higher than the seller's cost, the seller will sell that right and total surplus increases. If the market price for mineral rights is higher than the seller's cost, the seller will sell that right and total surplus increases. If the two rights, however, cannot be sold separately, a seller can only sell both rights or none at all. Imagine a situation in which the seller values the mineral right highly (that is, has a high cost of selling it) but values the above-ground right much less. If the two rights are separate, the owner may sell the above-ground right (increasing total surplus) but not the mineral right. If, however, the two rights cannot be sold separately, and the owner values the mineral right sufficiently highly, she may not sell either of the two rights. In this case, surplus could have been created through the sale of the above-ground right but goes unrealized because the two rights could not be sold separately.

2. There will be many sellers willing to sell their books but only a few buyers who want to buy books at that price. As a result, only a few transactions will actually occur, and many transactions that would have been mutually beneficial will not take place. This, of course, is inefficient.

3. Markets, alas, do not always lead to efficiency. When there is market failure, the market outcome may be inefficient. This can occur for three main reasons. Markets can fail when, in an attempt to capture more surplus, one party—a monopolist, for instance—prevents mutually beneficial trades from occurring. Markets can also fail when one individual's actions have side effects—externalities—on the welfare of others. Finally, markets can fail when the goods themselves—such as goods about which some relevant information is private—are unsuited for efficient management by markets. And when markets don't achieve efficiency, government intervention can improve society's welfare.

Chapter Five

Check Your Understanding

5-1

1. a. Fewer homeowners are willing to rent out their driveways because the price ceiling has reduced the payment they receive. This is an example of a fall in price leading to a fall in the quantity supplied. It is shown in the accompanying diagram by the movement from point E to point A along the supply curve, a reduction in quantity of 400 parking spaces.

b. The quantity demanded increases by 400 spaces as the price decreases. At a lower price, more fans are willing to drive and rent a parking space. It is shown in the diagram

by the movement from point E to point B along the demand curve.

c. Under a price ceiling, the quantity demanded exceeds the quantity supplied; as a result, shortages arise. In this case, there will be a shortage of 800 parking spaces. It is shown by the horizontal distance between points A and B.

d. Price ceilings result in wasted resources. The additional time fans spend to guarantee a parking space is wasted time.

e. Price ceilings lead to inefficient allocation of a good—here, the parking spaces—to consumers.

f. Price ceilings lead to black markets.

2. a. False. By lowering the price that producers receive, a price ceiling leads to a decrease in the quantity supplied.

b. True. A price ceiling leads to a lower quantity supplied than in an efficient, unregulated market. As a result, some people who would have been willing to pay the market price, and so would have gotten the good in an unregulated market, are unable to obtain it when a price ceiling is imposed.

c. True. Those producers who still sell the product now receive less for it and are therefore worse off. Other producers will no longer find it worthwhile to sell the product at all and so will also be made worse off.

3. a. Since the apartment is rented quickly at the same price, there is no change (either gain or loss) in producer surplus. So any change in total surplus comes from changes in consumer surplus. When you are evicted, the amount of consumer surplus you lose is equal to the difference between your willingness to pay for the apartment and the rent-controlled price. When the apartment is rented to someone else at the same price, the amount of consumer surplus the new renter gains is equal to the difference between his or her willingness to pay and the rent-controlled price. So this will be a pure transfer of surplus from one person to another only if both your willingness to pay and the new renter's willingness to pay are the same. Since under rent control apartments are not always allocated to those who have the highest willingness to pay, the new renter's willingness to pay may be either equal to, lower, or higher than your willingness to pay. If the new renter's willingness to pay is lower than yours, this will create additional deadweight loss: there is some additional consumer surplus that is lost. However, if the new renter's willingness to pay is higher than yours, this will create an increase in total surplus, as the new renter gains more consumer surplus than you lost.

b. This creates deadweight loss: if you were able to give the ticket away, someone else would be able to obtain consumer surplus, equal to their willingness to pay for the ticket. You neither gain nor lose any surplus, since you cannot go to the concert whether or not you give the ticket away. If you were able to sell the ticket, the buyer would obtain consumer surplus equal to the difference between their willingness to pay for the ticket and the price at which you sell the ticket. In addition, you would obtain producer surplus equal to the difference between the price at which you sell the ticket and your cost of selling the ticket (which, since you won the ticket, is presumably zero). Since the restriction to neither sell nor give away the ticket means that this surplus cannot be obtained by anybody, it creates deadweight loss. If you could give the ticket away, as described above, there would be consumer surplus that accrues to the recipient of the ticket; and if you give the ticket to the person with the highest willingness to pay, there would be no deadweight loss.

c. This creates deadweight loss. If students buy ice cream on campus, they obtain consumer surplus: their willingness to pay must have been higher than the price of the ice cream. Your college obtains producer surplus: the price is higher than your college's cost of selling the ice cream. Prohibiting the sale of ice cream on campus means that these two sources of total surplus are lost: there is deadweight loss.

d. Given that your dog values ice cream equally as much as you do, this is a pure transfer of surplus. As you lose consumer surplus, your dog gains equally as much consumer surplus.

Check Your Understanding 5-2

1. a. Some gas station owners will benefit from getting a higher price. Q_F indicates the sales made by these owners. But some will lose; there are those who make sales at the market equilibrium price of P_E but do not make sales at the regulated price of P_F. These missed sales are indicated on the graph by the fall in the quantity demanded along the demand curve, from point E to point A.

b. Those who buy gas at the higher price of P_F will probably receive better service; this is an example of *inefficiently high quality* caused by a price floor as gas station owners compete on quality rather than price. But opponents are correct to claim that consumers are generally worse off—those who buy at P_F would have been happy to buy at P_E, and many who were willing to buy at a price between P_E and P_F are now unwilling to buy. This is indicated on the graph by the fall in the quantity demanded along the demand curve, from point E to point A.

c. Proponents are wrong because consumers and some gas station owners are hurt by the price floor, which creates "missed opportunities"—desirable transactions between consumers and station owners that never take place. The deadweight loss, the amount of total surplus lost because of missed opportunities, is indicated by the shaded area in the accompanying figure. Moreover, the inefficiency of wasted resources arises as consumers spend time and money driving to other states. The price floor also tempts people to engage in black market activity. With the price floor, only Q_F units are sold. But at prices between P_E and P_F, there are drivers who cumulatively want to buy more than Q_F and owners who are willing to sell to them, a situation likely to lead to illegal activity.

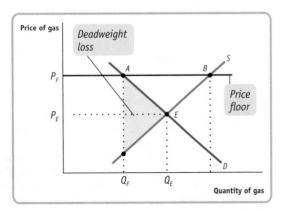

Check Your Understanding 5-3

1. a. The price of a ride is $7 since the quantity demanded at this price is 6 million: $7 is the *demand price* of 6 million rides. This is represented by point A in the accompanying figure.

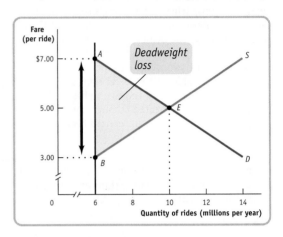

b. At 6 million rides, the supply price is $3 per ride, represented by point B in the figure. The wedge between the demand price of $7 per ride and the supply price of $3 per ride is the quota rent per ride, $4. This is represented in the figure above by the vertical distance between points A and B.

c. The quota discourages 4 million mutually beneficial transactions. The shaded triangle in the figure represents the deadweight loss.

d. At 9 million rides, the demand price is $5.50 per ride, indicated by point C in the accompanying figure, and the supply price is $4.50 per ride, indicated by point D. The quota rent is the difference between the demand price and the supply price: $1. The deadweight loss is represented by the shaded triangle in the figure. As you can see, the deadweight loss is smaller when the quota is set at 9 million rides than when it is set at 6 million rides.

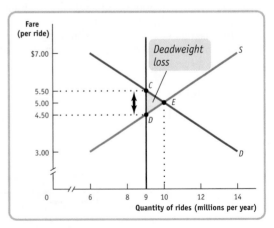

2. The accompanying figure shows a decrease in demand by 4 million rides, represented by a leftward shift of the demand curve from D_1 to D_2: at any given price, the quantity demanded falls by 4 million rides. (For example, at a price of $5, the quantity demanded falls from 10 million to 6 million rides per year.) This eliminates the effect of a quota limit of 8 million rides. At point E_2, the new market equilibrium, the equilibrium quantity is equal to the quota limit; as a result, the quota has no effect on the market.

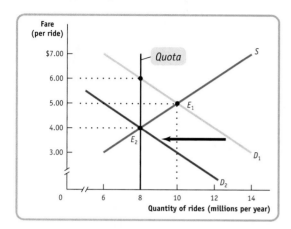

Chapter Six

Check Your Understanding
6-1

1. By the midpoint method, the percent change in the price of strawberries is

$$\frac{\$1.00 - \$1.50}{(\$1.50 + \$1.00)/2} \times 100 = \frac{-\$0.50}{\$1.25} \times 100 = -40\%$$

Similarly, the percent change in the quantity of strawberries demanded is

$$\frac{200,000 - 100,000}{(100,000 + 200,000)/2} \times 100 = \frac{100,000}{150,000} \times 100 = 67\%$$

Dropping the minus sign, the price elasticity of demand using the midpoint method is 67%/40% = 1.7.

2. By the midpoint method, the percent change in the quantity of movie tickets demanded in going from 4,000 tickets to 5,000 tickets is

$$\frac{5,000 - 4,000}{(4,000 + 5,000)/2} \times 100 = \frac{1,000}{4,500} \times 100 = 22\%$$

Since the price elasticity of demand is 1 at the current consumption level, it will take a 22% reduction in the price of movie tickets to generate a 22% increase in quantity demanded.

3. Since price rises, we know that quantity demanded must fall. Given the current price of $0.50, a $0.05 increase in price represents a 10% change, using the method in Equation 6-2. So the price elasticity of demand is

$$\frac{\% \text{ change in quantity demanded}}{10\%} = 1.2$$

so that the percent change in quantity demanded is 12%. A 12% decrease in quantity demanded represents 100,000 × 0.12, or 12,000 sandwiches.

Check Your Understanding
6-2

1. a. Elastic demand. Consumers are highly responsive to changes in price. For a rise in price, the quantity effect (which tends to reduce total revenue) outweighs the price effect (which tends to increase total revenue). Overall, this leads to a fall in total revenue.
   b. Unit-elastic demand. Here the revenue lost to the fall in price is exactly equal to the revenue gained from higher sales. The quantity effect exactly offsets the price effect.
   c. Inelastic demand. Consumers are relatively unresponsive to changes in price. For consumers to purchase a given percent increase in output, the price must fall by an even greater percent. The price effect of a fall in price (which tends to reduce total revenue) outweighs the quantity effect (which tends to increase total revenue). As a result, total revenue decreases.
   d. Inelastic demand. Consumers are relatively unresponsive to price, so a given percent fall in output is accompanied by an even greater percent rise in price. The price effect of a rise in price (which tends to increase total revenue) outweighs the quantity effect (which tends to reduce total revenue). As a result, total revenue increases.

2. a. Once bitten by a venomous snake, the victim's demand for an antidote is very likely to be perfectly inelastic because there is no substitute and it is necessary for survival. The demand curve will be vertical, at a quantity equal to the needed dose.
   b. Students' demand for green erasers is likely to be perfectly elastic because there are easily available substitutes: non-green erasers. The demand curve will be horizontal, at a price equal to that of non-green erasers.

Check Your Understanding
6-3

1. By the midpoint method, the percent increase in Chelsea's income is

$$\frac{\$18,000 - \$12,000}{(\$12,000 + \$18,000)/2} \times 100 = \frac{\$6,000}{\$15,000} \times 100 = 40\%$$

Similarly, the percent increase in her consumption of CDs is

$$\frac{40 - 10}{(10 + 40)/2} \times 100 = \frac{30}{25} \times 100 = 120\%$$

Chelsea's income elasticity of demand for CDs is therefore 120%/40% = 3.

2. Sanjay's consumption of expensive restaurant meals will fall more than 10% because a given percent change in income (a fall of 10% here) induces a larger percent change in consumption of an income-elastic good.

3. The cross-price elasticity of demand is 5%/20% = 0.25. Since the cross-price elasticity of demand is positive, the two goods are substitutes.

Check Your Understanding
6-4

1. By the midpoint method, the percent change in the number of hours of web-design services contracted is

$$\frac{500,000 - 300,000}{(300,000 + 500,000)/2} \times 100 = \frac{200,000}{400,000} \times 100 = 50\%$$

Similarly, the percent change in the price of web-design services is:

$$\frac{\$150 - \$100}{(\$100 + \$150)/2} \times 100 = \frac{\$50}{\$125} \times 100 = 40\%$$

The price elasticity of supply is 50%/40% = 1.25. Hence supply is elastic.

2. True. An increase in demand raises price. If the price elasticity of supply of milk is low, then relatively little additional supply will be forthcoming as the price rises. As a result, the price of milk will rise substantially to satisfy the increased demand for milk. If the price elasticity of supply is high, then a relatively large amount of additional supply will be produced as the price rises. As a result, the price of milk will rise only by a little to satisfy the higher demand for milk.

3. False. It is true that long-run price elasticities of supply are generally larger than short-run elasticities of supply. But this means that the short-run supply curves are generally steeper, not flatter, than the long-run supply curves.

4. True. When supply is perfectly elastic, the supply curve is a horizontal line. So a change in demand has no effect on price; it affects only the quantity bought and sold.

Chapter Seven

Check Your Understanding

7-1

1. The following figure shows that, after introduction of the excise tax, the price paid by consumers rises to $1.20; the price received by producers falls to $0.90. Consumers bear $0.20 of the $0.30 tax per pound of butter; producers bear $0.10 of the $0.30 tax per pound of butter. The tax drives a wedge of $0.30 between the price paid by consumers and the price received by producers. As a result, the quantity of butter bought and sold is now 9 million pounds.

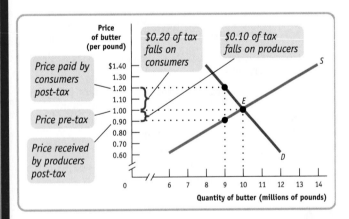

2. The fact that demand is very inelastic means that consumers will reduce their demand for textbooks very little in response to an increase in the price caused by the tax. The fact that supply is somewhat elastic means that suppliers will respond to the fall in the price by reducing supply. As a result, the incidence of the tax will fall heavily on consumers of economics

textbooks and very little on publishers, as shown in the accompanying figure.

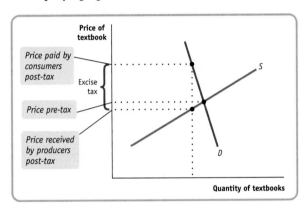

3. True. When a substitute is readily available, demand is elastic. This implies that producers cannot easily pass on the cost of the tax to consumers because consumers will respond to an increased price by switching to the substitute. Furthermore, when producers have difficulty adjusting the amount of the good produced, supply is inelastic. That is, producers cannot easily reduce output in response to a lower price net of tax. So the tax burden will fall more heavily on producers than consumers.

4. The fact that supply is very inelastic means that producers will reduce their supply of bottled water very little in response to the fall in price caused by the tax. Demand, on the other hand, will fall in response to an increase in price because demand is somewhat elastic. As a result, the incidence of the tax will fall heavily on producers of bottled spring water and very little on consumers, as shown in the accompanying figure.

5. True. The lower the elasticity of supply, the more the burden of a tax will fall on producers rather than consumers, other things equal.

Check Your Understanding

7-2

1. a. Without the excise tax, Zhang, Yves, Xavier, and Walter sell, and Ana, Bernice, Chizuko, and Dagmar buy one can of soda each, at $0.40 per can. So the quantity bought and sold is 4.

b. With the excise tax, Zhang and Yves sell, and Ana and Bernice buy one can of soda each. So the quantity bought and sold is 2.

c. Without the excise tax, Ana's individual consumer surplus is $0.70 – $0.40 = $0.30, Bernice's is $0.60 – $0.40 = $0.20, Chizuko's is $0.50 – $0.40 = $0.10, and Dagmar's is $0.40 – $0.40 = $0.00. Total consumer surplus is $0.30 + $0.20 + $0.10 + $0.00 = $0.60. With the tax, Ana's individual consumer surplus is $0.70 – $0.60 = $0.10 and Bernice's is $0.60 – $0.60 = $0.00. Total consumer surplus post-tax is $0.10 + $0.00 = $0.10. So the total consumer surplus lost because of the tax is $0.60 – $0.10 = $0.50.

d. Without the excise tax, Zhang's individual producer surplus is $0.40 – $0.10 = $0.30, Yves's is $0.40 – $0.20 = $0.20, Xavier's is $0.40 – $0.30 = $0.10, and Walter's is $0.40 – $0.40 = $0.00. Total producer surplus is $0.30 + $0.20 + $0.10 + $0.00 = $0.60. With the tax, Zhang's individual producer surplus is $0.20 – $0.10 = $0.10 and Yves's is $0.20 – $0.20 = $0.00. Total producer surplus post-tax is $0.10 + $0.00 = $0.10. So the total producer surplus lost because of the tax is $0.60 – $0.10 = $0.50.

e. With the tax, two cans of soda are sold, so the government tax revenue from this excise tax is 2 × $0.40 = $0.80.

f. Total surplus without the tax is $0.60 + $0.60 = $1.20. With the tax, total surplus is $0.10 + $0.10 = $0.20, and government tax revenue is $0.80. So deadweight loss from this excise tax is $1.20 – ($0.20 + $0.80) = $0.20.

2. a. The demand for gasoline is inelastic because there is no close substitute for gasoline itself and it is difficult for drivers to arrange substitutes for driving, such as taking public transportation. As a result, the deadweight loss from a tax on gasoline would be relatively small, as shown in the accompanying diagram.

b. The demand for milk chocolate bars is elastic because there are close substitutes: dark chocolate bars, milk chocolate kisses, and so on. As a result, the deadweight loss from a tax on milk chocolate

bars would be relatively large, as shown in the accompanying diagram.

Check Your Understanding 7-3

1. a. Since drivers are the beneficiaries of highway safety programs, this tax performs well according to the benefits principle. But since the level of the tax does not depend on ability to pay the tax, it does not perform well according to the ability-to-pay principle. Since higher-income car purchasers are likely to spend more on a new car, a tax assessed as a percentage of the purchase price of the car would perform better on the ability-to-pay principle. A $500-per-car tax will cause people to buy fewer new cars, while a percentage-based tax will cause people to buy fewer cars and less expensive cars.

b. This tax does not perform well according to the benefits principle because the payers are nonresidents of the local area, but the beneficiaries are local residents who will enjoy greater government services. But to the extent that people who stay in hotels have higher income compared to those who don't, the tax performs well according to the ability-to-pay principle. It will distort the action of staying in a hotel room in this area, resulting in fewer nights of hotel room stays.

c. This tax performs well according to the benefits principle because local homeowners are the users of local schools. It also performs well according to the ability-to-pay principle because it is assessed as a percentage of home value: higher-income residents, who own more expensive homes, will pay higher taxes. It will distort the action of buying a house in this area versus another area with a lower property tax rate or the action of making changes to a house that increase its assessed value.

d. This tax performs well according to the benefits principle because food consumers are the beneficiaries of government food safety programs. It does not perform well according to the ability-to-pay principle because food is a necessity, and lower-income people will pay approximately as much as higher-income people. This tax will distort the action of buying food, leading people to purchase cheaper varieties of food.

Check Your Understanding 7-4

1. a. The marginal tax rate for someone with income of $5,000 is 1%: for each additional $1 in income, $0.01 or 1%, is taxed away. This person pays total tax of $5,000 × 1% = $50, which is ($50/$5,000) × 100 = 1% of his or her income.

b. The marginal tax rate for someone with income of $20,000 is 2%: for each additional $1 in income, $0.02 or 2%, is taxed away. This person pays total tax of $10,000 × 1% + $10,000 × 2% = $300, which is ($300/$20,000) × 100 = 1.5% of his or her income.

c. Since the high-income taxpayer pays a larger percentage of his or her income than the low-income taxpayer, this tax is progressive.

2. A 1% tax on consumption spending means that a family earning $15,000 and spending $10,000 will pay a tax of 1% × $10,000 = $100, equivalent to 0.67% of its income; ($100/$15,000) × 100 = 0.67%. But a family earning $10,000 and spending $8,000 will pay a tax of 1% × $8,000 = $80, equivalent to 0.80% of its income; ($80/$10,000) × 100 = 0.80%. So the tax is regressive, since the lower-income family pays a higher percentage of its income in tax than the higher-income family.

3. a. False. Recall that a seller always bears some burden of a tax as long as his or her supply of the good is not perfectly elastic. Since the supply of labor a worker offers is not perfectly elastic, some of the payroll tax will be borne by the worker, and therefore the tax will affect the person's incentive to take a job.

b. False. Under a proportional tax, the percentage of the tax base is the same for everyone. Under a lump-sum tax, the total tax paid is the same for everyone, regardless of their income. A lump-sum tax is regressive.

Chapter Eight

Check Your Understanding 8-1

1. a. To determine comparative advantage, we must compare the two countries' opportunity costs for a given good. Take the opportunity cost of 1 ton of corn in terms of bicycles. In China, the opportunity cost of 1 bicycle is 0.01 ton of corn; so the opportunity cost of 1 ton of corn is 1/0.01 bicycles = 100 bicycles. The United States has the comparative advantage in corn since its opportunity cost in terms of bicycles is 50, a smaller number. Similarly, the opportunity cost in the United States of 1 bicycle in terms of corn is 1/50 ton of corn = 0.02 ton of corn. This is greater than 0.01, the Chinese opportunity cost of 1 bicycle in terms of corn, implying that China has a comparative advantage in bicycles.

b. Given that the United States can produce 200,000 bicycles if no corn is produced, it can produce 200,000 bicycles × 0.02 ton of corn/bicycle = 4,000 tons of corn when no bicycles are produced. Likewise, if China can produce 3,000 tons of corn if no bicycles are produced, it can produce 3,000 tons of corn × 100

bicycles/ton of corn = 300,000 bicycles if no corn is produced. These points determine the vertical and horizontal intercepts of the U.S. and Chinese production possibility frontiers, as shown in the accompanying diagram.

(a) U.S. Production Possibility Frontier

Quantity of corn (tons)

U.S. production with trade

4,000

Slope = −0.02

U.S. consumption with trade

1,000

PPF_{US}

0   200,000   Quantity of bicycles

(b) Chinese Production Possibility Frontier

Quantity of corn (tons)

Chinese consumption with trade

3,000

Slope = −0.01

Chinese production with trade

PPF_{China}

0   100,000   300,000   Quantity of bicycles

c. The diagram shows the production and consumption points of the two countries. Each country is clearly better off with international trade because each now consumes a bundle of the two goods that lies outside its own production possibility frontier, indicating that these bundles were unattainable in autarky.

2. a. According to the Heckscher–Ohlin model, this pattern of trade occurs because the United States has a relatively larger endowment of factors of production, such as human capital and physical capital, that are suited to the production of movies, but France has a relatively larger endowment of factors of production suited to wine-making, such as vineyards and the human capital of vintners.

b. According to the Heckscher–Ohlin model, this pattern of trade occurs because the United States has a relatively larger endowment of factors of production, such as human and physical capital, that are suited to making machinery, but Brazil has a relatively larger endowment of factors of production suited to shoe-making, such as unskilled labor and leather.

Check Your Understanding 8-2

1. In the accompanying diagram, P_A is the U.S. price of grapes in autarky and P_W is the world price of grapes under international trade. With trade, U.S. consumers pay a price of P_W for grapes and consume quantity Q_D, U.S. grape producers produce quantity Q_S, and the difference, $Q_D - Q_S$, represents imports of Mexican grapes. As a consequence of the strike by truckers, imports are halted, the price paid by American consumers rises to the autarky price, P_A, and U.S. consumption falls to the autarky quantity Q_A.

a. Before the strike, U.S. consumers enjoyed consumer surplus equal to areas $W + X + Z$. After the strike, their consumer surplus shrinks to W. So consumers are worse off, losing consumer surplus represented by $X + Z$.
b. Before the strike, U.S. producers had producer surplus equal to the area Y. After the strike, their producer surplus increases to $Y + X$. So U.S. producers are better off, gaining producer surplus represented by X.
c. U.S. total surplus falls as a result of the strike by an amount represented by area Z, the loss in consumer surplus that does not accrue to producers.

2. Mexican grape producers are worse off because they lose sales in the amount of $Q_D - Q_S$, and Mexican grape pickers are worse off because they lose the wages that were associated with the lost sales. The lower demand for Mexican grapes caused by the strike implies that the price Mexican consumers pay for grapes falls, making them better off. American grape pickers are better off because their wages increase as a result of the increase of $Q_A - Q_S$ in U.S. sales.

Check Your Understanding
8-3

1. a. If the tariff is $0.50, the price paid by domestic consumers for a pound of imported butter is $0.50 + $0.50 = $1.00, the same price as a pound of domestic butter. Imported butter will no longer have a price advantage over domestic butter, imports will cease, and domestic producers will capture all the feasible sales to domestic consumers, selling amount Q_A in the accompanying figure. But if the tariff is less than $0.50—say, only $0.25—the price paid by domestic consumers for a pound of imported butter is $0.50 + $0.25 = $0.75, $0.25 cheaper than a pound of domestic butter. American butter producers will gain sales in the amount of $Q_2 - Q_1$ as a result of the $0.25 tariff. But this is smaller than the amount

they would have gained under the $0.50 tariff, the amount $Q_A - Q_1$.

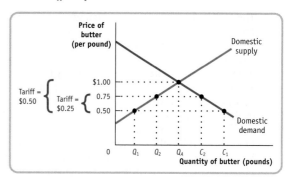

b. As long as the tariff is at least $0.50, increasing it more has no effect. At a tariff of $0.50, all imports are effectively blocked.

2. All imports are effectively blocked at a tariff of $0.50. So such a tariff corresponds to an import quota of 0.

Check Your Understanding
8-4

1. There are many fewer businesses that use steel as an input than there are consumers who buy sugar or clothing. So it will be easier for such businesses to communicate and coordinate among themselves to lobby against tariffs than it will be for consumers. In addition, each business will perceive that the cost of a steel tariff is quite costly to its profits, but an individual consumer is either unaware of or perceives little loss from tariffs on sugar or clothing. The tariffs were indeed lifted at the end of 2003.

2. Countries are often tempted to protect domestic industries by claiming that an import poses a quality, health, or environmental danger to domestic consumers. A WTO official should examine whether domestic producers are subject to the same stringency in the application of quality, health, or environmental regulations as foreign producers. If they are, then it is more likely that the regulations are for legitimate, non–trade protection purposes; if they are not, then it is more likely that the regulations are intended as trade protection measures.

Chapter Nine

Check Your Understanding
9-1

1. a. Supplies are an explicit cost because they require an outlay of money.
b. If the basement could be used in some other way that generates money, such as renting it to a student, then the implicit cost is that money forgone. Otherwise, the implicit cost is zero.
c. Wages are an explicit cost.
d. By using the van for their business, Karma and Don forgo the money they could have gained by selling it. So use of the van is an implicit cost.
e. Karma's forgone wages from her job are an implicit cost.

Check Your Understanding 9-2

1. a. The marginal cost of doing your laundry is the opportunity cost of your time spent doing laundry today—that is, the value you would place on spending time today on your next best alternative activity, like seeing a movie. The marginal benefit is having more clean clothes today to choose from.

b. The marginal cost of changing your oil is the opportunity cost of time spent changing your oil now as well as the explicit cost of the oil change. The marginal benefit is the improvement in your car's performance.

c. The marginal benefit of another jalapeno on your nachos is the pleasant taste that you receive from it. The marginal cost is the unpleasant feeling of a burning mouth that you receive from it plus any explicit cost of the jalapeno.

d. The marginal benefit of hiring another worker in your company is the value of the output that worker produces. The marginal cost is the wage you must pay that worker.

e. The marginal benefit of another dose of the drug is the value of the reduction in the patient's disease. The marginal cost is the value lost due to the increased side effects from this additional dose.

f. The marginal benefit of assigning one more soldier to your invasion force is the increased probability of a successful invasion generated by that extra soldier. The marginal cost is the decreased probability of success in the alternative project for which you could use that soldier, such as defending your borders.

2. The accompanying table shows Babette's new marginal cost and her new net gain. It also reproduces Babette's marginal benefit from Table 9-5.

Quantity of chicken wings	Total cost	Marginal cost (per wing)	Marginal benefit (per wing)	Net gain (per wing)
0	$4.00			
		$0.25	$4.30	$4.05
1	4.25			
		0.15	2.50	2.35
2	4.40			
		0.10	1.50	1.40
3	4.50			
		0.15	1.20	1.05
4	4.65			
		0.25	0.90	0.65
5	4.90			
		0.45	0.70	0.25
6	5.35			
		0.85	0.60	−0.25
7	6.20			

Babette's marginal cost is now decreasing at first, until the portion size is 3 wings. When Babette increases the portion size beyond 3 wings, marginal cost increases. The optimal quantity is 6 wings. For any quantities fewer than 6 wings, marginal benefit exceeds marginal cost; for any quantities greater than 6 wings, marginal cost exceeds marginal benefit.

Check Your Understanding 9-3

1. a. Your sunk cost is $8,000 because none of the $8,000 spent on the truck is recoverable.

b. Your sunk cost is $4,000 because 50% of the $8,000 spent on the truck is recoverable.

2. a. This is an invalid argument because the time and money already spent are a sunk cost at this point.

b. This is also an invalid argument because what you should have done two years ago is irrelevant to what you should do now.

c. This is a valid argument because it recognizes that sunk costs are irrelevant to what you should do now.

d. This is a valid argument given that you are concerned about disappointing your parents. But your parents' views are irrational because they do not recognize that the time already spent is a sunk cost.

Check Your Understanding 9-4

1. a. The net present value of project A is unaffected by the interest rate since it is money received today; its present value is still $100. The net present value of project B is now −$10 + $115/1.02 = $102.75. The net present value of project C is now $119 − $20/1.02 = $99.39. Project B is now preferred.

b. When the interest rate is lower, the cost of waiting for money that arrives in the future is lower. For example, at a 10% interest rate, $1 arriving 1 year from today is worth only 1/$1.10 = $0.91. But when the interest rate is 2%, $1 arriving 1 year from today is worth 1/$1.02 = $0.98, a sizable increase. As a result, project B, which has a benefit one year from today, becomes more attractive. And project C, which has a cost 1 year from today, becomes less attractive.

Chapter Ten

Check Your Understanding 10-1

1. Consuming a unit that generates negative marginal utility leaves the consumer with lower total utility than not consuming that unit at all. A rational consumer, a consumer who maximizes utility, would not do that. For example, from Figure 10-1 you can see that Cassie receives 64 utils if she consumes 8 clams; but if she consumes the 9th clam, she loses a util, netting her a total utility of only 63 utils. So whenever consuming a unit generates negative marginal utility, the consumer is made better off by not consuming that unit, even when that unit is free.

2. Since Marta has diminishing marginal utility of coffee, her first cup of coffee of the day generates the greatest increase in total utility. Her third and last cup of the day generates the least.

3. a. Mabel has increasing marginal utility of exercising since each additional unit consumed brings more additional enjoyment than the previous unit.

b. Mei has constant marginal utility of CDs because each additional unit generates the same additional enjoyment as the previous unit.

c. Dexter has diminishing marginal utility of restaurant meals since the additional utility generated by a good restaurant meal is less when he consumes lots of them than when he consumed few of them.

10-2

1. a. The accompanying table shows the consumer's consumption possibilities, *A* through *C*. These consumption possibilities are plotted in the accompanying diagram, along with the consumer's budget line.

Consumption bundle	Quantity of popcorn (buckets)	Quantity of movie tickets
A	0	2
B	2	1
C	4	0

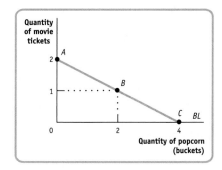

b. The accompanying table shows the consumer's consumption possibilities, *A* through *D*. These consumption possibilities are plotted in the accompanying diagram, along with the consumer's budget line.

Consumption bundle	Quantity of underwear (pairs)	Quantity of socks (pairs)
A	0	6
B	1	4
C	2	2
D	3	0

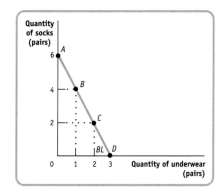

10-3

1. From Table 10-3 you can see that Sammy's marginal utility per dollar from increasing his consumption of clams from 3 pounds to 4 pounds and his marginal utility per dollar

from increasing his consumption of potatoes from 9 to 10 pounds are the same, 0.75 utils. But a consumption bundle consisting of 4 pounds of clams and 10 pounds of potatoes is not Sammy's optimal consumption bundle because it is not affordable given his income of $20; 4 pounds of clams and 10 pounds of potatoes costs $4 × 4 + $2 × 10 = $36, $16 more than Sammy's income. This can be illustrated with Sammy's budget line from Figure 10-3: a bundle of 4 pounds of clams and 10 pounds of potatoes is represented by point *X* in the accompanying diagram, a point that lies outside Sammy's budget line. If you look at the horizontal axis of Figure 10-4, it is quite clear that there is no such thing in Sammy's consumption possibilities as a bundle consisting of 4 pounds of clams and 10 pounds of potatoes.

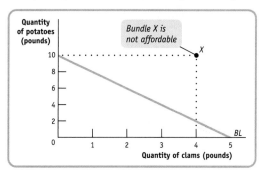

2. Sammy's maximum utility per dollar is generated when he goes from consuming 0 to 1 pound of clams (3.75 utils) and as he goes from 0 to 1 pound of potatoes (5.75 utils). But this bundle consisting of 1 pound of clams and 1 pound of potatoes generates only 26.5 utils for him. Instead, Sammy should choose the consumption bundle that satisfies his budget constraint and for which the marginal utility per dollar for both goods is equal.

10-4

1. a. Since spending on orange juice is a small share of Clare's spending, the income effect from a rise in the price of orange juice is insignificant. Only the substitution effect, represented by the substitution of lemonade in place of orange juice, is significant.
b. Since rent is a large share of Delia's expenditures, the increase in rent generates an income effect, making Delia feel poorer. Since housing is a normal good for Delia, the income and substitution effects move in the same direction, leading her to reduce her consumption of housing by moving to a smaller apartment.
c. Since a meal ticket is a significant share of the students' living costs, an increase in its price will generate an income effect. Students respond to the price increase by eating more often in the cafeteria. So the substitution effect (which would induce them to eat in the cafeteria less often as they substitute restaurant meals in place of meals at the cafeteria) and the income effect (which would induce them to eat in the cafeteria more often because they are poorer) move in opposite directions. This happens because cafeteria meals are an inferior good. In fact, since the income effect outweighs the

substitution effect (students eat in the cafeteria more as the price of meal tickets increases), cafeteria meals are a Giffen good.

Chapter Eleven

Check Your Understanding
11-1

1. **a.** As you can see from the accompanying diagram, the four bundles are associated with three indifference curves: B on the 10-util indifference curve, A and C on the 6-util indifference curve, and D on the 4-util indifference curve.

b. From comparing the quantities of chocolate kisses and licorice drops, you can predict that Samantha will prefer B to A because B gives her one more chocolate kiss and the same amount of licorice drops as A. Next, you can predict that she will prefer C to D because C gives her one more chocolate kiss and the same amount of licorice drops as D. You can also predict that she prefers B to D because B gives her two more licorice drops and the same amount of chocolate kisses as D. But without data about utils, you cannot predict how Samantha would rank A versus C or D because C and D have more chocolate kisses but fewer licorice drops than A. Neither can you rank B versus C, for the same reason.

2. Bundles A and B each generate 200 utils since they both lie on the 200-util indifference curve. Likewise, bundles A and C each generate 100 utils since they both lie on the 100-util indifference curve. But this implies that A generates 100 utils and also that A generates 200 utils. This is a contradiction and so cannot be true. It shows that indifference curves cannot cross.

Check Your Understanding
11-2

1. **a.** The marginal rate of substitution of books in place of games, MU_B/MU_G, is 2 for Lucinda and 5 for Kyle. This implies that Lucinda is willing to trade 1 more book for 2 fewer games and Kyle is willing to trade 1 more book for 5 fewer games. So starting from a bundle of 3 books and 6 games, Lucinda would be equally content with a bundle of 4 books and 4 games and Kyle would be equally content with a bundle of 4 books and 1 game. Lucinda finds it more difficult to trade games for books: she is willing to give up only 2 games for a book but Kyle is willing to give up 5 games for a book. If books are measured on the horizontal axis and games on the vertical axis, Kyle's indifference curve will be steeper than Lucinda's at the current consumption bundle.

b. Lucinda's current consumption bundle is optimal if P_B/P_G, the relative price of books in terms of games, is 2. Kyle's current consumption bundle is not optimal at this relative price; his bundle would be optimal only if the relative price of books in terms of games is 5. Since, for Kyle, $MU_B/MU_G = 5$ but $P_B/P_G = 2$, he should consume fewer games and more books to lower his MU_B/MU_G until it is equal to 2.

Check Your Understanding
11-3

1. **a.** Since Sanjay cares only about the number of jelly beans, not about whether they are banana- or pineapple-flavored, he is always willing to exchange one for the other at the same rate. This implies that his marginal rate of substitution of one flavor of jelly bean in place of another is constant. So they are perfect substitutes.

b. Cherry pie and vanilla ice cream are complements for Hillary since her marginal utility of cherry pie goes up as she has another scoop of vanilla ice cream. But they are ordinary goods, not perfect complements, because she gains some utility from having cherry pie without any vanilla ice cream.

c. Omnisoft's software programs and its operating system are perfect complements for its customers: they gain no utility from the software programs without the operating system. So their marginal rate of substitution of one good in place of the other is undefined, and their indifference curves have a right-angle shape.

d. Income and leisure are ordinary goods for Darnell: the more income he has made by working more hours, the less willing he is to earn yet more by giving up additional leisure time.

Check Your Understanding
11-4

1. **a.** Sammy's original budget line is illustrated in the accompanying diagram by BL_1. His original consumption is at point A. When the price of clams falls, his budget line rotates outward to BL_2, allowing him to achieve a higher level of total utility. The pure substitution effect would involve the same change in the slope of his budget line, but without any increase in total utility. So the pure substitution effect is illustrated by the movement from A to B. In fact, his total utility does rise, so his total consumption moves from A to C. The movement from B to C is the income effect.

b. Again, in the accompanying diagram Sammy's original budget line is BL_1, and his original consumption is at point A. The increase in the price of clams causes his budget line to rotate inward to BL_2. This reduces his total utility. The pure substitution effect is what would happen if the slope of the budget line changed but his total utility did not; it is shown as the movement from A to B. The full effect of the price change is the movement from A to C. The movement from B to C is the income effect.

Chapter Twelve

Check Your Understanding

12-1

1. **a.** The fixed input is the 10-ton machine, and the variable input is electricity.
   b. As you can see from the declining numbers in the third column of the accompanying table, electricity does indeed exhibit diminishing returns: the marginal product of each additional kilowatt of electricity is less than that of the previous kilowatt.

Quantity of electricity (kilowatts)	Quantity of ice (pounds)	Marginal product of electricity (pounds per kilowatt)
0	0	
		1,000
1	1,000	
		800
2	1,800	
		600
3	2,400	
		400
4	2,800	

   c. A 50% increase in the size of the fixed input means that Bernie now has a 15-ton machine. So the fixed input is now the 15-ton machine. Since it generates a 100% increase in output for any given amount of electricity, the quantity of output and marginal product are now as shown in the accompanying table.

Quantity of electricity (kilowatts)	Quantity of ice (pounds)	Marginal product of electricity (pounds per kilowatt)
0	0	
		2,000
1	2,000	
		1,600
2	3,600	
		1,200
3	4,800	
		800
4	5,600	

Check Your Understanding

12-2

1. **a.** As shown in the accompanying table, the marginal cost for each pie is found by multiplying the marginal cost of the previous pie by 1.5. Variable cost for each output level is found by summing the marginal cost for all the pies produced to reach that output level. So, for example, the variable cost of three pies is $1.00 + $1.50 + $2.25 = $4.75. Average fixed cost for Q pies is calculated as $9.00/Q since fixed cost is $9.00. Average variable cost for Q pies is equal to variable cost for the Q pies divided by Q; for example, the average variable cost of five pies is $13.19/5, or approximately $2.64. Finally, average total cost can be calculated in two equivalent ways: as TC/Q or as AVC + AFC.

Quantity of pies	Marginal cost of pie	Variable cost	Average fixed cost of pie	Average variable cost of pie	Average total cost of pie
0		$0.00	—	—	—
	$1.00				
1		1.00	$9.00	$1.00	$10.00
	1.50				
2		2.50	4.50	1.25	5.75
	2.25				
3		4.75	3.00	1.58	4.58
	3.38				
4		8.13	2.25	2.03	4.28
	5.06				
5		13.19	1.80	2.64	4.44
	7.59				
6		20.78	1.50	3.46	4.96

   b. The spreading effect dominates the diminishing returns effect when average total cost is falling: the fall in AFC dominates the rise in AVC for pies 1 to 4. The diminishing returns effect dominates when average total cost is rising: the rise in AVC dominates the fall in AFC for pies 5 and 6.
   c. Alicia's minimum-cost output is 4 pies; this generates the lowest average total cost, $4.28. When output is less than 4, the marginal cost of a pie is less than the average total cost of the pies already produced. So making an additional pie lowers average total cost. For example, the marginal cost of pie 3 is $2.25, whereas the average total cost of pies 1 and 2 is $5.75. So making pie 3 lowers average total cost to $4.58, equal to (2 × $5.75 + $2.25)/3. When output is more than 4, the marginal cost of a pie is greater than the average total cost of the pies already produced. Consequently, making an additional pie raises average total cost. So, although the marginal cost of pie 6 is $7.59, the average total cost of pies 1 through 5 is $4.44. Making pie 6 raises average total cost to $4.96, equal to (5 × $4.44 + $7.59)/6.

Check Your Understanding

12-3

1. **a.** The accompanying table shows the average total cost of producing 12,000, 22,000, and 30,000 units for each of the three choices of fixed cost. For example, if the firm makes choice 1, the total cost of producing 12,000 units of output is $8,000 + 12,000 × $1.00 = $20,000. The average total cost of producing 12,000 units of output is therefore $20,000/12,000 = $1.67. The other average total costs are calculated similarly.

	12,000 units	22,000 units	30,000 units
Average total cost from choice 1	$1.67	$1.36	$1.27
Average total cost from choice 2	1.75	1.30	1.15
Average total cost from choice 3	2.25	1.34	1.05

So if the firm wanted to produce 12,000 units, it would make choice 1 because this gives it the lowest average total cost. If it wanted to produce 22,000 units, it would make choice 2. If it wanted to produce 30,000 units, it would make choice 3.

b. Having historically produced 12,000 units, the firm would have adopted choice 1. When producing 12,000 units, the firm would have had an average total cost of $1.67. When output jumps to 22,000 units, the firm cannot alter its choice of fixed cost in the short run, so its average total cost in the short run will be $1.36. In the long run, however, it will adopt choice 2, making its average total cost fall to $1.30.

c. If the firm believes that the increase in demand is temporary, it should not alter its fixed cost from choice 1 because choice 2 generates higher average total cost as soon as output falls back to its original quantity of 12,000 units: $1.75 versus $1.67.

2. a. This firm is likely to experience constant returns to scale. To increase output, the firm must hire more workers, purchase more computers, and pay additional telephone charges. Because these inputs are easily available, their long-run average total cost is unlikely to change as output increases.

b. This firm is likely to experience decreasing returns to scale. As the firm takes on more projects, the costs of communication and coordination required to implement the expertise of the firm's owner are likely to increase.

c. This firm is likely to experience increasing returns to scale. Because diamond mining requires a large initial set-up cost for excavation equipment, long-run average total cost will fall as output increases.

3. The accompanying diagram shows the long-run average total cost curve (*LRATC*) and the short-run average total cost curve corresponding to a long-run output choice of 5 cases of salsa (*ATC₅*). The curve *ATC₅* shows the short-run average total cost for which the level of fixed cost minimizes average total cost at an output of 5 cases of salsa. This is confirmed by the fact that at 5 cases per day, *ATC₅* touches *LRATC*, the long-run average total cost curve.

If Selena expects to produce only 4 cases of salsa for a long time, she should change her fixed cost. If she does

not change her fixed cost and produces 4 cases of salsa, her average total cost in the short run is indicated by point *B* on *ATC₅*; it is no longer on the *LRATC*. If she changes her fixed cost, though, her average total cost could be lower, at point *A*.

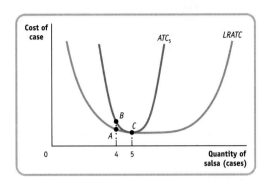

Chapter Thirteen

Check Your Understanding
13-1

1. a. With only two producers in the world, each producer will represent a sizable share of the market. So the industry will not be perfectly competitive.

b. Because each producer of natural gas from the North Sea has only a small market share of total world supply of natural gas, and since natural gas is a standardized product, the natural gas industry will be perfectly competitive.

c. Because each designer has a distinctive style, high-fashion clothes are not a standardized product. So the industry will not be perfectly competitive.

d. The market described here is the market in each city for tickets to baseball games. Since there are only one or two teams in each major city, each team will represent a sizable share of the market. So the industry will not be perfectly competitive.

Check Your Understanding
13-2

1. a. The firm should shut down immediately when price is less than minimum average variable cost, the shut-down price. In the accompanying diagram, this is optimal for prices in the range 0 to P_1.

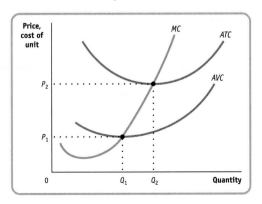

b. When price is greater than minimum average variable cost (the shut-down price) but less than minimum average total cost (the break-even price), the firm should continue to operate in the short run even though it is making a loss. This is optimal for prices in the range P_1 to P_2 and for quantities Q_1 to Q_2.

c. When price exceeds minimum average total cost (the break-even price), the firm makes a profit. This happens for prices in excess of P_2 and results in quantities greater than Q_2.

2. This is an example of a temporary shut-down by a firm when the market price lies below the shut-down price, the minimum average variable cost. In this case, the market price is the price of a lobster meal and variable cost is the variable cost of serving such a meal, such as the cost of the lobster, employee wages, and so on. In this example, however, it is the average variable cost curve rather than the market price that shifts over time, due to seasonal changes in the cost of lobsters. Maine lobster shacks have relatively low average variable cost during the summer, when cheap Maine lobsters are available; during the rest of the year, their average variable cost is relatively high due to the high cost of imported lobsters. So the lobster shacks are open for business during the summer, when their minimum average variable cost lies below price; but they close during the rest of the year, when price lies below their minimum average variable cost.

Check Your Understanding

13-3

1. a. A fall in the fixed cost of production generates a fall in the average total cost of production and, in the short run, an increase in each firm's profit at the current output level. So in the long run new firms will enter the industry. The increase in supply drives down price and profits. Once profits are driven back to zero, entry will cease.

b. An increase in wages generates an increase in the average variable and the average total cost of production at every output level. In the short run, firms incur losses at the current output level, and so in the long run some firms

will exit the industry. (If the average variable cost rises sufficiently, some firms may even shut down in the short run.) As firms exit, supply decreases, price rises, and losses are reduced. Exit will cease once losses return to zero.

c. Price will rise as a result of the increased demand, leading to a short-run increase in profits at the current output level. In the long run, firms will enter the industry, generating an increase in supply, a fall in price, and a fall in profits. Once profits are driven back to zero, entry will cease.

d. The shortage of a key input causes that input's price to increase, resulting in an increase in average variable and average total costs for producers. Firms incur losses in the short run, and some firms will exit the industry in the long run. The fall in supply generates an increase in price and decreased losses. Exit will cease when losses have returned to zero.

2. In the accompanying diagram, point X_{MKT} in panel (b), the intersection of S_1 and D_1, represents the long-run industry equilibrium before the change in consumer tastes. When tastes change, demand falls and the industry moves in the short run to point Y_{MKT} in panel (b), at the intersection of the new demand curve D_2 and S_1, the short-run supply curve representing the same number of egg producers as in the original equilibrium at point X_{MKT}. As the market price falls, an individual firm reacts by producing less—as shown in panel (a)—as long as the market price remains above the minimum average variable cost. If market price falls below minimum average variable cost, the firm would shut down immediately. At point Y_{MKT} the price of eggs is below minimum average total cost, creating losses for producers. This leads some firms to exit, which shifts the short-run industry supply curve leftward to S_2. A new long-run equilibrium is established at point Z_{MKT}. As this occurs, the market price rises again, and, as shown in panel (c), each remaining producer reacts by increasing output (here, from point Y to point Z). All remaining producers again make zero profits. The decrease in the quantity of eggs supplied in the industry comes entirely from the exit of some producers from the industry. The long-run industry supply curve is the curve labeled *LRS* in panel (b).

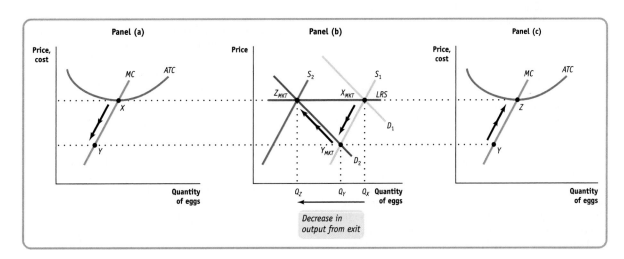

Chapter Fourteen

Check Your Understanding
14-1

1. a. This does not support the conclusion. Texas Tea has a limited amount of oil, and the price has risen in order to equalize supply and demand.

b. This supports the conclusion because the market for home heating oil has become monopolized, and a monopolist will reduce the quantity supplied and raise price to generate profit.

c. This does not support the conclusion. Texas Tea has raised its price to consumers because the price of its input, home heating oil, has increased.

d. This supports the conclusion. The fact that other firms have begun to supply heating oil at a lower price implies that Texas Tea must have earned profits—profits that attracted the other firms to Frigid.

e. This supports the conclusion. It indicates that Texas Tea enjoys a barrier to entry because it controls access to the only Alaskan heating oil pipeline.

2. a. Extending the length of a patent increases the length of time during which the inventor can reduce the quantity supplied and increase the market price. Since this increases the period of time during which the inventor can earn economic profits from the invention, it increases the incentive to invent new products.

b. Extending the length of a patent also increases the period of time during which consumers have to pay higher prices. So determining the appropriate length of a patent involves making a trade-off between the desirable incentive for invention and the undesirable high price to consumers.

Check Your Understanding
14-2

1. a. The price at each output level is found by dividing the total revenue by the number of emeralds produced; for example, the price when 3 emeralds are produced is $252/3 = $84. The price at the various output levels is then used to construct the demand schedule in the accompanying table.

b. The marginal revenue schedule is found by calculating the change in total revenue as output increases by one unit. For example, the marginal revenue generated by increasing output from 2 to 3 emeralds is ($252 − $186) = $66.

c. The quantity effect component of marginal revenue is the additional revenue generated by selling one more unit of the good at the market price. For example, as shown in the accompanying table, at 3 emeralds, the market price is $84; so, when going from 2 to 3 emeralds the quantity effect is equal to $84.

d. The price effect component of marginal revenue is the decline in total revenue caused by the fall in price when one more unit is sold. For example, as shown in the table, when only 2 emeralds are sold, each emerald sells at a price of $93. However, when Emerald, Inc. sells an additional emerald, the price must fall by $9 to $84. So the price effect component in going from 2 to 3 emeralds is (−$9) × 2 = −$18. That's because 2 emeralds can only be sold at a price of $84 when 3 emeralds in total are

sold, although they could have been sold at a price of $93 when only 2 in total were sold.

Quantity of emeralds demanded	Price of emerald	Marginal revenue	Quantity effect component	Price effect component
1	$100			
		$86	$93	−$7
2	93			
		66	84	−18
3	84			
		28	70	−42
4	70			
		−30	50	−80
5	50			

e. In order to determine Emerald, Inc.'s profit-maximizing output level, you must know its marginal cost at each output level. Its profit-maximizing output level is the one at which marginal revenue is equal to marginal cost.

2. As the accompanying diagram shows, the marginal cost curve shifts upward to $400. The profit-maximizing price rises and quantity falls. Profit falls from $3,200 to $300 × 6 = $1,800. Competitive industry profits, though, are unchanged at zero.

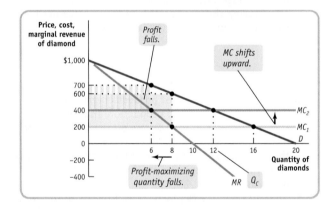

Check Your Understanding
14-3

1. a. Cable Internet service is a natural monopoly. So the government should intervene only if it believes that price exceeds average total cost, where average total cost is based on the cost of laying the cable. In this case it should impose a price ceiling equal to average total cost. Otherwise, it should do nothing.

b. The government should approve the merger only if it fosters competition by transferring some of the company's landing slots to another, competing airline.

2. a. False. As can be seen from Figure 14-8, panel (b), the inefficiency arises from the fact that some of the consumer surplus is transformed into deadweight loss (the yellow area), not that it is transformed into profit (the green area).

b. True. If a monopolist sold to all customers who have a valuation greater than or equal to marginal cost, all mutually beneficial transactions would occur and there would be no deadweight loss.

3. As shown in the accompanying diagram, a profit-maximizing monopolist produces Q_M, the output level at which $MR = MC$. A monopolist who mistakenly believes that $P = MR$ produces the output level at which $P = MC$ (when, in fact, $P > MR$, and at the true profit-maximizing level of output, $P > MR = MC$). This misguided monopolist will produce the output level Q_C, where the demand curve crosses the marginal cost curve—the same output level produced if the industry were perfectly competitive. It will charge the price P_C, which is equal to marginal cost, and make zero profit. The entire shaded area is equal to the consumer surplus, which is also equal to total surplus in this case (since the monopolist receives zero producer surplus). There is no deadweight loss since every consumer who is willing to pay as much as or more than marginal cost gets the good. A smart monopolist, however, will produce the output level Q_M and charge the price P_M. Profit equals the green area, consumer surplus corresponds to the blue area, and total surplus is equal to the sum of the green and blue areas. The yellow area is the deadweight loss generated by the monopolist.

Check Your Understanding
14-4

1. a. False. A price-discriminating monopolist will sell to some customers that a single-price monopolist will refuse to—namely, customers with a high price elasticity of demand who are willing to pay only a relatively low price for the good.
  b. False. Although a price-discriminating monopolist does indeed capture more of the consumer surplus, inefficiency is lower: more mutually beneficial transactions occur because the monopolist makes more sales to customers with a low willingness to pay for the good.
  c. True. Under price discrimination consumers are charged prices that depend on their price elasticity of demand. A consumer with highly elastic demand will pay a lower price than a consumer with inelastic demand.

2. a. This is not a case of price discrimination because all consumers, regardless of their price elasticities of demand, value the damaged merchandise less than undamaged merchandise. So the price must be lowered to sell the damaged merchandise.
  b. This is a case of price discrimination. Senior citizens have a higher price elasticity of demand for restaurant meals (their demand for restaurant meals is more responsive to price changes) than other patrons. Restaurants lower the price to high-elasticity consumers (senior citizens).

Consumers with low price elasticity of demand will pay the full price.
  c. This is a case of price discrimination. Consumers with a high price elasticity of demand will pay a lower price by collecting and using discount coupons. Consumers with a low price elasticity of demand will not use coupons.
  d. This is not a case of price discrimination; it is simply a case of supply and demand.

Chapter Fifteen

Check Your Understanding
15-1

1. a. The world oil industry is an oligopoly because a few countries control a necessary resource for production, oil reserves.
  b. The microprocessor industry is an oligopoly because two firms possess superior technology and so dominate industry production.
  c. The wide-bodied passenger jet industry is an oligopoly because there are increasing returns to scale in production.

2. a. The HHI in this industry is $44^2 + 29^2 + 13^2 + 6^2 + 5^2 + 3^2 = 3{,}016$.
  b. If Yahoo! and MSN were to merge, making their combined market $29\% + 13\% = 42\%$, the HHI in this industry would be $44^2 + 42^2 + 6^2 + 5^2 + 3^2 = 3{,}770$.

Check Your Understanding
15-2

1. a. The firm is likely to act noncooperatively and raise output, which will generate a negative price effect. But because the firm's current market share is small, the negative price effect will fall much more heavily on its rivals' revenues than on its own. At the same time, the firm will benefit from a positive quantity effect.
  b. The firm is likely to act noncooperatively and raise output, which will generate a fall in price. Because its rivals have higher costs, they will lose money at the lower price while the firm continues to make profits. So the firm may be able to drive its rivals out of business by increasing its output.
  c. The firm is likely to collude. Because it is costly for consumers to switch products, the firm would have to lower its price quite substantially (by increasing quantity a lot) to induce consumers to switch to its product. So increasing output is likely to be unprofitable given the large negative price effect.
  d. The firm is likely to collude. It cannot increase sales because it is currently at maximum production capacity.

Check Your Understanding
15-3

1. When Margaret builds a missile, Nikita's payoff from building a missile as well is −10; it is −20 if he does not. The same set of payoffs holds for Margaret when Nikita builds a missile: her payoff is −10 if she builds one as well, −20 if she does not. So it is a Nash (or noncooperative) equilibrium for both Margaret and Nikita to build missiles, and their total payoff is (−10) + (−10) = −20. But their total payoff is greatest when neither builds a missile: their total payoff is 0 + 0 = 0.

But this outcome—the cooperative outcome—is unlikely. If Margaret builds a missile but Nikita does not, Margaret gets a payoff of +8, rather than the 0 she gets if she doesn't build a missile. So Margaret is better off if she builds a missile but Nikita doesn't. Similarly, Nikita is better off if he builds a missile but Margaret doesn't: he gets a payoff of +8, rather than the 0 he gets if he doesn't build a missile. So both players have an incentive to build a missile. Both will build a missile, and each gets a payoff of −10. So unless Nikita and Margaret are able to communicate in some way to enforce cooperation, they will act in their own individual interests and each will build a missile.

2. a. Future entry by several new firms will increase competition and drive down industry profits. As a result, there is less future profit to protect by behaving cooperatively today. So each oligopolist is more likely to behave noncooperatively today.

   b. When it is very difficult for a firm to detect if another firm has raised output, then it is very difficult to enforce cooperation by playing "tit for tat." So it is more likely that a firm will behave noncooperatively.

   c. When firms have coexisted while maintaining high prices for a long time, each expects cooperation to continue. So the value of behaving cooperatively today is high, and it is likely that firms will engage in tacit collusion.

Check Your Understanding
15-4

1. a. This is likely to be interpreted as evidence of tacit collusion. Firms in the industry are able to tacitly collude by setting their prices according to the published "suggested" price of the largest firm in the industry. This is a form of price leadership.

   b. This is not likely to be interpreted as evidence of tacit collusion. Considerable variation in market shares indicates that firms have been competing to capture each others' business.

   c. This is not likely to be interpreted as evidence of tacit collusion. These features make it more unlikely that consumers will switch products in response to lower prices. So this is a way for firms to avoid any temptation to gain market share by lowering price. This is a form of product differentiation used to avoid direct competition.

   d. This is likely to be interpreted as evidence of tacit collusion. In the guise of discussing sales targets, firms can create a cartel by designating quantities to be produced by each firm.

   e. This is likely to be interpreted as evidence of tacit collusion. By raising prices together, each firm in the industry is refusing to undercut its rivals by leaving its price unchanged or lowering it. Because it could gain market share by doing so, refusing to do it is evidence of tacit collusion.

Chapter Sixteen
Check Your Understanding
16-1

1. a. Ladders are not differentiated as a result of monopolistic competition. A ladder producer makes different ladders (tall ladders versus short ladders) to satisfy different consumer needs, not to avoid competition with rivals. So two tall ladders made by two different producers will be indistinguishable by consumers.

   b. Soft drinks are an example of product differentiation as a result of monopolistic competition. For example, several producers make colas; each is differentiated in terms of taste, which fast-food chains sell it, and so on.

   c. Department stores are an example of product differentiation as a result of monopolistic competition. They serve different clienteles that have different price sensitivities and different tastes. They also offer different levels of customer service and are situated in different locations.

   d. Steel is not differentiated as a result of monopolistic competition. Different types of steel (beams versus sheets) are made for different purposes, not to distinguish one steel manufacturer's products from another's.

2. a. Perfectly competitive industries and monopolistically competitive industries both have many sellers. So it may be hard to distinguish between them solely in terms of number of firms. And in both market structures, there is free entry into and exit from the industry in the long run. But in a perfectly competitive industry, one standardized product is sold; in a monopolistically competitive industry, products are differentiated. So you should ask whether products are differentiated in the industry.

   b. In a monopoly there is only one firm, but a monopolistically competitive industry contains many firms. So you should ask whether or not there is a single firm in the industry.

Check Your Understanding
16-2

1. a. An increase in fixed cost raises average total cost and shifts the average total cost curve upward. In the short run, firms incur losses. In the long run, some will exit the industry, resulting in a rightward shift of the demand curves for those firms that remain in the industry, since each one now serves a larger share of the market. Long-run equilibrium is reestablished when the demand curve for each remaining firm has shifted rightward to the point where it is tangent to the firm's new, higher average total cost curve. At this point each firm's price just equals its average total cost, and each firm makes zero profit.

   b. A decrease in marginal cost lowers average total cost and shifts the average total cost curve and the marginal cost curve downward. Because existing firms now make profits, in the long run new entrants are attracted into the industry. In the long run, this results in a leftward shift of each existing firm's demand curve since each firm now has a smaller share of the market. Long-run equilibrium is reestablished when each firm's demand curve has shifted leftward to the point where it is tangent to the new, lower average total cost curve. At this point each firm's price just equals average total cost, and each firm makes zero profit.

2. If all the existing firms in the industry joined together to create a monopoly, they would achieve monopoly profits. But this would induce new firms to create new, differentiated products and then enter the industry and capture some of the monopoly profits. So in the long run it would be impossible to maintain a monopoly. The problem arises from the fact that because new firms can create new products, there is no barrier to entry that can maintain a monopoly.

Check Your Understanding 16-3

1. **a.** False. As can be seen from panel (b) of Figure 16-4, a monopolistically competitive firm produces at a point where price exceeds marginal cost—unlike a perfectly competitive firm, which produces where price equals marginal cost (at the point of minimum average total cost). A monopolistically competitive firm will refuse to sell at marginal cost. This would be below average total cost and the firm would incur a loss.

   b. True. Firms in a monopolistically competitive industry could achieve higher profits (monopoly profits) if they all joined together and produced a single product. In addition, since the industry possesses excess capacity, producing a larger quantity of output would lower the firm's average total cost. The effect on consumers, however, is ambiguous. They would experience less choice. But if consolidation substantially reduces industry-wide average total cost and therefore substantially increases industry-wide output, consumers may experience lower prices under monopoly.

   c. True. Fads and fashions are created and promulgated by advertising, which is found in oligopolies and monopolistically competitive industries but not in monopolies or perfectly competitive industries.

Check Your Understanding 16-4

1. **a.** This is economically useful because such advertisements are likely to focus on the medical benefits of aspirin.

   b. This is economically wasteful because such advertisements are likely to focus on promoting Bayer aspirin versus a rival's aspirin product. The two products are medically indistinguishable.

   c. This is economically useful because such advertisements are likely to focus on the health and enjoyment benefits of orange juice.

   d. This is economically wasteful because such advertisements are likely to focus on promoting Tropicana orange juice versus a rival's product. The two are likely to be indistinguishable by consumers.

   e. This is economically useful because the longevity of a business gives a potential customer information about its quality.

2. A successful brand name indicates a desirable attribute, such as quality, to a potential buyer. So, other things equal—such as price—a firm with a successful brand name will achieve higher sales than a rival with a comparable product but without a successful brand name. This is likely to deter new firms from entering an industry in which an existing firm has a successful brand name.

Chapter Seventeen

Check Your Understanding 17-1

1. **a.** The external cost is the pollution caused by the wastewater runoff, an uncompensated cost imposed by the poultry farms on their neighbors.

   b. Since poultry farmers do not take the external cost of their actions into account when making decisions about how much wastewater to generate, they will create more runoff than is socially optimal in the absence of government intervention or a private deal. They will produce runoff up to the point at which the marginal social benefit of an additional unit of runoff is zero; however, their neighbors experience a high, positive level of marginal social cost of runoff from this output level. So the quantity of wastewater runoff is inefficient: reducing runoff by one unit would reduce total social benefit by less than it would reduce total social cost.

   c. At the socially optimal quantity of wastewater runoff, the marginal social benefit is equal to the marginal social cost. This quantity is lower than the quantity of wastewater runoff that would be created in the absence of government intervention or a private deal.

2. Yasmin's reasoning is not correct: allowing some late returns of books is likely to be socially optimal. Although you impose a marginal social cost on others every day that you are late in returning a book, there is some positive marginal social benefit to you of returning a book late—for example, you get a longer period to use it in working on a term paper.

   The socially optimal number of days that a book is returned late is the number at which the marginal social benefit equals the marginal social cost. A fine so stiff that it prevents any late returns is likely to result in a situation in which people return books although the marginal social benefit of keeping them another day is greater than the marginal social cost—an inefficient outcome. In that case, allowing an overdue patron another day would increase total social benefit more than it would increase total social cost. So charging a moderate fine that reduces the number of days that books are returned late to the socially optimal number of days is appropriate.

Check Your Understanding 17-2

1. This is a misguided argument. Allowing polluters to sell emissions permits makes polluters face a cost of polluting: the opportunity cost of the permit. If a polluter chooses not to reduce its emissions, it cannot sell its emissions permits. As a result, it forgoes the opportunity of making money from the sale of the permits. So despite the fact that the polluter receives a monetary benefit from selling the permits, the scheme has the desired effect: to make polluters internalize the externality of their actions.

2. **a.** If the emissions tax is smaller than the marginal social cost at Q_{OPT}, a polluter will face a marginal cost of polluting (equal to the amount of the tax) that is less than the marginal social cost at the socially optimal quantity of pollution. Since a polluter will produce emissions up to the point where the marginal social benefit is equal to its marginal cost, the resulting amount of pollution will be larger than the socially optimal quantity. As a result, there is inefficiency: if the amount of pollution is larger than the socially optimal quantity, the marginal social cost exceeds the marginal social benefit, and society could gain from a reduction in emissions levels.

   If the emissions tax is greater than the marginal social cost at Q_{OPT}, a polluter will face a marginal cost of polluting (equal to the amount of the tax) that is greater than the marginal social cost at the socially optimal quantity of pollution. This will lead the polluter to reduce emissions below the socially optimal quantity. This also is inefficient: whenever the marginal social benefit is greater than the marginal social cost, society could benefit from an increase in emissions levels.

b. If the total amount of allowable pollution is set too high, the supply of emissions permits will be high and so the equilibrium price at which permits trade will be low. That is, polluters will face a marginal cost of polluting (the price of a permit) that is "too low"—lower than the marginal social cost at the socially optimal quantity of pollution. As a result, pollution will be greater than the socially optimal quantity. This is inefficient.

If the total level of allowable pollution is set too low, the supply of emissions permits will be low and so the equilibrium price at which permits trade will be high. That is, polluters will face a marginal cost of polluting (the price of a permit) that is "too high"—higher than the marginal social cost at the socially optimal quantity of pollution. As a result, pollution will be lower than the socially optimal quantity. This also is inefficient.

Check Your Understanding
17-3

1. The London congestion charge acts like a Pigouvian tax on driving in central London. If the marginal external cost in terms of pollution and congestion of an additional car driven in central London is indeed £8, then the scheme is an optimal policy.

2. a. Planting trees imposes an external benefit: the marginal social benefit of planting trees is higher than the marginal benefit to individual tree planters, since many people (not just those who plant the trees) can benefit from the increased air quality and lower summer temperatures. The difference between the marginal social benefit and the marginal benefit to individual tree planters is the marginal external benefit. A Pigouvian subsidy could be placed on each tree planted in urban areas in order to increase the marginal benefit to individual tree planters to the same level as the marginal social benefit.

b. Water-saving toilets impose an external benefit: the marginal benefit to individual homeowners from replacing a traditional toilet with a water-saving toilet is zero, since water is virtually costless. But the marginal social benefit is large, since fewer rivers and aquifers need to be pumped. The difference between the marginal social benefit and the marginal benefit to individual homeowners is the marginal external benefit. A Pigouvian subsidy on installing water-saving toilets could bring the marginal benefit to individual homeowners in line with the marginal social benefit.

c. Disposing of old computer monitors imposes an external cost: the marginal cost to those disposing of old computer monitors is lower than the marginal social cost, since environmental pollution is borne by people other than the person disposing of the monitor. The difference between the marginal social cost and the marginal cost to those disposing of old computer monitors is the marginal external cost. A Pigouvian tax on disposing of computer monitors, or a system of tradable permits for their disposal,

could raise the marginal cost to those disposing of old computer monitors sufficiently to make it equal to the marginal social cost.

Check Your Understanding
17-4

1. a. The voltage of an appliance must be consistent with the voltage of the electrical outlet it is plugged into. Consumers will want to have 110-volt appliances when houses are wired for 110-volt outlets, and builders will want to install 110-volt outlets when most prospective homeowners use 110-volt appliances. So a network externality arises because a consumer will want to use appliances that operate with the same voltage as the appliances used by most other consumers.

b. Printers, copy machines, fax machines, and so on are designed for specific paper sizes. Consumers will want to purchase paper of a size that can be used in these machines, and machine manufacturers will want to manufacture their machines for the size of paper that most consumers use. So a network externality arises because a consumer will want to use the size of paper used by most other consumers—namely, 8½-by-11-inch paper rather than 8-by-12½-inch paper.

2. Of the two competing companies, the company able to achieve the higher number of sales is likely to dominate the market. In a market with a network externality, new consumers will base their buying decisions on the number of existing consumers of a specific product. In other words, the more consumers a company can attract initially, the more consumers will choose to buy that company's product; therefore, the good exhibits *positive feedback*. So it is important for a company to make a large number of sales early on. It can do this by pricing its good cheaply and taking a loss on each unit sold. The company that can best afford to subsidize a large number of sales early on is likely to be the winner of this competition.

Chapter Eighteen
Check Your Understanding
18-1

1. a. Use of a public park is nonexcludable, but it may or may not be rival in consumption, depending on the circumstances. For example, if both you and I use the park for jogging, then your use will not prevent my use—use of the park is nonrival in consumption. In this case the public park is a public good. But use of the park is rival in consumption if there are many people trying to use the jogging path at the same time or when my use of the public tennis court prevents your use of the same court. In this case the public park is a common resource.

b. A cheese burrito is both excludable and rival in consumption. Hence it is a private good.

c. Information from a password-protected website is excludable but nonrival in consumption. So it is an artificially scarce good.

d. Publicly announced information on the path of an incoming hurricane is nonexcludable and nonrival in consumption. So it is a public good.

2. A private producer will supply only a good that is excludable; otherwise, the producer won't be able to charge a price for it that covers the costs of production. So a private producer would be willing to supply a cheese burrito and information from a password-protected website but unwilling to supply a public park or publicly announced information about an incoming hurricane.

Check Your Understanding 18-2

1. a. With 10 Homebodies and 6 Revelers, the marginal social benefit schedule of money spent on the party is as shown in the accompanying table.

Money spent on party	Marginal social benefit
$0	
	$(10 \times \$0.05) + (6 \times \$0.13) = \$1.28$
1	
	$(10 \times \$0.04) + (6 \times \$0.11) = \$1.06$
2	
	$(10 \times \$0.03) + (6 \times \$0.09) = \$0.84$
3	
	$(10 \times \$0.02) + (6 \times \$0.07) = \$0.62$
4	

The efficient spending level is $2, the highest level for which the marginal social benefit is greater than the marginal cost ($1).

b. With 6 Homebodies and 10 Revelers, the marginal social benefit schedule of money spent on the party is as shown in the accompanying table.

Money spent on party	Marginal social benefit
$0	
	$(6 \times \$0.05) + (10 \times \$0.13) = \$1.60$
1	
	$(6 \times \$0.04) + (10 \times \$0.11) = \$1.34$
2	
	$(6 \times \$0.03) + (10 \times \$0.09) = \$1.08$
3	
	$(6 \times \$0.02) + (10 \times \$0.07) = \$0.82$
4	

The efficient spending level is now $3, the highest level for which the marginal social benefit is greater than the marginal cost ($1). The efficient level of spending has increased from that in part a because with relatively more Revelers than Homebodies, an additional dollar spent on the party generates a higher level of social benefit compared to when there are relatively more Homebodies than Revelers.

c. When the numbers of Homebodies and Revelers are unknown but residents are asked their preferences, Homebodies will pretend to be Revelers to induce a higher level of spending on the public party. That's because a Homebody still receives a positive individual marginal benefit from an additional $1 spent, despite the fact that his or her individual marginal benefit is lower than that of a Reveler for every additional $1. In

this case the "reported" marginal social benefit schedule of money spent on the party will be as shown in the accompanying table.

Money spent on party	Marginal social benefit
$0	
	$16 \times \$0.13 = \$2.08$
1	
	$16 \times \$0.11 = \$1.76$
2	
	$16 \times \$0.09 = \$1.44$
3	
	$16 \times \$0.07 = \$1.12$
4	

As a result, $4 will be spent on the party, the highest level for which the "reported" marginal social benefit is greater than the marginal cost ($1). Regardless of whether there are 10 Homebodies and 6 Revelers (part a) or 6 Homebodies and 10 Revelers (part b), spending $4 in total on the party is clearly inefficient because marginal cost exceeds marginal social benefit at this spending level.

As a further exercise, consider how much Homebodies gain by this misrepresentation. In part a, the efficient level of spending is $2. So by misrepresenting their preferences, the 10 Homebodies gain, in total, $10 \times (\$0.03 + \$0.02) = \$0.50$—that is, they gain the marginal individual benefit in going from a spending level of $2 to $4. The 6 Revelers also gain from the misrepresentations of the Homebodies; they gain $6 \times (\$0.09 + \$0.07) = \$0.96$ in total. This outcome is clearly inefficient—when $4 in total is spent, the marginal cost is $1 but the marginal social benefit is only $0.62, indicating that too much money is being spent on the party.

In part b, the efficient level of spending is actually $3. The misrepresentation by the 6 Homebodies gains them, in total, $6 \times \$0.02 = \$0.12$, but the 10 Revelers gain $10 \times \$0.07 = \$0.70$ in total. This outcome is also clearly inefficient—when $4 is spent, marginal social benefit is only $0.12 + $0.70 = $0.82 but marginal cost is $1.

Check Your Understanding 18-3

1. When individuals are allowed to harvest freely, the government-owned forest becomes a common resource, and individuals will overuse it—they will harvest an inefficiently excessive number of trees. In economic terms, the marginal social cost of harvesting a tree is greater than a private logger's individual marginal cost.

2. The three methods consistent with economic theory are (i) Pigouvian taxes, (ii) a system of tradable licenses, and (iii) allocation of property rights.

i. *Pigouvian taxes.* You would enforce a tax on loggers that equals the difference between the marginal social cost and the individual marginal cost of logging a tree at the socially efficient harvest amount. In order to do this, you must know the marginal social cost schedule and the individual marginal cost schedule.

ii. *System of tradable licenses.* You would issue tradable licenses, setting the total number of trees harvested equal to the socially efficient harvest number. The market that arises in these licenses will allocate the right to log efficiently when loggers differ in their costs of logging: licenses will be purchased by those who have a relatively lower cost of logging. The market price of a license will be equal to the difference between the marginal social cost and the individual marginal cost of logging a tree at the socially efficient harvest amount. In order to implement this level, you need to know the socially efficient harvest amount.

iii. *Allocation of property rights.* Here you would sell or give the forest to a private party. This party will have the right to exclude others from harvesting trees. Harvesting is now a private good—it is excludable and rival in consumption. As a result, there is no longer any divergence between social and private costs, and the private party will harvest the efficient level of trees. You need no additional information to use this method.

Check Your Understanding
18-4

1. a. The efficient price to a consumer is $0, since the marginal cost of allowing a consumer to download it is $0.

   b. Xenoid will not produce the software unless it can charge a price that allows it at least to make back the $300,000 cost of producing it. So the lowest price at which Xenoid is willing to produce it is $150. At this price, it makes a total revenue of $150 × 2,000 = $300,000; at any lower price, Xenoid will not cover its cost. The shaded area in the accompanying diagram shows the deadweight loss when Xenoid charges a price of $150.

Chapter Nineteen

Check Your Understanding
19-1

1. a. A pension guarantee program is a social insurance program. The possibility of an employer declaring bankruptcy and defaulting on its obligation to pay employee pensions creates insecurity. By providing pension income to those employees, such a program alleviates this source of economic insecurity.

   b. The SCHIP program is a poverty program. By providing health care to children in low-income households, it targets its spending specifically to the poor.

   c. The Section 8 housing program is a poverty program. By targeting its support to low-income households, it specifically helps the poor.

   d. The federal flood program is a social insurance program. For many people, the majority of their wealth is tied up in the home they own. The potential for a loss of that wealth creates economic insecurity. By providing assistance to those hit by a major flood, the program alleviates this source of insecurity.

2. The poverty threshold is an absolute measure of poverty. It defines individuals as poor if their incomes fall below a level that is considered adequate to purchase the necessities of life, irrespective of how well other people are doing. And that measure is fixed: in 2007, for instance, it took $10,787 for an individual living alone to purchase the necessities of life, regardless of how well-off other Americans were. In particular, the poverty threshold is not adjusted for an increase in living standards: even if other Americans are becoming increasingly well-off over time, in real terms (that is, how many goods an individual at the poverty threshold can buy) the poverty threshold remains the same.

3. a. To determine mean (or average) income, we take the total income of all individuals in this economy and divide it by the number of individuals. Mean income is ($39,000 + $17,500 + $900,000 + $15,000 + $28,000)/5 = $999,500/5 = $199,900. To determine median income, look at the accompanying table, which lines up the five individuals in order of their income.

	Income
Vijay	$15,000
Kelly	17,500
Oskar	28,000
Sephora	39,000
Raul	900,000

The median income is the income of the individual in the exact middle of the income distribution: Oskar with an income of $28,000. So the median income is $28,000.

Median income is more representative of the income of individuals in this economy: almost everyone earns income between $15,000 and $39,000, close to the median income of $28,000. Only Raul is the exception: it is his income that raises the mean income to $199,900, which is not representative of most incomes in this economy.

   b. The first quintile is made up of the 20% (or one-fifth) of individuals with the lowest incomes in the economy. Vijay makes up the 20% of individuals with the lowest incomes. His income is $15,000, so that is the average income of the first quintile. Oskar makes up the 20% of individuals with the third-lowest incomes. His income is $28,000, so that is the average income of the third quintile.

4. As the Economics in Action pointed out, much of the rise in inequality reflects growing differences among highly educated workers. That is, workers with similar levels of education earn very dissimilar incomes. As a result, the principal source of rising inequality in the United States today is reflected by statement b: the rise in the bank CEO's salary relative to that of the branch manager.

Check Your Understanding
19-2

1. The Earned Income Tax Credit (EITC), a negative income tax, applies only to those workers who earn income; over a certain range of incomes, the more a worker earns, the

higher the amount of EITC received. A person who earns no income receives no income tax credit. By contrast, poverty programs that pay individuals based solely on low income still make those payments even if the individual does not work at all; once the individual earns a certain amount of income, these programs discontinue payments. As a result, such programs contain an incentive not to work and earn income, since earning more than a certain amount makes individuals ineligible for their benefits. The negative income tax, however, provides an incentive to work and earn income because its payments increase the more an individual works.

2. According to the data in Table 19-4, the U.S. welfare state reduces the poverty rate for every age group. It does so particularly dramatically for those aged 65 and over, where it cuts the poverty rate by more than 80%.

Check Your Understanding 19-3

1. a. The program benefits you and your parents because the pool of all college students contains a representative mix of healthy and less healthy people, rather than a selected group of people who want insurance because they expect to pay high medical bills. In that respect, this insurance is like *employment-based health insurance.* Because no student can opt out, the school can offer health insurance based on the health care costs of its average student. If each student had to buy his or her own health insurance, some students would not be able to obtain any insurance and many would pay more than they do to the school's insurance program.

b. Since all students are required to enroll in its health insurance program, even the healthiest students cannot leave the program in an effort to obtain cheaper insurance tailored specifically to healthy people. If this were to happen, the school's insurance program would be left with an adverse selection of less healthy students and so would have to raise premiums, beginning the adverse selection death spiral. But since no student can leave the insurance program, the school's program can continue to base its premiums on the average student's probability to require health care, avoiding the adverse selection death spiral.

2. According to critics, part of the reason the U.S. health care system is so much more expensive than that of other countries is its fragmented nature. Since each of the many insurance companies has significant administrative (overhead) costs—in part because each insurance company incurs marketing costs and exerts significant effort in weeding out high-risk insureds—the system tends to be more expensive than one in which there is only a single medical insurer. Another part of the explanation is that U.S. medical care includes many more expensive treatments than found in other wealthy countries, pays higher physician salaries, and has higher drug prices.

Check Your Understanding 19-4

1. a. Recall one of the principles from Chapter 1: one person's spending is another person's income. A high sales tax on consumer items is the same as a high marginal tax rate on income. As a result, the incentive to earn income by working or by investing in risky projects is reduced, since the payoff, after taxes, is lower.

b. If you lose a housing subsidy as soon as your income rises above $25,000, your incentive to earn more than $25,000 is reduced. If you earn exactly $25,000, you obtain the housing subsidy; however, as soon as you earn $25,001, you lose the entire subsidy, making you worse off than if you had not earned the additional dollar. The complete withdrawal of the housing subsidy as income rises above $25,000 is what economists refer to as a *notch.*

2. Over the past 30 years, polarization in Congress has increased. Thirty years ago, some Republicans were to the left of some Democrats. Today, the rightmost Democrats appear to be to the left of the leftmost Republicans.

Chapter Twenty

Check Your Understanding 20-1

1. Many college professors will depart for other lines of work if the government imposes a wage that is lower than the market wage. Fewer professors will result in fewer courses taught and therefore fewer college degrees produced. It will adversely affect sectors of the economy that depend directly on colleges, such as the local shopkeepers who sell goods and services to students and faculty, college textbook publishers, and so on. It will also adversely affect firms that use the "output" produced by colleges: new college graduates. Firms that need to hire new employees with college degrees will be hurt as a smaller supply results in a higher market wage for college graduates. Ultimately, the reduced supply of college-educated workers will result in a lower level of human capital in the entire economy relative to what it would have been without the policy. And this will hurt all sectors of the economy that depend on human capital. The sectors of the economy that might benefit are firms that compete with colleges in the hiring of would-be college professors. For example, accounting firms will find it easier to hire people who would otherwise have been professors of accounting, and publishers will find it easier to hire people who would otherwise have been professors of English (easier in the sense that the firms can recruit would-be professors with a lower wage than before). In addition, workers who already have college degrees will benefit; they will command higher wages as the supply of college-educated workers falls.

Check Your Understanding 20-2

1. a. As the demand for services increases, the price of services will rise. And as the price of the output produced by the industries increases, this shifts the *VMPL* curve upward—that is, the demand for labor rises. This results in an increase in both the equilibrium wage rate and the quantity of labor employed.

b. The fall in the catch per day means that the marginal product of labor in the industry declines. The *VMPL* curve shifts downward, generating a fall in the equilibrium wage rate and the equilibrium quantity of labor employed.

2. When firms from different industries compete for the same workers, then each worker in the various industries will be paid the same equilibrium wage rate, *W*. And since, by the marginal productivity theory of income distribution, $VMPL = P \times MPL = W$ for the last worker hired in equilibrium, the last worker hired in each of these different industries will have the same value of the marginal product of labor.

Check Your Understanding
20-3

1. **a.** False. Income disparities associated with gender, race, or ethnicity can be explained by the marginal productivity theory of income distribution provided that differences in marginal productivity across people are correlated with gender, race, or ethnicity. One possible source for such correlation is past discrimination. Such discrimination can lower individuals' marginal productivity by, for example, preventing them from acquiring the human capital that would raise their productivity. Another possible source of the correlation is differences in work experience that are associated with gender, race, or ethnicity. For example, in jobs where work experience or length of tenure is important, women may earn lower wages because on average more women than men take child-care-related absences from work.
   b. True. Companies that discriminate when their competitors do not are likely to hire less able workers because they discriminate against more able workers who are considered to be of the wrong gender, race, ethnicity, or other characteristic. And with less able workers, such companies are likely to earn lower profits than their competitors who don't discriminate.
   c. Ambiguous. In general, workers who are paid less because they have less experience may or may not be the victims of discrimination. The answer depends on the reason for the lack of experience. If workers have less experience because they are young or have chosen to do something else rather than gain experience, then they are not victims of discrimination if they are paid less. But if workers lack experience because previous job discrimination prevented them from gaining experience, then they are indeed victims of discrimination when they are paid less.

Check Your Understanding
20-4

1. **a.** Clive is made worse off if, before the new law, he had preferred to work more than 35 hours per week. As a result of the law, he can no longer choose his preferred time allocation; he now consumes fewer goods and more leisure than he would like.
   b. Clive's utility is unaffected by the law if, before the law, he had preferred to work 35 or fewer hours per week. The law has not changed his preferred time allocation.
   c. Clive can never be made better off by a law that restricts the number of hours he can work. He can only be made worse off (case a) or equally as well off (case b).

2. The substitution effect would induce Clive to work fewer hours and consume more leisure after his wage rate falls—the fall in the wage rate means the price of an hour of leisure falls, leading Clive to consume more leisure. But a fall in his wage rate also generates a fall in Clive's

income. The income effect of this is to induce Clive to consume less leisure and therefore work more hours, since he is now poorer and leisure is a normal good. If the income effect dominates the substitution effect, Clive will in the end work more hours than before.

Chapter Twenty-One
Check Your Understanding
21-1

1. The family with the lower income is likely to be more risk-averse. In general, higher income or wealth results in lower degrees of risk aversion, due to diminishing marginal utility. Both families may be willing to buy an "unfair" insurance policy. Most insurance policies are "unfair" in that the expected claim is less than the premium. The degree to which a family is willing to pay more than an expected claim for insurance depends on the family's degree of risk aversion.

2. **a.** Karma's expected income is the weighted average of all possible values of her income, weighted by the probabilities with which she earns each possible value of her income. Since she makes $22,000 with a probability of 0.6 and $35,000 with a probability of 0.4, her expected income is (0.6 × $22,000) + (0.4 × $35,000) = $13,200 + $14,000 = $27,200. Her expected utility is simply the expected value of the total utilities she will experience. Since with a probability of 0.6 she will experience a total utility of 850 utils (the utility to her from making $22,000), and with a probability of 0.4 she will experience a total utility of 1,260 utils (the utility to her from making $35,000), her expected utility is (0.6 × 850 utils) + (0.4 × 1,260 utils) = 510 utils + 504 utils = 1,014 utils.
   b. If Karma makes $25,000 for certain, she experiences a utility level of 1,014 utils. From the answer to part a, we know that this leaves her equally as well off as when she has a risky expected income of $27,200. Since Karma is indifferent between a risky expected income of $27,200 and a certain income of $25,000, you can conclude that she would prefer a certain income of $27,200 to a risky expected income of $27,200. That is, she would definitely be willing to reduce the risk she faces when this reduction in risk leaves her expected income unchanged. In other words, Karma is risk-averse.
   c. Yes. Karma experiences a utility level of 1,056 utils when she has a certain income of $26,000. This is higher than the expected utility level of 1,014 utils generated by a risky expected income of $27,200. So Karma is willing to pay a premium to guarantee a certain income of $26,000.

Check Your Understanding
21-2

1. **a.** An increase in the number of ships implies an increase in the quantity of insurance demanded at any given premium. This is a rightward shift of the demand curve, resulting in a rise in both the equilibrium premium and the equilibrium quantity of insurance bought and sold.
   b. An increase in the number of trading routes means that investors can diversify more. In other words, they can reduce risk further. At any given premium, there are now more investors willing to supply insurance. This is a

rightward shift of the supply curve for insurance, leading to a fall in the equilibrium premium and a rise in the equilibrium quantity of insurance bought and sold.

c. If shipowners in the market become even more risk-averse, they will be willing to pay even higher premiums for insurance. That is, at any given premium, there are now more people willing to buy insurance. This is a rightward shift of the demand curve for insurance, leading to a rise in both the equilibrium premium and the equilibrium quantity of insurance bought and sold.

d. If investors in the market become more risk-averse, they will be less willing to accept risk at any given premium. This is a leftward shift of the supply curve for insurance, leading to a rise in the equilibrium premium and a fall in the equilibrium quantity of insurance bought and sold.

e. As the overall level of risk increases, those willing to buy insurance will be more willing to buy insurance at any given premium; the demand curve for insurance shifts to the right. But since overall risk cannot be diversified away, those ordinarily willing to take on risk will be less willing to do so, leading to a leftward shift in the supply curve for insurance. As a result, the equilibrium premium will rise; the effect on the equilibrium quantity of insurance is uncertain.

f. If the wealth levels of investors fall, investors will become more risk-averse and so less willing to supply insurance at any given premium. This is a leftward shift of the supply curve for insurance, leading to a rise in the equilibrium premium and a fall in the equilibrium quantity of insurance bought and sold.

Check Your Understanding
21-3

1. The inefficiency caused by adverse selection is that an insurance policy with a premium based on the average risk of all drivers will attract only an adverse selection of bad drivers. Good (that is, safe) drivers will find this insurance premium too expensive and so will remain uninsured. This is inefficient. However, safe drivers are also those drivers who have had fewer moving violations for several years. Lowering premiums for only those drivers allows the insurance company to screen its customers and sell insurance to safe drivers, too. This means that at least some of the good drivers now are also insured, which decreases the inefficiency that arises from adverse selection. In a way, having no moving violations for several years is building a reputation for being a safe driver.

2. The moral hazard problem in home construction arises from private information about what the contractor does: whether she takes care to reduce the cost of construction or allows costs to increase. The homeowner cannot, or can only imperfectly, observe the cost-reduction effort of the contractor. If the contractor were fully reimbursed for all costs incurred during construction, she would have no incentive to reduce costs. Making the contractor responsible for any additional costs above the original estimate means that she now has an incentive to keep costs low. However, this imposes risk on the contractor. For instance, if the weather is bad, home construction will take longer, and will be more costly, than if the weather had been good. Since the contractor pays for any additional costs (such as weather-induced delays) above the original estimate, she now faces risk that she cannot control.

3. a. True. Drivers with higher deductibles have more incentive to take care in their driving, to avoid paying the deductible. This is a moral hazard phenomenon.

b. True. Suppose you know that you are a safe driver. You have a choice of a policy with a high premium but a low deductible or one with a lower premium but a higher deductible. In this case, you would be more likely to choose the cheap policy with the high deductible because you know that you will be unlikely to have to pay the deductible. When there is adverse selection, insurance companies use screening devices such as this to make inferences about people's private information about how skillful they are as drivers.

c. True. The wealthier you are, the less risk-averse you are. If you are less risk-averse, you are more willing to bear risk yourself. Having an insurance policy with a high deductible means that you are exposed to more risk: you have to pay more of any insurance claim yourself. This is an implication of how risk aversion changes with a person's income or wealth.

Chapter Twenty-Two
Check Your Understanding
22-1

1. a. This is a microeconomic question because it addresses decisions made by individual consumers.

b. This is a macroeconomic question because it addresses consumer spending in the overall economy.

c. This is a macroeconomic question because it addresses changes in the overall economy.

d. This is a microeconomic question because it addresses changes in a particular market, in this case the market for geologists.

e. This is a microeconomic question because it addresses choices made by individual consumers and producers about which mode of transportation to use.

f. This is a microeconomic question because it addresses changes in a particular market.

g. This is a macroeconomic question because it addresses changes in a measure of the economy's overall price level.

2. a. When people can't get credit to finance their purchases, they will be unable to spend money. This will weaken the economy, and as others see the economy weaken, they will also cut back on their spending in order to save for future bad times. As a result, the credit shortfall will spark a compounding effect through the economy as people cut back their spending, making the economy worse, leading to more cutbacks in spending, and so on.

b. If you believe the economy is self-regulating, then you would advocate doing nothing in response to the slump.

c. If you believe in Keynesian economics, you would advocate that policy makers undertake monetary and fiscal policies to stimulate spending in the economy.

Check Your Understanding
22-2

1. We talk about business cycles for the economy as a whole because recessions and expansions are not confined to a few industries—they reflect downturns and upturns for the economy as a whole. The data clearly show that in the steep downturns, almost every sector of the economy reduces output and the number of people employed. Moreover, business cycles are an international phenomenon, sometimes moving in rough synchrony across countries.

2. Recessions cause a great deal of pain across the entire society. They cause large numbers of workers to lose their jobs and make it hard to find new jobs. Recessions hurt the standard of living of many families and are usually associated with a rise in the number of people living below the poverty line, an increase in the number of people who lose their houses because they can't afford their mortgage payments, and a fall in the percentage of Americans with health insurance. Recessions also hurt the profits of firms.

Check Your Understanding 22-3

1. Countries with high rates of population growth will have to maintain higher growth rates of overall output than countries with low rates of population growth in order to achieve an increased standard of living per person because aggregate output will have to be divided among a larger number of people.

2. No, Argentina is not poorer than it was in the past. Both Argentina and Canada have experienced long-run growth. However, after World War II, Argentina did not make as much progress as Canada, perhaps because of political instability and bad macroeconomic policies. Canada's economy grew much faster than Argentina's. Although Canada is now about three times as rich as Argentina, Argentina still had long-run growth of its economy.

Check Your Understanding 22-4

1. a. As some prices have risen but other prices have fallen, there may be overall inflation or deflation. The answer is ambiguous.
   b. As all prices have risen significantly, this sounds like inflation.
   c. As most prices have fallen and others have not changed, this sounds like deflation.

Check Your Understanding 22-5

1. a. This situation reflects comparative advantage. Canada's comparative advantage results from the discovery of oil— Canada now has an abundance of oil.
   b. This situation reflects comparative advantage. China's comparative advantage results from an abundance of labor; China is good at labor-intensive activities such as assembly.
   c. This situation reflects macroeconomic forces. China has been running a huge trade surplus because of underlying decisions regarding savings and investment spending with its savings in excess of its investment spending.
   d. This situation reflects macroeconomic forces. The United States was able to begin running a large trade deficit because the technology boom made the United States an attractive place to invest, with investment spending outstripping U.S. savings.

Chapter Twenty-Three

Check Your Understanding 23-1

1. Let's start by considering the relationship between the total value added of all domestically produced final goods and services and aggregate spending on domestically produced final goods and services. These two quantities are equal because every final good and service produced in the economy is either purchased by someone or added to inventories. And additions to inventories are counted as spending by firms. Next, consider the relationship between aggregate spending on domestically produced final goods and services and total factor income. These two quantities are equal because all spending that is channeled to firms to pay for purchases of domestically produced final goods and services is revenue for firms. Those revenues must be paid out by firms to their factors of production in the form of wages, profit, interest, and rent. Taken together, this means that all three methods of calculating GDP are equivalent.

2. Firms make sales to other firms, households, the government, and the rest of the world. Households are linked to firms through the sale of factors of production to firms, through purchases from firms of final goods and services, and through lending funds to firms in the financial markets. Households are linked to the government through their payment of taxes, their receipt of transfers, and their lending of funds to the government to fund government borrowing via the financial markets. Finally, households are linked to the rest of the world through their purchases of imports and transactions with foreigners in financial markets.

3. You would be counting the value of the steel twice—once as it was sold by American Steel to American Motors and once as part of the car sold by American Motors.

Check Your Understanding 23-2

1. a. In 2006 nominal GDP was $(1,000,000 \times \$0.40) + (800,000 \times \$0.60) = \$400,000 + \$480,000 = \$880,000$. A 25% rise in the price of french fries from 2006 to 2007 means that the 2007 price of french fries was $1.25 \times \$0.40 = \$0.50$. A 10% fall in servings means that $1,000,000 \times 0.9 = 900,000$ servings were sold in 2007. As a result, the total value of sales of french fries in 2007 was $900,000 \times \$0.50 = \$450,000$. A 15% fall in the price of onion rings from 2006 to 2007 means that the 2007 price of onion rings was $0.85 \times \$0.60 = \$0.51$. A 5% rise in servings sold means that $800,000 \times 1.05 = 840,000$ servings were sold in 2007. As a result, the total value of sales of onion rings in 2007 was $840,000 \times \$0.51 = \$428,400$. Nominal GDP in 2007 was $\$450,000 + \$428,400 = \$878,400$. To find real GDP in 2007, we must calculate the value of sales in 2007 using 2006 prices: $(900,000 \text{ french fries} \times \$0.40) + (840,000 \text{ onion rings} \times \$0.60) = \$360,000 + \$504,000 = \$864,000$.
   b. A comparison of nominal GDP in 2006 to nominal GDP in 2007 shows a decline of $((\$880,000 - \$878,400) / \$880,000) \times 100 = 0.18\%$. But a comparison using real GDP shows a decline of $((\$880,000 - \$864,000) / \$880,000) \times 100 = 1.8\%$. That is, a calculation based on

real GDP shows a drop 10 times larger (1.8%) than a calculation based on nominal GDP (0.18%). In this case, the calculation based on nominal GDP underestimates the true magnitude of the change.

2. A price index based on 1990 prices will contain a relatively high price of electronics and a relatively low price of housing compared to a price index based on 2000 prices. This means that a 1990 price index used to calculate real GDP in 2007 will magnify the value of electronics production in the economy, but a 2000 price index will magnify the value of housing production in the economy.

Check Your Understanding
23-3

1. This market basket costs, pre-frost, $(100 \times \$0.20) + (50 \times \$0.60) + (200 \times \$0.25) = \$20 + \$30 + \$50 = \$100$. The same market basket, post-frost, costs $(100 \times \$0.40) + (50 \times \$1.00) + (200 \times \$0.45) = \$40 + \$50 + \$90 = \$180$. So the price index is $(\$100/\$100) \times 100 = 100$ before the frost and $(\$180/\$100) \times 100 = 180$ after the frost, implying a rise in the price index of 80%. This increase in the price index is less than the 84.2% increase calculated in the text. The reason for this difference is that the new market basket of 100 oranges, 50 grapefruit, and 200 lemons contains proportionally more of the items that have experienced relatively lower price increases (the lemons, whose price has increased by 80%) and proportionately fewer of the items that have experienced relatively large price increases (the oranges, whose price has increased by 100%). This shows that the price index can be very sensitive to the composition of the market basket. If the market basket contains a large proportion of goods whose prices have risen faster than the prices of other goods, it will lead to a higher estimate of the increase in the price level. If it contains a large proportion of goods whose prices have risen more slowly than the prices of other goods, it will lead to a lower estimate of the increase in the price level.

2. a. A market basket determined 10 years ago will contain fewer cars than at present. Given that the average price of a car has grown faster than the average prices of other goods, this basket will underestimate the true increase in the price level because it contains relatively too few cars.

b. A market basket determined 10 years ago will not contain broadband Internet access. So it cannot track the fall in prices of Internet access over the past few years. As a result, it will overestimate the true increase in the price level.

3. Using Equation 23-3, the inflation rate from 2006 to 2007 is $((207.3 - 201.6)/201.6) \times 100 = 2.8\%$.

Chapter Twenty-Four

Check Your Understanding
24-1

1. The advent of websites that enable job-seekers to find jobs more quickly will reduce the unemployment rate over time. However, websites that induce discouraged workers to begin actively looking for work again will lead to an increase in the unemployment rate over time.

2. a. Rosa is not counted as unemployed because she is not actively looking for work, but she is counted in broader measures of labor underutilization as a discouraged worker.

b. Anthony is not counted as unemployed; he is considered employed because he has a job.

c. Grace is unemployed; she is not working and is actively looking for work.

d. Sergio is not unemployed, but underemployed; he is working part-time for economic reasons. He is counted in broader measures of labor underutilization.

e. Natasha is not unemployed, but marginally attached. She is counted in broader measures of labor underutilization.

3. Both parts a and b are consistent with the relationship, illustrated in Figure 24-5, between above-average or below-average growth in real GDP and changes in the unemployment rate: during years of above-average growth, the unemployment rate falls, and during years of below-average growth, the unemployment rate rises. However, part c is not consistent: it implies that a recession is associated with a fall in the unemployment rate.

Check Your Understanding
24-2

1. a. When the pace of technological advance quickens, there will be higher rates of job creation and destruction as old industries disappear and new ones emerge. As a result, frictional unemployment will be higher as workers leave jobs in declining industries in search of jobs in expanding industries.

b. When the unemployment rate is low, frictional unemployment will account for a larger share of total unemployment because other sources of unemployment will be diminished. So the share of total unemployment composed of the frictionally unemployed will rise.

2. A binding minimum wage represents a price floor below which wages cannot fall. As a result, actual wages cannot move toward equilibrium. So a minimum wage causes the quantity of labor supplied to exceed the quantity of labor demanded. Because this surplus of labor reflects unemployed workers, it affects the unemployment rate. Collective bargaining has a similar effect—unions are able to raise the wage above the equilibrium level. This will act like a minimum wage by causing the number of job-seekers to be larger than the number of workers firms are willing to hire. Collective bargaining causes the unemployment rate to be higher than it otherwise would be, as shown in the accompanying diagram.

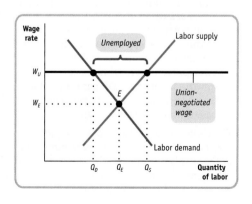

3. An increase in unemployment benefits reduces the cost to individuals of being unemployed, causing them to spend more time searching for new jobs. So the natural rate of unemployment would increase.

Check Your Understanding 24-3

1. Shoe-leather costs as a result of inflation will be lower because it is now less costly for individuals to manage their assets in order to economize on their money holdings. This reduction in the costs associated with converting nonmoney assets into money translates into lower shoe-leather costs.

2. If inflation came to a complete stop over the next 15 or 20 years, the inflation rate would be zero, which of course is less than the expected inflation rate of 2–3%. Because the real interest rate is the nominal interest rate minus the inflation rate, the real interest rate on a loan would be higher than expected, and lenders would gain at the expense of borrowers. Borrowers would have to repay their loans with funds that have a higher real value than had been expected.

Chapter Twenty-Five

Check Your Understanding 25-1

1. Economic progress raises the living standards of the average resident of a country. An increase in overall real GDP does not accurately reflect an increase in an average resident's living standard because it does not account for growth in the number of residents. If, for example, real GDP rises by 10% but population grows by 20%, the living standard of the average resident falls: after the change, the average resident has only $(110/120) \times 100 = 91.6\%$ as much real income as before the change. Similarly, an increase in nominal GDP per capita does not accurately reflect an increase in living standards because it does not account for any change in prices. For example, a 5% increase in nominal GDP per capita generated by a 5% increase in prices implies that there has been no change in living standards. Real GDP per capita is the only measure that accounts for both changes in the population and changes in prices.

2. Using the Rule of 70, the amount of time it will take for China to double its real GDP per capita is $(70/8.3) = 8$ years; India and Ireland, $(70/4.1) = 17.1$ years; the United States, $(70/2.0) = 35$ years; France, $(70/1.5) = 46.7$ years; and Argentina $(70/0.8) = 87.5$ years. Since the Rule of 70 can only be applied to a positive growth rate, we cannot apply it to the case of Zimbabwe, which experienced negative growth. If India continues to have a higher growth rate of real GDP per capita than the United States, then India's real GDP per capita will eventually surpass that of the United States.

3. The United States began growing rapidly over a century ago, but China and India have begun growing rapidly only recently. As a result, the living standard of the typical Chinese or Indian household has not yet caught up with that of the typical American household.

Check Your Understanding 25-2

1. a. Significant technological progress will result in a positive growth rate of productivity even though physical capital per worker and human capital per worker are unchanged.
   b. The growth rate of productivity will fall but remain positive due to diminishing returns to physical capital.

2. a. If the economy has grown 3% per year and the labor force has grown 1% per year, then productivity—output per person—has grown at approximately 3% – 1% = 2% per year.
   b. If physical capital has grown 4% per year and the labor force has grown 1% per year, then physical capital per worker has grown at approximately 4% – 1% = 3% per year.
   c. According to estimates, each 1% rise in physical capital, other things equal, increases productivity by 0.3%. So, as physical capital per worker has increased by 0.3%, productivity growth that can be attributed to an increase in physical capital per worker is $0.3 \times 3\% = 0.9\%$. As a percentage of total productivity growth, this is $0.9\%/2\% \times 100\% = 45\%$.
   d. If the rest of productivity growth is due to technological progress, then technological progress has contributed 2% – 0.9% = 1.1% to productivity growth. As a percentage of total productivity growth, this is $1.1\%/2\% \times 100\% = 55\%$.

3. It will take a period time for workers to learn how to use the new computer system and to adjust their routines. And because there are often setbacks in learning a new system, such as accidentally erasing your computer files, productivity at Multinomics may decrease for a period of time.

Check Your Understanding 25-3

1. A country that has high domestic savings is able to achieve a high rate of investment spending as a percent of GDP. This, in turn, allows the country to achieve a high growth rate.

2. It is likely that the United States will experience a greater pace of creation and development of new drugs because closer links between private companies and academic research centers will lead to work more directly focused on producing new drugs rather than on pure research.

3. It is likely that these events resulted in a fall in the country's growth rate because the lack of property rights would have dissuaded people from making investments in productive capacity.

Check Your Understanding 25-4

1. The conditional version of the convergence hypothesis says that countries grow faster, other things equal, when they start from relatively low GDP per capita. From this we can infer that they grow more slowly, other things equal, when their real GDP per capita is relatively higher. This points to lower future Asian growth. However, other things might not be equal: if Asian economies continue investing in human capital, if savings rates continue to be high, if governments invest in infrastructure, and so on, growth might continue at an accelerated pace.

2. As you can see from panel (b) of Figure 25-8, although it is important in determining the growth rate for some countries (such as those of Western Europe), the initial

level of GDP per capita isn't the only factor. High rates of savings and investment appear to be better predictors of future growth than today's standard of living.

3. The evidence suggests that both sets of factors matter: better infrastructure is important for growth, but so is political and financial stability. Policies should try to address both areas.

Check Your Understanding 25-5

1. Economists are typically more concerned about environmental degradation than resource scarcity. The reason is that in modern economies the price response tends to alleviate the limits imposed by resource scarcity through conservation and the development of alternatives. However, because environmental degradation involves a negative externality—a cost imposed by individuals or firms on others without the requirement to pay compensation—effective government intervention is required to address it. As a result, economists are more concerned about the limits to growth imposed by environmental degradation because a market response would be inadequate.

2. Growth increases a country's greenhouse gas emissions. The current best estimates are that a large reduction in emissions will result in only a modest reduction in growth. The international burden sharing of greenhouse gas emissions reduction is contentious because rich countries are reluctant to pay the costs of reducing their emissions only to see newly emerging countries like China rapidly increase their emissions. Yet most of the current accumulation of gases is due to the past actions of rich countries. Poorer countries like China are equally reluctant to sacrifice their growth to pay for the past actions of rich countries.

Chapter Twenty-Six

Check Your Understanding 26-1

1. **a.** As capital flows into the economy, the supply of loanable funds increases. This is illustrated by the shift of the supply curve from S_1 to S_2 in the accompanying diagram. As the equilibrium moves from E_1 to E_2, the equilibrium interest rate falls from r_1 to r_2, and the equilibrium quantity of loanable funds increases from Q_1 to Q_2.

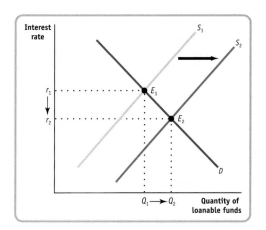

b. Savings fall due to the higher proportion of retired people, and the supply of loanable funds decreases. This is illustrated by the leftward shift of the supply curve from S_1 to S_2 in the accompanying diagram. The equilibrium moves from E_1 to E_2, the equilibrium interest rate rises from r_1 to r_2, and the equilibrium quantity of loanable funds falls from Q_1 to Q_2.

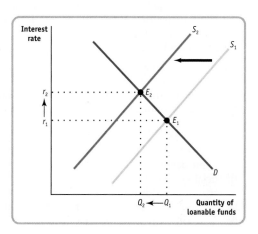

2. We know from the loanable funds market that as the interest rate rises, households want to save more and consume less. But at the same time, an increase in the interest rate lowers the number of investment spending projects with returns at least as high as the interest rate. The statement "households will want to save more money than businesses will want to invest" cannot represent an equilibrium in the loanable funds market because it says that the quantity of loanable funds offered exceeds the quantity of loanable funds demanded. If that were to occur, the interest rate must fall to make the quantity of loanable funds offered equal to the quantity of loanable funds demanded.

3. **a.** The real interest rate will not change. According to the Fisher effect, an increase in expected inflation drives up the nominal interest rate, leaving the real interest rate unchanged.

b. The nominal interest rate will rise by 3%. Each additional percentage point of expected inflation drives up the nominal interest rate by 1 percentage point.

c. As we saw in Figure 26-7, as long as inflation is expected, it does not affect the equilibrium quantity of loanable funds. Both the supply and demand curves for loanable funds are pushed upward, leaving the equilibrium quantity of loanable funds unchanged.

Check Your Understanding 26-2

1. The transaction costs for (a) a bank deposit and (b) a share of a mutual fund are approximately equivalent because each can typically be accomplished by making a phone call, going online, or visiting a branch office. Transaction costs are highest for (c) a share of a family business, since finding a buyer for the share consumes time and resources. The level of risk is lowest for (a) a bank deposit, since these deposits are insured by the Federal Deposit Insurance Corporation (FDIC) up to $250,000; somewhat higher for (b) a share of a mutual

fund, since despite diversification, there is still risk associated with holding stocks; and highest for (c) a share of a family business, since this investment is not diversified. The level of liquidity is highest for (a) a bank deposit, since withdrawals can usually be made immediately; somewhat lower for (b) a share of a mutual fund, since it may take a few days between selling your shares and the payment being processed; and lowest for (c) a share of a family business, since it can only be sold with the unanimous agreement of other members and it will take some time to find a buyer.

2. Economic development and growth are the result of, among other factors, investment spending on physical capital. Since investment spending is equal to savings, the greater the amount saved, the higher investment spending will be, and so the higher growth and economic development will be. So the existence of institutions that facilitate savings will help a country's growth and economic development. As a result, a country with a financial system that provides low transaction costs, opportunities for diversification of risk, and high liquidity to its savers will experience faster growth and economic development than a country that doesn't.

Check Your Understanding
26-3

1. a. Today's stock prices reflect the market's expectation of future stock prices, and according to the efficient markets hypothesis, stock prices always take account of all available information. The fact that this year's profits are low is not new information, so it is already built into the share price. However, when it becomes known that the company's profits will be high next year, the price of a share of its stock will rise today, reflecting this new information.

   b. The expectations of investors about high profits were already built into the stock price. Since profits will be lower than expected, the market's expectations about the company's future stock price will be revised downward. This new information will lower the stock price.

   c. When other companies in the same industry announce that sales are unexpectedly slow this year, investors are likely to conclude that sales will also be unexpectedly slow for this company. As a result, investors will revise downward their expectations of future profits and of the future stock price. This new information will result in a lower stock price today.

   d. This announcement will either have no effect on the company's stock price or will increase it only slightly. It does not add any new information, beyond removing some uncertainty about whether the profit forecast was correct. It should therefore result in either no increase or only a small increase in the stock price.

2. The efficient markets hypothesis states that all available information is immediately taken into account in stock prices. So if investors consistently bought stocks the day after the Dow rose by 1%, a smart investor would *sell* on that day because demand—and so stock prices—would be high. If a profit can be made that way, eventually many investors would be selling, and it would no longer be true that investors always bought stocks the day after the Dow rose by 1%.

Chapter Twenty-Seven
Check Your Understanding
Check Your Understanding
27-1

1. A decline in investment spending, like a rise in investment spending, has a multiplier effect on real GDP—the only difference in this case is that real GDP falls instead of rises. The fall in I leads to an initial fall in real GDP, which leads to a fall in disposable income, which leads to lower consumer spending, which leads to another fall in real GDP, and so on. So consumer spending falls as an indirect result of the fall in investment spending.

2. When the MPC is 0.5, the multiplier is equal to $1/(1 - 0.5) = 1/0.5 = 2$. When the MPC is 0.8, the multiplier is equal to $1/(1 - 0.8) = 1/0.2 = 5$.

3. The greater the share of GDP that is saved rather than spent, the lower the MPC. Disposable income that goes to savings is like a "leak" in the system, reducing the amount of spending that fuels a further expansion. So it is likely that Amerigo will have the larger multiplier.

Check Your Understanding
Check Your Understanding
27-2

1. a. Angelina's autonomous consumer spending is $8,000. When her current disposable income rises by $10,000, her consumer spending rises by $4,000 ($12,000 – $8,000). So her MPC is $4,000/$10,000 = 0.4 and her consumption function is $c = \$8,000 + 0.4 \times yd$. Felicia's autonomous consumer spending is $6,500. When her current disposable income rises by $10,000, her consumer spending rises by $8,000 ($14,500 – $6,500). So her MPC is $8,000/$10,000 = 0.8 and her consumption function is $c = \$6,500 + 0.8 \times yd$. Marina's autonomous consumer spending is $7,250. When her current disposable income rises by $10,000, her consumer spending rises by $7,000 ($14,250 – $7,250). So her MPC is $7,000/$10,000 = 0.7 and her consumption function is $c = \$7,250 + 0.7 \times yd$.

   b. The aggregate autonomous consumer spending in this economy is $8,000 + $6,500 + $7,250 = $21,750. A $30,000 increase in disposable income ($3 \times \$10,000$) leads to a $4,000 + $8,000 + $7,000 = $19,000 increase in consumer spending. So the economy-wide MPC is $19,000/$30,000 = 0.63 and the aggregate consumption function is $C = \$21,750 + 0.63 \times YD$.

2. If you expect your future disposable income to fall, you would like to save some of today's disposable income to tide you over in the future. But you cannot do this if you cannot save. If you expect your future disposable income to rise, you would like to spend some of tomorrow's higher income today. But you cannot do this if you cannot borrow. If you cannot save or borrow, your expected future disposable income will have no effect on your consumer spending today. In fact, your MPC must always equal 1: you must consume all your current disposable income today, and you will be unable to smooth your consumption over time.

Check Your Understanding
Check Your Understanding
27-3

1. a. An unexpected increase in consumer spending will result in a reduction in inventories as producers sell items from their inventories to satisfy this short-term increase in

demand. This is negative unplanned inventory investment: it reduces the value of producers' inventories.

   b. A rise in the cost of borrowing is equivalent to a rise in the interest rate: fewer investment spending projects are now profitable to producers, whether they are financed through borrowing or retained earnings. As a result, producers will reduce the amount of planned investment spending.

   c. A sharp increase in the rate of real GDP growth leads to a higher level of planned investment spending by producers, according to the accelerator principle, as they increase production capacity to meet higher demand.

   d. As sales fall, producers sell less, and their inventories grow. This leads to positive unplanned inventory investment.

2. Since the marginal propensity to consume is less than 1—because consumers normally spend part but not all of an additional dollar of disposable income—consumer spending does not fully respond to fluctuations in current disposable income. This behavior diminishes the effect of fluctuations in the economy on consumer spending. In contrast, by the accelerator principle, investment spending is directly related to the expected future growth rate of GDP. As a result, investment spending will magnify fluctuations in the economy: a higher expected future growth rate of real GDP leads to higher planned investment spending; a lower expected future growth rate of real GDP leads to lower planned investment spending.

3. When consumer spending is sluggish, firms with excess production capacity will cut back on planned investment spending because they think their existing capacities are sufficient for expected future sales. Similarly, when consumer spending is sluggish and firms have a large amount of unplanned inventory investment, they are likely to cut back their production of output because they think their existing inventories are sufficient for expected future sales. So an inventory overhang is likely to depress current economic activity as firms cut back on their planned investment spending and on their output.

27-4

1. A slump in planned investment spending will lead to a fall in real GDP in response to an unanticipated increase in inventories. The fall in real GDP will translate into a fall in households' disposable income, and households will respond by reducing consumer spending. The decrease in consumer spending leads producers to further decrease output, further lowering disposable income and leading to further reductions in consumer spending. So although the slump originated in investment spending, it will cause a reduction in consumer spending.

2. a. After an autonomous fall in planned aggregate spending, the economy is no longer in equilibrium: real GDP is greater than planned aggregate spending. The accompanying figure shows this autonomous fall in planned aggregate spending by the shift of the aggregate spending curve from AE_1 to AE_2. The difference between the two results in positive unplanned inventory investment: there is an unanticipated increase in inventories. Firms will respond by reducing production. This will eventually move the economy to a new equilibrium. In the accompanying figure, this is illustrated by the movement from

the initial income–expenditure equilibrium at E_1 to the new income–expenditure equilibrium at E_2. As the economy moves to its new equilibrium, real GDP falls from its initial income–expenditure equilibrium level at Y_1^* to its new lower level, Y_2^*.

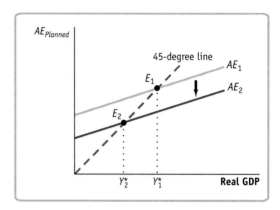

   b. We know that the change in income–expenditure equilibrium GDP is given by Equation 27-17: $\Delta Y^* =$ Multiplier $\times \Delta AAE_{Planned}$. Here, the multiplier $= 1/(1 - 0.5) = 1/0.5 = 2$. So a \$300 million autonomous reduction in planned aggregate spending will lead to a $2 \times \$300$ million $= \$600$ million (\$0.6 billion) fall in income–expenditure equilibrium GDP. The new Y^* will be \$500 billion $-$ \$0.6 billion $=$ \$499.4 billion.

Chapter Twenty-Eight

28-1

1. a. This is a shift of the aggregate demand curve. A decrease in the quantity of money raises the interest rate, since people now want to borrow more and lend less. A higher interest rate reduces investment and consumer spending at any given aggregate price level. So the aggregate demand curve shifts to the left.

   b. This is a movement up along the aggregate demand curve. As the aggregate price level rises, the real value of money holdings falls. This is the interest rate effect of a change in the aggregate price level: as the value of money falls, people want to hold more money. They do so by borrowing more and lending less. This leads to a rise in the interest rate and a reduction in consumer and investment spending. So it is a movement along the aggregate demand curve.

   c. This is a shift of the aggregate demand curve. Expectations of a poor job market, and so lower average disposable incomes, will reduce people's consumer spending today at any given aggregate price level. So the aggregate demand curve shifts to the left.

   d. This is a shift of the aggregate demand curve. A fall in tax rates raises people's disposable income. At any given aggregate price level, consumer spending is now higher. So the aggregate demand curve shifts to the right.

   e. This is a movement down along the aggregate demand curve. As the aggregate price level falls, the real value of assets rises. This is the wealth effect of a change in the aggregate price level: as the value of assets rises, people will increase their consumption plans. This leads to higher consumer spending. So it is a movement along the aggregate demand curve.

  f. This is a shift of the aggregate demand curve. A rise in the real value of assets in the economy due to a surge in real estate values raises consumer spending at any given aggregate price level. So the aggregate demand curve shifts to the right.

Check Your Understanding 28-2

1. a. This represents a movement along the *SRAS* curve because the CPI—like the GDP deflator—is a measure of the aggregate price level, the overall price level of final goods and services in the economy.

  b. This represents a shift of the *SRAS* curve because oil is a commodity. The *SRAS* curve will shift to the right because production costs are now lower, leading to a higher quantity of aggregate output supplied at any given aggregate price level.

  c. This represents a shift of the *SRAS* curve because it involves a change in nominal wages. An increase in legally mandated benefits to workers is equivalent to an increase in nominal wages. As a result, the *SRAS* curve will shift leftward because production costs are now higher, leading to a lower quantity of aggregate output supplied at any given aggregate price level.

2. You would need to know what happened to the aggregate price level. If the increase in the quantity of aggregate output supplied was due to a movement along the *SRAS* curve, the aggregate price level would have increased at the same time as the quantity of aggregate output supplied increased. If the increase in the quantity of aggregate output supplied was due to a rightward shift of the *LRAS* curve, the aggregate price level might not rise. Alternatively, you could make the determination by observing what happened to aggregate output in the long run. If it fell back to its initial level in the long run, then the temporary increase in aggregate output was due to a movement along the *SRAS* curve. If it stayed at the higher level in the long run, the increase in aggregate output was due to a rightward shift of the *LRAS* curve.

Check Your Understanding 28-3

1. a. An increase in the minimum wage raises the nominal wage and, as a result, shifts the short-run aggregate supply curve to the left. As a result of this negative supply shock, the aggregate price level rises and aggregate output falls.

  b. Increased investment spending shifts the aggregate demand curve to the right. As a result of this positive demand shock, both the aggregate price level and aggregate output rise.

  c. An increase in taxes and a reduction in government spending both result in negative demand shocks, shifting the aggregate demand curve to the left. As a result, both the aggregate price level and aggregate output fall.

  d. This is a negative supply shock, shifting the short-run aggregate supply curve to the left. As a result, the aggregate price level rises and aggregate output falls.

2. As long-run growth increases potential output, the long-run aggregate supply curve shifts to the right. If, in the short run, there is now a recessionary gap (aggregate output is less than potential output), nominal wages will fall, shifting the short-run aggregate supply curve to the right. This results in a fall in the aggregate price level and a rise in aggregate output. As prices fall, we move along the aggregate demand curve due to the wealth and interest rate effects of a change in the aggregate price level. Eventually, as long-run macroeconomic equilibrium is reestablished, aggregate output will rise to be equal to potential output.

Check Your Understanding 28-4

1. a. An economy is overstimulated when an inflationary gap is present. This will arise if an expansionary monetary or fiscal policy is implemented when the economy is currently in long-run macroeconomic equilibrium. This shifts the aggregate demand curve to the right, in the short run raising the aggregate price level and aggregate output and creating an inflationary gap. Eventually nominal wages will rise and shift the short-run aggregate supply curve to the left, and aggregate output will fall back to potential output. This is the scenario envisaged by the speaker.

  b. No, this is not a valid argument. When the economy is not currently in long-run macroeconomic equilibrium, an expansionary monetary or fiscal policy does not lead to the outcome described above. Suppose a negative demand shock has shifted the aggregate demand curve to the left, resulting in a recessionary gap. An expansionary monetary or fiscal policy can shift the aggregate demand curve back to its original position in long-run macroeconomic equilibrium. In this way, the short-run fall in aggregate output and deflation caused by the original negative demand shock can be avoided. So, if used in response to demand shocks, fiscal or monetary policy is an effective policy tool.

2. Those within the Fed who advocated lowering interest rates were focused on boosting aggregate demand in order to counteract the negative demand shock caused by the collapse of the housing bubble. Lowering interest rates will result in a rightward shift of the aggregate demand curve, increasing aggregate output, but raising the aggregate price level. Those within the Fed who advocated holding interest rates steady were focused on the fact that fighting the slump in aggregate demand in the face of a negative supply shock could result in a rise in inflation. Holding interest rates steady relies on the ability of the economy to self-correct in the long run, with the aggregate price level and aggregate output only gradually returning to their levels before the negative supply shock.

Chapter Twenty-Nine

Check Your Understanding 29-1

1. a. This is a contractionary fiscal policy because it is a reduction in government purchases of goods and services.

b. This is an expansionary fiscal policy because it is an increase in government transfers that will increase disposable income.

c. This is a contractionary fiscal policy because it is an increase in taxes that will reduce disposable income.

2. Federal disaster relief that is quickly disbursed is more effective than legislated aid because there is very little time lag between the time of the disaster and the time it is received by victims. So it will stabilize the economy after a disaster. In contrast, legislated aid is likely to entail a time lag in its disbursement, potentially destabilizing the economy.

29-2

1. A $500 million increase in government purchases of goods and services directly increases aggregate spending by $500 million, which then starts the multiplier in motion. It will increase real GDP by $500 million × $1/(1 - MPC)$. A $500 million increase in government transfers increases aggregate spending only to the extent that it leads to an increase in consumer spending. Consumer spending rises by $MPC × \$1$ for every $1 increase in disposable income, where MPC is less than 1. So a $500 million increase in government transfers will cause a rise in real GDP only MPC times as much as a $500 million increase in government purchases of goods and services. It will increase real GDP by $500 million × $MPC/(1 - MPC)$.

2. This is the same issue as in Problem 1, but in reverse. If government purchases of goods and services fall by $500 million, the initial fall in aggregate spending is $500 million. If there is a $500 million reduction in government transfers, the initial fall in aggregate spending is $MPC ×$ $500 million, which is less than $500 million.

3. Boldovia will experience greater variation in its real GDP than Moldovia because Moldovia has automatic stabilizers while Boldovia does not. In Moldovia the effects of slumps will be lessened by unemployment insurance benefits which will support residents' incomes, while the effects of booms will be diminished because tax revenues will go up. In contrast, incomes will not be supported in Boldovia during slumps because there is no unemployment insurance. In addition, because Boldovia has lump-sum taxes, its booms will not be diminished by increases in tax revenue.

29-3

1. The actual budget balance takes into account the effects of the business cycle on the budget deficit. During recessionary gaps, it incorporates the effect of lower tax revenues and higher transfers on the budget balance; during inflationary gaps, it incorporates the effect of higher tax revenues and reduced transfers. In contrast, the cyclically adjusted budget balance factors out the effects of the business cycle and assumes that real GDP is at potential output. Since, in the long run, real GDP tends to potential output, the cyclically adjusted budget balance is a better measure of the long-run sustainability of government policies.

2. In recessions, real GDP falls. This implies that consumers' incomes, consumer spending, and producers' profits also fall. So in recessions, states' tax revenue (which depends in large part on consumers' incomes, consumer spending, and producers' profits) falls. In order to balance the state budget, states have to cut spending or raise taxes. But that deepens the recession. Without a balanced-budget requirement, states could use expansionary fiscal policy during a recession to lessen the fall in real GDP.

29-4

1. a. A higher growth rate of real GDP implies that tax revenue will increase. If government spending remains constant and the government runs a budget surplus, the size of the public debt will be less than it would otherwise have been.

b. If retirees live longer, the average age of the population increases. As a result, the implicit liabilities of the government increase because spending on programs for older Americans, such as Social Security and Medicare, will rise.

c. A decrease in tax revenue without offsetting reductions in government spending will cause the public debt to increase.

d. Public debt will increase as a result of government borrowing to pay interest on its current public debt.

2. In order to stimulate the economy in the short run, the government can use fiscal policy to increase real GDP. This entails borrowing, increasing the size of the public debt further and leading to undesirable consequences: in extreme cases, governments can be forced to default on their debts. Even in less extreme cases, a large public debt is undesirable because government borrowing "crowds out" borrowing for private investment spending. This reduces the amount of investment spending, reducing the long-run growth of the economy.

Chapter Thirty

30-1

1. The defining characteristic of money is its liquidity: how easily it can be used to purchase goods and services. Although a gift certificate can easily be used to purchase a very defined set of goods or services (the goods or services available at the store issuing the gift certificate), it cannot be used to purchase any other goods or services. A gift certificate is therefore not money, since it cannot easily be used to purchase all goods or services.

2. Again, the important characteristic of money is its liquidity: how easily it can be used to purchase goods and services. M1, the narrowest definition of the money supply, contains only currency in circulation, traveler's checks, and checkable bank deposits. CDs aren't checkable—and they can't be made checkable without incurring a cost because there's a penalty for early withdrawal. This makes them less liquid than the assets counted in M1.

3. Commodity-backed money uses resources more efficiently than simple commodity money, like gold and silver coins, because commodity-backed money ties up fewer valuable resources. Although a bank must keep some of the commodity—generally gold and silver—on hand, it only has to keep enough to satisfy demand for redemptions. It can then lend out the remaining gold and silver, which allows society to use these resources for other purposes, with no loss in the ability to achieve gains from trade.

Check Your Understanding 30-2

1. Even though you know that the rumor about the bank is not true, you are concerned about other depositors pulling their money out of the bank. And you know that if enough other depositors pull their money out, the bank will fail. In that case, it is rational for you to pull your money out before the bank fails. All depositors will think like this, so even if they all know that the rumor is false, they may still rationally pull their money out, leading to a bank run. Deposit insurance leads depositors to worry less about the possibility of a bank run. Even if a bank fails, the FDIC will currently pay each depositor up to $250,000 per account. This will make you much less likely to pull your money out in response to a rumor. Since other depositors will think the same, there will be no bank run.

2. The aspects of modern bank regulation that would frustrate this scheme are *capital requirements* and *reserve requirements*. Capital requirements mean that a bank has to have a certain amount of capital—the difference between its assets (loans plus reserves) and its liabilities (deposits). So the con artist could not open a bank without putting any of his own wealth in because the bank needs a certain amount of capital—that is, it needs to hold more assets (loans plus reserves) than deposits. So the con artist would be at risk of losing his own wealth if his loans turn out badly.

Check Your Understanding 30-3

1. Since they only have to hold $100 in reserves, instead of $200, banks now lend out $100 of their reserves. Whoever borrows the $100 will deposit it in a bank, which will lend out $100 × (1 − rr) = $100 × 0.9 = $90. Whoever borrows the $90 will put it into a bank, which will lend out $90 × 0.9 = $81, and so on. Overall, deposits will increase by $100/0.1 = $1,000.

2. Silas puts $1,000 in the bank, of which the bank lends out $1,000 × (1 − rr) = $1,000 × 0.9 = $900. Whoever borrows the $900 will keep $450 in cash and deposit $450 in a bank. The bank will lend out $450 × 0.9 = $405. Whoever borrows the $405 will keep $202.50 in cash and deposit $202.50 in a bank. The bank will lend out $202.50 × 0.9 = $182.25, and so on. Overall, this leads to an increase in deposits of $1,000 + $450 + $202.50 + . . . But it decreases the amount of currency in circulation: the amount of cash is reduced by the $1,000 Silas puts into the bank. This is offset, but not fully, by the amount of cash held by each borrower. The amount of currency in circulation therefore changes by −$1,000 + $450 + $202.50 + . . . The money supply

therefore increases by the sum of the increase in deposits and the change in currency in circulation, which is $1,000 − $1,000 + $450 + $450 + $202.50 + $202.50 + . . . and so on.

Check Your Understanding 30-4

1. An open-market purchase of $100 million by the Fed increases banks' reserves by $100 million as the Fed credits their accounts with additional reserves. In other words, this open-market purchase increases the monetary base (currency in circulation plus bank reserves) by $100 million. Banks lend out the additional $100 million. Whoever borrows the money puts it back into the banking system in the form of deposits. Of these deposits, banks lend out $100 million × (1 − rr) = $100 million × 0.9 = $90 million. Whoever borrows the money deposits it back into the banking system. And banks lend out $90 million × 0.9 = $81 million, and so on. As a result, bank deposits increase by $100 million + $90 million + $81 million + . . . = $100 million/$rr$ = $100 million/0.1 = $1,000 million = $1 billion. Since in this simplified example all money lent out is deposited back into the banking system, there is no increase of currency in circulation, so the increase in bank deposits is equal to the increase in the money supply. In other words, the money supply increases by $1 billion. This is greater than the increase in the monetary base by a factor of 10: in this simplified model in which deposits are the only component of the money supply and in which banks hold no excess reserves, the money multiplier is $1/rr$ = 10.

Check Your Understanding 30-5

1. The Panic of 1907, the S&L crisis, and the crisis of 2008 all involved losses by financial institutions that were less regulated than banks. In the crises of 1907 and 2008, there was a widespread loss of confidence in the financial sector and collapse of credit markets. Like the crisis of 1907 and the S&L crisis, the crisis of 2008 exerted a powerful negative effect on the economy.

2. The creation of the Federal Reserve failed to prevent bank runs because it did not eradicate the fears of depositors that a bank collapse would cause them to lose their money. The bank runs eventually stopped after federal deposit insurance was instituted and the public came to understand that their deposits were now protected.

3. The balance sheet effect occurs when asset sales cause declines in asset prices, which then reduce the value of other firms' net worth as the value of the assets on their balance sheets declines. In the vicious cycle of deleveraging, the balance sheet effect on firms forces their creditors to call in their loan contracts, forcing the firms to sell assets to pay back their loans, leading to further asset sales and price declines. Because the vicious cycle of deleveraging occurs across different firms and no single firm can stop it, it is necessary for the government to step in to stop it.

Chapter Thirty-One

Check Your Understanding
31-1

1. **a.** By increasing the opportunity cost of holding money, a high interest rate reduces the quantity of money demanded. This is a movement up and to the left along the money demand curve.

   b. A 10% fall in prices reduces the quantity of money demanded at any given interest rate, shifting the money demand curve leftward.

   c. This technological change reduces the quantity of money demanded at any given interest rate. So it shifts the money demand curve leftward.

   d. Payment in cash require employers to hold more money, increasing the quantity of money demanded at any given interest rate. So it shifts the money demand curve rightward.

2. **a.** A 1% processing fee on debit/credit card transactions for purchases less than $50 reduces the opportunity cost of holding cash because consumers will save money by paying with cash.

   b. An increase in the interest paid on six-month CDs raises the opportunity cost of holding cash because holding cash requires forgoing the higher interest paid.

   c. A fall in real estate prices has no effect on the opportunity cost of holding cash because real estate is an illiquid asset and so isn't relevant in the decision of how much cash to hold. Also, real estate transactions are not done in cash.

   d. Because many purchases of food are made in cash, a significant increase in the cost of food reduces the opportunity cost of holding cash.

Check Your Understanding
31-2

1. In the accompanying diagram, the increase in the demand for money is shown as a rightward shift of the money demand curve, from MD_1 to MD_2. This raises the equilibrium interest rate from r_1 to r_2.

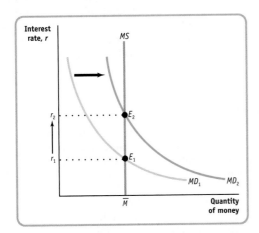

2. In order to prevent the interest rate from rising, the Federal Reserve must make an open-market purchase of Treasury bills, shifting the money supply curve rightward.

This is shown in the accompanying diagram as the move from MS_1 to MS_2.

Check Your Understanding
31-3

1. **a.** The money supply curve shifts to the right.

   b. The equilibrium interest rate falls.

   c. Investment spending rises, due to the fall in the interest rate.

   d. Consumer spending rises, due to the multiplier process.

   e. Aggregate output rises because of the rightward shift of the aggregate demand curve.

2. There are two pieces of evidence. (1) Actual monetary policy has been more consistent with a rule that includes consideration of both the inflation rate and the output gap than with a rule that considers only the inflation rate or a rule that considers only the output gap. (2) The changes in interest rates predicted by an application of the Taylor rule have always been in the same direction as actual changes in interest rates. The Fed is likely to respond more directly to a financial crisis than the Bank of England because, unlike the Bank of England, it does not have to set policy to meet a prespecified inflation target.

Check Your Understanding
31-4

1. **a.** Aggregate output rises in the short run, then falls back to equal potential output in the long run.

   b. The aggregate price level rises in the short run, but by less than 25%. It rises further in the long run, for a total increase of 25%.

   c. In the short run, the aggregate price level rises by less than 25%. So in the short run, the real value of the money supply increases. In the long run, however, the aggregate price level will fully adjust and rise by 25%, returning the real value of the money supply to its original level.

   d. The interest rate falls in the short run, then rises back to its original level in the long run.

2. In the short run, a change in the interest rate alters the economy because it affects investment spending, which in turn affects aggregate demand and real GDP through the multiplier process. However, in the long run,

changes in consumer spending and investment spending will eventually result in changes in nominal wages and the nominal prices of other factors of production. For example, an expansionary monetary policy will eventually cause a rise in factor prices; a contractionary policy will eventually cause a fall in factor prices. In response, the short-run aggregate supply curve will shift to move the economy back to long-run equilibrium. So in the long run monetary policy has no effect on the economy.

Chapter Thirty-Two

Check Your Understanding
32-1

1. The inflation rate is more likely to quickly reflect changes in the money supply when the economy has had an extended period of high inflation. That's because an extended period of high inflation sensitizes workers and firms to raise nominal wages and prices of intermediate goods when the aggregate price level rises. As a result, there will be little or no increase in real output in the short run after an increase in the money supply, and the increase in the money supply will simply be reflected in an equal-sized percent increase in prices. In an economy where people are not sensitized to high inflation because of low inflation in the past, an increase in the money supply will lead to an increase in real output in the short run. This illustrates the fact that the classical model of the price level best applies to economies with *persistently* high inflation, not those with little or no history of high inflation even though they may currently have high inflation.

2. Yes, there can still be an inflation tax because the tax is levied on people who hold money. As long as people hold money, regardless of whether prices are indexed or not, the government is able to use seignorage to capture real resources from the public.

Check Your Understanding
32-2

1. When real GDP equals potential output, cyclical unemployment is zero and the unemployment rate is equal to the natural rate. This is given by point E_1 in Figure 32-8. Assuming a 0% expected inflation rate, this also corresponds to a 6% unemployment rate on curve $SRPC_0$ in Figure 32-10. Any unemployment in excess of this 6% rate, or less than the 6% rate, represents cyclical unemployment. An increase in aggregate demand leads to a fall in the unemployment rate below the natural rate (negative cyclical unemployment) and an increase in the inflation rate. This is given by the movement from E_1 to E_2 in Figure 32-8 and traces a movement upward along the short-run Phillips curve. A reduction in aggregate demand leads to a rise in the unemployment rate above the natural rate (positive cyclical unemployment) and a fall in the inflation rate. This would be represented by a movement down along the short-run Phillips curve from point E_1. So for a given expected inflation rate, the short-run Phillips curve illustrates the relation-ship between cyclical unemployment and the actual inflation rate.

2. A fall in commodities prices leads to a positive supply shock, which lowers the aggregate price level and reduces inflation. As a result, any given level of unemployment can be sustained with a lower inflation rate now—meaning that the short-run Phillips curve has shifted downward. In contrast, a surge in commodities prices leads to a negative supply shock, which raises the aggregate price level and increases inflation. Any given level of unemployment can be sustained only with a higher inflation rate—meaning that the short-run Phillips curve has shifted upward.

Check Your Understanding
32-3

1. There is no long-run trade-off between inflation and unemployment because once expectations of inflation adjust, wages will also adjust, returning employment and the unemployment rate to their equilibrium (natural) levels. This implies that once expectations of inflation fully adjust to any change in actual inflation, the unemployment rate will return to the natural rate of unemployment, or NAIRU. This also implies that the long-run Phillips curve is vertical.

2. There are two possible explanations for this. First, negative supply shocks (for example, increases in the price of oil) will cause an increase in unemployment and an increase in inflation. Second, it is possible that British policy makers attempted to peg the unemployment rate below the natural rate of unemployment. Any attempt to peg unemployment below the natural rate will result in an increase in inflation.

3. Disinflation is costly because to reduce the inflation rate, aggregate output in the short run must typically fall below potential output. This, in turn, results in an increase in the unemployment rate above the natural rate. In general, we would observe a reduction in real GDP. The costs of disinflation can be reduced by not allowing inflation to increase in the first place. Second, the costs of any disinflation will be lower if the central bank is credible and it announces in advance its policy to reduce inflation. In this situation, the adjustment to the disinflationary policy will be more rapid, resulting in a smaller loss of aggregate output.

Check Your Understanding
32-4

1. If the nominal interest rate is negative, an individual is better off simply holding cash, which has a 0% nominal rate of return. If the options facing an individual are to lend and receive a negative nominal interest rate or to hold cash and receive a 0% nominal interest rate, the individual will hold cash. Such a scenario creates the possibility of a liquidity trap, in which monetary policy is ineffective because the nominal interest rate cannot fall below zero. Once the nominal interest rate falls to zero, further increases in the money supply will lead firms and individuals to simply hold the additional cash.

Chapter Thirty-Three

Check Your Understanding

33-1

1. **a.** The figure on the first page of Chapter 33 shows that the Fed pursued a policy that led to a rapid rise in the money supply during and after the 2001 recession. So the data support the first part of the quotation—that there was an "aggressive monetary policy." Whether this did in fact "reduce the depth" of that particular recession is a different question, one that cannot be answered just by looking at the data in the figure. To address the latter part of the quotation, we would have to ask what the size and depth of the 2001 recession would have been had the Fed not aggressively pursued an expansionary monetary policy.

   b. A classical economist would have said that the aggressive monetary expansion would have had no short-run effect on aggregate output and would simply have resulted in a proportionate increase in the aggregate price level.

Check Your Understanding

33-2

1. This is partly a Keynesian statement. Tax cuts will increase after-tax income and, from a Keynesian perspective, increase economic activity. A Keynesian would typically argue that a tax cut will increase disposable income, causing households to increase consumer spending. This increase in consumer spending will cause an increase in aggregate demand and, given an upward-sloping aggregate supply curve, will cause an increase in aggregate output. The Keynesian explanation of the way in which tax cuts affect economic activity, however, does not support the latter part of the quotation. The latter part of the quotation suggests that the tax cuts will increase economic activity by increasing "incentives to work, save, and invest." That part doesn't seem to have much to do with Keynesian ideas.

Check Your Understanding

33-3

1. Monetarists argue that central banks should implement policy so that the money supply grows at some constant rate. Had the Fed pursued a monetarist policy during this period, we would have observed movements in M1 that would have shown a fixed rate of growth during this period. We would not, therefore, have observed any of the reductions in M1 that are observed in the figure, nor would we have observed the acceleration in the rate of growth of M1 that occured in 2001.

2. As in Problem 1, a monetarist policy would have resulted in a constant rate of growth in M1. Between 1960 and 1980, the velocity of M1 rose smoothly. After 1980, the velocity of money experienced a number of shocks, where we observe increases and reductions in velocity. Given a constant rate of money growth, these changes in the velocity of M1 would have caused changes in aggregate demand and in economic activity, other things equal. In this situation, a monetarist policy would have allowed these shocks to the velocity of money to cause fluctuations in economic activity.

3. Fiscal policy is limited by time lags in recognizing economic problems, forming a response, passing legislation, and implementing the policies. Monetary policy is also limited by time lags, but not as severe as those for fiscal policy because the Federal Reserve tends to act more quickly than Congress. Attempts by both fiscal and monetary policy to reduce unemployment below the natural rate are limited by predictions of the natural rate hypothesis: that these attempts will result in accelerating inflation. Also, both fiscal and monetary policy are limited by concerns over the political business cycle: that they will be used to satisfy political ends and will end up destabilizing the economy.

Check Your Understanding

33-4

1. **a.** Rational expectations theorists would argue that only unexpected changes in the money supply would have any short-run effect on economic activity. They would also argue that expected changes in the money supply would affect only the aggregate price level, with no short-run effect on aggregate output. So such theorists would give credit to the Fed for limiting the severity of the 2001 recession only if the Fed's monetary policy had been more aggressive than individuals expected during this period.

   b. Real business cycle theorists would argue that the Fed's policy had no effect on ending the 2001 recession because they believe that fluctuations in aggregate output are caused largely by changes in total factor productivity.

Check Your Understanding

33-5

1. The Modern consensus has resolved the debate over the effectiveness of both expansionary fiscal and monetary policy. Expansionary fiscal policy is considered effective, although it is limited by the problem of time lags, making monetary policy the stabilization tool of choice except in special circumstances. Expansionary monetary policy is considered effective except in the case of a liquidity trap. The Modern consensus has not resolved, however, how monetary policy should be implemented: whether the Fed should adopt an inflation target, whether it should use monetary policy to manage asset price bubbles, and what, if any, kind of unconventional monetary policy it should use in the situation of a liquidity trap.

Chapter Thirty-Four

Check Your Understanding

34-1

1. **a.** The sale of the new airplane to China represents an export of a good to China and so enters the current account.

   b. The sale of Boeing stock to Chinese investors is a sale of a U.S. asset and so enters the financial account.

   c. Even though the plane already exists, when it is shipped to China it is an export of a good from the United States. So the sale of the plane enters the current account.

   d. Because the plane stays in the United States, the Chinese investor is buying a U.S. asset. So this is identical to the answer to part b: the sale of the jet enters the financial account.

2. As we saw in the Global Comparison in this chapter, between 1996 and 2007, the United States became the recipient of huge capital inflows from the rest

of the world. If China decides to embark on a huge program of infrastructure spending financed by borrowing, it is likely that other countries will decrease their lending to the United States and increase their lending to China. These capital outflows from the United States will reduce the U.S. surplus in the financial account and at the same time reduce the deficit in the current account.

Check Your Understanding 34-2

1. a. The increased purchase of Mexican oil will cause U.S. individuals (and firms) to increase their demand for the peso. To purchase pesos, individuals will increase their supply of U.S. dollars to the foreign exchange market, causing a rightward shift in the supply curve of U.S. dollars. This will cause the peso price of the dollar to fall (the amount of pesos per dollar will fall). The peso has appreciated and the U.S. dollar has depreciated as a result.

b. This appreciation of the peso means it will take more U.S. dollars to obtain the same quantity of Mexican pesos. If we assume that the price level (measured in Mexican pesos) of other Mexican goods and services does not change, other Mexican goods and services become more expensive to U.S. households and firms. The dollar cost of other Mexican goods and services will rise as the peso appreciates. So Mexican exports of goods and services other than oil will fall.

c. U.S. goods and services become cheaper in terms of pesos, so Mexican imports of goods and services will rise.

2. a. The real exchange rate equals

Pesos per U.S. dollar × $\dfrac{\text{Aggregate price level in the U.S.}}{\text{Aggregate price level in Mexico}}$

Today, the aggregate price levels in both countries are both equal to 100. The real exchange rate today is: $10 \times (100/100) = 10$. The aggregate price level in five years in the U.S. will be $100 \times (120/100) = 120$, and in Mexico it will be $100 \times (1{,}200/800) = 150$. The real exchange rate in five years, assuming the nominal exchange rate does not change, will be $10 \times (120/150) = 8$.

b. Today, a basket of goods and services that costs $100 costs 800 pesos, so the purchasing power parity is 8 pesos per U.S. dollar. In five years, a basket that costs $120 will cost 1,200 pesos, so the purchasing power parity will be 10 pesos per U.S. dollar.

Check Your Understanding 34-3

1. The accompanying diagram shows the supply of and demand for the yuan, with the U.S. dollar price of the yuan on the vertical axis. In 2005, prior to the revaluation, the exchange rate was pegged at 8.28 yuan per U.S. dollar or, equivalently, 0.121 U.S. dollars per yuan ($0.121). At the target exchange rate of $0.121, the quantity of yuan demanded exceeded the quantity of yuan supplied, creating the shortage depicted in the diagram. Without any intervention by the Chinese government, the U.S. dollar price of the yuan would be bid up, causing an appreciation of the yuan.

The Chinese government, however, intervened to prevent this appreciation.

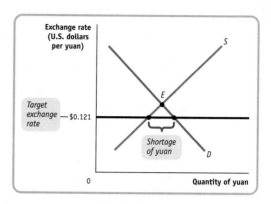

a. If the exchange rate were allowed to move freely, the U.S. dollar price of the exchange rate would move toward the equilibrium exchange rate (labeled XR* in the accompanying diagram). This would occur as a result of the shortage, when buyers of the yuan would bid up its U.S. dollar price. As the exchange rate increases, the quantity of yuan demanded would fall and the quantity of yuan supplied would increase. If the exchange rate were to increase to XR*, the disequilibrium would be entirely eliminated.

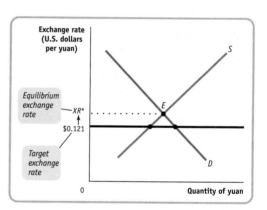

b. Placing restrictions on foreigners who want to invest in China would reduce the demand for the yuan, causing the demand curve to shift in the accompanying diagram from D_1 to something like D_2. This would cause a reduction in the shortage of the yuan. If demand fell to D_3, the disequilibrium would be completely eliminated.

c. Removing restrictions on Chinese who wish to invest abroad would cause an increase in the supply of the yuan and a rightward shift in the supply curve. This increase in supply would also cause a reduction in the size of the shortage. If, for example, supply increased from S_1 to S_2, the disequilibrium would be eliminated completely in the accompanying diagram.

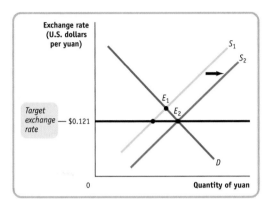

d. Imposing a tax on exports (Chinese goods sold to foreigners) would raise the price of these goods and decrease the amount of Chinese goods purchased. This would also decrease the demand for the yuan. The graphical analysis here is virtually identical to that found in the figure accompanying part b.

Check Your Understanding 34-4

1. The devaluations and revaluations most likely occurred in those periods when there was a sudden change in the franc–mark exchange rate: 1974, 1976, the early 1980s, 1986, and 1993–1994.

2. The high Canadian interest rates would likely have caused an increase in capital inflows to Canada. To obtain these assets (which yielded a relatively higher interest rate) in Canada, investors would first have had to obtain Canadian dollars. The increase in the demand for the Canadian dollar would have caused the Canadian dollar to appreciate. This appreciation of the Canadian currency would have raised the price of Canadian goods to foreigners (measured in terms of the foreign currency). This would have made it more difficult for Canadian firms to compete in other markets.

ability-to-pay principle the principle of tax fairness by which those with greater ability to pay a tax should pay more tax.

absolute advantage the advantage conferred on an individual in an activity if he or she can do it better than other people.

absolute value the value of a number without regard to a plus or minus sign.

accelerator principle the proposition that a higher rate of growth in *real GDP* results in a higher level of *investment spending*, and a lower growth rate in real GDP leads to lower planned investment spending.

accounting profit a business's revenue minus the *explicit cost* and depreciation.

actual investment spending the sum of *planned investment spending* and *unplanned inventory investment*.

AD–AS model the basic model used to understand fluctuations in *aggregate output* and the *aggregate price level*. It uses the *aggregate supply* curve and the *aggregate demand curve* together to analyze the behavior of the *economy* in response to shocks or government policy.

administrative costs (of a tax) the *resources* used (which is a cost) by government to collect the tax, and by taxpayers to pay it, over and above the amount of the tax, as well as to evade it.

adverse selection occurs when an individual knows more about the way things are than other people do. Adverse selection problems can lead to market problems: private information leads buyers to expect hidden problems in items offered for sale, leading to low prices and the best items being kept off the market.

aggregate consumption function the relationship for the *economy* as a whole between aggregate current *disposable income* and aggregate *consumer spending*.

aggregate demand curve a graphical representation that shows the relationship between the *aggregate price level* and the quantity of *aggregate output* demanded by *households*, *firms*, the government, and the rest of the world. The aggregate demand curve has a negative slope due to the *wealth effect of a change in the aggregate price level*

and the *interest rate effect of a change in the aggregate price level*.

aggregate output the total quantity of *final goods and services* the *economy* produces for a given time period, usually a year. *Real GDP* is the numerical measure of aggregate output typically used by economists.

aggregate price level a single number that represents the overall price level for *final goods and services* in the *economy*.

aggregate production function a hypothetical function that shows how productivity (*real GDP* per worker) depends on the quantities of *physical capital* per worker and *human capital* per worker as well as the state of technology.

aggregate spending the total flow of funds into markets for domestically produced *final goods and services*; the sum of *consumer spending, investment spending, government purchases of goods and services*, and *exports* minus *imports*.

aggregate supply curve a graphical representation that shows the relationship between the *aggregate price level* and the total quantity of *aggregate output* supplied.

antitrust policy legislative and regulatory efforts undertaken by the government to prevent oligopolistic industries from becoming or behaving like *monopolies*.

appreciation a rise in the value of one currency in terms of other currencies.

artificially scarce good a good that is *excludable* but *nonrival in consumption*.

autarky a situation in which a country does not trade with other countries.

automatic stabilizers government spending and taxation rules that cause *fiscal policy* to be automatically expansionary when the *economy* contracts and automatically contractionary when the economy expands without requiring any deliberate actions by policy makers. Taxes that depend on *disposable income* are the most important example of automatic stabilizers.

autonomous change in aggregate spending an initial rise or fall in *aggregate spending* at a given level of *real GDP*.

average cost an alternative term for *average total cost*; the *total cost* divided by the quantity of output produced.

average fixed cost the *fixed cost* per unit of output.

average total cost *total cost* divided by quantity of output produced. Also referred to as *average cost*.

average variable cost the *variable cost* per unit of output.

backward-bending individual labor supply curve an *individual labor supply curve* that slopes upward at low to moderate wage rates and slopes downward at higher wage rates.

balance of payments accounts a summary of a country's transactions with other countries, including two main elements: the *balance of payments on current account* and the *balance of payments on financial account*.

balance of payments on current account (current account) transactions that don't create liabilities; a country's *balance of payments on goods and services* plus net international transfer payments and factor income.

balance of payments on financial account (financial account) international transactions that involve the sale or purchase of assets, and therefore create future liabilities.

balance of payments on goods and services the difference between the value of *exports* and the value of *imports* during a given period.

balance sheet effects the reduction in a firm's net worth from falling asset prices.

bank a *financial intermediary* that provides *liquid* assets in the form of *bank deposits* to lenders and uses those funds to finance the *illiquid* investments or *investment spending* needs of borrowers.

bank deposit a claim on a *bank* that obliges the bank to give the depositor his or her cash when demanded.

bank reserves currency held by *banks* in their vaults plus their deposits at the Federal Reserve.

bank run a phenomenon in which many of a *bank*'s depositors try to withdraw their funds due to fears of a bank failure.

bar graph a graph that uses bars of varying height or length to show the comparative sizes of different observations of a *variable*.

barrier to entry something that prevents other firms from entering an industry. Crucial in protecting the profits of a *monopolist*. There are four types of barriers to entry: control over scarce *resources* or *inputs,* increasing returns to scale, technological superiority, and government-created barriers such as *licenses.*

barter a transaction in which people directly exchange goods or services that they have for goods or services that they want.

benefits principle the principle of tax fairness by which those who benefit from public spending should bear the burden of the tax that pays for that spending.

black market a market in which goods or services are bought and sold illegally, either because it is illegal to sell them at all or because the prices charged are legally prohibited by a *price ceiling.*

bond a legal document based on borrowing in the form of an IOU that pays interest.

brand name a name owned by a particular firm that distinguishes its products from those of other firms.

break-even price the market price at which a firm earns zero profits.

budget balance the difference between tax revenue and government spending. A positive budget balance is referred to as a *budget surplus*; a negative budget balance is referred to as a *budget deficit.*

budget constraint the cost of a consumer's *consumption bundle* cannot exceed the consumer's income.

budget deficit the difference between tax revenue and government spending when government spending exceeds tax revenue; dissaving by the government in the form of a budget deficit is a negative contribution to *national savings.*

budget line all the *consumption bundles* available to a consumer who spends all of his or her income.

budget surplus the difference between tax revenue and government spending when tax revenue exceeds government spending; saving by the government in the form of a budget surplus is a positive contribution to *national savings.*

business cycle the short-run alternation between economic downturns, known as *recessions,* and economic upturns, known as *expansions.*

business-cycle peak the point in time at which the *economy* shifts from *expansion* to *recession.*

business-cycle trough the point in time at which the *economy* shifts from *recession* to *expansion.*

capital the combined value of a business's assets; includes equipment, buildings, tools, inventory, and financial assets.

capital at risk funds that an insurer places at *risk* when providing insurance.

capital inflow the net inflow of funds into a country; the difference between the total inflow of foreign funds to the home country and the total outflow of domestic funds to other countries. A positive net capital inflow represents funds borrowed from foreigners to finance domestic investment; a negative net capital inflow represents funds lent to foreigners to finance foreign investment.

cartel an agreement among several producers to obey output restrictions in order to increase their joint profits.

causal relationship the relationship between two *variables* in which the value taken by one variable directly influences or determines the value taken by the other variable.

central bank an institution that oversees and regulates the banking system and controls the *monetary base.*

chained dollars method of calculating *real GDP* that splits the difference between growth rates calculated using early base years and the growth rates calculated using late base years.

checkable bank deposits *bank* accounts on which people can write checks.

circular-flow diagram a diagram that represents the transactions in an *economy* by two kinds of flows around a circle: flows of physical things such as goods or labor in one direction and flows of money to pay for these physical things in the opposite direction.

classical model of the price level a simplified financial model of the price level in which the real quantity of money, M/P, is always at its long-run *equilibrium* level. This model ignores the distinction between the short run and the long run but is useful for analyzing the case of high *inflation.*

Coase theorem the proposition that even in the presence of *externalities* an *economy* can always reach an *efficient* solution as long as *transaction costs* are sufficiently low.

collusion cooperation among producers to limit production and raise prices so as to raise one another's profits.

commercial bank a *bank* that accepts deposits and is covered by *deposit insurance.*

commodity output of different producers regarded by consumers as the same good; also referred to as a *standardized product.*

commodity-backed money a *medium of exchange* that has no intrinsic value whose ultimate value is guaranteed by a promise that it can be converted into valuable goods on demand.

commodity money a *medium of exchange* that is a good, normally gold or silver, that has intrinsic value in other uses.

common resource a *resource* that is *nonexcludable* and *rival in consumption.*

comparative advantage the advantage conferred on an individual or nation in producing a good or service if the *opportunity cost* of producing the good or service is lower for that individual or nation than for other producers.

compensating differentials wage differences across jobs that reflect the fact that some jobs are less pleasant or more dangerous than others.

competitive market a market in which there are many buyers and sellers of the same good or service, none of whom can influence the price at which the good or service is sold.

complements pairs of goods for which a rise in the price of one good leads to a decrease in the demand for the other good.

constant marginal cost each additional unit costs the same to produce as the previous one.

constant returns to scale long-run *average total cost* is constant as output increases.

consumer price index (CPI) a measure of prices; calculated by surveying market prices for a *market basket* intended to represent the consumption of a typical urban American family of four. The CPI is the most commonly used measure of prices in the United States.

consumer spending *household* spending on goods and services from domestic and foreign *firms.*

consumer surplus a term often used to refer both to *individual consumer surplus* and to *total consumer surplus.*

consumption bundle (of an individual) the collection of all the goods and services consumed by a given individual.

consumption function an equation showing how an individual *household*'s *consumer spending* varies with the household's current *disposable income*.

consumption possibilities the set of all *consumption bundles* that can be consumed, given a consumer's income and prevailing prices.

contractionary fiscal policy *fiscal policy* that reduces aggregate demand by decreasing government purchases, increasing taxes, or decreasing transfers.

contractionary monetary policy *monetary policy* that, through the raising of the *interest rate*, reduces aggregate demand and therefore output.

convergence hypothesis a principle of economic growth that holds that international differences in *real GDP per capita* tend to narrow over time because countries that start with lower real GDP per capita tend to have higher growth rates.

copyright the exclusive legal right of the creator of a literary or artistic work to profit from that work; like a *patent*, it is a temporary monopoly.

cost (of potential seller) the lowest price at which a seller is willing to sell a good.

cost-benefit analysis an estimate of the costs and benefits of providing a good. When governments use cost-benefit analysis, they estimate the social costs and social benefits of providing a public good.

cross-price elasticity of demand a measure of the effect of the change in the price of one good on the *quantity demanded* of the other; it is equal to the percent change in the quantity demanded of one good divided by the percent change in the price of another good.

crowding out the negative effect of *budget deficits* on private investment, which occurs because government borrowing drives up *interest rates*.

currency in circulation actual cash held by the public.

current account (balance of payments on current account) transactions that don't create liabilities; a country's *balance of payments on goods and services* plus net international transfer payments and factor income.

curve a line on a graph, which may be curved or straight, that depicts a relationship between two *variables*.

cyclical unemployment the difference between the actual rate of *unemployment* and the *natural rate of unemployment*.

cyclically adjusted budget balance an estimate of what the *budget balance* would be if *real GDP* were exactly equal to *potential output*.

deadweight loss the loss in total surplus that occurs whenever an action or a policy reduces the quantity transacted below the efficient market *equilibrium quantity*.

debt deflation the reduction in aggregate demand arising from the increase in the real burden of outstanding debt caused by *deflation*; occurs because borrowers, whose real debt rises as a result of deflation, are likely to cut spending sharply, and lenders, whose real assets are now more valuable, are less likely to increase spending.

debt–GDP ratio government debt as a percentage of GDP, frequently used as a measure of a government's ability to pay its debts.

decreasing marginal benefit the case in which each additional unit of an activity produces less benefit than the previous unit.

decreasing returns to scale long-run *average total cost* increases as output increases (also known as *diseconomies of scale*).

deductible a sum specified in an insurance policy that the insured individual must pay before being compensated for a claim; deductibles reduce *moral hazard*.

default the risk that the bond issuer fails to make payments as specified by the bond contract.

deflation a fall in the overall level of prices.

demand curve a graphical representation of the *demand schedule*, showing the relationship between *quantity demanded* and price.

demand price the price of a given quantity at which consumers will demand that quantity.

demand schedule a list or table showing how much of a good or service consumers will want to buy at different prices.

demand shock an event that shifts the *aggregate demand curve*. A positive demand shock is associated with higher demand for *aggregate output* at any price level and shifts the curve to the right. A negative demand shock is associated with lower demand for aggregate output at any price level and shifts the curve to the left.

dependent variable the determined *variable* in a *causal relationship*.

deposit insurance a guarantee that a *bank*'s depositors will be paid even if the bank can't come up with the funds, up to a maximum amount per account.

depreciation a fall in the value of one currency in terms of other currencies.

devaluation a reduction in the value of a currency that is set under a *fixed exchange rate regime*.

diminishing marginal rate of substitution the principle that the more of one good that is consumed in proportion to another, the less of the second good the consumer is willing to substitute for another unit of the first good.

diminishing returns to an input the effect observed when an increase in the quantity of an *input*, while holding the levels of all other inputs fixed, leads to a decline in the *marginal product* of that input.

diminishing returns to physical capital in an *aggregate production function* when the amount of *human capital* per worker and the state of technology are held fixed, each successive increase in the amount of *physical capital* per worker leads to a smaller increase in productivity.

discount rate the rate of interest the Federal Reserve charges on loans to *banks* that fall short of *reserve requirements*.

discount window a protection against *bank runs* in which the Federal Reserve stands ready to lend money to *banks* in trouble.

discouraged workers individuals who want to work but who have stated to government researchers that they aren't currently searching for a job because they see little prospect of finding one given the state of the job market.

discretionary fiscal policy *fiscal policy* that is the direct result of deliberate actions by policy makers rather than rules.

discretionary monetary policy policy actions, either changes in *interest rates* or changes in the *money supply*, undertaken by the *central bank* based on its assessment of the state of the *economy*.

disinflation the process of bringing down *inflation* that has become embedded in expectations.

disposable income income plus *government transfers* minus taxes; the total amount of *household* income available to spend on consumption and saving.

diversification investment in several different assets with unrelated, or independent, risks, so that the possible losses are *independent events*.

domestic demand curve a *demand curve* that shows how the quantity of a good demanded by domestic consumers depends on the price of that good.

domestic supply curve a *supply curve* that shows how the quantity of a good supplied by domestic producers depends on the price of that good.

dominant strategy in *game theory*, an action that is a player's best action regardless of the action taken by the other player.

duopolist one of the two firms in a *duopoly*.

duopoly an *oligopoly* consisting of only two firms.

economic growth the growing ability of the *economy* to produce goods and services.

economic profit a business's revenue minus the *opportunity cost* of *resources*; usually less than the *accounting profit*.

economic signal any piece of information that helps people make better economic decisions.

economics the social science that studies the production, distribution, and consumption of goods and services.

economy a system for coordinating society's productive activities.

efficiency wages wages that employers set above the *equilibrium* wage rate as an incentive for workers to deliver better performance.

efficiency-wage model a model in which some employers pay an above-equilibrium wage as an *incentive* for better performance.

efficient describes a market or *economy* that takes all opportunities to make some people better off without making other people worse off.

efficient allocation of risk the case in which those most willing to bear *risk* are those who end up bearing it.

efficient markets hypothesis a principle of asset price determination that holds that asset prices embody all publicly available information. The hypothesis implies that *stock* prices should be unpredictable, or follow a *random walk*, since changes should occur only in response to new information about fundamentals.

elastic demand when the *price elasticity of demand* is greater than 1.

emissions tax a tax that depends on the amount of pollution a firm produces.

employment the total number of people currently employed for pay in the *economy*, either full-time or part-time.

environmental standards rules established by a government to protect the environment by specifying actions by producers and consumers.

equilibrium an economic situation in which no individual would be better off doing something different.

equilibrium exchange rate the *exchange rate* at which the quantity of a currency demanded in the *foreign exchange market* is equal to the quantity supplied.

equilibrium price the price at which the market is in *equilibrium*, that is, the quantity of a good or service demanded equals the quantity of that good or service supplied; also referred to as the *market-clearing price*.

equilibrium quantity the quantity of a good or service bought and sold at the *equilibrium* (or *market-clearing*) *price*.

equilibrium value of the marginal product the additional value produced by the last unit of a factor employed in the *factor market* as a whole.

equity fairness; everyone gets his or her fair share. Since people can disagree about what's "fair," equity isn't as well defined a concept as efficiency.

European Union (EU) a customs union among 27 European nations.

excess capacity when firms produce less than the output at which *average total cost* is minimized; characteristic of *monopolistically competitive* firms.

excess reserves a *bank's reserves* over and above the reserves required by law or regulation.

exchange market intervention government purchases or sales of currency in the *foreign exchange market*.

exchange rate the price at which currencies trade, determined by the *foreign exchange market*.

exchange rate regime a rule governing policy toward the *exchange rate*.

excise tax a tax on sales of a good or service.

excludable referring to a good, describes the case in which the supplier can prevent those who do not pay from consuming the good.

expansion period of economic upturn in which output and employment are rising; most economic numbers are following their normal upward trend; also referred to as a *recovery*.

expansionary fiscal policy *fiscal policy* that increases aggregate demand by increasing government purchases, decreasing taxes, or increasing transfers.

expansionary monetary policy *monetary policy* that, through the lowering of the *interest rate*, increases aggregate demand and therefore output.

expected utility the expected value of an individual's total *utility* given uncertainty about future outcomes.

expected value in reference to a *random variable*, the weighted average of all possible values, where the weights on each possible value correspond to the probability of that value occurring.

explicit cost a cost that involves actually laying out money.

exporting industries industries that produce goods or services that are sold abroad.

exports goods and services sold to other countries.

external benefit an uncompensated benefit that an individual or firm confers on others; also known as *positive externalities*.

external cost an uncompensated cost that an individual or firm imposes on others; also known as *negative externalities*.

externalities *external benefits* and *external costs*.

factor distribution of income the division of total income among labor, land, and *capital*.

factor intensity the difference in the ratio of factors used to produce a good in various industries. For example, oil refining is capital-intensive compared to clothing manufacture because oil refiners use a higher ratio of capital to labor than do clothing producers.

factor markets markets in which *firms* buy the *resources* they need to produce goods and services.

factors of production the *resources* used to produce goods and services. Labor and capital are examples of factors.

fair insurance policy an insurance policy for which the *premium* is equal to the expected value of the claim.

federal funds market the *financial market* that allows *banks* that fall short of *reserve requirements* to borrow funds from banks with *excess reserves*.

federal funds rate the *interest rate* at which funds are borrowed and lent in the *federal funds market*.

fiat money a *medium of exchange* whose value derives entirely from its official status as a means of payment.

final goods and services goods and services sold to the final, or end, user.

financial account (balance of payments on financial account) international transactions that involve the sale of purchase of assets, and therefore create future liabilities.

financial asset a paper claim that entitles the buyer to future income from the seller. *Loans, stocks, bonds,* and *bank deposits* are types of financial assets.

financial intermediary an institution, such as a *mutual fund, pension fund, life insurance company,* or *bank,* that transforms the funds it gathers from many individuals into *financial assets*.

financial markets the banking, *stock,* and *bond* markets, which channel *private savings* and foreign lending into *investment spending, government borrowing,* and foreign borrowing.

financial risk uncertainty about future outcomes that involve financial losses and gains.

firm an organization that produces goods and services for sale.

fiscal policy changes in government spending and taxes designed to affect overall spending.

fiscal year the time period used for much of government accounting, running from October 1 to September 30.

Fiscal years are labeled by the calendar year in which they end.

Fisher effect the principle by which an increase in expected future *inflation* drives up the *nominal interest rate,* leaving the expected real interest rate unchanged.

fixed cost a cost that does not depend on the quantity of output produced; the cost of a *fixed input*.

fixed exchange rate an *exchange rate regime* in which the government keeps the *exchange rate* against some other currency at or near a particular target.

fixed input an *input* whose quantity is fixed for a period of time and cannot be varied (for example, land).

floating exchange rate an *exchange rate regime* in which the government lets the *exchange rate* go wherever the market takes it.

forecast a simple prediction of the future.

foreign exchange controls licensing systems that limit the right of individuals to buy foreign currency.

foreign exchange market the market in which currencies can be exchanged for each other.

foreign exchange reserves *stocks* of foreign currency that governments can use to buy their own currency on the *foreign exchange market*.

free entry and exit describes an industry that potential producers can easily enter or current producers can leave.

free trade *trade* that is unregulated by government *tariffs* or other artificial barriers; the levels of *exports* and *imports* occur naturally, as a result of supply and demand.

free-rider problem when individuals have no *incentive* to pay for their own consumption of a good, they will take a "free ride" on anyone who does pay; a problem with goods that are *nonexcludable*.

frictional unemployment *unemployment* due to time workers spend in *job search*.

gains from trade An economic principle that states that by dividing tasks and trading, people can get more of what they want through *trade* than they could if they tried to be self-sufficient.

game theory the study of behavior in situations of *interdependence*. Used to explain the behavior of an *oligopoly*.

GDP deflator a price measure for a given year that is equal to 100 times the ratio of *nominal GDP* to *real GDP* in that year.

GDP per capita GDP divided by the size of the population; equivalent to the average GDP per person.

Gini coefficient a number that summarizes a country's level of income inequality based on how unequally income is distributed across quintiles.

globalization the phenomenon of growing economic linkages among countries.

government borrowing the amount of funds borrowed by the government in *financial markets* to buy goods and services.

government purchases of goods and services total purchases by federal, state, and local governments on goods and services.

government transfers payments by the government to individuals for which no good or service is provided in return.

gross domestic product (GDP) the total value of all *final goods and services* produced in the *economy* during a given period, usually a year.

growth accounting estimates the contribution of each of the major factors (physical and human capital, labor, and technology) in the *aggregate production function*.

Heckscher–Ohlin model a *model* of international trade in which a country has a *comparative advantage* in a good whose production is intensive in the factors that are abundantly available in that country.

horizontal axis the horizontal number line of a graph along which values of the *x*-variable are measured; also referred to as the *x-axis*.

horizontal intercept the point at which a *curve* hits the *horizontal axis*; it indicates the value of the *x*-variable when the value of the *y*-variable is zero.

household a person or a group of people who share income.

human capital the improvement in labor created by the education and knowledge embodied in the workforce.

illiquid describes an asset that cannot be quickly converted into cash without much loss of value.

imperfect competition a market structure in which no firm is a *monopolist,* but producers nonetheless have *market power* they can use to affect market prices.

implicit cost a cost that does not require the outlay of money; it is measured by the value, in dollar terms, of forgone benefits.

implicit cost of capital the *opportunity cost* of the capital used by a business; that is, the income that could have been realized had the capital been used in the next best alternative way.

implicit liabilities spending promises made by governments that are effectively a debt despite the fact that they are not included in the usual debt statistics. In the United States, the largest implicit liabilities arise from Social Security and Medicare, which promise transfer payments to current and future retirees (Social Security) and to the elderly (Medicare).

import-competing industries industries that produce goods or services that are also imported.

import quota a legal limit on the quantity of a good that can be imported.

imports goods and services purchased from other countries.

incentive anything that offers rewards to people who change their behavior.

incidence (of a tax) a measure of who really pays a tax.

income distribution the way in which total income is divided among the owners of the various *factors of production.*

income effect the change in the quantity of a good consumed that results from the change in a consumer's purchasing power due to the change in the price of the good.

income-elastic demand when the *income elasticity of demand* for a good is greater than 1.

income elasticity of demand the percent change in the quantity of a good demanded when a consumer's income changes divided by the percent change in the consumer's income.

income–expenditure equilibrium a situation in which *aggregate output,* measured by *real GDP,* is equal to *planned aggregate spending* and *firms* have no incentive to change output.

income–expenditure equilibrium GDP the level of *real GDP* at which real GDP equals *planned aggregate spending.*

income-inelastic demand when the *income elasticity of demand* for a good is positive but less than 1.

income tax a tax on the income of an individual or family.

increasing marginal cost the case in which each additional unit costs more to produce than the previous one.

increasing returns to scale long-run *average total cost* declines as output increases (also referred to as *economies of scale*).

independent events events for which the occurrence of one does not affect the likelihood of occurrence of any of the others.

independent variable the determining *variable* in a *causal relationship.*

indifference curve a contour line showing all *consumption bundles* that yield the same amount of total *utility* for an individual.

indifference curve map a collection of *indifference curves* for a given individual that represents the individual's entire *utility function;* each curve corresponds to a different total *utility* level.

individual choice the decision by an individual of what to do, which necessarily involves a decision of what not to do.

individual consumer surplus the net gain to an individual buyer from the purchase of a good; equal to the difference between the buyer's *willingness to pay* and the price paid.

individual demand curve a graphical representation of the relationship between *quantity demanded* and price for an individual consumer.

individual labor supply curve a graphical representation showing how the quantity of labor supplied by an individual depends on that individual's wage rate.

individual producer surplus the net gain to an individual seller from selling a good; equal to the difference between the price received and the seller's *cost.*

individual supply curve a graphical representation of the relationship between *quantity supplied* and *price* for an individual consumer.

industrial policy a policy that supports industries believed to yield *positive externalities.*

industry supply curve a graphical representation that shows the relationship between the price of a good and the total output of the industry for that good.

inefficient describes a market or *economy* in which there are missed opportunities: some people could be made better off without making other people worse off.

inefficient allocation to consumers a form of inefficiency in which people who want a good badly and are willing to pay a high price don't get it, and those who care relatively little about the good and are only willing to pay a low price do get it; often a result of a *price ceiling.*

inefficient allocation of sales among sellers a form of inefficiency in which sellers who would be willing to sell a good at the lowest price are not always those who actually manage to sell it; often the result of a *price floor.*

inefficiently high quality a form of inefficiency in which sellers offer high-quality goods at a high price even though buyers would prefer a lower quality at a lower price; often the result of a *price floor.*

inefficiently low quality a form of inefficiency in which sellers offer low-quality goods at a low price even though buyers would prefer a higher quality at a higher price; often a result of a *price ceiling.*

inelastic demand when the *price elasticity of demand* is less than 1.

inferior good a good for which a rise in income decreases the demand for the good.

inflation a rise in the overall level of prices.

inflation rate the annual percent change in a price index—typically the *consumer price index.* The inflation rate is positive when the *aggregate price level* is rising (*inflation*) and negative when the aggregate price level is falling (*deflation*).

inflation targeting an approach to *monetary policy* that requires that the *central bank* try to keep the *inflation rate* near a predetermined target rate.

inflation tax the reduction in the value of money held by the public caused by *inflation.*

inflationary gap exists when *aggregate output* is above *potential output.*

infrastructure *physical capital*, such as roads, power lines, ports, information networks, and other parts of an *economy*, that provides the underpinnings, or foundation, for economic activity.

in-kind benefit a benefit given in the form of goods or services.

input a good or service used to produce another good or service.

interaction (of choices) my choices affect your choices, and vice versa; a feature of most economic situations. The results of this interaction are often quite different from what the individuals intend.

interdependence the relationship among firms when their decisions significantly affect one another's profits; characteristic of oligopolies.

interest rate the price, calculated as a percentage of the amount borrowed, charged by lenders to borrowers for the use of their savings for one year.

interest rate effect of a change in the aggregate price level the effect on *consumer spending* and *investment spending* caused by a change in the purchasing power of consumers' money holdings when the *aggregate price level* changes. A rise (fall) in the aggregate price level decreases (increases) the purchasing power of consumers' money holdings. In response, consumers try to increase (decrease) their money holdings, which drives up (down) interest rates, thereby decreasing (increasing) consumption and investment.

intermediate goods and services goods and services, bought from one *firm* by another firm, that are inputs for production of *final goods and services*.

internalize the externality when individuals take into account *external costs* and *external benefits*.

international trade agreements treaties by which countries agree to lower *trade protections* against one another.

inventories stocks of goods and raw materials held to satisfy future sales.

inventory investment the value of the change in total *inventories* held in the *economy* during a given period. Unlike other types of *investment spending*, inventory investment can be negative, if inventories fall.

investment bank a *bank* that trades in *financial assets* and is not covered by *deposit insurance*.

investment spending spending on productive *physical capital*, such as machinery and construction of structures, and on changes to *inventories*.

invisible hand a phrase used by Adam Smith to refer to the way in which an individual's pursuit of self-interest can lead, without the individual's intending it, to good results for society as a whole.

job search when workers spend time looking for *employment*.

Keynesian cross a diagram that identifies *income–expenditure equilibrium* as the point where the *planned aggregate spending* line crosses the 45-degree line.

Keynesian economics a school of thought emerging out of the works of John Maynard Keynes; according to Keynesian economics, a depressed *economy* is the result of inadequate spending and government intervention can help a depressed economy through *monetary policy* and *fiscal policy*.

kinked demand curve a model used to explain the stability of *oligopoly* pricing; a *demand curve* that kinks (bends) because the *oligopolist* will lose sales if output is reduced and price is increased but gain only a few additional sales if output is increased and price is lowered (because the lower price will be matched at once by other oligopolists), the curve will be very flat above the kink and very steep below the kink.

labor force the sum of *employment* and *unemployment*; that is, the number of people who are currently working plus the number of people who are currently looking for work.

labor force participation rate the percentage of the population age 16 or older that is in the *labor force*.

labor productivity output per worker; also referred to as simply *productivity*. Increases in labor productivity are the only source of *long-run economic growth*.

law of demand the principle that a higher price for a good or service, other things equal, leads people to demand a smaller quantity of that good or service.

leisure the time available for purposes other than earning money to buy marketed goods.

leverage the degree to which a financial institution is financing its investments with borrowed funds.

liability a requirement to pay income in the future.

license the right, conferred by the government, to supply a good.

life insurance company a *financial intermediary* that sells policies guaranteeing a payment to a policyholder's beneficiaries when the policyholder dies.

linear relationship the relationship between two *variables* in which the *slope* is constant and therefore is depicted on a graph by a *curve* that is a straight line.

liquid describes an asset that can be quickly converted into cash without much loss of value.

liquidity preference model of the interest rate a model of the market for money in which the *interest rate* is determined by the supply and demand for money.

liquidity trap a situation in which *monetary policy* is ineffective because *nominal interest rates* are up against the *zero bound*.

loan a lending agreement between an individual lender and an individual borrower. Loans are usually tailored to the individual borrower's needs and ability to pay but carry relatively high *transaction costs*.

loanable funds market a hypothetical market that brings together those who want to lend money (savers) and those who want to borrow (*firms with investment spending* projects).

loan-backed securities assets created by pooling individual *loans* and selling shares in that pool.

long run the time period in which all *inputs* can be varied.

long-run aggregate supply curve a graphical representation that shows the relationship between the *aggregate price level* and the quantity of *aggregate output* supplied that would exist if all prices, including *nominal wages*, were fully flexible. The long-run aggregate supply curve is vertical because the aggregate price level has no effect on aggregate output in the long run; in the long run, aggregate output is determined by the *economy's potential output*.

long-run average total cost curve a graphical representation showing the relationship between output and *average total cost* when *fixed cost* has been chosen to minimize average total cost for each level of output.

long-run economic growth the sustained rise in the quantity of goods and services the *economy* produces.

long-run industry supply curve a graphical representation that shows how *quantity supplied* responds to price once producers have had time to enter or exit the industry.

long-run macroeconomic equilibrium the point at which the *short-run macroeconomic equilibrium* is on the *long-run aggregate supply curve;* so short-run equilibrium aggregate output is equal to *potential output.*

long-run market equilibrium an economic balance in which, given sufficient time for producers to enter or exit an industry, the *quantity supplied* equals the *quantity demanded.*

long-run Phillips curve a graphical representation of the relationship between *unemployment* and *inflation* in the long run after expectations of inflation have had time to adjust to experience.

long-term interest rate the *interest rate* on *financial assets* that mature a number of years into the future.

lump-sum taxes taxes that don't depend on the taxpayer's income.

macroeconomic policy activism the use of *monetary policy* and *fiscal policy* to smooth out the *business cycle.*

macroeconomics the branch of *economics* that is concerned with the overall ups and downs in the *economy.*

marginal analysis the study of *marginal decisions.*

marginal benefit the additional benefit derived from producing one more unit of a good or service.

marginal benefit curve a graphical representation showing how the benefit from producing one more unit depends on the quantity that has already been produced.

marginal cost the additional cost incurred by producing one more unit of a good or service.

marginal cost curve a graphical representation showing how the cost of producing one more unit depends on the quantity that has already been produced.

marginal decision a decision made at the "margin" of an activity to do a bit more or a bit less of that activity.

marginal product the additional quantity of output produced by using one more unit of a given *input.*

marginal productivity theory of income distribution the proposition that every *factor of production* is paid its *equilibrium value of the marginal product.*

marginal propensity to consume (MPC) the increase in *consumer spending* when *disposable income* rises by $1. Because consumers normally spend part but not all of an additional dollar of disposable income, MPC is between 0 and 1.

marginal propensity to save (MPS) the fraction of an additional dollar of *disposable income* that is saved; MPS is equal to 1-MPC.

marginal rate of substitution (MRS) the ratio of the *marginal utility* of one good to the marginal utility of another.

marginal revenue the change in *total revenue* generated by an additional unit of output.

marginal revenue curve a graphical representation showing how *marginal revenue* varies as output varies.

marginal social benefit of a good or activity the *marginal benefit* that accrues to consumers plus the marginal *external benefit.*

marginal social benefit of pollution the additional gain to society as a whole from an additional unit of pollution.

marginal social cost of a good or activity the *marginal cost* of production plus the marginal *external cost.*

marginal social cost of pollution the additional cost imposed on society as a whole by an additional unit of pollution.

marginal tax rate the percentage of an increase in income that is taxed anyway.

marginal utility the change in total *utility* generated by consuming one additional unit of a good or service.

marginal utility curve a graphical representation showing how *marginal utility* depends on the quantity of the good or service consumed.

marginal utility per dollar the additional *utility* gained from spending one more dollar on a good or service.

marginally attached workers nonworking individuals who say they would like a job and have looked for work in the recent past but are not currently looking for work.

market basket a hypothetical consumption bundle of consumer purchases of goods and services, used to measure changes in overall price level.

market-clearing price the price at which the market is in *equilibrium,*

that is, the quantity of a good or service demanded equals the quantity of that good or service supplied; also referred to as the *equilibrium price.*

market economy an *economy* in which decisions about production and consumption are made by individual producers and consumers.

market failure the situation in which a market fails to be efficient.

markets for goods and services markets in which *firms* sell goods and services that they produce to *households.*

market power the ability of a producer to raise prices.

market share the fraction of the total industry output accounted for by a given producer's output.

maximum the highest point on a *nonlinear curve,* where the *slope* changes from positive to negative.

mean household income the average income across all households.

means-tested a program in which benefits are available only to individuals or families whose incomes fall below a certain level.

median household income the income of the household lying at the exact middle of the *income distribution.*

medium of exchange an asset that individuals acquire for the purpose of trading for goods and services rather than for their own consumption.

menu cost the real cost of changing a listed price.

merchandise trade balance (trade balance) the difference between a country's *exports* and *imports* of goods alone—not including services.

microeconomics the branch of *economics* that studies how people make decisions and how those decisions interact.

midpoint method a technique for calculating the percent change in which changes in a variable are compared with the average, or midpoint, of the starting and final values.

minimum the lowest point on a *nonlinear curve,* where the *slope* changes from negative to positive.

minimum-cost output the quantity of output at which the *average total cost* is lowest—the bottom of the *U-shaped average total cost curve.*

minimum wage a legal floor on the wage rate. The wage rate is the market price of labor.

model a simplified representation of a real situation that is used to better understand real-life situations.

monetarism a theory of *business cycles*, associated primarily with Milton Friedman, that asserts that GDP will grow steadily if the *money supply* grows steadily.

monetary aggregate an overall measure of the *money supply*. The most common monetary aggregates in the United States are M1, which includes *currency in circulation*, traveler's checks, and *checkable bank deposits*, and M2, which includes M1 as well as *near-moneys*.

monetary base the sum of *currency in circulation* and *bank reserves*.

monetary neutrality the concept that changes in the *money supply* have no real effects on the *economy* in the long run and only result in a proportional change in the price level.

monetary policy changes in the quantity of money in circulation designed to alter *interest rates* and affect the level of overall spending.

monetary policy rule a formula that determines the *central bank's* actions.

money any asset that can easily be used to purchase goods and services.

money demand curve a graphical representation of the relationship between the *interest rate* and the quantity of money demanded. The money demand curve slopes downward because, other things equal, a higher interest rate increases the *opportunity cost* of holding money.

money multiplier the ratio of the *money supply* to the *monetary base*.

money supply the total value of *financial assets* in the *economy* that are considered *money*.

money supply curve a graphical representation of the relationship between the quantity of money supplied by the Federal Reserve and the *interest rate*.

monopolist a firm that is the only producer of a good that has no close substitutes.

monopolistic competition a market structure in which there are many competing producers in an industry, each producer sells a differentiated product, and there is *free entry and exit* into and from the industry in the *long run*.

monopoly an industry controlled by a *monopolist*.

moral hazard the situation that can exist when an individual knows more about his or her own actions than other people do. This leads to a distortion of incentives to take care or to expend effort when someone else bears the costs of the lack of care or effort.

movement along the demand curve a change in the *quantity demanded* of a good that results from a change in the price of that good.

movement along the supply curve a change in the *quantity supplied* of a good that results from a change in the price of that good.

multiplier the ratio of total change in *real GDP* caused by an *autonomous change in aggregate spending* to the size of that autonomous change.

mutual fund a *financial intermediary* that creates a *stock* portfolio by buying and holding shares in companies and then selling shares of this portfolio to individual investors.

Nash equilibrium in *game theory*, the *equilibrium* that results when all players choose the action that maximizes their *payoffs* given the actions of other players, ignoring the effect of that action on the *payoffs* of other players; also known as *noncooperative equilibrium*.

national income and product accounts method of calculating and keeping track of *consumer spending*, sales of producers, business *investment spending*, government purchases, and a variety of other flows of money between different sectors of the *economy*; also referred to as *national accounts*.

national savings the sum of *private savings* and the government's *budget balance;* the total amount of savings generated within the *economy*.

natural monopoly a *monopoly* that exists when *increasing returns to scale* provide a large cost advantage to having all output produced by a single firm.

natural rate hypothesis the hypothesis that because *inflation* is eventually embedded into expectations, to avoid accelerating inflation over time the *unemployment rate* equals the expected inflation rate.

natural rate of unemployment the normal *unemployment rate* around which the actual unemployment rate fluctuates; the unemployment rate that arises from the effects of *frictional* and *structural unemployment*.

near-money a *financial asset* that can't be directly used as a *medium of exchange* but can be readily converted into cash or *checkable bank deposits*.

negative externalities *external costs*.

negative income tax a government program that supplements the income of low-income working families.

negative relationship a relationship between two *variables* in which an increase in the value of one variable is associated with a decrease in the value of the other variable. It is illustrated by a *curve* that slopes downward from left to right.

net exports the difference between the value of *exports* and the value of *imports*. A positive value for net exports indicates that a country is a net exporter of goods and services; a negative value indicates that a country is a net importer of goods and services.

net present value the *present value* of current and future benefits minus the present value of current and future costs.

network externality the increase in the value of a good to an individual is greater when a large number of others own or use the same good.

new classical macroeconomics an approach to the *business cycle* that returns to the classical view that shifts in the *aggregate demand curve* affect only the *aggregate price level*, not *aggregate output*.

new Keynesian economics theory that argues that market imperfections can lead to price stickiness for the *economy* as a whole.

nominal GDP the value of all *final goods and services* produced in the *economy* during a given year, calculated using the prices current in the year in which the output is produced.

nominal interest rate the *interest rate* in dollar terms.

nominal wage the dollar amount of any given wage paid.

nonaccelerating inflation rate of unemployment (NAIRU) the *unemployment rate* at which, other things equal, *inflation* does not change over time.

noncooperative behavior actions by firms that ignore the effects of those actions on the profits of other firms.

noncooperative equilibrium in *game theory*, the *equilibrium* that results when all players choose the action that maximizes their *payoffs* given the actions of other players, ignoring the effect of that action on the *payoffs* of other players; also known as *Nash equilibrium*.

nonexcludable referring to a good, describes the case in which the supplier cannot prevent those who do not pay from consuming the good.

nonlinear curve a *curve* in which the *slope* is not the same between every pair of points.

nonlinear relationship the relationship between two *variables* in which the *slope* is not constant and therefore is depicted on a graph by a *curve* that is not a straight line.

nonprice competition competition in areas other than price to increase sales, such as new product features and advertising; especially engaged in by firms that have a tacit understanding not to compete on price.

nonrival in consumption referring to a good, describes the case in which the same unit can be consumed by more than one person at the same time.

normal good a good for which a rise in income increases the demand for that good—the "normal" case.

normative economics the branch of economic analysis that makes prescriptions about the way the *economy* should work.

North American Free Trade Agreement (NAFTA) a *trade* agreement among the United States, Canada, and Mexico.

offshore outsourcing the practice of businesses hiring people in another country to perform various tasks.

Okun's law the negative relationship between the *output gap* and the *unemployment rate*, whereby each additional percentage point of output gap reduces the unemployment rate by about ½ of a percentage point.

oligopolist a firm in an industry with only a small number of producers.

oligopoly an industry with only a small number of producers.

omitted variable an unobserved *variable* that, through its influence on other variables, creates the erroneous appearance of a direct *causal relationship* among those variables.

open economy an *economy* that trades goods and services with other countries.

open-market operation a purchase or sale of U.S. Treasury bills by the Federal Reserve, normally through a transaction with a *commercial bank*.

opportunity cost the real cost of an item: what you must give up in order to get it.

optimal consumption bundle the *consumption bundle* that maximizes a consumer's total *utility*, given that consumer's *budget constraint*.

optimal consumption rule when a consumer maximizes *utility*, the *marginal utility per dollar* spent must be the same for all goods and services in the *consumption bundle*.

optimal output rule profit is maximized by producing the quantity of output at which the *marginal revenue* of the last unit produced is equal to its *marginal cost*.

optimal quantity the quantity that generates the maximum possible total net gain.

optimal time allocation rule an individual should allocate time so that the *marginal utility* gained from the income earned from an additional hour worked is equal to the marginal utility of an additional hour of *leisure*.

ordinary goods in a consumer's *utility function*, those for which additional units of one good are required to compensate for fewer units of another, and vice versa; and for which the consumer experiences a *diminishing marginal rate of substitution* when substituting one good in place of another.

origin the point where the axes of a two-*variable* graph meet.

other things equal assumption in the development of a model, the assumption that all relevant factors except the one under study remain unchanged.

output gap the percentage difference between the actual level of *real GDP* and *potential output*.

overuse the depletion of a *common resource* that occurs when individuals ignore the fact that their use depletes the amount of the resource remaining for others.

patent a temporary monopoly given by the government to an inventor for the use or sale of an invention.

payoff in *game theory*, the reward received by a player (for example, the profit earned by an *oligopolist*).

payoff matrix in *game theory*, a diagram that shows how the *payoffs* to each of the participants in a two-player game depend on the actions of both; a tool in analyzing *interdependence*.

payroll tax a tax on the earnings an employer pays to an employee.

pension fund a type of *mutual fund* that holds assets in order to provide retirement income to its members.

perfect complements goods a consumer wants to consume in the same ratio, regardless of their *relative price*.

perfect price discrimination when a *monopolist* charges each consumer the maximum that the consumer is willing to pay.

perfect substitutes goods for which the *indifference curves* are straight lines; the *marginal rate of substitution* of one good in place of another good is constant, regardless of how much of each an individual consumes.

perfectly competitive industry an industry in which all producers are price-takers.

perfectly competitive market a market in which all participants are price-takers.

perfectly elastic demand the case in which any price increase will cause the *quantity demanded* to drop to zero; the *demand curve* is a horizontal line.

perfectly elastic supply the case in which even a tiny increase or reduction in the price will lead to very large changes in the *quantity supplied*, so that the *price elasticity of supply* is infinite; the perfectly elastic *supply curve* is a horizontal line.

perfectly inelastic demand the case in which the *quantity demanded* does not respond at all to changes in the price; the *demand curve* is a vertical line.

perfectly inelastic supply the case in which the *price elasticity of supply* is zero, so that changes in the price of the good have no effect on the *quantity supplied*; the perfectly inelastic *supply curve* is a vertical line.

physical asset a claim on a tangible object that gives the owner the right to dispose of the object as he or she wishes.

physical capital manufactured resources, such as buildings and machines.

pie chart a circular graph that shows how some total, usually expressed in percentages, is divided among its components.

Pigouvian subsidy a payment designed to encourage activities that yield *external benefits*.

Pigouvian taxes taxes designed to reduce *external costs*.

planned aggregate spending the total amount of planned spending in the *economy*; includes *consumer spending* and *planned investment spending*.

planned investment spending the *investment spending* that *firms* intend to undertake during a given period. Planned investment spending may differ from actual investment spending due to *unplanned inventory investment*.

political business cycle a *business cycle* that results from the use of macroeconomic policy to serve political ends.

pooling a strong form of *diversification* in which an investor takes a small share of the risk in many *independent events*, so the *payoff* has very little total overall risk.

positive economics the branch of economic analysis that describes the way the *economy* actually works.

positive externalities *external benefits*.

positive feedback put simply, success breeds success, failure breeds failure; the effect is seen with goods that are subject to *network externalities*.

positive relationship a relationship between two *variables* in which an increase in the value of one variable is associated with an increase in the value of the other variable. It is illustrated by a *curve* that slopes upward from left to right.

positively correlated a relationship between events such that each event is more likely to occur if the other event also occurs.

potential output the level of *real GDP* the *economy* would produce if all prices, including *nominal wages*, were fully flexible.

poverty program a government program designed to aid the poor.

poverty rate the percentage of the population with incomes below the *poverty threshold*.

poverty threshold the annual income below which a family is officially considered poor.

premium a payment to an insurance company in return for the promise to pay a claim in certain states of the world.

present value the amount of money needed at the present time to produce, at the prevailing *interest rate*, a given amount of money at a specified future time.

price ceiling the maximum price sellers are allowed to charge for a good or service; a form of *price control*.

price controls legal restrictions on how high or low a market price may go.

price discrimination charging different prices to different consumers for the same good.

price elasticity of demand the ratio of the percent change in the *quantity demanded* to the percent change in the price as we move along the *demand curve* (dropping the minus sign).

price elasticity of supply a measure of the responsiveness of the quantity of a good supplied to the price of that good; the ratio of the percent change in the *quantity supplied* to the percent change in the price as we move along the *supply curve*.

price floor the minimum price buyers are required to pay for a good or service; a form of *price control*.

price index a measure of the cost of purchasing a given *market basket* in a given year, where that cost is normalized so that it is equal to 100 in the selected base year; a measure of overall price level.

price leadership a pattern of behavior in which one firm sets its price and other firms in the industry follow.

price regulation a limitation on the price a *monopolist* is allowed to charge.

price stability a situation in which the overall cost of living is changing slowly or not at all.

price-taking consumer a consumer whose actions have no effect on the market price of the good or service he or she buys.

price-taking firm's optimal output rule the profit of a price-taking firm is maximized by producing the quantity of output at which the market price is equal to the *marginal cost* of the last unit produced.

price-taking producer a producer whose actions have no effect on the market price of the good or service it sells.

price war a collapse of prices when *tacit collusion* breaks down.

principle of diminishing marginal utility the proposition that each successive unit of a good or service consumed adds less to total *utility* than did the previous unit.

principle of marginal analysis the proposition that the *optimal quantity* is the quantity at which *marginal benefit* is equal to *marginal cost*.

prisoners' dilemma a game based on two premises in which (1) each player has an incentive to choose an action that benefits itself at the other player's expense; and (2) both players are then worse off than if they had acted cooperatively.

private good a good that is both *excludable* and *rival in consumption*.

private health insurance program in which each member of a large pool of individuals pays a fixed amount to a private company that agrees to pay most of the medical expenses of the pool's members.

private information information that some people have that others do not.

private savings *disposable income* minus *consumer spending*; disposable income that is not spent on consumption but rather goes into *financial markets*.

producer price index (PPI) a measure of the cost of a typical basket of goods and services purchased by producers. Because these commodity prices respond quickly to changes in demand, the PPI is often regarded as a leading indicator of changes in the *inflation rate*.

producer surplus a term often used to refer to either *individual producer surplus* or *total producer surplus*.

product differentiation the attempt by firms to convince buyers that their products are different from those of other firms in the industry. If firms can so convince buyers, they can charge a higher price.

production function the relationship between the quantity of *inputs* a firm uses and the quantity of output it produces.

production possibility frontier a model that illustrates the trade-offs facing an *economy* that produces only two goods. It shows the maximum quantity of one good that can be produced for any given quantity produced of the other.

productivity output per worker; a shortened form of the term *labor productivity*.

profits tax a tax on the profits of a firm.

progressive tax a tax that takes a larger share of the income of high-income taxpayers than of low-income taxpayers.

property rights the rights of owners of valuable items, whether *resources* or goods, to dispose of those items as they choose.

property tax a tax on the value of property, such as the value of a home.

proportional tax a tax that is the same percentage of the *tax base* regardless of the taxpayer's income or wealth.

protection policies that limit *imports*; an alternative term for *trade protection*.

public debt government debt held by individuals and institutions outside the government.

public good a good that is both *nonexcludable* and *nonrival in consumption*.

public ownership when goods are supplied by the government or by a firm owned by the government to protect the interests of the consumer in response to *natural monopoly*.

purchasing power parity (between two countries' currencies) the nominal *exchange rate* at which a given basket of goods and services would cost the same amount in each country.

quantity control an upper limit, set by the government, on the quantity of some good that can be bought or sold; also referred to as a *quota*.

quantity demanded the actual amount of a good or service consumers are willing to buy at some specific price.

quantity supplied the actual amount of a good or service producers are willing to sell at some specific price.

quota an upper limit, set by the government, on the quantity of some good that can be bought or sold; also referred to as a *quantity control*.

quota limit the total amount of a good under a *quota* or *quantity control* that can be legally transacted.

quota rent the difference between the *demand price* and the *supply price* at the *quota limit*; this difference, the earnings that accrue to the license holder, is equal to the market price of the *license* when the license is traded.

random variable a *variable* with an uncertain future value.

random walk the movement over time of an unpredictable *variable*.

rate of return (of an investment project) the profit earned on an investment project expressed as a percentage of its cost.

rational expectations a theory of expectation formation that holds that individuals and *firms* make decisions optimally, using all available information.

real business cycle theory a theory of *business cycles* that asserts that fluctuations in the growth rate of *total factor productivity* cause the business cycle.

real exchange rate the *exchange rate* adjusted for international differences in *aggregate price levels*.

real GDP the total value of all *final goods and services* produced in the *economy* during a given year, calculated using the prices of a selected base year.

real income income divided by the price level.

real interest rate the *nominal interest rate* minus the *inflation rate*.

real wage the wage rate divided by the price level.

recession a period of economic downturn when output and unemployment are falling; also referred to as a contraction.

recessionary gap exists when *aggregate output* is below *potential output*.

regressive tax a tax that takes a smaller share of the income of high-income taxpayers than of low-income taxpayers.

relative price the ratio of the price of one good to the price of another.

relative price rule at the *optimal consumption bundle*, the *marginal rate of substitution* of one good in place of another is equal to the *relative price*.

rental rate the cost, implicit or explicit, of using a unit of land or capital for a given period of time.

reputation a long-term standing in the public regard that serves to reassure others that *private information* is not being concealed; a valuable asset in the face of *adverse selection*.

research and development (R&D) spending to create new technologies and prepare them for practical use.

reserve ratio the fraction of *bank deposits* that a *bank* holds as reserves. In the United States, the minimum required reserve ratio is set by the Federal Reserve.

reserve requirements rules set by the Federal Reserve that set the minimum *reserve ratio* for banks. For *checkable bank deposits* in the United States, the minimum reserve ratio is set at 10%.

resource anything, such as land, labor, and capital, that can be used to produce something else; includes natural resources (from the physical environment) and human resources (labor, skill, intelligence).

revaluation an increase in the value of a currency that is set under a *fixed exchange rate regime*.

reverse causality the error committed when the true direction of causality between two *variables* is reversed, and the *independent variable* and the *dependent variable* are incorrectly identified.

Ricardian model of international trade a model that analyzes international *trade* under the assumption that *opportunity costs* are constant.

risk uncertainty about future outcomes.

risk-averse describes individuals who choose to reduce *risk* when that reduction leaves the expected value of their income or wealth unchanged.

risk-neutral describes individuals who are completely insensitive to risk.

rival in consumption referring to a good, describes the case in which one unit cannot be consumed by more than one person at the same time.

Rule of 70 a mathematical formula that states that the time it takes *real GDP* per capita, or any other variable that grows gradually over time, to double is approximately 70 divided by that variable's annual growth rate.

run market equilibrium an economic balance in which, given sufficient time for producers to enter or exit an industry, the *quantity supplied* equals the *quantity demanded.*

sales tax a tax on the value of goods sold.

savings and loans (thrifts) deposit-taking *banks*, usually specialized in issuing home loans.

savings–investment spending identity an accounting fact that states that savings and *investment spending* are always equal for the *economy* as a whole.

scarce in short supply; a *resource* is scarce when there is not enough of the resource available to satisfy all the various ways a society wants to use it.

scatter diagram a graph that shows points that correspond to actual observations of the *x*- and *y*-variables; a *curve* is usually fitted to the scatter of points to indicate the trend in the data.

screening using observable information about people to make inferences about their *private information;* a way to reduce *adverse selection.*

securitization the pooling of loans and mortgages made by a financial institution and the sale of shares in such a pool to other investors.

self-correcting describes an *economy* in which shocks to aggregate demand affect *aggregate output* in the short run but not in the long run.

self-regulating economy an *economy* in which problems such as *unemployment* are resolved without government intervention, through the working of the *invisible hand*, and in which government attempts to improve the economy's performance would be ineffective at best, and would probably make things worse.

share a partial ownership of a company.

shift of the demand curve a change in the *quantity demanded* at any given price, represented graphically by the change of the original *demand curve* to a new position, denoted by a new demand curve.

shift of the supply curve a change in the *quantity supplied* of a good or service at any given price, represented graphically by the change of the original *supply curve* to a new position, denoted by a new supply curve.

shoe-leather costs (of inflation) the increased costs of transactions caused by *inflation.*

short run the time period in which at least one *input* is fixed.

shortage the insufficiency of a good or service that occurs when the *quantity demanded* exceeds the *quantity supplied*; shortages occur when the price is below the *equilibrium price.*

short-run aggregate supply curve a graphical representation that shows the positive relationship between the *aggregate price level* and the quantity of *aggregate output* supplied that exists in the short run, the time period when many production costs, particularly *nominal wages*, can be taken as fixed. The short-run aggregate supply curve has a positive slope because a rise in the aggregate price level leads to a rise in profits, and therefore output, when production costs are fixed.

short-run equilibrium aggregate output the quantity of *aggregate output* produced in *short-run macroeconomic equilibrium.*

short-run equilibrium aggregate price level the *aggregate price level* in *short-run macroeconomic equilibrium.*

short-run individual supply curve a graphical representation that shows how an individual producer's profit-maximizing output quantity depends on the market price, taking *fixed cost* as given.

short-run industry supply curve a graphical representation that shows how the *quantity supplied* by an industry depends on the market price, given a fixed number of producers.

short-run macroeconomic equilibrium the point at which the quantity of *aggregate output* supplied is equal to the *quantity demanded.*

short-run market equilibrium an economic balance that results when the *quantity supplied* equals the *quantity demanded*, taking the number of producers as given.

short-run Phillips curve a graphical representation of the negative short-run relationship between the *unemployment rate* and the *inflation rate.*

short-term interest rate the *interest rate* on *financial assets* that mature within less than a year.

shut-down price the price at which a firm ceases production in the short run because the market price has fallen below the minimum *average variable cost.*

signaling taking some action to establish credibility despite possessing *private information;* a way to reduce *adverse selection.*

single-payer system a health care system in which the government is the principal payer of medical bills funded through taxes.

single-price monopolist a *monopolist* that offers its product to all consumers at the same price.

slope the ratio of the "rise" (the change between two points on the *y-axis*) to the "run" (the difference between the same two points on the *x-axis*); a measure of the steepness of a *curve.*

social insurance government programs—like Social Security, Medicare, unemployment insurance, and food stamps—intended to protect families against economic hardship.

socially optimal quantity of pollution the quantity of pollution that society would choose if all the costs and benefits of pollution were fully accounted for.

specialization a situation in which different people each engage in the different task that he or she is good at performing.

stabilization policy the use of government policy to reduce the severity of *recessions* and to rein in excessively strong *expansions.* There are two main tools of stabilization policy: *monetary policy* and *fiscal policy.*

stagflation the combination of *inflation* and falling *aggregate output.*

standardized product output of different producers regarded by consumers as the same good; also referred to as a *commodity.*

state of the world a possible future event.

sticky wages *nominal wages* that are slow to fall even in the face of high *unemployment* and slow to rise even in the face of labor shortages.

stock a share in the ownership of a company held by a shareholder.

store of value an asset that is a means of holding purchasing power over time.

strategic behavior actions taken by a firm that attempt to influence the future behavior of other firms.

structural unemployment *unemployment* that results when there are more people seeking jobs in a labor market than there are jobs available at the current wage rate.

subprime lending lending to home buyers who don't meet the usual criteria for borrowing.

substitutes pairs of goods for which a rise in the price of one of the goods leads to an increase in the demand for the other good.

substitution effect the change in the quantity of a good consumed as the consumer substitutes a good that has become relatively cheaper in place of one that has become relatively more expensive.

sunk cost a cost that has already been incurred and is not recoverable.

supply and demand model a model of how a *competitive market* works.

supply curve a graphical representation of the *supply schedule,* showing the relationship between *quantity supplied* and price.

supply price the price of a given quantity at which producers will supply that quantity.

supply schedule a list or table showing how much of a good or service producers will supply at different prices.

supply shock an event that shifts the *short-run aggregate supply curve.* A negative supply shock raises production costs and reduces the *quantity supplied* at any *aggregate price level,* shifting the curve leftward. A positive supply shock decreases production costs and increases the quantity supplied at any aggregate price level, shifting the curve rightward.

surplus the excess of a good or service that occurs when the *quantity supplied* exceeds the *quantity demanded;* surpluses occur when the price is above the *equilibrium price.*

sustainable describes continued *long-run economic growth* in the face of the limited supply of natural resources and the impact of growth on the environment.

T-account a simple tool that summarizes a business's financial position by showing, in a single table, the business's assets and liabilities, with assets on the left and liabilities on the right.

tacit collusion cooperation among producers, without a formal agreement, to limit production and raise prices so as to raise one anothers' profits.

tangency condition on a graph of a consumer's *budget line* and available *indifference curves* of available *consumption bundles,* the point at which an indifference curve and the budget line just touch. When the indifference curves have the typical convex shape, this point determines the *optimal consumption bundle.*

tangent line a straight line that just touches a *nonlinear curve* at a particular point; the *slope* of the tangent line is equal to the slope of the nonlinear curve at that point.

target federal funds rate the Federal Reserve's desired level for the *federal funds rate.* The Federal Reserve adjusts the *money supply* through the purchase and sale of Treasury bills until the actual rate equals the desired rate.

tariff a tax levied on *imports.*

tax base the measure or value, such as income or property value, that determines how much tax an individual pays.

tax rate the amount of tax people are required to pay per unit of whatever is being taxed.

tax structure specifies how a tax depends on the *tax base;* usually expressed in percentage terms.

Taylor rule for monetary policy a rule for setting the *federal funds rate* that takes into account both the *inflation rate* and the *output gap.*

technology the technical means for the production of goods and services.

technology spillover an *external benefit* that results when knowledge spreads among individuals and firms.

theorem the proposition that even in the presence of *externalities* an *economy* can always reach an *efficient* solution as long as *transaction costs* are sufficiently low.

time allocation the decision about how many hours to spend on different activities, which leads to a decision about how much labor to supply.

time allocation budget line an individual's possible trade-off between consumption of *leisure* and the income that allows consumption of marketed goods.

time-series graph a two-*variable* graph that has dates on the *horizontal axis* and values of a variable that occurred on those dates on the *vertical axis.*

tit for tat in *game theory,* a strategy that involves playing cooperatively at first, then doing whatever the other player did in the previous period.

total consumer surplus the sum of the *individual consumer surpluses* of all the buyers of a good in a market.

total cost the sum of the *fixed cost* and the *variable cost* of producing a given quantity of output.

total cost curve a graphical representation of the *total cost,* showing how total cost depends on the quantity of output.

total factor productivity the amount of output that can be produced with a given amount of factor inputs.

total producer surplus the sum of the *individual producer surpluses* of all the sellers of a good in a market.

total product curve a graphical representation of the *production function,* showing how the quantity of output depends on the quantity of the *variable input* for a given quantity of the *fixed input.*

total revenue the total value of sales of a good or service (the price of the good or service multiplied by the quantity sold).

total surplus the total net gain to consumers and producers from trading in a market; the sum of the *consumer surplus* and the *producer surplus.*

tradable emissions permits *licenses* to emit limited quantities of pollutants that can be bought and sold by polluters.

trade when individuals provide goods and services to others and receive goods and services in return.

trade balance (merchandise trade balance) the difference between a country's *exports* and *imports* of goods alone—not including services.

trade deficit when the value of the goods and services bought from foreigners is more than the value of the goods and services sold to consumers abroad.

trade protection policies that limit *imports;* also known simply as *protection.*

trade surplus when the value of goods and services bought from foreigners is less than the value of the goods and services sold to them.

trade-off a comparison of the costs and benefits of doing something.

trade-off between equity and efficiency the dynamic whereby a well-designed tax system can be made more efficient only by making it less fair, and vice versa.

transaction costs the expenses of negotiating and executing a deal.

transfer a government payment to an individual or a family.

truncated cut; in a truncated axis, some of the range of values are omitted, usually to save space.

underemployment the number of people who work part-time because they cannot find full-time jobs.

unemployment the total number of people who are actively looking for work but aren't currently employed.

unemployment rate the percentage of the total number of people in the *labor force* who are unemployed, calculated as *unemployment/(unemployment + employment)*.

unions organizations of workers that try to raise wages and improve working conditions for their members by bargaining collectively.

unit of account a measure used to set prices and make economic calculations.

unit-of-account costs (of inflation) costs arising from the way *inflation* makes money a less reliable unit of measurement.

unit-elastic demand the case in which the *price elasticity of demand* is exactly 1.

unplanned inventory investment unplanned changes in *inventories*, which occur when actual sales are more or less than businesses expected.

U-shaped average total cost curve a distinctive graphical representation of the relationship between output and *average total cost*; the average total cost curve at first falls when output is low and then rises as output increases.

util a unit of *utility*.

utility (of a consumer) a measure of the satisfaction derived from consumption of goods and services.

utility function (of an individual) the total *utility* generated by an individual's *consumption bundle*.

value added (of a producer) the value of a producer's sales minus the value of input purchases.

value of the marginal product the value of the additional output generated by employing one more unit of a given factor, such as labor.

value of the marginal product curve a graphical representation showing how the *value of the marginal product* of a factor depends on the quantity of the factor employed.

variable a quantity that can take on more than one value.

variable cost a cost that depends on the quantity of output produced; the cost of a *variable input*.

variable input an *input* whose quantity the firm can vary at any time (for example, labor).

velocity of money the ratio of *nominal GDP* to the *money supply*.

vertical axis the vertical number line of a graph along which values of the *y*-variable are measured; also referred to as the *y-axis*.

vertical intercept the point at which a *curve* hits the *vertical axis*; it shows the value of the *y*-variable when the value of the *x*-variable is zero.

vicious cycle of deleveraging describes the sequence of events that takes place when a *firm's* asset sales to cover losses produce negative *balance sheet effects* on other firms and force creditors to call in their *loans*, forcing sales of more assets and causing further declines in asset prices.

wasted resources a form of inefficiency in which people expend money, effort, and time to cope with the shortages caused by a *price ceiling*.

wealth (of a *household*) the value of accumulated savings.

wealth effect of a change in the aggregate price level the effect on *consumer spending* caused by the change in the purchasing power of consumers' assets when the *aggregate price level* changes. A rise in the aggregate price level decreases the purchasing power of consumers' assets, so consumers decrease their consumption; a fall in the aggregate price level increases the purchasing power of consumers' assets, so consumers increase their consumption.

wealth tax a tax on the wealth of an individual.

wedge the difference between the *demand price* of the quantity transacted and the *supply price* of the quantity transacted for a good when the supply of the good is legally restricted. Often created by a *quantity control*, or *quota*.

welfare state the collection of government programs designed to alleviate economic hardship.

willingness to pay the maximum price a consumer is prepared to pay for a good.

world price the price at which a good can be bought or sold abroad.

World Trade Organization (WTO) an international organization of member countries that oversees *international trade agreements* and rules on disputes between countries over those agreements.

x-axis the horizontal number line of a graph along which values of the *x*-variable are measured; also referred to as the *horizontal axis*.

y-axis the vertical number line of a graph along which values of the *y*-variable are measured; also referred to as the *vertical axis*.

zero bound the lower bound of zero on the *nominal interest rate*.

zero-profit equilibrium an economic balance in which each firm makes zero profit at its profit-maximizing quantity.

Index

Note: Key terms appear in **boldface** type.

A

Applications in Economics

Indicates global example